MW00654271

THE ESSENTIAL WORKS OF
Andrew Murray

Updated in Today's Language

12 Complete Books
Covering the Entire
Christian Life

THE ESSENTIAL WORKS OF
Andrew Murray

Updated in Today's Language

BARBOUR
PUBLISHING

Published by Barbour Publishing, Inc., P.O. Box 719, Uhrichsville, Ohio 44683
www.barbourbooks.com

Our mission is to publish and distribute inspirational products offering exceptional value and biblical encouragement to the masses.

 Member of the
Evangelical Christian
Publishers Association

Printed in the United States of America.

May not a single moment of my life be spent
outside the light, love, and joy
of God's presence.

ANDREW MURRAY

CONTENTS

INTRODUCTION

THE remarkable life of the Reverend Andrew Murray began on May 9, 1828, in a Dutch Reformed parsonage in Graaff Reinet, South Africa.

Murray was born to and reared by parents whose passion for God colored his entire life and ministry. In the Murray home, Andrew enjoyed and benefited from regular prayer, worship, Bible study, and Christian love and fellowship—all of which were led by his father, the Rev. Andrew Murray Sr.

From his youth in Cape Town, Andrew Murray set his sights on following his father into full-time ministry. But it was only as he began theological training at Utrecht University in the Netherlands that his heart was fully turned toward Jesus Christ. "Your son has been born again," Murray wrote to his parents shortly after his conversion. "I have cast myself on Christ."

Murray never strayed from his commitment to Jesus Christ, or from serving men and women in the Lord's name. During his career, which began at age twenty-one, he pastored churches in Bloemfontein, Worcester, Cape Town, and Wellington, all in South Africa. His ministry stressed personal devotion to and unbending faith in Christ and reliance on the Holy Spirit. Murray wrote about those topics prolifically and with great ease and enthusiasm—and lived them out in every area of his personal life.

Though Murray was a minister of the Dutch Reformed Church, his own theology was oftentimes at odds with that of his Calvinist brethren. He attempted to align his own beliefs with those of the Reformed Church, but his writings demonstrated his belief that man was free to choose salvation and that God desires the salvation of all. While Murray acknowledged that the Bible teaches God's election, he also wrote that humans were free to claim for themselves the freely offered grace of God. That choice, he wrote, included the offer for every believer to walk more consistently, more fully, more confidently, and more victoriously in the power of God's Holy Spirit. That, he believed, was no contradiction of the biblical doctrine of divine election, but a divine mystery none could fully understand this side of heaven.

Despite criticism for some of his beliefs and writings, Murray attacked his life, his ministries, and his writing with a passion seldom seen in his time or since. His work reflected his deep conviction that all Christians should approach their faith with a wholehearted surrender to God, with full confidence in the anointing and power of the Holy Spirit, and with a passion for interaction with God through daily prayer.

Murray believed that any believer who wanted to experience *all* of God, *all* of Jesus Christ, and *all* of the Holy Spirit needed to understand, among other things, personal holiness and obedience, the importance of "abiding" in Christ, the power of personal prayer and intercession, and an attitude of complete surrender to God.

As a pastor, missionary, evangelist, educator, revival leader, and author, Andrew Murray became well-known throughout the world. After sixty-plus years of ministry in the Dutch Reformed Church of South Africa, the writing of more than 240 books and tracts, and considerable social and humanitarian work (including the founding of several educational institutions), Andrew Murray went home to his eternal reward on January 18, 1917, four months shy of his eighty-ninth birthday.

Though nearly a century has passed since Andrew Murray's death, his amazing legacy remains. To this day, his writings are readily available in several languages, and they continue to influence and inspire believers throughout the world. He is considered by many a forerunner of modern-day Pentecostalism.

"I must be filled; it is absolutely necessary," Murray wrote of his relationship with the Holy Spirit. "I may be filled; God has made it blessedly possible. I desire to be filled; it is eminently desirable. I will be filled; it is so blessedly certain."

These words, as much as anything, define and summarize Andrew Murray's writings. He gave a much-needed human voice to the absolute necessity for every believer to be filled with and walk in the power of God's Holy Spirit. Murray knew that nothing short of a life of faith in God's ability and willingness to give every believer more of the Holy Spirit would lead to the fuller life, the life of victory and power and love that Jesus promised all who place their faith in Him, who follow after Him as true disciples.

Choosing the twelve "essentials" from among Andrew Murray's vast writings is no easy task. But this collection includes the books—the *full* books, lightly edited and updated for ease of reading, but still maintaining the nineteenth-century "voice" of Andrew Murray—we believe best summarize what Murray consistently and repeatedly taught during his six-plus decades of ministry. They are, as best as can be done, ordered so that the "basics" come first, followed by the writings/teachings that, if followed, will lead to a fuller life in Christ, the life of daily abiding in, trusting in, and relying on Him, through His Holy Spirit, to give you the abundant life He promised.

Some, but not all, of the writings included in this collection originally ended with personal applications, some in the form of statements of the essentials, some in the form of questions for the reader to answer personally based on what he or she has just read. In the interest of consistency, we have added personal application questions to the ends of each of the writings that didn't originally include them— questions that will inspire you, challenge you toward self-examination, and give you the opportunity to make their truths yours, both practically and experientially.

One final note. As you read through these writings, make sure you have one other book readily available: the Bible. Every word of Andrew Murray's writing was based on the truths of the holy scriptures, and we—as well as Andrew Murray himself—would encourage you to weigh what you read against what God has said in His written Word. Prayerfully read God's own words, and not just Andrew Murray's, as you seek and claim the blessings God wants to give you when you apply His truth to your personal Christian life.

TRACY M. SUMNER
EDITOR

THE TWO COVENANTS

Contents

Introduction

IT is often said that the great aim of the preacher ought to be to translate scripture truth from its Jewish form into the language and the thought of the present century in order to make it intelligible and acceptable to ordinary Christians. It is to be feared that the experiment will do more harm than good. In the course of the translation, the force of the original is lost. The scholar who trusts to translations will never become a master of the language he wants to learn. A race of Christians will be raised up to whom the language of God's Word, and with that the God who spoke it, will be strange. In the scripture words, not a little of scripture truth will be lost. For the true Christian life, nothing is so healthy and invigorating as to have each man come and study for himself the very words the Holy Spirit has spoken.

One of the words of scripture, which is almost going out of fashion, is the word *covenant*. There was a time when it was the keynote of the theology and the Christian life of strong and holy men. We know how deep in Scotland it entered into the national life and thought. It made mighty men to whom God and His promise and power were wonderfully real. It will be found still to bring strength and purpose to those who will take the trouble to bring all their life under control of the inspiring assurance that they are living in covenant with a God who has sworn faithfully to fulfill in them every promise He has given.

This book is a humble attempt to show what exactly the blessings are that God has covenanted to bestow on us, what the assurance is that the Covenant gives that they must and can and will be fulfilled, what the hold on God Himself is that it thus gives us, and what the conditions are for the full and continual experience of its blessings. I feel confident that if I can lead any to listen to what God has to say to them about His Covenant, and to encourage them to deal with Him as a Covenant God, it will bring them strength and joy.

Not long ago I received from one of my correspondents a letter with the following passage in it: "I think you will excuse and understand me when I say there is one further note of power I would like so much to have introduced into your next book on Intercession. God Himself has, I know, been giving me some direct teaching this winter on the place the New Covenant is to have in intercessory prayer. . . . I know you believe in the Covenant and the Covenant rights we have on account of it. Have you followed out your views of the Covenant as they relate to this subject of intercession? Am I wrong in coming to the conclusion that we may come boldly into God's presence and not only ask, but claim a Covenant right through Christ Jesus to all the spiritual searching, cleansing, knowledge, and power promised in the three great Covenant promises? If you would take the Covenant and speak of it as God could enable you to speak, I think that would be the quickest way the Lord could take to make His Church wake up to the power He has put into our hands in giving us a Covenant. I would be so glad if you would tell God's people that *they have a Covenant*."

Though this letter was not the reason for the writing of the book, and our Covenant rights have been considered in a far wider aspect than their relationship to prayer, I am persuaded that nothing will help us more in our work of intercession than the entrance for ourselves personally into what it means that we have a Covenant God.

My one great desire has been to ask Christians whether they are really seeking to find out what exactly God wants them to be and is willing to make them. It is only as they wait so "that the mind of the LORD might be shown to them" (Lev. 24:12) that their faith can ever truly see, or accept, or enjoy what God calls "His salvation." As long as we expect God to do for us what we ask or think, we limit Him. When we believe that as high as the heavens are above the earth, His thoughts are above our thoughts (see Isa. 55:8–9) and wait on Him as God to do unto us *according to His Word,* as He means it, we shall be prepared to live the truly supernatural, heavenly life the Holy Spirit can work in us—the true Christ life.

May God lead every reader into the secret of His presence, and "show him His Covenant" (see Ps. 25:14).

ANDREW MURRAY
Wellington, South Africa,
November 1, 1898

1

A COVENANT GOD

*"Therefore know that the LORD your God, He is God,
the faithful God who keeps covenant and mercy for. . .
those who love Him and keep His commandments."*
DEUTERONOMY 7:9

MEN often make covenants. They know the advantages to be derived from them. As an end of hostility or uncertainty, as a statement of services and benefits to be rendered, as a security for their certain performance, as a bond of friendship and goodwill, as a ground for perfect confidence and friendship, a covenant has often been of unspeakable value.

In His infinite reaching down to our human weakness and need, there is no possible way in which men pledge their faithfulness that God has not sought to make use of to give us perfect confidence in Him and the full assurance of all that He, in His infinite riches and power as God, has promised to do to us. It is with this view that He has consented to bind Himself by covenant, as if He could not be trusted. Blessed is the man who truly knows God as his Covenant God, who knows what the Covenant promises him, and what unwavering confidence of expectation it secures so that all its terms will be fulfilled to him. What a claim and hold it gives him on the Covenant-keeping God Himself!

To many a man who has never thought much of the Covenant, a true and living faith in it would mean the transformation of his whole life. *The full knowledge of what God wants to do* for him, *the assurance that it will be done* by an almighty power, *the being drawn to God Himself* in personal surrender and dependence, and *the waiting to have it done*—all this would make the Covenant the very gate of heaven. May the Holy Spirit give us some vision of its glory.

When God created man in His image and likeness, it was so that he might have a life as like His own as it was possible for a creature to live. This was to be by God Himself living and working all in man. For this, man was to yield himself in loving dependence on the wonderful glory of being the recipient, the bearer, and the manifestation of a divine life. The one secret of man's happiness was to be a trustful surrender of his whole being to the willing and the working of God. When sin entered, this relationship to God was destroyed. When man had disobeyed, he feared God and fled from Him. He no longer knew, loved, or trusted God.

Man could not save himself from the power of sin. If his redemption was to be accomplished, God must do it all. And if God was to do it in harmony with the law of man's nature, man must be brought to desire it, to yield his willing consent and to entrust himself to God. All that God wanted man to do was to believe in Him. What a man believes moves and rules his whole being, enters into him, and becomes part of his very life.

Salvation could only be by faith: God restoring the life man had lost, and man in faith yielding himself to God's work and will. The first great work of God with man was to get him to believe. This work cost God more care and time and patience than we can easily conceive. All the dealings with individual men, and with the people of Israel, had just this one object: to teach men to trust Him. Where He found faith He could do anything. Nothing dishonored and grieved Him so much as unbelief. Unbelief was the root of disobedience and every sin and made it impossible for God to do His work. The one thing God sought to awaken in men by promise and threatening, by mercy and judgment, was faith.

> *Blessed is the man who truly knows God as his Covenant God, who knows what the Covenant promises him, and what unwavering confidence of expectation it secures so that all its terms will be fulfilled to him.*

Of the many devices of which God's patient and condescending grace made use to stir up and strengthen faith, one of the most important was the Covenant. In more than one way God sought to accomplish this by His Covenant. First of all, His Covenant was always *a revelation of His purposes,* a holding out in definite promise of what God was willing to work in those with whom the Covenant was made. It was a divine pattern of the work God intended to do in their behalf so that they might know what to desire and expect so that their faith might nourish itself with the very things, though as yet unseen, that God was working out. Then the Covenant was meant to be *a security and guarantee,* as simple and plain and humanlike as the divine glory could make it, that the very things that God had promised would indeed be brought to pass and produced in those with whom He had entered into covenant.

Amid all delay and disappointment and apparent failure of the divine promises, the Covenant was to be the anchor of the soul, pledging the divine authenticity and faithfulness and unchangeableness for the certain performance of what had been promised. And so the Covenant was, above all, to give man *a hold on God* as the Covenant-keeping God, to link him to God Himself in expectation and hope, and to bring him to make God Himself alone the portion and the strength of his soul.

Oh, that we knew how God longs that we should trust Him—and how surely His every promise must be fulfilled to those who do so! Oh, that we knew how it is because of nothing but our unbelief that we cannot enter into the possession of God's promises and that God cannot—yes, cannot—do His mighty works in us, for us, and through us! Oh, that we knew how one of the surest remedies for our unbelief—the divinely chosen cure for it—is the Covenant into which God has entered with us! The whole dispensation of the Spirit, the whole economy of grace in Christ Jesus, the whole

> *he Covenant was, above all, to give man a hold on God as the Covenant-keeping God, to link him to God Himself in expectation and hope, and to bring him to make God Himself alone the portion and the strength of his soul.*

of our spiritual life, and the whole of the health and growth and strength of the Church have been laid down and provided for and secured in the New Covenant. No wonder that where that Covenant, with its wonderful promises, is so little thought of, its plea for an abounding and unhesitating confidence in God is so little understood, its claim on the faithfulness of the omnipotent God so little tested. No wonder that Christian life misses the joy and the strength, the holiness and the heavenliness that God meant and so clearly promised that it should have.

Let us listen to the words in which God's Word calls us to know, worship, and trust our Covenant-keeping God—it may be that we will find what we have been looking for: the deeper, the full experience of all God's grace can do in us. In our text, Moses says: *"Therefore know* that the LORD your God, He *is* God, *the faithful God who keeps covenant* and mercy for a thousand generations with those who love Him."* Hear what God says in Isaiah: "'For the mountains shall depart and the hills be removed, but My kindness shall not depart from you, *nor shall My covenant of peace be removed,'* says the LORD, who has mercy on you" (54:10). Surer than any mountain is the fulfillment of every Covenant promise. Of the New Covenant, in Jeremiah God speaks: *"And I will make an everlasting covenant with them, that I will not turn away from doing them good; but I will put My fear in their hearts so that they will not depart from Me"* (32:40). The Covenant secures alike that God will not turn from us, nor we depart from Him. He undertakes both for Himself and us. Let us ask very earnestly whether the lack in our Christian life, and especially in our faith, is not due to the neglect of the Covenant. We have not worshiped nor trusted the Covenant-keeping God. Our soul has not done what God called us to—"to take hold of His Covenant" (see Isa. 56:6), "to remember the Covenant" (see Lev. 26:42), so is it any wonder that our faith has failed and come short of the blessing? God could not fulfill His promises in us. If we will begin to examine the terms of the Covenant as the title-deeds of our inheritance and the riches we are to possess even here on earth, if we will think of the certainty of their fulfillment as being surer than the foundations of the everlasting mountains, if we will turn to the God who has engaged to do all for us and who keeps covenant forever, our life will become different from what it has been. Then it can, and will, be all that God would make it.

The great lack of our religion is that we need more of God. We accept salvation as His gift, but we do not know that the only object of salvation—its chief blessing—is to make us fit for and bring us back to *that close relationship with God* for which we were created and in which our glory in eternity will be found. All that God has ever done for His people in making a covenant was always to bring them to Himself as their chief, their only good, to teach them to trust in Him, to delight in Him, and to be one with Him. It cannot be otherwise.

If God is indeed nothing but a very fountain of goodness and glory, of beauty and blessedness, then the more we can have of His presence, the more we conform to His will, the more we are engaged in His service, the more we have Him ruling and working all in us, the more truly happy shall we be. If God indeed is thereby Owner and Author of life and strength and of holiness and happiness, and can alone give and work it in us, the more we trust Him and depend and wait on Him, the stronger and the holier and the happier we shall be. And that only is a true and good religious life, which brings us every day nearer to this God, which makes us give up everything to have more of Him. No obedience can be too strict, no dependence too absolute, no submission too complete, no confidence too implicit to a soul that is learning to count God Himself its chief good, its exceeding joy.

In entering into covenant with us, God's one object is to draw us to Himself, to render us entirely dependent on Himself, and so to bring us into the right position and disposition in which He can fill us with Himself, His love, and His blessedness. Let us undertake our study of the New Covenant in which, if we are believers, God is at this moment living and walking with us with the honest purpose and surrender, at any price, to know what God wishes to be to us, to do in us, and to have us be and do to Him. The New Covenant may become to us one of the windows of heaven through which we see into the face, into the very heart, of God.

FOR FURTHER THOUGHT

1. *What was God's primary purpose for creating humankind in His image?*
2. *What, above all, is God's purpose for His covenant with humankind?*
3. *In what ways do God's covenant promises differ from those of man? In what ways are the two alike?*

2

THE TWO COVENANTS:
THEIR RELATION

For it is written that Abraham had two sons:
the one by a bondwoman, the other by a freewoman.
But he who was of the bondwoman was born according to the flesh,
and he of the freewoman through promise, which things
are symbolic. For these are the two covenants.
GALATIANS 4:22–24

THERE are two covenants, one called the Old, the other the New. God speaks of this very distinctly in Jeremiah, where He says: "The days are coming... when I will make a new covenant with the house of Israel and with the house of Judah—not according to the covenant that I made with their fathers" (31:31–32). This is quoted in Hebrews, with the addition: "In that He says, 'A new covenant,' He has made the first obsolete" (8:13). Our Lord spoke Himself of the New Covenant in His blood (see Luke 22:20). In His dealings with His people, in His working out His great redemption, it has pleased God that there should be two covenants.

It has pleased Him, not as an arbitrary appointment, but for good and wise reasons, which made it indispensably necessary that it should be so and no other way. The clearer our insight into the reasons, and the divine reasonableness, of there being two covenants, and into their relationship to each other, the fuller and truer can be our own personal understanding of what the New Covenant is meant to be to us. They indicate two stages in God's dealing with man—two ways of serving God, a lower or elementary one of preparation and promise, and a higher or more advanced one of fulfillment and possession. As that in which the true excellence of the second consists is opened up to us, we can spiritually enter into what God has prepared for us. Let us try to understand why there should have been two, neither less nor more.

The reason is to be found in the fact that in religion, in all interaction between God and man, there are two parties, and that each of these must have the opportunity to prove what their part is in the Covenant. In the Old Covenant, man had the opportunity given him to prove what he could do with the aid of all the means of grace God could bestow. That Covenant ended in man proving his own unfaithfulness and failure. In the New Covenant, God is to prove what He can do with man, as all unfaithful and weak as he is, when He is allowed and trusted *to do all the work*. The Old Covenant was one dependent on man's obedience, one that he could break and did break (Jer. 31:32). The New Covenant was one that God has promised shall never be broken, because *He Himself keeps it and ensures our keeping it, and so He makes it an Everlasting Covenant.*

> *The clearer our insight into the reasons, and the Divine reasonableness, of there being two covenants, and into their relationship to each other, the fuller and truer can be our own personal understanding of what the New Covenant is meant to be to us.*

It will reward us richly to look a little deeper into this. This relationship of God to fallen man in covenant is the same as it was to unfallen man as Creator. And what was that relationship? God proposed to make a man in His own image and likeness. The chief glory of God is that He has life in Himself, that He is independent of all else, and that He owes what He is to Himself alone. If the image and likeness of God were not to be a mere name, and man was really to be like God in the power to make himself what he was to be, then he needs to have the power of free will and self-determination. This was the problem God had to solve in man's creation in His image. Man was to be a creature made by God, and yet he was to be, as far as a creature could be, like God, self-made. In all God's treatment of man, these two factors were always to be taken into account. God was always to take the initiative and be to man the source of life. Man was always to be the recipient, and yet at the same time the disposer of the life God bestowed.

When man had fallen through sin, and God entered into a covenant of salvation, these two sides of the relationship had still to be maintained intact. God was always to be the first and man the second. And yet man, as made in God's image, was always, as second, to have full time and opportunity to appropriate or reject what God gave, to prove how far he could help himself and indeed be self-made. His absolute dependence on God was not to be forced on him. If it was really to be a thing of moral worth and true blessedness, it must be his deliberate and voluntary choice. And this now is the reason why there was a first and a second covenant, so that at first man's desires and efforts might be fully awakened and time given for him to make full proof of what his human nature, with the aid of outward instruction and miracles and means of grace, could accomplish. When his utter powerlessness, his hopeless captivity under the power of sin, had been discovered, there came the New Covenant, in which God was to reveal how man's true liberty from sin and self and the creature, his true nobility and Godlikeness, was to be found in the most entire and absolute dependence—*in God's being and doing all within him.*

In the very nature of things, there was no other way possible for God than this in dealing with a being He had endowed with the Godlike power of a will. And all the weight this reason for the divine procedure has in God's dealing with His people as a whole, it equally has in dealing with the individual. The two covenants represent two stages of God's education of man and of man's seeking after God. The progress and transition from the one to the other is not merely chronological or historical, but also organic and spiritual. In greater or lesser degree, it is seen in every member of the body, as well as in the body as a whole. Under the Old Covenant, there were men in whom, by anticipation, the powers of the coming redemption worked mightily. In the New Covenant, there are men in whom the spirit of the Old still makes itself manifest. The New Testament proves, in some of its most important epistles—especially those to the Galatians, Romans, and Hebrews—how possible it is within the New Covenant still to be held firmly in the bondage of the Old.

This is the teaching of the passage from which our text is taken. In the home of Abraham, the father of the faithful, Ishmael and Isaac are both found—the one born of a slave, the other of a free woman; the one after the flesh and the will of man, the other through the promise and the power of God; the one only for a time, then to be cast out, the other to be heir of all. A picture held up to the Galatians of the life they were leading as they trusted to the flesh and its religion, making a fair show, proved by their being led captive to sin to be not of the free but of the servant woman. Only through faith in the promise and the mighty quickening power of God could they—could any of them—be made truly and fully free and stand in the freedom with which Christ has made us free.

> *It is by the Holy Spirit—who came forth from that Holiest of all, where Christ had entered to bring its life to us and make us one with it—that we can have the power to live and walk always with the consciousness of God's presence in us.*

As we proceed to study the two covenants in the light of this and other scriptures, we shall see how they are indeed the divine revelation of two systems of religious worship, each with its spirit or life-principle ruling every man who professes to be a Christian. We shall see how the one great cause of the weakness of so many Christians is just this: that the Old Covenant spirit of bondage still has the mastery. And we shall see that nothing but a spiritual insight, with a whole-hearted acceptance and a living experience of all the New Covenant engages *that God will work in us,* can possibly enable us for walking as God would have us do.

This truth of there being two stages in our service of God, two degrees of nearness in our worship, is typified in many things in the Old Covenant worship—perhaps nowhere more clearly than in the difference between the Holy Place and the Most Holy Place in the temple, with the veil separating them. Into the former the priests might always enter to draw near to God. And yet they might not come too near, because the veil kept them at a distance. To enter within that was death. Once a year, the high priest might enter, as a promise of the time when the veil would be taken away and the full access to dwell in God's presence was given to His people. In Christ's death, the veil of the temple was torn in two, and His blood gives us boldness and power to enter into the Holiest of all and live there day by day in the immediate presence of God. It is by the Holy Spirit—who came forth from that Holiest of all, where Christ had entered to bring its life to us and make us one with it—that we can have the power to live and walk always with the consciousness of God's presence in us.

It is therefore not only in Abraham's home that there were the types of the two covenants—the spirit of bondage and the spirit of liberty—but even in God's home in the temple. The priests didn't yet possess the liberty of access into the Father's presence. Not only among the Galatians, but everywhere throughout the Church, there are to be found two classes of Christians. Some are content with the mingled life: half flesh and half spirit, half self-effort and half grace. Others are not content with this, but are seeking with their whole heart to fully know what the deliverance from sin and what the abiding full power for a walk in God's presence are, which the New Covenant has brought and can give. God help us all to be satisfied with nothing less.[1]

For Further Thought

1. *Why did God make two covenants with humankind—the Old Covenant and the New Covenant?*
2. *What is God's main glory? What does this teach you about His nature and His love?*
3. *What are the two classes of Christians in this chapter, and what is the most important way in which they differ in their approach to God?*

---

[1] See Note A, on the second blessing.

3

THE FIRST COVENANT

"Now therefore, if you will indeed obey My voice and keep
My covenant, then you shall be a special treasure to Me."
EXODUS 19:5

"He declared to you His covenant which He commanded
you to perform, the Ten Commandments."
DEUTERONOMY 4:13

"Because you listen to these judgments, and keep and do them. . .
the LORD your God will keep with you the covenant."
DEUTERONOMY 7:12

"I will make a new covenant with the house of Israel and with
the house of Judah—not according to the covenant that I made
with their fathers. . .My covenant which they broke."
JEREMIAH 31:31–32

WE have seen how the reason for there being two covenants is to be found in the need of giving the divine and the human will each their due place in the working out of man's destiny. God always takes the initiative. Man must then have the opportunity to do his part and to prove either what he can do or needs to have done for him. The Old Covenant was on the one hand indispensably necessary to awaken man's desires, to call forth his efforts, to deepen the sense of dependence on God, to convince of his sin and powerlessness, and so to prepare him to feel the need of the salvation of Christ.

In the significant language of Paul, "The law was our tutor *to bring us* to Christ" (Gal. 3:24). "We were kept under guard by the law, kept for the faith which would afterward be revealed" (3:23). To understand the Old Covenant correctly, we must always remember its two great characteristics—the one, that it was of divine appointment, filled with much true blessing, and *absolutely indispensable* for the working out of God's purposes; the other, that it was only provisional and preparatory for something higher, and therefore *absolutely insufficient* for giving that full salvation that man needs if his heart or the heart of God is to be satisfied.

Note now the terms of this first Covenant. "*If you* will indeed obey My voice and keep My covenant, then you shall be a special treasure to Me." Or, as it is expressed in Jeremiah, "Obey My voice, and I will be your God" (7:23; 11:4). Obedience everywhere, especially in the book of Deuteronomy, appears as the condition of blessing. "A blessing if you obey" (see 11:27).

Some may ask how God could make a covenant when He knew man could not keep it. The answer opens up to us the whole nature and object of the Covenant. All education, divine or human, deals with its pupils on the principle that faithfulness in the less is essential to the attainment of the greater. In taking Israel into His training, God dealt with them as men in whom, with all the ruin sin had brought, there still was a conscience to judge between good and evil, a heart capable of being stirred to long after God, and a will to choose the good and to choose Himself.

> *S*ome may ask how God could make a covenant when He knew man could not keep it. The answer opens up to us the whole nature and object of the Covenant.

Before Christ and His salvation could be revealed and understood and truly appreciated, these faculties of man had to be stirred and awakened. The law took men into its training, and sought, if I may use the expression, to make the very best that could be made of them by external instruction. In the provision made in the law for a symbolic atonement and pardon, in all God's revelation of Himself through priest and prophet and king, in His interposition in providence and grace, everything was done that He could do to touch and win the heart of His people and to give force to the appeal to their self-interest or their gratitude, their fear or their love.

Its work was not without fruit. Under the law, administered by the grace that always accompanied it, there was trained up a number of men whose great mark was the fear of God and a desire to walk blamelessly in all His commandments. And yet, as a whole, scripture represents the Old Covenant as a failure. The law had promised life, but it could not give it (Deut. 4:1; Gal. 3:21). The real purpose for which God had given it was the very opposite: It was meant by Him as a "ministry of death" (2 Cor. 3:7). He gave it that it might convince man of his sin and might so waken the confession of his powerlessness and of his need of a New Covenant and a true redemption.

It is in this view that scripture uses such strong expressions—"By the law is *the knowledge of sin. . .*that *every mouth* may be stopped, and *all the world* may become guilty before God" (Rom. 3:20, 19). "The law *brings about wrath*" (Rom. 4:15). "The law entered that the *offense might abound*" (Rom. 5:20). "That sin through the commandment might become *exceedingly sinful*" (Rom. 7:13). "For as many as are of the works of the law are *under the curse*" (Gal. 3:10). "We were kept under guard by the law, kept for the faith which would afterward be revealed" (Gal. 3:23). "Therefore the law was our tutor *to bring us* to Christ, that we might be justified by faith" (Gal. 3:24). The great work of the law was to reveal what sin was—its hatefulness as accursed of God, its misery in working temporal and eternal ruin, its power, binding man down in hopeless slavery, and the need of a divine interposition as the only hope of deliverance.

In studying the Old Covenant, we should always keep in mind the twofold aspect under which we have seen that scripture represents it. It was God's grace that gave Israel the law and fashioned the law to make it work out its purpose in individual believers and in the people as a whole. The whole of the Old Covenant was a school of grace, an elementary school to prepare for the fullness of grace and truth in Christ Jesus. A name is generally given to an object according to its most important feature. And so the Old Covenant is called a ministry of condemnation and death, not because there was no grace in it—it had its own glory (2 Cor. 3:10–12)—but because the law with its curse was the predominant element.

The combination of the two aspects we find with especial clearness in Paul's epistles. So he speaks of all who are of the works of the law as under the curse (Gal. 3:10). And then almost immediately after that, he speaks of the law as being our benefactor, a schoolmaster to bring us to Christ, into whose charge as to a tutor or governor we had been given until the time appointed by the Father. We are everywhere brought back to what we said above. The Old Covenant is absolutely indispensable for the preparatory work it had to do, but utterly insufficient to work for us a true or a full redemption.

The two great lessons God desires to teach us by it are very simple. The one is the lesson of *sin*, the other the lesson of *holiness*. The Old Covenant attains its objective only as it brings men to a sense of their utter sinfulness and their hopeless inability to deliver themselves. As long as they have not learned this, no offer of the New Covenant life can take hold of them. As long as an intense longing for deliverance from sinning has not been brought about, they will naturally fall back into the power of the law and the flesh. The holiness that the New Covenant offers will terrify rather than attract them. And the life in the spirit of bondage appears to make more allowance for sin, because obedience is declared to be impossible.

The other is the lesson of holiness. In the New Covenant, the Triune God engages to do all. He undertakes to give and keep the new heart, to give His own Spirit in it, and to give the will and the power to obey and do His will. As the one demand of the first Covenant was the sense of sin, the one great demand of the New is faith that the need created by the discipline of God's law will be met in a divine and supernatural way. The law cannot work out its purpose unless it brings a man to lie guilty and helpless before the holiness of God. There the New finds him and reveals that same God in His grace accepting him and making him partaker of His holiness.

This book is written with a very practical purpose. Its object is to help believers to know the wonderful New Covenant of grace that God has made with them and to lead them into the living and daily enjoyment of the blessed life it secures for them. The practical lesson taught to us by the fact that there was a first Covenant, that its one special work was to convince of sin, and that without it the New Covenant could not come is just what many Christians need. At conversion, they were convinced of sin by the Holy Spirit. But this had mainly reference to the guilt of sin and, in some degree, to its hatefulness. But a real knowledge of the power of sin, of their entire and utter inability to cast it out or to work in themselves what is good, is what they did not learn immediately. And until they have learned this, they cannot possibly enter fully into the blessing of the New Covenant. It is when a man sees that as little as he could raise himself from the dead can he make or keep his own soul alive that he becomes capable of appreciating the New Testament promise and is made willing to wait on God to do all in him.

Do you, my reader, feel that you are not fully living in the New Covenant, that there is still somewhat of the Old Covenant spirit of bondage in you? Then come and let the Old Covenant finish its work in you. Accept its teaching that all your efforts are failures. As, at conversion, you were content to fall down as a condemned, death-deserving sinner, be content now to sink down before God in the confession that as His redeemed child, you still feel yourself utterly unable to do and be what you see He asks of you. And begin to ask whether the New Covenant does not perhaps have a provision you have not yet understood for meeting your powerlessness and giving you the strength to do what is well-pleasing to God. You will find the wonderful answer in the assurance that God, by His Holy Spirit, undertakes to work everything in you. The longing to be delivered from the life of daily sinning, and the extinction of all hope to secure this by our efforts as Christians, will prepare us for understanding and accepting God's new way of salvation: Himself working in us all that is pleasing in His sight.

For Further Thought

1. *What was God's true purpose for the Old Covenant? For what did it prepare humankind?*
2. *What, according to scripture, is the Old Covenant's most important shortfall when it comes to bringing sinful man into the presence of a holy God?*
3. *In light of the Old Covenant, how should you see yourself in your relationship with God?*

4
THE NEW COVENANT

"But this is the covenant that I will make with the house of Israel
after those days, says the LORD: I will put My law in their minds,
and write it on their hearts; and I will be their God, and they shall
be My people. No more shall every man teach his neighbor, and every
man his brother, saying, 'Know the LORD,' for they all shall
know Me, from the least of them to the greatest of them,
says the LORD. For I will forgive their iniquity,
and their sin I will remember no more."
JEREMIAH 31:33–34

ISAIAH has often been called the evangelical prophet, because of the wonderful clearness with which he announces the coming Redeemer, both in His humiliation and suffering, and in the glory of the kingdom He was to establish. And yet it was given to Jeremiah, in this passage, and to Ezekiel, in the parallel one, to foretell what would actually be the outcome of the Redeemer's work and the essential character of the salvation He was to accomplish, and with a distinctness that is nowhere found in the older prophet.

In words that the New Testament (Hebrews 8) takes as the divinely inspired revelation of what the New Covenant is of which Christ is the Mediator, God's plan is revealed and we are shown what it is that He will do in us to make us fit and worthy of being the people of whom He is the God. Through the whole of the Old Covenant, there was always one trouble: man's heart was not right with God. In the New Covenant, the evil is to be remedied. Its central promise is a heart delighting in God's law and capable of knowing and holding fellowship with Him. Let us mark the fourfold blessing spoken of.

1. *"I will put My law in their minds, and write it on their hearts."* Let us understand this well. In our inward parts, or in our heart, there are no separate chambers in which the law can be put while the rest of the heart can be given up to other things. The heart is a unity. Nor are the inward parts and the heart like a house, which can be filled with things of an entirely different nature from what the walls are made of, without any living organic connection. No, the inward parts, the heart, are the disposition, the love, the will, the life. Nothing can be put into the heart, and especially by God, without entering and taking possession of it,

without securing its affection and controlling its whole being. And this is what God undertakes to do in the power of His divine life and operation: to breathe the very spirit of His law into and through the whole inward being.

hrough the whole of the Old Covenant, there was always one trouble: man's heart was not right with God. In the New Covenant, the evil is to be remedied.

"I will put My law in their minds, and write it on their hearts." At Sinai, the tablets of the Covenant, with the law written on them, were of stone, a lasting substance. It is easy to know what that means. The stone was set wholly apart for this one thing—to carry and show this divine writing. The writing and the stone were inseparably connected. And so the heart in which God gets His way and writes His law in power lives only and wholly to carry that writing, and is unchangeably identified with it. So alone can God realize His purpose in creation and have His child of one mind and one spirit with Himself, delighting in doing His will.

When the Old Covenant with the law engraved on stone had done its work in the discovering and condemning of *sin*, the New Covenant would give in its stead the life of obedience and true holiness of heart. The whole of the Covenant blessing centers in this—the heart being put right and made fit to know God: "Then I will give them *a heart to know Me*, that I *am* the LORD; and they shall be My people, and I will be their God, for they shall return to Me *with their whole heart*" (Jer. 24:7).

2. "*And I will be their God, and they shall be My people.*" Do not pass these words lightly. They occur chiefly in Jeremiah and Ezekiel in connection with the promise of the everlasting Covenant. They express the very highest experience of the Covenant relationship. It is only when God's people learn to love and obey His law, when their heart and life are together wholly devoted to Him and His will, that He can be to them the altogether inconceivable blessing that these words express, "*I will be your God.*" All I am and have as God shall be yours. All you can need or wish for in a God, I will be to you. In the fullest meaning of the word, I, the Omnipresent, will be always present with you in all My grace and love. I, the Almighty One, will each moment work all in you by My mighty power. I, the Three-times-Holy One, will reveal My sanctifying life within you. I will be your God. *And you shall be My people,* saved and blessed, ruled and guided and provided for by Me, known and seen to be indeed the people of the Holy One, the God of glory. Only let us give our hearts time to meditate and wait for the Holy Spirit to work in us all that these words mean.

3. "*No more shall every man teach his neighbor, and every man his brother, saying, 'Know the LORD,' for they all shall know Me, from the least of them to the greatest of*

them, says the LORD.*"* Individual personal fellowship with God, for the weakest and the least, is to be the wonderful privilege of every member of the New Covenant people. Each one will know the Lord. That does not mean the knowledge of the mind—that is not the equal privilege of all, and that in itself may hinder the fellowship more than help it—but with the knowledge that means appropriation and assimilation, and which is eternal life.

As the Son knew the Father because He was one with Him and dwelled in Him, the child of God will receive by the Holy Spirit that spiritual illumination that will make God to him the One he knows best because he loves Him most and lives in Him. The promise "They shall all be taught by God" (John 6:45; Isa. 54:13) will be fulfilled by the Holy Spirit's teaching. God will speak to each out of His Word what he needs to know.

4. *"For I will forgive their iniquity, and their sin I will remember no more."* The word *for* shows that this is the reason of all that precedes. Because the blood of this New Covenant was of such infinite worth, and its Mediator and High Priest in heaven of such divine power, there is promised in it such a divine blotting out of sin that God cannot remember it. It is this entire blotting out of sin that cleanses and sets us free from its power so that God can write His law in our hearts and show Himself in power as our God and, by His Spirit, reveal to us His deep things—the deep mystery of Himself and His love. It is the atonement and redemption of Jesus Christ accomplished outside us and for us that has removed every obstacle and made it fitting for God, and made us fit, that the law in the heart, and the claim on our God and the knowledge of Him, should now be our daily life and our eternal portion.

> *W*hen the Old Covenant with the law engraved on stone had done its work in the discovering and condemning of Sin, the New Covenant would give in its stead the life of obedience and true holiness of heart.

Here we now have the divine summary of the New Covenant inheritance. The last-named blessing, the pardon of sin, is the first in order and the root of all. The second, having God as our God, and the third, the divine teaching, are the fruit. The tree itself that grows on this root and bears such fruit is what is named first—the law in the heart.[2]

The central demand of the Old Covenant, "Obey My voice, and I will be your God," has now been met. With the law written in the heart, He can be our God and we shall be His people. Perfect harmony with God's will—holiness in heart and life—is the only thing that can satisfy God's heart or ours. And it is this the New Covenant gives in divine power: "Then I will give *them a heart* to know Me. . .and they shall be My people, and I will be their God, for they shall

---

[2] On the law written in the heart, see Note B.

return to Me *with their whole heart.*" It is on the state of the heart, it is on the new heart, as *given by God,* that the New Covenant life hinges.

But why, if all this is meant to be literally and exactly true of God's people, do we see so little of this life and experience so little of it in ourselves? There is only one answer: Because of your unbelief! We have spoken of the relationship of God and man in creation as what the New Covenant is meant to make possible and real. But the law that God will not compel cannot be repealed. He can only fulfill His purpose as the heart is willing and accepts His offer.

> *W*hen God teaches us the meaning of His promises in a heart yielded to His Holy Spirit, only then we can believe and receive them in a power that makes them a reality in our life.

In the New Covenant, all is of faith. Let us turn away from what human wisdom and human experience may say, and ask God Himself to teach us what His Covenant means. If we persevere in this prayer in a humble and teachable spirit, we can count most certainly on its promise: "No more shall every man teach his neighbor, and every man his brother, saying, 'Know the LORD,' for they all shall know Me." *The teaching of God Himself, by the Holy Spirit, to make us understand what He says to us in His Word is our Covenant right.* Let us count on it. It is only by a God-given faith that we can appropriate these God-given promises. And it is only by a God-given teaching and inward illumination that we can see their meaning in such a way that we believe them. When God teaches us the meaning of His promises in a heart yielded to His Holy Spirit, only then we can believe and receive them in a power that makes them a reality in our life.

But is it really possible, amid the wear and tear of daily life, to walk in the experience of these blessings? Are they really meant for all God's children? Let us rather ask the question, "Is it possible for God to do what He has promised?" The one part of the promise we believe—the complete and perfect pardon of sin. Why should we not believe the other part—the law written in the heart and the direct divine fellowship and teaching?

We have been so accustomed to separating what God has joined together—the objective, outward work of His Son, and the subjective, inward work of His Spirit—that we consider the glory of the New Covenant above the Old to consist chiefly in the redeeming work of Christ for us, and not equally in the sanctifying work of the Spirit in us. It is because of this ignorance and unbelief in the indwelling of the Holy Spirit, as the power through whom God fulfills the New Covenant promises, that we do not really expect them to be made true to us.

Let us turn our hearts away from all past experience of failure, *as caused by nothing but unbelief,* and let us admit fully and heartily what failure has taught us—namely the absolute impossibility of even a regenerate man walking in God's law in his own strength—and then turn our hearts quietly and trustfully to our own Covenant God. Let us hear *what* He says He will do for us, and believe Him. Let us rest on His unchangeable faithfulness and the surety of the Covenant, on His almighty power and the Holy Spirit working in us. And let us give up ourselves to Him as our God. He will prove that what He has done for us in Christ is not one bit more wonderful than what He will do in us every day by the Spirit of Christ.

FOR FURTHER THOUGHT

1. *What does God's New Covenant give you personally that the Old was incapable of giving?*
2. *How—or through whom—are you to personally receive the promises of God in His two covenants?*
3. *How do you think God intended for you to walk in and experience the blessings He promised His people through His covenants?*

5

THE TWO COVENANTS—
IN CHRISTIAN EXPERIENCE

*For these [women] are the two covenants: the one from Mount Sinai
which gives birth to bondage, which is Hagar—for this Hagar is
Mount Sinai in Arabia, and corresponds to Jerusalem which now is,
and is in bondage with her children—but the Jerusalem above is free,
which is the mother of us all. . . . So then, brethren, we are not
children of the bondwoman but of the free. . . . Stand fast therefore
in the liberty by which Christ has made us free,
and do not be entangled again with a yoke of bondage.*
GALATIANS 4:24–26, 31; 5:1

THE house of Abraham was the Church of God of that age. The division in his house—one son, his own son, but born after the flesh, the other after the promise—was a divinely ordained manifestation of the division there would be in all ages between the children of the bondwoman, those who served God in the spirit of bondage, and those who were children of the free and served Him in the Spirit of His Son.

The passage teaches us what the whole epistle confirms: that the Galatians had become entangled with a yoke of bondage and were not standing fast in the freedom with which Christ makes free indeed. Instead of living in the New Covenant, in the Jerusalem that is from above and in the liberty that the Holy Spirit gives, their whole walk proved that though they were Christians, they were of the Old Covenant, which produces children of bondage. The passage teaches us the great truth, which it is of the utmost importance for us to apprehend thoroughly: that a man with a measure of the knowledge and experience of the grace of God may prove, by a legalistic spirit, that he is yet practically to a large extent under the Old Covenant. And it will show us with wonderful clarity what the proofs are of the absence of the true New Covenant life.

A careful study of the epistle shows us that the difference between the two covenants is seen in three things. *The law and its works* are contrasted with the hearing of faith, *the flesh and its religion* with the flesh crucified, and *the inability toward good* with a walk in the liberty and the power of the Spirit. May the Holy Spirit reveal to us this twofold life.

The first antithesis we find in Paul's words, "Did you receive the Spirit by the works of the law, or by the hearing of faith?" (Gal. 3:2). These Galatians had indeed been born into the New Covenant and had received the Holy Spirit. But they had been led away by Jewish teachers and, though they had been justified by faith, they were seeking to be sanctified by works. They were looking to the observance of the law for the maintenance and the growth of their Christian life. They had not understood that, equally with the beginning, the progress of the divine life is alone by faith, that it day by day receives its strength from Christ alone, and that in Jesus Christ nothing benefits but faith working by love.

> The proof that our religion is very much that of the religious flesh is that the sinful flesh will be found to flourish along with it.

Almost every believer makes the same mistake as the Galatian Christians. Very few learn immediately at conversion that it is only by faith that we stand, walk, and live. They have no understanding of the meaning of Paul's teaching about being dead to the law and freed from the law—about the freedom with which Christ makes us free. "All who are led by the Spirit are not under the law" (see Gal. 5:18). Regarding the law as a divine ordinance for our direction, they consider themselves prepared and made fit by conversion to take up the fulfillment of the law as a natural duty. They do not know that in the New Covenant, the law written in the heart needs an unceasing faith in a divine power to enable us by a divine power to keep it. They cannot understand that it is not to the law but to a Living Person that we are now bound, and that our obedience and holiness are only possible by the unceasing faith in His power constantly working in us. It is only when this is seen that we are prepared truly to live in the New Covenant.

The second word that reveals the Old Covenant spirit is the word *flesh*. Its contrast is the flesh crucified. Paul asks: "Are you so foolish? Having begun in the Spirit, are you now being made perfect by the flesh?" (Gal. 3:2). "Flesh" means our sinful human nature. At his conversion, the Christian has generally no idea of the terrible evil of his nature and the subtlety with which it offers itself to take part in the service of God. It may be most willing and diligent in God's service for a time. It may devise numberless observances for making His worship pleasing and attractive. And yet this may all be only what Paul calls "mak(ing) a good showing in the flesh" (Gal. 6:12), "boasting in the flesh" (see Gal. 6:13), in man's will and man's efforts. This power of the religious flesh is one of the great marks of the Old Covenant religion. It misses the deep humility and spirituality of the true worship of God—a heart and life entirely dependent on Him.

The proof that our religion is very much that of the religious flesh is that the sinful flesh will be found to flourish along with it. It was that way with the Galatians. While they were making a fair show in the flesh, and boasting in it, their daily life was full of bitterness, envy, hatred, and other sins. They were biting and devouring one another. Religious flesh and sinful flesh are one, so it is no wonder that, with a great deal of religion, temper and selfishness and worldliness are so often found side by side. The religion of the flesh cannot conquer sin.

What a contrast to the religion of the New Covenant! What is the place the flesh has there? "Those *who are* Christ's have crucified the flesh with its passions and desires" (Gal. 5:24). Scripture speaks of the will of the flesh, the mind of the flesh, and the lust of the flesh—all this the true believer has seen to be condemned and crucified in Christ because he has given it over to the death. He not only accepts the Cross, with its bearing of the curse and its redemption from it, as his entrance into life, but he glories in it as his only power day by day to overcome the flesh and the world. "I have been crucified with Christ" (Gal. 2:20). "God forbid that I should boast except in the cross of our Lord Jesus Christ, by whom the world has been crucified to me, and I to the world" (Gal. 6:14). Even as nothing less than the death of Christ was needed to establish the New Covenant and the resurrection life that animates it, there is no entrance into the true New Covenant life other than by a partaking of that death.

> *A*s long as grace is principally connected with pardon and the entrance into the Christian life, the flesh is the only power in which to serve and work.

"Fallen from grace" (Gal. 5:4). This is a third word that describes the condition of these Galatians in that bondage in which they were really powerless to all true good. Paul is not speaking of a final falling away here, for he still addresses them as Christians, but of their having wandered from that walk in the way of enabling and sanctifying grace, in which a Christian can get the victory over sin. As long as grace is principally connected with pardon and the entrance into the Christian life, the flesh is the only power in which to serve and work. But when we know what exceeding abundance of grace has been provided and how God "is able to make all grace abound toward you, that you. . .may have an abundance for every good work" (2 Cor. 9:8), we know that as it is by faith, so too it is by grace alone that we stand a single moment or take a single step.

The contrast to this life of powerlessness and failure is found in the one word: "the Spirit." "If you are led by the Spirit, you are not under the law" (Gal. 5:18), with its demand on your own strength. "Walk in the Spirit, and you shall not"—a definite, certain promise—"you shall not fulfill the lust of the flesh" (Gal. 5:16).

The Spirit gives liberty from the law, from the flesh, from sin. "The fruit of the Spirit is love, joy, peace" (Gal. 5:22). Of the New Covenant promise, "I will put *My Spirit* within you and *cause* you to walk in My statutes, and *you will keep* My judgments and do them" (Ezek. 36:27), the Spirit is the center and the sum. He is the power of the supernatural life of true obedience and holiness.

And what would have been the course that the Galatians would have taken if they had accepted this teaching of St. Paul? As they hear his question, "But now after you have known God. . .how *is it that* you turn again to the weak and beggarly elements, to which you desire again to be in bondage?" (Gal. 4:9), they would have felt that there was only one course. Nothing else could help them but to immediately turn back again to the path they had left. At the point where they had left it, they could enter again. With any one of them who wished to do so, this turning away from the Old Covenant legal spirit and the renewed surrender to the Mediator of the New Covenant could be the act of a moment—one single step. As the light of the New Covenant promise dawned on him and he saw how Christ was to be all, and faith all, and the Holy Spirit in the heart all, and the faithfulness of a Covenant-keeping God all in all, he would feel that he had but one thing to do—in utter inability to yield himself to God, and in simple faith to count on Him to perform what He had spoken.

In Christian experience there may be still the Old Covenant life of bondage and failure. In Christian experience there may be a life that gives way entirely to the New Covenant grace and spirit. In Christian experience, when the true vision has been received of what the New Covenant means, a faith that rests fully on the Mediator of the New Covenant can enter immediately into the life that the Covenant secures.

I cannot too earnestly beg all believers who long to know to the utmost what the grace of God can accomplish in them to study carefully the question as to whether the acknowledgment that our being in the bondage of the Old Covenant is the reason of our failure, and whether a clear insight into the possibility of an entire change in how we relate to God is not what is needed to give us the help we seek. We may be seeking for our growth in a more diligent use of the means of grace and a more earnest striving to live in accordance with God's will, and yet entirely fail.

The reason is that there is a secret root of evil that must be removed. That root is the spirit of bondage, the legalistic spirit of self-effort, which hinders that humble faith that knows that God will accomplish all and yields to Him to do it. That spirit may be found amid very great zeal for God's service and very earnest prayer for His grace. It does not enjoy the rest of faith and cannot overcome sin because it does not stand in the liberty with which Christ has made us free, and because it does not know that where the Spirit of the Lord is, there is liberty. There the soul can say: "The law of the Spirit of life in Christ Jesus *has made me free* from the law of sin and death" (Rom. 8:2). When once we admit heartily not only that there are failings in our life but that there is something radically wrong that can be changed, we shall turn with a new interest, with a deeper confession of ignorance and powerlessness, and with a hope that looks to God alone for teaching and strength to find that in the New Covenant there is an actual provision for every need.

FOR FURTHER THOUGHT

1. *What evidence shows that a Christian, who is to live under God's New Covenant, still approaches his faith and his relationship with God under Old Covenant thinking and living?*
2. *What must your faith overcome in order for you to walk and live in God's New Covenant blessings? How is it to be overcome?*
3. *What specific blessings can you receive when you begin to live, walk, and worship under a New Covenant faith?*

6

THE EVERLASTING COVENANT
OF THE SPIRIT

"They shall be My people, and I will be their God. . . . And I will
make an everlasting covenant with them, that I will not turn
away from doing them good; but I will put My fear in their
hearts so that they will not depart from Me."
JEREMIAH 32:38, 40

"I will give you a new heart and put a new spirit
within you; I will take the heart of stone out of your flesh
and give you a heart of flesh. I will put My Spirit
within you and cause you to walk in My statutes,
and you will keep My judgments and do them. . . .
Moreover I will make a covenant of peace with them,
and it shall be an everlasting covenant with them."
EZEKIEL 36:26–27; 37:26

WE have had the words of the institution of the New Covenant. Let us listen
to the further teaching we have concerning it in Jeremiah and Ezekiel, where God
speaks of it as an everlasting covenant.

In every covenant there are two parties. And the very foundation of a covenant
rests on the thought that each party is to be faithful to the part it has undertaken
to perform. Unfaithfulness on either side breaks the covenant.

It was this way with the Old Covenant. God had said to Israel, "Obey My
voice, and I will be your God" (Jer. 7:23; 11:4). These simple words contained
the whole Covenant. And when Israel disobeyed, the Covenant was broken. The
question of Israel being able or not able to obey was not taken into consideration.
Disobedience forfeited the privileges of the Covenant.

If a New Covenant were to be made, and if that was to be better than the
Old, this was the one thing to be provided for. No New Covenant could be of any
profit unless provision was made for securing obedience. Obedience there must
be. God as Creator could never take His creatures into His favor and fellowship

unless they obeyed Him. The thing would have been an impossibility. If the New Covenant is to be better than the Old, if it is to be an everlasting covenant, never to be broken, it must make some sufficient provision for securing the obedience of the Covenant people.

And this is indeed the glory of the New Covenant, the glory that excels, that this provision has been made. In a way that no human thought could have devised, by a stipulation that never entered into any human covenant, by an undertaking in which God's infinite condescension and power and faithfulness are to be most wonderfully exhibited, by a supernatural mystery of divine wisdom and grace, the New Covenant provides a guarantee not only for God's faithfulness, *but for man's too*! And this in no other way than by God Himself undertaking to secure man's part as well as His own. Do try to grasp this.

It is just because this, the essential part of the New Covenant, so exceeds and confounds all human thoughts of what a covenant means that Christians, from the Galatians downward, have not been able to see and believe what the New Covenant really brings. They have thought that human unfaithfulness was a factor permanently to be understood as something utterly unconquerable and incurable, and that the possibility of a life of obedience, with the witness from within of a good conscience and from above of God's pleasure, was not to be expected. They have therefore sought to stir the mind to its utmost by arguments and motives, but never realized how the Holy Spirit is to be the unceasing, universal, all-sufficient worker of everything that has to be produced by the Christian.

> *When* the Old Covenant with the law engraved on stone had done its work in the discovering and condemning of sin, the New Covenant would give in its stead the life of obedience and true holiness of heart.

Let us ask God earnestly that He would reveal to us by the Holy Spirit the things that He has prepared for those who love Him, things that have not entered into the heart of man: the wonderful life of the New Covenant. All depends on our knowledge of what God will accomplish in us. Listen to what God says in Jeremiah of the two parts of His everlasting Covenant shortly after He had announced the New Covenant, and in further illumination of it. The central thought of that, *that the heart is to be made right,* is here repeated and confirmed. "I will make an everlasting covenant with them, *that I will not turn away from doing them good."* That is, God will be unchangeably faithful. He will not turn from us. "But *I will put My fear in their hearts so that they will not depart from Me."* This is the second half: Israel will be unchangeably faithful too. And that because God will so put His fear in their hearts that they will not depart from Him. *As little as God will turn from them, will they depart from Him!* As faithfully as He undertakes for the fulfillment of His part, will He undertake for the fulfillment of their part, so that they shall not depart from Him!

Listen to God's word in Ezekiel in regard to one of the terms of His Covenant of peace, His everlasting Covenant (Ezek. 34:25; 36:27; 37:26): "I will put My Spirit within you and *cause you to walk in My statutes, and you will keep* My judgments and do them." In the Old Covenant we have nothing of this sort. You have, on the contrary, from the story of the golden calf and the breaking of the Tablets of the Covenant onward the sad fact of continual departure from God. We find God longing for what He so desired to see but was not to be found. "Oh, that they had such a heart in them that they would fear Me and always keep all My commandments" (Deut. 5:29). We find throughout the book of Deuteronomy a thing without parallel in the history of any religion or religious lawgiver: that Moses most distinctly prophesies their forsaking of God, with the terrible curses and scattering that would come upon them. It is only at the close of his warnings that he gives the promise of the new time that would come: "And the LORD your God will circumcise your heart. . .to love the LORD your God with all your heart and with all your soul. . . . And *you will again obey* the voice of the LORD" (Deut. 30:6, 8).

The whole Old Covenant was dependent on man's faithfulness: "The LORD your God. . .*keeps covenant*. . .with those *who*. . .*keep* His commandments" (Deut. 7:9). God's keeping the Covenant accomplished little if man did not keep it. Nothing could help man until the "*If you earnestly keep*" of the law was replaced by the word of promise, "I will put My Spirit within you. . .and *you will keep* My judgments and do them." The one supreme difference of the New Covenant, the one thing for which the Mediator, the Blood, and the Spirit were given, the one fruit God sought and Himself engaged to bring forth was this: a heart filled with His fear and love, a heart to cling to Him and not depart from Him, a heart in which His Spirit and His law dwell, a heart that delights to do His will.

> *A* heart in perfect harmony with Himself, a life and walk in His way—God has engaged in Covenant to work this in us.

Here is the innermost secret of the New Covenant. It deals with the heart of man in a way of divine power. It doesn't just appeal to the heart by every motive of fear or love, of duty or gratitude. That the law also did. But it reveals God Himself cleansing our heart and making it new—changing it entirely from a stony heart into a heart of flesh, a tender, living, loving heart, putting His Spirit within it—and so, by His almighty power and love, breathing and working in it, making the promise true, "I *will*. . .*cause you* to walk in My statutes, and *you will keep* My judgments." A heart in perfect harmony with Himself, a life and walk in

His way—God has engaged in Covenant to work this in us. He undertakes for our part in the Covenant as much as for His own.

This is nothing but the restoration of the original relationship between God and the man He had made in His likeness. He was on earth to be the very image of God, because God was to live and to work all in him, and he to find his glory and blessedness in this way owing everything to God. This is the exceeding glory of the New Covenant, of the Pentecostal dispensation: that by the Holy Spirit, God could now again be the indwelling life of His people and so make the promise a reality: "I will. . .cause you to walk in My statutes."

With God's presence secured to us every moment of the day—"I will not turn away from them"—with God's "fear put into our heart" by His own Spirit, and our heart therefore responding to His holy presence, with our hearts therefore made right with God, we can and we shall walk in His statutes and keep His judgments.

Let us ask God earnestly that He would reveal to us by the Holy Spirit the things that He has prepared for those who love Him, things that have not entered into the heart of man: the wonderful life of the New Covenant.

My brethren, the great sin of Israel under the Old Covenant, by which they greatly grieved Him, was this: They "limited the Holy One of Israel" (Ps. 78:41). Under the New Covenant there is no less danger of this sin. *It makes it impossible for God to fulfill His promises.* Let us seek, above everything, for the Holy Spirit's teaching to show us exactly what God has established the New Covenant for so that we may honor Him by believing all that His love has prepared for us.

And if we ask for the cause of the unbelief that prevents the fulfillment of the promise, we shall find that it is not far to seek. It is, in most cases, the lack of desire for the promised blessing. In all who came to Jesus on earth, the intensity of their desire for the healing they needed made them ready and glad to believe in His word. Where the law has done its full work, where the actual desire to be freed from every sin is strong and masters the heart, the promise of the New Covenant, when it is really understood, comes like bread to a starving man.

The subtle unbelief that thinks it is impossible to be kept from sinning cuts away the power of accepting the provision of the everlasting Covenant. God's Word, "I will put My fear in their hearts so that *they will not* depart from Me," and "I will put My Spirit within you. . .and *you will* keep My judgments," is understood in some weak sense, according to our experience and not according to what the Word and what God means. And the soul settles down into despair or self-contentment that says it can never be otherwise and makes true conviction for sin impossible.

Let me say to every reader who desires to be able to believe fully all that God says. Cherish every whisper of the conscience and of the Spirit who convicts of sin. Whatever it be—a quick temper, a sharp word, an unloving or impatient thought, or anything of selfishness or self-will—cherish that which condemns it in you as part of the schooling that is to bring you to Christ and the full possession of His salvation.

The New Covenant is meant to meet the need for a power of not sinning, which the Old could not give. Come with that need, and it will prepare and open the heart for all the everlasting Covenant has given you. It will bring you to that humble and entire dependence on God in His omnipotence and His faithfulness, in which He can and will work all He has promised.

FOR FURTHER THOUGHT

1. *How do you know for certain that God will keep each and every one of His New Covenant promises?*
2. *What, according to this chapter, is the main reason so many believers fail to live under God's New Covenant blessings?*
3. *How does the New Covenant give you the power to defeat sin in your life?*

7

THE NEW COVENANT:
A MINISTRY OF THE SPIRIT

You are an epistle of Christ, ministered by us,
written not with ink but by the Spirit of the living God,
not on tablets of stone but on tablets of flesh, that is, of the heart. . . .
[God] also made us sufficient as ministers of the new covenant,
not of the letter but of the Spirit; for the letter kills, but the Spirit
gives life. But if the ministry of death, written and engraved on
stones, was glorious. . .how will the ministry of the Spirit not be more
glorious? For if the ministry of condemnation had glory, the ministry
of righteousness exceeds much more in glory. For even what was made
glorious had no glory in this respect, because of the glory that excels.
2 CORINTHIANS 3:3, 6–10

IN this wonderful chapter, Paul reminds the Corinthians, as he speaks of his ministry among them, of what its chief characteristics were. As a ministry of the New Covenant, he contrasts it, and the whole dispensation of which it is part, with that of the Old. The Old was graven in stone, the New in the heart. The Old could be written in ink and was in the letter that kills, the New of the Spirit that makes alive. The Old was a ministry of condemnation and death, the New of righteousness and life.

The Old indeed had its glory, for it was of divine appointment and brought its divine blessing. But it was a glory that passed away, and had no glory by reason of the glory that excels, the exceeding glory of that which remains. With the Old, there was the veil on the heart, but in the New, the veil is taken away from the face and the heart, the Spirit of the Lord gives liberty, and, reflecting with unveiled face the glory of the Lord, we are changed from glory to glory into the same image, as by the Spirit of the Lord. The glory that excels proved its power in this: that it not only marked the dispensation on its divine side, but so exerted its power in the heart and life of its subjects that it was seen in them, too, as they were changed by the Spirit into Christ's image, from glory to glory.

Think a moment of the contrast. The Old Covenant was of the letter that kills.

The law came with its literal instruction and sought by the knowledge it gave of God's will to appeal to man's fear and his love, to his natural powers of mind and conscience and will. It spoke to him as if he could obey so that it might convince him of what he did not know—that he could not obey. And so it fulfilled its mission: "And the commandment, which *was* to *bring* life, I found to *bring* death" (Rom. 7:10). In the New, on the contrary, how different was everything. Instead of the letter, the Spirit who gives life, who breathes the very life of God—the life of heaven into us. Instead of a law engraved in stone, the law written in the heart worked into the heart's affection and powers, making it one with them. Instead of the vain attempt to work from the outside in, the Spirit and the law are put into the inner parts, there to work outward in life and walk.

> With the Old, there was the veil on the heart, but in the New, the veil is taken away from the face and the heart, the Spirit of the Lord gives liberty, and, reflecting with unveiled face the glory of the Lord, we are changed from glory to glory.

This passage brings into view that which is the distinctive blessing of the New Covenant. In working out our salvation, God bestowed on us two wonderful gifts. We read: *"God sent forth His Son,* born of a woman, born under the law, to redeem those who were under the law, that we might receive the adoption as sons. And because you are sons, *God has sent forth the Spirit of His Son* into your hearts, crying out, 'Abba, Father!'"* (Gal. 4:4–6). Here we have the two parts of God's work in salvation. The one, the more objective, what He did that we might become His children: He sent forth His Son. The second, the more subjective, what He did that we might live like His children: He sent forth the Spirit of His Son into our hearts. In the former we have the external manifestation of the work of redemption. In the other, we have its inward appropriation—the former for the sake of the latter. These two halves form one great whole, which may not be separated.

In the promises of the New Covenant, as we find them in Jeremiah and Ezekiel as well as in our text and many other passages of scripture, it is obvious that God's great object in salvation is to get possession of the heart. The heart is the real life. With the heart a man loves, wills, and acts. The heart makes the man. God made man's heart for His own dwelling so that in it He might reveal His love and His glory. God sent Christ to accomplish a redemption by which man's heart could be won back to Him. Nothing but that could satisfy God. And that is what is accomplished when the Holy Spirit makes the heart of God's child what it should be.

The whole work of Christ's redemption—His atonement and victory, His exaltation and intercession, His glory at the right hand of God—is only preparatory to what is the chief triumph of His grace: the renewal of the heart to be the temple of God. Through Christ, God gives the Holy Spirit to glorify Him in the heart by working there all that He has done and is doing for the soul.

In a great deal of our religious teaching, a fear—unless we should detract from the honor of Christ—has been alleged as the reason for giving His work for us, on the cross or in heaven, a greater prominence than His work in our heart by the Holy Spirit. The result has been that the indwelling of the Holy Spirit, and His mighty work as the life of the heart, is very little known in true power. If we look carefully at what the New Covenant promises mean, we shall see how the "sending forth of the Spirit of His Son into our hearts" is indeed the consummation and crown of Christ's redeeming work. Let us just think of what these promises imply.

In the Old Covenant, man had failed in what he had to do. In the New, God is to do everything in him. The Old could only convict of sin. The New is to put it away and cleanse the heart from its filthiness. In the Old, it was the heart that was wrong. For the New, a new heart is provided, into which God puts His fear and His law and His love. The Old demanded but failed to secure obedience. In the New, God causes us to walk in His judgments. The New is to fit man for a true holiness, a true fulfillment of the law of loving God with the whole heart and our neighbors as ourselves, a walk truly well-pleasing to God. The New changes a man from glory to glory after the image of Christ. All because the Spirit of God's Son is given into the heart. The Old gave no power, but in the New, all is by the Spirit, the mighty power of God. As complete as the reign and power of Christ on the throne of heaven is His dominion on the throne of the heart by His Holy Spirit given to us.[3]

It is as we bring all these traits of the New Covenant life together into one focus, and look at the heart of God's child as the object of this mighty redemption, that we shall begin to understand what is secured to us and what it is that we are to expect from our Covenant God. We shall see in what the glory of the ministry of the Spirit consists, even in this: that God can fill our heart with His love and make it His home.

We are accustomed to saying, and truly so, that the worth of the Son of God, who came to die for us, is the measure of the worth of the soul in God's sight and of the greatness of the work that had to be done to save it. Let us even so see that the divine glory of the Holy Spirit, the Spirit of the Father and the Son, is the measure of God's longing to have our heart wholly for Himself, of the glory of the work that is to be produced within us, and of the power by which that work will be accomplished.

We shall see how the glory of the ministry of the Spirit is no other than the glory of the Lord, as it is not only in heaven but also resting on us and dwelling in us and changing us into the same image from glory to glory. The inconceivable glory of our exalted Lord in heaven has its counterpart here on earth in the exceeding glory of the Holy Spirit who glorifies Him in us, who lays His glory on

[3] See Note C, on George Müller.

us as He changes us into His likeness.

The New Covenant has no power to save and to bless except as it is a ministry of the Spirit. That Spirit works in lesser or greater degree as He is neglected and grieved, or yielded to and trusted. Let us honor Him and give Him His place as the Spirit of the New Covenant by expecting and accepting all He waits to do for us.

He is the great gift of the Covenant. His coming from heaven was the proof that the Mediator of the Covenant was on the throne in glory and could now make us partakers of the heavenly life.

He is the only Teacher of what the Covenant means: Dwelling in our heart, He awakens there the thought and the desire for what God has prepared for us.

He is the Spirit of faith, who enables us to believe the otherwise incomprehensible blessing and power in which the New Covenant works, and to claim it as our own.

He is the Spirit of grace and of power, by whom the obedience of the Covenant and the fellowship with God can be maintained without interruption.

He (the Holy Spirit) Himself is the Possessor and the Bearer and the Communicator of all the Covenant promises, the Revealer and the Glorifier of Jesus, its Mediator and Surety.

To believe fully in the Holy Spirit as the present and abiding and all-comprehending gift of the New Covenant has been to many an entrance into its fullness of blessing.

Begin now, child of God, to give the Holy Spirit the place in your religion He has in God's plan. Be still before God and believe that He is within you, and ask the Father to work in you through Him. Regard yourself, your spirit as well as your body, with holy reverence as His temple. Let the consciousness of His holy presence and working fill you with holy calm and fear. And be sure that all God calls you to be, Christ through His Spirit will accomplish in you.

For Further Thought

1. *How does God remove the veil that had for all of human history stayed between Himself and His own people?*

2. *How does the New Covenant allow and enable you to succeed in living the life God calls you to live as a believer?*

3. *How does God reveal and communicate His New Covenant blessings to believers today?*

8

THE TWO COVENANTS:
THE TRANSITION

*Now may the God of peace who brought up our Lord Jesus from
the dead, that great Shepherd of the sheep, through the blood of the
everlasting covenant, make you complete in every good work
to do His will, working in you what is well pleasing
in His sight, through Jesus Christ.*
HEBREWS 13:20–21

THE transition from the Old Covenant to the New was not slow or gradual,
but by a tremendous crisis. Nothing less than the death of Christ was the close of
the Old. Nothing less than His resurrection from the dead, through the blood of
the everlasting Covenant, the opening of the New. The path of preparation that
led up to the crisis was long and slow—the tearing of the veil, which symbolized
the end of the old worship, was the work of a moment. By a death, once for all,
Christ's work as fulfiller of law and prophets and as the end of the law was forever
finished. By a resurrection in the power of an endless life, the Covenant of Life
was ushered in.

These events have an infinite significance, as revealing the character of the covenants they are related to. The death of Christ shows the true nature of the Old
Covenant, which is elsewhere called a "ministry of death" (2 Cor. 3:7). It brought
forth nothing but death. It ended in death, because only by death could the life that
had been lived under it be brought to an end. The New was to be a Covenant of Life.
It had its birth in the omnipotent resurrection power that brought Christ from the
dead. Its one mark and blessing is that all it gives comes not only as a promise, but
as an experience in the power of an endless life. The death reveals the utter *ineffectiveness* and *insufficiency* of the Old. The life brings near and imparts to us forever all
that the New has to offer. An insight into the completeness of the transition, as seen
in Christ, prepares us for understanding the reality of the change in our life, when,
"just as Christ was raised from the dead by the glory of the Father, even so we also
should walk in newness of life" (Rom. 6:4).

The complete difference between the life in the Old and the New is remarkably illustrated by a previous passage in the epistle (Heb. 9:16). After having said that a death for the redemption of transgressions had to take place before the New Covenant could be established, the writer adds, "For where there is a testament, there must also of necessity be the death of the testator."[4] Before any heir can obtain the legacy, its first owner, the testator, must have died. The old proprietorship, the old life, must disappear entirely before the new heir, the new life, can enter into the inheritance. Nothing but death can work the transference of the property. It is even so with Christ, with the Old and the New Covenant life, with our own deliverance from the Old and our entrance into the New. Now, having been made dead to the law by the body of Christ, we have been discharged from the law, having died to that in which we were held—here is the completeness of the deliverance from Christ's side; "so that we should serve"—here is the completeness of the change in our experience—"in the newness of the Spirit and not *in* the oldness of the letter" (Rom. 7:6).

> By a death, once for all, Christ's work as fulfiller of law and prophets and as the end of the law was forever finished. By a resurrection in the power of an endless life, the Covenant of Life was ushered in.

The transition, if it is to be real and whole, must take place by a death. As with Christ the Mediator of the Covenant, so with His people, the heirs of the Covenant. In Him we are dead to sin; in Him we are dead to the law. Just as Adam died to God, and we inherit a nature actually and really dead in sin, dead to God and His kingdom, so in Christ we died to sin and inherit a nature actually dead to sin and its dominion. It is when the Holy Spirit reveals and makes real to us this death to sin and to the law, too, as the one condition of a life to God, that the transition from the Old to the New Covenant can be fully realized in us. The Old was, and was meant to be, a "ministry of death," and until it has completely done its work in us, there is no complete release from its power.

The man who sees that self is incurably evil and must die, who gives self utterly to death as he sinks before God in utter helplessness and in the surrender to His working, who consents to death with Christ on the cross as his desert, and who in faith accepts it as his only deliverance—he alone is prepared to be led by the Holy Spirit into the full enjoyment of the New Covenant life. He will learn to understand how completely death makes an end to all self-effort, and how, as he lives in Christ to God, everything from that moment on is to be the work of God Himself.

See how beautifully our text brings out this truth that just as much as Christ's resurrection out of death was the work of God Himself, our life is equally to be

[4] The Greek word for covenant and testament is the same. This is the only passage where the allusion to a testator makes the meaning of the word *testament* a necessity. Everywhere else, the King James Version has rightly used "covenant."

wholly God's own work. No more direct and wonderful than was in Christ the transition from death to life is to be in us the experience of what the New Covenant life is to bring. Notice the subject of the two verses. In verse 20 we have what God *has done* in raising Christ from the dead; in verse 21, what God *is to do in us*, working in us what is pleasing to Him: (20) "The God of peace who brought up our Lord Jesus from the dead, that great Shepherd of the sheep, (21) make you complete in every good work to do His will, working in you what is well pleasing in His sight, through Jesus Christ."

> *J*ust as He raised Christ from the dead, the God of the everlasting Covenant can and will now make you perfect in every good thing to do His will, working in you that which is well-pleasing in His sight through Jesus Christ.

We have the name of our Lord Jesus twice. In the first case, it refers to what God has done to Christ for us, raising Him, and in the second, to what God is doing through Christ in us, working His pleasure in us. Because it is the same God continuing in us the work He began in Christ, it is in us just what it was in Christ. In Christ's death, we see Him in utter helplessness allowing and counting on God to work all and give Him life. God accomplished the wonderful transition. In us we see the same. It is only as we give ourselves to that death, too, as we entirely cease from self and its works, and as we lie, as in the grave, waiting for God to work all, that the God of resurrection life can work in us all His good pleasure.

It was "through the blood of the everlasting covenant," with its atonement for sin and its destruction of sin's power, that God achieved that resurrection. It is through that same blood that we are redeemed and freed from the power of sin and made partakers of Christ's resurrection life. The more we study the New Covenant, the more we shall see that its one aim is to restore man out of the Fall and to the life in God for which he was created. It does this first by delivering him from the power of sin in Christ's death, and then by taking possession of his heart and his life for God to work all in him by the Holy Spirit.

The whole argument of the epistle to the Hebrews as to the Old and New Covenants is here summed up in these concluding verses. Just as He raised Christ from the dead, the God of the everlasting Covenant can and will now make you perfect in every good thing to do His will, working in you that which is well-pleasing in His sight through Jesus Christ. Your doing His will is the object of creation and redemption. God's working it all in you is what redemption has made possible. The Old Covenant of law and effort and failure has ended in condemnation and death. The New Covenant is coming to give, in all whom the law has slain and brought to bow in their utter powerlessness, the law written in the heart, the Spirit dwelling there, and God working all, both to will and to do, through Jesus Christ.

Oh, for a divine revelation that the transition from Christ's death, in its powerlessness, to His life in God's power, is the image, the pledge, the power of our transition out of the Old Covenant, when it has slain us, to the New, with God working in us all in all!

The transition from Old to New, as accomplished in Christ, was sudden. Is it so in the believer? Not always. In us it depends on a revelation. There have been cases in which a believer, sighing and struggling against the yoke of bondage, has in one moment had it revealed to him what a complete salvation the New Covenant brings to the heart and the inner life through the ministry of the Spirit. Then, by faith, he has entered immediately into his rest. There have been other cases in which, gradual as the dawn of day, the light of God has risen upon the heart. God's offer of entrance into the enjoyment of our New Covenant privileges is always urgent and immediate. Every believer is a child of the New Covenant and an heir of all its promises. The death of the Testator gives him full right to immediate possession. God longs to bring us into the land of promise. Let us not come short through unbelief.

There may be someone who can hardly believe that such a mighty change in his life is within his reach, and yet who desires to know what he is to do if there is to be any hope of his attaining it. I have just said the death of the testator gives the heir immediate right to the inheritance. And yet the heir, if he be a minor, does not enter into the possession. A term of years ends the stage of minority on earth, and he is no longer under guardians. In the spiritual life, the state of pupilage ends not with the expiration of years, but at the moment the minor proves his fitness for being made free from the law by accepting the liberty there is in Christ Jesus. The transition—as with the Old Testament, as with Christ, as with the disciples—comes when the time is fulfilled and all things are now ready.

But what is one to do who is longing to be made ready for this? Accept your death to sin in Christ, and act it out. Acknowledge the sentence of death on everything that is of nature. Take and keep the place before God of utter unworthiness and helplessness. Sink down before Him in humility, meekness, patience, and resignation to His will and mercy.[5] Fix your heart on the great and mighty God, who in His grace will work in you above what you can ask or think, and will make you a monument of His mercy. Believe that every blessing of the Covenant of grace is yours, because by the death of the Testator you are entitled to it all—and on that faith act, knowing that all is yours.

The new heart is yours. The law written in the heart is yours. The Holy Spirit, the seal of the Covenant, is yours. Act on this faith, and count on God as faithful and able and, oh, so loving, to reveal and make true in you all the power and glory of His everlasting Covenant.

May God reveal to us the difference between the two lives under the Old and

[5] If you want to understand the full meaning of this clause and know how to practice its teaching, consult a little book just published, *Dying to Self: A Golden Dialogue*, by William Law, with notes by Rev. Andrew Murray (Nisbet & Co.). See also Note D.

the New—the resurrection power of the New, with God working all in us, and the power of the transition secured to us in death with Christ and life in Him. And may He teach us at once to trust Christ Jesus for a full participation in all the New Covenant secures.

FOR FURTHER THOUGHT

1. *What events ushered in both the end of the Old Covenant and the beginning of the New?*
2. *What specific steps should you take in order to be made ready to receive the inheritance promised you under the New Covenant?*
3. *Under the New Covenant, what specific gifts from God are yours?*

9

THE BLOOD OF THE COVENANT

"This is the blood of the covenant
which the LORD has made with you."
EXODUS 24:8 (cf. HEBREWS 9:20)

"This cup is the new covenant in My blood."
1 CORINTHIANS 11:25 (cf. MATTHEW 26:28)

The blood of the covenant by which he was sanctified.
HEBREWS 10:29

The blood of the everlasting covenant.
HEBREWS 13:20

THE blood is one of the strangest, the deepest, the mightiest, and the most heavenly of the thoughts of God. It lies at the very root of both covenants, but especially of the New Covenant. The difference between the two covenants is the difference between the blood of animals and the blood of the Lamb of God! The power of the New Covenant has no lesser measure than the worth of the blood of the Son of God! Your Christian experience ought to know of no standard of peace with God, and purity from sin, and power over the world, than the blood of Christ can give! If we desire to enter truly and fully into all the New Covenant is meant to be to us, let us pray and ask God to reveal to us the worth and the power of the blood of the Covenant: the precious blood of Christ!

The First Covenant was not brought in without blood. There could be no covenant of friendship between a holy God and sinful men without atonement and reconciliation—and no atonement without a death as the penalty of sin. God said: "I have given [the blood] to you upon the altar to make atonement for your souls; for it is the blood that makes atonement for the soul" (Lev. 17:11). The blood shed in death meant the death of a sacrifice slain for sin of man, and the blood sprinkled on the altar meant that vicarious death accepted by God for the sinful one. No forgiveness, no covenant without blood-shedding.

All this was but a type and shadow of what was one day to become a mysterious reality. What no thought of man or angel could have conceived, what even now passes all understanding: the eternal Son of God took flesh and blood and then shed that blood as the blood of the New Covenant, not merely to ratify it, but to open the way for it and to make it possible. Yes, more, to be in time and eternity the living power by which entrance into the Covenant was to be obtained and all life in it to be secured. Until we learn to form our expectation of a life in the New Covenant according to the inconceivable worth and power of the blood of God's Son, we never can have even an insight into the entirely supernatural and heavenly life that a child of God may live. Let us think for a moment on the threefold light in which scripture teaches us to regard it.

In the passage from Hebrews, we read, "And for this reason He is the Mediator of the new covenant, by means of death, for the redemption of the transgressions under the first covenant, that those who are called may receive the promise of the eternal inheritance" (9:15). The sins of the ages, of the First Covenant, which had only figuratively been atoned for, had gathered up before God. A death was needed for the redemption of these. In that death and blood-shedding of the Lamb of God, not only were these atoned for, but the power of all sin was forever broken.

> *If we desire to enter truly and fully into all the New Covenant is meant to be to us, let us pray and ask God to reveal to us the worth and the power of the blood of the Covenant: the precious blood of Christ!*

The blood of the New Covenant is redemption blood, a purchase price and ransom from the power of sin and the law. In any purchase made on earth, the transference of property from the old owner to the new is complete. Its worth may be ever so great and the hold on it ever so strong that if the price is paid, it is gone forever from him who owned it. The hold sin had on us was terrible. No thought can realize its legitimate claim on us under God's law, its awful tyrant power in enslaving us. But the blood of God's Son has been paid. "You were not redeemed with corruptible things, *like* silver or gold, from your aimless conduct *received* by tradition from your fathers, but with the precious blood of Christ, as of a lamb without blemish and without spot" (1 Pet. 1:18–19).

We have been rescued, ransomed, and redeemed out of our old natural life under the power of sin—utterly and eternally. Sin has not the slightest claim on us, nor the slightest power over us, except when our ignorance or unbelief or half-heartedness allows it to have dominion. Our New Covenant birthright is to stand in the freedom with which Christ has made us free. Until the soul sees, desires, accepts, and claims the redemption and the liberty that has the blood of the Son of God for its purchase price, its measure, and its security, it never can fully live the New Covenant life.

As wonderful as the blood-shedding for our redemption is the blood-sprinkling for our cleansing. Here is indeed another of the spiritual mysteries of the New Covenant, which lose their power when understood in human wisdom, without the ministry of the Spirit of life. When scripture speaks of "having our hearts sprinkled from an evil conscience" (Heb. 10:22), of "the blood of Christ cleansing our conscience" (see Heb. 9:14), and of our singing here on earth "to Him who loved us and washed us from our sins in His own blood" (Rev. 1:5), it brings this mighty, quickening blood of the Lamb into direct contact with our hearts. It gives the assurance that that blood, in its infinite worth, in its divine sin-cleansing power, can keep us clean in our walk in the sight and the light of God. It is as this blood of the New Covenant is known, trusted, waited for, and received from God in the Spirit's mighty operation in the heart that we shall begin to believe that the blessed promise of a New Covenant life and walk can be fulfilled.

There is one more thing scripture teaches concerning this blood of the New Covenant. When the Jews contrasted Moses with our Lord Jesus, He said: "Unless you eat the flesh of the Son of Man and drink His blood, you have no life in you. . . . He who eats My flesh and drinks My blood abides in Me, and I in him" (John 6:53, 56). As if the redeeming, sprinkling, washing, and sanctifying do not sufficiently express the intense inwardness of its action and its power to permeate our whole being, the drinking of this precious blood is declared to be indispensable to having life. If we desire to enter deep into the Spirit and power of the New Covenant, let us, by the Holy Spirit, drink deeply of this cup—the cup of the New Covenant in His blood.

On account of sin there could be no covenant between man and God without blood. And no New Covenant without the blood of the Son of God. As the cleansing away of sins was the first condition in making a covenant, so it is equally the first condition of an entrance into it. It has always been found that a deeper appropriation of the blessings of the Covenant must be preceded by a new and deeper cleansing from sin. We know how in Ezekiel the words about God's causing us to walk in His statutes are preceded by "*I will cleanse you from all your filthiness*" (36:25). And then later we read, "They shall not defile themselves anymore with their idols, nor with their detestable things, nor with any of their transgressions; *I will but. . .cleanse them.* Then they shall be My people, and I will be their God. . . . Moreover I will make a covenant of peace with them, and it shall be an everlasting covenant with them" (37:23, 26). The confession and casting away, then the cleansing away of sin in the blood are the indispensable but all-sufficient preparation for a life in everlasting covenant with God.

Many feel that they do not understand or realize this wonderful power of the blood. Much thought does not help them, and even prayer does not appear to bring the light they seek. The blood of Christ is a divine mystery that passes all thought. Like every spiritual and heavenly blessing, this, too—but this especially—needs to be imparted to us by the Holy Spirit. It was "through the eternal Spirit" (Heb. 9:14) that Christ offered the sacrifice in which the blood was shed. The blood had the life of Christ, the life of the Spirit, in it. The outpouring of the blood for us was to prepare the way for the outpouring of the Spirit on us.

> *Until the soul sees, desires, accepts, and claims the redemption and the liberty that has the blood of the Son of God for its purchase price, its measure, and its security, it never can fully live the New Covenant life.*

It is the Holy Spirit, and He alone, who can minister the blood of the everlasting Covenant in power. Just as He leads the soul to the initial faith in the pardon that blood has purchased and the peace it gives, He leads further to the knowledge and experience of its cleansing power. Here again, too, by faith—a faith in a heavenly power, of which it does not fully understand and cannot define the action, but of which it knows that it is an operation of God's mighty power and accomplishes a cleansing that gives a clean heart. A clean heart, first known and accepted by the same faith—apart from signs or feelings, apart from sense or reason—and then experienced in the joy and the fellowship with God it brings. Oh, let us believe in the blood of the everlasting Covenant and the cleansing the Holy Spirit ministers. Let us believe in the ministry of the Holy Spirit, until our whole life in the New Covenant becomes entirely His work, to the glory of the Father and of Christ.

The blood of the Covenant—O mystery of mysteries! O grace above all grace! O mighty power of God, opening the way into the holiest, and into our hearts, and into the New Covenant, where the Holy One and our heart meet! Let us ask God much, by His Holy Spirit to make us know what it is and what it does within us. The transition from the death of the Old Covenant to the life of the New was, in Christ, "through the blood of the everlasting covenant." It will not be otherwise with us.

FOR FURTHER THOUGHT

1. *How has God not only atoned for your sins, but also broken the power of sin in you forever?*

2. *Read John 6:53–56. What condition does Jesus lay out for those who desire to live a life of abiding in Him? What does that condition mean to you?*

3. *How has God imparted to you the gift of the blood of the Second Covenant— Christ's blood? What does that say to you concerning your relationships with all three Persons of the Three-One God?*

10

JESUS, THE MEDIATOR OF
THE NEW COVENANT

"I will keep You and give You as a covenant to the people."
ISAIAH 42:6; (cf. 49:8)

"And the Lord, whom you seek,
will suddenly come to His temple, even the Messenger
of the covenant, in whom you delight."
MALACHI 3:1

By so much more Jesus has become a surety of a better covenant.
HEBREWS 7:22

He is also Mediator of a better covenant, which was established
on better promises. . . . The Mediator of the new covenant. . . .
You have come. . .to Jesus the Mediator of the new covenant.
HEBREWS 8:6; 9:15; 12:22, 24

WE have here four titles given to our Lord Jesus in connection with the New Covenant. He is Himself called a Covenant. The union between God and man, which the Covenant aims at, was accomplished in Him personally. In Him, the reconciliation between the human and divine was perfectly effected. In Him, His people find the Covenant with all its blessings. He is all that God has to give, and is the assurance that it is given. . . . He is called the Messenger of the Covenant, because He came to establish and to proclaim it. . . . He is the Surety of the Covenant, not only because He paid our debt, but as He is Surety to us for God that He will fulfill His part and Surety for us with God that we will fulfill our part. . . . And He is Mediator of the Covenant, because as the Covenant was established in His atoning blood, is administered and applied by Him, and is entered on alone by faith in Him, so it is experimentally known only through the power of His resurrection life and His never-ceasing intercession. All these names point to the one truth: that in the New Covenant Christ is all in all.

The subject is so large that it would be impossible to enter on all the various aspects of this precious truth. Christ's actions in atonement and intercession, in His giving of pardon and the Holy Spirit, and in His daily communication of grace and strength are truths that lie at the very foundation of the faith of Christians. We don't need to speak of them here. What especially needs to be made clear to many is how, by faith in Christ as the Mediator of the New Covenant, we actually have access to and enter into the enjoyment of all its promised blessings.

Christ's actions in atonement and intercession, in His giving of pardon and the Holy Spirit, and in His daily communication of grace and strength are truths that lie at the very foundation of the faith of Christians.

We have already seen, in studying the New Covenant, how all these blessings culminate in the one thing—that the heart of man is to be put right, as the only possible way of his living in the favor of God and of God's love finding its satisfaction in him. That he is to receive a heart to fear God, to love God with all his strength, to obey God, and to keep all His statutes. All that Christ did and does has this for its aim, and all the higher blessings of peace and fellowship flow from this. In this God's saving power and love find the highest proof of their triumph over sin. Nothing so reveals the grace of God, the power of Jesus Christ, the reality of salvation, and the blessedness of the New Covenant as the heart of a believer, where sin once abounded but where grace now abounds more exceedingly within it.

I do not know how I can better set forth the glory of our blessed Lord Jesus as He accomplishes this, the real object of His redeeming work—and as He takes entire possession of the heart He has bought and won and cleansed as a dwelling for His Father—than by pointing out the place He takes and the work He does in the case of a soul who is being led out of the Old Covenant bondage, with its failure, into the real experience of the promise and power of the New Covenant.[6] In studying the work of the Mediator in an individual this way, we may get a truer idea of the real glory and greatness of the work He actually accomplishes than when we only think of the work He has done for all. It is in the application of the redemption here in the life of earth, where sin abounded, that its power is seen. Let us see how the entrance into the New Covenant blessing is attained.

The first step toward it in one who has been truly converted and assured of his acceptance with God is the sense of sin. He sees that the New Covenant promises are not made true in his experience. There is not only indwelling sin, but he finds that he gives way to temper, self-will, worldliness, and other known transgressions of God's law. The obedience to which God calls and will enable him, the life of abiding in Christ's love, which is his privilege, the power for a

[6] For a practical illustration in the life of Canon Battersby, see Note D.

holy walk that is well-pleasing to God—in all this his conscience condemns him. It is in this conviction of sin that any thought or desire of the full New Covenant blessing must have its rise.

Where the thought that obedience is an impossibility and that nothing but a life of failure and self-condemnation is to be looked for has produced a secret despair of deliverance or contentment with our present state, it is vain to speak of God's promise or power. The heart does not respond, for it knows well enough, it is sure, that the liberty spoken of is a dream. But where the dissatisfaction with our state has produced a longing for something better, the heart is open to receive the message.

The New Covenant is meant to be the deliverance from the power of sin, and a keen longing for this is the indispensable preparation for entering fully into the Covenant.

> *The New Covenant is meant to be the deliverance from the power of sin, and a keen longing for this is the indispensable preparation for entering fully into the Covenant.*

Now comes the second step. As the mind is directed to the literal meaning of the terms of the New Covenant—on its promises of cleansing from sin and a heart filled with God's fear and God's law and a power to keep God's commands and never to depart from Him—and as the eye is fixed on Jesus the Surety of the Covenant—who will Himself make it all true—and as the voice is heard of witnesses who can declare how after years of bondage all this has been fulfilled in them, the longing begins to grow into a hope, and the inquiry is made as to what is needed to enter this blessed life.

Then follows another step. The heart-searching question comes whether we are willing to give up every evil habit, all our own self-will, and all that is of the spirit of the world and surrender ourselves to be wholly and exclusively for Jesus. God cannot take so complete possession of a man, and bless him so wonderfully and work in him so mightily, unless He has him very completely—yes, wholly—for Himself. Happy is the man who is ready for any sacrifice.

Now comes the last, the simplest, and yet often the most difficult step. And here it is that we need to know Jesus as Mediator of the Covenant. As we hear of the life of holiness, obedience, and victory over sin, which the Covenant promises, and hear that it will be done for us according to our faith—so that if we claim it in faith it will surely be ours—the heart often fails because of fear. I am willing, but do I have the power to make and, what is more, to maintain this full surrender? Do I have the power, the strong faith, to so grasp and hold this offered blessing that it shall indeed be and continue to be mine?

How such questions perplex the soul—until it finds the answer to them in the one word: Jesus! *It is He who will give the power to make the surrender and to believe.* This is as surely and as exclusively His work, because atonement and intercession are His alone. As sure as it was His to win and to ascend the throne, it is His to prove His dominion in the individual soul. It is He, the Living One, who is in divine power to work and maintain the life of communion and victory within us. He is the Mediator and Surety of the Covenant—He, the God-man, who has undertaken not only for all God requires, but for all that we need, too.

When this is seen, the believer learns that here, just as at conversion, it is all from faith. The one thing needed now is, with the eye firmly fixed on some promise of the New Covenant, to turn from self and anything it could or need do, to let go of self and fall into the arms of Jesus. He is the Mediator of the New Covenant. It is His to lead us into it. In the assurance that Jesus, and every New Covenant blessing, is already ours by virtue of our being God's children—with the desire now to appropriate and enjoy what we have before now allowed to lie unused, in the faith that Jesus now gives us the needed strength in faith to claim and accept our heritage as a present possession—the will dares boldly to do the deed and to take the heavenly gift: a life in Christ according to the better promises. By faith in Jesus, you have seen and received Him in full faith as your Mediator of the New Covenant, both in heaven and in your heart. He is the Mediator who makes it true between God *and you,* as your experience.

> *H*e is the Mediator and Surety of the Covenant—He, the God-man, who has undertaken not only for all God requires, but for all that we need, too.

The fear has sometimes been expressed that if we press so urgently the work that Christ through the Spirit does in the heart, we may be drawn away from trusting in what He has done, and always is doing, to what we are experiencing of its working. The answer is simple. It is *with the heart alone* that Christ can be truly known or honored. It is *in the heart* that the work of grace is to be done and the saving power of Christ to be displayed. It is *in the heart* alone that the Holy Spirit has His sphere of work. *There* He is to work Christ's likeness, and *there* alone He can glorify Christ. The Spirit can only glorify Christ by revealing His saving power *in us.*

If we were to speak of what *we are to do* in cleansing our heart and keeping it right, the fear would be well-grounded. But the New Covenant calls us to the very opposite. What it tells us of the Atonement, and the righteousness of God it has won for us, will be our only glory, even amid the highest holiness of heaven: Christ's work of holiness here in the heart can only deepen the consciousness of that righteousness as our only plea.

The sanctification of the Spirit as the fulfillment of the New Covenant promises is all a taking of the things of Christ and revealing and imparting them to us. The deeper our entrance into and our possession of the New Covenant gift of a new heart, the fuller will be our knowledge and our love of Him who is its Mediator, and the more we shall glory in Him alone. The Covenant deals with the heart—just that Christ may be found there, may *dwell there by faith*. As we look at the heart, not in the light of feeling or experience, but in the light of the faith of God's Covenant, we shall learn to think and speak of it as God does, and we will begin to know what it means that there Christ manifests Himself and there He and the Father come to make their home.

FOR FURTHER THOUGHT

1. *What are two blessings that Christ imparted to you through the shedding of His blood?*
2. *What is Christ's true purpose for shedding His blood for you at Calvary? How does knowing that purpose change your faith in and approach to Him?*
3. *What are the three steps you must take in order to receive the blessings of the New Covenant?*

11

JESUS, THE SURETY OF
A BETTER COVENANT

*And inasmuch as He was not made priest without an oath...
by so much more Jesus has become a surety of a better covenant. ...
Therefore He is also able to save to the uttermost those
who come to God through Him, since He always
lives to make intercession for them.*
HEBREWS 7:20, 22, 25

A surety is one who stands good for another so that a certain engagement will be faithfully performed. Jesus is the Surety of the New Covenant. He stands as surety with us for God—so that God's part in the Covenant will faithfully be performed. And He stands as surety with God for us so that our part will be faithfully performed, too. If we are to live in covenant with God, everything depends on our knowing correctly what Jesus secures for us. The more we know and trust Him, the more assured will our faith be that its every promise and every demand will be fulfilled, and that a life of faithful keeping of God's Covenant is indeed possible, because Jesus is the Surety of the Covenant. He makes God's faithfulness and ours equally sure.

We read that it was because His priesthood was confirmed by the oath of God that He became the Surety of a so much better Covenant. The oath of God gives us the security that His suretyship will secure all the better promises. The meaning and infinite value of God's oath had been explained in the previous chapter. "An oath for confirmation is for them an end of all dispute. Thus God, determining to show more abundantly to the heirs of promise the immutability of His counsel, confirmed it by an oath, that by two immutable things, in which it is impossible for God to lie, we might have strong consolation" (Heb. 6:16–18). We therefore have not only a Covenant, including certain definite promises; we have not only Jesus, the Surety of the Covenant; but at the back of that again, we have the living God—with a view to our having perfect confidence in the unchangeableness of His counsel and promise—coming in between with an oath.

Do we not begin to see that the one thing God aims at in this Covenant, and asks with regard to it, is an absolute confidence that He is going to do all He has promised, however difficult or wonderful it may appear? His oath is an end of all fear or doubt. Let no one think of understanding the Covenant, of judging or saying what may be expected from it, much less of experiencing its blessings, until he meets God with an Abraham-like faith that gives Him the glory and is fully assured that what He has promised He is able to perform. The Covenant is a sealed mystery, except to the soul that is going without reserve to trust God and abandon itself to His word and work.

Of the work of Christ as the Surety of the better Covenant, our passage tells us that because of this priesthood confirmed by oath, He is able to save completely those who draw near to God through Him. And this because "He always lives to make intercession for them." As Surety of the Covenant, He is ceaselessly engaged in watching their needs and presenting them to the Father, in receiving His answer and imparting its blessing. It is because of this never-ceasing mediation, receiving and transmitting from God to us the gifts and powers of the heavenly world, that He is able to save completely—to work and maintain in us a salvation as complete as God is willing it should be, as complete as the better Covenant has assured us it shall be, and in the better promises on which it was established. These promises are expounded (Heb. 8:7–13) as being none other than those of the New Covenant of Jeremiah, with the law written in the heart by the Spirit of God as our experience of the power of that salvation.

> *Do we not begin to see that the one thing God aims at in this Covenant, and asks with regard to it, is an absolute confidence that He is going to do all He has promised, however difficult or wonderful it may appear?*

Jesus, the Surety of a better Covenant, Jesus is to be our assurance that everything connected with the Covenant is unchangeably and eternally sure. In Jesus, the keynote is given of all our communication with God, of all our prayers and desires, and of all our life and walk, that with full assurance of faith and hope we may look for every word of the Covenant to be made fully true to us by God's own power. Let us look at some of these things of which we are to be fully assured, if we are to breathe the spirit of children of the New Covenant.

There is the love of God. The very thought of a covenant is an alliance of friendship. And it is as a means of assuring us of His love, of drawing us close to His heart of love, and of getting our hearts under the power of His love and filled with it—it is because God loves us with an infinite love, and wants us to know it, and to give it complete liberty to bestow itself on us and bless us, that the New Covenant has been made and God's own Son been made its Surety. This love of God is an infinite divine energy that does its utmost to fill the soul with itself and its blessedness. Of this love God's Son is the Messenger, and of the Covenant in which God reveals it to us He is the Surety. Let us learn that the chief need in studying the Covenant and keeping it, in seeking and claiming its blessings, is the exercise of a strong and confident assurance in God's love.

Then there is the assurance of the sufficiency of Christ's finished redemption. All that was needed to put away sin, to free us entirely and forever from its power, has been accomplished by Christ. His blood and death, His resurrection and ascension, have taken us out of the power of the world and transplanted us into a new life in the power of the heavenly world. All this is divine reality. Christ is Surety that the divine righteousness and the divine acceptance, that all-sufficient divine grace and strength, are always and forever ours. He is Surety that all these can and will be communicated to us in unbroken continuation.

It is also so with the assurance of what is needed on our part to enter into this life in the New Covenant. We shrink back, either from the surrender of all, because we don't know whether we have the power to let it go, or from the faith for all, because we fear ours will never be so strong or so bold that it takes all that is offered us in this wonderful Covenant.

> *Let us believe that by the Holy Spirit the heart is His home and His throne. Let us, if we have not done it yet in a definite act of faith, throw ourselves utterly on Him for the whole of the New Covenant life and walk.*

Jesus is Surety of a better Covenant. The better consists just in this very thing: that it undertakes to provide the children of the Covenant with the very dispositions they need to accept and enjoy it. We have seen how the heart is just the central object of the Covenant promise. A heart circumcised to love God with all the heart, a heart into which God's law and fear have been put so that it will not depart from Him—it is of all this Jesus is the Surety under the oath of God. Let us say it once more: Surely the one thing God asks of us and has given the Covenant and its Surety to secure—*the confident trust that all will be done in us that is needed*—is what we don't dare withhold.

I think some of us are beginning to see what has been our great mistake. We have thought and spoken great things of what Christ did on the cross and does on the throne as Covenant Surety. And we have stopped there. *But we have not expected Him to do great things in our hearts.* And yet it is there, in our heart, that the consummation takes place of the work on the cross and the throne. In the heart, the New Covenant has its full triumph. The Surety is to be known not by what the mind can think of Him in heaven, but by what He does to make Himself known in the heart. *There* is the place where His love triumphs and is enthroned.

Let us with the heart believe and receive Him as the Covenant Surety. Let us, with every desire we entertain in connection with it, with every duty it calls us to, and with every promise it holds out, look to Jesus, under God's oath the Surety of the Covenant. Let us believe that by the Holy Spirit the heart is His home and His throne. Let us, if we have not done it yet in a definite act of faith, throw ourselves utterly on Him for the whole of the New Covenant life and walk. No surety was ever so faithful to his undertaking *as Jesus will be to His on our behalf, in our hearts.*

And now, notwithstanding the strong confidence and consolation the oath of God and the Surety of the Covenant gives, there are some still looking longingly at this blessed life, and yet afraid to trust themselves to this wondrous grace. They have an idea of faith as something great and mighty, and they know and feel that theirs is not that kind. And so their weakness remains an insurmountable barrier to their inheriting the promise.

Let me try to say once again: Brother, the act of faith by which you accept and enter this life in the New Covenant is not commonly an act of power, but often of weakness and fear and much trembling. And even in the midst of all this weakness, it is not an act in your strength, but in a secret and perhaps unfelt strength that Jesus the Surety of the Covenant gives you. God has made Him Surety, with the very object of inspiring us with courage and confidence. He longs and delights to bring you into the Covenant. Why not bow before Him and humbly say, "He does hear prayer. He brings into the Covenant. He enables a soul to believe. I may trust Him confidently." And just begin quietly to believe that there is an almighty Lord, given by the Father to do everything needed to make *all* Covenant grace wholly true in you. Bow low and look up out of your low state to your glorified Lord, and maintain your confidence that a soul in its nothingness trusts in Him and will receive more than it can ask or think.

Dear believer, come and be a believer. Believe that God is showing you how entirely the Lord Jesus wants to have you and your life for Himself, how entirely He is willing to take charge of you and work all in you, how entirely you may even now commit your trust, your surrender, and your faithfulness to the Covenant with all you are and are to be to Him, your blessed Surety. If you believe, you will see the glory of God. *What Christ has undertaken, you may confidently count on His performing.*

In a sense, measure, and power that passes knowledge, Jesus Christ is Himself all that God can either ask or give, all that God wants to see in us. *"He who believes in Me. . .out of his heart will flow rivers of living water"* (John 7:38).

For Further Thought

1. *Reread Hebrews 7:20–25. What benefit do you receive, both personally and individually, because Jesus is the "surety of a better covenant"?*
2. *What personal benefits do you receive from studying and claiming for yourself God's New Covenant promises?*
3. *How does God make your heart His home and throne? How does God impart the faith it takes for you to allow Him to make your heart His home and throne?*

12

THE BOOK OF THE COVENANT

Then he took the Book of the Covenant and read in the hearing
of the people. And they said, "All that the LORD has said
we will do, and be obedient." And Moses took the blood,
sprinkled it on the people, and said, "This is the
blood of the covenant which the LORD has made
with you according to all these words."
EXODUS 24:7–8 (cf. HEBREWS 9:18–20)

HERE is a new aspect in which to regard God's blessed Book. Before Moses
sprinkled the blood, he read the Book of the Covenant and obtained the people's
acceptance of it. And when he had sprinkled it, he said, "This is the blood of the
covenant which the LORD has made with you *according to all these words.*" The
Book contained all the conditions of the Covenant, and only through the Book
could they know all that God asked of them and all that they might ask of Him.
Let us consider what new light may be thrown both on the Covenant and on the
Book by the one thought that the Bible is the Book of the Covenant.

The very first thought suggested will be this: that in nothing will the spirit of
our life and experience, as it lives either in the Old or the New Covenant, be more
revealed than in our dealings with the Book. The Old as well as the New had a
book. Our Bible contains both. The New was enfolded in the Old, and the Old is
unfolded in the New. It is possible to read the Old in the spirit of the New, and it
is possible to read the New as well as the Old in the spirit of the Old.

What this spirit of the Old is, we cannot see so clearly anywhere as just in Israel when the Covenant was made. They were now ready to promise: "All that the
LORD has said we will do, and be obedient" (Exod. 24:7). There was so little sense
of their own sinfulness, or of the holiness and glory of God, that with perfect
self-confidence they considered themselves able to undertake to keep the Covenant. They understood little of the meaning of that blood with which they were
sprinkled, or of that death and redemption of which it was the symbol. In their
own strength, in the power of the flesh, they were ready to engage to serve God.

It is just the spirit in which many Christians regard the Bible—as a system
of laws, a course of instruction to direct us in the way God would have us go.

All He asks of us is that we should do our utmost in seeking to fulfill them. We cannot do more, and we are sincerely ready to do this. They know little or nothing of what the death means through which the Covenant is established, or what the life from the dead is through which alone a man can walk in covenant with the God of heaven.

This self-confident spirit in Israel is explained by what had happened just previously. When God had come down on Mount Sinai in thunderings and lightnings to give the law, they were greatly afraid. They said to Moses: "You speak with us, and we will hear; but let not God speak with us, lest we die" (Exod. 20:19). They thought it was simply a matter of hearing and knowing, that they could for certain obey. They didn't know that it is only the presence, the fear, the nearness, and the power of God humbling us and making us afraid that can conquer the power of sin and give the power to obey.

> *True obedience and fellowship with God, for which man was created but which sin broke off, which the law demanded but could not work, and which God's own Son came from heaven to restore in our lives, is now brought within our reach and offered us.*

It is so much easier to receive the instruction from man and live than to wait and hear the voice of God and die to all our own strength and goodness. It is no different from many Christians seeking to serve God without ever seeking to live in daily contact with Him, and without the faith that it is only His presence that can keep from sin. Their religion is a matter of outward instruction from man, and the waiting to hear God's voice that they may obey Him and the death to the flesh and the world that comes with a close walk with God are unknown. They may be faithful and diligent in their study of the Bible and in reading or hearing Bible teaching. But to have as much as possible of that personal interaction with the Covenant God Himself, which makes the Christian life possible—this they do not seek.

If you want to be delivered from all this, learn to always read the Book of the New Covenant in the New Covenant Spirit. One of the very first articles of the New Covenant has reference to this matter. When God says, "I will put My law in their minds, and write it on their hearts" (Jer. 31:33), He establishes that the words of His Holy Book shall no longer be mere outward teaching, but that what they command shall be our very disposition and delight, fashioned in us as a birth and a life by the Holy Spirit. Every word of the New Covenant then becomes a divine assurance of what may be obtained by the Holy Spirit's working. The soul learns to see that "the letter kills" (2 Cor. 3:6), that "the flesh profits nothing" (John 6:63). The study and knowledge of and the delight in Bible words and thoughts cannot profit unless the Holy Spirit is waited on to make them life. The acceptance of holy scripture in the letter, the reception of it in the human understanding, is seen to be as fruitless as was Israel's at Sinai. But as the Word of God, spoken by the living God through the Spirit into the heart that waits on Him, it is found to be quick and powerful. It then is a word that works effectually in those who believe (see 1 Thess. 2:13), giving within the heart the actual possession of the very grace of which the Word has spoken.

The New Covenant is a ministry of the Spirit (see chap. 7). All its teaching is meant to be teaching by the Holy Spirit. The two most remarkable chapters in the Bible on the preaching of the gospel are those in which Paul expounds on the secret of this teaching (1 Cor. 2; 2 Cor. 3). Every minister ought to see whether he can pass his examination in them. They tell us that in the New Covenant the Holy Spirit is everything. It is the Holy Spirit entering the heart, writing, revealing, and impressing on it God's law and truth that alone works true obedience. No excellence of speech or human wisdom can in the least profit. God must reveal by His Holy Spirit to preacher and hearer the things He has prepared for us.

What is true of the preacher is equally true of the hearer. One of the great reasons that so many Christians never come out of the Old Covenant, never even know that they are in it and have to come out of it, is that there is so much head knowledge without the power of the Spirit in the heart being waited for. It is only when preachers and hearers and readers believe that the Book of the New Covenant needs the Spirit of the New Covenant to explain and apply it that the Word of God can do its work.

> *The study and knowledge of and the delight in Bible words and thoughts cannot profit unless the Holy Spirit is waited on to make them life.*

Learn the double lesson. What God has joined together, let not man separate (Matt. 19:6). The Bible is the Book of the New Covenant. And the Holy Spirit is the only minister of what belongs to the Covenant. Do not expect to understand or profit by your Bible knowledge without seeking continually the teaching of the Holy Spirit. Be careful that you don't let your earnest Bible study, your excellent books, or your beloved teachers *take the place of the Holy Spirit*! Pray daily and perseveringly and believingly for His teaching. He will write the Word in your heart.

The Bible is the Book of the New Covenant. Ask the Holy Spirit to specially reveal to you the New Covenant in it. It is inconceivable what loss the Church of our day is suffering because so few believers truly live as its heirs in the true knowledge and enjoyment of its promises. Ask God, in humble faith, to give you in all your Bible reading the spirit of wisdom and revelation, to enlighten the eyes of your heart to know what the promises are that the Covenant reveals and what the divine security in Jesus, the Surety of the Covenant, so that every promise will be fulfilled in you in divine power; and what the intimate fellowship to which it admits you with the God of the Covenant. The ministry of the Spirit, humbly waited for and listened to, will make the Book of the Covenant shine with new light—even the light of God's countenance and a full salvation.

All this applies especially to the knowledge of what the New Covenant is actually meant to work. Amid all we hear, read, and understand of the different promises of the New Covenant, it is quite possible that we never yet have had that heavenly vision of it as a whole, that with its overmastering power it compels acceptance. Just hear once again what it really is. *True obedience and fellowship with God,* for which man was created but which sin broke off, which the law demanded but could not work, and which God's own Son came from heaven to restore in our lives, *are now brought within our reach and offered us.*

Our Father tells us in the Book of the New Covenant that He now expects us to live in full and unbroken obedience and communion with Him. He tells us that by the mighty power of His Son and Spirit, *He Himself will work this in us,* that everything has been arranged for it. He tells us that such a life of unbroken obedience is possible because Christ, as the Mediator, will live in us and enable us each moment to live in Him. He tells us that all He wants is simply the surrender of faith, the yielding of ourselves to Him to do His work.

Oh, let us look and see *this holy life, with all its powers and blessings, coming down from God in heaven, in the Son and His Spirit.* Let us believe that the Holy Spirit can give us a vision of it as a prepared gift to be bestowed in living power and take possession of us. Let us look upward and look inward, in the faith of the Son and the Spirit, and God will show us that every word written in the Book of the Covenant is not only true, but that it can be made spirit and truth within us and in our daily life. *This can indeed be.*

FOR FURTHER THOUGHT

1. *What role do the holy scriptures play in your relationship with God, with living the life He wants you to live as a believer?*
2. *What is the key to making your personal study of the Bible life to you, to making the words real and alive and profitable?*
3. *What has God's New Covenant done with regard to true fellowship and obedience to Him in all things?*

13

NEW COVENANT OBEDIENCE

"Now therefore, if you will indeed obey My
voice and keep My covenant, then you shall be
a special treasure to Me above all people."
EXODUS 19:5

"And the LORD your God will circumcise your heart and the heart of
your descendants, to love the LORD your God with all your heart and
with all your soul. . . . And you will again obey the voice of the LORD
and do all His commandments which I command you today."
Deuteronomy 30:6, 8

"I will put My Spirit within you and cause you to walk
in My statutes, and you will keep My judgments and do them."
EZEKIEL 36:27

IN making the New Covenant, God said very definitely, "Not according to the covenant that I made with their fathers" (Jer. 31:32). We have learned what the fault was with that Covenant: it made God's favor dependent on the obedience of the people. *"If you obey*, I will be your God." We have learned how the New Covenant remedied the defect: God Himself provided for the obedience. It changes *"If you keep* My judgments" into "I will put My Spirit within you, and *you will keep."* Instead of the Covenant and its fulfillment depending on man's obedience, God undertakes to ensure the obedience. The Old Covenant proved the need and pointed out the path of holiness, but the New inspires the love and gives the power of holiness.

In connection with this change, a serious and most dangerous mistake is often made. Because in the New Covenant, obedience no longer occupies the place it had in the Old—as the condition of the Covenant—and free grace has taken its place—justifying the ungodly and bestowing gifts on the rebellious—many are under the impression that obedience is now *no longer as indispensable as it was then.* The error is a terrible one.

The whole Old Covenant was meant to teach the lesson of the absolute and indispensable necessity of obedience for a life in God's favor. The New Covenant comes not to provide a substitute for that obedience in faith, but through faith to secure the obedience by giving a heart that delights in it and has the power for it. And men abuse the free grace that without our own obedience accepts us for a life of new obedience when they rest content with the grace but without the obedience it is meant for. They boast of the higher privileges of the New Covenant, while its chief blessing—*the power of a holy life, a heart delighting in God's law,* and a life in which God causes and enables us by His indwelling Spirit to keep His commandments—is neglected. If there is one thing we need to know well, it is the place obedience takes in the New Covenant.

> *W*hen the law is written in the heart, it means that the love of God's law and of Himself has now become the moving power of our life.

Let our first thought be: *Obedience is essential.* At the very root of the relationship between a creature and his God, and of God's admitting the creature to His fellowship, lays the thought of obedience. It is the one and only thing God spoke of in Paradise when "the LORD God commanded the man" not to eat of the forbidden fruit (Gen. 2:16–17). In Christ's great salvation it is the power that redeemed us: "By one Man's obedience many will be made righteous" (Rom. 5:19). In the promise of the New Covenant it takes the first place. God engages to circumcise the hearts of His people—in the putting off of the body of the flesh, in the circumcision of Christ—to love God with all their heart and to obey His commandments. The crowning gift of Christ's exaltation was the Holy Spirit to bring salvation to us as an inward thing. The First Covenant demanded obedience and failed because it could not find it. *The New Covenant was expressly made to provide for obedience.* To a life in the full experience of the New Covenant blessing, obedience is essential.

It is this indispensable necessity of obedience that explains why so often the entrance into the full enjoyment of the New Covenant has depended on some single act of surrender. There was something in the life, some evil or doubtful habit, in regard to which conscience had often said that it was not in perfect accord with God's perfect will. Attempts were made to push aside the troublesome suggestion. Or unbelief said it would be impossible to overcome the habit and maintain the promise of obedience to the Voice within. Meantime, all our prayer appeared of no benefit. It was as if faith could not take hold of the blessing that was fully in sight until at last the soul consented to regard this little thing as the test of its surrender to obey in everything, and of its faith that in everything the Surety of the Covenant would give power to maintain the obedience. With the evil or doubtful thing given up, and with a good conscience restored, and the heart's confidence before God assured, the soul could receive and possess what it sought. Obedience is essential.

Obedience is possible. The thought of a demand that man cannot possibly submit to cuts at the very root of true hope and strength. The secret thought, *No man can obey God*, throws thousands back into the Old Covenant life and into a false peace that God does not expect more than that we do our best. But obedience is possible because the whole New Covenant promises and secures this.

Only understand correctly what obedience means. The renewed man still has the flesh, with its evil nature, out of which there arises involuntary evil thoughts and dispositions. These may be found in a truly obedient man. Obedience deals with the doing of what is known to be God's will as it is taught by the Word, the Holy Spirit, and conscience. When George Müller spoke of the great happiness he had had for more than sixty years in God's service, he attributed it two things: He had loved God's Word, and "he had maintained a good conscience, not willfully going on in a course he knew to be contrary to the mind of God." When the full light of God broke in upon Gerhard Tersteegen, he wrote: "I promise, with Your help and power, rather to give up the last drop of my blood than to knowingly and willingly in my heart or my life be untrue and disobedient to You." Such obedience is an attainable degree of grace.

> The Old Covenant demanded obedience with an inexorable *must*, and the threat that followed it. The New Covenant changes the *must* to *can* and *may.*

Obedience is possible. This love is no vague sentiment in man's imagination of something that exists in heaven, but a living, mighty power of God in the heart, working effectually according to His working, which works in us mightily. A life of obedience is possible.

This obedience is of faith. "By faith Abraham obeyed" (Heb. 11:8). By faith, the promises of the Covenant, the presence of the Surety of the Covenant, the hidden inworking of the Holy Spirit, and the love of God in His infinite desire and power to make true in us all His love and promises must live in us. Faith can bring them near and make us live in the very midst of them. Christ and His wonderful redemption need not remain at a distance from us in heaven, but can become our continual experience. However cold or weak we may feel, faith knows that the new heart is in us, that the love of God's law is our very nature, and that the teaching and power of the Spirit are within us. Such faith knows it can obey. Let us hear the voice of our Savior, the Surety of the Covenant, as He says, with a deeper, fuller meaning than when He was on earth: "Only believe. If you can believe, all things are possible to him who believes" (Mark 9:23).

And last of all, let us understand: *Obedience is blessedness.* Do not regard it only as *the way* to the joy and blessings of the New Covenant, but as itself, in its very nature, joy and happiness. To have the voice of God teaching and guiding you, to be united to God in desiring what He desires in working out what He works in you by His Spirit and in doing His holy will and pleasing Him—surely all this is joy unspeakable and full of glory.

To a healthy man, it is a delight to walk or work, to put forth his strength and conquer difficulties. To a slave or a hireling it is bondage and weariness. The Old Covenant demanded obedience with an inexorable *must,* and the threat that followed it. The New Covenant changes the *must* to *can* and *may.* Ask God, by the Holy Spirit, to show you how you have been "created in Christ Jesus for good works" (Eph. 2:10), and how, as made fit as a vine is for bearing grapes, your new nature is perfectly prepared for every good work. Ask Him to show you that He means obedience not only to be a possible thing, but the most delightful and attractive gift He has to give and the entrance into His love and all its blessedness.

In the New Covenant, the chief thing is not the wonderful treasure of strength and grace it contains, nor the divine security that this treasure can never fail. It is this: that the living God gives Himself and makes Himself known and takes possession of us as our God. For this man was created, for this he was redeemed again, for this so that it may be our actual experience, the Holy Spirit has been given and is dwelling in us. Between what God has already accomplished in us and what He waits to accomplish, obedience is the blessed link. Let us seek to walk before Him in the confidence that we are of those who live in the noble and holy consciousness: My one work is to obey God.[7]

What can be the reason, I ask once again, that so many believers have seen so little of the beauty of this New Covenant life, with its power of holy and joyful obedience? "Their eyes were restrained, so that they did not know Him" (Luke 24:16). The Lord was with the disciples, but their hearts were blind. It is so still. It is as with Elisha's servant: All heaven is around him and he doesn't know it. Nothing will help but the prayer, "Lord, open his eyes that he may see" (2 Kings 6:17). Lord, is there not someone who may be reading this who just needs one touch to see it all? Oh, give that touch!

Just listen, my brother. Your Father loves you with an infinite love and longs to make you, even today, His holy, happy, obedient child. Hear His message: He has for you an entirely different life from what you are living, *a life in which His grace shall actually work in you every moment all He asks you to be.* A life of simple childlike obedience, doing for the day just what the Father shows you to be His will. A life in which the abiding love of your Father, the abiding presence of your Savior, and the joy of the Holy Spirit can keep you and make you glad and strong. This is His message. This life is for you. Do not be afraid to accept this life, to give up yourself to it and its entire obedience. In Christ it is possible, it is sure.

Now, my brother, just turn heavenward and ask the Father, by the Holy Spirit, to show you the beautiful heavenly life. Ask and expect it. Keep your eyes fixed

---

[7] In *The School of Obedience,* the thoughts of this chapter are more fully worked out.

on it. *The great blessing of the New Covenant is obedience, the wonderful power to will and do as God wills.* It is indeed the entrance to every other blessing. It is paradise restored and heaven opened—the creature honoring his Creator, the Creator delighting in His creature; the child glorifying the Father, the Father glorifying the child, as He changes him, from glory to glory, into the likeness of His Son.

FOR FURTHER THOUGHT

1. *What part does personal obedience play in God's New Covenant with His people? How important is obedience in your daily Christian life?*
2. *How has the command for personal obedience changed from the Old Covenant to the New Covenant?*
3. *How should you pray in order to receive the motivation and the power for a life of personal obedience to your heavenly Father?*

14

The New Covenant:
A Covenant of Grace

For sin shall not have dominion over you,
for you are not under law but under grace.
Romans 6:14

THE phrase "covenant of grace," though not found in scripture, is the correct expression of the truth it abundantly teaches: that the contrast between the two covenants is none other than that of law and grace. Of the New Covenant, grace is the great characteristic: "The law entered that the offense might abound. But where sin abounded, grace abounded much more" (Rom. 5:20). It is to bring the Romans away entirely from under the Old Covenant and to teach them their place in the New, that Paul writes: "You are not under law but under grace" (Rom. 6:14). And he assures them that if they believe this and live in it, their experience would confirm God's promise: "Sin shall not have dominion over you." What the law could not do—give deliverance from the power of sin over us—grace would accomplish. The New Covenant was entirely a covenant of grace. In the wonderful grace of God it had its origin. It was meant to be a manifestation of the riches and the glory of that grace: of grace, and by grace working in us, all its promises can be fulfilled and experienced.

The word *grace* is used in two senses. It is first the gracious disposition in God *that moves Him* to love us freely without our merit and to bestow all His blessings on us. Then it also means that power through which this grace does its work in us. The redeeming work of Christ and the righteousness He won for us, equally with the work of the Spirit in us, as the power of the new life, are spoken of as grace. It includes all that Christ has done and still does, all He has and gives, all He is for us and in us. John says, "We beheld His glory, the glory as of the only begotten of the Father, full of grace and truth" (John 1:14). "The law was given through Moses, but grace and truth came through Jesus Christ" (1:17). "And of His fullness we have all received, and grace for grace" (1:16). What the law demands, grace supplies.

The contrast that John pointed out is expounded by Paul: "Moreover the law entered that the offense might abound" (Rom. 5:20), and the way is prepared for the abounding of grace more exceedingly. The law points the way but gives no strength to walk in it. The law demands but makes no provision for its demands being met. The law burdens and condemns and slays. It can waken desire but not satisfy it. It can rouse to effort but not secure success. It can appeal to motives but gives no inward power beyond what man himself has. And so, while warring against sin, it became its very ally in giving the sinner over to a hopeless condemnation. "The strength of sin is the law" (1 Cor. 15:56).

To deliver us from the bondage and the dominion of sin, grace came by Jesus Christ. Its work is twofold. Its exceeding abundance is seen in the free and full pardon there is of all transgression, in the bestowal of a perfect righteousness, and in the acceptance into God's favor and friendship. "In Him we have redemption through His blood, the forgiveness of sins, according to the riches of His grace" (Eph. 1:7). It is not only at conversion and our admittance into God's favor, but throughout all our life, at each step of our way and amid the highest attainments of the most advanced saint, that we owe everything to grace and grace alone. The thought of merit and work and worthiness is forever excluded.

> *It is in the fulfillment of this promise, in the maintenance of the heart in a state of fitness for God's indwelling, that the glory of grace is specially seen.*

The exceeding abundance of grace is equally seen in the work that the Holy Spirit every moment maintains within us. We have found that the central blessing of the New Covenant, flowing from Christ's redemption and the pardon of our sins, is the new heart in which God's law and fear and love have been put. It is in the fulfillment of this promise, *in the maintenance of the heart in a state of fitness for God's indwelling,* that the glory of grace is specially seen.

In the very nature of things this must be so. Paul writes: "Where sin abounded, grace abounded much more" (Rom. 5:20). And where, as far as I was concerned, did sin abound? All the sin in earth and hell could not harm me, were it not for its presence in my heart. It is there that it has exercised its terrible dominion. And it is there that the exceeding abundance of grace must be proved if it is to benefit me. All grace in earth and heaven could not help me. It is only in the heart that it can be received, known, and enjoyed. "Where sin abounded," in the heart, there "grace abounded much more, so that as sin reigned in death," working its destruction in the heart and life, "even so might grace reign," in the heart, too, "through righteousness to eternal life through Jesus Christ our Lord" (Rom. 5:20–21). As had been said just before, "Those who receive abundance of grace and of the gift of righteousness will reign in life through the One, Jesus Christ" (5:17).

Of this reign of grace in the heart scripture speaks wondrous things. Paul speaks of the grace that made him fit for his work, of "the gift of *the grace* of God given to me by the effective working of His power" (Eph. 3:7). "And the *grace* of our Lord was exceedingly abundant, with faith and love" (1 Tim. 1:14). *"His grace* toward me was not in vain; but *I labored more abundantly* than they all, yet not I, but *the grace* of God which was with me" (1 Cor. 15:10). "And He said to me, *'My grace* is sufficient for you, for My strength is made perfect in weakness'" (2 Cor. 12:9). He speaks in the same way of grace as working in the life of believers, when he exhorts them to "be strong in the grace that is in Christ Jesus" (2 Tim. 2:1), when he tells us of "the grace of God" exhibited in the liberality of the Macedonian Christians (see 2 Cor. 8:1–3), and "the exceeding grace of God" in the Corinthians, when he encourages them: "God is able to make all grace abound toward you, that you. . .may have an abundance for every good work" (2 Cor. 9:8).

> *L*et us pray and ask God to open our eyes by the Holy Spirit to see that in the New Covenant, everything—every movement and every moment of our Christian life—is of grace, abounding grace, grace abounding exceedingly and working mightily.

Grace is not only the power that moves the heart of God in its compassion toward us when He acquits and accepts the sinner and makes him a child, but it is equally the power that moves the heart of the saint and provides it each moment with just the disposition and the power it needs to love God and do His will.

It is impossible to speak too strongly of the need to know that as wonderful and free and alone sufficient is the grace that pardons and the grace that sanctifies, we are just as absolutely dependent on the latter as the former. We can do as little to the one as the other. The grace that works in us must just as exclusively do all in us and through us as the grace that pardons does all for us. In the one case as the other, everything is by faith alone.

Not understanding this brings a double danger. On the one hand, people think that grace cannot be more exalted than in the bestowal of pardon on the vile and unworthy. Then a secret feeling arises that if God is so magnified by our sins more than anything else, we must not expect to be freed from them in this life. With many this cuts at the root of the life of true holiness. On the other hand, from not knowing that grace is always and alone to do all the work in our sanctification and fruit-bearing, men are thrown on their own efforts, and their life remains one of weakness and bondage under the law, and they never yield themselves to let grace do all it would.

Let us listen to what God's Word says: *"By grace* you have been saved *through faith*. . .not of works, lest anyone should boast. For we are His workmanship, created in Christ Jesus for good works, which God prepared beforehand that we should walk in them" (Eph. 2:8–10). Grace stands in contrast to good works of our own not only before conversion, but after conversion, too. We are created *in*

Christ Jesus for good works, which God had prepared for us. It is grace alone that can work them in us and work them out through us.

Not only the commencement but the continuance of the Christian life is the work of grace. "And if by grace, then it is no longer of works; otherwise grace is no longer grace. . . . Therefore it is of faith that it might be according to grace" (Romans 11:6; 4:16). As we see that grace is literally and absolutely to do all in us, so that all our actions are the showing forth of grace in us, we shall consent to live the life of faith—a life in which, every moment, everything is expected from God. It is only then that we shall experience that sin shall not, never, not for a moment, have dominion over us.

"You are not under the law but under grace." There are three possible lives: one entirely under the law, one entirely under grace, and one a mixed life of partly law, partly grace. It is this last life against which Paul warns the Romans. It is this that is so common and works such ruin among Christians. Let us find out whether this is not our position and the cause of our low state. Let us pray and ask God to open our eyes by the Holy Spirit to see that in the New Covenant, everything— every movement and every moment of our Christian life—is of grace, abounding grace, grace abounding exceedingly and working mightily. Let us believe that our Covenant God waits to cause all grace to abound toward us. And let us begin to live the life of faith that depends on, trusts in, looks to, and always waits for God, through Jesus Christ and by the Holy Spirit, to work in us that which is pleasing in His sight.

Grace to you, and peace be multiplied!

For Further Thought

1. *In what two ways does God use the word* grace *in His written Word, the Bible?*
2. *How does God contrast obedience through our own power and effort with obedience through the grace He imparts to us?*
3. *What three approaches do believers take when it comes to personal obedience? Which is the correct one, and why?*

15

THE COVENANT OF AN
EVERLASTING PRIESTHOOD

*"That My covenant with Levi may continue. . . . My covenant was
with him, one of life and peace, and I gave them to him that he
might fear Me; so he feared Me and was reverent before My name.
The law of truth was in his mouth, and injustice was not
found on his lips. He walked with Me in peace and equity,
and turned many away from iniquity."*
MALACHI 2:4–6

ISRAEL was meant by God to be a nation of priests. In the first making
of the Covenant, this was distinctly stipulated. "If you will indeed obey My voice
and keep My covenant...you shall be to Me a kingdom of priests" (Exod. 19:5–6).
They were to be the stewards of the oracles of God, the channels through whom
God's knowledge and blessing were to be communicated to the world. In them all
nations were to be blessed.

Within the people of Israel, one tribe was specially set apart to embody and
emphasize the priestly idea. The firstborn sons of the whole people were to have
been the priests. But to secure a more complete separation from the rest of the
people, as well as the entire giving up of any share in their possessions and pursuits, God chose one tribe to be exclusively devoted to the work of proving what
constitutes the spirit and the power of priesthood. Just as the priesthood of the
whole people was part of God's Covenant with them, so the special calling of Levi
is spoken of as God's Covenant of life and peace being with Him, as the Covenant
of an everlasting priesthood. All this was to be a picture to help them and us, in
some measure, to understand the priesthood of His own blessed Son, the Mediator of the New Covenant.

Like Israel, all God's people are, under the New Covenant, a royal priesthood
(see 1 Pet. 2:9). The right of free and full access to God, the duty and power of
mediating for our fellow men and being God's channel of blessing to them, is the
inalienable birthright of every believer. Owing to the weakness and incapacity of
many of God's children, their ignorance of the mighty grace of the New Covenant,

they are utterly unable to take up and exercise their priestly functions.

To make up for this lack of service, to show forth the exceeding riches of His grace in the New Covenant and the power He gives men of becoming— just as the priests of old were the forerunners of the Great High Priest—His followers and representatives, God still allows and invites those of His redeemed ones who are willing to offer their lives to this blessed ministry. To him who accepts the call, the New Covenant brings in special measure what God has said: "My covenant was with him, one of life and peace" (Mal. 2:5). It then becomes to him in very deed "the Covenant of an everlasting priesthood." Just as the Covenant of Levi's priesthood issued and culminated in Christ's, ours issues from that again and receives from it its blessing to dispense to the world.

> *he right of free and full access to God, the duty and power of mediating for our fellow men and being God's channel of blessing to them, is the inalienable birthright of every believer.*

To those who desire to know the conditions on which, as part of the New Covenant, the Covenant of an everlasting priesthood can be received and carried out, a study of the conditions on which Levi received the priesthood will be most instructive. We are told not only that God chose that tribe, but what there specifically was in that tribe that fitted it for the work. Malachi says: "And I gave them to him that he might fear Me; so he feared Me and was reverent before My name" (2:5). The reference is to what took place at Sinai when Israel had made the molten calf. Moses called all who were on the Lord's side, who were ready to avenge the dishonor done to God, to come to him. The tribe of Levi did so, and at his bidding took their swords and killed three thousand of the idolatrous people (Exod. 32:26–29). In the blessing with which Moses blessed the tribes before his death, their absolute devotion to God, without considering relative or friend, is mentioned as the proof of their fitness for God's service (Deut. 33:8–11): "*Let* Your Thummim and Your Urim *be* with Your holy one. . .who says of his father and mother, 'I have not seen them'; nor did he acknowledge his brothers, or know his own children; for they have observed Your word and kept Your covenant."

The same principle is strikingly illustrated in the story of Aaron's grandson, Phinehas, where he, in his zeal for God, executed judgment on disobedience to God's command. The words are most suggestive. "Then the LORD spoke to Moses, saying: 'Phinehas the son of Eleazar, the son of Aaron the priest, has turned back My wrath from the children of Israel, because he was zealous with My zeal among them, so that I did not consume the children of Israel in My zeal. Therefore say, "Behold, I give to him My covenant of peace; and it shall be to him and his descendants after him a covenant of an everlasting priesthood, because he was zealous for his God, and made atonement for the children of Israel""" (Num. 25:10–13).

To be jealous (or zealous) with God's jealousy, to be jealous for God's honor and rise up against sin is the gate into the Covenant of an everlasting priesthood and the secret of being entrusted by God with the sacred work of teaching His people, burning incense before Him, and turning many from iniquity (Deut. 33:10; Mal. 2:6).

Even the New Covenant is in danger of being abused by the seeking of our own happiness or holiness more than the honor of God or the deliverance of men. Even where these are not entirely neglected, they do not always take the place they are meant to have—that first place that makes everything, even the dearest and best, secondary and subordinate to the work of helping and blessing men. A reckless disregard of everything that would interfere with God's will and commands, a being jealous with God's jealousy against sin, a witnessing and a fighting against it at any sacrifice—this is the school of training for the priestly office.

> *A* reckless disregard of everything that would interfere with God's will and commands, a being jealous with God's jealousy against sin, a witnessing and a fighting against it at any sacrifice—this is the school of training for the priestly office.

It is this the world needs nowadays—men of God in whom the fire of God burns, men who can stand and speak and act in power on behalf of a God who, amid His own people, is dishonored by the worship of the golden calf. Understand that as you will, of the place given to money and rich men in the church, of the prevalence of worldliness and luxury, or of the subtler danger of a worship meant for the true God, under forms taken from the Egyptians and suited to the wisdom and the carnal life of this world. A religion God cannot approve is often found even where the people still profess to be in covenant with God. "Consecrate yourselves to day to the LORD, even every man upon his son, and upon his brother" (Exod. 32:29 KJV). This call of Moses is as much needed today as ever. To each one who responds there is the reward of the priesthood.

Let all who desire to know fully what the New Covenant means remember God's covenant of life and peace with Levi. Accept the holy calling to be an intercessor and to burn incense before the Lord continually. Love, work, pray, and believe as one whom God has sought and found to stand in the gap before Him. The New Covenant was dedicated by a sacrifice and a death. Consider it your most wonderful privilege—your fullest entrance into its life as you reflect the glory of the Lord and are changed into the same image from glory to glory, as by the Spirit of the Lord—to let the Spirit of that sacrifice and death be the moving power in all your priestly functions. Sacrifice yourself; live and die for your fellow men.

One of the great objects with which God has made a Covenant with us is, as we have said so often, to awaken strong confidence in Himself and His faithfulness to His promise. And one of the objects that He has in awakening and so strengthening the faith in us is that He may use us as His channels of blessing to the world. In the work of saving men, He wants intercessory prayer to take the first place. He would have us come to Him to receive from Him in heaven the spiritual life and power that can pass out from us to them. He knows how difficult and hopeless it is in many cases to deal with sinners. He knows that it is no light thing for us to believe that in answer to our prayer, the mighty power of God will move to save those around us. He knows that it requires strong faith to persevere patiently in prayer in cases in which the answer is long delayed—and every year appears farther off than ever. And so He undertakes, in our own experience, to prove what faith in His divine power can do in bringing down all the blessings of the New Covenant on ourselves so that we may be able to expect confidently what we ask for others.

In our priestly life there is still another aspect. The priests had no inheritance with their brethren, for the Lord God was their inheritance. They had access to His dwelling and His presence so that there they might intercede for others and there testify of what God is and wills. Their personal privilege and experience prepared them for their work. If we desire to intercede in power, let us live in the full realization of New Covenant life. It gives us not only liberty and confidence with God and power to persevere, but also power with men because we can testify to and prove what God has done to us. Here is the full glory of the New Covenant: that like Christ its Mediator, we have the fire of the divine love dwelling in us and consuming us in the service of men. May for each of us the chief glory of the New Covenant be that it is the Covenant of an everlasting priesthood.

For Further Thought

1. *What inalienable right do you have as a believer, as a child of God?*
2. *What are the conditions for receiving the promise of the everlasting priesthood? What are the benefits of knowing and meeting those conditions?*
3. *What was one of God's most important objectives in making the New Covenant with those who believe in Him?*

16

THE MINISTRY OF
THE NEW COVENANT

*You are our epistle written in our hearts, known and read by all
men; clearly you are an epistle of Christ, ministered by us, written
not with ink but by the Spirit of the living God, not on tablets
of stone but on tablets of flesh, that is, of the heart. And we have
such trust through Christ toward God. Not that we are sufficient
of ourselves to think of anything as being from ourselves, but our
sufficiency is from God, who also made us sufficient as ministers
of the new covenant, not of the letter but of the Spirit;
for the letter kills, but the Spirit gives life.*
2 CORINTHIANS 3:2–6

WE have seen that the New Covenant is a ministry of the Spirit. The Holy
Spirit ministers all its grace and blessing in divine power and life.[8] He does this
through men who are called ministers of a New Covenant, ministers of the Spirit.
The divine ministry of the Covenant to men and the earthly ministry of God's
servants are equally to be in the power of the Holy Spirit. The ministry of the New
Covenant has its glory and its fruit in this: that it is all to be a demonstration of
the Spirit and of power.

What a contrast this is to the Old Covenant! Moses had indeed received of
the glory of God shining upon him, but had to put a veil on his face. Israel was
incapable of looking on it. In hearing and reading Moses, there was a veil on their
hearts. From Moses they might receive knowledge and thoughts and desires—the
power of God's Spirit to enable them to see the glory of what God speaks was not
yet given. This is the exceeding glory of the New Covenant: that it is a ministry
of the Spirit, that its ministers have their sufficiency from God, who makes them
ministers of the Spirit and makes them able so to speak the words of God in the
Spirit that they are written in the heart and that the hearers become legible, living
epistles of Christ, showing the law written in their heart and life.

The ministry of the Spirit! What a glory there is in it! What a responsibility

---

[8] It may be well to read again and compare chapter 7: "The New Covenant: A Ministry of the
Spirit."

it brings! What a sufficiency of grace there is provided for it! What a privilege to be a minister of the Spirit!

What tens of thousands we have throughout Christianity who are called ministers of the gospel! What an inconceivable influence they exert for life or for death over the millions who depend on them for their knowledge of and participation in the Christian life! What a power there would be if all these were ministers of the Spirit! Let us study the Word until we see what God meant the ministry to be and learn to take our part in praying and laboring to have it be nothing less.

God has made us ministers of the Spirit. The first thought is that a minister of the New Covenant must be a man personally possessed of the Holy Spirit. There is a twofold work of the Spirit: one in giving a holy disposition and character, the other in qualifying and empowering a man for work. The former must always come first. The promise of Christ to His disciples that they should receive the Holy Spirit for their service was very definitely given to those who had followed and loved Him and kept His commandments. It is by no means enough that a man has been born of the Spirit. If he is to be a "sufficient minister" of the New Covenant, he must know what it is to be led by the Spirit, to walk in the Spirit, and to say, "The law of the Spirit of life in Christ Jesus has made me free from the law of sin and death" (Rom. 8:2).

The divine ministry of the Covenant to men and the earthly ministry of God's servants are equally to be in the power of the Holy Spirit.

What man who wants to learn Greek or Hebrew would accept a professor who hardly knows the elements of these languages? And how can a man be a minister of the New Covenant, which is so entirely "a ministry of the Spirit" and a ministry of heavenly life and power, unless he knows by experience what it is to live in the Spirit? The minister must, before everything, be a personal proof and witness of the truth and power of God in the fulfillment of what the New Covenant promises. Ministers are to be picked men—the best specimens and examples of what the Holy Spirit can do to sanctify a man and, by the working of God's power in him, to prepare him for His service.

God has made us ministers of the Spirit. Next to this thought of being personally possessed by the Spirit comes the truth that all their work in the ministry can be done in the power of the Spirit. What an unspeakably precious assurance—Christ sends them to do a heavenly work, to do His work, to be the instruments in His hands by which He works. He clothes them with a heavenly power. Their calling is "to preach the gospel with the Holy Spirit sent down from heaven" (see 1 Pet. 1:12). As far as feelings are concerned, they may have to say as Paul: "I was with you in weakness, in fear, and in much trembling" (1 Cor. 2:3). That does not prevent their adding—no, rather, that may just be the secret of their being able to add: "My preaching was in demonstration of the Spirit and of power" (see 1 Cor. 2:4).

If a man is to be a minister of the New Covenant, a messenger and a teacher of its true blessing so as to lead God's children to live in it, nothing less will do than a full experience of its power in himself as the Spirit ministers it. Whether in his feeding on God's Word himself or his seeking in it for God's message for his people, whether in secret or intercessory prayer, whether in private interaction with souls or public teaching, he is to wait on, receive, and yield to the energizing of the Holy Spirit as the mighty power of God working with him. This is his sufficiency for the work. He may every day freshly claim and receive the anointing with fresh oil—the new inbreathing from Christ of His own Spirit and life.

> *What an unspeakably precious assurance—Christ sends them to do a heavenly work, to do His work, to be the instruments in His hands by which He works.*

God has made us ministers of the Spirit. There is something still of no less importance. The minister of the Spirit must especially see to it that *he leads men to the Holy Spirit.* Many will say, "If he is led by the Spirit in teaching men, is not that enough?" By no means. Men may become too dependent on him. They may take his scripture teaching at secondhand and, while there are power and blessing in his ministry, have reason to wonder why the results are not more definitely spiritual and permanent. The reason is simple. The New Covenant is: "No more shall every man teach his neighbor, and every man his brother, saying, 'Know the LORD,' for they all shall know Me, from the least of them to the greatest" (Jer. 31:34). The Father wants every child, from the least, to *live in continual personal interaction with Himself.* This cannot be unless he is taught and helped to know and wait on the Holy Spirit. Bible study and prayer, faith and love and obedience, the whole daily walk must be taught as entirely dependent on the teaching and working of the indwelling Spirit.

The minister of the Spirit very definitely and perseveringly points away from himself to the Spirit. This is what John the Baptist did. He was filled with the Holy Spirit from his birth but sent men away from himself to Christ to be by Him baptized with the Spirit. Christ did the same. In His farewell address, He called His disciples to turn from His personal instruction to the inward teaching of the Holy Spirit, who should dwell in them and guide them into the truth and power of all He had taught them.

There is nothing so needed in the Church today. All its weaknesses and formalities and worldliness, the lack of holiness and of personal devotion to Christ and of enthusiasm for His cause and kingdom, are due to one thing—the Holy Spirit is not known and honored and yielded to as the one only, as the one all-sufficient source of a holy life. The New Covenant is not known as a ministry of the Spirit in the heart of every believer. The one thing needed for the Church is the Holy

Spirit in His power dwelling and ruling in the lives of God's saints. And as one of the chief means to this there are needed ministers of the Spirit who themselves are living in the enjoyment and power of this great gift, who persistently labor to bring their brethren into the possession of their birthright: the Holy Spirit in the heart, maintaining, in divine power, an unceasing communion with the Son and with the Father. The inner ministry of the Spirit makes the ministry of the Spirit possible and effectual. And the ministry of the Spirit again makes the inner ministry of the Spirit an actual experimental reality in the life of the Church.

We know how dependent the Church is on its ministry. The converse is no less true. The ministers are dependent on the Church. They are its children. They breathe its atmosphere, share its health or sickliness, and are dependent on its fellowship and intercession. Let none of us think that all that the New Covenant calls us to is to see that we personally accept and rejoice in its blessings. No, indeed. God wants everyone who enters into it to know that its privileges are for all His children and to give himself to make this known. And there is no more effectual way of doing this than taking thought for the ministry of the Church.

Compare the ministry around you with its pattern in God's Word (see specially 1 Cor. 2; 2 Cor. 3). Join with others who know how the New Covenant is nothing if it is not a ministry of the Spirit, and cry to God for a spiritual ministry. Ask the leading of God the Holy Spirit to teach you what can be done, what you can do to have the ministry of your Church become a truly spiritual one. Human condemnation will do as little good as human approval. It is as the supreme place of the Holy Spirit as the representative and revealer of the Father and the Son is made clear to us that the one desire of our heart, and our continual prayer, will be that God would so reveal to all the ministers of His Word their heavenly calling, so that they may, above everything, seek this one thing—to be sufficient ministers of the New Covenant, not of the letter, but of the Spirit.

For Further Thought

1. *On what—specifically whom—are we to be dependant in order to receive and impart to others what God has promised in His New Covenant?*
2. *What is the twofold work of the Holy Spirit in the heart and in the life of every believer?*
3. *What must you do in order to live in continual, personal interaction and fellowship with God the Father?*

17
HIS HOLY COVENANT

*"To remember His holy covenant. . .to grant us that we, being
delivered from the hand of our enemies, might serve
Him without fear, in holiness and righteousness
before Him all the days of our life."*
LUKE 1:72, 74–75

WHEN Zacharias was filled with the Holy Spirit and prophesied, he spoke of
God's visiting and redeeming His people as a remembering of His holy Covenant.
He speaks of what the blessings of that Covenant would be, not in words that had
been used before, but in what is clearly a divine revelation to him by the Holy Spirit,
which gathers up all the former promises in these words: *"That we. . .might serve
Him without fear, in holiness and righteousness before Him all the days of our life."* Holiness in life and service is to be the great gift of the Covenant of God's holiness. As
we have seen before, the Old Covenant proclaimed and demanded holiness and the
New provides it. Holiness of heart and life is its great blessing.

There is no attribute of God so difficult to define, so peculiarly a matter of
divine revelation, so mysterious, incomprehensible, and inconceivably glorious, as
His holiness. It is that by which He is specially worshipped in His majesty on the
throne of heaven (Isa. 5:2; Rev. 4:8; 15:4). It unites His righteousness, which judges
and condemns, with His love, which saves and blesses. As the Holy One, He is a
consuming fire (Isa. 10:17). As the Holy One, He loves to dwell among His people
(Isa. 12:6). As the Holy One, He is at an infinite distance from us. As the Holy One,
He comes inconceivably near and makes us one with and makes us like Himself.
The one purpose of His holy Covenant is to make us holy as He is holy.

As the Holy One, He says: "I am holy; you be holy; I am the LORD who sanctifies you, who makes you holy" (see Lev. 11:44; 22:32). The highest conceivable
summit of blessedness is our being partakers of the divine nature, of the divine
holiness.

This is the great blessing Christ, the Mediator of the New Covenant,
brings. He has been made for us both "righteousness and sanctification" (1 Cor.
1:30)—righteousness in order to, as a preparation for, sanctification[9] or holiness.
He prayed to the Father: "Sanctify them. . . . For their sakes I *sanctify* Myself, that
they also may be *sanctified* by the truth" (John 17:17, 19). In Him we are sanctified,

---

[9] Remember that the words *sanctify*, *sanctity*, and *saint* are the same as *make holy*, *holiness*, *holy one*.

saints, holy ones (Rom. 1:7; 1 Cor. 1:2). We have put on the new man that after God is created in righteousness and holiness. Holiness is our very nature.

We are holy in Christ. As we believe it, as we receive it, as we yield ourselves to the truth and draw near to God to have the holiness drawn forth and revealed in fellowship with Him, its fountain, we shall know how divinely true it is.

It is for this that the Holy Spirit has been given in our hearts. He is the "Spirit of holiness" (Rom. 1:4). His every working is in the power of holiness. Paul says: "God. . .chose [us] for salvation *through sanctification by the Spirit* and belief in the truth" (2 Thess. 2:13). As simple and entire as is our dependence on the word of truth, as the external means, must our confidence be in the hidden power for holiness that the working of the Spirit brings.

> *There is no attribute of God so difficult to define, so peculiarly a matter of divine revelation, so mysterious, incomprehensible, and inconceivably glorious, as His holiness.*

The connection between God's electing purpose and the work of the Spirit, with the word we obey, comes out with equal clearness in Peter: "*Elect. . .in sanctification of the Spirit,* for obedience" (1 Pet. 1:2). The Holy Spirit is the Spirit of the life of Christ, and as we know and honor and trust Him, we shall learn and also experience that in the New Covenant, as the ministry of the Spirit, the sanctification, the holiness of the Holy Spirit is our covenant right. We shall be assured that as God has promised, so He will work it in us so that we should "serve Him without fear, in holiness and righteousness before Him all the days of our life." With a treasure of holiness in Christ, and the very Spirit of holiness in our hearts, we can live holy lives. That is, if we believe Him "who works in you both to will and to do" (Phil. 2:13).

In the light of this Covenant promise, with the blessed Son and the Holy Spirit to work it out in us, what new meaning is given to the teaching of the New Testament. Take the first epistle St. Paul ever wrote. It was directed to men who had only a few months previously been turned from idols to serve the living God and to wait for His Son from heaven. The words he speaks in regard to the holiness they might aim at and expect, because God was going to work it in them, are so grand that many Christians pass them by as practically unintelligible (1 Thess. 3:12–13): "And may the Lord make you increase and abound in love. . .so that *He may establish your hearts blameless in holiness* before our God and Father at the coming of our Lord Jesus Christ with all His saints." That promises holiness, blameless holiness, a heart blameless in holiness, a heart established in all this by God Himself. Paul might indeed say of a word like this: "Who has believed our report?" He had written of himself: "You are witnesses. . .how *devoutly* and *justly* and *blamelessly* we behaved ourselves" (2:10). Paul assures them that what God has done for him He will do for them—give them hearts blameless in holiness.

The Church believes so little in the mighty power of God and the truth of His holy Covenant that the grace of such heart-holiness is hardly spoken of. The verse is often quoted in connection with "the coming of our Lord Jesus with all His saints," but its real point and glory—that when He comes we may meet Him with *hearts established blameless in holiness* by God Himself—all too little this is understood or proclaimed or expected.

> *A*s simple and entire as is our dependence on the word of truth, as the external means, must our confidence be in the hidden power for holiness that the working of the Spirit brings.

Or take another verse in the epistle (5:21), also spoken to these young converts from heathenism, in reference to the coming of our Lord. Some think that to speak much of the coming of the Lord will make us holy. Sadly, how little it has done so in many cases. It is the New Covenant holiness, brought about by God Himself in us, believed in and waited for from Him, that can make our waiting differ from the carnal expectations of the Jews or the disciples. Listen—"THE GOD OF PEACE HIMSELF"—that is the keynote of the New Covenant—what you never can do God will work in you—"SANCTIFY YOU COMPLETELY"—this you may ask and expect—*"and may your whole spirit, soul, and body be preserved* BLAMELESS *at the coming of our Lord Jesus Christ"* (5:23). And now, as if to meet the doubt that will arise: *"He who calls you is faithful,* WHO ALSO WILL DO IT" (5:24).

Again, it is the secret of the New Covenant—what has not entered into the heart of man—GOD WILL WORK in those who wait for Him. Until the Church awakes to see and believe that our holiness is to be the *immediate almighty working of the Three-One God in us,* and that our whole religion must be an unceasing dependence to receive it *directly from Himself,* these promises remain a sealed book.

Let us now return to the prophecy of the Holy Spirit by Zacharias of God's remembering the Covenant of His holiness, to make us holy, to establish our hearts blameless in holiness, that we should serve Him IN HOLINESS AND RIGHTEOUSNESS. Note how every word is significant.

To grant us. It is to be a gift from above. The promise given with the Covenant was: "I, the LORD, have spoken it. . .*I will do it"* (Ezek. 24:14). We need to ask God to show us both what *He will do* and that *He will do it.* When our faith expects all from Him, the blessing will be found.

"That we, being delivered from the hand of our enemies." He had just before said: *And [He] has raised up a horn of salvation for us. . .that we should be saved from our enemies and from the hand of all who hate us* (Luke 1:69, 71). It is only a free people

who can serve a holy God or be holy. It is only as the teaching of Romans 6–8 is experienced and I know what it is that we are "freed from sin" and "freed from the law" and that "the Spirit of life in Christ Jesus has made me free from the law of sin and death" (Rom. 8:2) that in the perfect liberty from every power that could hinder, I can expect God to do His mighty work in me.

Might serve Him. My servant does not serve me by spending all his time in getting himself ready for work but in doing my work. The holy Covenant sets us free and endows us with divine grace so that God may have us for His work—the same work Christ began and we now carry on.

Without fear. In childlike confidence and boldness before God. And before men, too. A freedom from fear in every difficulty because, having learned to know that God works all in us, we can trust Him to work all for us and through us.

Before Him. With His continued unceasing presence all the day as the unceasing security of our obedience and our fearlessness, the never-failing secret of our being sanctified wholly.

All the days of our life. Not only all the day for one day, but for every day, because Jesus is a High Priest in the power of an endless life, and the mighty operation of God as promised in the Covenant is as unchanging as is God Himself. Is it not as if you begin to see that God's Word appears to mean more than you have ever conceived of or expected? It is well that it should be so. It is only when you begin to say, "*Glory to Him* who is able to do *exceeding abundantly above all* we can ask or think" (see Eph. 3:20), and expect God's almighty, supernatural, altogether immeasurable power and grace to work out the New Covenant life in you and to *make you holy,* that you will really come to the place of helplessness and dependence where God can work.

I ask you, my brother, to believe that God's Word is true, and say with Zacharias, "Blessed *is* the Lord God of Israel, for He has visited. . .His people. . .to remember *His holy covenant.* . .and to grant us that we, being delivered from the hand of our enemies, might serve Him without fear, *in holiness and righteousness before Him all the days of our life*" (Luke 1:68, 72, 74–75).

FOR FURTHER THOUGHT

1. *What different roles did the Old and New Covenants play when it comes to personal holiness before God?*
2. *What should you do in order to fully and completely understand the truth that you have been made holy in Jesus Christ?*
3. *God calls each of His people to service. What must you do in order to be prepared and empowered for service to God and to man?*

18

ENTERING THE COVENANT:
WITH ALL THE HEART

Then they entered into a covenant to seek the LORD
God of their fathers with all their heart and with all their soul.
2 CHRONICLES 15:12 (cf. 34:31; 2 KINGS 23:3)

"And the LORD your God will circumcise your heart and
the heart of your descendants, to love the LORD your
God with all your heart and with all your soul."
DEUTERONOMY 30:6

"Then I will give them a heart to know Me, that I am the LORD;
and they shall be My people, and I will be their God,
for they shall return to Me with their whole heart."
JEREMIAH 24:7 (cf. 29:13)

"And I will make an everlasting covenant with them, that
I will not turn away from doing them good; but I will put
My fear in their hearts so that they will not depart from Me.
Yes, I will rejoice over them to do them good. . .
with all My heart and with all My soul."
JEREMIAH 32:40–41

IN the accounts of the days of Asa, Hezekiah, and Josiah, we read of Israel entering into "the Covenant" with their whole heart, "to perform the words of the covenant that were written in this book" (2 Chron. 34:31). Of Asa's day, we read: "They took an oath before the LORD. . . . And all Judah rejoiced at the oath, for they had sworn *with all their heart* and sought Him *with all their soul*; and He was found by them" (2 Chron. 15:14–15).

Wholeheartedness is the secret of entering the Covenant, and of God being found by us in it. Wholeheartedness is the secret of joy in religion—a full entrance into all the blessedness the Covenant brings. God rejoices over His people to do them good, *with His whole heart and His whole soul*. This needs, on our part, *our whole heart and our whole soul* to enter into and enjoy this joy of God in doing us good with His whole heart and His whole soul. With what measure we give, it shall be given in like measure to us again.

If we have at all understood the teaching of God's Word in regard to the New Covenant, we know what it reveals in regard to the two parties who meet in it. On God's side, there is the promise to do for us and in us all that we need to serve and enjoy Him. He will rejoice in doing us good—with His whole heart. He will be our God, doing for us all that a God can do, giving Himself as God to be wholly ours. And on our side, there is the prospect held out of our being able, in the power of what He engages to do, to "turn to Him with our whole heart," "to love Him with all our heart and all our strength."

The first and great commandment, the only possible terms on which God can fully reveal Himself or give Himself to His creature to enjoy, is: "You shall love the LORD your God with all your heart" (Deut. 6:5; Mark 12:30). That law is unchangeable. The New Covenant comes and brings us the grace to obey by lifting us into the love of God as the air we breathe, and enabling us, in the faith of that grace, to rise and be of good courage, and with our whole heart to yield ourselves to the God of the Covenant and the life in His service.

> *W*holeheartedness is the secret of entering the Covenant, and of God being found by us in it. Wholeheartedness is the secret of joy in religion—a full entrance into all the blessedness the Covenant brings.

Wholeheartedness in the love and the service of God! How shall I speak of it? Of its imperative necessity? It is the one unalterable condition of true communion with God, of which nothing can supply the need. Of its infinite reasonableness? With such a God—a very fountain of all that is loving and lovely, of all that is good and blessed, the all-glorious God—surely there cannot for a moment be a thought of anything else being His due, or of our consenting to offer Him anything less than the love of the whole heart.

Of its unspeakable blessedness? To love Him with the whole heart is the only possible way of receiving His great love into our heart and rejoicing in it—yielding oneself to that mighty love and allowing God Himself, just as an earthly love enters into us and makes us glad, to give us the taste and the joy of the heavenliness of that love.

Of its terrible lack? Yes, what shall I speak of this? Where can I find words to open the eyes and reach the heart and show how almost universal is the lack of true wholeheartedness in the faith and love of God—in the desire to love Him with the whole heart, in the sacrifice of everything to possess Him, to please Him, and to be wholly possessed of Him?

And then of the blessed certainty of its attainability? The Covenant has provided for it. The Triune God will accomplish it by taking possession of the heart and dwelling there. The blessed Mediator of the Covenant undertakes for all we have to do. His constraining love shed abroad in our hearts by the Holy Spirit can bring it and maintain it.

Yes, I ask, how shall I speak of all this?

Have we not spoken enough of it already in this book? Do we not need something more than words and thoughts? Is not what we need rather this—to quietly turn to the Holy Spirit who dwells in us and, in the faith of the light and the strength our Lord gives through Him, accept and act out what God tells us of the God-given heart He has placed within us, the God-produced wholeheartedness He works? Surely the new heart that has been given us to love God with God's Spirit in it is wholly for God. Let our faith accept and rejoice in the wondrous gift and not fear to say: "I will love You, O Lord, with my whole heart." Just think for a moment of what it means that God has given us such a heart.

We know what God's giving means. *His giving depends on our taking.* He does not force on us spiritual possessions. He promises and gives in such measure as desire and faith are ready to receive. He gives in divine power, and as faith yields itself to that power and accepts the gift, it becomes consciously and experimentally our possession.

As spiritual gifts, God's impartings *are not recognized by sense or reason.* "Eye has not seen, nor ear heard, nor have entered into the heart of man *the things which God has prepared* for those who love Him.' But God has *revealed them to us through His Spirit....* Now we have received, not the spirit of the world, but the Spirit who is from God, that we might *know the things that have been freely given to us by God*" (1 Cor. 2:9–10, 12). It is as you yield yourself to be led and taught by the Spirit that your faith will be able, despite of all lack of feeling, to rejoice in the possession of the new heart and all that is given with it.

Then, *this divine giving is continuous.* I give a gift to a man, he takes it, and I never see him again. So God bestows temporal gifts on men, and they never think of Him. But spiritual gifts are only to be received and enjoyed in unceasing communication with God Himself. The new heart is not a power I have in myself, like the natural endowments of thinking or loving. No, it is only in unceasing dependence on and in close contact with God that the heavenly gift of a new heart can be maintained uninjured and can day by day become stronger. It is only in God's immediate presence, in unbroken direct dependence on Him, that spiritual endowments are preserved.

Then, further, *spiritual gifts can only be enjoyed by acting them out in faith.* None of the graces of the Christian life—like love, meekness, or boldness—can be felt or known, much less strengthened, until we begin to exercise them. We must not wait to feel them or to feel the strength for them. We must, in the obedience of the faith that they are given us and hidden within us, practice them. Whatever we read of the new heart and of all God has given into it in the New Covenant must be boldly believed and carried out into action.

All this is especially true of wholeheartedness and of loving God with all our heart. You may at first be very ignorant of all it implies. God has planted the new heart in the midst of the flesh, which, with its animating principle, *self*, has to be denied, to be kept crucified, and, by the Holy Spirit, to be put to death. God has placed you in the midst of a world from which, with all that is of it and its spirit, you are to come out and be entirely separate. God has given you your work in His kingdom, for which He asks all your interest, time, and strength. In all these three respects you need wholeheartedness to enable you to make the sacrifices that may be required.

If you take the ordinary standard of Christian life around you, you will find that wholeheartedness—or intense devotion to God and His service—is hardly thought of. How to make the best of both worlds, or innocently to enjoy as much as possible of this present life, is the ruling principle. As a natural consequence, the present world secures the larger share of interest. To please self is considered legitimate, and the Christlike life of *not pleasing self* has little place.

Wholeheartedness will lead you, and enable you, too, to accept Christ's command and sell all for the pearl of great price. Though at first you may be afraid of what it may involve, do not hesitate to speak the word frequently in the ear of your Father: *with my whole heart.* You may count on the Holy Spirit to open up its meaning, to show you to what service or what sacrifice God calls you in it, to increase its power, to reveal its blessedness, and to make it the very spirit of your life of devotion to your Covenant God.

> *A* redeeming God, rejoicing with His whole heart and whole soul to do us good and to accomplish in us all that is well-pleasing in His sight: This is the one side. Such is the God of the Covenant.

And now, who is ready to enter into this new and everlasting Covenant with his whole heart? Let each of us do it.

Begin by asking God very humbly to give you by the Spirit, who dwells in you, the vision of the heavenly life of wholehearted love and obedience, as it has actually been prepared for you in Christ. It is an existing reality, a spiritual endowment out of the life of God that can come upon you. It is secured to you in the Covenant, and in Christ Jesus, its Surety. Ask earnestly, definitely, believingly, that God reveal this to you. Do not rest until you know fully what your Father means you to be and has provided for your most certainly being.

When you begin to see why the New Covenant was given, what it promises, and how divinely certain its promises are, *offer yourself to God unreservedly to be taken up into it.* Offer, if He will take you in, to love Him with your whole heart and to obey Him with all your strength. Don't hold back, and don't be afraid. God has sworn to do you good *with His whole heart.* Do say, do not hesitate to say, that into this Covenant in which *He promises to cause you* to turn to Him and to love Him with your whole heart, you now with your whole heart enter. If there be any fear, just ask again and believingly for a vision of the Covenant life: God swearing to do you good with *His whole heart,* God undertaking to make and enable you to love and obey Him with *your whole heart.* The vision of this life will make you bold to say: "Into this Covenant of a wholehearted love in God and in me I do with my whole heart now enter: Here I will dwell."

Let us close and part with this one thought. A redeeming God, rejoicing with His whole heart and whole soul to do us good and to accomplish in us all that is well-pleasing in His sight: This is the one side. Such is the God of the Covenant. Gaze upon Him. Believe Him. Worship Him. Wait on Him until the fire begins to burn and your heart is drawn out with all its might to love this God. Then the other side. A redeemed soul, rejoicing with all its heart and all its soul in the love of this God, entering into the covenant of wholehearted love, and venturing, before it knows, to say to Him: "With my whole heart I love You, God, my exceeding joy." Such are the children of the Covenant.

Beloved reader: Do not rest until you have entered in through the Gate Beautiful, through Christ the door into this temple of the love, of the heart, of God.

FOR FURTHER THOUGHT

1. *God gives each man and woman who puts their faith in him a new heart. What is the only way you can maintain and strengthen that new heart?*

2. *What must you do before God will fully reveal Himself and give Himself unreservedly to you?*

3. *What is the key to acting out, acting on, and enjoying the spiritual gifts God imparts to each and every one of His children?*

The Second Blessing

IN the life of the believer there sometimes comes a crisis, as clearly marked as his conversion, in which he passes out of a life of continual weakness and failure to one of strength, victory, and abiding rest. The transition has been called "the second blessing." Many have objected to the phrase as being unscriptural or as tending to make a rule for all what was only a mode of experience in some. Others have used it as helping to express clearly in human words what should be taught to believers as a possible deliverance from the ordinary life of the Christian to one of abiding fellowship with God and entire devotion to His service. In introducing it into the title of this book, I have indicated my belief that, rightly understood, the words express a scriptural truth and may be a help to believers in putting clearly before them what they may expect from God. Let me try to make clear how I think we ought to understand it.

I have connected the expression with the two Covenants. Why was it that God made two Covenants—not one, and not three? Because there were two parties concerned. In the First Covenant, man was to prove what he could do and what he was. In the Second, God would show what He would do. The former was the time of needed preparation; the latter, the time of divine fulfillment. The same necessity as there was for this in the race exists in the individual, too.

Conversion makes of a sinner a child of God—full of ignorance and weakness, without any conception of what the wholehearted devotion is that God asks of him or the full possession God is ready to take of him. In some cases, the transition from the elementary stage is by a gradual growth and enlightenment. But experience teaches that in the great majority of cases this healthy growth is not found. To those who have never found the secret of a healthy growth, of victory over sin and perfect rest in God, and who have possibly given up ever finding it because all their efforts have been failures, it has often been a wonderful help to learn that it is possible by a single decisive step, namely bringing them into a right relationship to Christ, His Spirit, and His strength, to enter into an entirely new life.

What is needed to help a man to take that step is very simple. He must see and confess the wrongness, the sin, of the life he is living, which is not in harmony with God's will. He must see and believe in the life scripture holds out and Christ Jesus promises to work and maintain in him. As he sees that his failure has been due to his striving in his own strength, and as he believes that our Lord Jesus will actually work all in him in divine power, he takes courage and dares surrender himself to Christ anew. Confessing and giving up all that is of self and sin and yielding himself wholly to Christ and His service, he believes and receives a new power to live his life by the faith of the Son of God. The change is in many cases as clear, as marked, and as wonderful as conversion. For lack of a better name, that of "the second blessing" came most naturally.

When once it is seen how greatly this change is needed in the life of most Christians, and how entirely it rests on faith in Christ and His power, as revealed in the Word, all doubt as to its scripturalness will be removed. And when once its truth is seen, we shall be surprised to find how, throughout scripture, in history and teaching, we find what illustrates and confirms it.

Take the twofold passage of Israel through water, first out of Egypt, then into Canaan. The wilderness journey was the result of unbelief and disobedience, allowed by God to humble them, prove them, and show what was in their heart. When this purpose had been accomplished, a second blessing led them through Jordan as mightily into Canaan just as the first blessing had brought them through the Red Sea out of Egypt.

Or take the Holy Place and the Holiest of All as types of the life in the two covenants, and equally in the two stages of Christian experience. In the former, there was very real access to God and fellowship with Him, but always with a veil between. In the latter, the full access, through a torn veil, into the immediate presence of God and the full experience of the power of the heavenly life. As the eyes are opened to see how terribly the average Christian life comes short of God's purpose, and how truly the mingled life can be expelled by the power of a new revelation of what God waits to do, the types of scripture will shine with a new meaning.

Or look to the teachings of the New Testament. In Romans, Paul contrasts the life of the Christian under the law with that of the believer under grace—the spirit of bondage with the Spirit of adoption. What does this mean but that Christians may still be living under the law and its bondage, that they need to come out of this into the full life of grace and liberty through the Holy Spirit, and that when first they see the difference, nothing is needed but the surrender of faith to accept and experience what grace will do by the Holy Spirit.

To the Corinthians, Paul writes of some being carnal and still babies, walking as men after the flesh, and of others being spiritual, with spiritual discernment and character. To the Galatians, he speaks of the liberty with which Christ, by the Spirit, makes free from the law, in contrast to those who sought to perfect in the flesh what was begun in the Spirit, and who boasted in the flesh—all to call them to recognize the danger of the carnal, divided life and to come immediately to the life of faith, the life in the Spirit, which alone is according to God's will.

Everywhere we see in scripture what the state of the Church at the present day confirms: that conversion is only the gate that leads into the path of life, and that within that gate there is still great danger of mistaking the path, of turning aside or turning back, and that where this has taken place we are called now, and with our whole heart, to turn and give ourselves to nothing less than all Christ is willing to work in us.

Just as there are many who have always thought that conversion must be slow, gradual, and uncertain, who cannot understand how it can be sudden and final because they only take man's powers into account, so many cannot see how the revelation of the true life of holiness and the entrance into it by faith out of a life of self-effort and failure may be immediate and permanent. They look too much to man's efforts and don't know how the second blessing is nothing more nor less than a new vision of what Christ is willing to work in us and the surrender of faith that yields all to Him.

I would like to hope that what I have written in this book may help some to see that the second blessing is just what they need, is what God by His Spirit will work in them, is nothing but the acceptance of Christ in all His saving power as our strength and life, and is what will bring them into and fit them for that full life in the New Covenant, in which God works all in all.

Let me close this note with a quotation from the introduction to a little book just published, *Dying to Self: A Golden Dialogue,* by William Law, with notes by A. M.:

> A great deal has been said against the use of the terms, "the Higher Life" and "the Second Blessing." In Law, one finds nothing of such language, but of the deep truth of which they are the, perhaps defective, expression, his book is full. The points on which so much stress is laid in what is called Keswick teaching, stand prominently out in his whole argument. The low state of the average life of believers, the cause of all failure as coming from self-confidence, the need of an entire surrender of the whole being to the operation of God, the call to turn to Christ as the One and Sure Deliverer from the power of self, the Divine certainty of a better life for all who will in self-despair trust Christ for it, and the heavenly joy of a life in which the Spirit of Love fills the heart—these truths are common to both. What makes Law's putting of the truth of special value is the way in which he shows how humility and utter self-despair, with the resignation to God's mighty working in simple faith, is the infallible way to be delivered from self, and have the Spirit of Love born in the heart.

THE LAW WRITTEN

IN THE HEART

THE thought of the law written in the heart sometimes causes difficulty and discouragement because believers do not see or feel in themselves anything corresponding to it. An illustration may help to remove the difficulty. There are fluids by which you can write so that nothing is visible, either immediately or later, unless the writing is exposed to the sun or the action of some chemical. The writing is there, but one who is ignorant of the process cannot think it is there and doesn't know how to make it readable. The faith of a man who is in the secret believes in it though he doesn't see it.

It is like that with the new heart. God has put His law into it: "Blessed are the people in whose heart is God's law." But it is there invisibly. He who takes God's promise in faith knows that it is in his own heart. As long as there is not clear faith on this point, all attempts to find it or to fulfill that law will be vain. But when by a simple faith the promise is held firmly, the first step is taken to realize it. The soul is then prepared to receive instruction as to what the writing of the law in the heart means. It means, first, that God has implanted in the new heart a love of God's law and a readiness to do all His will. You may not feel this disposition there, but it is there. God has put it there. Believe this, and be assured that there is in you a divine nature that says—and you therefore do not hesitate to say it—"I delight to do Your will, O my God" (Ps. 40:8). In the name of God, and in faith, say it.

This writing of the law means, further, that in planting this principle in you, God has taken all that you know of God's will already and inspired that new heart with the readiness to obey it. It may as yet be written there with invisible writing, and you are not conscious of it. That does not matter. You have here to deal with a divine and hidden work of the Holy Spirit. Be not afraid to say: "Oh, how I love Your law!" (Ps. 119:97). God has put the love of it into your heart, the new heart. He has taken away the stony heart; it is by the new heart you have to live.

The next thing implied in this writing of the law is that you have accepted all God's will, even what you do not yet know, as the delight of your heart. In giving yourself up to God, you gave yourself wholly to His will. That was the one condition of your entering the Covenant, and Covenant grace will now provide for teaching you to know and strengthening you to do all your Father would have you do.

The whole life in the New Covenant is a life of faith. Faith accepts every promise of the Covenant, is certain that it is being fulfilled, and looks confidently to the God of the Covenant to do His work. Faith believes implicitly in the new heart, with the law written in it, because it believes in both the promise and in the God who gave and fulfills the promise.

It may be well to add here that the same truth holds good of all the promises concerning the new heart—they must be accepted and acted on by faith. When we read of "the love of God. . .poured out in our hearts by the Holy Spirit" (Rom. 5:5), of "Christ dwelling in the heart" (see Eph. 3:17), of "a clean heart," of "loving one another fervently with a pure heart" (see 1 Pet. 1:22), of "God establishing our heart blameless in holiness" (see 1 Thess. 3:13), we must, with the eye of faith, regard these spiritual realities as actually and in very deed existing within us. In His hidden unseen way, God is working them there. Not by sight or feeling, but by faith in the living God and His Word, we know they are as the power for the dispositions and inclinations of the new heart. In this faith we are to act, knowing that we have the power to love, to obey, to be holy. The New Covenant gives us a God who works all in us, and faith in Him gives us the assurance, above and beyond all feeling, that this God is doing His blessed work.

And if the question is asked, "What are we to think of all there is within us that contradicts this faith?" let us remember what scripture teaches us of it. We sometimes speak of an old and a new heart. Scripture does not do so. It speaks of the old, the stony, heart being taken away—the heart, with its will, disposition, affections, being made new with a divine newness. This new heart is placed in the midst of what scripture calls the flesh, in which there dwells nothing good.

We shall find it a great advantage to adhere as closely as possible to scripture language. It will greatly help our faith even to use the very words God by His Holy Spirit has used to teach us. And it will greatly clear our view for knowing what to think of the sin that remains in us if we think of it and deal with it in the light of God's truth. Every evil desire and affection comes from the flesh, man's sinful natural life. It owes its power greatly to our ignorance of its nature and to our trusting in its help and strength to cast out its evil.

I have already pointed out how sinful flesh and religious flesh are one, and how all failure in religion is due to a secret trust in ourselves. As we accept and make use of what God says of the flesh, we shall see in it the source of all evil in us. Then we shall say of its temptations: "It is no longer I who do it, but sin that dwells in me" (Rom. 7:20). Then we will maintain our integrity as we maintain a good conscience that condemns us for nothing knowingly done against God's will, and we will be strong in the faith of the Holy Spirit, who dwells in the new heart to strengthen so that we need not and "shall not fulfill the lust of the flesh" (Gal. 5:16).

I conclude with an extract of an address by Rev. F. Webster, at Keswick last year, in confirmation of what I have just said:

"Put on the Lord Jesus Christ, and make no provision for the flesh, to fulfill its lusts" (Rom. 13:14). "Make no provision for the flesh." The flesh is there, you know. To deny or ignore the existence of an enemy is to give him a great chance against you, and the flesh is in the believer to the very end a force of evil to be reckoned with continually, an evil force inside a man, and yet, thank God, a force that can be so dealt with by the power of God so that it shall have no power to defile the heart or deflect the will. The flesh is in you, but your heart may be kept clean moment by moment in spite of the existence of evil in your fallen nature. Every avenue, every opening that leads into the heart, every thought and desire and purpose and imagination of your being, may be closed against the flesh, so that there shall be no opening to come in and defile the heart or deflect the will from the will of God.

You say that is a very high standard. But it is the Word of God. There is to be no secret sympathy with sin. Although the flesh is there, you are to make it no excuse for sins. You are not to say, "I am naturally irritable, anxious, jealous, and I cannot help letting these things crop up, for they come from within." Yes, they come from within, but then there need be no provision, no opening in your heart for these things to enter. Your heart can be barricaded with an impassable barrier against these things. "No provision for the flesh." Not merely the front door barred and bolted so that you do not invite them to come in, but the side and back door closed, too. You may be so Christ-possessed and Christ-enclosed that you shall positively hate everything that is of the flesh.

"Make no provision for the flesh." The only way to do so is to "put on the Lord Jesus Christ." I spoke of the heart being so barricaded that there should be no entrance to it, that the flesh should never be able to defile it or deflect the will from the will of God. How can that be done? By putting on the Lord Jesus Christ. It has been such a blessing to me just to learn that one secret, just to learn the positive side of deliverance—putting on the Lord Jesus Christ.

NOTE C

GEORGE MÜLLER AND
HIS SECOND CONVERSION

IN the life of George Müller of Bristol, there was an epoch four years after his conversion, to which he always looked back afterwards, and of which he often spoke as his entrance into the true Christian life.

In an address given to ministers and workers after his ninetieth birthday, he spoke of it himself this way:

"That leads to another thought—the full surrender of the heart to God. I *was converted* in November 1825, but I only *came into the full surrender of the heart* four years later, in July 1829. The love of money was gone, the love of place was gone, the love of position was gone, the love of worldly pleasures and engagements was gone. God, God, God alone became my portion. I found my all in Him. I wanted nothing else. And by the grace of God this has remained and has made me a happy man, an exceedingly happy man, and it led me to care only about the things of God. I ask, affectionately, my beloved brethren, have you fully surrendered the heart to God, or is there this thing or that thing with which you are taken up irrespective of God? I read a little of the scriptures before, but preferred other books, but since that time the revelation He has made of Himself has become unspeakably blessed to me, and I can say from my heart, God is an infinitely lovely Being. Oh, do not be satisfied until in your innermost soul you can say, 'God is an infinitely lovely Being!'"

The account he gives of this change in his journal is as follows. He speaks of one whom he had heard preach at Teignmouth, where he had gone for the sake of his health:

"Though I did not like all he said, yet I saw a gravity and solemnity in him different from the rest. Through the instrumentality of this brother, the Lord bestowed a great blessing upon me for which I shall have cause to thank Him throughout eternity. God then began to show me that the Word of God alone is to be our standard of judgment in spiritual things, that it can only be explained by the Holy Spirit, and that in our day, as well as in former times, He is the Teacher of His people. *The office of the Holy Spirit I had not experimentally understood before that time.* I had not before seen that the Holy Spirit alone can teach us about our state by nature, show us our need of a Savior, enable us to believe in Christ, explain to us the scriptures, help us in preaching, etc.

"It was my beginning to understand this point in particular that had a great effect on me, for the Lord enabled me to put it to the test of experience by laying aside commentaries and almost every other book and simply reading the Word of God and studying it. The result of this was that the first evening that I shut myself into my room to give myself to prayer and meditation over the scriptures, I learned more in a few hours than I had done during a period of several months previously. *But the particular difference was that I received real strength in my soul in doing so.*

"In addition to this, it pleased the Lord to lead me to see a *higher standard of devotedness* than I had seen before. He led me, in a measure, to see what is my glory in this world, even to be despised, to be poor and mean with Christ. . . . I returned to London much better in body. And as to my soul, *the change was so great that it was like a second conversion.*"

In another passage he speaks this:

"I fell into the snare into which so many young believers fall: the reading of religious books is preferred to the scriptures. Now the scriptural way of reasoning would have been: God Himself has condescended to become an author, and I am ignorant of that precious Book that His Holy Spirit has caused to be written. Therefore I ought to read again this Book of books most earnestly, most prayerfully, and with much meditation.

"Instead of acting this way and being led by my ignorance of the Word to study it more, my difficulty of understanding it made me careless about reading it, and then, like many believers, I practically preferred for the first four years of my Christian life the works of uninspired men to the oracles of the living God. The consequence was that I remained a babe, both in knowledge and grace. In knowledge, I say, for all true knowledge must be derived by the Spirit from the Word. This lack of knowledge most sadly kept me back from walking steadily in the ways of God. For it is the truth that makes us free, by delivering us from the slavery of the lusts of the flesh, the lusts of the eyes, and the pride of life. The Word proves it, the experience of the saints proves it, and also my own experience most decidedly proves it. For when it pleased the Lord, in August 1829, to bring me really to the scriptures, my life and walk became very different.

"If anyone would ask me how he may read the scriptures most profitably, I would answer him:

"1. Above all he must seek to have it settled in his own mind *that God alone, by the Holy spirit, can teach him,* and that, therefore, as God will be inquired for all blessings, it becomes him to seek for God's blessing previous to reading, and also while reading.

"2. He should also have it settled in his mind that though *the Holy Spirit is the best and sufficient Teacher*, yet that He does not always teach immediately when we desire it, and that, therefore, *we may have to ask Him again and again* for the explanation of certain passages. But that *He will surely teach us* at last, if we will seek for light prayerfully, patiently, and for the glory of God."

Just one more passage, from an address given on his ninetieth birthday:

"For sixty-nine years and ten months he had been a very happy man. That he attributed to two things. He had maintained a good conscience, not willfully going on in a course he knew to be contrary to the mind of God. He did not, of course, mean that he was perfect. He was poor, weak, and sinful. Secondly, he attributed it to his love of holy scripture. Of late years, his practice had been four times every year to read through the scriptures, with application to his own heart, and with meditation. And that day he was a greater lover of God's Word than he was sixty-six years ago. It was this, and maintaining a good conscience, that had given him all these years peace and joy in the Holy Spirit."

In connection with what has been said about the New Covenant being a ministry of the Spirit, this narrative is most instructing. It shows us how George Müller's power lay in God's revealing to him the work of the Holy Spirit. He writes that up to the time of that change, he had "not experimentally understood the office of the Holy Spirit." We speak much of George Müller's power in prayer, and it is of importance to remember that that power was entirely due to his love of, and faith in, God's Word. But it is of still more importance to notice that his power to believe God's Word so fully was entirely due to his having learned to know the Holy Spirit as his Teacher. When the words of God are explained to us and made living within us by the Holy Spirit, they have a power to awaken faith that they otherwise don't have. The Word then brings us into contact with God, comes to us as from God direct, and binds our whole life to Him.

When the Holy Spirit feeds us on the Word this way, our whole life comes under His power, and the fruit is seen, not only in the power of prayer, but as much in the power of obedience. Notice how Müller tells us that the two secrets of his great happiness were his great love for God's Word and his always *maintaining a good conscience*, not knowingly doing anything against the will of God. In giving himself to the teaching of the Holy Spirit, as he tells us in his birthday address, he made a full surrender of the entire heart to God to be ruled by the Word. He gave himself to obey that Word in everything, he believed that the Holy Spirit gave the grace to obey, and so he was able to maintain a walk free from knowingly transgressing God's law. This is a point he always insisted on.

So he writes, in regard to a life of dependence on God: "It will not do—it is not possible—*to live in sin,* and at the same time, by communion with God, to draw down from heaven everything one needs for the life that now is."

Again, speaking of the strengthening of faith: "It is of the utmost importance that we seek to maintain an *upright heart and a good conscience,* and therefore do not knowingly and habitually indulge in those things that are contrary to the mind of God. All my confidence in God, all my leaning on Him in the hour of trial, will be gone if I have a guilty conscience, and do not seek to put away this guilty conscience but still continue to do things which are contrary to His mind."

A careful perusal of this testimony will show us how the chief points usually insisted upon in connection with the second blessing are all found here. There is the full surrender of the heart to be taught and led alone by the Spirit of God. There is the higher standard of holiness that is at once set up. There is the tender desire in nothing to offend God, but to have at all times a good conscience that testifies that we are pleasing to God. And there is the faith that where the Holy Spirit reveals to us in the Word the will of God, He gives the sufficient strength for the doing of it. "The particular difference," he says of reading with faith of the Holy Spirit's teaching, "was that I received real strength in my soul in doing so." No wonder that he said: *"The change was so great that it was like a second conversion."*

All centers in this: that we believe in the New Covenant and its promises as a ministry of the Spirit. That belief may come to some suddenly, as to George Müller, or it may dawn upon others by degrees. Let all say to God that they are ready to put their whole heart and life under the rule of the Holy Spirit dwelling in them, teaching them by the Word, and strengthening them by His grace. He enables us to live pleasing to God.

Note D

Canon Battersby

I do not know that I can find a better case by which to illustrate the place Christ, the Mediator of the Covenant, takes in leading into its full blessing than that of the founder of the Keswick Convention, the late Canon Battersby.

It was at the Oxford Convention in 1873 that he witnessed to having "received a new and distinct blessing to which he had been a stranger before." For more than twenty-five years he had been most diligent as a minister of the gospel and, as appears from his journals, most faithful in seeking to maintain a close walk with God. But he was always disturbed by the consciousness of being overcome by sin. So far back as 1853 he had written, "I feel again how very far I am from enjoying habitually that peace and love and joy that Christ promises. I must confess that I do not have it, and that very ungentle and unchristian tempers often strive within me for the mastery."

When in 1873 he read what was being published of the higher life, the effect was to render him utterly dissatisfied with himself and his state. There were indeed difficulties he could not quite understand in that teaching, but he felt that he must either reach forward to better things, nothing less than redemption from *all* iniquities, or fall back more and more into worldliness and sin.

At Oxford he heard an address on the rest of faith. It opened his eyes to the truth that a believer who really longs for deliverance from sinning must simply take Christ at His word and rely, without feeling, on Him to do His work of cleansing and keeping the soul. "I thought of the sufficiency of Jesus, and said, 'I will rest in Him,' and I did rest in Him. I was afraid that it might be a passing emotion, but I found that a presence of Jesus was graciously manifested to me in a way I did not know before, and that *I did abide in Him.* I do not want to rest in these emotions, but just to believe and to cling to Christ as my all." He was a man of very reserved nature, but felt it a duty before the close of the conference to confess publicly his past shortcoming and testify openly to his having entered upon a new and definite experience.

In a paper written not long after this, he pointed out what the steps are leading to this experience. *First,* a clear view of the possibilities of Christian attainment—a life in word and action habitually governed by the Spirit, in constant communion with God and continual victory over sin through abiding in Christ. *Then,* the deliberate purpose of the will for a full renunciation of all the idols of the flesh or spirit and a will-surrender to Christ. And then this last and important step: *We must look up to and wait on our ascended Lord for all that we need to enable us to do this.*

A careful perusal of this very brief statement will prove how everything centers here in Christ. The surrender for a life of continual communion and victory is to be to Christ. The strength for that life is to be in Him and from Him, by faith in Him. And *the power* to make the full surrender and rest in Him *is to be waited for from Him alone.*

In June 1875, the first Keswick Convention was held. In the circular calling it, we read: "Many are everywhere thirsting that they may be brought to enjoy more of the Divine presence in their daily life and a fuller manifestation of the Holy Spirit's power, whether in subduing the lusts of the flesh or in enabling them to offer more effective service to God. It is certainly God's will that His children should be satisfied in regard to these longings, and there are those who can testify that He has satisfied them, and does satisfy them with daily fresh manifestations of His grace and power."

The results of the very first convention were most blessed, so that after its close he wrote: "There is a very remarkable resemblance in the testimonies I have since received as to the nature of the blessing obtained, viz., *the ability given* to make a full surrender to the Lord, and the consequent experience of an abiding peace far exceeding anything previously experienced." Through all, the chief thought was Christ, first drawing and enabling the soul to rest in Him, and then meeting it with the fulfillment of its desire, the abiding experience of His power to keep it in victory over sin and communion with God.

And what was the fruit of this new experience? Eight years later, Canon Battersby spoke: "It is now eight years since that I knew this blessing as my own. I cannot say that I have never for a moment ceased to trust the Lord to keep me. But I can say that so long as I have trusted Him, He has kept me. He has been faithful."

NOTHING OF MYSELF

ONE would think that no words could make it plainer than the words of the Covenant state it—that the one difference between Old and New is that in the latter everything is to be done by God Himself. And yet believers and even teachers do not take it in. And even those who do find it hard to live it out. Our whole being is so blinded to the true relation to God, His inconceivable omnipresent omnipotence working every moment in us is so far beyond the reach of human conception, that our little hearts cannot rise to the reality of His infinite love making itself one with us and delighting to dwell in us and to work all in us that has to be done there—that when we think we have accepted the truth, we find it is only a thought.

We are such strangers to the knowledge of what a *God* really is, as the actual life by which His creatures live. *In Him* we live and move and have our being (Acts 17:28). And especially is the knowledge of the Triune God too high for us, in that wonderful, most real, and most practical indwelling, to make which possible the Son became Incarnate, and the Holy Spirit was sent forth into our hearts. Only they who confess their ignorance and wait very humbly and persistently on our blessed God to teach us by His Holy Spirit what that all-working indwelling is can hope to have it revealed to them.

It is not long since I had occasion, in preparing a series of Bible lessons for our Students Association here, to make a study of the Gospel of St. John and of the life of our Lord as set forth there. I cannot say how deeply I have been newly impressed with that which I cannot but regard as the deepest secret of His life on earth: *His dependence on the Father*. It has come to me like a new revelation. Some twelve times and more He uses the word *not* and *nothing* of Himself. *Not* My will. *Not* My words. *Not* My honor. *Not* My own glory. I can do *nothing* of Myself. I speak *not* of Myself. I came *not* of Myself. I do *nothing* of Myself.

Just think a moment what this means in connection with what He tells us of His life in the Father. "As the Father has life in Himself, so He has granted the Son to have life in Himself" (John 5:26). "That all should honor the Son just as they honor the Father" (5:23). And yet this Son, who has life in Himself just as the Father has, immediately adds: "I can of Myself do *nothing*" (5:30). We should have thought that with this life in Himself, He would have the power of independent action as the Father has. But no. "The Son can do nothing of Himself, but what He sees the Father do" (5:19). The chief mark of this divine life He has in Himself is evidently unceasing dependence—receiving from the Father, by the moment, what He had to speak or do.

Nothing of Myself is as distinctly true of Him as it ever could be of the weakest or most sinful man. The life of the Father dwelling in Christ, and Christ in the Father, meant that just as truly as when He was begotten of the Father, He received divine life and glory from Him, so the continuation of that life came only by an eternal process of giving and receiving, as absolute as is the eternal generation itself. The more closely we study this truth, and Christ's life in the light of it, the more we are compelled to say that the deepest root of Christ's relationship to the Father—the true reason why He was so well-pleasing, the secret of His glorifying the Father—was this: *He allowed God to do all in Him.* He only received and accomplished what God accomplished in Him. His whole attitude was that of the open ear, the servant spirit, the childlike dependence that waited for all on God.

The infinite importance of this truth in the Christian life is easily felt. The life Christ lived in the Father is the life He imparts to us. We are to abide in Him and He in us, *just as* He in the Father and the Father in Him. And if the secret of His abiding in the Father is this unceasing self-denial—"I can do nothing of Myself"—this life of most entire and absolute dependence and waiting on God, must it not far more be the most marked feature of our Christian life, the first and all-pervading disposition we seek to maintain?

In a little book of William Law's that has just been issued,[10] he specially insists upon this in his so-striking repetition of the call—if we would die to self in order to have the birth of divine love in our souls, to sink down in humility, meekness, patience, and resignation to God. I think that no one who at all enters into this advice but will feel what new emphasis is given to it by the remembrance of how this entire self-renunciation was not only one of the many virtues in the character of Christ, but, indeed, that first essential one without which God could have accomplished nothing in Him, through which God did work all.

Let us make Christ's words our own: "*I can do nothing of Myself.*" Take it as the keynote of a single day. Look up and see the infinite God waiting to do everything as soon as we are ready to give up all to Him and receive all from Him. Bow down in lowly worship and wait for the Holy Spirit to work some measure of the mind of Christ in you. Do not be disconcerted if you do not learn the lesson at once. There is the God of love waiting to do everything in him who is willing to be nothing. At moments, the teaching appears dangerous, at other times terribly difficult. The blessed Son of God teaches it to us—this was His whole life: I can do nothing of Myself. He is our life, and He will work it in us. And when as the Lamb of God He produces this His disposition in us, we shall be prepared for Him to rise on us and shine in us in His heavenly glory.

"Nothing of Myself"—that word spoken two thousand years ago, coming

---

[10] William Law, *Dying to Self: A Golden Dialogue.* The thought is worked out with exceeding power, and the lesson taught that the only thing man can do for his salvation is to deny and cease from himself, that God may work in him.

out of the innermost depths of the heart of the Son of God—is a seed in which the power of the eternal life is hidden. Take it straight from the heart of Christ and hide it in your heart. Meditate on it until it reveals the beauty of His divine meekness and humility and explains how all the power and glory of God could work in Him. Believe in it as containing the very life and disposition that you need, and believe in Christ, whose Spirit dwells in the seed to make it true in you. Begin, in single acts of self-emptying, to offer it to God as the one desire of your heart. Count on God accepting them, and meeting them with His grace, to make the acts into habits, and the habits into dispositions. And you may depend on it—there is nothing that will lift you so near to God, nothing that will unite you closer to Christ, nothing that will prepare you for the abiding presence and power of God working in you, as the death to self that is found in the simple word—*nothing of Myself.*

This word is one of the keys to the New Covenant life. As I believe that God is actually to work all in me, I shall see that the one thing that is hindering me is my doing something of myself. As I am willing to learn from Christ by the Holy Spirit to say truly, *Nothing of myself,* I shall have the true preparation to receive all God has engaged to work, and the power confidently to expect it. I shall learn that the whole secret of the New Covenant is just one thing: *God Works All!* The seal of the Covenant stands sure: "I, the LORD, have spoken it. . .*and I will do it*" (Ezek. 24:14).

THE WHOLE HEART

LET me give the principal passages in which the words "the whole heart" and "all the heart" are used. A careful study of them will show how wholehearted love and service are what God has always asked, because He can, in the very nature of things, ask nothing less. The prayerful and believing acceptance of the words will awaken the assurance that such wholehearted love and service are exactly the blessing the New Covenant was meant to make possible. That assurance will prepare us for turning to the omnipotence of God to work in us what may have hitherto appeared beyond our reach.

Hear, first, God's word in Deuteronomy—

4:29: "But from there you will seek the LORD your God, and you will find Him if you *seek Him* with all your heart and with all your soul."

6:4–5: "Hear, O Israel: The LORD our God, the LORD is one! You *shall love the LORD your God* with all your heart, with all your soul, and with all your strength."

10:12: "What does the LORD your God require of you, but to fear the LORD your God, to walk in all His ways and to love Him, to serve the LORD your God with all your heart and with all your soul."

11:13: "Earnestly obey My commandments which I command you today, *to love* the LORD your God and *serve Him* with all your heart and with all your soul."

13:3: "The LORD your God is testing you to know whether you love the LORD your God with all your heart and with all your soul."

26:16: "This day the LORD your God commands you to *observe these statutes and judgments.* . .to observe them with all your heart and with all your soul."

30:2: "Return to the LORD your God and *obey His voice.* . .with all your heart and with all your soul."

30:6: "The LORD your God will circumcise your heart. . .*to love* the LORD your God with all your heart and with all your soul" (see also 30:9–10).

Take these often-repeated words as the expression of God's will concerning His people, and concerning yourself; then ask if you could wish to give God anything less. Take the last-cited verse as the divine promise of the New Covenant—that He will circumcise, will so cleanse the heart to love Him with a wholehearted love, that obedience is within your reach, and then say whether you will not vow afresh to keep this His first and great commandment.

Listen to Joshua (22:5): "But take careful heed. . .*to love* the LORD your God, *to walk* in all His ways, *to keep* His commandments, *to hold fast* to Him, and *to serve* Him with all your heart and with all your soul."

Listen to Samuel (1 Sam. 12:20, 24): "Do not turn aside from following the LORD, but *serve the LORD* with all your heart. . . . Only fear the LORD, and *serve Him* in truth with all your heart."

Hear David repeating God's promise to Solomon (1 Kings 2:4): "If your sons take heed to their way, *to walk before Me* in truth with all their heart and with all their soul."

Hear God's word concerning David (1 Kings 14:8): "My servant David, who kept My commandments and *who followed Me* with all his heart, to do only what was right in My eyes."

Hear Solomon in his temple prayer (1 Kings 8:48–49): "When they *return to You* with all their heart and with all their soul. . .then hear in heaven Your dwelling place their prayer."

Listen to what is said of Jehu (2 Kings 10:30–31): "The LORD said to Jehu, 'Because you have done well in doing what is right in My sight. . .' But Jehu took no heed to walk in the law of the LORD God of Israel with all his heart."

Of Josiah we read (2 Kings 23:3, 25): "Then the king stood by a pillar and made a covenant before the LORD, *to follow the LORD*. . .with all his heart and all his soul, to perform the words of this covenant that were written in this book. And all the people took their stand for the covenant. . . . There was no king like him, *who turned to the LORD* with all his heart, with all his soul, and with all his might."

The words concerning Asa in 2 Chronicles 15:12, 15, we had as our text.

Of Jehoshaphat, men said (2 Chron. 22:9): "[He] *sought* the LORD with all his heart."

And of Hezekiah it is written (2 Chron. 31:21): "And in every work that he began. . .to seek his God, he did *it* with all his heart. So he prospered."

Oh, that all would ask God to give them, by the Holy Spirit, a simple vision of Himself!—claiming, giving, accepting, blessing, delighting in the love and service of the whole heart—the sacrifice of the whole burnt offering. Surely they would fall down and join the ranks of those who have given it, and refuse to think of anything as religious life, or worship, or service, but that in which their whole heart went out to God.

Turn to the Psalms. Hear David (9:1; 111:1; 138:1): "I will praise You with my whole heart." And in Psalm 119, the psalm of the way of blessedness: "Blessed are those. . .who seek Him with the whole heart! . . .With my whole heart have I sought You. . . . I shall keep Your law; indeed, I shall observe it with my whole heart. . . . I entreated Your favor with my whole heart. . . . I will keep Your precepts with my whole heart. . . . I cry out with my whole heart"(119:2, 10, 34, 58, 69, 145). Praise and prayer; seeking God and keeping His precepts; all equally with the whole heart.

Shall we not begin asking more earnestly than ever, as often as we see men engaged in their earthly pursuits in search of money, pleasure, fame, or power with their whole heart, "Is this the spirit in which Christians consider that God must be served? Is this the spirit in which I serve Him? *Is not this the one thing needed in our religion?*" Lord, reveal unto us Your will!

Now, just a few words more from the Prophets about the new time, the great change that can come into our lives.

Jer. 24:7: "*I will give them a heart* to know Me, that I am the LORD; and they shall be My people, and I will be their God, *for they shall return to Me* with their whole heart."

29:13–14: "You will seek Me and find Me, when you search for Me with all your heart. *I will be found by you,* says the LORD."

32:39–41—Let my reader not be weary of reading carefully these divine words. They contain the secret the seed, the living power of a complete transition out of a life in the bondage of halfhearted service to the glorious liberty of the children of God—"*I will give them one heart* and one way, that they may fear Me forever. . . . And I will make an everlasting covenant with them, that *I will not turn away* from doing them good; but *I will put* My fear in their hearts so that they *will not depart* from Me. Yes, I will rejoice over them to do them good, and I will assuredly plant them in this land, *with all My heart and with all My soul.*"

It is to be all God's doing. And He is to do it with His whole heart and His whole soul. It is the vision of this God with His whole heart loving us, longing and delighting to fulfill His promise and make us wholly His own, that we need. *This vision makes it impossible not to love Him with our whole heart.* Lord, open our eyes that we may see!

Joel 2:12: "'Now, therefore,' says the LORD, '*turn to* Me with all your heart.'"

Zeph. 3:14: "Shout, O Israel! *Be glad and rejoice with all your heart. The LORD has taken away your judgments. He has cast out your enemy. The King of Israel, the LORD, is in your midst; You shall see disaster no more.*"

Now one word from our Lord Jesus (Matt. 22:37): "Jesus said to him, '*You shall love the LORD your God with all your heart.*'" This is the first and great commandment. This is the sum of that law He came to fulfill for us and in us, *came to enable us to fulfill.* "For what the law could not do in that it was weak through the flesh, God. . .sending His own Son. . .condemned sin in the flesh, that the righteous requirement of the law might be fulfilled in us who do not walk according to the flesh but according to the Spirit" (Rom. 8:3–4).

Praise God! This righteousness of the law—loving God with all the heart, for love is the fulfilling of the law—this righteousness of the law is fulfilled *in us* who walk after the Spirit. Jesus came to make it possible. He gives His Spirit—the Spirit of life in Christ Jesus—to make it actual. Let us not fear to give ourselves a whole burnt offering, acceptable to God, and love Him with all our heart and mind and strength.

May I ask the reader just once again to peruse chapter 6, "The Everlasting

Covenant of the Spirit," and chapter 18, "Entering into the Covenant: With All the Heart." And say then, if you have never yet entered fully into this covenant of the whole heart, whether you are not ready to do it now. God demands, God works, God is, oh, so infinitely worthy of, the whole heart! Do not be afraid to say He shall have it. You may confidently count on the blessed Lord Jesus, the Surety of the Covenant, whose it is to make it true in you by His Spirit, to enable you to exercise the faith that knows that God's power will work what He has promised. In His name say: With my whole heart I do love You!

THE NEW LIFE

CONTENTS

Preface

I N communication with young converts, I have very frequently longed for a suitable book in which the most important truths that they have need of for the new life should be briefly and simply set forth. I could not find anything that entirely corresponded to what I desired. During the services in which, since Whitsuntide 1884, I have been permitted to take part, and in which I have been enabled to speak with so many who professed to have found the Lord and who were, nevertheless, still very weak in knowledge and faith, this need was felt by me still more keenly.

In the course of my journey, I felt myself moved to take the pen in hand. Under a vivid impression of the infirmities and the distorted thoughts concerning the new life with which, as was apparent to me from conversations I had with them, almost all young Christians have to wrestle, I wished, in some words of instruction and encouragement, to let them see what a glorious life of power and joy is prepared for them in their Lord Jesus, and how simple the way is to enjoy all this blessing.

I have confined myself in these reflections to some of the most important topics. The first is the *Word of God* as the glorious and sure guide, even for the simplest souls who will only surrender themselves to it. Then, as the chief element in the Word, there is *the Son*, the gift of the Father, to do all for us. After that follows what the scriptures teach concerning *sin*, as the only thing that we have to bring to Jesus, as that which we must give to Him, and from which He will set us free. Further, there is *faith*, the great word in which is expressed our inability to bring or to do anything and that teaches us that all our salvation must be received every day of our life as a gift from above. With the *Holy Spirit* also must the young Christian make acquaintance, as the Person through whom the Word and Jesus, with all His work and faith in Him, can become power and truth. Then there is the *holy life* of obedience and of fruitfulness, in which the Spirit teaches us to walk.

It is to these six leading thoughts of the new life that I have confined myself, with the ceaseless prayer that God may use what I have written to make His young children understand what a glorious and mighty life it is that they have received from their Father. It was often very unwillingly that I took leave of the young converts who had to go back to lonely places, where they could have little counsel or help and seldom mingle in the preaching of the Word. It is my sure and confident expectation that what the Lord has given me to write shall prove a blessing to many of these young confessors.

(I have, in some instances, attached the names of the places where the different portions of this manual were written; in others, the names of the towns where the substance of them was spoken, as a remembrance to the friends with whom I had fellowship.)

While writing this book I have had a second wish abiding with me. I have thought what I could possibly do to make sure my little book does not draw away attention from the Word of God, but rather help to make the Word more precious. I resolved to furnish the work with parenthetical references so that, on every point that was treated, the reader might be stirred up still to listen *to the Word itself,* to *God Himself.*

I hope that this arrangement will yield a double benefit. Many a one does not know, and had nobody to teach him, how to examine the scriptures properly. This book may help him in his loneliness. If he will only meditate on one and another point and then look up the texts that are quoted, he will get into the habit of consulting God's Word itself on that which he wishes to understand. But it may just as readily be of service in prayer meetings or social gatherings for the study of the Word. Let each one read the portion fixed on at home and review those texts that seem to him the most important. Let the leader of the meeting read the portion aloud once. Let him then request that each one who pleases should announce one and another text on that point which has struck him most.

We have found in my congregation that the benefit of such meetings for bringing and reading aloud texts on a point previously announced is very great. This practice leads to the searching of God's Word in a way that even preaching does not. It stirs up the members of the congregation, especially the young people, to independent dealing with the Word. It leads to a more living *fellowship* among the members of Christ's body, and helps also their building up in love. It prepares the way for a social recognition of the Word as the living communication of the thoughts of God, which with divine power shall accomplish in us what is pleasing to God. I am persuaded that there is many a believing man or woman who asks what they can accomplish for the Lord, who along this pathway could become the channels of great blessing. Let them once a week bring together some of their neighbors or friends (sometimes two or three households live on one farm) to hear read out texts for which all have been previously searching: The Lord shall certainly give His blessing there.

With respect to the use of this book in retirement, I would gladly request one thing more. I hope that no one will think it strange. Let every portion be read over at least three times. The great bane of all our conversation on divine things is superficiality. When we read anything and understand it somewhat, we think that this is enough. No, we must give *time* so that it may make an impression and wield its own influence on us. Read every portion *the first time* with consideration to understand the good that is in it, and then see if you receive benefit from the thoughts that are there expressed. Read it *the second time* to see if it is really in accordance with God's Word. Take some, if not all, of the texts that are cited on each point and ponder them in order to come under the full force of what God has said on the point. Let your God, through His Word, teach you what you must think and believe concerning Him and His will. Read it then *the third time* to find out the corresponding places, not in the Bible, but in your own life, so that you may know if your life has been in harmony with the new life, and to direct your life for the future entirely according to God's Word. I am fully persuaded that the time and efforts spent on such converse with the Word of God under the teaching of this or some book that helps you in dealing with it will be rewarded tenfold.

I conclude with a cordial brotherly greeting to all with whom I have been permitted to mingle during the past year in my speaking about the precious Savior and His glorious salvation. Also to all in other congregations who in this last season have learned to know the beloved Lord Jesus as their Redeemer. With a heart full of peace and love, I think of you all and I pray that the Lord may confirm His work in you. I have not become weary of crying to you. The blessedness and the power of the new life that is in you are greater than you know, are wonderfully great. Only learn to know correctly and trust in Jesus, *the gift of God*, and the scriptures, *the Word of God*. Only give Him time to communicate with you and to work in you, and your heart shall overflow with the blessedness of God.

Now to Him who is able to do more than exceedingly above all that we can ask or think, to Him be glory in the Church to all eternity.

ANDREW MURRAY
Wellington, South Africa,
August 12, 1885

They go from strength to strength;
each one appears before God in Zion.
PSALM 84:7

1

THE NEW LIFE

*"For God so loved the world that He gave His
only begotten Son, that whoever believes in Him
should not perish but have everlasting life."*

JOHN 3:16

*For you died, and your life is hidden with Christ in God.
When Christ who is our life appears. . .*

COLOSSIANS 3:3–4

*We. . .declare to you that eternal life which was with the Father
and was manifested to us. . . . God has given us eternal life,
and this life is in His Son. He who has the Son has life.*

1 JOHN 1:2; 5:11–12

HOW glorious, then, is the blessing everyone who believes in the Lord Jesus receives. Not only does there come a change in his disposition and manner of life, but he also receives from God out of heaven an entirely new life. He is born anew, born of God—he has passed from death into life (John 1:12–13; 3:5, 7; 5:24; 1 John 3:14; 5:1).

This new life is nothing less than eternal life (John 3:15–16, 36; 6:40, 51; 6:25–26; Rom. 6:11, 23; 8:2; 1 John 5:12–13). This does not mean, as many believe, that our life shall now no longer die but shall endure into eternity. No, eternal life is nothing else but the very life of God, the life that He has had in Himself from eternity and that has been visibly revealed in Christ. This life is now the possession of every child of God (1 John 1:3; 3:1; 5:11).

This is a life of inconceivable power. Whenever God gives life to a young plant or animal, that life has in itself the power of growth, whereby the plant or animal grows large on its own. Life is power. In the new life, that is, in your heart, there is the power of eternity (John 5:10, 28; Heb. 7:16, 29; 6:25–26; 2 Cor. 7:9; 8:4; Col. 3:3–4; Phil. 4:13). More certain than the healthy growth of any tree or animal is the growth and increase of the child of God, who, in reality, surrenders himself to the working of the new life.

What hinders this power and the reception of the new spiritual life is chiefly two things. The one is ignorance of its nature, its laws, and its workings. Man, even the Christian, has by himself not the least conception of the new life that comes from God—it surpasses all his thoughts. His own distorted thoughts of the way to serve and to please God—namely by what he does and is—are so deeply rooted in him that although he thinks he understands and receives God's Word, he yet thinks humanly and carnally on divine things (Josh. 3:4; Isa. 4:8–9; Matt. 16:23).

Not only must God give salvation and life; He must also give the Spirit to make us know what He gives. Not only must He point out the land of Canaan and the way to get there; we must also, like the blind, be led every day by Himself. The young Christian must try to cherish a deep conviction of his ignorance concerning the new life and of his inability to form right thoughts about it. This will bring him to the humility and to the childlike spirit of docility to which the Lord shall make His secret known (Pss. 25:5, 8–9; 143:8; Isa. 42:16; 64:4; Matt. 11:25; 1 Cor. 1:18–19; 2:7, 10, 12; Heb. 11:8).

There is a second hindrance in the way of faith. In the life of every plant and every animal and every child, there lies sufficient power by which it can become big. In the new life, God has made the most glorious provision of a sufficient power through which His child can grow and become all that he must be. Christ Himself is his life and his power of life (Pss. 18:2; 27:1; 34:8; 38:3, John 14:19; Gal. 2:20; Col. 3:3–4).

> *Let everyone who, therefore, has received this new life cultivate this great conviction: It is eternal life that works in me.*

Yet because this mighty life is not visible or cannot be felt but instead works in the midst of human weakness, the young Christian's mind often becomes filled with doubt. He then fails to believe that he will grow with divine power and certainty. He does not understand that the believing life is a life of faith in which he thinks on the life that is in Christ for him, although he neither sees, feels, nor experiences anything (Hab. 2:4; Matt. 6:27; Rom. 1:17; Gal. 3:11; Heb. 10:38).

Let everyone who, therefore, has received this new life cultivate this great conviction: It is eternal life that works in me. It works with divine power. I can and shall become what God wants me to be. Christ Himself is my life. I have to receive Him every day as my life given by God to me, and then He shall be my life in full power.

O my Father, who has given me Your Son that I may have life in Him, I thank You for the glorious new life that is now in me. I ask You, teach me to know acceptably this new life. I will acknowledge my ignorance and the wrong thoughts that are in me concerning Your service. I will believe in the heavenly power of the new life that is in me. I will believe that my Lord Jesus, who Himself is my life, will by His Spirit teach me to know how I can walk in that life. Amen.

FOR FURTHER THOUGHT:

1. *What is the nature of this new life? It is eternal life, the very life of God that you have now received through faith.*
2. *How are you to live this life? This new life is in Christ, and the Holy Spirit is in you to give to you all that is in Christ. Christ lives in you through the Holy Spirit.*
3. *How can you live this life, even though you are weak? This life is a life of wonderful power. However weak you may feel, you must believe in the Divine power of the life that is in you.*
4. *This life needs time to grow in you and to take possession of you. Give it time, and it will certainly grow.*
5. *Don't forget that all the laws and rules of this new life are in conflict with all human thoughts of the way to please God. Be very cautious when it comes to your thoughts, and let Christ, who is your life and also your wisdom, teach you all things.*

2

THE MILK OF THE
WORD OF GOD

*As newborn babes, desire the pure milk
of the word, that you may grow thereby.*
1 PETER 2:2

BELOVED young Christians, hear what your Father has to say in this word. You have just recently given yourselves to the Lord and have believed that He has received you. You have therefore received the new life from God. You are now like newborn infants, and He desires to teach in this word what is necessary for you to grow and become strong.

The first point is this: *You must know that you are God's children.* Hear how distinctly Peter says this to those just converted: "You have been born again" (see 1 Pet. 1:23); "You are newborn babes" (see 2:2); "You are now converted" (see 2:25); "You are now the people of God" (see 2:10).

A Christian—however young and weak he is—must know that he is God's child. Only then can he have the courage to believe that he will make progress and the boldness to use the food of the children provided in the Word. All scripture teaches us that we must know and can know that we are children of God (Rom. 8:16; 1 Cor. 3:1, 16; Gal. 4:6–7; 1 John 3:2, 14, 24; 4:13, 5:10, 13). The assurance of faith is indispensable to a healthy powerful growth in the Lord (Eph. 5:8; Col. 2:6; 1 Pet. 1:14, 19).

The second point this word teaches you is that *you are still very weak*, weak as newborn children. The joy and the love a young convert sometimes experiences do indeed make him think that he is very strong. He runs the risk of exalting himself and of trusting in what he experiences. He must all the same learn much of how he must become strong in his Lord Jesus. Endeavor to feel deeply that you are still young and weak (1 Cor. 3:1, 13; Heb. 5:13–14). Out of this sense of weakness comes the humility that has nothing (Matt. 5:3; Rom 12:3, 10; Eph. 4:2; Phil. 2:3–4; Col. 3:12) in itself, and therefore expects all from its Lord (Matt. 8:8, 15, 27–28).

The third lesson is this: *The young Christian must not remain weak* but must grow and increase in grace. He must make progress and become strong. God lays this upon us as a command. His Word gives us concerning this point the most glorious promises. It lies in the nature of the thing: A child of God must and can make progress. The new life is a life that is healthy and strong. When a disciple surrenders himself to it, the growth certainly comes (Judg. 5:31; Pss. 84:8; 92:13, 14; Prov. 4:18; Isa. 40:31; Eph. 4:14; 1 Thess. 4:1; 2 Pet. 3:18).

The fourth and principal lesson—the lesson young disciples of Christ have most need of is—is this: *It is through the milk of the Word that God's newborn infants can grow.* The new life from the Spirit of God can be sustained only by the word from the mouth of God. Your life, my young brother, will largely depend on whether you learn to deal wisely and well with God's Word, or whether you learn to use the Word from the beginning as your milk (Pss. 19:8, 11; 119:97, 100; Isa. 55:2–3; 1 Cor. 12:11).

See what a charming parable the Lord has given us here in the mother's milk. Out of her own life the mother yields food and life to her child. The feeding of the child is the work of the most tender love, in which the child is pressed to the breast and is held in the closest fellowship with the mother. And the milk is just what the weak child requires: gentle and yet strong food.

> *F* or the disciple who receives the Word and trustfully relies on Jesus to teach him by the Spirit, the Word of God shall practically prove to be gentle sweet milk for newborn infants.

Even so is there in the Word of God the very life and power of God (John 6:63; 1 Thess. 2:13; Heb. 4:12). His tender love will through the Word receive us into the gentlest and most intimate fellowship with Himself (John 10:4). His love will give us out of the Word what is, like warm soft milk, well fitted for our weakness. Let no one assume that the Word is too high or too hard for him. For the disciple who receives the Word and trustfully relies on Jesus to teach him by the Spirit, the Word of God shall practically prove to be gentle sweet milk for newborn infants (Ps 119:18; John 14:26; Eph. 1:17–18).

Dear young Christian, do you desire to continue standing? Do you desire to become strong? Do you desire to always live for the Lord? Then hear today the voice of your Father: "As newborn babes, desire the pure milk of the word." Receive this Word into your heart and hold it firmly as the voice of your Father. On your use of the Word of God will your spiritual life depend. Let the Word of God be precious to you above everything (Ps. 119:14, 47, 48, 111, 127).

Above all, don't forget this: The Word is the milk, and the sucking or drinking on the part of the little child is the inner, living, blessed fellowship with the mother's love. Through the Holy Spirit, your use of the milk of the Word can become warm, living fellowship with the living love of your God.

Oh, long then very eagerly for the milk. Do not take the Word as something that is difficult and troublesome to understand, for in that way you lose all delight in it. Receive it with trust in the love of the living God. With a tender, motherly love will the Spirit of God teach and help you in your weakness. Always believe that the Spirit will make the Word in you life and joy, and a blessed fellowship with your God.

Precious Savior, You have taught me to believe Your Word, and You have made me by that faith a child of God. Through that Word, as the milk for the newborn babes, You will also feed me. Lord, I shall be very eager for this milk. Every day I will long for it. Teach me, through the Holy Spirit and the Word, to walk and hold communication every day in living fellowship with the love of the Father. Teach me always to believe that the Spirit has been given to me with the Word. Amen.

FOR FURTHER THOUGHT

1. *What texts do you consider the best for proving that the scriptures teach us that we must know we are children of God?*
2. *What are the three points in which the nursing child is to us a type of the young child in Christ in his dealing with the Word?*
3. *What must a young Christian do when he has little blessing in the reading of God's Word? He must set himself through faith in fellowship with Jesus Himself and must believe that Jesus will teach him through the Spirit and more trustfully continue in the reading.*
4. *One verse chosen to meet our needs and read ten times and then laid up in the heart is better than ten verses read once. Only the amount of the Word I actually receive and inwardly apply for myself is food for my soul.*
5. *Choose for yourselves what you consider one of the most glorious promises about making progress and becoming strong; then learn it by heart and repeat it continually as the language of your positive expectation.*
6. *Have you learned well to understand what the great means for growth in grace is?*

3

GOD'S WORD IN OUR HEART

"Therefore you shall lay up these words
of mine in your heart and in your soul."
DEUTERONOMY 11:18

"Son of man, receive into your heart all My words
that I speak to you, and hear with your ears."
EZEKIEL 3:10

Your word I have hidden in my heart,
that I might not sin against You.
PSALM 119:11

DESIRE *the pure milk of the word, that you may grow thereby"* (1 Pet. 2:2). This charming word taught every young Christian that if he wants to grow, he must receive the Word as milk, as the living participation of the life and the love of God. On this account, it is very important to know well how we must deal with the Word. The Lord says that we must receive it and lay it in our heart (Deut. 30:14; Pss. 1:2; 119:34, 36; Isa. 51:7; John 5:38; 8:31; 15:7; Rom. 10:8–9; Col. 3:16). The Word must possess and fill the heart.

But what does that mean?

The heart is the temple of God. In the temple there was an outer court and an inner sanctuary. It's the same way in the heart. The gate of the court is the understanding, meaning that what I do not understand cannot enter into the heart. Through the outer gate of the understanding the Word comes into the court (Ps. 119:34; Matt. 13:19; Acts 8:30). There it is kept by memory and reflection (Ps. 119:15–16). Still it is not yet properly in the heart. From the court there is an entrance into the innermost sanctuary, meaning that the entrance of the door is *faith.* What I believe I receive into my heart (John 5:38; Acts 8:37; Rom. 10:10, 17). Here it then becomes held firmly in love and in the surrender of the will. Where this takes place, there the heart becomes the sanctuary of God. His law is there, as in the ark, and the soul cries out: "The law is within my heart" (see Exod. 25:16; Pss. 37:31, 40:9; Col. 3:16).

Young Christian, God has asked for your heart, your love, your whole self. You have given yourself to Him. He has received you and desires to have you and your heart entirely for Himself. He will make that heart full of His Word. What is in the heart one holds dear, because one thinks continually on that which gives joy. God desires to have the Word in the heart. Where His Word is, there He is Himself, along with His strength.

God considers Himself bound to fulfill His Word. When you have the Word, you have God Himself to work in you (Gen. 21:1; Josh. 23:14). He wills that you should receive and lay up His words in your heart: then He will greatly bless you (Deut. 11:10; 28:1–2; Pss. 1:2–3; 119:14, 45, 98, 165; John 17:6, 8, 17).

How I wish that I could persuade all young Christians to receive simply so that word of their Father, "Lay up these words of Mine in your heart," and to give their whole heart to become full of God's Word. Resolve then to do this. Take pains to understand what you read. When you understand it, take then always one or another word to keep in remembrance and to ponder. Learn words of God by heart and repeat them to yourself in the course of the day. The Word is seed, and as the seed must have time and must be kept in the ground, so must the Word be carried in the heart.

> *He who daily, faithfully opens his heart to God's voice to hear what God says, and who keeps and carries with him that word, will see how faithfully God also opens His heart to our voice to hear what we say to Him in prayer.*

Give the best powers of your heart, your love, your desire, and the willing and joyful activity of your will to God's Word. "Blessed is the man [whose]. . .delight is in the law of the LORD, and in His law he meditates day and night" (Ps. 1:1–2). Let the heart be a temple, not for the world and its thoughts, but for God and His thoughts (Ps. 119:69; John 15:3, 7; 17:6, 8, 17). He who daily, faithfully opens his heart to God's voice to hear what God says, and who keeps and carries with him that word, will see how faithfully God also opens His heart to our voice to hear what we say to Him in prayer.

Dear Christian, please read yet once again the words at the head of this section. Receive them as God's word to you—the word of the Father who has received you as a child, of Jesus who has made you God's child. God asks of you, as His child, to give your heart to become filled with His Word. Will you do this? What say you? The Lord Jesus desires to complete His holy work in you with power along this way (John 14:21, 23; 1 John 2:14, 24; Rev. 3:8, 10). Let your answer be distinct and continuous: "Your word I have hidden in my heart" (Ps. 119:11); "Oh, how I love Your law! It *is* my meditation all the day" (119:97). Even if it appears difficult for you to understand the Word, read it all the more. The Father has promised to make it a blessing in your heart. But you must first take it into your heart. Believe then that God will by the Holy Spirit make it living and powerful in you.

O my Father, who has said to me, "My son, give Me your heart," I have given You my heart. Now that You charge me to lay up and to keep Your Word in that heart, I answer: "I keep Your commands with my whole heart." Father, teach me every day to receive Your Word in my heart so that it can exercise there its blessed influence. Strengthen me in the deep conviction that even though I do not actually grasp its meaning and power, I can still depend on You to make the Word living and powerful in me. Amen.

For Further Thought

1. *What is the difference between the reading of the Word to increase knowledge and the receiving of it in faith?*

2. *The Word is like a seed. Seed requires time before it springs up. During this time it must be kept silently and constantly in the earth. I must not only read God's Word, but also ponder it and reflect upon it. Only then will it work in me. The Word must be in me the whole day, must abide in me, and must dwell in me.*

3. *What are the reasons that the Word of God sometimes has so little power in those who read it and really long for blessing? One of the principal reasons is surely that they do not give the seed time to grow, that they do not keep it and reflect upon it in the believing assurance that the Word itself shall do its work.*

4. *What is the pledge to His disciples that Jesus mentions first in the high-priestly prayer (John 17)?*

5. *What are the blessings of a heart filled with the Word of God?*

4

FAITH

"Blessed is she who believed,
for there will be a fulfillment of those things
which were told her from the Lord."
LUKE 1:45

"Therefore take heart, men, for I believe God
that it will be just as it was told me."
ACTS 27:25

[Abraham] was strengthened in faith . . .
being fully convinced that what He had
promised He was also able to perform.
ROMANS 4:20–21

GOD has asked you to take and lay up His words in your heart. Faith is the proper avenue through which the Word is taken and received into the innermost depths of the heart. Let the young Christian then make the effort always to understand better what faith is so that he may gain an insight into the reasons why such great things are bound up with faith. He will yield his perfect assent to the view that full salvation is daily made dependent on faith (1 Chron. 20:20; Mark 9:23; Heb. 11:33, 35; 1 John 5:4–5).

Let me now ask my reader to read over once again the three texts above, and to find out what the principal thought is that they teach about faith. Please read nothing beyond them, but read first these words of God, and then ask yourself what they teach you about faith. They make us see that faith always attaches itself to what God has said or promised.

When an honorable man says anything, he also does it; on the back of the saying follows the doing. So also is it with God. When He intends to do anything, He says so first through His Word. When the man of God becomes possessed with this conviction and established in it, God always does for him what He has said. With God, speaking and doing always go together. The deed follows the word. *Will God say it and not do it?* (See Gen. 21:1; 32:12; Num. 14:17–18, 20;

23:19; Josh. 21:45; 23:14; 2 Sam. 7:25, 29; 1 Chron. 8:15, 24; Ps. 119:49.)

When I have a word of God in which He promises to do something, I can always remain sure that He will do it. I need simply to take and hold firmly the word, and then wait on God, who will make sure that He fulfills His word to me. Before I ever feel or experience anything, I hold firmly the promise, and I know by faith that God will keep it for me (Luke 1:38, 45; John 3:33; 4:50; 11:40; 20:29; Heb. 11:11, 18).

> *Let the young Christian then make the effort always to understand better what faith is so that he may gain an insight into the reasons why such great things are bound up with faith.*

What, now, is faith? Nothing other than the certainty that what God says is true. When God says that something exists or is, then faith rejoices, even though it can't see anything of it (Rom. 1:17; 4:5; 5:1; Gal. 3:27; Eph. 1:19; 3:17). When God says that He has given me something, that something in heaven is mine. I know by faith with entire certainty that it is mine (John 3:16–17, 36; 1 John 5:12–13). When God says that something shall take place, or that He will do something for me, in faith this word is just as good as if I had seen it (Rom. 8:38; Phil. 3:21; 1 Thess. 5:24; 1 Pet. 1:4–5). Things that are but that I have not seen, and things that are not yet but shall come, are with faith entirely sure. "Now faith is the substance of things hoped for, the evidence of things not seen" (Heb. 11:1). Faith always asks only for what God has said, and then relies on His faithfulness and power to fulfill His word.

Let us now review again the words of scripture. Of Mary we read: "Blessed is she who believed, for there will be a fulfillment of those things which were told her from the Lord" (Luke 1:45). All things that have been spoken in the Word shall be fulfilled for me—so I believe them.

Of Abraham it is reported that he was fully assured that that which had been promised, God was also able to fulfill. This is assurance of faith: to be assured that God will do what He has promised.

That is the exact word of Paul: "I believe God that it will be just as it was told me" (Acts 27:25). It stood certain with him that God would do what He had spoken.

Young disciples in Christ, the new, the eternal life that is in you is a life of faith. And do you not see how simple and how blessed that life of faith is? I go every day to the Word and hear in it what God has said He has done and will do (Gal. 2:20; 3:2, 5; 5:5–6; Heb. 10:35; 1 Pet. 1:8). I take time to store in my heart the word in which God says that, and I hold it firmly, entirely assured that what God has promised, He is able to perform. And then in a childlike spirit I await the fulfillment of all the glorious promises of His Word. And my soul experiences: "Blessed is she who believed, for there will be a fulfillment of those things which were told her from the Lord." God promises, I believe, God fulfills. That is the secret of the new life.

O my Father, Your child thanks You for this blessed life of faith in which we have to walk. I can do nothing, but You can do everything. All that You can do You have spoken in Your Word. And every word that I take and trustfully bring to You, You fulfill. Father, in this life of faith, so simple, so glorious, I will walk with You. Amen.

FOR FURTHER THOUGHT

1. *What part should scripture reading play in your new faith and new life? The Christian must read and search the scriptures to increase his knowledge. For this purpose he daily reads one or more principal portions. But he reads the scriptures also to strengthen his faith. And to this end he must take one or two verses to make them the subject of special reflection, and to appropriate them trustfully for himself.*

2. *How should you see the nature of your new faith in Christ? I ask you, do not allow yourselves to be led astray by those who speak as if faith were something great and unintelligible. Faith is nothing other than the certitude that God speaks truth. Take some promises of God and say to Him: "I know for certain that this promise is truth, and that You will fulfill it." He will do it.*

3. *How are you to deal with your unbelief and weakness? Never mourn over unbelief as if it were only a weakness you cannot help. As God's child, however weak you may be, you have the power to believe, for the Spirit of God is in you. You have only to keep in mind this: No one understands anything before that he has the power to believe; he must simply begin and continue with saying to the Lord that he is sure that His Word is truth. He must hold firmly the promise and rely upon God for the fulfillment.*

5

THE POWER OF GOD'S WORD

So then faith comes by hearing,
and hearing by the word of God.
ROMANS 10:17

Receive with meekness the implanted word,
which is able to save your souls.
JAMES 1:21

We also thank God without ceasing, because when you received
the word of God which you heard from us, you welcomed it not
as the word of men, but as it is in truth, the word of God,
which also effectively works in you who believe.
1 THESSALONIANS 2:13

For the word of God is living and powerful.
HEBREWS 4:12

THE new life of a child of God depends so much on the right use of God's Word that I shall once again speak of it with my young brothers and sisters in the Lord.

It is a great thing when the Christian discerns that he can receive and accomplish everything only through faith. He needs only to believe, and God will see to the fulfilling of what is promised. He needs every morning to trust in Jesus and in the new life as given in Jesus and working in himself. Jesus will see to it that the new life works in him.

But now he runs the risk of another error. He thinks that the faith that does such great things must be something great, and that he must have a great power in order to exercise such a great faith (Luke 17:5–6; Rom. 10:6–8). And because he does not feel this power, he thinks he cannot believe as he should. This error may prove a loss to him during his entire life.

Come and hear, then, how in error this thought is. You must not bring this mighty faith to get the Word fulfilled, but the Word comes and brings you this faith, which you must have. "For the word...is living and powerful" (Heb. 4:12). The word works faith in you. The scripture says, "Faith comes...by the word" (Rom. 10:17).

Think on what we have said about the heart being like a temple, and of its two divisions. There is the outer court, with the understanding as its gate or entrance. There is the innermost sanctuary, with the faith of the heart as its entrance. There is a natural faith—the historic faith—that every man has. With this, I must first receive the Word into my possession and consideration. I must say to myself, "The Word of God is certainly true. I can make a stand upon it." That is how I bring the Word into the outer court. Then, from within, the heart desire reaches out to it, seeking to receive it into the heart. The Word now exercises its divine power of life, and it begins to grow and shoot out roots. As a seed that I place in the earth sends forth roots and presses still deeper into the soil, the Word presses inwardly into the holy place. This is how the Word works true saving faith (1 Thess. 2:13; James 1:21; 1 Pet. 1:23).

Young Christian, please understand this. The Word is living and powerful, for through the Word you are born again. The Word works faith in you, for through the Word comes faith. Receive the Word simply knowing that it will work in you. Keep yourselves occupied with the Word, and give it time. The Word has a divine life in itself. Carry it in your innermost parts, and it will work life in you. It will work in you a faith strong and able for anything.

> It is a great thing when the Christian discerns that he can receive and accomplish everything only through faith. He needs only to believe, and God will see to the fulfilling of what is promised.

Do be resolved, then, I ask you, never to say, "I cannot believe." You can believe. You have the Spirit of God in you. Even the natural man can say, "This word of God is certainly true or certainly not true." And when he with a desire of the soul says, "It is true; I will believe it," the living Spirit, through whom the Word is living and powerful, works this living faith. Besides, the Spirit is not only in the Word, but also in you. Although you do not feel as though you are believing, know for certain you can believe (Deut. 32:46–47; Josh. 1:7, 9). Begin actually to receive the Word, and it will work a mighty faith in you. Rely on it, so that when you have to do with God's Word, you have to do with a word that can be surely trusted that it of itself works faith in you.

And not only the promises, but also the commands have this living power. When I first receive a command from God, it is as if I felt no power to accomplish it. But if I then simply receive the word as God's Word, which works in those who believe—if I trust in the word to have its working and in the living God who gives it its operation—that commandment will work in me the desire and the power for obedience. When I weigh and hold firmly the command, it places within me the desire and the will to obey and urges me strongly toward the conviction that I can certainly do what my Father says.

The Word produces both faith and obedience of faith. I must believe that through the Spirit I have the power to do what God desires, for in the Word the power of God works in me. The Word, as the command of the living God who loves me, is my power (Rom. 1:3; 16:6; Gal. 6:6; 1 Thess. 1:3; James 1:21).

Therefore, young disciples in Christ, learn to receive God's Word trustfully. Although you do not at first understand it, continue to meditate on it. It has a living power in it. It will glorify itself. Although you feel no power to believe or to obey, the Word is living and powerful. Take it and hold it firmly, and it will accomplish its work with divine power. The Word rouses and strengthens for faith and obedience.

Lord God, I begin to understand how You are in Your Word with Your life and Your power, and how that Word itself produces faith and obedience in the heart that receives and keeps it. Lord, teach me to carry Your every word as a living seed in my heart, in the assurance that it shall accomplish in me all Your good pleasure. Amen.

For Further Thought

1. *How should you personally connect the Word of God with God Himself? Don't forget that it is one and the same to believe in the word, or in the person who speaks the word, or in the thing that is promised in the word. The very same faith that receives the promises receives also the Father who promises, as well as the Son with the salvation that is given in the promises. Please see to it that you never separate the Word and the living God from each other.*

2. *See to it also that you understand thoroughly the distinction between the reception of the Word "as the word of man" and "as the word of God, which also effectively works in you who believe."*

3. *What role does faith play in studying and meditating on the Word? I think you now know what is necessary to become strong in faith. Exercise as much faith as you have. Take a promise of God. Say to yourself that it is certainly true. Go to God and say to Him that you rely on Him for the fulfillment. Ponder the promise, and cling to it as you converse with God. Rely on Him to do for you what He says. He will certainly do it.*

4. *How do you obediently apply what you read in scripture? The Spirit and the Word always go together. I can be sure concerning all the Word says I must do, that I also can do it through the Spirit. I must receive the Word and also the command in the confidence that it is the living Word of the living God that also works in us who believe.*

6

GOD'S GIFT OF HIS SON

*"For God so loved the world that He gave His
only begotten Son, that whoever believes in Him
should not perish but have everlasting life."*
JOHN 3:16

Thanks be to God for His indescribable gift!
2 CORINTHIANS 9:15

THIS is how dear God holds the world. How dear? That He gave His only begotten Son for everyone in the world who will trust in Him. And how did He give? He gave Him in His birth as man, in order to be forever one with us. He gave Him in His death on the cross as a promise, in order to take our sin and curse upon Himself. He gave Him on the throne of heaven, in order to arrange for our welfare, as our Representative and Intercessor over all the powers of heaven. He gave Him in the outpouring of the Spirit, in order to dwell in us and to be entirely and altogether our own (John 1:14, 16; 14:23; Rom. 5:8; 8:32, 34; Eph. 1:22; 3:17; Col. 2:9–10; Heb. 7:24, 26; 1 John 4:9–10). Yes, that is the love of God: that He gave His Son to us, for us, in us.

Nothing less than His Son Himself. This is the love of God, not that He gives us some*thing*, but that He gives us some*one*—a living person—not one or another blessing, but Him in whom is all life and blessing—Jesus Himself. Not simply forgiveness, revival, sanctification, nor glory He gives us, but Jesus, His own Son. The Lord Jesus is the beloved, the equal, the intimate friend, and the eternal blessedness of the Father. And it is the will of the Father that we should have Jesus as ours, even as He has Him (Matt. 11:27; John 17:23, 25; Rom. 8:38–39; Heb. 2:11). For this purpose He gave Him to us. The whole of salvation consists in this: to have, to possess, to enjoy Jesus. God has given His Son wholly to become ours (Pss. 73:25; 142:6; John 20:28; Heb. 3:14).

So what are we to do? We are to take Him, to receive and possess to ourselves the gift, to enjoy Jesus as our own. This is eternal life. "He who has the Son has life" (1 John 5:12; also see John 1:12; 2 Cor. 3:13; 5:8; Col. 2:6).

How I wish, therefore, that all young Christians may understand this. The one great work of God's love for us is that He gives us His Son. In Him we have every-thing. For that reason, the one great work of our heart must be to receive this Jesus who has been given to us, to see Him and use Him as ours. I must begin every new day with the thought, *I have Jesus to do all for me* (John 15:5; Rom. 8:37; 1 Cor. 1:30; Eph. 1:3; 2:10; Phil. 4:13; 2 Tim. 1:12). In all weakness or darkness or danger, in the case of every desire or need, let your first thought always be, *I have Jesus to make everything right for me, for God has given Him to me.* Whether your need is forgiveness or comfort or confirmation, whether you have fallen or are tempted to fall into danger, whether you don't know what the will of God is in one or another matter (or know that you don't have the courage and the strength to do this will), let this always be your first thought: *The Father has given me Jesus to care for me.*

> *This is the love of God, not that He gives us something, but that He gives us someone—a living person—not one or another blessing, but Him in whom is all life and blessing—Jesus Himself.*

For this purpose, rely on this gift of God every day as yours. It has been presented to you in the Word. Take the Son as yours in faith in the Word. Take Him freshly every day. Through faith you have the Son (John 1:12; 1 John 5:9, 13). The love of God has given the Son. Take Him, and hold Him firmly in the love of your heart (1 John 4:4, 19). It is to bring life, eternal life, to you that God has given Jesus. Take Him up into your life, and let heart and tongue and whole walk be under the might and guidance of Jesus (2 Cor. 5:15; Phil. 3:8). Young Christian, so weak and so sinful, listen, I ask, to that Word. God has given you Jesus. He is yours. Taking is nothing else but the fruit of faith. The gift is for me. He will do all for you.

O my Lord Jesus, today anew, and every day, I take You. In all Your fullness, in all Your relations, without ceasing, I take You for myself. You who are my Wisdom, my Light, my Leader, I take as my Prophet. You who perfectly reconciles me and brings me near to God, who purifies and sanctifies me and prays for me, I take as my Priest. You who guides and keeps and blesses me, I take as my King. You, Lord, are All, and You are wholly mine. I give thanks to God for His unspeakable gift. Amen.

FOR FURTHER THOUGHT

1. *Think much about the word* give. *God gives in a wonderful way: from the heart, completely for nothing, to the unworthy. And He gives effectively. What He gives He will really make entirely our possession and inwardly apply for us. Believe this, and you shall have the certain assurance that Jesus will fully come into your possession, and with all He brings.*

2. *Think much also about that other word,* take. *To take Jesus and to hold Him firmly and use Him when received is our great work. And that taking is nothing but trusting. He is mine with all that He has. Take Jesus—the full Jesus—every day as yours: This is the secret of the life of faith.*

3. *Then weigh carefully also the word* have. *"He who has the Son has life." What I have is mine, for my use and service. I can use it and can have the full enjoyment of it. "He who has the Son has life."*

4. *Remember especially that what God gives, what you take, and what you now have is nothing less than the living Son of God. Do you receive this?*

7

Jesus' Surrender of Himself

Christ also loved the church and gave Himself for her, that He might
sanctify and cleanse her. . .that He might present her to Himself
a glorious church, not having spot or wrinkle or any such thing,
but that she should be holy and without blemish.
Ephesians 5:25–27

So great and wonderful was the work that Jesus had to do for the sinner that nothing less was necessary than that He should give Himself to do that work. So great and wonderful was the love of Jesus toward us that He actually gave Himself for us and to us. So great and wonderful is the surrender of Jesus that the very same thing for which He gave Himself can actually and completely come to pass in us. For Jesus, the Holy and the Almighty, has taken it upon Himself to do it: He gave *Himself* for us (Gal. 1:4; 2:20; Eph. 5:2, 25; 1 Tim. 2:6; Titus 2:14). And now the one thing that is necessary is that we should rightly understand and firmly believe this His surrender for us.

For what ultimate purpose, then, was it that He gave Himself for the Church? Hear what God says. In order that He might sanctify her, in order that she might be without blemish (Eph. 1:4; 5:27; Col. 1:22; 1 Thess. 2:10; 3:13; 5:23–24). This is the aim of Jesus. He will reach this aim in the soul as the soul accordingly surrenders to it in such a way that it makes it its highest portion, and then relies upon Jesus' surrender of Himself to do it.

Hear still a word of God: "Who gave Himself for us, that He might redeem us from every lawless deed and purify for Himself His own special people, zealous for good works" (Titus 2:14). Yes, it is to prepare for Himself a *pure* people, a people *of His own*, a *zealous* people to whom Jesus gives Himself. When I receive Him, when I believe that He gave Himself to do this for me, I shall certainly experience it. I shall be purified through Him, shall be held firmly as His possession, and shall be filled with zeal and joy to work for Him.

And notice further how the operation of this surrender of Himself will especially be that He shall then have us entirely for Himself: "that He might present (us) to Himself," "that He might. . .purify for Himself His own special people." The more I understand and contemplate Jesus' surrender of Himself for me, the more I give myself again to Him. The surrender is a mutual one. The love comes from both sides.

His giving of Himself makes such an impression on my heart that my heart with the self and the same love and joy becomes entirely His. Through giving Himself to me, He takes possession of me for Himself. He becomes mine and I His. I know that I have Jesus wholly for me and that He has me wholly for Him (Exod. 19:4–5; Deut. 26:17–18; Isa. 41:9–10; 1 Cor. 6:19–20; 1 Pet. 2:10).

> *The more I understand and contemplate Jesus' surrender of Himself for me, the more I give myself again to Him. The surrender is a mutual one.*

And how do I come then to the full enjoyment of this blessed life? "I live *by faith* in the Son of God, who loved me and gave Himself for me" (Gal. 2:20; also see John 6:29, 35; 7:38; 10:10, 38). Through faith I reflect on and contemplate His surrender to me as sure and glorious. Through faith I make it my own. Through faith I trust in Jesus to confirm this surrender and to communicate Himself to me and reveal Himself within me. Through faith I wait with certainty the full experience of salvation, which arises from having Jesus as mine to do all—all for me. Through faith, I live in this Jesus who loved me and gave Himself for me, and I say, "It is no longer I who live, but Christ lives in me" (Gal. 2:20). Christian, I want you to believe it with your whole heart: Jesus gives Himself for you. He is wholly yours, and He will do everything for you (Matt. 8:10; 9:2, 22; Mark 11:24; Luke 7:50; 8:48; 17:19; 18:42; Rom. 4:16, 21; 5:2; 11:20; Gal. 3:25–26; Eph. 1:19; 3:17).

My Lord Jesus, what wonderful grace is this, that You gave Yourself for me. In You is eternal life. You Yourself are the life, and You give Yourself to be in my life all that I need. You purify me and sanctify me and make me zealous in good works. You take me wholly for Yourself and give Yourself entirely for me. Yes, my Lord, in every way You are my life. Make me rightly understand this. Amen.

FOR FURTHER THOUGHT

1. *What motivated God to send His Son for you? It was in His great love that the Father gave the Son. It was out of love that Jesus gave Himself (Rom. 3:15; Eph. 5:26). The taking and the having of Jesus are the entrance to a life in the love of God. This is the highest life (John 14:21, 23; 17:23, 26; Eph. 3:17–18). Through faith we must press into love and dwell there (1 John 4:16–18).*
2. *Do you think you have now learned all the lesson: to begin every day with the childlike trust that says, "I take Jesus this day to be my life and to do all for me"?*
3. *What is the nature of your relationship with Jesus? Understand that to take and to have Jesus starts with a personal dealing with Himself. To have pleasure in Him, to gladly converse with Him, to rejoice in Him as my friend and in His love—this leads to the faith that truly takes Him.*

8

CHILDREN OF GOD

But as many as received Him,
to them He gave the right to become children of God,
to those who believe in His name.
John 1:12

W HAT is given must be received; otherwise it does no good for anyone. If the first great deed of God's love is the gift of His Son, the first work of man must be to receive this Son. And if all the blessings of God's love come to us only in the ever-new, ever-living Son of the Father, all these blessings enter into us from day to day through the always-new, always-continuing reception of the Son.

What is necessary for this reception, you, beloved young Christians, already know, for you have already received the Lord Jesus. But all that this reception involves must become clearer and stronger: the unceasing living action of your faith (2 Cor. 10:15; 1 Thess. 1:8; 3:10; 2 Thess. 1:3). In this especially is the increase of faith. Your first receiving of Jesus rested on the certainty that the Word gave you that He was for you. Through the Word your soul must be still further filled with the assurance that all that is in Him is literally and really for you—given by the Father in Him to be your life.

The impulse to your first receiving was found in your lack and your need. Through the Spirit you become still poorer in spirit, and you see everything every moment. This leads to a ceaseless, ever-active taking of Him as your all (Matt 5:3; 2 Cor. 3:10, 13, 16; 6:10; Eph. 4:14–15; Col. 2:6).

Your first receiving consisted of nothing but accepting for yourself by faith from what you could not yet see or feel. That same faith must be continually exercised in saying, "All I see in Jesus is for me. I take it as mine, although I do not yet experience it." The love of God is a communicating, a ceaseless outstreaming of His light of life over the soul, and a very powerful and veritable giving of Jesus. Our life is nothing but a continuous blessed understanding and reception of Him (John 1:16; Col. 2:9–10; 3:3).

And this is the way to live as children of God: "As many as received Him, to them He gave the right to become children of God." This holds true not only of conversion and regeneration, but of every day of my life. If to walk in all things as a child of God—and to exhibit the image of my Father—is indispensable, then I must take Jesus the only begotten Son, for it is He who makes me a child of God.

To have Jesus Himself, to have the heart and life full of Him, is the way to live as a child of God. I go to the Word and learn there all the characteristics of a child of God (Matt 5:9, 16, 44–45; Rom. 8:14; Eph. 1:4–5; 5:1–2; Phil. 2:15; Heb. 2:10; 1 Pet. 1:14, 17; 1 John 3:1, 10; 5:1, 3), and after each one of them I write: "This Jesus shall work in me: I *have* him to make me to be a child of God."

Beloved young Christian, I beg you to learn and to understand the simplicity and the glory of being a true Christian. It is to receive Jesus, to receive Him in all His fullness, to receive Him in all the glorious relations in which the Father gives Him to you. Take Him as your Prophet, as your Wisdom, as your Light, and as your Guide. Take Him as your Priest who renews you, purifies you, sanctifies you, brings you near to God, and takes you and forms you wholly for His service. Take Him as your King who governs you, protects you, and blesses you. Take him as your Head, your Example, your Brother, your Life, your All.

> *To every prayer, the answer of God is, "Jesus—all is in Him, all in Him is for you." Let your response always be, "Jesus, in Him I have all."*

The giving of God is a divine and ever-progressive and effectual communication to your soul. Let your taking be the childlike, cheerful, and continuous opening of mouth and heart for what God gives: the full Jesus and all His grace. To every prayer, the answer of God is, "Jesus—all is in Him, all in Him is for you." Let your response always be, "Jesus, in Him I have all." You are and you live in all things as "sons of God through faith in Christ Jesus" (Gal. 3:26).

O my Father, open the eyes of my heart to understand what it is to be a child of God: to live always as a child through always believing in Jesus, Your only Son. Let every breath of my soul be a faith in Jesus, a confidence in Him, a resting in Him, and a surrender to Him to work all in me.

For Further Thought

1. *What is your responsibility to others now that you have entered into the new life in Christ? If by the grace of God you now know you have received Jesus and are God's child, you must now make the effort to make His salvation known. There are many people who long to know and cannot find out how they can become children of God.*

2. *What do those around you need to know about the new life God has offered them, too? Endeavor to make two things plain to them: First, that the new birth is something so high and holy that they can do nothing in it. They must receive eternal life from God through the Spirit; they must be born from above. Jesus teaches this (John 3:1–8). Then make plain to them how low God has descended to us with this new life and how near He brings it to us. In Jesus there is life for everyone who believes in Him. Jesus teaches this also (John 3:14–18). And this Jesus and the life are in the Word.*

3. *What are you to tell those you know need salvation through Christ? Tell sinners that when they take the Word, they then have Jesus and life in the Word (Rom. 10:8). Do pray, but also make the effort to tell of the good news that we become children of God only through faith in Jesus.*

9

OUR SURRENDER TO JESUS

They first gave themselves to the Lord.
2 CORINTHIANS 8:5

IN the surrender of Jesus for me, I have the chief element of what He has done and always does for me. In my surrender to Him, I have the chief element of what He wants me to do. For young Christians who have given themselves to Jesus, it is a matter of great importance to always hold firmly to and to confirm and renew this surrender. This is the special life of faith, to say again every day: I have given myself to Him, to follow Him and to serve Him (Matt. 4:22; 10:24–25, 37–38; Luke 18:22; John 12:25–26; 2 Cor. 5:15). He has taken me, so I am His and entirely at His service (Matt. 28:20).

Young Christian, hold firm to your surrender and make it always firmer. When there happens a stumbling or a sin after you have surrendered yourself, don't think the surrender was not sincere. No! The surrender to Jesus does not make us perfect immediately. You have sinned because you were not thoroughly or firmly enough in His arms. Hold to this, although it is with shame: Lord, You know I have given myself to You; I am Yours (John 21:17; Gal. 6:1; 1 Thess. 5:24; 2 Tim. 2:13; 1 John 5:16). Confirm this surrender again. Say to Him that you now begin to see better how complete the surrender to Him must be, and renew every day the voluntary, entire, and undivided offering up of yourselves to Him (Phil. 3:7–8).

The longer we continue as Christians, the deeper will be our insight into that word: "Surrender to Jesus." We shall always see more clearly that we do not yet fully understand or contemplate it. The surrender must become, especially, more undivided and trustful. The language that Ahab once used must be ours: "My lord, O king, just as you say, I and all that I have are yours" (1 Kings 20:4). This is the language of undivided dedication: *I and all that I have are yours.*

Keep nothing back. Keep back no single sin that you do not confess and leave off. Without conversion, there can be no surrender (Matt. 7:21, 27; John 3:20–21; 2 Tim. 2:19, 21). Keep back no single power. Let your head with all its thinking, your mouth with all its speaking, your heart with all its feeling, your hand with all its working—let your time, your name, your influence, your property—let all be laid upon the altar (Rom. 6:13, 22; 12:1; 2 Cor. 5:15; Heb. 8:15; 1 Pet. 2:5). Jesus has a right to all, and He demands the whole. Give yourself, with all that you have, to be guided and used and kept, sanctified and blessed. "My lord, O king, just as you say, I and all that I have are yours."

That is the language of trustful dedication. It is on the Word of the Lord, which calls upon you to surrender yourself, that you have done this. That Word is your guarantee that He will take and guide and keep you. As surely as you give yourself, He takes you, and what He takes He can keep. Only we must not take it again out of His hand.

> *A*ccording to His Word, you are able to take a stand on this: What you give He takes, and what He takes He keeps.

Let it remain decided within you that your surrender is in the highest degree pleasing to Him. Be certain of it: Your offering is a sweet-smelling aroma. Not because of what you are or on what you experience or discover in yourselves can you say this, but on His Word. According to His Word, you are able to take a stand on this: What you give He takes, and what He takes He keeps (John 10:28; 2 Thess. 3:3; 2 Tim. 1:12). Therefore every new day, let this be the childlike, joyful activity of your life of faith: You surrender yourselves without ceasing to Jesus, and you are safe in the assurance that He in His love takes and holds you firmly and that His answer to your giving is the renewed and always-deeper surrender of Himself to you.

According to Your Word, my Lord and King, I and all that I have are Yours. This day and every day I will confirm that I am not my own, but am my Lord's. I ask You fervently to take full possession of Your property so that no one may doubt whose I am. Amen.

FOR FURTHER THOUGHT

1. *What is the connection in the new life of giving, taking, and having? Think now once again about the words* giving *and* taking *and* having. *What I give to Jesus, He takes with a divine taking. And what He takes, He has and from that time forward cares for. Now it is absolutely no longer mine. I must not think about it, and I may not use it. I encourage you, let your faith find expression in adoration: Jesus takes me. Jesus has me.*

2. *How can you effectively handle doubt? Should there overtake you a time of doubting or darkness during which your assurance that the Lord has received you has been lost, don't allow yourself to become disheartened. Come simply as a sinner, confess your sins, and believe in His promise that He will by no means cast out those who come to Him. Then begin simply, on the ground of the promise, to say: "I know that He has received me."*

3. *Don't forget what the chief element of surrender is: a surrender to Jesus and to His love. Fix your eye, not on your activity in surrender, but on Jesus, who calls you, who takes you, and who can do all for you. This is what makes faith strong.*

4. *What is the connection between your faith and your purposefully surrendering yourself to God? Faith is always a surrender. Faith is the eye for seeing the invisible. When I look at something, I surrender myself to the impression it makes on me. Faith is the ear that hears and listens to the voice of God. When I believe a message, I surrender myself to the influence—cheering or saddening—the message has on me. When I believe in Jesus, I surrender myself to Him, in reflection and in desire and in anticipation, in order that He may be in me and do that for which He has been given to me by God.*

10

A Savior from Sin

"And she will bring forth a Son, and you shall call His name JESUS, for He will save His people from their sins."
MATTHEW 1:21

And you know that He was manifested to take away our sins, and in Him there is no sin. Whoever abides in Him does not sin. Whoever sins has neither seen Him nor known Him.
1 JOHN 3:5–6

SIN is the cause of our misery. It is sin that provoked God and brought His curse upon man. He hates sin with a perfect hatred and will do everything to root it out (Deut. 27:26; Isa. 59:1–2; Jer. 44:4; Rom. 1:18). It is to take away sin that God gave His Son and that Jesus gave Himself (Gal. 2:4; Eph. 5:25, 27; 1 Pet. 2:24; 1 John 3:8). It is God's choice alone to set us free, not only from punishment and curse, from anxiety and terror, but from sin itself (Jer. 27:9; 1 Pet. 1:2, 15, 16; 2:14; 1 John 3:8). You know that He was revealed and sent so that He might take away our sins. Let us receive the thought deep into our hearts that it is God alone who can take away our sins from us. The better we understand this, the more blessed shall our life be.

Not all receive this. They seek chiefly to be freed from the consequences of sin—from fear and darkness and from the punishment sin brings (Gen. 27:34; Isa. 58:5–6; John 6:26; James 4:3). On this alone they do not come to the true rest of salvation. They do not understand that to save is to free from sin. Let us hold it firmly. Jesus saves through taking away sin. Then we shall learn two things.

The first is to come to Jesus with every sin (Ps. 32:5; Luke 7:38; 19:7–8, 10; John 8:11). The sin that still attacks and rules you even after you have given yourself over to the Lord must not make you lose heart. There must also be no endeavor in your own strength alone to take away and overcome sin. Bring every sin to Jesus. He has been ordained by God to take away sin. He has already brought it to nothing upon the cross and broken its power (Heb. 9:26). It is His work and His desire to set you free from it. Learn then always to come to Jesus with every sin. Sin is your deadly enemy, but if you confess it to Jesus and surrender it to Him, you shall certainly overcome it (Rom. 7:4, 9; 8:2; 2 Cor. 12:9; 2 Thess. 2:3).

The second point is to learn to believe this firmly. Understand that Jesus—Jesus Himself—is the Savior from sin. It is not you who must overcome sin with the help of Jesus, but Jesus Himself, Jesus in you (Deut. 8:17–18; Ps. 44:4, 8; John 16:33; 1 John 5:4–5). If you want to become free from sin, if you want to enjoy full salvation, let your life's one endeavor be to stand always in full fellowship with Jesus. Don't wait until you enter into temptation before you turn to Jesus. But let your life beforehand be always through Jesus. Let His nearness be your one desire. Jesus saves from sin, and to have Jesus is salvation from sin (1 Cor. 15:10; Gal. 2:20; Phil. 4:13; Col. 3:3–5). If only we could indeed rightly understand this! Jesus will not merely save from sin as a work that He will from time to time do in us, but He will give it as a blessing through Himself to us and in us (Exod. 29:43, John 15:4–5; Rom. 8:10; Eph. 3:17–18). When Jesus fills me, when Jesus is all for me, sin has no hold on me: "Whoever abides in Him does not sin" (1 John 3:6).

> Understand that Jesus—Jesus Himself—is the Savior from sin. It is not you who must overcome sin with the help of Jesus, but Jesus Himself, Jesus in you

Yes, sin is driven out and kept out only through the presence of Jesus. It is Jesus, Jesus Himself, who, through His giving Himself to me and through His living in me, is salvation from sin.

Precious Lord, let Your light stream over me, and let it become still clearer to my soul that You Yourself are my salvation. To have You with me and in me—this keeps sin out. Teach me to bring every sin to You. Let every sin drive me into a closer alliance with You. Then shall Your Jesus-name become truly my salvation from sin. Amen.

For Further Thought

1. *See of what moment it is that the Christian should always grow in the knowledge of sin. The sin that I do not know I cannot bring to Jesus. The sin that I do not bring to Him is not taken out of me.*

2. *What do you need in order to know your sin? To know sin better there are required: the constant prayer, "Examine me"—in other words, "Make known to me my transgression and my sin" (see Job 13:23; Ps. 139:23–24); a tender conscience that is willing to be convicted of sin through the Spirit, because He also uses the conscience for this end; and the very humble surrender to the Word so that we think concerning sin only as God thinks.*

3. *What personal effects will come when you know more deeply your own sin? The deeper knowledge of sin will be found in these results: That we shall see as sin things we previously did not regard in that way; that we shall perceive more the exceedingly sinful and detestable character of sin (Rom. 7:13); and that with the overcoming of external sins we become all the more encouraged over the deep sinfulness of our nature, of the hostility of our flesh against God. Then we give up all hope of being or of doing anything good, and we are turned wholly to live in faith through the Spirit.*

4. *What is the connection between Jesus and your sin? Let us thank God very heartily that Jesus is a Savior from sin. The power that sin has had over us, Jesus now has. The place that sin has taken in the heart, Jesus will now take. "The law of the Spirit of life in Christ Jesus has made me free from the law of sin and death" (Rom. 8:2).*

11

THE CONFESSION OF SIN

If we confess our sins,
He is faithful and just to forgive us our sins
and to cleanse us from all unrighteousness.

1 JOHN 1:9

THE one thing that God hates, that grieves Him, that He is provoked by, and that He will destroy is sin. The one thing that makes man unhappy is sin (Gen. 6:5–6; Isa. 43:24; Ezek. 33:6; Rev. 6:16–17). The one thing for which Jesus had to give His blood was sin. Therefore, in all the interaction between the sinner and God, the first thing that the sinner must bring to his God is his sin (Judg. 10:10, 15–16; 2 Chron. 17:14; Ezra 9:6; Neh. 2:33; 9:2, 33; Jer. 3:21, 25; Dan. 9:4–5, 20).

When you first came to Jesus, you perceived this in some measure. But you should learn to understand this lesson more deeply. The one counsel concerning sin is to bring it daily to the only One who can take it away—God Himself. You should learn that one of the greatest privileges of a child of God is the confession of sin. It is only the holiness of God that can consume sin. It is through confession that I must hand over my sin to God, lay it down in God, get rid of it to God, and cast it into the fiery oven of God's holy love, which burns against sin like a fire. Yes, God Himself, and He alone, takes away sin (Lev. 6:21; Num. 5:7; 2 Sam. 12:13; Pss. 32:5; 38:19; 51:5, 19).

The Christian does not always understand this. He has an inborn tendency to desire to cover sin, or to make it less, or to root it out only when he wants to draw near to God. He tries to cover sin with his repentance and self-blame, with scorn of the temptation that came to him, or otherwise with what he has done or still hopes to do (Gen. 3:12; Exod. 32:22, 24; Isa. 1:11, 15; Luke 13:26). Young Christian, if you desire to enjoy the gladness of a complete forgiveness and a divine cleansing of sin, see to it that you use correctly the confession of sin. In the true confession of sin you have one of the most blessed privileges of a child of God and one of the deepest roots of a powerful spiritual life.

For this result, let your confession be a definite one (Num. 12:11; 21:7; 2 Sam. 24:10, 17; Isa. 59:12–13; Luke 23:41; Acts 1:18–19; 22:19–20; 1 Tim. 1:13, 15). The continued indeterminate confession of sin does more harm than good. It is much better to say to God that you have nothing to confess than to confess what you don't know. Begin with one sin. Let it come to a complete harmony between God and you concerning this one sin. Let it be certain to you that this sin is through confession placed in God's hands. You shall experience that in such confession there are both power and blessing.

Let the confession be an upright one (Lev. 26:40–41; Prov. 28:13; Jer. 31:18–19). By it, deliver up the sinful deed to be laid aside. By it, deliver up the sinful feeling with a view to trusting in God. Confession implies renunciation, or the putting off of sin. Give up sin to God, to forgive you for it and to cleanse you from it. Do not confess if you are not prepared or if you do not heartily desire to be freed from it. Confession has value only as it is a giving up of sin to God.

Let the confession be trustful (2 Sam. 12:13; Ps. 32:5; Isa. 55:7). Believe firmly upon God actually to forgive you and also to cleanse you from sin. Continue in confession in casting the sin of which you desire to be rid into the fire of God's holiness until your soul has the firm confidence that God takes it on Himself to forgive and to cleanse away. It is this faith that really overcomes the world and sin—the faith that God in Jesus really frees from sin (1 John 2:12).

Brother, do you understand it now? What must you do with sin, with every sin? Bring it in confession to God and give it to God, because God alone takes away sin.

Lord God, what thanks shall I express for the unspeakable blessing that I may come to You with sin? You know, Lord, how sin before Your holiness causes terror and flight. You know it is our deepest thought first to have sin covered, and then to come to You with our desire and endeavor for good. Lord, teach me to come to You with sin, every sin, and in confession to lay it down before You and give it up to You. Amen.

FOR FURTHER THOUGHT

1. *What is the distinction between the covering of sin by God and by man? How does man do it? How does God do it?*

2. *What are the great hindrances in the way of the confession of sin? Ignorance about sin. Fear to come with sin to the holy God. The endeavor to come to God with something good. Unbelief in the power of the blood and in the riches of grace.*

3. *Must I immediately confess an oath or a lie or a wrong word, or wait until my feeling has first cooled and become rightly inclined? Please confess it immediately. Come in full sinfulness to God, without first desiring to make it less!*

4. *Is it also necessary or good to confess before man? It is indispensable if our sin has been against man. And, besides, it is often good, for it is often easier to acknowledge before God than before man that I have done something wrong? (James 5:16).*

12

THE FORGIVENESS OF SINS

Blessed is he whose transgression is forgiven,
whose sin is covered.
PSALM 32:1

Bless the LORD, O my soul. . .
who forgives all your iniquities.
PSALM 103:2–3

IN connection with surrender to the Lord, it was said that the first great blessing of the grace of God was this: the free, complete, everlasting forgiveness of all
your sins. For the young Christian, it is of great importance that he should stand
strong in this forgiveness of his sins and always carry the certainty of it with him.
To this end, he must especially consider the following truths.

The forgiveness of our sin is a complete forgiveness (Ps. 103:12; Isa. 38:17;
55:7; Mic. 7:18–19; Heb. 10:16–18). God does not forgive by halves. Even with
man, we understand that a half forgiveness is not true forgiveness. The love of God
is so great, and the atonement in the blood of Jesus is so complete and powerful,
that God always forgives completely. Take time with God's Word to come to the
full understanding that your guilt has been blotted out completely and altogether.
God thinks absolutely no more of your sins. "I will forgive their iniquity, and their
sin I will remember no more" (Jer. 31:34; also see Heb. 8:12; 10:17)

The forgiveness of our sin restores us entirely again to the love of God
(Hos. 14:5; Luke 15:22; Acts 26:18; Rom. 5:1, 5). Not only does God not attribute
sin anymore—that is but one half—but He assigns to us the righteousness of
Jesus also, so that for His sake we are as dear to God as He is. Not only is wrath
turned away from us, but the fullness of love now rests upon us. "I will love them
freely, for My anger has turned away from him" (Hos. 14:4). Forgiveness is access
to all the love of God. On this account, forgiveness is also the introduction to all
the other blessings of redemption.

Live in the full assurance of forgiveness and let the Spirit fill your heart with the
certainty and the blessedness of it, and then you shall have great confidence in expecting all from God. Learn from the Word of God, through the Spirit, to know God

rightly and to trust Him as the ever-forgiving God. That is His name and His glory.

To one to whom much—in fact, all—is forgiven, He will also give much. He will give all (Ps. 103:3; Isa. 12:1, 3; Rom. 5:10; 8:32; Eph. 1:7; 3:5). Let it therefore be your daily joyful thanksgiving. "Bless the LORD, O my soul. . .who forgives all your iniquities" (Ps. 103:2–3). Then forgiveness becomes the power of a new life: "He who is forgiven much, loves much" (see Luke 7:47). The forgiveness of sins, received anew in living faith every day, is a bond that binds anew to Jesus and His service (John 13:14–15; Rom. 12:1; 1 Cor. 6:20; Eph. 5:25–26; Titus 2:14; 1 Pet. 1:17–18).

> *It is not enough to know that I once received forgiveness. My life in the love of God, my living fellowship with Jesus by faith—this makes the forgiveness of sin again always new and powerful, and the joy and life of my soul.*

Then the forgiveness of former sins always gives courage to go immediately anew with every new sin and trustfully to take forgiveness (Exod. 34:6–7; Matt. 28:21; Luke 1:77–78). Look, however, to one thing: The certainty of forgiveness must not be a matter of memory or understanding, but the fruit of life—living fellowship with the forgiving Father and with Jesus, in whom we have forgiveness (Eph. 2:13, 18; Phil. 3:9; Col. 1:21–22). It is not enough to know that I once received forgiveness. My life in the love of God, my living fellowship with Jesus by faith—this makes the forgiveness of sin again always new and powerful, and the joy and life of my soul.

Lord God, this is the wonder of Your grace, that You are a forgiving God. Teach me every day to know freshly the glory of Your love. Let the Holy Spirit every day seal forgiveness to me as a blessing—everlasting, ever-fresh, living, and powerful. And let my life be as a song of thanksgiving. "Bless the LORD, O my soul. . .who forgives all your iniquities." Amen.

FOR FURTHER THOUGHT

1. *What does the Bible teach you about justification? In essence, forgiveness is one with justification. Forgiveness is the word that looks more to the relationship of God as Father. Justification looks more to His acquittal as Judge. Forgiveness is a word that is more easily understood by the young Christian. But he must also endeavor to understand the word justification, and to obtain part in all that the scripture teaches about it.*

2. *What do I need to know about justification? About justification we must understand: That man in himself is wholly unrighteous. That he cannot be justified by works—that is, pronounced righteous before the judgment seat of God. That Jesus Christ has brought in a righteousness in our place. His obedience is our righteousness. That we through faith receive Him and are united with Him, and then are pronounced righteous before God. That we through faith have the assurance of this, and, as justified, we draw near before God. That union with Jesus is a life by which we are not only pronounced righteous, but are also really righteous and act righteously.*

3. *How does knowing you are justified affect your relationship with God? Let the certainty of your part in justification—in the full forgiveness of your sins and in full restoration to the love of God—be every day your confidence in drawing near to God.*

13

THE CLEANSING OF SIN

But if we walk in the light. . .the blood of Jesus Christ His Son
cleanses us from all sin. . . . If we confess our sins, He is faithful and
just to forgive us our sins and to cleanse us from all unrighteousness.
1 JOHN 1:7, 9

THE same God who forgives sin also cleanses from it. Cleansing is no less a promise of God than forgiveness, and it is therefore a matter of faith. As it is indispensable, as it is impossible for man, so is cleansing as well as forgiveness certain to be obtained from God.

And what now is this cleansing? The word comes from the Old Testament. While forgiveness was a sentence of acquittal passed on the sinner, cleansing was something that happened to him and in him. Forgiveness came to him through the word, but in the case of cleansing, something was done to him that he could experience (Lev. 13:13; 14:7–8; Num. 19:12; 31:23–24; 2 Sam. 22:21, 25; 2 Chron. 5:10; Neh. 13:30; Ps. 21:4; Mal. 3:3). Consequently, with us also cleansing is the inner revelation of the power of God in which we are liberated from unrighteousness and from the pollution and working of sin. Through cleansing we obtain the blessing of a pure heart—a heart in which the Spirit can complete His operations with a goal of sanctifying us and revealing God within us (Pss. 51:12; 73:1; Matt. 5:8; 1 Tim. 1:5; 2 Tim. 2:22; 1 Pet. 1:22).

Cleansing is through the blood. Forgiveness and cleansing are both through the blood. The blood breaks the power sin has in heaven to condemn us. The blood thereby also breaks the power of sin in the heart to hold us captive. The blood has a ceaseless operation in heaven from moment to moment. The blood has likewise a ceaseless operation in our heart to purify and to keep pure the heart into which sin always seeks to penetrate from the flesh. The blood cleanses the conscience from dead works so it can serve the living God. The marvelous power that the blood has in heaven it has also in the heart (John 13:10–11; Heb. 9:14; 10:22; 1 John 1:7).

Cleansing is also through the Word, for the Word testifies of the blood and of the power of God (John 14:3). Therefore, cleansing is also through faith. It is a divine and effectual cleansing, but it must also be received in faith before it can be experienced and felt. I believe that I am cleansed with a divine cleansing, even while I still perceive sin in the flesh. Through faith in this blessing, cleansing itself shall be my daily experience.

Cleansing is credited sometimes to God or the Lord Jesus, but sometimes to man (Ps. 51:3; Ezek. 30:25; John 13:2; 2 Cor. 7:1; 1 Tim. 5:22; 2 Tim. 2:21; James 4:8; 1 John 3:3). That is because God cleanses us by making us active in our own cleansing. Through the blood, the lust that leads to sin is put down, the certitude of power against it is awakened, and the desire and the will are therefore made alive. Happy is he who understands this. He is protected against useless endeavors after self-purification in his own strength, for he knows God alone can do it. He is protected against discouragement, for he knows God will certainly do it.

What we have now to accordingly lay the chief stress upon is found in two things: the desire and the reception of cleansing. The desire must be strong for a real purification. Forgiveness must be only the gateway or beginning of a holy life. I have several times remarked that the secret of progress in the service of God is a strong yearning to become free from every sin and a hunger and thirst after righteousness (Ps. 19:13; Matt. 5:6). Blessed are those who learn this. They shall understand and receive the promise of a cleansing through God.

They learn also what it is to do this in faith. Through faith, they know that an unseen, spiritual, heavenly, but very real cleansing through the blood is accomplished in them by God Himself.

Beloved child of God, you remember how we have seen that it was to cleanse us that Jesus gave Himself (Eph. 5:26; Titus 2:14). Let Him, let God the Lord, cleanse you. Having these promises of a divine cleansing, cleanse yourselves. Believe that every sin, when it is forgiven you, is also cleansed away. It shall be to you according to your faith. Let your faith in God, in the Word, in the blood, and in your Jesus increase continually: "He is faithful and just to forgive us our sins and to cleanse us from all unrighteousness."

Lord God, I thank You for these promises. You give not only forgiveness, but also cleansing. As surely as forgiveness comes first, does cleansing follow for everyone who desires it and believes. Lord, let Your Word penetrate my heart, and let a divine cleansing from every sin that is forgiven me be the stable expectation of my soul. Beloved Savior, let the glorious, ceaseless cleansing of Your blood through Your Spirit in me be made known to me and shared by me every moment. Amen.

FOR FURTHER THOUGHT

1. *What is the connection between cleansing by God and cleansing by man himself?*
2. *What, according to 1 John 1:9, are the two things that must precede cleansing?*
3. *Is cleansing, as well as forgiveness, the work of God in us? If this is the case, of what inexpressible importance is it to trust God for it! To believe that God gives me a divine cleansing in the blood when He forgives me is the way to become partaker of it.*
4. *What, according to scripture, is the evidence of a pure heart?*
5. *What are "clean hands" (Ps. 24:4)?*

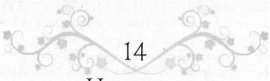

14

HOLINESS

As He who called you is holy, you also be holy in all your
conduct, because it is written, "Be holy, for I am holy."
1 PETER 1:15–16

But of Him you are in Christ Jesus,
who became for us. . .redemption.
1 CORINTHIANS 1:30

God from the beginning chose you for salvation through
sanctification by the Spirit and belief in the truth.
2 THESSALONIANS 2:13

NOT only salvation, but holiness—salvation in holiness. For this purpose God has chosen and called us. Not only safe in Christ, but holy in Christ must be the goal of the young Christian. Safety and salvation are in the long run found only in holiness. The Christian who thinks that his salvation consists merely in safety and not in holiness will find himself deceived. Young Christian, listen to the Word of God: Be holy.

And why must I be holy? Because He who called you is holy, and He summons you to fellowship and conformity with Himself. How should anyone be saved in God when he doesn't have the same disposition as God? (Exod. 19:6; Lev. 11:44; 19:2; 20:6–7)

God's holiness is His highest glory. In His holiness, His righteousness and love are united. His holiness is the flaming fire of His zeal against all that is sin, whereby He keeps Himself free from sin and, in love, also makes others free from it. It is as the Holy One of Israel that He is the Redeemer and that He dwells in the midst of His people (Exod. 15:11; Isa. 12:6; 41:14; 43:15; 49:7; 57:15; Hos. 11:9). Redemption is given to bring us to Himself and to the fellowship of His holiness. We cannot possibly have a part in the love and salvation of God if we are not holy as He is holy (Isa. 10:17; Heb. 12:15). Young Christians, be holy.

And what is this holiness that I must have? Answer: Of God are you in Christ, who of God is made unto you sanctification. Christ is your sanctification, and the life of Christ in you is your holiness (1 Cor. 1:30; Eph. 5:27). In Christ you are sanctified; you are holy. In Christ you must still be sanctified. The glory of Christ must penetrate your whole life.

Holiness is more than purity. In scripture we see that cleansing precedes holiness (2 Cor. 7:1; Eph. 5:26–27; 2 Tim. 2:21). Cleansing is the taking away of that which is wrong—liberation from sin. Holiness is the filling with that which is good, divine, and with the character of Jesus. Conformity to Him—this is holiness. Separation from the spirit of the world and the being filled with the presence of the holy God—this is holiness. The tabernacle was holy because God dwelled there. We are holy, as God's temple, after we have the indwelling of God. Christ's life in us is our holiness (Exod. 29:43, 45; 1 Cor. 1:2; 3:16–17; 6:19).

And how do we become holy? By the sanctification of the Spirit. The Spirit of God is named the Holy Spirit because He makes us holy. He reveals and glorifies Christ in us. Through Him Christ dwells in us, and His holy power works in us. Through this Holy Spirit the workings of the flesh are made dead and God works in us both the will and the accomplishment (Rom. 1:4; 8:2, 13; 1 Pet. 1:2).

> The Christian who thinks that his salvation consists merely in safety and not in holiness will find himself deceived. Young Christian, listen to the Word of God: Be holy.

And what is now the work that we have to do to receive this holiness of Christ through the Holy Spirit? "God from the beginning chose you for salvation through sanctification by the Spirit and belief in the truth" (2 Thess. 2:13). The holiness of Christ becomes ours through faith. There must naturally first be the desire to become holy. We must cleanse ourselves from all pollutions of flesh and spirit by confessing them, giving them up to God, and having them cleansed away in the blood. Only then can we perfect holiness (2 Cor. 7:1). Then, in belief of the truth that Christ Himself is our sanctification, we have to take and receive from Him what is prepared in His fullness for us (John 1:14, 16; 1 Cor. 2:9–10). We must be deeply convinced that Christ is wholly and alone our sanctification, just as He is our justification, and that He will actually and powerfully work in us that which is well-pleasing to God. In this faith, we must know that we have sufficient power for holiness and that our work is to receive this power from Him by faith every day (Gal. 2:21; Eph. 2:10; Phil. 2:13; 4:13). He gives His Spirit—the Holy Spirit—in us, and the Spirit communicates the holy life of Jesus to us.

Young Christian, the Three-One God is the Thrice-Holy (Isa. 6:3; Rev. 4:8; 15:3–4). And this Three-One God is the God who sanctifies you: the Father, by giving Jesus to you and confirming you in Jesus; the Son, by Himself becoming your sanctification and giving you the Spirit; and the Spirit, by revealing the Son in you, preparing you as a temple for the indwelling of God, and making the Son dwell in you. Oh, be holy, for God is holy.

Lord God, the Holy One of Israel, what thanks shall I present to You for the gift of Your Son as my sanctification—and that I am sanctified in Him? And what thanks for the Spirit of sanctification to dwell in me and transplant the holiness of Jesus into me. Lord, help me to understand this correctly and to long for the experience of it. Amen.

For Further Thought

1. *What is the distinction between forgiveness and cleansing, and between cleansing and holiness?*
2. *What made the temple a sanctuary? The indwelling of God. What makes us holy? Nothing less than this: the indwelling of God in Christ by the Holy Spirit. Obedience and purity are the way to holiness, but holiness itself is something higher.*
3. *In Isaiah 52:17, there is a description of the man who will become holy. It is he who, in poorness of spirit, acknowledges that even when he is living as a righteous man, he has nothing and looks to God to come and dwell in Him.*
4. *No one is holy but the Lord. You have as much of holiness as you have of God in you.*
5. *The word* holy *is one of the deepest words in the Bible and the deepest mystery of the Godhead. Do you desire to understand something of it and to obtain part in it? Then take these two thoughts, "I am holy," "Be holy," and carry them in your heart as a seed of God that has life.*
6. *What is the connection between the perseverance of the saints and perseverance in holiness?*

15

RIGHTEOUSNESS

He has shown you, O man, what is good;
and what does the LORD require of you but to do justly,
to love mercy, and to walk humbly with your God?
MICAH 6:8

Present yourselves to God as being alive from the dead,
and your members as instruments of righteousness. . . .
And having been set free from sin, you became slaves. . .
of righteousness for holiness.
ROMANS 6:13, 18–19

THE word of Micah teaches us that the fruit of the salvation of God is seen chiefly in three things. The new life must be characterized in my relationship to God and His will by righteousness and doing right; in my relation to my neighbor, by love and charity; and in relation to myself, by humility and lowliness. Today we meditate on righteousness.

Scripture teaches us that no man is righteous before God or has any righteousness that can stand before God (Pss. 14:3; 143:2; Rom. 3:10, 20); that man receives the rightness or righteousness of Christ for nothing; and that by this righteousness, which is received in faith, he is then justified before God (Rom. 3:22, 24: 10:3, 10; 1 Cor. 1:30; 2 Cor. 5:21; Gal. 2:16; Phil. 3:9) and right with God. This righteous sentence of God is something effectual, whereby the life of righteousness is implanted in man, who learns to live as a righteous man and to do righteousness (Rom. 5:17–18; 6:13, 18–19; 8:3; Titus 1:8; 2:12; 1 John 2:29; 3:9–10). *Being* right with God is followed by *doing* right. "The just shall live by faith" (Rom. 1:17) a righteous life.

It is to be feared that this is not always understood. One thinks sometimes more of justification than of righteousness in life and walk. To understand the will and the thoughts of God here, let us trace what scripture teaches us on this point. We shall be persuaded that the man who is clothed with a divine righteousness before God must also walk before God and man in a divine righteousness.

Consider how in the Word, the servants of God are praised as "righteous" (Gen.

6:9; 7:1; Matt. 1:19; Luke 1:6; 2:25; 2 Pet. 2:7), how the favor and blessing of God are pronounced upon the righteous (Pss. 1:6; 5:13; 14:5; 34:16, 20; 37:17, 39; 92:13; 97:11; 144:8), and how the righteous are called to confidence and joy (Pss. 32:11; 33:1; 58:11; 64:11; 68:4; 97:12). See this especially in the book of Psalms. See how in Proverbs, although you should take just one chapter only, all blessing is pronounced upon the righteous (Prov. 10:3, 6–7, 11, 16, 20–21, 24–25, 28, 30–32). See how everywhere men are divided into two classes: the righteous and the godless (Eccles. 3:17; Isa. 3:10; Ezek. 3:18, 20; 18:21, 23; 33:12; Mal. 3:18; Matt. 5:45; 12:49; 25:46). See how, in the New Testament, the Lord Jesus demands this righteousness (Matt. 5:6, 20; 6:33); how Paul, who announces most the doctrine of justification by faith alone, insists that this is the aim of justification: to form righteous men who do right (Rom. 3:31; 6:13, 22; 7:4, 6; 8:4; 2 Cor. 9:9–10; Phil. 1:11; 1 Tim. 6:11). See how John names righteousness along with love as the two indispensable marks of the children of God (1 John 2:4, 11, 29; 3:10; 5:2). When you put all these facts together, it will be very evident to you that a true Christian is a man who does righteousness in all things, even as God is righteous.

> *S*cripture teaches us that no man is righteous before God or has any righteousness that can stand before God, that man receives the rightness or righteousness of Christ for nothing,.

And scripture will also teach you what this righteousness is. It is a life in accordance with the commands of God, in all their breadth and height. The righteous man does what is right in the eyes of the Lord (Ps. 119:166, 168; Luke 1:6, 75; 1 Thess. 2:10). He does not take the rules of human action, and he doesn't ask what man considers lawful. As a man who stands right with God and who walks uprightly with God, he dreads above all things even the least unrighteousness. He is afraid, above all, of being partial to himself, of doing any wrong to his neighbor for the sake of his own advantage. In great and little things alike, he takes the scriptures as his measure and standard. As the ally of God, he knows that the way of righteousness is the way of blessing, life, and joy.

Consider, further, the promises of blessing and joy that God has for the righteous—he who lives as one who, in friendship with God and clothed with the righteousness of His Son through faith, has no alternative but to do righteousness.

O Lord, who has said, "There is no other God besides Me, a just God and a Savior" (see Isa. 45:21): You are my God. It is as a righteous God that You are my Savior who has redeemed me in Your Son. As a righteous God, You make me also righteous and say to me that the righteous shall live by faith. O Lord, let the new life in me be the life of faith, the life of a righteous man. Amen.

FOR FURTHER THOUGHT

1. *What is the connection between the doing of righteousness and sanctification? In Romans 6:19, 22 God tells us, "Present your members as slaves of righteousness for holiness [or sanctification]," and "Having become slaves of God, you have your fruit to holiness." The doing of righteousness—righteousness in conduct and action—is the way to holiness. Obedience is the way to become filled with the Holy Spirit. And the indwelling of God through the Spirit—this is holiness.*

2. *What must you do in order to be filled with God's Spirit? Jesus said, "Permit it to be so now, for thus it is fitting for us to fulfill all righteousness" (Matt. 3:15). It was when the Lord Jesus had spoken that word that He was baptized with the Spirit. Let us set aside every temptation not to walk in full obedience toward God, even as He did, and we, too, shall be filled with the Spirit. "Blessed are those who hunger and thirst for righteousness" (Matt. 5:6).*

3. *Make great efforts to set before yourselves the image of a man who so walks that the name of "righteous" is involuntarily given to him. Think of his uprightness, his conscientious care to cause no one to suffer the least injury, his holy fear and carefulness to transgress none of the commands of the Lord—righteous and walking blamelessly in all the commandments and ordinances of the Lord—and then say to the Lord that you want to live that way.*

4. *What is the most important result of your true faith in God? You understand now the great word, "The just shall live by faith." By faith, the godless is justified and becomes a righteous man. By faith, he lives as a righteous man.*

16

LOVE

"A new commandment I give to you, that you love one another;
as I have loved you, that you also love one another. By this all will
know that you are My disciples, if you have love for one another."
JOHN 13:34–35

Love does no harm to a neighbor;
therefore love is the fulfillment of the law.
ROMANS 13:10

Beloved, if God so loved us, we also ought to love one
another. . . . If we love one another, God abides in us,
and His love has been perfected in us.
1 JOHN 4:11–12

IN the word of Micah, in the previous chapter, righteousness was the first thing—to love mercy second—that God demands. Righteousness stood more in the foreground in the Old Testament. It is in the New Testament that it is first seen that love is supreme. Words to this effect are not difficult to find. It is in the advent of Jesus that the love of God is first revealed; that the new, the eternal life, is first given; that we become children of the Father, and brethren of one another. On this ground the Lord can then, for the first time, speak of the New Commandment—the commandment of brotherly love. Righteousness is not required any less in the New Testament than in the Old (Matt 5:6, 17, 20; 6:33). Yet the focus of the New Testament is that power has been given us for a love that in early days was impossible (John 13:34; Rom. 5:5; Gal. 5:22; 1 Thess. 4:9; 1 John 4:11).

Let every Christian take it deeply to heart that in the first and the great commandment, the new commandment given by Jesus at His departure, the peculiar characteristic of a disciple of Jesus is brotherly love. And let him with his whole heart yield himself to Him and obey that command. For the right exercise of this brotherly love, one must pay attention to more than one thing.

Love for the brethren arises from the love of the Father. By the Holy Spirit, the love of God is shed abroad in our hearts and the wonderful love of the Father is unveiled to us, so that His love becomes the life and the joy of our soul. Out of this fountain of the love of God to us springs our love for Him (Rom. 5:5; 1 John 4:19). And our love for Him works naturally toward love to the brethren (Eph. 4:2, 6; 5:1–2; 1 John 3:1; 4:7, 20; 5:1).

Do not attempt then to fulfill the commandment of brotherly love on your own. You are not in a position to do this. But believe that the Holy Spirit, who is in you to make known the love of God to you, also certainly enables you to demonstrate this love. Never say: "I feel no love," or "I do not feel as if I can forgive this man." Feeling is not the rule of your duty, but the command and the faith that God gives power to obey the command. In obedience to the Father, with the choice of your will and in faith that the Holy Spirit gives you power, begin to say: "I will love him; I do love him." The feeling will follow the faith. Grace gives power for all that the Father asks of you (Matt. 5:44–45; Gal. 2:20; 1 Thess. 3:12–13; 5:24; Phil. 4:13; 1 Pet. 1:22).

Let every Christian take it deeply to heart that in the first and the great commandment, the new commandment given by Jesus at His departure, the peculiar characteristic of a disciple of Jesus is brotherly love.

Brotherly love has its measure and rule in the love of Jesus. "This is My commandment, that you love one another as I have loved you" (John 15:12; also see Luke 22:26–27; John 13:14–15, 34; Col. 2:13). The eternal life that works in us is the life of Jesus. It knows no other law than what we see in Him. It produces with power in us what it demonstrated in Him. Jesus Himself lives in us and loves in and through us. We must believe in the power of this love in us and in that faith love as He loved. Oh, do believe that this is true salvation—to love even as Jesus loves.

Brotherly love must be in deed and in truth (Matt. 12:50; 25:40; Rom. 13:10; 1 Cor. 7:19; Gal. 5:6; James 2:15–16; 1 John 3:16–18). It is not mere feeling. Faith working by love is what has power in Christ. It demonstrates itself in all the attitudes and actions enumerated in the Word of God. Contemplate its glorious image in 1 Corinthians 13:4–7. Mark all the glorious encouragements to gentleness, to longsuffering, to mercy (Gal. 5:22; Eph. 4:2, 32; Phil. 2:2–3; Col. 3:12; 2 Thess. 1:3). In all your conduct, let others see that the love of Christ dwells in you. Let your love be a helpful, self-sacrificing love—like that of Jesus. Hold all children of God, however sinful or perverse they may be, fervently dear. Let your love for them teach you to love all men (Luke 6:32, 35; 1 Pet. 1:22; 2 Pet. 1:7). Let your household, the Church, and the world see in you one with whom "love is greatest" (see 1 Cor. 13:13), one in whom the love of God has a full dwelling and a free working.

Christian, God is love. Jesus is the gift of this love to bring love to you and to transplant you into that life of godlike love. Live in that faith, and you shall not complain that you have no power to love, because the love of the Spirit will be your power and your life.

Beloved Savior, I discern more clearly that the whole of the new life is a life in love. You Yourself are the Son of God's love and the gift of His love come to bring us into His love and give us a dwelling there. And the Holy Spirit is given to show abroad the love of God in our hearts and to open a spring out of which will stream love for You, for the brethren, and for all mankind. Lord, here am I, one redeemed by love, to love for it, and in its might to love all. Amen.

FOR FURTHER THOUGHT

1. *What is the true place love must have in your new life in Christ? Those who reject the Word of God sometimes say that it is of no importance what we believe as long as we but have love, thus making love the one condition of salvation. In their zeal against this view, the orthodox party has sometimes presented faith in justification, as if love were not of so much importance. This is likely to be very dangerous. God is love. His Son is the gift and the bringer of His love to us. The Spirit sheds abroad the love of God in the heart. The new life is a life in love. Love is the greatest thing. Let it be the chief element in our life: true love, that, namely, which is known in the keeping of God's commandments. (See 1 John 3:10, 23, 24; 5:2.)*

2. *How can you love others for whom you "feel" no love? Do not wonder that I have said to you that you must love even though you do not feel the least love. Not the feeling but the will is your power. It is not in your feeling but in faith that the Spirit in you is the power of your will to work in you all that the Father commands you. Therefore, although you feel absolutely no love for your enemy, say in the obedience of faith: "Father, I love him. In faith in the hidden working of the Spirit in my heart, I do love him."*

3. *How should you effectively and rightly demonstrate your love for others through Christ? Please don't think that it is love if you wish no evil to anyone, or if you should be willing to help if he were in need. No, love is much more: Love is love. Love is the disposition with which God addressed you when you were His enemy, and then afterwards ran to you with tender longing to bless you.*

17

HUMILITY

And what does the LORD require of you but to do justly,
to love mercy, and to walk humbly with your God?
MICAH 6:8

"Learn from Me, for I am gentle and lowly in heart,
and you will find rest for your souls."
MATTHEW 11:29

ONE of the most dangerous enemies against which the young Christian must watch is pride or self-exaltation. There is no sin that works more cunningly and more stealthily. It knows how to penetrate into everything, even into our service for God, our prayers—yes, even into our humility. There is nothing so small in the earthly life, nothing so holy in the spiritual life that self-exaltation does not know to extract its nourishment out of it (2 Chron. 26:5, 16; 32:26, 31; Isa. 65:5; Jer. 7:4; 2 Cor. 12:7). The Christian must therefore be on his guard against it and must listen to what scripture teaches about it—and about the lowliness through which it is driven out.

Man was created to have part in the glory of God. He obtains this by surrendering himself to the glorification of God. The more he seeks that the glory of God only is seen in him, the more this glory rests upon himself (Isa. 43:7, 21; John 12:28; 13:31–32; 1 Cor. 10:31; 2 Thess. 1:11–12). The more he forgets and loses himself, desiring to be nothing so that God may be all and be alone glorified, the happier he will be.

By sin this design has been thwarted. Man seeks himself and his own will (Rom. 1:21, 23). Grace has come to restore what sin has corrupted and to bring man to glory by the pathway of dying to himself and living solely for the glory of God. This is the humility or lowliness of which Jesus is the perfect example: He never thought of Himself but gave Himself over fully to glorify the Father (John 8:50; Phil. 2:7).

He who would be freed from self-exaltation must not think to obtain this by striving against its mere workings. No, pride must be driven out and kept out by humility. The Spirit of life in Christ—the Spirit of His lowliness—will work in us true lowliness (Rom. 8:2; Phil. 2:5).

The means He will chiefly use for this purpose is the Word. It is by the Word that we are cleansed from sin, by the Word that we are sanctified and filled with the love of God.

Observe what the Word says about this point. It speaks of God's aversion to pride and the punishment that comes upon it (Ps. 31:24; Prov. 16:5; Matt. 23:12; Luke 1:51; James 4:5; 1 Pet. 5:5). It gives the most glorious promises to the lowly (Ps. 34:19; Prov. 11:2; Isa. 57:15; Luke 9:48; 14:11; 18:14). In nearly every epistle, humility is highly praised to Christians as one of the first virtues (Rom. 12:3, 16; 1 Cor. 13:4; Gal. 5:22, 26; Eph. 4:2; Phil. 2:3; Col. 2:13). It is the feature in the image of Jesus that He seeks chiefly to impress on His disciples. His whole incarnation and redemption has its roots in His humiliation (Matt. 20:26, 28; Luke 22:27; John 13:14–15; Phil. 2:7–8).

> *D*on't attempt to hide your pride, or to forget it or to root it out yourself. Confess this sin, with every working of it that you find, in the sure confidence that the blood cleanses and the Spirit sanctifies.

Take singly some of these words of God from time to time and store them in your heart. The tree of life yields many different kinds of seed—the seed also of the heavenly plant, lowliness. The seeds are the words of God. Carry them in your heart, and they will grow up and yield fruit (1 Thess. 2:13; Heb. 4:12; James 1:21).

Consider, likewise, how lovely, how becoming, how well-pleasing to God lowliness is. As man who is created for the honor of God, you find it fitting for you (Gen. 1:27; 1 Cor. 11:7). As a sinner who is deeply unworthy, you have nothing more to battle against it (Job 40:6; Isa. 6:5; Luke 5:8). As a redeemed soul who knows that only through the death of the natural *I* does the way to the new life lie, you find it indispensable (Rom. 7:18; 1 Cor. 15:9–10; Gal. 2:20).

But here, as everywhere in the life of grace, let faith be the chief thing. Believe in the power of the eternal life that works in you. Believe in the power of Jesus, who is your life. Believe in the power of the Holy Spirit, who dwells in you. Don't attempt to hide your pride, or to forget it or to root it out yourself. Confess this sin, with every working of it that you find, in the sure confidence that the blood cleanses and the Spirit sanctifies. Learn from Jesus that He is humble and lowly in heart. Consider that He is your life, with all that He has. Believe that He gives His humility to you. The word "Do it to the Lord Jesus" means "Be clothed with the Lord Jesus." Be clothed with humility, so that you may be clothed with Jesus. It is Christ in you that shall fill you with humility.

Blessed Lord Jesus, there never was anyone among the children of men so high, so holy, so glorious as You. And never was there anyone who was so lowly and ready to deny himself as the servant of all. O Lord, when shall we learn that lowliness is the grace by which man can be most closely conformed to the divine glory? Oh teach me this. Amen.

FOR FURTHER THOUGHT

1. *How should you approach humility in yourself and in others? Be careful to do nothing to feed pride on the part of others. Be careful that you do not allow others to feed your pride. Be careful, above all, that you do nothing yourself to feed your pride. Let God alone always and in all things obtain the honor. Endeavor to observe all that is good in His children and to thank Him heartily for it. Thank Him for all that helps you to hold yourself in small esteem, whether it is sent through friend or foe. Resolve, especially, never on any account to be eagerly bent on your own honor, when this is not given to you as it should be. Commit this to the Father: Take heed only to His honor.*

2. *How is true humility different from weakness, fear, and doubt? By no means assume that faintheartedness or doubting is lowliness. Deep humility and strong faith go together. The centurion who said, "I am not worthy that You should come under my roof" (Matt. 8:8), and the woman who said, "Yes, Lord, yet even the little dogs eat the crumbs" (Matt. 15:27), were the most humble and the most trustful the Lord found. The reason is this: The nearer we are to God, the less we are in ourselves and the stronger we are in Him. The more I see of God, the less I become, and the deeper is my confidence in Him. To become lowly, let God fill your eye and heart. Where God is all, there is no time or place for man.*

3. *What do you see in the life of Jesus Christ—in His words and actions alike— that can serve as examples of true humility?*

18

STUMBLINGS

For we all stumble in many things.
JAMES 3:2

THIS word of God by James is the description of what man is—even the Christian—when he is not kept by grace. It serves to take away from us all hope in ourselves (Rom. 7:14, 23; Gal. 6:1). "Now to Him who is able to keep you from stumbling. . .be glory and majesty, dominion and power, both now and forever" (Jude 24–25). This word of God by Jude points to Him who can keep us from falling, and it stirs up the soul to credit to Him the honor and the power. It serves to confirm our hope in God (2 Cor. 1:9; 1 Thess. 5:24; 2 Thess. 2:16–17; 3:3). "Brethren, be even more diligent to make your call and election sure, for if you do these things you will never stumble" (2 Pet. 1:10). This word of God by Peter teaches us the way in which we can become partakers of the keeping of the Almighty: the confirmation of our election by God in a godlike walk (see 1:4, 8, 11). It serves to lead us into diligence and conscientious watchfulness (Matt. 26:41; Luke 12:35; 1 Pet. 1:13; 5:8–10).

For the young Christian, it is often a difficult question what he should think of his stumblings. On this point, he should especially be on his guard against two errors. Some become discouraged when they stumble, thinking that their surrender was not sincere, and lose their confidence toward God (Heb. 3:6, 14; 10:35). Others again take it too lightly, thinking that it cannot be otherwise, and so they concern themselves little with stumblings and continue to live in them (Rom. 6:1; Gal. 2:18; 3:3). Let us take these words of God to teach us what we should think of our stumblings. There are three lessons.

Let no stumblings discourage you. You are called to perfection, but this doesn't come all at once; time and patience are needed for it. Therefore James says: "Let patience have its perfect work, that you may be perfect and complete" (James 1:4; also see Matt. 5:48; 2 Tim. 3:17; Heb. 13:20–21; 1 Pet. 5:10). Don't think that your surrender was not sincere, but only acknowledge how weak you still are. Don't think, either, that you must only continue stumbling. Instead, acknowledge only how strong your Savior is.

Let stumbling rouse you to faith in the mighty Keeper. It is because you have not relied on Him with a sufficient faith that you have stumbled (Matt. 14:31; 17:20).

Let stumbling drive you to Him. The first thing you must do with a stumbling is go with it to your Jesus and tell Him about it (Pss. 38:18; 69:6; 1 John 1:9; 2:1). Confess it and receive forgiveness. Confess it and commit yourself with your weakness to Him, and rely on Him to keep you. Sing continually the song: "To Him who is able to keep you. . .be glory."

> *he first thing you must do with a stumbling is go with it to your Jesus and tell Him about it. Confess it and receive forgiveness. Confess it and commit yourself with your weakness to Him, and rely on Him to keep you.*

And then *let stumbling make you very careful* (Prov. 28:14; Phil. 2:12; 1 Pet. 1:17–18). By faith you will strive and overcome. In the power of your Keeper and the joy and security of His help, you shall have courage to watch. The surer you make your election, the stronger the certainty that He has chosen you and will not let you go, the more conscientious shall you become to live in all things only for Him, in Him, through Him (2 Chron. 20:15; Pss. 18:30, 37; 44:5, 9; John 5:4–5; Rom. 11:20; 2 Cor. 1:24; Phil. 2:13). When you do this, the Word of God says, you will never stumble.

Lord Jesus, a sinner who is ready to stumble every moment would give honor to You, who is mighty to keep him from stumbling: Yours is the might and the power, and I take You as my Keeper. I look to Your love that has chosen me and wait for the fulfillment of Your word: "You will never stumble." Amen.

FOR FURTHER THOUGHT

1. *Should you expect stumbling to be a consistent, unavoidable part of your new life in Christ? Let your thoughts about what the grace of God can do for you be taken only from the Word of God. Our natural expectations—that we must just always be stumbling—are wrong. They are strengthened by more than one thing. There is secret unwillingness to surrender everything. There is the example of so many sluggish Christians. There is the unbelief that cannot quite understand that God will really keep us. There is the experience of so many disappointments when we have striven in our own power.*
2. *Let no stumbling be tolerated for a trivial reason.*
3. *What must you do to avoid stumbling into sin?*
4. *What should be your response when you do stumble?*

19

JESUS THE KEEPER

The LORD is your keeper. . . .
The LORD shall preserve you from all evil;
He shall preserve your soul.
PSALM 121:5, 7

I know whom I have believed and am persuaded that
He is able to keep what I have committed to Him until that Day.[11]
2 TIMOTHY 1:12

FOR young disciples of Christ who are still weak, there is no lesson more necessary than this: That the Lord not only has received them, but also will keep them (Gen. 28:15; Deut. 7:9; 32:10; Pss. 17:8; 89:33–34; Rom. 12:2, 29). The lovely name "the Lord your Keeper" must for this purpose be carried in the heart until the assurance of an almighty keeping becomes as strong with us as it was with Paul when he spoke that glorious word: "I know whom I have believed and am persuaded that He is able to keep what I have committed to Him until that Day." Come and learn this lesson from him.

Learn from him *to deposit your pledge with Jesus.* Paul had surrendered himself, body and soul, to the Lord Jesus. That was his pledge, which he had deposited with the Lord. You have also surrendered yourselves to the Lord, but perhaps not with the clear understanding that it is in order to be *kept* every day. Do this now daily. Deposit your soul with Jesus as a costly pledge that He will keep you secure. Do this same thing with every part of your life. Is there something that you cannot rightly hold—your heart, because it is too worldly (Ps. 31:6; Jer. 31:33); your tongue, because it is too idle (Pss. 51:17; 141:8); your temper, because it is too passionate (Ps. 119:165; Jer. 26:3–4; John 14:27; Phil. 4:6–7; 2 Thess. 3:16); or your calling to confess the Lord, because you are too weak (Isa. 50:7; Jer. 1:9; Matt. 10:19–20)? Learn, then, to deposit it as a pledge for keeping with Jesus, so that He may fulfill in you the promise of God about it.

You often pray and strive too much in vain against a sin. That is because, although this is done with God's help, you want to be the person who would overcome. No! Entrust the matter wholly to Jesus: "The battle is not yours, but God's" (2 Chron.

---

[11] The Dutch verson has "My pledge, which I deposited with Him."—Tr.

20:15; also see Exod. 14:14; Deut. 3:22; 20:4). Leave it in His hands and believe in Him to do it for you: "And this is the victory that has overcome the world—our faith" (1 John 5:4; also see Matt. 9:23). But you must first take it wholly out of your hands and put it in His.

Learn from Paul *to place your confidence only on the power of Jesus*. I am persuaded that *He is able* to keep my pledge. You have an almighty Jesus to keep you. Faith keeps itself occupied only with His omnipotence (Gen. 17:1; 18:14; Jer. 32:17, 27; Matt. 8:27; 28:18; Luke 1:37, 49; 18:27; Rom. 4:21; Heb. 11:18). Let your faith especially be strengthened in what God is able to do for you (Rom. 4:21; 14:4; 2 Cor. 9:8; 2 Tim. 1:12). Expect with certainty from Him that He will do for you great and glorious things entirely above your own strength. See in the holy scriptures how constantly the power of God was the basis of the trust of His people. Take these words and hide them in your heart. Let the power of Jesus fill your soul. Ask only: "What is my Jesus able to do?" What you really trust Him with, He is able to keep (John 13:1; 1 Cor. 1:8–9).

> *For young disciples of Christ who are still weak, there is no lesson more necessary than this: that the Lord not only has received them, but also will keep them.*

And learn also from Paul where he obtained the assurance that this power would keep his pledge: *in his knowledge of Jesus.* "I know whom I have believed," and therefore I am assured (see John 10:14, 28; Gal. 2:20; 2 Tim. 4:18; 1 John 2:13–14). You can trust the power of Jesus if you *know* that He is yours, if you converse with Him as your friend. Then you can say: "I know whom I have believed. I know that He holds me very dear. I know and am assured that He is able to keep my pledge."

So runs the way to the full assurance of faith: Deposit your pledge with Jesus and give yourselves wholly. Give everything into His hands, think often of His might, and rely on Him. Then live with Him so that you may always know who He is in whom you have believed.

Young disciples of Christ, please receive this word: "The Lord is your Keeper." For every weakness and every temptation, learn to deposit your soul with Him as a pledge. You can rely on it and shout joyfully over it: The Lord will keep you from all evil (Josh. 1:9; Ps. 23:4; Rom. 8:35, 39).

Holy Jesus, I take You as my Keeper. Let Your name, "the Lord your Keeper," sound as a song in my heart the whole day. Teach me in every need to deposit my case as a pledge with You, and to be assured that You are able to keep it. Amen.

For Further Thought

1. *There was once a woman who for many long years, and with much prayer, had struggled against her temper but could not obtain the victory. On a certain day she resolved not to come out of her room until by earnest prayer she had the power to overcome. She went out believing that she would succeed. She was still in her household when something gave her offense and caused her to be angry. She was deeply ashamed, burst into tears, and hurried back to her room. A daughter, who understood the way of faith better than she, went to her and said, "Mother, I have observed your conflict. May I tell you what I think the hindrance is?" "Yes, my child." "Mother, you struggle against temper and pray that the Lord may help you to overcome. This is wrong. The Lord must do it alone. You must give temper wholly into His hands. Then He takes it wholly, and He keeps you." The mother could not at first understand this, but later it was made plain to her. And she enjoyed the blessedness of the life in which Jesus keeps us and we by faith have the victory. Do you understand the importance of allowing God to overcome temper and other sin? How do you allow that to happen?*

2. *How does God want you to overcome sin? "The Lord must help me to overcome sin." This expression is altogether outside of the New Testament. The grace of God in the soul does not become a help to us. He will do everything: "For. . .the Spirit. . .has made me free from the law of sin" (Rom. 8:2).*

3. *When you surrender anything to the Lord for keeping, be sure of two things: that you give it wholly into His hands, and that you leave it there. Let Him have it wholly, and He will carry out your case gloriously.*

20

POWER IN WEAKNESS

He said to me, "My grace is sufficient for you, for My strength is
made perfect in weakness." Therefore most gladly I will rather
boast in my infirmities, that the power of Christ may rest upon me.
Therefore I take pleasure in infirmities, in reproaches...
2 CORINTHIANS 12:9–10

THERE is almost no word so imperfectly understood in the Christian life as the word *weakness*. Sin and shortcoming, sluggishness and disobedience, are set to the account of our weakness. With this appeal to weakness, the true feeling of guilt and the sincere endeavor after progress are impossible. How, I ask, can I be guilty when I do not do what it is not in my power to do? The Father cannot demand of His child what He can certainly do independently. That, indeed, was done by the law under the Old Covenant. But that the Father, under the New Covenant, does not do. He requires of us nothing more than what He has prepared for us power to do in His Holy Spirit. The new life is a life in the power of Christ through the Spirit.

The error of this mode of thinking is that people estimate their weakness not too highly, but too lowly. They would still try to do something by the exercise of all their own powers—and with the help of God. They don't know that they must be nothing before God (Rom. 4:4–5; 11:6; 1 Cor. 1:27–28). You think that you still have a little strength and that the Father must help you by adding something of His own power to your feeble energy. This thought is wrong. Your weakness appears in the fact that you *can do nothing*. It is better to speak of utter inability—that is what the scriptures mean by the word *weakness*. "Without Me you can do nothing" (John 15:5), and "In us is no power" (see 2 Chron. 16:9; 20:12; John 5:19; 2 Cor. 1:9).

Whenever the young Christian acknowledges and agrees to this his weakness, then he learns to understand the secret of the power of Jesus. He then sees that he is not to wait and pray to become stronger or to feel stronger. No, in his inability he is to have the power of Jesus. By faith he is to receive it. He is to believe that it is for him and that Jesus Himself will work in and by him (John 15:5; 1 Cor. 1:24; 15:10; Eph. 1:18–19; Col. 1:11). It then becomes clear to him what the Lord means when He says, "My strength is made perfect in weakness." He knows to return the answer, "For when I am weak, then I am strong" (2 Cor. 12:10). Yes, the weaker I am, the stronger I become. And he learns to sing with Paul, "I shall glory in my weaknesses" (see 2 Cor. 11:30), "I take pleasure in weaknesses" (see 12:9), and "We rejoice when we are weak" (see 13:9).

It is wonderful how glorious that life of faith becomes for him who is content to have nothing or feel nothing in himself, and who always lives in the power of his Lord. He learns to understand what a joyful thing it is to know God as his strength. "The LORD is my strength and song" (Ps. 118:14; see also Ps. 89:18; Jer. 12:2). He lives in what the Psalms so often express: "I will love You, O LORD, my strength" (18:1); "I will sing of Your power.... To You, O my Strength, I will sing praises" (59:16; 17). He understands what is meant when a psalm says, "Give unto the LORD glory and strength.... The LORD will give strength to His people" (29:1, 11), and when another says, "Ascribe strength to God.... The God of Israel *is* He who gives strength and power to *His* people" (68:34–35) When we give or ascribe all the power to God, then He gives it to us again.

> *He* requires of us nothing more than what He has prepared for us power to do in His Holy Spirit. The new life is a life in the power of Christ through the Spirit.

"I have written to you, young men, because you are strong, and the word of God abides in you, and you have overcome the wicked one" (1 John 2:14). The Christian is strong in his Lord (Ps. 71:16)—not sometimes strong and sometimes weak, but always weak, and therefore always strong. He need only know and use his strength trustfully. To be strong is a command, an order that must be obeyed. On obedience there comes more strength. Be strong "and He shall strengthen your heart" (Ps. 27:14; also see Ps. 31:25; Isa. 40:31). In faith the Christian must simply obey the command to "be strong in the Lord and in the power of His might" (Eph. 6:10).

The God of the Lord Jesus, the Father of glory: Give us the spirit of wisdom and of revelation in the knowledge of Jesus, so that we may know what is the exceeding greatness of His power to us who believe. Amen.

FOR FURTHER THOUGHT

1. *How do you do those things God calls you to do, but you know are difficult or even impossible for you? So long as the Christian thinks of the service of God or of sanctification as something that is hard and difficult, he will make no progress in it. He must see that this very thing is for him impossible. Then he will cease still attempting to do something, but will instead surrender himself so that Christ may work all in him. See these thoughts set forth in detail in Professor Hofmeyr's book,* Out of Darkness into Light: A Course of Instruction on Conversion, the Surrender of Faith, and Sanctification, *chapter 3 and following.*

2. *The complaint about weakness is often nothing else than an apology for our idleness. There is power to be obtained in Christ for those who will make the effort to have it.*

3. *How do you acquire strength and power to do the things God calls you to do? "Be strong in the Lord and in the power of His might." Pay attention to that. I must abide in the Lord and in the power of His might. Only then will I become strong. To have His power I must have Himself. The strength is His and continues to be His, while the weakness continues to be mine. He, the Strong, works in me, the weak; I, the weak, abide by faith in Him, the Strong, so that I, in the same moment, know myself to be weak and strong.*

4. *For what purpose does God give you strength and power? Strength is for work. He who would be strong simply to be spiritual will not be so. He who in his weakness begins to work for the Lord shall become strong.*

21

THE LIFE OF FEELING

For we walk by faith, not by sight.
2 CORINTHIANS 5:7

"Blessed are those who have not seen and yet have believed."
JOHN 20:29

"Did I not say to you that if you would
believe you would see the glory of God?"
JOHN 11:40

IN connection with your conversion there was no greater hindrance in your way than feeling. You thought, perhaps for years, that you must experience something, must feel and perceive something in yourselves. It was to you as if it were too hazardous to so simply and without some feeling believe in the Word, be sure that God had received you, and know your sins were forgiven. But at last you have had to acknowledge that the way of faith—without feeling—is the way of the Word of God. And it has been to you the way of salvation. Through faith alone have you been saved, and your soul has found rest and peace (John 3:36; Rom. 3:28; 4:5, 16; 5:1).

In the further life of the Christian there is no temptation more persistent and more dangerous than this same feeling. We do not find the word *feeling* in scripture, but what we call "feeling" the scripture calls "seeing." And it tells us without ceasing that it is not seeing but believing, that believing right in opposition to what we see gives salvation. "And not being weak in faith, [Abraham] did not consider his own body" (Rom. 4:19). Faith adheres simply to what God says. The unbelief that wants to see shall not see, but the faith that will not see but has enough in God shall see the glory of God (2 Chron. 7:2; Ps. 27:13; Isa. 7:9; Matt. 14:30–31; Luke 5:5). The man who seeks for feeling and mourns about it shall not find it, but the man who doesn't care about feeling shall have it overflowing. "For whoever desires to save his life will lose it, but whoever loses his life for My sake will find it" (Matt. 16:25). Faith in the word becomes later on sealed with true feeling by the Holy Spirit (John 12:25; Gal. 3:2, 14; Eph. 1:13).

Child of God, learn to live by faith. Let it be fixed with you that faith is God's way to a blessed life. When there is no feeling of liveliness in prayer, when you feel cold and dull in the inner chamber, live by faith. Let your faith look upon Jesus as near, upon His power and faithfulness. And though you have nothing to bring to Him, believe that He will give you all. Feeling always seeks something in itself, but faith keeps itself occupied with what Jesus is (Rom. 4:20–21; 2 Tim. 1:12; Heb. 9:5–6; James 3:16). When you read the Word and have no feeling of interest or blessing, read it yet again in faith. The Word will work and bring blessing: "The word of God...also effectively works in you who believe" (1 Thess. 2:13).

When you feel no love, believe in the love of Jesus and say in faith that He knows that you still love Him. When you have no feeling of gladness, believe in the inexpressible joy that there is in Jesus for you. Faith is blessedness and will give joy to those who are not concerned about the self-sufficiency that springs from joy, but about the glorification of God that springs from faith (Rom. 15:13; Gal. 2:20; 1 Pet. 1:5, 7–8). Jesus will surely fulfill His word: "Blessed are those who have not seen and yet have believed." "Did I not say to you that if you would believe you would see the glory of God?"

> *F*aith adheres simply to what God says. The unbelief that wants to see shall not see, but the faith that will not see but has enough in God shall see the glory of God.

Between the life of feeling and the life of faith, the Christian has to choose every day. Happy is he who has once for all made the firm choice, and every morning renews the choice, not to seek or listen for feeling, but only to walk by faith, according to the will of God. The faith that keeps itself occupied with the Word—with what God has said—and, through the Word, with God Himself and Jesus His Son, shall taste the blessedness of a life in God above. Feeling seeks and aims at itself, but faith honors God and shall be honored by Him. Faith pleases God and shall receive from Him the witness in the heart of the believer that he is acceptable to God.

Lord God, the one and only thing You desire of Your children is that they should trust You and that they should always relate with You in that faith. Lord, let the one thing in which I seek my happiness be to honor and to please You by a faith that firmly holds You, the Invisible, and trusts You in all things. Amen.

FOR FURTHER THOUGHT

1. *What relationship do feelings have to the faith you are to walk in? There is indeed something marvelous in the new life. It is difficult to make it clear to the young Christian. The Spirit of God teaches him to understand it after he perseveres in grace. Jesus has laid the foundation of that life in the first word of the Sermon on the Mount: "Blessed are the poor in spirit, for theirs is the kingdom of heaven" (Matt. 5:3)—feelings of deep poverty and of royal riches, of utter weakness and of kingly might, exist together in the soul. To have nothing in itself, to have all in Christ is the secret of faith. And the true secret of faith is to bring this into exercise and, in hours of barrenness and emptiness, to still know that we have all in Christ.*

2. *How do you keep your feelings from holding you back from faith and from the things God calls you to do? Don't forget that faith, of which God's Word speaks so much, stands not only in opposition to works, but also in opposition to feeling, and therefore that for a pure life of faith, you must cease to seek your salvation not only in works, but also in feeling. Therefore let faith always speak against feeling. When feeling says, "In myself, I am sinful; I am dark; I am weak; I am poor; I am sad," let faith say, "In Christ, I am holy; I am light; I am strong; I am rich; I am joyful."*

3. *In what ways does the Word of God keep you from relying on your feelings instead of Him?*

22

The Holy Spirit

And because you are sons,
God has sent forth the Spirit of His Son
into your hearts, crying out, "Abba, Father!"
GALATIANS 4:6

THE great gift of the Father, through whom He obtained salvation and brought it near to us, is the Son. On the other hand, the great gift of the Son, whom He sends to us from the Father, to apply to us an inner and effectual salvation, is the Holy Spirit (John 7:38; 14:16, 26; Acts 1:4; 2:33; 1 Cor. 3:16). As the Son reveals and glorifies the Father, so the Spirit reveals and glorifies the Son (John 15:26; 16:14–15; 1 Cor. 2:8, 12; 12:3). The Spirit is in us to transfer to us the life and the salvation that are prepared in Jesus, and to make them wholly ours (Job 14:17, 21; Rom. 8:2; Eph. 3:17, 19). Jesus who is in heaven is made present in us and dwells in us by the Spirit.

We have seen that in order to become a partaker of Jesus, there are always two things necessary: the knowledge of the sin that is in us and of the redemption that is in Him. It is the Holy Spirit who continually promotes this double work in believers. He reproves and comforts, and He convicts of sin and glorifies Christ (John 16:9, 14).

The Spirit convicts of sin. He is the light and the fire of God, through whom sin is unveiled and consumed. He is "the Spirit of judgment and of burning" (see Isa. 4:4) by whom God purifies His people (Zech. 12:10–11; Matt. 3:11–12). To the anxious soul who complains that he does not feel his sin deeply enough, we must often say that there is no limit as to how deep his repentance must be. He must come daily just as he is. The deepest conviction oftentimes comes after conversion. To the young convert, we have simply to say: Let the Spirit who is in you convict you always of sin.

He will make you hate sin, which formerly you knew only by name. Sin, which you had not seen in the hidden depths of your heart, He will make you know and, with shame, confess. Sin, of which you believed that it was not with you and which you had judged severely in others, He will point out to you in yourself (Ps. 139:7, 23; Isa. 10:17; Matt. 7:5; Rom. 14:4; 1 Cor. 2:10; 14:24–25). And He will teach you with repentance and self-condemnation to cast yourself upon grace as entirely sinful, in order to be thereby redeemed and purified from it.

Beloved brother, the Holy Spirit is in you as the light and fire of God to unveil and to consume sin. The temple of God is holy, and you are this temple. Let the Holy Spirit in you have full mastery to point out and expel sin (Pss. 19:13; 139:23; Mic. 3:8; 1 Cor. 3:17; 2 Cor. 3:17; 6:16). After He makes you know sin, He will at every turn make you know Jesus as your life and your sanctification.

And then shall the Spirit who rebukes also comfort. He will glorify Jesus in you and will take what is in Jesus and make it known to you. He will give you knowledge concerning the power of Jesus' blood to cleanse (1 John 1:7; 5:6) and the power of Jesus' indwelling to keep (John 14:21, 23; Eph. 3:17; 1 John 3:24; 4:13). He will make you see how literally, how completely, how certainly Jesus is with you every moment, doing Himself all his own Jesus-work in you. Yes, in the Holy Spirit, the living, almighty, and ever-present Jesus shall be your portion, and you will also know this and have the full enjoyment of it. The Holy Spirit will teach you to bring all your sin and sinfulness to Jesus and to know Jesus with His complete redemption from sin as your own. As the Spirit of sanctification, He will drive out sin in order that He may cause Jesus to dwell in you (Rom. 1:4; 5:5; 8:2, 13; 1 Pet. 1:2).

> *We have seen that in order to become a partaker of Jesus, there are always two things necessary: the knowledge of the sin that is in us and of the redemption that is in Him.*

Beloved young Christian, take time to understand and to become filled with the truth: *The Holy Spirit is in you.* Review all the assurances of God's Word that this is so (Rom. 8:14, 16; 1 Cor. 6:19; 2 Cor. 1:22; 6:16; Eph. 1:13). Please don't think for a moment of living as a Christian without the indwelling of the Spirit. Take pains to have your heart filled with the faith that the Spirit dwells in you and will do His mighty work, for through faith the Spirit comes and works (Gal. 3:2, 5, 15; 5:5). Have a great reverence for the work of the Spirit in you. Seek Him every day to believe, to obey, to trust, and He will take and make known to you all that there is in Jesus. He will make Jesus very glorious to you and in you.

O my Father, I thank You for this gift that Jesus sent me from You, the Father. I thank You that I am now the temple of Your Spirit and that He dwells in me.

Lord, teach me to believe this with the whole heart and to live in the world as one who knows that the Spirit of God is in him to lead him. Teach me to think with deep reverence and with the awe of a son on this: that God is in me. Lord, in that faith I have the power to be holy.

Holy Spirit, reveal to me all that sin is in me. Holy Spirit, reveal to me all that Jesus is in me. Amen.

FOR FURTHER THOUGHT

1. *How important to you is the knowledge of the person and the work of the Holy Spirit? For us, this is just as important as the knowledge of the person and the work of Christ.*

2. *What is Jesus' purpose for giving you the Holy Spirit? Concerning the Holy Spirit, we must endeavor especially to hold firmly the truth that He is given as the fruit of the work of Jesus for us, that He is the power of the life of Jesus in us, and that through Him, Jesus Himself, with His full salvation, He dwells in us.*

3. *What must happen in order for you to receive all God's spiritual blessings? In order to enjoy all this, we must be filled with the Spirit. This simply means being emptied of all else and full of Jesus—to deny ourselves, to take up the cross, and to follow Jesus. Or rather, this is the way in which the Spirit leads us to His fullness. No one has the power to enter fully into the death of Jesus but he who is led by the Spirit. But He takes him who desires this by the hand and brings him.*

4. *What is needed for you to receive the gifts and power of the Holy Spirit? As the whole of salvation, the whole of the new life is by faith, so is this also true of the gift and the working of the Holy Spirit. By faith, not by works—not in feeling do I receive Him, am I led by Him, am I filled with Him.*

5. *As clear and definite as my faith is in the work that Jesus only and alone finished for me, so clear and definite must my faith be in the work that the Holy Spirit accomplishes in me: to work in me the willing and the performing of all that is necessary for my salvation.*

23

THE LEADING OF THE SPIRIT

For as many as are led by the Spirit of God, these are
sons of God. . . . The Spirit Himself bears witness with
our spirit that we are children of God,
ROMANS 8:14, 16

IT is the very same Spirit who leads us as children who also assures us that we are children. Without His leading, there can be no assurance of our status as God's children. True, full assurance of faith is enjoyed by him who surrenders himself entirely to the leading of the Spirit.

In what does this leading consist? Chiefly in this: that our whole hidden inner life is guided by Him to what it should be. This we must firmly believe. Our growth and increase, our development and progress are not our work but His, and we are to trust Him for it. As a tree or animal grows and becomes large by the spirit of life that God has given to it, so also does the Christian by the Spirit of life grow in Christ Jesus (Hos. 14:6–7; Matt. 6:28; Mark 4:26, 28; Luke 2:40; Rom. 8:2). We have to cherish the joyful assurance that the Spirit whom the Father gives to us with divine wisdom and power guides our hidden life and brings it where God wants it.

Then there are also special directions of this leading. "He will guide you into all the truth" (John 16:13). When we read the Word of God, we are to wait upon Him to make us experience the truth, the essential power of what God says. He makes the Word living and powerful. He leads us into a life corresponding to the Word (John 6:63; 14:26; 1 Cor. 2:10, 14; 1 Thess. 2:13).

When you pray, you can rely on His leading: "The Spirit also helps in our weaknesses" (Rom. 8:26). He leads us to what we must desire. He leads us into the way in which we are to pray—trustfully, persistently, and mightily (Zech. 12:10; Rom. 8:26–27; Jude 12, 20).

It is He who will lead in the way of sanctification. He leads us in the path of righteousness. He leads us into all the will of God (1 Cor. 6:19–20; 1 Pet 1:2, 15).

He will lead in our speaking and working for the Lord. Every child has the Spirit, and every child needs Him to know and to do the work of the Father. Without Him, no child can please or serve the Father. The leading of the Spirit is the blessed privilege, the sure gift, the only power of a child of God (Matt. 10:20;

Acts 1:8; Rom 8:9, 13; Gal. 4:6; Eph. 1:13).

And how then can you fully enjoy this leading? The first thing necessary for this is *faith*. You must take time, young Christian, to have your heart filled with the deep and living consciousness that the Spirit is in you. Read all the glorious declarations of your Father in His Word concerning what the Spirit is in you and for you, until the conviction wholly fills you so that you are really a temple of the Spirit. Ignorance or unbelief on this point makes it impossible for the Spirit to speak in you and to lead you. Cherish an ever-abiding assurance that the Spirit of God dwells in you (Acts 19:2; Rom. 5:5; 1 Cor. 3:16; 2 Cor. 5:5; Gal. 3:5, 14).

Then the second thing that is necessary is this: You are to *hold yourself still*, to listen to the voice of the Spirit. As the Lord Jesus acts, so does also the Spirit: "He will not cry out, nor raise His voice" (Isa. 42:2). He whispers gently and quietly, and only the soul that sets itself very silently toward God can perceive His voice and guidance. When we become to a needless extent engrossed with the world—with its business, its cares, its enjoyments, its literature, its politics—the Spirit cannot lead us. When our service to God is a bustling and working in our own wisdom and strength, the Spirit cannot be heard in us. It is the weak and the simple who are willing to have themselves taught in humility who receive the leading of the Spirit. Sit down every morning and often in the day to say: "Lord Jesus, I know nothing. I will be silent. Let the Spirit lead me" (1 Chron. 19:12; Pss. 62:2, 6; 131:2; Isa. 43:2; Hab. 2:20; Zech. 4:6; Acts 1:4).

> *It is the weak and the simple who are willing to have themselves taught in humility who receive the leading of the Spirit. Sit down every morning and often in the day to say: "Lord Jesus, I know nothing. I will be silent. Let the Spirit lead me."*

And then: *Be obedient*. Listen to the inner voice, and then do what it says to you. Fill your heart every day with the Word, and when the Spirit puts you in mind of what the Word says, commit yourself to the doing of it. This is how you become capable of further teaching. It is to the obedient that the full blessing of the Spirit is promised (John 14:15–16; Acts 5:32).

Young Christian, know that you are a temple of the Spirit, and that it is only through the daily leading of the Spirit that you can walk as a child of God, with the witness that you are pleasing the Father.

Precious Savior, imprint this lesson deeply on my mind. The Holy Spirit is in me. His leading is every day and everywhere indispensable for me. I cannot hear His voice in the Word when I do not wait silently upon Him. Lord, let a holy circumspectness keep watch over me so that I may always walk as a pupil of the Spirit. Amen.

FOR FURTHER THOUGHT

1. *It is often asked: How do I know that I shall continue standing, so that I shall be kept and that I shall increase? The question dishonors Him. The question indicates that you are seeking the secret of strength for perseverance in yourself, and not in the Holy Spirit, your heavenly Guide.*

2. *How does God maintain the new life you have entered into in faith? As God sees to it that every moment there is air for me to breathe, so shall the Holy Spirit unceasingly maintain life in the hidden depths of my soul. He will not break off his own work.*

3. *What are you to do once you receive the Holy Spirit? From the time we receive the Holy Spirit, we have nothing to do but to honor his work—to keep our hands off it, to trust Him, and to let Him work.*

4. *The beginning and the end of the work of the Spirit is to reveal Jesus to me and to cause me to abide in Him. As soon as I desire to look after the work of the Spirit in me, I hinder Him. He cannot work when I am not willing to look upon Jesus.*

5. *The voice of the Father, the voice of the Good Shepherd, and the voice of the Holy Spirit is very gentle. We must learn to become deaf to other voices— to the world and its news of friends and their thoughts, to our own ego and its desires. Then we will distinguish the voice of the Spirit. Let us often set ourselves silent in prayer—entirely silent—to offer up our will and our thoughts, and, with our eye on Jesus, to keep ear and heart open for the voice of the Spirit.*

24

GRIEVING THE SPIRIT

And do not grieve the Holy Spirit of God,
by whom you were sealed for the day of redemption.
EPHESIANS 4:30

IT is by the Holy Spirit that the child of God is sealed—separated and stamped and marked as the possession of God. This sealing is not a dead or external action that is finished once for all. It is a living process, which has power in the soul and gives firm assurance of faith, but only when it is experienced through the life of the Spirit in us. On this account, we are to take great care not to grieve the Spirit, for in Him alone can we have every day the joyful assurance and the full blessing of our childship. It is the very same Spirit who leads us who witnesses with our spirit that we are children of God.

And how can anyone grieve the Spirit? Above all by yielding to sin. He is the Holy Spirit who is given to sanctify us, and for every sin from which the blood cleanses us to fill us with the holy life of God, with God. Sin grieves Him (Isa. 53:10; Acts 7:51; Heb. 10:29). For this reason, the Word of God states by name the sins against which above all we are to be on our guard. Mark only the four great sins that Paul mentions in connection with our text.

There is first *lying*. There is no single sin the Bible so brings into connection with the devil as lying. Lying is from hell, and it goes on to hell. God is the God of truth. And the Holy Spirit cannot possibly carry forward His blessed working in a man or woman who lies, who is insincere, who does injury to the truth. Young Christian, review with care what the Word of God says about lying and liars, and ask God that you may never speak anything but the literal truth. Grieve not the Holy Spirit of God (Ps. 5:7; Prov. 12:22; 21:28; John 8:44; Rev. 21:8, 27; 22:15).

Then there is *anger*. "Let all bitterness, wrath, anger, clamor, and evil speaking be put away from you" (Eph. 4:31). Hastiness—proneness to anger, the sin of temper—is, along with lying, the most common sin by which the Christian is kept back from increase in grace (Matt. 5:22, 26–27; 1 Cor. 1:10–11; 3:3; 13:1, 3; Gal. 5:5; Col. 3:8, 12; 1 Thess. 5:15; James 3:14). Christian, put all passion toward anger away from you, because this follows on the command not to grieve the Spirit. Believe that the Holy Spirit, the great power of God, is in you. Surrender yourself every day to His indwelling, in the faith that Jesus can keep you by Him.

He will make and keep you gentle. Yes, believe, I tell you, in the power of God and of Jesus and of the Holy Spirit to overcome temper (Matt. 11:29; 1 Cor. 6:19–20; Gal. 6:1; Eph. 2:16–17; Col. 1:8; 2 Tim. 1:12). Confess the sin, and God will cleanse you from it. Don't grieve the Holy Spirit of God.

Then there is *stealing*: all sin against the property or possession of my neighbor, all deception and dishonesty in trade, whereby I do wrong to my neighbor and seek my own advantage at his cost. The law of Christ is love, whereby I seek the advantage of my neighbor as well as my own. Oh, the love of money and property, which is inseparable from self-seeking—it is incompatible with the leading of the Holy Spirit. The Christian must be a man who is known as honest to the backbone, righteous, and loving his neighbor as himself (Luke 6:31; Rom. 13:10; 1 Thess. 4:6).

> *E*ven the tongue of God's child belongs to his Lord. He must be known by his mode of speech. By his speaking, he can grieve or please the Spirit.

Then says the apostle: "*no corrupt word. . .but what is good for necessary edification*" (Eph. 4:29). Even the tongue of God's child belongs to his Lord. He must be known by his mode of speech. By his speaking, he can grieve or please the Spirit. The sanctified tongue is a blessing not only to his neighbors but to the speaker himself. Foul talk, idle words, and foolish jests all grieve the Holy Spirit and make it impossible for the Spirit to sanctify and to comfort and to fill the heart with the love of God (Prov. 10:19, 20–21, 31; 18:20; Eccles. 5:1–2; Matt. 12:36; Eph. 5:4; James 3:9–10).

Young Christian, I tell you, do not grieve the Holy Spirit of God by these or other sins. If you have committed such sins, confess them, and God will cleanse you from them. By the Holy Spirit you are sealed. If you would walk in the stability and joy of faith, listen to the word: "Do not grieve the Holy Spirit of God."

Lord God, my Father in heaven, I beg You to cause me to understand what marvelous grace You are demonstrating to me in that You have given to me Your Holy Spirit in my heart. Lord, let this faith be the argument and the power for cleansing me from every sin. Holy Jesus, sanctify me so that in my thinking, speaking, acting—in all things— Your image may appear. Amen.

FOR FURTHER THOUGHT

1. *The thought of the Christian about this word, "Do not grieve the Holy Spirit," is a standard as to whether he understands the life of faith. For some it is a word of terror and fear. A father once brought a child to the train to go on a journey with the new instructor with whom she was to remain. Before her departure he said: "I hear that she is very sensitive and takes things very wrong. Take care that you do nothing to grieve her." The poor child didn't have a pleasant journey. It was to her very difficult to be in anxious fear of one who was so prone to take anything wrong. This is the view of the Holy Spirit that many have: a Being it is difficult to satisfy, who thinks little of our weakness, and who, even though we try hard, is displeased when our work is not perfect. Have you done anything that could grieve Him? If so, what is it, and what will you do about it now?*

2. *Another father also brought his daughter to the train to go on a journey and to be away from home for a time—but with her mother, whom she loved very dearly. "You are to be a good child," said the father, "and do everything to please your mama. Otherwise you shall grieve her and me." "Oh, certainly, Papa!" was the joyful answer of the child. That's because she felt so happy to be with her mother, and was willing to do her utmost to please her. There are children of God to whom the Holy Spirit is so well known in His tender, helpful love, and as the Comforter and the Good Spirit, that the word, "Do not grieve the Spirit of God," has for them a gentle, encouraging power. May our fear of grieving Him always be the tender childlike fear that comes out of trusting love. What motivates you to please God and to avoid grieving the Holy Spirit?*

3. *How can you know if you have done, or are doing, anything that grieves the Holy Spirit of God?*

25

FLESH AND SPIRIT

And I, brethren, could not speak to
you as to spiritual people but as to
carnal, as to babes in Christ.
1 CORINTHIANS 3:1

I am carnal, sold under sin. . . .
For to will is present with me, but how to perform what is
good I do not find. . . . For the law of the Spirit of life in
Christ Jesus has made me free from the law of sin and death. . . .
But you are not in the flesh but in the Spirit,
if indeed the Spirit of God dwells in you.
ROMANS 7:14, 18; 8:2, 9

Having begun in the Spirit, are you now being
made perfect by the flesh? . . . If you are led by the Spirit,
you are not under the law. . . . If we live in the
Spirit, let us also walk in the Spirit.
GALATIANS 3:3; 5:18, 25

IT is of great importance for the young Christian to understand that there are in him two natures that strive against one another (Gal. 5:17, 24–25; 6:8; Eph. 4:22, 24; Col. 3:9–10; 1 Pet. 4:2). If we weigh the above texts, we shall see that the Word of God teaches us the following truths on this point.

Sin comes from the flesh. The reason the Christian still sins is that he yields to the flesh and does not walk by the Spirit. Every Christian has the Spirit and lives by the Spirit, but every Christian does not walk by the Spirit. If he walks by the Spirit, he will not fulfill the desires of the flesh (Rom. 8:7; 1 Cor. 3:1, 3; Gal. 5:16, 25).

So long as there are still in the Christian strife and envy, the Word of God calls him carnal. He would indeed do good, but he cannot. Instead, he does what he doesn't want to do, because he still strives in his own strength and not in the power of the Spirit (Rom. 7:18; 1 Cor. 3:3; Gal. 5:15, 26).

The flesh remains under the law and seeks to obey the law. But through the flesh the law is powerless, and the endeavor to do good is vain. Its language is: "I am carnal, sold under sin. . . . For to will is present with me, but how to perform what is good I do not find" (see Rom. 4:14–15; 7:4, 6; 8:3, 8; Gal. 5:18; 6:12–13; Heb. 7:18; 8:9, 13).

This is not the condition in which God would have his child remain. The Word says: "It is God who works in you both to will and to do" (Phil. 2:13). The Christian must not only live by the Spirit, but also walk by the Spirit. He must be a spiritual man and abide entirely under the leading of the Spirit (Rom. 8:14; 1 Cor. 2:15; 3:1; Gal. 6:1). If he walks that way, he will no longer do what he doesn't want to do. He will no longer remain in the condition of Romans 7, as a newborn babe still seeking to fulfill the law, but in that of Romans 8, as one who through the Spirit is made free from the law with its commandment, "Do this," which gives no power but brings death, and who walks not in the oldness of the letter, but in the newness of the Spirit (Rom. 7:6; 8:2, 13).

There are Christians who begin with the Spirit but end with the flesh. They are converted, born again through the Spirit, but they fall unconsciously into a life in which they endeavor to overcome sin and be holy through their own efforts, through doing their best. They ask God to help them in these endeavors and think that this is faith. They do not understand what it is to say, "In me (that is, in my flesh) nothing good dwells" (Rom. 7:18), and that therefore they are to cease from their own endeavors, in order to do God's will wholly and only through the Spirit (Gal. 3:3; 4:9; 5:4, 7).

> *S*in comes from the flesh. The reason the Christian still sins is that he yields to the flesh and does not walk by the Spirit.

Child of God, please learn what it is to say of yourself, just as you are, even after the new birth: "I am carnal, sold under sin." *Endeavor no longer to be doing your best, to be praying to God, and to be trusting Him to help you.* No, learn to say: "For the law of the Spirit of life in Christ Jesus has made me free from the law of sin and death." Let your work every day be to have the Spirit work in you, to walk by the Spirit. Then you will be redeemed from the life of complaining, "The good that I will to do, I do not do" (Rom. 7:19), into a life of faith, in which "it is God who works in you both to will and to do" (Phil. 2:13).

Lord God, teach me to acknowledge with all my heart that in me, that is, in my flesh, dwells nothing good. Teach me also to cease from every thought that I can with my own endeavors serve or please You. Teach me to understand that the Spirit is the Comforter who frees me from all anxiety and fear about my own powerlessness, in order that He may work the strength of Christ in me. Amen.

FOR FURTHER THOUGHT

1. *In what ways, exactly, are the flesh and the Spirit in conflict? In order to understand the conflict between flesh and Spirit, we must especially seek to have a clear insight into the connection between Romans 7 and 8. In Romans 7:6 Paul had spoken of the twofold way of serving God—the one in the oldness of the letter, the other in the newness of the Spirit. In Romans 7:14, 16 he describes the first, in Romans 8:1–16 the second. This appears clearly when we observe that in chapter 7 he mentions the Spirit only once, but the law more than twenty times; in Romans 8:1–16 he mentions the Spirit sixteen times. In Romans 7 we see the regenerate soul—just as he is in himself with his new nature—desiring but powerless to fulfill the law, mourning as one who "is captive under the law of sin." In Romans 8 we hear him say, "the law of the Spirit of life in Christ made me free from the law of sin." Romans 7 describes the ever-abiding condition of the Christian, renewed but not experiencing by faith the power of the Holy Spirit. In Romans 8 is his life in the freedom that the Spirit of God really gives from the power of sin.*

2. *How can you avoid the conflicts between the flesh and the Spirit? It is of very great importance to understand that the conflict between grace and works, between faith and one's own power, and between the Holy Spirit and confidence in ourselves and the flesh always continues to go on, not only in connection with conversion and the reception of the righteousness of God, but even further, into a walk in this righteousness. On this account the Christian has to watch very carefully against the deep inclination of his heart still to work on his own behalf when he sees in himself anything wrong or when he desires to follow after holiness—instead of always and only trusting in Jesus Christ and so serving God in the Spirit.*

3. *What does God's Word say about these conflicts, and what does it teach you concerning the overcoming of them? In order to make clear the opposition between the two methods of serving God, let me cite consecutively in their entirety the passages in which they are expressed with special distinctness. Compare them with care. Ask God for the Spirit in order to make you understand them. Take deeply to heart the lesson as to how you are to serve God well, and how not to. "Circumcision is that of the heart, in the Spirit, not in the letter" (Rom. 2:29). "But to him who does not work but believes on Him who justifies the ungodly, his faith is accounted for righteousness" (Rom. 4:5). "You are not under law but under grace" (Rom. 6:14). "We have been delivered from the law. . .so that we should serve in the newness of the Spirit and not in the oldness of the letter" (Rom. 7:6). "For we know that the law is spiritual, but I am carnal, sold under sin" (Rom. 7:14). "The righteous requirement of the law might be fulfilled in us who do not walk according to the flesh but according to the Spirit" (Rom. 8:4). "For you did not receive the spirit of*

*bondage again to fear, but you received the Spirit of adoption" (Rom. 8:15).
"For Moses writes about the righteousness which is of the law, 'The man
who does those things shall live by them.' But the righteousness of faith
speaks in this way, 'Do not say in your heart, "Who will ascend. . . Who will
descend. . .?"' . . . But what does it say? 'The word is near you, in your mouth
and in your heart'" (Rom. 10:5–8). "If by grace, then it is no longer of works"
(Rom. 11:6). "And I, brethren, could not speak to you as to spiritual people
but as to carnal, as to babes in Christ" (1 Cor. 3:1). "It is no longer I who
live, but Christ lives in me" (Gal. 2:20). "'The just shall live by faith.'
Yet the law is not of faith, but 'the man who does them shall live by them'"
(Gal. 3:11–12). "For if the inheritance is of the law, it is no longer of promise"
(Gal. 3:18). "Therefore you are no longer a slave but a son" (Gal. 4:7). "So
then, brethren, we are not children of the bondwoman but of the free" (Gal.
4:31). "Walk in the Spirit, and you shall not fulfill the lust of the flesh" (Gal.
5:16). "But if you are led by the Spirit, you are not under the law" (Gal. 5:18).
"For we. . .worship God in the Spirit, rejoice in Christ Jesus, and have no
confidence in the flesh" (Phil. 3:3). ". . .another priest who has come, not
according to the law of a fleshly commandment, but according to the power of
an endless life" (Heb. 7:15–16).*

4. *Beloved Christian, you have received the Holy Spirit from the Lord Jesus
to reveal Him and His life in you, and to put to death the working of the body
of sin. Pray much to be filled with the Spirit. Live in the joyful faith that the
Spirit is in you, as your Comforter and Teacher, and that through Him all will
come right. Learn by heart this text, and let it live in your heart and on your
lips: "For we are the circumcision, who worship God in the Spirit, rejoice in
Christ Jesus, and have no confidence in the flesh" (Phil. 3:3).*

26
THE LIFE OF FAITH

"The just shall live by his faith."
HABAKKUK 2:4

But now we have been delivered from the law,
having died to what we were held by,
so that we should serve in the newness of the
Spirit and not in the oldness of the letter.
ROMANS 7:6

It is no longer I who live, but Christ lives in me;
and the life which I now live in the flesh I live by faith in
the Son of God, who loved me and gave Himself for me.
GALATIANS 2:20

THE word from Habakkuk is quoted three times in the New Testament as the divine representation of salvation in Christ by faith alone (Rom. 1:17; Gal. 3:11; Heb. 10:38). But that word is oftentimes very imperfectly understood—as if it read: "Man shall on his conversion be justified by faith." The word includes this, but it signifies much more. It says that the righteous shall *live* by faith, meaning that the whole life of the righteous, from moment to moment, shall be by faith (Rom. 5:17, 21; 6:11; 8:2; Gal. 2:20; 1 John 5:11–12).

We all know how sharp is the contrast that God in His Word presents between the grace that comes by faith and the law that works—demands. This is generally admitted with reference to justification. But that distinction holds just as much of the whole life of sanctification. The righteous shall live by faith alone; that is, shall have power to live according to the will of God.

As at his conversion he found it necessary to understand that there was nothing good in him, that he must receive grace as one who was powerless and godless, so must a believer just as clearly understand that in him there is nothing good and that he must receive his power for good every moment from above (Rom. 7:18; 8:2, 13; Heb. 11:38). And his work must therefore be every morning and every hour to look up and believe and receive his power from above, out of his Lord in heaven. *I am not to do what I can and hope in the Lord to supply strength.* No, as one who has been dead, who is literally able for nothing in himself and whose life is in his Lord above, I am to rely by faith on Him who will work in me mightily (Rom. 4:17; 2 Cor. 1:9; Col. 1:20; 2:3).

Happy is the Christian who understands that his greatest danger every day is again to fall under the law and to desire to serve God in the flesh with his own strength. Happy when he understands that he is not under the law, which just demands and yet is powerless through the flesh, but is under grace, where we need simply to receive what has been given. Happy when he fully claims for himself the promise of the Spirit, who transfers all that is in Christ to him. Yes, happy when he understands what it is to live by faith and to serve not in the oldness of the letter but in the newness of the Spirit (Rom. 7:4, 6; 12:5–6; Gal. 5:18; Phil. 3:3).

> *The* righteous shall live by faith alone; that is, shall have power to live according to the will of God.

Let us make our own the words of Paul, because they present to us the true life of faith: "I have been crucified with Christ. . .and. . .I live" (Gal. 2:20). My flesh—not only my sin, but my flesh, all that is of myself, my own living and willing, my own power and working—I have given up to death. I live no longer—in myself, I cannot. I will not live or do anything (John 15:4–5; 1 Cor. 15:10; 2 Cor. 12:10). Christ lives in me. He Himself, by His Spirit, is my power, and He teaches and strengthens me to live as I should. And that life that I now live in the flesh, I live by faith in Him. My great work is to rely on Him, to work in Him, as well the willing as the accomplishment.

Young Christian, let this life of faith be your faith.

O my Lord Jesus, You are my life—yes, my life. You live in me and are willing to take my whole life as Yours. And my whole life may daily be a joyful trust and experience that You are working all in me. Precious Lord, to that life of faith I will surrender myself. Yes, to You I surrender myself, to teach me and to reveal Yourself fully in me. Amen.

FOR FURTHER THOUGHT

1. Do you discern the error of the expression "If the Lord helps me. . ." or "The Lord must help me"? In natural things we speak this way, for we have a certain measure of power, which the Lord will increase. But the New Testament never uses the expression "help" of the grace of God in the soul. We have absolutely no power—God is not to help us because we are weak. No! He is to give His life and His power in us who are entirely powerless. He who discerns this correctly will learn to live by faith alone.

2. "Without faith it is impossible to please [God]" (Heb. 11:6); "Whatever is not from faith is sin" (Rom. 14:23). Such works of the Spirit of God teach us how really every deed and disposition of our life is to be full of faith. What steps can you take to make sure that is true of your own life?

3. Therefore our first work every day is to newly exercise faith in Jesus as our life, to believe that He dwells in us and will do all for us and in us. This faith must be the mood of our soul all day. This faith cannot be maintained except in the fellowship and nearness of Jesus Himself.

4. What is the relationship between true faith and surrender? This faith has its power in the mutual surrender of Jesus and the believer to each other. Jesus first gives Himself wholly for us. The believer gives himself wholly in order to be taken into possession and guided by Jesus. Then the soul cannot even doubt if He will do all for it.

27

THE MIGHT OF SATAN

*"Simon, Simon! Indeed, Satan has asked for you,
that he may sift you as wheat. But I have prayed for you,
that your faith should not fail."*
LUKE 22:31–32

THERE is nothing that makes an enemy so dangerous as the fact that he remains hidden or forgotten. Of the three great enemies of the Christian— the world, the flesh, and the devil—the devil is the most dangerous, not only because it is he who, strictly speaking, lends to the others what power they have, but also because he is not seen and, therefore, little known or feared. The devil has the power of darkness. He darkens the eyes so that men do not know him. He surrounds himself with darkness so that he is not seen. Yes, he has even the power to appear as an angel of light (Matt. 4:6; 2 Cor. 4:4; 11:14). It is by the faith that recognizes things unseen that the Christian is to endeavor to know Satan as the scripture has revealed him.

When the Lord Jesus was living on earth, His great work was to overcome Satan. When at His baptism He was filled with the Spirit, this fullness of the Spirit brought him into contact with Satan, the head of the world of evil spirits, to combat him and to overcome him (Matt. 4:1, 10). After that time the eyes of the Lord were always open to the power and working of Satan. In all sin and misery He saw the revelation of the mighty kingdom of the very same ruler: the evil one. Not only in those who were demoniacs, but also in the sick He saw the enemy of God and man (Matt. 12:28; Mark 4:15; Luke 13:16; Acts 10:38).

In the advice of Peter to avoid the cross, and in his denial of his Lord, where we should think of the revelation of the natural character of Peter, Jesus saw the work of Satan (Matt. 26:23; Luke 22:31–32). In His own suffering, where we rather speak of the sin of man and the permission of God, Jesus perceives the power of darkness. His whole work in living and in dying was to destroy the works of Satan, just as He will also at His second coming utterly bruise Satan himself (Luke 10:18; 22:3, 53; John 12:31; 14:30; 16:11; Rom. 16:20; Col. 2:15; 2 Thess. 2:8–9; 1 John 3:8).

His word to Peter, compared with the personal experience of the Lord, gives us a fearful insight into the work of the enemy. "Satan has eagerly desired to have you," says Jesus. "Your adversary the devil walks about like a roaring lion, seeking whom he may devour" (1 Pet. 5:8), says Peter himself later on (also see 1 Cor. 7:5; 2 Cor. 2:10). He doesn't have unlimited power, but he is always eager to make use of every weak or unguarded moment.

"That he might sift you as wheat." What a picture! This world, yes, even the Church of Christ, is the threshing floor of Satan. The corn belongs to God, but the chaff is the devil's own. He sifts and sifts continually, and all that falls through with the chaff he tries to take for himself. And many a Christian there is who falls through in a terrible fashion, and who, were it not for the intercession of his Lord, would perish forever (1 Cor. 5:5; 1 Tim. 1:20).

Satan has more than one sieve. The first is generally worldly-mindedness—the love of the world. Many a one is spiritual in his time of poverty, but when he becomes rich he again eagerly strives to win the world. Or in the time of conversion and awakening he appears very zealous, but through the care of the world he is led astray (Matt. 4:9; 8:22; 1 Tim. 6:9–10; 2 Tim. 4:10).

A second sieve is self-love and self-seeking. Whenever anyone does not give himself undividedly to serve his Lord and his neighbor and to love his neighbor in the Lord, it soon appears that the principal evidence of discipleship is lacking in him. It will be obvious that many, with a fair profession of being devoted to the service of God, fail utterly on this point and must be counted with the chaff. Lovelessness is the sure evidence of the power of Satan (John 8:44; 1 John 3:10, 15; 4:20).

> *Happy are they who with deep humility, with fear and trembling, distrust themselves. Our only security is in the intercession and guidance of Him who overcame Satan.*

Yet another sieve, and a very dangerous one, is self-confidence. Under the name of following the Spirit, one may listen to the thoughts of his own heart. He is zealous for the Lord, but with a carnal zeal in which the gentleness of the Lamb of God is not seen. Without being observed, the movements of the flesh mingle with the workings of the Spirit, and while he boasts that he is overcoming Satan, he is being secretly ensnared by him (Gal. 3:3; 5:13).

Oh, it is a serious life here on the earth, where God gives permission for Satan to set his threshing floor even in the Church. Happy are they who with deep humility, with fear and trembling, distrust themselves. Our only security is in the intercession and guidance of Him who overcame Satan (Eph. 6:10, 12, 16). Far be from us the idea that we know all the depths of Satan and are a match for all his cunning plots. It is in the region of the spirit, in the invisible, that he works and has power—as well as in the visible. Let us fear that while we have known and overcome him in the visible, he should prevail over us in the spiritual. May our only security be the conviction of our frailty and weakness, and our confidence in

Him who certainly protects the lowly in heart.

Lord Jesus, open our eyes to know our enemy and his deceit. Cause us to see him and his realm so that we may dread all that is of him. And open our eyes to see how You have overcome him and how in You we are invincible. Oh, teach us what it is to be in You, to put to death all that is of the mere ego and the will of the flesh, and to be strong in weakness and lowliness. And teach us to bring into prayer the conflict of faith against every stronghold of Satan, because we know that You will bruise him under our feet. Amen.

FOR FURTHER THOUGHT

1. *What comfort does the knowledge of the existence of Satan give us? We know then that sin is derived from a foreign power that has thrust itself into our nature, and that it does not naturally belong to us. We know besides that he has been entirely defeated by the Lord Jesus, and therefore has no power over us so long as we abide trustfully in Christ.*

2. *What kind of power does the devil have today? The whole of this world, with all that is in it, is under the domination of Satan. Therefore there is nothing, even what appears good and fair, that may not be dangerous for us. In all things, even in what is lawful and right, we must be led and sanctified by the Spirit if we are to continue to be liberated from the power of Satan.*

3. *What is the only way you can overcome Satan in your new life? Satan is an evil spirit. Only by the good Spirit, the Spirit of God, can we offer resistance to him. He works in the invisible. In order to combat him, we must, by prayer, enter into the invisible. He is a mighty prince. Only in the name of One who is mightier and in fellowship with Him can we overcome.*

4. *What a glorious work is labor for souls, for the lost, for drunkards, for heathens, and what a conflict it is to rescue them from the might of Satan (Acts 26:18).*

5. *In the Book of Revelation, the victory over Satan is credited to the blood of the Lamb (12:11). Christians have also testified that there is no power in temptation, because Satan readily retreats when one appeals to the blood, by which one knows that sin has been entirely dealt with, and we are therefore also wholly freed from his power.*

28

THE CONFLICT OF THE CHRISTIAN

"Strive to enter through the narrow gate."
LUKE 13:24

Fight the good fight of faith.
1 TIMOTHY 6:12

I have fought the good fight,
I have finished the race, I have kept the faith.
2 TIMOTHY 4:7

THESE texts speak of a twofold conflict. The first is addressed to the unconverted: "Strive to enter through the narrow gate." Entrance by a gate is the work of a moment. The sinner is not to strive to enter during his whole lifetime, but is to strive and do it immediately. He is not to allow anything to hold him back. He must enter in (Gen. 19:22; John 10:9; 2 Cor. 6:2; Heb. 4:6–7).

Then comes the second, the lifelong conflict: By the narrow gate I come upon the new way. On the new way there are still always enemies. Of this lifelong conflict Paul says: "I have fought the good fight, I have finished the race, I have kept the faith." With respect to the continuous conflict, he gives the charge: "Fight the good fight of faith."

There is much misunderstanding about this twofold conflict. Many strive all their life against the Lord and His summons, and because they are not at rest but feel an inner conflict, they think that this is the conflict of a Christian. Assuredly not! This is the struggle against God by one who is not willing to abandon everything and surrender himself to the Lord (Acts 5:39; 1 Cor. 10:22). This is not the conflict that the Lord would have. What He says is that the conflict is concerned with entering in, but it is not a conflict for long years. No, He desires that you should break through the enemies that would hold you back and immediately enter in.

Then follows the second conflict, which endures for life. Paul twice calls this the fight of faith. The chief characteristic of it is faith. He who understands well that the principal element in the battle is to believe, and acts accordingly, does certainly endure and overcome, just as in another passage Paul says to the Christian combatant: "Above all, taking the shield of faith with which you will be able to quench all the fiery darts of the wicked one" (Eph. 6:16; also see 1 John 3:4–5).

And what then does this "fight of faith" mean? That while I strive, I am to believe that the Lord will help me? No, it is not so, although it often is understood this way.

In a conflict, it is of supreme importance that I should be in a stronghold or fortress that cannot be captured. With such a stronghold, a weak garrison can offer resistance to a powerful enemy. Our conflict as Christians is now no longer concerned with going into the fortress. No, we have gone in and are now in, and so long as we remain in it, we are invincible. The stronghold, this stable fort, is Christ (Pss. 18:3; 46:2; 62:2–3, 6–8; 144:2; Eph. 6:10). By faith we are in Him, and by faith we know that the enemy can make no progress against our fortress.

> *Entrance by a gate is the work of a moment. The sinner is not to strive to enter during his whole lifetime, but is to strive and do it immediately. He is not to allow anything to hold him back.*

The wiles of Satan all go forth on the line of enticing us out of our fortress, of engaging us in conflict with him on the open plain. There he always overcomes. But if we only strive in faith, abiding in Christ by faith, then we overcome. That's because Satan then has to deal with Him who fights and overcomes (Exod. 14:14; Josh. 5:14; 2 Chron. 23:15; Rom. 8:37; 2 Cor. 2:14). "And this is the victory that has overcome the world—our faith" (1 John 5:4). Our first and greatest work is to believe this. As Paul said before he mentions the warlike equipment of the Christian: "Finally, my brethren, be strong in the Lord and in the power of His might" (Eph. 6:10).

The reason why the victory is only by faith, and why the fight of faith is the good fight, is this: It is the Lord Jesus who purchased the victory, and who therefore alone gives power and dominion over the enemy. If we are, and abide, in Him and surrender ourselves to live in Him and by faith appropriate for ourselves what He is, then the victory is in itself our own. We then understand: "The battle is not yours, but God's. . . . The LORD will fight for you, and you shall hold your peace" (2 Chron. 20:15; Exod. 14:14). Just as we in opposition to God can achieve nothing good of ourselves but in Christ please Him, so also is it in our opposition to Satan: In ourselves we achieve nothing, but in Christ we are more than conquerors. By faith we stand in Him righteous before God, and just so in Him are we strong against our enemies (Ps. 44:4, 9; Isa. 45:24).

In this light we can read and take home for ourselves all the noble passages in the Old Testament, especially in the Psalms, where the glorious conflict of God in behalf of his people is spoken of. Fear or spiritlessness or uncertainty makes weak and cannot overcome, but faith in the living God is equal to everything (Deut. 20:3, 8; Josh. 6:20; Judges 7:3; Ps. 18:32–40; Heb. 11:23). In Christ this truth is now still more real. God has come near. His power works in us who believe, and it is really He who fights for us.

O Lord Jesus, who is the Prince of the army of the Lord, the Hero, and the Victor: Teach me to be strong in You my stronghold, and in the power of Your strength. Teach me to understand what the good fight of faith is, and how the one thing that I need is always to look to You, the supreme Guide of faith. And, consequently, in me, too, let this be the victory that overcomes the world—namely my faith. Amen.

For Further Thought

1. *What exactly is the nature of the conflict of faith with the devil and with the world? The conflict of faith is no civil war in which one half of the kingdom is divided against the other. This would be insurrection. This is the one conflict that many Christians know: the unrest of the conscience and the powerless wrestling of a will that agrees with what is good but does not perform it. The Christian is not to overcome himself. This his Lord does when he surrenders himself. Then he is free and strong to combat and overcome the enemies of his Lord and of the kingdom. No sooner, however, are we willing that God should have His way with us than we are found striving against God. This also is truly conflict, but it is not the good fight of faith.*

2. *What is the right way to overcome the power of the flesh? What is the wrong way? In Galatians 5, reference is made to the inner conflict, for the Galatians had not yet entirely surrendered themselves to the Spirit or to walk after the Spirit. "The connection," says Lange, "shows that this conflict between the flesh and the Spirit of God is not endless, but that there is expected of the Christian a complete surrender of himself, in order to be led only by the one principle—the Spirit; and then, further, a refusal to obey the flesh." The believer must not strive against the flesh in order to overcome it: this he cannot do. What he is to do is to choose to whom he will subject himself. By the surrender of faith to Christ, to strive in Him through the Spirit, he has a divine power for overcoming.*

3. *What one heart attitude and disposition is necessary for living an overcoming life? As we have seen in connection with the beginning of the new life, our one work every day and the whole day is to believe. Out of faith come all blessings and powers, and also the victory for overcoming.*

29

BE A BLESSING

"Get out of your country,
from your family and from your father's
house, to a land that I will show you.
I will make you a great nation;
I will bless you and make your name great;
and you shall be a blessing."

GENESIS 12:1–2

IN these first words that God spoke to Abraham, we have the short summary of all that God has to say to him—and to us as His children. We see what the goal is to which God calls us, what the power is that carries us to that goal, and what the place is where the power is found.

Be a blessing: That is the goal for which God separates Abraham and every believing child of His.

God wanted to have him and us made to understand that when He blesses us, it is certainly not simply to make us happy, but that we should still further communicate His blessing (Matt. 5:34–35; 10:8; 18:33). God Himself is love, and therefore He blesses. Love does not seek its own: When the love of God comes to us, it will seek others through us (Isa. 43:10–11; 1 Cor. 13:5; 1 John 4:11). The young Christian must from the beginning understand that he has received grace with the definite aim of becoming a blessing to others. I encourage you, don't keep for yourself what the Lord gives to you for others. Offer yourself expressly and completely to the Lord to be used by Him for others. That is the way to be blessed to overflowing yourself (Ps. 112:5, 9; Prov. 11:24–25; Matt. 25:40; 1 Cor. 15:58; 2 Cor. 9:6; Heb. 6:10).

The power for this work will be given. "Be a blessing," and "I will bless you," says the Lord. You are to be personally blessed yourself, personally sanctified and filled with the Spirit, peace, and power of the Lord. Then you have power to bless (Luke 24:49; John 7:38; 14:12). In Christ God has "blessed us with every spiritual blessing" (Eph. 1:3), so let Jesus fill you with these blessings and you shall certainly be a blessing—you need not doubt or fear. The blessing of God includes in it the power of life for multiplication, for expansion, for communication. See in the scriptures how blessing and multiplication go together (Gen. 1:22, 28; 9:1; 22:17; 26:24).

Blessing always includes the power to bless others. Only give the word of the almighty God, "I will bless you," time to sink into your spirit. Wait on God so that He Himself may say to you, "I will bless you." Let your faith hold firmly to this. God will make it truth to you above all asking and thinking (2 Cor. 9:8, 11; Eph. 1:3; Heb. 6:14).

But for this purpose you must also take yourself to the place of blessing: the land of promise, the simple life of faith in the promises. "Get out of your country . . .and from your father's house," says the Lord. Departure and separation from the life of nature and the flesh, in which we were born of our father Adam, are what God desires for you. The offering up of what is most precious to man is the way to the blessing of God (John 12:24–25; 2 Cor. 6:17–18). "Get. . .to a land that I will show you," says the Lord, out of the old life and into a new life, where I alone am your guide—that is, a life where God can have me wholly for Himself alone, where I walk only on the promises of God—a life of faith.

> *Be a blessing: That is the goal for which God separates Abraham and every believing child of His.*

Christian, God will in a divine fashion fulfill to you His promise, "I will bless you." Just go, I encourage you, out of your land and your father's house, out of the life of nature and the flesh, out of fellowship with the flesh and this world, to the new life: the life of the Spirit, the life in fellowship with God to which He will lead you. There you become receptive to His blessing; there your heart becomes open to full faith in His word, "I will bless you." There He can fulfill that word to you and make you full of His blessing and power to be a blessing to others. Live with God, separated from the world, and then shall you hear the voice of God speak with power: "I will bless you," and "Be a blessing."

O my Father, show me the way to that promised land where You bring Your people to have them fully for Yourself. I will abandon everything to follow You, to fellowship with You alone, in order that You may fill me with Your blessing. Lord, let Your word, "I will bless you," live in my heart as a word of God. Then I shall give myself fully to live for others and to be a blessing. Amen.

FOR FURTHER THOUGHT

1. *God is the great—the only—fountain of blessing. So as much of God as I have in me, only that much blessing can I bring. I can work much for others without blessing them. Actually to be a blessing, I must begin with that word, "I will bless you." Then the other, "Be a blessing," becomes easy.*

2. *In order to become a blessing, begin on a small scale. Give yourself up for others. Live to make others happy. Believe that the love of God dwells in you by the Spirit, and give yourself wholly to be a blessing and a joy to those around you. Ask God to shed abroad His love in you still further by the Spirit. And believe very firmly that God can make you a greater blessing than you can think—if you surrender yourself to Him for this purpose.*

3. *But this surrender must have time in solitary prayer so that God may obtain possession of your spirit. This is for you the departure from your father's house. Separate yourself from others so that God may speak with you.*

4. *Do you think Abraham was ever filled with regret that he placed himself so entirely under the leading of God? Then do you the same.*

5. *Do you now know the two words that are the source of all promises and all commands to the children of believing Abraham? The promise is: "I will bless you." The command is: "Be a blessing." I encourage you, take them both firmly for yourself.*

6. *And do you now understand where these two words to Abraham are fulfilled? In separation from his father's house—in the walk in fellowship with God.*

30
PERSONAL WORK

Restore to me the joy of Your salvation,
and uphold me by Your generous Spirit.
Then I will teach transgressors Your ways,
and sinners shall be converted to You.
PSALM 51:12–13

I believed, therefore I spoke.
PSALM 116:10

"But you shall receive power when the
Holy Spirit has come upon you."
ACTS 1:8

EVERY redeemed man is called to be a witness for his Lord. Not only by a godly walk, but by personal effort must I serve and make known my Lord. My tongue, my speech, is one of the principal means of interaction with others and influence on them. It is but a half dedication when I do not also bring the offering of the lips to speak for the Lord (Pss. 40:10–11; 66:16; 71:8, 15, 24; Heb. 13:15).

Of this work there is inconceivably real need. There are thousands of Christians who continually enjoy the preaching of the Word, and yet do not understand the way of salvation. The Lord Jesus not only preached to the multitudes, but He also spoke to individuals according to their needs (Luke 7:40; John 3:3; 4:7). Scripture is full of examples of those who told others what the Lord had done for them, and who therefore became a blessing to them (Exod. 18:8, 11; 2 Chron. 5:3). The teacher alone cannot do this work of personal speaking: Every ransomed soul must cooperate with him. He is in the world as a witness for his Lord. His own life cannot come to its full healthy increase if he does not confess his Lord and work for Him.

That witness for the Lord must be a personal witness. We must have the courage to say, "He has redeemed me, and He will also redeem you. Will you not accept this redemption? Come, let me show you the way" (John 1:42, 46; 4:28, 39; Acts 11:19). There are hundreds who would be glad if the personal question were put to them, "Are you redeemed? What keeps you back? Can I not help you to go to the Lord?" Parents ought to speak personally with their children and ask the question, "My child, have you already received the Lord Jesus?" Teachers in Sabbath schools and in day schools, when they teach the Word of God, ought to bring forward the personal question of whether the children have really received salvation, and ought to seek the opportunity of also putting the question to them separately. Friends must speak with their friends. Yes, before everything else this work should be done.

Such work must be the work of love. Let souls feel that you love them tenderly. Let the humility and gentleness of love, as they were seen in Jesus, be seen also in you. At every turn, surrender yourself to Jesus to be filled with His love—not by feeling but by faith in this love can you do your work. "Beloved. . .keep yourselves in the love of God. . . . And on some have compassion, making a distinction; but others save with fear" (Jude 20–23). The flesh often thinks that strength and force do more than love and patience. But that is not so: Love achieves everything. It has overcome on the cross (Heb. 3:13; 10:24).

> *Surrender yourself continually to God to be used for the rescue of souls, and take your stand on the fact that He who has redeemed you for this purpose will for this purpose bless you.*

Such work must be the work of faith, of faith working by love and faith that the Lord desires to use you and will use you. Do not be afraid on account of your weakness, but learn in the scriptures what glorious promises God from time to time gave to those who had to speak for Him (Exod. 4:11–12; Josh. 1:9; Isa. 50:4, 11; Jer. 1:6–7; Matt. 10:19–20). Surrender yourself continually to God to be used for the rescue of souls, and take your stand on the fact that He who has redeemed you for this purpose will for this purpose bless you.

Although your work is in weakness and fear, although no blessing appears to come, be of good courage: In His time, we shall reap (2 Chron. 15:7; Ps. 126:6–7; Hag. 2:5). Be filled with faith in the power of God, in His blessing upon you, and in the certainty of the hearing of prayer. "If anyone sees his brother sinning a sin which does not lead to death, he will ask, and He will give him life" (1 John 5:16). Whether it is the most miserable and neglected, or whether it is the decent but indifferent who does not know his sin, take courage. The Lord is mighty to bless, and He hears prayer.

But above all—for this is the principal point—carry out this work in fellowship with Jesus. Live closely with Him—live entirely for Him—and let Jesus be in all your own life, and He will speak and work in you (Acts. 4:13; 2 Cor. 3:5; 8:3). Be full of the blessing of the Lord, full of His Spirit and His love, and it cannot be otherwise than that you should be a blessing. You shall be able to tell what He is continually for you. You shall have the love and the courage, with all humility, to put to souls the question, "Is it well with you? Do you indeed have the Lord Jesus as your Savior?" And the Lord will make you experience the rich blessing that is promised to those who live to bless others.

Young Christian, be a witness for Jesus. Live as one who is fully given away to Him to watch and to work for His honor.

Blessed Lord, who has redeemed me to serve the Father in the proclamation of His love, I will with a free spirit offer myself to You for this purpose. Fill my heart for this purpose with love for Him, for You, and for souls. Cause me to see what an honor it is to do the work of redeeming love, just as You did it. Strengthen my confidence that You are working with Your power in my weakness. And let my joy be to help souls to come to You. Amen.

FOR FURTHER THOUGHT

1. *The question is often asked, "What can I do to work for the Lord?" Can you not teach a class in the Sabbath school? Perhaps you live in the country where there are children who have no hour of the Sabbath devoted to them. Perhaps there are unreached children, or even grown-up people of the farms who do not go to church. See whether you cannot gather them together in the name of Jesus. Make it a matter of prayer and faith. Although you do this work with trembling, you may be sure that to begin to work will make you strong. Or can you do something for the circulation of books and tracts? When you have a book that has been useful to you, order six or twelve copies of it. Speak of it and offer it for sale. You can do great service by this means. So also with tracts. If you are too poor to give them for nothing, have them to sell. You may acquire blessing by this method. It will especially help you to speak to others when you start with telling what is in a book.*

2. *But the principal thing is personal speaking. Do not hold back because you feel no freedom. The Lord will give you freedom in His own time. It is incredible how many are lost through ignorance. No one has ever personally made it clear to them how they can be saved. The thought that a change must first be sought and felt is so deeply rooted that the most faithful preaching is often of no use against it. By their erroneous ideas, people misunderstand everything. Begin then to speak and to help souls to understand that they are to receive Jesus just as they are, that they can certainly know that He receives them, and that this is the power of a new and holy life. How can you begin speaking out and not just living out your faith today?*

31

MISSIONARY WORK

And He said to them,
"Go into all the world and preach the gospel to every creature." . . .
And they went out and preached everywhere, the Lord working with
them and confirming the word through the accompanying signs.
MARK 16:15, 20

EVERY friend of Jesus is a friend of missions. Where there is a healthy spiritual life, there is a love for the missionary cause. When you consider the reasons of this, you obtain an insight into the glory of missions, and into your calling to embrace this cause as a part of your soul's life. Come and hear how much there is to make missionary work glorious and precious.

1. It is the cause for which Jesus left the throne of heaven. The heathen are His inheritance, given to Him by His Father. It is in heathendom that the power of Satan has been established. Jesus must have Himself vindicated as the conqueror. His glory, the coming and manifestation of His kingdom, depend on missions (Ps. 2:8; Matt. 24:14; 28:18, 28; Mark 13:10; Luke 21:24; Rom. 11:25).

2. Missionary work is the principal aim of the church on earth. All the last words of the Lord Jesus teach us this (Mark 16:15; Luke 24:47; John 17:18; Acts 1:8). The Lord is the head, and He has made himself dependent on His body—on His members, by whom alone He can do His work (1 Cor. 12:21). As a member of Christ, as a member of the church, shall I not give myself to take part in the work so that this goal may be reached?

3. It is the work for which the Holy Spirit was given. See this in the promise of the Spirit and in the leading of the Spirit granted to Peter and Barnabas and Saul (Acts 1:8; 11:12, 23–24; 8:2, 4; 22:21). In the history of the Church we find that times of revival go hand in hand with new zeal for the missionary cause. The Holy Spirit is always a holy enthusiasm for the extension of the kingdom.

4. Missionary work brings blessing on the Church. It rouses men to heroic deeds of faith and self-denial. It has furnished the most glorious instances of the wondrous power of the Lord. It gives heavenly joy over the conversion of sinners to those who watch for it with love and prayer. It cleanses the heart to understand God's great plans and to await the fulfillment of them in prayer. Missionary work is an evidence of life in a church, and it brings more life (Acts 14:27; 15:4–5;

Rom. 11:25, 33; 15:10; Eph. 3:5, 8, 10).

5. What a blessing it is for the world! What would we have been had missionaries not come to our heathen forefathers in Europe? What a glorious blessing has missionary work already won in some lands? What help is there for the hundreds of millions of heathens, if not in missions (Isa. 49:6, 12, 18, 22; 54:1–2; 60:1–22)? Heaven and hell look upon missions as the battlefield where the powers of Satan and of Jesus Christ encounter one another. It is sad that the conflict should be carried on so ineffectively.

6. There will be a blessing for your own soul in love for missionary work (Prov. 11:24–25, Isa. 58:7–8).

You will be strengthened in faith. Missionary work is a cause for faith, especially where everything goes on slowly and not according to the desires of men. You will learn to cleave to God and the Word.

Love will be awakened. You will learn to go more out of yourselves and your little circle and with an open eye and a large heart live in the interests of your Lord and King. You will feel how little true love you have, and you will receive more love.

> The Lord is the head, and He has made himself dependent on His body—on His members, by whom alone He can do His work.

You will be drawn into prayer. Your calling and power as an intercessor will become clearer to you, and through it you will receive the blessedness of this co-operation for the kingdom. You will discern how it is the highest conformity to Him who came to seek the lost to give up your own ease and rest to fight in love the fight of prayer against Satan in behalf of the heathen.

Young Christian, missionary work is more glorious and holy than you might believe. There is more blessing in it than you are aware of. The new life in you depends upon it more than you can as yet understand. Yield yourself up anew in obedience to the word to give missions a large place in your heart—yes, in your heart. The Lord Himself will further teach and bless you.

And if you desire to know how to have your love for missions, as the work of your Lord, increased, follow these hints: Become acquainted with the missionary cause. Endeavor by writings and books to know what the condition and need of heathendom is; what, by the blessing of the Lord, has been already done there; what the work is that is being done now. Speak with others about this cause. Perhaps there could be instituted in your neighborhood a little missionary society. Perhaps one of your prayer meetings—say, once a month—could be set apart for prayer in behalf of the missionary cause. Pray also for this in secret. Let the coming of the kingdom have a definite place in your secret prayers.

Endeavor to follow the material for prayer in the promises of the Word about the heathen, in the whole scriptures, especially in the prophet Isaiah (49:6, 18, 21–22; 54:1, 3; 60:1, 3, 11, 16; 62:2).

Give also to missions—not only when you are asked and not merely what you can spare without feeling it. Instead, set apart for this cause a portion of what you possess or earn. Let the Lord see that you are in earnest agreement with His work. If there is missionary work that is being done in your neighborhood, show yourself a friend to it. Although there is much imperfection in that work— and where is there work of man that is perfect?—don't complain about the imperfection, but look at the essence of the cause, the endeavor to obey the command of the Lord, and give your prayer and your help. A friend of Jesus is a friend of missions. Love for missionary work is an indispensable element of the new life.

Son of God, when You breathed Your Spirit upon Your disciples, saying, "Receive the Holy Spirit," You added, "As the Father has sent Me, I also send you" (John 20:21–22). Lord, here I am: Send me also. Breathe Your Spirit into me also so that I may live for Your kingdom. Amen.

FOR FURTHER THOUGHT

1. *In what can you find motivation for missions work? "Unknown makes unbeloved" is a word that is especially true of missionary work. He who is acquainted with the wonders that God has performed in some lands will praise and thank God for what the missionary enterprise has achieved and will be strengthened in his faith that missionary work is really God's own cause. Among the books that help to awaken interest in missions are biographies of missionaries.* The Life of Henry Martyn *is one, formerly issued by the Book Society.* Uncle Charles *is the name of a book with an account of missionary work in South Africa. Some books on missions are generally to be found in our Sabbath school libraries.*

2. *What specific gifts do you need to take your part in missions? We should never forget that the missionary cause is an enterprise of faith. It requires faith in the promises of God and in the power of God. It requires love—love for Jesus, through which the heart is filled with desire for His honor, and love for souls, which longs for their safety. It is a work of the Spirit of God, "whom the world cannot receive" (John 14:17). Therefore the world can approve of missions only when they go forward with the highest prosperity.*

3. *How do you respond when the work goes more slowly than you would have liked? Let no friend of missions become discouraged when the work proceeds slowly. Among our forefathers in Europe, a whole century was occupied with the introduction of Christianity. Sometimes a nation received Christianity to cast it off again after thirty or forty years. It required a thousand years to bring*

them up to the height at which we now stand. Let us not expect too much from the heathen at once, but with love and patience and firm faith, pray and work, and expect the blessing of God.

32

LIGHT AND JOYFULNESS

Blessed are the people who know the joyful sound!
They walk, O LORD, in the light of Your countenance.
In Your name they rejoice all day long.
PSALM 89:15–16

Light is sown for the righteous,
and gladness for the upright in heart.
PSALM 97:11

"I am the light of the world.
He who follows Me shall not walk
in darkness, but have the light of life."
JOHN 8:12

"I will see you again and your heart will rejoice,
and your joy no one will take from you."
JOHN 16:22

As sorrowful, yet always rejoicing.
2 CORINTHIANS 6:10

A father will always be eager to see his children joyful. He does all that he can to make them happy. Likewise, God also desires that His children should walk before Him in gladness of heart. He has promised them gladness, and He will give it (Ps. 89:16–17; Isa. 29:19; John 16:22; 1 Pet. 1:8). He has commanded it, and we must take it and walk in it at all times (Ps. 32:11; Isa. 12:5–6; Phil. 4:4; 1 Thess. 5:16).

The reason for this is not difficult to find. Gladness is always the evidence that something really satisfies me and has great value for me. More than anything else, gladness for what I possess is a recommendation of it to others. And gladness in God is the strongest proof that I have in God what satisfies and fills me: that I do not serve Him with dread or to be kept, but because He is my salvation.

Gladness is the evidence of the truth and the worth of obedience, and it shows whether I have pleasure in the will of God (Deut. 28:47; Pss. 40:9; 119:11). It is for this reason that joy in God is so acceptable to Him, so strengthening to believers themselves, and to all who are around the most eloquent testimony of what we think of God (Neh. 8:11; Ps. 68:4; Prov. 4:18).

In the scriptures, light and gladness are frequently connected with each other (Esther 8:16; Prov. 13:9; 15:30; Isa. 60:20). It is so in nature. The joyful light of the morning awakens the birds to their song and gladdens the watchers who in the darkness have longed for the day. It is the light of God's countenance that gives the Christian his gladness. In fellowship with his Lord, he can, and always will, be happy. The love of the Father shines like the sun on His children (Exod. 10:23; 2 Sam. 23:4; Ps. 36:10; Isa. 60:1, 20; 1 John 1:5; 4:16). When darkness comes over the soul, it is always through one of two things: sin or unbelief. Sin is darkness, and it makes dark. And unbelief also makes dark, for it turns us from Him, who alone is the light.

> *More than anything else, gladness for what I possess is a recommendation of it to others. And gladness in God is the strongest proof that I have in God what satisfies and fills me.*

The question is sometimes asked, "Can the Christian walk always in the light?" The answer of our Lord is clear: "He who follows Me shall not walk in darkness" (John 8:12). It is sin, the turning from behind Jesus to our own way, that makes dark. But at the moment we confess sin and have it cleansed in the blood, we are again in the light (Josh. 7:13; Isa. 58:10; 59:1, 2, 9; Matt. 15:14, 16; 2 Cor. 6:14; Eph. 5:8, 14; 1 Thess. 5:5; 1 John 2:10). Or it is unbelief that makes dark. We look to ourselves and our strength and try to seek comfort in our own feeling or our own works, and all becomes dark. As soon as we look to Jesus—to the fullness, to the perfect provision for our needs that is in Him—all is light. He says, "I am the light of the world. He who follows Me shall not walk in darkness, but have the light of life" (John 8:12). So long as I believe, I have light and gladness (John 12:36; 11:40; Rom. 15:13; 1 Pet. 1:8).

Christians who desire to walk according to the will of the Lord, hear what His Word says: "Finally, my brethren, rejoice in the Lord. . . . Rejoice in the Lord always. Again I will say, rejoice!" (Phil. 3:1; 4:4). In the Lord Jesus there is joy unspeakable and full of glory. Believing in Him, rejoice in this. Live the life of faith, for that life is salvation and glorious joy. A heart that gives itself undividedly to follow Jesus and that lives by faith in Him and His love shall have light and gladness. Therefore, soul, only believe. Do not seek gladness, for in that case you will not find it, because you are seeking feeling. But seek Jesus, follow Jesus, and believe in Jesus, and then gladness shall be added to you. "Though now you do not see Him, yet believing, you rejoice with joy inexpressible and full of glory" (1 Pet. 1:8).

Lord Jesus, You are the Light of the world, the brilliant radiance of the unapproachable light in whom we see the light of God. From Your countenance radiates upon us the illumination of the knowledge of the love and glory of God. And You are ours—our light and our salvation. Oh, teach us to believe more firmly that with You we can never walk in the darkness. Let gladness in You be the proof that You are all to us, including our strength to do all that You want us to do. Amen.

FOR FURTHER THOUGHT

1. *What is the basis of your gladness in your new life? The gladness that I have in anything is the measure of its worth in my eyes. The gladness I have in a person is the measure of my pleasure in him. The gladness in a work is the measure of my pleasure in it. Gladness in God and His service is one of the surest evidences of healthy spiritual life.*

2. *What keeps you from enjoying the gladness God promises those who enter into the new life? Gladness is hindered by ignorance, when we do not rightly understand God and His love and the blessedness of His service; by unbelief, when we still seek something in our own strength or feeling; and by double-heartedness, when we are not willing to give up and lay aside everything for Jesus.*

3. *Understand this saying: "He who seeks gladness shall not find it; he who seeks the Lord and His will shall find gladness unsought." Think over this. He who seeks gladness as a thing of feeling seeks himself. He would rather be happy, but he will not find happiness. He who forgets himself and lives in the Lord and His will shall learn to rejoice in the Lord. It is God, God Himself, who is the God of the gladness of our rejoicing. Seek God, and you have gladness. You need only to simply take and enjoy it by faith.*

4. *How can you find lasting gladness? To thank much for what God is and does and to believe much in what God says and will do is the way to lasting gladness.*

5. *"The light of the eyes rejoices the heart" (Prov. 15:30). God does not intend that His children should walk in the darkness. Satan is the prince of the darkness, but God is light. Christ is the Light of the world, and we are children of the light. Let us walk in the light. Let us believe in the promise, "The LORD will be to you an everlasting light. . . . Your sun shall no longer go down. . .for the LORD will be your everlasting light, and the days of your mourning shall be ended" (Isa. 60:19–20).*

33

CHASTISEMENT

Blessed is the man whom You instruct, O LORD,
and teach out of Your law, that You may
give him rest from the days of adversity.
PSALM 94:12

Before I was afflicted I went astray,
but now I keep Your word. . . .
It is good for me that I have been afflicted,
that I may learn Your statutes.
PSALM 119:67, 71

But He [chastens us] for our profit,
that we may be partakers of His holiness.
HEBREWS 12:10

My brethren, count it all joy when you fall
into various trials, knowing that the
testing of your faith produces patience.
JAMES 1:2–3

EVERY child of God must at one time or another enter the school of trial. What the scriptures teach us is confirmed by experience. And the scriptures teach us further that we are to count it a joy when God takes us into this school (see James 1:2). It is a part of our heavenly blessedness to be educated and sanctified by the Father through chastisement.

Not that trial in itself brings a blessing (Isa. 5:3; Hos. 7:14–15; 2 Cor. 7:10). Just as there is no profit in the ground's being made wet by rain or broken up by the plow when no seed is cast into it, so there are children of God who enter into trial and have little blessing from it. The heart is softened for a time, but they don't know how to obtain a lasting blessing from it. They don't know what the Father has in mind for them in the school of trial.

In a good school, there are four things necessary: a definite aim, a good textbook, a capable teacher, and a willing pupil.

1. Let the aim of trial be clear to you. Holiness is the highest glory of the Father, and also of the child. He chastens us "for our profit, that we may be partakers of *His holiness*" (see Isa. 27:8–9; 1 Cor. 11:32; Heb. 2:10; 12:11). In trial the Christian often only wants to have comfort. Or he seeks to be quiet and content under the special chastisement. This is indeed the beginning, but the Father desires something else, something higher. He would make him *holy, holy,* for his whole life. When Job said, "Blessed be the name of the LORD" (Job 1:21), this was still but the beginning of his school time, for the Lord had still more to teach him. God desires to unite our will with His holy will, not only on the one point in which He is testing us, but in everything. God wants to fill us with His Holy Spirit, with His holiness. This is the aim of God, and this also must be your aim in the school of trial.

> *God wants to fill us with His Holy Spirit, with His holiness. This is the aim of God, and this also must be your aim in the school of trial.*

2. Let the Word of God at this time be your reading book. See in our trials how in affliction God would teach us out of His law. The Word will reveal to you why the Father chastens or disciplines you, how deeply He loves you in the midst of it, and how rich are the promises of His comfort. Trial will give new glory to the promises of the Father. In chastisement, turn to the Word (Ps. 119:49–50, 92, 143; Isa. 40:1; 43:2; 1 Thess. 4:8).

3. Let Jesus be your Teacher. He Himself was sanctified by suffering, for it was in suffering that He learned full obedience. He has a wonderfully sympathetic heart. Have much fellowship with Him. Don't seek your comfort from much speaking on the part of men or with men. *Give Jesus the opportunity to teach you.* Have much conversation with Him in solitude (Isa. 26:16; 61:1–2; Heb. 2:10, 17–18; 5:9). The Father has given you the Word, the Spirit, and the Lord Jesus your sanctification in order to sanctify you. Affliction and chastisement are meant to bring you to the Word, to Jesus Himself, in order that He may make you a partaker of His holiness. It is in fellowship with Jesus that comfort comes as of itself (2 Cor. 1:3–4; Heb. 13:5–6).

4. Be a willing pupil. Acknowledge your ignorance. Don't think that you understand the will of God. Ask and expect that the Lord wants to teach you the lesson that you are to learn in affliction. To the humble there is the promise of teaching and wisdom. Seek to have the ear open, the heart very quiet and turned toward God. Know that it is the Father who has placed you in the school of trial, and yield yourself with all willingness to hear what He says, to learn what He would teach you. He will bless you greatly in this (Pss. 25:9; 39:2, 10; Isa. 50:4–5).

"Blessed is the man whom You instruct, O Lord, and teach out of Your law" (Ps. 94:12). "Count it all joy when you fall into various trials. . .that you may be perfect and complete, lacking nothing" (James 1:2, 4). Regard the time of trial as a time of blessing, as a time of close communication with the Father, of being made a partaker of His holiness, and you shall also rejoice and say: "It is good for me that I have been afflicted."

Father, what thanks shall I express to You for the glorious light that Your Word casts on the dark trials of this life. You will by this means teach me and make me a partaker of Your holiness. Have You considered the suffering and the death of Your beloved Son not too much to bring holiness near to me, and shall I not be willing to endure Your chastisement to be partaker of it? No! Father, I thank You for Your precious work. Only fulfill Your purpose in me. Amen.

For Further Thought

1. *How can you find joy or comfort during difficulties and trials? In chastisement it is first of all necessary that we should be possessed by the thought: This is the will of God. Although the trial comes through our own folly or the wickedness of men, we must acknowledge that it is the will of God that we should be in that suffering by means of that folly or wickedness. We see this clearly in Joseph and the Lord Jesus. Nothing will give us rest but the willing acknowledgment: This is the will of God.*

2. *The second thought is: God wills not only the trial, but also the comfort, the power, and the blessing in it. He who acknowledges the will of God in the chastisement itself is on the way to seeing and experiencing the accompaniments also as the will of God.*

3. *How can you overcome your fear of God's discipline and correction? The will of God is as perfect as He Himself, so let us not be afraid to surrender ourselves to it. No one suffers loss by seeing the will of God as unconditionally good.*

4. *This is holiness: to know and to adore the will of God and to unite one's self wholly with it.*

5. *To whom do you turn for comfort and assurance during a trial or test? Please don't seek comfort in trial in connection with men. Do not mingle too much with them but see to it that you deal with God and His Word. The object of a trial is just to draw you away from what is earthly, in order that you may turn to God and give Him time to unite your will with His perfect will.*

34

PRAYER

"But you, when you pray, go into your room,
and when you have shut your door, pray to your Father
who is in the secret place; and your Father who
sees in secret will reward you openly."
MATTHEW 6:6

THE spiritual life with its growth depends in great measure on prayer. Whether I pray much or little, pray with pleasure or as a duty, pray according to the Word of God or my own inclination, will life flourish or decay. In the word of Jesus quoted above, we have the leading ideas of true prayer.

Alone with God. That is the first thought. The door must be shut, with the world and man outside, because I am to talk with God undisturbed. When God met with His servants in the old days, He got them alone (Gen. 18:22–23; 22:5; 32:24; Exod. 33:11). Let the first thought in your prayer be: Here are God and I in the chamber with each other. Your conviction of the nearness of God will determine the power of your prayer.

In the presence of *your Father.* This is the second thought. You come to the inner chamber, because your Father with His love awaits you there. Although you are cold, dark, and sinful—although it is doubtful whether you can pray at all—come, because the Father is there and there He looks upon you. Set yourself beneath the light of His eye. Believe in His tender fatherly love, and out of this faith prayer will be born (Matt. 6:8; 7:11).

Count certainly on an answer. That is the third point in the word of Jesus. "Your Father. . .will reward you openly." There is nothing about which the Lord Jesus has spoken so positively as the certainty of an answer to prayer. Review the promises (Matt 6:7–8; 11:24; Luke 18:8; John 14:13–14; 15:7, 16; 16:23–24). Observe how constantly in the Psalms, that prayer book of God's saints, God is called upon as the God who hears prayer and gives answers (Pss. 3:5; 4:4; 6:10; 10:17; 17:6, 22, 25; 20:2, 7, 10; 34:5, 7, 18; 38:16; 40:2; 65:3; 66:19).

It may be that there is much in you that prevents the answer. Delay in the answer is a very blessed discipline. It leads to self-searching as to whether we are praying amiss, and whether our life is truly in harmony with our prayer. It rouses to a purer exercise of faith (Josh. 7:12; 1 Sam. 8:18; 14:37–38; 28:6, 15; Prov.

21:13; Isa. 1:15; Mic. 3:4; Hag. 1:9; James 1:6; 4:3; 5:16). It conducts to a closer and more persistent fellowship with God. The sure confidence of an answer is the secret of powerful praying. Let this always be with us the principal thing in prayer. When you pray, stop in the midst of your prayer to ask, "Do I believe that I am receiving what I pray for?" Let your faith receive and hold firmly the answer as given. It shall turn out according to your faith (Ps. 145:9; Isa. 30:19; Jer. 33:3; Mal. 3:10; Matt. 9:29; 15:28; 1 John 3:22; 5:14–15).

> *God is our salvation and our strength, and Christ is our life and our holiness. Only in personal fellowship with the living God is our blessedness found.*

Beloved young Christians, if there is one thing about which you must be conscientious, it is this: secret communication with God. Your life is hidden with Christ in God. Every day you must in prayer ask from above, and by faith receive in prayer what you need for that day. Every day must personal communication with the Father and the Lord Jesus be renewed and strengthened. God is our salvation and our strength, and Christ is our life and our holiness. Only in personal fellowship with the living God is our blessedness found.

Christian: Pray much, pray continually, pray without ceasing. When you have no desire to pray, *go just then to the inner chamber.* Go as one who has nothing to bring to the Father and set yourself before Him in faith in His love. That coming to the Father and abiding before Him is already a prayer He understands. Be assured that to appear before God, however passively, always brings a blessing. The Father not only hears; He sees in secret and will reward it openly.

O my Father, who has so certainly promised in Your Word to hear the prayer of faith, give to me the Spirit of prayer, so that I may know how to offer that prayer. Graciously reveal to me Your wonderful fatherly love: the complete blotting out of my sins in Christ, by which every hindrance in this direction is taken away, and the intercession of the Spirit in me, by which my ignorance or weakness cannot deprive me of the blessing. Teach me with faith in You, the Three-One, to pray in fellowship with You. And confirm me in the strong, living certitude that I receive what I believingly ask. Amen.

FOR FURTHER THOUGHT

1. *On what should all your prayer be based? In prayer, the principal thing is faith. The whole of salvation, the whole of the new life, is by faith, and therefore also by prayer. There is all too much prayer that brings nothing, because there is little faith in it. Before I pray, while I pray, and after I have prayed, I must ask: "Do I pray in faith?" I must say: "I believe with my whole heart."*

2. *How can you attain the faith it takes to pray effectively? To arrive at this faith, we must take time in prayer, time to set ourselves silently and trustfully before God and to become awake to His presence, time to have our soul sanctified in fellowship with God, and time for the Holy Spirit to teach us to hold firmly and use trustfully the word of promise. No earthly knowledge, no earthly possessions, no earthly food, and no fellowship with friends can we have without time—sufficient time. Let us not think to learn how to pray or how to enjoy the power and the blessedness of prayer without taking time with God.*

3. *And then there must be not only time every day, but perseverance from day to day. Time is required to grow in the certainty that we are acceptable to the Father, that our prayer has power in the confidence of beloved sons who know our prayer is according to His will and is heard. We must not assume that we know well enough how to pray and can just ask, and then it is over. No, prayer is communication and fellowship with God in which God has time and opportunity to work in us, and in which our souls die to their own will and power and become bound up and united with God. What steps can you take to make sure you pray consistently and perserveringly?*

4. *For encouragement in persistent prayer, the following instance may be of service. In an address delivered at Calcutta, George Müller recently said that in 1844, five persons were laid upon his heart and that he began to pray for their conversion. Eighteen months passed by before the first was converted. He prayed five more years, and then the second was converted. After twelve and a half years, yet another was converted. And now he also already prayed forty years for the other two, without letting slip a single day, and still they are not converted. He was, nevertheless, full of courage in the sure confidence that these two also would be given him in answer to his prayer. Are there people you have endeavored to pray for? Have you remained persistent in your faith and prayers for them?*

5. *In the book* With Christ in the School of Prayer: Thoughts on Our Training for the Ministry of Intercession, *I have endeavored in thirty-one meditations to explain the principal points in the life of prayer.*

35

THE PRAYER MEETING

*"Again I say to you that if two of you agree on earth
concerning anything that they ask, it will be done for them
by My Father in heaven. For where two or three are gathered
together in My name, I am there in the midst of them."*
MATTHEW 18:19–20

THE Lord Jesus has told us to go into the inner chamber and hold our personal communication with God by prayer in secret—and not to be seen by men. The very same voice tells us that we are also to pray in fellowship with one another (Matt. 6:6; Luke 9:18, 28). And when He went to heaven, the birth of the Christian Church took place in a prayer meeting that 120 men and women held for ten days (Acts 1:14). The day of Pentecost was the fruit of unanimous, persevering prayer.

Let everyone who wants to please the Lord Jesus, who desires the gift of the Spirit with power for his congregation or church, who wants to have the blessing of fellowship with the children of God, attach himself to a prayer meeting and prove whether the Lord will make good His word and bestow upon it a special blessing (2 Chron. 20:4, 17; Neh. 9:2–3; Joel 2:16–17; Acts 12:5). And let him give help in it, so that the prayer meeting may be such as the Lord presented it to us.

For a blessed prayer meeting, there must be, first of all, agreement concerning the thing we desire. There must be something that we really desire to have from God. Concerning this, we are to be in harmony. There must be inner love and unity among the suppliants—all that is strife, envy, wrath, lovelessness makes prayer powerless (Ps. 133:1, 3; Matt. 5:23–24; Mark 11:25)—and then agreement on the definite object that is desired (Jer. 32:39; Acts. 4:24).

For this purpose it is entirely proper that what people are to pray for should be stated in the prayer meeting. Whether it is that one of the members wants to have his particular needs brought forward, or whether others want to bring more general needs to the Lord—such as the conversion of the unconverted, the revival of God's children, the anointing of the teacher, the extension of the kingdom—let the objects be announced beforehand. And let no one then assume that there is unanimity whenever one is content to join in prayer for these objects. No, we are to take them into our heart and life, bring them continually before the Lord, and be inwardly eager that the Lord should give them. Then we are on the way to the prayer that has power.

The second feature that characterizes a right prayer meeting is the coming together in the name of Jesus and the consciousness of His presence. The scripture says, "The name of the LORD is a strong tower; the righteous run to it and are safe" (Prov. 18:10). The name is the expression of the person. When believers come together, they are to enter into the name of Jesus, to move themselves within this name as their fortress and home. In this name they mingle with one another before the Father, and out of this name they pray.

This name makes them also truly one with each other. And when they are in this name this way, the living Lord Himself is in their midst, and He says that this is the reason why the Father certainly hears them (John 14:13–14; 15:7, 16; 16:23–24). They are in Him, and He is in them, and out of Him they pray, and their prayer comes before the Father in His power. Oh, let the name of Jesus really be the point of union, the meeting place, in our prayer meetings, and we shall be conscious that He is in our midst.

> *For a blessed prayer meeting, there must be, first of all, agreement concerning the thing we desire. There must be something that we really desire to have from God.*

Then there is the third feature of united prayer of which the Lord has told us: Our request shall certainly be done by the heavenly Father. The prayer shall certainly be answered. We may well cry out in these days, "Where is the God of Elijah?" for He was a God who answered. "The God who answers...He is God," said Elijah to the people. And he said to God, "Hear me, O LORD, hear me, that this people may know that You are the LORD God" (1 Kings 18:24, 37; also see James 5:16).

When we are content with much and continuous praying without answer, then there will be little answer given. But when we understand that the answer as the proof of God's pleasure in our prayer is the principal thing, and are not willing to be content without it, we shall discover what is lacking in our prayer, and shall set ourselves to pray in such a way that an answer can come. And this surely we may firmly believe: The Lord takes delight in answering. It is a joy to Him when His people enter this way into the name of Jesus and pray out of it, so that He can give what they desire (Acts 12:5; 2 Cor. 1:11; James 4:8; 5:16–17).

Children of God, however young and weak you may still be, here is one of the institutions prepared for you by the Lord Jesus Himself to supply you with help in prayer. Let everyone make use of the prayer meeting. Let everyone go in a praying and believing frame of mind, seeking the name and the presence of the Lord. Let everyone seek to live and pray with his brethren and sisters. And let everyone expect surely to see glorious answers to prayer.

Blessed Lord Jesus, who has given us the commandment to pray as well in the solitary inner chamber as in public fellowship with one another, let the one habit always make the other more precious as complement and confirmation. Let the inner chamber prepare us and awaken the need for union with Your people in prayer. Let Your presence there be our blessedness. And let fellowship with Your people strengthen us with certainty to expect and receive answers. Amen.

FOR FURTHER THOUGHT

1. *What are some practical ways you can begin prayer meetings? There are many places of our country where prayer meetings might be a great blessing. A spiritual man or woman who should once a week, or on Sabbath at midday, gather together the inhabitants on a farm place or the neighbors of two or three places that are not far from one another, might be able to obtain great blessing. Let every believing reader of this portion ask if there isn't in his neighborhood this kind of need, and let him begin in the name of the Lord. Let me therefore earnestly put the question to every reader: Is there a prayer meeting in your district? Do you faithfully take part in it? Do you know what it is to come together with the children of God in the name of Jesus to experience His presence and His hearing of prayer?*

2. *There is a book,* The Hour of Prayer, *with suitable portions for reading out in such gatherings. Or let this book,* The New Life, *be taken and a portion read and some of the texts reviewed and spoken on. This will give material for prayer.*

3. *"Will the prayer meeting do no harm to the inner chamber?" is a question sometimes asked. My experience is just the reverse of this result. The prayer meeting is a school of prayer. The weak learn from more advanced petitioners. Material for prayer is given, as well as the opportunity for self-searching and the encouragement to more prayer.*

4. *How important are specific prayer requests to a prayer meeting? It should be more usual in prayer meetings for people to speak of definite objects for which to pray—things in which one can definitely and trustfully look out for an answer—and concerning which one can know when an answer comes. Such announcements would greatly further unanimity and believing expectation.*

36

THE FEAR OF THE LORD

Blessed is the man who fears the LORD. . . .
He will not be afraid of evil tidings. . . . His heart
is established; he will not be afraid.
PSALM 112:1, 7–8

And walking in the fear of the Lord
and in the comfort of the Holy Spirit,
they were multiplied.
ACTS 9:31

THE scriptures use the word *fear* in a twofold way. In some places it speaks of fear as something wrong and sinful, and in the strongest terms it forbids us to fear (Gen. 15:1; Isa. 8:13; Jer. 32:40; Rom. 8:15; 1 Pet. 3:14; 1 John 4:18). In nearly one hundred places occurs the word: "Fear not." In many other places, however, fear is praised as one of the surest evidences of true godliness, as acceptable to the Lord and fruitful for blessing to us (Pss. 22:24, 26; 33:18; 112:1; 115:13; Prov. 28:14). The people of God bear the name "those who fear the Lord."

The distinction between these two rests in this simple fact: The one is unbelieving fear, while the other is believing. Where fear is found connected with lack of trust in God, there it is sinful and very hurtful (Matt. 8:26; Rev. 21:9). On the other hand, the fear that is coupled with trust and hope in God is for the spiritual life entirely indispensable. The fear that has man and what is temporal as its object is condemned, but the fear that with childlike confidence and love honors the Father is commanded (Pss. 33:18; 147:11; Luke 12:4, 7).

It is the believing—not mindless but familiar—fear of the Lord that is presented in the scriptures as a source of blessing and power. He who fears the Lord will fear nothing else. The fear of the Lord will be the beginning of all wisdom. The fear of the Lord is the sure way to the enjoyment of God's favor and protection (Ps. 56:5, 12; Prov. 1:7; 9:10; 10:27; 19:23; Acts 9:31; 2 Cor. 7:1).

There are some Christians who by their upbringing are led into the fear of the Lord even before they come to faith. This is a very great blessing. Parents can give a child no greater blessing than to bring him up in the fear of the Lord. Those who are brought up this way have a great advantage, because they are, as it were, prepared to walk in the joy of the Lord. Conversely, when those who don't have this preparation come to conversion, they need special teaching and vigilance in order to pray for and awaken this holy fear.

The elements of which this fear is composed are many and glorious. The principal are the following:

There are holy reverence and awe before the glorious majesty of God and before the All Holy. These guard against the superficiality that forgets who God is and that make no efforts to honor Him as God (Job 42:6; Ps. 5:8; Isa. 6:2, 5; Hab. 2:20; Zech. 2:3).

> *He who fears the Lord will fear nothing else. The fear of the Lord will be the beginning of all wisdom.*

There is deep humility that is afraid of itself and couples deep confidence in God with an entire distrust in itself. Conscious weakness that knows the subtlety of its own heart always dreads doing anything contrary to the will or honor of God. But just because he fears God, such a one firmly relies on Him for protection. And this same humility inspires him in all his interaction with his fellow men (Luke 18:2, 4; Rom. 11:20; 1 Pet. 3:5).

There is circumspectness or vigilance. With holy forethought, it seeks to know the right path, to watch against the enemy, and to be guarded against all lightness or hastiness in speech, resolve, and conduct (Prov. 2:5, 11; 8:12–13; 13:33; 16:6; Luke 1:74).

And there are also in it holy zeal and courage in watching and striving. The fear of displeasing the Lord by not conducting one's self in everything as His servant motivates to being faithful in that which is least. The fear of the Lord takes all other fear away and gives inconceivable courage in the certainty of victory (Deut. 6:2; Isa. 12:2).

And out of this fear is then born joy. "Rejoice with trembling" (Ps. 2:11), for the fear of the Lord gives joy its depth and stability. Fear is the root, joy the fruit, and the deeper the fear, the higher the joy. On this account it is said: "You who fear the LORD, praise Him!" (Ps. 22:23); "You who fear the LORD, bless the LORD!" (Ps. 135:20).

Young disciples of Christ, hear the voice of your Father: "Oh, fear the LORD, you His saints!" (Ps. 34:9). Let deep fear of the Lord and dread of all that might displease or grieve Him fill you. Then you will never have any evil to fear. He who fears the Lord and seeks to do all that pleases Him, for him God shall also do all that he desires. The childlike believing fear of God will lead you into the love and joy of God, while mindless, unbelieving, cowardly fear is utterly cast out.

27

7

4

O my God, make my heart ready for the fear of Your name. May I always be among those who fear the Lord, who hope in His mercy. Amen.

FOR FURTHER THOUGHT

1. What are some of the blessings of the fear of God? (Pss. 31:20; 115:13; 127:11; 145:19; Prov. 1:1, 7–8, 13–14, 27; Acts 10:35)
2. What are the reasons we are to fear God? (Deut. 10:17, 20–21; Josh. 4:24; 1 Sam. 12:24; Jer. 5:22; 10:6–7; Matt. 10:28; Rev. 15:4)
3. It is especially the knowledge of God in His greatness, power, and glory that will fill the soul with fear. But for this purpose, we must set ourselves silent before Him and take time for our soul to come under the impression of His majesty.
4. "He...delivered me from all my fears" (Ps. 34:4). Does this apply to every different sort of fear by which you are hindered? There is the fear of man (Isa. 51:12–13; Heb. 13:16), the fear of heavy trial (Isa. 40:1–2), the fear of our own weakness (Isa. 41:10), fear for the work of God (1 Chron. 28:20), and the fear of death (Ps. 23:4).
5. Do you now understand the word: "Blessed is the man who fears the LORD.... His heart is established; he will not be afraid"?

37

UNDIVIDED CONSECRATION

*But Ittai answered the king and said, "As the LORD lives, and as my
lord the king lives, surely in whatever place my lord the king shall be,
whether in death or life, even there also your servant will be."*
2 SAMUEL 15:21

*"So likewise, whoever of you does not forsake
all that he has cannot be My disciple."*
LUKE 14:33

*"Come out from among them and be separate, says the
Lord. Do not touch what is unclean, and I will
receive you. I will be a Father to you."*
2 CORINTHIANS 6:17–18

*Yet indeed I also count all things loss for the excellence
of the knowledge of Christ Jesus my Lord.*
PHILIPPIANS 3:8

WE have already said that surrender to the Lord is something that for the
Christian always obtains newer and deeper significance. When this takes place,
he comes to understand how this surrender involves nothing less than a complete
and undivided consecration to live only, always, wholly for Jesus. As entirely as
the temple was dedicated to the service of God alone, so that everyone knew that
it existed only for that purpose; as entirely as the offering on the altar could be
used only according to the command of God, and no one had a right to use one
portion of it in any way other than God had said—so entirely do you belong to
your Lord, and so undivided must your consecration to Him be. God continually
reminded Israel that He had redeemed them to be His possession (Exod. 19:4–5;
Lev. 1:8–9; Deut. 7:6; Rom. 12:1; 1 Cor. 3:16–17). Let us see what this implies.

There is *personal attachment to Jesus,* and fellowship with Him in secret. He will
be and must be the beloved, the desire and the joy of our souls. It is not, in the first
instance, to the service of God, but to Jesus as our Friend and King, our Redeemer
and God, that we are to be consecrated (John 14:21; 15:14–15; 21:17; Gal. 2:10).

It is only the spiritual impulse of a personal, cordial love that can set us in a condition for a life of complete consecration. Continually Jesus used the words: "For My sake," "Follow Me," and "My disciple." He Himself must be the central point (Matt. 10:32–33, 37–38, 40; Luke 14:26–27, 33; 18:22). He gave Himself, and to desire to have Him, to love Him, and to depend on Him is the characteristic of a disciple.

Then there is *public confession*. What has been given to anyone, that he will have acknowledged by all as his property. His possessions are his glory. When the Lord Jesus manifests His great grace to a soul in redeeming it, He desires that the world should see and know it and that He would be known and honored as its proprietor. He desires that everyone who belongs to Him would confess Him, and that it should come out that Jesus is King (Exod. 33:16; Josh. 24:15; John 13:35). Apart from this public confession, the surrender is only a halfhearted one. As a part of this public confession, it is also required that we join His people and acknowledge them as our people. The one new commandment that the Lord gave, the sure proof by which all should recognize that we are His disciples, is brotherly love.

> *A*s entirely as the temple was dedicated to the service of God alone, so that everyone knew that it existed only for that purpose. . .so entirely do you belong to your Lord, and so undivided must your consecration to Him be.

Although the children of God in a locality are few—or despised or full of imperfection—you still join them. Love them and hold fellowship with them. Attach yourself to them in prayer meetings and otherwise. Love them fervently, because brotherly love has wonderful power to open the heart for the love and the indwelling of God (Ruth 1:16; John 15:12; Rom. 7:5; 1 Cor. 12:20–21; Eph. 4:14, 16; 1 Pet. 1:22).

To complete consecration there also belongs separation from sin and the world. Don't touch the unclean thing. Know that the world is under the power of the Evil One. Don't ask how much of it you can retain without being lost. Don't ask always what is sin and what is lawful. Even that which is lawful, the Christian must oftentimes willingly renounce to be able to live wholly for his God (1 Cor. 8:13; 9:25, 27; 10:23; 2 Cor. 6:16–17; 2 Tim. 2:4). Abstinence even from lawful things is often indispensable for the full imitation of the Lord Jesus. Live as one who is really separated for God and His holiness. He who renounces everything, who counts everything as loss for Jesus' sake, shall even in this life receive a hundredfold more (Gen. 22:16–17; 2 Chron. 25:9; Luke 18:29; John 12:24–25; Phil. 3:8).

And what I separate from everything, I will use. Entire consecration has its eye on making us useful and fit for God and His service. Do not let there be with you the least doubt as to whether God has need of you and will make you a great blessing. Only give yourself unreservedly into His hands. Present yourself to Him so that He may fill you with His blessing, His love, His Spirit. Then you shall be a blessing (2 Tim. 2:21).

Let no one fear that this demand for a complete consecration is too high for him. You are not under the law, which demands but gives no power. You are under grace, which itself works what it requires (2 Cor. 9:8; 2 Thess. 1:11–12). Like the first surrender, so is every fresh dedication yielded to this Jesus, whom the Father has given to do all things for you. Consecration is a deed of faith, a part of the glorious life of faith. It is on this account that you have to say: "It is not I, but the grace of God in me, that will do it. I live only by faith in Him who works in me as well the willing as the performance" (see 1 Cor. 15:10; Gal. 2:20; Phil. 2:13).

Blessed Lord, open the eyes of my heart so that I may see how completely You desire to have me for Yourself. Be in the hidden depths of my heart the one power that keeps me occupied and holds me in possession. Let all know of me that You are my King, and that I ask only for Your will. In my separation from the world, in my surrender to Your people and to Your will, let it be demonstrated that I am wholly—yes, wholly—the Lord's. Amen.

For Further Thought

1. *How important is entire consecration to God in your new life of faith? There is likely no point of the Christian life in connection with which I should more desire to urge you to pray to God that He may enlighten your eyes than this of the entire consecration that God desires. In myself and others, I discover that with our own thoughts we can form no conception of how completely God Himself would take possession of our will and live in us. The Holy Spirit must reveal this in us. Only then indeed does a conviction arise of how little we understand this. We are not to think: I see truly how entirely I must live for God, but I cannot accomplish this. No, we are to say: "I am still blind. I have still no view of what is the glory of a life in which God is all. If I should once see that, I would strongly desire and believe that, not I, but God should work it in me."*

2. *What steps do you think God wants you to take toward entire consecration? Let there not be in your mind the least doubt as to whether you have given yourself to God, to live wholly and only as His. Express this conviction often before Him. Acknowledge that you do not yet see or understand what it means, but abide by this: that you desire it to be so. Rely on the Holy Spirit to seal you, to stamp you as God's entire possession. Even if you stumble and discover self-will, hold firmly your integrity, and trustfully declare that the deep, firm choice of your heart is in all things—in all things—to live to God.*

3. *How has God enabled you to give yourself completely to Him? Always keep before your eyes that the power to give all to the Lord, and to be all for the Lord, arises from the fact that He has given all for you, that He is all for you. Faith in what He did for you is the power for what you do for Him.*

38

ASSURANCE OF FAITH

[Abraham] did not waver at the promise of God
through unbelief, but was strengthened in faith, giving glory to God,
and being fully convinced that what He had promised
He was also able to perform.
ROMANS 4:20–21

My little children, let us not love in word or in tongue,
but in deed and in truth. And by this we know that we are
of the truth, and shall assure our hearts before Him.
1 JOHN 3:18–19

And by this we know that He abides in us,
by the Spirit whom He has given us.
1 JOHN 3:24

EVERY child of God needs the assurance of faith: the full certainty of faith that the Lord has received him and made him His child. The holy scripture always speaks to Christians as those who know that they are redeemed, that they are now children of God, and that they have received eternal life (Deut. 26:27–28; Isa. 44:5; Gal. 4:7; 1 John 5:12). How can a child love or serve his father while he is uncertain whether his father will really acknowledge him as a child? We have already spoken on this point in a previous chapter; but oftentimes by ignorance or distrust a Christian again comes into darkness. For this reason we will now deal with it once again of set purpose.

Scripture names three things by which we have our certainty: first, *faith* in the Word; after that, *works*; and then, in and with both of these, *the Holy Spirit*.

First, faith in the Word. Abraham is to us the great example of faith, and also of the assurance of faith. And what then says the scripture about the certainty that he had? He was fully assured that what God had promised He was also able to perform. His expectation was only from God and what God had promised. He relied on God to do what He had said. The promise of God was for him his only but sufficient assurance of faith (John 3:33; 5:24; Acts. 27:25; Rom. 4:21–22; 1 John 5:10–11).

There are many young Christians who think that faith in the Word is not sufficient to give full assurance, and who would like to have something more. They imagine that assurance, a sure inward feeling or conviction, is what is given above or outside of faith. This is wrong. As I need nothing more than the word of a trustworthy man to give me complete certainty, so must the Word of God be my certainty. People err because they seek something in themselves and in their feeling. No, the whole of salvation comes from God. The soul must not be occupied with itself or its work, but with God. He who forgets himself to hear what God says, and to rely on His promise as something worthy of credit, has in this fact the fullest assurance of faith (Num. 23:19; Ps. 89:35). He does not doubt the promises, but is strong in faith, giving God the glory and being fully assured that what was promised God is also able to perform.

> *he more clearly I at the outset hold the assurance of faith, without works but on the Word alone, the more certainly shall works follow.*

Then the scripture names also works: By genuine love we shall assure our hearts (1 John 3:18–19). Here carefully observe this: Assurance by faith in the promise, without works, comes first. The godless man who receives grace knows this only from the Word. But then, later on, assurance is to follow from works. "By works faith was made perfect" (James 2:22; also see John 15:10, 14; Gal. 5:6; 1 John 3:14). The tree is planted in faith while it is without fruit. But when the time of fruit arrives and no fruit appears, then I may begin to doubt. The more clearly I at the outset hold the assurance of faith, without works but on the Word alone, the more certainly shall works follow.

And both—assurance by faith and by works—come by the Spirit. Not by the Word alone and not by works as something that I myself do, but by the Word as the instrument of the Spirit. And by works, which are the fruit of the Spirit, a child of God has the heavenly certification that he is the Lord's (John 4:13; Rom. 8:13–14; 1 John 3:24).

Oh, let us believe in Jesus as our life and abide in Him, and then assurance of faith shall never be lacking to us.

O my Father, teach me to find my assurance of faith in a life with You, in cordial reliance on Your promises, and in cordial obedience to Your commands. Let Your Holy Spirit also witness with my spirit that I am a child of God. Amen.

For Further Thought

1. *How important is it to you to be assured that God loves you? The importance of the assurance of faith lies in the fact that I cannot possibly love or serve as a child of God when I do not know whether He loves and acknowledges me as His child.*

2. *Where can you find proof and assurance that you are God's child? The whole Bible is one great proof for the assurance of faith. Just because it speaks this way of itself, it is not always named. Abraham and Moses knew well that God had received them—otherwise they could not serve or trust Him. The people of Israel knew that God had redeemed them, and for this reason they had to serve God. How much more must this be the case in the greater redemption of the New Testament? All the epistles are written to men of whom it is assumed that they know and confess that they are redeemed, holy children of God.*

3. *What part does obedience play in this kind of faith and assurance? Faith and obedience are inseparable, just as root and fruit. First, there must be the root, and the root must have time without fruits. Then later on certainly come the fruits—first assurance without fruits by living faith in the Word, then further assurance from fruits. It is in a life with Jesus that assurance of faith is lifted up firmly above all doubt.*

4. *Assurance of faith is much helped by confession. What I express becomes from me more evident; I am bound and confirmed by it.*

5. *It is at the feet of Jesus, looking up into His friendly countenance, listening to His loving promises—it is in communion with Jesus Himself in prayer— that all doubtfulness of mind falls away. Go to Him for the full assurance of faith.*

39

CONFORMITY TO JESUS

Predestined to be conformed to the image of His Son...
ROMANS 8:29

I have given you an example, that you
should do as I have done to you.
JOHN 13:15

THE Bible speaks of a twofold conformity, a twofold likeness that we bear. We may be conformed to the world or to Jesus. The one excludes and drives out the other. Conformity to Jesus, where it is sought, will be secretly prevented by conformity to the world more than anything else. And conformity to the world can be overcome by nothing but conformity to Jesus.

Young Christian, the new life of which you have become partaker is the life of God in heaven. In Christ that life is revealed and made visible. What the workings and fruits of eternal life were in Jesus, they shall also be in you. In His life you get to see what eternal life will do in you. It cannot be otherwise. If for this purpose you surrender yourself unreservedly to Jesus and the dominion of eternal life, it will bring forth in you a walk of wonderful conformity to that of Jesus (Matt. 20:27–28; Luke 6:40; John 6:57; 1 John 2:6; 4:17).

To the true imitation of Jesus in His example and growth in inward conformity to Him, two things especially are necessary. These are *a clear insight* that I am really called to this and *a firm trust* that it is possible for me.

One of the greatest hindrances in the spiritual life is that we do not know and do not see what God desires that we should be (Matt. 22:19; Luke 24:16; 1 Cor. 3:1–2; Heb. 5:11–12). Our understanding is still so little enlightened, we have still so many of our own human thoughts and imaginations about the true service of God, and we know so little about waiting for the Spirit who alone can teach us. We do not acknowledge that even the clearest words of God do not have for us the meaning and power that God desires. And as long as we do not spiritually discern what likeness to Jesus is, and how completely we are called to live like Him, there can be very little said of true conformity. If only we could simply understand our need for a special heavenly instruction on this point (1 Cor. 2:12–13; Eph. 1:17–18).

Let us for this purpose earnestly examine the scriptures in order to know what God says and desires about our conformity to Christ (John 13:15; 15:10, 12; Eph. 5:2; Phil. 2:5; Col. 3:13). Let us unceasingly ponder such words of scripture and keep our heart in contact with them. Let it remain fixed with us that we have given ourselves wholly to the Lord, to be all that He desires. And let us trustfully pray that the Holy Spirit would inwardly enlighten us and bring us to a full view of the life of Jesus so far as that can be seen in a believer (1 Cor. 11:1; 2 Cor. 3:18). The Spirit will convince us that we, no less than Jesus, are absolutely called to live only for the will and glory of the Father and to be in the world just as He is.

The other thing we need is the belief that it is really possible for us with some measure of exactness to bear the image of our Lord. Unbelief is the cause of powerlessness. But we see this matter otherwise. Because we are powerless, we think we don't dare believe that we can be conformed to our Lord. This thought is in conflict with the Word of God. We do not have it in our own power to carry ourselves after the image of Jesus. No, He is our head and our life. He dwells in us and will have His life work from within, outward, with divine power, through the Holy Spirit (John 14:23; 2 Cor. 13:3; Eph. 3:17–18).

Young Christian, the new life of which you have become partaker is the life of God in heaven. In Christ that life is revealed and made visible.

Yet this cannot happen apart from our faith. Faith is the consent of the heart, the surrender to Him to work, and the reception of His working. "According to your faith let it be to you" (Matt. 9:29) is one of the fundamental laws of the kingdom of God (also see Zech. 8:6; Luke 1:37, 45; 18:27; Gal. 2:20). It is something incredible what a power unbelief has to hinder the working and the blessing of the almighty God. The Christian who desires to be a partaker of conformity to Christ must specially cherish the firm trust that this blessing is within his reach and is entirely within the range of possibility. He must learn to look to Jesus as Him to whom he can, by the grace of God Almighty, in his measure, be truly conformable. He must believe that the same Spirit who was in Jesus is also in him, that the same Father who led and strengthened Jesus also watches over him, that the same Jesus who lived on earth now lives in him. He must cherish the strong assurance that this Three-One God is at work in changing him into the image of the Son (John 14:19; 17:19; Rom. 8:2; 2 Cor. 3:18; Eph. 1:9–10).

He who believes this shall receive it. It will not be without much prayer. It will require especially ceaseless communication with God and Jesus. Yet he who desires it and is willing to give time and sacrifice to it certainly receives it.

Son of God, radiance of the glory of God, the very image of His substance: I must be changed into Your image. In You I see the image and the likeness of God in which we are created, in which we are by You created anew. Lord Jesus, let conformity to You be the one desire, the one hope of my soul. Amen.

FOR FURTHER THOUGHT

1. *Conformity to Jesus: We think that we understand the word, but how little we understand that God really expects we should live even as Jesus. It requires much time with Him in prayer and pondering of His example to at all rightly conceive it. The writer of these principles has written a book on this theme and has often spoken of it, and yet he sometimes feels as if he must cry out, "Is it really true? Has God indeed called us to live even as Jesus?"*

2. *How can you avoid being conformed to the world and seek to be conformed to Jesus? Conformity to the world is strengthened especially by interaction with it, but it is through interaction with Jesus that we shall adopt His mode of thinking, His disposition, His manners.*

3. *The chief feature of the life of Jesus is this: He surrendered Himself wholly to the Father on behalf of men. This is the chief feature of conformity to Him: the offering up of ourselves to God for the redemption and blessing of the lost.*

4. *What dispositions of Christ should you seek to emulate in order to be conformed to Him? The chief feature of His inner disposition was childlikeness—absolute dependence on the Father, great willingness to be taught, cheerful preparedness to do the will of the Father. Be just like Him in this.*

40

CONFORMITY TO THE WORLD

*I beseech you therefore, brethren, by the mercies of God,
that you present your bodies a living sacrifice, holy,
acceptable to God, which is your reasonable service. And do not
be conformed to this world, but be transformed by the renewing
of your mind, that you may prove what is that good
and acceptable and perfect will of God.*
ROMANS 12:1–2

DO not be conformed to this world. But what is conformity to the world? The opposite of conformity to Jesus, for Jesus and the world stand directly opposed to each other. The world crucified Him. He and His disciples are not of the world. The spirit of this world cannot receive the Spirit of God, for it doesn't see Him or know Him (John 14:17; 17:14, 16; 1 Cor. 2:6, 8).

And what is the spirit of this world? The spirit of this world is the disposition that animates mankind in his natural condition, where the Spirit of God has not yet renewed him. The spirit of this world comes from the Evil One, who is the prince of this world, and who has dominion over all who are not renewed by the Spirit of God (John 14:30; 16:11; 1 Cor. 2:12).

And in what does the spirit of this world, or conformity to it, manifest itself? The Word of God gives the answer: "For all that is in the world—the lust of the flesh, the lust of the eyes, and the pride of life—is not of the Father but is of the world" (1 John 2:16). The craving for pleasure, or the desire to enjoy the world; the craving for property, or the desire to possess the world; the craving for glory, or the desire to be honored in the world—these are the three chief forms of the spirit of the world.

And these three are one in origin and essence. The spirit of this world is that man makes himself his own purpose, that he makes himself the central point of the world, that all creation, so far as he has power over it, must serve him, and that he seeks his life in the visible. This is the spirit of the world: to seek one's self and the visible (John 5:44). And this is the Spirit of Jesus: to live not for one's self and not for the visible, but for God and the things that are invisible (2 Cor. 4:18; 5:7, 15).

It is a very terrible and serious thought that one can carry on a busy, fashionable life, free from obvious sin or unrighteousness, and yet remain in the friendship of the world, and thereby in conflict against God (James 4:4).

Where the care for the earthly—for what we eat and what we should drink, for what we possess or may still possess, for what we can have brought forth in the earth and made to increase—is the chief element in our life, there we are conformed to this world. It is a terrible and a very serious thought that one can maintain in all appearance a Christian life and think that he is trusting in Christ, yet still be living with the world for self and the visible (Matt. 6:32–33). For this reason, the command comes to all Christians with great emphasis: Do not be conformed to this world, but to Jesus.

And how can I, for this purpose, come to be not conformed to the world? Read our text over again with consideration. We read there two things. Observe what goes before. It is those who have presented their bodies to God as a sacrifice on the altar who have it said to them: Do not be conformed to this world. Offer yourself to God—that is conformity to Jesus. Live every day as one that is offered up to God, crucified in Christ to the world. Then you will not be conformed to the world (see Gal. 6:14).

> *A* Christian who strives after the progressive renewal of his whole mind will not be conformed to the world because the Spirit of God makes him conformed to Jesus.

Observe also what follows: "Be transformed by the renewing of your mind, that you may prove what is that good and acceptable and perfect will of God." There must be a continuous growing renewal of our mind. This takes place by the Holy Spirit when we let ourselves be led by Him. Then we learn to judge spiritually what is according to the will of God and what is according to the spirit of the world. A Christian who strives after the progressive renewal of his whole mind will not be conformed to the world because the Spirit of God makes him conformed to Jesus (2 Cor. 6:14, 16; Eph. 5:17; Heb. 5:14).

Christians, by all means believe that Jesus has obtained for you the power to overcome the world and its deep, hidden seductions to live for ourselves. Believe this. Believe in Him as Victor, and you also will have the victory (John 16:33; 1 John 5:4–5).

Precious Lord, we have presented ourselves to You as living sacrifices. We have offered up ourselves to God. We are not of the world, even as You are not of the world. Lord, let our minds be enlightened by the renewing of the Holy Spirit, so that we may rightly see what the spirit of this world is. And let it be seen in us that we are not of this world, but are conformed to Jesus. Amen.

FOR FURTHER THOUGHT

1. *Worldly pleasures. Is dancing sin? What harm is there in playing billiards? Why may a Christian not go to the play? One has sometimes wished that there were in the scriptures a distinct law to forbid such things. God has intentionally not given this. If there were such a law, it would make men only externally religious. God would put each one upon trial whether his inner disposition is worldly or heavenly. Learn Romans 12:1–2 by heart, and ask the Spirit of God to make it living in you. The Christian who offers himself up to God and becomes transformed by the renewing of the mind to prove the perfect will of God will speedily learn whether he may dance or play billiards. The Christian who is afraid only of hell, but not of conformity to the world, cannot see what the Spirit of God gives His children to see.*

2. *It is remarkable that the trinity of the god of this world, in John's Epistle, is seen as well in the temptation in Paradise (Gen. 3) as in that of the Lord Jesus (Matt. 4). The lust of the flesh: The woman saw that the tree was good for food. Command that these stones become bread. The lust of the eyes: And that it was pleasant to the eyes. The devil showed Him all the kingdoms of the world. And the boastful pride of life: And that the tree was to be desired to make one wise. Throw Yourself down.*

3. *Consider what I say to you: It is only conformity to Jesus that will keep out conformity to the world. Let conformity to Jesus be the goal, the endeavor of your soul. What are you doing today to be conformed to Jesus Christ?*

41

THE LORD'S DAY

Then God blessed the seventh day and sanctified it,
because in it He rested from all His work
which God had created and made.
GENESIS 2:3

Then, the same day at evening, being the first day of the week,
when the doors were shut where the disciples were assembled,
for fear of the Jews, Jesus came and stood in the midst,
and said to them, "Peace be with you."
JOHN 20:19

I was in the Spirit on the Lord's Day. . . .
REVELATION 1:10

MAN abides under the law of time. He must have time for what he desires to do or obtain. In a wonderful way God gives him time for interaction with Himself. One day in seven God separated for fellowship with Himself.

The great object of God's gift of this day is said to be that it may serve as a proof that God desires to sanctify man (Exod. 31:13, 17; Ezek. 20:12, 20). Endeavor, I encourage you, to understand well that word *holy*. It is one of the most important words in the Bible. God is the Holy One. That alone is holy to which God communicates His holiness by revealing Himself through it.

We know that the temple was holy, because God dwelled there. God had taken possession of it. He gave Himself to dwell there. In that same way, God desires also to sanctify man, to take possession of him, and to fill him with Himself, with His own life, His disposition, and His holiness. For this purpose, God took possession of the seventh day, and, claiming it for Himself, He sanctified it. And He calls man also to sanctify it and to acknowledge it as the Lord's Day, the day of the Lord's presence and special working. He who does this, who sanctifies this day, shall, as God has promised, be sanctified by Him. (Read with attention Exod. 31:12–17, especially verse 13.)

God blessed the seventh day by sanctifying it. The blessing of God is the

240

power of life, placed by Him in anything through which it has a result full of blessing. Grass, cattle, and man He blessed with power to multiply (Gen. 1:22, 28; 22:17). And so He placed in the seventh day a power to bless and the promise that everyone who sanctifies this day shall be sanctified and blessed by it. We must train ourselves always to think of the Sabbath as a blessed day that certainly brings blessing. The blessing bound up with it is very great (Isa. 46:4–7; 48:13–14).

There is still a third word that is used concerning the institution of the Sabbath: "He rested on the seventh day" (Gen. 2:2), and, as pointed out in Exodus, "was refreshed" (31:17), or gladdened. God wants to sanctify and bless us by introducing us into His rest. He wants to bring us to see that we are not to burden ourselves with our cares and weakness. We are to rest in Him, in His finished work, in His rest, which He takes because all is in order. This rest is not the outward stopping of activities. No, it is the rest of faith, by which we cease from our works as God did from His, because all is finished. Into this rest we enter by faith in the finished work of Jesus and in surrender to be sanctified by God (Heb. 4:3, 10).

> *E*ndeavor, I encourage you, to understand well that word holy. It is one of the most important words in the Bible.

Because Jesus finished the second creation in His resurrection, and we, by the power of His resurrection, enter into life and rest, the seventh day is changed to the first day of the week. There is no specific statement on this point. Under the New Testament, the Spirit takes the place of the law. The Spirit of the Lord led His disciples to the celebration of this day. It was the day not only on which the Lord was raised, but also on which, in all likelihood, the Spirit was poured out; not only on which the Lord manifested Himself during the forty days, but on which the Spirit also specially worked (John 20:1, 19, 26; Acts. 1:8; 20:7; 1 Cor. 16:2; Rev. 1:10).

The principal lessons we have to learn about this day are the following:

The principal aim of the Sabbath is to make you holy, as God is holy. God desires for you to be holy. This is glory; this is blessedness. This is His blessing, this His rest. God desires for you to be holy, filled with Himself and His holiness (Exod. 29:43, 45; Ezek. 37:27–28; 1 Pet. 1:15–16).

In order to sanctify you, God must have you with Him—in His presence and fellowship. You are to come away from all your struggling and working to rest with Him and to rest quietly, without exertion or anxiety, in the certainty that the Son has finished everything, that the Father cares for you in everything, and that the Spirit will work everything in you. In the holy rest of a soul that is converted to God—that is silent toward God, that remains silent before His presence to hear what God speaks in him, and that relies on God to achieve all—God can reveal Himself (Ps. 62:2, 6; Hab. 2:20; Zech. 2:13; John 19:30). This is how He sanctifies us.

We sanctify the day of rest, first by withdrawing from all external business and distraction, and then especially by setting it aside as God's day, belonging to the Lord for what He destined it: fellowship with Himself.

Take heed, on the other hand, that you do not use the day of rest only as a day for the public observance of divine worship. It is especially in private personal interaction that God can bless and sanctify you. In the church, the understanding is kept active, and you have the ordinances of preaching, united prayer, and praise to keep you occupied. But we do not there always know whether the heart is really dealing with God and taking delight in Him. This takes place in solitude. Oh, become accustomed to, then, being alone with the Lord your God. And not only speak to Him, but let Him speak to you. Let your heart be the temple in whose holy silence His voice is heard. Rest in God, and then will God say of your heart: "This is My resting place. . .here I will dwell" (Ps. 132:14).

> The principal aim of the Sabbath is to make you holy,
> as God is holy. God desires for you to be holy. This is glory;
> this is blessedness. This is His blessing, this His rest.

Young Christian, make the holy, blessed day of rest a priority. Long for it. Thank God for it. Keep it very holy. And, above all, let it be a day of inner fellowship with your God, of a living association with His love.

Holy God, I thank You for the holy day You have given me as a guarantee that You will sanctify me. Lord God, it is You who sanctified the day by taking it for Yourself. Sanctify me in the same way by taking me for Yourself. Teach me to so enter into Your rest and to so find my rest in Your love that my whole soul will be silent before You, in order that You may make Yourself and Your love known in me. And let every Sabbath be to me a foretaste of the eternal rest with You. Amen.

FOR FURTHER THOUGHT

1. *Why did God institute the Sabbath? The Sabbath was first of all the means of God's grace, instituted even before the Fall. You cannot set too high a value upon it.*
2. *In what ways has the Three-One God revealed Himself in the day of rest? The Father rested on this day. The Son rose from the dead on it. The Spirit sanctified this day by His special workings. You may on this day expect the fellowship and the powerful workings of the Three-One.*
3. *What is meant by the word* holy? *Of what is the day of rest a sign, according to Exodus 31:13? How did God sanctify the day of rest? How does He sanctify us?*
4. *There are in this country specific difficulties in the way of the quiet celebration of the day of rest in a village, where the church is often very full. Yet one can lay aside*

that which is unnecessary and receive the influx of company. We can fix an hour in which there shall be reading and singing.

5. It is a matter of great importance to bring up children rightly when it comes to the sanctification of the Sabbath day by avoiding worldly society and conversation and by getting them used to reading something that may be useful for them. For the younger children, there should be in every place a Sabbath school. For the older children, it is good to come together in connection with such a book as this, everyone with a Bible, and to review texts.

6. There is no better day than the Lord's Day for doing good to body and soul. Let the works of Satan on this day come to an end, and work for the sinners and the ignorant be carried forward.

7. The principal point is this: The day of rest is the day of God's rest, of rest in and with God and of interaction with Him. It is God who will sanctify us. He does this by taking possession of us.

42

HOLY BAPTISM

"Go therefore and make disciples of all the nations,
baptizing them in the name of the Father and of the
Son and of the Holy Spirit, teaching them to observe
all things that I have commanded you."
MATTHEW 28:19–20

"He who believes and is baptized will be saved."
MARK 16:16

IN these words of the institution of baptism, we find its meaning comprehended as in a summary. The word *teach* means "make disciples of all the nations, baptizing them." The believing disciple, as he is baptized in the water, is also to be baptized or introduced into the name of the Three-One God. By the name of the Father, the new birth and life as a child in the love of the Father are given to him (Gal. 3:26–27; 4:6–7); by the name of the Son, participation in the forgiveness of sins and the life that is in Christ (Col. 2:12); and by the name of the Holy Spirit, the indwelling and progressive renewal of the Spirit (Titus 2:5–6). And every baptized believer must always look at baptism as his entrance into a covenant with the Three-One God and as a pledge that the Father, the Son, and the Spirit will over time do for him all that they have promised. It requires a lifelong study to know and enjoy all the blessing that is presented in baptism.

In other passages of scripture, the three-time twofold blessing is again set forth separately. We therefore find connected with it the new birth required to make a child of God. "Unless one is born of water and the Spirit, he cannot enter the kingdom of God" (John 3:5). The baptized disciple has in God a Father, and he has to live as a child in the love of this Father.

Then, again, baptism is brought more directly into connection with the redemption that is in Christ. Consequently, the first and simplest representation of it is the forgiveness or washing away of sins. Forgiveness is always the gateway or entrance into all blessing. Therefore, baptism is also the sacrament of the beginning of the Christian life—but of a beginning that is maintained through the whole life.

It is on this account that in Romans 6 baptism is represented as the secret of the whole of sanctification, the entrance into a life in union with Jesus. "Or do you not know that as many of us as were baptized into Christ Jesus were baptized into His death?" (6:3). And then follows in verses 4–11 the more precise explanation of what it is to be baptized into the death of Jesus and to arise out of this with Him for a new life in Him. This is elsewhere very powerfully comprehended in this one word: "For as many of you as were baptized into Christ have put on Christ" (Gal. 3:27). This alone is the right life of a baptized disciple: He has put on Christ (Rom. 6:3–4; Col. 2:12). Just as one is plunged into water and passes under it, so also is the believing confessor baptized into the death of Christ, so he can then live and walk clothed with the new life of Christ.

Every baptized believer must always look at baptism as his entrance into a covenant with the Three-One God and as a pledge that the Father, the Son, and the Spirit will over time do for him all that they have promised.

And there are other passages where again there is connected with baptism the promise of the Spirit, not only as the Spirit of regeneration, but as the gift given from heaven to believers for indwelling and sealing and for progressive renewal. "He saved us, through the washing of regeneration and renewing of the Holy Spirit, whom He poured out on us abundantly" (Titus 3:5–6). Renewal is here the activity of the Spirit, through which the new life that is planted during the new birth penetrates our whole being, so that all our thinking and doing are sanctified by Him (Rom. 12:2; Eph. 4:23).

And all this rich blessing that lies in baptism is received by faith. "He who believes and is baptized will be saved" (Mark 16:16). Baptism was not only a confession on man's part of the faith that he who desires to be a disciple already had, but equally on God's part a seal for the confirmation of faith, a covenant evidence in which the whole treasury of grace is based, to be enjoyed throughout life. As often as a baptized believer sees a baptism administered, or reflects on it, it is to be to him an encouragement to press on by an ever-growing faith into the full life of salvation that the Three-One desires to work in him. The Holy Spirit is given to appropriate within us all the love of the Father and all the grace of the Son. The believing candidate for baptism is baptized into the death of Christ and has put on Christ. The Holy Spirit is in him to give him all this as his daily experience (Eph. 4:14–15; Col. 2:6).

Lord God, make Your holy baptism always operative in my soul as the experience that I am baptized into the death of Christ. And let Your people everywhere understand by Your Spirit what rich blessing lies thrown open in the baptism of their children. Amen.

FOR FURTHER THOUGHT

1. *What does the word* baptism *mean to you in relation to your new life in Christ?*

2. *What does the Bible teach about the true meaning of baptism?*

3. *And what are we now to think of infant baptism? With the assurance that those who cleave only to God's Word, namely the Baptists, will say to us: "You cannot cite a single passage in scripture where the baptism of little children is spoken of." Our answer is that this is thoroughly taught us in scripture, not indeed by separate texts, but by its whole tenor. The reason why the Lord Jesus did not name children specially was that this was altogether unnecessary. From the time of Abraham onward, God had engrained it in His people that in His covenant He always reckoned parents and children together. He deals not with separate individuals alone, but with households: The faith of a father held good for the child, so long as the child did not violate the covenant.*

   - *In Abraham, Isaac obtained part; in every father among the people of Israel, his child obtained part in the covenant blessing, and therefore in the covenant promise. "I will establish My covenant between Me and you and your descendants after you in their generations, for an everlasting covenant, to be God to you and your descendants after you" (Gen. 17:7).*

   - *Even so in connection with the Passover, it was ordained that when a stranger would join the people, all his males should be circumcised (Exod. 12:48). Up to the time of Christ, it was unquestionably the case that when anyone belonged to the people of God or desired to become attached to them, his little children were received along with him. If the Lord had desired to change this, a very express injunction was needed for the purpose.*

   - *How expressly did the Lord Jesus declare of children: "Of such is the kingdom of God" (Mark 10:14). And under the kingdom should he not have as a Christian the privilege that he had as a Jew? Yes, the covenant of Abraham is still confirmed from child to child.*

   - *The answer of Paul to the jailer confirms the continuance of what God had instituted: "Believe on the Lord Jesus Christ, and you will be saved, you and your household" (Acts 16:31). Although there were no children in that house, this promise confirms the principle that God deals not merely with individuals, but with households.*

   - *"Therefore are your children holy." Since the child itself is holy, it has of itself a right to the holy token of the covenant.*

43

THE LORD'S SUPPER

*The cup of blessing which we bless,
is it not the communion of the blood of Christ?
The bread which we break, is it not the
communion of the body of Christ?*
1 CORINTHIANS 10:16

*He who eats My flesh and drinks My blood
abides in Me, and I in him. . . . He who feeds
on Me will live because of Me."*
JOHN 6:56–57

ALL life needs food. It is sustained by nourishment that it takes in from out-side itself. Likewise, the heavenly life must have heavenly food, and nothing less than Jesus Himself is the bread of life: "He who feeds on Me will live because of Me" (also see Ps. 42:3; Matt. 4:4; John 6:51).

This heavenly food, Jesus, is brought near to us in two of the means of grace: the Word and the Lord's Supper. The Word comes to present Jesus to us from the side of the intellectual life—by our thoughts. The Lord's Supper comes in like manner to present Jesus to us from the side of the emotional life—by the physical senses.

Man has a double nature: He has spirit and body. Redemption begins with the spirit, but it would also penetrate to the body (Rom. 8:23; 1 Cor. 6:13, 15, 19–20; Phil. 3:21). Redemption is not complete until this mortal body also shares in glory. The Supper is the pledge that the Lord will also change our body of humiliation and make it like His own glorified body by the work in which He subdues all things to Himself. It is not simply because all that is physical is clearer and more intelligible for us, or that the Lord gives Himself in the bread of the Supper. No, by "the body," scripture often means the whole man. In the Supper, Christ wants to take possession of the whole man, body and soul, to renew and sanctify him by the power of His holy body and blood. Even His body shares in His glory. Even His body is communicated by the Holy Spirit. Even our body is fed with His holy body and renewed by the working of the Holy Spirit (Matt. 26:26; John 6:54–55; Rom. 8:11, 13).

This feeding with the body of Christ takes place on the side of the Lord by the Spirit, and on our side by faith. On the side of the Lord by the Spirit, for the Spirit communicates to us the power of the glorified body, through which even our bodies, according to scripture, become members of His body (1 Cor. 6:15, 17; 12:13; Eph. 5:23, 30). The Spirit gives us to drink of the life-power of His blood, so that the blood becomes the life and the joy of our soul. The bread is a participation in the body, and the cup is a participation in the blood.

And this takes place on our side by faith: a faith that, above what can be seen or understood, relies on the wonder-working power of the Holy Spirit to unite us really, alike in soul and body, with our Lord, by communicating Him inwardly to us (Luke 1:37; 1 Cor. 2:9, 12).

This is what the Heidelberg Catechism intends in Question and Answer 76: "What is it to eat the glorified body of Christ and to drink His shed blood?"

"It is not only to receive with a believing heart the whole suffering and dying of Christ, and thereby to obtain forgiveness of sins and eternal life, but also therewith, by the Holy Spirit, who dwells alike in Christ and in us, to be so united more and more with His blessed body, that we, although He is in heaven and we are upon earth, are nevertheless flesh of His flesh and bone of His bone, and so live and are governed eternally by one Spirit, as the members of our body by a soul."[12]

> *It is readily understood that the blessing of the Supper depends very much on preparation within the inner chamber, on the hunger and thirst with which one longs for the living God.*

This deeply inward union with Jesus, even with His body and blood, is the great aim of the Lord's Supper. All that it teaches and gives us of the forgiveness of sins, of the remembrance of Jesus, of the confirmation of the divine covenant, of union with one another, and of the announcement of the Lord's death until He comes, must lead to this: complete oneness with Jesus through the Spirit (Matt. 26:28; Luke 22:19; John 6:56, 15:4; 1 Cor. 10:17; 11:25; Rev. 3:20). "He who eats My flesh and drinks My blood abides in Me, and I in him. . . . He who feeds on Me will live because of Me."

It is readily understood that the blessing of the Supper depends very much on preparation within the inner chamber, on the hunger and thirst with which one longs for the living God (Job 11:13; Isa. 55:1, 3; Matt. 5:6; Luke 1:53; 1 Cor. 11:8). Do not imagine, however, that the Supper is nothing but a symbolic gesture of what we already have by faith in the Word. No, it is an actual spiritual communication from the exalted Lord in heaven of the powers of His life—yet this only according to the measure of desire and faith. Prepare for the Lord's Supper,

---

[12] "Der Heidelbergische Catechismus," 28, 5:76.

therefore, with very earnest separation and prayer. And then expect that the Lord will, with His heavenly power and in a way incomprehensible to you, yet sure, renew your life.

Blessed Lord, who instituted the Supper in order to communicate Yourself to Your redeemed as their food and their power of life, teach us to use the Supper. Teach us at every opportunity to eat and to drink with great hunger and thirst for You and for full union with You, believing that the Holy Spirit feeds us with Your body and gives us to drink of Your blood. Amen.

FOR FURTHER THOUGHT

1. *In connection with the Supper let us be especially on our guard against the idea of a mere divine service of the congregation or of transitory emotion. Preaching and addresses may make an edifying impression, while there is little power or blessing.*

2. *What is the chief need or requirement for taking part in the Supper? For a meal, the first requisite is hunger. A strong hunger and thirst for God is indispensable.*

3. *In the Supper, Jesus desires to give Himself to us and desires to have us give ourselves to Him. These are great and holy things.*

4. *What are the lessons of the Supper? Many! It is a feast of remembrance, a feast of reconciliation, a covenant feast, a love feast, and a feast of hope. But all these separate thoughts are only subordinate parts of the principal element: The living Jesus wants to give Himself to us in the most inward union. The Son of God wants to descend into our innermost parts. He wants to come in to celebrate the Supper with us. "He who eats My flesh and drinks My blood abides in Me, and I in him."*

5. *And then union with Jesus is union with His people in love and sympathy.*

6. *The preparatory address is not itself the preparation; it is only a help to the private preparation that one must have in fellowship with Jesus.*

7. *To hold festival with God at His table is something of unspeakable importance. Please do not assume that because you are a Christian, it is easy for you to go and sit down. No, take yourself to solitude with Jesus so that He may speak to you and say how you are to prepare you heart to eat with Him, yes, with Himself.*

It is very useful to take the whole week before the Supper for preparation and the whole week after for reflection. You will find help for this in the book *The Table of the Lord: A Help to the Right Celebration of the Holy Supper.*

44

OBEDIENCE

*"Now therefore, if you will indeed obey My voice
and keep My covenant, then you shall be a
special treasure to Me above all people."*
EXODUS 19:5

*"The LORD will greatly bless you. . .
only if you carefully obey the voice of the LORD your God."*
DEUTERONOMY 15:4–5

By faith Abraham obeyed.
HEBREWS 11:8

*He learned obedience by the things which He suffered.
And having been perfected, He became the author
of eternal salvation to all who obey Him.*
HEBREWS 5:8–9

OBEDIENCE is one of the most important words in the Bible and in
the life of the Christian. It was in the way of disobedience that man lost the favor
and the life of God, and it is only in the way of obedience that that favor and that
life can again be enjoyed (Rom. 5:19; 6:16; 1 Pet. 1:2, 14, 22). God cannot possibly
take pleasure in those who are not obedient, nor can He bestow His blessing on
them. "If you will indeed obey My voice and keep My covenant, then you shall be
a special treasure to Me." "The LORD will greatly bless you. . .only if you carefully
obey the voice of the LORD your God." These are the eternal principles by which
alone man can enjoy God's favor and blessing.

We see this in the Lord Jesus. He says: "If you keep My commandments, you will
abide in My love, just as I have kept My Father's commandments and abide in His
love" (John 15:10). He was in the love of the Father, but could not abide there otherwise than by obedience. And He says that this is equally for us the one way to abide in
His love: We must keep His commandments. He came to open for us the way back
to God, and this way was the way of obedience. Only he who through faith in Jesus

walks in this way shall come to God (Gen. 22:17–18; 26:4–5; 1 Sam. 15:22).

How gloriously is this connection between the obedience of Jesus and our own expressed in Hebrews 5: "He learned obedience. . .and. . .became the author of eternal salvation" (5:8–9). This is the bond of unity between Jesus and His people, the point of conformity and inward unanimity. He was obedient to the Father, and they, on the other hand, are obedient to Him. He and they are both obedient. His obedience not only atones for but drives out their disobedience. He and they bear one sign: obedience to God (Rom. 6:17; 2 Cor. 10:5; Phil. 2:8).

This obedience is a characteristic of the life of faith. It is called the obedience of faith (Acts. 6:7; Rom. 1:5; 16:26). There is nothing in earthly things that so spurs on men to work as faith. The belief that there is advantage or joy to be found is the secret of all work. "By faith Abraham obeyed when he was called" (Heb. 11:8). According to what I believe shall my works be. The faith that Jesus made me free from the power of sin for obedience and sets me in a suitable condition for it has a mighty power to make me obedient. Faith in the overflowing blessing that the Father gives to it, faith in the promises of the love and indwelling of God and of the fullness of the Spirit, which comes by this channel, strengthens for obedience (Deut. 28:1; Isa. 63:5; John 14:15, 21, 23; Acts 5:32).

> *He* came to open for us the way back to God, and this way was the way of obedience. Only he who through faith in Jesus walks in this way shall come to God.

The power of this faith, again, as also of obedience lies especially in interaction with the living God Himself. There is only one Hebrew word for "*obeying* voice" and "*hearing* voice," so to hear correctly prepares to obey. It is when I learn the will of God—not in the words of a man or a book, but from God Himself—when I hear the *voice* of God that I shall surely believe what is promised and do what is commanded. The Holy Spirit is the voice of God, and when we hear the living voice speak, obedience becomes easy (Gen. 12:1, 4; 31:13, 16; Matt. 14:28; Luke 5:5; John 10:4, 27). Oh, let us then wait in silence upon God and set our soul open before Him so that He may speak by His Spirit. When in our Bible-reading and praying we learn to wait more upon God, so that we can say, "My God has spoken this to me, has given me this promise, and has commanded this," then shall we also obey. "To listen to the voice" earnestly and diligently is the sure way to obedience.

With a servant, a warrior, a child, or a subject, obedience is indispensable, the first sign of integrity. And shall God, the living, glorious God, find no obedience with us (Mal. 1:6; Matt. 7:21)? No, let cheerful, timely, precise obedience from the beginning be the evidence of the genuineness of our fellowship with the Son whose obedience is our life.

THE NEW LIFE

O Father, who makes us Your children in Christ, You make us in Him obedient children, just as He was obedient. Let the Holy Spirit make the obedience of Jesus so glorious and powerful in us that obedience shall be the highest joy of our life. Teach us in everything only to seek to know what You desire and then to do it. Amen.

For Further Thought

What must you bring to God in order to live a life of obedience? For a life of obedience these things are required:

1. *Decisive surrender. I must no longer have to ask in every single case, "Shall I or shall I not, must I, can I, be obedient?" No, it must be such an unquestionable thing that I shall know of nothing else than to be obedient. He who cherishes such a heart attitude and thinks of obedience as a thing that stands firm shall find it easy, yes, shall literally taste in it great joy.*

2. *The knowledge of God's will through the Spirit. Please do not imagine that because you know the Bible in some way that you know the will of God. The knowledge of God's will is something spiritual. Let the Holy Spirit make known to you the knowledge of God's will.*

3. *The doing of all that we know to be right. All doing teaches men, and all doing of what is right teaches men obedience. All that the Word, conscience, or the Spirit tells you is right, so actually do it. It helps to form doing into a holy habit, and is an exercise leading to more power and more knowledge. Do what is right, Christian, out of obedience to God, and you shall be blessed.*

4. *Faith in the power of Christ. Be sure of this: You have the power to obey. Although you do not feel it, you have it in Christ your Lord by faith.*

5. *The glad assurance of the blessing of obedience. It unites us with our God, wins His good pleasure and love, strengthens our life, and brings the blessedness of heaven into our heart.*

45

THE WILL OF GOD

"Your will be done on earth as it is in heaven."
MATTHEW 6:10

THE glory of heaven, where the Father dwells, is that His will is done there. He who desires to taste the blessedness of heaven must know the Father who is there, and do His will, as it is done in heaven (see Dan. 4:35).

Heaven is an unending holy kingdom, of which the throne of God is the central point. Around this throne there are innumerable multitudes of pure, free beings, all ordered under powers and dominions. An indescribably rich and many-sided activity fills their life. All the highest and noblest that keeps man occupied is but a faint shadow of what finds place in this invisible world. All these beings possess each their free personal will. The will, however, has in self-conscious freedom, by its own choice, become one with the holy will of the holy Father, so that, in the midst of a diversity that flashes out in a million forms, only one will is accomplished—the will of God. All the rich, blessed movement of the inhabitants of heaven has its origin and its aim in the will of God.

And why is it then that His children on earth do not regard this will as their highest joy? Why is it that the petition, "Your will be done on earth as it is in heaven," is for the most part coupled with thoughts of the severe and trying elements in the will of God and of the impossibility of our always rejoicing in God's will? The cause is this: We do not take pains to know the will of God in its glory and beauty as the giving out of love, as the source of power and joy, or as the expression of the perfection of God. We think of God's will only in the law that He gave and that we cannot keep, or in the trials in which this will appears in conflict with our own. Let us no longer do this, but make the effort to understand that in the will of God, all His love and blessedness are understood and can be possessed by us (Gal. 1:4; Eph. 1:5, 9, 11; Heb. 10:10).

Hear what the Word says about the will of God and the glorious things that are destined for us in this will.

"And this is the will of Him who sent Me, that everyone who sees the Son and believes in Him may have everlasting life" (John 6:40). The will of God is the rescue of sinners by faith in Christ. He who surrenders himself to this glorious will to seek souls shall have the assurance that God will bless his work to others;

for he carries out God's will, even as Jesus did it (John 4:34; 5:30; 6:38).

"It is not the will of your Father who is in heaven that one of these little ones should perish" (Matt. 18:14). The will of God is the maintenance, the strengthening, and the keeping of the weakest of His children. What courage shall he have who unites himself lovingly with this will!

"For this is the will of God, your sanctification" (1 Thess. 4:3; also see 4:23, 29). With His whole heart, with all the power of His will, God is willing to make us holy. If we simply open our heart to believe that it is not the law, but the will of God—something that He certainly gives and does where we permit Him—then we shall rejoice over our sanctification as stable and sure.

"In everything give thanks; for this is the will of God in Christ Jesus for you" (1 Thess. 5:18). A joyful, thankful life is what God has destined for us, what He will work in us, and what He desires. That He certainly does in those who do not resist Him, but receive and allow His will to work in them.

> *L*et us make the effort to understand that in the will of God, all His love and blessedness are understood and can be possessed by us.

What we require then is to surrender our spirit to be filled with the thought that what God desires to have, He will certainly bring to pass when we do not resist Him. And if we further consider how glorious, good, and perfect the will of God is, shall we not then yield ourselves with the whole heart so that this will may bring itself to accomplishment in us (Rom. 12:2)?

To this end, let us believe that the will of God is His love. Let us see what blessings in the Word are connected with the doing of this will (Matt. 7:21; 12:50; John 7:17; 9:31; Eph. 5:17; 6:6; 1 John 2:17). Let us think of the glory of heaven as consisting in the doing of God's will, and make the choice that that our life on earth shall be. And let us with prayer and meditation allow ourselves to be led of the Spirit to know this will correctly (Rom. 12:2; Col. 1:9; 4:12; Heb. 10:36; 13:21).

When we have therefore learned to know the will of God on its glorious heavenly side in the Word and have done it, it will not be difficult for us also to bear this will where it appears to be contrary to our nature. We shall be so filled with the adoration of God and His will that we shall resolve to see, accept, and love this will in everything. And it will be the most glorious thought of our life that there is to be nothing—nothing—in which the will of God must not be known and honored (Ps. 42:9; Matt. 26:39; Heb. 10:7, 9).

O my Father, this was the glory of the Lord Jesus, that He did not His own will, but the will of His Father. This, His glory, I desire to have as mine. Father, open my eyes and my heart to know the perfection and the glory of Your will and the glory of a life in this will. Teach me to understand Your will correctly, then willingly and cheerfully to execute it; and where I have to bear it, to do this also with the adoration of a son. Amen.

FOR FURTHER THOUGHT

1. *How important is it to you to do God's will even during the "good times" and not just when you are enduring difficulty? To do the will of God from the heart in times of prosperity is the only way to bear this will from the heart in times of suffering.*

2. *How are you to learn the will of God? To do the will of God, I must know it spiritually. The light and the power of the Spirit go together: What He teaches to see as God's will, He certainly teaches all to do. Meditate much on Romans 12:2, and pray earnestly to see God's will correctly.*

3. *How can you do the perfect will of God, even when others are mistreating or opposing you? Learn always to adore the will of God in the least and the worst thing that man does to you. It is the will of God that His child should be proved this way. Say then always in the least as well as the greatest trials: "It is the will of God that I am in this difficulty." This brings the soul to rest and silence, and teaches it to honor God in the trial.*

4. *When God gave a will to man, He gave him a power to accept or reject the will of God. Child of God, open your will to receive the will of God with its full power and to be filled with it. This is heavenly glory and blessedness: to be conscious every day that my will is in harmony with God's will and that God's will lives in me. It is the will of God to accomplish this in you.*

46
SELF-DENIAL

Then Jesus said to His disciples,
"If anyone desires to come after Me, let him deny himself,
and take up his cross, and follow Me."
MATTHEW 16:24

SELF-DENIAL was an exercise of which the Lord Jesus often spoke. He mentioned it several times as an indispensable characteristic of every true disciple. He connects it with cross-bearing and losing life (Matt. 10:38–39; Luke 9:23; 14:27; John 12:24–25).

Our old life is so sinful—and remains to the end so sinful—that it is never in a condition for anything good. It must therefore be denied and put to death in order that the new life, the life of God, may have free dominion over us (Rom. 6:6; 8:13; Gal. 2:20; 5:24; 6:14; Col. 3:5). Let the young Christian resolve from the very beginning to deny himself wholly, in accordance with the injunction of his Lord. At the outset, it seems severe, but he will find that it is the source of inconceivable blessing.

Let self-denial reach our carnal understanding. It was when Peter had spoken according to the thought of the natural understanding that the Lord had to say to him: "You are not mindful of the things of God, but the things of men" (Matt. 16:23). You must deny yourselves and your own thoughts. We must be careful that the activity of our understanding with the Word and prayer, in endeavoring to reach the knowledge of what is God's will, does not deceive us with a service of God that is not in spirit and in truth. Deny your carnal understanding and bring it to silence, and in that holy silence give place to the Holy Spirit and let the voice of God be heard in your heart (Matt. 16:28; 1 Cor. 1:17, 27; 2:6; Col. 2:18).

Deny also your own will, with all its lusts and desires. Let it be once for all unquestionable that the will of God in everything is your choice, and that therefore every desire that does not fall in with this will must be put to death. I urge you, believe that in the will of God there is heavenly blessedness, and that therefore self-denial appears severe only at the beginning, but that when you exercise yourself heartily in it, it becomes a great joy. Let the body with all its life abide under the law of self-denial (Matt. 26:39; Rom. 6:13; 1 Cor. 9:25, 27).

Deny also your own honor. Don't seek it, but seek the honor of God. This brings such a rest into the soul. "How can you believe," says Jesus, "who receive honor from one another?" (John 5:44). Although your honor may be hurt or insulted, commit it to God to watch over it. Be content to be little, to be nothing. "Blessed are the poor in spirit, for theirs is the kingdom" (Matt. 5:3; also see John 5:44; 7:18; 8:50; 1 Thess. 2:6).

Deny, in the same way, your own power. Cherish the deep conviction that it is those who are weak, those who are nothing, whom God can use. Be very much afraid of your own endeavors in the service of God, however sincere they may be. Although you feel as if you had power, say before God that you don't, that your power is nothing. Continuous denial of your own power is the way to enjoy the power of God. It is in the heart that dies to its own power that the Holy Spirit decides to dwell and bring the power of God (2 Cor. 3:5; 12:9).

Deny especially your own interests. Don't live to please yourself, but to please your neighbor. He who seeks his own life shall lose it, and he who desires to live for himself shall not find life. But he who would really imitate Jesus and share in His joy, let him give his life as He did and let him sacrifice his own interests (Luke 9:24; Rom. 15:1, 3; 1 Cor. 10:23–24; Eph. 2:4).

> *L*et the young Christian resolve from the very beginning to deny himself wholly, in acordance with the injunction of his Lord.

Beloved Christian, at conversion you had to make a choice between your own self and Christ when it came to which you should obey. You then said: "Not I, but Christ." Now you are to confirm this choice every day. The more you do so, the more joyful and blessed it will be for you to renounce the sinful self, to cast aside unholy self-working, and to allow Jesus to be all. The way of self-denial is a way of deep heavenly blessedness.

There are very many Christians who observe nothing of this way. They want Jesus to make them free from punishment, but not to liberate them from themselves and from their own will. But the invitation to discipleship still always rings: "If anyone desires to come after Me, let him deny himself, and take up his cross, and follow Me."

The reason as well as the power for self-denial we find in the little word *Me*. "If anyone desires to come after *Me*, let him deny *himself*, and follow *Me*." The old life is in ourselves, but the new life is in Jesus, and the new life cannot rule without driving out the old. Where one's own self had everything to say, it must now be nothing. This it would happily not be: On this account there must be all the day denial of one's self, imitation of Jesus. He, with His teaching, His will, His honor, and His interests, must fill the heart. But he who has and knows Him willingly denies himself, for Christ is so precious to him that he sacrifices everything, even himself, to win Him (Gal. 2:20; Phil. 3:7–8). This is the true life of faith. Not according to what nature sees or thinks to be acceptable do I live, but according to what Jesus says and desires to have. Every day and every hour I confirm the wonderful bargain: "Not I, but Christ"—I nothing, Christ everything. "You died," and no longer have power, or will, or honor; "and your life is hidden with Christ in God" (Col. 3:3). Christ's power and will alone prevail. O soul, cheerfully deny that sinful wretched self, in order that the glorious Christ may dwell in you.

Precious Savior, teach me what self-denial is. Teach me to so distrust my heart that in nothing shall I yield to its thoughts or desires. Teach me to so know You that it will be impossible for me to do anything but to offer up myself to possess You and Your life. Amen.

For Further Thought

1. *How important is self-denial to knowing God and His truth? Of the denial of the natural understanding, Tersteegen says: "God and His truth are never known rightly, except by one who, by the dying of his carnal nature, his inclinations, passions, and will, is made very earnest and silent, and by the abandonment of the manifold deliberations of the understanding, has become very simple and childlike. We must give our heart and our will entirely to God, forsaking our own will in all things, releasing ourselves especially from the manifold imaginations and activities of the understanding, even in spiritual things, that it may collect itself silently in the heart and dwell as in the heart with God. Not in the head, but in the heart is found the living truth itself, the anointing that teaches us all things. In the heart is found the living fountain of light. Anyone who lives in a heart entertained with God will often with a glance of the eye discern more truth than another with the greatest exertion."*

2. *Read the above passage with care and you will find in it the reason why we have several times said that when you read or pray you must at every opportunity keep quiet for a little and set yourself in entire silence before God. This is necessary to bring the activity of the natural understanding to silence and to set the heart open before God so that He may speak there. In the heart is the temple where worship in spirit and truth takes place. Distrust, deny your understanding in spiritual things. The natural understanding is in the head, the spiritual understanding in the heart, the temple of God. Preserve in the temple of God a holy silence before His face—then He will speak.*

3. *The peculiar mark of Christian self-denial is inward cheerfulness and joy in the midst of hardship. The word of God makes unceasing joy a duty. This joyful disposition, which, originating from eternity, has all change and changeability underfoot, and will hold its ground not only in times of severe suffering, but also in the self-denial of every day and hour that is inseparable from the Christian life.*

4. *What all am I to deny? Deny yourself. How shall I know where and when to deny myself? Do so always and in everything. And if you do not rightly understand that answer, know that no one can give you the right explanation of it but Jesus Himself. To imitate Him, to be taught by Him, is the only way to self-denial. Only when Jesus comes in does self go out.*

47

DISCRETION

When wisdom enters your heart,
and knowledge is pleasant to your soul,
discretion will preserve you."
PROVERBS 2:10–11

My son. . .keep sound wisdom and discretion;
so they will be life to your soul.
PROVERBS 3:21–22

"You ought to be quiet and do nothing rashly."
ACTS 19:36

INDISCRETION is not merely the sin of the unconverted: among the people of God, it is often the cause of much evil and misery. We read of Moses: "They angered Him also at the waters of strife, so that it went ill with Moses on account of them; because they rebelled against His Spirit, so that he spoke rashly with his lips" (Ps. 106:32–33). So of Uzzah's touching the ark: "And God struck him there for his error [margin, 'rashness']" (2 Sam. 6:7; also see Prov. 12:18).

What discretion is and why it is so necessary may be easily explained. When an army marches into the province of an enemy, its safety depends on the guards who are set, who are to be always on the watch and who are to know and to give warning when the enemy approaches. Advance guards are sent out so that the territory and power of the enemy may be known. This prudence, which looks out beforehand and looks around, is indispensable.

The Christian lives in the province of the enemy. All that surrounds him may become a snare or an occasion for sin. Therefore his whole walk is to be carried out in a holy reserve and watchfulness, in order that he may do nothing carelessly. He watches and prays that he may not enter into temptation (Matt. 26:41; Luke 21:36; Eph. 6:18; 1 Pet. 4:7; 5:8). Prudence keeps guard over him (1 Sam. 18:14; Matt. 10:16; Luke 1:17; 16:8; Eph. 5:15; Titus 2:4).

Discretion keeps watch over the lips. Oh, what loss many a child of God suffers by the thought that if he only speaks nothing wrong, he may speak what he will. He does not know how, through much speaking, the soul becomes ensnared in the distractions of the world, because in the multitude of words there is not lacking transgression. Discretion endeavors not to speak, except for the glory of God and blessing to neighbors (Pss. 39:2; 141:3; Prov. 10:19; Eccles. 5:1–2).

Over the ear also discretion keeps guard. Through the gate of the ear comes to me all the news of the world and all the indiscreet speech of others that would infect me. Very hurtful for the soul is eagerness for news. One can afterwards no longer look into one's self, because one lives wholly in the world around him. Corinth was much more godless than Athens. But in Athens, where they "spent their time in nothing else but either to tell or to hear some new thing" (Acts 17:21), very few were converted. Take heed, says Jesus, what you hear (Prov. 2:2; 18:15; Mark 4:24).

On this account, discretion keeps watch over the society in which the Christian mingles. "A man who isolates himself seeks his own desire" (Prov. 18:1). The child of God doesn't have the freedom to yield himself to the society of the world so much and so long as he would; he must know the will of his Father (Ps. 1:1; 2 Cor. 6:14; 2 Thess. 3:14; 2 John 10–11).

Discretion keeps watch over all lawful occupations and possessions. It knows how gradually and sneakily the love of money, worldly-mindedness, and the secret power of the flesh obtain the upper hand, and that it can never assume it is free from this temptation (Matt. 13:22; Luke 21:34; 1 Tim. 6:9, 17).

> The Christian lives in the province of the enemy. Therefore his whole walk is to be carried out in a holy reserve and watchfulness, in order that he may do nothing carelessly.

And, above all, it keeps watch over the heart, because there are the issues of life; there is the fountain out of which everything springs (Prov. 4:23). Remembering the word, "He who trusts in his own heart is a fool" (Prov. 28:26), it walks in deep humility and works out salvation with fear and trembling (Prov. 3:21, 23; Jer. 31:33).

And from where does the soul have the power to be with a never-resting watchfulness on its guard against the thousand dangers that surround it on all sides? Is it not fatiguing, exhausting, or harassing to have to watch always this way and never to be at rest in the certainty that there is no danger? No, absolutely not! Discretion brings just the highest restfulness. It has its security and strength in its heavenly Keeper, who never slumbers or sleeps. In confidence in Him, under the inspiration of His Spirit, discretion does its work. The Christian walks as one who is wise, and the dignity of a holy prudence adorns him in all his actions. The rest of faith, the faith that Jesus watches and guards, binds to Him in love, and holy discretion springs, as if on its own, from a love that would not grieve or abandon Him and from a faith that has its strength for everything in Him.

Lord my God, guard me so that I may not be like one who is indiscreet in heart. Let the prudence of the righteous always characterize me, in order that in everything I may be kept from giving offense. Amen.

FOR FURTHER THOUGHT

1. *To one who took great care to have his horse and cart in thoroughly good order, it was once said: "Come, it is not necessary to be always taking so many pains with this." His answer was: "I have always found my prudence paid." How many a Christian needs this lesson! How many a young Christian may well pray for this—that his conversion may be, according to God's Word, "to the prudence of the righteous." What can you do to keep your life of faith in thoroughly good order?*
2. *Discretion has its root in self-knowledge. The deeper my knowledge of my powerlessness and the sinfulness of my flesh, the greater the need of watchfulness. It is therefore our element of true self-denial. How do you think God wants to enable you to know yourself in this way?*
3. *How does God teach us or impart to us discretion? Discretion has its power in faith. The Lord is our Keeper, and He does His keeping through the Spirit keeping us in mind. It is from Him that our discretion comes.*
4. *Its activity is not limited to ourselves, but it reaches out especially to our neighbor in the way of giving him no offense and in laying no stumbling-block in his way (Rom. 14:13; 1 Cor. 8:9–10:32; Phil. 1:10).*
5. *It finds great delight in silence, so as to commit its way to the Lord with composure and deliberation. It esteems highly the word of the town-clerk of Ephesus: "You ought to be quiet and do nothing rashly."*
6. *In great generals and their victories, we see that discretion is not timidity; it is consistent with the highest courage and the most joyful certitude of victory. Discretion watches against rashness, but enhances the courage of faith.*

48

MONEY

Money answers everything.
ECCLESIASTES 10:19

*"I had wholly dedicated the silver
from my hand to the LORD."*
JUDGES 17:3

*"So you ought to have deposited my money with the bankers,
and at my coming I would have received
back my own with interest."*
MATTHEW 25:27

IT is in his dealing with the world and its possessions that the Christian finds one of the opportunities in which he is to demonstrate his self-denial and the spirit of discretion (John 17:15–16; 1 Cor. 7:31). Since it is in money that all value or property on earth finds its expression, so it is especially in his dealing with money that he can show whether he is free from worldliness to deny himself and to serve his God. In order rightly to understand this, we must consider for a time what is said about money.

What is money the symbol of? It is the symbol of the work by which a man earns it—of his industry, zeal, and ability in that work, and of his success and the blessing of God on the work. It is also the symbol of all that I can do with money: the symbol of the work that others would do for me, of the power that I thereby have to accomplish what I desire, and of the influence that I exercise on those who are dependent on me for my money. It is the symbol of all the possessions or enjoyments that are to be obtained by money, a symbol of all upon earth that can make life desirable—yes, a symbol of life itself, which without the purchase of indispensable food cannot be supported.

Money is therefore, of earthly things, indeed one of the most desirable and fruitful. No wonder that it is so greatly esteemed by all.

What is the danger of money? What is the sin that is done with it, that the Bible and experience should so warn us to be prudent in dealing with it? There is the anxiousness that doesn't know if there will be sufficient money (Matt. 6:31). There is the covetousness that longs too much for it (1 John 2:16). There is the dishonesty that, without gross deception or theft, does not give to a neighbor what belongs to him (James 5:4). There is the lovelessness that would draw everything to one's self and does not care for another (Luke 16:21). There is love of money, which seeks after riches and lands in greed (1 Tim. 6:9–10, 17). There is robbery of God and the poor in withholding the share that belongs to them (Prov. 7:24, 26; Mal. 3:8).

What is the blessing of money? If the danger of sin is so great, would it not be better if there were no money? Is it not better to be without money? No, for even in the spiritual life, money may be a great blessing. It can be a blessing as an exercise in industry and activity (Prov. 13:4; 18:19), in care and economy, as an evidence of God's blessing upon our work (Prov. 10:4, 22), as an opportunity for showing that we can possess and lay it out for God without withholding it or cleaving to it so that we can demonstrate our compassion to the poor and our overflowing love for God's cause (Isa. 57:7–8, 10–11; 2 Cor. 8:14–15). It can be a blessing as a means of glorifying God by our charity and of spreading among men the gold of heavenly blessing (2 Cor. 9:12–13)—as a thing that, according to the assurance of Jesus, we can exchange for a treasure in heaven (Matt. 19:21; Luke 12:33).

> *It is in his dealing with the world and its possessions that the Christian finds one of the opportunities in which he is to demonstrate his self-denial and the spirit of discretion.*

And what is now the way to be freed from the danger and to be led into the right blessing of money?

Let God be Lord over your money. Receive all your money with thanksgiving, as coming from God in answer to the prayer: "Give us this day our daily bread" (Matt. 6:11; also see 1 Chron. 29:14).

Lay it all down before God as belonging to Him. Say with the woman: "I had wholly dedicated the silver from my hand to the LORD" (see 1 Tim. 4:4–5).

Let your dealing with your money be a part of your spiritual life. Receive, possess, and give out your money as one who has been bought at a high price, who has been redeemed, not with silver and gold, but with the precious blood (Luke 19:2).

Make what the Word of God says about money as an earthly good a special study. The word of the Father alone teaches how the child of the Father is to use blessing.

Reflect much on the fact that it is not given to you for yourself alone, but for you and your brethren together. The blessing of money is to do good to others and make them rejoice (Acts 20:35).

Remember especially that it can be given up to the Father and the service of His kingdom for the building up of His spiritual temple, for the extension of His influence. Every time of spiritual blessing mentioned in scripture was a time of cheerful giving for God's cause. Even the outpouring of the Holy Spirit made itself known in the giving of money for the Lord (Exod. 36:5; 1 Chron. 29:6, 9; Acts. 2:15; 4:34).

Christian, understand it: All the deepest deliberations of the heart and its most spiritual activities can demonstrate themselves in the way in which we deal with our money. Love for God and for our neighbor, victory over the world by faith, the hope of everlasting treasure, faithfulness as a steward, joy in God's service, cheerful self-denial, holy discretion, and the glorious freedom of the children of God can all be seen in the use of money. Money can be the means of the most glorious fellowship with God, and the full enjoyment of the blessedness of being able to honor and serve Him.

Lord God, make me rightly discern in what close connection my money stands with my spiritual life. Let the Holy Spirit lead and sanctify me, so that all my earning and receiving, and my keeping and dispensing of money, may always be well-pleasing to You and a blessing to my soul. Amen.

FOR FURTHER THOUGHT

1. *How do you think God wants you to properly use the money He has given you? John Wesley always said that there were three rules about the use of money, which he gave to men in business and by which he was sure that they would experience benefit:*
     - *Make as much money as you can. Be industrious and diligent.*
     - *Save as much money as you can. Be no spendthrift, but live frugally and prudently.*
     - *Give away as much money as you can. That is the divine destination of money, and it makes it an everlasting blessing for yourselves and others.*
2. *Acquaint yourself with the magnificent prayer of David in 1 Chronicles 29. Receive it into your soul. It teaches us the blessedness and the glorification of God that spring from cheerful giving. What does that passage teach you personally about your use of money?*
3. *What does how you use your money tell you about the condition of your life of faith and obedience?*

49

THE FREEDOM OF THE CHRISTIAN

And having been set free from sin, you became slaves
of righteousness. . . . But now having been set free
from sin. . .you have your fruit to holiness.
ROMANS 6:18, 22

But now we have been delivered from the law.
ROMANS 7:6

For the law of the Spirit of life in Christ Jesus
has made me free from the law of sin and death.
ROMANS 8:2

FREEDOM is counted in scripture as one of the greatest privileges of the child of God. There is nothing in history for which nations have made such great sacrifices as freedom. Slavery is the lowest condition into which man can sink, for in it he no longer makes his own decisions. Freedom is the deepest need of his nature.

To be free, then, is the condition in which anything can develop itself according to the law of its nature, that is, according to its disposition. Without freedom, nothing can attain its destiny or become what it ought to be. This is true alike of animal and man, of the physical and the spiritual.

It was for this cause that God in Israel chose the redemption out of the slavery of Egypt into the glorious liberty of God's people as the everlasting type of redemption out of the slavery of sin into the liberty of the children of God (Exod. 1:14; 4:23; 6:5; 20:2; Deut. 24:8). On this account, Jesus said on earth: "If the Son makes you free, you shall be free indeed" (John 8:36). And the holy scriptures teach us to stand firmly in the freedom with which Christ made us free. A right insight into this freedom opens up to us one of the greatest glories of the life that the grace of God has prepared for us (John 8:32, 36; Gal. 4:21, 31; 5:1).

In the three passages from the Epistle to the Romans in which sanctification is dealt with, a threefold freedom is spoken of. There is freedom from sin in the sixth chapter, freedom from the law in the seventh, and freedom from the law of sin in the eighth.

There is freedom from sin (Rom. 6:7, 18, 22). Sin is represented as a power that rules over man, under which he is brought and taken captive, and which controls him as a slave to evil (John 8:34; Rom. 7:14, 23; 2 Pet. 2:19). By the death of Christ and in Christ of the believer, who is one with Him, he is made entirely free from the dominion of sin, and it has no more power over him. If, then, he still sins, it is because he, not knowing his freedom by faith, permits sin still to rule over him. But if by faith he fully accepts what the Word of God here confirms, then sin has no power over him. He overcomes it by the faith that he is made free from it (Rom. 5:21; 6:12, 14).

Then there is freedom from the law. This leads us deeper into the life of grace than freedom from sin. According to scripture, law and sin always go together. "The strength of sin is the law" (1 Cor. 15:56): The law does nothing but make the offense greater (Rom. 4:15; 5:13, 20; 7:13). The law is the indication of our sinfulness and cannot help us against sin, but with its demand for perfect obedience gives us over as hopeless to the power of sin. The Christian who does not discern that he is made free from the law will still always abide under sin (Rom. 6:15; 7:5). Christ and the law cannot rule over us together. In every endeavor to fulfill the law as believers, we are taken captive by sin (Rom. 7:5, 23). The Christian must know that he is entirely free from the law, from the *"you must"* that stands outside us and over us. Then, for the first time, he will know what it is to be free from sin.

> *he holy scriptures teach us to stand firmly in the freedom with which Christ made us free. A right insight into this freedom opens up to us one of the greatest glories of the life that the grace of God has prepared for us.*

Then there is also freedom from the law of sin—actual liberation from the power of sin in our bodies. What we have in Christ, namely freedom from sin and from the law, is inwardly appropriated for us by the Spirit of God: "The law of the Spirit of life in Christ Jesus has made me free from the law of sin and death" (Rom. 8:2). The Holy Spirit in us takes the place of the law over us: "But if you are led by the Spirit, you are not under the law" (Gal. 5:18). Freeing from the law is not anything external but takes place according to the measure that the Spirit obtains dominion in us and leads us: "Where the Spirit of the Lord is, there is liberty" (2 Cor. 3:17). According as the law of the Spirit rules in us, we are made free from the law, from the law of sin. We are then free to do what we, as God's children, would rather do, free to serve God.

Free expresses a condition in which nothing hinders me from being what I want to be and ought to be. In other words, *free* is to be able to do what I desire. The power of sin over us, the power of the law against us, and the power of the law of sin in us hinder us. But he who stands in the freedom of the Holy Spirit, he who is then truly free—nothing can prevent or hinder him from being what he wants to be and ought to be. Just as it is the nature of a tree to grow upward as it is free from all hindrances, so a child of God then grows to what he ought to be and shall be. And according as the Holy Spirit leads him into this freedom, there springs up the joyful consciousness of his strength for the life of faith. He joyfully shouts: "I can do all things through Christ who strengthens me" (Phil. 4:13). "Thanks be to God who always leads us in triumph in Christ" (2 Cor. 2:14).

Son of God, anointed with the Spirit to announce freedom to the captives, make me also truly free. Let the Spirit of life in You, my Lord, make me free from the law of sin and of death. I am Your ransomed one. Oh, let me live as Your freed one who is hindered by nothing from serving You. Amen.

For Further Thought

1. *What does freedom in Christ truly mean? The freedom of the Christian extends over his whole life. He is free in relation to the institutions and teachings of men. "You were bought at a price; do not become slaves of men." (1 Cor. 7:23; also see Col. 2:20). He is free in relation to the world, and in the use of what God gives. He has power to possess it or to use it, to enjoy it or to sacrifice it (1 Cor. 8:8; 9:4–5).*

2. *What does this freedom in Christ give you? What doesn't it give you? This freedom is no lawlessness. We are free from sin and the law to serve God in the Spirit. We are not under the law, but give ourselves, with free choice and in love, to Him who loved us (Rom. 6:18; Gal. 5:13; 1 Pet. 2:16). Not under the law, also not without law; but in the law; a new, a higher law, "the law of the Spirit of life," "the law of liberty," the law written in our hearts, is our rule and measure (1 Cor. 9:21; James 1:15; 2:12). In this last passage the translation ought to be: "bound by a law to Christ."*

3. *How can you walk in this freedom, and how can you make yourself even freer in Christ? This freedom has its continuation from the Word and also in it: The more the Word abides in me and the truth lives in me, the freer I become (John 8:31–32, 36).*

4. *Freedom manifests itself in love. I am free from the law, from men, and from institutions to be able now like Christ to surrender myself for others (Rom. 14:13, 21; Gal. 5:13; 6:1).*

5. *This glorious liberty to serve God and our neighbor in love is a spiritual thing. We cannot by any means seize it and draw it to us. It becomes known only by a life in the Holy Spirit. "Where the Spirit of the Lord is, there is liberty." "If you are led by the Spirit, you are not under the law." It is the Holy Spirit who makes free. Let us allow ourselves to be introduced by Him into the effectual glorious liberty of the children of God. "The Spirit of life in Christ Jesus has made me free from the law of sin and death."*

50

GROWTH

*"The kingdom of God is as if a man should scatter seed on the ground,
and should sleep by night and rise by day, and the seed should sprout
and grow, he himself does not know how. For the earth
yields crops by itself: first the blade, then the head,
after that the full grain in the head."*
MARK 4:26–28

*The Head, from whom all the body,
nourished and knit together by joints and ligaments,
grows with the increase that is from God.*
COLOSSIANS 2:19

*Speaking the truth in love, may [we] grow up in all things into
Him who is the head—Christ—from whom the whole body, joined
and knit together by what every joint supplies, according to the
effective working by which every part does its share,
causes growth of the body.*
EPHESIANS 4:15–16

DEATH is always a standing still, but life is always movement and progressiveness. Increase or growth is the law of all created life. Consequently, the new life in man is destined to increase, and always by becoming stronger. Just as there are in the seed and in the earth a life and power of growth by which the plant is impelled to have its full height and fruit, so is there in the seed of the eternal life an impelling force by which also that life always increases and grows with a divine growth, until we come to be a perfect man, to the measure of the stature of the fullness of Christ (Eph. 4:12; 2 Thess. 1:4).

In this parable of the seed that springs up by itself and becomes great and bears fruit, the Lord teaches us two of the most important lessons on the increase of the spiritual life. The one is that of its *self-sufficiency*, the other that of its *gradualness*.

The first lesson is for those who ask what they are to do in order to grow and advance more in grace. As the Lord said of the body, "Which of you by worrying can add one cubit to his stature?...Consider the lilies of the field, how they grow" (Matt. 6:27–28), so He says to us here that we can do nothing, and need to do nothing, to make the spiritual life grow (Hos. 14:16; Matt. 6:25, 27, 30). Do you not see how, while man slept, the seed sprang up and became high, though he didn't know how, and how the earth brought forth fruit by itself? When man has once sowed, he must believe that God cares for the growth. Man doesn't need to care for it but must trust and rest.

And must man then do nothing? He can do nothing, because it is from within that the power of life must come—from the life, from the Spirit implanted in him. To the growth itself he can contribute nothing. It shall be given him to grow (Ps. 92:14; Gal. 2:20; Col. 3:3).

All he can do is to let the life grow. All that can hinder the life he must take away and keep away. If there are thorns and thistles that take away place and power in the soil that the plant should have, he can take them away (Jer. 4:13, Matt. 13:22–23). The plant must have its place in the earth alone and undivided. For this the farmer can care, and then it grows further *of itself.* So must the Christian take away what can hinder the growth of the new life—to surrender the heart entire and undivided for the new life, to hold it alone in possession and to fill it, so that it may grow free and unhindered (Song of Sol. 2:15; Heb. 12:1).

> *When* man has once sowed, he must believe that God cares for the growth. Man doesn't need to care for it but must trust and rest.

The farmer can also bring forward what the plant requires in the way of food or drink; he can fertilize or moisten the soil as it is needed. So must the believer see to it that for the new life there is brought forward nourishment out of the word and the living water of the Spirit by prayer. It is in Christ that the new life is planted. From Him it increases with divine increase. So abide rooted in Him by the exercise of faith, and the life will grow by itself (John 15:4–5; Col. 2:6–7). Give it what it must have and take away what can hinder it. When you do that, the life will grow and increase by itself.

Then comes in the second lesson of the parable, the gradualness of the growth: "first the blade, then the head, after that the full grain in the head." Do not expect everything at once. Give God time. By faith and endurance we inherit the promises: the faith that knows that it has everything in Christ, and the endurance that expects everything in its time according to the rule and the order of the divine government. Give God time. Give the new life time. It is by continued abiding in the earth that the plant grows. Likewise, it is by continuous standing in grace, in Christ Himself, in whom God has planted us, that the new life grows (Heb. 3:13; 6:12, 15; James 5:7).

Yes, give the new life only sufficient time: time in prayer, time in fellowship with God, time in the continuous exercise of faith, and time in persistent separation from the world. Give it time. Slow but sure, hidden but real, in apparent weakness but with heavenly power, is the divine growth with which the life of God in the soul grows up to the perfect man in Christ.

Lord God, graciously strengthen the faith of Your children that their growth and progress are in Your hands. Enable them to see what a precious, powerful life was implanted in them by You—a life that increases with a divine increase. Enable them by faith and patience to inherit the promises. And teach them in that faith to take away all that can hinder the new life and to bring forward all that can further it, so that You may make Your work in them glorious. Amen.

FOR FURTHER THOUGHT

1. *What is the key for growth in the Christian life? For a plant, the principal thing is the soil in which it stands and out of which it draws its strength. For the Christian, this also is the principal thing: He is in Christ. Christ is all. He must grow up in Him, for out of Him the body obtains its growth. To abide in Christ by faith—that is the main thing.*

2. *Remember that faith must set itself toward a silent restfulness, that growth is just like that of the lilies in God's hands, and that He will see to it that we increase and grow strong.*

3. *What benefit do you receive from firm and joyful faith? Through it, you become "strengthened with all might, according to His glorious power, for all patience and longsuffering with joy" (Col. 1:11).*

4. *This faith in the fact that God cares for our growth takes away all anxiety and gives courage for doing the two things that we have to do: the taking away of what may be obstructive to the new life, and the bringing forward of what may be serviceable to it.*

5. *Observe well the distinction between planting and growing. Planting is the work of a moment; in a moment the earth receives the seed, and after that comes the slow growth. Without delay—immediately must the sinner receive the Word. Before conversion there is no delay. Then with time follows the growth of the seed.*

6. *The main thing is Christ: From Him and in Him is our growth. He is the soil that of itself brings forth fruit, though we don't understand how. Hold daily communication with Him.*

51

SEARCHING THE SCRIPTURES

Oh, how I love Your law!
It is my meditation all the day.
PSALM 119:97

"You search the Scriptures,
for in them you think you have eternal life;
and these are they which testify of Me."
JOHN 5:39

But the word which they heard did not profit them,
not being mixed with faith in those who heard it.
HEBREWS 4:2

AT the beginning of this book there is more than one passage on the use of God's Word in the life of grace. Before I leave my readers, I would like once again to come back to this all-important point. I cannot too earnestly and urgently address this call to my beloved young brothers and sisters: Upon your use of the Word of God your spiritual life in great measure depends. Man lives by the word that proceeds from the mouth of God (see Matt. 4:4). Therefore seek with your whole heart to learn how to use God's Word rightly. For that purpose, receive the following hints.

Read the Word *more with the heart than with the understanding*. With the understanding I will know and comprehend, but with the heart I desire, love, and hold firmly. Let the understanding be the servant of the heart. Be very aware of the understanding of the carnal nature that cannot receive spiritual things (1 Cor. 1:12, 27; 2:6, 12; Col. 2:18). Deny your understanding, and wait in humility on the Spirit of God. On every occasion, still keep silent during your reading of the Word, and say to yourselves: "This word I now receive in my heart, to love and to let it live in me" (see Ps. 119:10–11, 47; Rom. 10:8; James 1:21).

Read the Word always *in fellowship with the living God*. The power of a word depends on my conviction regarding the man from whom it comes. First set yourself in loving fellowship with the living God under the impression of His nearness and love. Deal with the Word under the full conviction that He, the eternal God, is speaking with you. And let the heart be silent to listen to God, to God Himself (Gen. 17:3; 1 Sam. 3:9–10; Isa. 50:4; 52:6; Jer. 1:2). Then the Word certainly becomes to you a great blessing.

Read the Word *as a living word in which the Spirit of God dwells and that certainly works in those who believe.* The Word is seed. Seed has life and grows and yields fruit of itself. The Word has life, and of itself grows and yields fruit (Mark 4:27–28; John 6:63; 1 Thess. 2:13; 1 Pet. 1:23). If you do not wholly understand it, if you do not feel its power, carry it in your heart. Ponder it and meditate on it, for it will by itself begin to yield a working and growth in you (Ps. 119:15, 40, 48, 69; 2 Tim. 3:16–17). The Spirit of God is with and in the Word.

Read it *with the resolve to be not only a hearer, but a doer of the Word.* Let the great question be: "What does God now want for me with this word?" If the answer is: "He desires to have me believe it and rely on Him to fulfill it," do this immediately from the heart. If the word is a command for what you are to do, yield yourself immediately to doing it (Matt. 5:19–20; 7:21, 24; Luke 11:28; James 1:21, 25). There is an unspeakable blessedness in the doing of God's Word and in the surrender of myself to be and to act just as the Word says and would have it. Be not hearers, but doers of the Word.

> *I* cannot too earnestly and urgently address this call to my beloved young brothers and sisters: Upon your use of the Word of God your spiritual life in great measure depends.

Read the Word *with time.* I see more and more that one obtains nothing on earth without time. Give the Word time. Give the Word time every time you sit down to read it to come into your heart. Give it time in the persistence with which you cleave to it from day to day and month after month (Deut. 6:5; Pss. 1:2; 119:97; Jer. 15:16). By perseverance you become exercised and more accustomed to the Word, and then the Word begins to work. And do not be disheartened when you do not understand the Word. Hold on; take courage and give the Word time, and later on the Word will explain itself. David had to meditate day and night to understand it.

Read the Word *with a searching of the scriptures.* The best explanation of the Bible is the Bible itself. Take three or four texts covering a point; then set them close to one another and compare them. See where they agree and where they differ; where they say the same thing or again something else. Let the Word of God at the same time be cleared up and confirmed by what He said at another time on the same subject. This is the safest and the best explanation.

Even the sacred writers used this method of instruction with the scriptures:

"and again" (Isa. 34:16; John 19:37; Acts 17:11; Heb. 2:13). Do not complain that this method takes too much time and effort. It is worthy of the efforts, and your efforts will be rewarded. On earth you have nothing without effort (Prov. 2:4–5; 3:13, 18; Matt. 13:44). Even the bread of life we have to eat by the sweat of our face. He who wants to go to heaven never goes without taking efforts. Search the scriptures: It will be richly rewarding to you.

Young Christian, let one of my last and most earnest words to you be this: On your dealing with the Word of God depends your growth, your power, your life. Love God's Word then. See it as sweeter than honey, better than thousands in gold or silver. In the Word, God can and will reveal His heart to you. In the Word, Jesus will communicate Himself and all His grace. In the Word, the Holy Spirit will come in to you to renew your heart and all your thoughts according to the mind and will of God. Don't read just enough of the Word to keep you from backsliding, but make it one of your chief occupations on earth to yield yourself so that God may fill you with His Word and that He may fulfill His Word in you.

Lord God, what grace it is that You speak to us in Your Word that we in Your Word have access to Your heart, to Your will, and to Your love. Forgive us our sins against Your precious Word. And, Lord, let the new life become so strong by the Spirit in us that all its desire shall be to abide in Your Word. Amen.

For Further Thought

Psalm 119. In the middle of the Bible stands this psalm, in which the praise and the love of God's Word are so strikingly expressed. It is not enough for us to read through the divisions of this psalm successively. We must take its principal points, and one with another seek what is said in different passages on each of them. Let us, for example, take the following points, observing the indications of the answers, and seek in this way to come under the full impression of what is taught us of the glory of God's Word:

1. *The blessing that the Word gives. Verses 1, 2, 6, 9, 11, 14, 24, 45, 46, 47, and so on.*
2. *The terms that in this psalm are given to God's Word.*
3. *How we have to handle the Word. (Observe—walk—keep—mark—and so on.)*
4. *Prayer for divine teaching. Verses 5, 10, 12, 18, 19, 26.*
5. *Surrender to obedience to the Word. Verses 93, 105, 106, 112, 128, 133.*
6. *God's Word the basis of our prayer. Verses 41, 49, 58, 76, 107, 116, 170.*
7. *Observance as the ground of confidence in prayer. Verses 77, 159, 176.*
8. *Observance as promised upon the hearing of prayer. Verses 8, 17, 33, 34, 44.*
9. *The power to observe the Word. Verses 32, 36, 41, 42, 117, 135, 146.*
10. *The praise of God's Word. Verses 54, 72, 97, 129, 130, 144.*
11. *The confident confession of obedience. Verses 102, 110, 121, 168.*
12. *Personal fellowship with God, seen in the use of You and I, Yours and Mine.*

I have merely mentioned a few points and a few verses. Seek out more and mark them, until your mind is filled with the thoughts about the Word, which the Spirit of God desires to give you.

Read with great thoughtfulness the words of that man of faith, George Müller. He says: "The power of our spiritual life will be according to the measure of the room that the word of God takes up in our life and in our thoughts. After an experience of fifty-four years, I can solemnly declare this. For three years after my conversion I used the word little. Since that time I searched it with diligence, and the blessing was wonderful. From that time, I have read the Bible through a hundred times in order, and at every time with increasing joy. Whenever I start freshly with it, it appears to me as a new book. I cannot express how great the blessing is of faithful, daily, regular searching of the Bible. The day is lost for me, on which I have used no rounded time for enjoying the word of God.

"Friends sometimes say: 'I have so much to do that I can find no time for regular Bible study.' I believe that there are few who have to work harder than I have. Yet it remains a rule with me never to begin my work until I have had real sweet fellowship with God. After that, I give myself heartily to the business of the day, that is, to God's work, with only intervals of some minutes of prayer." (See also the very remarkable words of his quoted in The School of Prayer.)

52

THE LORD THE PERFECTER

I will cry out to God Most High,
to God who performs all things for me.
PSALM 57:2

The LORD will perfect that which concerns me.
PSALM 138:8

Being confident of this very thing,
that He who has begun a good work in you
will complete it until the day of Jesus Christ.
PHILIPPIANS 1:6

For of Him and through Him and to Him
are all things, to whom be glory forever.
ROMANS 11:36

WE read that David was once disheartened by unbelief, and said: "I shall perish someday by the hand of Saul" (1 Sam. 27:1). So even the Christian may indeed fear that he shall one day perish. This is because he looks at himself and what is in him and does not set his trust wholly on God. It is because he does not yet know God as the Perfecter. He does not yet know what is meant by His name being "the Alpha and the Omega, the Beginning and the End, the First and the Last" (Rev. 22:13). If I really believe in God as the beginning out of whom all is, then must I also trust Him as the continuation by whom, as also the End to whom, all is.

God is the beginning: "He who began a good work in you." "You did not choose Me, but I chose you" (John 15:16). It is God's free choice, from before the foundation of the world, we have to thank that we became believers and have the new life (Rom. 8:29–30; Eph. 1:4, 11). Those who are still unconverted have nothing to do with this election. For them there is the offer of grace and the summons to surrender. Outside, over the door of the Father, stands the superscription: "The one who comes to Me I will by no means cast out." This everyone can see and understand. No sooner are they inside the door than they see and understand the

other superscription: "All that the Father gives Me will come to Me" (John 6:37).
Then they can discern how all things are of God: first obedience to the command
of God, then insight into the counsel of God.

But then it is of great importance to hold firmly this truth: He has begun the
good work. Then shall every thought of God strengthen the confidence that He will
also perfect it. His faithfulness, His love, and His power are all pledged that He will
perfect the good work that He began. Now read how God has taken more than one
oath regarding His unchangeable faithfulness, and then your soul will rest in it and
find courage (Gen. 28:15; Ps. 89:29, 34–36; Isa. 54:9–10; Jer. 33:25–26).

> *There is no part of your destiny as a child of God—even
> in things of which you have as yet not the least thought—
> that the Father will not continue and complete His work in it.*

And how shall He finish His work? What has its origin *from* Him is sustained
by Him and shall one day be brought *to* Him and His glory. There is nothing in
your life, temporal or spiritual, for which the Father will not care, because it has
influence upon you for eternity (Matt. 6:25, 34; 1 Pet. 5:7). There is no moment
of day or night in which the silent growth of your soul is not to go forward. The
Father will take care of this, if you believe. There is no part of your destiny as a child
of God—even in things of which you have as yet not the least thought—that the
Father will not continue and complete His work in it (Isa. 27:2–3; 51:12–13). Yet
upon one condition. You must trust Him for this. You must in faith allow Him to
work. You must trustfully say: "The LORD will perfect that which concerns me" (Ps.
138:8). You must trustfully pray: "I will cry out to God...who performs *all things*
for me" (Ps. 57:2). Christian, please let your soul become full of the thought that the
whole care for the continuation and the perfecting of God's work in me is in His
hands (Heb. 10:35; 13:5–6, 20–21; 1 Pet 5:10).

And how glorious shall the perfecting be! In our spiritual life, God is prepared
to exhibit His power in making us partakers of His holiness and the image of His
Son. He will make us fit and put us in a condition for all the blessed work in His
kingdom that He would have from us. Our body He will make like to the glorious
body of His Son. We may wait for the coming of the Son Himself from heaven to
take His own to Him. He will unite us in one body with all His chosen and will
receive us and make us dwell forever in His glory. How can we think that God will
not perfect His work? He will surely do it. He will gloriously do it for everyone
who trusts Him for it.

Child of God, say in deep assurance of faith, "The Lord will perfect that which
concerns me." In every need say continually with great boldness, "I will
cry out to God, who performs all things for me." And let the song of your life be

the joyful doxology: "For of Him and through Him and to Him are all things, to whom be glory forever." Amen.

Lord God, who will perfect that which concerns me, teach me to know You and to trust You. And let every thought of the new life go hand in hand with the joyful assurance: He who began a work in me will perfect it. Amen.

FOR FURTHER THOUGHT

1. *"He who endures to the end shall be saved" (Mark 13:13). It brings but little profit to begin well. We must hold the beginning of our hope firmly until the end (Matt. 10:27; 24:13; Heb. 3:14, 16; 11:12).*

2. *The perseverance of the saints—in holiness—is one of the characteristic articles of doctrine of the Reformed Church. The grace of regeneration is inadmissible.*

3. *How do we explain the falling away of some believers? They were only temporary believers, partakers only of the workings of the Spirit (Heb. 6:4).*

4. *How do I know whether I am partaker of the true new birth? "For as many as are led by the Spirit of God, these are sons of God" (Rom. 8:14). The faith that God has given me is matured and confirmed by works, by a walk under the leading of the Spirit.*

5. *How can anyone know for certain that he will persevere to the end? By faith in God the Perfecter. We may take the almighty God as our Keeper. He who gives himself in sincerity to Him and trusts wholly in Him to perfect His work obtains a divine certainty that the Lord has Him and will hold him firmly until the end. Child of God, live in fellowship with your Father. Live the life of faith in your Jesus with an undivided heart, and all fear of falling away shall be taken away from you. The living sealing of the Holy Spirit shall be your assurance of perseverance until the end.*

THE FULL BLESSING OF PENTECOST

CONTENTS

"He who believes in Me. . .out of his heart
will flow rivers of living water."
John 7:38

PREFACE

THE Dutch Reformed Church of South Africa has, during the past forty years, been in the habit of observing the ten days between Ascension and Whitsunday as days of prayer. The custom had its origin during the revival that passed over this country between 1860 and 1863 in the suggestion of the minister of a parish that at that time had received special blessing. The observance has in many cases been accompanied with blessing. The opportunity it gives for training Christians in the knowledge of what God's Word teaches concerning the Spirit, to the practice and the faith to which it calls, to prayer and fellowship and special efforts in behalf of the careless, has often been of the greatest value. Each year subjects for meditation and discourse have been published.

It was when I was about to proceed to England in 1895 that I was led to write and publish a little book with the title *The Full Pentecostal Blessing*. I never had any thoughts of translating it into English, as about that time there had been various books published on the subject. A request has lately come to me from Holland urging that it should appear in English, too, specially for the sake of some English friends with whom those in Holland had been in close communication. Though I was in doubt about the need, I gladly gave my consent.

I venture just one remark. In all our study of the work of the blessed Spirit, and in all our pursuit of a life in His fullness, we shall always find the sum of Christ's teaching in those wonderful words: "He who believes in Me, as the scripture has said, out of his heart will flow rivers of living water" (John 7:38). It is as we are convicted of the defectiveness of our faith in Christ and what He has promised to do in saving and keeping us from sin, and as we understand that believing in Him means a yielding up of the whole heart and life and will to let Him rule and live within us, that we can confidently count on receiving all that we need of the Holy Spirit's power and presence. It is as Christ becomes to us all that God has made Him to be that the Holy Spirit can flow from Him and do His blessed work of leading us back to know Him better and to believe in Him more completely.

My attention has lately again been directed by a brother to the Epistle to the Hebrews and to the way it speaks of Christ in His heavenly glory and power as the object of our faith. In my book *The Holiest of All*, I have tried to point out (see chaps. 65–70 and elsewhere) how the Holy Spirit reveals the way into the Holiest as opened by the blood of Christ and invites us by faith in Christ to have our life there.

It is as we yield our hearts to the leading of the Spirit to know Christ and look at Him, and believe in what is revealed, that the Spirit can take possession of us. The Spirit is given to reveal Christ, and every revelation of Christ fully accepted gives the Spirit room to dwell and work within us. This is the sure way in which the promise will be fulfilled: "He who believes in Me...out of his heart will flow rivers of living water" (John 7:38). May God lead us to this simple and full faith in Christ, our great High Priest and King in the heavens, and so into a life in the fullness of the Spirit.

ANDREW MURRAY
Wellington, South Africa

INTRODUCTION

THE message that this little book brings is simple but most solemn. It is to the effect that the one thing needed for the Church, and the thing that, above all others, men ought everywhere to seek for with one accord and with their whole heart is to be filled with the Spirit of God.

In order to secure attention to this message and attract the hearts of my readers to the blessing of which it speaks, I have laid particular emphasis on certain main points. These I briefly state here: (1) *It is the will of God that every one of His children should live entirely and unceasingly under the control of the Holy Spirit.* (2) *Without being filled with the Spirit, it is utterly impossible that an individual Christian or a church can ever live or work as God desires.* (3) *Everywhere and in everything we see the proofs, in the life and experience of Christians, that this blessing is but little enjoyed in the Church and, sadly, is but little sought for.* (4) *This blessing is prepared for us, and God waits to bestow it. Our faith may expect it with the greatest confidence.* (5) *The great hindrance in the way is that the self-life, and the world, which it uses for its own service and pleasure, usurp the place that Christ ought to occupy.* (6) *We cannot be filled with the Spirit until we are prepared to yield ourselves to be led by the Lord Jesus to forsake and sacrifice everything for this pearl of great price.*

I feel very deeply the imperfection that attaches to this little volume. Yet I am not without the hope that the Lord will make it a blessing to His people. We have such a feeble conception of the unspiritual and sinful state that prevails in the Church that unless we take time to devote our heart and our thoughts to the real facts of the case, the promise of God can make no deep impression upon us. I hope that the attempt I have made to exhibit the subject in various aspects will help to prepare the way for the conviction that this blessing is in truth the one thing needed, and that to get possession of this one thing we ought to bid farewell to everything else we hold dear.

I frankly invite Christian disciples into whose hands the book may fall to peruse it carefully more than once. Owing to the prevailing lack of the presence and operation of the Spirit, it takes a long time before these spiritual truths concerning the need, the fullness, and the reality of the Spirit's power can obtain entire mastery over us. It is only by the exercise of self-sacrifice and persistence in keeping our minds occupied with these thoughts that we can ever obtain what might otherwise come to us at once.

On reviewing what I have written, I am inclined to think that there is one point on which I ought to have spoken more definitely. I refer to the place that persevering prayer must occupy in connection with this blessing. This little book was not exclusively written for prayer at the season of Pentecost. Every day ought to be a Pentecostal season in the Church of Christ. For just as little as man can remain in sound health without the fresh air of heaven can Christians or the Church live according to the will of God without this blessing. The book is designed to point to what must prevail throughout all the year, and it seems to me now that, perhaps under the impression that in the season of Pentecost prayer for the blessing is practically unanimous, I have not strongly enough exhorted my readers to ceaseless calling on God in the confidence that He will answer. Let me call attention again to this point in a few sentences.

When we read the book of the Acts, we see that the filling with the Spirit and His mighty operation was always obtained by prayer. Recall, for example, what took place at Antioch. It was when the Christians there were engaged in fasting and prayer that God regarded them as prepared to receive the revelation that they must separate Barnabas and Saul; and it was only after they had once more fasted and prayed that these two men went forth, sent by the Holy Spirit (Acts 13:2–3). These servants of God felt that the benefit they needed must come only from above. To obtain the blessing we much need, from heaven and out of the hands of the living God Himself, we in like manner, even with fasting, must liberate ourselves as far as possible from the demands of the earthly life, even in that which otherwise appears quite lawful, and no less must we take ourselves wholly to God in prayer.

Let us therefore never become weary or discouraged, but in union with God's own elect, who call upon Him day and night, plead with Him and even weary Him by our incessant requests that the Holy Spirit may again assume His rightful place and exercise full dominion in ourselves and the Church as a whole—yes, more, that He may again have His true place in the Church, be held in honor by all, and in everything reveal the glory of our Lord Jesus. To the soul that in sincerity prays according to His Word, God's answer will surely come.

There is nothing so fitted to search and to cleanse the heart as true prayer. It teaches one to put to himself such questions as these: Do I really desire what above everything I pray for? Am I willing to cast out everything to make room for what God is prepared to give me? Is the prayer of my lips really the prayer of my life? Do I really continue in communication with God, waiting upon Him in quiet trust until He gives me this great, heavenly, supernatural gift, His own Spirit, to be my spirit, the spirit of my life every hour?

Oh, let us "pray always and not lose heart" (see Luke 18:1), setting ourselves before God with supplications and strong crying as His priests and the representatives of His Church. We may rely upon it that He will hear us.

> In my distress I called upon the LORD, and cried out to my God;
> He heard my voice from His temple, and my cry came before Him,
> even to His ears.... He delivered me from my strong enemy....
> He also brought me out into a broad place.
> PSALM 18:6, 17, 19

Brother, you know that the Lord is a God who often hides Himself. He desires to be trusted. He is oftentimes very near to us without our knowing it. He is a God who knows His own time. Yet "though He tarries, wait for Him; because He will surely come, He will not tarry" (see Hab. 2:3).

1

How It Is to Be Taught

And it happened. . .that Paul. . .came to Ephesus.
And finding some disciples he said to them, "Did you receive
the Holy Spirit when you believed?"
Acts 19:1–2

IT was about twenty years after the outpouring of the Holy Spirit that the incident that is referred to in the beginning of this chapter of Acts took place. In the course of his journey, Paul came to Ephesus and found in the Christian church there something lacking in their belief or experience. Accordingly, he put to them the question, "Did you receive the Holy Spirit when you believed?" Their reply was that they had not yet heard of the Holy Spirit. They had been baptized by disciples of John the Baptist with the baptism of repentance with a view to faith in Jesus as One who was to come, but with the great event of the outpouring of the Spirit or the significance of it they were still unacquainted. They came from a region of the country into which the full Pentecostal preaching of the exalted Savior had not yet penetrated.

Accordingly, Paul took them at once under his care and made them conversant with the full gospel of the glorified Lord, who had received the Spirit from the Father and had sent Him down to this world so that every one of His believing disciples might also receive Him. Hearing this glad tiding and consenting to it, they were baptized into the name of this Savior, who baptizes with the Holy Spirit. Paul then prayed for them and laid his hands on them, and they received the Holy Spirit. Then, as evidence of the fact that this whole transaction was a heavenly reality, they obtained a share in the Pentecostal miracle and spoke "with other tongues" (see Acts 19:6).

In these chapters, it is my desire to bring to the children of God the message that there is a twofold Christian life. The one is that in which we experience something of the operations of the Holy Spirit, just as many did under the Old Covenant, but do not yet receive Him as the Pentecostal Spirit, as the personal indwelling Guest, concerning whom we know that He has come to abide permanently in the heart. On the other hand, there is a more abundant life, in which the indwelling just referred to is known and the full joy and power of redemption are facts of personal experience.

It will be only when Christians come to understand fully the distinction between these two conditions and discern that the second of these is in very deed the will of God concerning them—and therefore a possible experience for each believer—when with shame and confusion of face they shall confess the sinful and inconsistent elements that still mark their life—that we shall dare to hope that the Christian community will once more be restored to its Pentecostal power. It is with our eye fixed on this distinction that we desire to ponder the lessons presented to us in the record of this incident at Ephesus.

1. *For a healthy Christian life, it is indispensable that we should be fully conscious that we have received the Holy Spirit to dwell in us.*

Had it been otherwise, Paul would never have put the question: "Did you receive the Holy Spirit when you believed?" These disciples were recognized as believers. This position, however, was not enough for them. The disciples who walked with the Lord Jesus on earth were also true believers, yet He commanded them not to rest satisfied until they had received the Holy Spirit from Himself in heaven. Paul, too, had seen the Lord in His heavenly glory and was by that vision led to conversion. Yet even in his case the spiritual work he required to have done in him was not thereby completed. Ananias had to go to him and lay his hands upon him that he might receive the Holy Spirit (see Acts 9:17). Only then could he become a witness for Christ.

> *he disciples who walked with the Lord Jesus on earth were also true believers, yet He commanded them not to rest satisfied until they had received the Holy Spirit from Himself in heaven.*

All these facts teach us that there are two ways in which the Holy Spirit works in us. The first is the preparatory operation in which He simply acts on us but does not yet take up His home within us, though leading us to conversion and faith and ever urging us to all that is good and holy. The second is the higher and more advanced phase of His working when we receive Him as an abiding gift, as an indwelling Person, concerning whom we know that He assumes responsibility for our whole inner being, working in it both to will and to do. This is the ideal of the full Christian life.

2. *There are disciples of Christ who know little or nothing of this conscious indwelling of the Holy Spirit.*

It is of the utmost importance to understand and hold firmly this statement. The more fully we come under the conviction of its truth, the better shall we understand the condition of the Church in our times and be at last enabled to discover where we ourselves really stand.

The condition I refer to becomes very plain to us when we consider what took place at Samaria. Philip the evangelist had preached there. Many had been led to believe in Jesus and were baptized into His name, and there was great joy in that city. When the apostles heard this news, they sent down Peter and John, who, when they came to Samaria, prayed that these new converts might receive the Holy Spirit (see Acts 3:16–17). This gift was therefore something quite different from the working of the Spirit that led them to conversion and faith and joy in Jesus as a Savior. It was something higher, for now from heaven, and by the glorified Lord Himself, the Holy Spirit was imparted in power with His abiding indwelling to consecrate and fill their hearts.

If this new experience had not been bestowed, the Samaritan disciples would still indeed have been Christians, but they would have remained weak, defective, and sickly. It is this way in our own days. There is still many a Christian life that knows nothing of this bestowment of the Holy Spirit. Amid much that is good and amiable, with even much earnestness and zeal, the life of such Christians is still hampered by weakness and stumbling and disappointment, simply because it has never been brought into vitalizing contact with power from on high, because such souls have not received the Holy Spirit as the Pentecostal gift, to be possessed, and kept, and filled by Him.

3. *It is the great work of the gospel ministry to lead believers to the Holy Spirit.*

Was it not the great aim of the Lord Jesus, after He had educated and trained His disciples for three years by His communication with them, to lead them up to the point of waiting for the promise of the Father and receiving the Holy Spirit sent down from heaven? Was not this the chief object of Peter on the day of Pentecost, when, after summoning those who were pricked in their hearts to repent and be baptized for the forgiveness of sins, he assured them that they should then receive the Holy Spirit? (see Acts 2:38). Was it not this also that Paul aimed at when in his epistles he asked his fellow Christians if they did not know that they were each one a "temple of the Holy Spirit" (1 Cor. 6:19), or reminded them that they had to be "filled with the Spirit" (Eph. 5:18)?

Yes, the supreme need of the Christian life is to receive the Holy Spirit and, when we have Him, to be conscious of the fact and to live in harmony with Him. An evangelical minister must not merely preach about the Holy Spirit from time to time or even oftentimes, but must also direct all his efforts toward teaching his congregation that there can be no true worship except through the indwelling and unceasing operation of the Holy Spirit.

4. *For believers to be led to the Holy Spirit, the great lack in their life must be pointed out to them.*

This was distinctly the intention in Paul's question: "Did you receive the Holy Spirit when you believed?" Just as only those who are thirsty will drink water with eagerness and only those who are sick will desire a physician, so it is that only when believers are prepared to acknowledge the defective and sinful character of their spiritual condition will the preaching of the full blessing of Pentecost find an entrance into their hearts.

So long as Christians imagine that the only thing lacking in their life is more earnestness, more persistence, or more strength, that if they only obtain these benefits they themselves will become all they ought to be, the preaching of a full salvation will be of little benefit. It is only when the discovery is made that they are not standing in a right attitude toward the Holy Spirit, that they have only His preparatory operations but do not yet know and honor Him in His indwelling, that the way to something higher will ever be open or even be desired. For this discovery, it is indispensable that the question should be put to each, man by man, as pointedly and as personally as may be: "Did you receive the Holy Spirit when you believed?" When the answer shall take the shape of a deeply felt and utterly sincere "Sadly, no!" then the time of revival is not far off.

5. *Believers must receive help to appropriate this blessing in faith.*

In the Acts of the Apostles we read often about laying on of hands and prayer. Even a man like Paul—whose conversion was due to the direct interposition of the Lord, and was therefore so effectual—had to receive the Spirit through laying on of hands and prayer on the part of Ananias (see Acts 9:17).

This implies that there must be among ministers of the gospel and believers generally a power of the Spirit that makes them the channel of faith and courage to others. Those who are weak must be helped to appropriate the blessing for themselves. But those who have and bring this blessing, as well as those who desire to have it, must realize and acknowledge their absolute dependence on the Lord and expect all from Him.

The gift of the Spirit is imparted only by God Himself. Every fresh bestowment of the Spirit comes from above. There must be frequent personal dealing with God. The minister of the Spirit whom God is to use for communicating the blessing, as well as the believer who is to receive it, must meet with God in immediate and closest interaction. Every good gift comes from above. It is faith in this truth that will give us courage to expect with confidence and gladness that the full Pentecostal blessing may confidently be looked for, and that a life under the continual leading of the Holy Spirit is within our reach.

6. *The proclamation and appropriation of this blessing will restore the Christian community to the primary Pentecostal power.*

On the day of Pentecost the speaking "with other tongues" (Acts 2:4) and the prophesying were the result of being filled with the Spirit. Here at Ephesus, twenty years later, the very same miracle is again witnessed as the visible evidence and pledge of the other glorious gifts of the Spirit. We may rely upon it that where the reception of the Holy Spirit and the possibility of being filled with Him are proclaimed and appropriated, the blessed life of the Pentecostal community will be restored in all its pristine power.

In our days there is an increasing acknowledgment of the lack of power in the Church of the Lord. In spite of all the multiplication of the means of grace, there is neither the power of the divine salvation in believers, nor the power for conversion in preaching, nor the power in the conflict of the Church with worldliness and unbelief and unrighteousness that, according to God's Word, we are bound to look for. The complaint is made with justice. Let us desire that the expression of it become so strong that the children of God, driven by a keen sense of need, may be led to cast themselves upon the great truth that the Word of God teaches—namely, that it is only when faith in the full Pentecostal blessing and the full enjoyment of it are found in the Christian Church that the members of it shall again find their strength and be able to do their first works.

7. *The most urgent need of the Church is that of men who shall be able to bear testimony to this blessing.*

Whether it be of teachers like Peter and Paul, of deacons like Philip, or of ordinary believers like Ananias, who came to Paul, this is our first need. It furnishes abundant reason why teachers and members of congregations should in unison call upon God, that alike in preaching and pastoral interaction there may be more apparent proof that those who preach Christ Jesus may preach Him as John the Baptist did, as the One who baptizes with the Holy Spirit (see Mark 1:8). It is only the minister who stands forth as a personal witness and living proof of the ministry of the Spirit whose word will have full entrance into the hearts of the people and exercise full influence over them. The first disciples obtained the baptism on their knees, and on their knees they obtained it for others. It will be on our knees also that the full blessing will be won today. On our knees—let this be the attitude in which we await the full blessing of our God, alike in our individual and collective life.

Have you received the Holy Spirit since you believed? Let every reader submit himself to this heart-searching question. To be filled with the Holy Spirit of God, to have the full enjoyment of the Pentecostal blessing, is the will of God concerning us. Let us judge our life and our work before the Lord in the light of this question, and return the answer to God.

Oh, do not be afraid, my brother, to confess before your Lord what is still lacking in you. Do not keep back, although you do not as yet fully understand what the blessing is or how it comes. The early disciples did not know that, yet they called upon their Lord and waited for it with prayer and supplications. Let your heart be filled with a deep conviction of what you lack, a desire for what God offers, a willingness to sacrifice everything for it, and you may rest assured that the marvel of Jerusalem and of Samaria, of Caesarea and Ephesus, will once again be repeated. We may, we shall, be filled with the Spirit. Amen.

FOR FURTHER THOUGHT

1. *What is the difference between the believer who has experienced some of the power of the Holy Spirit and one who has experienced the full indwelling of the Spirit?*
2. *What are the "symptoms" of your spiritual life that indicate your need for the full blessing of Pentecost, the full indwelling of God's Holy Spirit?*
3. *What is the first step in your making sure that you possess the Holy Spirit—and He possesses you—with all the power He has to give you?*

2
How Glorious It Is

They were all filled with the Holy Spirit.
ACTS 2:4

WHENEVER we speak of being filled with the Holy Spirit, and desire to know what it precisely is, our thoughts always turn back to the day of Pentecost. There we see as in a mirror how glorious the blessing is that is brought from heaven by the Holy Spirit and with which He can fill the hearts of men.

There is one fact that makes the great event of the day of Pentecost doubly instructive—this, namely, that we have learned to know very intimately the men, who were then filled with the Spirit, by their interaction for three years with the Lord Jesus. Their infirmities and defects, their sins and perversities, all stand open to our view. But the blessing of Pentecost brought about a complete transformation. They became entirely new men, so that one might say of them with truth: "Old things have passed away; behold, all things have become new" (2 Cor. 5:17).

Close study of them and their example helps us in more than one way. It shows us to what weak and sinful men the Spirit will come. It teaches us how they were prepared for the blessing. It teaches us also—and this is the principal thing—how mighty and complete the revolution is that is brought to pass when the Holy Spirit is received in His fullness. It lets us see how glorious the grace is that awaits us is if we press on to the full blessing of Pentecost.

1 *The ever-abiding presence and indwelling of the Lord Jesus.*

In this we have the first and principal blessing of the Pentecostal life. In the course of our Lord's communication with His disciples on earth, He spared no pains to teach and train them, to renew and sanctify them. In most respects, however, they remained just what they were. The reason was that up to this point He was always still nothing more than an external Christ who stood outside of them and from without sought to work upon them by His word and His personal influence.

With the advent of Pentecost this condition was entirely changed. In the Holy Spirit, He came down as the inward, indwelling Christ to become in the very innermost recesses of their being the life of their life. This is what He Himself had promised in the words: "I will not leave you orphans; *I will come to you*. . . . At that day you will know that I am in My Father, and you in Me, and I in you" (John 14:18, 20). This was the source of all the other blessings that came with

Pentecost. Jesus Christ, the Crucified, the Glorified, the Lord from heaven, came in spiritual power, by the Spirit, to impart to them that ever-abiding presence of their Lord that had been promised to them, and that indeed in a way was at the same time most intimate, all-powerful, and wholly divine: by the indwelling that makes Him in truth their life. Him whom they had had in the flesh, living with them on earth, they now received by the Spirit in His heavenly glory within them. Instead of an outward Jesus near them, they now obtained the inward Jesus within them.

2. *From this first and principal blessing sprang the second: The Spirit of Jesus came into them as the life and the power of sanctification.*

> *In the Holy Spirit, He came down as the inward, indwelling Christ to become in the very innermost recesses of their being the life of their life.*

Here I shall allude at the outset to only one feature in this change. We know how often the Lord had to rebuke them for their pride and exhort them to humility. It was all of no avail. Even on the last night of His earthly life, at the table of the Holy Supper, there was a conflict among them as to which of them should be the greatest (see Luke 22:24). The outward teaching of the outward Christ, whatever other influences it may have exercised, was not sufficient to redeem them from the power of indwelling sin. This could be achieved only by the indwelling Christ. Only when Jesus descended into them by the Holy Spirit did they undergo a complete change. They received Him in His heavenly humility and subjection to the Father, and in His self-sacrifice for others, as their life. From that time forward all was changed. From that moment onward they were animated by the Spirit of the meek and lowly Jesus.

This, in very truth, is still the only way to a real sanctification, to a life that actually overcomes sin. It is just because so many preachers and so many Christians keep their minds occupied only with the external Christ on the cross or in heaven, and wait for the blessing of His teaching and His working without understanding that the blessing of Pentecost brings Him *into us* to work Himself all *in us*, that they make so little progress in sanctification. Christ Himself is by God made for us sanctification, and that in no other way than by our living and moving and existing in Him, because He lives and abides in our heart and works all there.

3. *An overflowing of the heart with the love of God is also a part of the blessing of Pentecost.*

Next to pride, lack of love—or, as we may put it in one word, lovelessness—was the sin for which the Lord had so often to rebuke His disciples.

These two sins have in truth one and the same root: the self-seeking *I*, the desire for self-pleasing. The new commandment that He gave them, the proof through which all men should know that they were His disciples, was love to one another. How gloriously was it manifested on the day of Pentecost that the Spirit of the Lord shed abroad His love in the hearts of His own. The multitude of them who believed were as one heart, one soul: All things they possessed were held in common, and no one said that anything of that which he had was his own. The kingdom of heaven with its life of love had come down to them. The Spirit, the disposition, the wonderful love of Jesus, filled them, because He Himself had come into them.

How closely the mighty working of the Spirit and the indwelling of the Lord Jesus are bound up with a life in love appears from the prayer of Paul in behalf of the Ephesians, in which he asks that they might be strengthened with power by the Spirit, in order that Christ might dwell in their hearts (Eph. 3:16–17). Then he immediately makes this addition: "that you, being rooted and grounded in love, may be able to comprehend. . .the love of Christ which passes knowledge" (3:18–19). The filling with the Spirit and the indwelling of Christ bring by themselves a life that has its root, its joy, its power, its evidence in love, because the indwelling Christ Himself is Love.

Oh, how would the love of God fill the Church and convince the world that she has received a heavenly element into her life, if the filling with the Spirit and the indwelling of Christ in the heart were recognized as the blessing that the Father has promised us!

4. *The coming of the Spirit changed weakness and fear into courage and power.*

We all know how, from fear rising in his heart at the word of a woman, Peter denied his Lord, and how that same night all the disciples fled and forsook Him. Their hearts were really attached to Him, and they were sincerely willing to do what they had promised and go to die with Him. But when it came to the crisis, they had neither courage nor power. They had to say: "To will is present with me, but to perform I find not" (see Rom. 7:18).

After the blessing of the Spirit of Pentecost, there was no more question of merely willing apart from performing. By Christ dwelling in us, God works both the willing and the doing. With what confidence of spirit did Peter on the day of Pentecost dare to preach the Crucified One to thousands of hostile Jews. With what boldness was he able, in opposition to the leaders of the people, to say: "We must obey God rather than men" (Acts 5:29 NASB). With what courage and joy were Stephen and Paul and so many others enabled to encounter threatening and suffering and death. They did this even triumphantly. It was because the Spirit of Christ, the Victor—yes, the Christ Himself, who had been glorified—dwelled within them. It is the joy of the blessing of Pentecost that gives courage and power to speak for Jesus, because by it the whole heart is filled with Him.

5. *The blessing of Pentecost makes the whole Word of God new.*

How distinctly do we see this fact in the case of the disciples. As with all the Jews of that age, their ideas of the Messiah and the kingdom of God were utterly external and carnal. All the instruction of the Lord Jesus throughout three long years could not detach their minds from them. They were utterly unable to comprehend the doctrine of a suffering and dying Messiah or of the hope of His invisible spiritual dominion. Even after His resurrection, He had to rebuke them for their unbelieving spirit and their backwardness in understanding the scriptures.

With the coming of the day of Pentecost an entire change took place. The whole of their ancient scriptures opened up before them. The light of the Holy Spirit in them illuminated the Word. In the preaching of Peter and Stephen, in the addresses of Paul and James, we see how a divine light had shone upon the word of the Old Testament. They saw everything through the Spirit of this Jesus who had made His home with them.

So will it be also with ourselves. It is as necessary as it is helpful that we should study the scriptures and meditate upon them, and keep the Word of God alike in head and heart and daily walk. Let us, however, constantly remember that it is only when we are filled with the Spirit that we can rightly and fully experience the spiritual power and truth of the Word. He is "the Spirit of truth" (John 14:17; 15:26; 16:13). He alone guides into all truth when He dwells in us.

6. *It is the blessing of Pentecost that gives power to bless others.*

The divine power of the exalted Jesus to grant repentance and the forgiveness of sins is exercised by Him through His servants whom He sends forth to proclaim these blessings. The minister of the gospel who desires to preach repentance and forgiveness through Jesus with success in winning souls must do the work in the power of the Spirit of this Jesus. The chief reason why so much preaching of conversion and pardon is fruitless lies in the fact that these elements of truth are presented only as a doctrine, and that preachers endeavor to secure a way to the hearts of their audience in the power of merely human earnestness, reasoning, and eloquence. But little blessing is won by these means. It is the man who makes it his chief desire to be filled with the Spirit of God, and then by faith in the indwelling of Christ comes to be assured that the glorified Lord will speak and work in him, who will obtain blessing.

It is true, indeed, that this blessing will not always be given in the very same measure or in the very same manner, but it will always certainly come—just because the preacher permits the Lord to work in and through him. Alike in preaching and in the daily life of a servant of Christ, the full blessing of Pentecost is the sure way of becoming a blessing to others. "He who believes in Me," said Jesus, "out of his heart shall flow rivers of living water" (John 7:38). This He said of the Holy Spirit. A heart filled with the Spirit will overflow with the Spirit.

7. *It is the blessing of Pentecost that will make the Church of Christ what God desires her to be.*

We have spoken of what the Spirit will do in individual believers. We have also to think of what the blessing will be when the Church as a whole shall apprehend her calling to be filled with the Spirit and then to exhibit the life and the power—yes, and the very presence—of her Lord to the world. We must not only seek and receive this blessing, every one for himself, but also remember that the full manifestation of what the blessing itself is cannot be given until the whole body of Christ is filled with it.

"If one member suffers, all the members suffer with it" (1 Cor. 12:26). If many members of the Church of Christ are content to remain without this blessing, the whole Church will suffer. Even in individual disciples the blessing cannot come to its full manifestation. Therefore it is of the utmost importance that we should not only think of what being "filled with the Spirit" means for ourselves, but also consider what it will do for the Church, especially in our own neighborhood, and by her for all the world.

To this end, let us simply recall the morning of the day of Pentecost. At that juncture, the Christian Church in Jerusalem consisted only of 120 disciples, most of them poor unlearned fishermen, tax collectors, and humble women—an insignificant and despised gathering (see Acts 1:15). Yet it was just by these believers that the kingdom of God had to be proclaimed and extended. And they did it. By them, and those who were added to them, the power of Jewish prejudice and of pagan hardness of heart was overcome, and the Church of Christ won glorious triumphs.

> *L*et us constantly remember that it is only when we are filled with the Spirit that we can rightly and fully experience the spiritual power and truth of the Word.

This grand result was achieved simply and only because the first Christian church was filled with the Spirit. The members of it gave themselves wholly to their Lord. They allowed themselves to be filled and consecrated, governed and used, only by Him. They yielded themselves to Him as instruments of His power. He dwelled in them and accomplished in them all His wondrous deeds.

It is to this same experience that the Church of Christ in our age must be brought back. This is the only thing that will help her in the conflict with mere civilization or paganism, with sin or the world. She must be filled with the Spirit.

Beloved fellow Christians, this summons comes to you. "One thing is needed." Alike for yourselves and the whole Church of the Lord, this is the one thing that is needed: We have to be filled with the Spirit. Please do not imagine that you must comprehend or understand it all before you seek and find it. For those who wait upon Him, God will do even that which has not yet entered into their heart to conceive. If you desire to taste the happiness, if you desire to know by personal experience the unutterable blessedness of having Jesus in the heart, of having in you His Spirit of holiness and humility, of love and self-sacrifice, of courage and power, as naturally and continuously as you have your own spirit; if you want to have the Word of God in you as light and power, and be enabled to carry it about as a blessing for others; if you want to see the Church of Christ stand forth arrayed in her first splendor—then separate yourselves from everything that is evil, cast it utterly out of your heart, and fix your desire on this one thing: to be filled with the Spirit of God. Reckon on receiving this as your rightful heritage. Appropriate it and hold it fast by faith. It shall certainly be given to you.

For Further Thought

1. *What is the first—and greatest—benefit of having the Holy Spirit dwelling within you to the point He has full control and possession of you?*

2. *What will the Holy Spirit do within you when you fully and unreservedly yield yourself for Him to take complete possession of you and to make your heart His home?*

3. *How was the early Church affected when the people received the full blessing of the Holy Spirit at Pentecost? How do you think the Church today would be affected if she received that same blessing?*

3

HOW IT WAS

BESTOWED FROM HEAVEN

"If you love Me, keep My commandments.
And I will pray the Father, and He will give you another Helper,
that He may abide with you forever—the Spirit of truth."
JOHN 14:15–17

A tree lives always according to the nature of the seed from which it sprang. Every living being is always guided and governed by the nature that it received at its birth. Thus the Church of Christ received the promise and the law of her existence and her growth in that which was bestowed upon her in the Holy Spirit on the day of her birth. This is the reason why it is of such importance for us to turn back often to the day of Pentecost and not to rest until we thoroughly understand, and receive, and experience what God did for His people on that day. When we see how the blessing was then for the first time given from heaven, and what the disposition of heart was that fitted the disciples for receiving the Spirit, then we know for all coming time what remains to be done by ourselves to enjoy the same blessing. The first disciples serve us as examples and forerunners on the way to the fullness of the Spirit.

What, then, was there in them that enabled them to become the recipients of these heavenly gifts and made them fit objects of the unspeakable grace that in them first of all the Three-One God came to take up His home? The right answer to this question will help us not a little on the way to being filled with the Holy Spirit.

What do we find in these first disciples?

1. In the first place, there is the fact that *they were deeply attached to the Lord Jesus.*

The Son of God came into the world in order to unite the divine life that He had with the Father with the life of man, and thus to secure that the life of God should penetrate into the life of the creature. When He had completed the work in His own person by His obedience, death, and resurrection, He was exalted to the throne of God on high in order that in spiritual power, and not only apart from the limitations of earthly life but in the might of the all-penetrating sovereign presence of God, His disciples and His Church might participate in His very life.

We read that the Holy Spirit "was not yet," because Jesus was not yet glorified (John 7:39). It was only after His glorification that the Holy Spirit, as the Spirit of Godhead united with manhood, the Spirit of the complete indwelling of God in man, could be given. It is the Spirit of the glorified Jesus that the disciples received on the day of Pentecost, the Spirit of the Head, penetrating all the members of His body.

It is evident without proof that if the fullness of the Spirit thus dwells in Jesus, a personal relationship to Him is the first condition for the reception of the full gift of the Comforter. It was to attain this end that the Lord Jesus throughout all His three years' work on earth kept the disciples in such close communion with Himself. He desired to attach them to Himself. He wanted them to feel themselves truly one with Him. He wanted them to identify themselves with Him, as far as this was possible. By knowledge and communication, by love and obedience, they became inwardly knit to Him. This was the preparation for participating in the Spirit of His glorification.

The lesson that is here taught us is indeed extremely simple, but it is one of profound significance. There are not a few Christians who believe in the Lord and are very zealous in His service, who eagerly desire to become holy, and who yet do not succeed in their endeavor. It seems oftentimes as if they could not understand the promise of the Spirit. The thought of being filled with the Spirit exercises but little influence on them. The reason is obvious. There is lacking in their religion that personal relationship to the Lord Jesus, that inward attachment to Him, that perfectly natural reference to Him as the best and nearest Friend, as the beloved Lord, which was so characteristic of the disciples. This, however, is absolutely indispensable. It is a heart that is entirely occupied with the Lord Jesus and depends only on Him that can alone hope for the fullness of the Spirit.

2. *They had left all for Jesus.*

"Nothing for nothing." This proverb contains a deep truth. A thing that costs me nothing may nevertheless cost me much. It may bring me under an obligation to the giver, and so cost me more than it is worth. I may have so much trouble in appropriating it and keeping it that I may pay much more for it than the price that should be asked for it. "Nothing for nothing": The maxim holds good also in the life of the kingdom of heaven. The parables of the pearl of great price (Matt. 13:45–46) and the treasure hidden in a field (Matt. 13:44) teach us that in order to obtain possession of the kingdom within us, we must sell all that we have. This is the very renunciation that Jesus literally demanded of the disciples who had to follow Him. This is the requirement He so often repeated in His preaching: "Whoever of you does not forsake all that he has cannot be My disciple" (Luke 14:33).

The two worlds between which we stand are in such direct conflict with one another, and the world in which we by nature live exercises such a mighty influence over us, that it is often necessary for us, even by external and visible sacrifice, to withdraw from it. It was thus that Jesus trained His disciples to long for that which is heavenly. Only this way could He prepare them to desire and receive the heavenly gift with an undivided heart.

The Lord has left us no outward directions as to how much of the world we are to abandon or in what manner. But by His whole Word, He teaches us that without sacrifice, without a deliberate separation from the world and forsaking of it, we shall never make much progress in grace. The spirit of this world has penetrated so deeply into us that we do not notice it. We share in its desire for comfort and enjoyment, for self-pleasing and self-exaltation, without our knowing how impossible these things make it for us to be filled with the Spirit. Let us learn from the early disciples that to be filled from the heavenly world with the Spirit that dwells there, we must be entirely separate from the children of this world or from worldly Christians. We must be ready and eager to live as entirely different men, men who literally represent heaven upon earth, because we have received the Spirit of the King of heaven.

3. *They had despaired utterly of themselves and all that is of man.*

Man has two great enemies by which the devil tempts him and with which he has to contend. The one is the world without; the other is the self-life within. This last, the selfish *ego*, is much more dangerous and stronger than the first. It is quite possible for a man to have made much progress in forsaking the world while the self-life retains full dominion within him. You see this fact illustrated in the case of the disciples. Peter could say with truth: "See, we have left all and followed You" (Mark 10:28). Yet how manifestly did the selfish *ego*, with its self-pleasing and its self-confidence, still retain its full sway over him.

> The Son of God came into the world in order to unite the divine life that He had with the Father with the life of man, and thus to secure that the life of God should penetrate into the life of the creature.

As the Lord at their first calling led them up to the point of forsaking their outward possessions and following Him, so shortly afterwards He began to teach them that a disciple must deny himself and lose his own life if he wants to be worthy of receiving His. He must hate not only father and mother, where this was necessary, but even his own life. It was love for this self-life, more than all love for father and mother, that hindered the Lord Jesus from doing His work in the heart. It was to cost them more to be redeemed from the selfish *ego* within them than to get quit of the world around them. The self-life is the natural life of sinful man. He can be liberated from it by nothing save by death—that is, by first dying to it and then living in the strength of the new life that comes from God.

The forsaking of the world began at the outset of the three years' discipleship. It was at the end of that period, at the cross of Jesus, that dying to the self-life first took place. When they saw Him die, they learned to despair of themselves and of everything on which they had to that point based their hope. Whether they thought of their Lord and the redemption that they had expected, or whether they thought of themselves and their shameful unfaithfulness toward Him, everything tended to fill them with despair. Little did they know that it was just this despair that was to prove the breaking up of their hard hearts—the putting to death of the self-life and of confidence in themselves—which would enable them to receive something entirely new—namely a divine life through the Spirit of the glorified Jesus in the innermost depths of their souls.

Oh, that we understood better that there is nothing that so hampers us as secret reliance on something in ourselves or in the Church around us, which we imagine can help us! On the other hand, there is nothing that brings so much blessing as entire despair of ourselves and of all that is upon the earth, in the way of teaching us to turn our hearts only and wholly to heaven and to partake of the heavenly gift that comes from there.

4. *They received and held firmly the promise of the Spirit given by the Lord Jesus.*

We know how, in His farewell address on the last night of His stay on earth, Jesus comforted His disciples in their sorrow over His departure with one great promise—namely the mission of the Holy Spirit from heaven. This was to be better than His own bodily presence among them. It would be to them the full fruit and power of His redemption. The divine life—yes, He Himself, with the Father—was to make home within them. The unheard-of wonder, the mystery of the ages, was to be their portion. They were to know that they were in Him and He in them. At His ascension from the Mount of Olives, this promise of the Spirit was the subject of the last words He addressed to them.

It is evident that the disciples had still but little idea of what this promise signified. But however defective their understanding of it was, they held it fast—or rather, the promise held them fast and would not let them go. They all had only one thought: Something has been promised to us by our Lord. It will give us a share in His heavenly power and glory, and we know for certain that it is coming. Of what the thing itself was, or of what their experience of it was to be, they could give no account. It was enough for them that they had the word of the Lord. He would make it a blessed reality within them.

Now it is just the same disposition that we have so much need of now. To us also, even as to them, has the word of the Lord come concerning the Spirit who is to descend from the throne in the power of His glorified life. "He who believes in Me. . .out of his heart will flow rivers of living water" (John 7:38). For us also, it is the one thing needed to hold firmly that word, to set our whole desire upon the fulfillment of it, and to lay aside all else until we inherit the promise. The word from the mouth of Jesus concerning the reception of the Spirit in such measure that we shall be provided power from on high must animate and fill us with strong desire, with firm and joyful assurance.

5. *They waited on the Father until the performance of the promise came and they were filled with the Spirit.*

The ten days of waiting were for them days in which they were continually in the temple praising and blessing God and "continued with one accord in prayer and supplication" (Acts 1:14). It is not enough for us to endeavor to strengthen desire and to hold firmly our confidence. The principal thing is to set ourselves in close and abiding contact with God. The blessing must come from God. God Himself must give it to us, and we are to receive the gift directly from Him. What is promised us is a wonderful work of divine omnipotence and love. What we desire is the personal occupancy and indwelling of God the Holy Spirit. God Himself must bestow this personally upon us.

> *I*t is evident that the disciples had still but little idea of what this promise signified. But however defective their understanding of it was, they held it fast—or rather, the promise held them fast and would not let them go.

A man gives another a piece of bread or a piece of money. He gives it away from himself and has nothing further to do with it. It is not like that with God's gift of the Holy Spirit. No, the Spirit is God. God is in the Spirit who comes to us, even as He was in the Son. The gift of the Spirit is the most personal act of the Godhead, the gift of Himself unto us. We have to receive it in the very closest personal contact with God.

The clearer the insight we obtain into this principle, the more deeply shall we feel how little we can do to grasp the blessing by our own desiring, or endeavoring, or believing. No, all our desiring, and striving, and believing can only issue in a more complete acknowledgment that we ourselves can do nothing to win the benefit. It is the goodness of God alone that must give it. It is His omnipotence that must work it in us. Our disposition must be one of silent assurance that the Father desires to give it to us, that He will not keep us waiting one moment longer than is absolutely necessary, and that there shall not be a single soul that persists in waiting in the pathway of self-renunciation and dependence that shall not be filled with the glory of God.

Every tree continues always to grow from the root out of which it first sprang. The day of Pentecost was the planting of the Christian Church, and the Holy Spirit became the power of its life. Let us turn back to that experience. There is our power still. We learn from the disciples what is really necessary. Attachment to Jesus, the abandonment of everything in the world for Him, despair of self and of all help from man, holding on to the word of promise, and then waiting on God, "the living God"—this is the sure way of living in the joy and the power of the Holy Spirit.

For Further Thought

1. *What was Christ's main desire and objective in having the early believers filled with His Holy Spirit? What are His desires and objectives for the same thing today?*

2. *In order to receive the fullness of the Holy Spirit, how must you approach "self"— the love of self, the reliance on self, and the confidence in self?*

3. *What steps must you take today to receive the Holy Spirit in all His power? How are those steps like the ones the early disciples took before they received the full blessing of Pentecost?*

4

How Little It Is Enjoyed

My speech and my preaching were not with persuasive words
of human wisdom, but in demonstration of the Spirit
and of power, that your faith should not be in the
wisdom of men but in the power of God.
1 Corinthians 2:4–5

PAUL speaks here of two kinds of preaching and two kinds of faith. According to the spirit of the preacher will be the faith of the congregation. When the preaching of the Cross is given only in the words of human wisdom, then the faith of the hearers will be in the wisdom of men. When the preaching is in demonstration of the Spirit and of power, the faith of the Christian people will also be in the power of God, at once firm and strong.

Preaching in the demonstration of the Spirit will bring the double blessing of power in the word and power in the faith of those who receive that word. If we desire to know the measure of the working of the Spirit, we must consider the preaching and the faith that springs from it. In this way alone can we see whether the full blessing of Pentecost is truly manifested in the Church of Christ.

There are very few who are prepared to say that this is really the case. Everywhere among the children of God we hear complaints of weakness and sin. Among those who do not so complain, there is reason to fear that their silence is to be ascribed to the prevalence of ignorance or self-satisfaction. It is of the utmost importance that we should concentrate our thoughts upon this fact, until we come under the full conviction that the condition of the Church is marked by powerlessness, and that nothing can restore her but the return to a life in the full enjoyment of the blessing of Pentecost. The more deeply we feel our deficiency, the more speedily shall we desire and obtain restoration. It will help to awaken longing for this blessing, and to find out the way to obtain it, if we earnestly consider how little it is enjoyed in the Church and how far the Church is from being what her Lord has willingness and power to make her.

1. *Think, for example, what little power over sin there is among the children of God.*

The Spirit of Pentecost is the Holy Spirit, the Spirit of God's holiness. When

He came down upon the disciples, what a transformation was effected in them. Their carnal thoughts were changed into spiritual insight, their pride into humility, their selfishness into love, their fear of man into courage and fidelity. Sin was cast out by the inflowing of the life of Jesus and of heaven.

The life that the Lord has prepared for His people is a life of victory. It is not indeed victory to such an extent as that there shall be no temptation to evil, nor yet that the inclination toward sin, inward sinfulness, shall be utterly rooted out of the flesh. But there is to be victory of such a kind that the indwelling power of the Spirit who fills us, the presence of the indwelling Savior, shall keep sin in subjection as the light subdues the darkness.

Yet to what a small extent do we see power for victory over sin in the Church of Christ. On the contrary, how often, even among earnest Christians, do we see much untruthfulness and lack of honor, pride and self-esteem, selfishness and lack of love. How little are the traces of the image of Jesus—obedience, humility, love, and entire surrender to the will of God—seen even among the people of God. The truth is that we have become so accustomed to the confession of sin and unfaithfulness, of disobedience and backsliding, that it is no longer regarded as a matter for shame. We make the confession before each other, and then after the prayer rest comforted and content.

> *I*f we desire to know the measure of the working of the Spirit, we must consider the preaching and the faith that springs from it. In this way alone can we see whether the full blessing of Pentecost is truly manifested in the Church of Christ.

O brethren, let us rather feel humbled and mourn over it! It is because so little of the full blessing of the Spirit is enjoyed or sought for that the children of God still commit so much sin, and have therefore so much to confess. Let every sin, whether in ourselves or others, serve as a summons to notice how much is lacking of the Spirit of God among us. Let every instance of failure in the fear of the Lord, in love, holiness, and entire surrender to the will of God, only urge us more unceasingly to call upon God to bring His Spirit once more to full dominion over the whole Church of Christ.

2. *Think, too, how little there is of separation from the world.*

When the Lord Jesus promised the Comforter, He said: "Whom the world cannot receive" (John 14:17). The spirit of this world, which is devotion to the visible, is in irreconcilable antagonism with the Spirit of Jesus in heaven, where God and His will are everything. The world has rejected the Lord Jesus. And to whatever extent it may now usurp the Christian name, the world at heart is still the same untamable foe. It was for this reason that Jesus said of His disciples, and as indicating one of their chief distinctive marks: "They are not of the world, just as I am not of the world" (John 17:16). This, too, is the reason why Paul said: "We have received, not the spirit of the world, but the Spirit who is from God" (1 Cor. 2:12). The two spirits, the spirit of the world and the Spirit of God, are engaged in a life-and-death conflict with one another.

For this reason, God has always called upon His people to separate themselves from the world and to live as pilgrims whose treasure and whose heart are in heaven. But is this what is really seen among Christians? Who shall dare to say so? When they have attained to a measure of blamelessness in walk and assurance of heaven, most Christians consider that they are at liberty to enjoy the world as fully as others. There is little to be seen of true heavenly-mindedness in conversation and walk, in disposition and endeavor. Is not this the case just because the fullness of the Spirit is so little enjoyed and sought for? Nothing but light can drive out darkness, and nothing but the Spirit of heaven can expel the spirit of the world. Where a man does not surrender himself to be filled with the Spirit of Jesus and the Spirit of heaven, there can be no other issue than that, Christian though he may be, he must come under the power of the spirit of the world.

Oh, listen to the piercing cry that rises from the whole Church of Christ: "Who shall rescue us from the power of this spirit of the world?" And let your answer be: "Nothing, no one, but the Spirit of God. I must be filled with the Spirit."

3. *Think how little there is of steadfastness and growth in faith.*

There is nothing of which ministers, and especially those who labor for the salvation of souls, have to complain more than that there are so many who for a time are full of zeal and then fall away. We see, not only among the young or in times of awakening, but even among many who have for years maintained a good confession, that whenever they enter into another circle of influence, and are put to the proof by prosperity or any special form of temptation, they immediately cease to persevere.

From where does this unhappy result arise? From nothing but the fact that the preaching is more with the wisdom of persuasive words than in demonstration of the Spirit and of power. For that reason, their faith also stands in the wisdom and work of man rather than in the power of God. So long as such people have the benefit of earnest and instructive preaching, they continue to stand. But whenever they lose it, they begin to backslide. It is because the current preaching is so little in the demonstration of the Spirit that souls are brought so little into contact with the living God. For the same reason, far too much of the current faith is not in the power of God.

Even the Word of God—which ought always only to be a guide pointing *toward God Himself*—becomes all too frequently a veil with the study of which the soul becomes occupied and is thus kept back from meeting with God. The Word, and preaching, and means of grace become a hindrance in place of a help if they are not in demonstration of the Spirit. All external means of grace are things that inevitably change and fade. It is the Spirit alone who works a faith that stands in the power of God, and so remains strong and unwavering.

Why is it that there are so many who do not continue to stand? Let the answer of God to this question penetrate deeply into our hearts. There is a grave lack of the demonstration of the Spirit. Let every sad discovery of congregations, or of smaller circles, or of individuals who do not remain steadfast, or who do not grow in grace, serve as a summons to us to acknowledge that the full blessing of Pentecost is lost. This is what we long for and must have from God. Let all that is within us begin to thirst and cry out: "Come from the four winds, Spirit of God, and breathe upon these dead souls, that they may live" (see Ezek. 37:9).

4. *Think how little there is of power for service among the unconverted.*

What an immense host of workers there is in Christian countries. How varied and unceasing is the preaching of the Word. Sunday school teachers are to be numbered by hundreds of thousands. How great is the number of Christian parents who make their children acquainted with the Word of God and want also to bring them to the Lord as Savior.

Yet how widespread is the acknowledgment of the little fruit that springs from all this work. How many there are who, notwithstanding all they hear, and in spite of the fact that they are by no means indifferent, are yet never laid hold of with power and helped to make a definite choice of salvation. How many also there are who from youth to old age are conversant with the Word of God but are never seized by it in the depths of their heart. They find it good, pleasing, and instructive to attend church, but they have never felt the power of the Word as a hammer, a sword, and a fire. The reason why they are so little disturbed is that the preaching they listen to is so little in demonstration of the Spirit and of power. Sadly, there is evidence enough that there is but too great a lack of the full blessing of Pentecost.

Does the blame for this issue attach to preachers or to congregations? My belief is that it belongs to both together. The preachers are the offspring of the Christian community. By the children, we are enabled to see whether the mother is healthy or not. Preachers are very dependent on the life that is in their congregations. When a congregation finds satisfaction in the merely acceptable and instructive preaching of a young minister, it encourages him to go forward on the same path, while he should rather be helped by its elder or more advanced believers to seek earnestly the demonstration of the Spirit. When a minister does not lead his congregation, either in public worship or in private prayer, really to expect everything from the Spirit of God, then he is tempted, both for himself and his people, to put confidence in the wisdom of man and the work of man.

Oh, that we could lay it to heart that, in the midst of all our lamentation over increasing worldliness of spirit and widespread indifference, the great cause of all impenitence is the lack of the full blessing of Pentecost! This alone gives power from on high that can break down and quicken again the hard hearts of men.

5. *Think how little preparedness there is for self-sacrifice in behalf of the extension of the kingdom of God.*

When the Lord Jesus at His ascension promised the Holy Spirit, it was as a power in us to work for Him. "You shall receive power when the Holy Spirit has come upon you; and you shall be witnesses to Me. . .to the end of the earth" (Acts 1:8).

The aim of the Pentecostal blessing from the King in heaven was simply to complete the equipping of His servants for His work as King upon the earth. No sooner did the Spirit descend upon them than they began to witness for Him. The Spirit filled them with the desire and the impulse, with the courage and the power, to brave all hostility and danger and to endure all suffering and persecution, if only they could succeed in making Jesus known as Savior. The Spirit of Pentecost was that true missionary Spirit that seeks to win the whole world for Jesus Christ.

It is often said in our days that the missionary spirit is so much on the increase. Yet when we reflect carefully how little effort is expended on the missionary enterprise in comparison with what we bestow on our own interests, we shall see at once how weakly this question is still kindled in our hearts: "What more can I still sacrifice for Jesus? He offered Himself for me. I will offer myself wholly for Him and His work."

> The aim of the Pentecostal blessing from the King in heaven was simply to complete the equipping of His servants for His work as King upon the earth. No sooner did the Spirit descend upon them than they began to witness for Him.

It has been well said that the Lord measures our gifts not according to what we give, but according to what we retain. He who stands beside the treasury and observes what is cast into it still finds many who, like the widow, cast in all their living. But how sad it is how many are there who with their five shillings or their five pounds have given only what they could never miss and what costs them little or no sacrifice. How far different would it be if the full blessing of Pentecost began to flow in. How would the hearts of men burn with love to Jesus, and out of very joy be impelled to give everything that He might be known as the Savior all around, and that all might know His love.

Brother, contemplate the condition of the Church on earth, of the Christian community around you, and of your own heart, and then say if there is not grave reason for the cry: "The full blessing of Pentecost—how little is it known." Ponder the present lack of sanctification, of separation from the world, of steadfastness among professing Christians, of conversions among the unsaved, and of self-sacrifice for the kingdom of God, and let the sad reality deepen in your soul the conviction that the Church is at present suffering from one great evil, and that this is her lack of the blessing of Pentecost. There can be no healing of her breaches, no restoration from her fall, no renewing of her power, except by this one remedy—namely her being filled with the Spirit of God.

> *All external means of grace are things that inevitably change and fade. It is the Spirit alone who works a faith that stands in the power of God, and so remains strong and unwavering.*

Let us then never cease to speak, think, mourn, and pray over this trouble until this "one thing needed" becomes the one thing that occupies our hearts. The restoration is not easy. It will perhaps not come all at once, and it may not come speedily. The disciples of Jesus required every day with Jesus for three long years to prepare them for it. Let us not be unduly discouraged if the transformation we long for does not take place immediately. Let us feel the need and lay it to heart. Let us continue in prayer. Let us stand firmly in faith. The blessing of Pentecost is the birthright of the Church, the pledge of our inheritance, something that belongs to us here on the earth. Faith can never be put to shame. Cleaving to Jesus with purpose of heart can never be in vain. The hour will surely come when, if we believe perseveringly in Him, out of our hearts, too, will flow rivers of living water. Amen.

For Further Thought

1. *What do you think keeps you, as well as the Church at large, from fully enjoying and walking in the fullness of the Holy Spirit today?*
2. *What things does God want to do within you through filling you with the fullness of His Spirit? What things does He want to accomplish through you through that same infilling?*
3. *What is God's primary reason for giving believers, including you, the Holy Spirit in His fullness, the full blessing of Pentecost?*

5

HOW THE BLESSING IS HINDERED

Then Jesus said to His disciples, "If anyone desires to come after Me,
let him deny himself, and take up his cross, and follow Me.
For whoever desires to save his life will lose it,
but whoever loses his life for My sake will find it."
MATTHEW 16:24–25

THERE are many who seek the full blessing of Pentecost long and earnestly and yet do not find it. Often the question is put as to what may be the cause of this failure. To this inquiry more than one answer may be given. Sometimes the solution of the problem points in the direction of one or another sin that is still permitted. Worldliness, lovelessness, lack of humility, ignorance of the secret of walking in the way of faith—these, and indeed many more causes, may also be often mentioned with justice.

There are, however, many people who think that they have come to the Lord with what of these sources of failure still remains in them, and have sincerely confessed them and put them away, and yet complain that the blessing does not come. For all such, it is particularly necessary to point out that there remains still one great hindrance—namely the root from which all other hindrances have their beginning. This root is nothing else than our individual self, the hidden life of self with its varied forms of self-seeking, self-pleasing, self-confidence, and self-satisfaction. The more earnestly anyone strives to obtain the blessing and wants to know what prevents him, the more certainly will he be led to the discovery that it is here the great evil lies. He himself is his worst foe: He must be liberated from himself; the self-life to which he clings must be utterly lost. Only then can the life of God entirely fill him.

That is what is taught us in the words of the Lord Jesus to Peter. Peter had uttered such a glorious confession of his Lord that Jesus said to him: "Blessed are you, Simon Bar-Jonah, for flesh and blood has not revealed this to you, but My Father who is in heaven." But when the Lord began to speak of His death by crucifixion, the self-same Peter was seduced by Satan to say: "Far be it from You, Lord; this shall not happen to You!" (Matt. 16:17, 22). In answering, the Lord said to him that not only must He Himself lay down His life, but that this same sacrifice was to be made by every disciple. Every disciple must deny himself and take up his cross in order that he himself may be crucified and put to death on it. He who wants to save his life will lose it, and he who was prepared to lose his life for Christ's sake will find it (see Matt. 16:23–28).

You see, then, what the Lord here teaches and requires. Peter had learned through the Father to know Christ as the Son of God, but he did not yet know Him as the Crucified One. Of the absolute necessity of the cross, and death on the cross, he as yet knew nothing. It may be so with the Christian. He knows the Lord Jesus as his Savior. He desires to know Him better—yes, fully—but he does not yet understand that for this end it is necessary that he must have a deeper discernment of the death of the cross as a death that he himself must die, that he must actually deny, and hate, and lose his life—his whole life and being in the world—before he can receive the full life of God.

> *Every disciple must deny himself and take up his cross in order that he himself may be crucified and put to death on it. He who wants to save his life will lose it, and he who was prepared to lose his life for Christ's sake will find it.*

This requirement is hard and difficult. And why is this so? Why should a Christian be called upon always to deny himself, his own feeling, will, and pleasure? Why must he part with his life—that life to maintain that a man is prepared to make any sacrifice? Why should a man hate and lose his life? The answer is very simple. It is because that life is so completely under the power of sin and death that it has to be utterly denied and sacrificed. The self-life must be completely taken away to make room for the life of God. He who would have the full, the overflowing life of God, must utterly deny and lose his own life.

You see it now, do you not? There is only one great stumbling-block in the way of the full blessing of Pentecost. It lies in the fact that two diverse things cannot at one and the same time occupy the very same place. Your own life and the life of God cannot fill the heart at the same time. Your life hinders the entrance of the life of God. When your own life is cast out, the life of God will fill you. So long as *I myself* am still something, *Jesus Himself* cannot be everything. My life must be expelled. Then the Spirit of Jesus will flow in.

Let every seeker of the full blessing of Pentecost accept this principle and hold it firmly. The subject is of such importance that I would like to make it still clearer by pointing out the chief lessons that these words of the Lord Jesus teach us.

1. *Our life, our individual self, is entirely and completely under the power of sin.*

When God created the angels and man, He gave them a separate personality, a power over themselves, with the intention that they should of their own free will present and offer up that life, that individual self, to Him, in order that He in turn might fill them with His life and His glory. This was to be the highest blessedness of the creature. Man was to be a vessel filled with the life and the perfection of God.

The whole fall alike of angels and of men consisted of nothing but the perversion of their life, their will, their personality, away from God, in order to please themselves. This self-exaltation was the pride that changed the angels into demons and cast them out of heaven into hell. This pride was the infernal poison that the serpent breathed into the ear and the heart of Eve. Man turned himself away from God to find delight in himself and the world. His life, his whole individuality, was perverted and withdrawn from the control of God that he might seek and serve *himself*.

It was no wonder that Jesus said: "You must hate, you must utterly lose *that life*, before the full life of the Spirit of God can be yours. To the minutest details, always and in everything, you must deny that self-life; otherwise the life of God cannot possibly fill you. He who wants to come after Me, let him deny *himself*, take up his cross, and follow *Me*" (see Matt. 16:24).

> *S*o long as I myself am still something, Jesus Himself cannot be everything. My life must be expelled. Then the Spirit of Jesus will flow in.

A deep conviction of the entire corruption of our nature, demonstrating itself in the fact that even the Christian still pleases himself in many things, is an experience that is still lacking in many people. It appears to them both strange and harsh when we say that in nothing is the Christian free to follow his own feeling, that self-denial is a requirement that must prevail in every sphere of life and without any exceptions. The Lord has never withdrawn His words: "Whoever does not forsake all that he has cannot be My disciple—cannot walk with Me, cannot be as I am" (see Luke 14:33).

2. *Our own life must be utterly cast aside to make full room for the life of God.*

At the time of his conversion, the young Christian has but little understanding of this requirement. He receives the seed of the new life into his heart while the natural life is still strong. It was still like that with Peter when the Lord addressed to him the words that have been quoted. He was a disciple, but, sadly, how defective and incomplete. When his Lord was to die, instead of denying himself, he denied his Lord. But that grievous failure brought him at last to that despair of himself that caused him to go out and weep bitterly, and so prepared him for losing entirely his own life and for being wholly filled with the life of Jesus.

This, accordingly, is the point to which we must all in the long run come. So long as a Christian imagines that in some things—for example, in his eating and drinking, in the spending of his time or money, in his thinking and speaking about others—he has still the right and the liberty to follow his own wishes, to please himself, to maintain his own life, he cannot possibly attain to the full blessing of Pentecost.

My brethren, it is an unspeakably holy and glorious thing that a man can be filled with the Spirit of God. It demands inevitably that the present occupant and governor of the heart, our individual self, shall himself be cast out, and that everything within us, everything wholly and entirely, shall be surrendered into the hands of the new Inhabitant, the Spirit of God. We need to understand that the joy and power of being filled with the Spirit will come of themselves when once we comply with the first and principal condition—namely that He alone shall be acknowledged as our Life and our Leader.

3. *It is once for all impossible for the Christian to bring about this great transformation in himself.*

At no stage of our spiritual career are the power and the deceitfulness of our individual self and the self-life more obvious than in the attempt to grasp the full blessing of Pentecost. Many people endeavor to appropriate this blessing, and that by a great variety of efforts. They do not succeed, and they are not able to discover the reason why. They forget that self-will can never cast out self-will—that self can never really put itself to death.

Happy is the man who is brought up to the point of acknowledging his helplessness and powerlessness. He will here especially need to deny himself, and so cease to expect anything from his own life and strength, but will rather lay himself down in the presence of the Lord as one who is alike powerless and dead, that he may really receive the blessing from Him.

It was not Peter who prepared himself for the day of Pentecost or brought down the Pentecostal blessing from heaven. It was his Lord who did all this for him. His part was to despair of himself and yield himself to his Lord to accomplish in him what He had promised. For this reason also it is your part, believer, while yielding obedience to this call, to deny *yourself* and to lose *your own life*, and in the presence of the Lord to sink down in your nothingness and powerlessness.

Accustom yourself to set your heart before Him in deep humility, silent patience, and childlike submission. The humility that is prepared to be nothing, the patience that will wait for Him and His time, and the submission that will yield itself wholly so that He may do what seems to Him good is all that you can do to show that you are ready to lose your life. Jesus summons you to follow Him. Remember how He first sacrificed His will, and when He had laid down His life into the hands of the Father, and went down into the grave, waited until God raised Him again to life. Be you in like manner ready to lay down your life in weakness, and be assured that God will raise it up again in power with the fullness of the Spirit. Be done with the strength of mere personal efforts and abandon the dominion of your own power of understanding. "'Not by might nor by power, but by My Spirit,' says the LORD" (Zech. 4:6).

4. *It is the surrender of faith to Jesus in His self-humiliation and death that opens*

the way to the full blessing of Pentecost.

You of course say at once: "Who is sufficient for these things? Who can sacrifice everything and die and lay down his life utterly as Jesus did? To man, such a surrender is impossible." My reply is that it is indeed so. But "with God all things are possible" (Matt. 19:26). You cannot literally follow Jesus, and like Him go down into death and the grave. That always remains beyond your power. Never will our individual self yield itself up to death or rest quietly in the grave. But hear the good news. In Christ, you have died and have been buried. The power of His dying, of His willing surrender of His spirit into the hands of the Father, and of His silent resting in the grave works in you. In faith in this working, however little you may understand it—in faith in this working in you of the spirit and the power of the death and the life of the Lord Jesus, give up yourself willingly to lose your life.

For this end, begin to regard the denying of yourself as the first and most necessary work of every day. Accept the message I bring you. The great hindrance in the way of the life of Pentecost is the self-life. Believe in the sinfulness, the detestableness of that life—not on account of its gross external sins, but because it sets itself in the place of God, because it seeks, pleases, and honors itself more than God. Exercise yourself in what Jesus lays upon you, and hate your own life as your own worst foe and as the foe of God. Begin to see what the full blessing is that Jesus has prepared for you and that He bestowed at Pentecost—namely His own life, His own indwelling—and count nothing too precious or too costly to give as an exchange for this pearl of great price.

> *We need to understand that the joy and power of being filled with the Spirit will come of themselves when once we comply with the first and principal condition—namely that He alone shall be acknowledged as our Life and our Leader.*

Brother, are you really in earnest about having the full blessing of Pentecost and being filled with the Spirit of God? Is it your great desire to be made to know what hinders you from obtaining it? Take the word of our Lord and keep it in your heart. Take it and go with it to Himself. He is able to make you understand, consider, and experience it. It is He who baptizes with the Holy Spirit. Let everything in you that belongs to self be sacrificed to Him and be counted as loss and cast away to give place to Himself—He who by His death obtained the Spirit, who prepared Peter for Pentecost in the fellowship of His suffering, who has your guidance in His hands. Trust, oh, trust Him, your own Jesus. He baptizes with the Spirit, beyond doubt or question. Deny yourself and follow Him. Lose your own life and find His. Let Him impart Himself in the place you have before now retained for yourself. From Him there will flow rivers of living water. Amen.

For Further Thought

1. *Reread Matthew 16:24–25. What is Jesus' one condition for following Him and then receiving the fullness of the Holy Spirit?*
2. *In yourself, what specifically keeps you from enjoying the full blessing of Pentecost? What must you do to overcome what hinders God's Spirit from moving in and taking full control of you?*
3. *What personal decision can you make and what must you acknowledge today before the way is opened for you to receive the fullness of God's Holy Spirit?*

6

How It Is

Obtained by Us

And do not be drunk with wine,
in which is dissipation; but be filled with the Spirit.
Ephesians 5:18

THE command to be filled with the Spirit is just as peremptory as the prohibition not to be drunk with wine. As truly as we are not at liberty to be guilty of the vice are we bound not to be disobedient to the positive injunction. The same God who calls upon us to live in sobriety urges us with equal earnestness to be filled with the Spirit.

His command is tantamount to a promise: a sure pledge that He Himself will give what He wants to see us possess. With full confidence in this fact, let us in all simplicity ask for the way in which in this respect we should live in the will of God, as those who desire to be filled with the Spirit. I desire now to suggest to those who really long for this blessing some directions whereby they may obtain what is prepared for them.

1. *The full blessing of Pentecost is the inheritance of all the children of God.*

This is the first principle we have to enunciate. There are many of God's children who do not fully believe this. They imagine that the day of Pentecost was only the birthday feast of the Church, and that it was thus a time of blessing and of power that was not destined to endure. They do not reflect on the command to be filled with the Spirit. The result is that they never with earnestness seek to receive the full blessing. They take their ease and remain content with the weak and defective life in which the Church of the day exists.

Is not this the case with you, my reader? Far be it from us. In order to carry on her work in the world, the Church requires the full blessing. To please your Lord and to live a life of holiness and joy and power, you, too, have need of it. To manifest His presence, indwelling, and glory in you, Jesus counts it necessary that you should be filled with the Spirit. Believe firmly that the full blessing of Pentecost is a sacred reality. A child of God may and must have it. Take time to contemplate it and to allow yourself to be fully possessed by the thought of its glorious significance and power. A firm confidence that the blessing is actually within our reach is the first step toward obtaining it and a powerful impulse in the pursuit.

2. *I do not as yet have this blessing.*

This is the second step toward it. You may perhaps ask the question why it should be necessary to cherish this conviction. I will tell you briefly the reasons why I consider it of importance.

The first is that there are many Christians who think that they already have the Holy Spirit, and that all they require is to be more faithful in the endeavor to know and to obey Him. They think that they are already standing in God's grace, and that they only need to make a better use of the life they possess. They imagine that they have all that is necessary for continued growth. On the contrary, it is my deep conviction that such souls are in a sickly state and that they have need of a healing as divine and effective as that which the blind and lame received from the Lord on earth. Accordingly, just as the first condition of my recovery from disease is the knowledge that I am sick, so it is absolutely necessary for them to discover and acknowledge that they do not live the life of Pentecost, that they do not walk in the fullness and the joy of the Spirit, that they do not possess the full blessing, which is indispensable for them if they are to please God in everything.

> *In order to carry on her work in the world, the Church requires the full blessing. To please your Lord and to live a life of holiness and joy and power, you, too, have need of it.*

Once this first conviction is made thoroughly clear to them, they will be prepared for another consideration—namely that they ought to acknowledge the guiltiness of their condition. They ought to see that if they have not yet rendered obedience to the command to "be filled with the Spirit," this defect is to be ascribed to sluggishness, self-satisfaction, and unbelief. They should be persuaded to acknowledge with shame that they have despised what God has prepared for them. When once the confession that they have not yet received the full blessing is deeply rooted in them, there will spring from it a stronger impulse to attain it. Take, then, this thought and let it work in you with power: "No, it is true that I do not as yet have the full blessing."

3. The thought that will come next in succession is: *This blessing is for me.*

I have spoken of those who suppose that the full blessing of Pentecost was only for the first Christian community. There are others who are willing enough to acknowledge that it was intended also for the Church of later times but still think that all are not entitled to expect it. Eminent believers, the leaders of the Church, and such as have much leisure and abundant opportunity to occupy their

minds with such attainments may well cherish the hope of receiving this blessing, but it is not to be expected by ordinary members of the churches. Any one of
these might quite reasonably say: "My unfavorable circumstances, my unfortunate
disposition, my lack of real ability, and similar difficulties make it impossible for
me to realize this ideal. God will not expect this at my hands. He has not destined
me to obtain it."

O soul, do not permit yourself to be deceived by such shallow views. All the
members of a body, even to the very least, must be healthy before the body as a
whole can be healthy. The indwelling, the fullness of the Spirit, is nothing but the
entire healthfulness of the body of Christ. Be assured that even though you are
actually the most insignificant member of it, the blessing is for you. In your own
little measure, you can at least be full.

In this respect the Father makes no exceptions. A great distinction no doubt
prevails in point of gifts, calling, and circumstances, but there can be no distinction in the love of the Father and His desire to see every one of His children in full
health and in the full enjoyment of the Spirit of adoption. Learn, then, to express
and to repeat over again the conviction: "*This blessing is for me.* My Father desires
to have me so that He may fill me with His Spirit. The blessing lies before me, to
be taken with my full consent. I will no longer despise by unbelief what falls to me
as my birthright. With my whole heart I will say: 'This blessing is for me.'"

4. *I cannot grasp this blessing in my own power.*

Whenever a Christian begins to strive for this blessing, he generally makes a
variety of efforts to reach after the faith, obedience, humility, and submission that
are the conditions of obtaining it. Then, when he does not succeed, he is tempted
to blame himself, and if he does not become utterly discouraged, he rouses himself
to still stronger effort and greater zeal. All this struggling is not without its value
and its use. It has its use, however, in other ways than are commonly anticipated. It
does the very work that the law does—that is to say, it brings us to the knowledge
of our entire impotence; it leads us to that despair of ourselves in which we become willing to give to God the place that belongs to Him. This lesson is entirely
indispensable. "I can neither bestow this blessing on myself nor take it. It is God
alone who must work it in me."

The blessing of Pentecost is a supernatural gift, a wonderful act of God in the
soul. The life of God in every soul is just as truly a work of God as when that life
was first manifested in Jesus Christ. A Christian can do as little to bring the full
life of the Spirit to fruition in his soul as the Virgin Mary did to conceive her
supernatural child (see Luke 1:38). Like her, he can only receive it as the gift of
God; the impartation of this heavenly blessing is as entirely an act of God as the
resurrection of Christ from the dead was His divine work. As Christ Jesus had
wholly and entirely to go down to death, and lay aside utterly the life He had, in
order to receive a new life from God, so must the believer abandon all power and
hope of his own to receive this full blessing as a free gift of divine omnipotence.

This acknowledgment of our utter inability, this descent into true self-despair, is indispensable if we want to enjoy this supreme blessing.

5. *I must have this blessing at any cost.*

To get possession of the pearl of great price, the merchant had to sell all that he had. The full blessing of Pentecost is to be obtained at no smaller price. He who desires to have it must sell all, must forsake all. Sin to its smallest item, the love of the world in its most innocent forms, self-will in its simplest and most natural expressions, every faculty of our nature, every moment of our life, every pleasure that feeds our self-complacency, every exercise of our body, soul, and spirit—all must be surrendered to the power of the Spirit of God. In nothing can independent control or independent force have a place. Everything—everything, I say—must be under the leading of the Spirit. One must indeed say: "Whatever it costs, I am determined to have this blessing." Only the vessel that is utterly empty of everything can be filled and overflow with this living water.

We know that there is oftentimes a great gulf between the will and the deed. Even when God has produced the willing, the doing does not always come immediately. But it will come wherever a man surrenders himself to the will that God has produced, and openly expresses his consent in the presence of God. This, accordingly, is what must be done by the soul who intends to be sincerely ready to part with everything, even though he feels that he has no power to accomplish it. The selling price is not always paid at the moment. Nevertheless, the purchaser may become the possessor as soon as the sale is concluded and security is given for the payment.

O my brother, this very day speak the word: "Whatever it costs, I will have this blessing." Jesus is surety that you will have power to abandon everything. Express your decision in the presence of God with confidence and perseverance. Repeat it before your own conscience and say: "I am a purchaser of the pearl of great price. I have offered everything to obtain the full blessing of Pentecost. I have said to God that I must, I will have it. By this decision I abide. I must, I will have it."

6. *In faith that God accepts my surrender and bestows this blessing upon me, I appropriate it for myself.*

There is a great difference between the appropriation of a blessing by faith and the actual experience of it. It is because Christians do not understand this that they often become discouraged when they do not immediately experience the feeling and the enjoyment of what is promised them.

Whenever in response to the offer of Christ you have said that you forsake all and count it but loss for the full blessing of Pentecost, then from that moment you have to believe that He receives your offer and that He bestows upon you the fullness of the Spirit. Yet it may easily be that you cannot at that crossroad trace any marked change in your experience. It is as if everything in you remained in its old condition. Now, however, is just the very time to persevere in faith.

Learn by faith to be as sure as if you had seen it written in heaven that God has accepted your surrender of everything as a certain and completed transaction. In this faith look upon yourself as a man who is known to God as one who has sold everything to obtain this heavenly treasure. Believe that God has in heaven bestowed upon you the fullness of the Spirit. In this faith regard yourself as on the way to know the full blessing also in feeling and experience. Believe that God will order this blessing to break forth and be revealed in you. In this faith let your life be a life of joyful thanksgiving and expectation. God will not disappoint you.

7. *Now I count on God and wait on Him to reveal truly within me the blessing that He has bestowed upon me.*

Faith must lead me to the actual inheritance of the promise, to the experience and enjoyment of it. Do not rest content with a belief that does not lead to experience. Rest in God by faith in the full assurance that He can make Himself known to you in a manner that is truly divine. At times the whole process may appear to you too great and too wonderful, and really impossible. Do not be afraid. The more clearly you discern the amazing elements in the fact that you on your part have said to the eternal Holy God that He on His part may have you to make you full of His Holy Spirit here on earth, the more shall you feel what a miracle of the grace of God it must be.

> *W*henever in response to the offer of Christ you have said that you forsake all and count it but loss for the full blessing of Pentecost, then from that moment you have to believe that He receives your offer and that He bestows upon you the fullness of the Spirit.

There may be in you things you are not aware of that hinder the breaking forth of the blessing. God is determined to put them aside. Let them be consumed in the fire of strong burning desire. Let them be annihilated in the flame of God's countenance and His love. Let your expectation be fixed upon the Lord your God. He who in a frail woman revealed the divine life in the Infant Jesus, He who raised up the dead Jesus to the life of glory, He can—He will, indeed—just as miraculously bring this heavenly blessing to fruition in you, so that you may be filled with the Holy Spirit and that you may know, not by reasoning but by experience, that you have actually received the Holy Spirit.

Beloved brother, you who read all this, give answer, I encourage you, to the summons I bring you. God promises, God desires to make you full of the Holy Spirit. He desires to have your whole nature and life under the power of the Holy Spirit. He asks if you on your part are willing, if you really desire to have it. Let there be in your answer no uncertain sound, but let all that is within you cry out: "Yes, Lord, with all my heart." Let this promise of your God become the chief element in your life, the most precious, the chief, the only thing you seek. Do not be content to think and pray over it, but this very day enter into a transaction and a compact with God that will admit of no doubt concerning the choice you have made.

When once you have made this choice, cleave firmly to what is the chief element in it—namely the faith that expects this blessing as a miracle of divine omnipotence. The more earnestly you exercise that faith, the more will it teach you that your heart must be entirely emptied of everything and set free from every impediment to be filled with the Spirit, to be occupied by the indwelling Christ. Think of yourself in faith as a man between whom and God a firm compact has been made that you must receive the full blessing. You may take it for granted that it will surely come. Amen.

For Further Thought

1. *What personal acknowledgment is absolutely necessary for you to make before you can personally grasp the power and the blessings of the fullness of God's Spirit?*

2. *What part does your faith in God—faith that He can do all and you can do nothing—play in your receiving the promised fullness of His Holy Spirit's taking possession of you and working within and through you?*

3. *What part does a personal, consuming desire for the fullness of God's blessing play in your receiving it? What will God do when He sees that desire within you?*

7
HOW IT MAY BE KEPT

But you. . .praying in the Holy Spirit, keep yourselves in
the love of God. . . . Now to Him who is able to keep you
from stumbling. . .to God our Savior. . .be glory. . .
both now and forever. Amen.
JUDE 20–21, 24–25

CAN one who has the full blessing of Pentecost lose it again? Yes, undoubtedly! God does not bestow this benefit with such constraint that a man retains it
whether he will or not. No, this blessing also is entrusted to him as a talent that
must be used, and only by use does it become secure and win success. Just as the
Lord Jesus after He was baptized with the Holy Spirit had to be perfected by
obedience and submission to the leading of the Spirit, so the Christian who has
received the blessing of Pentecost has to see to it that he guards safely the deposit
that has been entrusted to him.

When we inquire how we can keep it, scripture points us to the fact that our
keeping of it consists in our entrusting it to the Lord to be kept by Him. Paul
places these two ideas alongside one another in his second letter to Timothy: "He
is able to keep what I have committed to Him"; "That good thing which was committed to you, keep by the Holy Spirit who dwells in us" (2 Tim. 1:12, 14). Jude
also, after saying, "Keep yourselves in the love of God" (21), adds the doxology:
"To Him who is able to keep you. . .be glory" (24–25).

The main secret of success in the preservation of the blessing is the exercise of
a humble dependence on the Lord, who keeps us, and on the Spirit, by whom He
keeps it in us and by whom we ourselves keep it in fellowship with Him. It is with
this blessing as with the manna that fell in the wilderness: It must be renewed from
heaven every day. It is with the new heavenly life as with the life we live on earth:
The fresh air that sustains it must be drawn in every moment from without and
from above. Let us see how this ever-abiding, uninterrupted keeping takes place.

1. *Jesus, who gave us the blessing, will keep it for us.*

Jesus is the Keeper of Israel. This is His name and this is His work. God not
only created the world but also keeps and upholds it. Jesus is not content with
merely giving the blessing of Pentecost: He will also maintain it every moment.

The Holy Spirit is not a power that in any sense is subordinate to us, that is entrusted to us, and that we must use. He is a power that is over and above us, that possesses and energizes us, a power by which Jesus in heaven will carry forward His work from moment to moment. Our right place and our proper attitude must always be that of the deepest dependence, a sinking down in our own nothingness and helplessness. Our chief concern is to let Jesus do His work within us.

> *Our right place and our proper attitude must always be that of the deepest dependence, a sinking down in our own nothingness and helplessness. Our chief concern is to let Jesus do His work within us.*

So long as the soul does not discern this truth, there will always be in it a certain dread of receiving the full blessing. Such a one will be inclined to say: "I shall not be able to continue in that holy life. I shall not be able to dwell always on such a lofty plane." But these thoughts only show what a weak grasp such a one has of the great reality. When Jesus comes by the Spirit to dwell in my heart and to live in me, He will actually work out the maintenance of the blessing and regard my whole inner life as His special care. He who believes this truth sees that the life in the joy of the blessing of Pentecost, while it can never be relieved of the necessity of watchfulness, is a life that is freed from anxiety and ought to be characterized by continued gladness. The Lord has come into His holy temple. There He will abide and work out everything. He desires only this one thing—namely that the soul shall know and honor Him as its faithful Shepherd, its almighty Keeper. Jesus, who gives the blessing of Pentecost, will certainly keep it in us.

2. Jesus will keep the blessing, as He gave it, by faith.

The law that prevails at every stage in the progress of the kingdom of God is: "According to your faith let it be to you" (Matt. 9:29). The faith that in the first reception of the Lord Jesus was as small as a grain of mustard seed must, in the course of the Christian life, become always so enlarged that it shall see more and receive and enjoy more of the fullness that is in the Lord.

Paul wrote to the Galatians: "It is no longer I who live, but Christ lives in me; and the life which I now live in the flesh I live by faith" (2:20). His faith was as broad and boundless and unceasing as were the needs of his life and work. In everything and at all times, without ceasing, he trusted in Jesus to do all. His faith was as wide and abundant as the energy that flows from Jesus for the enrichment of His people is mighty and glorious. He had given up his whole life to Jesus, and he himself lived no longer. By a continuous and unrestricted faith he gave to Jesus the liberty of energizing his life without ceasing and without limitation.

The fullness of the Spirit is not a gift that is bestowed once for all as a part of the heavenly life. No, it is not so. It is rather a constantly flowing stream of the river of the water of life that pours from beneath the throne of God and of the Lamb. It is an uninterrupted communication of the life and the love of Jesus, the most personal and intimate association of the Lord with His own upon the earth. It is by the faith that discerns this truth and assents to it and cleaves to it with joy that Jesus will certainly do His work of keeping.

3. *Jesus keeps this blessing in fellowship with Himself.*

The single aim of the blessing of Pentecost is to reveal Jesus as the Savior so that He may exhibit His power to redeem souls in us and by us here in the world. The Spirit did not come merely to occupy the place of Jesus, but only and wholly to unite the disciples with their Lord more closely, deeply, and completely than when He was on earth. The power from on high did not come as a power that they were from then on to rely on as their own. Rather, the power was inseparably bound up with the Lord Jesus and the Holy Spirit. Every operation of the power was a direct working of God in them. The fellowship that the disciples had with Jesus on earth, the following of Him, the reception of His teaching, the doing of His will, the participation in His suffering—all this was to be still their experience, only in greater measure.

> *The Spirit in us will always glorify Jesus, will always make it manifest that He alone is to be Lord, that all which is glorious comes only from Him.*

Not otherwise, accordingly, is it with us. The Spirit in us will always glorify Jesus, will always make it manifest that He alone is to be Lord, that all which is glorious comes only from Him. Close communion with God in the inner chamber, faithfulness in searching His Word and seeking to know His will in the scriptures, sacrifice of time and business and interaction with men, to bring us into touch with the Savior—all this is indispensable for the keeping of the blessing. Jesus keeps us through our closeness with Him, being occupied with Himself. He who loves His fellowship above everything shall have the experience of His keeping.

4. *Jesus keeps the blessing in the pathway of obedience.*

When the Lord Jesus promised the Holy Spirit, He said three times over that the blessing was for the obedient. "If you love Me, keep My commandments. And I will pray the Father, and He will give you another Helper" (John 14:15–16; cf. 20:21, 23). Peter speaks of "the Holy Spirit whom God has given to those who obey Him" (Acts 5:32). Of our Lord Himself, we read that He "became obedient to the point of death. . . . Therefore God also has highly exalted Him" (Phil. 2:8–9). Obedience is what God cannot but demand. It is the only true relationship and blessedness of the creature. It is obedience that attains what was lost by the Fall. It is the power of obedience Jesus came to restore. It is His own life. Apart from obedience the blessing of Pentecost can neither come nor abide.

There are two kinds of obedience. There is one that is very defective, like that of the disciples previous to Pentecost. They desired from the heart to do what the Lord said, but they did not have the power. Yet the Lord accounted their desire and purpose as obedience. On the other hand, there is a more abundant life, which comes with the fullness of the Spirit, where new power is given for full obedience. The characteristic of the full blessing of Pentecost, and the way to keep it, is a surrender to obedience in the minutest details. To listen to the voice of Jesus Himself, to the voice of the Spirit, to the voice of conscience—this is the way in which Jesus leads us. The method of making the life of Pentecost within us sure and strong is to know Jesus and to love Him, and receive Him in that aspect that made Him well-pleasing to the Father—namely as the Obedient One. The whole Jesus becomes the life of the soul.

> *I*t is obedience that attains what was lost by the Fall. It is the power of obedience Jesus came to restore. It is His own life. Apart from obedience the blessing of Pentecost can neither come nor abide.

It is the exercise of this obedience that gives to the soul a wonderful firmness and confidence and power to trust God and to expect all from Him. A strong will is necessary for a strong faith, and it is in obedience that the will is strengthened to trust God to the uttermost. This is the only way in which the Lord can lead us to ever-richer blessing.

5. *Jesus keeps the blessing in fellowship with His people.*

At the outset of His seeking for the full blessing, a Christian thinks for the most part only of himself. Even after he receives the blessing as a new experience, he is still rather disposed to see merely how he can keep it safely for himself. But very speedily the Spirit will teach him that a member of the body cannot enjoy the flow of healthful life in a state of separation from others. He begins to understand that "there is one body and one Spirit" (Eph. 4:4). The unity of the body must be realized to enjoy the fullness of the Spirit.

This principle teaches us some very important lessons about the condition on which the blessing received can be maintained. All that you have belongs to others and must be employed for their service. All that they have belongs to you and is in turn indispensable for you. The Spirit of the body of the Lord can work effectively only when the members of it work in unison. You should confess to others what the Lord has done for you, ask their intercession, seek their fellowship, and help them with what the Lord has given you. You should lay to heart the unhappy condition of the weakened Christian Church in our days, yet not in the spirit of judgment or bitterness, but rather in the spirit of humility and prayer, of gentleness and willingness to serve. Jesus will teach you what is meant by the saying that "love is the greatest" (see 1 Cor. 13:13), and by the very intensity of your surrender to the welfare of His Church He will both keep and increase the blessing in you.

6. Jesus keeps the blessing in the service of His kingdom.

We have said more than once that the Spirit came as the power for work. The very name of Jesus Christ involves entire consecration to God's work, utter devotion to the rescue of souls. It was for this end alone that He lived, and it is only for this cause that He lives in heaven. How can anyone ever dream of having the Spirit of Christ otherwise than as a Spirit who aims at the work of God and the salvation of souls? It is an impossibility. Therefore, from the outset we must keep these two aspects of the Spirit's operation closely knit together. What the Spirit works in us is for the sake of what He works by us. Our seeking for the blessing will miscarry, our initial possession of the blessing will be lost, if we do not as the dominant feature of our life present ourselves to be used by the Spirit in the doing of His work.

> *Although you do not understand everything, yet believe that the Lord Jesus has sent His Spirit with no other object in view than just to receive and keep you in His divine power. Trust Him for this.*

The blessing of Pentecost does not always come with equal power and not always instantly. God often gives preparatory experiences and awakenings that must lead to the full blessing. Every attempt to keep such gracious gifts for ourselves will entail loss. He who does not follow his own inclination, either in being silent or in speaking, but presents himself to the Lord and waits upon Him with an undivided spirit, will experience that work, so far from exhausting or weakening, is the sure way to keep the treasure.

7. One thought more. *It is as the indwelling Lord that Jesus keeps the blessing of Pentecost in us.*

Whenever mention is made of Jesus as our Keeper, it is oftentimes difficult to believe that we who are on the earth can really know ourselves to be always, without interruption, in His hands and under His power. How much clearer and more glorious does the truth become when the Spirit reveals to us the truth that Christ is in us, and that not only as a tenant in a house, or water in a glass, in such a fashion that they continue quite distinct, but rather as the soul is in the body animating and moving every part of it, and never to be separated from each other except by a violent death.

Yes, this is how Christ dwells in us: penetrating our whole nature with His nature. The Holy Spirit came for the purpose of making Him deeply present within us this way. As the sun is high in the sky above me, and yet by its heat penetrates my bones and marrow and awakens my whole life, so the Lord Jesus, who is exalted high in heaven, penetrates my whole nature by His Spirit in such a way that all my willing, thinking, and feeling are animated by Him. Once this fact is fully grasped, we no longer think of an external keeping through a person outside of us in heaven, but rather become convinced that our whole individual life is itself quickened and possessed by One who, not in a human but in a divine, all-penetrating manner, occupies and fills the heart. Then we see how natural, how certain, how blessed it is that the indwelling Jesus keeps the blessing and always maintains the fullness of the Spirit.

Brethren, is there anyone among you who is longing for this life in the fullness of blessing and yet is afraid to enter upon it because he does not know how he is to persevere? Please listen to what I say: Jesus will make this blessing continuous and sure. Is there any one of you who longs for it and yet cannot understand where the secret of it lies? Again listen to me: The blessing is this—that as Jesus Christ was daily with His disciples in bodily fashion, so He will by His Spirit every day and always be your life; yes, live His life in you.

No one can fully understand how things look on the top of a mountain until he himself has been there. Although you do not understand everything, yet believe that the Lord Jesus has sent His Spirit with no other object in view than just to receive and keep you in His divine power. Trust Him for this. Let all burdens be laid aside and give yourself up to receive from Him this full blessing of Pentecost as a fountain that He Himself will cause to spring up in you unto everlasting life.

For Further Thought

1. *What heart attitude must you have in order for Jesus Christ to keep and to maintain the blessing of the fullness of God's Holy Spirit within you?*
2. *What role does personal obedience play in your continuously and consistently walking in the fullness of God's indwelling Spirit?*
3. *To what must you consecrate yourself, or set yourself apart for, before Jesus Christ will maintain within you the full indwelling of His Spirit?*

8

HOW IT MAY BE INCREASED

"He who believes in Me shall never thirst."
JOHN 6:35

*"He who believes in Me...
out of his heart will flow rivers of living water."*
JOHN 7:38

CAN the full blessing of Pentecost be still further increased? Can anything that is full become still fuller? Yes, undoubtedly. It can become so full that it always overflows. This is especially the characteristic and law of the blessing of Pentecost.

The words of our blessed Lord Jesus that have been quoted point us to a double blessing. First, Jesus says that he who believes in Him shall never thirst, that he shall always have life in himself—that is to say, the satisfaction of all his needs. Then He speaks of something that is grander and more glorious: He who believes in Him, out of his heart will flow rivers of living water to quench the thirst of others. It is the distinction between full and overflowing.

A vessel may be full and yet have nothing over for others. When it continues full and yet has something over for others, there must be in it an over-brimming, ever-flowing supply. This is what our Lord promises to His believing disciples. At the outset, faith in Him gives them the blessing that they shall never thirst. But as they advance and become stronger in faith, it makes them a fountain of water out of which streams flow to others. The Spirit who at first only fills us will overflow out of us to souls around us.

It is with the rivers of living water as with many a fountain on earth. When we begin to open them, the stream is weak. The more the water is used, the more deeply the source is opened up, the more strongly does the water flow. I should like to inquire how far this principle holds good in the realm of the spiritual life and to discover what is necessary to secure that the fullness of the Spirit may constantly flow more abundantly from us. There are several simple directions that may help us in reaching this knowledge.

1. *Hold fast that which you have.*

See to it that you do not misunderstand the blessing that God has given you. Be sure that you do not form any wrong conceptions of what the full blessing is. Do not imagine that the animation, and joy, and power of Pentecost must be felt and seen immediately. No, the Church at present is in a dead-and-alive condition, and the restoration often comes slowly. At first, indeed, one receives the full blessing only as a seed: The full life is wrapped up in a little invisible capsule. The awakened soul has longed for it, has surrendered himself unreservedly for it, has believed in silence that God has accepted his consecration and fulfilled His promise. In that faith, he goes on his way, silent and happy, saying to himself: "The blessing of the fullness of the Spirit is for me."

But the actual experiences of the blessing did not come as he had anticipated, or they did come but lasted only for a short time. The result was that he began to fear that his surrender was not a reality, that he had been rejoicing in what was only a transient emotion, and that the real blessing was something greater and more powerful than he had yet received. The result is that very speedily the blessing becomes less instead of larger, and he moves farther back rather than forward through discouragement on account of his disappointment.

The cause of this condition is simply lack of faith. We are bent on judging God and His work in us by sight and feeling. We forget that the whole process is the work of faith. Even in its highest revelations in Christians who have made the greatest progress, faith does not rest on what is to be seen of the work of God or on the experiences of it, but on the work of God as spiritual, invisible, deeply hidden, and inconceivable.

To you, therefore, my brother, who desires in this time of discouragement to return to the true life according to the promise, my counsel is not to be greatly surprised if it comes to you slowly or if it appears to be involved in darkness. If you know that you have given yourself to God with a perfect heart, and if you know that God, really and with His whole heart, waits to fulfill His promise in you with divine power, then rest in silence before His face and hold fast your integrity. Although the cold of winter appears to bury everything in death, say with the prophet Habakkuk: "Though the fig tree may not blossom, nor fruit be on the vines...yet I will rejoice in the LORD, I will joy in the God of my salvation" (3:17–18). Do this, and you shall know God, and God will know you.

If you are sure that you have set yourself before God as an empty, separated, purified vessel, to become full of His Spirit, then continue still to regard yourself so and keep silence before Him. If you have believed that God has received you to fill you as a purified vessel—purified through Jesus Christ and by your entire surrender to Him—then abide in this attitude day by day, and you may rely on it that the blessing will grow and begin to flow. "He who believes will by no means be put to shame" (see Isa. 28:16; 1 Pet. 2:6).

2. *Persevere in the entire denial of yourself and the sacrifice of everything.*

If I wish to have a reservoir of water, the greater the excavation I make for it, the wider the space I occupy with it, the greater is the quantity of water I can collect, and the stronger is the stream that flows from it when the channels are opened. In your surrender for sanctification, or for the full blessing of the Spirit, you have said in truth and uprightness that you are prepared to sacrifice and forsake all in order to win this pearl of the kingdom of heaven—and this consecration was acceptable to God. But you have not yet fully understood the full significance of the words you have used. The Lord has still much to teach you concerning what the individual self is, how deeply rooted in your nature, how utterly corrupt as well as deeply hidden it is, as the secret source of many things you both say and do.

> *A vessel may be full and yet have nothing over for others. When it continues full and yet has something over for others, there must be in it an over-brimming, ever-flowing supply. This is what our Lord promises to His believing disciples.*

Be willing to make room for the Spirit by a constant, daily, and entire denial of the self-life, and you may be sure that He will always be willing to come and fill the empty place. You have forsaken and sacrificed everything so far as you know, but keep your mind open to the teaching of the Spirit, and He will lead you farther on and let you see that only when the entire sacrifice of everything after the example of Christ comes again to be the rule in His Church shall the full blessing again break forth like an overflowing stream.

It is surprising how sometimes a very little thing may hinder the continuance in the increase of the blessing. It may, for example, be a little conflict between friends, in which they show that they are not willing to forgive and to forbear at once according to the law of Christ. Or it may be some unobserved yielding to undue sensitiveness or to the ambition that is not prepared to take the lowest place. Or it may be the possession or use of earthly property as if it were our own. Or it may be some providing for the flesh in the enjoyment of eating and drinking without the self-denial that Christ always expects at our hands every day. Or it may be in connection with things that are lawful and in themselves innocent but which, however, do not befit us in our profession of being led by the Spirit of God. For here, like the Lord Jesus in His poverty, we are bound to show that the heavenly portion we possess is itself sufficient to satisfy all our desires. Or it may be in connection with doubtful things, in which we give way too easily to the lust of the flesh.

Christian brother, do you really desire to enjoy the full measure of the blessing of the Spirit? Then, before temptation comes, train yourself to understand the fundamental law of the imitation of Jesus and of full discipleship—namely, *Forsake all*. Allow yourself also to be strengthened and drawn into the observance of it by the sure promise of the "hundredfold in this life" (see Mark 10:30). A full blessing will be given to you, a measure shaken together and running over.

3. *Regard yourself as living only to make others happy.*

God is Love. His whole being is nothing but a surrender of Himself in love to be the life of the creature, to make the creature participate in His holiness and blessedness. He blesses and serves all that lives. His glory as God is that He puts all that He has at the disposal of His creatures.

Jesus Christ is the Son of God's love—the Bearer, the Bringer, the Dispenser of the love. What God is as invisible in heaven, He was as visible on earth. He came, He lived, He suffered and died only to glorify the Father—that is, to let it be seen how glorious the Father in His love is, and to show that in the Godhead there is no other purpose than to bless men and make them happy, to make it evident that the highest honor and blessedness of any being is to give and to sacrifice.

> *Jesus Christ is the Son of God's love—the Bearer, the Bringer, the Dispenser of the love. What God is as invisible in heaven, He was as visible on earth.*

The Holy Spirit came as the Spirit of the Father and the Son to make us partakers of this divine nature, to shed abroad the love of God in our hearts, to secure the indwelling of the Son and His love in our hearts to such an extent that Christ may truly be formed within us, and that our whole "inner man" shall bear the impression of His disposition and His likeness.

Therefore, when any soul seeks and receives the fullness of the Spirit and desires to have it increased, is it not perfectly evident that he can enjoy this blessing only according as he is prepared to give himself to a life in the service of love? The Spirit comes to expel the life of self and self-seeking. The fullness of the Spirit presupposes a willingness to consecrate ourselves to the blessing of others and as the servants of all, and that in a constantly increasing and unreserved measure. The Spirit is the outflowing of the life of God. If we will but yield ourselves to Him, He will become rivers of living water flowing from the depths of our heart.

Christian brother, if you will have the blessing increased, begin to live as a man who is left here on earth only in order that the love of God may work by you. Love all around you with the love of God that is in you through the Spirit. Love the children of God cordially, even the weakest and most perverse. Exercise and exhibit your love in every possibly way. Love the unsaved. Present yourself to the Spirit to love Him. Then will love constrain you to speak, to work, to give, and to pray. If there is no open door for working, or if you have not the strength for it, the door of prayer is always open, and power can be obtained at the mercy seat.

THE FULL BLESSING OF PENTECOST

Embrace the whole world in your love, for Christ, who is in your heart, belongs also to the heathen. The Spirit is the power of Christ for redeeming them.

4. *Let Jesus Christ for your faith be everything.*

You know what the scripture says: "For it pleased the Father that *in Him* all the fullness should dwell...that in all things *He* may have the preeminence" (Col. 1:18–19), and again: "All the promises of God *in Him* are Yes, and *in Him* Amen, to the glory of God through us" (2 Cor. 1:20). When the Lord spoke of "rivers of living water," He connected the promise with faith in Himself: "He who believes in *Me*...out of his heart will flow rivers." If we only understood that word *believes* rightly, we would require no other answer than this to the question as to how the blessing may be increased.

Faith is primarily a seeing by the Spirit that Jesus is nothing but a flowing fountain of the divine love, and that the Spirit Himself always flows from Him as the Bearer of the life that this love brings and that always streams forth in love. Then it is an embracing of the promise, an appropriation of the blessing as it is provided in Christ, a resting in the certainty of it, and a thanking of God for what He is yet to do. Thereafter, faith is a keeping open of the soul, so that Christ can come in with the blessing and take possession and fill all. Accordingly, faith becomes the most fervent and unbroken communion between the soul in which Christ obtains His place and Christ Himself, who by the silent, effectual blessing of the Spirit is enthroned in the heart.

Like God and Jesus and the Spirit, live wholly to bless others. Then the blessing shall stream forth and become overflowing.

Christian brother, I encourage you to learn the lesson that if you believe, you shall see the glory of God. Let every doubt, every weakness, every temptation find you trusting, rejoicing in Jesus, and relying on Him always to work all in you. You know that there are two ways in which a believer can encounter and strive against sin. One is to endeavor to ward it off with all his might, seeking his strength in the Word and in prayer. In this form of the conflict we use the power of the will. The other is to turn at the very moment of the temptation to the Lord Jesus in the silent exercise of faith and say to Him: "Lord, I have no strength. You are my Keeper" (see Ps. 121:5). This is the method of faith. "And this is the victory that has overcome the world—our faith" (1 John 5:4). Yes, this is indeed "the one thing needed," because it is the only way in which Jesus, who is in Himself "The One Thing Needed," can maintain the work of His Spirit in us. It is by the exercise of faith without ceasing that the blessing will flow without ceasing.

Christ must be all to us every moment. It is of no benefit to me that I have life on earth unless that life is renewed every moment by my inbreathing of fresh air. Even so must God actually renew, and uphold, and strengthen the divine life in me every moment. He does this for me in my union with Christ. Christ is simply the fullness of God, the life of God, and the love of God prepared for us and communicating itself to us. The Spirit is simply the fullness of Christ, the life of Christ, and the self-communicating love of Christ surrounding us as the air surrounds the body.

> *It is of no benefit to me that I have life on earth unless that life is renewed every moment by my inbreathing of fresh air. Even so must God actually renew, and uphold, and strengthen the divine life in me every moment.*

Oh, let us believe that we are in Christ, who surrounds us in His heavenly power, longing to make the rivers of His Spirit flow forth by us! Let us endeavor to obtain a heart filled with the joyful assurance that the almighty Lord will fulfill His word with power, and that our only choice is to see Him, to rejoice in Him, and to sacrifice all for Him. Then shall His word become true: "He who believes in Me...out of his heart will flow rivers of living water." Amen.

For Further Thought

1. *God calls you to entire, continual self-denial and self-sacrifice as a condition for the fullness of His Spirit. How can you know you are living in this kind of denial of self? How can you know if there are parts of your life in which you are not living in this kind of self-denial?*
2. *What should your attitude and actions toward others look like if you want to not just maintain but increase the fullness of the Holy Spirit's indwelling power in your life?*
3. *Faith in Jesus Christ is absolutely essential for the increasing of His Spirit's indwelling within you. What exactly must you believe God for when it comes to this kind of faith? How can you increase that kind of faith?*

9

How It Comes to Its Full Manifestation

I bow my knees to the Father...
[1] that He would grant you...to be strengthened
with might through His Spirit in the inner man,
[2] that Christ may dwell in your hearts through faith;
[3] that you, being rooted and grounded in love, may be
able to...know the love of Christ which passes knowledge;
[4] that you may be filled with all the fullness of God.
EPHESIANS 3:14–19

WE have remarked several times that every blessing that God gives is like a seed with the power of an indissoluble life hidden in it. Let no one therefore imagine that to be filled with the Spirit is a condition of perfection that leaves nothing more to be desired. In no sense can this be true.

It was after the Lord Jesus was filled with the Spirit at His baptism that He had to go forth to be still further perfected by temptations and the learning of obedience. When the disciples were filled with the Spirit on the day of Pentecost, this equipment with power from on high was given to them so that they might carry out the victory over sin in their own lives and all around them. The Spirit is the Spirit of truth, and He must guide us into it. It will only be by slow degrees that He will lead us into the eternal purpose of God, into the knowledge of Christ, into true holiness, into full fellowship with God. The fullness of the Spirit is simply the full preparation for living and working as a child of God.

When we consider the matter from this point of view, we see at a glance how entirely indispensable it is for every child of God to aim at obtaining this blessing. Then we begin to feel that this is the very blessing that is to be pressed on the acceptance of the weak and timid. We also understand why it is that Paul offers this prayer on which we are now to meditate, on behalf of all believers without distinction. He did not regard it as a spiritual distinction or special luxury that was intended only for those who were prominent or favored among the children of God. No, it was for all without distinction, for all who at their conversion had by faith received the Holy Spirit, that he prayed. And his request was that by the special, powerful, and ever-deepening work of the Spirit, God would bring them to what was their true destiny—namely to be filled to all the fullness of God. This prayer of Paul is everywhere regarded as one of the most glorious representations that the Word of God gives of what the life of a Christian ought to be. Let us then endeavor to learn what the full revelation and manifestation of this blessing of the Spirit may become.

1. *That the Father would grant you that you may be strengthened with power through the Spirit.*

That these Christians had received the Spirit when they believed in Christ is clear from a previous statement of the epistle (see Eph. 1:14). But he sees that they do not yet know or have all that the Spirit can do for them, and that there is a danger that, by their ignorance, they may make no further progress. For that reason, he bows his knees and prays without ceasing in their behalf that the Father would strengthen them with might by His Spirit in the inner man. This powerful strengthening with the Spirit is equivalent to being filled with the Spirit, is indeed this same blessing under another aspect. It is the indispensable condition of a healthy, growing, and fruitful life.

> *T*he Spirit is the Spirit of truth, and He must guide us into it. It will only be by slow degrees that He will lead us into the eternal purpose of God, into the knowledge of Christ, into true holiness, into full fellowship with God.

Paul prays that the Father would grant this benefit. He asks for a new, definite operation of God. He pleads that God would do this according to the riches of His glory. It is surely not any insignificant thing, anything very common, that he craves. He desires that God would remember and bring into play all the riches of His grace and, in a fashion commensurate with the divine glory of His power, do a heavenly wonder and as the living God strengthen these believers with might by His Spirit in the inner man.

O Christian, learn at this point that your life every day depends on God's will, on God's grace, on God's omnipotence. Yes, every moment God must work in your inner life and strengthen you by His Spirit; otherwise you cannot live as He would have you live. Just as no creature in the natural world can exist for a moment if God does not work in it to sustain its life, so the gift of the Holy Spirit is the pledge that God Himself is to work everything in us from moment to moment. Learn to know your entire, your blessed dependence on God, and the claim that you have on Him as your heavenly Father to begin in you a life in the mighty strengthening of the Spirit and to maintain it without the interruption of a single moment.

Paul tells these believers what he prays for on their behalf in order that they may know what they need and ask for it for themselves. Do you also learn to offer up this petition? Expect everything from God alone. Bow your knees and ask and expect from the Father that He would manifest to you—yes, in you—the riches of His glory. Ask and expect that He would strengthen you with might by His Spirit, that Spirit who in fact is already in you, but only as an unknown, hidden, and slumbering seed. Let this become the one desire, the strong confidence of your soul: "God will fill me with the Spirit: God will strengthen me through the Spirit with His almighty energy." Let your whole life every day be permeated by this prayer and this expectation.

2. *That Christ may dwell in your hearts through faith.*

This is the glorious fruit of the divine strengthening with might in the inner man by the Spirit. The great work of the Father in eternity is to bring forth the Son.

In Him alone is the good pleasure of God realized. The Father can have no fellowship with the creature except through the Son. He can have no joy in man except so far as He sees His Son in him. Therefore, it is His great work in redemption to reveal His Son in us, and so to obtain a home for Him in us so that our life shall be a visible expression of the life of Jesus.

That is the aim He has in view in strengthening us with might by the Spirit in the inner man. It is that Christ may dwell in our hearts by faith.

> *Just as no creature in the natural world can exist for a moment if God does not work in it to sustain its life, so the gift of the Holy Spirit is the pledge that God Himself is to work everything in us from moment to moment.*

This indwelling of Christ in us is not like that of a man who lives in a house but is nevertheless in no sense identified with it. No, His indwelling is a possession of our hearts that is truly divine, quickening and penetrating their inmost being with His life. The Father strengthens us inwardly with might by His Spirit so that the Spirit animates our will and brings it, like the will of Jesus, into entire sympathy with His own. The result is that our heart then, like the heart of Jesus, bows before Him in humility and surrender. Then our life seeks only His honor, and our whole soul thrills with desire and love for Jesus. This inward renewal makes the heart fit to be a dwelling place of the Lord. By the Spirit He is revealed within us and we come to know that He is actually in us as our life, in a deep, divine unity, one with us.

Brother, God longs to see Jesus in you. He is prepared to work mightily in you so that Christ may dwell in you. The Spirit has come, and the Father is willing to work mightily by Him that the living presence of His Son may always abide in you. Jesus loves you so dearly and longs so intensely for you that He cannot rest until He makes His home in your heart. This is the supreme blessing that the fullness of the Spirit brings you.

That Christ may dwell in your heart through faith. It is by faith that you receive and know the indwelling of the Spirit and the operation of the Father by Him. By faith, which discerns things invisible as clearly as the sun, you receive and know the living Jesus in your heart. As constantly as He was with His disciples on earth—yes, more constantly than with them, because more inwardly and more really—He will be in you and will grant you to enjoy His presence and His love.

> *As constantly as He was with His disciples on earth—yes, more constantly than with them, because more inwardly and more really—He will be in you and will grant you to enjoy His presence and His love.*

O soul, pray that the Father would strengthen you with might by the Spirit, would open your heart for the fullness of the Spirit and enable you to trustfully appropriate it. Then at last shall you know what it means to have Christ dwelling in your heart by faith.

3. *That you, being rooted and grounded in love, may be able to know the love of Christ which passes knowledge.*

Here is the glorious fruit of the indwelling of Christ in the heart. By the Spirit the love of God is shed abroad in the heart. By Christ who dwells in the heart, the love with which God loved Him comes into us. Then we learn that just as life in God between Father, Son, and Spirit is only infinite love, so the life of Christ in us is nothing but love. Thus we become rooted and grounded in love. We are implanted in the soil of love. We sink our roots into heavenly love, and from then on, we have our being in it and draw our strength from it. Love is the supreme element in our spiritual life. The Spirit in us and the Son in us bring us nothing but the love of God. Love is the first and the chief among the streams of living water that are to flow from us.

This is how we come to discover the truths that love is the fulfilling of the law, that love does no harm to one's neighbor (see Rom. 13:10), that love does not seek its own (1 Cor. 13:5), that love lays down its life for the brethren (1 John 3:16). Our heart becomes ever larger and larger, and so our friends, our enemies, the children of God and the children of the world, those who are worthy to be loved and those who are hateful, the ransomed and the lost, the world as a whole and every individual creature in particular—all are embraced in the love of God.

We find, then, that our happiness lies in the sacrifice of our own honor, our own advantage and comfort, in favor of others. Love takes no account of sacrifice, for it is its blessedness to love. It cannot do otherwise, for actual loving is its nature and its life. We are able so to love because the Father with His Spirit works mightily within us, because the Son, "who loved me and gave Himself for me" (Gal. 2:20), dwells in us, and He, who is crucified Love, has filled the heart completely with Himself. We are rooted in love, and in accordance with the nature of the root in God is the fruit from God—love.

That you may be able to know the love which passes knowledge: that is, to know love not with the knowledge of the understanding and its thoughts alone, but in the conscious blessedness of a heart in which Jesus dwells; to know love as something that cannot be known or conceived by the heart of itself; to be strong to know it fully, so far as this is possible before God, in order that He may fill you, an earthen vessel, with His own love to overflowing.

O souls, please listen to the word: "God is Love," and He has provided everything to the purpose that you may know love fully. It is for this object that the Spirit is in you, and that the Father will work mightily in you. It is with this aim that Christ desires to have your whole heart. O let us begin to pray, as never before, that the Father would strengthen us with might by the Spirit, that the Father would grant to us to be filled with the Spirit, that you may be strong to know the love of Christ.

4. *That you may be filled with all the fullness of God.*

What an expression! What an impenetrable mystery! What a divine blessedness! Filled with all the fullness of God: This is the experience to which the fullness of the Spirit is intended to bring us, and will bring us.

Filled with all the *fullness* of God: Who shall ever unfold the meaning of this expression to us? How shall we ever reach any definite idea of what it signifies? God has made provision for our enlightenment. In Christ Jesus we see a man full of God, a man who was perfected by suffering and obedience, filled with all the fullness of God—yes, a man who in the solitariness and poverty of an ordinary human life, with all its needs and infirmities, has nevertheless let us see on earth the life enjoyed by the inhabitants of heaven, as they are there filled unto all the fullness of God. The will and the honor, the love and the service of God were always visible in Him. God was all to Him.

When God called the world into existence, it was in order that it might reveal Him. In it, His wisdom and might and goodness were to dwell and be visibly manifested. We say continually that nature is full of God. God can be seen in everything by the believing eye. The Seraphim sing: "The whole earth is full of His glory!" (Isa. 6:3). When God created man after His image, it was in order that He Himself might be seen in man, that man should simply serve as a reflection of His likeness. The image of a man never serves any other purpose than to represent the man. As the image of God, man was destined simply to receive the glory of God in his own life, to bear it and make it visible. God was to be all to him, to be all in him: He was to be full of God.

By sin this divine purpose has been frustrated. Instead of being full of God, man became full of himself and the world, and to such an extent has sin blinded us that it appears an impossibility ever to become full of God again. Sadly, even many Christians see nothing desirable in this fullness. Yet it is back to this blessing that Jesus came to redeem and bring us. And this is the end for which God is prepared to work mightily within us by His Spirit. This is no less the result for which the Son of God desires to dwell in our heart and which He will bring to accomplishment. It is all that we may be filled unto the fullness of God.

Yes, this is the highest aim of the Pentecostal blessing. To attain this, we can count on the Spirit to make sure of our reaching it. He will open the way for us and guide us in it. He will work in us the deep humility of Jesus, who always said: "I can of Myself *do nothing*" (John 5:30), "I do *not* My own will" (see John 6:38), and "The words that I speak. . .I *do not* speak on My own authority" (14:10).

Amid this self-emptying and sense of dependence, He will work in us the assurance and the experience that for the soul that is nothing, God is surely *all*. By our faith, He will reveal to us Jesus, who was full of God, as our life. He will cause us to be rooted in the love in which God gives all, and we shall take God as all. Thus it will be with us as with Jesus: man nothing, and God's honor, God's will, God's love, God's power, everything. Yes, the issue will be that we shall be "filled with all the fullness of God" (Eph. 3:19).

> *As the image of God, man was destined simply to receive the glory of God in his own life, to bear it and make it visible. God was to be all to him, to be all in him: He was to be full of God.*

Christian, I beg of you by the love of God not to say that this is too high an experience for you, or that it is not for you. No, it is in truth the will of God concerning you—the will alike of His commandment and of His promise. He is bent on fulfilling His promise, and He Himself will work it out. Today, then, in humility and faith take this word, "filled with all the fullness of God," as the purpose and the watchword of your life, and see what it will do for you. It will become to you a mighty lever to raise you out of the self-seeking that is quite content with only being prepared for blessing. It will urge you to enter into and become firmly rooted in the love of God that gives everything to you, and thereby in the love that gives everything back to Him. It will convince you that nothing less than Christ Himself dwelling in your heart can keep such a love abiding in you or actually make the fullness of God a reality within you. It will train you to fix your only hope of all this blessing on the mighty operation of God Himself by the Spirit. It will also move you to go down upon your knees and summon to your aid the wealth of God's glory so that it may itself prepare you for this great wonder. This it will continue to do until your heart is enabled to utter the response: "Yes, *filled with all the fullness of God* is what my God has prepared for me."

With this glorious prospect before us, come and let us join with the apostle in the doxology: "Now to Him who is able to do exceedingly abundantly above all that we ask or think, according to the power that works in us [the power of His might], to Him be glory. . .forever and ever" (Eph. 3:20–21). Let us desire nothing less than these riches of the glory of God. Today, if we have never done it before, let us make a beginning and appropriate for ourselves the full blessing of the Spirit as the power that is sure to lead us to be "filled with all the fullness of God."

When God said to Abraham, "I am Almighty God" (Gen. 17:1), He invited him to trust His omnipotence to fulfill His promise. When Jesus went down into the grave and its powerlessness, it was in the faith that God's omnipotence could lift Him to the throne of His glory. It is that same omnipotence that waits to work out God's purpose in those who believe in Him to do so. Let our hearts say, "*To Him who is able* to do exceedingly abundantly above all that we ask or think, to Him be the glory." Amen.

For Further Thought

1. *Paul prays that God's Spirit may dwell within His people through faith. How is that "dwelling" like a man dwelling in his own home? How is it different?*

2. *One of the conditions and outgrowths of the full manifestation of God's Spirit in you is to "know the love of Christ which passes knowledge." How does that love demonstrate itself—from God to you, from you to God, and from you to others?*

3. *What does it mean to you to be "filled with all the fullness of God," and what can you do to ensure that you are filled with Him in every way?*

10

How Fully It Is
Assured to Us by God

*"If you then, being evil, know how to give good gifts
to your children, how much more will your heavenly Father
give the Holy Spirit to those who ask Him!"*
LUKE 11:13

WHEN Jairus came to the Lord Jesus to plead His help for his dying daughter, and he learned on the way the sorrowful news that she had already died, Jesus said: "Do not be afraid; only believe" (Luke 8:50). Face-to-face with a trial in which man was utterly helpless, the Lord called upon him to put his trust in Himself. There was but one thing that suited his case or could help him: "Only believe."

Many a thousand times has that word been the strength of God's children, where so far as man was concerned all hope was lost and success appeared to be impossible. So here also, while we are on our way to search for and know the full Pentecostal blessing, we have need of this word. In view of the inconceivable preciousness of the blessing, and of the divine element in it, it will indeed be only the wonder-working power of God that can make this exceeding grace a reality within us. Let us only be silent before God, and here also we shall hear the voice of Jesus saying to us: "Do not be afraid; only believe, and God will do it for you."

It is nothing less than this that is the aim of this word of our Lord concerning the divine assurance: that much more readily than an earthly father will give his children bread will God give the Holy Spirit to those who ask Him. We should regard it as quite unnatural on the part of a father if he did not give his child bread. How much more, then, shall not God give the Holy Spirit, yes, all the promised fullness of the Spirit, to those who ask Him? In the midst of all our thinking and speaking, all our praying and hoping, the fundamental element in our spiritual life must be the firm confidence that the Father will give His child His full heritage.

God is spirit. He desires in His eternal love to obtain full possession of us. But He can do this in no other manner than by giving us His Spirit. As surely as He is God will He, O child of God, fill you with His Holy Spirit. Without that faith you will never succeed in your quest of this blessing. That faith will give you the victory over every difficulty. Therefore, "do not be afraid; only believe." Hear the voice of Jesus: "Did I not say to you that if you would believe you would see the glory of God?" (John 11:40).

Let us listen to these three great lessons.

1. *Although you cannot comprehend or explain everything by the mere power of your understanding, still: "Only believe."*

There are many preliminary questions that arise at once in connection with this subject and that tempt us to resolve that we shall first take in and understand everything about it before we expect the blessing. Two of these questions I shall venture to mention now.

The first is: From where must this blessing come, from *within* or from *above*? Some earnest Christians will say immediately that "it must come from *within*." The Holy Spirit descended upon the earth on the day of Pentecost and was given to the Christian community. At the moment of conversion, He comes into our heart. We have therefore no longer to pray that He may be given to us. We are simply to recognize and use what we already have. It is not as if we had to seek to have more of the Spirit, for we have Him in the fullness of the gift as it is. It is rather the Holy Spirit who must have more of us. As we yield ourselves entirely to Him, He will entirely fill us. It is from *within* that the blessing must come. The fountain of living water is already there; the fountain has only to be opened and every obstruction cleared out of the way and the water shall stream forth. It must spring from *within*.

On the other hand, there are not a few who say, "No, it must come from *above*." When, on the arrival of the day of Pentecost, the Father bestowed the Spirit, He did not give Him away beyond His own control. The fullness of the Spirit still remains in God. God bestows nothing apart from Himself to work without or independently of His will. He Himself works only through the Spirit, and every new and greater manifestation of the Spirit's power comes directly from *above*. Long after the day of Pentecost, the Spirit came down again from heaven at Samaria and Caesarea. In His fullness He is in heaven still, and it is from God in heaven that the fullness of the Spirit is to be always waited for.

Brother Christian, I encourage you, do not linger until by reasonings of your own you have decided which of these representations is the right one. God can bless men in both ways. When the flood came, all the fountains of the abyss were broken up and the waterways of heaven were opened. It came simultaneously from beneath and from above. God is prepared to bless men in both of these methods. He desires to teach us to know and honor the Spirit who is already within us. He desires also to bring us to wait upon Himself in a spirit of utter dependence, beseeching Him that He as our Father would give us our daily bread, the new, the fuller influx of His Spirit. I beg you not to allow yourself to be held back by such a question as this. God understands your petition. He knows what you desire. Believe that God is prepared to fill you with His Spirit. Then let that faith look up to Him with unceasing prayer and confidence. He will give the blessing.

The other question is: Does this blessing come gradually or immediately? Will it manifest itself in the shape of a silent, unobserved increase of the grace of the Spirit, or as a momentary immediate outpouring of His power? It must suffice for me to say here again that God has already sent this blessing in both modes and will continue to do so still. What must take place immediately is this: There must be a definite resolve to place the whole life unreservedly under the control of the Spirit, and a conviction of faith that God has accepted this surrender. In the majority of cases this is done immediately. It must at last come to this, perhaps after a long course of seeking and praying, that the soul shall present itself to God for this blessing in one definite, irrevocable act, and shall believe that the offering is then sanctified and accepted upon the altar. From then on, whether the experience of the blessing comes at once and with power, or comes quietly and gradually, the soul must maintain its act of self-dedication and simply look to God to do His own work.

> *L*et us only be silent before God, and here also we shall hear the voice of Jesus saying to us: "Do not be afraid; only believe, and God will do it for you."

Therefore, in dealing with all such questions the chief concern is this: "Only believe" and rest in the *faithfulness of God*. Hold fast this one principle: God has given us a promise that He will fill us with His Spirit. It is His work to make His promise an accomplished fact. Thank God for the promise even as you would thank Him for the fulfillment of it. In the promise, God has already pledged Himself to you. Rejoice in Him and in His faithfulness. Be not held back by any questions whatsoever. Set your heart on what God will do and on Himself from whom the blessing must come. The result will be certain and glorious.

2. *Although you receive but little help from others, or even encounter opposition, still: "Only believe."*

It is one of the saddest evidences of the unspiritual condition of the Church that so many are content with things just as they are and have no desire to know more of this seeking for the reality of the Spirit's power. They point to the present purity of doctrine, to the prevailing earnestness of preaching, to the generous gifts that are made for the maintenance of religious works and the enterprises of philanthropy, to the interest that is manifested in the cause of education and of missions, and they say that we ought rather to give God thanks for the good we see around us.

Such people would condemn the language of Laodicea, and would refuse to say that they were rich and increased in goods, needing nothing (Rev. 3:17), and yet there are some traces of this spirit in what they say. They do not consider the injunction to be "filled with the Spirit." They have forgotten the command to prophesy to the Spirit and say: "Come from the four winds, O breath, and breathe on these slain, that they may live" (Ezek. 37:9). When you speak of these things you will receive little encouragement from them. They do not understand what you mean. They believe indeed in the Holy Spirit, but their eyes have not been opened to the fact that more of the Spirit, the fullness of the Spirit, is the one thing needed for the Church.

> *Your representation of the promise of God is glorious, and all that you expect from the mighty working of the Spirit is in the highest degree desirable.*

There are others who will agree with you when you speak of this need, and yet will really give you less encouragement. They have often both thought and prayed over the matter, but no benefit has accrued from the effort: They have made no real progress. They invite you to look to the Church of earlier times, and say that it was never much otherwise than it is now. What you say of the poverty and weakness of the Church in its relationship to the world is true. Your representation of the promise of God is glorious, and all that you expect from the mighty working of the Spirit is in the highest degree desirable. But—it is not to be obtained. These people belong to the generation of the ten spies who were sent to spy out Canaan. The land is glorious, but the enemy in possession is too strong. We are too weak to overcome them. Lack of consecration and of willingness to surrender everything for this blessing is the root of the unbelief, and it has made them incapable of exercising the courage of Caleb when he said: "Let us go up at once and take possession, for we are well able to overcome it" (Num. 13:30).

My brother, if you desire to be filled with the Spirit, do not allow yourself to be held back by such reasonings. "Only believe" and strengthen yourself in the omnipotence of God. Do not say: "Is God able?" Say rather: "God is able." The God who was able to raise Christ from the dead is still mighty in the midst of His people, and is able to reveal His divine life with power in your heart. Hear His voice saying to you as to Abraham: "I am Almighty God; walk before Me and be blameless" (Gen. 17:1). Set your heart without distraction on what God has said that He will do, and then on the omnipotence that is prepared to bring the promise to accomplishment. Pray to the Father that He would grant to you to be strengthened with might by His Spirit. Adore Him who is able to do for us exceedingly abundantly above all that we ask and think, and give Him the glory. Let faith in the omnipotence of God fill your soul, and you will be full of the assurance that however difficult, however improbable, however impossible it may seem, God can fill us with His Spirit. "Only believe."

3. *Although everything in you appears entirely unfit for this blessing and unworthy of it, still: "Only believe."*

When one prays for this blessing of being filled with the Spirit, the thought will spring up, unbidden, of what one's life as a Christian has already been. The believer thinks of all the workings of divine grace in his heart and of the incessant strivings of the Spirit. He thinks of all his efforts and prayers, of his past attempts at entire surrender and the appropriation of faith. He then looks on what he is at the moment, on his unfaithfulness and sin and helplessness, and he becomes discouraged. In the lapse of so many years so little progress has been made. The past testifies only of failure and unfaithfulness. What benefit is it to think that the future will be any better? If all his praying and believing of earlier days have been of so little value, why should he now dare to hope that everything is to be transformed at once? He presents to himself the life of a man full of the Holy Spirit, and alongside it he sets his own life as he has learned to know it, and it becomes impossible for him to imagine that he shall ever be able to live as a man full of the Spirit. For such a task he is once for all unfit, and he feels no courage to make the attempt.

> *God* will take upon Himself the responsibility of making you full of the Spirit, not as a treasure that you must carry and keep, but as a power that is to carry and keep you.

Christian, when such thoughts as these throng in upon you, there is but one counsel to follow, and that is: "Only believe." Cast yourself into the arms of your Father, who gives His children the Holy Spirit much more readily than an earthly father gives bread. Only believe, and count upon *the love of God.* All your self-dedication and surrender, all your faith and integrity is not a work by which you have to move God or make Him willing to bless you. Far from it. It is God who desires to bless you and who will Himself work everything in you. *God loves you as a father* and sees that in order for you to be able to live in perfect health and happiness as His child, you need nothing but this one thing—to be full of His Spirit.

Jesus has by His blood opened up the way to the full enjoyment of this love. You must learn to enter this love, to abide in this love, and by faith to acknowledge that it shines upon you and surrounds you, even as the light of the sun illumines and animates your body. Begin to trust this love. I do not say in its willingness: no—in its unspeakable longings to fill you entirely with itself. It is your Father, whose love waits to make you full of His Spirit. He Himself will do it for you.

And what does He crave at your hands? Simply this: that you yield yourself to Him in utter unworthiness, nothingness, and powerlessness, to let Him do this work in you. He is prepared to take charge of all the preparatory work. You may be sure that He will help you by His Spirit. He will strengthen you with might in the inner man—silently and hiddenly, yet nonetheless surely—to abandon everything that has to be given up and to receive this treasure. He will help you in the faith of appropriation to rest in His Word and to wait for Him. He will hold Himself responsible for all the future. He will make provision that you shall be able to walk in the fullness of this blessing.

> *Believe that God is prepared to fill you with His Spirit. Then let that faith look up to Him with unceasing prayer and confidence. He will give the blessing.*

You have perhaps already formed a very high idea of what a man must be who is filled with the Spirit of God, and you see no chance of your being able to live in such a fashion. Or it may be that you have not been able to form any idea of it whatever, and are on that account afraid to strive for a life that is so unknown to you. O Christian, abandon all such thoughts. The Spirit alone, when He is once in you, will Himself teach you what that life is, for He will work it in you. God will take upon Himself the responsibility of making you full of the Spirit, not as a treasure that you must carry and keep, but as a power that is to carry and keep you. Therefore, O soul, "only believe": *Count on the love of your Father.*

In His promise of the blessing and the power of the Spirit, the Lord Jesus always pointed to God the Father. He called it "the Promise of My Father" (Luke 24:49). He directed us to the faithfulness of God: "He who promised is faithful" (Heb. 10:23). He directed us to the power of God: The Spirit was, as power from on high, to come from God Himself (see Acts 1:8). He directed us to the love of God: It is as a Father that God is to give this benefit to His children. Let every thought of this blessing and every desire for it only lead us to God. Here is something that *He* must do, that He must give, that *He, He alone*, must work. Let us in silent adoration set our heart upon God: He will do something for us. Let us joyfully trust in Him: He is able to do above all praying and thinking. His love will, Oh so willingly, bestow upon us a full blessing. Therefore, "only believe": God will make me full of the Spirit. And say humbly: "Behold the servant of the Lord. Let Him do to me what is good in His sight. Let it be to me according to Your word" (see Luke 1:38). "He who calls you is faithful, *who also will do it*" (1 Thess. 5:24).

For Further Thought

1. How should you respond to God even though you do not fully understand what it means to have the fullness of the Holy Spirit within you?

2. How do you handle the indifference or opposition of others—even professing Christians—in your desire to have everything God has for you through His Holy Spirit?

3. Part of receiving the Holy Spirit is seeing your own unfitness and inability to understand His indwelling. What does God want you to do with that lack of fitness and understanding?

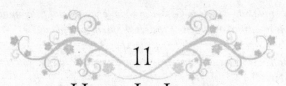

11

HOW IT IS TO
BE FOUND BY ALL

"Then I will sprinkle clean water on you,
and you shall be clean; I will cleanse you from all your filthiness
and from all your idols. . . . I will put My Spirit within
you and cause you to walk in My statutes, and you
will keep My judgments and do them."
EZEKIEL 36:25, 27

THE full Pentecostal blessing is for all the children of God. As many as are led by the Spirit of God, these are the children of God (see Rom. 8:14). God does not give a half portion to any one of His children. To every one He says: "Son, you are always with Me, and all that I have is yours" (see Luke 15:31). Christ is not divided; he who receives Him receives Him in all His fullness. Every Christian is destined by God, and is actually called, to be filled with the Spirit.

In the preceding chapters I have had in view especially those who are to some extent acquainted with these things, and have been already in search of the truth—such as have been already led after conversion to make a more complete renunciation of sin and to yield themselves wholly to the Lord. But it is quite conceivable that among those who read this book there may be Christians who have heard but little of the full Pentecostal blessing, and in whose hearts the desire has arisen to obtain a share in it. There is, however, so much that they do not as yet understand that they are willing indeed to have pointed out to them in the simplest possible fashion where they are to begin and what they have to do in order to succeed in their desire. They are prepared to acknowledge that their life is full of sin and that it seems to them as if they would have to strive long and earnestly before they can become full of the Spirit. I should like much to inspire them with fresh courage and to direct them to the God who has said: "I, the LORD, will hasten it in its time" (Isa. 60:22). I should like to take them and guide them to the place where God will bless them, and to point to them out of His Word what the disposition and the attitude must be in which they can receive this blessing.

1. *First of all, there must be a new discovery and confession and casting away of sin.*

In the message of Ezekiel, God first promised: "I will cleanse you," and then, "I will put My Spirit within you" (36:25–27). A vessel into which anything precious is to be poured must always first be cleansed. So if the Lord is to give you a new and full blessing, a new cleansing must also take place. In your conversion, it is true, there was a confession and putting away of sin. Yet this separation was only superficial and external. The soul was still half enveloped in darkness and thought more of its heinous sins and the punishment they might entail. After conversion, it did indeed endeavor to overcome sin, but the effort did not succeed. It did not know in what holiness the Lord desires His people to live, and it did not know how pure and holy the Lord would have it to be and would make it be.

> *Christ is not divided; he who receives Him receives Him in all His fullness. Every Christian is destined by God, and is actually called, to be filled with the Spirit.*

This new cleansing must come through new confession and discovery of sin. The old leaven cannot be purged away unless it be first searched for and found. Do not say that you already know sufficiently well that your Christian life is full of sin. Sit down in silent meditation and with the express purpose of seeing of what sort your life as a Christian has been. How much pride, self-seeking, worldliness, self-will, and impurity has been in it? Can such a heart receive the fullness of the Spirit? It is impossible.

Look into your home life. In your relationships with spouse and children, servants and friends, do not hastiness of temper, anxiety about yourself, bitterness, idle or harsh or unbecoming words testify how little you have been cleansed? Look into the current life of the Church. How much religion is there that is merely intellectual, or formal, or pleasing to men, without that real humiliation of spirit, that real desire for the living God, that real love for Jesus, that real subjection to the Word, which constitute worship in spirit and in truth? Look into your general course of conduct. Consider whether the people among whom you mingle can testify that they have observed, by your honorable spirit and disinterestedness and freedom from worldly-mindedness, that you are one who has been cleansed from sin by God. Contemplate all this in the light of what God expects from you and has offered to work in you, and take your place as a guilty, helpless soul that must be cleansed before God can bestow the full blessing upon you.

On the back of this discovery follows the actual putting away and casting out of what is impure. This is something that you are simply bound to do. You must come with these sins, and especially with those that are most strictly your own ensnaring sins, and acknowledge them before God in confession, and there and then make renunciation of them. You must be brought to the conviction that your life is a guilty and shameful life. You are not at liberty to take comfort from the consideration that you are weak, or that the majority of Christians live no higher life. It must become a matter of earnest resolve with you that your life is to undergo a complete transformation. The sins that still cleave to you are to be cast off and done away with.

Perhaps you may say in reply that you find yourself unable to do away with them or cast them off. I tell you that you are quite able to do this—and in this way. You can give these sins up to God. If there should happen to be anything in my house that I wish to have taken away, and that I myself am unable to carry, I call for men who shall do it for me, and I give it over into their hands, saying, "Look here—take that away," and they do it. So I am able to say that I have put away this thing out of my house. In like manner, you can give up to God those sins of yours, against which you feel yourself utterly helpless. You can give them up to Him to be dealt with as He desires, and He will fulfill His promise: "I will cleanse you from all your filthiness." There is nothing so needed as that there should be a very definite understanding between you and the Lord, that you on your part really confess your sin and bid it everlasting farewell and give it up, and that you wait on Him until He assures you that He has taken it, or rather has taken your heart and life, into His own hands to give you a complete victory.

Do not say that you already know sufficiently well that your Christian life is full of sin. Sit down in silent meditation and with the express purpose of seeing of what sort your life as a Christian has been.

2. *In this way you come to a new discovery, and reception, and experience of what Christ is and is prepared to do for you.*

If the knowledge of sin at conversion is superficial, so also is the faith in Jesus. Our faith, our reception of Jesus, never goes further or deeper than our insight into sin. If since your conversion you have learned to know the inward invincible power of sin in you, you are now prepared to receive from God a discovery of the inward invincible power of the Lord Jesus in your heart, such as you have until now had no idea of. If you really long for a complete deliverance from sin, so as to be able to live in obedience to God, God will reveal the Lord Jesus to you as a complete Savior. He will make you to know that although the flesh always remains in you, with its inclination to evil, the Lord Jesus will so dwell in your heart that the power of the flesh shall be kept in subjection by Him, in order that you may no longer do the will of the flesh. Through Jesus Christ, God will cleanse you from all unrighteousness (see 1 John 1:9), so that day by day you may walk before God with a pure heart. What you really need is the discovery that He is prepared to work this change in you and that you may receive it by faith, here and now.

Yes, this is what Jesus Christ desires to work in you through the Holy Spirit. He came to put away sin—not the guilt and punishment of it only, but sin itself. He has not only mastered the power and dominion of the law and its curse over you, but also completely broken and taken away the power and dominion of sin. He has completely rescued you as a newborn soul from beneath the power of sin, and He lives in His heavenly authority and all-pervading presence in order to work out this deliverance in you. In this power He will live in you and Himself carry out His work in you. As the indwelling Christ, He is bent on maintaining and manifesting His redemption in you. The sins that you have confessed—the pride and the lovelessness, the worldly-mindedness and vanity and all uncleanness—He will by His power take out of your heart so that, although the flesh may tempt you, the choice and the joy of your heart abide in Him and in His obedience to God's will. Yes, you may indeed become "more than a conqueror" through Him who loved you (see Rom. 8:37). As the indwelling Christ, He will overcome sin in you.

> *If the knowledge of sin at conversion is superficial, so also is the faith in Jesus. Our faith, our reception of Jesus, never goes further or deeper than our insight into sin.*

What then is required on our side? Only this, a thing that can be done immediately—namely that when the soul sees it to be true that Jesus will carry out this work, it shall then open the door before Him and receive Him into the heart as Lord and King. Yes, that can be done immediately. A house that has remained closely shut for twenty years can be penetrated by the light in a moment if the doors and windows are thrown open. In like manner, a heart that has remained enveloped in darkness and powerlessness for twenty years because it did not know that Jesus was willing to take the victory over sin into His own hands can have its whole experience changed in a moment. When it acknowledges its sinful condition and yields itself to God and believes that the Son of God is prepared to assume the responsibility of the inner life and its purification from sin, when it ventures to trust the Lord that He will do this work at the very moment, then it may firmly believe that it is done, and that Jesus takes all that is in me into His own hands.

This is indeed an act of faith that must be held firmly in faith. When doors and windows are thrown open and the light streaming in drives out the darkness, we discover immediately how much dust and impurity there is in the house. But the light shines just in order that we may see how to take it away. When we receive Christ into the heart, everything is not yet perfected. Light and gladness are not seen and experienced at once, but by faith the soul knows that He who is faithful will keep His word and will surely do His work. The faith that has up to this moment only sought and wrestled now rests in the Lord and His Word. It knows that what was begun by faith must be carried forward only by faith. It says: "I abide in Jesus. I know that He abides in me and that He will manifest Himself to me."

As Jesus cleansed the lepers with a word—and it was only when they were on their way to the priest that they found out they were clean—so He cleanses us by His Word. He who firmly holds that fact in faith will see the proofs of it.

3. *So the soul is prepared to receive the full blessing of the Spirit.*

The Lord gave first the promise, "I will cleanse you," and then the second promise, "I will put My Spirit within you." The Holy Spirit cannot come with power or fill the heart and continue to dwell in it unless a special and complete cleansing first takes place within it. The Spirit and sin are engaged in a mortal combat. The only reason why the Spirit works so weakly in the Church is sin, which is all too little known or dreaded or cast out.

Men do not believe in the power of Christ to cleanse, and therefore He cannot do His work of baptizing with the Spirit. It is from Christ that the Spirit comes, and to Christ the Spirit returns again. It is the heart that gives Christ liberty to exercise dominion in it that shall inherit the full blessing. Therefore, my reader, if you have understood the lesson of this chapter and have done what has been suggested to you, if you have believed in Jesus as the Lord who cleanses you and dwells in you to keep you clean, be assured that God will certainly fulfill His word: "I will cleanse you and put My Spirit within you." Cleave to Jesus, who cleanses you: Let Him be all within you; God will see to it that you are filled with the Spirit.

> *As Jesus cleansed the lepers with a word—and it was only when they were on their way to the priest that they found out they were clean—so He cleanses us by His Word.*

Only keep in view these two truths.

First, that the gift and the blessing and the fullness of the Spirit do not always come, as on the day of Pentecost, with external observation. God is often a God who hides Himself. Do not be surprised, therefore, if your heart does not at once feel as you should like it to feel immediately after your act of surrender or appropriation. Rest assured that if you fully trust Christ to do everything for you, He there and then begins to do it in secret by His Spirit. Count upon it that if you present yourself to God as a pure vessel, cleansed by Christ to be filled with the Spirit, God will take you at your word and say to you: "Receive the Holy Spirit. . . . According to your faith let it be to you" (John 20:22; Matt. 9:29). At that moment, bow down before Him, more and more silently, more and more deeply, in holy adoration and expectation, in the blessed assurance that the unseen God has now begun to carry on His work more mightily in you, and that He will also manifest it to you more gloriously than ever before.

The other thing you must keep in view is the purpose for which the Spirit is given. "I will put My Spirit within you and *cause you to walk in My statues, and you will keep My judgments and do them.*" The fullness of the Spirit must be sought and received and kept with the direct aim that you shall now simply and wholly live to do God's will and work on the earth—yes, only to be able to live like the Lord Jesus and to say to Him, "Behold, I have come to do Your will" (see Ps. 40:8; Heb. 10:7). If you cherish this disposition, the fullness of the Spirit may be positively expected. Be full of courage and yield yourself to walk in God's statutes and to keep His judgments and do them, and you may trust God to keep His word that He *will cause you* to keep and do them. He, the living God, will work in you. Even before you are aware how the Spirit is in you, He will enable you to experience the full blessing.

> Be full of courage and yield yourself to walk in God's statutes and to keep His judgments and do them, and you may trust God to keep His word that He will cause you to keep and do them.

My brother, have you never yet known the fullness of the Spirit, or have you perhaps been really seeking it for a long time while without finding it? Here you have at last the sure method of winning it. Acknowledge the sinfulness of your condition as a Christian and make renunciation of it, once and for all, by yielding it up to God. Acknowledge that the Lord Jesus is ready and able to cleanse your heart from its sin, to conquer these sins by His entrance into it, and to set you free—and that His purpose is to do this at once. Take Him now as your Lord, immediately and forever. Then you may be assured that God will put His Spirit within you in a way and a measure and a power of which you have before now had no idea. Be assured that He will do it. Oh, permit Him to begin. Let Him do it in you now. Amen.

For Further Thought

1. *What steps can and should you take in order to have your sin revealed and cast away, so that you can receive all that God has for you?*
2. *How does God accomplish the inner cleansing from sin needed before you can receive the full blessing of His Spirit?*
3. *How can you know that you have received God's Holy Spirit in all His fullness, even when there are no "external" evidences?*

12

HOW EVERYTHING MUST
BE GIVEN UP FOR IT

Now when all things are made subject to Him, then the
Son Himself will also be subject to Him who put all
things under Him, that God may be all in all.
1 CORINTHIANS 15:28

WHEN we speak of entire consecration, we are frequently asked what
the precise distinction is between the ordinary doctrine of sanctification and the
preaching of that gracious work that has begun to prevail in the Church in recent
years. One answer that may be given is that the distinction lies solely in the little
word *all*. That word is the key of the secret. The ordinary method of proclaiming
the necessity of holiness is true so far as it goes. But sufficient emphasis is not laid
on this one point of the "all."

So is it also with the question as to the reasons why the fullness of the Spirit
is not more widely enjoyed. That little word *all* suggests the explanation. So long
as the "all" of God, of sin, of Christ, of surrender, of the Spirit, and of faith is not
fully understood, the soul cannot enjoy all that God desires to give and be, all that
God would have it be.

In this our last meditation, let us consider the full Pentecostal blessing from
this standpoint. We want to do this in a spirit of humble waiting on God, and
with the prayer that He would make us by His Spirit feel so deeply where the evil
lies and what the remedy is that we shall be ready to give up everything in order
to receive nothing less than everything.

1. *The All of God*

It lies in the very being and nature of God that He must be all. From Him
and through Him and to Him are all things. As God, He is the life of everything:
All life is only the effect of His direct and continuous operation. It is because all is
through Him and from Him that it is also to Him. Everything that exists serves
only as a means for the manifestation of the goodness and wisdom and power of
God.

Sin consists in nothing but this: that man determined to be something and would not allow God to be everything. And the redemption of Jesus has no other aim than that God should again become everything in our heart and life. At the end, even the Son shall be subjected to the Father so that God may be all in all. Nothing less than this is what redemption is to secure. Christ Himself has shown in His life what it means to be nothing and to allow God to be everything. And as He once lived on the earth, so does He still live in the hearts of His people. According to the measure in which they receive and rejoice in the truth that God is all, will the fullness of the blessing be able to find its way into their life.

The All of God: That is what we must seek. In His will, His honor, His power must He be everything for us. No moment of our time, no word of our lips, no movement of our heart, no satisfying of the needs of our physical life, should there be that is not the expression of the will, the glory, the power of God. Only the man who discerns this and consents to it, who desires and seeks after it, and who believes and appropriates it, can rightly understand what the fullness of the Spirit must effect, and why it is necessary that we should forsake everything if we desire to obtain it. God must be not merely *something*, not merely *much*, but literally *All*.

2. The All of Sin

What is sin? It is the absence of God and separation from God. Where man is guided by his own will, his own honor, his own power, where the will, the honor, the operation of God are not manifested, there sin must be at work. Sin is death and misery, only because it is a turning away from God to the creature.

> It is because all is through Him and from Him that it is also to Him. Everything that exists serves only as a means for the manifestation of the goodness and wisdom and power of God.

Sin is in no sense a thing that may exist in man along with other things that are good. No, as God was once everything, so has sin in fallen man become everything. It now dominates and penetrates his whole being, just as God should have been allowed to do. His nature in every part of it is corrupt. We still have our natural existence in God, and doubtless with not a few good inclinations in nature and character, just as these are to be found in the lower creatures. But of what is good in the spiritual and heavenly sense of the word, of what is done out of inward harmony with God or the direction of His Spirit—of all this there is nothing that has its origin in His nature. All is in sin, and under the influence of sin.

The All of sin: Some small measure of the knowledge of this fact was necessary even at the time of conversion. This, however, was still very imperfect. If a Christian is to make progress and become fully convinced of the necessity of being filled with the Spirit, his eyes must be opened to the extent to which sin dominates over everything within him. Everything in him is tainted with sin—his will, his power, his heart—and therefore the omnipotence of God must take in hand the renewal of everything by the Holy Spirit. Man is utterly powerless to do that which is good in the highest sense. He can do no more of what is good than what the Spirit actually works in him at any moment. He learns also to see the All of sin just as distinctly in the world around him, for the fairest, the most useful, and the most legitimate possessions or enjoyments are all under the power of sin. Everything must be sacrificed and given over to death. The All of God must expel the All of sin. God must again live wholly and entirely within us and take inwardly and continuously the place that sin usurped. He who desires this change will rightly understand and desire the fullness of the Spirit, and as he believes will certainly receive it.

3. The All of Christ

The Son is the revelation of the Father: The All of God is exhibited to our view and made accessible to us in the Son. On this account the *All* of Christ is just as necessary and infinite as that of God. Christ is God come upon the earth to undo the All of sin, to win back and restore in man the lost All of God. To this end, we must know thoroughly the All of Christ.

The idea that most believing disciples have of the All of Christ is that He alone does everything in the atonement and the forgiveness of sin. This is indeed the glorious beginning of His redemptive work, but still only the beginning. God has given in Him all that we have need of life and all grace. Christ Himself desires to be our life and strength, the Indweller of our heart who animates that heart and makes it what it ought to be before God. To know the All of Christ and to understand how intensely and how completely and how really Christ is prepared to be everything in us is the secret of true sanctification. He who discerns the will of God in this principle and from the heart yields himself to its operation has found the pathway to the full blessing of Pentecost.

The All of Christ: Acknowledge this in humble, joyful thanksgiving. Confess that everything has been given by God in Him. Receive with firm confidence the fact that Christ is all and the promise that He will work all, yes, *all* in you. Consent from the heart that this must be so, and confirm it by laying everything at His feet and offering it up to Him. The two things go together: Let Him be and do all; let Him reign and rule all. Let there be nothing in which He does not rule and operate. It is not impossible for you to accomplish this change. Let Him be everything—let Him have everything, in order that by His almighty energy He may fill everything with Himself.

4. The All of Surrender

Leave all, sell all, forsake all: That was the Lord's requirement when He was here on earth. The requirement is in force still.

The discernment of the fact that Christ is all leads of itself to the acknowledgment that He must have all. The chief hindrance of the Christian life is that because men do not believe that Christ is all, they consequently never think of the necessity of giving Him all.

Everything must be given to Him, because everything is under sin. He cannot cleanse and keep a thing when it is not so yielded up to Him that He can take full possession of it and fill it. All must be given up to Him, because He alone can bring the All of God to its rightful supremacy within us. Even what appears useful or lawful or innocent becomes defiled by the stain of our selfishness when it is held tightly in our own possession and for our own enjoyment. We must surrender it into the hands and the power of Christ, for only there can it be sanctified.

The All of surrender. Oh, it is because Christians are so ignorant of the requirement that all their praying and hearing accomplishes so little. If then, O soul, you are really prepared to turn to God for the fullness of the Spirit; if you have turned to Christ to have your heart purified and kept pure, then be assured that it is your blessed privilege to regard and deal with everything—everything that you have to strive for or do—as given up to Him.

> *Every glance at my own powerlessness or sin, every glance at the promise of God and His power to fulfill it, must rouse me to the gladness of faith, to the willing, cheerful acknowledgment that God is able to work all, to the assurance that He will do it.*

The All of surrender will be the measure of your experience of the All of Christ. In a preceding chapter, we have seen that surrender may be carried out instantly and as a whole. Let us not merely read and think of this, but actually do it. Yes, this very day, let the All of Christ be the power of a surrender on our part that shall be immediate, complete, and everlasting.

5. *The All of the Spirit*

The All of God and the All of Christ demand as a necessary consequence the All of the Spirit. It is the work of the Spirit to glorify the Son as dwelling in us, and by Him to reveal the Father. How can He do this if He Himself is not all and has not all and does not possess and penetrate all with His own power? To be filled with the Spirit, to let the Spirit have all, is indispensable to a true, healthy Christian life.

It is a source of great loss in the life of Christianity today that the truth is not discerned that the Three-One God must have all. Even the professing Christian oftentimes makes it his very first aim to find out what he is and what he desires, what pleases him and makes him happy. Then he brings in God in the second place to secure this happiness. The claim of God is not the primary or main consideration. He does not discern that God must have him at His disposal even in the most trivial details of his life to manifest His divine glory in him. He is not aware that this entire filling with the will and the operation of God would prove to be the highest happiness. He does not know that the very same Christ who once lived on the earth as the obedient, lowly Servant of God entirely surrendered to the will of the Father is prepared to abide and work in like manner in his heart and life now. It is on this account that he can never fully comprehend how necessary it is that the Spirit must be all and must fill him completely.

O my brother, if these thoughts have had any influence with you, allow yourself to be brought without delay to the acknowledgment that the Spirit must be all in you. Say from the heart: "I am not at liberty to make any, even the least, exception: The Spirit must have all." Then add to this confession the simple thought that Christ has come to restore the All of God, that the Spirit is given to reveal the All of Christ within us so that God may again be all, that the love of the Father is eagerly longing to secure again His own supreme place with us—and then your heart will be filled with the sure confidence that the Father actually gives you the fullness of the Spirit.

6. *The All of Faith*

"All things are possible to him who believes" (Mark 9:23). "*All things* for which you pray and ask, believe that you have received them, and they will be granted you" (Mark 11:24 NASB). The preceding sections of this chapter have taught us to understand why it is that faith is all. It is because God is all. It is because man is nothing, and therefore has nothing good in him except the capacity for receiving God. When he becomes a believer, that which God reveals becomes of itself a heavenly light that illumines him. He sees then what God is prepared to be for him. He keeps his soul silent before God and open to God and gives God the opportunity of working all by the Spirit. The more unceasingly and undividedly he believes, the more fully can the All of God and Christ prevail and work in him.

> *All things are possible to him who believes." "All things for which you pray and ask, believe that you have received them, and they will be granted you."*

The All of Faith: How little is it understood in the Church that the one and the only thing I have to do is without ceasing to keep my soul in its nothingness and dependence silent and open before God so that He may be free to work in me, that faith as the willing acceptance and expectation of God's working receives all and can achieve all. Every glance at my own powerlessness or sin, every glance at the promise of God and His power to fulfill it, must rouse me to the gladness of faith, to the willing, cheerful acknowledgment that God is able to work all, to the assurance that He will do it.

Let such a faith, as the act of a moment, look upon Christ even today and move you on the one hand to make renunciation of every known sin, and on the other to receive Him as One who purifies you, who keeps you, who dwells in your heart. Oh, that faith might receive the All of Christ and take Him with all that He is! Oh, that your faith might then see that the All of the Spirit is your rightful heritage and that your hope is sure that the full blessing has been bestowed upon you by God Himself, and will be revealed in you!

O soul, if the All of God, the All of Christ, the All of the Spirit be so immeasurable, if the dominion and power of the terrible All of sin be so unlimited, if the All of your surrender to God and your decision to live completely for Him be also so real, then let your faith in what God will do for you be also unlimited. "He who believes in Me. . .out of his heart will flow rivers of living water" (John 7:38).

> *ake Christ anew today as One who has given His life so that God may be all, and do also yield your life for this supreme end. God will fill you also with His Holy Spirit. Amen.*

My reader, the time has now come when we must part. Before this takes place, let me press on your heart one thing. There is something that can be done *today*. As the Holy Spirit says: "Today, if you will hear His voice, do not harden your hearts" (Heb. 3:15; cf. Ps. 95:8). I cannot promise that you shall immediately over-flow with the light and joy of the Holy Spirit. I do not promise you that you shall today feel very holy and truly blessed. But what can take place is this: Today you may receive Christ as One who purifies you, and baptizes, and fills with the Spirit. Yes, today you may surrender your whole being to Him to be from now on wholly under the mastery of the Spirit. Today you may acknowledge and appropriate the All of the Spirit as your personal possession. Today you may submit to the requirement of the All of faith and begin to live only and completely in the faith of what Christ will do in you through the Spirit. This you may do; this you ought to do. Kneel down at the mercy seat and do it. Read once more the earlier chapter with its directions as to what Christ is prepared to do, and surrender yourself this very hour as an empty vessel to be filled with the Spirit so that your whole life may be carried out under the leading of the Spirit. In His own time God will certainly accomplish it in you.

There is also something, however, that He on His part is prepared to do. To-day He is ready to give you the assurance that He accepts your surrender and to seal on your heart the conviction that the fullness of the Spirit belongs to you. Oh, wait on Him to give you this today!

My brother, please listen to my last words. The All of God summons you. The All of sin summons you. The All of Christ summons you. The All of the surrender that Jesus requires summons you. The All of the Spirit, His indispensableness and His glory, summons you. The All of faith summons you. Come and let the love of God conquer you. Come and let the glorious salvation master you. Do not fail to listen to the glorious news that the Triune God, with all that He is, is prepared to be your All, but be silent and listen to it until your soul becomes constrained to give the answer, "Even in me God shall be all." Take Christ anew today as One who has given His life so that God may be all, and do also yield your life for this supreme end. God will fill you also with His Holy Spirit. Amen.

For Further Thought

1. Is your relationship with God "all" in your life? What must you do in order to make that a reality so that you can receive His "all"?
2. Are there parts of your life that you have not fully surrendered to God in order to receive all He has for you? If so, what are they?
3. What is required of you to have all of the full blessing of Pentecost? What steps can you take today to see that you receive all God has for you?

HOLY IN CHRIST

CONTENTS

*For I am the Lord your God. You shall therefore
consecrate yourselves, and you shall be holy; for I am holy.
Neither shall you defile yourselves with any
creeping thing that creeps on the earth.*
LEVITICUS 11:44

PREFACE

THERE is not in scripture a word more distinctively divine in its origin and meaning than the word *holy*. There is not a word that leads us higher into the mystery of Deity, nor deeper into the privilege and the blessedness of God's children. And yet it is a word that many a Christian have never studied or understood.

There are not a few who can praise God that during the past twenty years the watchword *be holy* has been taken up in many a church and Christian circle with greater earnestness than before. In books and magazines, in conventions and conferences, in the testimonies and the lives of believers, we have abundant evidences that what is called the Holiness Movement is a reality.

And yet how much is still lacking! What multitudes of believing Christians there are who have none but the very vaguest thoughts of what holiness is! And of those who are seeking after it, how many who have hardly learned what it is to come to God's Word and to God Himself for the teaching that can alone reveal this part of the mystery of Christ and of God! To many, holiness has simply been a general expression for the Christian life in its more earnest form, without much thought of what the term really means.

In writing this little book, my object has been to discover in what sense God uses the word, that so it may mean to us what it means to Him. I have sought to trace the word through some of the most important passages of holy scripture where it occurs, there to learn what God's holiness is, what ours is to be, and what the way by which we attain it. I have been specially anxious to point out how many and various the elements are that go to make up true holiness as the divine expression of the Christian life in all its fullness and perfection. I have at the same time striven continually to keep in mind the wonderful unity and simplicity there is in it, as centered in the person of Jesus. As I proceeded in my work, I felt ever more deeply how high the task was I had undertaken in offering to guide others even into the outer courts of the Holy Place of the Most High. And yet the very difficulty of the task convinced me of how needed it was.

I fear there are some to whom the book may be a disappointment. They have heard that the entrance to the life of holiness is often but a step. They have heard of or seen believers who could tell of the blessed change that has come over their lives since they found the wonderful secret of holiness by faith. And now they are seeking for this secret. They cannot understand that the secret comes to those who do not seek it but only seek Jesus. They might want to have a book in which all they need to know of holiness and the way to it is gathered into a few simple lessons—easy to learn, to remember, and to practice. This they will not find. There is such a thing as a pentecost still to the disciples of Jesus, but it comes to him who has forsaken all to follow Jesus only, and in following fully has allowed the Master to reprove and instruct him. There are often very blessed revelations of Christ, as a savior from sin, both in the secret chamber and in the meetings of the saints.

But these are given to those for whom they have been prepared, and who have been prepared to receive.

Let all learn to trust in Jesus and rejoice in Him, even though their experiences are not what they would wish. He will make us holy. But whether we have entered the blessed life of faith in Jesus as our sanctification, or are still longing for it from afar, we all need one thing: the simple, believing, and obedient acceptance of each word that our God has spoken. It has been my earnest desire that I might be a helper of the faith of my brethren in seeking to trace with them the wondrous revelation of God's holiness through the ages as recorded in His blessed Word. It has been my continual prayer that God might use what is written to increase in His children the conviction that we must be holy, the knowledge of how we are to be holy, the joy that we may be holy, and the faith that we can be holy. And may He stir us all to cry day and night to Him for a visitation of the Spirit and the power of holiness on all His people, that the name of Christian and of saint may be synonymous, and that every believer be a vessel made holy and fit for the Master's use.

A. M.

Wellington, November 16, 1887

DAY 1
GOD'S CALL TO HOLINESS

But as He who called you is holy, you also be
holy in all your conduct, because it is written,
"Be holy, for I am holy."
I PETER 1:15–16

THE call of God is the manifestation in time of the purpose of eternity: "Whom He predestinated, these He also *called*" (Rom. 8:30). Believers are "the *called* according to His purpose" (Rom. 8:28). In His call, He reveals to us what His thoughts and His will concerning us are, and what the life is to which He invites us. In His call, He makes clear to us what the hope of our calling is, and as we spiritually apprehend and enter into this, our life on earth will be the reflection of His purpose in eternity.

Holy scripture uses more than one word to indicate the object or aim of our calling, but none more frequently than what Peter speaks of here—God has called us *to be holy as He is holy*. Paul addresses believers twice as "called to be *holy*" (Rom. 1:7, 1 Cor. 1:2). "God did not call us," he says, "to uncleanness, but *in holiness*" (1 Thess. 4:7). When he writes, "The God of peace. . .*sanctify* you completely," he adds, "He who *calls* you is faithful, who also will do it" (1 Thess. 5:23, 24). The calling itself is spoken of as "a *holy* calling" (2 Tim. 1:9).

The eternal purpose of which the calling is the outcome is continually also connected with holiness as its aim. "He *chose* us in Him. . .that we should be holy and without blame" (Eph. 1:4). "God from the beginning *chose* you for *salvation* through *sanctification* (2 Thess. 2:13). "*Elect* according to the foreknowledge of God the Father, in *sanctification* of the Spirit" (1 Pet. 1:2). The call is the unveiling of the purpose that the Father from eternity had set His heart on: that we should be holy.

It needs no proof that it is of infinite importance to know rightly what God has called us to. A misunderstanding here may have fatal results. You may have heard that God calls you to salvation or to happiness, to receive pardon or to obtain heaven, and yet never noticed that all these were subordinate. It was to "salvation through *sanctification*," it was to holiness in the first place, as the element in which salvation and heaven are to be found. The complaints of many Christians as to lack of joy and strength, as to failure and lack of growth, are simply due to this—the place God gave holiness in His call they have not given it in their response. God and they have never yet come to an agreement on this.

No wonder that Paul, in the chapter in which he has spoken to the Ephesians of their being "chosen to be holy," prays for the spirit of wisdom and revelation in the knowledge of God to be given to believers, that they might know "the hope of their *calling*" (1:17, 18). Let all of us who feel that we have too little realized that we are called to holiness pray this prayer. It is just what we need. Let us ask God to show us how, as He who has called us is Himself holy, so we are to be holy too. Our calling is a holy calling, a calling before and above everything, to holiness. Let us ask Him to show us what holiness is, His holiness first and then our holiness, to show us how He has set His heart on it as the one thing He wants to see in us, as being His own image and likeness, and to show us too the unutterable blessedness and glory of sharing with Christ in His holiness. Oh that God by His Spirit would teach us what it means that we are called to be holy as He is holy! We can easily conceive what a mighty influence it would exert.

"But as He who called you is holy, you also be holy" (1 Pet. 1:15). How this call of God shows us the true *motive* to holiness. "Be holy, for I am holy." It is as if God said, "Holiness is My blessedness and My glory. Without this you cannot, in the very nature of things, see Me or enjoy Me. Holiness is My blessedness and My glory, and there is nothing higher to be conceived. I invite you to share with Me in it. I invite you to likeness to Myself. 'Be holy, for I am holy.' Is it not enough, has it no attraction, does it not move and draw you mightily, the hope of being with Me, partakers of My Holiness? I have nothing better to offer—I offer you Myself: 'Be holy, for I am holy.'"

Shall we not cry earnestly to God to show us the glory of His holiness, so that our souls may be made willing to give everything in response to this wondrous call?

As we listen to the call, it shows also the *nature* of true holiness. "*As* He is holy, you also be holy." To be holy is to be Godlike, to have a disposition, a will, and a character like God. The thought almost looks like blasphemy, until we listen again, "He has chosen us *in Christ* to be holy." In Christ, the holiness of God appeared in a human life. In Christ's example, in His mind and Spirit, we have the holiness of the Invisible One translated into the forms of human life and conduct. To be Christlike is to be Godlike; to be Christlike is to be holy as God is holy.

The call equally reveals the *power* of holiness. "No one is holy like the Lord" (1 Sam. 2:2)—there is no holiness but what He has, or rather what He is and gives. Holiness is not something we do or attain. It is the communication of the divine life, the inbreathing of the divine nature, the power of the divine presence resting on us. And our power to become holy is to be found in the call of God. The Holy One calls us to Himself, that He may make us holy in possessing Himself. He not only says "I am holy," but "I am the Lord, who makes holy" (see Lev. 22:32). It is because the call to holiness comes from the God of infinite power and love that we may have the confidence that we can be holy.

The call no less reveals the *standard* of holiness. "*But as He. . .is holy, you also be holy,*" or (as in margin, English Revised Version), "Like the Holy One who calls you, be yourselves also holy." There is not one standard of holiness for God and another for man. The nature of light is the same, whether we see it in the sun or in a candle. Likewise, the nature of holiness remains unchanged, whether it is God or man in whom it dwells. The Lord Jesus could say nothing less than, "You shall be perfect, just as your Father in heaven is perfect" (Matt. 5:48). When God calls us to holiness, He calls us to Himself and His own life. The more carefully we listen to the voice and let it sink into our hearts, the more will all human standards fall away, and only the words be heard, "Holy, as I am holy."

> *hall we not cry earnestly to God to show us the glory of His Holiness, so that our souls may be made willing to give everything in response to this wondrous call?*

And the call shows us the *path* to holiness. The calling of God is one of mighty efficacy, an effectual calling. Oh, let us but listen to it, let us but listen to Him, and the call will with divine power work what it offers. He calls the things that are not as though they were. His call gives life to the dead and holiness to those whom He has made alive. He calls us to listen as He speaks of His holiness, and of our holiness like His. He calls us to Himself, to study, to fear, to love, to claim His holiness. He calls us to Christ, in whom divine holiness became human holiness, to see and admire, to desire and accept what is all for us. He calls us to the indwelling and the teaching of the Spirit of holiness, to yield ourselves so that He may bring home to us and breathe within us what is ours in Christ. Christian! Listen to God calling you to holiness. Come and learn what His holiness is, and what yours is and must be.

Yes, be very silent and listen. When God called Abraham, he answered, "Here I am" (Gen. 22:1). When God called Moses from the bush, he answered, "Here I am" (Exod. 3:4), and he hid his face, for he was afraid to look at God. God is calling you to holiness, to Himself the Holy One, so that He may make you holy. Let your whole soul answer, "Here I am, Lord! Speak, Lord! Show Yourself, Lord! Here I am." As you listen, the voice will sound ever deeper and ever stiller: Be holy, *as* I am holy. Be holy, *for* I am holy. You will hear a voice coming out of the great eternity, from the council-chamber of redemption, and as you catch its distant whisper, it will be, "Be holy, I am holy." You will hear a voice from paradise, the Creator making the seventh day holy for man whom He had created, and saying, "Be holy." You will hear the voice from Sinai, amid thunderings and lightnings, and still it is, "Be holy, as I am holy." You will hear a voice from Calvary, and there above all it is, "Be holy, for I am holy."

Child of God, have you ever realized it, our Father is calling us to Himself, to be holy as He is holy ? Must we not confess that happiness has been to us more than holiness, salvation than sanctification? Oh, it is not too late to correct the error. Let us now band ourselves together to listen to the voice that calls, to draw near, and to find out and know what holiness is, or rather, find out and know Himself the Holy One. And if the first approach to Him fills us with shame and confusion, makes us fear and shrink back, let us still listen to the voice and the call, "Be holy, as I am holy." "He who *calls* you is faithful, who also *will do it*." All our fears and questions will be met by the Holy One who has revealed His holiness, with this one purpose in view, so that we might share it with Him. As we yield ourselves in deep stillness of soul to listen to the holy voice that calls us, it will awaken within us new desire and strong faith, and the most precious of all promises will be to us this word of divine command:

BE HOLY, FOR I AM HOLY

O Lord, the alone Holy One! You have called us to be holy, even as You are holy. Lord! How can we, unless You reveal to us Your holiness. Show us, we pray, how You are holy, how holy You are, what Your holiness is, so that we may know how we are to be holy, how holy we are to be. And when the sight of Your holiness only shows us the more how unholy we are, teach us that You make partakers of Your own holiness those who come to You for it.

O God, we come to You, the Holy One. It is in knowing and finding and having You that the soul finds holiness. We do beg You, as we now come to You, establish it in the thoughts of our heart that the one object of Your calling us, and of our coming to You, is holiness. You desire to have us be like Yourself, partakers of Your holiness. If ever our heart becomes afraid, as if it were too high, or rests content with a salvation less than holiness, blessed God, let us hear Your voice calling again, "Be holy, I am holy." Let that call be our motive and our strength, because You who calls us will also do it. Let that call mark our standard and our path. Oh, let our life be everything You are able to make it.

Holy Father! I bow in lowly worship and silence before You. Let now Your own voice sound in the depths of my heart calling me, "Be holy, as I am holy." Amen.

FOR FURTHER THOUGHT

1. *Where—or in whom—does all holiness begin? Let me press it upon every reader of this little book, that if it is to help him in the pursuit of holiness, he must begin with God Himself. You must go to Him who calls you. it is only in the personal revelation of God to you, as He speaks, "I am holy," that the command, "Be holy," can have life or power.*

2. *Remember, as a believer you have already accepted God's call, even though you did not fully understand it. Let it be a settled matter that whatever you see to be the meaning of the call, you will immediately accept and carry out. If God calls me to be holy, holy I will be.*

3. *Do you strive to make yourself holy, or do you rely on God to do it for you? Take firm hold of the word: "The God of peace Himself sanctify you completely: He who calls you is faithful, who also will do it." In that faith, listen to God calling you.*

4. *How can you understand the meaning of the word* holiness*? Do be still now and listen to your Father calling you. Ask for and count on the Holy Spirit, the spirit of holiness, to open your heart to understand this holy calling. And then speak out the answer you have to give to this call.*

DAY 2
GOD'S PROVISION FOR HOLINESS

To those who are sanctified in
Christ Jesus, called to be saints [holy].
1 CORINTHIANS 1:2

To all the saints [holy ones]
in Christ Jesus who are in Philippi.
Greet every saint [holy one] *in Christ Jesus.*
PHILIPPIANS 1:1, 4:21 [13]

HOLY! *In Christ!* In these two expressions we have perhaps the most wonderful words of all the Bible.

Holy! The word of unfathomable meaning, which the seraphs utter with veiled faces. *Holy!* The word in which all God's perfections center, and of which His glory is but the streaming forth. *Holy!* The word that reveals the purpose with which God from eternity thought of man, and tells what man's highest glory in the coming eternity is to be: to be partaker of His holiness!

In Christ! The word in which all the wisdom and love of God are unveiled! The Father giving His Son to be one with us! The Son dying on the cross to make us one with Himself! The Holy Spirit of the Father dwelling in us to establish and maintain that union! *In Christ!* What a summary of what redemption has done, and of the inconceivably blessed life in which the child of God is permitted to dwell. *In Christ!* The one lesson we have to study on earth. God's one answer to all our needs and prayers. *In Christ!* The guarantee and the foretaste of eternal glory.

What wealth of meaning and blessing in the two words combined: *Holy in Christ!* Here is God's provision for our holiness, God's response to our question, How to be holy? Often and often as we hear the call, Be holy *as I* am holy, it is as

---

[13] There is one disadvantage in English in our having synonyms of which some are derived from Saxon and others from Latin. Ordinary readers are apt to forget that in our translation of the Bible we may use two different words for what in the original is expressed by one term. This is the case with the words *holy*, *holiness*, *keep holy*, *hallow*, *saint*, *sanctify*, and *sanctification*. When God or Christ is called the Holy One, the word in Hebrew and Greek is exactly the same that is used when the believer is called a saint: he too is a holy one. So the three words *hallow*, *keep holy*, and *sanctify*, all represent but one term in the original, of which the real meaning is to make holy, as it is in Dutch, *heiliging* (holying), and *heiligmaking* (holy-making).

if there is and always must be a great gulf between the holiness of God and man. *In Christ!* is the bridge that crosses the gulf—no, rather His fullness has filled it up. *In Christ!* God and man meet. *In Christ!* the holiness of God has found us and made us its own, has become human and can indeed become our very own.

To the anxious cries and the heart yearnings of thousands of thirsty souls who have God's provision for holiness believed in Jesus and yet don't know how to he holy, here is God's answer: *You are holy in Christ Jesus.* Would they but listen and believe, would they but take these divine words and say them over, if need be, a thousand times, how God's light would shine and fill their hearts with joy and love as they echo them back: Yes, now I see it. Holy in Christ! Made holy in Christ Jesus!

As we set ourselves to study these wondrous words, let us remember that it is only God Himself who can reveal to us what holiness truly is. Let us fear our own thoughts and crucify our own wisdom. Let us give up ourselves to receive, in the power of the life of God Himself, working in us by the Holy Spirit, that which is deeper and truer than human thought: Christ Himself as our holiness. In this dependence on the teaching of the spirit of holiness, let us seek simply to accept what holy scripture sets before us. As the revelation of the Holy One of old was a very slow and gradual one, so let us be content patiently to follow step by step the path of the shining light through the Word. Then it will shine more and more unto the perfect day.

We shall first have to study the word *holy* in the Old Testament. In Israel as the holy people, the type of us who now are holy in Christ, we shall see with what fullness of symbol God sought to work into the very constitution of the people some understanding of what He would have them be. In the law we shall see how *holy* is the great keyword of the redemption that it was meant to serve and prepare for. In the prophets we shall hear how the holiness of God is revealed as the source from where the coming redemption should spring, for it is not so much holiness as the Holy One they speak of, who would, in redeeming love and saving righteousness, make Himself known as the God of His people.

And when the meaning of the word has been somewhat opened up, and the deep need of the blessing made manifest in the Old Testament, we shall come to the New to find how that need was fulfilled. In Christ, the Holy One of God, divine holiness will be found in human life and human nature—a truly human will being made perfect and growing up through obedience into complete union with all the holy will of God. In the sacrifice of Himself on the cross, that holy nature gave itself up to the death, that, like the seed-corn, it might through death live again and reproduce itself in us. In the gift from the throne of the spirit of God's holiness, representing and revealing and communicating the unseen Christ, the holy life of Christ descends and takes possession of His people, and they become one with Him.

As the Old Testament had no higher word than that *holy*, the New has none deeper than this: *in Christ*. The being in Him, the abiding in Him, the being rooted in Him, the growing up in Him and into Him in all things, are the divine expressions in which the wonderful and complete oneness between us and our Savior are brought as near us as human language can do.

And when Old and New Testament have each given their message, the one in teaching us what *holy* means, the other what *in Christ* means, we have in the Word of God, which unites the two, the most complete summary of the great redemption that God's love has provided. The everlasting certainty, the wonderful sufficiency, the infinite effectiveness of the holiness that God has prepared for us in His Son are all revealed in this blessed, *Holy in Christ*.

> *What wealth of meaning and blessing in the two words combined:* Holy in Christ! *Here is God's provision for our holiness, God's response to our question, How to be holy?*

"The Holy Ones in Christ Jesus!" Such is the name, beloved fellow believers, that we bear in holy scripture, in the language of the Holy Spirit. It is no mere statement of doctrine that we are holy in Christ, and it is no deep theological discussion to which we are invited. But out of the depths of God's loving heart there comes a voice addressing His beloved children this way. It is the name by which the Father calls His children. That name tells us of God's provision for our being holy. It is the revelation of what God has given us and what we already are, of what God waits to work in us and what can be ours in personal practical possession. That name, gratefully accepted, joyfully confessed, trustfully pleaded, will be the pledge and the power of our attainment of the holiness to which we have been called.

And so we shall find that as we go along, all our study and all God's teaching will be comprised in three great lessons. The first a revelation, "*I am Holy*;" the second a command, "*Be holy*;" the third a gift, the link between the two, "*You are holy in Christ*."

First comes the revelation, "I am holy." Our study must be on bended knee, in the spirit of worship and deep humility. God must reveal Himself to us if we are to know what Holy is. The deep unholiness of our nature and all that is of nature must be shown us. As with Moses and Isaiah, when the Holy One revealed Himself to them, we must fear and tremble, and confess how utterly unfit we are for the revelation or the fellowship, without the cleansing of fire.

In the consciousness of the utter powerlessness of our own wisdom or understanding to know God, our souls must in contrition, brokenness from ourselves and our power or efforts, yield to God's Spirit, the spirit of holiness, to reveal God as the Holy One. And as we begin to know Him in His infinite righteousness, in His fiery burning zeal against all that is sin, and His infinite self-sacrificing love to free the sinner from his sin and to bring him to His own perfection, we shall learn to wonder at and worship this glorious God, to feel and deplore our terrible unlikeness to Him, and to long and cry for some share in the divine beauty and blessedness of this holiness.

And then will come with new meaning the command, "Be holy, as I am holy." Oh, my brethren! You who profess to obey the commands of your God, do give this all-surpassing and all-including command that first place in your heart and life that it claims. Do be holy with the likeness of God's holiness. Do be holy as He is holy. And if you find that the more you meditate and study, the less you can grasp this infinite holiness—that the more you at moments grasp of it, the more you despair of a holiness so divine—remember that such breaking down and such despair is just what the command was meant to accomplish. Learn to cease from your own wisdom as well as your own goodness, and then draw near in poverty of spirit to let the Holy One show you how utterly above human knowledge or human power is the holiness He demands. To the soul that ceases from self and has no confidence in the flesh, He will show and give the holiness He calls us to.

> *In the gift from the throne of the Spirit of God's Holiness, representing and revealing and communicating the unseen Christ, the holy life of Christ descends and takes possession of His people, and they become one with Him.*

It is to such that the great gift of holiness in Christ becomes intelligible and acceptable. Christ brings the holiness of God near by showing it in human conduct and interaction. He brings it near by removing the barrier between it and us, between God and us. He brings it near because He makes us one with Himself. "Holy in Christ": Our holiness is a divine bestowment, held for us, communicated to us, working mightily in us because we are *in Him.*

"In Christ!" Oh, that wonderful *in!* Our very life rooted in the life of Christ. That holy Son and servant of the Father, beautiful in His life of love and obedience on earth, sanctifying Himself for us—that life of Christ, the ground in which I am planted and rooted, the soil from which I draw as my nourishment its every quality and its very nature. How that word sheds its light both on the revelation, "I am holy," and on the command, "Be holy, as I am," and binds them in one! In Christ I see what God's holiness is, and what my holiness is. In Him both are one, and both are mine. In Him I am holy. Abiding and growing up in Him, I can be holy in all manner of living, as God is holy.

Be holy, as I am holy

O Most Holy God! We do beg You, reveal to Your children what it means that You have not only called them to holiness but even called them by this name, "the holy ones in Christ Jesus." Oh that every child of Yours might know that He bears this name, might know what it means and what power there is in it to make Him what it calls Him. Holy Lord God! Oh that the time of Your visitation might speedily come, and each child of Yours on earth be known as a holy one!

To this end we pray and ask You to reveal to Your saints what Your holiness is. Teach us to worship and to wait until You have spoken unto our souls with divine power Your word, "I am holy." Oh that it may search out and convict us of our unholiness! And reveal to us, we pray, that as holy as You are, even a consuming fire, so holy is Your command in its determined and uncompromising purpose to have us holy. O God! Let Your voice sound through the depth of our being with a power from which there is no escape: Be holy, be holy.

And let us, between Your infinite holiness on the one hand and our unholiness on the other, be driven and be drawn to accept of Christ as our sanctification, to abide in Him as our life and our power to be what You desire to have us— "Holy in Christ Jesus."

O Father! Let Your Spirit make this precious word life and truth within us. Amen.

For Further Thought

1. *How do you receive the teaching and understanding of holiness? You are entering anew on the study of a divine mystery. "Trust not it your own understanding" (see Prov. 3:5), but wait for the teaching of the Spirit of truth.*

2. In Christ. *A commentator says, "The phrase denotes two moral facts—first, the act of faith whereby a man lays hold of Christ; second, the community of life with Him contracted by means of this faith." There is still another fact, the greatest of all, that it is by an act of divine power that I am in Christ and am kept in Him. It is this I want to realize: the divineness of my position in Jesus. How does that position of being in Christ relate to being holy before Him?*

3. *Grasp the two sides of the truth. You are holy in Christ with a divine holiness. In the faith of that, you are to be holy, to become holy with a human holiness, the divine holiness manifest in all the conduct of a human life.*

4. *How can you know you can fully rely on Christ to make you holy? This Christ is a living person, a loving Savior. How He will delight to get complete possession and do all the work in you! Keep hold of this all along as we go on: you have a claim on Christ, on His love and power, to make you holy. As His redeemed one, you are at this moment, whatever and wherever you be, in*

Him. His holy presence and love are around you. You are in Him, in the enclosure of that tender love, which always encircles you with His holy presence. In that presence, accepted and realized, is your holiness.

DAY 3

HOLINESS AND CREATION

Then God blessed the seventh day and sanctified it,
because in it He rested from all His work
which God had created and made.
GENESIS 2:3

IN Genesis we have the book of beginnings. To its first three chapters we are specially indebted for a divine light shining on the many questions to which human wisdom never could find an answer. In our search after holiness, we are led there too. In the whole book of Genesis, the word *holy* occurs but once. But that once in such a connection as to open to us the secret spring from which flows all that the Bible has to teach or to give us of this heavenly blessing. The full meaning of the precious word we want to master, of the priceless blessing we want to get possession of, "Sanctified in Christ," takes its rise in what is here written of that wondrous act of God by which He closed His creation work and revealed how wonderfully it would be continued and perfected.

When God blessed the seventh day and *sanctified* it, He lifted it above the other days and set it apart to a work and a revelation of Himself, excelling in glory all that had preceded. In this simple expression, scripture reveals to us the character of God as the Holy One who *makes holy*; the way in which He makes holy, by entering in and resting; and the power of *blessing* with which God's making holy is always accompanied. These three lessons we shall find of the deepest importance to study well, as they contain the root principles of all the scripture will have to teach us in our pursuit of holiness.

1. God *sanctified* the Sabbath day. Of the previous six days the keyword was, from the first calling into existence of the heaven and the earth, down to the making of man: *God created*. All at once a new word and a new work of God is introduced: *God sanctified*. Something higher than creation, that for which creation is to exist, is now to be revealed: God Almighty is now to be known as God Most Holy. And just as the work of creation shows His power, without that power being mentioned, so His making holy the seventh day reveals His character as the Holy One. As omnipotence is the chief of His natural, so holiness is the first of His moral attributes. And just as He alone is Creator, so He alone is Sanctifier, and to make holy is His work as truly and exclusively as to create. Blessed is the child of

God who truly and fully believes this!

God sanctified the Sabbath day. The word can teach us what the nature is of the work God does when He makes holy. Sanctification in paradise cannot be essentially different from sanctification in redemption. God had pronounced all His works, and man the chief of them, very good. And yet they were not holy. The six days' work had none of defilement or sin, and yet it was not holy. The seventh day needed to be specially made holy, for the great work of making holy man, who was already very good. In Exodus, God says distinctly that He sanctified the Sabbath day, with a view to man's sanctification. "That you may know that I am the LORD *who sanctifies you*" (Exod. 31:13).

Goodness, innocence, purity, and freedom from sin is not holiness. Goodness is the work of omnipotence, an attribute of nature, as God creates it, but holiness is something infinitely higher. We speak of the holiness of God as His infinite moral perfection. Man's moral perfection could only come in the use of his will, consenting freely to and abiding in the will of God. Only this way could he become holy. The seventh day was made holy by God as a pledge that He would make man holy. In the ages that preceded the seventh day, the creation period, God's power, wisdom, and goodness had been displayed. The age to come, in the seventh day period, is to be the dispensation of holiness: God made holy the seventh day.

> *When* God blessed the seventh day and sanctified it, He lifted it above the other days and set it apart to a work and a revelation of Himself, excelling in glory all that had preceded.

2. God sanctified the Sabbath day, *because in it He rested* from all His work. This rest was something real. In creation, God had, as it were, gone out of Himself to bring forth something new, and in resting He now returns from His creating work into Himself, to rejoice in His love over the man He has created and to communicate Himself to him. This opens up to us the way in which God makes holy. The connection between the resting and making holy was no arbitrary one. The making holy was no afterthought. In the very nature of things, it could not be otherwise. He sanctified *because* He rested in it; He sanctified by resting. As He regards His finished work—more especially man—rejoices in it and, as we have it in Exodus, "is refreshed" (31:17), this time of His divine rest is the time in which He will carry on to perfection what He has begun, and make man, created in His image, in very deed partaker of His highest glory, His holiness.

Where God rests in contentment and love, He makes holy. The presence of God revealing itself, entering in, and taking possession, is what constitutes true holiness. As we go down the ages, studying the progressive unfolding of what holiness is, this truth will continually meet us. In God's indwelling in heaven, in His temple on earth, in His beloved Son, and in the person of the believer through the Holy Spirit, we shall everywhere find that Holiness is not something that man is or does, but that it always comes where God comes.

In the deepest meaning of the words: Where God enters to rest, there He sanctifies. And when we come to study the New Testament revelation of the way in which we are to be holy, we shall find in this one of our earliest and deepest lessons. It is as we enter into the rest of God that we become partakers of His holiness. "We who have believed do enter that rest" (Heb. 4:3); "He who has entered His rest has himself also ceased from his works as God did from His" (Heb. 4:10). It is as the soul ceases from its own efforts and rests in Him who has finished all for us, and will finish all in us, as the soul yields itself in the quiet confidence of true faith to rest in God, that it will know what true holiness is.

Where the soul enters into the Sabbath stillness of perfect trust, God comes to keep His Sabbath holy, and the soul where He rests He sanctifies. Whether we speak of His own day, "He sanctified it," or His own people "sanctified in Christ," the secret of holiness is always the same: "He sanctified because He rested."

3. And then we read, "*He blessed* and sanctified it." As used in the first chapter and throughout the book of Genesis, the word "God blessed" is one of great significance. "Be fruitful and multiply" (1:28) was, as to Adam, so later to Noah and Abraham, the divine exposition of its meaning. The blessing with which God blessed Adam and Noah and Abraham was that of fruitfulness and increase, the power to reproduce and multiply. When God blessed the seventh day, He filled it so with the living power of His holiness that in it that holiness might increase and reproduce itself in those who, like Him, seek to enter into its rest and sanctify it.

The seventh day is that in which we are still living. Of each of the creation days it is written, up to the last, "And the evening and the morning were the sixth day" (1:31). Of the seventh the record has not yet been made, because we are living in it now, God's own day of rest and holiness and blessing. Entering into it in a very special manner, taking possession of it as the time for His rejoicing in His creature, and manifesting the fullness of His love in sanctifying him, He has made the dispensation we now live in one of divine and mighty blessing.

And He has at the same time taught us what the blessing is. Holiness is blessedness. Fellowship with God in His holy rest is blessedness. And as all God's blessings in Christ have but one fountain, God's holiness, so they all have but one aim: making us partakers of that holiness. God created *and blessed* with the creation blessing, and God sanctified *and blessed* with the Sabbath blessing of His rest. The Creation blessing, of goodness and fruitfulness and dominion, is to be crowned by the Sabbath blessing of rest in God and holiness in fellowship with Him.

God's finished work of creation was marred by sin, and our fellowship with Him in the blessing of His holy rest was cut off. The finished work of redemption opened for us a truer rest and a surer entrance into the holiness of God. As He rested in His holy day, so He now rests in His holy Son. In Him we now can enter fully into the rest of God. "Made holy in Christ," let us rest in Him. Let us rest, because we see that as wonderfully as God by His mighty power finished His work of creation, so will He complete and perfect His work of sanctification. Let us yield ourselves to God in Christ, to rest where He rested, to be made holy with His own holiness, and to be blessed with God's own blessing. God the sanctifier is the name now inscribed on the throne of God the Creator. At the threshold of the history of the human race there shines this word of infinite promise and hope: "God blessed the seventh day and sanctified it, because in it He rested."

BE HOLY, FOR I AM HOLY

Blessed Lord God! I bow before You in humble worship. I adore You as God the Creator and God the sanctifier. You have revealed Yourself as God Almighty and God Most Holy. I ask You, teach me to know and to trust You as such.

I humbly ask You for grace to learn and hold firmly the deep spiritual truths You have revealed in making holy the Sabbath day. Your purpose in man's creation is to show forth Your holiness and make him partaker of it. Oh, teach me to believe in You as God my creator and sanctifier, to believe with my whole heart that the same almighty power that gave the sixth-day blessing of creation secures to us the seventh-day blessing of sanctification. Your will is our sanctification.

And teach me, Lord, to understand better how this blessing comes. It is where You enter into rest, to refresh and reveal Yourself, that You make holy. O my God! May my heart be Your resting place. I desire, in the stillness and confidence of a restful faith, to rest in You, believing that You do all in me. Let such fellowship with You, Your love, and Your will be to me the secret of a life of holiness. I ask it in the name of our Lord Jesus, in whom You have sanctified us. Amen.

FOR FURTHER THOUGHT

1. *How exactly can God make you holy? God the creator is God the sanctifier. The Omnipotence that did the first work does the second too. I can trust God Almighty to make me holy. God is holy, and if God is everything to me, His presence will be my holiness.*
2. *Rest is ceasing from work, not to work no more, but to begin a new work. God rests and begins at once to make holy that in which He rests. He created by the word of His power; He rests in His love. Creation was the building of the temple, but sanctification is the entering in and taking possession. Oh, that wonderful entering into human nature!*
3. *What position must you assume in order to allow God to make you holy? God rests only in what is restful and wholly at His disposal. It is in the restfulness of faith that we must look to God the sanctifier. Then He will come*

in and keep His holy Sabbath in the restful soul. We rest in God's rest; God rests in our rest.

4. *How do you know you can fully trust God the creator to be God your sanctifier? The God who rests in man whom He made, and in resting sanctifies, and in sanctifying blesses: this is our God. Praise and worship Him. And trust Him to do His work.*

5. *Rest! What a simple word. The rest of God! What an incomprehensible fullness of life and love in that word! Let us meditate on it and worship before Him until it overshadows us and we enter into it—the rest of God. Rest belongs to God, and He alone can give it, by making us share His own.*

Day 4
Holiness and Revelation

So when the LORD saw that he turned aside to look, God called to
him from the midst of the bush and said, "Moses, Moses!" And he
said, "Here I am." Then He said, "Do not draw near this place.
Take your sandals off your feet, for the place where
you stand is holy ground."...And Moses hid his face,
for he was afraid to look upon God.
EXODUS 3:4–6

AND why was it holy ground? Because God had come there and occupied it. Where God is, there is holiness—it is the presence of God makes holy. This is the truth we met with in paradise when man was just created. Here, where scripture uses the word *holy* for the second time, it is repeated and enforced. A careful study of the word in the light of the burning bush will further open its deep significance. Let us see what the sacred history, what the revelation of God, and what Moses teaches us of this holy ground.

1. Note the place this first direct revelation of God to man as the Holy One takes in sacred history. In paradise we found the word *holy* used of the seventh day. Since that time twenty-five centuries have elapsed. We found in God's sanctifying the day of rest a promise of a new dispensation—the revelation of the Almighty Creator to be followed by that of the Holy One making holy. And yet throughout the book of Genesis the word never occurs again. It is as if God's holiness has been temporarily suspended, for only in Exodus, with the calling of Moses, does it make its appearance again.

This is a fact of deep importance. Just as a parent or teacher seeks, in early childhood, to impress one lesson at a time, so God deals in the education of the human race. After having in the flood exhibited His righteous judgment against sin, He calls Abraham to be the father of a chosen people. And as the foundation of all His dealings with that people, He teaches him and his seed first of all the lesson of *childlike trust*—trust in Him as the Almighty, with whom nothing is too wonderful, and trust in Him as the Faithful One whose oath could not be broken. With the growth of Israel to a people, we see the revelation advancing to a new stage. The simplicity of childhood gives way to the waywardness of youth, and God must now interfere with the discipline and restriction of law. Having gained a right to a place in their confidence as the God of their fathers, He prepares them for a further revelation. Of the God of Abraham the chief attribute was that He was the Almighty One; of the God of Israel, Jehovah, that He is the Holy One.

And what is to be the special mark of the new period that is now about to be inaugurated and that is introduced by the word *holy*? God tells Moses that He is now about to reveal Himself in a new character. He had been known to Abraham as God Almighty, the God of promise (Exod. 6:3). He would now manifest Himself as Jehovah, the God of fulfillment, especially in the redemption and deliverance of His people from the oppression He had foretold to Abraham.

God Almighty is the God of creation. Abraham believed in God, "who gives life to the dead and calls those things which do not exist as though they did" (Rom. 4:17). Jehovah is the God of redemption and of holiness. With Abraham there was not a word of sin or guilt, and therefore not of redemption or holiness. To Israel the law is to be given to convince of sin and prepare the way for holiness. It is Jehovah, the Holy One of Israel, the Redeemer, who now appears. And it is the presence of this Holy One that makes the holy ground.

2. And how does this presence reveal itself? In the burning bush God makes Himself known as dwelling in the midst of the fire. Elsewhere in holy scripture the connection between fire and the holiness of God is clearly expressed: "The Light of Israel will be for a fire, and his Holy One for a flame" (Isa. 10:17).

The nature of fire may be either beneficial or destructive. The sun, the great central fire, may give life and fruitfulness or may scorch to death. All depends on occupying the right position, upon the relation in which we stand to it. And so wherever God the Holy One reveals Himself, we shall find the two sides together: God's holiness as judgment against sin, destroying the sinner who remains in it, and as mercy freeing His people from it. Judgment and mercy always go together.

Of the elements of nature, there is none of such spiritual and mighty energy as fire. What it consumes it takes and changes into its own spiritual nature, rejecting as smoke and ashes what cannot be assimilated. And likewise the holiness of God is that infinite perfection by which He keeps Himself free from all that is not divine, and yet has fellowship with the creature and takes it up into union with Himself, destroying and casting out all that will not yield itself to Him.

It is that way as One who dwells in the fire, who is a fire that God reveals Himself at the opening of this new redemption period. With Abraham and the patriarchs, as we have said, there had been little teaching about sin or redemption. The nearness and friendship of God had been revealed. Now the law will be given, sin will be made manifest, the distance from God will be felt, so that man, in learning to know himself and his sinfulness, may learn to know and long for God to make him holy.

In all God's revelation of Himself, we shall find the combination of the two elements—the one repelling, the other attracting. In His house He will dwell in the midst of Israel, and yet it will be in the awful, unapproachable solitude and darkness of the holiest of all within the veil. He will come near to them, and yet keep them at a distance. As we study the holiness of God, we shall see in increasing clearness how, like fire, it repels and attracts, how it combines into one His infinite distance and His infinite nearness.

3. But the distance will be that which comes out first and most strongly. This we see in Moses, who hid his face, for He feared to look at God. The first impression that God's holiness produces is that of fear and awe. Until man, both as a creature and a sinner, learns how high God is above him, how different and distant he is from God, the holiness of God will have little real value or attraction. Moses hiding his face shows us the effect of the drawing near of the Holy One, and the path to His further revelation.

> *O*ur utter unfitness to draw near or have any dealings with the Holy One is the very first lesson we have to learn if we are ever to participate in His holiness.

How distinctly this comes out in God's own words: "Do not draw near this place. Take your sandals off your feet." Yes, God had drawn near but Moses may not. God comes near but man must stand back. In the same breath God says, "Draw near" and "Do not draw near." There can be no knowledge of God or nearness to Him where we have not first heard His, "Do not draw near." The sense of sin, of unfitness for God's presence, is the groundwork of true knowledge or worship of Him as the Holy One.

"Take your sandals off your feet." The sandals are the means of interaction with the world, the aids through which the flesh or nature does its will, moves about, and does its work. In standing on holy ground, all this must be put away. It is with naked feet, naked and stripped of every covering, that man must bow before a holy God. Our utter unfitness to draw near or have any dealings with the Holy One is the very first lesson we have to learn if we are ever to participate in His holiness.

That *take off* must exercise its condemning power through our whole being, until we come to realize the full extent of its meaning in the great, "*Put off* the old man; put on the Lord Jesus" (Eph. 4:22, Rom. 14), and what the "*putting off* the body of the sins of the flesh, by the circumcision of Christ" (Col. 2:11) is. Yes, all that is of nature and the flesh, all that is of our own doing or willing or working—our very life—must be put off and given to the death if God, as the Holy One, is to make Himself known to us.

We have seen before that holiness is more than goodness or freedom from sin, that even unfallen nature is not holy. Holiness is that awful glory by which Divinity is separated from all that is created. Therefore even the seraphs veil their faces with their wings when they sing the Thrice Holy (see Isa. 6:1–3). But oh!

when the distance and the difference is not that of the creature only but of the sinner, who can express, who can realize the humiliation, the fear, the shame with which we ought to bow before the voice of the Holy One?

Sadly, this is one of the most terrible effects of sin: that it blinds us. We don't know how unholy, how abominable sin and the sinful nature are in God's sight. We have lost the power of recognizing the holiness of God—worldly philosophy had not even the idea of using the word as expressive of the moral character of its gods. In losing the light of the glory of God, we have lost the power of knowing what sin is. And now God's first work in drawing near to us is to make us feel that we may not draw near as we are, that there will have to be a very real and a very solemn putting or taking off, and even giving up to the death, of all that appears most lawful and most needed.

Not only our shoes are soiled with contact with this unholy earth, even our face must be covered and our eyes closed in recognition that the eyes of our heart, all our human wisdom and understanding, are incapable of beholding the Holy One. The first lesson in the school of personal holiness is to fear and hide our face before the holiness of God. "For thus says the High and Lofty One. . .whose name is Holy: 'I dwell in the high and holy place, with him who has a contrite and humble spirit'" (Isa. 57:15). Contrition, brokenness of spirit, fear, and trembling are God's first demand of those who desire to see His holiness.

Moses was to be the first preacher of the holiness of God. Of the full communication of God's holiness to us in Christ, His first revelation to Moses was the type and the pledge. From Moses' lips the people of Israel, from his pen the Church of Christ, was to receive the message, "Be holy. I am holy. I make holy." His preparation for being the messenger of the Holy One was here, where he hid his face, because he was afraid to look at God. It is with the face in the dust, it is in the putting off not only of the shoes but of all that has been in contact with the world and self and sin, that the soul draws near to the fire in which God dwells, and which burns but does not consume (Exod. 3:2).

Oh that every believer who seeks to witness for God as the Holy One might learn how the fulfillment of the type of the burning bush is the crucified Christ, and how, as we die with Him, we receive that baptism of fire, which reveals in each of us what it means: the Holy One dwelling in a burning bush. Only this way can we learn what it is to be holy, as He is holy.

BE HOLY, FOR I AM HOLY

Most Holy God! I have seen You who dwells in the fire. I have heard Your voice, "Do not draw near this place. Take your sandals off your feet." And my soul has feared to look upon God, the Holy One.

And yet, O my God, I must see You! You created me for Your likeness. You have taught that this likeness is Your holiness: "Be holy, as I am holy." O my God!

How shall I know to be holy unless I may see You, the Holy One? To be holy, I must look upon God.

I bless You for the revelation of Yourself in the flames of the thorn-bush, in the fire of the accursed tree. I bow in amazement and deep abasement at the great sight: Your Son in the weakness of His human nature, in the fire, burning but not consumed. O my God! In fear and trembling I have yielded myself as a sinner to die like Him. Oh, let the fire consume all that is unholy in me! Let me too know You as the God who dwells in the fire, to melt down and purge out and destroy what is not of You, to save and take up into Your own holiness what is Your own.

O Holy Lord God! I bow in the dust before this great mystery. Reveal to me Your Holiness so that I too may be its witness and its messenger on earth. Amen.

FOR FURTHER THOUGHT

1. *Holiness as the fire of God. Praise God that there is a power that can consume the vile and the dross, a power that will not leave it undisturbed. "The bush burning but not consumed" is not only the motto of the Church in time of persecution; it is the watchword of every soul in God's sanctifying work.*

2. *There is a new theology that only speaks of the love of God as seen in the cross. It doesn't see the glory of His righteousness and His righteous judgment. This is not the God of scripture. "Our God is a consuming fire" is New Testament theology. To "offer service with reverence and awe" is New Testament religion. In holiness, judgment and mercy meet. How do you rightly offer God that kind of service?*

3. *Holiness as the fear of God. Hiding the face before God in fear, not daring to look or speak—this is the beginning of rest in God. It is not yet the true rest, but on the way to it. May God give us a deep fear of whatever could grieve or anger Him. May we have a deep fear of ourselves and all that is of the old, the condemned nature, lest it rise again. "The spirit of the fear of the Lord" (Isa. 11:1–2) is the first manifestation of the spirit of holiness, and it prepares the way for the joy of holiness. Walking in the fear of the Lord, and in the comfort of the Holy Spirit—these are the two sides of the Christian life.*

4. *The holiness of God was revealed to Moses so that he might be its messenger. The Church needs nothing so much today as men and women who can testify for the holiness of God. Will you be one? How do you believe you can best testify to His holiness?*

THE connection between the fear of God and holiness is most intimate. There are some who seek most earnestly for holiness and yet never exhibit it in a light that will attract the world or even believers because this element is lacking. It is the fear of the Lord that works that meekness and gentleness, that deliverance from self-confidence and self-consciousness, which form the true groundwork of a saintly character.

The passages of God's Word in which the two words are linked together are well worthy of a careful study. "Who is like You, glorious in *holiness, fearful* in praises" (Exod. 15:11). "In *fear* of You I will worship toward Your *holy* temple" (Ps. 5:7). "Oh, fear the LORD, you His *holy ones*" (Ps. 34:9). "Oh, worship the LORD in the beauty of *holiness*! *Tremble* before Him, all the earth" (Ps. 96:9). "Let them praise Your great and *awesome* name—He is *holy*" (Ps. 99:3). "The *fear* of the LORD is the beginning of wisdom, and the knowledge of the *Holy One* is understanding" (Prov. 9:10). "The LORD of hosts, Him you shall *hallow*; let Him be your *fear*, and let Him be your *dread*" (Isa. 8:13). "Perfecting *holiness* in the *fear* of God" (1 Cor. 7:1). "But as He who *called you* is holy, you also be *holy*. . .and if *you call on the Father*. . .conduct yourselves throughout the time of your stay here in *fear*" (1 Pet. 1:15, 17).

And so on through the whole of scripture, from the Song of Moses on to the Song of the Lamb: "Who shall not *fear* You, O Lord, and glorify Your name? For You alone are *holy*" (Rev. 15:4). If we yield ourselves to the impression of such passages, we shall feel more deeply that the fear of God—the tender fear of in any way offending Him, the fear especially of entering into His holy presence with what is human and carnal, with nothing of our own wisdom and effort—is of the very essence of the holiness we are to follow after. It is this fear of God that will make us, like Moses, fall down and hide our face in God's presence, and wait for His own Holy Spirit to open in us the eyes, and breathe in us the thoughts and the worship, with which we draw near to Him, the Holy One. It is in this holy fear that that stillness of soul is produced that leads it to rest in God and opens the way for what we saw in paradise to be the secret of holiness: God keeping His Sabbath and sanctifying the soul in which He rests.

DAY 5

HOLINESS AND REDEMPTION

"Consecrate to Me all the firstborn."
EXODUS 13:2

*"All the firstborn are Mine. On the day that I struck all
the firstborn in the land of Egypt, I sanctified to Myself all
the firstborn in Israel. . . . For all the firstborn among
the children of Israel are Mine: I am the LORD.*
NUMBERS 3:13, 8:17

*"For I am the LORD who brings you up out of the land of Egypt,
to be your God. You shall therefore be holy, for I am holy."*
LEVITICUS 11:45

I have redeemed you. . . . You are Mine.
ISAIAH 43:1

AT Horeb we saw how the first mention of the word *holy* in the history of
fallen man was connected with the inauguration of a new period in the revelation
of God—that of redemption. In the Passover we have the first manifestation of
what redemption is, and here the more frequent use of the word *holy* begins. In
the feast of unleavened bread we have the symbol of the putting off of the old
and the putting on of the new, to which redemption through blood is to lead. Of
the seven days we read: "On the first day there shall be a holy convocation, and
on the seventh day there shall be a holy convocation" (Exod. 12:16). The meeting of the redeemed people to commemorate its deliverance is a holy gathering,
and they meet under the covering of their Redeemer, the Holy One. As soon as
the people had been redeemed from Egypt, God's very first word to them was,
"Consecrate—make holy to Me all the firstborn: it is mine" (see Exod. 13:2). The
word reveals how ownership is one of the central thoughts both in redemption
and in sanctification, the link that binds them together. And though the word is
here only used of the firstborn, they are regarded as the type of the whole people.

We know how all growth and organization commence from a center, around which in ever-widening circles the life of the organism spreads. If holiness in the human race is to be true and real, free as that of God, it must be the result of a self-appropriating development. And so the firstborn are sanctified, and afterwards the priests in their place, as the type of what the whole people is to be as God's firstborn among the nations, His peculiar treasure, "a holy nation." This idea of ownership as related to redemption and sanctification comes out with special clearness when God speaks of the exchange of the priests for the firstborn (Num. 3:12–13, 8:16–17): "They (the Levites) are *wholly given to Me*; instead of the firstborn I have *taken them for Myself*; for all the firstborn *are Mine*; on the day that I struck all the firstborn in the land of Egypt *I sanctified them to Myself*."

Let us try to realize the relationship existing between redemption and holiness. In paradise we saw what God's sanctifying the seventh day was: He took possession of it. He blessed it. He rested in it and refreshed Himself. Where God enters and rests, there is holiness, and the more perfectly the object is fitted for Him to enter and dwell, the more perfect the holiness. The seventh day was sanctified as the period for man's sanctification. At the very first step God took to lead him to His holiness—the command not to eat of the tree—man fell. God did not give up His plan, but had now to pursue a different and slower path.

After twenty-five centuries' slow but necessary preparation, He now reveals Himself as the Redeemer. A people whom He had chosen and formed for Himself He gives up to oppression and slavery so that their hearts may be prepared to long for and welcome a deliverer. In a series of mighty wonders, He proves Himself the conqueror of their enemies, and then, in the blood of the paschal lamb on their doors, teaches them what redemption is, not only from an unjust oppressor here on earth, but from the righteous judgment their sins had deserved. The Passover is to be to them the transition from the seen and temporal to the unseen and spiritual, revealing God not only as the Mighty but as the Holy One, freeing them not only from the house of bondage but the destroying angel.

And having redeemed them this way, He tells them that they are now His own. During their stay at Sinai and in the wilderness, the thought is continually pressed upon them that they are now the Lord's people, whom He has made His own by the strength of His arm so that He may make them holy for Himself, even as He is holy. The purpose of redemption is possession, and the purpose of possession is likeness to Him who is redeemer and owner, is holiness.

In regard to this holiness, and the way it is to be attained as the result of redemption, there is more than one lesson the sanctifying of the firstborn will teach us.

First of all, we want to realize how inseparable redemption and holiness are. Neither can exist without the other. *Only redemption leads to holiness.* If I am seeking holiness, I must abide in the clear and full experience of being a redeemed one, and as such of being owned and possessed by God. Redemption is too often looked at from its negative side as deliverance from, but its real glory is the positive element of being redeemed to Himself.

Full possession of a house means occupation. If I own a house without occupying it, it may be the home of all that is foul and evil. God has redeemed me and made me His own with the view of getting complete possession of me. He says of my soul, "It is Mine," and seeks to have His right of ownership acknowledged and made fully manifest. That will be perfect holiness, where God has entered in and taken complete and entire possession. It is redemption that gives God His right and power over me. It is redemption that sets me free for God now to possess and bless. It is redemption realized and filling my soul that will bring me the assurance and experience of all His power will work in me. In God, redemption and sanctification are one, so the more redemption as a divine reality possesses me, the closer I am linked to the Redeemer-God, the Holy One.

> *A*t the very first step God took to lead him to His holiness—the command not to eat of the tree—man fell. God did not give up His plan, but had now to pursue a different and slower path.

And just so, *only holiness brings the assurance and enjoyment of redemption.* If I am seeking to hold firmly redemption on lower ground, I may be deceived. If I have become unwatchful or careless, I should tremble at the very idea of trusting in redemption apart from holiness as its object. To Israel God spoke, "I brought you up out of the land of Egypt. You shall therefore be holy, for I am holy." It is God the redeemer who made us His own, who calls us too to be holy. So let holiness be to us the most essential, the most precious part of redemption—the yielding of ourselves to Him who has taken us as His own and has undertaken to make us His own entirely.

A second lesson suggested is the connection between God's and man's working in sanctification. To Moses the Lord speaks, "*Consecrate* to Me all the firstborn." He afterwards says, "*I sanctified* all the firstborn for Myself." What God does, He does to be carried out and appropriated through us. When He tells us that we are made holy in Christ Jesus, that we are His holy ones, He speaks not only of His purpose, but of what He has really done. We have been sanctified in the one offering of Christ, and in our being created anew in Him. But this work has a human side. To us comes the call to be holy, to follow after holiness, to perfect holiness. God has made us His own and allows us to say that we are His, but He waits for us now to yield Him an enlarged entrance into the secret places of our inner being, for Him to fill it all with His fullness.

Holiness is not something we bring to God or do for Him. Holiness is what there is of God in us. God has made us His own in redemption so that He might make Himself our own in sanctification. And our work in becoming holy is the bringing our whole life, and every part of it, into subjection to the rule of this holy

God, putting every member and every power upon His altar.

And this teaches us the answer to the question as to the connection between the sudden and the gradual in sanctification—between its being a thing once and for all complete, and yet imperfect and needing to be perfected. What God sanctifies is holy with a divine and perfect holiness as His gift, but man has to sanctify by acknowledging and maintaining and carrying out that holiness in relation to what God has made holy. God sanctified the Sabbath day, but man has to sanctify it, that is, to keep it holy. God sanctified the firstborn as His own, but Israel had to sanctify them, to treat them and give them up to God as holy. God is holy, but we are to sanctify Him in acknowledging and adoring and honoring that holiness. God has sanctified His great name, His name is holy, and we sanctify or hallow that name as we fear and trust and use it as the revelation of His holiness. God sanctified Christ, and Christ sanctified Himself, manifesting in His personal will and action perfect conformity to the holiness with which God had made Him holy. God has sanctified us in Christ Jesus, and we are to be holy by yielding ourselves to the power of that holiness, by acting it out and manifesting it in all our life and walk. The objective divine gift, bestowed once for all and completely, must be appropriated as a subjective personal possession; we must cleanse ourselves, perfecting holiness. Redeemed to holiness: as the two thoughts are linked in the mind and work of God, they must be linked in our heart and life.

> *Holiness is not something we bring to God or do for Him. Holiness is what there is of God in us. God has made us His own in redemption so that He might make Himself our own in sanctification.*

When Isaiah announced the second, the true redemption, it was given to him, even more clearly and fully than to Moses, to reveal the name of God as "Your Redeemer, the Holy One of Israel" (Isa. 48:17). The more we study this name, hallow it, and worship God by it, the more inseparably will the words become connected, and we shall see how, as the Redeemer is the Holy One, the redeemed are holy ones too. Isaiah says of the "Highway of Holiness," the "redeemed shall walk there" (35:8, 9). The redemption that comes out from the holiness of God must lead up into it too. We shall understand that to be redeemed in Christ is to be holy in Christ, and the call of our redeeming God will acquire new meaning: "I am *holy: you be holy.*"

Be holy, for I am holy

O Lord God, the Holy One of Israel and his Redeemer! I worship before You in deep humility. I confess with shame that I so long sought You more as the Redeemer than as the Holy One. I did not know that it was as the Holy One You had redeemed, that redemption was the outcome and the fruit of Your holiness, that a participation in Your holiness was its one purpose and its highest beauty. I only thought of being redeemed from bondage and death. Like Israel, I did not understand that without fellowship and conformity to Yourself, redemption would lose its value.

Most holy God! I praise You for the patience with which You bear with the selfishness and the slowness of Your redeemed ones. I praise You for the teaching of the Spirit of Your holiness, leading Your saints, and me too, to see how it is Your holiness, and the call to become partaker of it, that gives redemption its value, and how it is for Yourself as the Holy One, to be Your own, possessed and sanctified of You, that we are redeemed.

O my God! With a love and a joy and a thanksgiving that cannot be uttered, I praise You for Christ, who has been made for us by You sanctification and redemption. In Him You are my redeemer, my Holy One. In Him I am Your redeemed, Your holy one. O God! In speechless adoration I fall down to worship the love that passes understanding, that has done this for us, and to believe that in one who is now before You holy in Christ, You will fulfill all Your glorious purposes according to the greatness of Your power. Amen.

FOR FURTHER THOUGHT

1. *In what heart attitude should you think or pray for holiness? "Redemption through His blood." The blood we meet at the threshold of the pathway of holiness. For it is the blood of the sacrifice that the fire of God consumed, and yet could not consume. That blood has such power of holiness in it that we read, "Sanctified by His own blood." Always think of holiness, or pray for it, as one redeemed by blood. Live under the covering of the blood in its daily cleansing power.*

2. *How can you rightly approach God's holiness and righteous judgment if you hope to be holy? It is only as we know the holiness of God as fire, and bow before His righteous judgment, that we can appreciate the preciousness of the blood or the reality of the redemption. As long as we only think of the love of God as goodness, we may aim at being good; faith in God who redeems will awaken in us the need and the joy of being holy in Christ.*

3. *Have you understood the right of property God has in what He has redeemed? Have you heard a voice say, Mine. You are Mine? Ask God very humbly to speak it to you. Listen very gently for it.*

4. *The holiness of the creature has its origin in the divine will, in the divine election, redemption, and possession. Give yourself up to this will of God and rejoice in it.*

5. *As God created, so He redeemed, to sanctify. Have great faith in Him for this.*

6. *Let God have the entire possession and disposal of you. Holiness is His. Our holiness is to let Him, the Holy One, be all.*

DAY 6
HOLINESS AND GLORY

"Who is like You, O LORD, among the gods?
Who is like You, glorious in holiness, fearful in praises, doing
wonders? You in Your mercy have led forth the people whom
You have redeemed; You have guided them in Your strength
to Your holy habitation. . . . In. . .the sanctuary,
O Lord, which Your hands have established."
EXODUS 15:11–17

IN these words we have another step in advance in the revelation of holiness.
We have here for the first time holiness predicated of God Himself. *He is* glorious
in holiness, and it is to the dwelling place of *His holiness* that He is guiding His
people.

Let us first note the expression used here: glorious in holiness. Throughout
scripture we find the glory and the holiness of God mentioned together. In Exodus 29:43 we read, "and the tabernacle shall be *made holy by My glory*," that glory
of the Lord of which we afterwards read that it filled the house.

The glory of an object, of a thing or person, is its intrinsic worth or excellence, and to glorify is to remove everything that could hinder the full revelation
of that excellence. In the holiness of God, His glory is hidden, but in the glory
of God, His holiness is manifested. His glory, the revelation of Himself as the
Holy One, would make the house holy. In the same way the two are connected
in Leviticus 10:3: "By those who come near Me I must *be regarded as holy*; and
before all the people I must be *glorified*." The acknowledgment of His holiness in
the priests would be the manifestation of His glory to the people. So, too, in the
song of the seraphim, "*Holy, holy, holy* is the LORD of hosts; the whole earth is full
of His *glory*" (Isa. 6:3), God is He who dwells in a light that is unapproachable,
whom no man has seen or can see. It is the *light* of the knowledge of the glory
of God that He gives into our hearts. The glory is that which can be seen and
known of the invisible and unapproachable light. That light itself, and the glorious fire of which that light is the shining out, that light is the holiness of God.
Holiness is not so much an attribute of God as it is the comprehensive summary
of all His perfections.

It is on the shore of the Red Sea that Israel this way praises God: "Who is like You, O LORD? Who is like You, glorious in holiness?" He is the Incomparable One; there is none like Him. And where has He proved this and revealed the glory of His holiness? With Moses in Horeb, we saw God's glory in the fire, in its double aspect of salvation and destruction—consuming what could not be purified, purifying what was not consumed. We see it here too in the song of Moses. Israel sings of judgment and of mercy. The pillar of fire and of the cloud came between the camp of the Egyptians and the camp of Israel. It was a cloud and darkness to those, but it gave light by night to these.

The two thoughts run through the whole song. But in the two verses that follow the ascription of holiness, we find the sum of the whole. "You stretched out Your right hand; the earth swallowed them" (Exod. 15:12). "The LORD looked down upon the army of the Egyptians through the pillar of fire and cloud, and He troubled the army of the Egyptians" (Exod. 14:24). This is the glory of holiness as judgment and destruction of the enemy. "You in Your mercy have led forth *the people* whom You have redeemed; You have guided *them* in Your strength to Your holy habitation" (Exod. 15:13). This is the glory of holiness in mercy and redemption—a holiness that not only delivers but guides to the habitation of holiness, where the Holy One is to dwell with and in His people. In the inspiration of the hour of triumph, it is early revealed in this that the great object and fruit of redemption, as accomplished by the Holy One, is to be His indwelling. With nothing short of this can the Holy One rest content, or the full glory of His holiness be made manifest.

And now, observe further how as it is in the redemption of His people that God's holiness is revealed, so it is in the song of redemption that the personal ascription of holiness to God is found. We know how in scripture, after some striking special interjection of God as Redeemer, the special influence of the Spirit is manifested in some song of praise. It is remarkable how it is in these outbursts of holy enthusiasm God is praised as the Holy One. See it in the song of Hannah (1 Sam. 2:2), "No one is holy like the LORD." The language of the seraphim (Isa. 6:1–13) is that of a song of adoration. In the great day of Israel's deliverance the song will be, "For YAH, the LORD, is my strength and song. . . . Sing to the LORD, for He has done excellent things. Cry out and shout, O inhabitant of Zion, for great is the *Holy One* of Israel in your midst!" (Isa. 12:2, 5, 6). Mary sings, "For He who is mighty has done great things for me, and *holy* is His name" (Luke 1:49). The book of Revelation reveals the living creatures giving glory and honor and thanks to Him who sits on the throne: "And they do not rest day or night, saying: 'Holy, holy, holy, Lord God Almighty, Who was and is and is to come!'" (Rev. 4:8). And when the song of Moses and of the Lamb is sung by the sea of glass, it will still be, "Who shall not fear You, O Lord, and glorify Your name? For You alone are holy" (15:4).

It is in the moments of highest inspiration, under the fullest manifestation of God's redeeming power, that His servants speak of His holiness. In Psalm 97:12 we read, "Rejoice in the LORD, you righteous, and give thanks at the remembrance of His holy name." And in Psalm 99, which has, with its thrice-repeated *holy*, been called the echo on earth of the Thrice Holy of heaven, we sing—

> *Let them praise Your great and awesome name—He is holy.*
> *Exalt the LORD our God, And worship at His footstool—He is holy.*
> *Exalt the LORD our God, And worship at His holy hill;*
> *For the LORD our God is holy.*

It is only under the influence of high spiritual elevation and joy that God's holiness can be fully understood or rightly worshipped. The sentiment that becomes us as we worship the Holy One, that fits us for knowing and worshipping Him rightly, is the spirit of praise that sings and shouts for joy in the experience of His full salvation.

But is not this at odds with the lesson we learned at Horeb, when God said, "Do not draw near; Take your sandals off," and where Moses feared and hid his face? And is not this in very deed the posture fitting us as creatures and sinners? It is indeed. And yet the two sentiments are not at variance; rather they are indispensable to each other, for the fear is the preparation for the praise and the glory.

> *Holiness is not so much an attribute of God as it is the comprehensive summary of all His perfections.*

Or is it not that same Moses who hid his face and feared to look at God, who afterwards beheld His glory until his own face shone with a brightness that men could not bear to look upon (see Exod. 33:29–32)? And is not the song that sings here of God as glorious in holiness also the song of Moses, who feared and hid his face? Have we not seen in the fire, and in God, and specially in His holiness the twofold aspect: consuming and purifying, repelling and attracting, judging and saving, with the latter in each case not only the accompaniment but the result of the former?

And so we shall find that the deeper the humbling and the fear in God's holy presence, and the more real and complete the putting off of all that is of self and of nature—even to the putting off, the complete death of the old man and his will—the more hearty the giving up to be consumed of what is sinful, the deeper and fuller will be the praise and joy with which we daily sing our song of redemption: "Who is like You, O LORD?. . .glorious in holiness, fearful in praises, doing wonders?"

"*Glorious* in holiness, *fearful* in praises": The song itself harmonizes the apparently conflicting elements. Yes, I will sing of judgment and of mercy. I will rejoice with trembling as I praise the holy One. As I look at the two sides of His holiness as revealed to the Egyptians and the Israelites, I remember that what was there separated is in me united. By nature I am the Egyptian, an enemy doomed to destruction; by grace an Israelite chosen for redemption. In me the fire must consume and destroy. Only as judgment does its work can mercy fully save. It is only as I tremble before the searching light and the burning fire and the consuming heat of the Holy One, as I yield the Egyptian nature to be judged and condemned and slain, that the Israelite will be redeemed to know rightly his God as the God of salvation and to rejoice in Him.

Blessed be God! The judgment is past. In Christ, the burning bush, the fire of the divine holiness did its double work. In Him, sin was condemned in the flesh. In Him, we are free. In giving up His will to the death and doing God's will, Christ sanctified Himself, and in that will we are sanctified too. His crucifixion, with its judgment of the flesh, His death, with its entire putting off of what is of nature, is not only for us, but is really ours—a life and a power working within us by His Spirit.

Day by day we abide in Him. Tremblingly but rejoicingly we take our stand in Him, for the power of holiness as judgment to vindicate within us its fierce vengeance against what is sin and flesh, and so to let the power of holiness as redemption accomplish that glorious work that makes us give thanks at the remembrance of His holiness. And so the shout of salvation rings ever deeper and truer and louder through our life, "Who is like You, O LORD, among the gods? Who is like You, glorious in holiness, fearful in praises, doing wonders?"

BE HOLY, AS I AM HOLY

"*Who* is like You, O Lord! Who is like You, glorious in holiness, fearful in praises, doing wonders?" With my whole heart would I join in this song of redemption and rejoice in You as the God of my salvation.

O my God! Let Your Spirit, from whom these words of holy joy and triumph came, so reveal within me the great redemption as a personal experience that my whole life may be one song of trembling and adoring wonder.

I ask You especially, let my whole heart be filled with Yourself, glorious in holiness, fearful in praises, who alone does wonders. Let the fear of Your holiness make me tremble at all there is within me of self and flesh, and lead me in my worship to deny and crucify my own wisdom, so that the Spirit of Your holiness may breathe in me. Let the fear of the Lord give its deep undertone to all my coming in and going out in Your holy presence. Prepare me in this way for giving praise without ceasing at the remembrance of Your holiness. O my God! I want to rejoice in You as my redeemer, my Holy One, with a joy unspeakable and full of glory. As my redeemer, You make me holy. With my whole heart I trust You to do it, to sanctify me wholly. I do believe in Your promise. I do believe in You, and believing I receive You, the Holy One, my redeemer.

Who is like You, O Lord! Who is like You, glorious in holiness, fearful in praises, doing wonders?

FOR FURTHER THOUGHT

1. *God's holiness as glory. How do you think God is best glorified? It is in the holiness of His people that He is glorified. True holiness always gives glory to God alone. Live to the glory of God—that is holiness. Live holily—that will glorify God. To lose sight of self and seek only God's glory is holiness.*

2. *Our holiness as praise. Praise gives glory to God, and is thus an element of holiness. "But You are holy, enthroned in the praises of Israel" (Ps. 22:3). How does seeing the connection between praise and holiness affect your approach to your heavenly Father?*

3. *When you think of God's holiness and love, do you feel a sense of dread and hopelessness, or a sense of joy and praise? God's holiness, His holy redeeming love, is cause of unceasing joy and praise. Praise God every day for it. But you cannot do this unless you live in it. May God's holiness become so glorious to us, as we understand that whatever we see of His glory is just the outshining of His holiness, that we cannot help rejoicing in it, and in Him the Holy One.*

4. *The spirit of the fear of the Lord and the spirit of praise may, at first sight, appear to be at odds. But it is not so. The humility that fears the Holy One will also praise Him: "You who fear the LORD, praise Him!" (Ps. 22:3). The lower we lie in the fear of God, and the fear of self, the more surely will He lift us up in due time to praise Him.*

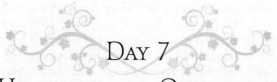

Day 7

Holiness and Obedience

"You have seen what I did to the Egyptians, and how I bore
you on eagles' wings and brought you to Myself. Now therefore,
if you will indeed obey My voice and keep My covenant,
then you shall be a special treasure to Me above all people. . . .
And you shall be to Me. . .a holy nation."
Exodus 19:4–6

ISRAEL has reached Horeb. The law is to be given and the covenant made. Here are God's first words to the people; He speaks of redemption and its blessing, fellowship with Himself: "You have seen how I brought you *to Myself*." He speaks of holiness as His purpose in redemption: "You shall be to Me a holy nation." And as the link between the two He places obedience: "If you will indeed *obey* My voice, you shall be to Me a *holy* nation." God's will is the expression of His holiness, and as we do His will, we come into contact with His holiness. The link between redemption and holiness is obedience.

This takes us back to what we saw in paradise. God sanctified the seventh day as the time for sanctifying man. And what was the first thing He did with this purpose? He gave him a commandment. Obedience to that commandment would have opened the door, would have been the entrance into the holiness of God. Holiness is a moral attribute, and moral is that which a free will chooses and determines for itself. What God creates and gives is only naturally good, and what man wills to have of God and His will, and really appropriates, has moral worth and leads to holiness. In creation, God manifested His wise and good will. His holy will He speaks in His commands. As that holy will enters man's will, as man's will accepts and unites itself with God's will, he becomes holy.

After creation, in the seventh day, God took man up into His work of sanctification to make him holy. Obedience is the path to holiness, because it is the path to union with God's holy will. With man unfallen, as with fallen man, in redemption here and in glory above, in all the holy angels, in Christ the Holy One of God Himself, obedience is the path of holiness. It is not itself holiness, but as the will opens itself to accept and to do the will of God, God communicates Himself and His holiness. To obey His voice is to follow Him as He leads in the way to the full revelation and communication of Himself and His blessed nature as the Holy One.

Obedience. Not knowledge of the will of God, not even approval, not even the will to do it, but the doing of it. Knowledge, and approval, and will must lead to action; the will of God must be done. "If you indeed obey My voice, you shall be to Me a holy nation." It is not faith, and not worship, and not profession that God here asks in the first place from His people when He speaks of holiness. It is obedience. God's will must be done on earth, as in heaven. "Remember *and do* all My commandments, and be holy for your God" (Num. 15:40). "Consecrate yourselves therefore, and be holy.... And you shall keep My statutes, and perform them: I am the LORD who sanctifies you" (Lev. 20:7, 8). "Therefore you shall keep My commandments, *and perform them*: I am the LORD. . . . I will be hallowed among the children of Israel. I am the LORD who sanctifies you, who brought you out of the land of Egypt" (Lev. 21:31, 32–33).

> *I*n creation, God manifested His wise and good will. His holy will He speaks in His commands. As that holy will enters man's will, as man's will accepts and unites itself with God's will, he becomes holy.

A moment's reflection will make the reason for this clear to us. It is in a man's work that he reveals what he is. I may know what is good, and yet not understand it. I may understand, and yet not will it. I may in a certain sense will it, and yet be lacking in the energy, or the self-sacrifice, or the power that will rouse and do the thing. Thinking is easier than willing, and willing is easier than doing. Action alone proves whether the object of my interest has complete mastery over me. God wants His will *done*. This alone is obedience. In this alone is it seen whether the whole heart, with all its strength and will, has given itself over to the will of God, whether we live it and are ready at any sacrifice to make it our own by doing it. God has no other way for making us holy. "You shall keep My statutes *and do them*: I am the Lord who makes you holy."

To all seekers after holiness, this is a lesson of deep importance. Obedience is not holiness. Holiness is something far higher, something that comes from God to us, or rather, something of God coming into us. But obedience is *indispensable* to holiness—it cannot exist without it. While, therefore, your heart seeks to follow the teaching of God's word and looks in faith to what God has done, as He has made you *holy in Christ*, and to what God is still to do through the Spirit of holiness as He fulfills the promise, "Now may the God of peace make you holy in every way," never for one moment forget to be obedient.

"If you will indeed obey My voice, you shall be a holy nation to Me." Begin by doing now whatever appears right to do. Give up immediately whatever conscience tells that you dare not say is according to the will of God. Not only pray for light and strength, *but act*—do what God says. "Whoever *does* the will of God is My brother," Jesus says (Mark 3:35). Every son of God has been born of the will of God—in it he has his life. To do the Father's will is the nourishment, the strength, the mark, of every son of God.

It is nothing less than the surrender to such a life of simple and entire obedience that is implied in becoming a Christian. Sadly, there are too many Christians who, from the lack either of proper instruction or of proper attention to the teaching of God's word, have never realized the place of supreme importance that obedience takes in the Christian life. They don't know that Christ, and redemption, and faith all lead to it, because through it alone is the way to the fellowship of the love, and the likeness, and the glory of God.

We have all, possibly, suffered from it ourselves. In our prayers and efforts after the perfect peace and the rest of faith, after the abiding joy and the increasing power of the Christian life, there has been a secret something hindering the blessing, or causing the speedy loss of what had been grasped. A wrong understanding as to the absolute necessity of obedience was probably the cause. It cannot too earnestly be insisted on that the freeness and mighty power of grace has this for its object from our conversion onwards: the restoring us to the active obedience and harmony with God's will from which we had fallen through the first sin in paradise. Obedience leads to God and His holiness. It is in obedience that the will is molded, the character fashioned, and an inner man built up whom God can clothe and adorn with the beauty of holiness.

When a Christian discovers that this has been the missing link, the cause of failure and darkness, there is nothing for it but, in a grand act of surrender, deliberately to choose obedience—universal, wholehearted obedience—as the law of his life in the power of the Holy Spirit. Let him not fear to make his own the words of Israel at Sinai, in answer to the message of God we are considering: "All that the LORD has spoken *we will do*" (Exod. 19:8), and "All that the LORD has said *we will do*, and be obedient."

What the law could not do, in that it was weak through the flesh, God has done by the gift of His Son and Spirit (see Rom. 8:3). The law-giving of Sinai on tablets of stone has been succeeded by the law-giving of the Spirit on the tablet of the heart. The Holy Spirit is the power of obedience, and is so the Spirit of Holiness, who, in obedience, prepares our hearts for being the dwelling of the Holy One. Let us in this faith yield ourselves to a life of obedience, for it is the New Testament path to the realization of the promise: "If you will *obey* My voice indeed, you shall be to Me a *holy* nation."

We have already seen how holiness in its very nature assumes the personal relationship to God, His personal presence. "I have brought you *to Myself*. If you obey, you shall be *to Me* a holy nation." It is as we understand and hold firmly this personal element that obedience will become possible and will lead to holiness. Mark well God's words: "If you will indeed obey My *voice* and keep My covenant" (Exod. 19:5). The voice is more than a law or a book; it always implies a living person and personal interaction with him. It is this that is the secret of gospel obedience: hearing the voice and following the lead of Jesus as a personal friend, a living Savior. It is being led by the Spirit of God—having Him to reveal the presence, and the will, and the love of the Father—that will work in us that personal relationship that the New Testament means when it speaks of doing everything for the Lord, as pleasing God.

Such obedience is the pathway of holiness. Its every act is a link to the living God, a surrender of the being for God's will, for God Himself to take possession. In the process of assimilation, slow but sure, by which the will of God, as the nourishment of our souls, is taken up into our innermost being, our spiritual nature is strengthened, is spiritualized, growing up into a holy temple in which God can reveal Himself and take up His home.

Let every believer study to realize this. When God sanctified the seventh day as His period of making holy, He taught us that He could not do it instantly. The revelation and communication of holiness must be gradual, as man is prepared to receive it. God's sanctifying work with each of us, as with the race, needs time. The time it needs and seeks is the life of daily, hourly obedience. All that is spent in self-will, and not in the living relation to the Lord, is lost. But when the heart seeks day by day to listen to the voice and to obey it, the Holy One Himself watches over His words to fulfill them: "You shall be to me a holy nation." In a way of which the soul beforehand can have but little conception, God will overshadow and make His home in the obedient heart. The habit of always listening for the voice and obeying it will only be the building or the temple: the living God Himself, the Holy One, will come to make His home. The glory of the Lord will fill the house, and the promise be made true, "I will sanctify it by My glory."

"I brought you *to Myself*; if you will indeed obey *My voice*, you shall be *to Me* a holy nation." Seekers after holiness! God has brought you to Himself. And now His voice speaks to you all the thoughts of His heart, so that as you take them in, make them your own, and make His will your own by living and doing it, you may enter into the most complete union with Himself, the union of will as well as of life, and so become a holy people to Him. Let obedience, the listening to and the doing the will of God, be the joy and the glory of your life, for it will give you access to the holiness of God.

BE HOLY, AS I AM HOLY

O my God! You have redeemed me for Yourself, so that You might have me wholly as Your own, possessing, filling my innermost being with Your own likeness, Your perfect will, and the glory of Your holiness. And You seek to train me, in the power of a free and loving will, to take Your will and make it my own, so that in the very center of my being I may have Your own perfection dwelling in me. And in Your words You reveal Your will, so that as I accept and keep them I may master their divine contents, and desire all that You desire.

O my God! Let me live day by day in such fellowship with You, so that I may indeed in everything hear Your voice, the living voice of the living God, speaking to me. Let the Holy Spirit, the Spirit of Your holiness, be to me Your voice guiding me in the path of simple, childlike obedience. I do praise You that I have seen that Christ, in whom I am holy, was the obedient One, that in obedience He sanctified Himself to become my sanctification, and that abiding in Him, Your obedient, holy Child, is abiding in Your will as once done by Him, and now to be done by me. O my God! I will indeed obey Your will. Make me one of Your holy nation, a special treasure above all people. Amen.

FOR FURTHER THOUGHT

1. *"He became obedient to the point of death" (Phil. 2:8). "Though He was a Son, yet He learned obedience by the things which He suffered" (Heb. 5:8). "I have come to do Your will" (Heb. 10:9). "By that will, we have been sanctified" (Heb. 10:10). Christ's example teaches us that obedience is the only path to the holiness or the glory of God. Let this be your consecration: a surrender in everything to seek and do the will of God. In what ways does reading and knowing these things change your attitude toward obedience to God?*

2. *We are "holy in Christ"—in this Christ who did the will of God and was obedient to the death. In Him it is we are; in Him we are holy. His obedience is the soil in which we are planted and must be rooted. "My food is to do the will of Him who sent Me" (John 4:34)—obedience was the sustenance of His life. In doing God's will He drew down divine nourishment. It must be so with us, too.*

3. *As you study what it is to be and abide in Christ, as you rejoice that you are in Him, what comes to mind? Always remember it is Christ who obeyed in whom God has planted you.*

4. *If ever you feel perplexed about holiness, just yield yourself again to do God's will and go and do it. It is ours to obey, it is God's to sanctify.*

5. *Holy in Christ. Christ sanctified Himself by obedience, by doing the will of God, and in that will, as done by Him, we have been sanctified. In accepting that will as done by Him, in accepting Him, I am holy. In accepting that will of God, as to be done by me, I become holy. I am in Him, and in every act of living obedience, I enter into living fellowship with Him and draw the power of His life into mine.*

6. *You can only obey what you know to be God's will, but how can you know that will? Obedience depends on hearing the voice. Do not imagine you know the will of God. Pray and wait for the inward teaching of the Spirit.*

Day 8

Holiness and Indwelling

"And let them make Me a sanctuary,
that I may dwell among them."
Exodus 25:8

"And there I will meet with the children of Israel,
and the tabernacle shall be sanctified by My glory....
I will dwell among the children of Israel and will be their God."
Exodus 29:43, 45

THE presence of God makes holy, even when it descends but for a little while, as at Horeb, in the burning bush. How much more must that presence make holy the place where it dwells, where it makes its permanent home! So much is this the case that the place where God dwells came to be called the holy place, "the holy place of the habitation of the Most High" (Ps. 46:4). All around where God dwelled was holy: the holy city, the mountain of God's holiness, His holy house, until we come within the veil to the most holy place, the holy of holies. It is *as the indwelling God* that He sanctifies His house, that He reveals Himself as the Holy One in Israel, that He makes us holy too.

Because God is holy, *the house* in which He dwells is holy too. This is the only attribute of God that He can communicate to His house—but this one He can and does communicate. Among men there is a very close link between the character of a house and its occupants. When there is no obstacle to prevent it, the house unintentionally reflects the master's likeness. Holiness expresses not so much an attribute as the very being of God in His infinite perfection, and His house testifies to this one truth: that He is holy, that where He dwells He must have holiness, that His indwelling makes holy.

In His first command to His people to build Him a holy place, God distinctly said that it was that He might dwell among them. The dwelling in the house was to be the shadowing forth of His dwelling in the midst of His people. The house with its holiness leads us this way on to the holiness of His dwelling among His redeemed ones.

The holy place, the habitation of God's holiness, was the center of all God's work in making *Israel* holy. Everything connected with it was holy. The altar, the priests, the sacrifices, the oil, the bread, the vessels—all were holy, because they belonged to God. From the house there came the twofold voice—God's call to be holy and God's promise to make holy. God's claim was manifested in the demand for cleansing, for atonement, and for holiness in all who were to draw near, whether as priests or worshippers. And God's promise shone forth from His house in the provision for making holy, in the sanctifying power of the altar, of the blood and the oil. The house embodied the two sides that are united in holiness: the repelling and the attracting, the condemning and the saving. Now by keeping the people at a distance, then by inviting and bringing them near, God's house was the great symbol of His own holiness. He had come near even to dwell among them, and yet they might not come near, they might never enter the secret place of His presence.

> *It is as the indwelling God that He sanctifies His house, that He reveals Himself as the Holy One in Israel, that He makes us holy too.*

All these things are written on our behalf. It is as the Indwelling One that God is the sanctifier of *His people* still. The indwelling presence alone makes us holy. This comes out with special clearness if we note how the nearer the presence was, the greater the degree of holiness. Because God dwelled among them, the camp was holy, and all uncleanness was to be removed from it. But the holiness of the court of the tabernacle was greater—uncleanness that did not exclude from the camp would not be tolerated there. Then the holy place was still holier, because still nearer God. And the inner sanctuary, where the presence dwelled on the mercy-seat, was the holiest of all, was most holy.

The principle still holds true: holiness is measured by nearness to God. The more of His presence, the more of true holiness. Perfect indwelling will be perfect holiness. There is none holy but the Lord. There is no holiness but in Him. He cannot part with a portion of His holiness and give it to us apart from Himself. We have only so much of holiness as we have of God Himself. And to have Himself truly and fully, we must have Him as the Indwelling One. And His indwelling in a house or locality, without life or spirit, is only a faint shadow of the true indwelling as the Living One, when He enters into and penetrates our very being and fills us, our very selves, with His own life.

There is no union so intimate, so real, so perfect, as that of an indwelling life. Think of the life that circulates through a large and fruitful tree. How it penetrates and fills every portion! How inseparably it unites the whole as long as it really is to exist! In wood and leaf, in flower and fruit, everywhere the indwelling life flows and fills. This life is the life of nature, the life of the Spirit of God who dwells in nature. It is the same life that animates our bodies: the spirit of nature pervading every portion of them with the power of sensibility and action.

Not less intimate—yes rather, far more wonderful and real—is the indwelling of the Spirit of the new life, through whom God dwells in the heart of the believer. And it is as this indwelling becomes a matter of conscious longing and faith that the soul obeys the command, "Let them make Me a sanctuary (a holy place), that I may dwell among them," and experiences the truth of the promise, "The tabernacle shall be sanctified by My glory. . .and I will dwell among the children of Israel" (Exod. 29:43, 45).

It was as the Indwelling One that God revealed Himself in the Son, whom He sanctified and sent into the world. More than once our Lord insisted on it: "Believe Me that I am in the Father and *the Father in Me*; the Father who *dwells in Me* does the works" (John 14:10–11). It is specially as the temple of God that believers are more than once called holy in the New Testament: "The temple of God is *holy*, which temple you are" (1 Cor. 3:17). "Your body is a temple of the *Holy* Spirit" (1 Cor. 6:19). "The whole building, being fitted together, grows into a *holy* temple in the Lord" (Eph. 2:21). It is—we shall later on learn to understand this better—just because it is through the Spirit that the heart is prepared for the indwelling, and the indwelling effected and maintained, that the Spirit so peculiarly takes the attribute of holy. The indwelling Spirit is the Holy Spirit. The measure of His indwelling, or rather of His revealing the indwelling Christ, is the measure of holiness.

> *We have only so much of holiness as we have of God Himself. And to have Himself truly and fully, we must have Him as the Indwelling One.*

We have seen what the various degrees of nearness to God's presence in Israel were. They are still to be found. You have Christians who dwell in the camp, but know little of drawing near to the Holy One. Then you have outer court Christians: They long for pardon and peace, they come repeatedly to the altar of atonement; but they know little of true nearness or holiness or of their privilege as priests to enter the holy place. Others there are who have learned that this is their calling and long to draw near, and yet they hardly understand the boldness they have to enter into the holiest of all and to dwell there. Blessed are they to whom this, the secret of the Lord, has been revealed. *They know* what the torn veil means, and the access into the immediate presence. The veil has been taken away from their hearts, and they have found the secret of true holiness in the indwelling of the Holy One, the God who is holy and makes holy.

Believer! The God who calls you to holiness is the God of the indwelling life. The tabernacle typifies it, the Son reveals it, the Spirit communicates it, the eternal glory will fully manifest it. And you may experience it. It is your calling as a believer to be God's holy temple. Oh, do but yield yourself to His full indwelling! Don't seek holiness in the first place in what you are or do, but seek it in God. Don't seek it even as a gift from God, seek it in God Himself, in His indwelling presence. Worship Him in the beauty of holiness, as He dwells in the high and holy place. And as you worship, listen to His voice: "For thus says the High and Lofty One who inhabits eternity, whose name is Holy: 'I dwell in the high and holy place, *with him* who has a contrite and humble spirit'" (Isa. 57:15).

> *It is your calling as a believer to be God's holy temple. Oh, do but yield yourself to His full indwelling! Don't seek holiness in the first place in what you are or do, but seek it in God.*

It is as the Spirit strengthens us mightily in the inward man, so that Christ dwells in our heart by faith, and the Father comes and makes with Him His home in us, that we are truly holy. Oh, let us but, in true, true-hearted consecration, yield ourselves to be, as distinctly as was the tabernacle or the temple, given up entirely to be the dwelling of the Most High, the habitation of His holiness. A house filled with the glory of God, a heart filled with all the fullness of God, is God's promise, is our portion. Let us in faith claim and accept and hold firmly the blessing: Christ, the Holy One of God, will in His Father's name enter and take possession. Then faith will bring the solution of all our difficulties, the victory over all our failures, the fulfillment of all our desires: "The tabernacle—the heart—shall be sanctified by my glory, and I will dwell among them." The open secret of true holiness, the secret of the joy unspeakable, is Christ dwelling in the heart by faith.

BE HOLY, AS I AM HOLY

We bow our knees to the Father of our Lord Jesus, so that He would grant to us, according to the riches of His glory, what He Himself has taught us to ask for. We ask nothing less than this: that Christ may dwell in our hearts by faith. We long for that most blessed, permanent, conscious indwelling of the Lord Jesus in the heart, which He so distinctly promised as the fruit of the Holy Spirit's coming. Father! We ask for what He meant when He spoke of the loving, obedient disciple: "I will come and manifest Myself to him. . . . We will come and make Our home with him" (John 14:21, 23). Oh, grant to us this indwelling of Christ in the heart by faith!

And for this, we ask You, grant us to be strengthened with power by Your Spirit in the inner man. O most mighty God! Let the spirit of Your divine power work mightily within us, renewing our mind, will, and affections, so that the heart be all prepared and furnished as a temple, as a home, for Jesus. Let that blessed Spirit strengthen us to the faith that receives the blessed Savior and His indwelling presence.

O most gracious Father! Hear our cry. We bow our knee to You. We plead the riches of Your glory. We praise You who are mighty to do above what we can ask or think. We wait on You, our Father: Grant us a mighty strengthening by the Spirit in the inner man, so that this bliss may be ours in its full blessedness, our Lord Jesus dwelling in the heart.

We ask it in His name. Amen.

For Further Thought

1. *What is the connection between holiness and God's dwelling within you? God's dwelling in the midst of Israel was the great central fact to which all the commands concerning holiness were but preparatory and subordinate. So the work of the Holy Spirit also culminates in the personal indwelling of Christ (John 14:21, 23; Eph. 3:16–17). Aim at this and expect it.*

2. *The tabernacle with its three divisions was, as of other spiritual truths, so the image of man's threefold nature. Our spirit is the holiest of all, where God is meant to dwell, where the Holy Spirit is given. The life of the soul, with its powers of feeling, knowing, and willing, is the holy place. And the outer life of the body, of conduct and action, is the outer court. How can you allow God to dwell in and have control of all three? Begin by believing that the Spirit dwells in the inmost sanctuary, where His workings are secret and hidden. Honor Him by trusting Him to work, by yielding to Him in silent worship before God. From within He will take possession of thought and will; He will even fill the outer court, the body, with the holiness of God. "Now may the God of peace Himself sanctify you completely; and may your whole spirit, soul, and body be preserved blameless at the coming of our Lord Jesus Christ. He who calls you is faithful, who also will do it" (1 Thess. 5:23–24).*

3. *God's indwelling was within the veil, in the unseen, the secret place. Faith knew it, and served Him with holy fear. Our faith knows that God the Holy Spirit has His home in the hidden place of our inner life. How should you invite Him to dwell there? Set open your innermost being to Him; bow in lowly reverence before the Holy One as you yield yourself to His working. Holiness is the presence of the indwelling One.*

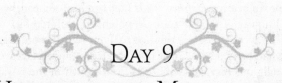

DAY 9

HOLINESS AND MEDITATION

*"You shall also make a plate of pure gold and engrave on it, like the
engraving of a signet: HOLINESS TO THE LORD.... So it shall
be on Aaron's forehead, that Aaron may bear the iniquity of the
holy things which the children of Israel hallow in all their
holy gifts; and it shall always be on his forehead,
that they may be accepted before the LORD."*
EXODUS 28:36, 38

GOD'S house was to be the dwelling place of His holiness, the place where
He was to reveal Himself as the Holy One, not to be approached but with fear
and trembling, and as the holy-making One, drawing to Himself all who would
be made partakers of His holiness.

Of the revelation of His holy and His holy-making presence, the center is
found in the person of the high priest, in his double capacity of representing
God with man, and man with God. He is the embodiment of the divine holiness in human form, and of human holiness as a divine gift, as far as the dispensation of symbol and shadow could offer and express it. In him God came
near to sanctify and bless the people. In him the people came their very nearest
to God. And yet the very Day of Atonement, in which he might enter into the
most holy, was but the proof of how unholy man was, and how unfit to abide in
God's presence. In himself a proof of Israel's unholiness, he yet was a type and
picture of the coming Savior, our blessed Lord Jesus, a wondrous exhibition of
the way in which hereafter the holiness of God should become the portion of
His people.

Among the many points in which the high priest typified Christ as our
sanctification, there is, perhaps, none more suggestive or beautiful than the *holy
crown* he wore on his forehead. Everything about him was to be holy. His garments
were holy garments. But there was to be one thing in which this holiness reached
its fullest manifestation. On his forehead he was always to wear a plate of gold
with the words engraved on it, *Holiness to the Lord.* Everyone was to read there
that the whole object of his existence, the one thing he lived for, was to be the
embodiment and the bearer of the divine holiness, the chosen one through whom

God's holiness might flow out in blessing on the people.

The way in which the blessing of the holy crown was to act was a most remarkable one. In bearing *Holiness to the LORD* on his forehead, he was, we read, "To bear the iniquity of the holy things which the children of Israel hallow. . . that they may be accepted before the LORD." For every sin some sacrifice or way of atonement had been devised. But how about the sin that cleaves to the very sacrifice and religious service itself? "You desire truth in the inward parts" (Ps. 51:6). How painfully the worshipper might be oppressed by the consciousness that his penitence, his faith, his love, his obedience, and his consecration were all imperfect and defiled! For this need, too, of the worshipper, God had provided.

The holiness of the high priest covered the sin and the unholiness of his holy things. The holy crown was God's pledge that the holiness of the high priest rendered the worshipper acceptable. If he was unholy, there was one among his brethren who was holy, who had a holiness that could avail for him too, a holiness he could trust in. He could look to the high priest not only to effect atonement by his blood-sprinkling, but in his person to secure a holiness too that made him and his gifts most acceptable. In the consciousness of personal unholiness, he might rejoice in a mediator, in the holiness of another than himself, the priest whom God had provided.

> To our question, How God makes holy, we have the divine answer: through a man whom the divine holiness has chosen to rest on, and whose holiness belongs to us, as His brethren, the very members of His own body.

Don't we have here a most precious lesson, leading us a step farther on in the way of holiness? To our question, How God makes holy, we have the divine answer: through a man whom the divine holiness has chosen to rest on, and whose holiness belongs to us, as His brethren, the very members of His own body. Through a holiness that is of such effectiveness that the very sins of our holy things disappear, and we can enter the holy presence with the assurance of being altogether well-pleasing.

And is not just this the lesson that many earnest seekers after holiness need? They know all that the Word teaches of the blessed atonement and the full pardon it has brought. They believe in the Father's wonderful love and in what He is ready to do for them. And yet, when they hear of the childlike simplicity, the assurance of faith, the loving obedience, and the blessed surrender with which the Father expects them to come and receive the blessing, their heart fails for fear. It is as if the blessing were all beyond their reach. What avails that the Holy One is said to come so near? Their unholiness renders them incapable of claiming or grasping the presence that offers itself to them. Just see how the Holy One here reveals His way of making holy and preparing for the fellowship of His holiness. In His Elect One as mediator, holiness is prepared and treasured up enough for all who come through Him.

As I bow to pray or worship and feel how much there is still lacking of that humility, fervency, and faith—which God has a right to demand—I may look up to the high priest in His holiness, to the holy crown on His forehead, and believe that the iniquity of my holy things is borne and taken away. I may, with all my deficiency and unworthiness, know most assuredly that my prayer is acceptable, a sweet-smelling savor. I may look up to the Holy One to see Him smiling on me, for the sake of His Anointed One. "The holy crown shall always be on His forehead, that they may be accepted before the LORD." It is the blessed truth of substitution—one for all—of mediatorship, God's way of making us holy. The sacrifice of the worshipping Israelite is holy and acceptable in virtue of the holiness of Another.

> *We* shall find that the holiness of Jesus our sanctification is not only imputed but imparted, because we are in Him, and the new man we have put on is created in true holiness.

The Old Testament shadow can never adequately set forth the New Testament reality with its fullness of grace and truth. As we proceed in our study, we shall find that the holiness of Jesus our sanctification is not only imputed but imparted, because we are *in Him*, and the new man we have put on is created in true holiness. We are not only counted holy; we *are* holy, because we have received a new holy nature in Christ Jesus.

"For both He who sanctifies and those who are being sanctified are all *of one*, for which reason He is not ashamed to call them brethren" (Heb. 2:11). It is our living union with Jesus, God's Holy One, that has given us the new and holy nature, and with that a claim and a share in all the holiness there is in Jesus. And so, as often as we are conscious of how unholy we are, we have only to come under the covering of the holiness of Jesus to enjoy the full assurance that we and our gifts are most acceptable. However great is the weakness of our faith, the shortcoming in our desire for God's glory, the lack in our love or zeal, as we see Jesus, with holiness to the Lord on His forehead, we lift up our faces to receive the divine smile of full approval and perfect acceptance.

This is God's way of making holy. Not only with the holy place, as we have seen, but with the holy persons too. He begins with a center, and from that in ever-widening circle makes holy. And that this divine method will be crowned with success we may be sure. In the Word we find a most remarkable illustration of the extent to which it will be realized. We find the words on the holy crown once again in the Old Testament at its close. In the day of the Lord, "'HOLINESS TO THE LORD' shall be engraved on the bells of the horses" (Zech. 14:20). The high priest's motto shall then have become the watchword of daily life. Every article of beauty or of service shall be holy too, and from the head it shall have extended to the skirts of the garments.

> *L*et us believe that we and our holy things are acceptable, because in Christ holy to the Lord. Let us live in this consciousness of acceptance and enter into fellowship with the Holy One.

Let us begin with realizing the holiness of Jesus in its power to cover the iniquity of our holy things. Let us make proof of it, and no longer allow our unworthiness to keep us back or make us doubt. Let us believe that we and our holy things are acceptable, because in Christ holy to the Lord. Let us live in this consciousness of acceptance and enter into fellowship with the Holy One. As we enter in and abide in the holiness of Jesus, it will enter in and abide in us. It will take possession and spread its conquering power through our whole life, until with us too upon everything that belongs to us the word shall shine, HOLINESS TO THE LORD. And we shall again find how God's way of holiness is always from a center, here the center of our renewed nature, throughout the whole circumference of our being, to make His holiness prove its power. Let us just dwell under the covering of the holiness of Jesus, as He takes away the iniquity of our holy things. He will make us and our life holy to the Lord.

BE HOLY, FOR I AM HOLY

O my God and Father! My soul blesses You for this wondrous revelation of what Your way and Your grace is with those whom You have called "Holy in Christ." You know, O Lord, how continually our hearts have limited our acceptance with You by our attainments, and conscious shortcoming has brought about condemnation. We knew too little how, in the holiness of Him who makes us holy, there is a divinely infinite effectiveness to cover our iniquities and to give us the assurance of perfect acceptance. Blessed Father! Open our eyes to see and our hearts to understand this holy crown of our blessed Jesus, with its wondrous and most blessed, *Holiness to the Lord.*

And when our hearts condemn us, because our prayers are so little consciously according to the will or to the glory of God, or truly in the name of Jesus, O most Holy Father, be pleased by Your Spirit to show us how bright the smile and how hearty the welcome is we still have with You. Teach us to come in the holiness of our high priest and enter into Yours until it takes possession of us and permeates our whole being, and all that is in us be holy to the Lord. Amen.

FOR FURTHER THOUGHT

1. *In what respect do you see yourself as holy? Holiness is not something I can see or admire in myself. Rather, it is covering myself, losing myself, in the holiness of Jesus. How wonderfully this is typified in Aaron and the holy crown. And the more I see and have understood of the holiness of Jesus, the less I will see or seek of holiness in myself.*

2. *What changes do you think take place in you when God makes you holy? He will make me holy. My tempers and dispositions will be renewed, my heart and mind cleansed and sanctified. Holiness will be a new nature, and yet there will be all along the consciousness, humbling and yet full of joy, that "It is no longer I who live, but Christ lives in me" (Gal. 2:20).*

3. *What attitude and disposition of heart invites God to reveal what holiness really means? Let us be very humble and tender before God, so that the Holy Spirit may reveal to us what it is to be holy in the holiness of another, in the holiness of Jesus, that is, in the holiness of God.*

4. *How can you obtain holiness, even when you don't fully understand it? Do not trouble or weary too much to grasp this with the intellect. Just believe it, and look in simplicity and trust to Jesus to make it all right for you.*

5. *Holy in Christ, in childlike faith I take Christ's holiness afresh as my covering before God. In loving obedience, I take it into my will and life. I trust and I follow Jesus, for this is the path of holiness.*

6. *If we gather up the lessons we have found in the Word from paradise downward, we see that the elements of holiness in us are these, each corresponding to some special aspect of God's holiness: deep restfulness (ch. 3), humble reverence (ch. 4), entire surrender (ch. 5), joyful adoration (ch. 6), simple obedience (ch. 7). These all prepare for the divine indwelling (ch. 8), and this again we have through the abiding in Jesus with the crown of holiness on His head.*

DAY 10

HOLINESS AND SEPARATION

"I am the LORD your God, who has separated
you from the peoples. . . . And you shall be holy to Me,
for I the LORD am holy, and have separated
you from the peoples, that you should be Mine."
LEVITICUS 20:24, 26

Until the days are fulfilled for which he separated himself
to the LORD, he shall be holy. Then he shall let the locks
of the hair of his head grow. . . . All the days of his
separation he shall be holy to the LORD.
NUMBERS 6:5, 8

Therefore Jesus also, that He might sanctify the people
with His own blood, suffered outside the gate.
Therefore let us go forth to Him,
outside the camp, bearing His reproach.
HEBREWS 13:12–13

SEPARATION is not holiness, but is the way to it. Though there can be no holiness without separation, there can be separation that does not lead to holiness. It is of deep importance to understand both the difference and the connection, so that we may be kept from the right-hand error of counting separation alone as holiness, as well as the left-hand error of seeking holiness without separation.

The Hebrew word for holiness possibly comes from a root that means to separate. But where we have in our translation "separate" or "sever" or "set apart," we have quite different words. The word for holy is used exclusively to express that special idea. And though the idea of holy always includes that of separation, it is itself something infinitely higher.

It is of great importance to understand this well, because the being set apart to God, the surrender to His claim, the devotion or consecration to His service, is often spoken of as if this constituted holiness. We cannot too earnestly press the thought that this is only the beginning, the presupposition, but that holiness itself is infinitely more—not what I am, or do, or give, is holiness, but what God is, and gives, and does to me. It is God's taking possession of me that makes me holy. It is the presence and the glory of God that really makes holy.

A careful study of God's words to Israel will make this clear to us. Eight times we find the expression in Leviticus, "You shall be holy, for I am holy." Holiness is the highest attribute of God, expressive not only of His relationship to Israel, but of His very being and nature, His infinite moral perfection. And though it is by very slow and gradual steps that He can teach the worldly, darkened mind of man what this means, yet from the very commencement He tells His people that His purpose is that they should be like Himself—holy because and as He is holy.

To tell me that God separates men for Himself to be His, even as He gives Himself to be theirs, tells me of a relationship that exists, but it tells me nothing of the real nature of this Holy Being or of the essential worth of the holiness He will communicate to me. Separation is only the setting apart and taking possession of the vessel to be cleansed and used, but it is the filling of it with the precious contents we entrust to it that gives it its real value. Holiness is the divine filling, without which the separation leaves us empty. Separation is not holiness.

God has separated us for Himself in the deepest sense of the word, so that He might enter into us and show forth Himself in us. His holiness is the sum and the center of all His perfections.

But separation is essential to holiness. "I. . .have separated you from other peoples, and you shall be holy." Until I have chosen out and separated a vessel from those around it and, if need be, cleansed it, I cannot fill or use it. I must have it in my hand, full and exclusive command of it for the time being, or I will not pour into it the precious milk or wine. And in just this way, God separated His people when He brought them out of Egypt—separated them *to Himself* when He gave them His covenant and His law, so that He might have them under His control and power, to work out His purpose of making them holy. This He could not do until He had them apart and had wakened in them the consciousness that they were His special people, wholly and only His, until He had so taught them also to separate themselves to Him. Separation is essential to holiness.

The institution of the Nazarite will confirm this, and will also bring out very clearly what separation means. Israel was meant to be a holy nation. Its holiness was specially typified in its priests. With regard to the individual Israelite, we nowhere read in the books of Moses of his being holy. But there were ordinances through which the Israelite who desired to prove his desire to be entirely holy could do so. He might separate himself from the ordinary life of the nation

415

around him and live the life of a Nazarite, a separated one. This separation was accepted, in those days of shadow and type, as holiness. "All the days of his separation he is holy to the LORD" (Num. 6:8).

The separation consisted specially in three things—temperance, in abstinence from the fruit of the vine; humiliation, in not cutting or shaving his hair ["if a man has long hair, it is a dishonor to him" (1 Cor. 11:14)]; self-sacrifice, in not defiling himself for even father or mother on their death. What we must specially note is that the separation was not from things unlawful, but things lawful. There was nothing sinful in itself in Abraham living in his father's house or in Israel dwelling in Egypt. It is in giving up not only what can be proved to be sin, but all that may hinder the full intensity of our surrender into God's hands to make us holy that the spirit of separation is manifested.

Let us learn the lessons this truth suggests. We must know *the need* for separation. It is no arbitrary demand of God, but has its ground in the very nature of things. To separate a thing is to set it free for one special use or purpose, so that it may with undivided power fulfill the will of him who chose it, and so realize its destiny. It is the principle that lies at the root of all division of labor—complete separation to one branch of study or labor is the way to success and perfection. I have before me an oak forest with the trees all shooting up straight and close to each other. On the outskirts there is one tree separated from his fellows. Its heavy trunk and wide-spreading branches prove how its being separated, and having a large piece of ground separated for its own use, over which roots and branches can spread, is the secret of growth and greatness. Our human powers are limited, so if God is to take full possession, if we are fully to enjoy Him, separation to Him is nothing but the simple, natural, indispensable requisite. God wants us all to Himself, so that He may give Himself all to us.

> It is God's taking possession of me that makes me holy. It is the presence and the glory of God that really makes holy.

We must know the *purpose* of separation. It is to be found in what God has said, "You shall be holy to Me, for I the LORD am holy, and have separated you from the peoples, that you should be *mine*." God has separated us *for Himself* in the deepest sense of the word, so that He might enter into us and show forth Himself in us. His holiness is the sum and the center of all His perfections. It is that He may make us holy like Himself that He has separated us. Separation never has any value in itself. It may become most wrong or hurtful. Everything depends on the object proposed. It is as God gets and takes full possession of us— as the eternal life in Christ has the mastery of our whole being, as the Holy Spirit flows fully and freely through us, so that we dwell in God, and God in us—that separation will not be a thing of ordinances and observances, but a spiritual reality.

And it is as this purpose of God is seen and accepted and followed after that difficult questions as to what we must be separated from, and how much sacrifice separation demands, will find an easy answer. God separates from all that does not lead us into His holiness and fellowship.

We need, above all, to know *the power* of separation, the power that leads us into it in the spirit of desire and of joy, of liberty, and of love. The great separating word in human language is the word *Mine*. In this we have the great spring of effort and of happiness: in the child with its toys, in labor with its gains and rewards, in the patriot who dies for his country, it is this *Mine* that lays its hand on what it sets apart from all else. It is the great word that love uses. Be it the child who says to its mother, "My own mamma," and calls forth the response, "My own child"; the bridegroom who draws the daughter from her beloved home and parents to become his; or the Holy God who speaks, "I have separated you from the people, that you should be *Mine*,'" it is always with that *Mine* that love exerts its mighty power and draws from all else to itself.

God Himself knows no mightier argument, can put forth no more powerful attraction than this, "that you should be *Mine*." And the power of separation will come to us and work in us just as we yield ourselves to study and realize that holy purpose, to listen to and appropriate that wondrous *Mine*, to be apprehended and possessed of that almighty love.

Let us study step by step the wondrous path in which divine love does its separating work. In redemption it prepares the way. Israel is separated from Egypt by the blood of the Lamb and the guiding pillar of fire. In its command, "Come out and be separate," it wakens man to action; in its promises, "I will be your God," it stirs desire and strengthens faith. In all the holy saints and servants of God, and at last in Him who was holy, harmless, undefiled, separate from sinners, it points the way. In the power of the Holy Spirit, the spirit of holiness, it seals the separation by the presence of the indwelling God. This is indeed the power of separation.

The separating power of the presence of God—this it is we need to know. "For how then will it be known that Your people and I have found grace in Your sight," said Moses, "*except You go with us? So we shall be separate*, Your people and I, from all the people who are upon the face of the earth" (Exod. 33:16). It is the consciousness of God's indwelling presence, making and keeping us His very own, that works the true separateness from the world and its spirit, from ourselves and our own will. And it is as this separation is accepted and prized and persevered in by us that the holiness of God will enter in and take possession. And we shall realize that to be the Lord's property, a people of His own, is infinitely more than merely to be accounted or acknowledged as His, that it means nothing less than that God, in the power and indwelling of the Holy Ghost, fills our being, our affections, and our will with His own life and holiness. He separates us for Himself and sanctifies us to be His dwelling. He comes Himself to take personal possession by the indwelling of Christ in the heart. And we are then truly separate, and kept separate, by the presence of God within us.

BE HOLY, FOR I AM HOLY

O my God, who has separated me for Yourself, I ask You, by Your mighty power, to make this divine separation deed and truth to me. May within, in the depths of my own spirit, and without, in all my relationships, the crown of separation of my God be on me.

I ask You especially, O my God, to perfect in power the separation from self! Let Your presence in the indwelling of my Lord Jesus be the power that banishes self from the throne. I have turned from it with abhorrence. Oh, my Father, reveal Your Son fully in me! It is His enthronement in my heart that can keep me as Your own, as He Himself takes the place of myself.

And give me grace; Lord, in my outward life to wait for a divine wisdom, so that I may know to witness, for Your glory and for what Your people need, to the blessedness of an entire giving up of everything for God, a separation that holds back nothing, to be His and His alone.

Holy Lord God! Visit Your people. Oh, withdraw them from the world and conformity to it. Separate, Lord, separate Your own for Yourself. Separate, Lord, the wheat from the chaff. Separate, as by fire, the gold from the dross, so that it may be seen who are the Lord's, even His holy ones. Amen.

FOR FURTHER THOUGHT

1. *What connection is there between love and separation to God? Love separates effectually. With what jealousy a husband claims his wife, a mother her children, a miser his possessions! Pray that the Holy Spirit may show how God brought you to Himself, that you should be His. "He is a holy God. He is a jealous God" (Josh. 24:19). God's love shed abroad in the heart makes separation easy.*

2. *How must you reckon yourself in order to be separated to God? Death separates effectually. If I reckon myself to be indeed dead in Christ, I am separated from self by the power of Christ's death. Life separates still more mightily. As I say, "It is no longer I who live, but Christ lives in me" (Gal. 2:20), I am lifted up out of the life of self.*

3. *What is the benefit of this separation, both to yourself and to those around you? Separation must be evident. It is meant as a witness to others and ourselves. It must find expression in the external, if internally it is to be real and strong. It is the characteristic of a symbolic action that it not merely expresses a feeling but nourishes and strengthens the feeling to which it corresponds. When the soul enters the fellowship of God, it feels the need of*

external separation, sometimes even from what appears to others harmless. If animated by the spirit of lowly consecration to God, the external may be a great strengthening of the true separateness.

4. Separation to God and appropriation by Him go together. This has been the blessing that has come to martyrs, confessors, missionaries—all who have given distinct expression to the forsaking of all.

5. Separation begins in love and ends in love. The spirit of separation is the spirit of self-sacrifice, of surrender to the love of God. The truly separate one will be the most loving and love-winning, given up to serve God and man. Is not what separates, what distinguishes Jesus from all others, His self-sacrificing love? This is His separateness, in which we are to be made like Him.

6. God's holiness is His separateness. Let us enter into His separateness from the world—that will be our holiness. Unite yourself to God. Then are you separate and holy. God separates for Himself, not by an act from without, but as His will and presence take possession of us.

Day 11

The Holy One of Israel

"For I am the LORD who brings you up out of
the land of Egypt, to be your God.
You shall therefore be holy, for I am holy."
LEVITICUS 11:45

"For I am the LORD your God, the Holy One of Israel,
your Savior;. . . Thus says the LORD, your Redeemer,
The Holy One of Israel: I am the LORD, your Holy One,
The Creator of Israel, your King."
ISAIAH 43:3, 14–15

IN the book of Exodus we found God making provision for the holiness of His people. In the holy times and holy places, holy persons, holy things, and holy services, He had taught His people that everything around Him, that all that would come near Him, must be holy. He would only dwell in the midst of holiness, so His people must be a holy people. But there is no direct mention of God Himself as holy.

In the book of Leviticus we are led on a step further. Here first we have God speaking of His own holiness and making it the plea for the holiness of His people, as well as its pledge and power. Without this, the revelations of holiness were incomplete, and the call to holiness powerless. True holiness will come to us as we learn that God Himself alone is holy. It is He alone makes holy. It is as we come to Himself, and in obedience and love are linked to Himself, that His holiness can rest on us.[14]

From the books of Moses onwards, we shall find that the name of God as

[14] "I am the Lord your God. You shall therefore consecrate yourselves, and you shall be holy; for I am holy" (Lev. 11:44). "I am the Lord who brings you up out of the land of Egypt, to be your God. You shall therefore be holy, for I am holy" (Lev. 11:45). "You shall be holy, for I the Lord your God am holy" (Lev. 19:2). "Consecrate yourselves therefore, and be holy, for I am the Lord your God. And you shall keep My statutes, and perform them: I am the Lord who [makes you holy]" (Lev. 20:7–8). "And you shall be holy to Me, for I the Lord am holy, and have separated you from the peoples, that you should be Mine" (Lev. 20:26). "He [the priest] shall be holy to you, for I the Lord, who sanctify you, am holy" (Lev. 21:8). "I will be hallowed among the children of Israel. I am the Lord who [makes you holy]" (Lev. 22:32). "I the Lord do [make them holy]" (Lev. 21:15, 23; 22:9, 16).

holy is found but seldom in the inspired writings, until we come to Isaiah, the evangelist prophet. There it occurs twenty-six times, and has its true meaning opened up in the way in which it is linked with the name of Savior and Redeemer. The sentiments of joy and trust and praise, with which a redeemed people would look upon their deliverer, are all mentioned in connection with the name of the Holy One. "Cry out and shout, O inhabitant of Zion, for great is the *Holy One of Israel* in your midst!" (Isa. 12:6). "The poor among men shall rejoice in the *Holy One of Israel*" (29:19). "You shall rejoice in the LORD, and glory in the *Holy One of Israel*" (41:16).

In paradise we saw that God the creator was God the sanctifier, perfecting the work of His hands. In Israel we saw that God the redeemer was always God the sanctifier, making holy the people He had chosen for Himself. Here in Isaiah we see how it is God the sanctifier, the Holy One, who is to bring about the great redemption of the New Testament. As the Holy One, He is the redeemer. God redeems because He is holy and loves to make holy. Holiness will be redemption perfected. Redemption and holiness together are to be found in the personal relation to God. The key to the secret of holiness is offered to each believer in that word: "Thus says the LORD, your Redeemer, The Holy One of Israel: I am the LORD, your Holy One." To come near, to know, to possess the Holy One, and be possessed by Him, is holiness.

If God's holiness is thus the only hope for ours, it is right that we seek to know what that holiness is. And though we may find it indeed to be something that passes understanding, it will not be in vain to gather up what has been revealed in the Word concerning it. Let us do so in the spirit of holy fear and worship, trusting to the Holy Spirit to be our teacher.

And let us first notice how this holiness of God, though it is often mentioned as one of the divine attributes, can hardly be counted such, on a level with the others. The other attributes all refer to some special aspect or characteristic of the divine nature, but holiness appears to express what is the very essence or perfection of the divine being Himself. None of the attributes can be predicated of all that belongs to God. But scripture speaks of His holy name, His holy day, His holy habitation, His holy Word. In the word *holy* we have the nearest possible approach to a summary of all the divine perfections, the description of what divinity is. We speak of the other attributes as divine perfections, but in this we have the only human expression for the divine perfection itself. It is for this reason that theologians have found such difficulty in framing a definition that can express all the word means.

The original Hebrew word, whether derived from a root signifying to separate, or another with the idea of shining, expressed the idea of something distinguished from others, separate from them by superior excellence. God is separate and different from all that is created, and He keeps Himself separate from all that is not God. As the Holy One, He maintains His divine glory and perfection against whatever might interfere with it: "No one is holy like the LORD" (1 Sam. 2:2). " 'To whom then will you liken Me, or to whom shall I be equal?' says the Holy One" (Isa. 40:25). As holy, God is indeed the Incomparable One. Holiness is His alone. There is nothing like it in heaven or earth, except when He gives it. And so our holiness will consist not in a human separation in which we attempt to imitate God's—no, but in entering into His separateness, in belonging entirely to Him, in being set apart by Him and for Himself.

Closely connected with this is the idea of exaltation: "For thus says the High and Lofty One who inhabits eternity, whose name is Holy" (Isa. 57:15). It was the Holy One who was seen sitting on a throne high and lifted up, the object of the worship of the seraphim. In Psalm 99, God's holiness is specially spoken of in connection with His exaltation. For this reason, too, His holiness is so often connected with His glory and majesty (see Day 6). And here our holiness will be seen to be nothing but the poverty and humility that comes when "the loftiness of man...is brought low, and the LORD alone will be exalted" (Isa. 2:17).

If we inquire more closely as to what the infinite excellence of this separateness and exaltation consists, we are led to think of the divine purity and that not only in its negative aspect—as hatred of sin—but with the more positive element of perfect beauty. Because we are sinners, and the revelation of God's holiness is in a world of sin, it is natural, right, and fitting that the first and abiding impression of God's holiness should be that of an infinite purity that cannot look on sin, in whose presence it is fitting for the sinner to hide his face and tremble.

The righteousness of God, forbidding and condemning and punishing sin, has its root in His holiness and is one of its two elements—the devouring and destroying power of the consuming fire. "God who is holy shall be hallowed in righteousness" (Isa. 5:16), and in righteousness the holiness of the Holy One is maintained and revealed. But light not only discovers what is impure so that it may be purified but is in itself a thing of infinite beauty. And so some of our holiest men have not hesitated to speak of God's holiness as the infinite pulchritude or beauty of the Divine Being, the perfect purity and beauty of that light in which God dwells. And if the holiness of God is to become ours, to rest on us and enter into us, there must be, without ceasing, the holy fear that trembles at the thought of grieving the infinite sensitiveness of this Holy One by our sins, and yet side by side, and in perfect harmony with it, the deep longing to behold the beauty of the Lord, an admiration of its divine glory, and a joyful surrender to be His alone.

We must go one step further. When God says, "I am holy: I *make holy*," we see that one of the chief elements of His holiness is this: that it seeks to communicate itself, to make partaker of its own perfection and blessedness. This is nothing but love. In the wonderful revelation in Isaiah of what the Holy One is to His people, we must beware of misreading God's precious Word. It is not said that *though* God is the Holy One and hates sin and ought to punish and destroy, that notwithstanding this He will save. By no means. But we are taught that *as* the Holy One, *just because* He is the Holy One who delights to make holy, He will be the deliverer of His people (see Hos. 11:9).

It is holiness above everything else that we are invited to look to, to trust in, to rejoice in. The Holy One is the Holy-making One. He redeems and saves so that He may win our confidence for Himself, so that He may draw us to Himself as the Holy One, so that in the personal attachment to Himself we may learn to obey, to become of one mind with Him, to be holy as He is holy.

> The righteousness of God, forbidding and condemning and punishing sin, has its root in His holiness and is one of its two elements—the devouring and destroying power of the consuming fire.

The divine holiness is therefore that infinite perfection of divinity in which righteousness and love are in perfect harmony, out of which they proceed, and which together they reveal. It is that energy of the divine life in the power of which God not only keeps Himself free from all creature weakness or sin, but unceasingly seeks to lift the creature into union with Himself and the full participation of His own purity and perfection. The glory of God as God, as the God of creation and redemption, is His holiness. It is in this that the separateness and exaltation of God, even above all thought of man, really consists. "God is light" (1 John 1:5), and in His infinite purity, He reveals all darkness and yet has no fellowship with it. He judges and condemns it, He saves out of it, and lifts up into the fellowship of His own purity and blessedness. This is the Holy One of Israel.

It is this God who speaks to us, "I am the Lord your God: I am holy: I make holy." It is in the adoring contemplation of His holiness, in the trustful surrender to it, in the loving fellowship with Himself, the Holy One, that we can be made holy. My brother! Would you be holy? Listen again and let, in the deep silence of trust, God's words sink into your heart—"Your Holy One." Come to Him and claim Him as your God, and claim all that He, as the Holy One who makes holy, can do for you. Just remember that holiness is Himself. Come to *Him*, worship *Him*, give *Him* the glory. Don't seek, even from Him, holiness in yourself. Let self be abased and be content that the holiness is His. As *His* presence fills your heart, as *His* holiness and glory are your one desire, as *His* holy will and love are your delight—as the Holy One becomes all in all to you—you will be holy with the holiness He loves to see. And as, to the end, you see nothing to admire in self, and only beauty in Him, you will know that He has laid of His glory on you, and your holiness will be found in the song, "There is none holy, but the Lord."

Be holy, as I am holy

O God! We have again heard the wonderful revelation of Yourself, "I am holy." And as we felt how infinitely exalted above all our conceptions Your holiness is, we heard Your call, almost still more wonderful, "Be holy, as I am holy." And as every thought of how we were to be holy, as You are holy, failed us, we heard Your voice once again, in this most wonderful word of all, "I make you holy." I am "your Holy One."

Most holy God! We do beg You, help us in some due measure to realize how unholy we are, and so to take the place that becomes us in Your presence. Oh that the sinfulness of our nature, and all that is of self, may be so revealed to us that it may be no longer possible to live in it! May the light that reveals this reveal too how Your holiness is our only hope, our sure refuge, our complete deliverance. O Lord! Speak into our souls the word, "The Holy One, your Redeemer," "Your Holy One," with such power by Your Spirit that our faith may grow into the assured confidence that we can be holy as You are holy.

Holy Lord God! We wait for You. Reveal Yourself in power within us, and fit us to be the messengers of Your holiness, to tell Your people how holy You are, and how holy we must be, and how holy You make us. Amen.

For Further Thought

1. *How do you view the one the Bible calls "the Holy One."? This Holy One is God Almighty. Before He revealed Himself to Israel as the Holy One, He made Himself known to Abraham as the Almighty, "who gives life to the dead" (Rom. 4:17). In all your dealings with God for holiness, remember He is the Almighty One who can do wonders in you. Say often, "Glory to Him who is able to do exceedingly abundantly above all we ask or think" (Eph. 3:20).*

2. *What can you expect God to do when you present yourself to Him to be made holy? This Holy One is the righteous God, a consuming fire. Cast yourself into it so that all that is sinful may be destroyed. As you lay yourself on the altar, expect the fire. "And present. . .your members as instruments of righteousness to God" (Rom. 6:13).*

3. *What is to be your approach to the Holy One? This Holy One is the God of love. He is your Father. Yield yourself to let the Holy Spirit cry in you, "Abba Father!"—that is, to let Him shed abroad and fill your heart with God's father-love. God's holiness is His fatherliness; our holiness is childlikeness. Be simple, loving, trustful.*

4. *This Holy One is God. Let Him be God to you—ruling all, filling all, working all. Worship Him, come near to Him, live with and in and for Him. He will be your holiness.*

DAY 12
THE THRICE HOLY ONE

I saw the Lord sitting on a throne, high and lifted up,
and the train of His robe filled the temple. Above it stood seraphim. . . .
And one cried to another and said: "Holy, holy, holy is the LORD
of hosts; The whole earth is full of His glory!"
ISAIAH 6:1–3

The four living creatures, each having six wings,
were full of eyes around and within. And they do not rest day
or night, saying: "Holy, holy, holy, Lord God Almighty,
Who was and is and is to come!"
REVELATION 4:8

IT is not only on earth, but in heaven too, that the holiness of God is His chief and most glorious attribute. It is not only on earth, but in heaven too, that the highest inspiration of adoration and praise makes mention of His holiness. The brightest of living beings, they who are always before and around and above the throne, find their glory in adoring and proclaiming the holiness of God. Surely there can be for us no higher honor than to study and to know, to worship and adore, to proclaim and show forth the glory of the Thrice Holy One.

After Moses, as we know, Isaiah was the chief messenger of the holiness of God. Each had a special preparation for his commission to make known the Holy One. Moses saw the Holy One in the fire and hid his face and feared to look at God, and so was prepared for being His messenger, and for praising Him as "glorious in holiness" (Exod. 15:11). Isaiah, as he heard the song of the seraphim, and saw the fire on the altar and the house filled with the smoke, cried out, "Woe is me" (Isa. 6:5). It was not until, in the deep sense of the need of cleansing, he had received the touch of the fire and the purging of his sin that he might bear to Israel the gospel of the Holy One as its redeemer. May it be in the spirit of fear and lowly worship that we listen to the song of the seraphim and seek to know and worship the Thrice Holy One. And may ours too be the cleansing with the fire, so that we may be found fit to tell God's people that He is the Holy One of Israel, their Redeemer.

The threefold repetition of the *holy* has at all times by the Church of Christ been connected with the Holy Trinity. The song of the living creatures around the throne (Rev. 4) is evidence of the truth of this thought. We there find it followed by the adoration of Him who was, and is, and is to come, the Almighty: the eternal source, the present manifestation in the Son, the future perfecting of the revelation of God in the Spirit's work in His Church.

The truth of the Holy Trinity is often regarded as an abstract doctrine, with little direct bearing on practical life. So far is this from being the case that a living faith must root in it: some spiritual insight into the relationship and the operation of each of the three, and the reality of their living oneness, is an essential element of true growth in knowledge and spiritual understanding.[15] Let us here regard the Trinity especially in its relationship to God's holiness and as the source of ours. What does it mean that we adore the Thrice Holy One? God is not only holy, but makes holy, and in the revelation of the three persons we have the revelation of the way in which God makes holy.

May it be in the spirit of fear and lowly worship that we listen to the song of the seraphim and seek to know and worship the Thrice Holy One.

The Trinity teaches us that God has revealed Himself in two ways. The Son is the *form of God*, His manifestation as He shows Himself to man, the image in which His unseen glory is embodied and to which man is to be conformed. The Spirit is the *power of God*, working in man and leading him up to that image. In Jesus, He who had been in the form of God took the form of man, and the divine holiness was literally manifested in the form of a human life and the members of a human body.

A new holy human nature was formed in Christ, to be communicated to us. In His death His own personal holiness was perfected as human obedience, and so the power of sin conquered and broken. Therefore in the resurrection, through the Spirit of Holiness, He was declared to be the Son of God with power to impart His life to us. There the Spirit of Holiness was set free from the veil of the flesh, the shackles that hindered it, and obtained power to enter and dwell in man. The Holy Spirit was poured out as the fruit of resurrection and ascension. And the Spirit is now the power of God in us, working upwards toward Christ to reproduce His life and holiness in us, to fit us for fully receiving and showing

---

[15] The divine necessity and meaning of the doctrine of the Trinity is seen from the counterpart we have of it in nature. In every living object that exists, we distinguish first the life, then the form or shape in which that life manifests itself, then the power or effect as seen in the result which the life acting in its form or manifestation produces. And so we have God as the Unseen One, the fountain of life; the Son as the form or image of God, the manifestation of the unseen life; and the Holy Spirit as the power of that life proceeding from the Father and the Son, and working out the purpose of God's will in the Church. Applying this thought to God as the Holy One, we shall understand better the place of the Son and the Spirit as they bring to us the holiness of God.

forth Him in our lives. Christ from above comes to us as the embodiment of the unseen holiness of God, and the Spirit from within lifts us up to meet Him, and fits us to receive and make our own all that is in Him.

The Triune God whom we adore is the Thrice Holy One, and the mystery of the Trinity is the mystery of holiness. The glory and the power of the Trinity is the glory and power of God who makes us holy. There is God, dwelling in light inaccessible, a consuming fire of holy love, destroying all that resists, glorifying into its own purity all that yields. There is the Son, casting Himself into that consuming fire, whether in its eternal blessedness in heaven or its angry wrath on earth, a willing sacrifice, to be its food and its satisfaction as well as the revelation of its power to destroy and to save. And there is the Spirit of holiness, the flames of that mighty fire spreading on every side, convicting and judging as the Spirit of burning, and then transforming into its own brightness and holiness all that it can reach. All the relationships of the Three Persons to each other and to us have their root and their meaning in the revelation of God as the Holy One. As we know and partake of Him, we shall know and partake of holiness.

> *Christ from above comes to us as the embodiment of the Unseen Holiness of God, and the Spirit from within lifts us up to meet Him, and fits us to receive and make our own all that is in Him.*

And how shall we know Him? Let us learn to know the holiness of God as the seraphs do: in the worship of the Thrice Holy One. Let us with veiled faces join in the ceaseless song of adoration: "Holy, holy, holy is the Lord of hosts" (Isa. 6:3). Each time we meditate on the Word, each prayer to the holy God, each act of faith in Christ the Holy One, each exercise of waiting dependence on the Holy Spirit, let it be in the spirit of worship: Holy, holy, holy.

Let us learn to know the holiness of God as Isaiah did. He was to be the chosen messenger to reveal and interpret to the people the name, the Holy One of Israel. His preparation was the vision that made him cry out, "Woe is me! For my eyes have seen the King, the Lord of hosts" (6:5). Let us bow in silence before the Holy One, until our beauty too be turned into corruption. And then let us believe in the cleansing fire from the altar, the touch of the live coals of the burning holiness, which not only consumes, but purges lips and heart to say, "Here am I, send me" (6:8). Yes, let us worship, whether like the adoring seraphim or like the trembling prophet, until we know that our service too is accepted, to tell forth the praise of the Thrice Holy One.

Holy, holy, holy: If we are indeed to be the messengers of the Holy One, let us seek to enter fully into what this Thrice Holy means. *Holy*, the Father, *God above us*, high and lifted up, whom no man has seen or can see, whose holiness none dare approach, but who Himself in His holiness draws near to make holy. *Holy*, the Son, *God with us*, revealing divine holiness in human life, maintaining it amid the suffering of death for us, and preparing a holy life and nature for His people. *Holy*, the Spirit, *God in us*, the power of holiness within us, reaching out to and embracing Christ, and transforming our inner life into the union and communion of Him in whom we are holy. Holy, holy, holy! It is all holiness. It is only holiness—perfect holiness. This is divine holiness: holiness hidden and unapproachable, holiness manifested and maintained in human nature, holiness communicated and made our very own.

> *This is divine holiness: holiness hidden and unapproachable, holiness manifested and maintained in human nature, holiness communicated and made our very own.*

The mystery of the Holy Trinity is the mystery of the Christian life, the mystery of holiness. The three are one, and we need to enter ever more deeply into the truth that neither of the three ever works separate or independent of the other. The Son reveals the Father, and the Father reveals the Son. The Father does not give Himself, but the Spirit. The Spirit does not speak of Himself, but cries *Abba Father!* The Son is our sanctification, our life, our all—the fullness is in Him. And yet we must always bow our knees to the Father for Him to reveal Christ in us, for Him to establish us in Christ. And the Father doesn't do this without the Spirit—so that we have to ask to be strengthened mightily by the Spirit so that Christ may dwell in us. Christ gives the Spirit to those who believe and love and obey. The Spirit again gives Christ, formed within and dwelling in the heart. And so in each act of worship, and each step of growth, and each blessed experience of grace, all the three persons are actively engaged. The one is always three, the three are always one.

If you desire to apply this in the life of holiness, then let faith in the Holy Trinity be a living practical reality. In every prayer to *the Father* to sanctify you, take up your position *in Christ*, and do it in the power of *the Spirit within you*. In every exercise of faith *in Christ* as your sanctification, let your posture be that of prayer to *the Father* and trust in Him as He delights to honor the Son, and of quiet expectancy of *the Spirit's* working, through whom the Father glorifies the Son. In every surrender of the soul to the sanctification of *the Spirit*, to His leading as the Spirit of Holiness, look to *the Father* who grants His mighty working and who sanctifies through faith in *the Son*, and expect the Spirit's power to manifest itself in showing the will of God, and Jesus as your sanctification. If for a time this appears at odds with the simplicity of childlike faith and prayer, be assured that as God has revealed Himself this way, He will teach you so to worship and believe.

And so the Holy, holy, holy will become the deep undertone of all our worship and all our life.

Children of God, called to be holy as He is holy, oh, come let us bow down and worship in His holy presence! Come and veil the face. Withdraw eye and mind from gazing on what passes knowledge, and let the soul be gathered into that inner stillness in which the worship of the heavenly sanctuary alone can be heard. Come and cover the feet. Withdraw from the rush of work and haste, be it worldly or religious, and learn to worship. Come, and as you fall down in self-abasement, the glory of the Holy One will shine on you. And as you hear and take up and sing the song, *Holy, Holy, Holy*, you will find how in such knowledge and worship of the Thrice Holy One is the power that makes you holy.

Be holy, for I am holy

Holy, holy, holy, the Lord God Almighty! The One who is and who was and who is to come! I worship You as the Triune God. With face veiled and feet covered, I want to bow in deep humility and silence until Your mercy lifts me as on eagles' wings to see Your glory.

Most merciful God, who has called me to be holy as You are holy: oh, reveal to me some part of Your holiness! As it shines on me and strikes death into the creature and the flesh, may even the most involuntary taint of sin, and its slightest movement, become unbearable. As it shines and revives the hope of being partaker of Your holiness, may the confidence grow strong that You Yourself are making me holy, will even make me a messenger of Your holiness.

Thrice Holy God ! I worship You as my God. *Holy! the Father*, holy and making holy; making holy His own Son and sending Him into the world so that we might behold the very glory of God in human face, the face of Jesus Christ. Holy! the Son; the Holy One of God, fulfilling the will of the Father, and so making holy Himself that He might be our holiness. *Holy! the Spirit*, the Spirit of Holiness, dwelling within us, making the Son and His holiness our own, and so making us partakers of the holiness of God. O my God! I bow down, and worship, and adore.

May even now the worship of heaven that rests not day or night be the worship my soul gives You without ceasing. May its song be, down in the depths of the heart, the keynote of my life: Holy, Holy, Holy, Lord God Almighty! The One who is and who was and who is to come. Amen.

For Further Thought

1. *How can you better understand the thought of the Three-One God? Thought always needs to distinguish and separate: in life alone there is perfect unity. The more we know the living God, the more we shall realize how truly the three are one. In each act of one person the other two are present. There is not a prayer that rises in which the presence of the Holy Three is needed; through Christ, in the Spirit, we speak to the Father.*

2. *How does understanding in faith the Three-One God relate to holiness. It is to have the secret of holiness. The Holy God above us, always giving and working; the Holy One of God, the living gift, who has possession of us, in whom we are; the Holy Spirit, God within us, through whom the Father works and the Son is revealed: this is the God who says, "I am holy, I make holy." In the perfect unity of the work of the three, holiness is found.*

3. *What must you learn in order to know God and to be holy? No wonder that the love of the Father and the grace of the Son do not accomplish more, when the fellowship of the Holy Spirit is little understood or sought or accepted. The Holy Spirit is the fruit and crown of the divine revelation, through whom the Son and the Father come to us. If you desire to know God, if you desire to be holy, you must be taught and led by the Spirit.*

4. *As often as you worship the Thrice Holy One, listen if no voice is heard: Whom shall I send, and who will go for us? Let the answer rise, "Here am I, send me!" and offer yourself to be a messenger of the holiness of God to those around you.*

5. *When in meditation and worship you have sought to take in and express what God's word has taught, then comes the time for confessing how you know nothing, and for waiting on God to reveal Himself.*

DAY 13

HOLINESS AND HUMILITY

*For thus says the High and Lofty One Who inhabits
eternity, whose name is Holy: "I dwell in the high and
holy place, with him who has a contrite and humble
spirit, to revive the spirit of the humble,
and to revive the heart of the contrite ones."*
ISAIAH 57:15

VERY wonderful is the revelation we have in Isaiah of God, the Holy One as
the Redeemer and the Savior of His people. In the midst of the people whom He
created and formed for Himself, He will as the Holy One dwell, showing forth
His power and His glory, filling them with joy and gladness.

All these promises have, however, reference to the people as a whole. Our
text today reveals a new and specially beautiful feature of the divine holiness in
its relation to the individual. The High and Lofty One, whose name is Holy, and
whose only fit dwelling place is eternity. He looks to the man who is of a humble
and contrite heart; with him will He dwell. God's holiness is His condescending love. As it is a consuming fire against all who exalt themselves before Him,
it is to the spirit of the humble like the shining of the sun, heart-reviving and
life-giving.

The deep significance of this promise comes out clearly when we connect it
with the other promises of New Testament times. The great feature of the New
Covenant, in its superiority to the Old, is this: that whereas in the law and its institution all was external, in the New the kingdom of God would be within. God's
laws given and written into the heart, a new spirit put within us, God's own Spirit
given to dwell within our spirit, and so the heart and the inner life fitted to be the
temple and home of God—it is this that constitutes the peculiar privilege of the
ministry of the Spirit.

Our text is perhaps the only one in the Old Testament in which this indwelling of the Holy One, not among the people only, but in the heart of the individual
believer, is clearly brought out. In this the two aspects of the divine holiness would
reach their full manifestation: "I dwell in the high and holy place, and with him
who has a contrite and humble spirit." In His heaven above, the high and lofty
place, and in our heart, contrite and humble, God has His home. God's holiness is

His glory that separates Him by an infinite distance, not only from sin, but even from the creature, lifting Him high above it. God's holiness is His love, drawing Him down to the sinner so that He may lift him into His fellowship and likeness and make him holy as He is holy. The Holy One seeks the humble, and the humble find the Holy One: such are the two lessons we have to learn today.

The Holy One seeks the humble. There is nothing that has such an attraction for God, that has such affinity with holiness, as a contrite and humble spirit. The reason is evident. There is no law in the natural and the spiritual world more simple than that two bodies cannot at the same moment occupy the same space. Only so much as the new occupant can expel of what the space was filled with can it really possess. In man, self has possession, and self-will the mastery, and there is no room for God. It is simply impossible for God to dwell or rule when self is on the throne. As long as, through the blinding influence of sin and self-love, even the believer is not truly conscious of the extent to which this self-will reigns, there can be no true contrition or humility. But as it is revealed by God's Spirit, and the soul sees how it has just been self that has been secretly keeping out God, with what shame it is broken down, and how it longs to break utterly away from self so that God may have His place!

> *T*he great feature of the New Covenant, in its superiority to the Old, is this: that whereas in the law and its institution all was external, in the New the kingdom of God would be within.

It is this brokenness, and continued breaking down, that is expressed by the word *contrition*. And as the soul sees what folly and guilt it has been, by its secret honoring of self, to keep the Holy One from the place that He alone has a right to—and that He would so blessedly have filled—it casts itself down in utter self-abasement, with the one desire to be nothing and to give God the place and the praise that is His due.

Such breaking down and humiliation is painful. Its intense reality consists in this: that the soul can see nothing in itself to trust or hope in. And least of all can it imagine that it should be an object of divine satisfaction or a fit vessel for the divine blessing. And yet just this is the message that the Word of the Lord brings to our faith. It tells us that the Holy One, who dwells in the high and lofty place, is seeking and preparing for Himself a dwelling here on this earth. It tells us, just what the truly contrite and humble never could imagine and even now can hardly believe, that it is even, that it is only, with such that He will dwell. These are they in whom God can be glorified, in whom there is room for Him to take the place of self and to fill the emptied place with Himself. The Holy One seeks the humble. Just when we see that there is nothing in us to admire or rest in, God sees in us everything to admire and to rest in, because there is room for Himself.

The lowly one is the home of the Holy One.

The humble find the Holy One. Just when the consciousness of sin and weakness, and the discovery of how much of self there is, makes you fear that you can never be holy, the Holy One gives Himself. Not as you look at self and seek to know whether now you are contrite and humble enough—no, but when no longer looking at self, because you have given up all hope of seeing anything in it but sin, you look up to the Holy One, you will see how His promise is your only hope.

> *God's holiness is His love, drawing Him down to the sinner so that He may lift him into His fellowship and likeness and make him holy as He is holy.*

It is in faith that the Holy One is revealed to the contrite soul. Faith is always the opposite of what we see and feel, for it looks to God alone. And it believes that in its deepest consciousness of unholiness and its fear that it never can be holy, God, the Holy One who makes holy, is near as Redeemer and Savior. And it is content to be low, in the consciousness of unworthiness and emptiness, and yet to rejoice in the assurance that God Himself does take possession and revive the heart of the contrite one. Happy is the soul who is willing at once to learn the lesson that, all along, it is going to be the simultaneous experience of weakness and power, of emptiness and filling, of deep, real humiliation, and the as real and most wonderful indwelling of the Holy One.

This is indeed the deep mystery of the divine life. To human reason it is a paradox. When Paul says of himself, "as dying, and behold we live. . .as sorrowful, yet always rejoicing. . .as having nothing, and yet possessing all things" (2 Cor. 6:9, 10), he only gives expression to the law of the kingdom: that as self is displaced and man becomes nothing, God will become all. Side by side with deepest sense of nothingness and weakness, the sense of infinite riches and the joy unspeakable can fill the heart.

However deep and blessed the experience becomes of the nearness, the blessing, the love, the actual indwelling of the Holy One, it is never an indwelling in the old self. Rather, it is always a divine presence humbling self to make place for God alone to be exalted. The power of Christ's death, the fellowship of His cross, works each moment side by side with the power and the joy of His resurrection. "He who humbles himself will be exalted" (Luke 14:11). In the blessed life of faith, the humiliation and the exaltation are simultaneous, each dependent on the other.

The humble find the Holy One, and when they have found, the possession only humbles all the more. Not that there is no danger or temptation of the flesh exalting itself in the possession, but, once knowing the danger, the humble soul seeks for grace to fear continually with a fear that only clings more firmly to God alone. Never for a moment imagine that you attain a state in which self or the flesh are absolutely dead. No! By faith you enter into and abide in a fellowship with Jesus, in whom they are crucified, and abiding in Him, you are free from their power, but only as you believe, and, in believing, have gone out of self and dwell in Jesus. Therefore, the more abundant God's grace becomes, and the more blessed the indwelling of the Holy One, keep yourself so much the lower. Your danger is greater, but your help is now nearer, so be content in trembling to confess the danger, and then it will make you bold in faith to claim the victory.

> The High and Lofty One whose name is Holy, who dwells in the holy place, and who can dwell nowhere but in a holy place seeks a dwelling here on earth. Will you give it to Him?

Believers, who profess to be nothing and to trust in grace alone, I encourage you, do listen to the wondrous message. The High and Lofty One whose name is Holy, who dwells in the holy place, and who can dwell nowhere but in a holy place seeks a dwelling here on earth. Will you give it to Him? Will you not fall down in the dust so that He may find in you the humble heart He loves to dwell in? Will you not now believe that even in you, however low and broken you feel, He delights to make His dwelling?

"Blessed are the poor in spirit, for theirs is the kingdom" (Matt. 5:3)—with them the King dwells. Oh, this is the path to holiness! Be humble, and then the holy nearness and presence of God in you will be your holiness. As you hear the command, Be holy, as I am holy, let faith claim the promise and answer, "I will be holy, O Most Holy God, if You, the Holy One, will dwell with me!"

BE HOLY, AS I AM HOLY

O Lord! You are the High and Lofty One whose name is Holy. And yet You speak, "I dwell in the high and holy place, with him who has a contrite and humble spirit." Yes, Lord! When the soul takes the low place and has low thoughts of itself, that it feels it is nothing, You love to come and comfort, to dwell with it and revive it.

O my God! My creature nothingness humbles me, my many transgressions humble me, and my innate sinfulness humbles me. But this humbles me most of all: Your infinite condescension and the indescribable indwelling You grant. It is Your holiness, in Christ bearing our sin, Your holy love bearing with our sin and consenting to dwell in us. O God, it is this love that passes understanding that humbles me. I do ask You, let it do its work until self hides its head and flees away at the presence of Your glory and You alone are all.

Holy Lord God! I ask You to humble me. Did You not of old meet Your servants and show Yourself to them until they fell on their faces and feared? You know, my God, I have no humility that I can bring You. In my blessed Savior, who humbled Himself in the form of a servant and to the death of the cross, I hide myself. In Him, in His spirit and likeness, I would live before You. Work it in me, by the Holy Spirit dwelling in me, and as I am dead to self in Him and His cross makes me nothing, let Your holy indwelling revive and make me alive. Amen.

FOR FURTHER THOUGHT

1. *What is the connection between lowliness and holiness? Keep a firm hold on the intimate connection. Lowliness is taking the place that fits me, and holiness is, giving God the place that becomes Him. If I am nothing before Him, and God all to me, I am on the sure path of holiness. Lowliness is holiness, because it gives all the glory to God.*

2. *"Blessed are the poor in spirit, for theirs is the kingdom of heaven." These first words of the Master when He opened His lips to proclaim the kingdom are often the last in the hearts of His disciples. "The Kingdom is in Holy Spirit" (see Rom. 14:17): to the poor in spirit, those who know they have nothing that is really spiritual, the Holy Spirit comes to be their life. The poor in spirit are the kingdom of the saints: in them the Holy Spirit reveals the King. How can you know that you are among the poor in spirit?*

3. *Many strive hard to be humble with God but with men they maintain their rights and nourish self. Remember that the great school of humility before God is to accept the humbling from man. Christ sanctified Himself in accepting the humiliation and injustice that evil men laid upon Him. What is your response when God tried to humble you using others?*

4. *Humility never sees its own beauty, because it refuses to look to itself. It only wonders at the condescension of the Holy God and rejoices in the humility of Jesus, God's Holy One, our Holy One.*

5. *The link between holiness and humility is indwelling. The lofty One, whose name is Holy, dwells with the contrite one. And where He dwells is the holy place.*

Day 14

The Holy One of God

"The Holy Spirit will come upon you,
and the power of the Highest will overshadow you;
therefore, also, that Holy One who is to
be born will be called the Son of God."
Luke 1:35

"Also we have come to believe and know
that You are the Christ, the Son of the living God."
John 6:69

"THE holy one of the Lord"—only once (Ps. 106:16) the expression is found in the Old Testament. It is spoken of Aaron, in whom holiness, as far as it could then be revealed, had found its most complete embodiment. The title waited for its fulfillment in Him who alone, in His own person, could perfectly show forth the holiness of God on earth—Jesus the Son of the Father. In Him we see holiness, as divine, as human, as our very own.

1. In Him we see wherein that incomparable excellence of the divine nature consists. "You love righteousness and hate wickedness; therefore God, Your God, has anointed You with the oil of gladness more than Your companions" (Ps. 45:7). God's infinite hatred of sin, and His maintenance of the right, might appear to have little moral worth, as being a necessity of His nature. In the Son we see divine holiness tested. He is tried and tempted. He suffers, being tempted. He proves that holiness has indeed a moral worth: it is ready to make any sacrifice, yes to give up life and cease to be, rather than consent to sin. In giving Himself to die, rather than yield to the temptation of sin; in giving Himself to die so that the Father's righteous judgment may be honored, Jesus proved how righteousness is an element of the divine holiness, and how the Holy One is sanctified in righteousness.

But this is only one side of holiness. The fire that consumes also purifies. It makes partakers of its own beautiful light-nature all that is capable of assimilation. So divine holiness not only maintains its own purity, it communicates it too. In this was Jesus indeed seen to be the Holy One of God, that He never said,

"Stand aside, for I am holier than you." His holiness proved itself to be the very incarnation of Him who had spoken, "For thus says the High and Lofty One who inhabits eternity, whose name is Holy: 'I dwell in the high and holy place, with him who has a contrite and humble spirit'" (Isa. 57:15). In Him was seen the affinity holiness has for all that is lost and helpless and sinful. He proved that holiness is not only the energy that in holy anger separates itself from all that is impure, but that in holy love separates to itself even what is most sinful, to save and to bless. In Him we see how the divine holiness is the harmony of infinite righteousness with infinite love.

2. Such is the divine aspect of the character of Christ, as He shows in human form what God's holiness is. But there is another aspect, to us no less interesting and important. We not only want to know how God is holy, but how man must act to be holy as God is holy. Jesus came to teach us that it is possible to be men and yet to have the life of God dwelling in us. We ordinarily think that the glory and the infinite perfection of Deity are the proper setting in which the beauty of holiness is to be seen. But Jesus proved the perfect adaptation and suitability of human nature for showing forth that which is the essential glory of Deity. He showed us how, in choosing and doing the will of God and making it his own will, man may truly be holy as God is holy.

> *He proves that holiness has indeed a moral worth: it is ready to make any sacrifice, yes to give up life and cease to be, rather than consent to sin.*

The value of this aspect of the Incarnation depends on our realizing intensely the true humanity of our Lord. The awful separating and purifying process that is always being carried on in the fiery furnace of the divine holiness, always consuming and always assimilating, we expect to see in Him in the struggles of a truly human will. Holiness, to be truly human, must not only be a gift, but an acquirement. Coming from God, it must be accepted and personally appropriated, in the voluntary surrender of all that is not in accordance with it. In Jesus, as He distinctly gave up His own will and did and suffered the Father's will, we have the revelation of what human holiness is, and how truly man, through the unity of will, can be holy as God is holy.

3. But what benefits us that we have seen in Jesus that a man can be holy? His example were indeed a mockery if He didn't show us the way and didn't give us the power to become like Himself. To bring us this was indeed the supreme object of the Incarnation. The divine nature of Christ did not simply make His humanity partaker of its holiness, leaving Him still nothing more than an individual man. His divinity gave the human holiness He accomplished, and the holy human nature that He perfected, an infinite value and power of communication. With Him a new life,

the eternal life, was grafted into the stem of humanity. For all who believe in Him, He sanctified Himself so that they themselves might also be sanctified in truth. Because His death was the great triumph of His obedience to the will of the Father, it broke forever the dominion of sin, atoned for our guilt, and won for Him from the Father the power to make His people partakers of His own life and holiness. In His resurrection and ascension, the power of the new life, and its right to universal dominion, were made reality, and He is now in full truth the Holy One of God, holding in Himself as head the power of a holiness, at the same divine and human, to communicate to every member of His body.

The Holy One of God! In a fullness of meaning that passes knowledge, in spirit and in truth, Jesus now bears this title. He is now the One Holy One whom God sees, of such an infinite compass and power of holiness, that He can be holiness to each of His brethren. And even as He is to God the Holy One in whom He delights, and for whose sake He delights in all who are in Him, so Christ may now be to us too the One Holy One in whom we delight, in whom the holiness of God has become ours. "We have come to believe and know that You are the Christ, *the Son of the living God*" (John 6:69)— blessed are they who can say this, and who know themselves to be holy in Christ.

> In Jesus, as He distinctly gave up His own will and did and suffered the Father's will, we have the revelation of what human holiness is, and how truly man, through the unity of will, can be holy as God is holy.

In speaking of the mystery of the Holy Trinity, we saw how Christ stands midway between the Father and the Spirit as the point of union in which they meet. In the Son, "the very image of His substance" (Heb. 1:3), we have the objective revelation of Deity, the divine holiness embodied and brought near. In the Holy Spirit, we have the same revelation subjectively, *the divine holiness entering our innermost being and revealing itself there.* The work of the Holy Spirit is to reveal and glorify Christ as the Holy One of God as He takes of His holiness and makes it ours. He shows us how all is in Christ, how Christ is all for us, how we are in Christ, and how, as a living savior, Christ through His Spirit takes and keeps charge of us and our life of holiness. He makes Christ indeed to be to us the *Holy One of God.*

My brother! If you desire to be holy, if you desire to know God's way of holiness—learn to know Christ as the Holy One of God. You are in Him "holy in Christ." You have been placed, by an act of divine power, in Christ, and that same power keeps you there, planted and rooted in that divine fullness of life and holiness that there is in Him. His holy presence, and the power of His eternal life, surround you. Let the Holy Spirit reveal this to you. The Holy Spirit is within you as the power of Christ and His life. Secretly, silently, but mightily, if you will look to the Father for His working, will He strengthen the faith that you are in Christ and that the divine life, which therefore encircles you on every side, will enter in and take possession of you. Study and pray to believe and realize that it is in Christ as the Holy One of God, in Christ in whom the holiness of God is prepared for you as a holy nature and holy living, that you are, and that you may abide.

> *If you desire to be holy, if you desire to know God's way of holiness— learn to know Christ as the Holy One of God. You are in Him "holy in Christ.*

And then remember, also, that this Christ is your savior, the most patient and compassionate of teachers. Study holiness in the light of His countenance, looking up into His face. *He came from heaven for the very purpose of making you holy.* His love and power are more than your slowness and sinfulness. Do learn to think of holiness as the inheritance prepared for you, as the power of a new life that Jesus waits and lives to dispense. Just think of it as all in Him, and of its possession as being dependent on the possession of Himself. And as the disciples, though they hardly understood what they confessed or knew where the Lord was leading them, became His saints, His holy ones, in virtue of their intense attachment to Him, so will you find that to love Jesus fervently, and obey Him simply, is the sure path to holiness and the fullness of the Holy Spirit.

BE HOLY, AS I AM HOLY

Most holy Lord God! I do bless You that Your beloved Son, whom You sanctified and sent into the world, is now to us the Holy One of God. I ask You that my inner life may so be enlightened by the Spirit that I may in faith fully know what this means.

May I know Him as the revelation of Your holiness, the incarnation in human nature, even to the point of the death, of Your infinite and unconquerable hatred of sin, as of Your amazing love to the sinner. May my soul be filled with great fear of and trust in You.

May I know Him as the exhibition of the holiness in which we are now to walk before You. He lived in Your holy will. May I know Him as He worked out that holiness, to be communicated to us in a new human nature, making it possible for us to live a holy life.

May I know Him as You have placed me in Him in heaven, holy in Christ, and as I may abide in Him by faith.

May I know Him, as He dwells in me, the Holy One of God on the throne of my heart, breathing His Holy Spirit and maintaining His holy rule. So shall I live holy in Christ.

O my Father! It pleased You that in Your Son should all the fullness dwell. In Him are hidden all the treasures of wisdom and knowledge, in Him dwell the unsearchable riches of grace and holiness. I ask You, reveal Him to me, reveal Him in me so that I may not have to satisfy myself with thoughts and desires, without the reality, but that in the power of an endless life I may know Him and be known by Him, the Holy One of God. Amen.

FOR FURTHER THOUGHT

1. *What should be your example of holiness? In the holiness of Jesus we see what ours must be: righteousness that hates sin and gives everything to have it destroyed, love that seeks the sinner and gives everything to have him saved. "Whoever does not practice righteousness is not of God, nor is he who does not love his brother" (1 John 3:10).*

2. *What does having more of Jesus do within a man when it comes to holiness? It is a solemn thought that we may be studying earnestly to know what holiness is, and yet have little of it because we have little of Jesus. It is a blessed thought that a man may directly be little occupied with the thought of holiness, and yet have much of it because he is full of Jesus.*

3. *We need the whole of what God teaches in His Word in regard to holiness in all its different aspects. We need still more to be always returning to the living center where God imparts holiness. Jesus is the Holy One of God: to have Him truly, to love Him fervently, to trust and obey Him, to be in Him—this makes us holy.*

4. *Your holiness is thus treasured up in this divine, almighty, and most gentle Savior—surely there needs to be no fear that He will not be ready or able to make you holy.*

5. *With such a sanctifier, why do so many seekers after holiness fail so sadly and know so little of the joy of a holy life? I am sure it is with very many this one thing: They seek to grasp and hold this Christ in their own strength, and do not know how it is the Holy Spirit within them who must be waited for to reveal this divine being, the Holy One of God, in their hearts.*

Day 15

The Holy Spirit

But this He spoke concerning the Spirit,
whom those believing in Him would receive;
for the Holy Spirit was not yet given,
because Jesus was not yet glorified.
John 7:39

"But the Helper, the Holy Spirit,
whom the Father will send in My name,
He will teach you all things, and bring to your
remembrance all things that I said to you."
John 14:26

God from the beginning chose you for salvation
through sanctification by the Spirit and belief in the truth.
2 Thessalonians 2:13 (also see 1 Peter 1:2)

It has sometimes been said that while the holiness of God stands out more prominently in the Old Testament, in the New it has to give way to the revelation of His love. The remark could hardly be made if it were fully realized that the Spirit is God, and that when He takes up the title *Holy* as His own proper name, it is to teach us that now the holiness of God is to come nearer than ever and to be specially revealed as the power that makes us holy.

In the Holy Spirit, God the Holy One of Israel, and He who was the Holy One of God, come near for the fulfillment of the promise, "I am the Lord who makes you holy." The unseen and unapproachable holiness of God had been revealed and brought near in the life of Christ Jesus, and all that hindered our participation in it had been removed by His death. The name of Holy Spirit teaches us that it is specifically the Spirit's work to impart it to us and make it our own.

Try to realize the meaning of this: The title that through the whole Old Testament has belonged to the Holy God is now appropriated to that Spirit who is within you. The holiness of God in Christ becomes holiness in you, because this Spirit is in you. The words and the divine realities the words express, *Holy* and

Spirit, are now inseparably and eternally united. You can only have as much of the Spirit as you are willing to have of holiness. You can only have as much holiness as you have of the indwelling Spirit.

There are some who pray for the Spirit because they long to have His light and joy and strength. And yet their prayers bring little increase of blessing or power. It is because they do not rightly know or desire Him as the *Holy* Spirit. His burning purity, His searching and convicting light, His making dead of the deeds of the body, of self with its will and its power, His leading into the fellowship of Jesus as He gave up His will and His life to the Father—of all this they have not thought. The Spirit cannot work in power in them because they don't receive Him as the *Holy* Spirit, in *sanctification* of the Spirit.

At times, in seasons of revival, as among the Corinthians and Galatians, He may indeed come with His gifts and mighty workings, while His sanctifying power is but little manifest (1 Cor. 3:1–3, 13:8, 14:4; Gal. 3:3, 5:15–26). But unless that sanctifying power is acknowledged and accepted, His gifts will be lost. His gifts coming on us are only meant to prepare the way for the sanctifying power within us. We must take the lesson to heart that we can have as much of the Spirit as we are willing to have of His holiness. "Be full of the Spirit" must mean to us, "Be fully holy."

> *You* can only have as much of the Spirit as you are willing to have of holiness. You can only have as much holiness as you have of the indwelling Spirit.

The converse is equally true. We can only have as much holiness as we have of the Spirit. Some souls very earnestly seek to be holy, but it is very much in their own strength. They will read books and listen to addresses most earnestly; they will use every effort to lay hold of every thought and act out every advice. And yet they must confess that they are still very much strangers to the true, deep rest and joy and power of abiding in Christ, and to being holy in Him. They sought for holiness more than for the Spirit. They must learn how even all the holiness that is so near and clear in Christ is beyond our reach, except when the Holy Spirit dwells within and imparts it. They must learn to pray for Him and His mighty strengthening (Eph. 3:16), to believe for Him (John 4:14, 7:37), and in faith to yield to Him as indwelling (1 Cor. 3:14, 6:19). They must learn to cease from self-effort in thinking and believing, in willing and in running, and begin to hope in God and wait patiently for Him. He will by His Holy Spirit make us holy. "Be holy" means, "be filled with the Spirit."

If we inquire more closely how it is that this Holy Spirit makes holy, the answer is—He reveals and imparts the holiness of Christ. Scripture tells us that

Christ is made for us sanctification (1 Cor. 1:30). He sanctified Himself for us so that we ourselves might also be sanctified in truth. We have been sanctified through the offering of the body of Jesus Christ once for all. We are sanctified in Christ Jesus. The whole living Christ is just a treasury of holiness for man. In His life on earth, He exchanged the divine holiness He possessed into the current coin needed for this human earthly life, obedience to the Father, and humility, and love, and zeal. As God, He has a sufficiency of it for every moment of the life of every believer.

> *We have been sanctified through the offering of the body of Jesus Christ once for all. We are sanctified in Christ Jesus. The whole living Christ is just a treasury of holiness for man.*

And yet, it is all beyond our reach, except when the Holy Spirit brings it to us and inwardly communicates it. But this is the very work for which He bears the divine name, the *Holy* Spirit, to glorify Jesus, the Holy One of God, within us, and so make us partakers of His holiness. He does it by revealing Christ so that we begin to see what is in Him. He does it by discovering the deep unholiness of our nature (Rom. 7:14–23). He does it by mightily strengthening us to believe, to receive Jesus Himself as our life. He does it by leading us to utter despair of self, to absolute surrender of obedience to Jesus as Lord, to the assured confidence of faith in the power of an indwelling Christ. He does it by, in the secret silent depths of the heart and life, imparting the dispositions and graces of Christ, so that from the inner center of our life, which has been renewed and sanctified in Christ, holiness should flow out and pervade all to the utmost circumference. Where the desire has once been awakened, and the delight in the law of God after the inward man been created, there, as the Spirit of this life in Christ Jesus, He makes free from the law of sin and death in the members, and He leads into the glorious liberty of the sons of God. As God within us, He communicates what God in Christ has prepared.

And if we ask once more how the working of this Holy Spirit, who thus makes holy, is to be secured, the answer is very simple and clear. He is the Spirit of the Holy Father and of Christ, the Holy One of God, and from them He must be received. "He showed me a pure river of water of life. . .proceeding from the throne of God and of the Lamb" (Rev. 22:1). Jesus speaks of "the Holy Spirit, whom the Father will send in my name" (John 14:26). He taught us to ask the Father. Paul prays for the Ephesians: "I bow my knees to the Father. . .that He would grant you, according to the riches of His glory, to be strengthened with might through His Spirit in the inner man" (Eph. 3:14–16).

It is as we look to God in His holiness, and all its revelation from creation downward, and see how the Spirit now flows out from the throne of His holiness as the water of life, that our hope will be awakened that God will give Him to work mightily in us. And as we then see Jesus revealing that holiness in human nature—ripping the veil in His atoning death so that the Spirit from the holiest of all may come forth and, as the Holy Spirit, be His representative, making Him present within us—we shall become confident that faith in Jesus will bring the fullness of the Spirit.

As He told us to ask the Father, He told us to believe in Himself. "He who believes in Me...out of his heart will flow rivers of living water" (John 7:38). Let us bow to the Father in the name of Christ, His Son, and let us believe very simply in the Son as Him in whom we are well-pleasing to the Father and through whom the Father's love and blessing reach us. Then we may be sure the Spirit, who is already within us, will, as the Holy Spirit, do His work in ever-increasing power. The mystery of holiness is the mystery of the Trinity: As we bow to the Father, believing in the Son, the Holy Spirit will work. And we shall see the true meaning of what God spoke in Israel: "*I am holy,*" thus speaks the Father; "be holy," as My Son and in my Son; "I make holy," through the Spirit of My Son dwelling in you. Let our souls worship and cry out, "Holy, holy, holy is the Lord God of hosts."

> *L*et the Holy Spirit, in quietness, and dependence, in the surrender of obedience and trust, have the rule, the free disposal of every faculty. Wait for Him—He can, He will in power reveal and impart the Holiness of the Father and the Son.

The Holy Spirit. All true knowledge of the Father in His adorable holiness, and of the Son in His, which is meant to be ours, and all participation of it, depend on our life in the Spirit, on our knowing and owning Him as abiding in us as our life. Oh, what can it be that, with such a Thrice Holy God, His holiness does not more cover His Church and children? The Holy Spirit is among us, is in us, so it must be we grieve and resist Him. If *you* desire not to do so, at once bow the knee to the Father so that He may grant you the Spirit's mighty workings in the inner man. Believe that the Holy Spirit, bearer to you of all the holiness of God and of Jesus, is indeed in you. Let Him take the place of self, with its thoughts and efforts. Set your soul still before God in holy silence, for Him to give you wisdom. Rest, in emptiness and poverty of spirit, in the faith that He will work in His own way.

As divine as is the holiness that Jesus brings, so divine is the power in which the Holy Spirit communicates it. Yield yourself day by day in growing dependence and obedience, to wait on and be led by Him. Let the fear of the Holy One be on you. Sanctify the Lord God in your heart, and let Him be your fear and dread. Fear not only sin, but fear above all self, as it thrusts itself in before God with its service. Let self die, in refusing and denying its work. Let the Holy Spirit, in quietness, and dependence, in the surrender of obedience and trust, have the rule, the free disposal of every faculty. Wait for Him—He can, He will in power reveal and impart the holiness of the Father and the Son.[16]

BE HOLY, AS I AM HOLY

Holy, holy, holy, Lord God of hosts! The whole earth is full of Your glory! Let that glory fill the heart of Your child as he bows before You. I come now to drink of the river of the water of life that flows from under the throne of God and of the Lamb. Glory be to God and to the Lamb for the gift that has not entered into the heart of man to conceive—the gift of the Holy indwelling Spirit.

O my Father! In the name of Jesus I ask You that I may be strengthened with might by Your Spirit in the inner man. Teach me, I ask You, to believe that You have given Him, to accept and expect Him to fill and rule my whole inner being. Teach me to give up to Him—not to will or to run, not to think or to work in my strength, but in quiet confidence to wait and to know that He works in me. Teach me what it is to have no confidence in the flesh, and to serve You in the Spirit. Teach me what it is in all things to be led by Your Holy Spirit, the Spirit of Thy holiness.

And grant, gracious Father, that through Him I may hear You speak and reveal Yourself to me in power: *I am holy.* May He glorify to me and in me Jesus, in whom Your command "Be holy" has been so blessedly fulfilled on my behalf. And let the Holy Spirit give me the anointing and the sealing that brings the perfect assurance that in Him Your promise is being gloriously fulfilled, "I make you holy." Amen.

---

[16] I cannot say how deeply I feel that one of the great wants of believers is that they do not know the Holy Spirit, who is within them, and thereby lose the blessed life He would work in them. If it please God, I hope that the next volume of this series may be on *The Spirit of Christ.* May the Father give me a message that shall help His children to know what the Holy Spirit can be to them.

FOR FURTHER THOUGHT

1. *It is universally admitted that the Holy Spirit doesn't have, in the teaching of the Church or the faith of believers, that place of honor and power that becomes Him as the revealer of the Father and the Son. Seek a deep conviction that without the Holy Spirit, the dearest teaching on holiness, the most fervent desires, the most blessed experiences even, will only be temporary, will produce no permanent result, and will bring no abiding rest. What place does the vital importance of having the Holy Spirit leading, guiding, and dwelling within you have in your life of faith?*

2. *What should you do to ensure that God's Spirit is working within you? The Holy Spirit dwells within and works within, in the hidden deep of your nature. Seek above everything the dear and habitual assurance that He is within you, doing His work.*

3. *To this end, deny self and its work in serving God. Your own power to think and pray and believe and strive—lay it all down expressly and distinctly in God's presence; claim, accept, and believe in the hidden workings of the indwelling Spirit.*

4. *How can you best learn and apply the truth that Christ is your holiness? As the Son always spoke of the Father, so the Spirit always points to Christ. The soul that yields itself to the Spirit will from Him learn to know how Christ is our holiness, how we can always abide in Christ our Sanctification. What a vain effort it has often been without the Spirit! "As the same anointing. . .has taught you, you will abide in Him" (1 John 2:27).*

5. *In the temple of your heart, beloved believer, there is a secret place, within the veil, where dwells, often all unknown, the Spirit of God. Bow in deep reverence before the Father and ask that He may work mightily. Expect the Spirit to do His work; He will make your inner man a fit home, your heart a throne for Jesus, and reveal Him there.*

Day 16

HOLINESS AND TRUTH

"Sanctify them by Your truth.
Your word is truth."
JOHN 17:17

God from the beginning chose you for salvation
through sanctification by the Spirit and belief in the truth.
2 THESSALONIANS 2:13

THE chief means of sanctification that God uses is His Word. And yet how much there is of reading and studying, of teaching and preaching the Word, that has almost no effect in making men holy. It is not the Word that sanctifies; it is God Himself who alone can sanctify. Nor is it simply through the Word that God does it, but through the truth that is in the Word. As a means, the Word is of unspeakable value as the vessel that contains the truth if God uses it; as a means it is of no value if God does not use it. Let us strive to connect God's holy Word with the holy God Himself. God sanctifies in the truth through His Word.

Jesus had just said, "I have given to them the words which You have given Me" (John 17:8). Let us try to realize what that means. Think of that great transaction in eternity: the Infinite Being, whom we call God, giving *His words* to His Son—in His words opening up His heart, communicating His mind and will, revealing Himself and all His purpose and love. In a divine power and reality passing all conception, God gave Christ His words. In the same living power, Christ gave them to His disciples, all full of a divine life and energy to work in their hearts, as they were able to receive them. And just as in the words of a man on earth we expect to find all the wisdom or all the goodness there is in him, so the Word of the Thrice Holy One is all alive with the holiness of God. All the holy fire, along with His burning zeal and His burning love, dwells in His words.

And yet men can handle these words, study them, and speak them, and be entire strangers to their holiness or to their power to make holy. It is God Himself, the Holy One, who must make holy through the Word. Every seed in which the life of a tree is contained has around it a husk or shell that protects and hides the inner life. Only where the seed finds a place in agreeable soil, and the husk is burst

447

and removed, can the seed germinate and grow up. And it is only where there is a heart in harmony with God's holiness, longing for it and yielding itself to it, that the Word will really make holy. It is the heart that is not content with the Word but seeks the living, Holy One in the Word to which He will reveal the truth, and in it Himself. It is the Word given to us by Christ as God gave it to Him, and received by us as it was by Him, to rule and fill our life, that has power to make holy.

But we must notice very specially how our Savior says, sanctify them, not in the word but in the truth. Just as in man there is body, soul, and spirit, so in truth too. There is first *word-truth*: A man may have the correct form of words while he does not really understand the truth they contain. Then there is *thought-truth*: There may be a clear intellectual understanding of truth without the experience of its power. The Bible speaks of truth as a living reality: this is the *life-truth* in which the very Spirit of the truth we profess has entered and possessed our inner being.

> *T*hink of that great transaction in eternity: the Infinite Being, whom we call God, giving His words to His Son—in His words opening up His heart, communicating His mind and will, revealing Himself and all His purpose and love.

Christ calls Himself *the truth* (John 14:6). He is said to be full of grace and truth (John 1:14). The divine life and grace are in Him as an actually substantial existence and *reality*. He not only acts on us by thoughts and motives, but communicates, as a reality, the eternal life He brought for us from the Father. The Holy Spirit is called the Spirit of truth (John 14:17, 15:26, 16:13), for what He imparts is all real and actual, the very substance of unseen things. He guides into the truth, not thought-truth or doctrine only, but life-truth, the personal possession of the truth as it is in Jesus. As the Spirit of truth He is the Spirit of holiness, and the life of God, which is His holiness, He brings to us as an actual possession. It is now of this living truth, which dwells in the Word, as the seed-life dwells in the husk, that Jesus says, "Sanctify them by Your truth. Your word is truth" (John 17:17). He desires that we mark the intimate connection, as well as the wide difference, between the word and the truth. The connection is one willed by God and meant to be inseparable.

"Your word is truth"—with God they are one. But not with man. Just as there were men in close contact and continual interaction with Jesus, to whom He was only a man and nothing more, so there are Christians who know and understand the Word, and yet are strangers to its true spiritual power. They have the letter but not the spirit, so the truth comes to them in word but not in power. The Word does not make them holy, because they do not hold it in Spirit and in truth. To others, on the contrary, who know what it is to receive the truth in the love of it, who yield themselves, in all their dealings with the Word, to the Spirit of truth who dwells in it and in them too, the Word comes indeed as truth, as a divine reality, communicating and working what it speaks of. And it is of such a use of the Word that the Savior says, "Make them holy by Your truth. Your word is truth." As the words, which God gave Him, were all in the power of the eternal life and love and will of God, the revelation and communication of the Father's purpose, as God's Word was truth to Him and in Him, so it can be in us. And as we receive it this way, we are made holy in the truth.

> *A*s the words, which God gave Him, were all in the power of the eternal life and love and will of God, the revelation and communication of the Father's purpose, as God's Word was truth to Him and in Him, so it can be in us.

And what now are the lessons we have to learn here for the path of holiness? The first is this: Let us see to it that in all our contact with God's blessed Word we rest content with nothing short of the experience of it, as truth of God, as spirit and as power. Jesus said, "If you abide in My word. . .you shall know the truth" (John 8:31, 32). No analysis can ever find or prove the life of a seed: plant it in its proper soil, and the growth will testify to the life. It is only as the word of God is received in the love of it, as it grows and works in us, that we can know its truth, can know that it is the truth of God. It is as we live in the words of Jesus in love and obedience, keeping and doing them, that the truth from heaven, the power of the divine life that there is in them, will unfold itself to us. Christ is the truth, and in Him the love and grace, the very life of God, has come to earth as a substantial existence, a living, mighty power, something new that was never on earth before (John 1:17). Let us yield ourselves to the living Christ to possess us and to rule us as the living truth, then God's Word will be truth to us and in us.

The Spirit of Christ is the Spirit of truth, and that actual heavenly reality of divine life and love in Christ, the truth, has a Spirit who comes to communicate and impart it. Let us beware of trying to study or understand or take possession of God's Word without that Spirit through whom the Word was spoken of old. When we do that, we will find only the husk, the truth or thought and sentiment, very beautiful perhaps, but with no power to make us holy. We must have *the Spirit* of the truth within us. He will lead us *into* the truth, and when we are in the truth, God makes us holy in it and by it.

The truth must be in us, and we in it. God desires truth in the inward parts. We must be of the people of whom Christ says, "If you were of the truth," "he who is of the truth knows Me." In the lower sphere of daily life and conduct, of thought and action, there must be an intense love of truth, and a willingness to sacrifice everything for it; in the spiritual life, a deep hungering to have all our religion every day, every moment, stand fully in the truth of God. It is to the simple, humble, childlike spirit that the truth of the Word will be unsealed and revealed. In such the Spirit of truth comes to dwell. In such, as they daily wait before the Holy One in silence and emptiness, in reverence and holy fear, His Holy Spirit works and gives the truth within. In thus imparting Christ as revealed in the Word, in His divine life and love and as their own life, He makes them holy with the holiness of Christ.

> *I*t is the Father who establishes us in Christ, who gives, in a daily fresh giving, the Holy Spirit. It is to the Father, the Holy Father, the soul must look up continually in the prayer, "Make me holy by Your truth."

There is another lesson. Listen to that prayer, the earthly echo of the prayer that He always lives to pray, "Holy Father! Make them holy by Your truth" (see John 17:11, 17). Do you desire to be holy, child of God? Cast yourself into that mighty current of intercession always flowing into, always reaching the Father's bosom. Let yourself be borne on it until your whole soul cries, with the unutterable groanings too deep and too intense for human speech, "Holy Father! Make me holy by Your truth." As you trust in Christ as the truth, the reality of what you long for and in His all-prevailing intercession; as you wait for the Spirit within as the Spirit of truth, look up to the Father and expect His own direct and almighty working to make you holy. The mystery of holiness is the mystery of the Triune One. The deeper entrance into the holy life rests in the fellowship of the Three in One. It is the Father who establishes us in Christ, who gives, in a daily fresh giving, the Holy Spirit. It is to the Father, the Holy Father, the soul must look up continually in the prayer, "Make me holy by Your truth."

It has been well said that in the word *holy* we have the central thought of the high-priestly prayer. As the Father's attribute (John 17:11), as the Son's work for Himself and us (17:19), as the direct work of the Father through the Spirit (17:17, 20), it is the revelation of the glory of God in Himself and in us. Let us enter into the holiest of all, and as we bow with our Great High Priest, let the deep, unceasing cry go up for all the Church of God, "Holy Father! Make them holy by Your truth. Your word is truth." The word in which God makes holy is summed up in this: *Holy in Christ.* May God make it truth in us!

BE HOLY, AS I AM HOLY

Blessed Father! To Israel You said, "I the Lord am holy and make holy." But it is only in Your beloved Son that the full glory of Your holiness, as making us holy, has been revealed. You are our Holy Father who makes us holy by Your truth.

We thank You that Your Son has given us the words You gave Him, and that as He received them from You in life and power, we may receive them too. O Father! With our whole heart we do receive them. Let the Spirit make them truth and life within us. That is how we shall know You as the Holy One, consuming the sin, renewing the sinner.

We bless You most for Your blessed Son, the Holy One of God, the Living Word in whom the truth dwells. We thank You that in His never-ceasing intercession, this cry always reaches You, "Father, sanctify them by Your truth," and that the answer is always streaming forth from Your glory. Holy Father! Make us holy by Your truth, in Your wonderful revelation of Yourself in Him who is the truth. Let Your Holy Spirit so have dominion in our hearts that Your holy child Jesus, sanctifying Himself for us so that we may be sanctified in the truth, may be to us the way, the truth, and the life. May we know that we are in Him in Your presence, and that Your one word in answer to our prayer to make us holy is—Holy in Christ. Amen.

FOR FURTHER THOUGHT

1. *What vital connection do you see between God Himself and His truth? God is the God of truth—not truth in speaking only, or truth of doctrine—but truth of existence, or life in its divine reality. And Christ is the truth, the actual embodiment of this divine life. And there is a kingdom of truth, of divine spiritual realities, of which Christ is King. And of all this truth of God in Christ, the very essence is the Spirit. He is the Spirit of truth: He leads us into it, so that we are of the truth and walk in it. Of the truth, the reality there is in God, holiness, is the deepest root. The Spirit of truth is the Holy Spirit.*

2. *How can you become "holy in truth?" It is the work of the Father to make us holy in the truth. Let us bow very low in childlike trust as we breathe the prayer: "Holy Father! Make us holy by Your truth." He will do it.*

3. *It is the intercession of the Son that asks and obtains this blessing. Let us take our place in Him and rejoice in the assurance of an answer. How can you best position yourself to receive the blessings the Son intercedes for on your behalf?*

4. *It is the Spirit of truth through whom the Father does this work, so that we dwell in the truth, and the truth in us. Let us yield very freely and very fully to the leading of the Spirit, in our contact with God's Word, so that, as the Son prays, the Father may make us holy in the truth.*

5. *Let us, in the light of this work of the Three-One, never read the Word but with this aim: to be made holy in the truth by God.*

DAY 17

HOLINESS AND CRUCIFIXION

*"And for their sakes I sanctify Myself,
that they also may be sanctified by the truth."*
JOHN 17:19

*Then He said, "Behold, I have come to do Your will, O God."
He takes away the first that He may establish the second.
By that will we have been sanctified through the offering of
the body of Jesus Christ once for all. . . . For by one offering
He has perfected forever those who are being sanctified.*
HEBREWS 10:9–10, 14

IT was in His high-priestly prayer, on His way to Gethsemane and Calvary, that Jesus spoke this to the Father: "I sanctify Myself." He had not long before spoken of Himself as "the Son whom the Father sanctified and sent into the world" (John 10:36). From the language of holy scripture we are familiar with the thought that what God has sanctified, man has to sanctify too. The work of the Father, in sanctifying the Son, is the basis and groundwork of the work of the Son in sanctifying Himself. If His holiness as man was to be a free and personal possession, accepted and assimilated in voluntary and conscious self-determination, it was not enough that the Father sanctify Him: He must sanctify Himself too.

This self-sanctifying of our Lord found place through His whole life, but culminates and comes out in special distinctness in His crucifixion. What it consists of is made clear by the words from the Epistle to the Hebrews. The Messiah said: "Behold, I have come to do Your will" (Heb. 10:9). And then it was added, "By that will we have been sanctified through the offering of the body of Jesus Christ" (10:10). It was the offering of the body of Christ that was the will of God, and in doing that will He sanctified us. It was of the doing that will in the offering His body that He said, "I sanctify Myself, that they also may be sanctified by the truth." The giving up of His will to God's will in the agony of Gethsemane, and then the doing of that will in the obedience to the point of death: This was Christ's sanctifying Himself and us too. Let us try to understand this.

The holiness of God is revealed in His will. Holiness even in the Divine Being has no moral value except as it is freely willed. In speaking of the Trinity, theologians have pointed out how as the Father represents the absolute necessity of everlasting goodness, the Son proves its liberty: within the Divine Being it is willed in love. And this now was the work of the Son on earth, amid the trials and temptations of a human life, to accept and hold firmly at any sacrifice, with His whole heart to desire the will of the Father.

"Though He was a Son, yet He learned obedience in that He suffered" (Heb. 5:8). In Gethsemane the conflict between the will of human nature and the divine will reached its height and manifests itself in language that almost makes us tremble at His sinlessness as He speaks of His will in antithesis to God's will. But the struggle is a victory, because in presence of the clearest consciousness of what it means to have His own will, He gives it up, and says, "Your will be done" (Matt. 26:42). To enter into the will of God, He gives up His very life. In His crucifixion He thus reveals the law of sanctification. Holiness is the full entrance of our will into God's will. Or rather, holiness is the entrance of God's will to be the death of our will. The only end of our will, and deliverance from it, is death to it under the righteous judgment of God. It was in the surrender to the death of the cross that Christ sanctified Himself and sanctified us so that we also might be sanctified in truth.

> The giving up of His will to God's will in the agony of Gethsemane, and then the doing of that will in the obedience to the point of death: this was Christ's sanctifying Himself and us too.

And now, just as the Father sanctified Him, and He in virtue thereof appropriated it and sanctified Himself, so we, whom He has sanctified, have to appropriate it to ourselves. In no other way than crucifixion, the giving up of Himself to the death, could Christ realize the sanctification He had from the Father. And in no other way can we realize the sanctification we have in Him. His own and our sanctification bears the common stamp of the cross. We have seen before that obedience is the path to holiness. In Christ we see that the path to perfect holiness is perfect obedience. And that is obedience to the point of death, even to the giving up of life, even the death of the cross (see Phil. 2:8). As the sanctification that Christ accomplished for us, even to the point of the offering of His body, bears the death mark, we cannot partake of it, we cannot enter it, unless we die to self and its will. Crucifixion is the path to sanctification.

This lesson is in harmony with all we have seen. The first revelation of God's holiness to Moses was accompanied with the command, "Put off" (Exod. 3:5). God's praise, as glorious in holiness, fearful in praises, was sounded over the dead bodies of the Egyptians. When Moses on Sinai was commanded to sanctify the Mount, it was said, "Whoever touches the mountain. . .whether man or beast, he shall not live" (Exod. 19:12, 13). The holiness of God is death to all that is in contact with sin. Only through death, through blood-shedding, was there access to the holiest of all. Christ chose death, even death as a curse so that He might sanctify Himself for us and open to us the path to holiness, to the holiest of all, to the Holy One.

And so it is still. No man can see God and live (Exod. 33:20). It is only in death, the death of self and of nature, that we can draw near and behold God. Christ led the way. No man can see God and live. "Then let me die, Lord," one has cried, "but see You I must." Yes, blessed be God, so real is our interest in Christ and our union to Him that we may live in His death. As day by day self is kept in the place of death, the life and the holiness of Christ can be ours.

And where is the place of death? And how can the crucifixion that leads to holiness and to God be accomplished in us? Thank God! It is no work of our own, no weary process of self-crucifixion. The crucifixion that is to sanctify us is an accomplished fact. The cross bears the banner, "It is finished" (John 19:30). On it Christ sanctified Himself for us so that we might be sanctified in truth. Our crucifixion, as our sanctification, is something that in Christ has been completely and perfectly finished. "We have been sanctified through the offering of the body of Jesus Christ once for all" (Heb. 10:10). "By one offering He has perfected forever those who are being sanctified" (Heb. 10:14).

> *Holiness is the full entrance of our will into God's will. Or rather, Holiness is the entrance of God's will to be the death of our will.*

In that fullness, which it is the Father's good pleasure should dwell in Christ, the crucifixion of our old man, of the flesh, of the world, of ourselves, is all a spiritual reality. He who desires and knows and accepts Christ fully receives all this in Him. And as the Christ, who had previously been known more in His pardoning, quickening, and saving grace, is again sought after as a real deliverer from the power of sin, as a sanctifier, He comes and takes up the soul into the fellowship of the sacrifice of His will. "He. . .put away sin *by the sacrifice of Himself*" (Heb. 9:26) must become true of us as it is of Him. He reveals how it is a part of His salvation to make us partakers of a will entirely given up to the will of God, of a life that had yielded itself to the death and had then been given back from the dead by the power of God, a life of which the crucifixion of self-will was the spirit and the power. He reveals this, and the soul that sees it, consents to it, yields its will and its life, and believes in Jesus as its death and its life and in His crucifixion as its possession and its inheritance, enters into the enjoyment and experience of it. The language is now, "I...died...that I might live. I have been crucified with Christ; it is no longer I who live, but Christ lives in me" (Gal. 2:19, 20). And the life it now lives is by the faith on the Son of God, the daily acceptance in faith of Him who lives within us in the power of a death that has been passed through and forever finished.

"For their sakes I sanctify Myself, that they also may be sanctified by the truth." "I have come to do Your will, O God. ... By that will," the will of God accomplished by Christ, "we have been sanctified through the offering of the body of Christ." Let us understand and hold it firmly: Christ's giving up His will in Gethsemane and accepting God's will in dying, Christ's doing that will in the obedience to the death of the cross—this is His sanctifying Himself, and this is our being sanctified in truth. "By that will we have been sanctified." The death to self, the utter and most absolute giving up of our own life, with its will and its power and its aims, to the cross, and into the crucifixion of Christ, the daily bearing the cross—not a cross on which we are yet to be crucified, but the cross of the crucified Christ in its power to kill and make dead—this is the secret of the life of holiness—this is true sanctification.

> *O*nly through death, through blood-shedding, was there access to the holiest of all. Christ chose death, even death as a curse so that He might sanctify Himself for us and open to us the path to holiness, to the holiest of all, to the Holy One.

Believer! Is this the holiness you are seeking? Have you seen and consented that God alone is holy, that self is all unholy, and that there is no way to be made holy but for the fire of the divine holiness to come in and be the death of self? "Always carrying about in the body the dying of the Lord Jesus, that the life of Jesus also may be manifested in our body" (2 Cor. 4:10)—that is the pathway for each one who seeks to be sanctified in truth, even as He sanctified Himself; sanctified just like Jesus.

He sanctified Himself for us so that we ourselves also might be sanctified in truth. Yes, our sanctification rests and roots in His, in Himself. And we are in Him. The secret roots of our being are planted into Jesus. Deeper down than we can see or feel, there is He our vine, bearing and making us alive. Let us by faith understand that, in a manner and a measure which are far beyond our comprehension, intensely divine and real, we are in Him who sanctified Himself for us. Let us dwell there, where we have been placed by God. And let us bow our knees to the Father that He would grant us to be mightily strengthened by His Spirit, that Christ as our sanctification may dwell in our hearts, that the power of His death and His life may be revealed in us, and that God's will be done in us as it was in Him.

Be holy, for I am holy

Holy Father! I bless You for this precious blessed Word, for this precious blessed work of Your beloved Son. In His never-ceasing intercession, You always hear the wonderful prayer, "For their sakes I sanctify Myself, that they also may be sanctified by the truth."

Blessed Father! I ask You to strengthen me mightily by Your Spirit so that in living faith I may be able to accept and live the holiness prepared for me in my Lord Jesus. Give me spiritual understanding to know what it means that He sanctified Himself, that my sanctification is secured in His, that as by faith I abide in Him, its power will cover my whole life. Let His sanctification indeed be the law as it is the life of mine. Let His surrender to Your fatherly will, His continual dependence and obedience, be its root and its strength. Let His death to the world and to sin be its daily rule.

Above all, *let Himself*, O my Father! *let Himself*, as sanctified for me, the living Jesus, be my only trust and support. He sanctified Himself for me so that I myself also may be sanctified in truth.

Beloved Savior! How shall I rightly bless and love and glorify You for this wondrous grace! You gave Yourself so that now I am holy in You. I give myself so that in You I myself may be made holy in truth. Amen, Lord Jesus! Amen.

For Further Thought

1. *"If anyone desires to come after Me, let him deny himself, and take up his cross, and follow Me" (Matt. 16:24). Jesus means that our life shall be the exact counterpart of His, including even the crucifixion. The beginning of such a life is the denial of self, to give Christ its place. The Jews would not deny self, but "denied the Holy One. . .and killed the Prince of life" (Acts 3:14, 15). The choice is still between Christ and self. Let us deny the unholy one, and give him to the death.*

2. *What are the steps of fully denying self? First, the deliberate decision that self shall be given up to the death; then, the surrender to Christ crucified to make us partakers of His crucifixion; then, "knowing that our old man was crucified" (Rom. 6:6), the faith that says, "I am crucified with Christ;" and then, the power to live as a crucified one, to glory in the cross of Christ.*

3. *How can you daily maintain true self-denial, self-crucifixion? This is God's way of holiness, a divine mystery, which the Holy Spirit alone can daily maintain in us. Blessed be God, it is the life a Christian can live, because Christ lives in us.*

4. *The central thought is: We are in Christ, who gave up His will and did the will of God. By the Holy Spirit the mind that was in Him is in us, the will of self is crucified, and we live in the will of God.*

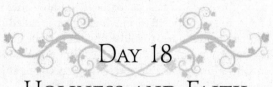

Day 18

Holiness and Faith

"That they may receive forgiveness of sins
and an inheritance among those who are
sanctified by faith in Me."
Acts 26:18

THE more we study scripture in the light of the Holy Spirit, or practice the Christian life in His power, the deeper becomes our conviction of the unique and central place faith has in God's plan of salvation. And we learn, too, to see that it is fitting and right that it should be so, that the very nature of things demands it. Because God is a spiritual and invisible being, every revelation of Himself, whether in His works, His Word, or His Son, calls for faith. Faith is the spiritual sense of the soul, being to it what the senses are to the body. By it alone we enter into communication and contact with God.

Faith is that humbleness of soul that waits in stillness to hear, to understand, to accept what God says, and to receive, to retain, and to possess what God gives or works. By faith we allow, we welcome God Himself, the Living Person, to enter in to make His home with us, to become our very life. However well we think we know it, we always have to learn the truth afresh, for a deeper and fuller application of it, that in the Christian life faith is the first thing, the one thing that pleases God and brings blessing to us. And because holiness is God's highest glory, and the highest blessing He has for us, it is especially in the life of holiness that we need to live by faith alone.

Our Lord speaks here of "those who that are sanctified by faith in Me."[17] He Himself is our sanctification as He is our justification. For the one as for the other it is faith that God asks, and both are equally given at once. The participle used here is not the present, denoting a process or work that is being carried on, but the aorist, indicating an act done once for all. When we believe in Christ, we receive the whole Christ, our justification and our sanctification, and we are at once accepted by God as righteous in Him and as holy in Him. God counts and calls us, what we really are, sanctified ones in Christ. It is as we are led to

---

[17] The best commentators connect the expression, "by faith in me," not with the word *sanctified*, but with the whole clause, "that by faith in me they may receive." This will, however, in no way affect the application to the word *sanctified*. Read this way, the text tells us that the remission of sin, and the inheritance, and the sanctification that qualifies for the inheritance are all received by faith.

see what God sees, as our faith grasps that the holy life of Christ is ours in actual possession, to be accepted and appropriated for daily use, that we shall really be able to live the life God calls us to: the life of holy ones in Christ Jesus. We shall then be in the right position in which what is called our progressive sanctification can be worked out. It will be, the acceptance and application in daily life of the power of a holy life, which has been prepared in Jesus, which has in the union with Him become our present and permanent possession, and which works in us according to the measure of our faith.

From this point of view it is evident that faith has a twofold operation. Faith is the evidence of things not seen, though *now actually existing*, the substance of things hoped for, *but not yet present* (see Heb. 11:1). It deals with the unseen present, as well as with the unseen future. As the evidence of things not seen, it rejoices in Christ our complete sanctification as a present possession. Through faith I simply look to what Christ is, as revealed in the Word by the Holy Spirit. Claiming all He is as my own, I know that His holiness, His holy nature and life, are mine. I am a holy one, because by faith in Him I have been sanctified.

> *B*ecause holiness is God's highest glory, and the highest blessing He has for us, it is especially in the life of holiness that we need to live by faith alone.

This is the first aspect of sanctification: It looks to what is a complete and finished thing, an absolute reality. As the substance of things hoped for, this faith reaches out in the assurance of hope to the future, to things I do not yet see or experience, and claims, day by day, out of Christ our sanctification, what it needs for practical holiness, "to be holy in all conduct" (1 Pet. 1:15). This is the second aspect of sanctification: I depend on Jesus to supply, in personal experience, gradually and unceasingly, for the need of each moment, what has been treasured up in His fullness. "Of God you are in Christ Jesus, who became for us. . .sanctification" (1 Cor. 1:30). Under its first aspect, faith says, "I know I am in Him and that all His holiness is mine." In its second aspect it speaks, "I trust in Him for the grace and the strength I need each moment to live a holy life."

And yet, it need hardly be said, these two are one. It is one Jesus who is our sanctification, whether we look at it in the light of what He is made for us once for all, or what, as the fruit of that He becomes to our experience day by day. And so it is one faith that, the more it studies and adores and rejoices in Jesus as made of God for us sanctification and as Him in whom we have been sanctified, becomes the bolder to expect the fulfillment of every promise for daily life and the stronger to claim the victory over every sin. Faith in Jesus is the secret of a holy life. All holy conduct, all really holy deeds, are the fruit of faith in Jesus as our holiness.

We know how faith acts, and what its great hindrances are, in the matter of justification. It is good that we remind ourselves that there are the same dangers in the exercise of sanctifying as of justifying faith. Faith *in God* stands opposed to trust *in self*, especially to its willing and working. Faith is hindered by every effort to do something ourselves. Faith looks to God working and yields itself to His strength as revealed in Christ through the Spirit. It allows God to work both to will and to do. Faith must work, for without works it is dead and by works alone can it be perfected (see James 2:20–22). In Jesus Christ, as Paul says, nothing benefits but "faith working through love" (Gal. 5:6).

> *F*aith in Jesus is the secret of a holy life. All holy conduct, all really holy deeds, are the fruit of faith in Jesus as our holiness.

But these works, which faith in God's working inspires and performs, are very different from the works in which a believer often puts forth his best efforts, only to find that he fails. The true life of holiness—the life of those who are sanctified in Christ—has its root and its strength in an abiding sense of utter powerlessness, in the deep restfulness that trusts to the working of a divine power and life, in the entire personal surrender to the loving Savior, and in that faith that to be nothing so that He may be all. It may appear impossible to discern or describe the difference between the working that is of self and the working that is of Christ through faith. But if we but know that there is such a difference, if we learn to distrust ourselves and to count on Christ working, the Holy Spirit will lead us into this secret of the Lord too. Faith's works are Christ's works.

And as by effort, so faith is also hindered by the desire to see and feel. "If you would believe, you would see" (John 11:40). The Holy Spirit will seal our faith with a divine experience, and we will see the glory of God. But this is His work. Ours is, when all appears dark and cold, in the face of all that nature or experience testifies, still each moment to believe in Jesus as our all-sufficient sanctification in whom we are perfected before God. Complaints as to lack of feeling, as to weakness or deadness, seldom profit, but it is the soul that refuses to occupy itself with itself, either with its own weakness or the strength of the enemy, but only looks to what Jesus is and has promised to do, to whom progress in holiness will be a joyful march from victory to victory. "The LORD your God. . .He will fight for you" (Deut. 1:30). This thought, so often repeated in connection with Israel's possession of the promised land, is the food of faith. In conscious weakness, in the presence of mighty enemies, it sings the conqueror's song. When God appears to be *not doing* what we trusted Him for, then is just the time for faith to glory in Him.

There is perhaps nothing that more reveals the true character of faith than joy and praise. When you give a child the promise of a present tomorrow, at once it says, "Thank you," and is glad. The joyful thanks are the proof of how really your promise has entered the heart. You are told by a friend of a rich inheritance he has left you in his will, and though it may not come true for years, even now it makes you glad. We have already seen what an element of holiness joy is: It is especially an element of holiness by faith.

Each time I really see how beautiful and how perfect God's provision is by which my holiness is in Jesus and by which I am to allow Him to work in me, my heart ought to rise up in praise and thanks. Instead of allowing the thought that it is, after all, a life of such difficult attainment and such continual self-denial, this life of holiness through faith, we ought to praise Him exceedingly that He has made it possible and sure for us that we can be holy, because Jesus the mighty and the loving one is our holiness. Praise will express our faith; praise will prove it; praise will strengthen it. "Then believed they His words; they sang His praise" (Ps. 106:12). Praise will commit us to faith. We shall see that we have but one thing to do: to go on in a faith that always trusts and always praises. It is in a living, loving attachment to Jesus that rejoices in Him and praises Him continually for what He is to us that faith proves itself and receives the power of holiness.

"Sanctified by faith in Me." Yes, "by faith *in Me*." It is the personal living Jesus who offers Himself, Himself in all the riches of His power and love, as the object, the strength, the life of our faith. He tells us that if we desire to be holy, always and in everything holy, we must just see to one thing: to be always and altogether full of faith in Him. Faith is the eye of the soul, the power by which we discern the presence of the Unseen One as He comes to give Himself to us. Faith not only sees but appropriates and assimilates. Let us set our souls very still for the Holy Spirit who dwells in us to awaken and strengthen that faith for which He has been given us. Faith is surrender, and yielding ourselves to Jesus to allow Him to do His work in us, giving up ourselves to Him to live out His life and work out His will in us, we shall find Him giving Himself entirely *to us* and taking complete possession. So faith will be power, the power of obedience to do God's will: "our most holy faith" (Jude 20), "the faith delivered to the holy ones" (Jude 3). And we shall understand how simple, to the single-hearted, is the secret of holiness: just Jesus. We are in Him, our sanctification. He personally is our holiness, and the life of faith in Him, that receives and possesses Him, must necessarily be a life of holiness. Jesus says, "Sanctified by faith in Me."

BE HOLY, AS I AM HOLY

Beloved Lord! Again have I seen, with adoring wonder, what You are willing to be to me. It is in You, and a life of living fellowship with You, that I am to become holy. It is in the simple life of personal attachment, of trust and love, of surrender and consecration, that You become my all and make me partaker of Yourself and Your holiness.

Blessed Lord Jesus! I do believe in You, help my unbelief. I confess what still remains of unbelief and count on Your presence to conquer and cast it out. My soul is opening up continually to see more how You Yourself are my life and my holiness. You are enlarging my heart to rejoice in You as my all and to be assured that You Yourself take possession and fill the temple of my being with Your glory. You are teaching me to understand that, however weak and human and disappointing experiences may be, Your Holy Spirit is the strength of my faith, leading me on to grow up into a stronger and a larger confidence in You in whom I am holy. O my Savior! I take Your Word this day, "Sanctified by faith in Me," as a new revelation of Your love and its purpose with me. In You Yourself is the power of my holiness, in You is the power of my faith. Bless Your name that You have given me too a place among them of whom You speak: "Sanctified by faith in Me." Amen.

FOR FURTHER THOUGHT

1. *What are the specific links between faith and holiness? Let us remember that it is not only the faith that is dealing specially with Christ for sanctification, but all living faith that has the power to sanctify. Anything that casts the soul wholly on Jesus, that calls forth intense and simple trust, be it the trial of faith, the prayer of faith, or the work of faith, helps to make us holy, because it brings us into living contact with the Holy One.*

2. *How does God reveal His holiness and make it ours? It is only through the Holy Spirit that Christ and His holiness are day by day revealed and made ours in actual possession. And so the faith that receives Him is of the Spirit too. Yield yourself in simplicity and trust to His working. Do not be afraid, as if you cannot believe, for you have "the Spirit of faith" within you, so you have the power to believe. And you may ask God to strengthen you mightily by His Spirit in the inner man, for the faith that receives Christ in the indwelling that knows no break.*

3. *I have only so much of faith as I have of the Spirit. Is not this then what I most need—to live entirely under the influence of the Spirit? How can you live under the Holy Spirit's influence?*

4. *Just as the eye in seeing is receptive and yields to let the object placed before it make is impression, so faith is the impression God makes on the soul when He draws near. Was not the faith of Abraham the fruit of God's drawing near and speaking to him and the impression God made on him? Let us be still to gaze on the divine mystery of Christ our holiness. Then His presence, waited for and worshipped, will work the faith. That is, the Spirit who proceeds from Him into those who cling to Him, will be faith.*

DAY 19

HOLINESS AND RESURRECTION

Concerning His Son Jesus Christ our Lord, who was born
of the seed of David according to the flesh, and declared to
be the Son of God with power according to the Spirit
of holiness, by the resurrection from the dead.
ROMANS 1:3–4

THESE words speak of a twofold birth of Christ. According to the flesh, He was born of the seed of David. According to the Spirit, He was the first begotten from the dead. As He was a Son of David in virtue of His birth through the flesh, so He was declared to be the Son of God with power, in virtue of His resurrection-birth through the Spirit of holiness. As the life He received through His first birth was a life in and after the flesh with its weakness, so the new life He received in the resurrection was a life in the power of the Spirit of holiness.

The expression "the Spirit of holiness" is a peculiar one. It is not the ordinary word for God's holiness that is here used as in Hebrews 12:10, describing holiness in the abstract as the attribute of an object, but another word (also used in 2 Cor. 7:1 and 1 Thess. 3:13) expressing the habit of holiness in its action—practical holiness or sanctity. Paul used this word because He wished to emphasize the thought that Christ's resurrection was distinctly the result of that life of holiness and self-sanctifying that had culminated in His death. It was the spirit of the life of holiness that He had lived, in the power of which He was raised again. He teaches us that that life and death of self-sanctification, in which alone our sanctification stands, was the root and ground of His resurrection and of its declaration that He was the Son of God with power, the first begotten from the dead. The resurrection was the fruit that that life of holiness bore.

And so the life of holiness becomes the property of all who are partakers of the resurrection. The resurrection life and the spirit of holiness are inseparable. Christ sanctified Himself in death so that we ourselves might he sanctified in truth. And when in virtue of the Spirit of sanctity He was raised from the dead, that Spirit of holiness was proved to be the power of resurrection life, and the resurrection life to be a life of holiness.

As a believer you have part in this resurrection life. You have been "begotten again through the resurrection of Jesus Christ from the dead" (1 Pet. 1:3). You are "risen with Christ" (Col. 3:1). You are commanded "to reckon yourself. . .to be alive to God in Christ Jesus" (Rom. 6:11). But the life can work in power only as you seek to know it, to yield to it, to let it have full possession and mastery. And if it is to do this, one of the most important things for you to realize is that as it was in virtue of the Spirit of holiness that Christ was raised, so the Spirit of that same holiness must be in you the mark and the power of your life. Study to know and possess the Spirit of holiness as it was seen in the life of your Lord.

And in what did it consist? Its secret was, we are told: "Behold, I have come to do Your will, O God" (Heb. 10:9). "By that will," as done by Christ, "we have been sanctified through the offering of the body of Jesus Christ" (Heb. 10:10). This was Christ's sanctifying Himself, in life and in death. This was what the Spirit of holiness accomplished in Him. This is what the same Spirit, the Spirit of the life in Christ Jesus, will work in us: a life in the will of God is a life of holiness.

Seek earnestly to grasp this clearly. Christ came to reveal what true holiness would be in the conditions of human life and weakness. He came to work it out for you so that He might communicate it to you by His Spirit. Unless you intelligently apprehend and heartily accept it, the Spirit cannot work it in you. Do seek with your whole heart to take hold of it: the will of God unhesitatingly accepted is the power of holiness.

> *The life of holiness becomes the property of all who are partakers of the resurrection. The Resurrection life and the spirit of holiness are inseparable.*

It is in this that any attempt to be holy as Christ is holy, with and in His holiness, must have its starting point. Many seek to take single portions of the life or image of Christ for imitation, and yet fail greatly in others. They have not seen that the self-denial, to which Jesus calls, really means the denial of self in the full meaning of that word. In not one single thing is the will of self to be done. Rather, Jesus, as He did the will of the Father only, must rule, and not self. To "stand perfect and complete in all the will of God" (Col. 4:12) must be the purpose, the prayer, the expectation of the disciple.

There need be no fear that it is not possible to know the will of the Father in everything. "If any man wills to do. . .he shall know" (John 7:17). The Father will not keep the willing child in ignorance of His will. As the surrender to the Spirit of holiness, to Jesus and the dominion of His holy life, becomes more simple, sin and self-will will be discovered, the spiritual understanding will be opened up, and the law written in the inward parts become legible and intelligible.

There need be no fear that it is not possible to do the will of the Father when it is known. When once the grief of failure and sin has driven the believer into the experience of Romans 7, and the "delight in the law of God according to the inward man" (Rom. 7:22) has proved its earnestness in the cry, "O wretched man that I am," (7:24) deliverance will come through Jesus Christ. The Spirit works not only to will but to do, and where the believer could only complain, "To perform what is good I do not find" (7:18), He gives the strength and song, "The law of the Spirit of life in Christ Jesus has made me free from the law of sin and death" (8:2).

In this faith, that it is possible to know and do the will of God in all things, take over from Him, in whom alone you are holy, as your life-principle, "I come to do Your will, O God." It is the principle of the resurrection life, and without it Jesus had never been raised again. It is the principle of the new life in you. Accept it, study it, realize it, act it out. Many a believer has found that some simple words of dedication, expressive of the purpose in everything to do God's will, have been an entrance into the joy and power of the resurrection life previously unknown. The will of God is the complete expression of His moral perfection, His divine holiness. To take one's place in the center of that will, to live it out, to be borne and sustained by it, was the power of that life of Jesus that could not be held of death, that could not but burst out in resurrection glory. What it was to Jesus it will be to us.

> *C*hrist came to reveal what true holiness would be in the conditions of human life and weakness. He came to work it out for you so that He might communicate it to you by His Spirit.

Holiness is life: this is the simplest expression of the truth our text teaches. There can be no holiness until there is a new life implanted. The new life cannot grow and break forth in resurrection power, cannot bring forth fruit, until it grows in holiness. As long as the believer is living the mixed life, part in the flesh and part in the spirit, with some of self and some of Christ, he seeks in vain for holiness. It is the new life that is the holy life. The full grasping of it in faith and the full surrender to it in conduct will be the highway of holiness. Jesus lived and died and rose again to prepare for us a new nature to be received day by day in the obedience of faith: we "have put on the new man which was created according to God, in true righteousness and holiness" (Eph. 4:24). Let the inner life, hidden with Christ in God, hidden also deep in the recesses of our innermost being, be acknowledged, be waited on, be yielded to, and then it will work itself out in all the beauties of holiness.

There is more. This life is not like the life of nature, a blind, non-conscious principle, involuntarily working out its ideal in unresisting obedience to the law of its being. There is the Spirit of the life in Christ Jesus—the Spirit of holiness—the Holy Spirit dwelling in us as a divine person, entering into fellowship with us, and leading us into the fellowship of the Living Christ. It is this that fills our life with hope and joy. The risen Savior breathed the Holy Spirit on His disciples, and the Spirit brings the Risen One into the field, into our hearts, as a personal friend, as a living guide and strengthener. The Spirit of holiness is the Spirit, the presence, and the power of the living Christ. Jesus said of the Spirit, "You know Him" (John 14:17). Is not our great need to know this Holy Spirit, the Spirit of Christ, of His holiness and of ours? How can we "walk according to the Spirit" (Rom. 8:1) and follow His leading if we don't know Him and His voice and His way?

> *There can be no holiness until there is a new life implanted. The new life cannot grow and break forth in resurrection power, cannot bring forth fruit, until it grows in holiness.*

Let us learn one more lesson from our text. *It is out of the grave of the flesh and the will of self that the Spirit of holiness breaks out in resurrection power.* We must accept death to the flesh, death to self with its willing and working, as the birthplace of our experience of the power of the Spirit of holiness. In view of each struggle with sin, in each exercise of faith or prayer, we must enter into the death of Jesus, the death to self and, as those who say, "we are not sufficient to think anything as being from ourselves" (2 Cor. 3:5), in quiet faith expect the Spirit of Christ to do His work.

The Spirit will work, strengthening you mightily in the inner man and building up within you a holy temple for the Lord. And the time will come, if it has not come to you yet—and it may be nearer than you dare hope—when the conscious indwelling of Christ in your heart by faith, the full revelation and enthronement of Him as ruler and keeper of heart and life, shall have become a personal experience. According to the Spirit of holiness, by the resurrection from the dead, will the Son of God be declared with power in the kingdom that is within you.

BE HOLY, FOR I AM HOLY

Most holy Lord God! We bless You that You raised Your Son from the dead and give Him glory so that our faith and hope might be in You. You made His resurrection the power of eternal life in us and now, even as He was raised, so we may walk in newness of life. As the Spirit of holiness dwelled and shaped in Him, it dwells and works in us, and becomes in us the Spirit of life.

O God! We ask You to perfect Your work in Your saints. Give them a deeper sense of the holy calling with which You have called them in Christ, the Risen One. Allow all to accept the Spirit of His life on earth, to delight in the will of

God as the spirit of their life. May those who have never yet fully accepted this be brought to do it, and in faith of the power of the new life to say, "I accept the will of God as my only law." May the Spirit of holiness be the spirit of their lives!

> *A*ccording to the Spirit of holiness, by the resurrection from the dead, will the Son of God be declared with power in the kingdom that is within you.

Father! We ask You, let Christ, in ever-increasing experience of His resurrection power, be revealed in our hearts as the Son of God, Lord and ruler within us. Let His life within inspire all the outer life so that in the home and society, in thought and speech and action, in religion and in business, His life may shine out from us in the beauty of holiness. Amen.

FOR FURTHER THOUGHT

1. *What is the specific importance of the resurrection? Scripture regards the resurrection in two different aspects. In one view, it is the title to the new life, the source of our justification (Rom. 4:25, 1 Cor. 15:17). In another, it is our regeneration, the power of the new life working in us, the source of our sanctification (Rom. 6:4; 1 Pet. 1:3). Pardon and holiness are inseparable. They have the same source: union with the risen, living Christ.*

2. *How can you possess the actual holiness of the risen Christ? The blessedness to the disciples of having a risen Christ was this: He, whom they thought dead, came and revealed Himself to them. Christ lives to reveal Himself to you and to me. Wait on Him, trust Him for this. He will reveal Himself to you as your sanctification. See to it that you have Him in living possession, and you have His holiness.*

3. *The life of Christ is the holiness of Christ. The reason we so often fail in the pursuit of holiness is that the old life, the flesh, in its own strength seeks for holiness as a beautiful garment to wear and enter heaven with. It is the daily death to self out of which the life of Christ rises up.*

4. *To die this way, to live this way in Christ, to be holy. How can we attain it? It all comes "according to the Spirit of holiness." Have the Holy Spirit within you. Say daily, "I believe in the Holy Spirit."*

5. *Holy in Christ. When Christ lives in us, and His mind, as it found expression in His words and work on earth, enters and fills our will and personal consciousness, then our union with Him becomes what He meant it to be. It is the Spirit of His holy conduct, the Spirit of His sanctity, that must be in us.*

DAY 20

HOLINESS AND LIBERTY

And having been set free from sin, you became slaves
of righteousness. . .so now present your members as slaves
of righteousness for holiness. . . . But now having been set free
from sin, and having become slaves of God, you have
your fruit to holiness, and the end, everlasting life.
ROMANS 6:18–19, 22

Our liberty which we have in Christ Jesus
GALATIANS 2:4

Stand fast therefore in the liberty by which Christ has made us free,
and do not be entangled again with a yoke of bondage.
GALATIANS 5:1

THERE is no possession more precious or priceless than liberty. There is nothing more inspiring and elevating, and nothing, on the other hand, more depressing and degrading than slavery. It robs a man of what constitutes his manhood, of the power of self-decision, of self-action, and of being and doing what he desires.

Sin is slavery, the bondage to a foreign power that has obtained the mastery over us and compels often a most reluctant service. The redemption of Christ restores our liberty and sets us free from the power of sin. If we are truly to live as redeemed ones, we need not only to look at the work Christ did to accomplish our redemption, but to accept and realize fully how complete, how sure, how absolute the liberty is with which He has made us free. It is only as we "*stand fast* in our liberty in Christ Jesus" (see Gal. 5:1) that we can have our fruit to sanctification.

It is remarkable how seldom the word *holy* occurs in the great argument of the Epistle to the Romans, and how, where twice used in chapter 6 in the expression "to holiness," it is distinctly set forth as the aim and fruit to be reached through a life of righteousness. The twice-repeated "to holiness," pointing to a result to be obtained, is preceded by a twice-repeated "having been set free from sin, you became slaves of righteousness." It teaches us how the liberty from the power of sin and the surrender to the service of righteousness are not yet of themselves holiness, but the sure and only path by which it can be reached. A true insight and a full entering into our freedom from sin in Christ are indispensable to a life of holiness. It was when Israel was freed from Pharaoh that God began to reveal Himself as the Holy One: it is as we know ourselves "freed from sin," delivered from the hand of all our enemies, that we shall serve God in righteousness and holiness all the days of our life.

"Having been set free from sin": To understand this word correctly, we must beware of a twofold error. We must neither narrow it down to less, nor infer into it more than the Holy Spirit means by it here. Paul is speaking neither of an imputation nor an experience. We must not limit it to being made free from the curse or punishment of sin. The context shows that he is speaking not of our judicial standing, but of a spiritual reality, our being in living union with Christ in His death and resurrection, and so being entirely taken out from under the dominion or power of sin. "Sin shall not have dominion over you" (Rom. 6:14). Nor is he as yet speaking of an experience, that we feel that we are free from all sin. He speaks of the great objective fact, Christ's having finally delivered us from the power that sin had to compel us to do its will and its works, and urges us, in the faith of this glorious fact, boldly to refuse to listen to the bidding or temptation of sin. To know our liberty that we have in Christ, our freedom from sin's mastery and power, is the way to realize it as an experience.

> It is only as we "stand fast in our liberty in Christ Jesus" (see Gal. 5:1) that we can have our fruit to sanctification.

In olden times, when Turks or Moors often made slaves of Christians, large sums were frequently paid for the ransom of those who were in bondage. But it happened more than once, away in the interior of the slave country, that the ransomed ones never got the news, for the masters were only too glad to keep it from them. Others, again, got the news, but had grown too accustomed to their bondage to rouse themselves for the effort of reaching the coast. Laziness or hopelessness kept them in slavery. They could not believe that they would be able ever in safety to reach the land of liberty. The ransom had been paid, and in truth they were free, but in their experience, by reason of ignorance or lack of courage, they were still in bondage.

Christ's redemption has so completely made an end of sin and the legal power it had over us—for "the strength of sin is the law" (1 Cor. 15:56)—that in very deed, in the deepest reality, sin has no power to compel our obedience. It is only as we allow it again to reign, as we yield ourselves again as its servants, that it can exercise the mastery. Satan does his utmost to keep believers in ignorance of the completeness of this, their freedom from his slavery. And because believers are so content with their own thoughts of what redemption means—and so little long and plead to see it and possess it in its fullness of deliverance and blessing—the experience of the extent to which the freedom from sin can be realized is so weak. "Where the Spirit of the Lord is, there is liberty" (2 Cor. 3:17). It is by the Holy Spirit, His light and leading within, humbly watched for and yielded to, that this liberty becomes our possession.

In the sixth chapter of Romans, Paul speaks of freedom from sin, in chapter 7 (Rom. 7:3–4, 6) of freedom from the law as both being ours in Christ and union with Him. In chapter 8, he speaks of this freedom as becoming ours in experience. He says, "the Spirit of life in Christ Jesus has made me free from the law of sin and death" (8:2). The freedom that is ours in Christ must become ours in personal appropriation and enjoyment through the Holy Spirit. The latter depends on the former: the fuller the faith, the clearer the insight, the more triumphant the glorying in Christ Jesus and the liberty with which He has made us free, the speedier and the fuller the entrance into the glorious liberty of the children of God.

> *Christ's redemption has so completely made an end of sin and the legal power it had over us—for "the strength of sin is the law"—that in very deed, in the deepest reality, sin has no power to compel our obedience.*

As the liberty is in Christ alone, so it is the Spirit of Christ alone that makes it ours in practical possession and keeps us dwelling in it: "the Spirit of life in Christ Jesus *has made me free* from the law of sin and death." "Where the Spirit of the Lord is, there is liberty." As the Spirit reveals Jesus to us as Lord and master—the new master, who alone has anything to say over us and leads us to yield ourselves, to present our members, to surrender our whole life to the service of God in Christ—our faith in the freedom from sin becomes a consciousness and a realization. Believing in the completeness of the redemption, the captive goes forth as "the Lord's freedman" (1 Cor. 7:22). He knows now that sin no longer has power for one moment to command obedience. It may seek to assert its old right, may speak in the tone of authority, may frighten us into fear and submission, but power, it has none over us unless we, forgetting our freedom, yield to its temptation and ourselves give it power.

We are the Lord's freedmen. "We have our liberty in Christ Jesus." In Romans 7, Paul describes the terrible struggles of the soul that still seeks to fulfill the law, but finds itself utterly helpless—sold under sin, a captive and a slave, without the liberty to do what the whole heart desires. But when the Spirit takes the place of the law, the complaint, "O wretched man that I am" (Rom. 7:24) is changed into the song of victory: "I thank God—through Jesus Christ. . . . the law of the Spirit of life has made me free" (7:25, 8:2).

What numberless complaints of insufficient strength to do God's will, of unsuccessful effort and disappointed hopes, of continual failure, re-echo in a thousand different forms the complaint of the captive, "O wretched man that I am!" Thank God! There is deliverance. "Stand fast therefore in the liberty by which Christ has made us free, and do not be entangled again with a yoke of bondage" (Gal. 5:1).

Satan is constantly seeking to lay on us again the yoke either of sin or the law, to produce again the spirit of bondage, as if sin or the law with their demands somehow had power over us. It is not so! Do not be entangled, but stand firm in the liberty with which Christ has made you free. Let us listen to the message: "And having been set free from sin, you became slaves of righteousness. . . . so now present your members *as* slaves *of* righteousness *for holiness.*" "But now having been set free from sin, and having become slaves of God, you have your fruit *to holiness.*"

To be holy, you must be free, perfectly free—free for Jesus to rule you, to lead you, free for the Holy Spirit to dispose of you, to breathe in you, to work His secret, gentle, but mighty work so that you may grow up unto all the liberty Jesus has won for you. The temple could not be sanctified by the indwelling of God unless as it was free from every other master and every other use, to be for Him and His service alone. The inner temple of our heart cannot be truly and fully sanctified unless we are free from every other master and power, from every yoke of bondage, or fear, or doubt, to let His Spirit lead us into the perfect liberty which has its fruit in true holiness.

> *To* be holy, you must be free, perfectly free—free for Jesus to rule you, to lead you, free for the Holy Spirit to dispose of you, to breathe in you, to work His secret, so that you may grow up unto all the liberty Jesus has won for you.

Having been set free from sin, you became slaves of righteousness, you have your fruit to holiness, and the end, everlasting life. Freedom, righteousness, holiness—these are the steps on the way to the coming glory. The more deeply we enter by faith into our liberty, which we have in Christ, the more joyfully and confidently we present our members to God as instruments of righteousness. The God is the Father whose will we delight to do, whose service is perfect liberty. The Redeemer is the master, to whom love binds us in willing obedience. The liberty is not lawlessness: "We, being delivered from the hand of our enemies, might serve Him. . .in holiness and righteousness before Him all the days of our life" (Luke 1:74, 75).

The liberty is the condition of the righteousness, and this again of the holiness. The doing of God's will leads up into that fellowship, that heart sympathy with God Himself, out of which comes that reflection of the Divine Presence, which is holiness. Being made free from sin, being made the slaves of righteousness and of God, we have our fruit to holiness, and the end—the fruit of holiness becomes, when ripe, the seed of—everlasting life.

BE HOLY, AS I AM HOLY

Most glorious God! I ask You to open my eyes to this wonderful liberty with which Christ has made me free. May I enter fully into Your Word so that sin shall have no dominion over me because I am not under the law but under grace. May I know my liberty that I have in Christ Jesus, and stand firm in it.

Father! Your service is perfect liberty: reveal this too to me. You are the infinitely free, and Your will knows no limits but what its own perfection has placed. And You invite us into Your will so that we may be free as You are. O my God! Show me the beauty of Your will as it frees me from self and from sin, and let it be my only blessedness. Let the service of righteousness so be a joy and a strength to me, having its fruit to sanctification, leading me into Your holiness.

Blessed Lord Jesus! My deliverer and my liberty, I belong to You. I give myself to Your will, to know no will but Yours. Master! You and You alone will I serve. I have my liberty in You! Be my keeper. I cannot stand for one moment out of You. In You I can stand firm. In You I put my trust.

Most holy God! As Your free, obedient, loving child, You will make me holy. Amen.

FOR FURTHER THOUGHT

1. *How should you walk in liberty so that you consistently act out of the law of your new nature in Christ? Liberty is the power to carry out unhindered the impulse of our nature. In Christ, the child of God is free from every power that could hinder his acting out the law of his new nature.*

2. *This liberty is of faith (Gal. 5:5–6). By faith in Christ, I enter into it and stand in it.*

3. *This liberty is of the Holy Spirit. "Where the Spirit of the Lord is, there is liberty." "If you are led by the Spirit, you are not under the law" (Gal. 5:18). A heart filled with the Spirit is made free indeed. But we are not made free that we may do our own will. No, made free to follow the leading of the Holy Spirit. "Where the Spirit is, there is liberty."*

4. *What is the connection between this liberty and love? "You, brethren, have been called to liberty; only do not use liberty as an opportunity for the flesh, but through love serve one another" (Gal. 5:13). The freedom with which the Son*

471

makes free is a freedom to become like Himself, to love and to serve. "Though I am free from all men, I have made myself a servant to all, that I might win the more" (1 Cor. 9:19). This is the liberty of love.

5. What is the relationship between your holiness and your actions? "Having been set free from sin, you became slaves of righteousness. . .for holiness." "Let my people go, that they may serve Me" (Exod. 8:1). It is only the man who does righteousness who can become holy.

6. This liberty is a thing of joy and singing. Knowing this, what words of praise and thanksgiving can you give to God for His gift?

7. This liberty is the groundwork of holiness. The Redeemer who makes free is God the Holy One. As the Holy Spirit, He leads into the full possession of it. To be so free from everything that God can take complete possession is to be holy.

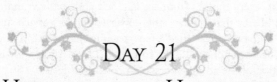

DAY 21

HOLINESS AND HAPPINESS

For the kingdom of God is not eating and drinking,
but righteousness and peace and joy in the Holy Spirit.
ROMANS 14:17

And the disciples were filled with joy
and with the Holy Spirit.
ACTS 13:52

Then he said to them, ". . .this day is holy to our Lord.
Do not sorrow, for the joy of the LORD is your strength."
So the Levites quieted all the people, saying, "Be still, for the day
is holy; do not be grieved." And all the people went their way to
eat and drink, to send portions and rejoice greatly, because
they understood the words that were declared to them."
NEHEMIAH 8:10–12

THE deep significance of joy in the Christian life is hardly understood. It is too often regarded as something secondary, but its presence is essential as the proof that God does indeed satisfy us, and that His service is our delight.

In our domestic life, we do not feel satisfied if all the proprieties of deportment are observed and each does his duty to the other. True love makes us happy in each other. As love gives out its warmth of affection, gladness is the sunshine that fills the home with its brightness. Even in suffering or poverty, the members of a loving family are a joy to each other. Without this gladness, especially, there is no true obedience on the part of the children. It is not the mere fulfillment of a command or performance of a service that a parent looks to. Rather, it is the willing, joyful enthusiasm with which it is done that makes it pleasing.

It is just so in the interaction of God's children with their Father. Even in the effort after a life of consecration and gospel obedience, we are continually in danger of coming under the law again, with its *You shall*. The consequence always is failure. The law only brings about wrath (Rom. 4:15); it gives neither life nor strength. It is only as long as we are standing in the joy of our Lord, in the joy

473

of our deliverance from sin, in the joy of His love and what He is for us, and in the joy of His presence that we have the power to serve and obey. It is only when made free from every master, from sin and self and the law, and only when rejoicing in this liberty that we have the power to render service that is satisfying either to God or to ourselves. "I will see you again," Jesus said, "and your heart will rejoice, and your joy no one will take from you" (John 16:22). Joy is the evidence and the condition of the abiding personal presence of Jesus.

> *I*t is only when made free from every master, from sin and self and the law, and only when rejoicing in this liberty that we have the power to render service that is satisfying either to God or to ourselves.

If holiness is the beauty and the glory of the life of faith, it is obvious that here especially the element of joy must not be lacking. We have already seen how the first mention of God as the Holy One was in the song of praise on the shore of the Red Sea, how Hannah and Mary in their moments of inspiration praised God as the Holy One, how the name of the Thrice Holy in heaven comes to us in the song of the seraphs, and how before the throne both the living creatures and the conquering multitude, who sing the song of the Lamb, adore God as the Holy One.

We are to "worship the LORD in the beauty of holiness" (Ps. 29:2), to "sing praise...at the remembrance of His holy name" (Ps. 30:4). It is only in the spirit of worship and praise and joy that we fully can know God as holy. Much more, it is only under the inspiration of adoring love and joy that we can ourselves be made holy. It is as we cease from all fear and anxiety, from all strain and effort, and rest with singing in what Jesus is in His finished work as our sanctification, as we rest and rejoice in Him, that we shall be made partakers of His holiness. It is the day of rest, is the day that God has blessed, the day of blessing and gladness, and it is the day He blessed that is His holy day. Holiness and blessedness are inseparable.

But is not this at odds with the teaching of scripture and the experience of the saints? Are not suffering and sorrow among God's chosen means of sanctification? Are not the promises to the broken in heart, the poor in spirit, and the mourner? Are not self-denial and the forsaking of all we have, the crucifixion with Christ and the dying daily, the path to holiness? And is not all this more a matter of sorrow and pain than of joy and gladness?

The answer will be found in the right understanding of the life of faith. Faith lifts above, and gives possession of, what is the very opposite of what we feel or experience. In the Christian life there is always a paradox: What appear irreconcilable opposites are found side by side at the same moment. Paul expresses it in the words, "As dying, and behold we live...as sorrowful, yet always rejoicing; as poor, yet making many rich; as having nothing, and yet possessing all things" (2 Cor. 6:9, 10). And elsewhere this way, "*When* I am weak, *then* am I strong" (2 Cor. 12:10). The apparent contradiction has its reconciliation, not only in the union of the two lives, the human and the divine, in the person of each believer, but specially in our being, at one and the same moment, partakers of the death and the resurrection of Christ. Christ's death was one of pain and suffering, a real and terrible death, a tearing apart of the bonds that united soul and body, spirit and flesh. The power of that death works in us: We must let it work mightily if we are to live holy, for in that death He sanctified Himself so that we ourselves might be sanctified in truth.

> *Faith lifts above, and gives possession of, what is the very opposite of what we feel or experience. In the Christian life there is always a paradox: What appear irreconcilable opposites are found side by side at the same moment.*

Our holiness is, like His, in the death to our own will, and to all our own life. But—this we must seek to grasp—we do not approach death from the side from which Christ met it, as an enemy to be conquered, as a suffering to be borne before the new life can be entered on. No, the believer who knows what Christ is as the Risen One approaches death, the crucifixion of self and the flesh and the world, from the resurrection side, the place of victory, in the power of the Living Christ.

When we were baptized into Christ, we were baptized into His death and resurrection as ours. And Christ Himself, the risen, living Lord, leads us triumphantly into the experience of the power of His death. And so, to the believer who truly lives by faith and doesn't seek in his own struggles to crucify and put to death the flesh, but knows the living Lord, the deep resurrection joy never for a moment forsakes Him but is his strength for what may appear to others to be only painful sacrifice and cross-bearing. He says with Paul, "I boast in the cross through which I have been crucified" (see Gal. 6:14). He never, as so many do, asks Paul's question, "Who will deliver me from this body of death?" (Rom. 7:24) without sounding the joyful and triumphant answer as a present experience, "I thank God—through Jesus Christ our Lord" (7:25). "Thanks be to God who always leads us in triumph in Christ" (2 Cor. 2:14).

It is the joy of a present Savior, of the experience of a perfect salvation, the joy of a resurrection life, that alone gives the power to enter deeply and fully into the death that Christ died and yield our will and our life to be wholly sanctified to God. In the joy of that life, from which the power of the death is never absent, it is possible to say with the apostle each moment, "As dying, and, behold, we live... as sorrowful, yet always rejoicing."

Let us seek to learn the two lessons: Holiness is essential to true happiness; happiness essential to true holiness. *Holiness is essential to true happiness.* If you want to have joy, the fullness of joy, an abiding joy that nothing can take away, be holy as God is holy. Holiness is blessedness. Nothing can darken or interrupt our joy but sin. Whatever is our trial or temptation, the joy of Jesus, of which Peter says, "you rejoice with joy inexpressible" (1 Pet. 5:8), can more than compensate and outweigh.

If we lose our joy, it must be sin. It may be an actual transgression, or an unconscious following of self or the world. It may be the stain on conscience of something doubtful, or it may be unbelief that would live by sight and thinks more of itself and its joy than of the Lord alone. Whatever it is, nothing can take away our joy but sin. If we would live lives of joy, assuring God and man and ourselves that our Lord is everything, is more than all to us, oh, let us be holy! Let us glory in Him who is our holiness, for in His presence is fullness of joy (Ps. 16:11). Let us live in the kingdom that is joy in the Holy Spirit. The Spirit of holiness is the Spirit of joy, because He is the Spirit of God. It is the saints, God's holy ones, who will shout for joy.

And *happiness is essential to true holiness.* If you desire to be a holy Christian, you must be a happy Christian. Jesus was anointed by God with "the oil of gladness" (Ps. 45:7, Heb. 1:9) so that He might give us "the oil of joy" (Isa. 61:3). In all our efforts after holiness, the wheels will move heavily if there is not the oil of joy—this alone removes all strain and friction and makes the onward progress easy and delightful.

Study to understand the divine worth of joy. It is the evidence of your being in the Father's presence and dwelling in His love. It is the proof of your being consciously free from the law and the strain of the spirit of bondage. It is the proof of your freedom from care and responsibility, because you are rejoicing in Christ Jesus as your sanctification, your keeper, and your strength. It is the secret of spiritual health and strength, filling all your service with the childlike happy assurance that the Father asks nothing that He does not give strength for, and that He accepts all that is done, however feebly, in this spirit.

True happiness is always self-forgetful: It loses itself in the object of its joy. As the joy of the Holy Spirit fills us, as we rejoice in God the Holy One through our Lord Jesus Christ, and as we lose ourselves in the adoration and worship of the Thrice Holy, we become holy. This is, even here in the wilderness, the highway of holiness: The ransomed of the Lord shall come with singing; the redeemed shall walk there; with everlasting joy on their heads; they shall obtain joy and gladness (see Isa. 35:8, 10).

Do all God's children understand this? That holiness is just another name, the true name, that God gives for happiness, that it is indeed unutterable blessedness to know that God does make us holy, that our holiness is in Christ, that Christ's Holy Spirit is within us? There is nothing so attractive as joy, but have believers understood that this is the joy of the Lord—to be holy? Or is not the idea of strain, sacrifice, and sighing, of difficulty and distance so prominent that the thought of being holy has hardly ever made the heart glad? If it has been so, let it be so no longer. "You shall glory in the Holy One of Israel" (Isa. 41:16).

Let us claim this promise. Let the believing assurance that our loving Father, and our beloved Lord Jesus, and the Holy Spirit, who in dovelike gentleness rests within us, have engaged to do the work and are doing it, fill us with gladness. Let us not seek our joy in what we see in ourselves of holiness. Rather, let us rejoice in the holiness of God in Christ as ours. Let us rejoice in the Holy One of Israel. So shall our joy be unspeakable and unceasing. So shall we give Him the glory.

Be holy, as I am holy

Most blessed God! I ask You to reveal to me and to all Your children the secret of rejoicing in You, the Holy One of Israel. You see how much of the service of Your own dear children is still in the spirit of bondage, and how many have never yet believed that the highway of holiness is one on which they may walk with singing and shall obtain joy and gladness.

O Father! Teach Your children to rejoice in You. I ask You especially to teach us that, in deep poverty of spirit, in humility and contrition and utter emptiness, in the consciousness that there is no holiness in us, we can sing all the day of Your holiness as ours, of Your glory that You lay upon us and that yet all the time is Yours alone. O Father! Open wide to Your children the blessed mystery of the kingdom, even the faith that sees all in Christ and nothing in itself, that indeed has and rejoices in all in Him, that never has or rejoices in anything in itself.

Blessed God, in Your Word You have said, "The humble also shall increase their joy in the LORD, and the poor among men shall rejoice in the Holy One of Israel" (Isa. 29:19). Oh, allow us, by Your Holy Spirit, in humility and poorness of spirit, to live so in Christ that His holiness may be our ever-increasing joy, and that in Yourself, the Holy One of Israel, we may rejoice all the day. And may all see in us what blessedness it is to live as God's holy ones. Amen.

For Further Thought

1. *How can you make sure you consistently walk in the joy of God? The great hindrance to joy in God is expecting to find something in ourselves to rejoice over. At the commencement of this pursuit of holiness, we always expect to see a great change accomplished in ourselves. As we are led deeper into what faith and the faith-life is, we understand how, though we do not see the change as we expected, we may yet rejoice with joy unspeakable in what Jesus is. This is the secret of holiness.*
2. *Joy must be cultivated. To rejoice is a command more frequently given than we*

know. It is part of the obedience of faith—to rejoice when we do not feel like doing so. Faith rejoices and sings, because God is holy. What will you do today to cultivate that joy?

3. "Filled with joy and with the Holy Spirit." "The kingdom is joy in the Holy Spirit." The Holy Spirit, the blessed Spirit of Jesus is within you, a very fountain of living water, of joy and gladness. Oh, seek to know Him who dwells in you to work all Jesus has for you. He will be in you the Spirit of faith and of joy. What can you do today and every day to seek to know the Holy Spirit of God?

4. Love and joy always keep company. Love, denying and forgetting itself for the brethren and for the lost, living in them, finds the joy of God. "The kingdom of God is joy in the Holy Spirit."

DAY 22

IN CHRIST OUR SANCTIFICATION

*But of Him you are in Christ Jesus, who became
for us wisdom from God—and righteousness and
sanctification and redemption—that, as it is written,
"He who glories, let him glory in the LORD."*

1 CORINTHIANS 1:30–31

THESE words lead us on now to the very center of God's revelation of the way of holiness. We know the steps of the road leading there. He is holy, and holiness is His. He makes holy by coming near. His presence is holiness. In Christ's life, the holiness that had only been revealed in symbol, and as a promise of good things to come, had really taken possession of a human will and been made one with true human nature. In His death, every obstacle had been removed that could prevent the transmission of that holy nature to us. Christ had truly become our sanctification. In the Holy Spirit, the actual communication of that holiness took place.

And now we want to understand what the work is the Holy Spirit does and how He communicates this holy nature to us, what our relationship is to Christ as our sanctification and what the position we have to take up toward Him so that in its fullness and its power it may do its work for us.

The divine answer to this question is, "Of God you are *in Christ*." The one thing we need to grasp is what our position and life in Christ is and how that position and life may on our part be accepted and maintained. Of this we may be sure, that it is not something that is high and beyond our reach. There need be no exhausting effort or hopeless sighing, "Who will ascend into heaven? (that is, to bring Christ down from above)?" (Rom. 10:6). It is a life that is meant for the sinful and the weary, for the unworthy and the powerless. It is a life that is the gift of the Father's love, and that He Himself will reveal in each one who comes in childlike trust to Him. It is a life that is meant for our everyday life, that in every varying circumstance and situation will make and keep us holy.

"Of God you are *in Christ*!" Before our blessed Lord left the world, He promised, "Lo! I am with you always, even to the end of the age" (Matt. 28:20). And it is written of Him: "He who descended is also the One who ascended far above all the heavens, that He might fill all things" (Eph. 4:10). "The church. . .is His body, the fullness of Him who fills all in all" (Eph. 1:22, 23).

In the Holy Spirit, the Lord Jesus is with His people here on earth. Though unseen, and not in the flesh, His personal presence is as real on earth as when He walked with His disciples. In regeneration, the believer is taken out of his old place "in the flesh." He is no longer in the flesh, but in the spirit (Rom. 8:9). He is really and actually in Christ. The living Christ is around him by His holy presence. Wherever and whatever he be, however ignorant of his position or however unfaithful to it, there he is in Christ. By an act of divine and omnipotent grace, he has been planted into Christ, encircled on every side by the power and the love of Him who fills all things, whose fullness specially dwells in His body here below, the Church.

> *he one thing we need to grasp is what our position and life in Christ is and how that position and life may on our part be accepted and maintained.*

And how can one who is longing to know Christ fully as his sanctification come to live out what God means and has provided in this—"in Christ?" The first thing that must be remembered is that it is a thing of faith and not of feeling. The promise of the indwelling and the quickening of the Holy One is to the humble and contrite. Just when I feel most deeply that I am not holy and can do nothing to make myself holy, when I feel ashamed of myself, just then is the time to turn from self and very quietly to say: "I am in Christ." Here He is all around me. Like the air that surrounds me, like the light that shines on me, here is my Lord Jesus with me in His hidden but divine and most real presence. My faith must in quiet rest and trust bow before the Father, of whom and by whose mighty grace I am in Christ, and He will reveal it to me with ever-growing clearness and power. He does it as I believe, and in believing open my whole soul to receive what is implied in it: The sense of sinfulness and unholiness must become the strength of my trust and dependence. In such faith, I abide in Christ.

But because it is of faith, therefore it is of the Holy Spirit. *Of God* you are *in Christ.* It is not as if God placed and planted us in Christ and left it to us now to maintain the union. No, God is the Eternal One, the God of the everlasting life who works every moment in a power that does not for one moment cease. What God gives, He continues with a never-ceasing giving. It is He who by the Holy Spirit makes this life in Christ a blessed reality in our consciousness.

"We have received. . .the Spirit who is from God, that we might know the things that have been freely given to us by God" (1 Cor. 2:12). Faith is not only dependent on God for the gift it is to accept, but for the power to accept. Faith not only needs the Son as its filling and its food, it needs the Spirit as its power to receive and hold. And so the blessed possession of all that it means to be in Christ our sanctification comes as we learn to bow before God in believing prayer for the mighty workings of the Spirit, and in the deep childlike trust that He will reveal and glorify in us this Christ our sanctification in whom we are.

And how will the Spirit reveal this Christ in who we are? It will specially be as the Living One, the personal friend and master. Christ is not only our example and our ideal. His life is not only an atmosphere and an inspiration, as we speak of a man who mightily influences us by his writings. Christ is not only a treasury and a fullness of grace and power, into which the Spirit is to lead us. But Christ is the living Savior, with a heart that beats with a love that is most tenderly human and yet divine. It is in this love He comes near, and into this love He receives us when the Father plants us into Him. In the power of a personal love He wishes to exercise influence, and to attach us to Himself. In that love of His we have the guarantee that His holiness will enter us; in that love the great power by which it enters.

As the Spirit reveals to us where we are dwelling, in Christ and His love, and that this Christ is a living Lord and Savior, there awakens within us the enthusiasm of a personal attachment and the devotion of a loving allegiance that make us wholly His. And it becomes possible for us to believe that we can be holy. We feel sure that in the path of holiness we can go from strength to strength (see Ps. 84:7).

> *W*hat God gives, He continues with a never-ceasing giving. It is He who by the Holy Spirit makes this life in Christ a blessed reality in our consciousness.

Such believing insight into our relationship to Christ as being in Him, and such personal attachment to Him who has received us into His love and keeps us abiding there, becomes the spring of a new obedience. The will of God comes to us in the light of Christ's life and His love—each command first fulfilled by Him, and then passed on to us as the sure and most blessed help to more perfect fellowship with the Father and His holiness. Christ becomes Lord and King in the soul, in the power of the Holy Spirit, guiding the will into all the perfect will of God and proving Himself to be its sanctification, as He crowns its obedience with ever larger inflow of the presence and the holiness of God.

Is there any dear child of God at all disposed to lose heart as he thinks of what manner of man he ought to be in all holy living? Let me call him to take courage. Could God have devised anything more wonderful or beautiful for such sinful, helpless creatures? Just think, Christ, God's own Son, made to be sanctification to you. The mighty, loving, holy Christ, sanctified through suffering so that He might have sympathy with you, given to make you holy. What more could you desire?

Yes, there is more: *"Of God you are in Him."* Whether you understand it or not, however feebly you realize it, there it is, a thing most divinely true and real. You are in Christ by an act of God's own mighty power. And there, in Christ, God Himself longs to establish and confirm you to the end. And you have, greatest wonder of all, the Holy Spirit within you to teach you to know, believe, and receive all that there is in Christ for you. And if you will but confess that there is in you no wisdom or power for holiness, none at all, and allow Christ, "the power of God and the wisdom of God" (1 Cor. 1:24), by the Holy Spirit within you to lead you on and prove how completely, how faithfully, how mightily He can be your sanctification, He will do it most gloriously.

> *he mighty, loving, holy Christ, sanctified through suffering so that He might have sympathy with you, given to make you holy. What more could you desire?*

O my brother! Come and consent more fully to God's way of holiness. Let Christ be your sanctification. Not a distant Christ to whom you look, but a Christ very near, all around you, in whom you are. Not a Christ after the flesh or a Christ of the past, but a present Christ in the power of the Holy Spirit. Not a Christ whom you can know by your wisdom, but the Christ of God, who is a Spirit and whom the Spirit within you, as you die to the flesh and self, will reveal in power. Not a Christ such as your little thoughts can frame a conception of, but a Christ according to the greatness of the heart and the love of God.

Oh, come and accept this Christ, and rejoice in Him! Be content now to leave all your weakness, foolishness, and faithlessness to Him, in the quiet confidence that He will do for you more than you can think. And so let it from this time forth be, as it is written. "He who glories, let him glory in the LORD" (1 Cor. 1:31).

BE HOLY, AS I AM HOLY

Most blessed Father! I bow in speechless adoration before the holy mystery of Your divine love. . . .

Oh, forgive me, that I have known and believed it so little as it is worthy of being known and believed.

Accept my praise for what I have seen and tasted of its divine blessedness. Accept, Lord God, of the praise of a glad and loving heart that only knows that it never can praise You as is fitting.

And hear my prayer, O my Father, that in the power of Your Holy Spirit, who dwells in me, I may each day accept and live out fully what You have given me in Christ my sanctification. May the unsearchable riches there are in Him be the daily supply for my every need. May His holiness, His delight in Your will, indeed become mine. Teach me, above all, how this can most surely be, because I am, through the work of Your almighty quickening power, in Him, kept there by Yourself. My Father! My faith cries out: I can be holy, blessed be my Lord Jesus!

In this faith I yield myself to You, Lord Jesus, my king and master, to do Your will alone. In everything I do, great or small, I would act as one sanctified in Jesus, united to God's will in Him. It is You alone who can teach me to do this, who can give me strength to perform it. But I trust in You—are You not Christ my sanctification? Blessed Lord! I do trust You. Amen.

For Further Thought

1. *What should your relationship to Christ look like in order for you to be holy? Christ, as He lived and died on earth, is our sanctification. His life, the Spirit of His life, is what constitutes our holiness. To be in perfect harmony with Christ, to have His mind, is to be holy.*

2. *What should you do to follow and seek after perfect holiness? Christ's holiness had two sides. God sanctified Him by His Spirit, and Christ sanctified Himself by following the leading of the Spirit, by giving up His will to God in everything. So God has made us holy in Christ, and so we follow after and perfect holiness by yielding ourselves to God's Spirit, by giving up our will and living in the will of God.*

3. *It is well that we take in every aspect of what God has revealed about holiness in His Word. But let us never weary ourselves by seeking to grasp all completely. Let us even return to the simplicity that is in Jesus. To bow at His feet, to believe that He knows all we need, and has it all, and loves to give it all, is rest. And holiness is resting in Jesus, the rest of God. Let all our thoughts be gathered up into this one: Jesus, blessed Jesus.*

4. *How can you know that God's holiness is for you individually? This holy life in Christ is for today, as you read this. For today He is made of God for you sanctification, today He will indeed be your holiness. Believe in Him for it. Trust Him, praise Him. And remember: you are in Him.*

Day 23

Holiness and the Body

Your body is the temple of the Holy Spirit who is in you. . . .
Now the body is. . .for the Lord, and the Lord for the body. . . .
Do you not know that your body is the temple of the
Holy Spirit who is in you, whom you have from
God. . . . Therefore glorify God in your body.
1 Corinthians 3:16; 6:13, 19–20

The unmarried woman cares about the things of the Lord,
that she may be holy both in body and in spirit.
1 Corinthians 7:34

Present your bodies a living sacrifice,
holy, acceptable to God.
Romans 7:1

COMING into the world, our blessed Lord spoke: "A body You have prepared for Me. . . . Behold, I have come to do Your will, O God" (Heb. 10:5, 7). Leaving this world again, it was in His own body that He bore our sins upon the tree. So it was in the body, no less than in soul and spirit, that He did the will of God. And therefore it is said, "By that will we have been sanctified through the offering *of the body* of Jesus Christ once for all" (Heb. 10:10).

When praying for the Thessalonians and their sanctification, Paul says, "Now may the God of peace Himself sanctify you completely; and may your whole spirit, soul, and body be preserved blameless at the coming of our Lord Jesus Christ" (1 Thess. 5:23). Of himself he had spoken as "always carrying about *in the body* the dying of the Lord Jesus, that the life of Jesus also may be manifested *in our body*. For we who live are always delivered to death for Jesus' sake, that the life of Jesus also may be manifested *in our mortal flesh*" (2 Cor. 4:10–11). His earnest expectation and hope was that "Christ will be magnified *in my body*, whether by life or by death" (Phil. 1:20).

The relationship between body and spirit is so intimate, the power of sin in the spirit comes so much through the body, the body is so distinctly the object both of Christ's redemption and the Holy Spirit's renewal that our study of holiness will be seriously defective if we do not take in the teaching of scripture on holiness in the body.

It has been well said that the body is, to the soul and spirit dwelling and acting within it, like the walls of the city. Through them the enemy enters in. In time of war, everything yields to the defense of the walls. It is often because the believer does not know the importance of keeping the walls defended, keeping the body sanctified, that he fails in having the soul and spirit preserved blameless. Or it is because he does not understand that the guarding and sanctifying of the body in all its parts must be as distinctly a work of faith, and as directly through the mighty power of Jesus and the indwelling of the Spirit, as the renewing of the inner life, that progress in holiness is so feeble.

> *It is the God of peace Himself, who sanctifies completely, who must preserve spirit and soul and body entire and without blame.*

The rule of the city we entrust to Jesus, but the defense of the walls we keep in our own hands. The king does not keep us as we expected, and we cannot discover the secret of failure. It is the God of peace *Himself,* who sanctifies completely, who must preserve spirit and soul and body entire and without blame. The tabernacle with its wood, the temple with its stone, were as holy as all included within their walls: God's holy ones need the body to be holy.

To realize the full meaning of this, let us remember how it was through the body sin entered. "The woman saw that the tree was good for food." This was the temptation in the flesh, and through this the soul was reached: "it was a delight to the eyes." Through the soul it then passed into the spirit, "and to be desired to make one wise" (Gen. 3:6). In John's description of what is in the world (1 John 2:16), we find the same threefold division, "the lust of the flesh, the lust of the eyes, and the pride of life." And the three temptations of Jesus by Satan correspond exactly: he first sought to reach Him through the body, in the suggestion to satisfy His hunger by making bread; the second (see Luke 4) appealed to the soul, in the vision of the kingdoms of this world and their glory; the third to the spirit, in the call to assert and prove His divine Sonship by casting Himself down.

Even to the Son of God the first temptation came, as to Adam and all in the world, as lust of the flesh, the desire to gratify the natural and lawful appetite of hunger. We cannot note too carefully that it was on a question of eating what appeared good for food that man's first sin was committed, and that that same question of eating to satisfy hunger was the battleground on which the Redeemer's first encounter with Satan took place.

It is on the question of eating and drinking what is good and lawful that more Christians than are aware of it are foiled by Satan. To have every appetite of the body under the rule and regulation of the Holy Spirit appears to some needless, to others too difficult. And yet it must be, if the body is to be holy, as God's temple, and we are to glorify Him in our body and our spirit. The first approaches of sin are made through the body, so in the body the complete victory will be gained.

What scripture teaches as to the intimacy of the connection between the body and spirit, physiology confirms. What appear at first merely physical transgressions leave a stain and have a degrading influence on the soul, and through it drag down the spirit. And on the other side, spiritual sins, sins of thought and imagination and disposition, pass through the soul into the body, fix themselves in the nervous constitution, and express themselves even in the countenance and in the habits or tendencies of the body.

Sin must be combated not only in the region of the spirit. If we are to perfect holiness, we must cleanse ourselves from all defilement of flesh *and* spirit. "If by the Spirit you put to death the deeds of *the body*, you will live" (Rom. 8:13). If we are indeed to be cleansed from sin and made holy to God, the body, as the outworks, must very specially be secured from the power of Satan and of sin.

> *If we are indeed to be cleansed from sin and made holy to God, the body, as the outworks, must very specially be secured from the power of Satan and of sin.*

And how is this to be done? God has made very special provision for this. holy scripture speaks so explicitly of the Holy Spirit, the Spirit that communicates holiness, in connection with the body. At first sight it looks as if the words, "your bodies," were simply used as equivalent to, your persons, yourselves. But as the deeper insight into the power of sin in the body, and the need of a deliverance specially there, quickens our perception, we see what is meant by the body being the temple of the Holy Spirit. We notice how very specially it is of sins in the body that Paul speaks as defiling God's holy temple—and how it is through the power of the Holy Ghost in the body that he would have us glorify God.

"Do you not know that *your body* is the temple of the Holy Spirit. . .therefore glorify God in *your body* and in your spirit, which are God's" (1 Cor. 6:19, 20). The Holy Spirit must not only exercise a restraining and regulating influence on the appetites of the body and their gratification so that they be in moderation and temperance—this is only the negative side—but there must be a positively spiritual element, making the exercise of natural functions a service of holy joy and liberty to the glory of God—no longer a threatened hindrance to the life of obedience and fellowship, but a means of grace, a real help to the spiritual life. It is only in a body that is full of the holy life, very entirely possessed of God's Spirit, that this will be the case.

And how can this be obtained? In the true Christian life, self-denial is the path to enjoyment, renunciation to possession, death to life. As long as there is something that we think we have liberty and power to use or enjoy rightly, if we but do so in moderation, we have not yet seen or confessed our own unholiness or the need of the entire renewing of the Holy Spirit. It is not enough to say, "Every creature of God is good...if it is received with thanksgiving." We must remember the addition, "for it is sanctified by the word and prayer" (1 Tim. 4:4, 5). This sanctifying of every creature and its use is a thing as real and solemn as the sanctifying of ourselves. And this will only be where, if need be, we sacrifice the gift and the liberty to use it, until God gives us the power truly to use it to His glory alone.

Of one of the most sacred of divine institutions, marriage, Paul, who so denounces those who would forbid to marry, says distinctly that there may be cases in which a voluntary celibacy may be the surest and acceptable way of being "holy both in body and spirit" (1 Cor. 7:34). When to be holy as God is holy indeed becomes the great desire and aim of life, everything will be cherished or given up as it promotes the chief end. The actual and active presence of the Holy Spirit in the life of the body will be the fire that is kept burning continually on the altar.

And how is this to be attained? Of the body as of the spirit it is God, God in Christ, who is our keeper and our sanctifier. The guarding of the walls of the city must be entrusted to Him who rules within. "I am persuaded that He is able to guard my deposit" (see 2 Tim. 1:12), to keep that which I have committed to Him, must become as definitely true of the body, and of each of its functions of which we are conscious that it is the occasion of doubt or of stumbling, as it has been of the soul we entrusted to Him for salvation.

A fixed deposit in a bank is money given away out of my hands to be kept there. Likewise, the body or any part of it that needs to be made holy must be a deposit with Jesus. Faith must trust His acceptance and guarding of it, and prayer and praise must daily afresh renew the assurance, must confirm the committal of the deposit, and maintain the fellowship with Jesus. Abiding in Him and His holiness, we shall receive, in a life of trust and joy, the power to prove, even in the body, how fully and wholly we are in Him who is made for us sanctification, how real and true the holiness of God is in His people.

BE HOLY, AS I AM HOLY

Blessed Lord, who is my sanctification, I come to You now with a very special request. O You who in Your own body bear our sins on the tree, and of whom it is written, "We have been sanctified through the offering of the body of Jesus Christ once for all" (Heb. 10:10), be pleased to reveal to me how my body may to the full experience the power of Your wonderful redemption. I do desire in soul and body to be holy to the Lord.

Lord! I have too little understood that my body is the temple of the Holy Spirit, that there is nothing in it that can be a matter of indifference, that its every state and function is to be holiness to the Lord. And where I saw that this should be so, I have still sought myself to guard from the enemy's approaches these the walls of the city. I forgot how this part of my being too could alone be kept and sanctified by faith, by Your taking and keeping charge of what faith entrusted to You.

Lord Jesus! I come now to surrender this body with all its needs into Your hands. In weariness and nervousness, in excitement and enjoyment, in hunger and need, in health and plenty, O my holy Savior, let my body be in Your keeping every moment. You call us, "having been set free from sin...so now present your members *as* slaves *of* righteousness for holiness" (Rom. 6:18, 19). Savior! In the faith of the freedom from sin that I have in You, I present every member of my body to You. I believe the Spirit of life in You makes me free from the law of sin in my members. Whether living or dying, be magnified in my body. Amen.

For Further Thought

1. *How must you approach and present your body when it comes to God's holiness? In the tabernacle and temple, the material part was to be in harmony with, and the embodiment of, the holiness that dwelled within. It was therefore all made according to the pattern shown in the mount. In the two last chapters of Exodus, we have eighteen times "as the Lord commanded." Everything, even in the exterior, was the embodiment of the will of God. Even so our body, as God's temple, must in everything be regulated by God's Word, quickened and sanctified by the Holy Spirit.*

2. *As part of this holiness in the body, scripture mentions dress. Speaking of the "arranging the hair, wearing gold, or putting on fine apparel," as being inconsistent with "the incorruptible beauty of a gentle and quiet spirit," Peter says, "For in this manner, in former times, the holy women who trusted in God also adorned themselves" (1 Pet. 3:3–5). Holiness was seen in their dressing; their body was the temple of the Holy Spirit. How does knowing this affect the way you dress or adorn your body?*

3. *"If by the Spirit you put to death the deeds of the body, you will live" (Rom. 8:13). His quickening energy must reign through the whole. We are so accustomed to connect the spiritual with the ideal and invisible that it will need time and thought and faith to realize how the physical and the sensible influence our spiritual life, and must be under the mastery and inspiration of God's Spirit. Even Paul says, "I discipline my body and bring it into subjection, lest...I myself should become disqualified" (1 Cor. 9:27). In what ways would God have you bring your own body into subjection?*

4. *If God actually breathed His Spirit into the body of Adam formed out of the ground, let it not be thought strange that the Holy Spirit should now animate our bodies too with His sanctifying energy.*

5. *"Corporeality [physical existence] is the end of the ways of God." This deep saying of an old divine reminds us of a much-neglected truth. The great work of God's Spirit is to ally Himself with matter and form it into a spiritual body for a dwelling for God. In our body the Holy Spirit will do it, if He gets complete possession.*

6. *It is on this truth of the Holy Spirit's power in the body that what is called faith-healing rests. Through all ages, in times of special spiritual quickening, God has given it to some to see how Christ would make, even here, the body partaker of the life and power of the Spirit. To those who do see it, the link between holiness and healing is a very close and blessed one, as the Lord Jesus takes possession of the body for Himself.*

Day 24

Holiness and Cleansing

Therefore, having these promises, beloved, let us cleanse
ourselves from all filthiness of the flesh and spirit,
perfecting holiness in the fear of God.
2 Corinthians 7:1

THAT holiness is more than cleansing, and must be preceded by it, is taught us in more than one passage of the New Testament. "Christ also loved the church and gave Himself for her, that He might *sanctify* and *cleanse* her with the washing of water by the word" (Eph. 5:25–26). "If anyone *cleanses* himself from the latter, he will be a vessel *for honor*" (2 Tim. 2:21).

The cleansing is the negative side, the being separate and not touching the unclean thing, the removal of impurity, but the sanctifying is the positive union and fellowship with God and the participation of the graces of the divine life and holiness (2 Cor. 6:17–18). So we read too of the altar, that God told Moses: "You shall *cleanse* the altar when you make atonement for it, and you shall anoint it to *sanctify* it" (Exod. 29:36). Cleansing must always prepare the way, and ought always to lead on to holiness.

Paul speaks of a twofold defilement, of flesh and spirit, from which we must cleanse ourselves. The connection between the two is so close that in every sin both are partakers. The lowest and most carnal form of sin will enter the spirit, and, dragging it down into partnership in crime, will defile and degrade it. And so will all defilement of spirit in course of time show its power in the flesh. Still, we may speak of the two classes of sins as they owe their origin more directly to the flesh or the spirit.

"Let us cleanse ourselves from all filthiness of the flesh." The functions of our body may be classed under the three heads of the nourishment, the propagation, and the protection of our life. Through the first, the world daily solicits our appetite with its food and drink. As the fruit good for food was the temptation that overcame Eve, so the pleasures of eating and drinking are among the earliest forms of defilement of the flesh. Closely connected with this is what we named second, and which is in scripture specially connected with the word *flesh*. We know how in paradise the sinful eating was at once followed by the

awakening of sinful lust and of shame. In his first Epistle to the Corinthians, Paul closely connects the two (1 Cor. 6:13, 15), as he also links drunkenness and impurity (1 Cor. 6:9, 10). Then comes the third form in which the vitality of the body displays itself: the instinct of self-preservation, setting itself against everything that interferes with our pleasures and comfort. What is called temper, with its fruits of anger and strife, has its roots in the physical constitution, and is one among the sins of the flesh.

From all this the Christian who desires to be holy must most determinedly cleanse himself. He must yield himself to the searching of God's Spirit, to be taught what there is in the flesh that is not in harmony with the temperance and self-control demanded both by the law of nature and the law of the Spirit. He must believe what Paul felt that the Corinthians so emphatically needed to be taught: that the Holy Spirit dwells in the body, making its members the members of Christ, and in this faith put off the works of the flesh. He must cleanse himself from all defilement of flesh.

> *The lowest and most carnal form of sin will enter the spirit, and, dragging it down into partnership in crime, will defile and degrade it. And so will all defilement of spirit in course of time show its power in the flesh.*

"And spirit." As the source of all defilement of the flesh is self-gratification, so self-seeking is at the root of all defilement of the spirit. In relation to God, it manifests itself in idolatry, be it in the worship of other gods after our own heart, the love of the world more than God, or the doing our will rather than His. In relation to our fellowmen, it shows itself in envy, hatred, and lack of love, cold neglect or harsh judging of others. In relation to ourselves, it is seen as pride, ambition, or envy, the disposition that makes self the center around which all must move and by which all must be judged.

For the discovery of such defilement of spirit, no less than of the sins of the flesh, the believer needs the light of the Holy Spirit so that the uncleanness may indeed be cleansed out and cast away forever. Even unconscious sin, if we are not earnestly willing to have it shown to us, will most effectually prevent our progress in the path of holiness.

"Beloved! Let us cleanse ourselves." The cleansing is sometimes spoken of as the work of God (Acts 15:9, 1 John 1:9), sometimes as that of Christ (John 15:3, Eph. 5:26, Titus 2:14). Here we are commanded to cleanse ourselves. God does His work in us by the Holy Spirit. The Holy Spirit does His work by stirring us up and enabling us to do. The Spirit is the strength of the new life, and in that strength we must set ourselves determinedly to cast out whatever is unclean. "Come out... and be separate...do not touch what is unclean" (2 Cor. 6:17). It is not only the

doing what is sinful, it is not only the willing of it, that the Christian must avoid, but even the touching it. The involuntary contact with it must be so unbearable as to force the cry, "O wretched man that I am!" and to lead on to the deliverance that the Spirit of the life of Christ does bring.

And how is this cleansing to be done? When Hezekiah called the priests to sanctify the temple that had been defiled, we read (2 Chron. 29:16), "The priests went into the inner part of the house of the LORD to cleanse it, and brought out all the debris that they found." Only then could the sin offering of atonement and the burnt offering of consecration, with the thank offerings, be brought, and God's service be restored.

> However deeply rooted the sin may appear, rooted in constitution and habit, we must cleanse ourselves of it if we desire to be holy.

In this way must all that is unclean be found, brought out, and utterly cast out. However deeply rooted the sin may appear, rooted in constitution and habit, we must cleanse ourselves of it if we desire to be holy. "If we walk in the light as He is in the light. . .the blood of Jesus Christ His Son cleanses us from all sin" (1 John 1:7). As we bring out every sin from the inner part of the house into the light of God and walk in the light, the precious blood that justifies will work mightily to cleanse too, for the blood brings into living contact with the life and the love of God.

Let us come into the light with the sin. Then the blood will prove its mighty power. Let us cleanse ourselves in yielding ourselves to the light to reveal and condemn, to the blood to cleanse and sanctify.

"Let us cleanse ourselves. . .*perfecting holiness in the fear of God.*" We read in Hebrews (10:14), "He has perfected forever those who are being sanctified." As we have so often seen that what God has made holy man must make holy too, as he accepts and appropriates the holiness God has bestowed, so here with the perfection that the saints have in Christ.

We must perfect holiness. Holiness must be carried out into the whole of life, and carried on even to its end. As God's holy ones, we must go on to perfection, perfecting holiness. Do not let us be afraid of the word. Our blessed Lord used it when He gave us the command, "You shall be perfect, just as your Father in heaven is perfect" (Matt. 5:48).

A child striving after the perfection in knowledge of his profession, which he hopes to attain when he has finished school, is told by his teacher that the way to the perfection he hopes for at the end of his course is to seek to be perfect in the lessons of each day. To be perfect in the small portion of the work that each hour brings is the path to the perfection that will crown the whole. The Master calls us to a perfection like that of the Father: He has already perfected us in Himself, and He holds out the prospect of perfection ever growing. His Word calls us here day by day to be perfecting holiness. Let us seek in each duty to be wholehearted and entire. Let us, as teachable students, in every act of worship or obedience, in every temptation and trial, do the very best that God's Spirit can enable us to do. "Let patience have its perfect work, that you may be perfect and complete, lacking nothing" (James 1:4). "The God of peace. . . make you perfect in every good work to do His will" (Heb. 13:20, 21 KJV).

"*Therefore, having these promises,* beloved, let us cleanse ourselves from all filthiness of the flesh and spirit, perfecting holiness in the fear of God." It is faith that gives the courage and the power to cleanse from all filthiness, perfecting holiness in the fear of God. It is as the promises of the divine love and indwelling (2 Cor. 6:16–18) are made ours by the Holy Spirit that we shall share the victory that overcomes the world, even our faith.

> *B*lessed is Your name for the wonderful love. Blessed is Your Name for the wonderful cleansing. Through the washing by the word and the washing in the blood, You have made us clean in every way.

In the path along which we have already come, from the rest in paradise down through holy scripture, we have seen the wondrous revelation of these promises in ever-growing splendor. That God the Holy One will make us holy, that God the Holy One will dwell with the lowly, that God in His Holy One has come to be our holiness, that God has planted us in Christ that He may be our sanctification, that God, who chose us in sanctification of the Spirit, has given us the Holy Spirit in our hearts, and now watches over us in His love to work out through Him His purposes and to perfect our holiness: such are the promises that have been set before us. "Having therefore these promises, beloved, let us cleanse ourselves from all filthiness of flesh and spirit, perfecting holiness in the fear of God."

Beloved brother! See here again God's way of holiness. Arise and step on to it in the faith of the promise, fully persuaded that what He has promised He is mighty to perform. Bring out of the inner part of the house all uncleanness, and bring it into the light of God. Confess it and cast it at His feet, who takes it away and cleanses you in His blood. Yield yourself in faith to perfect, in Christ your strength, the holiness to which you are called.

As your Father in heaven is perfect, give yourself to Him as a little child to be perfect too in your daily lessons and your daily walk. Believe that your surrender is accepted, that the charge committed to Him is undertaken. And give glory to Him who is able to do above what you can ask or think.

Be holy, as I am holy

Holy Lord Jesus! You gave Yourself for us so that, having cleansed us for Yourself as Your own, You might sanctify us and present us to Yourself a glorious Church, not having spot or wrinkle or any such thing. Blessed is Your name for the wonderful love. Blessed is Your name for the wonderful cleansing. Through the washing by the Word and the washing in the blood, You have made us clean in every way. And as we walk in the light, You cleanse every moment.

With these promises, in the power of Your Word and blood, You call us to cleanse ourselves from all filthiness of flesh and spirit. Blessed Lord! Graciously reveal in Your holy light all that is unclean, even its most secret working. Let me live as one who is to be presented to You without spot or wrinkle or any such thing—cleansed with a divine cleansing, because You gave Yourself to do it. Under the living power of Your word and blood, applied by the Holy Spirit, let my way be clean, and my hands clean, my lips clean, and my heart clean. Cleanse me thoroughly so that I may walk with You in white here on earth, keeping my garments unspotted and undefiled. For Your great love's sake, my blessed Lord. Amen.

For Further Thought

1. *Cleansing has almost always one aim: a cleansed vessel is fit for use. Spiritual work done for God, with the honest desire that He may through His Spirit use us, will give urgency to our desire for cleansing. A vessel not cleansed cannot be used. Is not this the reason that there are some workers God cannot bless? What does God want you to cleanse from your life today so that He can more fully bless you?*

2. *All defilement: one stain defiles. "Let us cleanse ourselves from all filthiness." Are there sins, even what you might think of as small or insignificant, that God wants you to cleanse from your body?*

3. *No cleansing without light. Open the heart for the light to shine in.*

4. *No cleansing like fire. Give the uncleanness over to the fire of His holiness, the fire that consumes and purifies. Give it into the death of Jesus, to Jesus Himself. What do you believe will happen to your uncleanness once you have given it over to Jesus for Him to cleanse?*

5. *"Perfecting holiness in the fear of God": it is a solemn work. Rejoice with trembling—work out your own salvation with fear and trembling (Phil. 2:12).*

6. *"Having these promises," it is a blessed work to cleanse ourselves—entering into the promises, the purity, the love of our Lord. The fear of God need never hinder the faith in Him. And true faith will never hinder this practical work of cleansing.*

7. *If we walk in the light, the blood cleanses us. The light reveals, we confess and forsake and accept the blood: so we cleanse ourselves. Let there be a very determined purpose to be clean from all uncleanness, everything that our Father considers a stain.*

Day 25

Holiness and Blamelessness

You are witnesses, and God also, how devoutly and justly
and blamelessly we behaved ourselves among you who believe. . . .
And may the Lord make you increase and abound in love
to one another and to all, just as we do to you, so that He
may establish your hearts blameless in holiness before
our God and Father at the coming of our
Lord Jesus Christ with all His saints.
1 Thessalonians 2:10, 3:12–13

He chose us in Him before the foundation
of the world, that we should be holy and
without blame before Him in love
Ephesians 1:4

THERE are two Greek words, signifying nearly the same, used frequently along with the word *holy*, and following it, to express what the result and effect of holiness will be as manifested in the visible life. The one is translated "without blemish," spotless, and is that also used of our Lord and His sacrifice: the Lamb without blemish (Heb. 9:14, 1 Pet. 1:19). It is then used of God's children with *holy*—holy and without blemish (Eph. 1:4–5, 27; Col. 1:22; Phil. 2:15; Jude 24; 2 Pet. 3:14). The other is without blame, faultless (as in Luke 1:6; Phil. 2:15, 3:6), and is also found in conjunction with *holy* (1 Thess. 2:10, 3:13, 23).

In answer to the question as to whether this blamelessness has reference to God's estimate of the saints or men's, scripture clearly connects it with both. In some passages (Eph. 1:4, 5:27; Col. 1:22; 1 Thess. 3:15; 2 Pet. 3:14), the words "before Him," "to Himself," and "before our God and Father" indicate that the first thought is of the spotlessness and faultlessness in the presence of a holy God, which is held out to us as His purpose and our privilege. In others (such as Phil. 2:15, 1 Thess. 2:10), the blamelessness in the sight of men stands in the foreground. In each case the word may be considered to include both aspects: without blemish and without blame must stand the double test of the judgment of God and man too.

And what is now the special lesson that this linking together of these two words in scripture, and the exposition of *holy* by the addition of *blameless*, is meant to teach us? A lesson of deep importance. In the pursuit of holiness, the believer, the more clearly he realizes what a deep spiritual blessing it is to be found only in separation from the world and direct fellowship with God, to be possessed fully only through a real divine indwelling, may be in danger of looking too exclusively to the divine side of the blessing, in its heavenly and supernatural aspect. He may forget how repentance and obedience, as the path leading up to holiness, must cover every, even the minutest, detail of daily life. He may not understand how faithfulness to the leadings of the Spirit, in such measure as we have Him already, faithfulness to His faintest whisper in reference to ordinary conduct, is essential to all fuller experience of His power and work as the Spirit of holiness. He may, above all, not have learned how not only obedience to what he knows to be God's will, but a very tender and willing teachableness to receive all that the Spirit has to show him of his imperfections and the Father's perfect will concerning him, is the only condition on which the holiness of God can be more fully revealed to us and in us. And so, while most intent on trying to discover the secret of true and full holiness from the divine side, he may be tolerating faults that all around him can notice, or remaining—and that not without sin, because it comes from the lack of perfect teachableness—ignorant of graces and beauties of holiness with which the Father wants to have had him adorn the doctrine of holiness before men. He may seek to live a very holy life, and yet think little of a perfectly blameless life.

> *In* linking holy *and* without blemish *(or* without blame*) so closely, the Holy Spirit would have led us to seek for the embodiment of holiness as a Spiritual power in the blamelessness of practice and of daily life.*

There have been such saints, holy but hard, holy but distant, holy but sharp in their judgments of others, holy, but men around them said, "unloving and selfish." The half-heathen Samaritan, for example, was more kind and self-sacrificing than the holy Levite and priest (see Luke 10:30–37). If this is true, it is not the teaching of holy scripture that is to blame. In linking *holy* and *without blemish* (or *without blame*) so closely, the Holy Spirit would have led us to seek for the embodiment of holiness as a spiritual power in the blamelessness of practice and of daily life. Let every believer who rejoices in God's declaration that he is holy in Christ seek also to perfect holiness, to reach out after nothing less than to be "blameless in holiness."

That this blamelessness has very special reference to our interactions with our fellowmen we see from the way in which it is linked with love. So in Ephesians 1:4, "That we should be holy and without blame before Him *in love*." But specially in that remarkable passage: "And may the Lord make you *increase and abound in love* to one another and to all...*so that He may establish your hearts blameless in holiness*" (1 Thess. 3:12–13). The holiness and the blamelessness, the positive hidden divine life-principle, and the external and human life-practice—both are to find their strength, by which we are to be established in them, in our abounding and ever-flowing love.

Holiness and lovingness—it is of deep importance that these words should be inseparably linked in our minds, as their reality in our lives. We have seen in the study of the holiness of God how love is the element in which it dwells and works, drawing to itself and making like itself all that it can get possession of. Of the fire of divine holiness love is the beautiful flame, reaching out to communicate itself and assimilate to itself all it can lay hold of. In God's children true holiness is the same. The divine fire burns to bring into its own blessedness all that comes within its reach.

When Jesus sanctified Himself so that we might be sanctified in truth, that was nothing but love giving itself to the death so that the sinful might share His holiness. Selfishness and holiness are irreconcilable. Ignorance may think of sanctity as a beautiful garment with which to adorn itself before God, while underneath there is a selfish pride saying, "I am holier than you," and quite content that the other should lack what it boasts of. True holiness, on the contrary, is the expulsion and the death of selfishness, taking possession of heart and life to be the ministers of that fire of love that consumes itself, to reach and purify and save others. Holiness is love. Abounding love is what Paul prays for as the condition of blameless holiness. It is as the Lord makes us to increase and abound in love that He can establish our hearts blameless in holiness.

> *rue holiness, is the expulsion and the death of selfishness, taking possession of heart and life to be the ministers of that fire of love that consumes itself, to reach and purify and save others.*

The apostle speaks of a twofold love: "love to one other and to all." Love to the brethren was what our Lord Himself commanded as the chief mark of discipleship. And He prayed to the Father for it as the chief proof to the world of the truth of His divine mission. It is in the holiness of love, in a loving holiness, that the unity of the body will be proved and promoted and prepared for the fuller workings of the Holy Spirit. In the epistles to the Corinthians and Galatians, division and distance among believers are named as the sure proof of the life of self and the flesh.

Oh, let us, if we desire to be holy, begin by being very gentle, and patient, and forgiving, and kind, and generous in our interactions with all the Father's children. Let us study the divine image of the love that does not seek its own (see 1 Cor. 13:5), and pray unceasingly that the Lord may make us to abound in love to each other. The holiest will be the humblest and most self-forgetting, the gentlest and most self-denying, the kindest and most thoughtful of others for Jesus' sake. "Therefore, as the elect of God, *holy and beloved*, put on tender mercies, kindness, humility, meekness, longsuffering" (Col. 3:12).

And then the love toward all men. A love proved in the conduct and relationships of daily life. A love that not only avoids anger and evil temper and harsh judgments, but exhibits the more positive virtue of active devotion to the welfare and interests of all. A charitable love that cares for the bodies as well as the souls. A love that not only is ready to help when it is called, but that really gives itself up to self-denial and self-sacrifice to seek out and relieve the needs of the most wretched and unworthy. A love that does indeed take Christ's love, which brought Him from heaven and led Him to choose the cross, as the only law and measure for its conduct, and makes everything subordinate to the Godlike blessedness of giving, of doing good, of embracing and saving the needy and lost. Abounding in this kind of love, we shall be blameless in holiness.

> *It is in Christ we are holy. It is of God we are in Christ, who is made by God for us sanctification.*

It is in Christ we are holy. It is of God we are in Christ, who is made by God for us sanctification. It is in this faith that Paul prays that the Lord, our Lord Jesus, may make us increase and abound in love. The Father is the fountain, He is the channel, and the Holy Spirit is the living stream. And He is our Life, through the Spirit. It is by faith in Him, by abiding in Him and in His love, by allowing, in close union with Him, the Spirit to shed abroad the love of God, that we shall receive the answer to our prayer, and shall by Himself be established blameless in holiness.

Let it be with us a prayer of faith that changes into praise: Blessed is the Lord, who will make us increase and abound in love and will establish us blameless in holiness before our God and Father at the coming of our Lord Jesus with His holy ones.

Be holy, as I am holy

Most gracious God and Father! Again I thank You for that wondrous salvation, through sanctification of the Spirit, that has made us holy in Christ. And I thank You that the Spirit can so make us partakers of the life of Christ that we too may be blameless in holiness. And that it is the Lord Himself who makes us to increase and abound in love, for the purpose that our hearts may be so established, and that the abounding love and the blameless holiness are both from Him.

Blessed Lord and Savior! I come now to claim and take as my own what You are able to do for me. I am holy only in You; in You I am holy. In You there is for me the power to abound in love. O Lord, in whom the fullness of God's love abides and in whom I abide, the Lord, my Lord, make me to abound in love. In union with You, in the life of faith in which You live in me, it can be and it shall be. By the teaching of Your Holy Spirit, lead me in all the footsteps of Your self-denying love so that I too may be consumed in blessing others.

And therefore, Lord, mightily establish my heart to be blameless in holiness. Let self perish in Your presence. Let Your holiness, giving itself to make the sinner holy, take entire possession, until my heart and life are sanctified completely and my whole spirit and soul and body be preserved blameless at Your coming. Amen.

FOR FURTHER THOUGHT

1. *How can you gain favor with both God and with others around you? Let us pray very earnestly that our interest in the study of holiness may not be a thing of the intellect or the emotions, but of the will and the life, seen by all men in the daily walk and conversation. "Abounding in love," "blameless in holiness" will give favor with God and man.*

2. *"God is love" (1 John 4:8), and creation is the outflow of love. Redemption is the sacrifice and the triumph of love. Holiness is the fire of love. The beauty of the life of Jesus is love. All we enjoy of the divine we owe to love. Our holiness is not God's, is not Christ's, if we do not love. What unloving actions and attitudes do you engage in that need to be replaced by those of love?*

3. *"Love does not seek its own" (1 Cor. 13:5). "Love never fails" (1 Cor. 13:8). "Love is the fulfilling of the law" (Rom. 13:10). "The greatest of these is love" (1 Cor. 13:13). "The purpose of the commandment is love" (1 Tim. 1:5). To love God and man is to be holy. In the interactions of daily life, holiness can have its simple and sweet beginnings and its exercise. So, in its highest attainment, holiness is love made perfect. Is your love for God and for man perfect? How can you make sure that it is today?*

4. *Faith has all its worth from love, from the love of God, from where it draws and drinks, and the love to God and man that streams out of it. Let us be strong in faith, then shall we abound in love.*

5. *"The love of God has been poured out in our hearts by the Holy Spirit who was given to us" (Rom. 5:5). Let this be our confidence.*

DAY 26

HOLINESS AND THE WILL OF GOD

For this is the will of God, your sanctification.
1 THESSALONIANS 4:3

"Behold, I have come to do Your will. . . ."
By that will we have been sanctified through the
offering of the body of Jesus Christ once for all.
HEBREWS 10:9–10

IN the will of God we have the union of His wisdom and power. The wisdom decides and declares what is to be, and the power secures the performance. The declarative will is only one side, but its complement, the executive will, is the living energy in which everything good has its origin and existence. So long as we only look at the will of God in the former light, as law, we feel it a burden, because we don't have the power to perform—it is too high for us. When faith looks to the power that works in God's will and carries it out, it has the courage to accept it and fulfill it, because it knows God Himself is working it out. The surrender in faith to the divine will as wisdom thus becomes the pathway to the experience of it as a power. "He does according to His will" (Dan. 4:35) is then the language not only of forced submission but of joyful expectation.

"This is the will of God, your sanctification." In the ordinary meaning of these words, they simply mean that among many other things that God has willed, sanctification is one—it is something in accordance with His will. This thought contains teaching of great value. God very distinctly and definitely has willed your sanctification, and your sanctification has its source and certainty in its being God's will. We are "elect in sanctification of the Spirit" (1 Pet. 1:2), "chosen to be holy" (Eph. 1:4)—the purpose of God's will from eternity, and His will now, our sanctification. We have only to think of what we said, of God's will being a divine power that works out what His wisdom has chosen, to see what strength this truth will give to our faith that we shall be holy: God wills it and will work it out for all and in all who do not resist it but yield themselves to its power. Seek your sanctification, not only in the will of God, as a declaration of what He wants you to be, but as a revelation of what He Himself will work out in you.

There is, however, another most precious thought suggested. If our sanctification is God's will, its central thought and its contents, *every part of that will* must bear upon it, and the sure entrance to sanctification, will be the hearty acceptance of the will of God in all things. To be one with God's will is to be holy. Let him who desires to be holy take his place there and "stand in all the will of God" (Col. 4:12). He will there meet God Himself and be made partaker of His holiness, because His will works out its purpose in power to each one who yields himself to it. Everything in a life of holiness depends on our being in the right relation to the will of God.

> *Seek your sanctification, not only in the will of God, as a declaration of what He wants you to be, but as a revelation of what He Himself will work out in you.*

There are many Christians to whom it appears impossible to think of their accepting all the will of God, or of their being one with it. They look at the will of God in its thousand commands and its numberless providential orderings. They have sometimes found it so hard to obey one single command or to give up willingly to some light disappointment. They imagine that they would need to be a thousandfold holier and stronger in grace before venturing to say that they do accept all God's will, whether to do or to endure. They cannot understand that all the difficulty comes from their not occupying the right standpoint. They are looking at God's will as at odds with their natural will, and they feel that that natural will shall never delight in all God's will. They forget that the new man has a renewed will. This new will delights in the will of God, because it is born of it. This new will sees the beauty and the glory of God's will, and is in harmony with it. If they are indeed God's children, the very first impulse of the spirit of a child is surely to do the will of the Father in heaven. And they need only yield themselves heartily and wholly to this spirit of sonship, and then they need not fear to accept God's will as theirs.

The mistake they make is a very serious one. Instead of living by faith, they judge by feeling, in which the old nature speaks and rules. It tells them that God's will is often a burden too hard to be borne, and that they never can have the strength to do it. Faith speaks differently. It reminds us that God is love, and that His will is nothing but Love revealed. It asks if we do not know that there is nothing more perfect or beautiful in heaven or earth than the will of God. It shows us how in our conversion we have already professed to accept God as Father and Lord. It assures us, above all, that if we will just definitely and trustingly give ourselves to that will which is love, it will as love fill our hearts and make us delight in it, and so become the power that enables us joyfully to do and to bear. Faith reveals to us that the will of God is the power of His love, working out its plan in divine beauty in each one who wholly yields to it.

And which shall we now choose? And where shall we take our place? Shall we attempt to accept Christ as a Savior without accepting His will? Shall we profess to be the Father's children, and yet spend our life in debating how much of His will we shall perform? Shall we be content to go on from day to day with the painful consciousness that our will is not in harmony with God's will? Or shall we not now and forever give up our will as sinful to His—to that will that He has already written on our heart? This is a thing that is possible. It can be done. In a simple, definite transaction with God, we can say that we do accept His holy will to be ours. Faith knows that God will not pass such a surrender unnoticed but will accept it. In the trust that He now takes us up into His will and undertakes to breathe it into us, with the love and the power to perform it—in this faith let us enter into God's will and begin a new life, standing in, abiding in the very center of this most holy will.

> *aith reveals to us that the will of God is the power of His love, working out its plan in divine beauty in each one who wholly yields to it.*

Such an acceptance of God's will prepares the believer, through the Holy Spirit, to recognize and know that will in whatever form it comes. The great difference between the carnal and the spiritual Christian is that the latter acknowledges God, under whatever low and poor and human appearances He manifests Himself. When God comes in trials that can be traced to no hand but His, he says, "Your will be done." When trials come through the weakness of men or his own folly, when circumstances appear unfavorable to his religious progress and temptations threaten to be too much for him and to overcome him, he learns first of all to see God in everything, and still to say, "Your will be done." He knows that a child of God cannot possibly be in any situation without the will of his Heavenly Father, even when that will has been to leave him to his own willfulness for a time, or to suffer the consequences of his own or others' sin. He sees this, and in accepting his circumstances as the will of God to try and prove him, he is in the right position for now knowing and doing what is right. Seeing and honoring God's will this way in everything, he learns always to abide in that will.

He does so also by doing that will. As his spiritual discernment grows to say of whatever happens, "All things are of God," so he grows too in wisdom and spiritual understanding to know the will of God as it is to be done. In the indications of conscience and of providence, in the teaching of the Word and the Spirit, he learns to see how God's will has reference to every part and duty of life, and it becomes his joy, in all things, to live, "doing the will of God from the heart...as to the Lord, and not to men" (Eph. 6:6, 7). "Laboring fervently in prayer to stand perfect and complete in all the will of God" (see Col. 4:12), he finds how blessedly the Father has accepted his surrender and supplies all the light and strength that is needed so that His will may be done by him on earth as it is in heaven.

Let me ask every reader to say to a holy God whether he has indeed given himself to Him to be made holy? Whether he has accepted, has entered into, and is living in the good and perfect will of God? The question is not whether when affliction comes he accepts the inevitable and submits to a will he cannot resist, but whether he has chosen the will of God as his chief good and has taken the life-principle of Christ to be his: "I delight to do Your will, O my God" (Ps. 40:8). This was the holiness of Christ, in which He sanctified Himself and us: the doing God's will. "By that will we have been sanctified." It is this will of God that is our sanctification.

> *This was the holiness of Christ, in which He sanctified Himself and us: the doing God's will. "By that will we have been sanctified." It is this will of God that is our sanctification.*

Brother! Are you in earnest to be holy? Wholly possessed of God? Here is the path. I plead with you not to be afraid or to hold back. You have taken God to be your God, but have you really taken His will to be your will? Oh, think of the privilege, the blessedness, of having one will with God! And fear not to surrender yourself to it most unreservedly. The will of God is, in every part of it and in all its divine power, your sanctification.

BE HOLY, AS I AM HOLY

Blessed Father! I come to say that I see that Your will is my sanctification, and there alone I would seek it. Graciously grant that by Your Holy Spirit who dwells in me, the glory of that will, and the blessedness of abiding in it, may be fully revealed to me.

Teach me to know it as the will of love, purposing always what is the very best and most blessed for Your child. Teach me to know it as the will of omnipotence, able to work out its every counsel in me. Teach me to know it in Christ, fulfilled perfectly on my behalf. Teach me to know it as what the Spirit wills and works in each one who yields to Him.

O my Father! I acknowledge Your claim to have Your will alone done, and I am here for it to do with me as You please. With my whole heart I enter into it, to be one with it forever. Your Holy Spirit can maintain this oneness without interruption. I trust You, my Father, step by step, to let the light of Your will shine in my heart and on my path, through that Spirit. May this be the holiness in which I live so that I forget and lose self in pleasing and honoring You. Amen.

FOR FURTHER THOUGHT

1. *What must you do to fully live in the will of God? Make it a study, in meditation and prayer and worship, to get a full impression of the majesty, the perfection, the glory of the will of God, with the privilege and possibility of living in it.*

2. *Study it, too, as the expression of an infinite love and fatherliness; its every manifestation full of lovingkindness. Every providence is God's will; whatever happens, meet God in it in humble worship. Every precept is God's will; meet God in it with loving obedience. Every promise is God's will; meet God in it with full trust. A life in the will of God is rest and strength and blessing.*

3. *And don't forget, above all, to believe in its omnipotent power. He works all things according the counsel of His will (Eph. 1:11). In nature and those who resist Him, without their consent. In His children, according to their faith, and as far as they will it. Do believe that the will of God will work out its counsel in you, as you trust it to do so.*

4. *This will is infinite benevolence and charitableness revealed in the self-sacrifice of Jesus. Live for others. So can you become an instrument for the divine will to use (Matt. 18:14, John 6:39–40). Yield yourselves to this redeeming will of God so that it may get full possession and work out through you too its saving purpose. Have you asked God how you can live for others?*

5. *What is the true definition of a Christian when it comes to being submitted to God's will? Christ is just the embodiment of God's will: He is God's will done. Abide in Him, by abiding in, by doing heartily and always, the will of God. A Christian is, like Christ, a man given up to the will of God.*

DAY 27

HOLINESS AND SERVICE

Therefore if anyone cleanses himself from the latter,
he will be a vessel for honor, sanctified and useful
for the Master, prepared for every good work.
2 TIMOTHY 2:21

A holy priesthood, to offer up spiritual sacrifices . . . .
a holy nation, His own special people, that you may
proclaim the praises of Him who called you out of
darkness into His marvelous light.
1 PETER 2:5, 9

THROUGH the whole of scripture we have seen that whatever God sanctifies is to be used in the service of His holiness. His holiness is an infinite energy that only finds its rest in making holy. To the revelation of what He is in Himself, "I, the Lord, *am holy*," God continually adds the declaration of what He does: "I am the Lord who *makes holy!*"

Holiness is a burning fire that extends itself, that seeks to consume what is unholy, and that communicates its own blessedness to all who will receive it. Holiness and selfishness, holiness and inactivity, holiness and laziness, holiness and helplessness, are utterly irreconcilable. Whatever we read of as holy was taken into the service of the holiness of God.

Let us just look back on the revelation of what is holy in scripture. The seventh day was made holy, so that in it God might make His people holy. The tabernacle was holy, to serve as a dwelling for the Holy One, as the center from where His holiness might reveal itself to the people. The altar was most holy, so that it might sanctify the gifts laid on it. The priests with their garments, the house with its furniture and vessels, the sacrifices and the blood—whatever bore the name of holy had a use and a purpose. Of Israel, whom God redeemed from Egypt that they might be a *holy* nation, God said, "Let My people go, that they may *serve* Me" (Exod. 9:1). The holy angels, the holy prophets and apostles, the holy scriptures— all bore the title as having been sanctified for the service of God.

Our Lord speaks of Himself "as Him whom the Father *sanctified and sent* into the world" (John 10:36). And when He says, "I sanctify Myself," He adds at once the purpose: it is in the service of the Father and His redeemed ones—"that they also may be sanctified by the truth" (John 17:19).

And can it be thought possible, now that God, in Christ the Holy One, and in the Holy Spirit, is accomplishing His purpose and gathering a people of saints, "holy ones," "made holy in Christ," that now holiness and service would be separated? Impossible! Here first we shall fully realize how essential they are to each other. Let us try to grasp their mutual relationship. We are only made holy that we may serve. We can only serve as we are holy.

> *H*oliness and selfishness, holiness and inactivity, holiness and laziness, holiness and helplessness, are utterly irreconcilable.

Holiness is essential to effective service. In the Old Testament we see degrees of holiness, not only in the holy places, but as much in the holy persons. In the nation, the Levites, the priests, and then the high priest, there is an advance from step to step: As in each succeeding stage the circle narrows and the service is more direct and entire, so the holiness required is higher and more distinct. It is even so in this more spiritual dispensation: the more of holiness, the greater the fitness for service. The more there is of true holiness, the more there is of God, and the more true and deep is the entrance He has had into the soul. The hold He has on the soul to use it in His service is more complete.

In the Church of Christ there is a vast amount of work done that yields very little fruit. Many throw themselves into work in whom there is but little true holiness, little of the Holy Spirit. They often work most diligently and, as far as human influence is concerned, most successfully. And yet true spiritual results in the building up of a holy temple in the Lord are but few. The Lord cannot work in them because He does not have the mastery of their inner life. His personal indwelling and fellowship, the rest of His holy presence, His holiness reigning and ruling in the heart and life—to all these they are comparative strangers.

It has been rightly said that work is the cure for spiritual poverty and disease. To some believers who had been seeking holiness apart from service, the call to work has been an unspeakable blessing. But to many, it has only been an additional blind to cover up the terrible lack of heart-holiness and heart-fellowship with the living God. They have thrown themselves into work more earnestly than ever, and yet do not have in their heart the rest-giving and refreshing witness that their work is acceptable and accepted.

My brother! Listen to the message. "Therefore if anyone *cleanses* himself from the latter, he will be a vessel for honor, *sanctified* and *useful* for the Master, *prepared* for every good work" (2 Tim. 2:21). You cannot have the law of service more clearly or beautifully laid down. A vessel of honor, one whom the King will delight to honor, must be a vessel cleansed from all defilement of flesh and spirit. Then only can it be a sanctified vessel, possessed and indwelt by God's Holy Spirit. So it becomes fit for the Master's use. He can use it, work in it, and wield it. And so, clean and holy and yielded into the Master's hands, we are divinely prepared for every good work. Holiness is essential to service.

If service is to be acceptable to God, effective for its work on souls, and to be a joy and a strength to ourselves, we must be holy. The will of God must first live in us if it is to be done by us. How many faithful workers there are, mourning the lack of power, longing and praying for it, and yet not obtaining it! They have spent their strength more in the outer court of work and service than in the inner life of fellowship and faith. They truly have never understood that only as the Master gets possession of them, as the Holy Spirit has them at His disposal, can He use them, can they have true power. They often long and cry for what they call a baptism of power. They forget that the way to have God's power in us is for ourselves to be in His power.

Put yourself into the power of God. Let His holy will live in you. Live in it and in obedience to it, as one who has no power to dispose of himself. Let the Holy Spirit dwell within, as in His holy temple, revealing the Holy One on the throne, ruling all. Then He will without fail use you as a vessel of honor, sanctified and fit for the Master's use. Holiness is essential to effectual service.

> The more there is of true holiness, the more there is of God, and the more true and deep is the entrance He has had into the soul.

And service is no less essential to true holiness. We have repeated it so often: Holiness is an energy, an intense energy of desire and self-sacrifice, to make others partakers of its own purity and perfection. Christ sacrificed Himself—in what did that sacrifice consist, and what was its aim? He sanctified Himself so that we might be sanctified too.

A holiness that is selfish is a delusion. True holiness, God's holiness in us, works itself out in love, in seeking and loving the unholy so that they may become holy too. Self-sacrificing love is of the very essence of holiness. The Holy One of Israel is its redeemer. The Holy One of God is the dying Savior. The Holy Spirit of God makes holy. There is no holiness in God but what is most actively engaged in loving and saving and blessing. It must be so in us too.

Let every thought of holiness, every act of faith or prayer, every effort in pursuit of it, be animated by the desire and the surrender to the holiness of God for use in the attaining of its object. Let your whole life be one distinctly and definitely given up to God for His use and service. Your circumstances may appear to be unfavorable. God may appear to keep the door closed against your working for Him in the way you would wish, and then your sense of unfitness may be painful. Still, let it be a matter settled between God and the soul that your longing for holiness is that you may be fitter for Him to use, and that what He has given you of His holiness in Christ and the Spirit is all at His disposal, waiting to be used. Be ready for Him to use. Live out, in a daily life of humble, self-denying, loving service of others, what grace you have received. You will find that in the union and interchange of worship and work, God's holiness will rest on you.

"The Father *sanctified* the Son, and *sent* Him into the world." The world is the place for the sanctified one, to be its light, its salt, its life. We are "sanctified in Christ Jesus" (1 Cor. 1:2) and sent into the world too. Oh, let us not fear to accept our position—our double position: in the world and in Christ! In the world, with its sin and sorrow, with its thousands of needs touching us at every point, and its millions of souls all waiting for us. And in Christ too. For the sake of that world, we "have been sanctified in Christ," we are "holy in Christ," we have "the spirit of sanctification" dwelling in us.

> *Put yourself into the power of God. Let His holy will live in you. Live in it and in obedience to it, as one who has no power to dispose of himself.*

As a holy salt in a sinful world, let us give ourselves to our holy calling. Let us come nearer and nearer to God who has called us. Let us root deeper and deeper in Christ our sanctification, in whom we are of God. Let us enter more firmly and more fully into that faith in Him in whom we are, by which our whole life will be covered and taken up in His. Let us ask the Father to teach us that His Holy Spirit does dwell in us every moment, making, if we live by faith, Christ with His holiness our home, our abode, our sure defense, and our infinite supply. As He who has called us is holy, let us be holy in His own Son, through His own Spirit, and then the fire of His holy love will work through us its work of judging and condemning, of saving and sanctifying. A sanctified soul God will use to save.

BE HOLY, AS I AM HOLY

Blessed Master! I thank You for reminding me anew of the purpose of Your redeeming love. You gave Yourself so that You might cleanse for Yourself a people of Your own, zealous in good works. You desire to make of each of us a vessel of honor, cleansed and sanctified, fit for Your use and prepared for every good work.

Blessed Lord! Write the lessons of Your Word deep in my heart. Teach me and all Your people that if we desire to work for You, if we desire to have You work in us and use us, we must be very holy, holy as God is holy. And that if we desire to be holy, we must be serving You. It is Your own Spirit, by which You sanctify us to use us, and sanctify in using. To be entirely possessed by You is the path to sanctity and service both.

Most holy Savior! We are in You as our sanctification, and in You we would abide. In the rest of a faith that trusts You for all, in the power of a surrender that would have no will but Yours, in a love that would lose itself to be wholly Yours, blessed Jesus, we do abide in You. In You we are holy, in You we shall bear much fruit. Oh, be pleased to perfect Your own work in us! Amen.

For Further Thought

1. *How do you think holiness should demonstrate itself in your life? It is difficult to make it clear in words how growth in holiness will simply reveal itself as an increasing simplicity and self-forgetfulness, accompanied by the restful and most blessed assurance that God has complete possession of us and will use us. We pass from the stage in which work presses as an obligation. Then it becomes the joy of fruit-bearing, faith's assurance that He is working out His will through us.*

2. *It has sometimes been said that people might be better employed in working for God than attending Holiness Conventions. This is surely a misunderstanding. It was before the throne of the Thrice Holy One, and as he heard the seraphim sing of God's holiness, that the prophet said, "Here am I; send me" (Isa. 6:8). Just as the mission of Moses, and Isaiah, and the Son, whom the Father sanctified and sent, each had its origin in the revelation of God's holiness, our missions will receive new power as they are more directly born out of the worship of God as the Holy One and baptized into the Spirit of Holiness.*

3. *What is God's two-way connection between doing His work and holiness? Let every worker take time to hear God's double call. If you desire to work, be very holy. If you desire to be holy, give yourself to God to use in His work.*

4. *What is the connection between "sanctified" and "fit for the Master's use?" True holiness is being possessed by God, and true service being used by God. How much service there is in which we are the chief agents, and ask God to help and to bless us. True service is being yielded up to the Master for Him to use. Then the Holy Spirit is the agent, and we are the instruments of His will. Such service is holiness.*

5. *"I sanctify Myself, that they also": a reference to others is the root principle of all true holiness.*

Day 28

The Way into the Holiest

*Therefore, brethren, having boldness to enter the Holiest
by the blood of Jesus, by a new and living way which He consecrated
for us, through the veil, that is, His flesh, and having a
High Priest over the house of God, let us draw near
with a true heart in full assurance of faith.*
HEBREWS 10:19–22

WHEN the high priest once a year entered into the second tabernacle within the veil, it was, we are told in the Epistle to the Hebrews, "the Holy Spirit indicating this, that the way into the holiest of all was not yet made manifest" (Heb. 9:8). When Christ died, the veil was torn, and all who were serving in the holy place had free access immediately into the most holy; the way into the holiest of all was opened up.

When the epistle passes over to its practical application (10:19), all its teaching is summed up in the words: "Therefore, brethren, having boldness to enter *the Holiest. . .*let us draw near." Christ's redemption has opened the way to the holiest of all, and our acceptance of it must lead to nothing less than our drawing near and entering in. The words of our text suggest to us four very precious thoughts in regard to the place of access, the right of access, the way of access, the power of access.

The place of access. Where are we invited to draw near? "Having boldness to enter into *the Holiest.*" The priests in Israel might enter the holy place, but they were always kept excluded from the holiest, God's immediate presence. The torn veil proclaimed liberty of access into that presence. It is there that believers as a royal priesthood are now to live and walk. Within the veil, in the very holiest of all, in the same place, the heavenlies, in which God dwells, in God's very presence, is to be our abode—our home.

Some speak as if the "Let us draw near" meant prayer, and that in our special approach to God in acts of worship we enter the holiest. No, for as great as this privilege is, God has meant something for us infinitely greater. We are to draw near and dwell always, to live our life and do our work within the sphere, the atmosphere, of the inner sanctuary. It is God's presence that makes holy ground. God's immediate presence in Christ makes any place the holiest of all, and this

511

is it into which we are to draw near and in which we are to abide. There is not a single moment of the day, not a circumstance or surrounding in which the believer may not be kept dwelling in the secret place of the Most High. As by faith he enters into the completeness of his reconciliation with God and into the reality of his oneness with Christ, as he in this way, abiding in Christ, yields to the Holy Spirit to reveal within the presence of the Holy One, the holiest of all is around him, he is indeed in it. With an uninterrupted access he draws near.[18]

The right of access. The thought comes up and the question is asked: Is this not simply an ideal? Can it be a reality, an experience in daily life to those who know how sinful their nature is? Blessed be God! It is meant to be. It is possible, because our right of access rests not in what we are, but in the blood of Jesus. "Having *boldness* to enter the Holiest *by the blood* of Jesus. . .let us draw near."

> *C*hrist's redemption has opened the way to the Holiest of all, and our acceptance of it must lead to nothing less than our drawing near and entering in.

In the Passover, we saw how redemption, and the holiness it aimed at, were dependent on the blood. In the sanctuary, God's dwelling, we know how in each part—the court, the holy place, the most holy—the sprinkling of blood was what alone secured access to God. And now that the blood of Jesus has been shed—oh, in what divine power, what intense reality, what everlasting efficacy, we now have access into the holiest of all, the most holy of God's heart and His love! We are indeed brought near by the blood. We have boldness to enter by the blood. "The worshipers, once purified, would have had no more consciousness of sins" (Heb. 10:2). Walking in the light, the blood of Jesus cleanses in the power of an endless life with a cleansing that never ceases. No consciousness of unworthiness or remaining sinfulness need hinder the boldness of access: the liberty to draw near rests in the never-failing, ever-acting, ever-living effectiveness of the precious blood. It is possible for a believer to dwell in the holiest of all.

The way of access. It is often thought that what is said of *the new and living way*, dedicated for us by Jesus, means nothing different from the boldness through His blood. This is not the case. The words mean a great deal more. "Having boldness. . .by the blood of Jesus, let us draw near by the way which He consecrated for us." That is, He opened for us a way to walk in, as He walked in it, "a new and living way. . .through the veil, that is, His flesh."

The way in which Christ walked when He gave His blood is the very same in which we must walk too. That way is the way of the Cross. There must not only be faith in Christ's sacrifice, but fellowship with Him in it. That way led to

[18] So near, so very near to God, I cannot nearer be; For in the person of His Son, I am as near as He.

the tearing of the veil of the flesh, and so through the torn veil of the flesh, in to God. And was the veil of Christ's holy flesh torn so that the veil of our sinful flesh might be spared? Truly, no. He meant us to walk in the very same way in which He did, following closely after Himself. He dedicated for us a new and living way through the veil, that is, His flesh. As we go in through the torn veil of *His flesh*, we find in it both the need and the power for our flesh being torn too. Following Jesus always means conformity to Jesus. It is Jesus with the torn flesh, in whom we are, in whom we walk.[19]

There is no way to God but through the tearing of the flesh. In acceptance of Christ's life and death by faith as the power that works in us, in the power of the Spirit that makes us truly one with Christ, we all follow Christ as He passes on through the torn veil, that is, His flesh, and become partakers with Him of His crucifixion and death. The way of the cross, "by which I have been crucified" (see Gal. 2:20), is the way through the torn veil. Man's destiny, fellowship with God in the power of the Holy Spirit, is only reached through the sacrifice of the flesh.

> *Walking in the light, the blood of Jesus cleanses in the power of an endless life with a cleansing that never ceases.*

And here we find now the solution of a great mystery—why so many Christians remain standing far off and never enter this holiest of all, why the holiness of God's presence is so little seen on them. They thought that it was only in Christ that the flesh needed to be torn, not in themselves. They thought that the liberty they had in the blood was the new and living way. They did not know that the way into true and full holiness, into the holiest of all, that the full entrance into the fellowship of the holiness of the great high priest, was only to be reached through the torn veil of the flesh, through conformity to the death of Jesus. This is in very deed the way He dedicated for us. He is Himself the way, and into His self-denial, His self-sacrifice, His crucifixion, He takes up all who long to be holy with His holiness, holy as He is holy.

The power of access. Does anyone shrink back from entering the very holiest for fear of this tearing of the flesh, because he doubts whether he could bear it, whether he could indeed walk in such a path? Let him listen once more. Hear what follows: "And *having a great priest* over the house of God, let us draw near." We have not only the holiest of all inviting us, and the blood giving us boldness, and the way through the torn veil consecrated for us, but the great priest over the house of God, the blessed living Savior, to draw, to help, and to welcome us. He is our Aaron. On His heart we see our name, because He only lives to think

---

[19] "Christ suffered...that He might bring us to God, being put to death in the flesh but made alive in the Spirit" (1 Pet. 3:18). "Therefore, since Christ suffered for us in the flesh, arm yourselves also with the same mind" (1 Pet. 4:1). The flesh and the Spirit are antagonistic: As the flesh dies, the Spirit lives.

of us and pray for us. On His forehead we see God's name, "Holy to the Lord," because in His holiness the sins of our holy things are covered. *In Him* we are accepted and sanctified: God receives us as holy ones. In the power of His love and His Spirit, in the power of Him the Holy One, in the joy of drawing nearer to Him and being drawn by Him, we gladly accept the way He has dedicated and walk in His holy footsteps of self-denial and self-sacrifice.

> *Man's destiny, fellowship with God in the power of the Holy Spirit, is only reached through the sacrifice of the flesh.*

We see how the flesh is the thick veil that separates from the Holy One who is a spirit, and it becomes an unceasing and most fervent prayer, that the crucifixion of the flesh may, in the power of the Holy Spirit, be in us a blessed reality. With the glory of the holiest of all shining out on us through the opened veil, and the precious blood speaking so loudly of boldness of access, and the Great Priest beckoning us with His loving presence to draw near and be blessed—with all this, we dare no longer fear, but choose the way of the torn veil as the path we love to tread, and give ourselves to enter in and dwell within the veil, in the very holiest of all.

And so our life here will be the earnest of the glory that is to come, as it is written—note how we have the four great thoughts of our text over again—"These are the ones who come out of the great tribulation," that is, by the way of the torn flesh; "and washed their robes and made them white in the blood of the Lamb," their boldness through the blood; "therefore they are before the throne of God," their dwelling in the holiest of all; "the Lamb who is in the midst of the throne will shepherd them," the great priest still the shepherd, Jesus Himself their all in all (see Rev. 7:14–17).

Brother! Do you see what holiness is and how it is to be found? It is not something placed within yourself? It is not something put on you from without? Holiness is the presence of God resting on you. Holiness comes as you consciously abide in that presence, doing all your work and living all your life as a sacrifice to Him, acceptable through Jesus Christ, sanctified by the Holy Ghost. Oh, no longer be fearful, as if this life were not for you! Look to Jesus! Having a great priest over the house of God, let us draw near. Be occupied with Jesus. Our Brother has charge of the temple, and He has liberty to show us all, to lead us into the secret of the Father's presence. The entire management of the temple has been given into His hands with this very purpose, that all the feeble and doubting ones might come with confidence. Only trust yourself to Jesus, to His leading and keeping. Only trust Jesus, God's Holy One, your Holy One. It is His delight to reveal to you what He has purchased with His blood. Trust Him to teach you the ordinances of the sanctuary. "That you may know how you ought to conduct yourself in the house of God" (1 Tim. 3:15), He has been given. *Having a great priest*, let us enter in, let us dwell in the holiest of all. In the power of the blood, in the power of the new and living way, in the power of the living Jesus, let the holiest of all, the presence of God, be the home of our soul. You are "Holy in Christ." In Christ you are in God's holy presence and love. Just stay there.

Be holy, for I am holy

Most holy God! How shall I praise You for the liberty to enter into the holiest of all and dwell there? And for the precious blood that brings us near? And for the new and living way, through the torn veil of that flesh, which had separated us from You, in which my flesh now too has been crucified? And for the great priest over the house of God, our living Lord Jesus, with Whom and in Whom we appear before You? Glory to Your holy name for this wonderful and most complete redemption.

> *H*aving a Great Priest over the house of God, let us draw near. Be occupied with Jesus. Our Brother has charge of the temple, and He has liberty to show us all, to lead us into the secret of the Father's presence.

I ask You, O my God, give me, and all Your children, some right sense of how really and surely we may live each day, may spend our whole life, within the veil, in Your own immediate presence. Give us the spirit of revelation, I ask You, that we may see how, through the torn veil, the glory of Your presence streams forth from the most holy into the holy place; how, in the pouring out of the Holy Spirit, the kingdom of heaven came to earth, and all who yield themselves to that Spirit may know that in Christ they are indeed so near, so very near to You. O Blessed Father! Let Your Spirit teach us that this indeed is the holy life—a life in Christ the Holy One, always in the light and the presence of Your holy majesty.

Most holy God! I draw near. In the power of the Holy Spirit I enter in. I am now in the holiest of all. And here I would abide in Jesus, my great priest—here, in the holiest of all. Amen.

FOR FURTHER THOUGHT

1. *What should be our response to knowing that you are "holy in Christ?" To abide in Christ is to dwell in the holiest of all. Christ is not only the sacrifice, and the way, and the great priest, but also Himself the temple, "The Lamb is the Temple" (Rev. 21:22). As the Holy Spirit reveals my union to Christ more clearly, and heart and will lose themselves in Him, I dwell in the holy presence, which is the holiest of all. You are "holy in Christ"—draw near, enter in with boldness and take possession—have no home but in the Holiest of all.*
2. *"Christ loved the Church, and gave Himself for her, that He might sanctify her" (Eph. 5:25–26). He gave Himself! Have you caught the force of that word? Do you grasp what it means to you? Because He would have no one else do it, because none could do it, to sanctify His Church, He gave Himself to do it. And so it is His own special beloved work to sanctify the Church He loved. Just accept Himself to do it. He can and will make you holy so that He may present you to Himself glorious, without spot or wrinkle. Let that word* Himself *live in you. The whole life and walk in the house of God is in His charge. Having a great priest, let us draw near.*
3. *What steps must you take to rest in the Father's presence? This entrance into the holiest of all—an ever-fresh and ever-deeper entrance—is, at the same time, an ever-blessed resting in the Father's presence. Faith in the blood, following in the way of the torn flesh, and fellowship with the living Jesus, are the three chief steps.*
4. *Enter into the holiest of all and dwell there. It will enter into you, and transform you, and dwell in you. And your heart will be the holiest of all, in which He dwells.*
5. *Have we not at times been lifted by an effort of thought and will, or in the fellowship of the saints, into what seemed the holiest of all, and speedily felt that the flesh had entered there too? It was because we did not enter by the new way of life—the way through death to life—the way of the torn veil of the flesh. O our crucified Lord! Teach us what this means. Give it to us. Be it Yourself to us.*
6. *Let me remember that my access into the holiest is as a priest. Let me dwell before the Lord all the day as an intercessor, offering, unceasingly, pleadings that are acceptable in Christ. May God's Church be like her of whom it is written, "this woman. . .did not depart from the temple, but served God with fastings and prayers night and day" (Luke 2:37). It is for this we have access to the holiest of all.*

Day 29

Holiness and Chastisement

For they indeed for a few days chastened us as seemed best to them,
but He for our profit, that we may be partakers of His holiness.
Pursue. . .holiness, without which no one will see the Lord.
Hebrews 12:10, 14

THERE is perhaps no part of God's word that sheds such divine light on suffering as the Epistle to the Hebrews. It does this because it teaches us what suffering was to the Son of God. It perfected His humanity. It so fitted Him for His work as the compassionate high priest. It proved that He, who had fulfilled God's will in suffering obedience, was indeed worthy to be its executor in glory, and to sit down on the right hand of the Majesty on high. "It was fitting for Him. . .in bringing many sons to glory, to make the captain of their salvation *perfect* through *sufferings*" (Heb. 2:10). "Though He was a Son, yet He *learned obedience* by the things which He *suffered*. And having been *perfected*, He became the author of eternal salvation to all who obey Him" (5:8–9). As He said Himself of His suffering, "I sanctify Myself," so we see here that His sufferings were indeed to Him the pathway to perfection and holiness.

What Christ was and won was all for us. The power that suffering was proved to have in Him to work out perfection, the power that He imparted to it in sanctifying Himself through suffering is the power of the new life that comes from Him to us. In the light of His example, we can see—in the faith of His power we too can prove—that suffering is to God's child the evidence of the Father's love and the channel of His richest blessing. To such faith, the apparent mystery of suffering is seen to be nothing but a divine need—the light affliction that works out—yes, *works out* and actually effects the exceeding weight of glory. We agree not only to what is written, "It *was fitting* for Him. . .to make the captain of their salvation perfect through sufferings," but understand somewhat how divinely becoming and fitting it is that we too should be sanctified by suffering.

"He chastens us for our profit, that we should be made partakers of His holiness." Of all the precious words holy scripture has for the sorrowful, there is hardly one that leads us more directly and more deeply into the fullness of blessing that suffering is meant to bring. It is *His holiness*, God's own holiness, we are to be made partakers of. The epistle had spoken very clearly of our sanctification from its divine side, as accomplished for us, and to be accomplished in us, by Jesus Himself. "He who sanctifies and those who are being sanctified are all of one" (Heb. 2:11). "We have been sanctified through the offering of the body of Jesus Christ" (10:10).

In our text we have the other side: the progressive work by which we are personally to accept and voluntarily to appropriate this divine holiness. In view of all there is in us that is at odds with God's will, and that must be discovered and broken down before we understand what it is to give up our will and delight in God's, in view of the personal fellowship of suffering that alone can lead to the full appreciation of what Jesus bore and did for us, and in view also of the full personal entrance into and satisfaction with the love of God as our sufficient portion—chastisement and suffering are indispensable elements in God's work of making holy. In these three aspects we shall see how what the Son needed is what we need, how what was of such unspeakable value to the Son will to us be no less rich in blessing.

> *As He said Himself of His suffering, "I sanctify Myself," so we see here that His sufferings were indeed to Him the pathway to perfection and holiness.*

Chastisement leads to the acceptance of God's will. We have seen how God's will is our sanctification, how it is in the will of God Christ has sanctified us, and, yes more, how He found the power to sanctify us in sanctifying Himself by the entire surrender of His will to God. His "I delight to do Your will" (Ps. 40:8) derived its worth from His continual "Not as I will" (Matt. 26:39). And wherever God comes with chastisement or suffering, the very first object He has in view is to ask and to work in us union with His own blessed will so that through it we may have union with Himself and His love. He comes in some one single point in which His will crosses our most cherished affection or desire and asks the surrender of what we desire to what He desires. When this is done willingly and lovingly, He leads the soul on to see how the claim for the sacrifice in the individual matter is the assertion of a principle—that in everything His will is to be our one desire. Happy is the soul to whom affliction is not a series of single acts of conflict and submission to single acts of His will, but an entrance into the school where we prove and approve all the good and perfect and acceptable will of God.

It has sometimes appeared, even to God's children, as if affliction were not a blessing. It so rouses the evil nature and calls forth all the opposition of the heart against God's will that it has brought the loss of the peace and the piety that once appeared to reign. Even in such cases, it is working out God's purpose. "To humble you and test you, to know what was in your heart" (Deut. 8:2) is still His object in leading into the wilderness. To an extent we are not aware of, our religion is often selfish and superficial, but when we accept the teaching of chastisement in discovering the self-will and love of the world that still prevails, we have learned one of its first and most necessary lessons.

This lesson has special difficulty when the trial does not come directly from God, but through men or circumstances. In looking at second causes, and in seeking for their removal, in the feeling of indignation or of grief, we often entirely forget to see God's will in everything His providence allows. As long as we do so, the chastisement is fruitless, and perhaps only hardens all the more. If, in our study of the pathway of holiness, there has been awakened in us the desire to accept and adore and stand complete in *all the will* of God, let us in the very first place seek to recognize that will in everything that comes our way. The sin of him who aggravates us is not God's will. But it is God's will that we should be in that position of difficulty to be tried and tested. Let our first thought be: This position of difficulty is my Father's will for me. I accept that will as my place now where He sees it fit to try me. Such acceptance of the trial is the way to turn it into blessing. It will lead on to an ever clearer abiding in all the will of God all the day.

> *Happy is the soul to whom affliction is not a series of single acts of conflict and submission to single acts of His will, but an entrance into the school where we prove and approve all the good and perfect and acceptable will of God.*

Chastisement leads to the fellowship of God's Son. The will of God out of Christ is a law we cannot fulfill. The will of God in Christ is a life that fills us. He came in the name of our fallen humanity and accepted all God's will as it rested on us, both in the demands of the law and in the consequences that sin had brought on man. He gave Himself entirely to God's will, whatever it cost Him. And so He paved for us a way through suffering, not only through it in the sense of past it and out of it, but by means and in virtue of it, into the love and glory of the Father. And it is in the power that Christ gives in fellowship with Himself that we too can love the way of the cross as the best and most blessed way to the crown.

Scripture says that the will of God is our sanctification, and also that Christ is our sanctification. It is only in Christ that we have the power to love and rejoice in the will of God. In Him we have the power. He became our sanctification once for all by delighting to do that will, and He becomes our sanctification in personal experience by teaching us to delight to do it. He learned to do it; He could not become perfect in doing it in any other way than by suffering. In suffering He draws near. He makes our suffering the fellowship of His suffering, and in it makes Himself, who was perfected through suffering, our sanctification.

O you suffering ones! All you whom the Father is chastening! Come and see Jesus suffering, giving up His will, being made perfect, sanctifying Himself. *His suffering is the secret of His holiness, of His glory, of His life.* Will you not thank God for anything that can admit you into the nearer fellowship of your blessed Lord? Shall we not accept every trial, great or small, as the call of His love to be one with Himself in living only for God's will. This is holiness: to be one with Jesus as He does the will of God, to abide in Jesus who was made perfect through suffering.

Chastisement leads to the enjoyment of God's love. Many a father has been surprised as he made his first experience of how a child, after being punished in love, began to cling to him more tenderly than before. Likewise, while to those who live at a distance from their Father, the misery in this world appears to be the one thing that shakes their faith in God's love, it is just through suffering that His children learn to know the reality of that love.

The chastening is so distinctly a father's prerogative, it leads so directly to the confession of its needfulness and its lovingness, it wakens so powerfully the longing for pardon and comfort and deliverance that it does indeed become, strange though this may seem, one of the surest guides into the deeper experience of the divine love. Chastening is the school in which the blessed lesson is learned that the will of God is all love, and that holiness is the fire of love, consuming that it may purify, destroying the dross only that it may assimilate into its own perfect purity all that yields itself to the wondrous change.

> The sin of him who aggravates us is not God's will. But it is God's will that we should be in that position of difficulty to be tried and tested.

"We have known and believed the love that God has for us. God is love, and he who abides in love abides in God, and God in him" (1 John 4:16). Man's destiny is fellowship with God, the fellowship, the mutual indwelling of love. It is only by faith that this love of God can be known. And faith can only grow by exercise, can only thrive in trial. When visible things fail, faith's energy is roused to yield itself to be possessed by the invisible, by the divine. Chastisement is the nurse of faith, one of its chosen attendants to lead deeper into the love of God. This is the new and living way, the way of the torn flesh in fellowship with Jesus leading up into the holiest of all. There it is seen how the justice that will not spare the child, and the love that sustains and sanctified it, are both one in the holiness of God.

O you chastened saints who are so specially being led in the way that goes through the torn veil of the flesh! You have boldness to enter in. Draw near. Come and dwell in the holiest of all. Make your home in the holiest of all, for there you are made partakers of *His* holiness. Chastisement is bringing your heart into unity with God's will, God's Son, God's love. Abide in God's will. Abide in God's Son. Abide in God's love. Dwell within the veil, in the holiest of all.

BE HOLY, AS I AM HOLY

Most holy God! Once again I bless You for the wondrous revelation of Your holiness. Not only have I heard You speak, "I am holy," but You have invited me to fellowship with Yourself: "Be holy, as I am holy." Blessed be Your name! I have heard more even: "I make holy," is Your word of promise, pledging Your own power to work out the purpose of Your love. I thank You for what You have revealed in Your Son, in Your Spirit, in Your Word, of the path of holiness. But how shall I bless You for the lesson of this day: that there is not a loss or sorrow, not a pain or care, not a temptation or trial, but Your love also means it and makes it to be a help in working out the holiness of Your people? Through each, You draw to Yourself so that they may taste how, in accepting Your will of love, there is blessing and deliverance.

Blessed Father! You know how often I have looked at the circumstances and the difficulties of this life as hindrances. Oh, let them all, in the light of Your holy purpose to make us partakers of Your holiness, in the light of Your will and Your love, from this hour be helps. Let, above all, the path of Your blessed Son, proving how suffering is the discipline of a Father's love, surrender the secret of holiness, and sacrifice the entrance to the holiest of all, be so revealed that in the power of His Spirit and His grace that path may become mine. Let even chastening, even the least, be from Your own hand, making me partaker of Your holiness. Amen.

FOR FURTHER THOUGHT

1. *What is God's ultimate goal in allowing—even causing—suffering into your life? How wonderful the revelation in the Epistle to the Hebrews of the holiness and the holy-making power of suffering, as seen in the Son of God! "He learned obedience by the things which He suffered" (Heb. 5:8). "It was fitting for Him to make the captain of our salvation perfect through suffering, for both He who sanctifies and they who are sanctified are all of one" (2:10–11). "In that He Himself has suffered, He is able to aid" (10:18). "We see Jesus. . .for the suffering of death crowned with glory and honor" (2:9). Suffering is the way of the torn veil, the new and living way Jesus walked in and opened for us. Let all sufferers study this. Let all who are "holy in Christ" here learn to know the Christ in whom they are holy, and the way in which He sanctified Himself and sanctifies us.*

2. *How can suffering affect and grow your relationship with Jesus Christ? If we begin by realizing the sympathy of Jesus with us in our suffering, it will lead*

us on to what is more: sympathy with Jesus in His suffering, fellowship with Him to suffer even as He did.

3. How does God use suffering to bring about your holiness? Let suffering and holiness be inseparably linked, as in God's mind and in Christ's person, so in your life through the Spirit. "It was fitting for Him to make the captain of our salvation perfect through suffering, for both He who sanctifies and they who are sanctified are all of one" Let every trial, small or great, be the touch of God's hand, laying hold on you to lead you to holiness. Give yourself into that hand.

4. "Rejoice to the extent that you partake of Christ's sufferings. . .for the Spirit of glory and of God rests upon you" (1 Pet. 4:13–14).

DAY 30

THE ANOINTING FROM
THE HOLY ONE

But you have an anointing from the Holy One,
and you know all things. . . . But the anointing which you have
received from Him abides in you, and you do not need that anyone
teach you; but as the same anointing teaches you concerning all
things, and is true, and is not a lie, and just as it has
taught you, you will abide in Him.
1 JOHN 2:20, 27

IN the revelation by Moses of God's holiness and His way of making holy, the priests, and especially the high priests, were the chief expression of God's holiness in man. In the priests themselves, the holy anointing oil was the one great symbol of the grace that made holy. Moses was to make a holy anointing oil: "And you shall take. . .some of the anointing oil, and sprinkle it on Aaron and. . .on his sons. . .and he. . .shall be hallowed, and his sons with him" (Exod. 29:21). "It shall be a holy anointing oil. . . . It shall not be poured on man's flesh; nor shall you make any other like it, according to its composition. It is holy, and it shall be holy to you" (Exod. 30:25, 32). With this the priests, and specially the high priests, were to be anointed and consecrated: "He who is the high priest among his brethren, on whose head the anointing oil was poured. . . shall not go out of the sanctuary, nor profane the sanctuary of his God; for the consecration of the anointing oil of his God is upon him" (Lev. 21:10, 12). And even so it is said of David, as type of the Messiah, "Our king *to the Holy One of Israel*. . .I have found My servant David; with My *holy oil* I have anointed him" (Ps. 89:18, 20).

We know how the Hebrew name *Messiah*, and the Greek *Christ*, has reference to this. So, in the passage just quoted, the Hebrew is, "with My holy oil I have *messiahed* him." And so in a passage like Acts 10:38, "How God *christed* Jesus of Nazareth with the Holy Spirit and with power." Or Psalm 45:7, "Your God has *messiahed* You with the oil of gladness more than Your companions." Or Hebrews 1:9, "God, Your God, has *christed* You with the oil of gladness." And so (as one of our Reformed Catechisms, the Heidelberg, has it, in answer to the question, Why are you called a Christian?) we are called Christians, because we are fellow-partakers with Him of His christing, His anointing. This is the anointing of which John speaks, the *chrisma* or christing of the Holy One. The Holy Spirit is the holy anointing that every believer receives: What God did to His Son to make Him the Christ, He does to me to make me a Christian. "You have the anointing from the Holy One."

1. *You have an anointing from the Holy One.* It is as the Holy One that the Father gives the anointing, and that with which He anoints is called the oil of holiness, the Holy Spirit. Holiness is indeed a divine ointment. Just as there is nothing so subtle and penetrating as the odor with which the ointment fills a house, so holiness is an indescribable, all-pervading breath of heavenliness that pervades the man on whom the anointing rests. Holiness does not consist in certain actions: This is righteousness. Holiness is the unseen and yet manifest presence of the Holy One resting on His anointed. Direct from the Holy One, the anointing is alone received, or rather, only in the abiding fellowship with Him in Christ, who is the Holy One of God.

> *The Holy Spirit is the holy anointing that every believer receives: What God did to His Son to make Him the Christ, He does to me to make me a Christian.*

And who receives it? Only he who has given himself entirely to be holy as God is holy. It was the priest who was separated to be holy to the Lord, who received the anointing. On other men's flesh it was not to be poured. How many would desire to have the precious ointment for the sake of its perfume to themselves! No, only he who is wholly consecrated to the service of the Holy One, to the work of the sanctuary, may receive it. If anyone had said: "I would desire to have the anointing but not be made a priest, for I am not ready to go and always be at the call of sinners seeking their God," he could have no share in it. Holiness is the energy that only lives to make holy and to bless in so doing. The anointing of the Holy One is for the priest, the servant of God Most High. It is only in the intensity of a soul truly roused and given up to God's glory, God's kingdom, and God's work that holiness becomes a reality. The holy garments were only prepared for priests and their service. In all our seeking after holiness, let us remember this. As we are careful of the error of thinking that work for Christ will make holy, let us also watch against the other, the straining after holiness without work. It is the priest who is set apart for the service of the holy place and the Holy One, it is the believer who is ready to live and die so that the holiness of God may triumph among men around him, who will receive the anointing.

2. *"The anointing teaches you."* The new man is created in *knowledge*, as well as in

righteousness and holiness. Christ is made for us *wisdom*, as well as righteousness and sanctification. God's service and our holiness are above all to be a free and full, an intelligent and most willing approval of His blessed will. And so the anointing, to make us fit for the service of the sanctuary, teaches us to know all things. Just as the perfume of the ointment is the most subtle essence, something that has never yet been found or felt, except as it is smelled, so the spiritual faculty that the anointing gives is the most subtle there can be. It makes "of quick understanding in the fear of the LORD" (Isa. 11:3). It teaches us by a divine instinct, by which the anointed one recognizes what has the heavenly fragrance in it and what is of earth. It is the anointing that makes the Word and the name of Jesus in the Word to be indeed as ointment poured forth.

The great mark of the anointing is, therefore, teachableness. It is the great mark of Christ, the Holy One of God, the Anointed One, that He listens: "I do not speak on My own authority; as I hear, so I speak" (John 14:10). And so it is of the Holy Spirit too: "He will not speak on His own authority, but whatever He hears He will speak" (John 16:13). It cannot be otherwise, for one anointed with the anointing of this Christ, with this Holy Spirit, will be teachable, will listen to be taught. "The anointing teaches." "And you do not need that anyone teach you; but the anointing teaches you concerning all things." "They shall be all taught by God" (John 6:45) includes every believer.

> *I*t is the anointing that makes the Word and the name of Jesus in the Word to be indeed as ointment poured forth.

The secret of true holiness is a very direct and personal relationship to the Holy One: all the teaching through the word or men made entirely dependent on and subordinate to the personal teaching of the Holy Spirit. The teaching comes through the anointing. Not, in the first place, in the thoughts or feelings, but in that all-pervading fragrance that comes from the fresh oil having penetrated the whole inner man.

3. *"The anointing abides in you." "In you."* In the spiritual life, it is of deep importance always to maintain the harmony between the objective and the subjective: God in Christ above me, God in the Spirit within me. In us, not as in a locality, but in us, as one with us, entering into the most secret part of our being and pervading all, dwelling in our very body, the anointing abides *in us*, forming part of our very selves. And this just in proportion to how we know it and yield ourselves to it, as we wait and are still to let the secret fragrance permeate our whole being. And this, again, not interruptedly, but as a continuous and unvarying experience.

Above circumstances and feelings, "the anointing abides." Not, indeed, as a fixed state or as something in our own possession, but according to the law of the new life, in the dependence of faith on the Holy One, and in the fellowship of Jesus. "I am anointed with fresh oil"—this is the objective side; every new morning the believer waits for the renewal of the divine gift from the Father. "The anointing abides in you"—this is the subjective side; the holy life, the life of faith and fellowship, the anointing, is always, from moment to moment, a spiritual reality. The holy anointing oil, always fresh, the anointing abiding always, is the secret of holiness.

> *In Christ, the unseen holiness of God was set before us and brought near. It became human, clothed in a human nature so that it might be communicated to us.*

4. *"And just as it has taught you, you will abide in Him."* Here we have again the Holy Trinity: the Holy One, from whom the holy anointing comes; the Holy Spirit, who is Himself the anointing; and Christ, the Holy One of God, in whom the anointing teaches us to abide. In Christ, the unseen holiness of God was set before us and brought near. It became human, clothed in a human nature so that it might be communicated to us. Within us dwells and works the Holy Spirit, drawing us out to the Christ of God, uniting us in heart and will to Him, revealing Him, and forming Him within us so that His likeness and mind are embodied in us. This is how we abide in Christ, for the holy anointing of the Holy One teaches it to us. It is this that is the test of the true anointing: abiding in Christ, as He meant it, becomes truth in us. Here is the life of holiness as the Thrice Holy gives it: the Father, the first, the Holy One, making holy; the Son, the second, His Holy One, in whom we are; the Spirit, the third, who dwells in us, and through whom we abide in Christ and Christ in us. This is how the Thrice Holy makes us holy.

Let us study the divine anointing. It comes from the Holy One. There is no other like it. It is God's way of making us holy—His holy priests. It is God's way of making us partakers of holiness in Christ. The anointing, received from Him day by day, abiding in us, teaching us all things, especially teaching us to abide in Christ, must be on us every day. Its subtle, all-pervading power must go through our whole life. The odor of the ointment must fill the house. Blessed be God, it can do so! The anointing that abides makes the abiding in Christ a reality and a certainty. And God Himself, the Holy One, makes the abiding anointing a reality and a certainty too. To His holy name is the praise!

BE HOLY, FOR I AM HOLY

My God, who is the Holy One, I come to You now for the renewed anointing.

O Father! This is the one gift Your child may most surely count on—the gift of Your Holy Spirit. Grant me now to sing, "You anoint my head" (Ps. 23:5); "I have been anointed with fresh oil" (Ps. 92:10).

I desire to confess with deep shame that Your Spirit has been sorely grieved and dishonored. How often the fleshly mind has usurped His place in Your worship! How much the fleshly will has sought to do His work! O my Father! Let Your light shine through me to convince me very deeply of this. Let Your judgment come on all that there is of human willing and running.

Blessed Father! Grant me, according to the riches of Your glory, even now to be strengthened with might by Your Spirit in the inner man. Strengthen my faith to believe in Christ for a full share in His anointing. Oh, teach me day by day to wait for and receive the anointing with fresh oil!

O my Father! Draw me and all Your children to see that for the abiding in Christ we need the abiding anointing. Father! We want to walk humbly, in the dependence of faith, counting on the inner and ever-abiding anointing. May we so be a sweet savor of Christ to all. Amen.

FOR FURTHER THOUGHT

1. *I think I know now the reason why at times we fail in the abiding. We think and read, we listen and pray, we try to believe and strive to look to Jesus only, and yet we fail. What was lacking was this: "His anointing teaches you; even as it taught you, abide in Him;" so far, and no farther.*

2. *What specifically must you do before you can have God's anointing? The washing always precedes the anointing. We cannot have the anointing if we fail in the cleaning. When cleaned and anointed, we are fit for use.*

3. *What steps can you take to have God's abiding anointing? Yield yourself wholly to be sanctified and made fit for the Master's use. Dwell in the holiest of all, in God's presence. Accept every chastisement as a fellowship in the way of the torn flesh. Be sure the anointing will flow in union with Jesus. "It is like the precious ointment upon the. . .head of Aaron. . .running down on the edge of his garments" (Ps. 133:2).*

4. *What will God's anointing accomplish in your spiritual life, in your relationship with Him? The anointing is the divine eye-salve, opening the eyes of the heart to know Jesus. So it teaches to abide in Him. I am sure most Christians have no idea of the danger and deceitfulness of a thought religion, with sweet and precious thoughts coming to us in books and preaching, and little power. The teaching of the Holy Spirit is in the heart first; man's teaching in the mind. Let all our thinking always lead us to cease from thought and to open the heart and will to the Spirit to teach there in His own divine way, deeper than thought and feeling. Unseen, within the veil, the Holy Spirit abides. Be silent and still, believe and expect, and cling to Jesus.*

5.   *Oh that God would visit His Church and teach His children what it is to wait for, to receive, and to walk in the full anointing, the anointing that abides and teaches to abide! Oh that the truth of the personal leading of the Holy Spirit in every believer were restored in the Church! He is doing it; He will do it.*

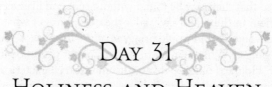

Day 31

Holiness and Heaven

Therefore, since all these things will be dissolved,
what manner of persons ought you to be
in holy conduct and godliness.
2 Peter 3:11

Pursue peace. . .and holiness,
without which no one will see the Lord.
Hebrews 12:14

He who is holy, let him be holy still. . . .
The grace of our Lord Jesus Christ be with you all. Amen.
Revelation 22:11, 21

O my brother, we are on our way to see God. We have been invited to meet the Holy One face to face. The infinite mystery of holiness, the glory of the invisible God, before which the seraphim veil their faces, is to be unveiled, to be revealed to us. And that not as a thing we are to look upon and to study. But we are to see the Thrice Holy One, the living God Himself. God, the Holy One, will show Himself to us: We are to see God. Oh, the infinite grace, the inconceivable blessedness! We are to see God.

We are to see God, the Holy One. And all our schooling here in the life of holiness is simply the preparation for that meeting and that vision. "Blessed are the pure in heart, for they shall see God" (Matt. 5:8). "Pursue. . .holiness, without which no one will see the Lord" (Heb. 12:14). Since the time when God said to Israel, "Be holy, as I am holy," holiness was revealed as the only meeting place between God and His people. To be holy was to be the common ground on which they were to stand with Him, the one attribute in which they were to be like God, the one thing that was to prepare them for the glorious time when He would no longer need to keep them away but would admit them to the full fellowship of His glory, to have the Word fulfilled in them: "He who is holy, let him be holy still."

In his second epistle, Peter reminds believers that the coming of the day of the

Lord is to be preceded and accompanied by the most tremendous catastrophe—the dissolution of the heavens and the earth. He makes it a plea with them to give diligence so that they may be found without spot and blameless in His sight. And he asks them to think and say, under the deep sense of what the coming of the day of God would be and would bring, what the life of those ought to be who look for such things: "What manner of persons ought you to be in holy conduct and godliness?" Holiness must be its one, its universal characteristic. At the close of our meditations on God's call to holiness, we may take Peter's question, and in the light of all that God has revealed of His holiness, and all that waits still to be revealed, ask ourselves, "What manner of persons ought we to be in holy conduct and godliness?"

We are to see God, the Holy One. And all our schooling here in the life of holiness is simply the preparation for that meeting and that vision.

Note first the meaning of the question. In the original Greek, the words *conduct* and *godliness* are plural. Alford says, "*In holy behaviors and pieties*; the plurals mark the holy behavior and piety *in all its forms and examples*." Peter would plead for a life of holiness pervading the whole man—in our behavior toward men and in our pieties toward God. True holiness cannot be found in anything less. Holiness must be the one, the universal characteristic of our Christian life. In God we have seen that holiness is the central attribute, the comprehensive expression for divine perfection, the attribute of all the attributes, the all-including label by which He Himself, as redeemer and Father, His Son and His Spirit, His day, His house, His law, His servants, His people, His name, are marked and known. Always and in everything, in judgment as in mercy, in His exaltation and His condescension, in His hiddenness and His revelation—always and in everything, God is the Holy One. And the Word would teach us that the reign of holiness, to be true and pleasing to God, must be supreme, must be in all holy living and godliness.

There must not be a moment of the day nor a relationship in life, there must be nothing in the outer conduct nor in the inmost recesses of the heart, there must be nothing belonging to us, whether in worship or in business, that is not holy. The holiness of Jesus, the holiness that comes of the Spirit's anointing, must cover and pervade all. Nothing, nothing may be excluded if we are to be holy. It must be as Peter said when he spoke of God's call—holy in all conduct; it must be as he says here: "in holy conduct and godliness." To use the significant language of the Holy Spirit: Everything must be done, "in a manner worthy of the holy ones," "as is fitting for holy ones" (Rom. 16:2, Eph. 5:3).

Note, too, the force of the question. Peter says, "Therefore, beloved, looking forward to these things" (2 Pet. 3:14). Yes, let us think what that means.

We have been studying, down through the course of Revelation, the wondrous grace and patience with which God has made known and made partaker of His holiness, all in preparation for what is to come. We have heard God, the Holy One, calling us, pleading with us, commanding us to be holy, as He is holy. And we expect to meet Him and to dwell through eternity in His light, holy as He is holy. It is not a dream; it is a living reality. We are looking forward to it as the only one thing that makes life worth living. We are looking forward to love to welcome us, as with the confidence of childlike love we come as His holy ones to cry, Holy Father!

> *he Word would teach us that the reign of holiness, to be true and pleasing to God, must be supreme, must be in all holy living and godliness.*

We have learned to know Jesus, the Holy One of God, our sanctification. We are living in Him, day by day, as those who are holy in Christ Jesus. We are drawing on His holiness without ceasing. We are walking in that will of God that He did, and that He enables us to do. And we are looking forward to meet Him with great joy, "when He comes, in that Day, to be glorified in His holy ones and to be admired among all those who believe" (2 Thess. 1:10). We have within us the Holy Spirit, the holiness of God in Christ come down to be at home within us, as the guarantee of our inheritance. He, the Spirit of Holiness, is secretly transforming us within, sanctifying our spirit, soul, and body, to be blameless at His coming, and making us fit for the inheritance of the holy ones in light. We are looking forward to the time when He shall have completed His work, when the body of Christ shall be perfected, and the bride, all filled and streaming with the life and glory of the Spirit within her, shall be set with Him on His throne, just as He sat with the Father on His throne. We hope through eternity to worship and adore the mystery of the Thrice Holy One. Even here it fills our souls with trembling joy and wonder. When God's work of making holy is complete, how we shall join in the song, "Holy, Holy, Holy, Lord God Almighty, the One who is and who was and who is to come!" (Rev. 11:17).

In preparation for all this, the most wonderful events are to take place. The Lord Jesus Himself is to appear, the power of sin and the world is to be destroyed. This visible system of things is to be broken up, and the power of the Spirit is to triumph through all creation. There is to be a new heaven and a new earth, in which dwells righteousness. And holiness is then to be unfolded in ever-growing blessedness and glory in the fellowship of the Thrice Holy: "He who is holy, let him be holy still." Surely it but needs the question to be put for each believer to feel and acknowledge its force: "Therefore, since all these things will be dissolved, what manner of persons ought you to be in holy conduct and godliness?"

And note now the need and the point of the question. "What manner of persons ought you to be?" But is such a question needed? Can it be that God's holy ones, made holy in Christ Jesus, with the very spirit of holiness dwelling with them, on the way to meet the Holy One in His glory and love—can it be that they need the question? How sad it is that what was so in the time of Peter is too much so in our days too! How sad it is how many Christians there are to whom the very word *holy*, though it be the name by which the Father, in His New Testament, loves to call His children more than any other, is strange and unintelligible. And again, how sad it is how many Christians there are for whom, when the word is heard, it has but little attraction, because it has never yet been shown to them as a life that is indeed possible, and unutterably blessed. And yet again, how sad it is how many there are, even workers in the Master's service, to whom the "all holy living and godliness" is yet a secret and a burden, because they have not yet consented to give up all, both their will and their work, for the Holy One to take and fill with His Holy Spirit. And yet once more, how sad it is that the cry comes, even from those who do know the power of a holy life, lamenting their unfaithfulness and unbelief as they see how much richer their entrance into the holy life might have been, how much fuller the blessing they still feel so unable to communicate to others. Oh, the question is needed! Shall not each of us take it, keep it, and answer it by the Holy Spirit through whom it came, and then pass it on to our brethren so that we and they may help each other in faith and live in joy and hope to give the answer our God would have?

We are looking forward to love to welcome us, as with the confidence of childlike love we come as His holy ones to cry, Holy Father!

"Therefore, since all these things will be dissolved, what manner of persons ought you to be in holy conduct and godliness?" Brethren, the time is short! The world is passing away. The sinners are perishing. Christians are sleeping. Satan is active and mighty. God's holy ones are the hope of the Church and the world. It is they their Lord can use. "What manner of persons shall we be in all holy conduct and godliness!" Shall we not seek to be such as the Father commands, "Holy, as He is holy"? Shall we not yield ourselves afresh and undividedly to Him who is our sanctification, and to His blessed Spirit, to make us holy in all behaviors and pieties? Oh, shall we not, in thought of the love of our Lord Jesus, in thought of the coming glory, in view of the coming end, of the need of the church and the world, give ourselves to be holy as He is holy, so that we may have power to bless each believer we meet with the message of what God will do, and that in concert with them we may be a light and a blessing to this perishing world?

I close with the closing words of God's blessed book: "He who testifies to these things says, 'Surely I am coming quickly.' Amen. Even so, come, Lord Jesus! The grace of our Lord Jesus Christ be with you all. Amen" (Rev. 22:20–21).

BE HOLY, AS I AM HOLY

Most holy God, who has called us to be holy, we have heard Your voice asking, What manner of persons ought we to be in all holy conduct and godliness? With our whole soul we answer in deep contrition and humility, holy Father! We ought to be so different from what we have been. In faith and love, in zeal and devotion, in Christlike humility and holiness. O Father! We have not been, before You and the world, what we ought to be, what we could be. Holy Father! We now pray for all who unite with us in this prayer and implore of You to grant a great revival of true holiness in us and in all Your Church. Visit, we ask You, visit all ministers of Your word, that in view of Your coming they may take up and sound abroad the question, What manner of persons ought you to be? Lay on them, and all Your people, such a burden surrounding unholiness and worldliness, that they may not cease to cry to You. Grant them such a vision of the highway of holiness, the new and living way in Christ, that they may preach Christ our sanctification in the power and the joy of the Holy Spirit, with the confident and triumphant voice of witnesses who rejoice in what You do for them. O God! Roll away the reproach of Your people so that their profession does not make them humbler or holier, more loving, and more heavenly than others.

O holy God! Give Yourself the answer to Your question and teach us and the world what manner of persons Your people can be, in the day of Your power, in the beauty of holiness. We bow our knees to You, O Father, that You would grant us, according to the riches of Your glory, to be mightily strengthened in the inner man by the Spirit of holiness. Amen.

FOR FURTHER THOUGHT

1. *What manner of men ought you to be in all holy conduct? That is a question God has written down for us. Might it not help us if we were to write down the answer and say how holy we think we ought to be? The dearer and more distinct our views are of what God wishes, of what He has made possible, of what in reality ought to be, the more definite our acts of confession, of surrender, and of faith can become.*

2. *How should you pray in order to receive God's outpouring of the Spirit of holiness? Let every believer who longs to be holy join in the daily prayer that God would visit His people with a great outpouring of the Spirit of Holiness. Pray without ceasing that every believer may live as a holy one.*

3. *On what should you focus in order to be the kind of Christian you should be*

in all holy living and godliness? "Therefore, beloved, looking forward to these things" (2 Pet. 3:14). Our life depends, in more than one sense, on what we look at. "We do not look at the things which are seen" (2 Cor. 4:18). It is only as we look at the invisible and spiritual and come under its power that we shall be what we ought to be in all holy living and godliness.

4.   Holy in Christ. Let this be our parting word. However strong the branch becomes, however far away it reaches around the home, out of sight of the vine, all its beauty and all its fruitfulness always depend on that one point of contact where it grows out of the vine. So be it with us too. All the outer circumference of my life has its center in the ego—the living, conscious "I myself," in which my being roots. And this "I" is rooted in Christ. Down in the depths of my inner life, there is Christ holding, bearing, guiding, quickening me into holiness and fruitfulness. In Him I am, in Him I will abide. His will and commands will I keep, His love and power will I trust. And I will daily seek to praise God that I am holy in Christ.

ABIDE IN CHRIST

Contents

Preface

DURING the life of Jesus on earth, the word He chiefly used when speaking of the relations of the disciples to Himself was: "*Follow Me*" (John 1:43, 21:19). When about to leave for heaven, He gave them a new word, in which their more intimate and spiritual union with Himself in glory should be expressed. That chosen word was: "*Abide in Me*" (John 15:4).

It is to be feared that there are many earnest followers of Jesus from whom the meaning of this word, with the blessed experience it promises, is very much hidden. While trusting in their Savior for pardon and for help, and seeking to some extent to obey Him, they have hardly realized to what closeness of union, to what intimacy of fellowship, to what wondrous oneness of life and interest, He invited them when He said, "Abide in Me." This is not only an unspeakable loss to themselves, but the Church and the world suffer in what they lose.

If we ask the reason why those who have indeed accepted the Savior and been made partakers of the renewing of the Holy Spirit thus come short of the full salvation prepared for them, I am sure the answer will in very many cases be that ignorance is the cause of the unbelief that fails of the inheritance. If, in our orthodox churches, the abiding in Christ, the living union with Him, the experience of His daily and hourly presence and keeping, were preached with the same distinctness and urgency as His atonement and pardon through His blood, I am confident that many would be found to accept with gladness the invitation to such a life, and that its influence would be manifest in their experience of the purity and the power, the love and the joy, the fruit-bearing and all the blessedness that the Savior connected with the abiding in Him.

It is with the desire to help those who have not yet fully understood what the Savior meant with His command, or who have feared that it was a life beyond their reach, that these meditations are now published. It is only by frequent repetition that a child learns its lessons. It is only by continuously fixing the mind for a time on some one of the lessons of faith that the believer is gradually helped to take and thoroughly assimilate them. I have the hope that to some, especially young believers, it will be a help to come and for a month day after day spell over the precious words, "Abide in Me," with the lessons connected with them in the parable of the vine. Step by step we shall get to see how truly this promise-precept is meant for us, how surely grace is provided to enable us to obey it, how indispensable the experience of its blessing is to a healthy Christian life, and how unspeakable the blessings are that flow from it. As we listen, and meditate, and pray—as we surrender ourselves, and accept in faith the whole Jesus as He offers Himself to us in it—the Holy Spirit will make the word to be spirit and life. Then, this word of Jesus, too, will become to us the power of God for salvation, and through it will come the faith that grasps the long desired blessing.

I pray earnestly that our gracious Lord may be pleased to bless this little book, to help those who seek to know Him fully, as He has already blessed it in its original issue in a different (the Dutch) language. I pray still more earnestly that He would, by whatever means, make the multitudes of His dear children who are still living divided lives to see how He claims them wholly for Himself, and how the wholehearted surrender to abide in Him alone brings the joy unspeakable and full of glory.

Oh, let each of us who has begun to taste the sweetness of this life yield himself wholly to be a witness to the grace and power of our Lord to keep us united with Himself, and seek by word and walk to win others to follow Him fully. It is only in such fruit-bearing that our own abiding can be maintained.

In conclusion, I ask to be permitted to give one word of advice to my reader. It is this. It *needs time* to grow into Jesus the vine. Do not expect to abide in Him unless you will give Him that time. It is not enough to read God's Word or meditations as here offered, and when we think we have hold of the thoughts and have asked God for His blessing, to go out in the hope that the blessing will abide. No, it needs day-by-day time with Jesus and with God. We all know the need of time for our meals each day—every worker claims his hour for dinner; the hurried eating of so much food is not enough. If we are to live through Jesus, we must feed on Him (John 6:57). We must thoroughly take in and assimilate that heavenly food the Father has given us in His life. Therefore, my brother, who would learn to abide in Jesus, take time each day, before you read, while you read, and after you read, to put yourself into living contact with the living Jesus, to yield yourself distinctly and consciously to His blessed influence. That his how you give Him the opportunity of taking hold of you, of drawing you up and keeping you safe in His almighty life.

And now, to all God's children whom He allows me the privilege of pointing to the heavenly vine, I offer my fraternal love and salutations, with the prayer that to each one of them may be given the rich and full experience of the blessedness of abiding in Christ. And may the grace of Jesus, and the love of God, and the fellowship of the Holy Spirit be their daily portion. Amen.

A. M.

1. *I am the true vine, and My Father is the vinedresser.*
2. *Every branch in Me that does not bear fruit He takes away; and every branch that bears fruit He prunes, that it may bear more fruit.*
3. *You are already clean because of the word which I have spoken to you.*
4. *Abide in Me, and I in you. As the branch cannot bear fruit of itself, unless it abides in the vine, neither can you, unless you abide in Me.*
5. *I am the vine, you are the branches. He who abides in Me, and I in him, bears much fruit; for without Me you can do nothing.*
6. *If anyone does not abide in Me, he is cast out as a branch and is withered; and they gather them and throw them into the fire, and they are burned.*
7. *If you abide in Me, and My words abide in you, you will ask what you desire, and it shall be done for you.*
8. *By this My Father is glorified, that you bear much fruit; so you will be My disciples.*
9. *As the Father loved Me, I also have loved you; abide in My love.*
10. *If you keep My commandments, you will abide in My love, just as I have kept My Father's commandments and abide in His love.*
11. *These things I have spoken to you, that My joy may remain in you, and that your joy may be full.*
12. *This is My commandment, that you love one another as I have loved you.*

Day 1
All You Who Have Come to Him

"Come to Me."
Matthew 11:28

"Abide in Me."
John 15:4

IT is to you who have heard and answered to the call, *"Come to Me,"* that this new invitation comes: *"Abide in Me."* The message comes from the same loving Savior. You doubtless have never regretted having come at His call. You experienced that His word was truth. All His promises He fulfilled, and He made you partakers of the blessings and the joy of His love. Was not His welcome most hearty, His pardon full and free, His love most sweet and precious? You more than once, at your first coming to Him, had reason to say, "The half was not told me."

And yet you have had to complain of disappointment. As time went on, your expectations were not realized. The blessings you once enjoyed were lost, and the love and joy of your first meeting with your Savior, instead of deepening, have become faint and weak. And often you have wondered what the reason could be, that with such a Savior, so mighty and so loving, your experience of salvation should not have been a fuller one.

The answer is very simple. You wandered from Him. The blessings He bestows are all connected with His "Come to *Me*," and are only to be enjoyed in close fellowship with Him. You either did not fully understand, or did not rightly remember, that the call meant, "Come to *Me* to stay with *Me*." And yet this was in very deed His object and purpose when first He called you to Himself. It was not to refresh you for a few short hours after your conversion with the joy of His love and deliverance, and then to send you off to wander in sadness and sin. He had destined you to something better than a short-lived blessedness to be enjoyed only in times of special earnestness and prayer, and then to pass away as you had to return to those duties in which far the greater part of life has to be spent.

No, indeed! He had prepared for you an abiding dwelling with Himself, where your whole life and every moment of it might be spent, where the work of your daily life might be done, and where all the while you might be enjoying unbroken communion with Himself. It was even this He meant when to that first word, "*Come to Me,*" He added this, "*Abide in me.*" As earnest and faithful, as loving and tender as was the compassion that breathed in that blessed "*Come*" was the grace that added this no less blessed "*Abide.*" As mighty as the attraction with which that first word drew you were the bonds with which this second, had you but listened to it, would have kept you. And as great as were the blessings with which that coming was rewarded, so large—yes, and much greater—were the treasures to which that abiding would have given you access.

And observe especially, it was not that He said, "Come to Me and abide with Me" but "*Abide in Me.*" The relationship was not only to be unbroken, but to remain most intimate and complete. He opened His arms to press you to His bosom, He opened His heart to welcome you there, He opened up all His divine fullness of life and love and offered to take you up into its fellowship, to make you wholly one with Himself. There was a depth of meaning you cannot yet realize in His words: "Abide in *Me.*"

> *he blessings He bestows are all connected with His "Come to Me," and are only to be enjoyed in close fellowship with Him.*

And with no less earnestness than He had cried, "Come to Me," did He plead, had you but noticed it, "*Abide in Me.*" By every motive that had induced you to come, did He ask you to abide. Was it the fear of sin and its curse that first drew you? The pardon you received on first coming could, with all the blessings flowing from it, only be confirmed and fully enjoyed on abiding in Him. Was it the longing to know and enjoy the infinite love that was calling you? The first coming gave but single drops to taste—it is only the abiding that can really satisfy the thirsty soul and give to drink of the rivers of pleasure that are at His right hand. Was it the weary longing to be made free from the bondage of sin, to become pure and holy, and so to find rest, the rest of God for the soul? This too can only be realized as you abide in Him—only abiding in Jesus gives rest in Him. Or if it was the hope of an inheritance in glory and an everlasting home in the presence of the Infinite One: The true preparation for this, as well as its blessed foretaste in this life, are granted only to those who abide in Him.

In very truth, there is nothing that moved you to come that does not plead with thousandfold greater force: "Abide in Him." You did well to come, but you do better to abide. Who would, after seeking the king's palace, be content to stand in the door, when he is invited in to dwell in the king's presence and share with Him in all the glory of His royal life? Oh, let us enter in and abide and enjoy to the full all the rich supply His wondrous love has prepared for us!

And yet I fear that there are many who have indeed come to Jesus, but who yet have sorrowfully to confess that they know but little of this blessed abiding in Him. With some, the reason is that they never fully understood that this was the meaning of the Savior's call. With others, that though they heard the word, they did not know that such a life of abiding fellowship was possible, and indeed within their reach. Others will say that though they did believe that such a life was possible, and seek after it, they have never yet succeeded in discovering the secret of its attainment. And others, again, sadly will confess that it is their own unfaithfulness that has kept them from the enjoyment of the blessing. When the Savior would have kept them, they were not found ready to stay. They were not prepared to give up everything and always, only, wholly to abide in Jesus.

To all such, I come now in the name of Jesus, their Redeemer and mine, with the blessed message: "*Abide in Me.*" In His name I invite them to come, and for a season meditate with me daily on its meaning, its lessons, its claims, and its promises. I know how many, and to the young believer, how difficult, the questions are that suggest themselves in connection with it. There is especially the question, with its various aspects, to the possibility, in the midst of wearying work and continual distraction, of keeping up—or rather being kept in—the abiding communion.

> *In very truth, there is nothing that moved you to come that does not plead with thousandfold greater force: "Abide in Him."*

I do not undertake to remove all difficulties—this Jesus Christ Himself alone must do by His Holy Spirit. But what I would desire by the grace of God to be permitted to do is to repeat day by day the Master's blessed command, "Abide in Me," until it enter the heart and find a place there, no more to be forgotten or neglected. I would desire that in the light of holy scripture we should meditate on its meaning until the understanding, that gate to the heart, opens to understand something of what it offers and expects. So we shall discover the means of its attainment and learn to know what keeps us from it—and what can help us to it. So we shall feel its claims and be compelled to acknowledge that there can be no true allegiance to our King without simply and heartily accepting this one, too, of His commands. So we shall gaze on its blessedness, until desire is inflamed and the will with all its energies is roused to claim and possess the unspeakable blessing.

Come, my brethren, and let us day by day set ourselves at His feet and meditate on this word of His, with an eye fixed on Him alone. Let us set ourselves in quiet trust before Him, waiting to hear His holy voice—the still small voice that is mightier than the storm that slits the rocks—breathing its quickening spirit within us, as He speaks: "Abide in Me." The soul that truly hears *Jesus Himself speak the word* receives with the word the power to accept and to hold the blessing He offers.

And it may please You, blessed Savior, indeed, to speak to us. Let each of us hear Your blessed voice. May the feeling of our deep need and the faith of Your wondrous love, combined with the sight of the wonderfully blessed life You are waiting to freely give us, move us to listen and to obey, as often as You speak: "Abide in Me." Let day by day the answer from our heart be clearer and fuller: "Blessed Savior, I do abide in You."

FOR FURTHER THOUGHT

1. *What is the condition for receiving the blessings connected with Jesus' call to "Come to Me"? What must you do in order to meet that condition?*

2. *What do you think actual "abiding in Christ" looks like in the believer who truly, constantly abides in Him? What are the visible evidences of that abiding?*

3. *What are some of the spiritual benefits and blessings associated with the decision first to come to Christ, and then to abide in Christ?*

DAY 2
AND YOU SHALL FIND
REST FOR YOUR SOULS

"Come to Me, all you who labor and are heavy laden,
and I will give you rest. Take My yoke upon you and
learn from Me, for I am gentle and lowly in heart,
and you will find rest for your souls."
MATTHEW 11:28–29

REST *for the soul*: Such was the first promise with which the Savior sought to win the heavy-laden sinner. Simple though it appears, the promise is indeed as large and comprehensive as can be found. Rest for the soul—does it not imply deliverance from every fear, the supply of every need, and the fulfillment of every desire? And now nothing less than this is the prize with which the Savior woos back the wandering one— who is mourning that the rest has not been so abiding or so full as it had hoped—to come back and abide in Him. Nothing but this was the reason that the rest has either not been found or, if found, has been disturbed or lost again: You did not abide with, you did not abide in Him.

Have you ever noticed how, in the original invitation of the Savior to come to Him, the promise of rest was repeated twice, and with such a variation in the conditions as might have suggested that abiding rest could only be found in abiding nearness. First the Savior says, "Come to me, and I will give you rest"; the very moment you come and believe, I will give you rest—the rest of pardon and acceptance—the rest in My love. But we know that all that God bestows needs time to become fully our own. It must be held firmly, and appropriated, and assimilated into our innermost being. Without this, not even Christ's giving can make it our very own in full experience and enjoyment.

And so the Savior repeats His promise, in words that clearly speak not so much of the initial rest with which He welcomes the weary one who comes, but of the deeper and personally appropriated rest of the soul that abides with Him. He now not only says, "Come to Me," but "Take My yoke upon you and learn from Me," or become my students, yield ourselves to my training, submit in all things to my will, let your whole life be one with mine—in other words, Abide in Me. And then He adds, not only, "I will give," but "you will find rest for your souls." The rest He gave at coming will become something you have really found and made your very own—the deeper the abiding rest that comes from longer acquaintance and closer fellowship, from entire surrender and deeper sympathy. "Take my yoke, and learn from Me," "Abide in Me"—this is the path to abiding rest.

Do not these words of the Savior show what you have perhaps often sought in vain to know how it is that the rest you at times enjoy is so often lost? It must have been this: you had not understood how *entire surrender to Jesus is the secret of perfect rest*. Giving up one's whole life to Him for Him alone to rule and order it, taking up His yoke and submitting to be led and taught, to learn of Him, to abide in Him to be and do only what He wills—these are the conditions of discipleship without which there can be no thought of maintaining the rest that was received on first coming to Christ. The rest is in Christ, and it is not something He gives apart from Himself, and so it is only in having Him that the rest can really be kept and enjoyed.

> *The rest He gave at coming will become something you have really found and made your very own—the deeper the abiding rest that comes from longer acquaintance and closer fellowship, from entire surrender and deeper sympathy.*

It is because so many a young believer fails to lay hold of this truth that the rest so speedily passes away. With some it is that they really did not know. They were never taught how Jesus claims the undivided allegiance of the whole heart and life, how there is not a spot in the whole of life over which He does not wish to reign, or how in the very least things His disciples must only seek to please Him. They did not know how entire the consecration was that Jesus claimed. With others, those who had some idea of what a very holy life a Christian ought to lead, the mistake was a different one: they could not believe such a life to be a possible attainment. Taking, and bearing, and never for a moment laying aside the yoke of Jesus appeared to them to require such a strain of effort and such an amount of goodness so as to be altogether beyond their reach. The very idea of always, all the day, abiding in Jesus, was too high—something they might attain to after a life of holiness and growth, but certainly not what a weak beginner was to start with. They did not know how that when Jesus said, "My yoke is easy," He spoke the truth, how just *the yoke gives the rest*, because the moment the soul yields itself to obey, the Lord Himself gives the strength and joy to do it. They did not notice how, when He said, "Learn from Me," He added, "I am gentle and lowly in heart," to assure them that His gentleness would meet their every need and bear them as a mother bears her feeble child. Oh, they did not know that when He said, "Abide in Me," He only asked the surrender to Himself and that His almighty love would hold them firmly and keep and bless them. And so, as some had erred from the lack of full consecration, so these failed because they did not fully trust. These two, consecration and faith, are the essential elements of the Christian life—the giving up all to Jesus and the receiving all from Jesus. They are implied in each other; they are united in the one word: surrender. A full surrender is to obey as well as to trust, to trust as well as to obey.

With such misunderstanding at the outset, it is no wonder that the disciple life was not one of such joy or strength as had been hoped. In some things you were led into sin without knowing it, because you had not learned how completely Jesus wanted to rule you, and how you could not keep right for a moment unless you had Him very near you. In other things you knew what sin was, but did not have the power to conquer it, because you did not know or believe how entirely Jesus would take charge of you to keep and to help you. Either way, it was not long before the bright joy of your first love was lost and your path, instead of being like the path of the just, shining more and more on the perfect day, became like Israel's wandering in the desert along the way—never very far, and yet always coming short of the promised rest. Weary soul, since so many years driven to and fro like the panting deer, O come and learn this day the lesson that there is a spot where safety and victory, where peace and rest, are always sure, and that that spot is always open to you—the heart of Jesus.

> *I*t is not the yoke but resistance to the yoke that makes the difficulty. The wholehearted surrender to Jesus, as at the same time our Master and our keeper, finds and secures the rest.

But, sadly, I hear someone say, "It is just this abiding in Jesus, always bearing His yoke, to learn from Him, that is so difficult, and the very effort to attain to this often disturbs the rest even more than sin or the world." What a mistake to speak this way, and yet how often the words are heard! Does it weary the traveler to rest in the house or on the bed where he seeks rest from his fatigue? Or is it a labor to a little child to rest in its mother's arms? Is it not the house that keeps the traveler within its shelter? Do not the arms of the mother sustain and keep the little one? And so it is with Jesus. The soul needs only to yield itself to Him, to be still and rest in the confidence that His love has undertaken, and that His faithfulness will perform, the work of keeping it safe in the shelter of His bosom.

Oh, it is because the blessing is so great that our little hearts cannot rise to grasp it. It is as if we cannot believe that Christ, the Almighty One, will in very deed teach and keep us all the day. And yet this is just what He has promised, for without this He cannot really give us rest. It is as our heart takes in this truth that when He says, "Abide in Me," "Learn from Me," He really means it, and that it is His own work to keep us abiding when we yield ourselves to Him, so that we shall venture to cast ourselves into the arms of His love and abandon ourselves to His blessed keeping. It is not the yoke but resistance to the yoke that makes the difficulty. The wholehearted surrender to Jesus, as at the same time our Master and our keeper, finds and secures the rest.

Come, my brother, and let us this very day begin to accept the word of Jesus in all simplicity. It is a distinct command, this: "Take my yoke, and learn from Me," "Abide in Me." A command has to be obeyed. The obedient student asks no questions about possibilities or results. He accepts every order in the confidence that his teacher has provided for all that is needed. The power and the perseverance to abide in the rest and the blessing in abiding—it belongs to the Savior to see to this: It is mine to obey, it is His to provide.

Abiding in Jesus is nothing but the giving up of oneself to be ruled and taught and led, and so resting in the arms of everlasting love.

Let us this day in immediate obedience accept the command and answer boldly, "Savior, I abide in You. At Your command I take Your yoke. I undertake the duty without delay. I abide in You." Let each consciousness of failure only give new urgency to the command and teach us to listen more earnestly than ever until the Spirit again allows us to hear the voice of Jesus saying, with a love and authority that inspire both hope and obedience, "Child, abide in Me." That word, listened to as coming from Himself, will be an end of all doubting—a divine promise of what shall surely be granted. And with ever-increasing simplicity its meaning will be interpreted. Abiding in Jesus is nothing but the giving up of oneself to be ruled and taught and led, and so resting in the arms of everlasting love.

Blessed rest! The fruit and the foretaste and the fellowship of God's own rest! Found of those who come to Jesus to abide in Him. It is the peace of God, the great calm of the eternal world, that passes all understanding and that keeps the heart and mind. With this grace secured, we have strength for every duty, courage for every struggle, a blessing in every cross, and the joy of life eternal in death itself.

O my Savior! If ever my heart should doubt or fear again, as if the blessing were too great to expect or too high to attain, let me hear Your voice to stir my faith and obedience: "Abide in Me," "Take My yoke upon you and learn from Me. You will find rest for your souls."

For Further Thought

1. *What do you think Jesus meant when He said, "You will find rest for your souls?" How do you think that kind of "rest" would demonstrate it in your daily life of faith?*
2. *What factors could, if you allowed it, keep you from fully abiding in Christ and finding the rest for your soul that He promises those who will simply abide daily?*
3. *How would a decision to abide in Christ daily change your daily life? What would you lose in that abiding? What would you gain?*

DAY 3
TRUSTING HIM TO KEEP YOU

*I press on, that I may lay hold of that for
which Christ Jesus has also laid hold of me.*
PHILIPPIANS 3:12

MORE than one admits that it is a sacred duty and a blessed privilege to abide in Christ, but shrinks back continually before the question: Is it possible, a life of unbroken fellowship with the Savior? Eminent Christians, to whom special opportunities of cultivating this grace have been granted, may attain to it, but for the large majority of disciples, whose life, by a divine appointment, is so fully occupied with the affairs of this life, it can scarcely be expected. The more they hear of this life, the deeper their sense of its glory and blessedness, and there is nothing they would not sacrifice to be made partakers of it. But they are too weak, too unfaithful—they never can attain to it.

Dear souls! How little they know that the abiding in Christ is just meant for the weak, and that it is so beautifully suited to their weakness. It is not the doing of some great thing, and it does not demand that we first lead a very holy and devoted life. No, it is simply weakness entrusting itself to a Mighty One to be kept—the unfaithful one casting self on One who is altogether trustworthy and true. Abiding in Him is not a work that we have to do as the condition for enjoying His salvation, but a consenting to let Him do all for us, in us, and through us. It is a work He does for us—the fruit and the power of His redeeming love. Our part is simply to yield, to trust, and to wait for what He has engaged to perform.

It is this quiet expectation and confidence, resting on the word of Christ that *in Him* there is an abiding place prepared, which is so sadly lacking among Christians. They rarely take the time or the trouble to realize that when He says "*Abide in Me,*" He offers Himself, the keeper of Israel who neither slumbers nor sleeps, with all His power and love, as the *living home* of the soul, where the mighty influences of His grace will be stronger to keep than all their weakness to lead astray.

The idea they have of grace is this: that their conversion and pardon are God's work, but that now, in gratitude to God, it is their work to live as Christians and follow Jesus. There is always the thought of a work that has to be done, and even though they pray for help, still the work is theirs. They fail continually and become hopeless, and the despondency only increases the helplessness. No, wandering one: As it was Jesus who drew you when He said, "*Come,*" so it is Jesus who keeps you when He says "*Abide.*"

The grace to come and the grace to abide are alike from Him alone. That word *come,* when it was heard, meditated on, and accepted was the cord of love that drew you near; that word *abide* is even so the band with which He holds you fast and binds you to Himself. Let the soul just take time to listen to the voice of Jesus. "*In Me,*" He says, "is your place—in My almighty arms. It is I who love you so, who speaks *Abide in Me.* Surely you can trust me." The voice of Jesus entering and dwelling in the soul cannot but call for the response: "Yes, Savior, *in You* I can, I will abide."

> *A*biding in Him is not a work that we have to do as the condition for enjoying His salvation, but a consenting to let Him do all for us, in us, and through us.

Abide in Me: These words are no law of Moses, demanding from the sinful what they cannot perform. They are the command of love, which is always only a promise in a different shape. Think of this until all feeling of burden and fear and despair pass away, and the first thought that comes as you hear of abiding in Jesus be one of bright and joyous hope: It is for me, I know I will enjoy it. You are not under the law, with its inexorable *do,* but under grace, with its blessed *believe* what Christ will do for you.

And if the question is asked, "But surely there is something for us to do?" the answer is, "Our doing and working are just the fruit of Christ's work in us." It is when the soul becomes utterly passive, looking and resting on what Christ is to do, that its energies are stirred to their highest activity, and that we work most effectually because we know that He works in us. It is as we see in that word *in Me* that the mighty energies of love reaching out after us to have us and to hold us, that all the strength of our will is roused to abide in Him.

This connection between Christ's work and our work is beautifully expressed in the words of Paul: "I press on, that I may lay hold of that for which Christ Jesus has also laid hold of me." It was because he knew that the mighty and the faithful One had grasped him with the glorious purpose of making him one with Himself that he did his utmost to grasp the glorious prize. The faith, the experience, and the full assurance that "Christ has laid hold of me," gave him the courage and the strength to press on and lay hold of that which had laid hold of him. Each new insight of the great end for which Christ had laid hold of and was holding him roused him afresh to aim at nothing less.

Paul's expression, and its application to the Christian life, can be best understood if we think of a father helping his child to mount the side of some steep precipice. The father stands above and has taken the son by the hand to help him on. He points him to the spot on which he will help him to plant his feet as he leaps upward. The leap would be too high and dangerous for the child alone, but the father's hand is his trust, and he leaps to get hold of the point for which his father has taken hold of him. It is the father's strength that secures him and lifts him up and so urges him to use his utmost strength.

Such is the relationship between Christ and you, O weak and trembling believer! Fix first your eyes on that *that for which* He has laid hold of you. It is nothing less than a life of abiding, unbroken fellowship with Himself to which He is seeking to lift you up. All that you have already received—pardon and peace, the Spirit and His grace—are but preliminary to this. And all that you see promised to you in the future—holiness and fruitfulness and glory everlasting—are but its natural outcome. Union with Himself, and so with the Father, is His highest object. Fix your eye on this and gaze until it stands out before you clear and unmistakable: Christ's aim is to have me abiding in Him.

> *It is as we see in that word "in Me" that the mighty energies of love reaching out after us to have us and to hold us, that all the strength of our will is roused to abide in Him.*

And then let the second thought enter your heart: *That for which Christ Jesus has also laid hold of me.* His almighty power has laid hold on me and offers now to lift me up to where He would have me. Fix your eyes on Christ. Gaze on the love that beams in those eyes and that asks whether you cannot trust Him who sought and found and brought you near now to keep you. Gaze on that arm of power, and say whether you have reason to be assured that He is indeed able to keep you abiding in Him.

And as you think of the spot from where He points—the blessed *that for which* Christ Jesus has laid hold of you—and keep your gaze fixed on Himself, holding you and waiting to lift you up, could you not this very day take the upward step and rise to enter into this blessed life of abiding in Christ? Yes, begin right now, and say, "O my Jesus, if You command me, and if You desire to lift and keep me there, I will venture. Trembling, but trusting, I will say: Jesus, I do abide in You."

My beloved fellow believer, go and take time alone with Jesus, and say this to Him. I don't dare speak to you about abiding in Him for the mere sake of calling forth a pleasing religious sentiment. God's truth must immediately be acted on. O yield yourself this very day to the blessed Savior in the surrender of the one thing He asks of you: Give up yourself to abide in Him. He Himself will accomplish it in you. You can trust Him to keep you trusting and abiding.

And if ever doubts again arise, or the bitter experience of failure tempts you to despair, just remember where Paul found His strength: "I am laid hold of by Jesus Christ." In that assurance you have a fountain of strength. From there you can look up to the *that which* He has set His heart, and set yours there too. From there you gather confidence that the good work He has begun He will also complete. And in that confidence you will gather courage, day by day, afresh to say, "'I press on, that I may lay hold of that for which Christ Jesus has also laid hold of me.' It is because Jesus has taken hold of me, and because Jesus keeps me, that I dare to say: Savior, I abide in You."

FOR FURTHER THOUGHT

1. *What is Christ's answer to those who refuse or fail to abide in Him because they believe they are too weak or too unfaithful—in the present or in the past— to constantly and consistently abide in Him?*

2. *From where must you receive the grace and the strength in order to abide in Christ every day of your Christian life?*

3. *What should you do with your doubts, your failures, and your inabilities in consistently abiding in Christ, as He has called you to do?*

Day 4

As the Branch in the Vine

"I am the vine, you are the branches."
John 15:5

It was in connection with the parable of the vine that our Lord first used the expression "Abide in me." That parable, so simple and yet so rich in its teaching, gives us the best and most complete illustration of the meaning of our Lord's command, and the union to which He invites us.

The parable teaches us the *nature* of that union. The connection between the vine and the branch is a living one. No external, temporary union will suffice, and no work of man can effect it: the branch, whether an original or an engrafted one, is such only by the Creator's own work, in virtue of which the life, the sap, the fatness, and the fruitfulness of the vine communicate themselves to the branch. And just so it is with the believer, too. His union with his Lord is no work of human wisdom or human will, but an act of God, by which the closest and most complete life-union is effected between the Son of God and the sinner. "God has sent forth the *Spirit of His Son into your hearts*" (Gal. 4:6). The same Spirit who dwelled in and still dwells in the Son becomes the life of the believer. In the unity of that one Spirit, and the fellowship of the same life that is in Christ, he is one with Him. As between the vine and branch, it is a life-union that makes them one.

The parable teaches us the *completeness* of the union. So close is the union between the vine and the branch that each is nothing without the other, that each is wholly and only for the other.

Without the vine the branch can do nothing. To the vine it owes its right of place in the vineyard, its life, and its fruitfulness. And so the Lord says, "Without Me you can do nothing" (John 15:5). The believer can each day be pleasing to God only in that which he does through the power of Christ dwelling in him. The daily inflowing of the life-sap of the Holy Spirit is his only power to bring forth fruit. He lives alone in Him and is for each moment dependent on Him alone.

Without the branch the vine can also do nothing. A vine without branches can bear no fruit. No less indispensable than the vine to the branch is the branch to the vine. Such is the wonderful condescension of the grace of Jesus, that just as His people are dependent on Him He has made Himself dependent on them.

Without His disciples He cannot dispense His blessing to the world; He cannot offer sinners the grapes of the heavenly Canaan. Don't marvel at this! It is His own appointment, and this is the high honor to which He has called His redeemed ones: that as indispensable as He is to them in heaven, that from Him their fruit may be found, so indispensable are they to Him on earth, that through them His fruit may be found. Believers, meditate on this until your soul bows to worship in presence of the mystery of the perfect union between Christ and the believer.

There is more: as neither vine nor branch is anything *without* the other, so is neither anything except *for* the other.

> *S*o close is the union between the vine and the branch that each is nothing without the other, that each is wholly and only for the other.

All the vine possesses belongs to the branches. The vine does not gather from the soil its fatness and its sweetness for itself—all it has is at the disposal of the branches. As it is the parent, so it is the servant of the branches. And Jesus, to whom we owe our life, how completely does He give Himself for us and to us: "The glory which You gave Me I have given them" (John 17:22); "He who believes in Me, the works that I do he will do also; and greater works than these he will do" (John 14:12). All His fullness and all His riches are for you, O believer, for the vine does not live for itself and keeps nothing for itself but exists only for the branches. All that Jesus is in heaven, He is for us. He has no interest there separate from ours. As our representative, He stands before the Father.

And all the branch possesses belongs to the vine. The branch does not exist for itself, but to bear fruit that can proclaim the excellence of the vine. It has no reason for existence except to be of service to the vine. Glorious image of the calling of the believer, and the entireness of his consecration to the service of his Lord. As Jesus gives Himself so wholly over to him, he feels himself urged to be wholly his Lord's. Every power of his being, every moment of his life, every thought and feeling, belong to Jesus, so that from Him and for Him he may bring forth fruit. As he realizes what the vine is to the branch, and what the branch is meant to be to the vine, he feels that he has but one thing to think of and to live for, and that is the will, the glory, the work, the kingdom of his blessed Lord—the bringing forth of fruit to the glory of His name.

The parable teaches us the *object* of the union. The branches are for fruit and fruit alone. "Every branch in Me that does not bear fruit He takes away" (John 15:2). The branch needs leaves for the maintenance of its own life and the perfection of its fruit, and the fruit itself it bears to give away to those around. As the believer enters into his calling as a branch, he sees that he has to forget himself and to live entirely for his fellowmen. To love them, to seek for them, and to save them, Jesus came—for this every branch on the vine has to live as much as the vine itself. It is for fruit, much fruit, that the Father has made us one with Jesus.

Wondrous parable of the vine—unveiling the mysteries of the divine love, of the heavenly life, of the world of Spirit—how little have I understood you! Jesus the living vine in heaven and, I the living branch on earth! How little have I understood how great my need, but also how perfect my claim, to all His fullness! How little understood, how great His need, but also how perfect His claim to my emptiness! Let me, in its beautiful light, study the wondrous union between Jesus and His people until it becomes to me the guide into full communion with my beloved Lord. Let me listen and believe until my whole being cries out, "Jesus is indeed to me the true vine, bearing me, nourishing me, supplying me, using me, and filling me to the full to make me bring forth fruit abundantly." Then I won't be afraid to say, "I am indeed a branch to Jesus, the true vine, abiding in Him, resting on Him, waiting for Him, serving Him, and living only that through me, too, He may show forth the riches of His grace, and give His fruit to a perishing world."

> *All His fullness and all His riches are for you, O believer, for the vine does not live for itself and keeps nothing for itself but exists only for the branches.*

It is when we therefore try to understand the meaning of the parable that the blessed command spoken in connection with it will come home to us in its true power. The thought of what the vine is to the branch, and Jesus to the believer, will give new force to the words, "Abide in Me!" It will be as if He says, "Think, soul, how completely I belong to you. I have joined Myself inseparably to you, and all the fullness and fatness of the vine are yours in very deed. Now that you once are in Me, be assured that all I have is wholly yours. It is My interest and My honor to have you be a fruitful branch; only *Abide in Me*. You are weak, but I am strong; you are poor, but I am rich. Only abide in Me. Yield yourself wholly to My teaching and rule. Simply trust My love, My grace, My promises. Only believe. I am wholly yours. I am the vine, you are the branch. Abide in Me."

What do you say, O my soul? Shall I any longer hesitate or withhold consent? Or shall I not, instead of only thinking how hard and how difficult it is to live like a branch of the true vine, because I thought of it as something I had to accomplish—shall I not now begin to look upon it as the most blessed and joyful thing under heaven? Shall I not believe that, now I once am in Him, He Himself will keep me and enable me to abide? On my part, abiding is nothing but the acceptance of my position, the consent to be kept there, the surrender of faith to the strong vine still to hold the weak branch. Yes, I will, I do abide in You, blessed Lord Jesus.

O Savior, how unspeakable is Your love! "Such knowledge is too wonderful for me; it is high, I cannot attain it" (Ps. 139:6). I can only yield myself to Your love with the prayer that, day by day, You would reveal to me somewhat of its precious mysteries, and so encourage and strengthen Your loving disciple to do what his heart longs to do indeed —always, only, wholly to abide in You.

For Further Thought

1. *In the parable of the vine, what is the nature of the union or the personal relationship between Jesus and those who abide in Him? How does this apply to your personal relationship with God through Jesus Christ?*
2. *What, according to the parable of the vine, is God's purpose in commanding you to abide in Jesus Christ?*
3. *As your true vine, in what ways does Jesus care for and bless you as you continue to abide in Him?*

DAY 5

AS YOU CAME TO HIM,

BY FAITH

As you therefore have received Christ Jesus the Lord,
so walk in Him, rooted and built up in Him and
established in the faith, as you have been taught,
abounding in it with thanksgiving.
COLOSSIANS 2:6–7

IN these words the apostle teaches us the weighty lesson that it is not only by faith that we first come to Christ and are united to Him, but that it is by faith that we are to be rooted and established in our union with Christ. Not less essential than for the commencement is faith for the progress of the spiritual life. Abiding in Jesus can only be by faith.

There are earnest Christians who do not understand this or, if they admit it in theory, they fail to realize its application in practice. They are very zealous for a free gospel, with our first acceptance of Christ, and justification by faith alone. But after this, they think everything depends on our diligence and faithfulness. While they firmly grasp the truth, "The sinner shall be justified by faith," they have hardly found a place in their scheme for the larger truth, "The just shall live by faith" (Rom. 1:17). They have never understood what a perfect savior Jesus is, and how He will each day do for the sinner just as much as He did the first day when he came to Him. They do not know that the life of grace is always and only a life of faith, and that in the relationship to Jesus the one daily and unceasing duty of the disciple is *to believe*, because believing is the one channel through which divine grace and strength flow out into the heart of man.

The old nature of the believer remains evil and sinful to the last, and it is only as he daily comes, all empty and helpless, to his Savior to receive of His life and strength that he can bring forth the fruits of righteousness to the glory of God. Therefore it is: "As *you* therefore have received Christ Jesus the Lord, so *walk in Him*, rooted and built up *in Him* and established in the faith. . .abounding in it with thanksgiving." As you came to Jesus, so abide in Him, by faith.

And if you want to know how faith is to be exercised in abiding in Jesus this way, to be rooted more deeply and firmly in Him, you have only to look back to the time when first you received Him. You remember well what obstacles at that time there appeared to be in the way of your believing. There was first your vileness and guilt; it appeared impossible that the promise of pardon and love could be for such a sinner. Then there was the sense of weakness and death; you didn't feel the power for the surrender and the trust to which you were called. And then there was the future; you dared not undertake to be a disciple of Jesus while you felt so sure that you could not remain standing but would speedily again be unfaithful and fall.

These difficulties were like mountains in your way. And how were they removed? Simply by the Word of God. That Word, as it were, compelled you to believe that, notwithstanding guilt in the past and weakness in the present and unfaithfulness in the future, the promise was sure that Jesus would accept and save you. On that Word you ventured to come, and you were not deceived. You found that Jesus did indeed accept and save.

Apply this, your experience in coming to Jesus, to the abiding in Him. Now, as then, the temptations to keep you from believing are many. When you think of your sins since you became a disciple, your heart is cast down with shame, and it looks as if it were too much to expect that Jesus should indeed receive you into perfect intimacy and the full enjoyment of His holy love. When you think how utterly, in times past, you have failed in keeping the most sacred vows, the consciousness of present weakness makes you tremble at the very idea of answering the Savior's command with the promise, "Lord, from now on I will abide in You." And when you set before yourself the life of love and joy, of holiness and fruitfulness, which in the future are to flow from abiding in Him, it is as if it only serves to make you still more hopeless. You, at least, can never attain to it. You know yourself too well. It is no use expecting it, only to be disappointed. A life fully and wholly abiding in Jesus is not for you.

> The old nature of the believer remains evil and sinful to the last, and it is only as he daily comes, all empty and helpless, to his Savior to receive of His life and strength that he can bring forth the fruits of righteousness to the glory of God.

Oh that you would learn a lesson from the time of your first coming to the Savior! Remember, dear soul, how you then were led, contrary to all that your experience, your feelings, and even your sober judgment said, to take Jesus at His word, and how you were not disappointed. He did receive you and pardon you. He did love you and save you—you know it. And if He did this for you when you were an enemy and a stranger, what think you now that you are His own?

Will He not much more fulfill His promise? Oh that you would come and begin simply to listen to His Word and to ask only the one question: Does He really mean that I should abide in Him? The answer His Word gives is so simple and so sure: By His almighty grace you now are in *Him*, and that same almighty grace will indeed enable you to abide in Him. By faith you became partakers of the initial grace, and by that same faith you can enjoy the continuous grace of abiding in Him.

And if you ask what exactly it is that you now have to believe that you may abide in Him, the answer is not difficult. Believe first of all what He says: "I am the vine." The safety and the fruitfulness of the branch depend upon the strength of the vine. Think not so much of yourself as a branch, nor of the abiding as your duty, until you have first had your soul filled with the faith of what Christ as the vine is. *He really will be to you all that a vine can be*—holding you firmly, nourishing you, and making Himself every moment responsible for your growth and your fruit.

Take time to know, and set yourself heartily to believe: My vine, on whom I can depend for all I need, is Christ. A large, strong vine bears the weak branch, and holds it more than the branch holds the vine. Ask the Father by the Holy Spirit to reveal to you what a glorious, loving, mighty Christ this is, in whom you have your place and your life. *It is the faith in what Christ is*, more than anything else, that will keep you abiding in Him. A soul filled with large thoughts of the vine will be a strong branch and will abide confidently in Him. Be much occupied with Jesus, and believe much in Him, as the true vine.

> *Remember, dear soul, how you then were led, contrary to all that your experience, your feelings, and even your sober judgment said, to take Jesus at His word, and how you were not disappointed.*

And then, when faith can well say, "He is my vine," let it further say, "I am His branch, I am in Him." I speak to those who say they are Christ's disciples, and on them I cannot too earnestly press the importance of exercising their faith in saying, "I am in Him." It makes the abiding so simple. If I realize clearly as I meditate: Now I am in Him, I see at once that there is nothing lacking but just my consent to be what He has made me, to remain where He has placed me. *I am in Christ.* This simple thought, carefully, prayerfully, believingly uttered, removes all difficulty as if there were some great attainment to be reached. No, *I am in Christ*, my blessed Savior. His love has prepared a home for me with Himself, when He says, "Abide in my love," and His power has undertaken to keep the door, and to keep me in, if I will but consent. *I am in Christ*: I have now but to say, "Savior, I bless You for this wondrous grace. I consent—I yield myself to Your gracious keeping. I do abide in You."

It is astonishing how such a faith will work out all that is further implied in abiding in Christ. There is in the Christian life great need of watchfulness and of prayer, of self-denial and of striving, of obedience and of diligence. But "all things are possible to him who believes" (Mark 9:23). "This is the victory that has overcome the world—our faith" (1 John 5:4).

> *A* soul filled with large thoughts of the vine will be a strong branch and will abide confidently in Him. Be much occupied with Jesus, and believe much in Him, as the true vine.

It is the faith that continually closes its eyes to the weakness of the creature, and finds its joy in the sufficiency of an almighty Savior, that makes the soul strong and glad. It gives itself up to be led by the Holy Spirit into an ever-deeper appreciation of that wonderful Savior whom God has given us—the infinite Immanuel. It follows the leading of the Spirit from page to page of the blessed Word, with the one desire to take each revelation of what Jesus is and what He promises as its nourishment and its life. In accordance with the promise, "If what you heard from the beginning abides in you, you also will abide in the Son and in the Father" (1 John 2:24), it lives by every word that proceeds out of the mouth of God. And so it makes the soul strong with the strength of God, to be and to do all that is needed for abiding in Christ.

Believer, you want to abide in Christ: only believe. Believe always, believe now. Bow even now before your Lord, and say to Him in childlike faith, that because He is your vine and you are His branch, you will this day abide in Him.

For Further Thought

1. *The Bible teaches that your old nature remains evil, even after you have come to Christ for salvation. What is necessary for you to bear the fruits of righteousness God has called you to bear for Him?*
2. *In His Word, God teaches you that it is through His grace that you are in Him, that it is by faith that you received His gift of salvation. What now is required of you to enjoy His continuous grace you receive when you abide in Him?*
3. *How can you know that you can depend on Jesus, as your true vine, to keep you, protect you, and enable and prepare you to bear fruit for Him?*

NOTE

I am the true vine. He who offers us the privilege of an actual union with Himself is the great *I am*, the almighty God who upholds all things by the word of His power. And this almighty God reveals Himself as our perfect Savior, even to the unimaginable extent of seeking to renew our fallen natures by grafting them into His own divine nature.

"To realize the glorious Deity of Him whose call sounds forth to longing hearts with such exceeding sweetness is no small step towards gaining the full privilege to which we are invited. But longing is by itself of no use. Still less can there be any profit in reading of the blessed results to be gained from a close and personal union with our Lord, *if we believe that union to be practically beyond our reach*. His words are meant to be a living, an eternal, precious reality. And this they can never become unless *we are sure that we may reasonably expect their accomplishment*. But what could make the accomplishment of such an idea possible—what could make it reasonable to suppose that we poor, weak, selfish creatures, full of sin and full of failures, might be saved out of the corruption of our nature and made partakers of the holiness of our Lord—except the fact, the marvelous, unalterable fact, that He who proposes to us so great a transformation is Himself the everlasting God, as able as He is willing to fulfill His own word.

"In meditating, therefore, upon these utterances of Christ, containing as they do the very essence of His teaching, the very concentration of His love, let us, at the outset, *put away all tendency to doubt*. Let us *not allow ourselves so much as to question whether* such erring disciples as we are *can be enabled to attain the holiness to which we are called* through a close and intimate union with our Lord. If there is any impossibility, any falling short of the proposed blessedness, it will arise from the lack of earnest desire on our part. There is no lack in any respect on His part who puts forth the invitation; with GOD there can be no shortcoming in the fulfillment of His promise."— *The Life of Fellowship; Meditations on John 15:1, 11*, by A. M. James.

It is perhaps necessary to say, for the sake of young or doubting Christians, that there is something more necessary than the effort to exercise faith in each separate promise that is brought under our notice. What is of even greater importance is the cultivation of a trustful disposition toward God, the habit of always thinking of Him, of His ways and His works, with bright confiding hopefulness. In such soil alone can the individual promises take root and grow up.

In a little work published by the Tract Society, *Encouragements to Faith*, by James Kimball, there will be found many most suggestive and helpful thoughts, all pleading for the right God has to claim that He shall be trusted. *The Christian's Secret of a Happy Life* is another little work that has been a great help to many. Its bright and buoyant tone, its loving and unceasing repetition of the keynote—we may indeed depend on Jesus to do all He has said, and more than we can think— has breathed hope and joy into many a heart that was almost ready to despair of ever getting on. In Frances Havergal's *Kept for the Master's Use*, there is the same healthful, hope-inspiring tone.

DAY 6

GOD HIMSELF HAS
UNITED YOU TO HIM

But of Him you are in Christ Jesus, who became
for us wisdom from God—and righteousness
and sanctification and redemption.
1 CORINTHIANS 1:30

"My Father is the vinedresser."
JOHN 15:1

"YOU are in Christ Jesus." The believers at Corinth were still weak and carnal, only babes in Christ. And yet Paul wants them, at the outset of his teaching, to know distinctly that they are in Christ Jesus. The whole Christian life depends on the clear consciousness of our position in Christ. Most essential to the abiding in Christ is the daily renewal of our faith's assurance, "I am in Christ Jesus." All fruitful preaching to believers must take this as its starting point: "You are in Christ Jesus."

But the apostle has an additional thought, of almost greater importance: *"Of Him* (God) you are in Christ Jesus." He would have us not only remember our union to Christ, but especially that it is not our own doing but the work of God Himself. As the Holy Spirit teaches us to realize this, we shall see what a source of assurance and strength it must become to us. If it is of God alone that I am in Christ, then God Himself, the Infinite One, becomes my security for all I can need or wish in seeking to abide in Christ.

Let me try to understand what it means, this wonderful *"of God"* in Christ." In becoming partakers of the union with Christ, there is a work God does and a work we have to do. God does His work by moving us to do our work. The work of God is hidden and silent, but what we do is something distinct and tangible. Conversion and faith, prayer and obedience, are conscious acts of which we can give a clear account, while the spiritual quickening and strengthening that come from above are secret and beyond the reach of human sight.

And so it comes that when the believer tries to say, "I am in Christ Jesus," he looks more to the work he did than to that wondrous secret work of God by which he was united to Christ. Nor can it well be otherwise at the commencement of the Christian course. "I know that I have believed" is a valid testimony. But it is of great consequence that the mind should be led to see that at the back of our turning, believing, and accepting of Christ, there was God's almighty power doing its work—inspiring our will, taking possession of us, and carrying out its own purpose of love in planting us into Christ Jesus. As the believer enters into this, the divine side of the work of salvation, he will learn to praise and to worship with new exultation, and to rejoice more than ever in the divineness of that salvation he has been made partaker of. At each step he reviews, the song will come, "This is the Lord's doing"—divine omnipotence working out what eternal love had devised. "*Of God* I am in Christ Jesus."

> *I*f it is of God alone that I am in Christ, then God Himself, the Infinite One, becomes my security for all I can need or wish in seeking to abide in Christ.

The words will lead him even further and higher, even to the depths of eternity. "Whom He predestined, these He also called" (Rom. 8:30). The calling in time is the manifestation of the purpose in eternity. Before the world was, God had fixed the eye of His sovereign love on you in the election of grace and had chosen you in Christ. That you know yourself to be in Christ is the stepping-stone by which you rise to understand in its full meaning the word, "*Of God* I am in Christ Jesus." With the prophet, your language will be, "The LORD has appeared of old to me, saying: 'Yes, I have loved you with an everlasting love; therefore with lovingkindness I have drawn you'" (Jer. 31:3). And you will recognize your own salvation as a part of that "mystery of His will, according to His good pleasure which He purposed in Himself" (Eph. 1:9), and join with the whole body of believers in Christ as these say, "In Him also we have obtained an inheritance, being predestined according to the purpose of Him who works all things according to the counsel of His will" (Eph. 1:11). Nothing will more exalt free grace and make man bow very low before it than this knowledge of the mystery "*Of God* in Christ."

It is easy to see what a mighty influence it must exert on the believer who seeks to abide in Christ. What a sure standing-ground it gives him as he rests his right to Christ and all His fullness on nothing less than the Father's own purpose and work! We have thought of Christ as the vine, and the believer as the branch, but let us not forget that other precious word, "My Father is the vinedresser." The Savior said, "Every plant which My heavenly Father has not planted will be uprooted" (Matt. 15:13), but every branch grafted by Him in the true vine shall never be plucked out of His hand. As it was the Father to whom Christ owed all He was, and in whom He had all His strength and His life as the vine, so to the Father the believer owes his place and his security in Christ. The same love and delight with which the Father watched over the beloved Son Himself, watch over every member of His body, every one who is in Christ Jesus.

What confident trust this faith inspires—not only as to the being kept in safety to the end, but specially as to the being able to fulfill in every point the object for which I have been united to Christ. The branch is as much in the charge and keeping of the vinedresser as the vine; his honor as much concerned in the well-being and growth of the branch as of the vine. The God who chose Christ to be the vine fitted Him thoroughly for the work He had as vine to perform. The God who has chosen me and planted me in Christ has thereby engaged to secure, if I will but let Him, by yielding myself to Him, that I in every way be worthy of Jesus Christ.

Oh that I did but fully realize this! What confidence and urgency it would give to my prayer to the God and Father of Jesus Christ! How it would quicken the sense of dependence and make me see that praying without ceasing is indeed the one need of my life—an unceasing waiting, moment by moment, on the God who has united me to Christ, to perfect His own divine work, to work in me both to will and to do of His good pleasure.

> Nothing will more exalt free grace and make man bow very low before it than this knowledge of the mystery "of God in Christ."

And what a motive this would be for the highest activity in the maintenance of a fruitful branch-life! Motives are mighty powers, and it is of infinite importance to have them high and clear. Here surely is the highest: "We are His workmanship, created in Christ Jesus for good works" (Eph. 2:10)—grafted by Him into Christ, unto the bringing forth of much fruit. Whatever God creates is exquisitely suited for its purpose. He created the sun to give light: How perfectly it does its work! He created the eye to see: How beautifully it fulfills its object! He created the new man unto good works: How admirably it is fitted for its purpose.

Of God I am in Christ—created anew, made a branch of the vine, prepared for fruit-bearing. God desires that believers would cease looking most at their old nature and complaining of their weakness, as if God called them to what they were unprepared for! He desires that they would believingly and joyfully accept the wondrous revelation of how God, in uniting them to Christ, has made Himself responsible for their spiritual growth and fruitfulness! How all sickly hesitancy and apathy would disappear, and under the influence of this mighty motive—the faith in the faithfulness of Him of whom they are in Christ—their whole nature would rise to accept and fulfill their glorious destiny!

O my soul! Yield yourself to the mighty influence of this word: "*Of God* you are in Christ Jesus." It is the same *God of whom* Christ is made all that He is for us, of *whom* we also are in Christ and will most surely be made what we must be to Him. Take time to meditate and to worship, until the light that comes from the throne of God has shone into you and you have seen your union to Christ as indeed the work of His almighty Father. Take time, day after day, and let, in your whole religious life—with all it has of claims and duties, of needs and wishes—God be everything. See Jesus, as He speaks to you, "Abide in Me," pointing upward and saying, "*My Father is the Vinedresser. Of Him* you are in Me, *through Him* you abide in Me, and *to Him* and to His glory shall be the fruit you bear." And let your answer be, Amen, Lord! So be it. From eternity, Christ and I were ordained for each other. Inseparably we belong to each other: it is God's will that I shall abide in Christ. It is of God I am in Christ Jesus.

FOR FURTHER THOUGHT

1. *What does it mean to you personally that it is of God that you are in Christ, that it is God who has united you to Christ and to Himself?*
2. *Read Ephesians 2:10. For what purpose has the Father united You to Christ and to Himself? What steps will you take to live out that purpose?*
3. *What does God desire you to look away from and to look at in order that you can live out your destiny as one who He has united to Christ?*

DAY 7

AS YOUR WISDOM

But of Him you are in Christ Jesus,
who became for us wisdom from God—
and righteousness and sanctification and redemption.
1 CORINTHIANS 1:30

JESUS Christ is not only priest to purchase and king to secure, but also prophet to reveal to us the salvation that God has prepared for those who love Him. Just as at the creation the light was first called into existence, so that in it all God's other works might have their life and beauty, so in our text wisdom is mentioned first as the treasury in which are to be found the three precious gifts that follow.

The life is the light of man. It is in revealing to us and making us behold the glory of God in His own face that Christ makes us partakers of eternal life. It was by the tree of knowledge that sin came, but it is through the knowledge that Christ gives that salvation comes. He is made of God for us wisdom. *In Him* are hidden all the treasures of wisdom and knowledge.

And of God you are in *Him*, and you need only to abide in Him to be made partaker of these treasures of wisdom. *In Him* you are, and *in Him* the wisdom is. Dwelling in Him, you dwell in the very fountain of all light. Abiding in Him, you have Christ the wisdom of God leading your whole spiritual life and ready to communicate, in the form of knowledge, just as much as you need to know. Christ is made for us wisdom: You are in Christ.

It is this connection between what Christ has been made of God for us, and how we have it only as we are also in Him, that we must learn to understand better. We shall thus see that the blessings prepared for us in Christ cannot be obtained as special gifts in answer to prayer *apart from the abiding in Him.* The answer to each prayer must come in the closer union and the deeper abiding in Him. In Him, the unspeakable gift, all other gifts are treasured up, including the gift of wisdom and knowledge.

How often have you longed for wisdom and spiritual understanding that you might *know* God better—whom to know is life eternal! Abide in Jesus so that your life in Him will lead you to that fellowship with God in which the only true knowledge of God is to be had. His love, His power, and His infinite glory will, as you abide in Jesus, be so revealed as it has not entered into the heart of man to conceive. You may not be able to grasp it with the understanding or to express it in words, but the knowledge that is deeper than thoughts or words will be given—the knowing of God that comes of being known by Him. "We preach Christ crucified. . .to those who are called. . .Christ the power of God and the wisdom of God" (1 Cor. 1:23, 24).

Or you would desire to count all things loss for the excellence of the *knowledge of Jesus Christ* your Lord (see Phil. 3:8). Abide in Jesus and be found in Him. You will know Him in the power of His resurrection and the fellowship of His sufferings. Following Him, you shall not walk in darkness, but have the light of life. It is only when God shines into the heart, and Christ Jesus dwells there, that the light of the knowledge of God in the face of Christ can be seen.

Or would you understand his blessed *work*, as He accomplished it on earth, or works it from heaven by His Spirit? Do you desire to know how Christ can become our righteousness and our sanctification and redemption? It is just as bringing, revealing, and communicating these that He is made for us wisdom from God. There are a thousand questions that at times come up, and the attempt to answer them becomes a weariness and a burden. It is because you have forgotten you are in Christ, whom God has made to be your wisdom. Let it be your first care to abide in Him in undivided, fervent devotion of heart. When the heart and the life are right, rooted in Christ, knowledge will come in such measure as Christ's own wisdom sees fitting.

> *I*t was by the tree of knowledge that sin came, but it is through the knowledge that Christ gives that salvation comes.

And without such abiding in Christ, the knowledge does not really profit, but is often most hurtful. The soul satisfies itself with thoughts that are but the forms and images of truth without receiving the truth itself in its power. God's way is always first to give to us, even though it be but as a seed, the thing itself, the life and the power, and then the knowledge. Man seeks the knowledge first, and often, sadly, never gets beyond it. God gives us Christ, and in Him *hid* the treasures of wisdom and knowledge. O let us be content to possess Christ, to dwell in Him, to make Him our life and, only in a deeper searching into Him, to search and find the knowledge we desire. Such knowledge is life indeed.

Therefore, believer, abide in Jesus as your wisdom, and expect from Him most confidently whatever teaching you may need for a life for the glory of the Father. In all that concerns your *spiritual life*, abide in Jesus as your wisdom. The life you have in Christ is a thing of infinite sacredness, far too high and holy for you to know how to act it out. It is He alone who can guide you, as by a secret spiritual instinct, to know what is becoming of your dignity as a child of God, what will help and what will hinder your inner life, and especially your abiding in Him.

Do not think of it as a mystery or a difficulty you must solve. Whatever questions come up as to the possibility of abiding perfectly and uninterruptedly in Him, and of really obtaining all the blessing that comes from it, always remember: He knows, all is perfectly clear to Him, and He is my wisdom. Just as much as you need to know and are capable of grasping will be communicated, *if you only trust Him*. Never think of the riches of wisdom and knowledge hidden in Jesus as treasures without a key, or of your way as a path without a light. Jesus your wisdom is guiding you in the right way, even when you do not see it.

> *I*t is only when God shines into the heart, and Christ Jesus dwells there, that the light of the knowledge of God in the face of Christ can be seen.

In all your interaction with the *blessed Word*, remember the same truth: Abide in Jesus, your wisdom. Study much to know the written Word, but study more to know the living Word, in whom you are of God. Jesus, the wisdom of God, is only known by a life of implicit confidence and obedience. The words He speaks are spirit and life to those *who live in Him*. Therefore, each time you read, or hear, or meditate on the Word, be careful to take up your true position. Realize first your oneness with Him who is the wisdom of God, know yourself to be under His direct and special training, and go to the Word abiding in Him, the very fountain of divine light—*in His light* you shall see light.

In all *your daily life*, in its ways and its work, abide in Jesus as your wisdom. Your body and your daily life share in the great salvation. In Christ, the wisdom of God, provision has been made for their guidance too. Your body is His temple, your daily life the sphere for glorifying Him. It is to Him a matter of deep interest that all your earthly concerns should be guided rightly. Only trust His sympathy, believe His love, and wait for His guidance—it will be given. Abiding in Him, the mind will be calmed and freed from passion, the judgment cleared and strengthened, the light of heaven will shine on earthly things, and your prayer for wisdom, like Solomon's, will be fulfilled above what you ask or think.

And so, especially in any *work* you do for God, abide in Jesus as your wisdom. "We are. . .created in Christ Jesus for good works, which God prepared beforehand that we should walk in them" (Eph. 2:10), so let all fear or doubt, unless we should not know exactly what these works are, be put far away. In Christ we are created for them. He will show us what they are and how to do them. Cultivate the habit of rejoicing in the assurance that the divine wisdom is guiding you, even where you do not yet see the way.

All that you can wish to know is perfectly clear to Him. As man, as mediator, He has access to the counsels of Deity, to the secrets of providence—in your interest and on your behalf. If you will just trust Him fully and abide in Him entirely, you can be confident of having unerring guidance.

Yes, abide in Jesus as your wisdom. Seek to maintain the spirit of waiting and dependence, which always seeks to learn and will not move unless the heavenly light leads on. Withdraw yourself from all needless distraction, close your ears to the voices of the world, and be as a docile learner, always listening for the heavenly wisdom the Master has to teach. Surrender all your own wisdom. Seek a deep conviction of the utter blindness of the natural understanding in the things of God, and both as to what you have to believe and have to do, wait for Jesus to teach and to guide. Remember that the teaching and guidance don't come from without. Rather, it is by *His life* in us that the divine wisdom does His work.

> *N*ever think of the riches of wisdom and knowledge hidden in Jesus as treasures without a key, or of your way as a path without a light. Jesus your wisdom is guiding you in the right way, even when you do not see it.

Retire frequently with Him into the inner chamber of the heart, where the gentle voice of the Spirit is heard only if all is still. Hold firmly with unshaken confidence, even in the midst of darkness and apparent desertion, His own assurance that He is the light and the leader of His own. And live, above all, day by day in the blessed truth that as He Himself, the living Christ Jesus, is your wisdom, your first and last care must always be this alone—to abide in Him. Abiding in Him, His wisdom will come to you as the spontaneous outflowing of a life rooted in Him. I am, I abide in Christ, who was *made for us* wisdom from God, so wisdom will be given to me.

FOR FURTHER THOUGHT

1. *What three "offices" does Christ hold in your life as a believer, and what does He accomplish in each?*
2. *What must you do in order to receive the wisdom and knowledge God wants you to have as a believer, as one who is in Christ?*
3. *What connection is there between the biblical teaching that Christ has been made for you wisdom and the work He calls you to do for Him and His kingdom?*

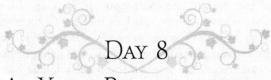

DAY 8

AS YOUR RIGHTEOUSNESS

But of Him you are in Christ Jesus, who became for
us wisdom from God—and righteousness
and sanctification and redemption.
1 CORINTHIANS 1:30

THE first of the great blessings that Christ our wisdom reveals to us as prepared in Himself is righteousness. It is not difficult to see why this must be first.

There can be no real prosperity or progress in a nation, a home, or a soul, unless there is peace. As not even a machine can do its work unless it is in rest, secured on a good foundation, quietness and assurance are indispensable to our moral and spiritual well-being. Sin had disturbed all our relations. We were out of harmony with ourselves, with men, and with God. The first requirement of a salvation that should really bring blessedness to us was peace. And peace can only come with right. Where everything is as God would have it—in God's order and in harmony with His will—there alone can peace reign.

Jesus Christ came to restore peace on earth and peace in the soul by restoring righteousness. Because He is Melchizedek, king of righteousness, He reigns as king of Salem, king of peace (Heb. 7:2). He so fulfills the promise the prophets held out: "A king will reign in righteousness. . .The work of righteousness will be peace, and the effect of righteousness, quietness and assurance forever" (Isa. 32:1, 17). Christ is made of God for us righteousness, of God we are in Him as our righteousness, and we are made the righteousness of God in Him. Let us try to understand what this means.

When first the sinner is led to trust in Christ for salvation, he, as a rule, looks more to His work than His person.

As he looks at the cross, and Christ suffering there, the Righteous One *for* the unrighteous, he sees in that atoning death the only but sufficient foundation for his faith in God's pardoning mercy. The substitution, the curse-bearing, and the atonement of Christ dying in the stead of sinners are what give him peace. And as he understands how the righteousness that Christ brings becomes his very own and how, in the strength of that, he is counted righteous before God, he feels that he has what he needs to restore him to God's favor: "Having been justified by faith, we have peace with God" (Rom. 5:1). He seeks to wear this robe of righteousness in the ever-renewed faith in the glorious gift of righteousness that has been bestowed upon him.

But as time goes on, and he seeks to grow in the Christian life, new needs arise. He wants to understand more fully how it is that God can somehow justify the ungodly on the strength of the righteousness of another. He finds the answer in the wonderful teaching of scripture as to the true union of the believer with Christ as the second Adam. He sees that it is because Christ had made Himself one with His people, and they were one with Him, that it was in perfect accordance with all law in the kingdom of nature and of heaven that each member of the body should have the full benefit of the doing and the suffering as of the life of the head. And so he is led to feel that it can only be in fully realizing his personal union with Christ as the head that he can fully experience the power of His righteousness to bring the soul into the full favor and fellowship of the Holy One. The work of Christ does not become less precious, but the person of Christ more so, and the work leads up into the very heart, the love, and the life of the God-man.

> *C*hrist is made of God for us righteousness, of God we are in Him as our righteousness, and we are made the righteousness of God in Him.

And this experience sheds its light again on scripture. It leads him to notice what he had scarcely remarked before: how distinctly the righteousness of God, as it becomes ours, is connected with the person of the Redeemer. "Now this is His name by which *He* will be called: *The Lord our righteousness*" (Jer. 23:6). "*In the Lord* I have righteousness and strength" (Isa. 45:24). "Of Him. . . *Christ Jesus*. . .became for us. . .righteousness" (1 Cor. 1:30). "That we might become the righteousness of *God in Him*" (2 Cor. 5:21). "That I may. . .be found *in Him*. . .having. . .the righteousness of God" (Phil. 3:8, 9). He sees how inseparable righteousness and life in Christ are from each other: "Through one Man's righteous act the free gift came to all men, resulting in *justification of life*" (Rom. 5:18). "Those who receive. . .the gift of righteousness *will reign in life* through the One, Jesus Christ" (Rom. 5:17). And he understands what deep meaning there is in the keyword of the Epistle to the Romans: "The just shall *live* by faith" (1:17). He is not now content with only thinking of the imputed righteousness as his robe but, putting on Jesus Christ and seeking to be wrapped up in, to be clothed upon with *Himself and His life*, he feels how completely the righteousness of God is his, because the Lord our righteousness is his.

Before he understood this, he too often felt it difficult to wear his white robe all the day. It was as if he specially had to put it on when he came into God's presence to confess his sins and seek new grace. But now the living Christ Himself is his righteousness—that Christ who watches over and keeps and loves us as His own. It is no longer an impossibility to walk all the day enrobed in the loving presence with which He covers His people.

Such an experience leads still further. The life and the righteousness are inseparably linked, and the believer becomes more conscious than before of a righteous nature planted within him. The new man created in Christ Jesus, is "created. . .in true righteousness and holiness" (Eph. 4:24). "He who practices righteousness is righteous, just as He is righteous" (1 John 3:7). The union to Jesus has effected a change not only in the relation to God, but in the personal state before God. And as the intimate fellowship to which the union has opened up the way is maintained, the growing renewal of the whole being makes righteousness to be his very nature.

> *The work of Christ does not become less precious, but the person of Christ more so, and the work leads up into the very heart, the love and the life of the God-man.*

To a Christian who begins to see the deep meaning of the truth, "*He* is made for us righteousness," it is hardly necessary to say, "Abide in Him." As long as he only thought of the righteousness of the substitute, and of our being counted judicially righteous for His sake, the absolute necessity of *abiding in Him* was not apparent. But as the glory of "the Lord our righteousness" unfolds to the view, he sees that abiding in Him personally is the only way to stand, at all times, complete and accepted before God, as it is the only way to realize how the new and righteous nature can be strengthened from Jesus our head. To the penitent sinner, the chief thought was *the righteousness* that comes through Jesus dying for sin, but to the learned and advancing believer, *Jesus*, the Living One, through whom the righteousness comes, is everything, because having Him, he has the righteousness, too.

Believer, abide in Christ as your righteousness. You carry with you a nature altogether corrupt and vile, always seeking to rise up and darken your sense of acceptance and of access to unbroken fellowship with the Father. Nothing can enable you to dwell and walk in the light of God, without even the shadow of a cloud between, but the habitual abiding in Christ as your righteousness. To this you are called. Seek to walk worthy of that calling. Yield yourself to the Holy Spirit to reveal to you the wonderful grace that permits you to draw near to God, clothed in a divine righteousness. Take time to realize that the king's own robe has indeed been put on, and that in it you need not fear entering His presence. It is the proof that you are the man whom the king delights to honor.

Take time to remember that as much as you need it in the palace, no less do you require it when He sends you forth into the world, where you are the king's messenger and representative. Live your daily life in the full consciousness of being righteous in God's sight, an object of delight and pleasure in Christ. Connect every view you have of Christ in His other graces with this first one: "Of God He became for you righteousness." This will keep you in perfect peace. That way, you shall enter into and dwell in the rest of God. So shall your inmost being be transformed into being righteous and doing righteousness. In your heart and life it will become manifest where you dwell. Abiding in Jesus Christ, the Righteous One, you will share His position, His character, and His blessedness: "You love righteousness and hate wickedness; therefore God, Your God, has anointed You with the oil of gladness more than Your companions" (Ps. 45:7). Joy and gladness above measure will be your portion.

FOR FURTHER THOUGHT

1. *What does it mean to you that Christ is made of God for you righteousness, of God you are in Him as our righteousness, and that you are made the righteousness of God in Him?*
2. *What changes in your life and your relationship to God will or has a full union with Jesus Christ accomplished?*
3. *What must you do to dwell and to live consistently and uninterruptedly in the light of God?*

DAY 9

AS YOUR SANCTIFICATION

But of Him you are in Christ Jesus, who became
for us wisdom from God—and righteousness
and sanctification and redemption.
1 CORINTHIANS 1:30

"PAUL...to the church of God which is at Corinth, to those who are sanctified in Christ Jesus, called to be saints"—thus the chapter opens in which we are taught that Christ is our sanctification.

In the Old Testament, believers were called the righteous; in the New Testament, they are called saints, the holy ones, sanctified in Christ Jesus. Holy is higher than righteous.[20] Holy in God has reference to His innermost being; righteous, to His dealings with His creatures. In man, righteousness is but a stepping stone to holiness. It is in this he can approach most near to the perfection of God (compare Matt. 5:48, 1 Pet.1:16). In the Old Testament righteousness was found, while holiness was only typified; in Jesus Christ, the Holy One, and in His people, His saints or holy ones, it is first realized.

As in scripture, and in our text, so in personal experience righteousness precedes holiness. When first the believer finds Christ as his righteousness, he has such joy in the new-made discovery that the study of holiness hardly has a place. But as he grows, the desire for holiness makes itself felt, and he seeks to know what provision his God has made for supplying that need.

A superficial acquaintance with God's plan leads to the view that while justification is God's work, by faith in Christ, sanctification is our work, to be performed under the influence of the gratitude we feel for the deliverance we have experienced, and by the aid of the Holy Spirit. But the earnest Christian soon finds how little gratitude can supply the power. When he thinks that more prayer will bring it, he finds that, indispensable as prayer is, it is not enough. Often the believer struggles hopelessly for years, until he listens to the teaching of the Spirit, as He glorifies Christ again and reveals Christ, our sanctification, to be appropriated by faith alone.

Christ is made by God for us sanctification. Holiness is the very nature of God, and *that alone is holy that God takes possession of and fills with Himself.* God's

---

[20] "Holiness may be called spiritual perfection, as righteousness is legal completeness." Horatius Bonar in *God's Way of Holiness.*

answer to the question, "How could sinful man become holy?" is, "Christ, the Holy One of God." In Him, whom the Father sanctified and sent into the world, God's holiness was revealed incarnate and brought within reach of man. "For their sakes I sanctify Myself, that they also may be sanctified by the truth" (John 17:19). There is no other way of our becoming holy but by becoming partakers of the holiness of Christ.[21] And there is no other way of this taking place than by our personal spiritual union with Him, so that through His Holy Spirit His holy life flows into us. "Of Him you are in Christ Jesus, who became for us. . .sanctification." Abiding by faith in Christ our sanctification is the simple secret of a holy life. The measure of sanctification will depend on the measure of abiding in Him. As the soul learns wholly to abide in Christ, the promise is increasingly fulfilled: "May the God of peace Himself sanctify you completely" (1 Thess. 5:23).

Often the believer struggles hopelessly for years, until he listens to the teaching of the Spirit, as He glorifies Christ again and reveals Christ, our sanctification, to be appropriated by faith alone

To illustrate this relationship between the measure of the abiding and the measure of sanctification experienced, let us think of the grafting of a tree, that instructive symbol of our union to Jesus. The illustration is suggested by the Savior's words, "Make the tree good and its fruit good" (Matt. 12:33). I can graft a tree so that only a single branch bears good fruit, while many of the natural branches remain and bear their old fruit—a type of believer in whom a small part of the life is sanctified, but in whom, from ignorance or other reasons, the carnal life still in many respects has full dominion. I can graft a tree so that every branch is cut off, and the whole tree becomes renewed to bear good fruit. And yet, unless I watch over the tendency of the stems to give sprouts, they may again rise and grow strong and, robbing the new graft of the strength it needs, make it weak. Such are Christians who, when apparently powerfully converted, forsake all to follow Christ, and yet after a time, through unwatchfulness, allow old habits to regain their power, and whose Christian life and fruit are but feeble. But if I want a tree fully made good, I take it when it is young and, cutting the stem clean off on the ground, I graft it just where it emerges from the soil. I watch over every bud that the old nature could possibly put forth, until the flow of sap from the old roots into the new stem is so complete that the old life has, as it were, been entirely conquered and covered by the new. Here I have a tree entirely renewed—an emblem of the Christian who has learned in entire consecration to surrender everything for Christ, and in a wholehearted faith wholly to abide in Him.

If, in this last case, the old tree were a reasonable being who could cooperate with the gardener, what would his language be to it? Would it not be this: "Yield

[21] See note at end of chapter.

yourself now entirely to this new nature with which I have provided you. Repress every tendency of the old nature to grow buds or sprouts. Let all your sap and all your life powers rise up into this graft from that beautiful tree, which I have put on you. That way you shall bring forth sweet and much fruit." And the language of the tree to the gardener would be: "When you graft me, don't spare a single branch. Let everything of the old self, even the smallest bud, be destroyed, so that I may no longer live in my own, but in that other life that was cut off and brought and put on me, so that I might be wholly new and good."

And, once again, if you could afterwards ask the renewed tree, as it was bearing abundant fruit, what it could say about itself, its answer would be this: "In me, that is, in my roots, there dwells no good thing. I am always inclined to evil. The sap I collect from the soil is in its nature corrupt and ready to show itself in bearing evil fruit. But just when the sap rises into the sunshine to ripen into fruit, the wise gardener has clothed me with a new life, through which my sap is purified and all my powers are renewed to the production of good fruit. I need only to abide in that which I have received. He cares for the immediate repression and removal of every bud that the old nature still would put forth."

If you desire to live a holy life, abide in Christ your sanctification. Look upon Him as the Holy One of God, made man that He might communicate to us the holiness of God

Christian, don't be afraid to claim God's promises to make you holy. Don't listen to the suggestion that the corruption of your old nature would render holiness an impossibility. In your flesh dwells no good thing, and that flesh, though crucified with Christ, is not yet dead but will continually seek to rise and lead you to evil. But the Father is the vinedresser. He has grafted the life of Christ on your life. That holy life is mightier than your evil life, and under the watchful care of the vinedresser, that new life can keep down the workings of the evil life within you. The evil nature is there, with its unchanged tendency to rise up and show itself. But the new nature is there too—the living Christ, your sanctification, is there—and through Him all your powers can be sanctified as they rise into life, and be made to bear fruit to the glory of the Father.

And now, if you desire to live a holy life, abide in Christ your sanctification. Look upon Him as the Holy One of God, made man that He might communicate to us the holiness of God. Listen when scripture teaches that there is within you a new nature, a new man, created in Christ Jesus in righteousness *and true holiness*. Remember that this holy nature that is in you is singularly fitted for living a holy life, and for performing all holy duties, as much so as the old nature is for doing evil. Understand that this holy nature within you has its root and life in Christ in heaven and can only grow and become strong as the interaction between it and its source is uninterrupted. And above all, believe most confidently that Jesus Christ Himself delights in maintaining that new nature within you, and imparting to it His own strength and wisdom for its work.

Let that faith lead you daily to the surrender of all self-confidence, and the confession of the utter corruption of all there is in you by nature. Let it fill you with a quiet and assured confidence that you are indeed able to do what the Father expects of you as His child, under the covenant of His grace, because you have Christ strengthening you. Let it teach you to lay yourself and your services on the altar as spiritual sacrifices, holy and acceptable in His sight, a sweet-smelling savor. Don't look at a life of holiness as a burden and an effort, but as the natural outgrowth of the life of Christ within you. And let ever again a quiet, hopeful, joyful faith hold itself assured that all you need for a holy life will most assuredly be given you out of the holiness of Jesus. Then will you understand and demonstrate what it is to abide in Christ our sanctification.

For Further Thought

1. *What do you think God means when He refers to you as "sanctified" in and through Jesus Christ? What are the practical outgrowths of a life of holiness and sanctification?*

2. *God wants you to live a life of gratitude for every blessing He has bestowed upon you, including giving you Christ as your righteousness. But what, according to this reading, are the limitations of gratitude in your life? What can it not accomplish?*

3. *The Bible teaches that in your flesh there dwells nothing good. So how can you, who lives a life in your flesh, be made righteous and sanctified before God?*

THE thought that in the personal holiness of our Lord a new holy nature was formed to be communicated to us, and that we make use of it by faith, is the central idea of Marshall's invaluable work, *The Gospel Mystery of Sanctification:*

"One great mystery is that the holy frame and disposition whereby our souls are furnished and enabled for immediate practice of the law must be obtained by receiving it out of Christ's fullness, as a thing already prepared and brought to an existence for us in Christ and treasured up in Him; and that, as we are justified by a righteousness provided in Christ and imputed to us, so we are sanctified by such a holy frame and qualification as are first accomplished and completed in Christ for us, and then imparted to us. As our natural corruption was produced originally in the first Adam and propagated from him to us, so our new nature and holiness is first produced in Christ and derived from Him to us, or, as it were, propagated. So that we are not at all to work together with Christ in making or producing that holy frame in us, but only to take it to ourselves and use it in our holy practice, as made ready to our hands. Thus we have fellowship with Christ, in receiving that holy frame of spirit that was originally in Him—for fellowship is where several persons have the same things in common. This mystery is so great that, notwithstanding all the light of the Gospel, we commonly think that we must get a holy frame by producing it anew in ourselves and by pursuing it and working it out of our own heart."[22]

---

[22] I have felt so strongly that the teaching of Marshall is just what the Church needs to bring out clearly what the scripture path of holiness is that I have prepared an abridgment (all in the author's own words) of his work. By leaving out what was not essential to his argument and shortening when he appeared diffuse, I hoped to bring his book within reach of many who might never read the larger work. It is published by Nisbet & Co. under the title, *The Highway of Holiness.* I cannot too earnestly urge every student of theology and of scripture and the art of holy living to make himself master of the teaching of Marshall's third, fourth, and twelfth chapters.

DAY 10
AS YOUR REDEMPTION

But of Him you are in Christ Jesus, who became
for us wisdom from God—and righteousness
and sanctification and redemption.
1 CORINTHIANS 1:30

HERE we have the top of the ladder, reaching into heaven—the blessed end to which Christ and life in Him is to lead. The word *redemption*, though sometimes applied to our deliverance from the guilt of sin, here refers to our complete and final deliverance from all its consequences, when the Redeemer's work shall become fully manifest, even to the redemption of the body itself (compare Rom. 8:21–23; Eph. 1:14, 4:30).

The expression points us to the highest glory to be hoped for in the future, and therefore also to the highest blessing to be enjoyed in the present in Christ. We have seen how, as a prophet, Christ is our wisdom, revealing to us God and His love, with the nature and conditions of the salvation that love has prepared. As a priest, He is our righteousness, restoring us to right relations to God and securing us His favor and friendship. As a king, He is our sanctification, forming and guiding us into the obedience to the Father's holy will. As these three offices work out God's one purpose, the grand consummation will be reached, the complete deliverance from sin and all its effects will be accomplished, and ransomed humanity will regain all that it had ever lost.

Christ is made of God for us *redemption*. The word invites us to look upon Jesus, not only as He lived on earth—teaching us by word and example, as He died, to reconcile us with God, as He lives again, a victorious king, rising to receive His crown—but as, sitting at the right hand of God, He takes again the glory that He had with the Father before the world began and holds it there for us. It consists in this, that there His human nature—yes, His human body—freed from all the consequences of sin to which He once had been exposed, is now admitted to share the divine glory. As Son of Man, He dwells on the throne and in the bosom of the Father, and the deliverance from what He had to suffer from sin is complete and eternal. The complete redemption is found embodied in His own person, and what He as man is and has in heaven is the complete redemption. *He* is made of God to us redemption.

We are in Him as such. And the more intelligently and believingly we abide in Him as our redemption, the more shall we experience, even here, of "the powers of the age to come" (Heb. 6:5). As our communion with Him becomes more intimate and intense, and as we let the Holy Spirit reveal Him to us in His heavenly glory, the more we realize how the life in us is the life of One who sits upon the throne of heaven. We feel the power of an endless life working in us. We taste the eternal life. We have the foretaste of the eternal glory.

The blessings flowing from abiding in Christ as our redemption are great. The soul is delivered from all fear of death. There was a time when even the Savior feared death. But now no longer. He has triumphed over death—even His body has entered into the glory. The believer who abides in Christ as his full redemption realizes even now his spiritual victory over death. It becomes to him the servant that removes the last rags of the old carnal garments, before he is clothed upon with the new body of glory. It carries the body to the grave, to lie there as the seed from which the new body will arise the worthy companion of the glorified spirit.

The resurrection of the body is no longer a barren doctrine, but a living expectation, and even a developing experience, because the Spirit of Him who raised Jesus from the dead dwells in the body as the pledge that even our mortal bodies shall be made alive (Rom. 8:11–23). This faith exercises its sanctifying influence in the willing surrender of the sinful members of the body to be put to death and completely subjected to the dominion of the Spirit, as preparation for the time when the frail body shall be changed and fashioned like to His glorious body.

As these three offices work out God's one purpose, the grand consummation will be reached, the complete deliverance from sin and all its effects will be accomplished, and ransomed humanity will regain all that it had ever lost.

This full redemption of Christ as extending to the body has a depth of meaning not easily expressed. It was of man as a whole, soul and body, that it is said that he was made in the image and likeness of God. In the angels, God had created spirits without material bodies; in the creation of the world, there was matter without spirit. Man was to be the highest specimen of divine art, the combination in one being of matter and spirit in perfect harmony, as an example of the most perfect union between God and His own creation. Sin entered in and appeared to thwart the divine plan. The material obtained a fearful supremacy over the spiritual. The Word was *made flesh*, the divine fullness received an *embodiment* in the humanity of Christ, so that the redemption might be a complete and perfect one, so that the whole creation, which now groans and labors in pain together, might be delivered from the bondage of corruption into the liberty of the glory of the children of God (see Rom. 8:22).

God's purpose will not be accomplished and Christ's glory will not be manifested fully until the body, with that whole of nature of which it is part and head, has been transfigured by the power of the spiritual life and made the transparent clothing for showing forth the glory of the infinite Spirit. Then only shall we understand: "Christ Jesus is made for us (complete) redemption."

In the meantime we are taught to believe: "Of God are you in Christ, as your redemption." This is not meant as a revelation, to be left to the future. For the full development of the Christian life, our present abiding in Christ must seek to enter into and appropriate it. We do this as we learn to triumph over death. We do it as we learn to look upon Christ as the Lord of our body, claiming its entire consecration, securing even here, if faith will claim it (Mark 16:17–18), victory over the terrible dominion sin has had in the body. We do this as we learn to look on all nature as part of the kingdom of Christ, destined, even though it is through a baptism of fire, to partake in His redemption. We do it as we allow the powers of the coming world to possess us, and to lift us up into a life in the heavenly places, to enlarge our hearts and our views, to anticipate, even here, the things that have never entered into the heart of man to conceive.

> *The believer who abides in Christ as his full redemption realizes even now his spiritual victory over death. It becomes to him the servant that removes the last rags of the old carnal garments, before he is clothed upon with the new body of glory.*

Believer, abide in Christ as your redemption. Let this be the crown of your Christian life. Don't seek it first or only, apart from the knowledge of Christ in His other relations. But seek it truly as that to which they are meant to lead you up. Abide in Christ as your redemption. Nothing will make you fit for this but faithfulness in the previous steps of the Christian life. Abide in Him as your wisdom, the perfect revelation of all that God is and has for you. Follow, in the daily ordering of the inner and the outer life, with humble docility His teaching, and you shall be counted worthy to have secrets revealed to you that to most disciples are a sealed book. The wisdom will lead you into the mysteries of complete redemption.

Abide in Him as your righteousness and dwell clothed upon with Him in that inner sanctuary of the Father's favor and presence to which His righteousness gives you access. As you rejoice in your reconciliation, you shall understand how it includes all things, and how they too await the full redemption: "For it pleased the Father. . .by Him to reconcile all things to Himself, by Him, whether things on earth or things in heaven" (Col. 1:19, 20).

And abide in Him as your sanctification. The experience of His power to make you holy in spirit and soul and body will awaken your faith in a holiness that shall not cease its work until the bells of the horses and every pot in Jerusalem shall be holiness to the Lord (see Zech. 14:21). Abide in Him as your redemption and live, even here, as the heir of the future glory. And as you seek to experience in yourself to the full the power of His saving grace, your heart shall be enlarged to realize the position man has been destined to occupy in the universe, as having all things made subject to him, and you shall for your part be prepared to live worthy of that high and heavenly calling.

FOR FURTHER THOUGHT

1. *As your own prophet, priest, and king, what great purposes does Jesus Christ fulfill for you in your life, both here on earth and in eternity?*
2. *What specific—and great—blessings and knowledge do you receive when you abide in Christ your redemption?*
3. *You know that having Christ as your redemption seals your eternity with Him in heaven. But how does having Christ as your redemption affect your daily life and walk here on earth?*

Day 11

The Crucified One

I have been crucified with Christ;
it is no longer I who live, but Christ lives in me.
GALATIANS 2:20

We have been planted together in the likeness of his death.
ROMANS 6:5 KJV

"I have been crucified with Christ." Thus the apostle expresses his assurance of his fellowship with Christ in His sufferings and death, and his full participation in all the power and the blessing of that death. And so really did he mean what he said, and know that he was now indeed dead, that he adds: "It is *no longer I who live*, but Christ lives in me."

How blessed must be the experience of such a union with the Lord Jesus! To be able to look upon His death as mine, just as really as it was His—upon His perfect obedience to God, His victory over sin, and complete deliverance from its power, as mine! To realize that the power of that death does by faith work daily with a divine energy in putting to death the flesh, and renewing the whole life into the perfect conformity to the resurrection life of Jesus! Abiding in Jesus, the Crucified One, is the secret of the growth of that new life, which is always begotten of the death of nature.

Let us try to understand this. The suggestive expression, "*Planted into* the likeness of His death," will teach us what the abiding in the Crucified One means. When a graft is united with the stock on which it is to grow, we know that it must be kept fixed, that it must abide in the place where the stock has been cut, been wounded, to make an opening to receive the graft. No graft without wounding— the laying bare and opening up of the inner life of the tree to receive the stranger branch. It is only through such wounding that access can be obtained to the fellowship of the sap and the growth and the life of the stronger stem.

It is just like that with Jesus and the sinner. Only when we are planted into the likeness of His death shall we also be in the likeness of His resurrection, partakers of the life and the power there are in Him. In the death of the cross Christ was wounded, and in His opened wounds a place prepared where we might be grafted in. And just as one might say to a graft, and does practically say as it is fixed in its place, "Abide here in the wound of the stem, that is now to bear you," so to the believing soul the message comes, "Abide in the wounds of Jesus. There is the place of union, and life, and growth. There you shall see how His heart was opened to receive you, how His flesh was wounded so that the way might be opened for your being made one with Him, and having access to all the blessings flowing from His divine nature."

You have also noticed how the graft has to be torn away from the tree where it by nature grew, and to be cut into conformity to the place prepared for it in the wounded stem. Likewise, the believer has to be made conformable to Christ's death—to be crucified and to die with Him. The wounded stem and the wounded graft are cut to fit into each other, into each other's likeness.

There is a fellowship between Christ's sufferings and your sufferings. His experiences must become yours. The disposition He demonstrated in choosing and bearing the cross must be yours. Like Him, you will have to give full assent to the righteous judgment and curse of a holy God against sin. Like Him, you have to consent to yield your life, as laden with sin and curse, to death, and through it to pass to the new life. Like Him, you shall experience that it is only through the self-sacrifice of Gethsemane and Calvary that the path is to be found to the joy and the fruit-bearing of the resurrection life. The more clear the resemblance between the wounded stem and the wounded graft, the more exactly their wounds fit into each other, the surer and the easier, and the more complete will be the union and the growth.

> *A*bide in the wounds of Jesus. There is the place of union, and life, and growth. There you shall see how His heart was opened to receive you, how His flesh was wounded so that the way might be opened for your being made one with Him

It is in Jesus, the Crucified One, I must abide. I must learn to look upon the cross as not only an atonement to God, but also a victory over the devil—not only a deliverance from the guilt, but also from the power of sin. I must gaze on Him on the cross as wholly mine, offering Himself to receive me into the closest union and fellowship, and to make me partaker of the full power of His death to sin and the new life of victory to which it is but the gateway. I must yield myself to Him in an undivided surrender, with much prayer and strong desire, imploring to be admitted into the ever-closer fellowship and conformity of His death, of the Spirit in which He died that death.

Let me try to understand why the cross is therefore the place of union. *On the cross* the Son of God enters into the fullest union with man—enters into the fullest experience of what it says to have become a son of man, a member of a race under the curse. It is in death that the prince of life conquers the power of death, in death alone that He can make me partaker of that victory. The life He imparts is a life from the dead, and each new experience of the power of that life depends on the fellowship of the death. The death and the life are inseparable. All the grace that Jesus the Saving One gives is given only in the path of fellowship with Jesus the Crucified One.

Christ came and took my place. I must put myself in His place and abide there. And there is but one place that is both His and mine—that place is the cross. His in virtue of His free choice, mine by reason of the curse of sin. He came there to seek me, and there alone I can find Him. When He found me there, it was the place of cursing. This He experienced, for "cursed is everyone who hangs on a tree" (Gal. 3:13). He made it a place of blessing. This I experienced, for Christ has delivered us from the curse, being made a curse for us.

> It is as I abide daily, deeply in Jesus the Crucified One that I shall taste the sweetness of His love, the power of His life, and the completeness of His salvation.

When Christ comes in my place, He remains what He was—the beloved of the Father. But in the fellowship with me He shares my curse and dies my death. When I stand in His place, which is still always mine, I am still what I was by nature: the accursed one who deserves to die. But as united to Him, I share His blessing and receive His life. When He came to be one with me, He could not avoid the cross, for the curse always points to the cross as its end and fruit. And when I seek to be one with Him, I cannot avoid the cross either, for nowhere but on the cross are life and deliverance to be found.

As inevitably as my curse pointed Him to the cross as the only place where He could be fully united to me, His blessing points me to the cross too as the only place where I can be united to Him. He took my cross for His own, and I must take His cross as my own—I must be crucified with Him. It is as I abide daily, deeply in Jesus the Crucified One that I shall taste the sweetness of His love, the power of His life, and the completeness of His salvation.

Beloved believer! It is a deep mystery, this of the cross of Christ. I fear there are many Christians who are content to look upon the cross, with Christ on it dying for their sins, but who have little heart for fellowship with the Crucified One. They hardly know that He invites them to it. Or they are content to consider the ordinary afflictions of life, which the children of the world often have as much as they, as their share of Christ's cross. They have no conception of what it is to be crucified with Christ, that bearing the cross means likeness to Christ in the principles that animated Him in His path of obedience. The entire surrender of all self-will, the complete denial to the flesh of its every desire and pleasure, the perfect separation from the world in all its ways of thinking and acting, the losing and hating of one's life, the giving up of self and its interests for the sake of others—this is the disposition that marks him who has taken up Christ's cross, who seeks to say, "I am crucified with Christ; I abide in Christ, the Crucified One."

Would you in very deed please your Lord and live in as close fellowship with Him as His grace could maintain you in? O pray that His Spirit lead you into this blessed truth, this secret of the Lord for them who fear Him. We know how Peter knew and confessed Christ as the Son of the living God while the cross was still an offense (Matt. 16:16–17, 21, 23). The faith that believes in the blood that pardons and the life that renews can only reach its perfect growth as it abides beneath the cross and in living fellowship with Him seeks for perfect conformity with Jesus the crucified.

O Jesus, our crucified Redeemer, teach us not only to believe in You, but to abide in You, to take Your cross not only as the ground of our pardon, but also as the law of our life. O teach us to love it, not only because on it You bore our curse, but because on it we enter into the closest fellowship with You and are crucified with You. And teach us that as we yield ourselves wholly to be possessed by the Spirit in which You bore the cross, we shall be made partakers of the power and the blessing to which the cross alone gives access.

FOR FURTHER THOUGHT

1. *What specifically did the apostle Paul mean when he wrote, "I have been crucified with Christ"? What does being crucified with Jesus Christ, the Crucified One, mean to you?*

2. *"There is a fellowship between Christ's sufferings and your sufferings. His experiences must become yours." How does this play itself out daily in your life of faith?*

3. *What happens to you—within you—when you abide deeply in Jesus Christ, the Crucified One?*

Day 12

God Himself Will
Establish You in Him

He who establishes us with you in
Christ and has anointed us is God.
2 Corinthians 1:21

THESE words of Paul teach us a much needed and most blessed truth: that just as our first being united with Christ was the work of divine omnipotence, so we may look to the Father, too, for being kept and being fixed more firmly in Him. "The Lord will perfect that which concerns me"—this expression of confidence should always accompany the prayer, "Do not forsake the works of Your hands" (Ps. 138:8). In all his longings and prayers to attain to a deeper and more perfect abiding in Christ, the believer must hold fast his confidence: "He who has begun a good work in you will complete it until the day of Jesus Christ" (Phil. 1:6). There is nothing that will so help to root and ground him in Christ as this faith: "He who establishes us in Christ is God."

How many there are who can witness that this faith is just what they need! They continually mourn over the variableness of their spiritual life. Sometimes there are hours and days of deep earnestness, and even of blessed experience of the grace of God. But how little is needed to mar their peace, to bring a cloud over the soul! And then, how their faith is shaken! All efforts to regain their standing appear utterly fruitless, and neither solemn vows nor watching and prayer help to restore to them the peace they for a while had tasted.

They need to but understand how just their own efforts are the cause of their failure, because it is God alone who can establish us in Christ Jesus. They would see that just as in justification they had to cease from their own working, and to accept in faith the promise that God would give them life in Christ, so now, in the matter of their sanctification, their first need is to *cease from striving themselves to establish the connection with Christ more firmly and to allow God to do it.* "God is faithful, by whom you were called into the fellowship of His Son, Jesus Christ" (1 Cor. 1:9). What they need is the simple faith that the establishing in Christ, day by day, is God's work—a work that He delights to do, in spite of all our weakness and unfaithfulness, if we will but trust Him for it.

To the blessedness of such a faith, and the experience it brings, many can testify. What peace and rest to know that there is a vinedresser who cares for the branch to see that it grows stronger and that its union with the vine becomes more perfect, who watches over every hindrance and danger, and who supplies every needed aid! What peace and rest, fully and finally to give up our abiding into the care of God, and never have a wish or thought, never to offer a prayer or engage in an exercise connected with it without first having the glad remembrance that what we do is only the manifestation of what God is doing in us!

The establishing in Christ is His work. He accomplishes it by stirring us to watch, and wait, and work. But this He can do with power only as we cease interrupting Him by our self-working—as we accept in faith the dependent posture that honors Him and opens the heart to let Him work. How such a faith frees the soul from care and responsibility! In the midst of the rush and bustle of the world's stirring life, amid the subtle and ceaseless temptations of sin, amid all the daily cares and trials that so easily distract and lead to failure, how blessed it would be to be an established Christian always abiding in Christ! How blessed even to have the faith that one can surely become it—that the attainment is within our reach!

> The establishing in Christ is His work. He accomplishes it by stirring us to watch, and wait, and work.

Dear believer, the blessing is indeed within your reach. He who establishes you with us in Christ *is God*. What I want you to take in is this—that believing this promise will not only give you comfort, but will be the means of your obtaining your desire. You know how scripture teaches us that in all God's leadings of His people, faith has everywhere been the one condition of the manifestation of His power. Faith is the ceasing from all nature's efforts, and all other dependence. Faith is confessed helplessness casting itself upon God's promise and claiming its fulfillment. Faith is the putting ourselves quietly into God's hands for Him to do His work. What you and I need now is to take time, until this truth stands out before us in all its spiritual brightness: It is God Almighty, God the faithful and gracious One, who has undertaken to establish me in Christ Jesus.

Listen to what the Word teaches you— "*The LORD will establish* you as a holy people to Himself" (Deut. 28:9); "O LORD God. . .*fix* their heart toward You" (1 Chron. 29:18); "Your God has loved Israel, to *establish* them forever" (2 Chron. 9:8); "You *will establish* the heart of the humble" (see Ps. 10:17); "Now to Him who is able *to establish you*. . .be glory through Jesus Christ forever"

(Rom. 16:25, 27); "So that He may *establish your hearts blameless in holiness*" (1 Thess. 3:13); "*The Lord is faithful*, who *will establish you* and guard you from the evil one" (2 Thess. 3:3); "The God of all grace, who called us to His eternal glory by Christ Jesus...perfect, *establish*, strengthen, and settle you" (1 Pet. 5:10).

Can you take these words to mean anything less than that you too—however inconsistent your spiritual life has up until now been, however unfavorable your natural character or your circumstances may appear—can be established in Christ Jesus, can become an established Christian? Let us but take time to listen, in simple childlike teachableness, to these words as the truth of God and the confidence will come: As surely as I am in Christ, I shall also, day by day, be established in Him.

The lesson appears so simple, and yet the most of us take so long to learn it. The chief reason is that the grace the promise offers is so large, so Godlike, so beyond all our thoughts, that we do not take it really to mean what it says. The believer who has once come to see and accept what it brings can bear witness to the wonderful change there comes over the spiritual life. Before, he had taken charge of his own welfare, but now he has a God to take charge of it. He now knows himself to be in the school of God, a teacher who plans the whole course of study for each of His pupils with infinite wisdom, and delights to have them come daily for the lessons He has to give. All he asks is to feel himself constantly in God's hands and to follow His guidance, neither lagging behind nor going before. Remembering that it is God who works both to will and to do, he sees his only safety to be in yielding himself to God's working. He lays aside all anxiety about his inner life and its growth, because the Father is the vinedresser under whose wise and watchful care each plant is well secured. He knows that there is the prospect of a most blessed life of strength and fruitfulness to everyone who will take God alone and wholly as his hope.

> What you and I need now is to take time, until this truth stands out before us in all its spiritual brightness: It is God Almighty, God the faithful and gracious One, who has undertaken to establish me in Christ Jesus.

Believer, you can do nothing but admit that such a life of trust must be a most blessed one. You say, perhaps, that there are times when you do, with your whole heart, consent to this way of living, and do wholly abandon the care of your inner life to your Father. But somehow it does not last. You forget again, and instead of beginning each morning with the joyous transference of all the needs and cares of your spiritual life to the Father's care, you again feel anxious, burdened, and helpless.

Is it not, perhaps, my brother, because you have not committed to the Father's care this matter of daily remembering to renew your entire surrender? Memory is one of the highest powers in our nature. By it day is linked to day, the unity of life through all our years is kept up, and we know that we are still ourselves. In the spiritual life, recollection is of infinite value. For the sanctifying of our memory, in the service of our spiritual life, God has provided most beautifully. The Holy Spirit is the remembrancer, the Spirit of recollection. Jesus said, "He will. . .bring to your remembrance" (John 14:26). "Now He who *establishes* us with you in Christ. . . is God, who also has sealed us and *given us the Spirit in our hearts as a guarantee*" (2 Cor. 1:21, 22). It is just for the establishing that the Holy Remembrancer has been given. God's blessed promises, and your unceasing acts of faith and surrender accepting of them—He will enable you to remember these each day. The Holy Spirit is—blessed be God—the memory of the new man.

> *In the spiritual life, recollection is of infinite value. For the sanctifying of our memory, in the service of our spiritual life, God has provided most beautifully.*

Apply this to the promise of the text: "He who establishes us in Christ. . .is God." As you now, at this moment, abandon all anxiety about your growth and progress to the God who has undertaken to establish you in the vine, and feel what a joy it is to know that God alone has charge, ask and trust Him by the Holy Spirit always to remind you of this your blessed relation to Him. He will do it, and with each new morning your faith may grow stronger and brighter: I have a God to see that each day I become more firmly united to Christ.

And now, beloved fellow-believer, "may the God of all grace, who called us to His eternal glory by Christ Jesus. . .*perfect, establish, strengthen, and settle you*" (1 Pet. 5:10). What more can you desire? Expect it confidently; ask it fervently. Count on God to do His work. And learn in faith to sing the song, the notes of which each new experience will make deeper and sweeter: "Now to Him who is able to *establish you*. . .be glory through Jesus Christ forever. Amen." Yes, glory to God, who has undertaken to establish us in Christ!

FOR FURTHER THOUGHT

1. *What does it mean to be "established in Christ?" What will your life of faith look like when you are established in Him?*
2. *Read Philippians 1:6. What specific kind of encouragement does that give you as you long and strive for a more perfect abiding in Jesus Christ?*
3. *How specifically does Christ establish us in Himself? What is your role in His work of establishing you? What must you do to ensure that this happens?*

DAY 13

EVERY MOMENT

In that day sing to her,
"A vineyard of red wine! I, the LORD, keep it,
I water it every moment; lest any hurt it,
I keep it night and day."
ISAIAH 27:2–3

THE vineyard was the symbol of the people of Israel, in whose midst the true vine was to stand. The branch is the symbol of the individual believer who stands in the vine. The song of the vineyard is also the song of the vine and its every branch. The command still goes forth to the watchers of the vineyard—if only they obeyed it and sang until every feeble-hearted believer had learned and joined the joyful strain—"Sing to her: I, *the LORD, keep it,* I water it *every moment*; lest any hurt it, I KEEP it night and day" (Isa. 27:2–3).

What an answer from the mouth of God Himself to the question so often asked: Is it possible for the believer always to abide in Jesus? Is a life of unbroken fellowship with the Son of God indeed attainable here in this earthly life? Truly not, if the abiding is our work, to be done in our strength. But the things that are impossible with men are possible with God. If the Lord Himself will keep the soul night and day, yes, will watch and water it every moment, then surely the uninterrupted communion with Jesus becomes a blessed possibility to those who can trust God to mean and to do what He says. Then surely the abiding of the branch of the vine day and night, summer and winter, in a never-ceasing life-fellowship, is nothing less than the simple but certain promise of your abiding in your Lord.

In one sense, it is true that there is no believer who does not always abide in Jesus, for without this there could not be true life. "If anyone does not abide in Me, he is cast out" (John 15:6). But when the Savior gives the command, "Abide in me," with the promise, "He who abides in Me. . .bears much fruit" (John 15:5), He speaks of that willing, intelligent, and wholehearted surrender by which we accept His offer and consent to the abiding in Him as the only life we choose or seek.

The objections raised against our right to expect that we shall always be able voluntarily and consciously to abide in Jesus are chiefly two. The one is derived from the nature of man. It is said that our limited powers prevent our being occupied with two things at the same moment. God's providence places many Christians in business, where for hours at a time, the closest attention is required to the work they have to do. How can such a man, it is asked, with his whole mind in the work he has to do, be at the same time occupied with Christ and keeping up fellowship with Him? The consciousness of abiding in Jesus is regarded as requiring such an effort and such a direct occupation of the mind with heavenly thoughts that to enjoy the blessing would imply a withdrawing of oneself from all the ordinary avocations of life. This is the same error as drove the first monks into the wilderness.

Blessed be God, there is no necessity for such a going out of the world. Abiding in Jesus is not a work that needs each moment the mind to be engaged, or the affections to be directly and actively occupied with it. It is an entrusting of oneself to the keeping of the eternal love, in the faith that it will abide near us and with its holy presence watch over us and ward off the evil, even when we have to be most intently occupied with other things. And so the heart has rest and peace and joy in the consciousness of being kept when it cannot keep itself.

> *I*s a life of unbroken fellowship with the Son of God indeed attainable here in this earthly life? Truly not, if the abiding is our work, to be done in our strength.

In ordinary life, we have abundant illustrations of the influence of a supreme affection reigning in and guarding the soul while the mind concentrates itself on work that requires its whole attention. Think of the father of a family, separated for a time from his home so that he may secure for his loved ones what they need. He loves his wife and children and longs much to return to them. There may be hours of intense occupation when he doesn't have a moment to think of them, and yet his love is as deep and real as when he can call up their images. All the while his love and the hope of making them happy urge him on and fill him with a secret joy in his work. Think of a king: in the midst of work, pleasure, and trial, he all the while acts under the secret influence of the consciousness of royalty, even while he does not think of it. A loving wife and mother never for one moment loses the sense of her relationship to the husband and children. The consciousness and the love are there, amid all her engagements.

And shall it be thought impossible for the everlasting love so to take and keep possession of our spirits so that we too shall never for a moment lose the secret consciousness that we are in Christ, kept in Him by His almighty power. Oh, it is possible—we can be sure it is. Our abiding in Jesus is even more than a fellowship of love—it is a fellowship of life. In work or in rest, the consciousness of life never leaves us. And even so can the mighty power of the eternal life maintain within us the consciousness of its presence. Or rather, Christ, who is our life, Himself dwells within us, and by His presence maintains our consciousness that we are in Him.

The second objection has reference to our sinfulness. Christians are so accustomed to looking at sinning daily as something absolutely inevitable that they regard it as a matter of course that no one can keep up abiding fellowship with the Savior: we must sometimes be unfaithful and fail. As if it was not just because we have a nature that is nothing but a very fountain of sin that the abiding in Christ has been ordained for us as our only but our sufficient deliverance! As if it were not the heavenly vine, the living, loving Christ, in whom we have to abide, and whose almighty power to hold us fast is to be the measure of our expectations! As if He would give us the command, "Abide in Me," without securing the grace and the power to enable us to perform it! As if, above all, we didn't have the Father as the vinedresser to keep us from falling, and that not in a large and general sense, but according to His own precious promise: "night and day, every moment!"

Oh, if we will but look to our God as the keeper of Israel, of whom it is said, "The LORD shall preserve you from all evil; He shall preserve your soul" (Ps. 121:7), we shall learn to believe that conscious abiding in Christ every moment, night and day, is indeed what God has prepared for those who love Him.

Abiding in Jesus is not a work that needs each moment the mind to be engaged, or the affections to be directly and actively occupied with it.

My beloved fellow Christians, let nothing less than this be your aim. I know well that you may not find it easy to attain, that there may come more than one hour of weary struggle and bitter failure. Were the Church of Christ what it should be— were older believers to younger converts what they should be: witnesses to God's faithfulness, like Caleb and Joshua, encouraging their brethren to go up and possess the land with their, "We are well able to overcome it. . . . If the LORD delights in us, then *He will bring us* into this land and give it to us" (Num. 13:30, 14:8)—were the atmosphere that the young believer breathes as he enters the fellowship of the saints that of a healthy, trustful, joyful consecration, abiding in Christ would come as the natural outgrowth of being in Him.

But in the sickly state in which such a great part of the body is, souls that are pressing after this blessing are sorely hindered by the depressing influence of the thought and the life around them. It is not to discourage that I say this, but to warn and to urge to a more entire casting of ourselves upon the word of God Himself. There may come more than our hour in which you are ready to yield to despair. But be of good courage. Only believe. He who has put the blessing within your reach will assuredly lead to its possession.

The way in which souls enter into the possession may differ. To some it may come as the gift of a moment. In times of revival, in the fellowship with other believers in whom the Spirit is working effectually, under the leading of some servant of God who can guide, and sometimes in solitude too, it is as if all at once a new revelation comes upon the soul. It sees, as in the light of heaven, the strong vine holding and bearing the weak branches so securely that doubt becomes impossible. It can only wonder how it ever could have understood the words to mean anything else than this: To abide unceasingly in Christ is the portion of every believer. It sees it, and to believe, rejoice, and love, come as of itself.

> *There may come more than our hour in which you are ready to yield to despair. But be of good courage. Only believe. He who has put the blessing within your reach will assuredly lead to its possession.*

To others it comes by a slower and more difficult path. Day by day, amid discouragement and difficulty, the soul has to press forward. Be of good cheer, for this way too leads to the rest. Seek only to keep your heart set on the promise: "I, *the LORD, keep it*. . .night and day." Take from His own lips the watchword: "*Every moment.*" In that, you have the law of His love and the law of your hope. Be content with nothing less. Think no longer that the duties and the cares, that the sorrows and the sins of this life must succeed in hindering the abiding life of fellowship. Take rather for the rule of your daily experience the language of faith: I am persuaded that neither death with its fears, nor life with its cares, nor things present with their pressing claims, nor things to come with their dark shadows, nor height of joy, nor depth of sorrow, nor any other created thing, shall be able, for one single moment, to separate us from the love of God, which is in Christ Jesus our Lord, and in which He is teaching me to abide (see Rom. 8:38–39).

If things look dark and faith would fail, sing again the song of the vineyard: In that day sing to her, "I, the LORD, keep it, I water it every moment; lest any hurt it, I keep it night and day." And be assured that if Jehovah keeps the branch night and day and waters it every moment, a life of continuous and unbroken fellowship with Christ is indeed our privilege.

FOR FURTHER THOUGHT

1. *Abiding in Jesus is not a work that needs each moment the mind to be engaged, or the affections to be directly and actively occupied with it. When is it then? How can you abide every moment in Christ?*
2. *Most Christians see daily sinning as inevitable, and therefore they believe it is not possible to maintain unbroken abiding in Christ. However, God wants you to live a life of conscious abiding in Christ every moment. How has He made this possible for you now?*

3.   *Read Roman 8:38–39. How does that passage relate to your constant, moment by moment abiding in Christ? What encouragement do you take from this passage, even during times when you feel that your faith might fail you in this abiding?*

DAY 14

DAY BY DAY

"And the people shall go out and gather a certain quota every day."
EXODUS 16:4

THE *day's quota in its day*: Such was the rule for God's giving and man's working in the gathering of the manna. It is still the law in all the dealings of God's grace with His children. A clear insight into the beauty and application of this arrangement is a wonderful help in understanding how one who feels himself utterly weak can have the confidence and the perseverance to hold on brightly through all the years of his earthly course.

A doctor was once asked by a patient who had met with a serious accident: "Doctor, how long shall I have to lie here?" The answer, "Only a day at a time," taught the patient a precious lesson. It was the same lesson God had recorded for His people of all ages long before: The day's quota every day.

It was, without doubt, with a view to this and to meet man's weakness that God graciously appointed the change of day and night. If time had been given to man in the form of one long unbroken day, it would have exhausted and overwhelmed him. The change of day and night continually recruits and recreates his powers.

As a child, who easily makes himself master of a book when each day only the lesson for the day is given him, would be utterly hopeless if the whole book were given him at once, so it would be with man if there were no divisions in time. Broken small and divided into fragments, he can bear them, for only the care and the work of each day have to be undertaken—the day's quota in its day. The rest of the night prepares him for making a fresh start with each new morning. The mistakes of the past can be avoided, its lessons improved. And he needs only each day to be faithful for the one short day, and long years and a long life take care of themselves, without the sense of their length or their weight ever being a burden.

Most sweet is the encouragement to be derived from this truth in the life of grace. Many a soul is disquieted with the thought as to how it will be able to gather and to keep the manna needed for all its years of travel through such a barren wilderness. It has never learned what unspeakable comfort there is in the word: The day's quota every day. That word takes away all care for tomorrow most completely.

Only today is yours; tomorrow is the Father's. The question, "What security do you have that during all the years in which you have to contend with the coldness, temptations, or trials of the world, you will always abide in Jesus?" is one you need, yes, you may not ask. Manna, as your food and strength, is given only by the day—faithfully to fill the present is your only security for the future. Accept, enjoy, and fulfill with your whole heart the part you have this day to perform. His presence and grace enjoyed today will remove all doubt whether you can entrust tomorrow to Him too.

How great the value that this truth teaches us to attach to each single day! We are so easily led to look at life as a great whole and to neglect the little today, to forget that the single days do indeed make up the whole and that the value of each single day depends on its influence on the whole. One day lost is a link broken in the chain, which it often takes more than another day to mend. One day lost influences the next and makes its keeping more difficult. Yes, one day lost may be the loss of what months or years of careful labor had secured. The experience of many a believer could confirm this.

Believer! If you desire to abide in Jesus, let it be day by day. You have already heard the message: moment by moment. The lesson of day by day has something more to teach. Of the moments, there are many when there is no direct exercise of the mind on your part. The abiding is in the deeper recesses of the heart, kept by the Father, to whom you entrusted yourself. But just this is the work that with each new day has to be renewed for the day—the distinct renewal of surrender and trust for the life of moment by moment.

It was, without doubt, with a view to this and to meet man's weakness that God graciously appointed the change of day and night.

God has gathered up the moments and bound them up into a bundle for the very purpose that we might take measure of them. As we look forward in the morning, or look back in the evening, and weigh the moments, we learn how to value and how to use them rightly. And even as the Father, with each new morning, meets you with the promise of just sufficient manna for the day for yourself and those who have to partake with you, meet Him with the bright and loving renewal of your acceptance of the position He has given you in His beloved Son. Accustom yourself to look upon this as one of the reasons for the appointment of day and night.

God thought of our weakness and sought to provide for it. Let each day have its value from your calling to abide in Christ. As its light opens on your waking eyes, accept it on these terms: A day, just one day only, but still a day, given to abide and grow up in Jesus Christ. Whether it be a day of health or sickness, joy or sorrow, rest or work, of struggle or victory, let the chief thought with which you receive it in the morning thanksgiving be this: "A day that the Father gave—in it I may, I must, become more closely united to Jesus." As the Father asks, "Can you trust Me just for this one day to keep you abiding in Jesus, and Jesus to keep you fruitful?" you can do nothing but give the joyful response: "I will trust and not be afraid."

The day's quota for its day was given to Israel in the morning very early. The portion was for use and nourishment during the whole day, but the giving and the getting of it was the morning's work. This suggests how greatly the power to spend a day rightly, to abide all the day in Jesus, depends on the morning hour. If the firstfruits are holy, the lump is holy (Rom. 11:16). During the day, there come hours of intense occupation in the rush of business or the crowd of men when only the Father's keeping can maintain the connection with Jesus unbroken. The morning manna fed all the day, and it is only when the believer in the morning secures his quiet time in secret to renew distinctly and effectually loving fellowship with his Savior that the abiding can be kept up all the day.

> *A*ccept, enjoy, and fulfill with your whole heart the part you have this day to perform. His presence and grace enjoyed today will remove all doubt whether you can entrust tomorrow to Him too.

But what cause for thanksgiving that it may be done! In the morning, with its freshness and quiet, the believer can look out on the day. He can consider its duties and its temptations, and pass them through beforehand, as it were, with his Savior, throwing all upon Him who has undertaken to be everything to him. Christ is his manna, his nourishment, his strength, his life, and he can take the day's quota for the day—Christ as his for all the needs the day may bring—and go on in the assurance that the day will be one of blessing and of growth.

And then, as the lesson of the value and the work of the single day is being taken to heart, the learner is all unconsciously being led on to get the secret of "day by day continually" (Exod. 29:38). The blessed abiding grasped by faith for each individual day is an unceasing and ever-increasing growth. Each day of faithfulness brings a blessing for the next and makes both the trust and the surrender easier and more blessed. And so the Christian life grows: as we give our whole heart to the work of each day, it becomes all the day, and from that every day. And so each day separately, all the day continually, day by day successively, we abide in Jesus. And the days make up the life. What once appeared too high and too great to attain is given to the soul that was content to take and use "every day his portion" (Ezra 3:4) "in the number required by ordinance for each day." Even here on earth, the voice is heard: "Well done, good and faithful servant; you have been faithful over a few things, I will make you ruler over many things. Enter into the joy of your Lord" (Matt. 25:23). Our daily life becomes a wonderful interchange of God's daily grace and our daily praise: "The Lord, who daily loads us with benefits" (Ps. 68:19), "that I may daily perform my vows" (Ps. 61:8).

We learn to understand God's reason for daily giving, as He most certainly gives, only enough but also fully enough for each day. And we get into His way, the way of daily asking and expecting only enough, but most certainly fully enough, for the day. We begin to number our days not from the sun's rising over the world, or by the work we do or the food we eat, but by the daily renewal of the miracle of the manna—the blessedness of daily fellowship with Him who is the life and the light of the world. The heavenly life is as unbroken and continuous as the earthly, because the abiding in Christ each day has for that day brought its blessing. We abide in Him every day and all the day. Lord, make this the portion of each one of us.

For Further Thought

1. *What connection to abiding in Christ did God intend when He separated night and day, when He gave you one new day after another?*
2. *What additional blessing for tomorrow do you think God wants to give you for abiding in Christ in faith just today?*
3. *God gives grace for abiding in Christ each day for that day? Why do you think that is?*

Day 15

At This Moment

Behold, now is the accepted time;
behold, now is the day of salvation.
2 Corinthians 6:2

THE thought of living moment by moment is of such central importance—looking at the abiding in Christ from our side—that we want once more to speak of it. And to all who desire to learn the blessed art of living only a moment at a time, we want to say: The way to learn it is to exercise yourself in living in the present moment. Each time your attention is free to occupy itself with the thought of Jesus—whether it is with time to think and pray, or only for a few passing seconds—let your first thought be to say: "Now, at this moment, I do abide in Jesus." Use such time, not in useless regrets that you have not been abiding fully, or still more hurtful fears that you will not be able to abide, but just at once take the position the Father has given you: "I am in Christ. This is the place God has given me. I accept it. Here I rest. I do now abide in Jesus." This is the way to learn to abide continually.

You may be yet so weak as to fear to say of each day, "I am abiding in Jesus." But the weakest can, each single moment, say, as he consents to occupy his place as a branch in the vine, "Yes, I do abide in Christ." It is not a matter of feeling—it is not a question of growth or strength in the Christian life—it is the simple question whether the will at the present moment desires and consents to recognize the place you have in your Lord, and to accept it. If you are a believer, you are in Christ. If you are in Christ and wish to stay there, it is your duty to say, though it is but for a moment, "Blessed Savior, I abide in You now; You keep me now."

It has been well said that in that little word *now* lays one of the deepest secrets of the life of faith. At the close of a conference on the spiritual life, a minister of experience rose and spoke. He did not know that he had learned any truth he did not know before, but he had learned how to use rightly what he had known. He had learned that it was his privilege at each moment, whatever surrounding circumstances might be, to say, "Jesus saves me *now*." This is indeed the secret of rest and victory. If I can say, "Jesus is to me at this moment all that God gave Him to be—life, and strength, and peace"—I have but as I say it to hold still, and rest, and realize it, and for that moment I have what I need. As my faith sees how of

God I am in Christ and takes the place in Him my Father has provided, my soul can peacefully settle down: Now I abide in Christ.

Believer! When striving to find the way to abide in Christ from moment to moment, remember that the gateway is: Abide in Him at this present moment. Instead of wasting effort in trying to get into a state that will last, just remember that it is Christ Himself—the living, loving Lord—who alone can keep you, and is waiting to do so. Begin now and act in faith in Him for the present moment, for this is the only way to be kept the next.

To attain the life of permanent and perfect abiding is not ordinarily given at once as a possession for the future. Rather, it comes mostly step by step. Make use, therefore, of every opportunity of exercising the trust of the present moment. Each time you bow in prayer, let there first be an act of simple devotion: "Father, I am in Christ. I now abide in Him." Each time you have, amid the bustle of duty, the opportunity of self-recollection, let its first involuntary act be: "I am still in Christ, abiding in Him now." Even when overtaken by sin, and the heart within is all disturbed and excited, O let your first look upwards be with the words: "Father, I have sinned. And yet I come—though I blush to say it—as one who is in Christ. Father, here I am! I can take no other place. Of God I am in Christ. I *now* abide in Christ." Yes, Christian in every possible circumstance, every moment of the day, the voice is calling: "Abide in Me. Do it now." And even now, as you are reading this, come at once and enter upon the blessed life of always abiding, by doing it at once. Do it now.

> *You* may be yet so weak as to fear to say of each day, "I am abiding in Jesus." But the weakest can, each single moment, say, as he consents to occupy his place as a branch in the vine, "Yes, I do abide in Christ."

In the life of David there is a beautiful passage that may help to make this thought clearer (2 Sam. 3:17–18). David had been anointed king in Judah. The other tribes still followed Ishbosheth, Saul's son. Abner, Saul's chief captain, resolves to lead the tribes of Israel to submit to David, the God-appointed king of the whole nation. He speaks to the elders of Israel: "In time past you were seeking for David to be king over you. Now then, do it! For the Lord has spoken of David, saying, 'By the hand of My servant David, I will save My people Israel from the hand of the Philistines and the hand of all their enemies.'" And they did it, and anointed David a second time to be king, now over all Israel, as at first only over Judah (2 Sam. 5:3)—a most instructive type of the way in which a soul is led to the life of entire surrender and undivided allegiance, to the full abiding.

First you have the *divided kingdom*: Judah faithful to the king of God's appointment, and Israel still clinging to the king of its own choosing. As a consequence, the nation divided against itself, and no power to conquer the enemies. Picture of the divided heart. Jesus accepted as king in Judah, the place of the holy mount, in the inner chamber of the soul; but the surrounding territory, the everyday life, not yet brought to subjection; more than half the life still ruled by self-will and its hosts. And so no real peace within and no power over the enemies.

Then there is the *longing desire* for a better state: "In time past you were seeking for David to be king over you." There was a time, when David had conquered the Philistines, when Israel believed in him, but they had been led astray. Abner appeals to their own knowledge of God's will, that David must rule over all. Likewise the believer, when first brought to Jesus, did indeed want Him to be Lord over all, had hoped that He alone would be king. But, sadly, unbelief and self-will had come in, and Jesus could not assert His power over the whole life. And yet the Christian is not content. How he longs—sometimes without daring to hope that it can be—for a better time.

> Yes, Christian in every possible circumstance, every moment of the day, the voice is calling: "Abide in Me. Do it now."

Then follows *God's promise*. Abner says: "The LORD has spoken. . .'By the hand of My servant David, I will save My people Israel from the hand. . .of all their enemies.'" He appeals to God's promise: As David had conquered the Philistines, the nearest enemy in time past, so he alone could conquer those farther off. He should save Israel from the hand of all their enemies. Beautiful type of the promise by which the soul is now invited to trust Jesus for the victory over every enemy and a life of undisturbed fellowship.

"The LORD has spoken"—this is our only hope. On that word rests the sure expectation (Luke 1:70–75): "As *He spoke*. . .that we should be saved from. . .the hand of *all* who hate us, to perform. . .the oath which He swore. . .to grant us that we, being delivered from the hand of our enemies, might serve Him without fear, in holiness and righteousness before Him all the days of our life." David reigning over every corner of the land and leading a united and obedient people on from victory to victory: This is the promise of what Jesus can do for us, as soon as in faith in God's promise all is surrendered to Him and the whole life given up to be kept abiding in Him.

"In time past you were seeking for David to be king over you," Abner said, and added, "Now then, do it!" *Do it now* is the message that this story brings to each one of us who longs to give Jesus unreserved supremacy. Whatever the present moment be, however unprepared the message finds you, however sad the divided and hopeless state of the life may be, still I come and urge Christ's claim to an immediate surrender—this very moment.

I know well that it will take time for the blessed Lord to assert His power and order all within you according to His will—to conquer the enemies and train all your powers for His service. This is not the work of a moment. But there are things that are the work of a moment—of this moment. The one is your surrender of all to Jesus, your surrender of yourself entirely to live only in Him. As time goes on, and exercise has made faith stronger and brighter, that surrender may become clearer and more intelligent. But for this no one may wait. The only way ever to attain to it is to begin immediately. *Do it now.* Surrender yourself this very moment to abide wholly, only, always in Jesus. It is the work of a moment.

> *Christ's renewed acceptance of you is the work of a moment. Be assured that He has you and holds you as His own, that each new "Jesus, I do abide in You," meets with an immediate and most hearty response from the Unseen One.*

And likewise, Christ's renewed acceptance of you is the work of a moment. Be assured that He has you and holds you as His own, that each new "Jesus, I do abide in You," meets with an immediate and most hearty response from the Unseen One. No act of faith can be in vain. He does indeed freshly take hold on us and draw us close to Himself. Therefore, as often as the message comes or the thought comes that Jesus says, "Abide in Me," do it immediately. Each moment there is the whisper: Do it now.

Let any Christian begin, then, and he will speedily experience how the blessing of the present moment is passed on to the next. It is the unchanging Jesus to whom he links himself. It is the power of a divine life, in its unbroken continuity, that takes possession of him. The *do it now* of the present moment—a little thing though it seems—is nothing less than the beginning of the ever-present now, which is the mystery and the glory of eternity. Therefore, Christian, abide in Christ: *do it now.*

For Further Thought

1. *Why is living moment by moment abiding in Christ important? How can you learn to live your life of faith that way—by the moment?*
2. *What is the remedy for those—perhaps yourself—who feel unprepared to abide in Christ, whose lives have been divided between Christ and the world?*
3. *What are the spiritual benefits of obeying Christ's command to "Abide in Me" moment by moment, of doing it right now, this instant?*

Day 16

Forsaking All for Him

*I have suffered the loss of all things,
and count them as rubbish, that I may
gain Christ and be found in Him.*
PHILIPPIANS 3:8–9

WHEREVER there is life, there is a continual interchange of taking in and giving out, of receiving and restoring. The nourishment I take is given out again in the work I do, in the impressions I receive, and in the thoughts and feelings I express. The one depends on the other—the giving out always increases the power of taking in. In the healthy exercise of giving and taking is all the enjoyment of life.

It is so in the spiritual life too. There are Christians who look on its blessedness as consisting all in the privilege of always receiving. They don't know how the capacity for receiving is only kept up and enlarged by continual giving up and giving out—how it is only in the emptiness that comes from the parting with what we have that the divine fullness can flow in. It was a truth our Savior continually insisted on. When He spoke of selling all to secure the treasure, of losing our life to find it, of the hundredfold to those who forsake all, He was expounding the need of self-sacrifice as the law of the kingdom for Himself as well as for His disciples. If we are really to abide in Christ, and to be found in Him—to have our life always and wholly in Him—we must each in our measure say with Paul, "I also count *all things loss* for the excellence of the knowledge of Christ Jesus my Lord. . .that I may gain Christ and be *found in Him*" (Phil. 3:8–9).

Let us try to see what there is to be forsaken and given up. First of all, there is sin. There can be no true conversion without the giving up of sin. And yet, due to the ignorance of the young convert of what really is sin, of what the claims of God's holiness are, and what the extent to which the power of Jesus can enable us to conquer sin, the giving up of sin is but partial and superficial. With the growth of the Christian life, there comes the need of a deeper and more entire purging out of everything that is unholy. And it is especially when the desire to abide in Christ uninterruptedly—to be always found in Him—becomes strong that the soul is led to see the need of a new act of surrender, in which it newly accepts and ratifies its death to sin in Christ and parts indeed with everything that is sin. Availing himself, in the strength of God's Spirit, of that wonderful power of our nature by which the whole of one's future life can be gathered up and disposed of in one act of the will, the believer yields himself to sin no more—to be only and wholly a servant of righteousness. He does it in the joyful assurance that every sin surrendered is gain indeed—room for the inflowing of the presence and the love of Christ.

Next to the parting with unrighteousness is the giving up of self-righteousness. Though contending most earnestly against our own works or merits, it is often long before we come really to understand what it is to refuse self the least place or right in the service of God. Unconsciously, we allow the actings of our own mind and heart and will free scope in God's presence. In prayer and worship, in Bible reading and working for God, instead of absolute dependence on the Holy Spirit's leading, self is expected to do a work it never can do. We are slow to learn the lesson, "In me, (that is, in my flesh) nothing good dwells" (Rom. 7:18). As it is learned and we see how corruption extends to everything that is of nature, we see that there can be no entire abiding in Christ without the giving up of all that is of self in religion—without giving it up to the death and waiting for the breathings of the Holy Spirit as alone able to do in us what is acceptable in God's sight.

> *With the growth of the Christian life, there comes the need of a deeper and more entire purging out of everything that is unholy.*

Then, again, there is our whole natural life, with all the powers and endowments bestowed on us by the Creator, with all the occupations and interests with which providence has surrounded us. It is not enough that when once you are truly converted, you have the earnest desire to have all these devoted to the service of the Lord. The desire is good, but can neither teach the way nor give the strength to do it acceptably.

Incalculable harm has been done to the deeper spirituality of the Church by the idea that when once we are God's children, the using of our gifts in His service follows as a matter of course. No, for this there is indeed needed very special grace. And the way in which the grace comes is again that of sacrifice and surrender. I must see how all my gifts and powers are, even though I am a child of God, still defiled by sin and under the power of the flesh. I must feel that I cannot instantly proceed to use them for God's glory. I must first lay them at Christ's feet, to be accepted and cleansed by Him. *I must feel myself utterly powerless to use them rightly.* I must see that they are most dangerous to me, because through them the flesh, the old nature, self, will so easily exert its power. In this conviction I must part with them, giving them entirely up to the Lord. When He has accepted them and set His stamp upon them, I receive them back, to hold them as His property, to wait on Him for the grace to use them rightly day by day, and *to have them act only under His influence.*

And so experience proves it true here too, that the path of entire consecration is the path of full salvation. Not only is what is given up received back again to become doubly our own, but the forsaking all is followed by the receiving all. We abide in Christ more fully as we forsake all and follow Him. As I count all things loss for His sake, I am found *in Him.*

The same principle holds true of all the lawful occupations and possessions with which we are entrusted by God. Such were the fishnets on the Sea of Galilee, and the household duties of Martha of Bethany—the home and the friends of many a one among Jesus' disciples. Jesus taught them in very deed to forsake all for Him. It was no arbitrary command, but the simple application of a law in nature to the kingdom of His grace—that the more perfectly the old occupant is cast out, the more complete can be the possession of the new, and the more entire the renewal of all within.

> *I* must see how all my gifts and powers are, even though I am a child of God, still defiled by sin and under the power of the flesh. I must feel that I cannot instantly proceed to use them for God's glory.

This principle has a still deeper application. The truly spiritual gifts that are the working of God's own Holy Spirit within us—don't these surely need to be given up and surrendered? They do indeed! The interchange of giving up and taking in is a life process, which may not cease for a moment. No sooner does the believer begin to rejoice in the possession of what he has than the inflow of new grace is retarded and stagnation threatens.

It is only into the thirst of an empty soul that the streams of living waters flow. *Always* thirsting is the secret of *never* thirsting. Each blessed experience we receive as a gift of God must immediately be returned back to Him from whom it came, in praise and love, in self-sacrifice and service. Only this way can it be restored to us again, fresh and beautiful with the bloom of heaven. Is not this the wonderful lesson Isaac on Moriah teaches us? (Gen. 22:1–19). Was he not the son of promise, the God-given life, the wonder-gift of the omnipotence of Him who gives life to the dead? (Rom. 4:17). And yet even he had to be given up and sacrificed so that he might be received back again a thousandfold more precious than before—a type of the only-begotten of the Father, whose pure and holy life had to be given up before He could receive it again in resurrection power, and could make His people partakers of it. A type, too, of what takes place in the life of each believer as, instead of resting content with past experiences or present grace, he presses on, forgetting and giving up all that is behind, and reaches out to the fullest possible laying hold of Christ His life.

And such surrender of all for Christ—is it a single step, the act and experience of a moment? Or is it a course of daily renewed and progressive attainment? It is both. There may be a moment in the life of a believer when he gets a first sight, or a deeper insight, of this most blessed truth, a moment when, made willing in the day of God's power, he does indeed, in an act of the will, gather up the whole of life yet before him into the decision of a moment and lay himself on the altar a living and an acceptable sacrifice.

Such moments have often been the blessed transition from a life of wandering and failure to a life of abiding and power divine. But even then his daily life becomes what the life must be of each one who has no such experience: the unceasing prayer for more light on the meaning of entire surrender, and the ever-renewed offering up of all he has to God.

> *And such surrender of all for Christ—is it a single step, the act and experience of a moment? Or is it a course of daily renewed and progressive attainment? It is both.*

Believer, if you desire to abide in Christ, see here the blessed path. Nature shrinks back from such self-denial and crucifixion in its rigid application to our life in its whole extent. But what nature does not love and cannot perform, grace will accomplish, and make to you a life of joy and glory. When you just yield up yourself to Christ your Lord, the conquering power of His incoming presence will make it joy to cast out all that before was most precious.

"A hundredfold in this life" (Mark 10:30): This word of the Master comes true to all who, with wholehearted faithfulness, accept His commands to forsake all. The blessed receiving soon makes the giving up most blessed too. And the secret of a life of close abiding will be seen to be simply this: As I give myself wholly to Christ, I find the power to take Him wholly for myself, and as I lose myself and all I have for Him, He takes me wholly for Himself, and gives Himself wholly to me.

FOR FURTHER THOUGHT

1. *Read Philippians 3:8–9. What was Paul's motivation for willingly and joyfully suffering the loss of all things he was and had in himself, and of considering them rubbish?*
2. *What is the spiritual connection between forsaking something for Christ and receiving something from Christ? What do you believe God is calling you to forsake for Him now?*
3. *What must you do to receive the grace it takes for you to use your gifts and powers—the very ones God Himself has given you individually—for God's glory?*

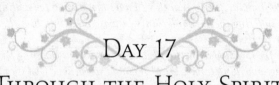

DAY 17
THROUGH THE HOLY SPIRIT

But the anointing which you have received from Him
abides in you. . .and just as it has taught you,
you will abide in Him.
1 JOHN 2:27

HOW beautiful the thought of a life always abiding in Christ! The longer we think of it, the more attractive it becomes. And yet how often it is that the precious words, "Abide in Me," are heard by the young disciple with a sigh! It is as if he understands so little what they really mean, can realize so little how this full enjoyment can be attained. He longs for someone who could make it perfectly clear and continually again remind him that the abiding is in very deed within his reach. If such a one would just listen to the word we have from John this day, what hope and joy it would bring! It gives us the divine assurance that we have the anointing of the Holy Spirit to teach us all things, also to teach us how to abide in Christ.

Sadly, someone answers, "This word does not give me comfort. It only depresses me more. For it tells of another privilege I so little know how to enjoy. I do not understand how the teaching of the Spirit is given—where or how I can discern His voice. If the teacher is so unknown, no wonder that the promise of His teaching about the abiding does not help me much."

Thoughts like these come from an error that is very common among believers. They imagine that the Spirit, in teaching them, must reveal the mysteries of the spiritual life first to their intellect, and afterwards in their experience. And God's way is just the contrary of this. What holds true of all spiritual truth is especially true of the abiding in Christ: *We must live and experience truth in order to know it.* Life-fellowship with Jesus is the only school for the science of heavenly things. "What I am doing you do not understand now, but you will know after this" (John 13:6) is a law of the kingdom, especially true of the daily cleansing of which it first was spoken, and the daily keeping. Receive what you do not comprehend, submit to what you cannot understand, accept and expect what to reason appears a mystery, believe what looks impossible, walk in a way which you know not—such are the first lessons in the school of God.

"*If you abide* in My word. . .*you shall know* the truth" (John 8:31, 32): In these and other words of God, we are taught that there is a habit of mind and life that precedes the understanding of the truth. True discipleship consists in *first* following, and then knowing the Lord. The believing surrender to Christ and the submission to His word to expect what appears most improbable is the only way to the full blessedness of knowing Him.

These principles hold especially true in regard to the teaching of the Spirit. That teaching consists *in His guiding the spiritual life within us to that which God has prepared for us, without our always knowing how.* On the strength of God's promise, and trusting in His faithfulness, the believer yields himself to the leading of the Holy Spirit, without claiming to have it first made clear to the intellect what He is to do, but consenting to let Him do His work in the soul, and afterwards to know what He has brought about there. Faith trusts the working of the Spirit unseen in the deep recesses of the inner life. And so the word of Christ and the gift of the Spirit are to the believer sufficient guarantee that He will be taught of the Spirit to abide in Christ. By faith he rejoices in what he does not see or feel: He knows and is confident that the blessed Spirit within is doing His work silently but surely, guiding him into the life of full abiding and unbroken communion.

> *What* holds true of all spiritual truth is especially true of the abiding in Christ: We must live and experience truth in order to know it.

The Holy Spirit is the Spirit of life in Christ Jesus. It is His work not only to breathe, but ever to foster and strengthen, and so to perfect the new life within. And just in proportion as the believer yields himself in simple trust to the unseen but most certain law of the Spirit of life working within him, will his faith pass into knowledge. It will be rewarded by the Spirit's light revealing in the Word what has already been accomplished by the Spirit's power in the life.

Apply this now to the promise of the Spirit's teaching us to abide in Christ. The Holy Spirit is indeed the mighty power of God. And He comes to us from the heart of Christ. He is the bearer of Christ's life, the revealer and communicator of Christ Himself within us. In the expression "the fellowship of the Spirit," we are taught what His highest work is. He is the bond of fellowship between the Father and the Son—by Him they are one. He is the bond of fellowship between all believers—by Him they are one. Above all, He is the bond of fellowship between Christ and believers. He is the life-sap through which vine and branch grow into real and living oneness—by Him we are one.

And we can be assured that if we simply believe in His presence and working, if we simply watch not to grieve Him, because we know that He is in us, and if we wait and pray to be filled with Him, He will teach us how to abide. First guiding our will to a wholehearted cleaving to Christ, then quickening our faith into ever larger confidence and expectation, then breathing into our hearts a peace and joy that pass understanding, He teaches us to abide, though we scarcely know how. Then coming through the heart and life into the understanding, He makes us know the truth—not as mere thought-truth, but as the truth that is in Christ Jesus, the reflection into the mind of the light of what He has already made a reality in the life. "The life was the light of men" (John 1:4).

In view of such teaching, it is clear how, if we desire to have the Spirit to guide us into the abiding life, our first need is quiet, restful faith. Amid all the questions and difficulties that may come up in connection with our striving to abide in Christ—amid all the longing we may sometimes feel to have a Christian of experience to aid us, amid the frequent painful consciousness of failure, of ignorance, of helplessness—do let us hold firmly the blessed confidence: *We have the anointing of the Holy One to teach us to abide in Him.* "*The anointing* which you have received from Him *abides in*. . .and just as it has taught you, *you will abide in Him*" (1 John 2:27).

> *W*hat holds true of all spiritual truth is especially true of the abiding in Christ: We must live and experience truth in order to know it. Life-fellowship with Jesus is the only school for the science of heavenly things.

Make this teaching of His in connection with the abiding a matter of special exercise of faith. Believe that as surely as you have part in Christ, you have His Spirit too. Believe that He will do His work with power, if only you do not hinder Him. Believe that He is working, even when you cannot discern it. Believe that He will work mightily if you ask this from the Father. *It is impossible to live the life of full abiding without being full of the Holy Spirit*, so believe that the fullness of the Spirit is indeed your daily portion. Be sure and take time in prayer to dwell at the footstool of the throne of God and the Lamb, from where flows the river of the water of life. It is *there, and only there*, that you can be filled with the Spirit. Cultivate carefully the habit of daily, yes, continually honoring Him by the quiet, restful confidence that He is doing His work within. Let faith in His indwelling make you careful of whatever could grieve Him—the spirit of the world or the actings of self and the flesh. Let that faith seek its nourishment in the Word and all it says of the Spirit, His power, His comfort, and His work. Above all, let that faith in the Spirit's indwelling lead you especially to look away to Jesus, for as we have received the anointing *of Him*, it comes in ever stronger flow from Him as we are occupied with Him alone. Christ is the Anointed One. As we look up to Him, the holy anointing comes, "the precious oil upon the head. . .of Aaron, running down on the edge of his garments" (Ps. 133:2). It is faith in Jesus that brings the anointing—the anointing leads to

Jesus and to the abiding in Him alone.

Believer, abide in Christ and in the power of the Spirit. Do you think the abiding should longer be a fear or a burden? Surely not! Oh, if we just knew the graciousness of our Holy Comforter and the blessedness of wholly yielding ourselves to His leading, we should indeed experience the divine comfort of having such a teacher to secure our abiding in Christ. The Holy Spirit was given for this one purpose—that the glorious *redemption and life in Christ might with divine power be conveyed and communicated to us.*

We have the Holy Spirit to make the living Christ, in all His saving power and in the completeness of His victory over sin, always present within us. It is this that constitutes Him the Comforter, and with Him we need never mourn an absent Christ. Let us therefore, as often as we read or meditate or pray in connection with this abiding in Christ, rely on it as a settled thing that we have the Spirit of God Himself within us, teaching, guiding, and working. Let us rejoice in the confidence that we must succeed in our desires, because the Holy Spirit is working all the while with secret but divine power in the soul that does not hinder Him by its unbelief.

FOR FURTHER THOUGHT

1. *"We must live and experience truth in order to know it." What steps must you take in order to live and experience God's truth?*
2. *In what does the teaching of the Holy Spirit consist? What must you as a believer do to receive that teaching?*
3. *What is God's reason for giving you the Holy Spirit? How does having the Holy Spirit within you change you and mold you?*

Day 18

In Stillness of Soul

"In returning and rest you shall be saved;
in quietness and confidence shall be your strength."
ISAIAH 30:15

Rest in the LORD, and wait patiently for Him.
PSALM 37:7

Truly my soul silently waits for God.
PSALM 62:1

THERE is a view of the Christian life that regards it as a sort of partnership, in which God and man have each to do their part. It admits that it is but little that man can do, and that little is defiled with sin. Still he must do his utmost—then only can he expect God to do His part.

To those who think this way, it is extremely difficult to understand what scripture means when it speaks of our being still and doing nothing, of our resting and waiting to see the salvation of God. It appears to them a perfect contradiction when we speak of this quietness and ceasing from all effort as the secret of the highest activity of man and all his powers. And yet this is just what scripture does teach.

The explanation of the apparent mystery is to be found in this: that when God and man are spoken of as working together, there is nothing of the idea of a partnership between two partners who each contribute their share to a work. The relationship is a very different one. The true idea is that of cooperation founded on subordination.

As Jesus was entirely dependent on the Father for all His words and all His works, so the believer can do nothing of himself. What he can do of himself is altogether sinful. He must therefore cease entirely from his own doing, and wait for the working of God in him. As he ceases from self-effort, faith assures him that God does what He has undertaken, and works in him. And what God does is to renew, to sanctify, and waken all his energies to their highest power. So that just in proportion as he yields himself a truly passive instrument in the hand of

God will he be wielded by God as the active instrument of His almighty power. The soul in which the wondrous combination of perfect passivity with the highest activity is most completely realized has the deepest experience of what the Christian life is.

Among the lessons to be learned by those who are studying the blessed art of abiding in Christ, there is none more necessary and more profitable than this one of stillness of soul. In it alone can we cultivate that teachableness of spirit, to which the Lord will reveal His secrets—that meekness to which He shows His ways. It is the spirit exhibited so beautifully in all the three Marys: In her whose only answer to the most wonderful revelation ever made to human being was, "Behold the maidservant of the Lord! Let it be to me according to your word" (Luke 1:38), and of whom, as mysteries multiplied around her, it is written: "Mary kept all these things and pondered *them* in her heart" (Luke 2:19). And in her who "sat at Jesus' feet and heard His word" (Luke 10:39), and who showed, in anointing Him for His burial, how she had entered more deeply into the mystery of His death than even the beloved disciple (John 12:3–7). And in her, too, who sought her Lord in the house of the Pharisee, with tears that spoke more than words (Luke 7:36–39). It is a soul silent before God that is the best preparation for knowing Jesus and for holding firmly the blessings He bestows. It is when the soul is hushed in silent awe and worship before the holy presence that reveals itself within that the still small voice of the blessed Spirit will be heard.

> *As Jesus was entirely dependent on the Father for all His words and all His works, so the believer can do nothing of himself. What he can do of himself is altogether sinful.*

Therefore, beloved Christian, as often as you seek to understand better the blessed mystery of abiding in Christ, let this be your first thought (Ps. 62:5): "My soul, *wait silently for God alone*, for my expectation is from Him." Do you in very deed hope to realize the wondrous union with the heavenly vine? Know that flesh and blood cannot reveal it unto you, but only the Father in heaven. "Cease from thine own wisdom" (Prov. 23:4 KJV). You need only bow in the confession of your own ignorance and powerlessness and the Father will delight to give you the teaching of the Holy Spirit. If your ear is only open, your thoughts brought into subjection, and your heart prepared in silence to wait upon God to hear what He speaks, He will reveal to you His secrets. And one of the first secrets will be the deeper insight into the truth that as you sink low before Him in nothingness and helplessness, in a silence and a stillness of soul that seeks to catch the faintest whisper of His love, teachings will come to you that you had never heard before over the rush and noise of your own thoughts and efforts. You shall learn how your great work is to listen and hear and believe what He promises, to watch and wait and see what He does, and then, in faith and worship and obedience, to yield yourself to His working who works in you mightily.

One would think that no message could be more beautiful or welcome than this: that we may rest and be quiet, and that our God will work for us and in us. And yet how far this is from being the case! And how slow many are to learn that quietness is blessedness, that quietness is strength, that quietness is the source of the highest activity—the secret of all true abiding in Christ! Let us try to learn it and to watch against whatever interferes with it. The dangers that threaten the soul's rest are not a few.

There is the wasting of soul that comes from entering needlessly and too deeply into the interests of this world. Every one of us has his divine calling, and within the circle pointed out by God Himself, interest in our work and its surroundings is a duty. But even here the Christian needs to exercise watchfulness and sobriety. And still more do we need a holy self-control in regard to things not absolutely imposed on us by God. If abiding in Christ really is our first aim, let us beware of all needless excitement. Let us watch even in lawful and necessary things against the wondrous power these have to keep the soul so occupied that there remains but little power or zest for fellowship with God. Then there is the restlessness and worry that come of care and anxiety about earthly things—these eat away the life of trust and keep the soul like a troubled sea. There the gentle whispers of the Holy Comforter cannot be heard.

> If your ear is only open, your thoughts brought into subjection, and your heart prepared in silence to wait upon God to hear what He speaks, He will reveal to you His secrets.

No less hurtful is the spirit of fear and distrust in spiritual things. With its apprehensions and its efforts, it never comes really to hear what God has to say. Above all, there is the unrest that comes from seeking in our own way and in our own strength the spiritual blessing that comes alone from above. *The heart occupied with its own plans and efforts for doing God's will, and in securing the blessing of abiding in Jesus, must fail continually.* God's work is hindered by our interference. He can do His work perfectly only when the soul ceases from its work. He will do His work mightily in the soul that honors Him by expecting Him to work both to will and to do.

And, last of all, even when the soul seeks truly to enter the way of faith, there is the impatience of the flesh, which forms its judgment of the life and progress of the soul not after the divine but the human standard.

In dealing with all this, and so much more, blessed is the man who learns the lesson of stillness and fully accepts God's word: "In quietness and confidence shall be your strength" (Isa. 30:15). Each time he listens to the word of the Father, or asks the Father to listen to his words, he doesn't dare begin his Bible reading or prayer without first pausing and waiting, until the soul be hushed in the presence of the eternal majesty. Under a sense of the divine nearness, the soul, feeling how self is always ready to assert itself and intrude even into the holiest of all with its thoughts and efforts, yields itself in a quiet act of self-surrender to the teaching and working of the divine Spirit. It is still and waits in holy silence until all is calm and ready to receive the revelation of the divine will and presence. Its reading and prayer then indeed become a waiting on God with ear and heart opened and purged to receive fully only what He says.

> *In dealing with all this, and so much more, blessed is the man who learns the lesson of stillness and fully accepts God's word: "In quietness and confidence shall be your strength"*

"Abide in Christ!" Let no one think that he can do this if he has not daily his quiet time, his seasons of meditation and waiting on God. In these, a habit of soul must be cultivated in which the believer goes out into the world and its distractions, the peace of God that passes all understanding, keeping the heart and mind. It is in such a calm and restful soul that the life of faith can take deep root, that the Holy Spirit can give His blessed teaching, and that the Holy Father can accomplish His glorious work.

May each one of us learn every day to say, "Truly my soul silently waits for God" (Ps. 62:1). And may every feeling of the difficulty of attaining this only lead us simply to look and trust to Him whose presence makes even the storm a calm. Cultivate the quietness as a means to the abiding in Christ, and expect the ever-deepening quietness and calm of heaven in the soul as the fruit of abiding in Him.

FOR FURTHER THOUGHT

1. *What attitude and disposition of Jesus is absolutely essential in your life if you are to walk as He walked, live as He lived, and accomplish the things He promised you would accomplish in this world for Him?*
2. *God's promise of revealing His secrets to you is a conditional one. What are the conditions for receiving that promise?*
3. *Why is it necessary for you to learn to be still and to listen to God when you need Him to speak to you? What are the blessings associated with that stillness and listening?*

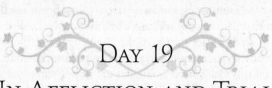

Day 19

In Affliction and Trial

"Every branch that bears fruit He prunes,
that it may bear more fruit."
JOHN 15:2

IN the whole plant world, there is not a tree to be found so specially suited to the image of man in his relation to God as the vine. There is none of which the fruit and its juice are so full of spirit, so quickening and stimulating. But there is also none of which the natural tendency is so entirely evil—none where the growth is so ready to run into wood that is utterly worthless except for the fire. Of all plants, not one needs the pruning knife so unsparingly and so unceasingly. None is so dependent on cultivation and training, but with this none yields a richer reward to the vinedresser.

In His wonderful parable, the Savior, with a single word, refers to this need of pruning in the vine and the blessing it brings. But from that single word what streams of light pour in upon this dark world, so full of suffering and of sorrow to believers! What treasures of teaching and comfort to the bleeding branch in its hour of trial: "Every branch that bears fruit *He prunes*, that it may bear more fruit." And so He has prepared His people, who are so ready when trial comes to be shaken in their confidence and to be moved from their abiding in Christ, to hear in each affliction the voice of a messenger that comes to call them to abide still more closely. Yes, believer, most especially in times of trial, abide in Christ.

Abide in Christ! This is indeed the *Father's object* in sending the trial. In the storm the tree sinks deeper roots in the soil. In the hurricane the inhabitants of the house abide within and rejoice in its shelter. Similarly, by suffering the Father desires to lead us to enter more deeply into the love of Christ. Our hearts are continually prone to wander from Him. Prosperity and enjoyment all too easily satisfy us, dull our spiritual perception, and make us unfit for full communion with Himself. It is an unspeakable mercy that the Father comes with His chastisement, makes the world around us all dark and unattractive, leads us to feel more deeply our sinfulness and for a time lose our joy in what was becoming so dangerous.

He does it in the hope that when we have found our rest in Christ in time of trouble, we shall learn to choose abiding in Him as our only portion and, when the affliction is removed, we have so grown more firmly into Him that in prosperity

He still shall be our only joy. So much has He set His heart on this that though He has indeed no pleasure in afflicting us, He will not keep back even the most painful chastisement if He can but thereby guide His beloved child to come home and abide in the beloved Son. Christian! Pray for grace to see in every trouble, small or great, the Father's finger pointing to Jesus and saying, "Abide in Him."

> *It is an unspeakable mercy that the Father comes with His chastisement, makes the world around us all dark and unattractive, leads us to feel more deeply our sinfulness and for a time lose our joy in what was becoming so dangerous.*

Abide in Christ, and then you will become *partaker of all the rich blessings God designed for you* in the affliction. The purposes of God's wisdom will become clear to you, your assurance of the unchangeable love will become stronger, and the power of His Spirit will fulfill for you the promise: "He for our profit [chastens us] that we may be partakers of His holiness" (Heb. 12:10). Abide in Christ, and then your cross becomes the means of fellowship with His cross and access into its mysteries—the mystery of the curse that He bore for you, of the death to sin in which you partake with Him, of the love in which, as sympathizing high priest, He descended into all your sorrows. Abide in Christ, growing in conformity to your blessed Lord in His sufferings, and then deeper experience of the reality and the tenderness of His love will be yours. Abide in Christ, and then in the fiery oven, one like the Son of Man will be seen as never before. The purging away of the dross and the refining of the gold will be accomplished, and Christ's own likeness reflected in you. O abide in Christ, and then the power of the flesh will be put to death, the impatience and self-will of the old nature be humbled to make place for the meekness and gentleness of Christ. A believer may pass through much affliction, and yet secure only a little blessing from it all. Abiding in Christ is the secret of securing all that the Father meant the chastisement to bring us.

Abide in Christ. In Him you shall find *sure and abundant consolation*. With the afflicted, comfort is often first and the profit of the affliction second. The Father loves us so much that with Him our real and abiding profit is His first object, but He does not forget to comfort too. When He comforts, it is so that He may turn the bleeding heart to Himself to receive the blessing in fellowship with Him. When He refuses comfort, His object is still the same. It is in making us partakers of His holiness that true comfort comes.

The Holy Spirit is the Comforter, not only because He can suggest comforting thoughts of God's love, but far more because He makes us holy and brings us into close union with Christ and with God. He teaches us to abide in Christ, and because God is found there, the truest comfort will come there too. *In Christ* the heart of the Father is revealed, and higher comfort there cannot be than to rest in the Father's bosom. *In Him* the fullness of the divine love is revealed, combined with the tenderness of a mother's compassion—and what can comfort like this? *In Him* you see a thousand times more given you than you have lost. See how God only took from you that you might have room to take from Him what is so much better. *In Him* suffering is consecrated, and it becomes the foretaste of eternal glory. In suffering it is that the Spirit of God and of glory rests on us. Believer! Would you have comfort in affliction?—Abide in Christ.

Abide in Christ so that will you *bear much fruit*. Not a vine is planted without the owner thinking of the fruit, and the fruit only. Other trees may be planted for ornament, for the shade, for the wood—the vine *only for the fruit*. And of each vine the vinedresser is continually asking how it can bring forth more fruit, much fruit. Believer! Abide in Christ in times of affliction, and then you shall bring forth more fruit. The deeper experience of Christ's tenderness and the Father's love will urge you to live to His glory. The surrender of self and self-will in suffering will prepare you to sympathize with the misery of others, while the softening that comes from chastisement will prepare you for becoming, as Jesus was, the servant of all.

The thought of the Father's desire for fruit in the pruning will lead you to yield yourself afresh, and more than ever, to Him, and to say that now you have but one object in life—making known and conveying His wonderful love to fellowmen. You shall learn the blessed art of forgetting self, and, even in affliction, availing yourself of your separation from ordinary life to plead for the welfare of others.

> The Holy Spirit is the Comforter, not only because He can suggest comforting thoughts of God's love, but far more because He makes us holy and brings us into close union with Christ and with God.

Dear Christian, in affliction abide in Christ. When you see it coming, meet it in Christ. When it is come, feel that you are more in Christ than in it, for He is nearer you than affliction ever can be. And when it is passing, still abide in Him. And let the one thought of the Savior, as He speaks of the pruning, and the one desire of the Father as He does the pruning, be yours too: "Every branch that bears fruit He prunes, that it may bear more fruit."

So shall your times of affliction become your times of choicest blessing—preparation for richest fruitfulness. Led into closer fellowship with the Son of God, and deeper experience of His love and grace—established in the blessed confidence that He and you entirely belong to each other—more completely satisfied with Him and more fully given up to Him than ever before—with your own will crucified afresh, and the heart brought into deeper harmony with God's will—you shall be a vessel cleansed, fit for the Master's use, prepared for every good work.

True believer! O try and learn the blessed truth that in affliction your first, your only, your blessed calling is to abide in Christ. Be much with Him alone. Beware of the comfort and the distractions that friends so often bring. Let Jesus Christ Himself be your chief companion and comforter. Delight yourself in the assurance that closer union with Him—and more abundant fruit through Him— are sure to be the results of trial, because it is the vinedresser Himself who is pruning, and who will ensure the fulfillment of the desire of the soul that yields itself lovingly to His work.

For Further Thought

1. *What are God's objectives in allowing afflictions and trials into your life—of even causing them? How does knowing those objectives change the way you approach and respond to difficulties?*
2. *In what ways is the Holy Spirit a comforter in times of difficulty? What does He teach you during those times?*
3. *For what specifically does affliction prepare you?*

DAY 20
THAT YOU MAY
BEAR MUCH FRUIT

"He who abides in Me, and I in him,
bears much fruit. . . . By this My Father is glorified,
that you bear much fruit; so you will be My disciples."
JOHN 15:5, 8

WE all know what fruit is. The produce of the branch, by which men are refreshed and nourished. The fruit is not for the branch, but for those who come to carry it away. As soon as the fruit is ripe, the branch gives it off to commence afresh its work of benefiting men, and anew prepare its fruit for another season. A fruit-bearing tree doesn't live for itself, but wholly for those to whom its fruit brings refreshment and life. And so the branch exists only and entirely for the sake of the fruit. To make glad the heart of the vinedresser is its object, its safety, and its glory.

Beautiful image of the believer, abiding in Christ! He not only grows in strength, the union with the vine becoming ever surer and firmer, but he also bears fruit—yes, much fruit. He has the power to offer that to others which they can eat and live. Amid all who surround him, he becomes like a tree of life, of which they can taste and be refreshed. He is in his circle a center of life and of blessing, and that simply because he abides in Christ and receives from Him the Spirit and the life of which he can impart to others. Learn then, if you wish to bless others, to abide in Christ, and that if you do abide, you shall surely bless. As surely as the branch abiding in a fruitful vine bears fruit, so surely, yes, *much more surely*, will a soul abiding in Christ with His fullness of blessing be made a blessing.

The reason for this is easily understood. If Christ, the heavenly vine, has taken the believer as a branch, then He has pledged Himself, in the very nature of things, to supply the sap and spirit and nourishment to make it bring forth fruit. "Your fruit is found in *Me*" (Hos. 14:8): These words derive new meaning from our parable. The soul needs to have one care—to abide closely, fully, wholly. He will give the fruit. He works all that is needed to make the believer a blessing.

Abiding in Him, you receive of Him *His Spirit of love and compassion toward sinners*, making you desirous to seek their good. By nature, the heart is full of self-ishness. Even in the believer, his own salvation and happiness are often too much his only object. But abiding in Jesus, you come into contact with His infinite love, and as its fire begins to burn within your heart, you see the beauty of love and you learn to look upon loving and serving and saving your fellowmen as the highest privilege a disciple of Jesus can have. Abiding in Christ, your heart learns to feel the wretchedness of the sinner still in darkness and the fearfulness of the dishonor done to your God. With Christ you begin to bear the burden of souls, the burden of sins not your own. As you are more closely united to Him, some of that passion for souls that urged Him to Calvary begins to breathe within you, and you are ready to follow His footsteps, to forsake the heaven of your own happiness, and devote your life to win the souls Christ has taught you to love. The very spirit of the vine is love. The spirit of love streams into the branch that abides in Him.

> *As surely as the branch abiding in a fruitful vine bears fruit, so surely, yes, much more surely, will a soul abiding in Christ with His fullness of blessing be made a blessing.*

The desire to be a blessing is just the beginning. As you undertake to work, you speedily become conscious of your own weakness and the difficulties in your way. Souls are not saved at your bidding. You are ready to be discouraged and to relax your effort. But abiding in Christ, you receive *new courage and strength* for the work. Believing what Christ teaches, that it is *He* who through you will give His blessing to the world, you understand that you are but the weak instrument through which the hidden power of Christ does its work, so that His strength may be perfected and made glorious in your weakness.

It is a great step when the believer fully acknowledges his own weakness, and the abiding consciousness of it, and so works faithfully on, fully assured that his Lord *is working* through him. He rejoices that the excellence of the power is of God, and not of us. Realizing his oneness with his Lord, he considers no longer his own weakness, but counts on the power of Him of whose hidden working within he is assured. It is this secret assurance that gives a brightness to his look, a gentle firmness to his tone, and a perseverance to all his efforts, which of themselves are great means of influencing those he is seeking to win. He goes forth in the spirit of one to whom victory is assured—for this is the victory that overcomes—our faith (see 1 John 5:4). He no longer counts it humility to say that God cannot bless his unworthy efforts. He claims and expects a blessing, because it is not he, but Christ in him, who works.

The great secret of abiding in Christ is the deep conviction that we are nothing and that He is everything. As this is learned, it no longer seems strange to believe that our weakness need be no hindrance to His saving power. The believer who yields himself wholly up to Christ for service in the spirit of a simple, childlike trust will assuredly bring forth much fruit. He will not fear even to claim his share in the wonderful promise: "He who believes in Me, the works that I do he will do also; and *greater works* than these he will do, because I go to My Father" (John 14:12). He no longer thinks that He cannot have a blessing and must be kept unfruitful, so that he may be kept humble. He sees that the most heavily laden branches bow the lowest down. Abiding in Christ, he has yielded assent to the blessed agreement between the vine and the branches, that of the fruit all the glory shall be to the vinedresser, the blessed Father.

Let us learn two lessons. If we are abiding in Jesus, let us begin to work. Let us first seek to influence those around us in daily life. Let us accept distinctly and joyfully our holy calling: that we are even now to live as the servants of the love of Jesus to our fellowmen. Our daily life must have for its object the making of an impression favorable to Jesus. When you look at the branch, you see right away the likeness to the vine. We must live so that somewhat of the holiness and the gentleness of Jesus may shine out in us. We must live to represent Him.

As was the case with Him when on earth, the life must prepare the way for the teaching. What the Church and the world both need is this: men and women full of the Holy Spirit and of love, who, as the living embodiments of the grace and power of Christ, witness for Him, and for His power on behalf of those who believe in Him. Living so, with our hearts longing to have Jesus glorified in the souls He is seeking after, let us offer ourselves to Him for direct work.

There is work in our own home. There is work among the sick, the poor, and the outcast. There is work in a hundred different paths that the Spirit of Christ opens up through those who allow themselves to be led by Him. There is work perhaps for us in ways that have not yet been opened up by others. Abiding in Christ, let us work. Let us work, not like those who are content if they now follow the fashion and take some share in religious work. No, let us work as those who are growing more like Christ, because they are abiding in Him, and who, like Him, count the work of winning souls to the Father the very joy and glory of heaven begun on earth.

And the second lesson is: If you work, abide in Christ. This is one of the blessings of work if done in the right spirit—it will deepen your union with your blessed Lord. It will reveal your weakness and throw you back on His strength. It will stir you to much prayer—and in prayer for others is the time when the soul, forgetful of itself, unconsciously grows deeper into Christ. It will make clearer to you the true nature of branch-life: its absolute dependence, and at the same time its glorious sufficiency—independent of all else, because dependent on Jesus.

If you work, abide in Christ. There are temptations and dangers. Work for Christ has sometimes drawn away from Christ and taken the place of fellowship with Him. Work can sometimes give a form of godliness without the power. As you work, abide in Christ. Let a living faith in Christ working in you be the secret spring of all your work. This will inspire at the same time humility and courage. Let the Holy Spirit of Jesus dwell in you as the Spirit of His tender compassion and His divine power. Abide in Christ, and offer every faculty of your nature freely and unreservedly to Him, to sanctify it for Himself.

If Jesus Christ is really to work through us, it needs an entire consecration of ourselves to Him, daily renewed. But we understand now, just this is abiding in Christ, just this it is that constitutes our highest privilege and happiness. To be a branch bearing much fruit—nothing less, nothing more—be this our only joy.

For Further Thought

1. *What is the connection between abiding in Christ, working for Christ, and bearing much fruit for Christ?*
2. *What additional important spiritual lesson do you learn when you approach your abiding in Jesus Christ with the conviction that you are nothing and that He is everything?*
3. *If you want to bear much fruit for Christ, what must be your relationship with Him look like? How can you attain that kind of relationship?*

DAY 21

SO WILL YOU HAVE

POWER IN PRAYER

*"If you abide in Me, and My words abide
in you, you will ask what you desire,
and it shall be done for you."*
JOHN 15:7

PRAYER is both one of the means and one of the fruits of union to Christ. As a means it is of unspeakable importance. All the things of faith, all the pleadings of desire, all the yearnings after a fuller surrender, all the confessions of shortcoming and of sin, all the exercises in which the soul gives up self and clings to Christ, find their utterance in prayer.

In each meditation on abiding in Christ, as some new feature of what scripture teaches concerning this blessed life is understood, the first impulse of the believer is to at once look up to the Father and pour out the heart into His, and ask from Him the full understanding and the full possession of what he has been shown in the Word. And it is the believer who is not content with this spontaneous expression of his hope but who takes time in secret prayer to wait until he has received and laid hold of what he has seen who will really grow strong in Christ. However weak the soul's first abiding, its prayer will be heard, and it will find prayer one of the great means of abiding more abundantly.

But it is not so much as a means, but as a fruit of the abiding, that the Savior mentions it in the parable of the vine. He does not think so much of prayer—as we, sadly, too exclusively do—as a means of getting blessing for ourselves, but as one of the chief channels of influence by which, through us as fellow workers with God, the blessings of Christ's redemption are to be dispensed to the world. He sets before Himself and us the glory of the Father, in the extension of His kingdom, as the object for which we have been made branches, and He assures us that if we but abide in Him, we shall be Israels, having power with God and man. Ours shall be the effectual, fervent prayer of the righteous man, accomplishing much, like Elijah's for ungodly Israel. Such prayer will be the fruit of our abiding in Him and the means of bringing forth much fruit.

To the Christian who is not abiding wholly in Jesus, the difficulties connected with prayer are often so great that they rob him of the comfort and the strength it could bring. Under the guise of humility, he asks how one so unworthy could expect to have influence with the Holy One. He thinks of God's sovereignty, His perfect wisdom and love, and cannot see how his prayer can really have any distinct effect. He prays, but it is more because he cannot rest without prayer than from a loving faith that the prayer will be heard. But what a blessed release from such questions and perplexities is given to the soul who is truly abiding in Christ! He realizes increasingly how it is in the real spiritual unity with Christ that we are accepted and heard. The union with the Son of God is a life union: We are in very deed one with Him—our prayer ascends like His prayer. It is because we abide in Him that we can ask what we desire, and it is given to us.

> *However weak the soul's first abiding, its prayer will be heard, and it will find prayer one of the great means of abiding more abundantly.*

There are many reasons why this must be so. One is that abiding in Christ and having His words abiding in us teach us to pray *in accordance with the will of God*. With the abiding in Christ, our self-will is kept down, the thoughts and wishes of nature are brought into captivity to the thoughts and wishes of Christ. Then like-mindedness to Christ grows upon us—all our working and willing become transformed into harmony with His. There is deep and often-renewed heart-searching to see whether the surrender has indeed been entire, fervent prayer to the heart-searching Spirit so that nothing may be kept back. Everything is yielded to the power of His life in us so that it may exercise its sanctifying influence even on ordinary wishes and desires. His Holy Spirit breathes through our whole being. And without our being conscious how, our desires, as the breathings of the divine life, are in conformity with the divine will, and are fulfilled. Abiding in Christ renews and sanctifies the will. We ask what we desire, and it is given to us.

In close connection with this is the thought that the abiding in Christ teaches the believer in prayer only to seek the glory of God. In promising to answer prayer, Christ's one thought (see John 14:13) is this: *that the Father may be glorified in the Son*. In His intercession on earth (John 17), this was His one desire and plea. In His intercession in heaven, it is still His great object. As the believer abides in Christ, the Savior breathes this desire into him. The thought, *only the glory of God*, becomes more and more the keynote of the life hidden in Christ.

At first this subdues, and quiets, and makes the soul almost afraid to dare entertain a wish, lest it should not be to the Father's glory. But when once its supremacy has been accepted, and everything yielded to it, it comes with mighty power to elevate and enlarge the heart and open it to the vast field open to the glory of God. Abiding in Christ, the soul learns not only to desire, but spiritually to discern what will be for God's glory. And one of the first conditions of acceptable prayer is fulfilled in it when, as the fruit of its union with Christ, the whole mind is brought into harmony with that of the Son as He said: "Father, glorify Your name" (John 12:28).

Once more: Abiding in Christ, we can fully avail ourselves *of the name of Christ.* Asking in the name of another means that that other has authorized me, sent me to ask, and wants to be considered as asking himself: He wants the favor done to him. Believers often try to think of the name of Jesus and His merits and to argue themselves into the faith that they will be heard, while they painfully feel how little they have of the faith of His name. They are not living wholly in Jesus' name, and it is only when they begin to pray that they want to take up that name and use it. This cannot be. The promise "*Whatever you ask in My name*" (John 14:13) may not be severed from the command, "Whatever you do. . .*do all in the name* of the Lord Jesus" (Col. 3:17). If the name of Christ is to be wholly at my disposal, so that I may have the full command of it for all I desire, it must be because I first put myself wholly at His disposal, so that He has free and full command of me. It is the abiding in Christ that gives the right and power to use His name with confidence.

To Christ, the Father refuses nothing. Abiding in Christ, I come to the Father as one with Him. His righteousness is in me, His Spirit is in me. The Father sees the Son in me, and gives me my request. It is not—as so many think—by a sort of imputation that the Father looks upon us as if we were in Christ, though we are not in Him. No, the Father wants to see us living in Him. That is how our prayers really have power to prevail. Abiding in Christ not only renews the will to pray rightly, but secures the full power of His merits to us.

> *T*he union with the Son of God is a life union: We are in very deed one with Him—our prayer ascends like His prayer. It is because we abide in Him that we can ask what we desire, and it is given to us.

Again: Abiding in Christ also works in us *the faith that alone can obtain an answer.* "According to your faith let it be to you" (Matt. 9:29): This is one of the laws of the kingdom. "Believe that you receive. . .and you will have" (Mark 11:24). This faith rests on and is rooted in the Word, but is something infinitely higher than the mere logical conclusion: "God has promised, I shall obtain." No, faith, as a spiritual act depends on the words abiding in us as living powers, and so on the state of the whole inner life.

Without fasting and prayer (Mark 9:29), without humility and a spiritual mind (John 5:44), without a wholehearted obedience (1 John 3:22), there cannot be this living faith. But as the soul abides in Christ, grows into the consciousness of its union with Him, and sees how entirely it is He who makes it and its petition acceptable, it dares to claim an answer because it knows itself one with Him. It was by faith it learned to abide in Him, and as the fruit of that faith, it rises to a larger faith in all that God has promised to be and to do. It learns to breathe its prayers in the deep, quiet, confident assurance: We know that we have the petitions that we ask of Him (see 1 John 5:14–15).

Abiding in Christ, further, keeps us in the place where the answer can be bestowed. Some believers pray earnestly for blessing, but when God comes and looks for them to bless them, they are not to be found. They never thought that the blessing must not only be asked for, but also waited for and received in prayer. Abiding in Christ is the place for receiving answers. Out of Him the answer would be dangerous—we should consume it on our pleasures (see James 4:3). Many of the richest answers—say for spiritual grace, or for power to work and to bless—can only come in the shape of a larger experience of what God makes Christ to us. The fullness is *in Him*, and abiding in Him is the condition of power in prayer, because the answer is treasured up and bestowed in Him.

> o Christ, the Father refuses nothing. Abiding in Christ, I come to the Father as one with Him. His righteousness is in me, His Spirit is in me.

Believer, abide in Christ, for there is the school of prayer—mighty, effectual, answer-bringing prayer. Abide in Him, and you shall learn what to so many is a mystery: *that the secret of the prayer of faith is the life of faith*—the life that abides in Christ alone.

For Further Thought

1. *Most believers think of prayer as a means to obtaining blessings for themselves. How does Christ's approach to prayer, as well as His example in it, differ from that of most Christians?*
2. *How and why does abiding in Christ, or being one with Him, benefit you in your life of prayer and make your prayer life an effective one?*
3. *Read Matthew 9:29. What essential heart condition does abiding in Christ accomplish within you when it comes to consistent answer-bringing prayer?*

Day 22

And in His Love

"As the Father loved Me,
I also have loved you; abide in My love."
John 15:9

BLESSED Lord, enlighten our eyes to rightly see the glory of this wondrous word. Open to our meditation the secret chamber of *Your Love* so that our souls may enter in and find there their everlasting dwelling place. How else shall we know anything of a love that passes knowledge?

Before the Savior speaks the word that invites us to abide in His love, He first tells us what that love is. What He says of it must give force to His invitation, and make the thought of not accepting it an impossibility: "As the Father loved Me, I also have loved you!"

"As the Father loved Me." How shall we be able to form right conceptions of this love? Lord, teach us. God is love. Love is His very being. Love is not an attribute of His, but the very essence of His nature, the center around which all His glorious attributes gather. It was because He was love that He was the Father and that there was a Son. Love needs an object to whom it can give itself away, in whom it can lose itself, with whom it can make itself one. Because God is love, there must be a Father and a Son. The love of the Father to the Son is that divine passion with which He delights in the Son, and speaks, "My beloved Son, in whom I am well pleased" (Matt. 3:17).

The divine love is as a burning fire. In all its intensity and infinity it has but one object and but one joy, and that is the only begotten Son. When we gather together all the attributes of God—His infinity, His perfection, His immensity, His majesty, His omnipotence—and consider them but as the rays of the glory of His love, we still fail in forming any conception of what that love must be. It is a love that passes understanding.

And yet this love of God to His Son must serve, O my soul, as the glass in which you are to learn how Jesus loves you. As one of His redeemed ones, you are His delight, and all His desire is to you, with the longing of a love that is stronger than death and that many waters cannot quench. His heart yearns after you and seeks your fellowship and your love. Were it needed, He could die again to possess you. As the Father loved the Son and could not live without Him, could not be God the blessed without Him—so Jesus loves you. His life is bound up in yours. You are to Him inexpressibly more indispensable and precious than you ever can know. You are one with Himself. "As the Father loved me, I also have I loved you." What a love!

It is an eternal love. From before the foundation of the world—God's Word teaches us this—the purpose had been formed that Christ should be the head of His Church, that He should have a body in which His glory could be set forth. In that eternity He loved and longed for those who had been given Him by the Father. And when He came and told His disciples that He loved them, it was indeed not with a love of earth and of time, but with the love of eternity. And it is with that same infinite love that His eye still rests upon each of us here seeking to abide in Him, and in each breathing of that love there is indeed the power of eternity. "I have loved you with an everlasting love" (Jer. 31:3).

It is a perfect love. It gives all and holds nothing back. "The Father loves the Son, and has given all things into His hand" (John 3:35). And just so Jesus loves His own: All He has is theirs. When it was needed, He sacrificed His throne and crown for you. He did not count His own life and blood too dear to give for you. His righteousness, His Spirit, His glory, even His throne—all are yours. This love holds nothing, nothing back, but, in a manner that no human mind can fathom, makes you one with itself. O wondrous love—to love us even as the Father loved Him and to offer us this love as our everyday dwelling!

> *God is love. Love is His very being. Love is not an attribute of His, but the very essence of His nature, the center around which all His glorious attributes gather.*

It is a gentle and most tender love. As we think of the love of the Father for the Son, we see in the Son everything so infinitely worthy of that love. When we think of Christ's love for us, there is nothing but sin and unworthiness to meet the eye. And the question comes: How can that love within the bosom of the divine life and its perfections be compared to the love that rests on sinners? Can it indeed be the same love? Blessed be God, we know it is so!

The nature of love is always one, however different the objects. Christ knows of no other law of love but that with which His Father loved Him. Our wretchedness only serves to call out more distinctly the beauty of love, such as could not be seen even in heaven. With the most tender compassion He bows to our weakness, with patience inconceivable He bears with our slowness, with the gentlest loving-kindness He meets our fears and our follies. It is the love of the Father to the Son, beautified, glorified, in its condescension, in its exquisite adaptation to our needs.

And it is an unchangeable love. "Having loved His own who were in the world, He loved them to the end" (John 13:1). "For the mountains shall depart and the hills be removed, but My kindness shall not depart from you" (Isa. 54:10). The promise with which it begins its work in the soul is this: "I will not leave you until I have done what I have spoken to you" (Gen. 28:15). And just as our wretchedness was what first drew it to us, so the sin, with which it is so often grieved, and which may well cause us to fear and doubt, is but a new motive for it to hold to us all the more. And why? We can give no reason but this: "As the Father loved me, I also have loved you."

And now, does not this love suggest the *motive*, the *measure*, and the *means* of that surrender by which we yield ourselves wholly to abide in Him?

This love surely supplies a motive. Only look and see how this love stands and pleads and prays. Gaze, O gaze on the divine form, the eternal glory, the heavenly beauty, the tenderly pleading gentleness of the crucified love, as it stretches out its pierced hands and says, "Oh, will you not abide with Me? Will you not come and abide in Me?" It points you up to the eternity of love from where it came to seek you. It points you to the cross and all it has borne to prove the reality of its affection and to win you for itself. It reminds you of all it has promised to do for you, if you will but throw yourself unreservedly into its arms. It asks you whether, so far as you have come to dwell with it and taste its blessedness, it has not done well by you. And with a divine authority, mingled with such an inexpressible tenderness that one might almost think he heard the tone of reproach in it, it says, "Soul, as the Father loved me, I also have loved you. Abide in My love." Surely there can be but one answer to such pleading: Lord Jesus Christ! Here I am. From now on, Your love shall be the only home of my soul. In Your love alone will I abide.

> *How can that love within the bosom of the divine life and its perfections be compared to the love that rests on sinners? Can it indeed be the same love? Blessed be God, we know it is so!*

That love is not only the motive but also the measure of our surrender to abide in it. Love gives all but asks all. It does so, not because it grudges us anything, but because without this it cannot get possession of us to fill us with itself. In the love of the Father and the Son, it was so. In the love of Jesus to us, it was so. In our entering into His love to abide there, it must be so too. Our surrender to it must have no other measure than its surrender to us.

O that we understood how the love that calls us has infinite riches and fullness of joy for us, and that what we give up for its sake will be rewarded a hundredfold in this life! Or rather, would that we understood that it is a *love* with a height and a depth and a length and a breadth that passes understanding!

How all thought of sacrifice or surrender would pass away, and our souls be filled with wonder at the unspeakable privilege of being loved with such a love, of being allowed to come and abide in it forever.

And if doubt again suggests the question, "But is it possible—can I always abide in His love?", listen how that love itself supplies the only means for the abiding in Him. It is faith in that love that will enable us to abide in it. If this love is indeed so divine, such an intense and burning passion, then surely I can depend on it to keep me and to hold me firmly. Then surely all my unworthiness and weakness can be no hindrance. If this love is indeed so divine, with infinite power at its command, I surely have a right to trust that it is stronger than my weakness, and that with its almighty arm it will clasp me to its bosom and allow me to go out no more.

> *If this love is indeed so divine, such an intense and burning passion, then surely I can depend on it to keep me and to hold me firmly*

I see how this is the one thing my God requires of me. Treating me as a reasonable being endowed with the wondrous power of willing and choosing, He cannot force all this blessedness on me, but waits until I give the willing consent of the heart. And the token of this consent He has in His great kindness ordered faith to be—that faith by which utter sinfulness casts itself into the arms of love to be saved, and utter weakness to be kept and made strong. O infinite love! Love with which the Father loved the Son! Love with which the Son loves us! I can trust you, I do trust you. O keep me abiding in Yourself.

FOR FURTHER THOUGHT

1. Jesus told His disciples, "As the Father loved Me, I also have loved you." Just how does the Father love the Son? What is the nature and attributes of that love?
2. How does Jesus demonstrate His love to us, though we are sinners undeserving of His love?
3. How can you know that Jesus loves you with the same love with which the Father loved Him? How can you know that He loves sinners with that same love?

Day 23

As Christ in the Father

"As the Father loved Me, I also have loved you;
abide in My love. . .just as I. . .abide in His love."
John 15:9, 10

CHRIST had taught His disciples that to abide in Him was to abide in His love. The hour of His suffering is near, and He cannot speak much more to them. They doubtless have many questions to ask as to what that abiding in Him and His love is. He anticipates and meets their wishes, and gives them His *own life* as the best exposition of His command. As example and rule for their abiding in His love, they have to look to His abiding in the Father's love. In the light of His union with the Father, their union with Him will become clear. *His life in the Father is the law of their life in Him.*

The thought is so high that we can hardly take it in, and is yet so clearly revealed that we dare not neglect it. Do we not read in John 6:57, "I live because of the Father, *so* he who feeds on Me will live because of Me"? And the Savior prays so distinctly (John 17:22–23), "that they may be one *just* as We are one: I in them, and You in Me." The blessed union of Christ with the Father and His life in Him is the only rule of our thoughts and expectations in regard to our living and abiding in Him.

Think first of the *origin* of that life of Christ in the Father. They were *one*—one in life and one in love. In this His abiding in the Father had its root. Though dwelling here on earth, He knew that He was one with the Father that the Father's life was in Him, and His love on Him. Without this knowledge, abiding in the Father and His love would have been utterly impossible. And it is this way only that you can abide in Christ and His love. Know that you are one with Him—one in the unity of nature. By His birth He became man and took your nature so that He might be one with you. By your new birth, you become one with Him and are made partaker of His divine nature. The link that binds you to Him is as real and close as the one that bound Him to the Father—the link of a divine life. Your claim on Him is as sure and always availing as was His on the Father. Your union with Him is as close.

And as it is the union of a divine life, it is one of an infinite love. In His life of humiliation on earth, He tasted the blessedness and strength of knowing Himself the object of an infinite love and of dwelling in it all the day. From His own example, He invites you to learn that herein is the secret of rest and joy. You are one with Him: Yield yourself now to be loved by Him; let your eyes and heart open to the love that shines and presses in on you on every side. Abide in His love.

Think then too of *the mode* of that abiding in the Father and His love that is to be the law of your life "I have kept My Father's commandments and abide in His love" (John 15:10). His was a life of subjection and dependence, and yet most blessed. To our proud, self-seeking nature, the thought of dependence and subjection suggests the idea of humiliation and servitude, but in the life of love that the Son of God lived, and to which He invites us, they are the secret of blessedness.

> *T*he blessed union of Christ with the Father and His life in Him is the only rule of our thoughts and expectations in regard to our living and abiding in Him.

The Son is not afraid of losing anything by giving up all to the Father, for He knows that the Father loves Him and can have no interest apart from that of the beloved Son. He knows that as complete as is the dependence on His part is the communication on the part of the Father of all He possesses. Therefore, when He had said, "The Son can do nothing of Himself, but what He sees the Father do," He adds at once, "Whatever He does, the Son also does in like manner. For the Father loves the Son, and shows Him all things that He Himself does" (John 5:19–20).

The believer who studies this life of Christ as the pattern and the promise of what his may be learns to understand how the "Without Me you can do nothing" (John 15:5) is but the forerunner of "I can do all things through Christ who strengthens me" (Phil. 4:13). We learn to glory in infirmities, to take pleasure in necessities and distresses for Christ's sake, for "when I am weak, then I am strong" (2 Cor. 12:10). He rises above the ordinary tone in which so many Christians speak of their weakness, while they are content to abide there, because he has learned from Christ that in the life of divine love, the emptying of self and the sacrifice of our will is the surest way to have all we can wish or will. Dependence, subjection, and self-sacrifice are for the Christian as for Christ the blessed path of life. Just as Christ lived through and in the Father, even so the believer lives through and in Christ.

Think of the *glory* of this life of Christ in the Father's love. Because He gave Himself wholly to the Father's will and glory, the Father crowned Him with glory and honor. He acknowledged Him as His only representative, made Him partaker of His power and authority, and exalted Him to share His throne as God. And even so will it be with him who abides in Christ's love. If Christ finds us willing to trust ourselves and our interests to His love, if in that trust we give up all care for our own will and honor, if we make it our glory to exercise and confess absolute dependence on Him in all things, if we are content to have no life but in Him, *He will do for us what the Father did for Him.* He will lay His glory on us: As the name of our Lord is Jesus is glorified in us, we are glorified in Him (2 Thess. 1:12). He acknowledges us as His true and worthy representatives, entrusts us with His power, and admits us to His counsels as He allows our intercession to influence His rule of His Church and the world, and makes us the vehicles of His authority and His influence over men. His Spirit knows no other dwelling than such, and seeks no other instruments for His divine work. Blessed life of love for the soul that abides in Christ's love, even as He in the Father's!

> *Y*ou are one with Him: yield yourself now to be loved by Him; let your eyes and heart open to the love that shines and presses in on you on every side.

Believer! Abide in the love of Christ. Take and study His relationship to the Father as pledge of what your own can become. As blessed, as mighty, as glorious as was His life in the Father, so can yours be in Him. Let this truth, accepted under the teaching of the Spirit in faith, remove every vestige of fear, as if abiding in Christ were a burden and a work. In the light of His life in the Father, let it from now on be to you a blessed rest in the union with Him, an overflowing fountain of joy and strength.

To abide in His love, His mighty, saving, keeping, satisfying love, even as He abided in the Father's love—surely the very greatness of our calling teaches us that it never can be a work we have to perform. Rather, it must be with us as with Him, the result of the spontaneous outflowing of a life from within, and the mighty inworking of the love from above. What we only need is this: to take time and study the divine image of this life of love set before us in Christ. We need to have our souls still before God, gazing upon that life of Christ in the Father until the light from heaven falls on it and we hear the living voice of our Beloved whispering gently to us personally the teaching He gave to the disciples.

Soul, be still and listen. Let every thought be hushed until the word has entered your heart too: "Child! I love you, just as the Father loved Me. Abide in My love, even as I abide in the Father's love. Your life on earth in Me is to be the perfect counterpart of mine in the Father."

And if the thought will sometimes come: Surely this is too high for us; can it be really true? only remember that the greatness of the privilege is justified by the greatness of the object He has in view. *Christ was the revelation of the Father on earth.* He could not be this if there were not the most perfect unity, the most complete communication of all the Father had to the Son. He could be it because the Father loved Him, and He abided in that love. *Believers are the revelation of Christ on earth.* They cannot be this unless there is perfect unity, so that the world can know that He loves them and has sent them. But they can be it if Christ loves them with the infinite love that gives itself and all it has, and if they abide in that love.

Lord, show us Your love. Make us with all the saints to know the love that passes understanding. Lord, show us in Your own blessed life what it is to abide in Your love. And the sight shall so win us that it will be impossible for us one single hour to seek any other life than the life of abiding in Your love.

FOR FURTHER THOUGHT

1. *As you look at the life of Jesus Christ on earth, in what specific ways did He constantly abide in loving union with the Father in heaven?*
2. *What three attributes of Christ's relationship with the Father in heaven are the path to a life of blessing in Christ?*
3. *What must you do to abide in Jesus' love just as He abides in the love of the Father?*

Day 24

Obeying His Commandments

*"If you keep My commandments, you will abide
in My love, just as I have kept My Father's
commandments and abide in His love."*
John 15:10

How clearly we are taught here the place that good works are to occupy in the life of the believer! Christ as the beloved Son was in the Father's love. He kept His commandments, and so He abided in the love. So the believer, without works, receives Christ and is in Him. He keeps the commandments, and so *abides* in the love.

When the sinner, in coming to Christ, seeks to prepare himself by works, the voice of the gospel sounds, *"Not of works."* When once in Christ, in case flesh should abuse the word, "Not of works," the gospel lifts its voice as loud: "Created in Christ Jesus *for good works*" (see Eph. 2:9–10). To the sinner out of Christ, works may be his greatest hindrance, keeping him from the union with the Savior. To the believer in Christ, works are strength and blessing, for by them faith is made perfect (James 2:22), the union with Christ is cemented, and the soul established and more deeply rooted in the love of God. "If anyone loves Me, he will keep My word; and My Father will love him" (John 14:23). "If you keep My commandments, you shall abide in My love."

The connection between this keeping the commandments and the abiding in Christ's love is easily understood. Our union with Jesus Christ is not a thing of the intellect or sentiment, but a real vital union in heart and life. The holy life of Jesus, with His feelings and disposition, is breathed into us by the Holy Spirit. The believer's calling is to think and feel and desire just what Jesus thought and felt and desired. He desires to be partaker not only of the grace but also of the holiness of His Lord—or rather, he sees that holiness is the chief beauty of grace. To live the life of Christ means to him to be delivered from the life of self. The will of Christ is to him the only path of liberty from the slavery of his own evil self-will.

To the ignorant or apathetic believer, there is a great difference between the promises and commands of scripture. The former he counts his comfort and his food, but to him who is really seeking to abide in Christ's love, the commands become no less precious. As much as the promises, they are the revelation of the divine love, guides into the deeper experience of the divine life, and blessed helpers in the path to a closer union with the Lord. He sees how the harmony of our will with His will is one of the chief elements of our fellowship with Him.

The will is the central faculty in the divine as in the human being. The will of God is the power that rules the whole moral as well as the natural world. How could there be fellowship with Him without delight in His will? It is only as long as salvation is to the sinner nothing but a personal safety, that he can be careless or afraid of the doing of God's will. No sooner is it to him what scripture and the Holy Spirit reveal it to be—the restoration to communion with God and conformity to Him—than he feels that there is no law more natural or more beautiful than this: Keeping Christ's commandments is the way to abide in Christ's love. His innermost soul approves when he hears the beloved Lord make the larger measure of the Spirit, with the manifestation of the Father and the Son in the believer, entirely dependent on the keeping of His commandments (John 14:15–16, 21, 23).

> *Our union with Jesus Christ is not a thing of the intellect or sentiment, but a real vital union in heart and life. The holy life of Jesus, with His feelings and disposition, is breathed into us by the Holy Spirit.*

There is another thing that opens to him a deeper insight and secures a still more cordial acceptance of this truth. It is this, that in no other way did Christ Himself abide in the Father's love. In the life that Christ led on earth, obedience was a solemn reality. The dark and awful power that led man to revolt from his God came upon Him too, to tempt Him. To Him as man, its offers of self-gratification were not matters of indifference. To refuse them, He had to fast and pray. He suffered, being tempted. He spoke very distinctly of not seeking to do His own will as a surrender He had continually to make. He made the keeping of the Father's commandments the distinct object of His life, and so abided in His love. Does He not tell us, "I do nothing of Myself; but as My Father taught Me, I speak these things. And He who sent Me is with Me. The Father has not left Me alone, for I always do those things that please Him" (John 8:28–29)? He thus opened to us the only path to the blessedness of a life on earth in the love of heaven. And when, as from our vine, His Spirit flows in the branches, this keeping the commands is one of the surest and highest elements of the life He inspires.

Believer! If you desire to abide in Jesus, be very careful to keep His commandments. Keep them in the love of your heart. Don't be content to have them in the Bible for reference, but have them transferred by careful study, by meditation and by prayer, by a loving acceptance, by the Spirit's teaching, to the fleshy tablets of the heart. Do not be content with the knowledge of some of the commands, those most commonly received among Christians, while others remain unknown and neglected. Surely, with your New Covenant privileges, you would not be behind the Old Testament saints who spoke so fervently: "*All* Your precepts concerning *all* things I consider to be right" (Ps. 119:128).

Be assured that there is still much of your Lord's will that you do not yet understand. Make Paul's prayer for the Colossians yours for yourself and all believers, "that you might be *filled* with the knowledge of His will in all wisdom and spiritual understanding" (Col. 1:9 KJV), and that of wrestling Epaphras, "that you may stand perfect and complete in all the will of God" (Col. 4:12 KJV). Remember that this is one of the great elements of spiritual growth—a deeper insight into the will of God concerning you. Don't imagine that entire consecration is the end—it is only the beginning—of the truly holy life. See how Paul, after having (Rom. 12:1) taught believers to lay themselves upon the altar, whole and holy burnt offerings to their God, immediately proceeds (12:2) to tell them what the true altar-life is: being ever more and more "renewed in their mind to prove what is the good and perfect and acceptable will of God."

> When, as from our vine, His Spirit flows in the branches, this keeping the commands is one of the surest and highest elements of the life He inspires.

The progressive renewal of the Holy Spirit leads to growing like-mindedness to Christ. Then comes a delicate power of spiritual perception—a holy instinct—by which the soul "quick of understanding in the fear of the Lord" (Isa. 11:3 KJV) knows to recognize the meaning and the application of the Lord's commands to daily life in a way that remains hidden to the ordinary Christian. Keep them dwelling richly within you, hide them within your heart, and you shall taste the blessedness of the man whose "delight is in the law of the LORD, and in His law he meditates day and night" (Ps. 1:2). Love will assimilate into your innermost being the commands as food from heaven. They will no longer come to you as a law standing outside and against you, but as the living power that has transformed your will into perfect harmony with all your Lord requires.

And keep them in the obedience of your life. It has been your solemn vow—has it not?—no longer to tolerate even a single sin: "I have sworn and confirmed that I will keep Your righteous judgments" (Ps. 119:106). Labor earnestly in prayer to stand perfect and complete in all the will of God. Ask earnestly for the discovery of every secret sin—of anything that is not in perfect harmony with the will of God. Walk up to the light you have faithfully and tenderly, yielding yourself in an unreserved surrender to obey all that the Lord has spoken. When Israel took that vow (Exod. 19:8, 24:7), it was only to break it all too soon. The New Covenant gives the grace to make the vow and to keep it too (Jer. 31). Be careful of disobedience, even in little things. Disobedience dulls the conscience, darkens the soul, deadens our spiritual energies—therefore keep the commandments of Christ with implicit obedience. Be a soldier who asks for nothing but the orders of the commander.

> *L*abor earnestly in prayer to stand perfect and complete in all the will of God. Ask earnestly for the discovery of every secret sin— of anything that is not in perfect harmony with the will of God.

And if even for a moment the commandments appear tedious, just remember whose they are. They are the commandments of Him who loves you. They are all love, they come from His love, and they lead to His love. Each new surrender to keep the commandments, each new sacrifice in keeping them, leads to deeper union with the will, the Spirit, and the love of the Savior. The double portion of reward shall be yours—a fuller entrance into the mystery of His love—a fuller conformity to His own blessed life. And you shall learn to prize these words as among your choicest treasures: "If you keep My commandments, you will abide in My love, *just as* I have kept My Father's commandments and abide in His love."

FOR FURTHER THOUGHT

1. *What did Jesus say was the evidence that you truly love Him?*
2. *What should you do in order to see to it that there is no hint of sin or disobedience in your life? What do you do once you recognize those things that are not pleasing to God?*
3. *How does disobedience to the commands of Christ affect the soul? Knowing that, what should you do in order to keep from being affected that way?*

DAY 25

THAT YOUR JOY MAY BE FULL

"These things I have spoken to you, that My joy
may remain in you, and that your joy may be full."
JOHN 15:11

ABIDING fully in Christ is a life of exquisite and overflowing happiness. As Christ gets more complete possession of the soul, it enters into the joy of its Lord. His own joy, the joy of heaven, becomes its own, and that in full measure, and as an ever-abiding portion. Just as joy on earth is everywhere connected with the vine and its fruit, so joy is an essential characteristic of the life of the believer who fully abides in Christ, the heavenly vine.

We all know the value of joy. It alone is the proof that what we have really satisfies the heart. As long as duty, self-interest, or other motives influence me, men cannot know what the object of my pursuit or possession is really worth to me. But when it gives me joy, and they see me delight in it, they know that to me at least it is a treasure. Therefore, there is nothing so attractive as joy, no preaching so persuasive as the sight of hearts made glad. Just this makes gladness such a mighty element in the Christian character: There is no proof of the reality of God's love and the blessing He bestows, which men so soon feel the force of, as when the joy of God overcomes all the trials of life. And for the Christian's own welfare, joy is no less indispensable. The joy of the Lord is his strength; confidence, courage, and patience find their inspiration in joy. With a heart full of joy no work can weary and no burden can depress, for God Himself is strength and song.

Let us hear what the Savior says of the joy of abiding in Him. He promises us *His own joy*: "My joy." As the whole parable refers to the life His disciples should have in Him when He ascended to heaven, the joy is that of His resurrection life. This is clear from those other words of His (John 16:22): "I will see you again and your heart will rejoice, and your joy no one will take from you." It was only with the resurrection and its glory that the power of the never-changing life began, and only in it that the never-ceasing joy could have its rise. With it was fulfilled the word: "Therefore...Your God has anointed You with the oil of gladness more than Your companions" (Ps. 45:7, Heb. 1:9). The day of His crowning was the day of the gladness of His heart. That joy of His was the joy of a work fully and forever completed, the joy of the Father's bosom regained, and the joy of souls redeemed.

These are the elements of His joy, and of them the abiding in Him makes us partakers.

The believer shares so fully His victory and His perfect redemption that his faith can without ceasing sing the conqueror's song: "Thanks be to God who always leads us in triumph" (2 Cor. 2:14). As the fruit of this, there is the joy of the undisturbed dwelling in the light of the Father's love—not a cloud to intervene if the abiding is unbroken. And then, with this joy in the love of the Father, as a love received, the joy of the love of souls, as love going out and rejoicing over the lost.

Abiding in Christ, penetrating into the very depths of His life and heart, and seeking for the most perfect oneness—these, the three streams of His joy, flow into our hearts. Whether we look backward and see the work He has done, or upward and see the reward He has in the Father's love that passes understanding, or forward in the continual accessions of joy as sinners are brought home, His joy is ours. With our feet on Calvary, our eyes on the Father's face, and our hands helping sinners home, we have His joy as our own.

> For the Christian's own welfare, joy is no less indispensable. The joy of the Lord is his strength; confidence, courage, and patience find their inspiration in joy.

And then He speaks of this joy as *abiding*—a joy that is never to cease or to be interrupted for a moment: "That My joy may remain in you." "Your joy no one will take from you." This is what many Christians cannot understand. Their view of the Christian life is that it is a succession of changes, now joy and now sorrow. And they appeal to the experiences of a man like the Apostle Paul as a proof of how much there may be of weeping, sorrow, and suffering. They have not noticed how just Paul gives the strongest evidence as to this unceasing joy. He understood the paradox of the Christian life as the combination at one and the same moment of all the bitterness of earth and all the joy of heaven. "As sorrowful, yet *always rejoicing*" (2 Cor. 6:10): These precious golden words teach us how the joy of Christ can overrule the sorrow of the world, can make us sing while we weep, and can maintain in the heart, even when cast down by disappointment or difficulties, a deep consciousness of a joy that is unspeakable and full of glory.

There is but one condition: "*I will see you again* and your heart will rejoice, and your joy no one will take from you." The presence of Jesus, distinctly manifested, can do nothing but give joy. Abiding in Him consciously, how can the soul help but rejoice and be glad? Even when weeping for the sins and the souls of others, there is the fountain of gladness springing up in the faith of His power and love to save.

And this, His own joy abiding with us, He wants to be *full*. Of the full joy our Savior spoke three times on the last night. Once here in the parable of the vine:

"*These things I have spoken* to you. . .that your joy may be *full*"—and every deeper insight into the wonderful blessedness of being the branch of such a vine confirms His Word. Then He connects it (John 16:24) with our prayers being answered: "*Ask, and you will receive*, that your joy may be *full*."

To the spiritual mind, answered prayer is not only a means of obtaining certain blessings, but something infinitely higher. It is evidence of our fellowship with the Father and the Son in heaven, of their delight in us, and of our having been admitted and having had a voice in that wondrous interchange of love in which the Father and the Son hold counsel and decide the daily guidance of the children on earth.

To a soul abiding in Christ, one that longs for manifestations of His love and that understands to take an answer to prayer in its true spiritual value—as a response from the throne to all its utterances of love and trust—the joy that it brings is truly unutterable. The word is found true: "Ask, and you will receive, that your joy shall be full." And then the Savior says, in His high priestly prayer to the Father (John 17:13), "*These things I speak*. . .that they may have My joy *fulfilled* in themselves." It is the sight of the great high priest entering the Father's presence for us, always living to pray and carry on His blessed work in the power of an endless life, that removes every possible cause of fear or doubt and gives us the assurance and experience of a perfect salvation.

> *W*ith our feet on Calvary, our eyes on the Father's face, and our hands helping sinners home, we have His joy as our own.

Let the believer who seeks, according to the teaching of John 15, to possess the full joy of abiding in Christ, and according to John 16, the full joy of prevailing prayer, press forward to John 17. Let him there listen to those wondrous words of intercession spoken so that his joy might be full. Let him, as he listens to those words, learn the love that even now pleads for him in heaven without ceasing, the glorious objects for which it is pleading, and which through its all-prevailing pleading are hourly being realized, and then Christ's joy will be fulfilled in him.

Christ's own joy, abiding joy, fullness of joy—such is the portion of the believer who abides in Christ. Why, O why is it that this joy has so little power to attract? The reason simply is that men, yes, even God's children, do not believe in it. Instead of the abiding in Christ being looked on as the happiest life that ever can be led, it is regarded as a life of self-denial and of sadness. They forget that the self-denial and the sadness are due to the not abiding, and that to those who once yield themselves unreservedly to abide in Christ as a bright and blessed life, their faith comes true—the joy of the Lord is theirs. The difficulties all arise from the lack of the full surrender to a full abiding.

Child of God who seeks to abide in Christ, remember what the Lord says. At the close of the parable of the vine, He adds these precious words: "*These things I have spoken to you, that My joy may remain in you, and that your joy may be full.*" Claim the joy as part of the branch life—not the first or chief part, but as the blessed proof of the sufficiency of Christ to satisfy every need of the soul. Be happy. Cultivate gladness.

> *I*t is the sight of the great high priest entering the Father's presence for us, that removes every possible cause of fear or doubt and gives us the assurance and experience of a perfect salvation.

If there are times when it comes of itself and the heart feels the unutterable joy of the Savior's presence, praise God for it and seek to maintain it. If at other times feelings are dull and the experience of the joy is not such as you could wish it, still praise God *for the life of unutterable blessedness to which you have been redeemed.* In this, too, the word holds good: "According to your faith let it be to you" (Matt. 9:29). As you claim all the other gifts in Jesus, always claim this one too— not for your own sake, but for His and the Father's glory. "*My joy* in you," "that *My joy* may *remain* in you," "*My joy fulfilled* in themselves"—these are Jesus' own words. It is impossible to take Him wholly and heartily and not to get His joy too. Therefore, "Rejoice in the Lord always. Again I will say, rejoice!" (Phil. 4:4).

FOR FURTHER THOUGHT

1. *In what way can your outer demonstrations of joy attract the world around you to the message of salvation through Jesus Christ? What does that joy prove to those around you?*
2. *What are the personal benefits you receive from walking and living with a heart attitude of joy in the Lord?*
3. *Jesus told His disciples, "These things I have spoken to you, that My joy may remain in you, and that your joy may be full." How can you daily cultivate that joy within you? How can you make sure it remains in you?*

Day 26

And in Love

to the Brethren

*"This is My commandment, that you love
one another as I have loved you."*
John 15:12

"As the Father loved Me, I *also* have loved you. . .love one another *as* I have loved you" (John 15:9, 12). God became man, and divine love began to run in the channel of a human heart. It becomes the love of man to man. The love that fills heaven and eternity is always to be daily seen here in the life of earth and of time.

"This is My commandment," the Savior says, "that you love one another as I have loved you." He sometimes spoke of commandments, but the love, which is the fulfilling of the law, is the all-including one, and therefore is called His commandment—the new commandment (see John 13:34). It is to be the great evidence of the reality of the New Covenant, of the power of the new life revealed in Jesus Christ. It is to be the one convincing and indisputable proof of discipleship: "*By this all will know* that you are My disciples" (John 13:35); "That they also may be one in Us, *that the world may believe*" (John 17:21); "that they may be made perfect in one, and *that the world may know* that You have. . .loved them as You have loved Me" (John 17:23). To the believer seeking perfect fellowship with Christ, the keeping of this commandment is both the blessed proof that he is abiding in Him, and the path to a fuller and more perfect union.

Let us try to understand how this is so. We know that God is love, and that Christ came to reveal this, not as a doctrine but as a life. His life, in its wonderful self-abasement and self-sacrifice was, above everything, the embodiment of divine love, the showing forth to men, in such human manifestations as they could understand, how God loves. In His love to the unworthy and the ungrateful, in His humbling Himself to walk among men as a servant, in His giving Himself up to death, He simply lived and acted out the life of the divine love that was in the heart of God. He lived and died to show us the love of the Father.

And now, just as Christ was to show forth God's love, believers are to show forth to the world the love of Christ. *They* are to prove to men that Christ loves them, and in loving fills them with a love that is not of earth. They, *by living and by loving just as He did*, are to be perpetual witnesses to the love that gave itself to die. He loved so that even the Jews cried out, as at Bethany, "See how He loved!" (John 11:36). Christians are to live so that men are compelled to say, "See how these Christians love one another."

In their daily fellowship with each other, Christians are made a spectacle to God, and to angels, and to men, and in the Christlikeness of their love to each other are to prove what manner of spirit they are of. Amid all diversity of character or of creed, of language, or of station, they are to prove that love has made them members of one body and of each other, and has taught them each to forget and sacrifice self for the sake of the other. Their life of love is the chief evidence of Christianity, the proof to the world that God sent Christ and that He has shed abroad in them the same love with which He loved Him. Of all the evidences of Christianity, this is the mightiest and most convincing.

> *And now, just as Christ was to show forth God's love, believers are to show forth to the world the love of Christ.*

Between their love to God and to all men. Of their love to God, whom they cannot see, it is the test. The love to one unseen may so easily be a mere sentiment, or even an imagination, but in the fellowship with God's children, love to God is really called into exercise and shows itself in deeds that the Father accepts as done to Himself. So alone can it be proved to be true.

The love to the brethren is the flower and fruit of the root, unseen in the heart, of love to God. And this fruit again becomes the seed of love to all men: fellowship with each other is the school in which believers are trained and strengthened to love their fellowmen who are yet out of Christ, not simply with the liking that rests on points of agreement, but with the holy love that takes hold of the unworthiest and bears with the most disagreeable for Jesus' sake. It is love to each other as disciples that is always put in the foreground as the link between love to God alone and to men in general.

In Christ's interaction with His disciples, this brotherly love finds the law of its conduct. As it studies His forgiveness and patience toward His friends, with the seven times seven as its only measure—as it looks to His unwearied patience and His infinite humility—as it sees the gentleness and lowliness with which He seeks to win for Himself a place as their servant, wholly devoted to their interests—it accepts with gladness His command, "You should do as I have done" (John 13:15). Following His example, each lives not for Himself but for the other.

The law of kindness is on the tongue, for love has vowed that never shall one unkind word cross its lips. It refuses not only to speak, but even to hear or to think evil. Of the name and character of the fellow Christian it is more jealous than of its own. My own good name I may leave to the Father; but my brother's name my Father has entrusted to me. In gentleness and lovingkindness, in courtesy and generosity, in self-sacrifice and charity, in its life of blessing and of beauty the divine love, which has been shed abroad in the believer's heart, shines out as it shone in the life of Jesus.

Christian! What do you say about this, your glorious calling to love like Christ? Does not your heart leap at the thought of the unspeakable privilege of this way showing forth the likeness of the eternal love? Or are you rather ready to sigh at the thought of the inaccessible height of perfection to which you are called to climb? Brother, do not sigh at what is in very deed the highest proof of the Father's love, or that He has called us to be like Christ in our love, just as He was like the Father in His love. Understand that He who gave the command in such close connection with His teaching about the vine and the abiding in Him gave us in that the assurance that we need only to abide in Him to be able to love like Him.

Accept the command as a new motive to a fuller abiding in Christ. Regard the abiding in Him more than ever as an abiding in His love. Then, rooted and grounded daily in a love that passes understanding, you receive of its fullness, and you learn to love. With Christ abiding in you, the Holy Spirit sheds abroad the love of God in your heart, and you love the brethren, the most trying and unlovable, with a love that is not your own, but the love of Christ in you. And the command about your love to the brethren is changed from a burden into a joy, if you but keep it linked, as Jesus linked it, to the command about His love to you: "*Abide in My love*; love one another, as I have loved you."

> *Let the love that does not seek its own but is always ready to wash others' feet, or even to give its life for them, be our aim as we abide in Jesus.*

"This is My commandment, that you love one another as I have loved you." Is not this now some of the "much fruit" that Jesus has promised we shall bear—in very deed a cluster of the grapes of Eshcol, with which we can prove to others that the land of promise is indeed a good land? Let us try in all simplicity and honesty to go out to our home to translate the language of high faith and heavenly enthusiasm into the plain prose of daily conduct, so that all men can understand it. Let our temper be under the rule of the love of Jesus: He cannot alone curb it—He can make us gentle and patient. Let the vow that not an unkind word about others shall ever be heard from our lips be laid trustingly at His feet. Let the gentleness that refuses to take offense, that is always ready to excuse and to think and hope the best, mark our interaction with all. Let the love that does not seek its own but is always ready to wash others' feet, or even to give its life for them, be our aim as we abide in Jesus.

Let our life be one of self-sacrifice, always seeking the welfare of others, finding our highest joy in blessing others. And let us, in studying the divine art of doing good, yield ourselves as obedient learners to the guidance of the Holy Spirit. By His grace, the most commonplace life can be transfigured with the brightness of a heavenly beauty, as the infinite love of the divine nature shines out through our frail humanity. Fellow Christian, let us praise God! We are called to love as Jesus loves, as God loves.

"Abide in My love, and love as I have loved." Bless God, it is possible. The new holy nature we have—and which grows ever stronger as it abides in Christ the vine—can love as He did. Every discovery of the evil of the old nature, every longing desire to obey the command of our Lord, and every experience of the power and the blessedness of loving with Jesus' love will urge us to accept with fresh faith the blessed injunctions: "Abide in Me, and I in you"; "Abide in My love."

FOR FURTHER THOUGHT

1. *Read John 13:34–35. Why did Christ refer to His commandment to the disciples to love one another as "a new commandment"?*
2. *How should Christ's law of love and kindness affect how you speak to and about others? What kinds of words demonstrate that kind of love?*
3. *How can you love those for whom you don't "feel" love, those who are, in simple human terms, unlovable?*

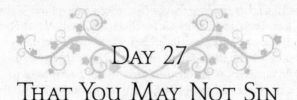

DAY 27
THAT YOU MAY NOT SIN

In Him there is no sin.
Whoever abides in Him does not sin.
1 JOHN 3:5–6

"YOU know," the apostle had said, "that He was manifested to take away our sins" (1 John 3:5), and had thus indicated salvation from sin as the great object for which the Son was made man. The connection shows clearly that the taking away has reference not only to the atonement and freedom from guilt, but to deliverance from the power of sin, so that the believer no longer does it.

It is Christ's personal holiness that constitutes His power to effect this purpose. He admits sinners into life union with Himself. The result is that their life becomes like His. "*In Him* there is no sin. Whosoever abides *in Him* does not sin." As long as he abides, and as far as he abides, the believer does not sin. Our holiness of life has its roots in the personal holiness of Jesus. "If the root is holy, so are the branches" (Rom. 11:16).

The question at once arises: How is this consistent with what the Bible teaches of the abiding corruption of our human nature, or with what John himself tells of the utter falsehood of our profession if we say that we have no sin, or that we have not sinned? (see 1 John 1:8, 10). It is just this passage that, if we look carefully at it, will teach us to understand our text correctly.

Note the difference in the two statements (1:8), "If we say that *we have no sin*," and (1:10), "If we say that *we have not sinned*." The two expressions cannot be equivalent, because the second would then be an unmeaning repetition of the first. *Having sin* in verse 8 is not the same as *doing sin* in verse 10. *Having sin* is having a sinful nature. The holiest believer must each moment confess that he has sin within him—the flesh, namely, in which dwells nothing good. Sinning or *doing sin* is something very different. It is yielding to indwelling sinful nature and falling into actual transgression.

And so we have two admissions that every true believer must make. The one is that he has still sin within him (1:8), the second that that sin has in former times broken out into sinful actions (1:10). No believer can say either, "I have no sin in me," or "I have in time past never sinned." If we say we have no sin at present, or that we have not sinned in the past, we deceive ourselves. But no confession, though we have sin in the present, is demanded that we are doing sin in the present, too. The confession of actual sinning refers to the past. It may, as appears from 1 John 2:2, be in the present also, but is expected not to be. And so we see how the deepest confession of sin in the past (as Paul's of his having been a persecutor), and the deepest consciousness of having still a vile and corrupt nature in the present, may consist with humble but joyful praise to Him who keeps us from stumbling.

But how is it possible that a believer, having sin in him—sin of such intense vitality and such terrible power as we know the flesh to have—that a believer *having sin* should yet not be *doing sin*? The answer is: "In Him there is no sin. He who abides in Him does not sin." When the abiding in Christ becomes close and unbroken, so that the soul lives from moment to moment in the perfect union with the Lord its keeper, He does, indeed, keep down the power of the old nature, so that it does not regain dominion over the soul.

We have seen that there are degrees in the abiding. With most Christians, the abiding is so weak and intermittent that sin continually obtains the dominance and brings the soul into subjection. The divine promise given to faith is: "Sin shall not have dominion over you" (Rom. 6:14). But with the promise is the command: "Do not let sin reign in your mortal body" (Rom. 6:12). The believer who claims the promise in full faith has the power to obey the command, and sin is kept from asserting its supremacy. Ignorance of the promise, or unbelief, or unwatchfulness opens the door for sin to reign. And so the life of many believers is a course of continual stumbling and sinning. But when the believer seeks full admission into, and a permanent home in Jesus, the Sinless One, then the life of Christ keeps from actual transgression. "In Him there is no sin. He who abides in Him does not sin." Jesus does indeed save him from his sin—not by the removal of his sinful nature, but by keeping him from yielding to it.

> *H*e admits sinners into life union with Himself. The result is that their life becomes like His. "In Him there is no sin. Whosoever abides in Him does not sin."

I have read of a young lion that nothing could awe or keep down but the eye of his keeper. With the keeper you could come near him, and he would crouch—his savage nature all unchanged and thirsting for blood—trembling at the keeper's feet. You might put your foot on his neck, as long as the keeper was with you. To approach him without the keeper would be instant death. And so it is that the believer can *have sin* and yet *not do sin*. The evil nature, the flesh, is unchanged in its enmity against God, but the abiding presence of Jesus keeps it down. In faith, the believer entrusts himself to the keeping, to the indwelling, of the Son of

God. He abides in Him, and counts on Jesus to abide in him too. The union and fellowship is the secret of a holy life: "In Him there is no sin. He who abides in Him does not sin."

And now another question will arise: Admitted that the complete abiding in the Sinless One will keep us from sinning, is such abiding possible? May we hope to be able so to abide in Christ, say, even for one day, so that we may be kept from actual transgressions? The question has only to be fairly stated and considered—it will suggest its own answer. When Christ commanded us to abide in Him, and promised us such rich fruit-bearing to the glory of the Father and such mighty power in our intercessions, can He have meant anything but the healthy, vigorous, complete union of the branch with the vine? When He promised that as we abide in Him He would abide in us, could He mean anything but that His dwelling in us would be a reality of divine power and love? Is not this way of saving from sin just that which will glorify Him?—keeping us daily humble and helpless in the consciousness of the evil nature, watchful and active in the knowledge of its terrible power, dependent and trustful in the remembrance that only His presence can keep the lion down.

O let us believe that when Jesus said, "Abide in Me, and I in you," He did indeed mean that while we were not to be freed from the world and its tribulation, from the sinful nature and its temptations, we were at least to have this blessing fully secured to us—grace to abide wholly, only, even in our Lord. The abiding in Jesus makes it possible to keep from actual sinning, and Jesus Himself makes it possible to abide in Him.

> *The abiding in Jesus makes it possible to keep from actual sinning, and Jesus Himself makes it possible to abide in Him.*

Beloved Christian! I do not wonder if the promise of the text appears almost too high. Do not, I encourage you, let your attention be diverted by the question as to whether it would be possible to be kept for your whole life, or for so many years, without sinning. Faith has always only to deal with the present moment. Ask this: Can Jesus at the present moment, as I abide in Him, keep me from those actual transgressions that have been the stain and the weariness of my daily life? You can say nothing but, "Surely He can."

Take Him then at this present moment, and say, "Jesus keeps me now, Jesus saves me now." Yield yourself to Him in the earnest and believing prayer to be kept abiding, by His own abiding in you—and go into the next moment, and the succeeding hours, with this trust continually renewed. As often as the opportunity occurs in the moments between your occupations, renew your faith in an act of devotion: "Jesus keeps me now; Jesus saves me now."

Let failure and sin, instead of discouraging you, only urge you still more to seek your safety in abiding in the Sinless One. Abiding is a grace in which you can grow wonderfully, if you will but make right away the complete surrender and then persevere with ever larger expectations. Regard it as His work to keep you abiding in Him, His work to keep you from sinning. It is indeed your work to abide in Him. But it is that only because it is His work as vine to bear and hold the branch. Gaze upon *His holy human nature as what He prepared for you to be partaker of with Himself,* and you will see that there is something even higher and better than being kept from sin—that is but the restraining from evil. There is the positive and larger blessing of being now a vessel purified and cleansed, of being filled with His fullness and made the channel of showing forth His power, His blessing, and His glory.

FOR FURTHER THOUGHT

1. *Read 1 John 3:5–6. What is the connection between abiding in Christ and not sinning? How does abiding in Him keep you from sin?*
2. *The apostle Paul wrote, "Sin shall not have dominion over you" (Rom. 6:14). What can keep the believer, even one who wants to defeat the power of sin in his life, from fully walking in the promise that sin will have no power over him?*
3. *How is it possible for you to continually abide in Christ and, therefore, continually be kept from sinning?*

NOTE

IS DAILY SINNING AN INEVITABLE NECESSITY?

WHY is it that, when we possess a Savior whose love and power are infinite, we are so often filled with fear and despondency? We are wearied and faint in our minds, because we do not look steadfastly to Jesus, the author and finisher of faith, who is set down at the right hand of God—to Him whose omnipotence embraces both heaven and earth, who is strong and mighty in His feeble saints.

"While we remember our weakness, we forget His all-sufficient power. While we acknowledge that apart from Christ we can do nothing, we do not rise to the height or depth of Christian humility: 'I can do all things through Christ who strengthens me' (Phil. 4:13). While we trust in the power of the death of Jesus to cancel the guilt of sin, we do not exercise a reliant and appropriating faith in the omnipotence of the living Savior to deliver us from the bondage and power of sin in our daily life. We forget that Christ works in us mightily, and that, one with Him, we possess strength sufficient to overcome every temptation.

"We are apt either to forget our nothingness, and imagine that in our daily path we can live without sin, that the duties and trials of our everyday life can be performed and borne in our own strength, or we do not avail ourselves of the omnipotence of Jesus, who is able to subdue all things to Himself and to keep us from the daily infirmities and falls that we are apt to imagine an inevitable necessity.

"If we really depended in all things and at all times on Christ, we would in all things and at all times gain the victory through Him whose power is infinite, and who is appointed by the Father to be the Captain of our salvation. Then all our deeds would be accomplished, not merely before but in God. We would then do all things to the glory of the Father, in the all-powerful name of Jesus, who is our sanctification. Remember that to Him all power is given in heaven and on earth, and live by the constant exercise of faith in His power. Let us most fully believe that we have and are nothing, that with man it is impossible, that in ourselves we have no life that can bring forth fruit; but that Christ is all—that abiding in Him, and His word dwelling in us, we can bring forth fruit to the glory of the Father."

—From Christ and the Church: Sermons by Adolph Saphir

Day 28

As Your Strength

"All power is given unto me
in heaven and in earth."
Matthew 28:18 KJV[23]

Be strong in the Lord
and in the power of His might.
Ephesians 6:10

"My strength is made perfect in weakness."
2 Corinthians 12:9

THERE is no truth more generally admitted among earnest Christians than that of their utter weakness. There is no truth more generally misunderstood and abused. Here, as elsewhere, God's thoughts are heaven-high above man's thoughts.

The Christian often tries to forget his weakness, but God wants us to remember it, to feel it deeply. The Christian wants to conquer his weakness and to be freed from it, but God wants us to rest and even rejoice in it. The Christian mourns over his weakness, but Christ teaches His servant to say, "I take pleasure in infirmities. . .most gladly I will rather boast in my infirmities" (2 Cor. 12:9, 10). The Christian thinks his weakness is his greatest hindrance in the life and service of God, but God tells us that it is the secret of strength and success. It is our weakness, heartily accepted and continually realized, that gives us our claim and access to the strength of Him who has said, "*My strength* is made perfect *in weakness.*"

When our Lord was about to take His seat on the throne, one of His last words was: "All power is given unto me in heaven and in earth." Just as His taking His place at the right hand of the power of God was something new and true—a real advance in the history of the God-man—so was this clothing with all power. Omnipotence was now entrusted to the man Christ Jesus, that from that time forward through the channels of human nature it might put forth its mighty energies. That is why He connected with this revelation of what He was to receive, the promise of the share that His disciples would have in it: "When I have ascended, you shall receive power from on high" (Luke 24:49, Acts 1:8). It

[23] The word *power* in this verse is properly *authority*, but the two ideas are so closely linked, and the authority as a living divine reality is so inseparable from the power that I have felt at liberty to retain the word *power*.

is in the power of the omnipotent Savior that the believer must find his strength for life and for work.

It was that way with the disciples. During ten days they worshipped and waited at the footstool of His throne. They gave expression to their faith in Him as their savior, to their adoration of Him as their Lord, to their love to Him as their friend, to their devotion and readiness to work for Him as their master. Jesus Christ was the one object of thought, of love, of delight. In such worship of faith and devotion, their souls grew up into the most intense communion with Him on the throne, and when they were prepared, the baptism of power came. It was power within and power around.

> *It is our weakness, heartily accepted and continually realized, that gives us our claim and access to the strength of Him who has said, "My strength is made perfect in weakness."*

The power came to qualify for the work to which they had yielded themselves— of testifying by life and word to their unseen Lord. With some the chief testimony was to be that of a holy life, revealing the heaven and the Christ from whom it came. The power came to set up the kingdom within them, to give them the victory over sin and self, to prepare them by living experience to testify to the power of Jesus on the throne, to make men live in the world as saints. Others were to give themselves up entirely to the speaking in the name of Jesus. But all needed and all received the gift of power, to prove that now Jesus had received the kingdom of the Father, all power in heaven and earth was indeed given to Him, and by Him imparted to His people just as they needed it, whether for a holy life or effective service. They received the gift of power, to prove to the world that the kingdom of God, to which they professed to belong, was not in word but in power. By having power within, they had power without and around. The power of God was felt even by those who would not yield themselves to it (Acts 2:43, 4:13, 5:13).

And what Jesus was to these first disciples, He is to us too. Our whole life and calling as disciples find their origin and their guarantee in the words: "All power is given unto Me in heaven and in earth." What He does in and through us, He does with almighty power. What He claims or demands, He works Himself by that same power. All He gives, He gives with power. Every blessing He bestows, every promise He fulfills, every grace He works—all is to be with power. Everything that comes from this Jesus on the throne of power is to bear the stamp of power. The weakest believer may be confident that in asking to be kept from sin, to grow in holiness, to bring forth much fruit, he may count on these his petitions being fulfilled with divine power. The power is in Jesus; Jesus is ours with all His fullness. It is in us His members that the power is to work and be made manifest.

And if we want to know how the power is bestowed, the answer is simple: Christ gives His power in us by giving His life in us. He does not, as so many believers imagine, take the powerless life He finds in them and impart a little strength to aid them in their feeble efforts. No—it is in giving His own life in us that He gives us His power. The Holy Spirit came down to the disciples directly from the heart of their exalted Lord, bringing down into them the glorious life of heaven into which He had entered.

And so His people are still taught to be strong in the *Lord* and in the power of *His* might. When He strengthens them, it is not by taking away the sense of weakness and giving in its place the feeling of strength. By no means. But in a very wonderful way leaving and even increasing the sense of utter powerlessness, He gives them along with it the consciousness of strength in Him. "We have this treasure in earthen vessels, that the excellence of the power may be of God, and not of us" (2 Cor. 4:7). The weakness and the strength are side by side. As the one grows, the other grows too, until they understand the saying, "When I am weak, then am I strong; I boast in my infirmities, that the power of Christ may rest on me" (see 2 Cor. 12:9, 10).

The believing disciple learns to look at Christ on the throne, Christ the omnipotent, as his life. He studies that life in its infinite perfection and purity, in its strength and glory, for it is the eternal life dwelling in a glorified man. And when he thinks of his own inner life and longs for holiness, to live well pleasing to God, or for power to do the Father's work, he looks up, and, rejoicing that Christ is his life, he confidently reckons that that life will accomplish mightily in him all he needs. In things little and things great—in the being kept from sin from moment to moment for which he has learned to look, or in the struggle with some special difficulty or temptation—*the power of Christ* is the measure of his expectation. He lives a most joyous and blessed life, not because he is no longer weak, but because, being utterly helpless, he consents and expects to have the mighty Savior work in him.

> *O*ur whole life and calling as disciples find their origin and their guarantee in the words: "All power is given unto Me in heaven and in earth." What He does in and through us, He does with almighty power.

The lessons these thoughts teach us for practical life are simple, but very precious. The first is that all our strength is in Christ, laid up and waiting for use. It is there as an almighty life, which is in Him for us, is ready to flow in according to the measure in which it finds the channels open. But whether its flow is strong or weak, whatever our experience of it be, there it is in Christ: all power in heaven and earth. Let us take time to study this. Let us get our minds filled with the thought: So that Jesus might be to us a perfect Savior, the Father gave Him all power. That is the qualification that fits Him for our needs—all the power of heaven over all the powers of earth, over every power of earth in our heart and life too.

The second lesson is: This power flows into us as we abide in close union with Him. When the union is weak, little valued or cultivated, the inflow of strength will be weak. When the union with Christ is rejoiced in as our highest good, and everything sacrificed for the sake of maintaining it, the power will work: "His strength will be made perfect in our weakness." Our one care must therefore be to abide in Christ as our strength. Our one duty is to be strong in the Lord and in the power of His might.

> *L*et our faith cultivate large and clear expectations of the exceeding greatness of God's power in those who believe, even that power of the risen and exalted Christ by which He triumphed over every enemy

Let our faith cultivate large and clear expectations of the exceeding greatness of God's power in those who believe, even that power of the risen and exalted Christ by which He triumphed over every enemy (Eph. 1:19–21). Let our faith consent to God's wonderful and most blessed arrangement: nothing but weakness in us *as our own*, all the power in Christ, and yet within our reach as surely as if it were in us. Let our faith daily go out of self and its life into the life of Christ, placing our whole being at His disposal for Him to work in us. Let our faith, above all, confidently rejoice in the assurance that He will in very deed, with His almighty power, perfect His work in us. As we abide this way in Christ, the Holy Spirit, the Spirit of His power, will work mightily in us, and we too shall sing, "For. . .the LORD is *my strength* and song; in the LORD I have righteousness *and strength*" (Isa. 12:2, 45:24). "*I can do all things* through Christ who strengthens me" (Phil. 4:13).

FOR FURTHER THOUGHT

1. *Jesus told the apostle Paul, "My strength is made perfect in weakness." How can you personally claim and apply that promise in your own life of faith? What must you recognize about yourself in order for that to happen?*
2. *What do Jesus' words, "All power is given unto Me in heaven and in earth," mean to you in your own life as a disciple of Christ?*
3. *Read Ephesians 1:19–21. What power is it that works within you to strengthen you in your life of abiding in Christ?*

DAY 29
AND NOT IN SELF

For I know that in me
(that is, in my flesh) nothing good dwells.
ROMANS 7:18

TO have life in Himself is the prerogative of God alone, and of the Son, to whom the Father has also given it. To seek life, not in itself, but in God, is the highest honor of the creature. To live in and to himself is the folly and guilt of sinful man, but to live to God in Christ is the blessedness of the believer. To deny, to hate, to forsake, to lose his own life, such is the secret of the life of faith. "It is *no longer* I who live, but Christ lives in me" (Gal. 2:20), and "*Not* I, but the grace of God which was with me" (1 Cor. 15:10): This is the testimony of each one who has found out what it is to give up his own life and to receive instead the blessed life of Christ within us. There is no path to true life, to abiding in Christ, than that on which our Lord went before us—through death.

At the first commencement of the Christian life, very few see this. In the joy of pardon, they feel constrained to live for Christ and trust with the help of God to be enabled to do so. They are as yet ignorant of the terrible enmity of the flesh against God and its absolute refusal in the believer to be subject to the law of God. They don't yet know that nothing but death, the absolute surrender to death of all that is of nature, will suffice if the life of God is to be manifested in them with power. But bitter experience of failure soon teaches them the insufficiency of what they have yet known of Christ's power to save, and deep heart-longings are awakened to know Him better.

He lovingly points them to His cross. He tells them that as there, in the faith of His death as their substitute, they found their title to life, so there they shall enter into its fuller experience too. He asks them if they are indeed willing to drink of the cup of which He drank—to be crucified and to die with Him. He teaches them that in Him they are indeed already crucified and dead—all unknowing, at conversion, that they became partakers of His death. But what they need now is to give a full and intelligent consent to what they received before they understood it, by an act of their own choice to will to die with Christ.

This demand of Christ's is one of unspeakable solemnity. Many a believer shrinks back from it. He can hardly understand it. He has become so accustomed to a low life of continual stumbling that he hardly desires, and still less expects, deliverance. Holiness, perfect conformity to Jesus, and unbroken fellowship with His love can scarcely be counted distinct articles of his creed. Where there is not intense longing to be kept to the utmost from sinning and to be brought into the closest possible union with the Savior, the thought of being crucified with Him can find no entrance. The only impression it makes is that of suffering and shame. Such a one is content that Jesus bore the cross, and so won for him the crown he hopes to wear.

How different the light in which the believer who is really seeking to abide fully in Christ looks at it. Bitter experience has taught him how, both in the matter of entire surrender and simple trust, his greatest enemy in the abiding life is *self*. Now it refuses to give up its will, and, then again by its working, it hinders God's work. Unless this life of self, with its willing and working, is displaced by the life of Christ, with *His* willing and working, to abide in Him will be impossible.

> *To* seek life, not in itself, but in God, is the highest honor of the creature. To live in and to himself is the folly and guilt of sinful man, but to live to God in Christ is the blessedness of the believer.

And then comes the solemn question from Him who died on the cross: "Are you ready to give up self to the death?" You yourself, the living person born of God, are already in Me dead to sin and alive to God—but are you ready now, in the power of this death, to put to death your members, to give up self entirely to its death of the cross, to be kept there until it is completely destroyed? The question is a heart-searching one. Am I prepared to say that the old self shall no longer have a word to say, that it shall not be allowed to have a single thought, however natural—not a single feeling, however gratifying—not a single wish or work, however right?

Is this in very deed what He requires? Is not our nature God's handiwork, and may not our natural powers be sanctified to His service? They may and must indeed. But perhaps you have not yet seen how the only way they can be sanctified is that they be taken from under the power of self and brought under the power of the life of Christ. Don't think that this is a work that you can do, because you earnestly desire it and are indeed one of His redeemed ones. No, there is no way to the altar of consecration but through death. As you yielded yourself a sacrifice on God's altar as one alive from the dead (Rom. 6:13, 7:1), so each power of your nature—each talent, gift, possession, that is really to be holiness to the Lord—must be separated from the power of sin and self and laid on the altar to be consumed by the fire that is always burning there.

It is in the putting to death, the slaying of self, that the wonderful powers with which God has prepared you to serve Him can be set free for a complete surrender to God and offered to Him to be accepted, sanctified, and used. And though, as long as you are in the flesh, there is no thought of being able to say that self is dead, yet when the life of Christ is allowed to take full possession, self can be so kept in its crucifixion place and under its sentence of death that it shall have no dominion over you, not for a single moment. Jesus Christ becomes your second self.

Believer! Do you desire to truly and fully abide in Christ? Then prepare yourself to part forever from self and not to allow it, even for a single moment, to have anything to say in your inner life. If you are willing to come entirely away out of self and to allow Jesus Christ to become your life within you, inspiring all your thinking, feeling, acting, in things temporal and spiritual, He is ready to undertake the charge. In the fullest and widest sense the word *life* ever can have, He will be your *life*, extending His interest and influence to each one, even the minutest, of the thousand things that make up your daily life. To do this He asks but one thing: Come away out of self and its life, abide in Christ and the Christ life, and then Christ will be your life. The power of His holy presence will cast out the old life.

> *In* this faith, abide in Christ! Cling to Him, rest on Him, and hope on Him. Daily renew your consecration. Daily accept afresh your position as ransomed from your tyrant, and now in turn made a conqueror.

For this purpose, give up self at once and for ever. If you have never yet dared to do it, out of fear you might fail of your engagement, do it now, in view of the promise Christ gives you that His life will take the place of the old life. Try to realize that though self is not dead, you are indeed dead to self. Self is still strong and living, but it has *no power over you*. You, your renewed nature—you, your new self, begotten again in Jesus Christ from the dead—are indeed dead to sin and alive to God. Your death in Christ has freed you completely from the control of self, and it has no power over you, except as you, in ignorance, or unwatchfulness, or unbelief, consent to yield to its usurped authority.

Come and accept by faith simply and heartily the glorious position you have in Christ. As one who, in Christ, has a life dead to self, as one who is freed from the dominion of self and has received His divine life to take the place of self, to be the animating and inspiring principle of your life, venture boldly to plant the foot on the neck of this enemy of yours and your Lord's. Be of good courage. Only believe, and don't be afraid to take the irrevocable step and to say that you have once for all given up self to the death for which it has been crucified in Christ

(Rom.6:6). And trust Jesus the Crucified One to hold self to the cross and to fill its place in you with His own blessed resurrection life.

In this faith, abide in Christ! Cling to Him, rest on Him, and hope on Him. Daily renew your consecration. Daily accept afresh your position as ransomed from your tyrant, and now in turn made a conqueror. Daily look with holy fear on the enemy, self, struggling to get free from the cross, seeking to tempt you into giving it some little liberty, or else ready to deceive you by its profession of willingness now to do service to Christ.

Remember, self seeking to serve God is more dangerous than self refusing obedience. Look at it with holy fear, and hide yourself in Christ—in Him alone is your safety. Abide this way in Him. He has promised to abide in you. He will teach you to be humble and watchful. He will teach you to be happy and trustful. Bring every interest of your life, every power of your nature, all the unceasing flow of thought, will, and feeling that makes up life, and trust Him to take the place that self once filled so easily and so naturally. Jesus Christ will indeed take possession of you and dwell in you, and in the restfulness and peace and grace of the new life, you shall have unceasing joy at the wondrous exchange that has been made—the coming out of self to abide in Christ alone.

FOR FURTHER THOUGHT

1. *What must you intensely long for in order for the importance of being crucified with Christ to take hold of you and make a difference in your life of faith?*

2. *What is required of you before God can prepare you and give you the power to serve Him as a wholly surrendered disciple of Christ?*

3. *What part should "self" play if you want to abide in Christ? What will Christ do with "self" in the believer who is committed to abiding in Him daily?*

NOTE

IN his work on *Sanctification*, Marshall, in the twelfth chapter, on "Holiness through faith alone," puts with great force the danger in which the Christian is of seeking sanctification in the power of the flesh, with the help of Christ, instead of looking for it to Christ alone and receiving it from Him by faith. He reminds us how there are two natures in the believer, and so two ways of seeking holiness, according as we allow the principles of the one or other nature to guide us. The one is the carnal way, in which we put forth our utmost efforts and resolutions, trusting Christ to help us in doing so. The other the spiritual way, in which, as those who have died and can do nothing, our one care is to receive Christ day by day, and at every step to let Him live and work in us.

"Despair of purging the flesh or natural man of its sinful lusts and inclinations, and of practicing holiness *by your willing and resolving to do the best that rests in your own power and trusting in the grace of God and Christ to help you in such resolutions and endeavors*. Rather, resolve to trust in Christ to work in you to will and to do by His own power according to His own good pleasure. Those who are convinced of their own sin and misery do commonly first think to tame the flesh, to subdue and root out its lusts, and to make their corrupt nature to be better-natured and inclined to holiness *by their struggling and wrestling with it*. And if they can but bring their hearts to a *full purpose and resolution* to do the best that rests in them, they hope that by such a resolution they shall be able to achieve great enterprises in the conquests of their lusts and performance of the most difficult duties.

"It is the great work of some zealous divines in their preachings and writings to stir up people *to this resolution*, wherein they place the chiefest turning point from sin to godliness. And they think that this is not contrary to the life of faith, *because they trust in the grace of God through Christ to help them in all such resolutions and endeavors*. Thus they endeavor to reform their old state and to be made perfect in the flesh, instead of putting it off and walking according to the new state in Christ. They trust in low carnal things for holiness and in the acts of their own will, their purposes, resolutions, and endeavors, instead of Christ. And *they trust in Christ to help them* in this carnal way, whereas true faith would teach them that they are nothing and that they labor in vain."

DAY 30

AS THE SURETY

OF THE COVENANT

Jesus has become a surety of a better covenant.
HEBREWS 7:22

OF the Old Covenant, scripture speaks as not being faultless, and God complains that Israel had not continued in it, and so He disregarded them (see Heb. 8:7–9). It had not secured its apparent object of uniting Israel and God. Israel had forsaken Him, and He had disregarded Israel. Therefore God promises to make a New Covenant, free from the faults of the first and effectual to realize its purpose.

If the New Covenant were to accomplish its end, it would need to secure God's faithfulness to His people, and His people's faithfulness to God. And the terms of the New Covenant expressly declare that these two objects shall be attained. "I will put My laws in their mind"—thus God proposes to secure their unchanging faithfulness to Him. "Their sins and their lawless deeds I will remember no more" (see Heb. 8:10–12)—thus He assures His unchanging faithfulness to them. A pardoning God and an obedient people: these are the two parties who are to meet and to be eternally united in the New Covenant.

The most beautiful provision of this New Covenant is that of the surety in whom its fulfillment on both parts is guaranteed. Jesus was made the surety of the better covenant. To man He became surety that God would faithfully fulfill His part, so that man could confidently depend upon God to pardon, accept, and never again to forsake. And to God He likewise became surety that man would faithfully fulfill his part, so that God could bestow on him the blessing of the covenant. And the way in which He fulfills His suretyship is this: As one with God, and having the fullness of God dwelling in His human nature, He is personally security to men that God will do what He has engaged. All that God has is secured to us in Him as man. And then, as one with us, and having taken us up as members into His own body, He is security to God that His interests shall be cared for. All that man must be and do is secured in Him. It is the glory of the New Covenant that it has in the person of the God-man its living surety, its everlasting security. And it can easily be understood how, in proportion as we abide in Him as the surety of the covenant, its objects and its blessings will be realized in us.

We shall understand this best if we consider it in the light of one of the promises of the New Covenant. Take that in Jeremiah 32:40: "I will make an everlasting covenant with them, that *I will not turn away from doing them good*; but I will put My fear in their hearts so that *they will not depart from Me*."

With what wonderful condescension the infinite God here bows Himself to our weakness! He is the faithful and unchanging One whose word is truth—and yet more abundantly to show to the heirs of the promise the immutability of His counsel, He binds Himself in the covenant that He will never change: "I will make an everlasting covenant, that I will not turn away from doing them good." Blessed is the man who has thoroughly appropriated this and finds his rest in the everlasting covenant of the Faithful One!

A pardoning God and an obedient people: these are the two parties who are to meet and to be eternally united in the New Covenant.

But in a covenant there are two parties. And what if man becomes unfaithful and breaks the covenant? Provision must be made, if the covenant is to be well ordered in all things and sure, that this cannot be, and that man too remain faithful. Man never can undertake to give such an assurance. And see, here God comes to provide for this too. He not only undertakes in the covenant that He will never turn from His people, but also to put His fear in their heart so that they do not depart from Him.

In addition to His own obligations as one of the covenanting parties, He undertakes for the other party too: "I *will. . .cause* you to walk in My statutes, and *you will keep* My judgments and do them" (Ezek. 36:27). Blessed is the man who understands this half of the covenant too! He sees that his security is not in the covenant that he makes with His God, and that he would only continually break again. He finds that a covenant has been made in which God stands good, not only for Himself, but for man too. He grasps the blessed truth that his part in the covenant is to accept what God has promised to do and to expect the sure fulfillment of the divine engagement to secure the faithfulness of His people to their God: "I will put My fear in their hearts so that *they will not depart from Me*."

It is just here that the blessed work comes in of the surety of the covenant, appointed by the Father to see to its maintenance and perfect fulfillment. To Him the Father has said, "I will keep You and give You as a covenant to the people" (Isa. 42:6). And the Holy Spirit testifies, "All the promises of God *in Him* are Yes, and in Him Amen, to the glory of God through us" (2 Cor. 1:20). The believer who abides in Him has a divine assurance for the fulfillment of every promise the covenant ever gave.

Christ was made surety of a better testament. It is as our Melchizedek that Christ is surety (see Heb. 7). Aaron and his sons passed away, but of Christ it is witnessed that *He lives*. He is priest in the power of an *endless life*. Because He *continues forever*, He has an unchangeable priesthood. And because He *always lives* to make intercession (Heb. 7:25), He can save to the uttermost, He can save completely.

It is because Christ is the Ever-living One that His suretyship of the covenant is so effectual. He lives always to make intercession, and can therefore save completely. Every moment there rises up from His holy presence to the Father the unceasing pleadings that secure to His people the powers and the blessings of the heavenly life. And every moment there goes out from Him downward to His people the mighty influences of His unceasing intercession, conveying to them uninterruptedly the power of the heavenly life. As surety with us for the Father's favor, He never ceases to pray and present us before Him. As surety with the Father for us, He never ceases to work and reveal the Father within us.

> *It is because Christ is the Ever-living One that His suretyship of the covenant is so effectual. He lives always to make intercession, and can therefore save completely.*

The mystery of the Melchizedek priesthood, which the Hebrews were not able to receive (Heb. 5:10–14), is the mystery of the resurrection life. It is in this that the glory of Christ as surety of the covenant consists: He always lives. He performs His work in heaven in the power of a divine, an omnipotent life. He always lives to pray, and not a moment that as surety His prayers do not rise Godward to secure the Father's fulfillment to us of the covenant. He performs His work on earth in the power of that same life. Not a moment that His answered prayers—the powers of the heavenly world—do not flow downward to secure for His Father our fulfillment of the covenant. In the eternal life there are no breaks—never a moment's interruption. Each moment has the power of eternity in it. He always, every moment, lives to pray. He always, every moment, lives to bless. He can save to the uttermost, completely and perfectly, because He always lives to pray.

Believer! Come and see here how the possibility of abiding in Jesus every moment is secured by the very nature of this ever-living priesthood of your surety. Moment by moment, as His intercession rises up, its effectiveness descends. And because Jesus stands good for the fulfillment of the covenant—"I will put My fear in their heart, and they will not depart from Me"—He cannot afford to leave you one single moment to yourself. He dare not do so, or He fails in His undertaking. Your unbelief may fail in realizing the blessing, but He cannot be unfaithful. If you will just consider Him and the power of that endless life after which He was made and is a high priest, your faith will rise to believe that an endless, ever-continuing, unchangeable life of abiding in Jesus is nothing less than what is waiting you.

It is as we see what Jesus is, and is to us, that the abiding in Him will become the natural and spontaneous result of our knowledge of Him. If His life unceasingly, moment by moment, rises to the Father for us and descends to us from the Father, then to abide moment by moment is easy and simple. Each moment of conscious fellowship with Him we simply say, "Jesus, surety, keeper, ever-living Savior, in whose life I dwell, I abide in You." Each moment of need, or darkness, or fear, we still say, "O You, the great High Priest, in the power of an endless, unchangeable life, I abide in You." And for the moments when direct and distinct communion with Him must give place to needed occupations, we can trust His suretyship, His unceasing priesthood, in its divine effectiveness, and the power with which He saves to the uttermost still to keep us abiding in Him.

FOR FURTHER THOUGHT

1. *How has God's relationship to His people changed from the Old Covenant to the New? In what specific ways are the two different?*
2. *In what ways does God tend to the weaknesses of His people under the New Covenant? How does He deal with your personal weaknesses?*
3. *What are the natural and spontaneous effects of your seeing who and what Jesus really is to you personally?*

Day 31

The Glorified One

Your life is hidden with Christ in God.
When Christ who is our life appears,
then you also will appear with Him in glory.
COLOSSIANS 3:3–4

HE who abides in Christ the Crucified One learns to know what it is to be crucified with Him, and in Him to be indeed dead to sin. He who abides in Christ the risen and glorified One becomes in the same way partaker of His resurrection life and of the glory with which He has now been crowned in heaven. Unspeakable are the blessings that flow to the soul from the union with Jesus in His glorified life.

This life is a life of *perfect victory and rest*. Before His death, the Son of God had to suffer and to struggle, could be tempted and troubled by sin and its assaults. But as the Risen One, He has triumphed over sin. And as the Glorified One, His humanity has entered into participation of the glory of Deity. The believer who abides in Him as such, as led to see how the power of sin and the flesh are indeed destroyed: the consciousness of complete and everlasting deliverance becomes increasingly clear, and the blessed rest and peace, the fruit of such a conviction that victory and deliverance are an accomplished fact, takes possession of the life. Abiding in Jesus, in whom he has been raised and set in the heavenly places, he receives of that glorious life streaming from the head through every member of the body.

This life is a life *in the full fellowship of the Father's love and holiness*. Jesus often gave prominence to this thought with His disciples. His death was a going to the Father. He prayed: "O Father, glorify Me together with Yourself, with the glory which I had with You" (John 17:5). As the believer, abiding in Christ the Glorified One, seeks to realize and experience what His union with Jesus on the throne implies, he understands how the unclouded light of the Father's presence is His highest glory and blessedness, and in Him the believer's portion too. He learns the sacred art of always, in fellowship with His exalted head, dwelling in the secret of the Father's presence. Further, when Jesus was on earth, temptation could still reach Him, but in glory, everything is holy and in perfect harmony with the will of God. And so the believer who abides in Him experiences that in this high fellowship his spirit is sanctified into growing harmony with the Father's will. The heavenly life of Jesus is the power that casts out sin.

This life is a life of *loving charity and activity*. Seated on His throne, He dispenses His gifts, bestows His Spirit, and never ceases in love to watch and to work for those who are His. The believer cannot abide in Jesus the Glorified One without feeling himself stirred and strengthened to work. The Spirit and the love of Jesus breathe the will and the power to be a blessing to others. Jesus went to heaven with the very object of obtaining power there to bless abundantly. He does this as the heavenly vine only through the medium of His people as His branches. Whoever, therefore, abides in Him, the Glorified One, bears much fruit, for he receives of the Spirit and the power of the eternal life of his exalted Lord and becomes the channel through which the fullness of Jesus, who has been exalted to be a prince and a Savior, flows out to bless those around him.

> *T*he believer cannot abide in Jesus the Glorified One without feeling himself stirred and strengthened to work. The Spirit and the love of Jesus breathe the will and the power to be a blessing to others.

There is one more thought in regard to this life of the Glorified One and ours in Him. It is a life of *wondrous expectation and hope*. It is so with Christ. He sits at the right hand of God, expecting until all His enemies be made His footstool, looking forward to the time when He shall receive His full reward, when His glory shall be made manifest, and His beloved people are forever with Him in that glory. The hope of Christ is the hope of His redeemed: "I will come again and receive you to Myself; that where I am, there you may be also" (John 14:3). This promise is as precious to Christ as it ever can be to us. The joy of meeting is surely no less for the coming bridegroom than for the waiting bride. The life of Christ in glory is one of longing expectation, and the full glory only comes when His beloved are with Him.

The believer who abides closely in Christ will share with Him in this spirit of expectation. Not so much for the increase of personal happiness, but from the spirit of enthusiastic allegiance to his king, he longs to see Him come in His glory, reigning over every enemy, the full revelation of God's everlasting love. "Until He comes" is the watchword of every true-hearted believer. Christ will appear, and we shall appear with Him in glory (see Col. 3:4).

There may be very serious differences in the exposition of the promises of His coming. To one, it is plain as day that He is coming very speedily in person to reign on earth, and that speedy coming is his hope and his stay. To another, loving his Bible and his Savior no less, the coming can mean nothing but the judgment day—the solemn transition from time to eternity, the close of history on earth, the beginning of heaven—and the thought of that manifestation of his Savior's glory is no less his joy and his strength. It is Jesus, Jesus coming again, Jesus taking us to Himself, Jesus adored as Lord of all that is to the whole Church the sum and the center of its hope.

It is by abiding in Christ the Glorified One that the believer will be awakened to that truly spiritual looking for His coming, which alone brings true blessing to the soul. There is an interest in the study of the things that are to be, in which the discipleship of a school is often more marked than the discipleship of Christ the meek, in which contending for opinions and condemnation of brethren are more striking than any signs of the coming glory. It is only the humility that is willing to learn from those who may have other gifts and deeper revelations of the truth than we, and the love that always speaks gently and tenderly of those who do not see these things as we do, and the heavenliness that shows that the Coming One is indeed already our life that will persuade either the Church or the world that this our faith is not in the wisdom of men, but in the power of God.

> To testify of the Savior as the Coming One, we must be abiding in and bearing the image of Him as the Glorified One.

To testify of the Savior as the Coming One, we must be abiding in and bearing the image of Him as the Glorified One. To testify of the Savior as the Coming One, we must be abiding in and bearing the image of Him as the Glorified One. Not the correctness of the views we hold, nor the earnestness with which we advocate them, will prepare us for meeting Him, but only the abiding in Him. Then only can our being manifested in glory with Him be what it is meant to be—a transfiguration, a breaking out and shining forth of the indwelling glory that had been waiting for the day of revelation.

Blessed life! "The life hidden with Christ in God" (Col. 3:3), "set in the heavenlies in Christ" (Eph. 1:20), abiding in Christ the glorified! Once again the question comes: Can a weak child of dust really dwell in fellowship with the king of glory? And again the blessed answer has to be given: To maintain that union is the very work for which Christ has all power in heaven and earth at His disposal.

The blessing will be given to him who will trust his Lord for it, who in faith and confident expectation does not cease to yield himself to be wholly one with Him. It was an act of wondrous though simple faith, in which the soul yielded itself at first to the Savior. That faith grows up to clearer insight and faster hold of God's truth that we are one with Him in His glory. In that same wondrous faith, wondrously simple but wondrously mighty, the soul learns to abandon itself entirely to the keeping of Christ's almighty power and the actings of His eternal life. Because it knows that it has the Spirit of God dwelling within to communicate all that Christ is, it no longer looks at it as a burden or a work, but allows the divine life to have its way, to do its work. Its faith is the increasing abandonment of self, the expectation and acceptance of all that the love and the power of the Glorified One can perform. In that faith, unbroken fellowship is maintained and growing conformity realized. As with Moses, the fellowship makes partakers of the glory, and the life begins to shine with a brightness not of this world.

Blessed life! *It is ours*, for Jesus is ours. Blessed life! We have the possession within us in its hidden power, and we have the prospect before us in its fullest glory. May our daily lives be the bright and blessed proof that the hidden power dwells within, preparing us for the glory to be revealed. May our abiding in Christ the Glorified One be our power to live to the glory of the Father, our fitness to share to the glory of the Son.

AND NOW,

LITTLE CHILDREN,

ABIDE IN HIM,

THAT WHEN HE APPEARS, WE MAY HAVE

CONFIDENCE AND NOT BE ASHAMED

BEFORE HIM AT HIS COMING.

FOR FURTHER THOUGHT

1. *What, according to this writing, will be the God-inspired results of your truly abiding in Jesus Christ the Glorified One—day by day, moment by moment? What kinds of changes will that mean in your personal life of faith? How will it change your approach to your relationships with others?*
2. *What is the connection between your abiding in Jesus Christ the Glorified One and your looking for His coming? What blessings will God give you as you look for His coming?*
3. *What is necessary for you to be a true, living witness to the power and love of the glorified Christ to those around you?*

THE SCHOOL OF OBEDIENCE

To the Members of
The Students' Christian Association of South Africa
and All Christian Students Throughout the World
This Volume Is Prayerfully Dedicated

CONTENTS

Preface

THESE addresses on obedience are issued with the very fervent prayer that it may please our gracious Father to use them for the instruction and strengthening of the young men and women, on whose obedience and devotion so much depends for the Church and the world. To all of them who read this I send my loving greeting. The God of all grace bless them abundantly!

It often happens after a conference, or even after writing a book, that it is as if one only then begins to see the meaning and importance of the truth with which one has been occupied. So I do indeed feel as if I had utterly failed in grasping or expounding the spiritual character, the altogether indispensable necessity, the divine and actual possibility, the inconceivable blessedness of a life of true and entire obedience to our Father in heaven. Let me, therefore, just in a few sentences gather up the main points which have come home to myself with special power, and ask every reader at starting to take note of them as some of the chief lessons to be learned in Christ's school of obedience.

The Father in heaven asks and requires, and actually expects, that every child of His yield Him wholehearted and entire obedience, day by day, and all the day.

To enable His child to do this, He has made a most abundant and altogether sufficient provision in the promise of the New Covenant, and in the gift of His Son and Spirit.

This provision can alone, but can most certainly, be enjoyed, and these promises fulfilled, in the soul that gives itself up to a life in the abiding communion with the Three-One God, so that His presence and power work in it all the day.

The very entrance into this life demands the vow of absolute obedience, or the surrender of the whole being, to be, think, speak, do, every moment, nothing but what is according to the will of God, and well-pleasing to Him.

If these things are indeed true, it is not enough to assent to them: We need the Holy Spirit to give us such a vision of their glory and divine power, and the demand they make on our immediate and unconditional submission, that there may be no rest until we accept all that God is willing to do for us.

Let us all pray that God may, by the light of His Spirit, so show His loving and almighty will concerning us that it may be impossible for us to be disobedient to the heavenly vision.

ANDREW MURRAY
Wellington, August 9, 1898

1

OBEDIENCE: ITS PLACE
IN HOLY SCRIPTURE

IN undertaking the study of a Bible word, or of a truth of the Christian life, it is a great help to take a survey of the place it takes in scripture. As we see where, and how often, and in what connections it is found, its relative importance may be apprehended as well as its bearing on the whole of revelation. Let me try in this first chapter to prepare the way for the study of what obedience is, by showing you where to go in God's Word to find the mind of God concerning it.

1. TAKE THE SCRIPTURE AS A WHOLE

We begin with paradise. In Genesis 2:16, we read: "And *the Lord God commanded the man*, saying." And later (3:11), "Have you eaten from the tree of which *I commanded you* that you should not eat?"

Note how obedience to the command is the one virtue of paradise, the one condition of man's abiding there, the one thing his Creator asks of him. Nothing is said of faith, or humility, or love: Obedience includes all. As supreme as is the claim and authority of God is the demand for obedience as the one thing that is to decide his destiny. In the life of man, to obey is the one necessary thing.

Turn now from the beginning to the close of the Bible. In its last chapter you read, "Blessed are those who *do His commandments*, that they may have the right to the tree of life" (Rev. 22:14). Or, if we accept the English Revised Version, which gives another reading, we have the same thought in chapters 12 and 14, where we read of the seed of the woman, "which *keep the commandments of God*, and hold the testimony of Jesus" (12:17) and of the patience of the saints: "Here are they that *keep the commandments of God*, and the faith of Jesus" (14:12).

From beginning to end, from paradise lost to paradise regained, the law is unchangeable—it is only obedience that gives access to the tree of life and the favor of God.

And if you ask how the change was effected out of the disobedience at the beginning that closed the way to the tree of life, to the obedience at the end that again gained entrance to it, turn to that which stands midway between the beginning and the end—the cross of Christ. Read a passage like Romans 5:19, "*By one*

Man's obedience many will be made righteous" or Philippians 2:8–9 "He. . .*became obedient to the point of* death. . .*Therefore* God also has highly exalted Him," or Hebrews 5:8–9 "*He learned obedience*. . .*and became* the author of eternal salvation *to all who obey Him*," and you see how the whole redemption of Christ consists in restoring obedience to its place. The beauty of His salvation consists in this: that He brings us back to the life of obedience, through which alone the creature can give the Creator the glory due to Him, or receive the glory of which his Creator desires to make him partaker.

> *From beginning to end, from paradise lost to paradise regained, the law is unchangeable—it is only obedience that gives access to the tree of life and the favor of God.*

Paradise, Calvary, heaven, all proclaim with one voice: "Child of God! The first and the last thing your God asks of you is simple, universal, unchanging obedience."

2. LET US TURN TO THE OLD TESTAMENT

Here let us specially notice how, with any new beginning in the history of God's kingdom, obedience always comes into special prominence.

A. Take Noah, the new father of the human race, and you will find four times written (Gen. 6:22; 7:5, 9, 16): "According to all that God commanded him, so he did."

It is the man who does what God commands, to whom God can entrust His work, whom God can use to be a savior of men.

B. Think of Abraham, the father of the chosen race. "By faith Abraham *obeyed*" (Heb. 11:7).

When Abraham had been forty years in this school of faith-obedience, God came to perfect his faith and to crown it with His fullest blessing. Nothing could prepare him for this but a crowning act of obedience. When he had bound his son on the altar, God came and said, "By Myself I have sworn. . .blessing I will bless you, and multiplying I will multiply your descendants. . .*because you have obeyed My voice*" (Gen. 22:17, 18).

And to Isaac He said, "I will perform the oath which I swore to Abraham your father. . .*because Abraham obeyed My voice*" (26:3, 5)

Oh, when shall we learn how unspeakably pleasing obedience is in God's sight, and how unspeakable is the reward He bestows on it! The way to be a blessing to the world is to be men of obedience, to be known by God and the world by this one mark: a will completely given up to God's will. Let all who profess to walk in Abraham's footsteps walk this way.

C. Go on to Moses. At Sinai, God gave him the message to the people: "*If you* *will indeed obey My voice. . .*you shall be a special treasure to Me above all people" (Exod. 19:5).

In the very nature of things it cannot be otherwise. God's holy will is His glory and perfection, and it is only by an entrance into His will, by obedience, that it is possible to be His people.

D. Take the building of the sanctuary in which God was to dwell. In the last three chapters of Exodus you have the expression nineteen times, "Thus Moses did; according to all that the Lord had commanded him, so he did," and *then*, "The glory of the Lord filled the tabernacle" (40:35). Just so again in Leviticus 8 and 9, you have, with reference to the consecration of the priests and the tabernacle, the same expression appears twelve times. And *then*, "Then the glory of the LORD appeared to all the people, and fire came out from before the LORD and consumed the burnt offering" (Lev. 9:23, 24).

> *Y*es, "a blessing if you obey!" That is the keynote of the blessed life. Canaan, just like paradise and heaven, can be the place of blessing as it is the place of obedience. God desires that we fully understand this.

Words cannot make it plainer, that it is in the results of His people's obedience that God delights to dwell, that it is the obedient He crowns with His favor and presence.

E. After the forty years wandering in the wilderness, and its terrible revelation of the fruit of disobedience, there was again a new beginning when the people were about to enter Canaan. Read Deuteronomy, with all Moses spoke in sight of the land, and you will find there is no book of the Bible that uses the word *obey* so frequently, or speaks so much of the blessing obedience will assuredly bring. The whole is summed up in the words, "Behold, I set before you today *a blessing. . .if you obey. . .*and the curse, if you do not obey" (Deut. 11:26, 27, 28).

Yes, "*a blessing if you obey!*" That is the keynote of the blessed life. Canaan, just like paradise and heaven, can be the place of blessing as it is the place of obedience. God desires that we fully understand this. But beware of praying only for a blessing. Let us be careful to obey, and God will give the blessing. Let my one thought as a Christian be how I can obey and please my God perfectly.

F. The next new beginning we have is in the appointment of kings in Israel. In the story of Saul we have the most solemn warning of the need of exact and entire obedience in a man whom God is to trust as ruler of His people. Samuel had commanded Saul to wait seven days for him to come and sacrifice, and to show him what to do (see 1 Sam. 10:8). When Samuel delayed Saul took it upon himself to sacrifice (13:8–14).

When Samuel came he said: "You have not kept the commandment of the LORD your God, *which He commanded you*. . . . your kingdom shall not continue. . . because you have not kept what *the* LORD *commanded you*" (13:13–14).

God will not honor the man who is not obedient.

> *M*ay God reveal to us whether we are indeed going all lengths with Him, seeking to utterly destroy all and spare nothing that is not in perfect harmony with His will.

Saul has a second opportunity given him of showing what is in his heart. He is sent to execute God's judgment against Amelek. He obeys. He gathers an army of two hundred thousand men, undertakes the journey into the wilderness, and destroys Amelek. But while God had commanded him "utterly destroy all that they have, and do not spare them" (1 Sam. 15:3), he spared the best of the cattle and Agag.

God speaks to Samuel, "I greatly regret that I have set up Saul *as* king, for he. . .*has not performed My commandments*" (15:11).

When Samuel comes, Saul twice over says, "I have performed the commandment of the LORD" (15:13); "I have obeyed the voice of the LORD" (15:20).

And so he had, as many would think. But his obedience had not been complete. God claims exact, full obedience. God had said, "*Utterly destroy all! Do not spare!*" This he had not done. He had spared the best sheep for a sacrifice to the Lord. And Samuel said, "*To obey* is better than sacrifice. . .Because you have rejected the word of the LORD, He also has rejected you" (15:22–23).

This is a sad example of obedience, which in part performs God's commandment and yet is not the obedience God asks! God says of all sin and all disobedience: "Utterly destroy all! Do not spare!" May God reveal to us whether we are indeed going all lengths with Him, seeking to utterly destroy all and spare nothing that is not in perfect harmony with His will. It is only a wholehearted obedience, down to the smallest details, that can satisfy God. Let nothing less satisfy you, so that you can never say, "I have obeyed," while God says, "You have rejected the word of the Lord."

G. Just one word more from the Old Testament. Next to Deuteronomy, Jeremiah is the book most filled with the word *obey*—though, sadly, it is mostly in connection with the people's disobedience. God sums up all His dealings with the fathers in the one word, "For I did not speak to your fathers. . .concerning burnt offerings or sacrifices. But this is what I commanded them, saying, '*Obey My voice, and I will be your God*'" (Jeremiah 7:22, 23).

God wants us to learn that all that He speaks of sacrifices, even of the sacrifice of His beloved Son, is subordinate to the one thing—to have His creature restored to full obedience. Into all the inconceivable meaning of the words, "I *will be your*

God," there is no gateway but this: "*Obey My voice.*"

3. WE COME TO THE NEW TESTAMENT

A. Here we think at once of our blessed Lord and the prominence He gives to obedience as the one thing for which He was come into the world. He who entered it with His "Behold, I have come to do Your will, O God" (Heb. 10:9) always confessed to men, "I do not seek My own will but the will of the Father who sent Me" (John 5:30).

Of all He did and of all He suffered, even to the death, He said, "This commandment have I received from My Father."

If we turn to His teaching, we find everywhere that the obedience He rendered is what He claims from everyone who desires to be His disciple.

During His whole ministry, from beginning to end, obedience is *the very essence of salvation.*

In the Sermon on the Mount He began with it: No one could enter the kingdom, "but he who does the will of My Father in heaven" (Matt. 7:21). And in the farewell discourse, how wonderfully He reveals the spiritual character of true obedience as it is born of love and inspired by it, and as it also opens the way into the love of God. Do take into your heart the wonderful words, "If you love Me, keep My commandments. . . . And I will pray the Father, and He will give you another Helper. . .He who has My commandments and keeps them, it is he who loves Me. And he who loves Me will be loved by My Father, and I will love him and manifest Myself to him. . . . If anyone loves Me, he will keep My word; and My Father will love him, and We will come to him and make Our home with him" (John 14:15–16, 21, 23).

> *A*s disobedience in Adam and in us was the one thing that brought death, so obedience, in Christ and in us, is the one thing that the gospel makes known as the way of restoration to God and His favor.

No words could express more simply or more powerfully the inconceivably glorious place Christ gives to obedience, with its twofold possibility: (1) as only possible to a loving heart; (2) as making possible all that God has to give of His Holy Spirit, of His wonderful love, of His indwelling in Christ Jesus. I know of no passage in scripture that gives a higher revelation of the spiritual life, or the power of loving obedience as its one condition. Let us pray God very earnestly that by His Holy Spirit its light may transfigure our daily obedience with its heavenly glory.

See how all this is confirmed in the next chapter. How well we know the parable of the vine! How often and how earnestly we have asked how to be able to abide continually in Christ! We have thought of more study of the Word, more faith, more prayer, more communion with God, and we have overlooked the simple truth that Jesus teaches so clearly, "*If you keep My commandments*, you will abide in My love," with its divine sanction, "*just as I have kept* My Father's commandments and abide in His love" (John 15:10).

For Him as for us, the only way under heaven to abide in divine love is to *keep the commandments*. Do let me ask, have you known it, have you heard it preached, have you believed it and proved it true in your experience: obedience on earth is the key to a place in God's love in heaven? Unless there be some correspondence between God's wholehearted love in heaven and our wholehearted, loving obedience on earth, Christ cannot manifest Himself to us, God cannot abide in us, we cannot abide in His love.

> he obedience that keeps His commandments: this is the garment in which the hidden, invisible love reveals itself, and whereby it is known.

B. If we go on from our Lord Jesus to His apostles, we find in the Acts two words of Peter's that show how our Lord's teaching had entered into him. In the one, "the Holy Spirit whom God has given to those who obey Him" (Acts 5:32), he proves how he knew what had been the preparation for Pentecost, the surrender to Christ. In the other, "*We ought to obey* God rather than men (5:29)—we have the man-ward side: Obedience is to be to death; nothing on earth dare or can hinder it in the man who has given himself to God.

C. In Paul's Epistle to the Romans, we have, in the opening and closing verses the expression, "*the obedience to the faith among all nations*" (1:5; 16:26), as that for which he was made an apostle. He speaks of what God had produced "to make the Gentiles obedient" (15:18). He teaches that, as the obedience of Christ makes us righteous, we become *the servants of obedience* to righteousness. As disobedience in Adam and in us was the one thing that brought death, so obedience, in Christ and in us, is the one thing that the gospel makes known as the way of restoration to God and His favor.

D. We all know how James warns us not to be hearers of the Word only but doers, and expounds how Abraham was justified, and his faith perfected, by his works (James 1:20–24).

E. In Peter's first epistle we have only to look at the first chapter to see the place obedience has in his system. In 1:2 he speaks to the "*elect according to the foreknowledge of God the Father, in sanctification of the Spirit, for obedience and sprinkling of the blood of Jesus Christ,*" and so points us to obedience as the eternal purpose of the Father, as the great object of the work of the Spirit, and a chief part of the salvation of Christ. In 1:14 he writes, "*As obedient children,*" born of it, marked by it, subject to it, "you also be holy in all your conduct" (1 Pet. 1:15). Obedience is the very starting point of true holiness.

In 1:22 we read, "Since you have purified your souls in obeying the truth. . ." —the whole acceptance of the truth of God was not merely a matter of intellectual assent or strong emotion. Rather, it was a subjection of the life to the dominion of the truth of God. The Christian life was in the first place obedience.

F. Of John we know how strong his statements are. "He who says, 'I know Him,' and *does not keep His commandments*, is a liar" (1 John 2:4). Obedience is the one certificate of Christian character.

"Let us not love in word or in tongue, but in deed and in truth. And by this we know that we are of the truth, and shall assure our hearts before Him. . . . And whatever we ask we receive from Him, *because we keep His commandments* and do those things that are pleasing in His sight" (1 John 3:18–19, 22). Obedience is the secret of good conscience, and of the confidence that God hears us. "For this is the love of God, that we *keep His commandments*" (1 John 5:3). The obedience that keeps His commandments: this is the garment in which the hidden, invisible love reveals itself, and whereby it is known.

> *L*et us unite in praying that the Holy Spirit may show us how defective the Christian's life is when obedience does not rule all, how that life can be exchanged for one of full surrender to absolute obedience

Such is the place obedience has in holy scripture, in the mind of God, in the hearts of His servants. We may well ask, "Does it take that place in my heart and life?" Have we indeed given obedience that supreme place of authority over us that God means it to have, as the inspiration of every action and of every approach to Him? If we yield ourselves to the searching of God's Spirit, we may find that we never gave it its true proportion in our scheme of life, and that this lack is the cause of all our failure in prayer and in work. We may see that the deeper blessings of God's grace and the full enjoyment of God's love and nearness have been beyond our reach, simply because obedience was never made what God would have it be—the starting point and the goal of our Christian life.

Let this, our first study, awaken in us an earnest desire to know God's will fully concerning this truth. Let us unite in praying that the Holy Spirit may show us how defective the Christian's life is when obedience does not rule all, how that life can be exchanged for one of full surrender to absolute obedience, and how sure it is that God in Christ will enable us to live it out.

For Further Thought

1. *What does an overview of the Bible—Old Testament and New Testament alike—teach you about the importance of obedience, of the blessings in obedience?*
2. *What, according to the Bible, is the connection between obedience to God and blessings from God?*
3. *The disobedience of Adam in the garden of Eden, as well as our own disobedience, brings death. What does the Bible teach brings about restoration to God and His favor?*

2

THE OBEDIENCE OF CHRIST

For as by one man's disobedience many were made sinners,
so also by one Man's obedience many will be made righteous....
Do you not know that to whom you present yourselves slaves to obey,
you are that one's slaves whom you obey, whether of sin leading
to death, or of obedience leading to righteousness?
ROMANS 5:19, 6:16

By one Man's obedience many will be made righteous." These words tell us what we owe to Christ. As in Adam we were made sinners, in Christ we are made righteous.

The words tell us, too, to what in Christ it is we owe our righteousness. As Adam's disobedience made us sinners, the obedience of Christ makes us righteous. To the obedience of Christ we owe everything.

Among the treasures of our inheritance in Christ, this is one of the richest. How many have never studied it, so as to love it and delight in it and get the full blessing of it! May God, by His Holy Spirit, reveal its glory and make us partakers of its power.

You are familiar with the blessed truth of justification by faith. In the section of the Epistle to the Romans preceding our passage (Rom. 3:21–5:11), Paul had taught what its ever-blessed foundation was—the atonement of the blood of Christ and its way and condition—faith in the free grace of a God who justifies the ungodly and its blessed fruits—the bestowing of the righteousness of Christ, with an immediate access into the favor of God, and the hope of glory.

In our passage he now proceeds to unfold the deeper truth of the union with Christ by faith, in which justification has its root, and which makes it possible and right for God to accept us for His sake. Paul goes back to Adam and our union with him, with all the consequences that flowed from that union, to prove how reasonable, how perfectly natural (in the higher sense of the word) it is that those who receive Christ by faith, and are so united with Him, become partakers of His righteousness and His life. It is in this argument that he specially emphasizes the contrast between the disobedience of Adam, with the condemnation and death it brought, and the obedience of Christ, with the righteousness and life it brings. As we study the place the obedience of Christ takes in His work for our salvation and see in it the very root of our redemption, we shall know what place to give it in our heart and life.

"By one man's disobedience many were made sinners." How was this?

There was a twofold connection between Adam and his descendants—the *judicial* and the *vital*.

1. Judicial and Vital Connection

Through the judicial, the whole race, though yet unborn, came immediately under the sentence of death. "Death reigned from Adam to Moses, even over those"—such as little children—"who had not sinned according to the likeness of the transgression of Adam" (Rom. 5:14).

This judicial relation was rooted in the vital connection. The sentence could not have come upon them if they had not been in Adam. And the vital again became the manifestation of the judicial, as each child of Adam enters life under the power of sin and death. "By one man's disobedience many were made sinners" both by position subject to the curse of sin and by nature subject to its power.

"Adam, who is a type of Him who was to come" (5:14), and who is called the Second Adam, the Second Father of the race. Adam's disobedience in its effects is the exact likeness of what the obedience of Christ becomes to us. When a sinner believes in Christ, he is united to Him, and is at once, by a judicial sentence, pronounced and accepted as righteous in God's sight. The judicial relationship is rooted in the vital. He has Christ's righteousness only by having Christ Himself, and being in Him. Before he knows anything of what it is to be in Christ, he can know himself acquitted and accepted. But he is then led on to know the vital connection, and to understand that as real and complete as was his participation in Adam's disobedience with the death as well as the sinful nature that followed on it, is his participation in Christ's obedience, with both the righteousness and the obedient life and nature that come from it.

2. Let us See and Understand This

Through Adam's disobedience we are made sinners. The one thing God asked of Adam in paradise was obedience. The one thing by which a creature can glorify God, or enjoy His favor and blessing, is obedience. The one cause of the power sin has over the world, and the ruin it has brought, is disobedience. The whole curse of sin has on us is due to disobedience imputed to us. The whole power of sin working in us is nothing but this—that as we receive Adam's nature, we inherit his disobedience—we are born "the children of disobedience" (Eph. 2:2).

It is evident that the one work a Christ was needed for was to remove this disobedience—its curse, its dominion, its evil nature and workings. Disobedience was the root of all sin and misery. The first object of His salvation was to cut away the evil root, and restore man to his original destiny—a life in obedience to his God.

3. HOW DID CHRIST DO THIS?

First of all, by coming as the Second Adam to undo what the first had done. Sin had made us believe that it was a humiliation always to be seeking to know and do God's will. Christ came to show us the nobility, the blessedness, the heavenliness of obedience.

When God gave us the robe of creaturehood to wear, we did not know that its beauty, its unspotted purity, was obedience to God. Christ came and put on that robe so that He might show us how to wear it and how with it we could enter into the presence and glory of God. Christ came to overcome, and so take away our disobedience and to replace it by His own obedience on us and in us. As universal, as mighty, as all-pervading as was the disobedience of Adam, even far more so was to be the power of the obedience of Christ.

The object of Christ's life of obedience was threefold: (1) as an example, to show us what true obedience was; (2) as our Surety, by His obedience to fulfill all righteousness for us; (3) as our head, to prepare a new and obedient nature to impart to us.

So He died, too, to show us that His obedience means a readiness to obey to the uttermost, to die for God, that it means the vicarious endurance and atonement of the guilt of our disobedience, and that it means a death to sin as an entrance to the life of God for Him and for us.

> *When a sinner believes in Christ, he is united to Him, and is at once, by a judicial sentence, pronounced and accepted as righteous in God's sight.*

The disobedience of Adam, in all its possible consequences, was to be put away and replaced by the obedience of Christ. Judicially, by that obedience we are made righteous. Just as we were made sinners by Adam's disobedience, we are at once and completely justified and delivered from the power of sin and death: We stand before God as righteous men. Vitally—for the judicial and the vital are as inseparable as in the case of Adam—we are made one with Christ in His death and resurrection, so that we are as truly dead to sin and alive to God as He is. And the life we receive in Him is no other than a life of obedience.

Let every one of us who desires to know what obedience is consider well: It is the obedience of Christ that is the secret of the righteousness and salvation I find in Him. The obedience is the very essence of that righteousness: Obedience is salvation. His obedience, first of all to be accepted, and trusted to, and rejoiced in, as covering and swallowing up and making an end of my disobedience, is the one unchanging, never-to-be-forsaken ground of my acceptance. And then, His obedience—just as Adam's disobedience was the power that ruled my life, the power of death in me—becomes the life-power of the new nature in me. Then I understand why Paul in this passage so closely links the righteousness and the life. "For if by the one man's offense death reigned through the one, much more those who receive abundance of grace and of the gift of righteousness will *reign in life through the One*" (Rom. 5:17), even here on earth. "*The free gift came* to all men, resulting in justification *of life*" (5:18).

The more carefully we trace the parallel between the first and Second Adam, and see how in the former the death and disobedience reigned in his seed equally with himself, and how both were equally transmitted, through union with him, the more we will be forced to recognize that the obedience of Christ is equally to be ours, not only by imputation, but by personal possession. It is so inseparable from Him that to receive Him and His life is to receive His obedience. When we receive the righteousness God offers us so freely, it immediately points us to the obedience out of which it was born, with which it is inseparably one, in which alone it can live and flourish.

> *L*et every one of us who desires to know what obedience is consider well: It is the obedience of Christ that is the secret of the righteousness and salvation I find in Him

See how this connection comes out in the next chapter. After having spoken of our life-union to Christ, Paul, for the first time in the epistle, gives an injunction, "Do not let sin reign. . .present yourselves to God" (6:12, 13); and then immediately proceeds to teach how this means nothing but obedience: "Do you not know that. . .you are that one's *slaves*. . .whether of sin leading to death, or *of obedience leading to righteousness?*" (6:16). Your relationship to obedience is a practical one. You have been delivered from disobedience (Adam's and your own) and are now servants of obedience—and that "leading to righteousness." Christ's obedience was to righteousness—the righteousness that is God's gift to you. Your subjection to obedience is the one way in which your relationship to God and to righteousness can be maintained.

Christ's obedience leading to righteousness is the only beginning of life for you; your obedience leading to righteousness is its only continuance. There is but one law for the head and the members. As surely as it was with Adam and his seed, disobedience and death, it is with Christ and his seed, obedience and life. The one bond of union, the one mark of likeness between Adam and his seed was disobedience. The one bond of union between Christ and His seed, the one mark of resemblance, is obedience.

It was obedience that made Christ the object of the Father's love (John 10:17–18) and our Redeemer, and it is *obedience alone* that can lead us in the way to dwell in that love (John 14:21, 23) and enjoy that redemption.

"By one Man's obedience many will be made righteous." Everything depends on our knowledge of and participation in the obedience as the gateway and path to the full enjoyment of the righteousness. At conversion the righteousness is given to faith, once for all, completely and forever, with but little or no knowledge of the obedience. But as the righteousness is indeed believed in and submitted to, and its full dominion over us, as "slaves of righteousness," sought after, it will open to us its blessed nature, as born out of obedience, and therefore always leading us back to its divine origin. The truer our hold of the righteousness of Christ, in the power of the Spirit, the more intense will be our desire to share in the obedience out of which it sprang. In this light let us study the obedience of Christ, so that like Him we may live as servants of obedience leading to righteousness.

1. *In Christ this obedience was a life principle.* Obedience with Him did not mean a single act of obedience now and then, not even a series of acts, but the spirit of His whole life. "I have come down from heaven, not to do My own will" (John 6:38). "Behold, I have come to do Your will, O God" (Heb. 10:9). He had come into the world for one purpose. He only lived to carry out God's will. The one supreme, all-controlling power of His life was obedience.

He is willing to make it so in us. This was what He promised when He said, "Whoever *does the will* of My Father in heaven is My brother and sister and mother" (Matt. 12:50).

The link in a family is a common life shared by all and a family likeness. The bond between Christ and us is that He and we together do the will of God.

2. *In Christ this obedience was a joy.* "I delight to do Your will, O my God" (Ps. 50:8). "My food is to do the will of Him who sent Me" (John 4:34).

Our food is refreshment and invigoration. The healthy man eats his bread with gladness. But food is more than enjoyment—it is a necessity of life. And so, doing the will of God was the food that Christ hungered after and without which He could not live, the one thing that satisfied His hunger, the one thing that refreshed and strengthened Him and made Him glad.

It was something of this David meant when he spoke of God's words being "sweeter also than honey and the honeycomb" (Ps. 19:10). As this is understood and accepted, obedience will become more natural to us and necessary to us, and more refreshing than our daily food.

3. *In Christ this obedience led to a waiting on God's will.* God did not reveal all His will to Christ at once, but day by day, according to the circumstances of the hour. In His life of obedience there was growth and progress; the most difficult lesson came the last. Each act of obedience prepared Him for the new discovery of the Father's further command. He said, "My ears You have opened. . . . I delight

to do Your will, O my God" (Ps. 40:6, 8).

It is as obedience becomes the passion of our life that the ears will be opened by God's Spirit to wait for His teaching, and we are content with nothing less than a divine guidance into the divine will for us.

4. *In Christ this obedience was to the point of death.* When He said, "I have come down from heaven, not to do My own will, but the will of Him who sent Me," He was ready to go all lengths in denying His own will and doing the Father's. He meant it: "In nothing My will, at all costs God's will."

This is the obedience to which He invites and for which He empowers us. This wholehearted surrender to obedience in everything is the only true obedience, is the only power that will avail to carry us through. God wants Christians to understand that nothing less than this brings the soul gladness and strength!

> The truer our hold of the righteousness of Christ, in the power of the Spirit, the more intense will be our desire to share in the obedience out of which it sprang.

As long as there is a doubt about universal obedience, and with that a lurking sense of the possibility of failure, we lose the confidence that secures the victory. But when once we set God before us, as really asking full obedience and engaging to work it, and see that we dare offer Him nothing less, we give up ourselves to the working of the divine power, which by the Holy Spirit can master our whole life.

5. *In Christ this obedience sprang from the deepest humility.* "Let this mind be in you which was also in Christ Jesus, who...*made Himself of no reputation*, taking the form of a bondservant and...*humbled Himself* and became obedient to the point of death (Phil. 2:5, 6, 7, 8).

It is the man who is willing for entire self-emptying, willing to be and live as the servant, "a servant of obedience," willing to be humbled very low before God and man, to whom the obedience of Jesus will unfold its heavenly beauty and its constraining power. There may be a strong will that secretly trusts in self and that strives for the obedience, and fails. It is as we sink low before God in humility, meekness, patience, and entire resignation to His will—and are willing to bow in an absolute helplessness and dependence on Him, as we turn away wholly from self—that it will be revealed to us how it is the one and only duty and blessing of a creature to obey this glorious God.

6. *In Christ this obedience was of faith*—in entire dependence upon God's strength. "I can of Myself do nothing" (John 5:30). "The Father who dwells in Me does the works" (John 14:10).

The Son's unreserved surrender to the Father's will was met by the Father's unceasing and unreserved bestowing of His power working in Him.

It will be the same with us. If we learn that our giving up our will to God is always the measure of His giving His power in us, we shall see that a surrender to full obedience is nothing but a full faith that God will work all in us.

God's promises of the New Covenant all rest on this: "The LORD your God will circumcise your heart and the heart...to love the LORD your God *with all your heart*...And you *will again obey* the voice of the LORD" (Deut. 30:6, 8). "I will put My Spirit within you and cause you to walk in My statutes, and *you will keep* My judgments" (Ezek. 36:27).

> *I*t is as obedience becomes the passion of our life that the ears will be opened by God's Spirit to wait for His teaching, and we are content with nothing less than a divine guidance into the divine will for us.

Let us, like the Son, believe that God works all in us, and we shall have the courage to yield ourselves to an unreserved obedience—an obedience to the point of death. That yielding ourselves up to God will become the entrance into the blessed experience of conformity to the Son of God in His doing the Father's will, because He counted on the Father's power. Let us give our all to God. He will work His all in us.

Do you not know that you are made righteous by *the obedience of One*, are like Him and in Him servants of obedience leading to righteousness? It is in the obedience of the One the obedience of the many has its root, its life, its security. Let us turn and gaze on, and study, and believe in Christ, as the obedient One, as never before. Let this be the Christ we receive and love, and seek to conform to. As His righteousness is our one hope, let His obedience be our one desire. Let our faith in Him prove its sincerity and its confidence in God's supernatural power working in us by accepting Christ, the obedient One, as in very deed our life, as the Christ who dwells in us.

FOR FURTHER THOUGHT

1. *What were and are the consequences of Adam's disobedience in the garden of Eden, and how does his disobedience contrast with the perfect obedience of Jesus Christ?*
2. *What benefits do you as a believer receive because of Christ's perfect obedience? What are the benefits of studying and observing the obedience of Christ to the Father in all things?*
3. *What was the Father's response to Jesus' unreserved surrender to His will? Of what benefit is that response to you today?*

3

THE SECRET OF TRUE OBEDIENCE

He learned obedience.
HEBREWS 5:8

THE secret of true obedience—let me say at once what I believe it to be—is the clear and close personal relationship to God. All our attempts after full obedience will be failures until we get access to His abiding fellowship. *It is God's holy presence, consciously abiding with us, that keeps us from disobeying Him.*

Defective obedience is always the result of a defective life. To rouse and spur on that defective life by arguments and motives has its use, but their chief blessing must be that they make us feel the need for a different life, a life so entirely under the power of God that obedience will be its natural outcome. The defective life, the life of broken and irregular fellowship with God, must be healed, and way made for a full and healthy life. Then full obedience will become possible. The secret of a true obedience is *the return to close and continual fellowship with God.*

"He learned obedience" (Heb. 5:8). And why was this needed? And what is the blessing He brings us? Listen, "He learned obedience by the things which He suffered. And having been perfected, He became the author of eternal salvation to all who obey Him" (Heb. 5:8–9).

Suffering is unnatural to us, and therefore calls for the surrender of our will.

Christ needed suffering so that in it He might learn to obey and give up His will to the Father at any cost. He needed to learn obedience so that as our great high priest He might be made perfect. He learned obedience, He became obedient to the point of death, so that He might become the author of our salvation. He became the author of salvation *through obedience*, that He might save those *"who obey Him."*

As obedience was with Him absolutely necessary to procure, it is with us absolutely necessary to inherit salvation. The very essence of salvation is obedience to God. Christ as the obedient One saves us as His obedient ones. Whether in His suffering on earth, or in His glory in heaven, whether in Himself or in us, obedience is what the heart of Christ is set on.

On earth Christ was a learner in the school of obedience, and in heaven He teaches it to His disciples here on earth. In a world where disobedience reigns to the point of death, the restoration of obedience is in Christ's hands. As in His own

THE SECRET OF TRUE OBEDIENCE

life, so in us He has undertaken to maintain it. He teaches and works it in us.

Let us try to think what and how He teaches: It may be we shall see how little we have given ourselves to be pupils in this school, where alone obedience is to be learned. When we think of an ordinary school, the principal things we ask about often are—(1) the teacher, (2) the class books, and (3) the pupils. Let us see what each of these is in Christ's school of obedience.

1. THE TEACHER

"He learned obedience." And now that He teaches it, He does so first and most by unfolding the secret of His own obedience to the Father.

I have said that the power of true obedience is to be found in the clear personal relationship to God. It was so with our Lord Jesus. Of all His teaching He said, "For I have not spoken on My own authority; but the Father who sent Me gave Me a command, what I should say and what I should speak. And I know that His command is everlasting life. Therefore, whatever I speak, just as the Father has told Me, so I speak" (John 12:49–50).

This does not mean that Christ received God's commandment in eternity as part of the Father's commission to Him on entering the world. No. Day by day, each moment as He taught and worked, He lived, as man, in continual communication with the Father and received the Father's instructions just as He needed them. Does He not say, "The Son can do nothing of Himself, but what He *sees* the Father do. . .For the Father loves the Son, and *shows* Him all things that He Himself does; and He *will show* Him greater works than these" (John 5:19, 20), "as I hear, I judge" (John 5:30), "I am not alone, but I *am* with the Father who sent Me" (John 8:16), and "The words that I speak to you I do not speak on My own *authority;* but the Father who dwells in Me" (John 14:10)? It is everywhere a dependence on a present fellowship and operation of God, a hearing and a seeing of what God speaks and does and shows.

> *he defective life, the life of broken and irregular fellowship with God, must be healed, and way made for a full and healthy life. Then full obedience will become possible.*

Our Lord often spoke of His relationship to the Father as the type and the promise of our relationship to Him, and to the Father through Him. With us as with Him, *the life of continual obedience is impossible without continual fellowship and continual teaching*. It is only when God comes into our lives, in a degree and a power that many never consider possible, when His presence as the eternal and Ever-present One is believed and received, just as the Son believed and received it, that there can be any hope of a life in which every thought is brought into captivity to the obedience of Christ.

The imperative need of the continual receiving our orders and instructions from God Himself is what is implied in the words: "*Obey My voice, and I will be your God*" (Jer. 7:23).

The expression "obeying the commandments" is very seldom used in scripture; it is almost always obeying *Me*, or obeying or listening to *My voice*. With the commander of an army, the teacher of a school, or the father of a family, it is not the code of laws, however clear and good, with its rewards or threats, that secures true obedience; it is the personal living influence, wakening love and enthusiasm. It is the joy of always hearing the Father's voice that will give the joy and the strength of true obedience. It is the voice that gives power to obey the word. The word without the living voice is of no benefit.

How clearly this is illustrated by the contrast of what we see in Israel. The people had heard the voice of God on Sinai, and were afraid. They asked Moses that God might no more speak to them. Let Moses receive the word of God and bring it to them. They only thought of the command, but they didn't know that *the only power to obey* is in the presence of God and His voice speaking to us. And so with only Moses to speak to them—and the stone tablets—their whole history is one of disobedience, because they were afraid of direct contact with God.

> *D*ay by day, each moment as He taught and worked, He lived, as man, in continual communication with the Father and received the Father's instructions just as He needed them.

It is still that way. Many, many Christians find it so much easier to take their teaching from godly men than to wait on God to receive it directly from Him. Their faith stands in the wisdom of men, and not in the power of God.

Let's learn the great lesson our Lord, "who learned obedience" by every moment waiting to see and hear the Father, has to teach us. *It is only when, like Him, with Him, in and through Him, we always walk with God and hear His voice* that we can possibly attempt to offer God the obedience He asks and promises to work.

Out of the depths of His own life and experience, Christ can give and teach us this. Pray earnestly that God show you the foolishness of attempting to obey without the same strength Christ needed, and that He may make you willing to give up everything for the Christlike joy of the Father's presence all the day.

2. The Textbook

Christ's direct communication with the Father did not render Him independent of holy scripture.

In the divine school of obedience there is but one textbook, whether for the elder brother or the younger children. In His learning obedience, He used the same textbook we have. Not only when He had to teach or to convince others did He appeal to the Word—He needed it and He used it for His own spiritual life and guidance.

From the commencement of His public life to its close, He lived by the Word of God. "*It is written*" was the sword of the Spirit with which He conquered Satan. "The Spirit of the LORD GOD *is* upon Me" (Isa. 61:1): This word of scripture was the consciousness with which He opened His preaching of the gospel. "That the Scripture might be fulfilled" was the light in which He accepted all suffering, and even gave Himself to the death. After the resurrection He expounded to the disciples "in all the Scriptures the things *concerning Himself*" (Luke 24:27).

> *I*t is the joy of always hearing the Father's voice
> that will give the joy and the strength of true obedience.
> It is the voice that gives power to obey the word.

In scripture He had found God's plan and path for Him marked out. He gave Himself to fulfill it. It was in and with the use of God's Word that He received the Father's continual direct teaching.

In God's school of obedience the Bible is the only textbook. That shows us the disposition in which we are to come to the Bible—with the simple desire in it to find what is written concerning us as to God's will, and to do it.

Scripture was not written to increase our knowledge but to guide our conduct: "that the man of God may be complete, thoroughly equipped *for every good work*" (2 Tim. 3:17). "If anyone wills to *do* His will, he shall know" (John 7:17). Learn from Christ to consider all there is in scripture of the revelation of God, and His love, and His counsel, as simply auxiliary to God's great purpose: That the man of God may be prepared to do His will, as it is done in heaven, that man may be restored to that perfect obedience on which God's heart is set, and in which alone is blessedness.

In God's school of obedience God's Word is the only textbook. To apply that Word in His own life and conduct, to know when each different portion was to be taken up and carried out, Christ needed and received a divine teaching. It is He who speaks in Isaiah, "The Lord GOD. . .awakens Me morning by morning, He awakens My ear to hear as the learned. The Lord GOD has opened My ear" (Isa. 50:4–5).

Even so does He who learned obedience this way teach it to us, by giving us the Holy Spirit in our heart as the divine interpreter of the Word. This is the great work of the indwelling Holy Spirit—to draw the Word we read and think upon *into our heart,* and make it quick and powerful there so that God's living Word may work effectually in our will, our love, our whole being. It is because this is not understood that the Word has no power to work obedience.

Let me try to speak very plainly about this. We rejoice in increased attention given to Bible study and in testimonies as to the interest awakened and benefit received. But let us not deceive ourselves. We may delight in studying the Bible, and we may admire and be charmed with the views we get of God's truth. The thoughts suggested may make a deep impression and waken the most pleasing religious emotions. And yet the practical influence in making us holy or humble, loving, patient, ready either for service or suffering, is very small. The one reason for this is that we do not receive the Word, as it is in very deed, as the Word of a living God, who must Himself speak to us and into us if it is to exert its divine power.

The letter of the Word, however we study and delight in it, has no saving or sanctifying power. Human wisdom and human will, however strenuous their effort, cannot give and cannot command that power. The Holy Spirit is the mighty power of God, so *it is only as the Holy Spirit teaches you,* only as the gospel is preached to you by man or by book, "by the Holy Spirit sent down from heaven" (1 Pet. 1:12), that it will really give you, with every command, the strength to obey, and work in you the very thing commanded.

> The only way of learning to do a thing is to do it. The only way of learning obedience from Christ is to give up your will to Him, and to make the doing of His will the one desire and delight of your heart.

With man, knowing and willing, knowing and doing, even willing and performing are, for lack of power, often separate, and even at odds. *Never in the Holy Spirit.* He is both the light and the might of God. All He is and does and gives has in it equally the truth and the power of God. When He shows you God's command, He always shows it to you as a possible and a certain thing, a divine life and gift prepared for you, which He who shows is able to impart.

Beloved Bible students: Learn to believe that it is only when Christ, through the Holy Spirit, teaches you to understand and take the Word into your heart that He can really teach you to obey as He did. Do believe, every time you open your Bible, that just as sure as you listen to the divine, Spirit-breathed Word, so surely will our Father, in answer to the prayer of faith and passive waiting, give the Holy Spirit's living operation in your heart.

Let all your Bible study be a thing of faith. Do not only try to believe the truths or promises you read. This may be in your own power. Before that, *believe in the Holy Spirit, in His being in you, in God's working in you through Him.* Take the Word into your heart, in the quiet faith that He will enable you to love it, and yield to it and keep it. Then our blessed Lord Jesus will make the book to you what it was to Him when He spoke of "the things which are written concerning Me." All scripture will become the simple revelation of what God is going to do for you, and in you, and through you.

3. THE PUPIL

We have seen how our Lord teaches us obedience by unfolding the secret of His learning it, in unceasing dependence on *the Father*. We have seen how He teaches us to use the sacred book as He used it, as a divine revelation of what God has ordained for us, with the *Holy Spirit* to expound and enforce. If we now consider the place the believer takes in the school of obedience as a pupil, we shall better understand what Christ the Son requires to do His work in us effectually.

In a faithful student there are several things that go to make up his feelings toward a trusted teacher. He submits himself entirely to his leading. He reposes perfect trust in him. He gives him just as much time and attention as he asks.

When we see and consent that Jesus Christ has a right to all this, we may hope to experience how wonderfully He can teach us an obedience like His own.

A. *The true pupil,* say of some great musician or painter, *yields his master a wholehearted and unhesitating submission.*

In practicing his scales or mixing the colors, in the slow and patient study of the elements of his art, he knows that it is wisdom simply and fully to obey.

It is this wholehearted surrender to His guidance, this implicit submission to His authority, Christ asks. We come to Him asking Him to teach us the lost art of obeying God as He did. He asks us if we are ready to pay the price. It is entirely and utterly to deny self! It is to give up our will and our life to the death! It is to be ready to do whatever He says!

The only way of learning to do a thing is to do it. The only way of learning obedience from Christ is to give up your will to Him, and to make the doing of His will the one desire and delight of your heart.

Unless you take the vow of absolute obedience as you enter this class of Christ's school, it will be impossible for you to make any progress.

B. The true student of a great master finds it easy to render him this implicit obedience, simply because *he trusts him.*

He gladly sacrifices his own wisdom and will to be guided by a higher.

We need this confidence in our Lord Jesus. He came from heaven to learn obedience so that He might be able to teach it well. His obedience is the treasury out of which, not only the debt of our past disobedience is paid, but out of which the grace for our present obedience is supplied. In His divine love and perfect human sympathy, in His divine power over our hearts and lives, He invites, He deserves, He wins our trust.

It is by the power of a personal admiration and attachment to Himself, it is by the power of His divine love, in every deed shed into our heart by the Holy Spirit and wakening within us a responsive love, that He awakens our confidence and communicates to us the true secret of success in His school. As absolutely as we have trusted Him as a savior to atone for our disobedience, so let us trust him as a Teacher to lead us out of it. Christ is our prophet or teacher. A heart that enthusiastically believes in His power and success as a teacher will, in the joy of that faith, find it possible and easy to obey. It is the presence of Christ with us all the day that will be the secret of true obedience.

C. A student gives his master just as much of *his attendance and attention* as he asks. The master fixes how much time must be devoted to personal communication and instruction.

Obedience to God is such a heavenly art, our nature is so utterly strange to it, and the path in which the Son Himself learned it was so slow and long that we must not wonder if it does not come instantly. Nor must we wonder if it needs more time at the Master's feet in meditation, prayer, and waiting, in dependence and self-sacrifice, than the most are ready to give. But let us give it.

In Christ Jesus, heavenly obedience has become human again, obedience has become our birthright and our life's breath. Let us cling to Him, let us believe and claim His steadfast presence. With Jesus Christ who learned obedience as our Savior, with Jesus Christ who teaches obedience as our Master, we can live lives of obedience. His obedience—we cannot study the lesson too earnestly—His obedience is our salvation, and in Him, the living Christ, we find it and partake of it moment by moment.

Let us ask God to show us how Christ and His obedience are actually to be our life every moment. That will then make us pupils who give Him all our heart and all our time. And He will teach us to keep His commandments and remain in His love, *just as He* kept His Father's commandments and remains in His love.

For Further Thought

1. *What must happen in the life of a human before full obedience is possible? How has Christ provided for it?*
2. *What must you allow Christ to do and to teach you before you can fully obey the Father as He did? What is required of you for that to happen?*
3. *What is the only way you can learn obedience from Christ? What steps should you take for that to happen?*

4

THE MORNING WATCH IN THE LIFE OF OBEDIENCE

If the firstfruit is holy, the lump is also holy;
and if the root is holy, so are the branches.
ROMANS 11:16

HOW wonderful and blessed is the divine appointment of the first day of the week as a holy day of rest. Not, as some think, that we might have at least one day of rest and spiritual refreshment amid the weariness of life, but that that one holy day, at the opening of the week, might sanctify the whole, might help and prepare us to carry God's holy presence into all the week and its work. With the firstfruit holy, the whole lump is holy; with the root holy, all the branches are holy too (see Rom. 11:16).

How gracious, too, is the provision suggested by so many types and examples of the Old Testament, by which a morning hour at the opening of the day can enable us to secure a blessing for all its work and give us the assurance of power for victory over every temptation. How unspeakably gracious, that in the morning hour the bond that unites us with God can be so firmly tied that during hours when we have to move amid the rush of men or duties, and can scarcely think of God, the soul can be kept safe and pure, that the soul can so give itself away, in the time of secret worship, into His keeping so that temptation shall only help us to unite it closer with Him. What cause for praise and joy, that the morning watch can so each day renew and strengthen the surrender to Jesus and the faith in Him that the life of obedience cannot only be maintained in fresh vigor, but can indeed go on from strength to strength.

I would gladly point out how intimate and vital the connection between obedience and the morning watch is. The desire for a life of entire obedience will give new meaning and value to the morning watch, even as this again can alone give the strength and courage needed for the former.

1. THE MOTIVE PRINCIPLE

Think first of *the motive principle* that will make us love and faithfully keep the morning watch.

If we take it upon us simply as a duty, and a necessary part of our religious life, it will very soon become a burden. Or if the chief thought is our own happiness and safety, that will not supply the power to make it truly attractive. There is only one thing will suffice—*the desire for fellowship with God.*

It is for that we were created in God's likeness. It is that in which we hope to spend eternity. It is that alone that can prepare us for a true and blessed life, either here or hereafter. To have more of God, to know Him better, to receive from Him the communication of His love and strength, to have our life filled with His—it is for this He invites us to enter the inner chamber and shut the door.

It is in the closet, in the morning watch, that our spiritual life is both tested and strengthened. *There* is the battlefield where it is to be decided every day whether God is to have all, whether our life is to be absolute obedience. If we truly conquer there, getting rid of ourselves into the hands of our Almighty Lord, the victory during the day is sure. It is *there,* in the inner chamber, proof is to be given whether we really delight in God and make it our aim to love Him with our whole heart.

Let this, then, be our first lesson: The presence of God is the chief thing in our devotions. To meet God, to give ourselves into His holy will, to know that we are pleasing to Him, to have Him give us our orders, and lay His hand upon us and bless us, and say to us, "Go in this your strength"—it is when the soul learns that this is what is to be found in the morning watch, day by day, that we shall learn to long for it and delight in it.

2. READING THE BIBLE

Let us next speak of *the reading of God's Word* as part of what occupies us there. With regard to this, I have more than one thing I wish to say.

A. One is that *unless we beware, the Word, which is meant to point us away to God, may actually intervene and hide Him from us.*

The mind may be occupied and interested and delighted at what it finds, and yet, because this is more head knowledge than anything else, it may bring little good to us. If it does not lead us to wait on God, to glorify Him, to receive His grace and power for sweetening and sanctifying our lives, it becomes a hindrance instead of a help.

B. Another lesson that cannot be repeated too often, or learned too urgently, is that *it is only by the teaching of the Holy Spirit that we can get at the real meaning of what God means by His Word and that the Word will really reach into our inner life and work in us.*

The Father in heaven, who gave us His Word from heaven, with its divine mysteries and message, has given us His Holy Spirit in us to explain and internally apply that Word. The Father wants us each time to ask that He teach us by His Spirit. He wants us to bow in a meek, teachable frame of mind and believe that the Spirit will, in the hidden depth of our heart, make His Word live and work. He wants us to remember that the Spirit is given us so that we should be led by Him, should walk after Him, should have our whole life under His rule, and that therefore He cannot teach us in the morning unless we honestly give up ourselves to His leading. But if we do this and patiently wait on Him, not to get new thoughts but to get the power of the Word in our heart, we can count on His teaching.

Let your closet be the classroom and your morning watch be the study hour in which your relationship of entire dependence on, and submission to, the Holy Spirit's teaching is proved to God.

C. A third remark I want to make, in confirmation of what was said above, is this: *Always study in God's Word in the spirit of an unreserved surrender to obey.*

You know how often Christ, and His apostles in their epistles, speaks of hearing and not doing. If you accustom yourself to study the Bible without an earnest and very definite purpose to obey, you are getting hardened in disobedience.

> *I*t is only by the teaching of the Holy Spirit that we can get at the real meaning of what God means by His Word and that the Word will really reach into our inner life and work in us.

Never read God's will concerning you without honestly giving up yourself to do it immediately, and asking grace to do so. God has given us His Word to tell us what He wants us to do and what grace He has provided to enable us to do it. How sad to think it a pious thing just to read that Word without any earnest effort to obey it! May God keep us from this terrible sin!

Let us make it a sacred habit to say to God, "*Lord, whatever I know to be Your will, I will immediately obey.*" Always read with a heart yielded up in willing obedience.

D. One more remark. I have here spoken of such commands as we already know and as are easily understood. But remember, there are a great many commands to which your attention may never have been directed, or others of which the application is so wide and unceasing that you have not taken them in.

Read God's Word with a deep desire to know all His will. If there are things that appear difficult, commands that look too high or for which you need a divine guidance to tell you how to carry them out—and there are many like that—let them drive you to seek a divine teaching.

It is not the text that is easiest and most encouraging that brings most blessing but the text, whether easy or difficult, that throws you most upon God. God wants to have you "filled with the knowledge of His will in all wisdom and spiritual understanding" (Col. 1:9), and it is in the closet this wonderful work is to be done.

Do remember, it is only when you know that *God is telling you to do a thing* that you feel sure He gives the strength to do it. It is only as we are willing to know all God's will that He will from time to time reveal more of it to us and that we will be able to do it all.

What a power the morning watch may be in the life of one who makes a determined resolve to meet God there to renew the surrender to absolute obedience, to humbly and patiently wait on the Holy Spirit to be taught all God's will, and to receive the assurance that every promise given him in the Word will infallibly be made true! He who prays that way for himself will become a true intercessor for others.

3. PRAYER

It is in the light of these thoughts I want now to say a few words on *what prayer is to be* in the morning watch.

A. First of all, *see that you secure the presence of God.*

Do not be content with anything less than seeing the face of God, having the assurance that He is looking on you in love, and listening and working in you.

If our daily life is to be full of God, how much more the morning hour, where the life of the day alone can have God's seal stamped upon it. In our religion we want nothing so much as *more of God*—His love, His will, His holiness, His Spirit living in us, His power working in us for men. Under heaven there is no way of getting this but by close personal communion. And there is no time so good for securing and practicing it as the morning watch.

> *I*f our daily life is to be full of God, how much more the morning hour, where the life of the day alone can have God's seal stamped upon it.

The superficiality and weakness of our religion and religious work all come from having so little real contact with God. If it is true that God alone is the fountain of all love and good and happiness, and that to have as much as possible of His presence and His fellowship, of His will and His service, is our truest and highest happiness, surely then to meet Himself alone in the morning watch ought to be our first care.

To have had God appear to them and speak to them was all the Old Testament saints' secret of their obedience and their strength. Do give God time in secret so to reveal Himself that your soul may call the name of the place Peniel— "for I have seen God face to face" (Gen. 32:30).

B. My next thought is: *Let the renewal of your surrender to absolute obedience for that day be a chief part of your morning sacrifice.*

Let any confession of sin be very definite—a plucking out and cutting off of everything that has been grieving to God. Let any prayer for grace for a holy walk be just as definite—an asking and accepting in faith of the very grace and strength you are in particular need of. Let your outlook on the day you are entering be a very determined resolve that obedience to God shall be its controlling principle.

Do understand that there is no surer way—rather, that there is no other possible way—of getting into God's love and blessing in prayer than by getting into His will. In prayer, give up yourself most absolutely to the blessed will of God. This will benefit more than much asking. Plead with God to show you this great mercy (that He allows you) that He will enable you to enter into His will and remain there. That will make the knowing and doing His will in your life a blessed certainty. Let your prayer indeed be a "morning sacrifice," a placing yourself as a whole burnt offering on the altar of the Lord.

The measure of surrender to full obedience will be the measure of confidence toward God.

C. Then remember that *true prayer and fellowship with God cannot be all from one side.*

We need to be still, to wait and hear what response God gives. *This is the office of the Holy Spirit: to be the voice of God to us.* In the hidden depths of the heart, He can give a secret but most certain assurance that we are heard, that we are well-pleasing, that the Father engages to do for us what we have asked. What we need, to hear the voice, to receive this assurance is the quiet stillness that waits on God, the quiet faith that trusts in God, the quiet heart that bows in nothingness and humility before God, and allows Him to be all in all.

It is when we wait on God to take His part in our prayer that the confidence will come to us that we receive what we ask, that our surrender of ourselves in the sacrifice of obedience is accepted, and that we can therefore count on the Holy Spirit to guide us into all the will of God, as He means us to know and do it.

What glory would come to us in the morning watch—and through it into our daily life—if it were made an hour spent with the Triune God, for the Father, through the Son and the Spirit, to take conscious possession of us for the day. How little need there then would be to urge and plead with God's children to watch the morning watch!

D. And now comes the last and the best of all. *Let your prayer be intercessional, on behalf of others.*

In the obedience of our Lord Jesus, as in all His fellowship with the Father, the essential element was this: It was all for others. This Spirit flows through every member of the body, and the more we know it and yield to it, the more our life will be what God wants to make it.

The highest form of prayer is intercession. The chief object for which God chose Abraham and Israel and us was to make us a blessing to the world. We are a royal priesthood—a priestly people (see 1 Pet. 2:9). As long as prayer is only a means of personal improvement and happiness, we cannot know its full power. Let intercession be a real longing for the souls of those around us, a real bearing of the burden of their sin and need, a real pleading for the extension of God's kingdom, a real labor in prayer for definite purposes to be realized. Let such intercession be what the morning watch is consecrated to, and see what new interest and attraction it will have.

Intercession! If we could just realize what it means! To take the name and the righteousness and the worthiness of Christ and put them on and in them to appear before God! "In Christ's stead," now that He is no longer in the world, to ask God, by name, for the individual men and needs, where His grace can do its work! In the faith of our own acceptance and of the anointing with the Spirit to prepare us for the work, to know that our prayer can avail to "save a soul from death," can bring down and dispense the blessing of heaven upon earth! To think that in the hour of the morning watch this work can be renewed and carried on day by day, each inner chamber maintaining its own separate communication with heaven, and helping together in bringing down its share of the blessing.

> Never read God's will concerning you without honestly giving up yourself to do it immediately, and asking grace to do so. God has given us His Word to tell us what He wants us to do and what grace He has provided to enable us to do it.

It is in intercession, more than in the zeal that works in its own strength with little prayer, that the highest type of piety, the true Christlikeness is cultivated. It is in intercession that a believer rises to his true nobility in the power of imparting life and blessing. It is to intercession we must look for any large increase of the power of God in the Church and its work for men.

One word in conclusion. Turn back and think now again about the intimate and vital connection between obedience and the morning watch.

Without obedience there cannot be the spiritual power to enter into the knowledge of God's Word and will. Without obedience there cannot be the confidence, the boldness, the liberty that knows that it is heard. Obedience is fellowship with God in His will—without it there is not the capacity for seeing and claiming and holding the blessings He has for us.

And so, on the other side, without very definite living communion with God in the morning watch, the life of obedience cannot possibly be maintained. It is there that the vow of obedience can every morning be renewed in power and confirmed from above. It is there that the presence and fellowship can be secured which make obedience possible. It is there that in the obedience of the One, and in the union with Himself, the strength is received for all that God can ask. It is there that the spiritual understanding of God's will is received, which leads to walk worthy of the

Lord to all well-pleasing.

God has called His children to live a wonderful, heavenly, altogether supernatural life. Let the morning watch each day be to you as the open gate of heaven, through which its light and power streams in on your waiting heart, and from which you go out to walk with God all the day.[24]

For Further Thought

1. *What must absolutely be your whole motivation for spending time with God in "the morning watch?" What are some of the wrong motivations, and how do you overcome them?*

2. *What is the relationship between surrendering yourself to God for full obedience and the confidence you have before God when you approach Him in prayer?*

3. *God calls you to be not just a praying man but also a man who intercedes on behalf of others. What does the Bible teach you about the privilege and the responsibility you have toward God and toward humankind when it comes to intercession?*

[24] See note, p. 739–740.

5

THE ENTRANCE TO THE
LIFE OF FULL OBEDIENCE

Obedient to the point of death.
PHILIPPIANS 2:8

AFTER all that has been said on the life of obedience, I want to speak in this address of the entrance into that life.

You might think it is a mistake to take this text, in which you have obedience in its very highest perfection, as our subject in speaking of the entrance on the course of obedience. But it is no mistake. The secret of success in a race is to have the goal clearly defined and aimed at from the very outset.

"He became obedient to the point of death." There is no other Christ for any of us, no other obedience that pleases God, no other example for us to copy, no other teacher from whom to learn to obey. Christians suffer inconceivably because they do not at once and heartily accept this as the only obedience they are to aim at. The youngest Christian will find it a strength in the school of Christ to make nothing less from the commencement his prayer and his vow: *obedient to the point of death.* It is at the same time the beauty and the glory of Christ. A share in it is the highest blessing He has to give. The desire for and the surrender to it is possible to the youngest believer.

If you want to be reminded of what it means, think of the story in ancient history. A proud king, with a great army following him, demands the submission of the king of a small but brave nation. When the ambassadors have delivered their message, he calls one of his soldiers to stab himself. Immediately he does it. A second is called, and he too obeys at once. A third is summoned, and he too is obedient to death.

"Go and tell your master that I have three thousand such men; let him come."

The king dared count on men who held their life not dear to them when the king's word called for it.

It is that kind of obedience God wants. It is that kind of obedience Christ gave. It is that kind of obedience He teaches. Be it is such obedience and nothing less that we seek to learn. From the very outset of the Christian life, let this be our aim, so that we may avoid the fatal mistake of calling Christ Master and yet not doing what He says.

Let all who by these addresses have in any degree been convicted of the sin of disobedience listen as we study from God's Word the way to escape from that and gain access to the life Christ can give—the entrance to the life of full obedience.

1. The Confession and Cleansing of the Disobedience

It is easy to see that this must be the first step. In Jeremiah, the prophet who more than any other speaks of the disobedience of God's people, God says, "'Return, backsliding Israel,' says the LORD. . . . *'Only acknowledge your iniquity. . .that you have not obeyed My voice,'* says the LORD. . . . 'Return, O backsliding children,' says the LORD" (Jer. 3:12–14).

As little as there can be pardon at conversion without confession can there be, after conversion, deliverance from the overcoming power of sin and the disobedience it brings without a new and deeper conviction and confession.

The thought of our disobedience must not be a vague generality. The special things in which we actually disobey must be definitely found out and, in confession, given up and placed in the hands of Christ and by Him cleansed away. Then only can there be the hope of entering into the way of true obedience.

Let us search our life by the light of the teaching of our Lord.

A. *Christ appealed to the law.*

He did not come to destroy the law, but to secure its fulfillment. To the young ruler, He said, "You know the commandments" (Luke 18:20). Let the law be our first test.

Let us take a single sin—such as that of lying. I had a note from a young lady once saying that she wished to obey fully and that she felt urged to confess an untruth she had told me. It was not a matter of importance, and yet she rightly judged that the confession would help her to cast it from her.

How much there is in ordinary society, how much in school life, too, that will not stand the test of strict truthfulness!

And so, there are other commandments, up to the very last, with its condemnation of all coveting and lusting after what is not ours, in which too frequently the Christian gives way to disobedience.

All this must come to a complete end. We must confess it, and in God's strength put it away forever if there is to be any thought of our entering a life of full obedience.

B. *Christ revealed the new law of love.*

To be merciful as the Father in heaven, to forgive just as He does, to love enemies and to do good to those who hate us, and to live lives of self-sacrifice and compassion—this was the religion Jesus taught on earth.

Let us look at an unforgiving spirit when we are provoked or wrongly used, at unloving thoughts and sharp or unkind words, at the neglect of the call to show mercy and do good and bless, all as so much disobedience, which must be felt and mourned over and plucked out like a right eye (see Matt. 18:9), so that the power of a full obedience can be ours.

C. *Christ spoke much of self-denial.*

Self is the root of all lack of love and obedience. Our Lord called His disciple to deny himself and to take up his cross and to forsake all (Mark 8:34), to hate and lose his own life (Luke 14:26), to humble himself and become the servant of all (Mark 10:43–44). He did so, because self, self-will, self-pleasing, and self-seeking are simply the source of all sin.

> *There is no other Christ for any of us, no other obedience that pleases God, no other example for us to copy, no other teacher from whom to learn to obey.*

When we indulge the flesh in such a simple thing as eating and drinking, when we gratify self by seeking or accepting or rejoicing in what indulges our pride, when self-will is allowed to assert itself and we make provision for the fulfillment of its desire, we are guilty of disobedience to His command. This gradually clouds the soul and makes the full enjoyment of His light and peace an impossibility.

D. *Christ claimed for God the love of the heart.*

For Himself He equally claimed the sacrifice of all to come and follow Him. The Christian who has not definitely at heart made this his aim, who has not determined to seek for grace so to live, is guilty of disobedience. There may be much in his religion that appears good and earnest, but he cannot possibly have the joyful consciousness of knowing that he is doing the will of his Lord and keeping His commandments.

When the call is heard to come and now begin anew a true life of obedience, there are many who feel the desire to do so, and try quietly to slip into it. They think that by more prayer and Bible study they will grow into it—it will gradually come. They are greatly mistaken. The word God uses in Jeremiah might teach them their mistake: "Return, you backsliding children. . .Return to Me" (Jer. 3:22, 4:1).

A soul that is fully earnest and has taken the vow of full obedience may grow out of a feeble obedience into a fuller one. But there is no growing out of disobedience into obedience. A turning back, a turning away, a decision, a crisis, is needed. And that only comes by the very definite insight into what has been wrong, and its confession with shame and repentance. Then alone will the soul seek for that divine and mighty cleansing from all its filthiness, which prepares for the consciousness of the gift of the new heart and God's Spirit in it causing us to walk in His statutes.

If you would hope to lead a different life, to become a man or a woman of a Christlike obedience to the point of death, begin by asking God for the Holy Spirit of conviction to show you all your disobedience and to lead you in humble confession to the cleansing God has provided. Do not rest until you have received it.

2. Faith That Obedience Is Possible

This is the second step. To take that step, we must try to understand clearly what obedience is.

A. For this purpose, we must attend carefully to the difference between *voluntary* and *involuntary* sin. It is with voluntary sin alone that obedience deals.

We know that the new heart God gives His child is placed in the midst of the flesh with its sinfulness. Out of this there often arises, even in one who is walking in true obedience, evil suggestions of pride, unlovingness, and impurity, over which he has no direct control. They are in their nature utterly sinful and vile, but they are not charged to a man as acts of transgression. They are not acts of disobedience, which he can break off and cast out, as he can the disobedience of which we have spoken. The deliverance from them comes in another way, not through the will of the regenerate man, by which obedience always comes, but through the cleansing power of the blood and the indwelling Christ. As the sinful nature rises, all he can do is to despise it and trust in the blood that both cleanses him and keeps him clean. It is of great consequence to note the distinction. It keeps the Christian from thinking that obedience is impossible. It encourages him to seek and offer his obedience in the sphere where it can avail. And it is just in proportion as in its own sphere the power of the will for obedience is maintained that the power of the Spirit can be trusted and obtained to do the cleansing work in what is beyond the reach of the will.

> *A* soul that is fully earnest and has taken the vow of full obedience may grow out of a feeble obedience into a fuller one. But there is no growing out of disobedience into obedience.

B. When this difficulty has been removed, there is often a second one that arises to make us doubt whether obedience is indeed possible.

Men connect it with the idea of absolute perfection. They put together all the commands of the Bible, and they think of all the graces these commands point to in their highest possible measure. Then they think of a man with all those graces, every moment in their full perfection, as an obedient man.

How different is the demand of the Father in heaven! He takes account of the different powers and attainments of each child of His. He asks of him only the obedience of each day, or rather, each hour at a time. He sees whether I have indeed chosen and given myself up to the wholehearted performance of every known command. He sees whether I am really longing and learning to know and do all His will. And when His child does this in simple faith and love, the obedience is acceptable. The Spirit gives us the sweet assurance that we are well-pleasing to Him and enables us to "have confidence toward God. . .because we keep His commandments and do those things that are pleasing in His sight" (1 John 3:21, 22).

This obedience is indeed an attainable degree of grace. The faith that it is, is indispensable to the obedient walk.

You ask for the ground of that faith in God's Word? You find it in God's New Covenant promise, "I will put My law in their minds, and write it on their hearts. . .I will put My fear in their hearts so that they will not depart from Me" (Jer. 31:33, 32:40).

The great defect of the Old Covenant was that it demanded but did not provide the power for obedience. This the New Covenant did. The heart means the love and the life. The law put in and written on the heart means that it has taken possession of the innermost life and love of the renewed man. The new heart delights in the law of God and is willing and able to obey it.

You doubt this because your experience does not confirm it. No wonder! A promise of God is a thing of faith: You do not believe it and so cannot experience it.

You know what invisible writing fluid is. You write with it on paper, and nothing can be seen by a man who is not in on the secret. Tell him of it, and by faith he knows it. Hold it up to the sun, or put some chemical on it, and out comes the secret writing. That is how God's law is written in your heart. If you believe this firmly, and come and say to God that His law is there in your innermost part, and hold up that heart to the light and heat of the Holy Spirit, you will find it true. The law written in the heart will mean to you the fervent love of God's commands, with the power to obey them.[25]

A story is told of one of Napoleon's soldiers. The doctor was seeking to extract a bullet that had lodged in the region of the heart, when the soldier cried, "Cut deeper, you will find Napoleon graven there."

Christian! Believe that the law lives in your innermost being! Speak in faith the words of David and of Christ, "I delight to do Your will, O my God, and Your law *is* within my heart" (Ps. 40:8).

The faith of this will assure you that obedience is possible. Such faith will help you into the life of true obedience.

---

[25] In a volume being published about the same time, *The Two Covenants and the Second Blessing,* I have tried to show how plain, how certain, how all sufficient the provision is that has been made in the New Covenant, the covenant of grace, for securing our obedience.

3. THE STEP OUT OF DISOBEDIENCE TO OBEDIENCE IS BY SURRENDER TO CHRIST

"Return, you backsliding children, and I will heal your backslidings," God said to Israel (Jer. 3:22). They were His people but had turned from Him; the return must be immediate and entire. To turn our back upon the divided life of disobedience and, in the faith of God's grace, to say "I will obey" may be the work of a moment.

The power for it, to take the vow and to maintain it, comes from the living Christ. We have said before, the power of obedience lies in the mighty influence of a living personal presence. As long as we took our knowledge of God's will from a book or from men, we could only fail. If we take Jesus, in His unchanging nearness, as both our Lord and our strength, we can obey. The voice that commands is the voice that inspires. The eye that guides is the eye that encourages. Christ becomes all in all to us: the Master who commands, the example who teaches, the helper who strengthens. Turn from your life of disobedience to Christ. Give up yourself to Him in surrender and faith.

> *Christ becomes all in all to us: the Master who commands, the example who teaches, the helper who strengthens. Turn from your life of disobedience to Christ. Give up yourself to Him in surrender and faith.*

In surrender. Let Him have all. Give up your life to be as full of Him, of His presence, of His will, and of His service as He can make it. Give up yourself to Him, not to be saved from disobedience, that now you may be happy and live your own life without sinning and trouble. No! Do so in order that He may have you wholly for Himself as a vessel, as a channel, which He can fill with Himself and with His life and love for men, and me in His blessed service.

In faith too. In a new faith. When a soul sees this new thing in Christ—the power for continual obedience—it needs a new faith to take in the special blessing of His great redemption. The faith that only understood "He became obedient to the point of death" of His atonement, as a motive to love and obedience, now learns to take the word as scripture speaks it, "Let this mind be in you which was also in Christ Jesus, who...humbled Himself and became obedient to the point of death" (Phil. 2:5, 6). It believes that Christ has put His own mind and Spirit into us, and in the faith of that prepares to live and act it out.

God sent Christ into the world to restore obedience to its place in our heart and life, to restore man to His place in the obedience to God. Christ came, and becoming obedient to the point of death proved what the only true obedience is. He lived it out and perfected it in Himself as a life that He won through death, and now He communicates to us. The Christ who loves us, who leads and teaches and strengthens us, who lives in us, is the Christ who was obedient to the point of death. "Obedient to the point of death" is the very essence of the life He imparts. Shall we not accept it and trust Him to manifest it in us?

Do you desire to enter into the blessed life of obedience? See here the open gate—Christ says, "I am the door" (John 10:9). See here the new and living way—Christ says, "I am the way" (14:6).

We begin to see it: Our disobedience was due to our not rightly knowing Christ. We see it: Obedience is only possible in a life of unceasing fellowship with Himself. The inspiration of His voice, the light of His eyes, and the grasp of His hand make it possible, make it certain.

Come and let us bow down and yield ourselves to this Christ. Obedient to the point of death, in the faith that He makes us partakers with Himself of all He is and has.

For Further Thought

1. *What is the connection between a new and deeper conviction and confession of sin and the deliverance from the overcoming power of sin and disobedience?*
2. *How can you know that obedience to God is possible in your own life? Is it really possible to live a life of obedience, and if so, what must you do to live that way?*
3. *God sent His Son into the world to save whoever would believe in Him (see John 3:16). But what is the role Christ is to play in restoring God's people to lives of obedience?*

6

THE OBEDIENCE OF FAITH

By faith Abraham obeyed.
HEBREWS 11:8

BY faith Abraham obeyed when he was called to go out to the place which he would receive as an inheritance. And he went out, not knowing where he was going" (Heb. 11:8). He believed that there was a land of Canaan, of which God had spoken. He believed in it as a "land of promise," secured to him as an inheritance. He believed that God would bring him there, would show it to him, and give it to him. In that faith he dared to go out, not knowing where he was going. In the blessed ignorance of faith, he trusted God, obeyed, and received the inheritance.

The land of promise that has been set before us is *the blessed life of obedience*. We have heard God's call to go out and dwell there—about that there can be no mistake. We have heard the promise of Christ to bring us there and to give us possession of the land—that, too, is clear and sure. We have surrendered ourselves to our Lord, and asked our Father to make all this true in us.

Our desire now is that all our life and work in it may be lifted up to the level of a holy and joyful obedience, and that through us God may make obedience the keynote of the Christian life we aim at promoting in others. Our aim is high, and we can only reach it by a new inflow of the power that comes from above. It is only by a faith that gets a new vision and hold of the powers of the heavenly world, secured to us in Christ, that we can obey and obtain the promise.

As we think of all this, of cultivating in ourselves and others the conviction that we only live to please Him to serve His purposes, some are ready to say: "This is not a land of promise we are called to enter, but a life of burden and difficulty and certain failure."

Do not say so, my brother! God calls you indeed to a land of promise. Come and prove what He can accomplish in you. Come and experience what the nobility is of a Christlike obedience to the point of death. Come and see what blessing God will give to him who, with Christ, gives himself the utmost to the ever-blessed and most holy will of God. Only believe in the glory of this good land of wholehearted obedience: in God, who calls you to it; in Christ, who will bring you in; in the Holy Spirit, who dwells and works all there. He who believes enters in.

I wish, then, to speak of the obedience of faith, and of faith as the sufficient power for all obedience. I give you these five simple words as expressive of the disposition of a believing heart entering into that life in the good land: I see it, I desire it, I expect it, I accept it, I trust Christ for it.

1. FAITH SEES IT

We have been trying to show you the map of the land, and to indicate the most important places in that land—the points at which God meets and blesses the soul. What we need now is in faith quietly and definitely to settle the question: Is there really such a land of promise, in which continuous obedience is certainly, is divinely, possible?

As long as there is any doubt on this point, it is out of the question to go up and possess the land.

> *There can be no strong faith without strong desire. Desire is the great motive-power in the universe. It was God's desire to save us that moved Him to send His Son.*

Just think of Abraham's faith. It rested in God, in His omnipotence and His faithfulness. We have put before you the promises of God. Hear another of them: "I will give you a new heart. . .and *I will put My Spirit within you* and *cause* you to walk in My statutes, and you will *keep My judgments and do them*" (Ezek. 36:26, 27). Here is God's covenant engagement. He adds, "I, the LORD, have spoken it. . . and I will do it" (24:14). He undertakes to cause and enable you to obey. In Christ and the Holy Spirit, He has made the most wonderful provision for fulfilling His engagement.

Just do what Abraham did—fix your heart on God. "He. . .was strengthened in faith, giving glory to God, and being fully convinced that what He had promised He was also able to perform" (Rom. 4:20–21). God's omnipotence was Abraham's strength. Let it be yours. Look out on all the promises God's Word gives of a clean heart, of a heart established blameless in holiness, of a life in righteousness and holiness, of a walk in all the commandments of the Lord blameless and well-pleasing to Him, of God's working in us to will and to do, of His working in us that which is well-pleasing in His sight, in the simple faith that if God says it, His power can do it.

Let the assurance that a life of full obedience is possible possess you. Faith can see the invisible and the impossible. Gaze on the vision until your heart says: "It must be true. It is true. There is a life promised I have never yet known."

2. FAITH DESIRES IT

When I read the gospel story and see how ready the sick and the blind and the needy were to believe Christ's word, I often ask myself what made them so much more ready to believe than we are. The answer I get in the Word is this: that one great difference lies in the honesty and intensity of the desire. They indeed desired deliverance with their whole heart. There was no need of pleading with them to make them willing to take His blessing.

How sad that it is so different with us! All indeed wish, in a sort of way, to be better than they are. But how few there are who really "hunger and thirst for righteousness" (Matt. 5:6), how few who intensely long and cry after a life of close obedience and the continual consciousness of being pleasing to God.

There can be no strong faith without strong desire. Desire is the great motive-power in the universe. It was God's desire to save us that moved Him to send His Son. It is desire that moves one to study and work and suffer. It is alone the desire for salvation that brings a sinner to Christ. It is the desire for God and the closest possible fellowship with Him, the desire to be just what He desires us to be and to have as much of His will as possible that will make the promised land attractive to us. It is this that will make us forsake everything to get our full share in the obedience of Christ.

And how can the desire be awakened?

> The land of promise that has been set before us is the blessed life of obedience. We have heard God's call to go out and dwell there—about that there can be no mistake.

Shame on us, that we need to ask the question, that the most desirable of all things—likeness to God in the union with His will and doing it—has so little attraction for us! Let us take it as a sign of our blindness and dullness, and beg God to give us by His Spirit "enlightened eyes of the understanding," that we may see and know "the riches of the glory of our inheritance" (see Eph. 1:8) waiting on the life of true obedience.

Let us turn and gaze, in this light of God's Spirit, and gaze again on the life as possible, as certain, as divinely secured and divinely blessed, until our faith begins to burn with desire, and to say: "I do long to have it. With my whole heart will I seek it."

3. FAITH EXPECTS IT

The difference between desire and expectation is great. There is often a strong desire after salvation in a soul who has little hope of really obtaining it. It is a great step in advance when desire passes into expectation, and the soul begins to savor spiritual blessing: "I am sure it is for me, and, though I do not see how, I confidently expect to obtain it."

The life of obedience is no longer an unattainable ideal held out by God to make us strive at least to get a little nearer it. It has become a reality, meant for the life in flesh and blood here on earth. Expect it as most certainly meant for you. Expect God to make it true.

There is much indeed to hinder this expectation: your past failure, your unfavorable temperament or circumstances, your feeble faith, your difficulty as to what such a devotion—obedient to the point of death—may demand, your conscious lack of power for it. All these things make you say, "It may be for others, but it is not for me, I fear."

I beg you not to talk that way. You are leaving God out of the equation. Expect to get it. Look up to His power and His love and begin to say, "It is for me."

> The life of obedience is no longer an unattainable ideal held out by God to make us strive at least to get a little nearer it. It has become a reality, meant for the life in flesh and blood here on earth.

Take courage from the lives of God's saints who have gone before you. Saint Teresa writes that after her conversion she spent more than eighteen years of her life in that miserable attempt to reconcile God and her life of sin. But at last she was able to write:

"I have made a vow never to offend God in the very least matter. I have vowed that I would rather die a thousand deaths than do anything of that kind, knowing I was doing it—this was obedience unto death. I am resolved never to leave anything whatever undone that I consider still to be more perfect, and more for the honor of my Lord."[26]

Gerhard Tersteegen had from his youth sought and served the Lord. After a time, the sense of God's grace was withdrawn from him, and for five long years he was like one far away on the great sea where neither sun nor stars appear. "But my hope was in Jesus." All at once, a light broke on him that never went out, and he wrote, with blood drawn from his veins, that letter to the Lord Jesus in which he said:

"From this evening to all eternity, Your will, not mine be done. Command and rule and reign in me. I yield up myself without reserve, and I promise, with Your help and power, rather to give up the last drop of my blood than knowingly or willingly be untrue or disobedient to You."

[26] She says further: "We are so long and so slow in giving up our hearts to You. And then You will not permit our possession of You without our paying well for so precious a possession. There is nothing in all the world with which to buy the shedding abroad of Your love in our hearts, but our heart's love. God never withholds Himself from them who pay this price and persevere in seeking Him. He will, little by little, and now and then, strengthen and restore that soul, until it is at last victorious."

That was his obedience to the point of death.

Set your heart on it and expect it. The same God lives still. Set your hope on Him and He will do it.

4. FAITH ACCEPTS IT

To accept is more than to expect. Many wait and hope and never possess because they do not accept.

To all who have not accepted and feel as if they were not ready to accept, we say, Expect. If the expectation is from the heart and set indeed on God Himself, it will lead the soul to accept.

To all who say they do expect, we urgently say, Accept. Faith has the wondrous God-given power of saying, "I accept, I take, I have."

It is because of the lack of this definite faith, which claims and appropriates the spiritual blessing we desire, that so many prayers appear to be fruitless. For such an act of faith all are not ready. Where there is no true conviction of the sin of disobedience and, sadly, no true sorrow for it, where there is no strong longing or purpose really in everything to obey God, where there is no deep interest in the message of holy scripture—that God wants to "make us complete in every good work to do His will" by Himself "working in us what is well pleasing in His sight" (see Heb. 13:21)—there is not the spiritual capacity to accept the blessing. The Christian is content to be a baby. He wants only to suck the milk of comfort. He is not able to eat the strong meat of which Jesus ate, "doing the will of His Father."

> *A*ccept the grace for this wondrous new life of obedience—
> accept it now. Without this, your act of consecration will do little.
> Without this, your purposing to try to be more obedient will fail.

And yet we come to all with the plea: Accept the grace for this wondrous new life of obedience—accept it now. Without this, your act of consecration will do little. Without this, your purposing to try to be more obedient will fail. Has not God shown you that there is an entirely new position for you to take—a possible position of simple childlike obedience, day by day, to every command His voice speaks to you through the Spirit, a possible position of simple childlike dependence on and experience of His all-sufficient grace, day by day, for every command He gives?

I ask you even now to take that position, make that surrender, and take that grace. Accept and enter into the true life of faith and the unceasing obedience of faith. Let your faith be as unlimited and as sure as God's promise and power are. As unlimited as your faith is, will your simple childlike obedience be. Oh, ask God for His aid, and accept all He has offered you!

5. Faith Trusts Christ for All

"For all the promises of God in Him are Yes, and in Him Amen, to the glory of God through us" (2 Cor. 1:20). It is possible that as we have spoken of the life of obedience, there have been questions and difficulties rising to which you cannot at once give answer. You may feel as if you cannot take it all in at once, or reconcile it with all the old habits of thought and speech and action. You fear you will not be able at once to bring all into subjection to this supreme all-controlling principle, "Do everything as the will of God: do all as obedience to Him."

To all these questions there is one answer, one deliverance from all these fears: Jesus Christ, the living Savior, knows all, and He asks you to trust in Him for the wisdom and the power to walk always in the obedience of faith.

We have seen more than once how His whole redemption, as He accomplished it, is nothing but obedience. As He communicates it, it is still the same. He gives us the Spirit of obedience as the Spirit of our life. This Spirit comes to us each moment through Him. He Himself keeps charge of our obedience. There is nothing under heaven but what He has and gives and works. He offers Himself to us as a guarantee for its maintenance, and He asks us to trust Him for it. It is in Jesus Himself that all our fears are removed, all our needs supplied, all our desires met. As He the righteous One is your righteousness, He the obedient One is your obedience.

> *J*esus Christ, the living Savior, knows all, and he asks you to trust in Him for the wisdom and the power to walk always in the obedience of faith.

Will you not trust Him for it? What faith sees and desires and expects and accepts, surely it dares to trust Christ to give and to work.

Will you not today take the opportunity to give glory to God and His Son by trusting Jesus now to lead you into the promised land? Look up to your glorified Lord in heaven, and in His strength renew, with new meaning, your vow of allegiance, your vow never to do anything knowingly or willingly that would offend Him. Trust Him for the faith to make the vow, for the heart to keep it, for the strength to carry it out. Trust Him, the loving One, by His living presence, to secure both your faith and obedience. Trust Him, and venture to join in an act of consecration, in the assurance that He undertakes to be its Yes and Amen, to the glory of God by us.

FOR FURTHER THOUGHT

1. *In what ways was Abraham an example of obedience that you can follow? What did Abraham do that you can do today to be a person of obedience to God?*
2. *What does God have to say to the believer who somehow thinks that a life of obedience may be for others but not for him, because he is too weak to be able to consistently obey?*
3. *What is Jesus Christ asking you to do today so that you may be empowered to live a life of obedience and faith?*

7

THE SCHOOL OF OBEDIENCE:

A BASKET OF FRAGMENTS

"Gather up the fragments that remain,
so that nothing is lost."
JOHN 6:12

IN this closing chapter I wish to gather up some points not yet touched on or not expressed with sufficient clarity, in the hope that they may help someone who has indeed enrolled himself in Christ's school of obedience.

1. ON LEARNING OBEDIENCE

First, let me warn against a misunderstanding of the expression "learning obedience."

We are apt to think that absolute obedience as a principle—obedience to the point of death—is a thing that can only be gradually learned in Christ's school. This is a great and most hurtful mistake. What we have to learn, and do learn gradually, is the practice of obedience in new and more difficult commands. But as to the principle, Christ wants us from the very entrance into His school to make the vow of entire obedience.

A little child of five can be implicitly obedient as a youth of eighteen. The difference between the two lies not in the principle, but in the nature of the work demanded.

Though externally Christ's obedience to the point of death came at the end of His life, the spirit of His obedience was the same from the beginning. Whole-hearted obedience is not the end but the beginning of our school life. The end is fitness for God's service, when obedience has placed us fully at God's disposal. A heart yielded to God in unreserved obedience is the one condition of progress in Christ's school—and of growth in the spiritual knowledge of God's will.

Young Christian, do get this matter settled at once! Remember God's rule: all for all. Give Him all, and He will give you all. Consecration benefits nothing unless it means presenting yourself as a living sacrifice to do nothing but the will of God. The vow of entire obedience is the entrance fee for him who would be enrolled by no assistant teacher, but by Christ Himself, in the school of obedience.

2. OF LEARNING TO KNOW GOD'S WILL

This unreserved surrender to obey, as it is the first condition of entering Christ's school, is the only fitness for receiving instruction as to the will of God for us.

There is a general will of God for all His children, which we can, in some measure, learn out of the Bible. But there is a special individual application of these commands—God's will concerning each of us personally, which only the Holy Spirit can teach. And He will not teach it, except to those who have taken the vow of obedience.

This is the reason why there are so many unanswered prayers for God to make known His will. Jesus said, "If anyone wills to do His will, he shall know concerning the doctrine, whether it is from God" (John 7:17). If a man's will is really set on doing God's will—that is, if his heart is given up to do it and he consequently does it as far as he knows it—he shall know what God has further to teach him.

> *A* heart yielded to God in unreserved obedience is the one condition of progress in Christ's school—and of growth in the spiritual knowledge of God's will.

It is simply what is true of every student with the art he studies, of every apprentice with his trade, of every man in business: Doing is the one condition of truly knowing. And so obedience, the doing of God's will as far as we know, and the will and the vow to do it all as He reveals it, is the spiritual organ, the capacity for receiving the true knowledge of what is God's will for each of us.

In connection with this, let me press upon you three things.

A. *Seek to have a deep sense of your very great ignorance of God's will and of your inability by any effort to fully know it.*

The consciousness of ignorance lies at the root of true teachableness. "And the humble He teaches His way" (Ps. 25:9)—those who humbly confess their need of teaching. Head knowledge only gives human thoughts without power. God by His Spirit gives a living knowledge that enters the love of the heart and works effectually.

B. *Cultivate a strong faith that God will make you know wisdom in the hidden part—in the heart.*

You may have known so little of this in your Christian life to this point that the thought of it appears strange. Learn that God's working, that the place where He gives His life and light is in the heart, deeper than all our thoughts. Any uncertainty about God's will makes a joyful obedience impossible. Believe most confidently that the Father is willing to make known what He wants you to do. Count on Him for this. Expect it with certainty.

C. In view of the darkness and deceitfulness of the flesh and fleshly mind, *ask God very earnestly for the searching and convincing light of the Holy Spirit.*

There may be many things that you have been accustomed to thinking as lawful or allowable, but that your Father wants different. To consider it settled that they are the will of God because others and you think so may effectually shut you out from knowing God's will in other things. Bring everything, without reserve, to the judgment of the Word, explained and applied by the Holy Spirit. Wait on God to lead you to know that everything you are and do is pleasing in His sight.

3. ON OBEDIENCE TO THE POINT OF DEATH

There is one of the deeper and more spiritual aspects of this truth to which I have not alluded. It is something that, as a rule, does not come up in the early stages of the Christian life, and yet it is necessary that every believer know what privileges that await him. There is an experience into which wholehearted obedience will bring the believer, in which he will know that, as surely as with his Lord, obedience leads to death.

> *elieve most confidently that the Father is willing to make known what He wants you to do. Count on Him for this. Expect it with certainty.*

Let us see what this means. During our Lord's life, His resistance to sin and the world was perfect and complete. And yet His final deliverance from their temptations and His victory over their power, His obedience, was not complete until He had died to the earthly life and to sin. In that death, He gave up His life in perfect helplessness into the Father's hands, waiting for Him to raise Him up. It was through death that He received the fullness of His life and glory. Through death alone, the giving up of the life He had, could obedience lead Him into the glory of God.

The believer shares with Christ in this death to sin. In regeneration he is baptized by the Holy Spirit into it. Due to ignorance and unbelief, he may know little experimentally of this entire death to sin. When the Holy Spirit reveals to him what he possesses in Christ, and he appropriates it in faith, the Spirit works in him the very same disposition that animated Christ in His death. With Christ, it was an entire ceasing from His own life, a helpless committal of His spirit into the Father's hands. This was the complete fulfillment of the Father's command: Lay down Your life in My hands. Out of the perfect self-oblivion of the grave He entered the glory of the Father.

It is into the fellowship of this a believer is brought. He finds that in the most unreserved obedience for which God's Spirit fits him there is still a secret element of self and self-will. He longs to be delivered from it. He is taught in God's Word that this can only be by death. The Spirit helps him to claim more fully that he is indeed dead to sin in Christ, and that the power of that death can work mightily in him. He is made willing to be obedient to the point of death, this entire death to self, which makes him truly nothing. In this he finds a full entrance into the life of Christ.

To see the need of this entire death to self, to be made willing for it, to be led into the entire self-emptying and humility of our Lord Jesus—this is the highest lesson that our obedience has to learn—this is, indeed, the Christlike obedience to the point of death.

There is no room here to enlarge on this. I thought it well to say this much on a lesson that God Himself will, in due time, teach those who are entirely faithful.

4. OF THE VOICE OF CONSCIENCE

In regard to the knowledge of God's will, we must see and give conscience its place, and submit to its authority.

There are a thousand little things in which the law of nature or education teaches us what is right and good, and in regard to which even earnest Christians do not hold themselves bound to obey. Now, remember, if you are unfaithful in that which is least, who will entrust you with the greater? Not God. If the voice of conscience tells you of some course of action that is the nobler or the better, and you choose another because it is easier or pleasing to self, you disqualify yourself for the teaching of the Spirit by disobeying the voice of God in nature.

> To see the need of this entire death to self, to be made willing for it, to be led into the entire self-emptying and humility of our Lord Jesus—this is the highest lesson that our obedience has to learn

A strong will always to do the right, to do the very best, as conscience points it out, is a will to do God's will. Paul writes, "I am not lying, my conscience also bearing me witness in the Holy Spirit" (Rom. 9:1). The Holy Spirit speaks through conscience, and if you disobey and hurt conscience, you make it impossible for God to speak to you.

Obedience to God's will shows itself in tender sensitivity to the voice of conscience. This holds true with regard to eating and drinking, sleeping and resting, spending money and seeking pleasure—let everything be brought into subjection to the will of God.

This leads to another thing of great importance in this area. If you desire to live the life of true obedience, see that you maintain a good conscience before God, and never knowingly indulge in anything which is contrary to His mind. George Müller attributed all his happiness during seventy years to this, along with his love of God's Word. He had maintained a good conscience in all things, not going on in a course he knew to be contrary to the will of God.

Conscience is the guardian or monitor God has given you to warn you when anything goes wrong. Up to the light you have, give heed to conscience. Ask God, by the teaching of His will, to give it more light. Seek the witness of conscience that you are acting up to that light. Conscience will become your encouragement and your helper, and it will give you the confidence, both that your obedience is accepted and that your prayer for ever-increasing knowledge of the will is heard.

5. OF LEGAL AND EVANGELICAL OBEDIENCE

Even when the vow of unreserved obedience has been taken, there may still be two sorts of obedience—that of the law, and that of the gospel. Just as there are two Testaments, an old and a new, so there are two styles of religion, two ways of serving God.

This is what Paul speaks of in Romans when he says, "For sin shall not have dominion over you, for you are *not under law* but under grace" (6:14), and further speaks of our being "delivered from the law," so "that we should serve in the newness of the Spirit and *not in the oldness of the letter*" (7:6), and then again reminds us, "You did *not receive the spirit of bondage again* to fear, but you received the Spirit of adoption" (8:15).

> *C*onscience will become your encouragement and your helper, and it will give you the confidence, both that your obedience is accepted and that your prayer for ever-increasing knowledge of the will is heard.

The threefold contrast points very evidently to a danger existing among those Christians of still acting as if they were under the law, serving in the oldness of the letter and in the spirit of bondage. One great cause of the weakness of so much Christian living is because it is more under law than under grace. Let us see what the difference is.

What the law demands from us, grace promises and performs for us.

The law deals with what we ought to do, whether we can or not, and by the appeal to motives of fear and love stirs us to do our best. But it gives no real strength, and so only leads to failure and condemnation. Grace points to what we cannot do, and offers to do it for us and in us.

The law comes with commands on stone or in a book. Grace comes in a living, gracious person who gives His presence and His power.

The law promises life if we obey. Grace gives life, even the Holy Spirit, with the assurance that we can obey.

Human nature is always prone to slip back out of grace into the law, and secretly to trust to trying and doing its utmost. The promises of grace are so divine, the gift of the Holy Spirit *to do all in us* is so wonderful, that few believe it. This is the reason they never dare take the vow of obedience or, having taken it, turn back again.

I encourage you, study well what gospel obedience is. The gospel is good news. Its obedience is part of that good news—*that grace, by the Holy Spirit, will do all in you.* Believe that, and let every undertaking to obey be in the joyous hopefulness that comes from faith in the exceeding abundance of grace, in the mighty indwelling of the Holy Spirit, in the blessed love of Jesus, whose abiding presence makes obedience possible and certain.

6. OF THE OBEDIENCE OF LOVE

This is one of the special and most beautiful aspects of gospel obedience. The grace that promises to work all through the Holy Spirit is the gift of eternal love. The Lord Jesus (who takes charge of our obedience, teaches it, and by His presence secures it to us) is He who loved us to the point of the death, who loves us with a love that passes knowledge.

Nothing can receive or know love but a loving heart. And it is this loving heart that enables us to obey. Obedience is the loving response to the divine love resting on us, and the only access to a fuller enjoyment of that love.

How our Lord insisted on that in His farewell discourse! Three times He repeats it in John 14—"*If you love Me*, keep My commandments" (John 14:15). "He who has My commandments and keeps them, it is he *who loves Me*" (14:21). "If anyone *loves Me*, he will keep My word" (14:23). Is it not clear that love alone can give the obedience Jesus asks, and receive the blessing Jesus gives to obedience? The gift of the Spirit, the Father's love and His own, with the manifestation of Himself; the Father's love and His own making their dwelling with us: into these, loving obedience gives the assured access.

In the next chapter He approaches it from the other side and shows how obedience leads to the enjoyment of God's love—He kept His Father's commandments, and *abides in His love.* If we keep His commandments, we shall *abide in His love.* He proved His love by giving His life for us, so *we are His friends* and we shall enjoy His love if we do what He commands us. Between His first love and our love in response to it, between our love and His fuller love in response to ours, *obedience is the one indispensable link.* True and full obedience is impossible, except as we live and love. "This is the love of God, that we keep His commandments" (1 John 5:3).

Do beware of a legal obedience, of striving after a life of true obedience under a sense of duty. Ask God to show you the "newness of life" that is needed for a new and full obedience. Claim the promise, "And I will circumcise your heart. . . to love the LORD your God with all your heart. . .And you will. . .obey the voice of the LORD" (see Deut. 30:6, 8). Believe in the love of God and the grace of our Lord Jesus. Believe in the Spirit given in you, enabling you to love, and so causing you to walk in God's statutes. In the strength of this faith, in the assurance of sufficient grace, made perfect in weakness, enter into God's love and the life of living obedience it works. For nothing but the continual presence of Jesus in His love can prepare you for continual obedience.

7. Is Obedience Possible?

I close with once again, and most urgently, pressing home this question. It lies at the very root of our life. The secret, half-unconscious thought that to live always well-pleasing to God is beyond our reach eats away the very root of our strength. I ask you to give a definite answer to the question.

> *T*he gospel is good news. Its obedience is part of that good news—that grace, by the Holy Spirit, will do all in you.

If in the light of God's provision for obedience—of His promise of working all His good pleasure in you, of His giving you a new heart, with the indwelling of His Son and Spirit—you still fear that obedience is not possible, ask God to open your eyes truly to know His will.[27] If your judgment is convinced and you acknowledge the truth theoretically, and yet fear to give up yourself to such a life, I say to you too, Do ask God to open your eyes and bring you to know *His will for yourself.* Do be careful not to let the secret fear of having to give up too much and of having to become too peculiar and entirely devoted to God keep you back. Beware of seeking just religion enough to give ease to the conscience, and then not desiring to do and be and give God all He is worthy of. And beware, above all, of "limiting" God, of making Him a liar by refusing to believe what He has said He can and will do.

If our study in the school of obedience is to be of any profit, don't rest until you have written it down—daily obedience to all that God wills of me is possible, is possible to me. In His strength I yield myself to Him for it.

But, remember, only on one condition. Not in the strength of your resolve or effort, but *that the unceasing presence of Christ and the unceasing teaching of the Spirit of all grace and power be your portion.* Christ, the obedient One, living in you, will secure your obedience. Obedience will be to you a life of love and joy in His fellowship.

---

[27] I once again refer to a new book, *The Two Covenants and the Second Blessing,* for further exposition of the sufficiency of the grace of the New Covenant to prepare us for entire obedience.

FOR FURTHER THOUGHT

1. *What does it mean to you to "learn obedience?" What part do the mind, the heart, and the will play in learning to obey God?*
2. *What part does the voice of conscience play in living obediently to God? How can you train your conscience to obey?*
3. *What is the relationship between love and obedience—love for God and for humankind?*

8

OBEDIENCE TO THE
LAST COMMAND

"Go therefore and make disciples of all the nations."
MATTHEW 28:19

*"Go into all the world and preach
the gospel to every creature."*
MARK 16:15

*"As You sent Me into the world,
I also have sent them into the world."*
JOHN 17:18

*But you shall receive power when the Holy Spirit
has come upon you; and you shall be witnesses
to Me. . .to the end of the earth."*
ACTS 1:8

ALL these words breathe nothing less than the spirit of world conquest. "All the nations," "all the world," "every creature," "the end of the earth"—each expression indicates that the heart of Christ was set on claiming His rightful dominion over the world He had redeemed and won for Himself. He counts on His disciples to undertake and carry out the work.

As Jesus stands at the foot of the throne, ready to ascend and reign, He tells them, "All authority has been given to Me in heaven and on earth" (Matt. 28:18), and points them at once to "all the world," to "the end of the earth" as the object of His and their desire and efforts. As the king on the throne, He Himself will be their helper: "I am with you always" (Matt. 28:20). They are to be the advance-guard of His conquering hosts, even to the end of the world. He Himself will carry on the war. He seeks to inspire them with His own assurance of victory, with His own purpose to make this the only thing to be thought of as worth living or dying for—the winning back of the world to its God.

Christ does not teach or argue, ask or plead: He simply commands. He has trained His disciples to obedience. He has attached them to Himself in a love that can obey. He has already breathed His own resurrection Spirit into them. He can count on them. He dares to say to them: "Go into all the world."

Before, during Jesus' life on earth, they had more than once expressed their doubt about the possibility of fulfilling His commands. But here, as quietly and simply as He speaks these divine words, they accept them. And no sooner has He ascended than they go to the appointed place to wait for the equipment of a heavenly power from their Lord in heaven for the heavenly work of making all the nations His disciples. They accepted the command and passed it on to those who through them believed on His name. And within a generation, simple men, whose names we do not even know, had preached the gospel in Antioch and Rome and the regions beyond. The command was passed on, and taken up into the heart and life, as meant for all ages, as meant for every disciple.

> *Christ does not teach or argue, ask or plead: He simply commands. He has trained His disciples to obedience. He has attached them to Himself in a love that can obey.*

The command is for us, too, for each one of us. There is in the Church of Christ no privileged class to which alone belongs the honor, nor any servile class on which alone rests the duty of carrying the gospel to every creature. The life Christ imparts is His own life, the spirit He breathes is His very own Spirit—the one disposition He works is His own self-sacrificing love. It lies in the very nature of His salvation that every member of His body, in full and healthy access with Him, feels himself urged to impart what he has received. The command is no arbitrary law from outside. It is simply the revelation, for our intelligent and voluntary consent, of the wonderful truth that we are His body, that we now occupy His place on earth, and that His will and love now carry out through us the work He began, and that now in His place we live to seek the Father's glory in winning a lost world back to Him.

How terribly the Church has failed in obeying the command! How many Christians there are who never knew that there is such a command! How many who hear of it, but do not in earnest set themselves to obey it! And how many who seek to obey it in such way and measure as seems to them fitting and convenient.

We have been studying what obedience is. We have professed to give ourselves up to a wholehearted obedience. Surely we are prepared gladly to listen to anything that can help us to understand and carry out this our Lord's last and great command: *the gospel to every creature.*

Let me give you what I have to say under the three simple headings: *Accept*

His command. Place yourself entirely at His disposal. Begin immediately to live for His kingdom.

1. ACCEPT HIS COMMAND

There are various things that weaken the force of this command. There is the impression that a command given to all, and general in its nature, is not as binding as one that is entirely personal and specific; that if others don't do their part, our share of the blame is comparatively small; that where the difficulties are very great, obedience cannot be an absolute demand; that if we are willing to do our best, this is all that can be asked of us.

Brothers and sisters, this is not obedience! This is not the spirit in which the first disciples accepted it. This is not the spirit in which we wish to live with our beloved Lord. We want to say, each one of us: "Even if there is no one else, I, by His grace, will give myself and my life to live for His kingdom. Let me for a moment separate myself from all others, and think of my personal relationship to Jesus."

I am a member of Christ's body. He expects every member to be at His disposal, to be animated by His Spirit, to live for what He is and does. It is so with my body. I carry every healthy member with me day by day, in the assurance that I can count upon it to do its part. Our Lord has taken me so truly up into His body that He can ask and expect nothing else from me. And I have so truly yielded myself to Him that there can be no idea of my wanting anything but just to know and do His will.

> *It lies in the very nature of His salvation that every member of His body, in full and healthy access with Him, feels himself urged to impart what he has received.*

Or let me take the illustration of "the vine and the branches" (see John 15:5). The branch has just as much only one object for its being as the vine—bearing fruit. If I really am a branch, I am just as much as He was in the world—only and wholly to bring forth fruit, to live and labor for the salvation of men.

Take still another illustration. Christ has bought me with His blood. No slave conquered by force or purchased by money was ever so entirely the property of his master as my soul—redeemed and won by Christ's blood, given up and bound to Him by love, and His property for Him alone to do with it what He pleases. He claims by divine right, working through the Holy Spirit in an infinite power, and I have given full consent, that I live wholly for His kingdom and service. This is my joy and my glory.

There was a time when it was different. There are two ways in which a man can bestow his money or service on another. In olden times, there was once a slave, who by his trade earned much money. All the money came to the master. The master was kind and treated the slave well. At length the slave, from earnings his master had allowed him, was able to purchase his liberty. In course of time the master became impoverished, and had to come to his former slave for help. He was not only able, but most willing to give it, and gave liberally, in gratitude for former kindness.

You see at once the difference between the bringing of his money and service when he was a slave, and his gifts when he was free. In the former case, he gave all, because it and he belonged to the master. In the latter, he only gave what he chose.

In which way ought we to give to Christ Jesus? I fear many, many give as if they were free to give what they chose or what they think they can afford. The believer, to whom the right that the purchase price of the blood has acquired, has been revealed by the Holy Spirit, and he delights to know that he is the bond slave of redeeming love and to lay everything he has at his Master's feet, because he belongs to Him.

> *He claims by divine right, working through the Holy Spirit in an infinite power, and I have given full consent, that I live wholly for His kingdom and service. This is my joy and my glory.*

Have you ever wondered why the disciples accepted the great command so easily and so heartily? They came fresh from Calvary, where they had seen the blood. They had met the risen One, and He had breathed His Spirit into them. During the forty days, "through the Holy Spirit had given commandments to the apostles whom He had chosen" (Acts 1:2). Jesus was to them Savior, Master, Friend, and Lord. His word was with divine power, and they could do nothing but obey.

Oh, let us bow at His feet and yield to the Holy Spirit to reveal and assert His mighty claim, and let us unhesitatingly and with the whole heart accept the command as our one life purpose: the gospel to every creature!

2. PLACE YOURSELF AT HIS DISPOSAL

The last great command has been so prominently urged in connection with foreign missions that many are inclined exclusively to confine it to them. This is a great mistake. Our Lord's words, "Make disciples of all the nations. . .teaching them to observe all things that I have commanded you" (Matt. 28:19–20) tell us what our aim is to be: nothing less than to make every man a true disciple who lives in holy obedience to all Christ's will.

What a work there is to be done in our Christian churches and our so-called Christian communities before it can be said that the command has been carried out! And what a need that the whole Church, with every believer in it, realizes that to do this work is the sole object of its existence! The gospel brought fully, perseveringly, savingly to every creature: This is the mission, this ought to be the passion, of every redeemed soul. For this alone is the Spirit and likeness and life of Christ formed in you.

If there is one thing that the Church needs to preach—in the power of the Holy Spirit—it is the absolute and immediate duty of every child of God not only to take some part in this work, as he may think fit or possible, but to give himself to Christ the Master to be guided and used as He would have. And therefore I say to every reader who has taken the vow of full obedience—and dare we count ourselves true Christians if we have not done so?—place yourself at once and wholly at Christ's disposal.

As binding, as is the first great command on all God's people, "You shall love the LORD your God with all your heart" (Deut. 6:5, Mark 12:30) is this, the last great command too—"The gospel to every creature." Before you know what your work may be, before you feel any special desire or call or fitness for any work, if you are willing to accept the command, place yourself at His disposal. It is His as Master to train and fit and guide and use you.

> *Before you know what your work may be, before you feel any special desire or call or fitness for any work, if you are willing to accept the command, place yourself at His disposal.*

Don't be afraid. Come at once and forever out of the selfish religion that puts your own will and comfort first and gives Christ what you see fit. Let the Master know that He can have you wholly. Enroll yourself at once with Him as a volunteer for His service. God has in these few past years filled our hearts with joy and thanksgiving at what He has done through the Student Volunteer Movement. The blessing it is bringing the Christian Church is as great as that coming to the heathen world. I sometimes feel as if there were only one thing still needed to perfect its work. Is there not a need of an enrollment of Volunteers for Home Service, helping its members to feel that as intense and undivided as is the consecration to which the volunteer for foreign work is stirred and helped is the devotion Christ asks of everyone He has bought with His blood for His service in saving the world?

What blessings have not these simple words, "It is my purpose, if God permit, to become a foreign missionary," brought into thousands of lives! It helped them into the surrender of obedience to the great command, and it became an era in their history. What blessings might not come to many who can never go abroad—

or who think so, because they have not asked their Master's will—if they could take the simple resolve: *By the grace of God I devote my life wholly to the service of Christ's kingdom!*

The external forsaking of home to go abroad is often a great help to the foreign volunteer, through the struggle it costs him, and the breaking away from all that could hinder him. The home volunteer may have to live in his calling and not have the need of such an external separation—he needs all the more the help that a pledge, given in secret or in union with others, can bring. The blessed Spirit can make it a crisis and a consecration that leads to a life utterly devoted to God.

Students in the school of obedience, study the last and great commandment well. Accept it with your whole heart. Place yourselves entirely at His disposal.

3. AND IMMEDIATELY TO ACT ON YOUR OBEDIENCE

In whatever circumstances you are, it is your privilege to have within your reach souls who can be won for God. All around you there are numberless forms of Christian activity that invite your help and offer you theirs. Look on yourself as redeemed by Christ for His service, as blessed with His Spirit to give you the very outlooks that were in Himself, and take up, humbly but boldly, your life calling to take part in the great work of winning back the world to God.

Whether you are led by God to join some of the many agencies already at work, or to walk in a more solitary path, don't regard the work as that of your church or of society or as your own, but as the Lord's. Cherish carefully the consciousness of "doing it for the Lord," of being a servant who is under orders and simply carrying them out. Your work will then not, as so often, come between you and the fellowship with Christ, but link you inseparably to Him, His strength, and His approval.

> *I*t is not only Christ on the throne—*glorious vision!*— that we need, but Christ with us here below, in His abiding presence, Himself working for us and through us.

It is so easy to get so engrossed in the human interest there is in our work that its spiritual character, the supernatural power needed for it, the direct working of God in us and through us—all that can fill us with true heavenly joy and hope is lost out of sight. Keep your eye on your Master, on your King, on His throne.

Before He gave the command and pointed His servants to the great field of the world, He first drew their eyes to Himself on the throne: "*All authority has been given to Me in heaven and on earth*" (Matt. 28:18). It is the vision of and the faith in Christ on the throne that reminds of the need and assures us of the sufficiency of His divine power. Obey not a command, but the living almighty Lord of glory.

Faith in Him will give you heavenly strength.

These words preceded the command, and then there followed, *"Lo, I am with you always"* (Matt. 28:20). It is not only Christ on the throne—glorious vision!—that we need, but Christ with us here below, in His abiding presence, Himself working for us and through us. Christ's power in heaven, Christ's presence on earth—between these two pillar promises stands the gate through which the Church enters to the conquest of the world. Let each of us follow our leader, receive from Him our orders as to our share in the work, and never falter in the vow of obedience that has given itself to live wholly for His will and His work alone.

Such a beginning will be a training time, preparing us fully to know and follow His leading. If His call for the millions of dying heathen come to us, we shall be ready to go. If His providence does not permit our going, our devotion at home will be as complete and intense as if we had gone. Whether it is at home or abroad, if only the ranks of the obedient, the servants of obedience, the obedient to the point of death, are filled up, Christ shall have His heart's desire, and His glorious thought—the gospel to every creature—will be accomplished!

Blessed Son of God! Here I am. By Your grace, I give my life to the carrying out of Your last great command. Let my heart be as Your heart. Let my weakness be as Your strength. In Your name, I take the vow of entire and everlasting obedience. Amen.

For Further Thought

1. *What are the steps you must take before you can take part in obeying Christ's command to preach the gospel to the whole world? What first step can you take today?*

2. *What do you need to do before God can reveal to you how and where you are to take part in the work of preaching the gospel?*

3. *How should you view the work of spreading the gospel, whatever it may be, that God has called you to? How will viewing it correctly affect how you approach that work?*

Morning Watch

By the observance of the morning watch is commonly meant the spending of *at least* the first half-hour of every day alone with God, in personal devotional Bible study and prayer.

"There are Christians who say that they do not have time to devote a full half-hour to such a spiritual exercise. It is a striking fact that the busiest Christians constitute the class who plead this excuse the least, and most generally observe the morning watch. Any Christian who will honestly and persistently follow this plan for a month or two will become convinced that it is the best possible use of his time, that it does not interfere with his regular work, and that it promotes the wisest economy of time....

"In India, in China, in Japan, hundreds of students have agreed to keep the morning watch....

"The practical question for each of us is, Why should not I keep the morning watch? Next to receiving Christ as Savior, and claiming the baptism of the Holy Spirit, *we know of no act attended with larger good to ourselves and to others* than the formation of an undiscourageable resolution to keep the morning watch."

These quotations are from an address by John R. Mott. At first sight, the closing statement appears too strong. But think a moment what such a revelation implies.

It means the deep conviction that the only way to maintain and carry out the surrender to Christ and the Holy Spirit is by meeting God very definitely at the beginning of each day and receiving from Him the grace needed for a walk in holy obedience.

It means an insight into the folly of attempting to live a heavenly life without rising up into close communion with God in heaven, and receiving from Him the fresh bestowal of spiritual blessings.

It means the confession that it is alone in personal fellowship with God, and in delight in His nearness, that proof can be given that our love responds to His, and that we count His nearness our chief joy.

It means the faith that if time enough is given for God to lay His hands on us and renew the inflowings of His Spirit, our soul may be so closely united to Him that no trials or duties can separate us from Him.

It means a purpose to live wholly and only for God, and by the sacrifice of time and ease to prove that we are willing to pay any price to secure the first of all blessings the presence of God for all the day.

Let us now look again at that sentence—"Next to receiving Christ as our Savior, and claiming the baptism of the Holy Spirit, *we know of no act attended with larger good to ourselves or to others* than the formation of an undiscourageable resolution to keep the morning watch." If our acceptance of Christ as Lord and Master was wholehearted, if our prayer for and claiming of the Holy Spirit to guide and control was sincere, surely there can be no thought of not giving God each day sufficient time, our very best time, for receiving and increasing in us what is indispensable to a life for Christ's glory and in His service.

You tell me there are many Christians who are content with ten minutes or a quarter of an hour. There are, but you will certainly not as a rule find them strong Christians. And the Students' Movement is pleading with God, above everything, that He would meet to train a race of devoted, wholehearted young men and women.

Christ asked great sacrifices of His disciples; He has perhaps asked little of you as yet. But now He allows, He invites, He longs for you to make some. Sacrifices make strong men. Sacrifices help wonderfully to wrench us away from earth and self-pleasing, and lift us heavenward. Do not try to pare down the time limit of the morning watch to less than the half hour. There can be no question about the possibility of finding the time. Ten minutes from sleep, ten from company or amusement, ten from lessons. How easy where the heart is right, hungering to know God and His will perfectly!

If you feel that you do not feel the need of so much time and don't know how to wait, we are content you should speak of your quiet time, or your hour of prayer. God may graciously, later on, draw you out to the morning watch. But do not undertake it unless you feel your heart stirred with the determination to make a sacrifice, and have full time for intimate fellowship with God. But if you are ready to do this, we urge you to join.

The very fact of setting apart such a period helps to awaken the feeling: *I have a great work to do, and I need time for it.* It strengthens in your heart the conviction: *If I am to be kept all this day without sin I must have time to get near to God.* It will give your Bible study new point, as you find time between the reading, to be still and bow in humility for the Holy Spirit's hidden working, and wait until you get some real understanding of God's will for you, through the Word. And, by the grace of God, it may help you to begin that habit of specific and definite intercession of which the Church so surely stands in need.

Students! You don't know whether in your future life your time may be more limited, your circumstances more unfavorable, your Christian earnestness weaker. Now is the accepted time. Today, as the Holy Spirit says. Listen to the invitation of your brethren in all lands, and don't be afraid to make an undiscourageable resolution to spend at least half an hour each morning *with God alone.*

THE SCHOOL OF PRAYER

CONTENTS

PREFACE

OF all the promises connected with the command "Abide in Me," there is none higher, and none that sooner brings the confession, "Not that I have already attained, or am already perfected" (Phil. 3:12), than this: "If you abide in Me, and My words abide in you, *you will ask what you desire, and it shall be done for you*" (John 15:17). Power with God is the highest attainment of the life of full abiding.

And of all the traits of a life like Christ, there is none higher and more glorious than conformity to Him in the work that now engages Him without ceasing in the Father's presence—His all-prevailing intercession. The more we abide in Him and grow unto His likeness, will His priestly life work in us mightily, and our life becomes what His is: a life that always pleads and prevails for men.

"You. . .have made us kings and priests to our God" (Rev. 5:9, 10). Both in the king and the priest, the chief thing is power, influence, and blessing. In the king it is the power coming downward; in the priest the power rising upward, prevailing with God. In our blessed Priest-King, Jesus Christ, the kingly power is founded on the priestly "*He is also* able to save to the uttermost. . .*since* He always lives to make intercession for them" (Heb. 7:25). In us, His priests and kings, it is no different: It is in intercession that the Church is to find and wield its highest power so that each member of the Church is to prove his descent from Israel, who as a prince had power with God and with men, and prevailed.

It is under a deep impression that the place and power of prayer in the Christian life is too little understood that this book has been written. I feel sure that as long as we look on prayer chiefly as the means of maintaining our own Christian life, we shall not know fully what it is meant to be. But when we learn to regard it as the highest part of the work entrusted to us, the root and strength of all other work, we shall see that there is nothing that we so need to study and practice as the art of praying rightly.

If I have at all succeeded in pointing out the progressive teaching of our Lord in regard to prayer, and the distinct reference the wonderful promises of the last night (John 14:16) have to the works we are to do in His name, to the greater works and to the bearing much fruit, we shall all admit that it is only when the Church gives herself up to this holy work of intercession that we can expect the power of Christ to manifest itself on her behalf. It is my prayer that God may use this little book to make clearer to some of His children the wonderful place of power and influence that He is waiting for them to occupy, and for which a weary world is waiting, too.

In connection with this, there is another truth that has come to me with wonderful clearness as I studied the teaching of Jesus on prayer. It is this: that the Father waits to hear every prayer of faith, to give us whatever we desire and whatever we ask in Jesus' name. We have become so accustomed to limiting the wonderful love and the large promises of our God that we cannot read the simplest and clearest statements of our Lord without the qualifying clauses by which we guard and expound them.

If there is one thing I think the Church needs to learn, it is that God means prayer to have an answer, and that it has not entered into the heart of man to conceive what God will do for His child who gives himself to believe that his prayer will be heard. *God hears prayer.* This is a truth universally admitted, but of which very few understand the meaning or experience the power. If what I have written stirs my reader to go to the Master's words and take His wondrous promises simply and literally as they stand, my object has been attained.

And then just one thing more. Thousands have in these last years found an unspeakable blessing in learning how completely Christ is our life, and how He undertakes to be and to do all in us that we need. I don't know if we have yet learned to apply this truth to our prayer life. Many complain that they don't have the power to pray in faith, to pray the effectual prayer that accomplishes much. The message I would gladly bring them is that the blessed Jesus is waiting, is longing, to teach them this.

Christ is our life: In heaven He always lives to pray, and His life in us is an ever-praying life, if we will just trust Him for it. Christ teaches us to pray not only by example, by instruction, by command, by promises, but *by showing* us *Himself, the ever-living Intercessor, as our Life.* It is when we believe this, then go and abide in Him for our prayer life, too, that our fears of not being able to pray rightly will vanish. Then we shall joyfully and triumphantly trust our Lord to teach us to pray, to be Himself the life and the power of our prayer.

May God open our eyes to see what the holy ministry of intercession is, to which, as His royal priesthood, we have been set apart. May He give us a large and strong heart to believe what mighty influence our prayers can exert. And may all fear as to our being able to fulfill our calling vanish as we see Jesus, living always to pray, the living and standing guarantee for our prayer life.

ANDREW MURRAY
Wellington, August 28, 1885

Lesson 1

"Lord, Teach Us to Pray,"
or, The Only Teacher

Now it came to pass, as He was praying in a certain place,
when He ceased, that one of His disciples said to Him,
"Lord, teach us to pray, as John also taught his disciples."
LUKE 11:1

THE disciples had been with Christ, and they had seen Him pray. They had learned to understand something of the connection between His wondrous life in public and His secret life of prayer. They had learned to believe in Him as a Master in the art of prayer—no one could pray like Him. And so they came to Him with the request, "Lord, teach us to pray." And in later years they would have told us that there were few things more wonderful or blessed He taught them than His lessons on prayer.

And now still it comes to pass, as He is praying in a certain place that the disciples who see Him engaged this way feel the need to repeat the same request, "Lord, teach us to pray." As we grow in the Christian life, the thought and the faith of the beloved Master in His never-failing intercession becomes more and more precious, and the hope of being *like Christ* in His intercession gains an attractiveness before unknown. And as we see Him pray, as we remember that there is no one who can pray like Him, no one who can teach like Him, we feel the request of the disciples, "Lord, teach us to pray" is just what we need. And as we think how all He is and has, how He Himself is our very own, how He is Himself our life, we feel assured that we need only ask, and He will be delighted to take us up into closer fellowship with Himself and teach us to pray just as He prays.

Come, my brothers! Shall we not go to the blessed Master and ask Him to enroll our names, too, anew in that school that He always keeps open for those who long to continue their studies in the divine art of prayer and intercession? Yes, let us this very day say to the Master, as they did of old, "Lord, teach us to pray." As we meditate, we shall find each word of the request we bring to be full of meaning.

"Lord, teach us *to pray*." Yes, *to pray*. This is what we need to be taught. Though in its beginnings prayer is so simple that the most helpless child can pray, yet it is at the same time the highest and holiest work to which man can rise. It is fellowship with the Unseen and most holy One. The powers of the eternal world have been placed at its disposal. It is the very essence of true religion, the channel of all blessings, the secret of power and life. Not only for ourselves, but for others, for the Church for the world, it is to prayer that God has given the right to take hold of Him and His strength. It is on prayer that the promises wait for their fulfillment, the kingdom for its coming, the glory of God for its full revelation. And for this blessed work, how lazy and unfit we are. It is only the Spirit of God who can enable us to do it rightly. How speedily we are deceived into resting in the form, while the power is lacking. Our early training, the teaching of the Church, the influence of habit, the stirring of the emotions—how easily these lead to prayer that has no spiritual power and benefits but little. True prayer that takes hold of God's strength, that benefits much, to which the gates of heaven are really opened wide—who would not cry, "Oh for someone to teach me to pray this way?"

> *Though in its beginnings prayer is so simple that the most helpless child can pray, yet it is at the same time the highest and holiest work to which man can rise.*

Jesus has opened a school, in which He trains His redeemed ones who specifically desire it to have power in prayer. Shall we not enter it with the request, "Lord, it is just this we need to be taught! O teach us to *pray*."

"Lord, teach *us* to pray." Yes, *us*, Lord. We have read in Your Word with what power Your believing people of old used to pray, and what mighty wonders were done in answer to their prayers. And if this took place under the Old Covenant, in the time of preparation, how much more will You not now, in these days of fulfillment, give Your people this sure sign of Your presence in their midst? We have heard the promises given to Your apostles of the power of prayer in Your name, and we have seen how gloriously they experienced their truth: We know for certain they can become true to us, too. We hear continually, even in these days, what glorious proofs of Your power You still give to those who trust You fully. Lord, these all are men with passions like our own; teach *us* to pray so, too. The promises are for us, as are the powers and gifts of the heavenly world. O teach *us* to pray so that we may receive abundantly. To us, too, You have entrusted Your work. On our prayer, too, the coming of Your kingdom depends. In our prayer, too, You can glorify Your name. "Lord, teach *us* to pray." Yes, us, Lord, for we offer ourselves as learners. We desire indeed to be taught by You. "Lord, teach *us* to pray."

"Lord, teach *us* to pray." Yes, we feel the need now of being *taught* to pray.

At first, there is no work that appears so simple, but later on, none that is more difficult. And the confession is forced from us: We don't know how to pray as we should. It is true we have God's Word, with its clear and sure promises. But sin has so darkened our mind that we don't always know how to apply the Word. In spiritual things we do not always seek the things most needed, or we fail in praying according to the law of the sanctuary. In earthly things we are still less able to avail ourselves of the wonderful liberty our Father has given us to ask what we need. And even when we know what to ask, how much there is still needed to make prayer acceptable.

> *At first, there is no work that appears so simple, but later on, none that is more difficult. And the confession is forced from us: We don't know how to pray as we should.*

It must be to the glory of God, in full surrender to His will, in full assurance of faith, in the name of Jesus, and with a perseverance that, if it is needed, refuses to be denied. All this must be learned. It can only be learned in the school of much prayer, for practice makes perfect. Amid the painful consciousness of ignorance and unworthiness, in the struggle between believing and doubting, the heavenly art of effectual prayer is learned. Because, even when we do not remember it, there is One, the beginner and finisher of faith and prayer, who watches over our praying and sees to it that *in all who trust Him* for their education in the school of prayer shall be carried on to perfection. Let just the deep undertone of all our prayer be the teachableness that comes from a sense of ignorance, and from faith in Him as a perfect teacher, and then we may be sure we shall be taught, we shall learn to pray in power. Yes, we may depend upon it, *He teaches* to pray.

"*Lord*, teach us to pray." No one can teach like Jesus, no one but Jesus. Therefore we call on Him, "Lord, teach us to pray." A pupil needs a teacher who knows his work, who has the gift of teaching, who in patience and love will descend to the pupil's needs. Blessed be God! Jesus is all this and much more. He knows what prayer is. It is Jesus, praying Himself, who teaches to pray. He knows what prayer is. He learned it amid the trials and tears of His earthly life. In heaven it is still His beloved work: His life there is prayer. Nothing delights Him more than to find those whom He can take with Him into the Father's presence, whom He can clothe with power to pray down God's blessing on those around them, whom He can train to be His fellow workers in the intercession by which the kingdom is to be revealed on earth. He knows how to teach. Now by the urgency of felt need, then by the confidence with which joy inspires. Here by the teaching of the Word, there by the testimony of another believer who knows what it is to have prayer heard.

By His Holy Spirit, He has access to our heart, and He teaches us to pray by showing us the sin that hinders the prayer, or giving us the assurance that we please God. He teaches by giving not only thoughts of what to ask or how to ask, but by breathing within us the very spirit of prayer, by living within us as the great Intercessor. We may indeed and most joyfully say, "Who teaches like Him?" Jesus never taught His disciples how to preach, only how to pray. He did not speak much of what was needed to preach well, but much of praying well. To know how to speak to God is more than knowing how to speak to man. Not power with men, but power with God is the first thing. Jesus loves to teach us how to pray.

> *A*s the members of His body, as a holy priesthood, we shall take part in His priestly work of pleading and prevailing with God for men.

What do you think, my beloved fellow disciples! Would it not be just what we need, to ask the Master for a month to give us a course of special lessons on the art of prayer? As we meditate on the words He spoke on earth, let us yield ourselves to His teaching in the fullest confidence that with such a teacher, we shall make progress. Let us take time not only to meditate, but to pray, to wait at the foot of the throne and be trained to the work of intercession. Let us do so in the assurance that amid our stammerings and fears, He is carrying on His work most beautifully. He will breathe His own life, which is all prayer, into us. As He makes us partakers of His righteousness and His life, He will of His intercession, too. As the members of His body, as a holy priesthood, we shall take part in His priestly work of pleading and prevailing with God for men. Yes, let us joyfully say, ignorant and weak though we are, "*Lord*, teach us to pray."

"LORD, TEACH US TO PRAY."

Blessed Lord who always lives to pray! You can teach me, too, to pray, me, too, to live always to pray. In this You love to make me share Your glory in heaven so that I should pray without ceasing and always stand as a priest in the presence of my God.

Lord Jesus! I ask You today to enroll my name among those who confess that they don't know how to pray as they should and specially ask You for a course of teaching in prayer. Lord! Teach me to wait with You in the school, and to give You time to train me. May a deep sense of my ignorance, of the wonderful privilege and power of prayer, of my need for the Holy Spirit as the Spirit of prayer, lead me to cast away my thoughts of what I think I know, and make me kneel before You in true teachableness and poorness of spirit.

And fill me, Lord, with the confidence that with such a teacher as You, I shall learn to pray. In the assurance that I have as my teacher Jesus, who is always praying to the Father, and by His prayer rules the destinies of His Church and the world, I will not be afraid. As much as I need to know of the mysteries of the prayer world, You will reveal to me. And when I may not know, You will teach me to be strong in faith, giving glory to God.

Blessed Lord! You will not put to shame Your student who trusts You, nor, by Your grace, would he You either. Amen.

For Further Thought

1. *Why did the disciples ask Jesus to teach them to pray? How did Jesus answer them? What is your motivation for wanting to know how to pray?*
2. *What is your blessed privilege and solemn responsibility as a member of Christ's body and as a member of what the Bible calls His holy priesthood?*
3. *How does Jesus gain access to your heart so that He can teach you to pray by first showing you what sins hinder your prayer?*

LESSON 2

"IN SPIRIT AND TRUTH,"
OR, THE TRUE WORSHIPPERS

"But the hour is coming, and now is, when the true worshipers
will worship the Father in spirit and truth; for the Father
is seeking such to worship Him. God is Spirit, and those who
worship Him must worship in spirit and truth."
JOHN 4:23–24

THESE words of Jesus to the woman of Samaria are His first recorded teaching on the subject of prayer. They give us some wonderful first glimpses into the world of prayer. The Father *seeks* worshippers: Our worship satisfies His loving heart and is a joy to Him. He seeks *true worshippers*, but finds many not such as He would have them. True worship is that which is *in spirit and truth*. The Son has *come* to open the way for this worship in spirit and in truth, and teach it to us. And so, one of our first lessons in the school of prayer must be to understand what it is to pray in spirit and in truth, and to know how we can accomplish it.

To the woman of Samaria our Lord spoke of a threefold worship. There is first, the ignorant worship of the Samaritans: "You worship what you do not know" (John 4:22). The second, intelligent worship of the Jew, having the true knowledge of God: "We know what we worship, for salvation is of the Jews" (4:22). And then the new, the spiritual worship which He Himself has come to introduce: "The hour is coming, and now is, when the true worshipers will worship the Father in spirit and truth."

From the connection, it is evident that the words "in spirit and truth" do not mean, as is often thought, earnestly, from the heart, in sincerity. The Samaritans had the five books of Moses and some knowledge of God, so there was no doubt more than one among them who honestly and earnestly sought God in prayer. The Jews had the true full revelation of God in His Word, as He had given it so far, and there were among them godly men who called upon God with their whole heart. And yet not "in spirit and truth," in the full meaning of the words. Jesus says, "The hour is coming, and now is": it is only in and through Him that the worship of God will be in spirit and truth.

Among Christians one still finds the three classes of worshippers. Some who in their ignorance hardly know what they ask: They pray earnestly, and yet receive little. Others there are who have more correct knowledge, who try to pray with all their mind and heart, and often pray more earnestly, and yet do not attain to the full blessedness of worship in spirit and truth. It is into this third class we must ask our Lord Jesus to take us. We must be taught by Him how to worship in spirit and truth. This alone is spiritual worship, for it makes us the kind of worshippers the Father seeks. In prayer, everything will depend on our understanding well and practicing the worship in spirit and truth.

"God is *Spirit*, and those who worship Him must worship *in spirit* and truth." The first thought suggested here by the Master is that there must be harmony between God and His worshippers; such as God is, so must His worship be. This is according to a principle that prevails throughout the universe: we look for correspondence between an object and the organ to which it reveals or yields itself. The eye has an inner fitness for the light, the ear for sound. The man who wants to truly worship God, who wants to find and know and possess and enjoy God, must be in harmony with Him, must have the capacity for receiving Him. Because God is *Spirit*, we must worship *in spirit*. As God is, so is His worshipper.

And what does this mean? The woman had asked our Lord whether Samaria or Jerusalem was the true place of worship. He answers that from now on worship is no longer to be limited to a certain place: "Woman, believe Me, *the hour is coming* when you will neither on this mountain, nor in Jerusalem, worship the Father" (John 4:21). As God is Spirit, not bound by space or time, but in His infinite perfection always and everywhere the same, so His worship would from that time forward no longer be confined by place or form, but spiritual as God Himself is spiritual.

> *True worship is that which is in spirit and truth. The Son has come to open the way for this worship in spirit and in truth, and teach it to us.*

A lesson of deep importance: How much our Christianity suffers from this— that it is confined to certain times and places. A man who seeks to pray earnestly in the church or in the closet spends the greater part of the week or the day in a spirit entirely at odds with that in which he prayed. His worship was the work of a fixed place or hour, not of his whole being. God is a Spirit: He is the everlasting and unchangeable One. What He is, He is always and in truth. Our worship must likewise be in spirit and truth: His worship must be the spirit of our life and our life must be worship in spirit as God is Spirit.

"*God is Spirit, and those who worship Him must worship in spirit and truth.*" The second thought that comes to us is that this worship in the spirit must come from God Himself. God is Spirit, and He alone has Spirit to give. It was for this that He sent His Son: to fit us for spiritual worship by giving us the Holy Spirit. It is of His own work that Jesus speaks when He says twice, "The hour is coming," and then adds, "and is now." He came to baptize with the Holy Spirit. The Spirit could not stream forth until He was glorified (John 1:33, 7:37–38, 16:7). It was when He had made an end of sin, and entering into the Holiest of all with His blood, had there on our behalf *received* the Holy Spirit (Acts 2:33), that He could send Him down to us as the Spirit of the Father. It was when Christ redeemed us, and we in Him had received the position of children, that the Father sent forth the Spirit of His Son into our hearts to cry, "Abba, Father" (Rom. 8:15). The worship in spirit is the worship of the Father in the Spirit of Christ, the spirit of sonship.

---

*O*ur worship must likewise be in spirit and truth: His worship must be the spirit of our life and our life must be worship in spirit as God is Spirit.

This is the reason why Jesus here uses the name of "Father." We never find one of the Old Testament saints personally use the name of child or call God his Father. The worship *of the Father* is only possible to those to whom the Spirit of the Son has been given. The worship *in spirit* is only possible to those to whom the Son has revealed the Father, and who have received the spirit of sonship. It is only Christ who opens the way and teaches the worship in spirit.

And *in truth*. That does not only mean, *in sincerity*. Nor does it only signify, *in accordance with the truth of God's Word*. The expression is one of deep and divine meaning. Jesus is "the only begotten of the Father, *full* of grace and *truth*" (John 1:14). "For the law was given through Moses, but grace and *truth came* through Jesus Christ" (John 1:17). Jesus says, "I am the way, *the truth*, and the life" (John 14:6). In the Old Testament, all was shadow and promise, but Jesus brought and gives the reality, *the substance*, of things hoped for. In Him the blessings and powers of the eternal life are our actual possession and experience. Jesus is full of grace and truth, and the Holy Spirit is the Spirit of truth, and through Him the grace that is in Jesus is ours in deed and truth, a positive communication out of the divine life. And so worship in spirit is worship *in truth*; actual living fellowship with God, a real correspondence and harmony between the Father, who is a Spirit, and the child praying in the spirit.

What Jesus said to the woman of Samaria, she could not immediately understand. Pentecost was needed to reveal its full meaning. We are hardly prepared at our first entrance into the school of prayer to grasp such teaching. We shall understand it better later on. Let us only begin and take the lesson as He gives it. We are carnal and cannot bring God the worship He seeks. But Jesus came to give the Spirit; He has given Him to us.

Let the disposition in which we set ourselves to pray be what Christ's words have taught us. Let there be the deep confession of our inability to bring God the worship that is pleasing to Him, the childlike teachableness that waits on Him to instruct us, or the simple faith that yields itself to the breathing of the Spirit. Above all, let us hold fast the blessed truth—we shall find that the Lord has more to say to us about it—that the knowledge of the fatherhood of God, the revelation of His infinite fatherliness in our hearts, the faith in the infinite love that gives us His Son and His Spirit to make us children, is indeed the secret of prayer in spirit and truth. This is the new and living way Christ opened up for us. To have Christ the Son, and *the Spirit of the Son*, dwelling within us, and revealing the Father— this makes us true, spiritual worshippers.

"LORD, TEACH US TO PRAY."

Blessed Lord! I adore the love with which You taught a woman, who had refused You a cup of water, what the worship of God must be. I rejoice in the assurance that You will no less now instruct Your disciple who comes to You with a heart that longs to pray in spirit and in truth. O my holy Master! Do teach me this blessed secret.

> *Jesus is full of grace and truth, and the Holy Spirit is the Spirit of truth, and through Him the grace that is in Jesus is ours in deed and truth, a positive communication out of the divine life.*

Teach me that the worship in spirit and truth is not of man but only comes from You, that it is not only a thing of times and seasons but the outflowing of a life in You. Teach me to draw near to God in prayer under the deep sense of my ignorance and my having nothing in myself to offer Him, and at the same time of the provision You, my Savior, make for the Spirit's breathing in my childlike stammerings. I do bless You that in You I am a child, and have a child's liberty of access, that in You I have the spirit of sonship and of worship in truth. Teach me, above all, blessed Son of the Father, how it is the revelation of the Father that gives confidence in prayer. And let the infinite fatherliness of God's heart be my joy and strength for a life of prayer and of worship. Amen.

For Further Thought

1. *What are the three kinds of worship listed in this chapter, and which of them is the true worship, the worship Jesus Christ came to teach?*
2. *What does worshipping "in spirit and in truth" truly mean to you today?*
3. *In whom and through whom will the worship of God be in spirit and in truth? What must your relationship to that person be in order for you to worship in spirit and in truth?*

LESSON 3

"PRAY TO YOUR FATHER WHO IS IN THE SECRET PLACE," OR, ALONE WITH GOD

"But you, when you pray, go into your room,
and when you have shut your door, pray to your Father
who is in the secret place; and your Father who
sees in secret will reward you openly."
MATTHEW 6:6

AFTER Jesus had called His first disciples, He gave them their first public teaching in the Sermon on the Mount. He there expounded to them the kingdom of God, its laws and its life. In that kingdom, God is not only King, but Father; He not only gives all, but is Himself all. In the knowledge and fellowship of Him alone is its blessedness. That's why it came as a matter of course that the revelation of prayer and the prayer life was a part of His teaching concerning the new kingdom He came to set up. Moses gave neither command nor regulation with regard to prayer, and even the prophets say little directly of the duty of prayer. It is Christ who teaches to pray.

And the first thing the Lord teaches His disciples is that they must have a secret place for prayer. Everyone must have some solitary spot where he can be alone with his God. Every teacher must have a schoolroom. We have learned to know and accept Jesus as our only teacher in the school of prayer. He has already taught us at Samaria that worship is no longer confined to times and places, that worship, true spiritual worship, is a thing of the spirit and the life; the whole man must in his whole life be worshipping in spirit and truth.

And yet He wants each one to choose for himself the fixed spot where He can daily meet him. That inner chamber, that solitary place, is Jesus' schoolroom. That spot may be anywhere. That spot may change from day to day if we have to change our living situation. But that secret place there must be, with the quiet time in which the pupil places himself in the Master's presence, to be prepared by Him to worship the Father. There alone, but there most surely, Jesus comes to us to teach us to pray.

A teacher always wants his schoolroom to be bright and attractive, filled with the light and air of heaven—a place where pupils long to come and love to stay. In His first words on prayer in the Sermon on the Mount, Jesus seeks to set the inner chamber before us in its most attractive light. If we listen carefully, we soon notice what the chief thing is He has to tell us of our waiting there. Three times He uses the name of Father: "Pray to *your Father*" (Matt. 6:6), "*Your Father. . .*will reward you openly" (Matt. 6:6), and "*Your Father* knows the things you have need of" (Matt. 6:8). The first thing in closet prayer is: I must meet my Father. The light that shines in the closet must be the light of the Father's countenance. The fresh air from heaven with which Jesus desires to have it filled, the atmosphere in which I am to breathe and pray, is God's Father-love and God's infinite fatherliness. Therefore, each thought or request we breathe out will be simple, hearty, childlike trust in the Father. This is how the Master teaches us to pray: He brings us into the Father's living presence. What we pray there must benefit. Let us listen carefully to hear what the Lord has to say to us.

First, *"Pray to your Father who is in the secret place."* God is a God who hides Himself from the carnal eye. As long as in our worship of God we are chiefly occupied with our own thoughts and exercises, we shall not meet Him who is a Spirit, the unseen One. But to the man who withdraws himself from all that is of the world and man, and prepares to wait upon God alone, the Father will reveal Himself. As he forsakes and gives up and shuts out the world, and the life of the world, and surrenders himself to be led by Christ into the secret of God's presence, the light of the Father's love will rise upon him.

> The first thing the Lord teaches His disciples is that they must have a secret place for prayer. Everyone must have some solitary spot where he can be alone with his God.

The secrecy of the inner chamber and the closed door, the entire separation from all around us, is an image of, and so a help to, that inner spiritual sanctuary— the secret of God's tabernacle, within the veil—where our spirit truly comes into contact with the invisible One. And so we are taught, at the very outset of our search after the secret of effectual prayer, to remember that it is in the inner chamber, where we are alone with the Father, that we shall learn to pray rightly.

The Father is in the secret place: In these words Jesus teaches us where He is waiting for us, where He is always to be found. Christians often complain that private prayer is not what it should be. They feel weak and sinful, and the heart is cold and dark. It is as if they have so little to pray, and in that little no faith or joy. They are discouraged and kept from prayer by the thought that they cannot come to the

Father as they should or as they wish.

Child of God, listen to your Teacher! He tells you that when you go to private prayer, your first thought must be: The Father is in the secret place and waits for me there. Just because your heart is cold and prayerless, get into the presence of the loving Father. As a father has compassion his children, so the Lord has compassion for you. Do not be thinking of how little you have to bring God, but of how much He wants to give you. Just place yourself before Him and look up into His face and think of His love—His wonderful, tender, compassionate love. Just tell Him how sinful and cold and dark all is. It is the Father's loving heart that will give light and warmth to yours.

O do what Jesus says: Just shut the door, and pray to your Father who is in the secret place. Is it not wonderful to be able to go alone with God, the infinite God, and then to look up and say: My Father!

"And your Father who sees in secret will reward you openly." Here Jesus assures us that secret prayer cannot be fruitless, that its blessing will show itself in our life. We have only in secret, alone with God, to entrust our life before men to Him, and then He will reward us openly. He will see to it that the answer to prayer be revealed in His blessing on us. Our Lord wants to thus teach us that as infinite fatherliness and faithfulness is that with which God meets us in secret, so on our part there should be the childlike simplicity of faith, the confidence that our prayer does bring down a blessing.

> We have only in secret, alone with God, to entrust our life before men to Him, and then He will reward us openly.

"He who comes to God must believe that He is, and that *He is a rewarder* of those who diligently seek Him" (Heb. 11:6). Not on the strong or the fervent feeling with which I pray does the blessing of the closet depend, but on the love and the power of the Father to whom I there entrust my needs. And therefore the Master has only one desire: Remember that your Father is and that He sees and hears in secret; go there and stay there, and go again from there in the confidence that He will reward. Trust Him for it, and depend on Him. Prayer to the Father cannot be vain. He will reward you openly.

Still further to confirm this faith in the Father-love of God, Christ speaks a third word: *"Your Father knows the things you have need of before you ask Him."* At first sight, it might appear as if this thought made prayer less needed: God knows far better than we what we need. But as we get a deeper insight into what prayer really is, this truth will help much to strengthen our faith. It will teach us that we do not need, as the heathen, with the multitude and urgency of our words, to compel an unwilling God to listen to us. It will lead to a holy thoughtfulness and silence in prayer as it suggests the question: Does my Father really know that I need this? It will—when once we have been led by the Spirit to the certainty that our request is indeed something that, according to the Word, we do need for God's glory—give us wonderful confidence to say, "My Father knows I need it and must have it." And if there is any delay in the answer, it will teach us in quiet perseverance to hold on: *Father, you know* I need it.

O the blessed liberty and simplicity of a child that Christ our Teacher would gladly cultivate in us as we draw near to God. Let us look up to the Father until His Spirit works it in us. Let us sometimes in our prayers, when we are in danger of being so occupied with our fervent, urgent petitions that we forget that the Father knows and hears, let us hold still and just quietly say: "My Father sees, my Father hears, my Father knows." It will help our faith to take the answer, and to say: "We know that we have what we have requested of Him" (see 1 John 5:15).

And now, all you who have recently entered the school of Christ to be taught to pray, take these lessons, practice them, and trust Him to perfect you in them. Dwell often in the inner chamber with the door shut—shut in from men, shut up with God. It is there *the Father* waits for you, there Jesus will teach you to pray. To be alone in secret with *the Father*: this is your highest joy. To be assured that *the Father* will openly reward the secret prayer so that it cannot remain unblessed: this is your strength day by day. And to know that *the Father* knows that you need what you ask: this is your liberty to bring every need, in the assurance that your God will supply it according to His riches in glory in Christ Jesus (see Eph. 4:19).

"LORD, TEACH US TO PRAY."

Blessed Savior! With my whole heart I bless You for the appointment of the inner chamber, as the school where You meet each of Your pupils alone and reveal to him the Father. O my Lord! Strengthen my faith so that in the Father's tender love and kindness that as often as I feel sinful or troubled, the first instinctive thought may be to go where I know the Father waits for me and where prayer never can go unblessed. Let the thought that He knows my need before I ask bring me, in great restfulness of faith, to trust that He will give what His child requires. O let the place of secret prayer become to me the most beloved spot of earth.

And, Lord! Hear me as I pray that You would everywhere bless the closets of Your believing people. Let Your wonderful revelation of a Father's tenderness free all young Christians from every thought of secret prayer as a duty or a burden, and lead them to regard it as the highest privilege of their life, a joy and a blessing. Bring back all who are discouraged because they cannot find strength to bring You in prayer. O teach them to understand that they need only come with their emptiness to Him who has all to give and delights to do it. Not what they have to bring the Father, but what the Father waits to give them is their one thought.

And bless especially the inner chamber of all Your servants who are working for You as the place where God's truth and God's grace are revealed to them, where they are daily anointed with fresh oil, where their strength is renewed, and where the blessings are received in faith, with which they are to bless their fellowmen. Lord, draw us all in the closet nearer to Yourself and the Father. Amen.

FOR FURTHER THOUGHT

1. *What is the first thing Jesus taught His disciples about their place of prayer? Why is that first lesson important to them then and to you today?*

2. *What are the conditions for you to be openly rewarded by your heavenly Father for your life of prayer?*

3. *Why do you think it is important for you to dwell often in the "inner chamber"—away from other people and with God only?*

LESSON 4

"IN THIS MANNER, THEREFORE, PRAY" OR, THE MODEL PRAYER

"In this manner, therefore, pray:
Our Father in heaven. . ."
MATTHEW 6:9

EVERY teacher knows the power of example. He not only tells the child what to do and how to do it, but shows him how it really can be done. In condescension to our weakness, our heavenly Teacher has given us the very words we are to take with us as we draw near to our Father. We have in them a form of prayer in which there breathe the freshness and fullness of the eternal life. So simple that the child can speak it, so divinely rich that it comprehends all that God can give. A form of prayer that becomes the model and inspiration for all other prayer, and yet always draws us back to itself as the deepest utterance of our souls before our God.

"Our Father in heaven!" To appreciate this word of adoration fully, I must remember that none of the saints in scripture had ever ventured to address God as their Father. The invocation places us at once in the center of the wonderful revelation the Son came to make of His Father, our Father, too.

It comprehends the mystery of redemption—Christ delivering us from the curse so that we might become the children of God. The mystery of regeneration—the Spirit in the new birth giving us the new life. And the mystery of faith—before the redemption is accomplished or understood, the word is given on the lips of the disciples to prepare them for the blessed experience still to come. The words are the key to the whole prayer, to all prayer. It takes time, it takes life to study them, and it will take eternity to understand them fully. The knowledge of God's Father-love is the first and simplest, but also the last and highest lesson in the school of prayer. It is in the personal relationship to the living God, and the personal conscious fellowship of love with Himself, that prayer begins.

It is in the knowledge of God's fatherliness, revealed by the Holy Spirit, that the power of prayer will be found to root and grow. In the infinite tenderness and compassion and patience of the infinite Father, in His loving readiness to hear and to help, the life of prayer has its joy. O let us take time, until the Spirit has made these words to us spirit and truth, filling heart and life: "Our Father in heaven." Then we are indeed within the veil, in the secret place of power where prayer always prevails.

"Hallowed be Your name" (Matt. 6:9). There is something here that strikes us at once. While we ordinarily first bring our own needs to God in prayer, and then think of what belongs to God and His interests, the Master reverses the order. First, *Your* name, *Your* kingdom, *Your* will; then, give *us*, forgive *us*, lead *us*, deliver *us*. The lesson is of more importance than we think. In true worship, the Father must be first, must be all. The sooner I learn to forget myself in the desire that *He* may be glorified, the richer will the blessing be that prayer will bring to me. No one ever loses by what he sacrifices for the Father.

This must influence all our prayer. There are two sorts of prayer: personal and intercessory. The latter ordinarily occupies the lesser part of our time and energy. This must not be. Christ has opened the school of prayer specifically to train intercessors for the great work of bringing down, by their faith and prayer, the blessings of His work and love on the world around them. There can be no deep growth in prayer unless this is made our aim.

> *T*he knowledge of God's Father-love is the first and simplest, but also the last and highest lesson in the school of prayer.

The little child may ask of the father only what it needs for itself; and yet it soon learns to say, "Give some for sister, too." But the grownup son, who only lives for the father's interest and takes charge of the father's business, asks more largely and gets all that is asked. And Jesus wants to train us to the blessed life of consecration and service, in which our interests are all subordinate to the name, and the kingdom and the will of the Father. O let us live for this and let, on each act of adoration, "Our Father!" there follow in the same breath, *Your* name, *Your* kingdom, *Your* will—for this we look up and long.

"Hallowed be Your name." What name? This new name of Father. The word *holy* is the central word of the Old Testament, the *name* Father of the New. In this name of love, all the holiness and glory of God are now to be revealed. And how is the name to be hallowed? By God Himself: "And I will sanctify My great name. . .which you have profaned" (Ezek. 36:23). Our prayer must be that in ourselves, in all God's children, in the presence of the world, that God Himself would reveal the holiness, the divine power, the hidden glory of the name of Father. The Spirit of the Father is the *Holy* Spirit, and it is only when we yield ourselves to be led by Him that the name will be hallowed in our prayers and our lives. Let us learn the prayer: "Our Father, hallowed be Your name."

"*Your kingdom come*" (Matt. 6:10). The Father is a King, and He has a kingdom. The son and heir of a king has no higher ambition than the glory of his father's kingdom. In time of war or danger, this becomes his passion; he can think of nothing else. The children of the Father are here in the enemy's territory, where the kingdom, which is in heaven, is not yet fully revealed. What is more natural than that, when they learn to hallow the Father-name, they should long and cry with deep enthusiasm: "Your kingdom come."

> he Spirit of the Father is the Holy Spirit, and it is only when we yield ourselves to be led by Him that the name will be hallowed in our prayers and our lives.

The coming of the kingdom is the one great event on which the revelation of the Father's glory, the blessedness of His children, and the salvation of the world depends. On our prayers, too, the coming of the kingdom waits. Shall we not join in the deep longing cry of the redeemed: "Your kingdom come"? Let us learn it in the school of Jesus.

"*Your will be done on earth as it is in heaven*" (Matt. 6:10). This request is too frequently applied alone to the *suffering* of the will of God. In heaven God's will is *done*, and the Master teaches the child to ask that the will may be done on earth just as in heaven: in the spirit of adoring submission and ready obedience. Because the will of God is the glory of heaven, the doing of it is the blessedness of heaven. As the will is done, the kingdom of heaven comes into the heart. And wherever faith has accepted the Father's love, obedience accepts the Father's will. The surrender to and the prayer for a life of heaven-like obedience, is the spirit of childlike prayer.

"*Give us this day our daily bread.*" (Matt. 6:11). When first the child has yielded himself to the Father in the care for His name, His kingdom, and His will, he has full liberty to ask for his daily bread. A master cares for the food of his servant, a general of his soldiers, a father of his child. And will not the Father in heaven care for the child who has in prayer given himself up to His interests?

We may indeed in full confidence say: "Father, I live for Your honor and Your work. I know You care for me." Consecration to God and His will gives wonderful liberty in prayer for temporal things. Then the whole earthly life is given to the Father's loving care.

"*And forgive us our debts, as we forgive our debtors*" (Matt. 6:12). As bread is the first need of the body, so forgiveness is for the soul. And the provision for the one is as sure as for the other. We are children, but sinners, too, and our right of access to the Father's presence we owe to the precious blood and the forgiveness it has won for us. Let us beware of the prayer for forgiveness becoming a formality. Only what is really confessed is really forgiven.

Let us in faith accept the forgiveness as promised: as a spiritual reality, as an actual transaction between God and us, as the entrance into all the Father's love and all the privileges of children. Such forgiveness, as a living experience, is impossible without a forgiving spirit to others. As *forgiven* expresses the heavenward, so *forgiving* the earthward, the relation of God's child. In each prayer to the Father, I must be able to say that I know of no one whom I do not heartily love.

"And do not lead us into temptation, but deliver us from the evil one" (Matt. 6:13). Our daily bread, the pardon of our sins, and then our being kept from all sin and the power of the evil one—in these three requests all our personal need is understood. The prayer for bread and pardon must be accompanied by the surrender to live in all things in holy obedience to the Father's will, and the believing prayer in everything to be kept by the power of the indwelling Spirit from the power of the evil one.

> *O*ur daily bread, the pardon of our sins, and then our being kept from all sin and the power of the evil one—in these three requests all our personal need is understood.

Children of God! It is in this way that Jesus wants to have us pray to the Father in heaven. O let His name and kingdom and will have the first place in our love. Then His providing and pardoning and keeping love will be our sure portion. So the prayer will lead us up to the true childlife: the Father all to the child, the Father all for the child.

We shall understand how Father and child, the *Your* and the *our*, are all one, and how the heart that begins its prayer with the God-devoted *Your* will have the power in faith to speak out the *Our*, too. Such prayer will, indeed, be the fellowship and interchange of love, always bringing us back in trust and worship to Him who is not only the Beginning but the End: *"For Yours is the kingdom and the power and the glory forever. Amen"* (Matt. 6:13). Son of the Father, teach us to pray, "*Our Father.*"

"LORD, TEACH US TO PRAY."

You who are the only begotten Son, teach us, we ask you, to pray, "*Our Father.*" We thank You, Lord, for these living, blessed words You have given us. We thank You for the millions who in them have learned to know and worship the Father, and for what they have been to us. Lord, it is as if we needed days and weeks in Your school with each separate request; so deep and full are they. But we look to You to lead us deeper into their meaning. Do it, we pray, for Your Name's sake;

Your name is Son of the Father.

Lord! You once said, "No one knows who the Son is except the Father, and who the Father is except the Son, and the one to whom the Son wills to reveal Him" (Luke 10:22). And again, "I have declared to them Your name, and will declare it, that the love with which You loved Me may be in them, and I in them" (John 17:26). Lord Jesus, reveal to us the Father. Let His name, His infinite Father-love, the love with which He loved You, according to Your prayer, *be in us*. Then will we rightly say, "*Our Father!*" Then shall we understand Your teaching, and the first spontaneous breathing of our heart will be: "Our Father, Your name, Your kingdom, Your will." And we shall bring our needs and our sins and our temptations to Him in the confidence that the love of such a Father cares for all.

Blessed Lord! We are Your students, and we trust You. Teach us to pray, "*Our Father.*" Amen.

FOR FURTHER THOUGHT

1. *Why is the knowledge of God's Father-love so important for your life of prayer? How can you best attain that knowledge and live in it in every way?*
2. *What is the one condition under which your prayers and your life will hallow, or lift up as holy, the name of your heavenly Father?*
3. *What are your three personal needs to be brought to God in prayer? Why are they so important?*

LESSON 5

"ASK, AND IT WILL BE GIVEN TO YOU," OR, THE CERTAINTY OF THE ANSWER TO PRAYER

"Ask, and it will be given to you; seek, and you will find;
knock, and it will be opened to you. For everyone
who asks receives, and he who seeks finds,
and to him who knocks it will be opened."
MATTHEW 7:7–8

You ask and do not receive, because you ask amiss.
JAMES 4:3

OUR Lord returns here in the Sermon on the Mount a second time to speak of prayer. The first time, He had spoken of the Father who is to be found in secret, and rewards openly, and had given us the pattern prayer (Matt. 6:5–15). Here He wants to teach us what in all scripture is considered the chief thing in prayer: the assurance that prayer will be heard and answered.

Observe how He uses words that mean almost the same thing, and each time repeats the promise distinctly: "You *will* receive, you *will* find, it *will* be opened to you," and then gives as ground for such assurance the law of the kingdom: "Everyone who asks *receives*, and he who seeks *finds*, and to him who knocks *it will be opened*." We cannot but feel how in this six-fold repetition He wants to impress deep on our minds this one truth: that we may and must most confidently expect an answer to our prayer. Next to the revelation of the Father's love, there is, in the whole course of the school of prayer, not a more important lesson than this: Everyone who asks receives.

In the three words the Lord uses—*ask, seek, knock*—a difference in meaning has been sought. If such was indeed His purpose, then the first, *ask*, refers to the gifts we pray for. But I may ask and receive the gift without the Giver. *Seek* is the word scripture uses of God Himself; Christ assures me that I can find Him. But it is not enough to find God in time of need without coming to abiding fellowship:

Knock speaks of admission to dwell with Him and in Him. Asking and receiving the gift would therefore lead to seeking and finding the Giver, and this again to the knocking and opening of the door of the Father's home and love. One thing is sure: The Lord wants us to count most certainly on it that asking, seeking, and knocking cannot be in vain. Receiving an answer, finding God, and the opened heart and home of God are the certain fruit of prayer.

That the Lord should have thought it necessary in so many forms to repeat the truth is a lesson of deep importance. It proves that He knows our heart—how doubt and distrust toward God are natural to us, and how easily we are inclined to rest in prayer as a religious work without an answer. He knows, too, how even when we believe that God is the hearer of prayer, believing prayer that lays hold of the promise is something spiritual, too high and difficult for the halfhearted disciple. He, therefore, at the very outset of His instruction to those who wanted to learn to pray seeks to lodge this truth deep into their hearts: Prayer does benefit much; ask and you *will* receive; *everyone* who asks receives.

This is the fixed eternal law of the kingdom: If you ask and do not receive, it must be because there is something missing or needed in the prayer. Hold on. Let the word and Spirit teach you to pray rightly, but do not let go of the confidence He seeks to waken in you: Everyone who asks receives.

> Next to the revelation of the Father's love, there is, in the whole course of the school of prayer, not a more important lesson than this: Everyone who asks receives.

"Ask, and it will be given to you." Christ has no mightier stimulus to persevering prayer in His school than this. As a child has to prove a sum to be correct, so the proof that we have prayed rightly is *the answer*. If we don't ask and receive, it is because we have not learned to pray rightly. Let every learner in the school of Christ therefore take the Master's word in all simplicity: Everyone who asks receives.

He had good reasons for speaking so unconditionally. Let us beware of weakening the Word with our human wisdom. When He tells us heavenly things, let us believe Him. His Word will explain itself to him who believes it fully. If questions and difficulties arise, let us not seek to have them settled before we accept the Word. No! Let us entrust them all to Him as His to solve. Our work is first and fully to accept and hold firmly His promise. Let in our inner chamber, in the inner chamber of our heart, too, the Word be inscribed in letters of light: Everyone who asks receives.

According to this teaching of the Master, prayer consists of two parts and has two sides: a human and a divine. The human is the asking, the divine is the giving. Or, to look at both from the human side, there is the asking and the receiving—the two halves that make up a whole. It is as if He wanted to tell us that we are not to rest without an answer, because this is the will of God, the rule in the Father's family: Every childlike, believing petition is granted. If no answer comes, we are not to sit down in the laziness that calls itself resignation and suppose that it is not God's will to give an answer. No! There must be something in the prayer that is not as God wants to have it: childlike and believing. We must seek for grace to pray so that the answer may come. It is far easier to the flesh to submit without the answer than to yield itself to be searched and purified by the Spirit until it has learned to pray the prayer of faith.

> *According to this teaching of the Master, prayer consists of two parts and has two sides: a human and a divine. The human is the asking, the divine is the giving.*

It is one of the terrible marks of the diseased state of Christian life in these days that there are so many who rest content without the distinct experience of answer to prayer. They pray daily, they ask many things, and trust that some of them will be heard, but know little of direct, definite answer to prayer as the rule of daily life! And it is this that the Father desires: He seeks daily communication with His children in listening to and granting their petitions. He desires that I should come to Him day by day with distinct requests, and He desires day by day to do for me what I ask. It was in His answer to prayer that the saints of old learned to know God as the living One and were stirred to praise and love (Psalm 34, 66:19, 116:1). Our Teacher waits to imprint this upon our minds: Prayer and its answer—the child asking and the father giving—belong to each other.

There may be cases in which the answer is a refusal because the request is not according to God's Word, as when Moses asked to enter Canaan. But still there was an answer. God did not leave His servant in uncertainty concerning His will. The gods of the heathen are dumb and cannot speak. Our Father lets His child know when He cannot give him what he asks, and he withdraws his petition, even as the Son did in Gethsemane. Both Moses the servant and Christ the Son knew that what they asked was not according to what the Lord had spoken. Their prayer was the humble request to see if it was not possible for the decision to be changed.

God will teach those who are teachable and give Him time, by His Word and Spirit, whether their request is according to His will or not. Let us withdraw the request if it is not according God's mind, or persevere until the answer comes. Prayer is appointed to obtain the answer. It is in prayer and its answer that the interchange of love between the Father and His child takes place.

How deep the estrangement of our heart from God must be that we find it so difficult to grasp such promises. Even while we accept the words and believe their truth, the faith of the heart that fully has them and rejoices in them comes so slowly. It is because our spiritual life is still so weak, and the capacity for taking God's thoughts is so feeble. But let us look to Jesus to teach us as no one but He can teach. If we take His words in simplicity and trust Him by His Spirit to make them within us life and power, they will so enter into our inner being so that the spiritual divine reality of the truth they contain will indeed take possession of us, and we shall not rest content until every petition we offer is taken heavenward on Jesus' own words: "Ask, and it will be given to you."

> *L*et us take these words just as they were spoken. Let us not allow human reason to weaken their force. Let us take these words as Jesus gives them and believe them.

Beloved fellow disciples in the school of Jesus, let us set ourselves to learn this lesson well. Let us take these words just as they were spoken. Let us not allow human reason to weaken their force. Let us take these words as Jesus gives them and believe them. He will teach us in due time how to understand them fully. Let us begin by implicitly believing them. Let us take time, as often as we pray, to listen to His voice: Everyone who asks receives. Let us not make the feeble experiences of our unbelief the measure of what our faith may expect. Let us seek, not only just in our seasons of prayer but at all times, to hold firmly the joyful assurance: Man's prayer on earth and God's answer in heaven are meant for each other. Let us trust Jesus to teach us so to pray so that the answer can come. He will do it if we hold firmly the word He gives today: "Ask, and you will receive."

"Lord, teach us to pray."

Lord Jesus! Teach me to understand and believe what You have now promised me. It is not hidden from You, my Lord, with what the reasonings my heart seeks to satisfy itself when no answer comes. There is the thought that my prayer is not in harmony with the Father's secret plan, that there is perhaps something better You would give me, or that prayer as fellowship with God is blessing enough without an answer. And yet, my blessed Lord, I find in Your teaching on prayer that You did not speak of these things but said plainly that prayer may and must expect an answer. You assure us that this is the fellowship of a child with the Father: The child asks and the Father gives.

Blessed Lord! Your words are faithful and true. It must be because I pray wrongly that my experience of answered prayer is not clearer. It must be because I live too little in the Spirit that my prayer is too little in the Spirit, that the power for the prayer of faith is lacking.

Lord! Teach me to pray. Lord Jesus, I trust You for it. Teach me to pray in faith. Lord, teach me this lesson of today! Everyone who asks receive. Amen.

FOR FURTHER THOUGHT

1. *In His teaching on prayer, Jesus used the words* ask, seek, *and* knock. *What is the significance of these three words, and how do they apply to your personal prayer life?*
2. *According to Jesus' teaching, prayer consists of what two parts. What are they, who fulfills them, and what role do they play in your life of prayer?*
3. *Why is it important for you to take specific requests to God, rather than just praying a general "Your will be done" prayer?*

LESSON 6

"HOW MUCH MORE," OR,
THE INFINITE FATHERLINESS OF GOD

*"Or what man is there among you who, if his son asks for bread, will
give him a stone? Or if he asks for a fish, will he give him a serpent?
If you then, being evil, know how to give good gifts to your
children, how much more will your Father who is in
heaven give good things to those who ask Him!"*
MATTHEW 7:9–11

IN these words our Lord proceeds further to confirm what He said of the certainty of an answer to prayer. To remove all doubt, and to show us on what sure ground His promise rests, He appeals to what everyone has seen and experienced here on earth.

We are all children, and we know what we expected of our fathers. We are fathers (or continually see them), and everywhere we see it as the most natural thing there can be for a father to hear his child. And the Lord asks us to look up from earthly parents, of whom the best are but evil, and to calculate *How much more* the heavenly Father will give good gifts to those who ask Him.

Jesus wants to lead us up to see that as much greater as God is than sinful man, *so much greater* our assurance ought to be that He will more surely than any earthly father grant our childlike petitions. As much greater as God is than man, *so much surer* is that prayer will be heard with the Father in heaven than with a father on earth.

As simple and easily understood as this parable is, so deep and spiritual is the teaching it contains. The Lord wants to remind us that the prayer of a child owes its influence entirely to the relationship in which he stands to the parent. The prayer can exert that influence only when the child is really living in that relationship—in the home, in the love, in the service of the Father. The power of the promise, "Ask, and it will be given to you" lies in the loving relationship between us as children and the Father in heaven. When we live and walk in that relationship, the prayer of faith and its answer will be the natural result. And so the lesson we have today in the school of prayer is this: Live as a child of God;

then you will be able to pray as a chi... a child you will m... ssuredly be heard.

And what is the true child-life? The... child who by choice forsakes the father's can be found in a... me. The presence and love and obedience of the fat who finds no pl... in the obtain what he wants and needs will surely b... who still think... and to whom the interaction and will and honor a...pointed. On the ...k and his life will find that it is the father's joy to grant... of the father are, he ...of

Scripture says, "For as many as are *led* by the Sp...uests. God" (Rom. 8:14). The childlike privilege of asking... of God, these a... childlike life under the leading of the Spirit. He who ... is inseparable f... the Spirit in his life will be led by Him in his prayers, too. And he will fin... Fatherlike giving is the divine response to childlike living.

> *T*he Lord asks us to look up from earthly parents, of whom the best are but evil, and to calculate how much more the heavenly Father will give good gifts to those who ask Him.

To see what this childlike living is, in which childlike asking and believing have their ground, we need only notice what our Lord teaches in the Sermon on the Mount about the Father and His children. In it, the prayer promises are imbedded in the life precepts; the two are inseparable. They form one whole, and he alone can count on the fulfillment of the promise who accepts, too, all that the Lord has connected with it. It is as if in speaking the word, "Ask, and you will receive," He says: I give these promises to those whom in the beatitudes I have pictured in their childlike poverty and purity, and of whom I have said, "They shall be called the children of God" (see Matt. 5: 3–9), to children who "Let your light so shine before men, that they may see your good works and glorify your Father in heaven" (5:16); to those who walk in love, "that you may be sons of your Father in heaven" (5:45) and who seek to be perfect "just as your Father in heaven is perfect" (5:48); to those whose fasting and praying and charity (6:1–18) is not before men, but before "your Father who sees in secret"; who forgive even as "your heavenly Father will also forgive you" (6:14); who trust the heavenly Father in all earthly need, seeking first the kingdom of God and His righteousness (6:26–32); who not only say, "'Lord, Lord'. . .but does the will of My Father in heaven" (7:21). Such are the children of the Father, and such is the life in the Father's love and service. In such a child-life answered prayers are certain and abundant.

But will not such teaching discourage the weak one? If we are first to conform to this portrait of a child, must not many give up all hope of answers to prayer? The difficulty is removed if we think again of the blessed name of father and child.

A child is wea...d there is a ...rence among children in age and gift. The
Lord does n...mand of us ...fulfillment of the law but only the childlike
and wholeh...d surrender ...as a child with Him in obedience and truth.
Nothing n... ...ut also, no...ss.

The ...must have ...ole heart. When this is given, and He sees the
child wit... ...est purpose...eady will seeking in everything to be and live as
a child...is prayer w...nt with Him as the prayer of a child. Let anyone
simply...nestly beg...study the Sermon on the Mount and take it as his
guide...nd then h...l find, notwithstanding weakness and failure, an ever-
gro...rty to clai...e fulfillment of its promises in regard to prayer. In the
na...her and...d he has the pledge that his petitions will be granted.

> *The Lord does not demand of us a perfect fulfillment of
> the law but only the childlike and wholehearted surrender to
> live as a child with Him in obedience and truth.*

is the one chief thought on which Jesus dwells here, and which He would
His students take in. He wants us to see that the secret of effectual prayer
to have the heart filled with the Father-love of God. It is not enough for
know that God is a Father, He would have us take time to come under the
impression of what that name implies. We must take the best earthly father
know, and we must think of the tenderness and love with which he regards the
request of his child, the love and joy with which he grants every reasonable desire.
We must then, as we think in adoring worship of the infinite love and fatherliness of God, consider with how much more tenderness and joy He sees us come
to Him, and gives us what we ask rightly. And then, when we see how much this
divine arithmetic is beyond our comprehension, we feel how impossible it is for us
to apprehend God's readiness to hear us. Then He would have us come and open
our heart for the Holy Spirit to shed abroad God's Father-love there.

Let us do this not only when we want to pray, but let us yield heart and life
to dwell in that love. The child who only wants to know the love of the father
when he has something to ask will be disappointed. But he who lets God be
Father always and in everything, who desires to desperately live his whole life in
the Father's presence and love, who allows God in all the greatness of His love to be
a Father to him—he will experience most gloriously that a life in God's infinite
fatherliness and continual answers to prayer are inseparable.

Beloved fellow disciple, we begin to see why we know so little of daily answers
to prayer, and what the chief lesson is that the Lord has for us in His school. It is
all in the name of Father. We thought of new and deeper insight into some of the
mysteries of the prayer world as what we should get in Christ's school. He tells

us the first is the highest lesson: We must learn to say well, "Abba, Father!" and "Our Father in heaven." He who can say this has the key to all prayer. In all the compassion with which a father listens to his weak or sickly child, in all the joy with which he hears his stammering child, in all the gentle patience with which he bears with a thoughtless child, we must, as in so many mirrors, study the heart of our Father until every prayer is borne upward on the faith of this divine word: "*How much more* will your Father who is in heaven give good things to those who ask Him."

"LORD, TEACH US TO PRAY."

Blessed Lord! You know that this, though it is one of the first and simplest and most glorious lessons in Your school, is to our hearts one of the hardest to learn. We know so little of the love of the Father. Lord, teach us to so live with the Father that His love may be to us nearer, clearer, dearer than the love of any earthly father. And let the assurance of His hearing our prayer be as much greater than the confidence in an earthly parent, as the heavens are higher than earth, as God is infinitely greater than man. Lord, show us that it is only our unchildlike distance from the Father that hinders the answer to prayer, and lead us on to the true life of God's children. Lord Jesus, it is fatherlike love that wakens childlike trust. Reveal to us the Father and His tender, compassionate love so that we may become childlike and experience how in the child-life rests the power of prayer.

This is the one chief thought on which Jesus dwells here, and which He would have all His students take in. He wants us to see that the secret of effectual prayer is this: to have the heart filled with the Father-love of God.

Blessed Son of God! The Father loves You and has given You all things. And You love the Father and have done all things He commanded You, and therefore have the power to ask all things. Lord, give us Your own Spirit, the Spirit of the Son. Make us childlike, as You were on earth. And let every prayer be breathed in the faith that as the heaven is higher than the earth, so God's Father-love and His readiness to give us what we ask surpasses all we can think or conceive. Amen.

FOR FURTHER THOUGHT

1. *God calls you to live as His child. When you do that, you will be able to pray as a child and be heard as a child. What should that child-life look like?*
2. *Do you believe that God demands perfect fulfillment of His law in order for Him to hear and answer your prayers? If not, what do you think He demands?*
3. *What does Jesus teach is the key to effectual prayer?*

YOUR *Father in heaven."* Sadly, we speak of it only as the utterance of a reverential homage. We think of it as a figure borrowed from an earthly life, and only in some faint and shallow meaning to be used by God. We are afraid to take God as our own tender and compassionate father. He is a schoolmaster, or almost farther off than that, and knowing less about us—as inspector, who knows nothing about us except through our lessons. His eyes are not on the student, but on the book, and all alike must come up to the standard.

Now open the ears of the heart, timid child of God. Let it go sinking right down into the innermost depths of the soul. Here is the starting point of holiness, in the love and patience and compassion of our heavenly Father. We need not learn to be holy as a hard lesson at school, so that we may make God think well of us. We are to learn it at home with the Father to help us. God loves you not because you are clever, not because you are good, but because He is *your Father.* The Cross of Christ does not make God love us; it is the outcome and measure of His love to us. He loves all His children, the clumsiest, the dullest, the worst of His children. His love lies at the back of everything, and we must get upon that as the solid foundation of our religious life, not growing up into that, but growing up *out of it.* We must begin there, or our beginning will come to nothing. Do take hold of this mightily. We must go out of ourselves for any hope, or any strength, or any confidence. And what hope, what strength, what confidence may be ours now that we begin here, *your Father in heaven!*

We need to get in at the tenderness and helpfulness that lie in these words, and to rest upon it—*your Father.* Speak them over to yourself until something of the wonderful truth is felt by you. It means that I am bound by God by the closest and most tender relationship, that I have a right to His love and His power and His blessing, such as nothing else could give me. O the boldness with which we can draw near! O the great things we have a right to ask for! *Your Father.* It means that all His infinite love and patience and wisdom bend over *me* to help *me.* In this relationship lies not only the possibility of holiness; there is infinitely more than that.

We are to begin in the patient love of our Father. Think how He knows us apart, and by ourselves, in all our peculiarities, and in all our weaknesses and difficulties. The master judges by the result, but our Father judges by the effort. Failure does not always mean fault. He knows how much things cost, and weighs them where others only measure. *Your Father.* Think how great store His love sets by the poor beginnings of the little ones, clumsy and unmeaning as they may be to others. All this lies in this blessed relationship and infinitely more. Do not fear to take it all as your own.

---

[28] From *Thoughts on Holiness*, by Mark Guy Pearse. What is so beautifully said of the knowledge of God's fatherliness as the starting point of holiness is no less true of prayer.

LESSON 7

"HOW MUCH MORE THE HOLY SPIRIT," OR, THE ALL-COMPREHENSIVE GIFT

"If you then, being evil, know how to give good gifts to your children,
how much more will your heavenly Father give the Holy Spirit to
those who ask Him!"
LUKE 11:13

IN the Sermon on the Mount, the Lord had already given utterance to His wonderful *How much more?* Here in Luke, where He repeats the question, there is a difference. Instead of speaking, as then, of giving *good gifts*, He says, "How much more will your heavenly Father give the *Holy Spirit?*" He thus teaches us that the chief and the best of these gifts is the Holy Spirit, or rather, that in this gift all others are comprised. The Holy Spirit is the first of the Father's gifts, and the one He delights most to give. The Holy Spirit is therefore the gift we should first and chiefly to seek.

The unspeakable worth of this gift we can easily understand. Jesus spoke of the Spirit as "*the* Promise of the Father" (Acts 1:4), the one promise in which God's fatherhood revealed itself. The best gift a good and wise father can give a child on earth is his own spirit. This is the great object of a father in education—to reproduce in his child his own disposition and character. If the child is to know and understand his father; if, as he grows up, he is to enter into all his will and plans; if he is to have his highest joy in the father, and the father in him, he must be of one mind and spirit with him. And so it is impossible to conceive of God bestowing any higher gift on His child than this, His own Spirit. God is what He is through His Spirit; the Spirit is the very life of God. Just think what it means—God giving His own Spirit to His child on earth.

Or was not this the glory of Jesus as a Son on earth that the Spirit of the Father was in Him? At His baptism in the Jordan the two things were united: the voice proclaiming Him the beloved Son, and the Spirit descending on Him. And so the apostle says of us, "And because you are sons, God has sent forth the Spirit of His Son into your hearts, crying out, 'Abba, Father!'" (Gal. 4:6).

A king seeks in the whole education of his son to call forth in him a kingly spirit. Our Father in heaven desires to educate us as His children for the holy, heavenly life in which He dwells. For this He gives us, from the depths of His heart, His own Spirit. It was this which was the whole aim of Jesus when, after having made atonement with His own blood, He entered for us into God's presence so that He might obtain for us, and send down to dwell in us, the Holy Spirit. As the Spirit of the Father and the Son, the whole life and love of the Father and the Son are in Him, and coming down into us, He lifts us up into their fellowship. As Spirit of the Father, He sheds abroad the Father's love, with which He loved the Son, in our hearts and teaches us to live in it. As Spirit of the Son, He breathes in us the childlike liberty and devotion and obedience in which the Son lived upon earth. The Father can impart no higher or more wonderful gift than this: His own Holy Spirit, the Spirit of sonship.

> *he Holy Spirit is the first of the Father's gifts, and the one He delights most to give. The Holy Spirit is therefore the gift we should first and chiefly seek.*

This truth naturally suggests the thought that this first and chief gift of God must be the first and chief object of all prayer. For every need of the spiritual life this is the one thing we need: the Holy Spirit. All the fullness is in Jesus—the fullness of grace and truth, out of which we receive grace for grace. The Holy Spirit is the appointed communicator, whose special work it is to make Jesus and all there is in Him for us ours in personal appropriation and in blessed experience. He is the Spirit of life in Christ Jesus, and as wonderful as the life is, so wonderful is the provision by which such an agent is provided to communicate it to us. If we just yield ourselves entirely to the disposal of the Spirit and let Him have His way with us, He will reveal the life of Christ within us. He will do this with a Divine power, maintaining the life of Christ in us in uninterrupted continuity. Surely, if there is one prayer that should draw us to the Father's throne and keep us there, it is this: for the Holy Spirit, whom we as children have received, to stream into us and out from us in greater fullness.

In the variety of the gifts that the Spirit has to dispense, He meets the believer's every need. Just think of the names He bears. The Spirit of grace (Heb. 10:29), to reveal and impart all of grace there is in Jesus. The Spirit of faith (2 Cor. 4:13), teaching us to begin and go on and increase in ever believing. The Spirit of adoption and assurance (Gal. 4:6), who witnesses that we are God's children and inspires the confiding and confident Abba Father! The Spirit of truth (John 14:17), to lead into all truth and to make each word of God ours in deed and in truth. The

Spirit of prayer (Zech. 12:10), through whom we speak with the Father; prayer that must be heard. The Spirit of judgment and burning (Isa. 28:6), to search the heart, and convince of sin. The Spirit of holiness (Rom. 1:4), revealing and communicating the Father's holy presence within us. The Spirit of power (2 Tim. 1:7), through whom we are strong to testify boldly and work effectually in the Father's service. The Spirit of glory (1 Pet. 4:14), the pledge of our inheritance, the preparation and the foretaste of the glory to come. Surely the child of God needs just one thing to be able really to live as a child: It is to be filled with this Spirit.

And now, the lesson Jesus teaches us today in His school is this: that the Father is just longing to give Him to us if we will but ask in the childlike dependence on what He says: "If you. . .know how to give good gifts to your children, *how much more* will your heavenly Father give the Holy Spirit to those who ask Him." In the words of God's promise, "I will pour out my spirit" *abundantly* (see Joel 2:28), and of His command, "Be *filled* with the Spirit" (Eph. 5:18), we have the measure of what God is ready to give and what we may obtain.

> The Father can impart no higher or more wonderful gift than this: His own Holy Spirit, the Spirit of sonship.

As God's children, we have already received the Spirit. But we still need to ask and pray for His special gifts and operations as we require them. And not only this, but for Himself to take complete and entire possession and for His unceasing momentary guidance. Just as the branch, already filled with the sap of the vine, is always crying for the continued and increasing flow of that sap so that it may bring its fruit to perfection, so the believer, rejoicing in the possession of the Spirit, always thirsts and cries for more. And what the great Teacher wants us to learn is, that nothing less than God's promise and God's command may be the measure of our expectation and our prayer. We must be filled abundantly. He wants to have us ask this in the assurance that the wonderful *how much more* of God's Father-love is the pledge that when we ask we do most certainly receive.

Let us now believe this. As we pray to be filled with the Spirit, let us not seek for the answer in our feelings. All spiritual blessings must be received, that is, accepted or taken in faith.[29] Let me believe, the Father *gives* the Holy Spirit to His praying child. Even now, while I pray, I must say in faith: "I have what I ask, so the fullness of the Spirit is mine." Let us continue steadfast in this faith. On the strength of God's Word we know that we have what we ask. Let us, with thanksgiving that we have been heard, with thanksgiving for what we have

[29] The Greek word for receiving and taking is the same. When Jesus said, "Everyone who asks *receives,*" He used the same verb as at the Supper, "*Take,* eat," or on the resurrection morning, "*Receive,*" accept, take, "the Holy Spirit." Receiving not implies God's bestowment, but our acceptance.

received and taken and now hold as ours, continue steadfast in believing prayer that the blessing, *which has already been given* us, and which we hold in faith, may break through and fill our whole being. It is in such believing thanksgiving and prayer that our soul opens up for the Spirit to take entire and undisturbed possession. It is such prayer that not only asks and hopes, but takes and holds and inherits the full blessing. In all our prayer, let us remember the lesson the Savior wants to teach us today—that, *if there is one thing on earth we can be sure of, it is this: that the Father desires to have us filled with His Spirit, that He delights to give us His Spirit.*

> *H*e who has once learned to know the Father in prayer for himself learns to pray most confidently for others, too.

And when once we have learned to believe this for ourselves, and each day to take out of the treasure we hold in heaven, what liberty and power to pray for the outpouring of the Spirit on the Church of God, on all flesh, on individuals, or on special efforts! He who has once learned to know the Father in prayer for himself learns to pray most confidently for others, too. The Father gives the Holy Spirit to those who ask Him, not least, but most, when they ask for others.

"LORD, TEACH US TO PRAY."

Father in heaven! You sent Your Son to reveal Yourself to us, Your Father-love, and all that that love has for us. And He has taught us that the gift above all gifts that you would give in answer to prayer is the Holy Spirit.

O my Father, I come to You with this prayer; there is nothing I would—may I not say, I do—desire so much as to be filled with the Spirit, the Holy Spirit. The blessings He brings are so unspeakable, and they are just what I need. He sheds abroad Your love in the heart and fills it with Yourself. I long for this. He breathes the mind and life of Christ in me so that I live as He did, in and for the Father's love. I long for this. He provides power from on high for all my walk and work. I long for this. O Father! I ask You, give me this day the fullness of Your Spirit.

Father, I ask this, resting on the words of my Lord: "*How much more the Holy Spirit!*" I do believe that You hear my prayer, and I receive now what I ask. Father! I claim and I take it: the fullness of Your Spirit as mine. I receive the gift this day again as a faith gift. In faith I believe my Father works through the Spirit all He has promised. The Father delights to breathe His Spirit into His waiting child as He waits in fellowship with Himself. Amen.

FOR FURTHER THOUGHT

1. *What is the very first of the gifts of the Father through Jesus Christ? What is the gift you should seek first and above all others? Why should you so earnestly seek this gift?*

2. *As the Spirit of the Father, and as the Spirit of the Son, what gifts does the Holy Spirit impart to those who walk in childlike faith in Him?*

3. *What part do feelings play in being filled with the Spirit? Should you seek "feelings" when you ask God to fill you with His Spirit? If so, why? If not, why not?*

Lesson 8

"Because of His Persistence," or,

The Boldness of God's Friends

And He said to them, "Which of you shall have a friend,
and go to him at midnight and say to him, 'Friend, lend me three
loaves; for a friend of mine has come to me on his journey, and I have
nothing to set before him'; and he will answer from within and say,
'Do not trouble me; the door is now shut, and my children are with
me in bed; I cannot rise and give to you'? I say to you, though he will
not rise and give to him because he is his friend, yet because of his
persistence he will rise and give him as many as he needs."

Luke 11:5–8

THE first teaching to His disciples was given by our Lord in the Sermon on the Mount. It was nearly a year later that the disciples asked Jesus to teach them to pray. In answer He gave them a second time the Lord's Prayer, so teaching them what to pray. He then speaks of *how* they ought to pray, and repeats what He formerly said of God's fatherliness and the certainty of an answer. But in between He adds the beautiful Parable of the Friend at Midnight to teach them the twofold lesson that God does not only want us to pray for ourselves, but for the perishing around us, and that in such intercession great boldness of request is often needed, always lawful, and, yes, pleasing to God.

The parable is a perfect storehouse of instruction in regard to true intercession. There is, first, *the love* that seeks to help the needy around us: "*a friend of mine* has come to me." Then *the need* that urges to the cry: "*I have nothing* to set before him." Then follows the *confidence* that help is to be had: "Which of you shall have a *friend*. . .and say to him, '*Friend*, lend me three loaves.'" Then comes the unexpected *refusal*, "I *cannot* rise and give to you." Then again the *perseverance* that takes no refusal: "Because of his *persistence*." And lastly, the reward of such prayer: "He will rise and give him *as many as he needs*." A wonderful setting forth of the way of prayer and faith in which the blessing of God has so often been sought and found.

Let us confine ourselves to the chief thought that prayer as an appeal to the friendship of God. Then we shall find that two lessons are specially suggested. The one, that if we are God's friends, and come as such to Him, we must prove ourselves the friends of the needy. God's friendship to us and ours to others go hand in hand. The other, that when we come that way, we may use the utmost liberty in claiming an answer.

There is a twofold use of prayer: the one, to obtain strength and blessing for our own life, the other—the higher, the true glory of prayer, for which Christ has taken us into His fellowship and teaching—is intercession, where prayer is the royal power a child of God exercises in heaven on behalf of others and even of the kingdom.

We see it in scripture, how it was in intercession for others that Abraham and Moses, Samuel and Elijah, with all the holy men of old, proved that they had power with God and prevailed. It is when we give ourselves to be a blessing that we can specially count on the blessing of God. It is when we draw near to God as the friend of the poor and the perishing that we may count on His friendliness. The righteous man who is the friend of the poor is very specially the friend of God. This gives wonderful liberty in prayer. Lord! I have a needy friend I must help. As a friend I have undertaken to help him. In You I have a Friend whose kindness and riches I know to be infinite. I am sure You will give me what I ask. If I, being evil, am ready to do for my friend what I can, how much more will You, my heavenly Friend, now do for Your friend what he asks?

> If we are God's friends, and come as such to Him,
> we must prove ourselves the friends of the needy. God's
> friendship to us and ours to others go hand in hand.

The question might suggest itself whether the fatherhood of God does not give such confidence in prayer, that the thought of His friendship can hardly teach us anything more: a father is more than a friend. And yet, if we consider it, this pleading the friendship of God opens new wonders to us. That a child obtains what he asks of his father looks so perfectly natural that we almost count it the father's duty to give. But with a friend it is as if the kindness is more free and dependent, not on nature, but on sympathy and character. And then the relationship of a child is more that of perfect dependence: Two friends are more nearly on a level. And so our Lord, in seeking to unfold to us the spiritual mystery of prayer, would gladly have us approach God in this relationship, too, as those whom He has acknowledged as His friends, whose mind and life are in agreement with His.

But then we must be living as His friends. I am still a child even when I am a wanderer. But friendship depends upon the conduct. "You are My friends if you do whatever I command you" (John 15:14). "Do you see that faith was working together with his works, and by works faith was made perfect? And the Scripture was fulfilled which says, 'Abraham believed God. . .' And he was called *the friend of God*" (James 2:22–23). It is the Spirit, "*the same* Spirit," who leads us who also bears witness to our acceptance with God. "*Likewise*," the same Spirit helps us in prayer (see Rom. 8:26).

It is a life as the friend of God that gives the wonderful liberty to say, "I have a friend to whom I can go even at midnight." And how much more when I go in the very spirit of that friendliness, manifesting myself the very kindness I look for in God, seeking to help my friend as I want God to help me. When I come to God in prayer, He always looks to what the aim is of my petition. If it is merely for my own comfort or joy I seek His grace, I do not receive. But if I can say that it is that He may be glorified in my dispensing His blessings to others, I shall not ask in vain. Or if I ask for others, but want to wait until God has made me so rich, so that it is no sacrifice or act of faith to aid them, I shall not obtain. But if I can say that I have already undertaken for my needy friend, that in my poverty I have already begun the work of love, because I know I had a friend who wants to help me, my prayer will be heard. Oh, how we don't know how much the plea benefits—the friendship of earth looking in its need to the friendship of heaven: "He will give him as much as he needs."

> *It is a life as the friend of God that gives the wonderful liberty to say, "I have a friend to whom I can go even at midnight."*

But not always immediately. The one thing by which man can honor and enjoy his God is *faith*. Intercession is part of faith's training school. There our friendship with men and with God is tested. There it is seen whether my friendship with the needy is so real that I will take time and sacrifice my rest, will go even at midnight and not cease until I have obtained for them what I need. There it is seen whether my friendship with God is so clear that I can depend on Him not to turn me away and therefore pray on until He gives.

O what a deep heavenly mystery this is of persevering prayer. The God who has promised, who longs, whose fixed purpose it is to give the blessing, holds it back. It is to Him a matter of such deep importance that His friends on earth should know and fully trust their rich Friend in heaven that He trains them, in the school of delayed answer, to find out how their perseverance really does prevail, and what the mighty power is they can wield in heaven, if they simply set themselves to it.

There is a faith that sees the promise and embraces it, and yet does not receive it (Hebrews 11:13, 39). It is when the answer to prayer does not come, and the promise we are most firmly trusting appears to be of no effect, that the trial of faith, more precious than of gold, takes place. It is in this trial that the faith that has embraced the promise is purified and strengthened and prepared in personal, holy fellowship with the living God, to see the glory of God. It takes and holds the promise until it has received the fulfillment of what it had claimed in a living truth in the unseen but living God.

Let each child of God who is seeking to work the work of love in his Father's service take courage. The parent with his child, the teacher with his class, the visitor with his district, the Bible reader with his circle, the preacher with his hearers—each one who, in his little circle, has accepted and is bearing the burden of hungry, perishing souls—let them all take courage. Nothing is at first so strange to us as that God should really require persevering prayer, that there should be a real spiritual need for persistence. To teach us this, the Master uses this almost strange parable. If the unfriendliness of a selfish earthly friend can be conquered by persistence, how much more will it succeed with the heavenly Friend, who does so love to give, but is held back by our spiritual unfitness, our inability to possess what He has to give.

> *It is when the answer to prayer does not come, and the promise we are most firmly trusting appears to be of no effect, that the trial of faith, more precious than of gold, takes place.*

O let us thank Him that in delaying His answer He is educating us of our true position and the exercise of all our power with Him and training us to live with Him in the fellowship of undoubting faith and trust to be indeed the friends of God. And let us hold firmly to the threefold cord that cannot be broken: the hungry friend needing the help, the praying friend seeking the help, and the mighty Friend, loving to give as much as he needs.

"LORD, TEACH US TO PRAY."

My Blessed Lord and Teacher! I must come to You in prayer. Your teaching is so glorious, and yet too high for me to grasp. I must confess that my heart is too little to take in these thoughts of the wonderful boldness I may use with Your Father as my Friend. Lord Jesus, I trust You to give me Your Spirit with Your Word, and to make the Word living and powerful in my heart. I desire to keep Your Word of this day: "Because of his persistence he will rise and give him as many as he needs."

Lord, teach me more to know the power of persevering prayer. I know that in it the Father suits Himself to our need of time for the inner life to attain its growth and maturity, so that His grace may indeed be assimilated and made our very own. I know that He desires to train us as to the exercise of that strong faith that does not let Him go even in the face of seeming disappointment. I know He wants to lift us to that wonderful liberty, in which we understand how really He has made the dispensing of His gift dependent on our prayer. Lord, I know this: Teach me to see it in spirit and truth.

And may it now be the joy of my life to become the distributor of my rich Friend in heaven, to care for all the angry and perishing, even at midnight, because I know *my Friend* who always gives to him who perseveres, because of his persistence, as many as he needs. Amen.

FOR FURTHER THOUGHT

1. What is the relationship between being a friend of God and being a friend of those who need you to demonstrate His love to them?
2. Read John 15:14 and James 2:22–23. What must you do in order to be counted a "friend of God"? What are the prayer benefits of friendship with God?
3. What should be your response when an answer to prayer does not come—at least when you want it to come or in the manner you think it should come?

LESSON 9

"PRAY THE LORD OF THE HARVEST,"
OR, PRAYER PROVIDES LABORERS

Then He said to His disciples, "The harvest truly is plentiful,
but the laborers are few. Therefore pray the Lord of the
harvest to send out laborers into His harvest."
MATTHEW 9:37–38

THE Lord frequently taught His disciples *that* they must pray and *how*, but seldom *what* to pray. This He left to their sense of need and the leading of the Spirit. But here we have one thing He expressly enjoins them to remember: In view of the abundant harvest and the need for reapers, they must cry to the Lord of the harvest to send out laborers. Just as in the parable of the friend at midnight, He wants them to understand that prayer is not to be selfish. Here it is the power through which blessing can come to others. The Father is Lord of the harvest, and when we pray for the Holy Spirit, we must pray for Him to prepare and send laborers for the work.

Isn't it strange that He should ask His disciples to pray for this? Couldn't He have prayed Himself? And wouldn't one prayer of His accomplish more than a thousand of theirs? And God, the Lord of the harvest, did He not see the need? And wouldn't He, in His own good time, send laborers without their prayer? Such questions lead us into the deepest mysteries of prayer and its power in the kingdom of God. The answer to such questions will convince us that prayer is indeed a power on which the gathering of the harvest and the coming of the kingdom do in very truth depend.

Prayer is not about form or show. The Lord Jesus was Himself the truth, and everything He spoke was the deepest truth. It was when "He saw the multitudes, He was moved with compassion for them, because they were weary and scattered, like sheep having no shepherd" (Matt. 9:36) that He called on the disciples to pray for laborers to be sent among them. He did so because He really believed their prayer was needed and would help.

The veil that hides the invisible world from us was wonderfully transparent to the holy human soul of Jesus. He had looked long and deep and far into the hidden connection of cause and effect in the spiritual world. He had pointed out how in God's Word how, when God called men like Abraham and Moses, Joshua and Samuel and Daniel, and given them authority over men in His name, He had at the same time given them authority and right to call the powers of heaven to their aid when they needed them. He knew that as to these men of old, and to Himself for His time here on earth, the work of God had been entrusted, so it was now about to pass over into the hands of His disciples. He knew that when they were charged with this work, it would not be a mere matter of form or show, but that on them, and their being faithful or unfaithful, the success of the work would actually depend.

As a single individual, within the limitations of a human body and a human life, Jesus feels how little a short visit can accomplish among these wandering sheep He sees around Him, and He longs for help to have them properly cared for. And so He tells His disciples to begin to pray, and, when they have taken over the work from Him on earth, to make this one of their chief petitions in their prayer: that the Lord of the harvest Himself would send out laborers into His harvest. The God who entrusted them with the work, and made it to so large an extent dependent on them, gave them authority to apply to Him for laborers to help and made the supply dependent on their prayer.

> *The veil that hides the invisible world from us was wonderfully transparent to the holy human soul of Jesus. He had looked long and deep and far into the hidden connection of cause and effect in the spiritual world.*

How little Christians really feel and mourn the need for laborers in the fields of the world, which are so ripe for the harvest. And how little they believe that our labor supply depends on prayer, that prayer will really provide "as many as he needs" (Luke 11:8). Not that the lack of labor is not known or discussed. Not that efforts are not sometimes made to supply the need. But how little the burden of the sheep wandering without a Shepherd is really demonstrated in the faith that the Lord of the harvest *will*, in answer to prayer, send out the laborers, and in the solemn conviction that without this prayer, fields ready for reaping will be left to perish. And yet it is so. So wonderful is the surrender of His work to His Church, so dependent has the Lord made Himself on them as His Body through whom His work can be done, so real is the power the Lord gives His people to exercise in heaven and earth, that the number of laborers and the measure of the harvest actually depends on their prayer.

Solemn thought! O why do we not obey the command of the Master more heartily, and cry more earnestly for laborers? There are two reasons for this. The one is that we miss the compassion of Jesus, which pointed out the need for this request for prayer. When believers learn that to love their neighbors as themselves, that to live entirely for God's glory in their fellowmen, is the Father's first commandment to His redeemed ones, they will accept the perishing ones as the charge their Lord entrusted to them. And, accepting them not only as a field of labor but as the objects of loving care and interest, it will not be long before compassion toward the hopelessly perishing will touch their heart, and the cry will ascend with an earnestness until then unknown: Lord! Send laborers.

The other reason for the neglect of the command—the lack of faith—will then make itself felt but will be overcome as our compassion pleads for help. We believe too little in the power of prayer to bring about definite results. We do not live close enough to God, and we are not given up entirely enough to His service and kingdom to be capable of the confidence that He will give it in answer to our prayer. Let us pray for a life so one with Christ that His compassion may stream into us, and that His Spirit be able to assure us that our prayer avails.

> *Let us pray for a life so one with Christ that His compassion may stream into us, and that His Spirit be able to assure us that our prayer avails.*

Such prayer will ask and obtain a twofold blessing. There will first be a desire for an increase in the number of men entirely given up to the service of God. It is a terrible blot on the Church of Christ that there are times when men actually cannot be found for the service of the Master as ministers, missionaries, or teachers of God's Word. As God's children make this a matter of prayerful request in their own circle or church, it will be given. The Lord Jesus is now Lord of the harvest. He has been exalted to bestow the gifts—the gifts of the Spirit. His chief gifts are men filled with the Spirit. But the supply and distribution of these gifts depend on the cooperation between the Head and the members. It is only prayer that will lead to such cooperation. The believing requesters will be stirred to find the men and the means for the work.

The other blessing to be asked for will not be less. Every believer is a laborer. Not one of God's children has not been redeemed for service and has not his work waiting. It must be our prayer that the Lord would so fill all His people with the spirit of devotion that no one may be found standing idle in the vineyard. Wherever there is a complaint of the lack of helpers, or of fit helpers in God's work, prayer has the promise of a supply. There is no Sunday school or district visiting, no Bible reading or rescue work, where God is not ready and able to provide. It may take time and persistence in prayer, but the command of Christ to ask the Lord of the harvest is the pledge that the prayer will be heard. "I say to you, he will rise and give him as many as he needs."

Solemn, blessed thought! This power has been given to us in prayer to provide in the need of the world, to secure the servants for God's work. The Lord of the harvest will hear. Christ, who called us so specifically to pray this way, will support the prayers offered in His Name and interest. Let us set apart time and give all of ourselves to this part of our intercessory work. It will lead us into the fellowship of that compassionate heart of His that led Him to call for our prayers. It will elevate us to the insight of our royal position as those whose will counts for something with the great God in the advancement of His Kingdom. It will make us feel how we really are God's fellow workers on earth, to whom a share in His work has in downright earnest been entrusted. It will make us partakers in the anguish of the soul, but also in the soul satisfaction of Jesus, as we know how, in answer to our prayer, blessing has been given that otherwise would not have come.

"LORD, TEACH US TO PRAY."

Blessed Lord! You have today again given us another of Your wondrous lessons to learn. We humbly ask You to allow us to see accurately the spiritual realities of which You have been speaking. There is the harvest, which is so large and perishing, as it waits for sleepy disciples to give the signal for laborers to come. Lord, teach us to look out on it with a heart full of compassion and pity. There are so few laborers. Lord, show us how terrible is the sin of the lack of prayer and faith, of which this is the evidence. And there is the Lord of the harvest, so able and ready to send them out. Lord, show us how He indeed waits for the prayer for which He has promised His answer. And there are the disciples to whom the commission to pray has been given. Lord, show us how You can pour down Your Spirit and breathe upon them, so that Your compassion and the faith in Your promise will move us to unceasing, prevailing prayer.

> *This power has been given to us in prayer to provide in the need of the world, to secure the servants for God's work. The Lord of the harvest will hear.*

O our Lord! We cannot understand how You can entrust such work and give such power to men so apathetic and unfaithful. We thank You for all those whom You are teaching day and night to cry for laborers to be sent out. Lord, breathe Your Spirit on all Your children so that they may learn to live for this one thing alone—the kingdom and glory of their Lord—and become fully awake to the faith in what their prayer can accomplish. And let our hearts be filled with the assurance that prayer offered in living faith in the living God will bring certain and abundant answer. Amen.

For Further Thought

1. What, according to Jesus' command to pray for laborers, is the connection between your asking and God sending them?
2. Where can you find motivation and inspiration to pray for God to send laborers into the fields of the world, which are so ripe for harvest? What must you recognize about the need for laborers and God's promise to send them?
3. How can you be assured that God will hear your prayer for more laborers? How does that assurance motivate you to pray?

LESSON 10

"WHAT DO YOU WANT,"
OR, PRAYER MUST BE DEFINITE

So Jesus answered and said to him,
"What do you want Me to do for you?"
MARK 10:51, LUKE 18:41

THE blind man had been crying out loudly, and that a great deal, "Son of David, have mercy on me!" (Mark 10:47). The cry had reached the ear of the Lord, and He knew what the man wanted and was ready to grant it to him. But before He does it, He asks him, "*What do you want* Me to do for you?" He wants to hear from his own lips, not only the general request for mercy, but the distinct expression of what his desire was. Until he speaks it out, he is not healed.

There is now still many a petitioner to whom the Lord puts the same question, and who cannot, until it is answered, get the aid he asks. Our prayers must not be a vague appeal to His mercy or an indefinite cry for blessing, but a distinct expression of definite need. Not that His loving heart does not understand our cries, or is not ready to hear. But He desires it for our own sakes. Such definite prayer teaches us to know our own needs better. It demands time, thought, and self-examination to find out what our greatest need really is. It searches us and puts us to the test as to whether our desires are honest and real, such as we are ready to persevere in. It leads us to judge whether our desires are according to God's Word and whether we really believe we shall receive the things we ask for. It helps us to wait for the specific answer and to recognize it when it comes.

And yet how much of our prayer is vague and pointless. Some cry for mercy, but don't take the trouble to know what mercy must do for them. Others ask, perhaps, to be delivered from sin, but do not begin by bringing any sin by name from which the deliverance can be claimed. Still others pray for God's blessing on those around them, for the outpouring of God's Spirit on their land or on the world, and yet they have no special field where they wait and expect to see the answer. To every one of these the Lord says, "What do you want Me to do for you?"

Every Christian has only limited powers, and just as he must have his own specific field of labor in which he works, so it is with his prayers, too. Each believer has his own circle, family, friends, and neighbors. If he were to take one or more of these by name, he would find this really brings him into the training school of faith, which leads to personal and pointed dealing with his God. It is when in such distinct matters we have in faith claimed and received answers that our more general prayers will be believing and effective.

We all know with what surprise the whole civilized world heard of the way in which trained troops were repulsed by the Transvaal Boers at Majuba. And to what did they owe their success? In the armies of Europe, the solider fires on the enemy standing in large masses and never thinks of seeking an aim for every bullet. In hunting game, the Boer had learned a different lesson: His practiced eye knew to send every bullet on its special mission, to seek and find its man. Such aiming must gain the day in the spiritual world, too. As long as in prayer we just pour out our hearts in a multitude of petitions without taking time to see whether every petition is sent with the purpose and expectation of getting an answer, not many will reach the mark. But if, as in silence of the soul we bow before the Lord, we were ready to answer questions such as these: What is now really my desire? Do I desire it in faith, expecting to receive? Am I now ready to place and leave it there in the Father's bosom? Is it settled between God and me that I am to have the answer?—we should learn to pray in such a way that God will see and we would know what we really expect.

> *Our prayers must not be a vague appeal to His mercy or an indefinite cry for blessing, but a distinct expression of definite need.*

It is for this reason, among others, that the Lord warns us against the vain repetitions of the Gentiles, who expect to be heard because they pray so much (see Matt. 6:7–8). We often hear prayers of great earnestness and fervor, in which a multitude of petitions are poured forth, but to which the Savior would undoubtedly answer, "What do you want Me to do for you?"

If I am in a strange land, in the interests of the business my father owns, I would certainly write two different sorts of letters home. There will be family letters giving expression to the interaction to which affection prompts, and there will be business letters containing orders for what I need. There may also be letters in which both are found. The answers will correspond to the letters. To each sentence of the letters containing the family news I do not expect a special answer. But for each order I send, I am confident of an answer as to whether the desired article has been sent. In our dealings with God, the business element must not be lacking. With our expressions of need and sin, of love and faith and consecration, there must be the specific statement of what we ask and expect to receive. It is in the answer that the Father loves to give us a proof of His approval and acceptance.

But the word of the Master teaches us more. He does not say, "What do you *wish*?" but "What do you *want*?" One often wishes for a thing without willing it. I wish to have a certain item, but I find the price is too high, so I decide not take it. I *wish* but do not *will* to have it. The lazy man wishes to be rich, but does not will it. Many a man wishes to be saved, but perishes because he does not will it. The will rules the whole heart and life. If I really will to have something that is within my reach, I do not rest until I have it. When Jesus asks us, "What do you want?" He asks whether it is indeed our purpose to have what we ask for at any price, however great the sacrifice. Do you really will to have it enough that, though He waits to answer, you will not hold your peace until He hears you? Sadly, many prayers are wishes sent up for a short time and then forgotten, or sent up year after year as a matter of duty, while we remain content with the prayer without the answer.

> *With our expressions of need and sin, of love and faith and consecration, there must be the specific statement of what we ask and expect to receive.*

But, it may be asked, is it not best to make our wishes known to God, and then leave it to Him to decide what is best, without our seeking to assert our will? By no means! This is the very essence of the prayer of faith, to which Jesus sought to train His disciples, that it does not only make known its desire and then leave the decision to God. That would be the prayer of submission for cases in which we cannot know God's will. But the prayer of faith, finding God's will in some promise of the Word, pleads for that until it comes.

In Matthew 9:28, we read that Jesus said to the blind man, "*Do you believe that I am able to do this?*" In Mark He said, "*What do you want* Me to do for you?*" (10:51). In both cases, He said that faith had saved them. And He said to the Syrophenician woman, too, "great is your *faith*! Let it be to you as you *desire*" (Matt. 15:28). Faith is nothing but the purpose of the will resting on God's Word and saying, "I must have it." To believe truly is to will firmly.

But is not such a will at odds with our dependence on God and our submission to Him? By no means! Rather, it is the true submission that honors God. It is only when the child has yielded his own will in entire surrender to the Father that he receives from the Father the liberty and power to will what he desires. But when once the believer has accepted the will of God, as revealed through the Word and the Spirit, as his will, too, then it is the will of God that His child should use this renewed will in His service. The will is the highest power of the soul. Grace wants above everything to sanctify and restore this will, one of the chief traits of God's image, to full and free exercise. As a son who lives only for his father's interests, who seeks not his own but his father's will, is trusted by the father with his business, so God speaks to His child in all truth, "What do you want?"

It is often spiritual complacency that, under the appearance of humility, professes to have no will, because it fears the trouble of searching for the will of God, or, when that will is found, the struggle of claiming it in faith. True humility is always accompanied by strong faith, which only seeks to know what is according to the will of God, and then boldly claims the fulfillment of the promise: "You will ask *what you desire*, and it shall be done for you" (John 15:7).

"LORD, TEACH US TO PRAY."

Lord Jesus! Teach me to pray with all my heart and strength so that there may be no doubt with You or with me about what I have asked. May I know so well what I desire that, even as my requests are recorded in heaven, I can also record them on earth and note each answer as it comes. And may my faith in what Your Word has promised be so clear that the Spirit may indeed work within me the liberty to will that it will come. Lord! Renew, strengthen, and sanctify wholly my will for the work of effectual prayer.

> *I*t is only when the child has yielded his own will in entire surrender to the Father that he receives from the Father the liberty and power to will what he desires.

Blessed Savior! I pray that You will reveal to me the wonderful grace You show us, thus asking us to say what we desire that You should do, and promising to do whatever we desire. Son of God! I cannot fully understand it. I can only believe that You have indeed redeemed us wholly for Yourself, and that You seek to make the will, as our noblest part, Your most effective servant. Lord! I most unreservedly yield my will to You as the power through which Your Spirit is to rule my whole being. Let Him take possession of it, lead it into the truth of Your promises, and make it so strong in prayer that I may always hear Your voice saying, "Great is your faith! Let it be to you as you desire." Amen.

FOR FURTHER THOUGHT

1. Knowing that Jesus asks, "What do you want Me to do for you," how will you now pray when you have needs and burdens to bring before Him?

2. What is the benefit of praying for your family, friends, and neighbors by name, rather than praying a general prayer for the salvation of those around you without naming names?

3. Specific prayers are not at odds with our dependence on and submission to God. How does this kind of praying truly honor God?

LESSON 11

"BELIEVE THAT YOU RECEIVE,"
OR, THE FAITH THAT TAKES

"Therefore I say to you, whatever things you ask when you pray,
believe that you receive them, and you will have them."
MARK 11:24

WHAT a promise! So large, so divine, that our little hearts cannot take it in, and in every possible way we seek to limit it to what we think is safe or probable, instead of allowing it, in its quickening power and energy, just as He gave it, to enter in and to enlarge our hearts to the measure of what His love and power are really ready to do for us.

Faith is very far from being a mere conviction of the truth of God's Word or a conclusion drawn from certain premises. It is the ear that has heard God say what He will do, the eye that has seen Him doing it. Therefore, where there is true faith, it is impossible for the answer not to come. If we only see to it that we do the one thing that he asks of us as we pray: *Believe that you receive*, He will see to it that He does the thing He has promised: *"You will have them."*

The keynote of Solomon's prayer (2 Chronicles 6:4), "Blessed be the LORD God of Israel, *who has fulfilled with His hands* what *He spoke with His mouth* to my father David," is the keynote of all true prayer. It is the joyful adoration of a God whose *hand* always secures the fulfillment of what His *mouth* has spoken. Let us in this spirit listen to the promise Jesus gives, for each part of it has a divine message.

"Whatever things." At this first word our human wisdom begins to doubt and ask, "Can this possibly be literally true?" But if it isn't, why did the Master speak it, using the very strongest expression He could find: "Whatever things." And it is not as if this were the only time He spoke that way. Is it not He who also said, "If you can believe, *all things* are possible to him who believes" (Mark 9:23) and, "If you have faith as a mustard seed. . .*nothing* will be impossible for you" (Matt. 17:20)? Faith is so wholly the work of God's Spirit through His word in the prepared heart of the believing disciple that it is impossible for the fulfillment not to come. Faith is the pledge and forerunner of the coming answer.

Yes, "*Whatever things* you ask in prayer, *believing, you will receive*" (Matt. 21:22). The tendency of human reason is to interpose here with certain qualifying clauses, such as "if expedient" or "if according to God's will," to break the force of a statement that appears dangerous. Let us beware of dealing this way with the Master's words. His promise is most literally true. He wants His often-repeated "*whatever things*" to enter into our hearts and reveal to us how mighty the power of faith is, how truly the Head calls the members to share with Him in His power, how wholly our Father places His power at the disposal of the child who wholly trusts Him. In this "whatever things," faith is to have its food and strength: as we weaken it, we weaken faith.

The *whatever* is unconditional. The only condition is what is implied in the believing. Before we can believe, we must find out and know what God's will is. Believing is the exercise of a soul surrendered and given up to the influence of the Word and the Spirit. But when we believe, nothing shall be impossible. God forbid that we should try to bring down His *all things* to the level of what we think is possible. Rather, let us now simply take Christ's *whatever* as the measure and the hope of our faith. It is a seed word that will, if taken just as He gives it and kept in the heart, germinate and take root, fill our life with its fullness, and bring forth abundant fruit.

> Blessed be the Lord God of Israel, who has fulfilled with His hands what He spoke with His mouth to my father David." It is the joyful adoration of a God whose hand always secures the fulfillment of what His mouth has spoken.

"Whatever things *you ask when you pray.*" It is in prayer that these "whatever things" are to be brought to God, to be asked for and received from Him. The faith that receives them is the fruit of the prayer. In one aspect, there must be faith before there can be prayer, but in another, the faith is the result and the growth of prayer. In the personal presence of the Savior, and in communication with Him, faith rises to grasp what at first appeared too high. It is in prayer that we hold up our desire to the light of God's holy will, that our motives are tested, and that proof is given whether we ask indeed in the name of Jesus and only for the glory of God. It is in prayer that we wait for the leading of the Spirit to show us whether we are asking for the right thing and in the right spirit. It is in prayer that we become aware of our lack of faith, that we are led to say to the Father that we do believe, and that we prove the reality of our faith by the confidence with which we persevere. It is in prayer that Jesus teaches and inspires faith. He who waits to pray, or loses heart in prayer because he doesn't yet feel the faith needed to get the answer, will never learn to believe. He who begins to pray and ask will find the Spirit of faith is given nowhere so surely as at the foot of the throne.

"Believe that you receive." It is clear that what we are to believe is that we receive the very things we ask. The Savior does not hint that because the Father knows what is best, He may give us something else. The very mountain that faith tells to depart is cast into the sea.

There is a prayer in which in everything we make our requests known with prayer and supplication, and the reward is the sweet peace of God in our hearts and minds (see Phil. 4:6–7). This is the prayer of trust. It has reference to things of which we cannot find out if God is going to give us. As children, we make known our desires in countless things of daily life, and then leave it to the Father to give or not as He thinks best. But the prayer of faith of which Jesus speaks is something higher, something different. When, whether in the greater interests of the Master's work or in the lesser concerns of our daily life, the soul is led to see how there is nothing that so honors the Father like the faith that is assured that He will do what He has said in giving us whatever we ask for—and takes its stand on the promise as brought home by the Spirit—it may know with certainty that it receives exactly what it asks. Observe how clearly the Lord states this in Mark 11:23: "Whoever. . .does not doubt in his heart, but believes that *those things he says* will be done, he will have whatever he says." This is the blessing of the prayer of faith of which Jesus speaks.

> *T*here is a prayer in which in everything we make our requests known with prayer and supplication, and the reward is the sweet peace of God in our hearts and minds. This is the prayer of trust.

"Believe that *you receive.*" This is the word of central importance, of which the meaning is too often misunderstood. Believe that you receive! now, while praying, the thing you ask for. It may only be later that you shall have it in personal experience, that you shall see what you believe. But now, without seeing, you are to believe that it has already been given to you by the Father in heaven. The receiving or accepting of an answer to prayer is just like receiving or accepting Jesus or of pardon: It is a spiritual thing, an act of faith separate from all feeling. When I come as a supplicant and ask for forgiveness, I believe Jesus in heaven is for me, and so I receive or take from Him. When I come as a supplicant for a specific gift that is according to God's Word, I must believe that what I ask is given to me. I believe that I have it, I hold it in faith, and I thank God that it is mine. "And if we know that He hears us, whatever we ask, we know that we have the petitions that we have asked of Him" (1 John 5:15).

"And you will have them." That is, the gift that we first hold in faith as bestowed on us in heaven will also become ours in personal experience. But

will it be necessary to pray longer once we know we have been heard and have received what we asked? There are cases in which such prayer will not be needed, in which the blessing is ready to break through at once, if we simply hold firmly our confidence, and prove our faith by praising for what we have received, even in the face of our not yet having it in experience. There are other cases in which the faith that has received needs to be still further tested and strengthened in persevering prayer. Only God knows when everything in and around us is fully ripe for the manifestation of the blessing that has been given to faith. Elijah knew for certain that rain would come, for God had promised it. And yet he had to pray the seven times. And that prayer was no show or play. It was an intense spiritual reality both in the heart of him who lay there pleading and in heaven where it has its effectual work to do.

It is "through faith *and patience* (we) inherit the promises" (Hebrews 6:12). Faith says most confidently, "I have received it." Patience perseveres in prayer until the gift bestowed in heaven is seen on earth. "Believe that *you receive them*, and *you will have.*" Between the *you receive* in heaven and the *will have* of earth is the keyword *believe*. Believing praise and prayer is the link.

> *I*t is "through faith and patience (we) inherit the promises." Patience perseveres in prayer until the gift bestowed in heaven is seen on earth. "Believe that you receive them, and you will have."

And now, remember one more thing: It is Jesus who said this. As we see heaven opened to us and the Father on the throne offering to give us whatever we ask for in faith, our hearts feel full of shame that we have so little made use of our privilege and full of fear that our weak faith still fails to grasp what is so clearly placed within our reach. There is one thing that must make us strong and full of hope: It is Jesus who brought us this message from the Father. He Himself, when He was on earth, lived the life of faith and prayer. It was when the disciples expressed their surprise at what He had done to the fig tree that He told them that the very same life He led could be theirs, that they could not only command the fig tree but the very mountain, and it must obey. And He is our life. All He was on earth, He is in us now. All He teaches, He really gives. He is Himself the Author and the Perfecter of our faith. He gives the spirit of faith.

Let us not be afraid that such faith isn't meant for us. It is meant for every child of the Father and it is within reach of anyone who will be childlike, yielding himself to the Father's will and love and trusting the Father's word and power. Dear fellow Christian! Let the thought that this word comes through Jesus, God's Son and our Brother, give us courage. And let our answer be, "Yes, blessed Lord, we do believe Your Word. We do believe so that we may receive."

"Lord, teach us to pray."

Blessed Lord! You came from the Father to show us all His love and all the treasures of blessing that love is waiting to bestow. Lord, You have this day again thrown the gates so wide open and given us such promises concerning our liberty in prayer that we must blush that our poor hearts have so little taken it in. It has been too large for us to believe.

Lord! We now look up to You to teach us to take and keep and use Your precious Word: "Whatever things you ask when you pray, believe that you receive them." Blessed Jesus! It is in You our faith must be rooted if it is to grow strong. Your work has freed us wholly from the power of sin and has opened the way to the Father. Your love always longs to bring us into the full fellowship of Your glory and power. Your Spirit is constantly drawing us upward into a life of perfect faith and confidence. We are assured that in Your teaching we will learn to pray the prayer of faith. You will train us to pray so that we believe that we receive, to believe that we really have what we ask for. Lord! Teach me to know and trust and love You, to live and abide in You such a way that all my prayers rise up and come before God in You, that my soul may have in You the assurance that I am heard. Amen.

For Further Thought

1. *Read Solomon's prayer in 2 Chronicles 6:4. How can you apply the principle of this prayer in your own prayer life?*
2. *When you pray, do you pray "Lord, if it is Your will," or do you make sure you are praying according to God's will, claiming Jesus' promise of "whatever things you ask"?*
3. *How can you know that you are praying in accordance with God's will, and not your own fleshly desires?*

LESSON 12

"HAVE FAITH IN GOD," OR,
THE SECRET OF BELIEVING PRAYER

So Jesus answered and said to them, "Have faith in God. For
assuredly, I say to you, whoever says to this mountain, 'Be removed
and be cast into the sea,' and does not doubt in his heart, but believes
that those things he says will be done, he will have whatever he says."
MARK 11:22–23

THE promise of answer to prayer, which formed our yesterday's lesson, is one of the most wonderful in all scripture. In how many hearts it has raised the question, How can I attain the faith that knows it receives all it asks?

It is this question our Lord will answer today. Before He gave that wonderful promise to His disciples, He spoke another word, in which He points out where the faith in the answer to prayer comes from and always finds its strength. *Have faith in God*: this word precedes the other, Have faith is the promise of an answer to prayer. The power to believe *a promise* depends entirely, but only, on faith in *the promiser*. Trust in the person leads to trust in his word. It is only where we live and associate with God in a personal, loving relationship, where *God Himself* is all to us, where our whole being is continually opened and exposed to the mighty influences that are at work where His holy presence is revealed, that He gives whatever we ask.

This connection between faith in God and faith in His promise will become clear to us if we think about what faith really is. It is often compared to the hand or the mouth, by which we take and use what is offered to us. But it is important that we should understand that faith is also the ear by which I hear what is promised and the eye by which I see what is offered me. The power to take depends on this. I must *hear* the person who gives me the promise, because the very tone of his voice gives me courage to believe. I must *see* him, because in the light of his eye and countenance all fear as to my right to take passes away. The value of the promise depends on the promiser. It is on my knowledge of what the promiser is that faith in the promise depends.

It is for this reason that Jesus, before He gives that wonderful prayer-promise, first says, "*Have faith in God.*" That is, let your eye be open to the living God, and gaze on Him, seeing Him who is invisible. It is through the eye that I yield myself to the influence of what is before me. I just allow it to enter and to exert its influence and leave its impression on my mind. So believing God is just looking to God and what He is, allowing Him to reveal His presence, and giving Him time and yielding the whole being to take in the full impression of what He is as God. That's the soul opened up to receive and rejoice in the overshadowing of His love. Yes, faith is the eye to which God shows what He is and does. Through faith the light of His presence and the workings of His mighty power stream into the soul. And that which I see lives in me, so by faith God lives in me, too.

> *T*he power to believe a promise depends entirely, but only, on faith in the promiser. Trust in the person leads to trust in his word.

Likewise, faith is also the ear through which the voice of God is always heard and fellowship with Him is kept up. It is through the Holy Spirit that the Father speaks to us. The Son is the Word—the substance of what God says—and the Spirit is the living voice. This the child of God needs to lead and guide him. The secret voice from heaven must teach him, as it taught Jesus, what to say and what to do. An ear opened toward God—that is, a believing heart waiting on Him—will hear Him speak. The words of God will be not only the words of a Book, but, proceeding from the mouth of God, they will be spirit and truth, life and power. They will bring in deed and living experience what are otherwise only thoughts. Through this opened ear, the soul abides under the influence of the life and power of God Himself. Just as the words I hear enter the mind and dwell and work there, so through faith God enters the heart and dwells and works there.

When faith now is in full exercise as eye and ear—as the faculties of the soul by which we see and hear God—then it will be able to exercise its full power as hand and mouth, by which we appropriate God and His blessings. The power of reception will depend entirely on the power of spiritual perception. For this reason, before Jesus gave the promise that God would answer believing prayer, He said, "*Have faith in God.*" Faith is simply surrender. I yield myself to the impression the news I hear makes on me. By faith *I yield myself to the living God.* His glory and love fill my heart and have mastery over my life.

Faith is fellowship. I give myself up to the influence of the friend who makes me a promise and become linked to him by it. And it is when we enter into this living fellowship *with God Himself,* in a faith that always sees and hears Him, that it becomes easy and natural to believe His promise regarding prayer. Faith in the promise is the fruit of faith in the promiser. The prayer of faith is rooted in the life of faith. And in this way the faith that prays effectively is indeed a gift of God.

Not something He bestows or infuses all at once, but, in a far deeper and truer sense, as the blessed disposition or habit of the soul that is formed and grows up in us in a life of fellowship with Him. Surely for one who knows his Father well and lives in constant close fellowship with Him, it is a simple thing to believe the promise that He will do the will of His child who lives in union with Himself.

It is because so many of God's children do not understand this connection between the life of faith and the prayer of faith that their experience of the power of prayer is so limited. When they desire earnestly to obtain an answer from God, they set their whole heart on the promise and try their best to grasp that promise in faith. When they do not succeed, they are ready to give up hope. The promise is true, but it is beyond their power to accept it in faith. Listen to the lesson Jesus teaches us today: *Have faith in God*, the Living God. Let faith look to God more than on the thing promised, because it is His love, His power, His living presence that will awaken and work the faith.

> *I*t is when we enter into this living fellowship with God Himself, in a faith that always sees and hears Him, that it becomes easy and natural to believe His promise regarding prayer.

A physician would say to one asking for some means to get more strength in his arms and hands to seize and hold, so that his whole constitution can be built up and strengthened. Likewise, the cure of weak faith can be found only in the invigoration of our whole spiritual lives through fellowship with God. Learn to believe in God, to take hold of God, and to let God take possession of your life, and it will be easy to take hold of the promise. He who knows and trusts God finds it easy to also trust the promise.

Just note how distinctly this comes out in the saints of old. Every special exhibition of the power of faith was the fruit of a special revelation from God. We see it in Abraham: "*The word of the LORD came* to Abram in a vision, saying, 'Do not be afraid, Abram. *I am your shield*'...*Then He brought him* outside *and said...And he believed* in the LORD" (Gen. 15:1, 5–6). And later again: "The LORD *appeared to Abram and said* to him, 'I am Almighty God...' Then Abram fell on his face, and *God talked with him*, saying: 'As for Me, behold, My covenant is with you'" (Gen. 17:1, 3–4). It was the revelation of God Himself that gave the promise its living power to enter the heart and cultivate the faith. Because they knew God, these men of faith could do nothing but trust His promise.

God's promise will be to us what God Himself is. It is the man who walks before the Lord and falls on his face to listen while the living God speaks to him who really will receive the promise. Though we have God's promises in the Bible, with full liberty to claim them, the spiritual power is lacking, unless *God Himself speaks them to us. He speaks to those who walk and live with Him.*

Therefore, *have faith in God.* Let faith be all eye and ear and the surrender to let God make His full impression and reveal Himself fully in the soul. Count it one of the chief blessings of prayer to exercise faith in God as the living mighty God who waits to fulfill in us all the good pleasure of His will, and the work of faith with power. See in Him the God of love, whose delight it is to bless and impart Himself. In such worship of faith in God, the power will speedily come to believe the promise too: "*And whatever things you ask in prayer, believing, you will receive*" (Matt. 21:22). Yes, see that you in faith make God your own, and then the promise will be yours, too.

> *Have faith in God. Let faith be all eye and ear and the surrender to let God make His full impression and reveal Himself fully in the soul.*

Jesus teaches us a precious lesson today. We seek God's gifts, but God wants to give us *Himself* first. We think of prayer as the power to draw good gifts from heaven, and Jesus as the means to draw ourselves up to God. We want to stand at the door and cry, but Jesus wants us first to enter in and realize that we are friends and children. Let us accept the teaching. Let every experience of the smallness of our faith in prayer move us to have and exercise more faith in the living God, and in such faith to yield ourselves to Him. A heart full of God has power for the prayer of faith. Faith in God fosters faith in the promise, too, of an answer to prayer.

Therefore, child of God, take time to bow before *Him* and wait for *Him* to reveal *Himself.* Take time, and let your soul in holy awe and worship exercise and express its faith in the infinite One, and as He imparts Himself and takes possession of you, the prayer of faith will crown your faith in God.

"LORD, TEACH US TO PRAY."

O my God! I do believe in You. I believe in You as the Father, infinite in Your love and power. And as the Son, my Redeemer and my Life. And as the Holy Spirit, my Comforter, my Guide, and Strength. Three-One God, I have faith in You. I know and am sure that all You are, You are to me, that all You have promised You will perform.

Lord Jesus! Increase this faith! Teach me to take time and wait and worship in the holy presence until my faith takes in all there is in my God for me. Let it see Him as the Fountain of all life, working with almighty strength to accomplish His will in the world and in me. Let it see Him in His love longing to meet and fulfill my desires. Let it so take possession of my heart and life that through faith,

God alone may dwell there. Lord Jesus, help me! With my whole heart, I want to believe in God. Let faith in God fill me each moment.

O my blessed Savior! How can Your Church glorify You, how can it fulfill the work of intercession through which Your kingdom must come, unless our whole life is *faith in God*. Blessed Lord! Speak Your Word, *"Have faith in God,"* into the depths of our souls. Amen.

FOR FURTHER THOUGHT

1. *How can you overcome the prayer-hindering doubts that present themselves when you go before God in prayer?*
2. *What is God's attitude when it comes to answering His children's prayer and giving them the things they ask for in Jesus' name?*
3. *What should you do to make it easier and more natural for yourself to believe God's promises, and therefore claim them for yourself and for others in prayer?*

LESSON 13

"PRAYER AND FASTING,"
OR, THE CURE OF UNBELIEF

Then the disciples came to Jesus privately and said, "Why could we
not cast it out?" So Jesus said to them, "Because of your unbelief;
for assuredly, I say to you, if you have faith as a mustard seed, you
will say to this mountain, 'Move from here to there,' and it will
move; and nothing will be impossible for you. However,
this kind does not go out except by prayer and fasting."
MATTHEW 17:19–21

WHEN the disciples saw Jesus cast the evil spirit out of the epileptic whom "they could not cure," they asked the Master for the cause of their failure. He had given them "power and authority over all demons, and to cure diseases" (Luke 9:1). They had often exercised that power, and then joyfully told Him how the demons were subject to them. But now, while He was on the Mount, they had completely failed.

That there had been nothing in the will of God or in the nature of the case to render deliverance impossible had been proved: At Christ's command, the evil spirit had left. From their expression, "Why could we not?" it is evident that the disciples had wished and attempted to do so. They had probably used the Master's name and called on the evil spirit to leave. Their efforts had been in vain, and, in the presence of the multitude, they had been put to shame. "Why could we not?"

Christ's answer was direct and plain: "Because of your unbelief." The cause of His success and their failure was not because He had a special power to which they had no access. No! The reason was not hard to see. He had so often taught them that there is one power—the power of faith—to which, in the kingdom of darkness as in the kingdom of God, everything must bow. In the spiritual world, failure has only one cause: the lack of faith.

Faith is the one condition on which all divine power can enter into man and work through him. It is the sensitivity of the unseen, of man's will yielded to and molded by the will of God. The power they had received to cast out demons they did not hold in themselves as a permanent gift or possession. The power was in

808

Christ, to be received, held, and used by faith alone, living faith in Himself. Had they been full of faith *in Him* as Lord and Conqueror in the spirit world, had they been full of faith *in Him* as having given them authority to cast out in His name, this faith would have given them the victory. "Because of your unbelief" was, for all time, the Master's explanation and reprimand for powerlessness and failure in His Church.

But such a lack of faith must have a cause, too. The disciples might well have asked, "And why couldn't we believe? Our faith has cast out demons before this. Why have we now failed in believing this time?" The Master proceeds to tell them before they ask: "This kind does not go out except by prayer and fasting."

As faith is the simplest, so it is the highest exercise of the spiritual life, where our spirit yields itself to perfect receptivity to God's Spirit, and so is strengthened to its highest activity. This faith depends entirely on the state of the spiritual life. Only when this is strong and in good health, when the Spirit of God has total influence in our life, is there the power of faith to do its mighty deeds.

> *Faith is the one condition on which all divine power can enter into man and work through him. It is the sensitivity of the unseen, of man's will yielded to and molded by the will of God.*

And therefore Jesus adds, "However, this kind does not go out except by prayer and fasting." The faith than can overcome such stubborn resistance such as you have just seen in this evil spirit, Jesus tells them, is not possible except for men living in very close fellowship with God and in very special separation from the world—in prayer and fasting. And so He teaches us two lessons of deep importance in regard to prayer. The one, that faith needs a life of prayer in which to grow and keep strong. The other, that prayer needs fasting for its full and perfect development.

Faith needs a life of prayer for its full growth. In all the different parts of the spiritual life, there is such a close union, such unceasing action and reaction, that each may be both cause and effect. So it is with faith. There can be no true prayer without faith. Some measure of faith must precede prayer. And yet prayer is also the way to more faith. There can be no higher degrees of faith except through much prayer. This is the lesson Jesus teaches here.

There is nothing that needs so much to grow as our faith. "Your faith grows exceedingly," is said of one church (see 2 Thess. 1:3). When Jesus spoke the words, "According to your faith let it be to you" (Matthew 9:29), He announced the law of the kingdom, which tells us that not all people have equal degrees of faith, that one person may have varying degrees, and that the amount of faith must always determine the amount of power and of blessing. If we want to know where and how our faith is to grow, the Master points us to the throne of God. It is in prayer, in the exercise of the faith I have in fellowship with the living God, that faith can increase. Faith can only live by feeding on what is divine—on God Himself.

It is in the adoring worship of God—the waiting on Him and for Him, the deep silence of soul that yields itself for God to reveal Himself—that the capacity for knowing and trusting God will be developed. It is as we take His Word from the blessed Book and bring it to Him and ask Him to speak it to us with His living, loving voice, that the power will come fully to believe and receive the word as God's own word to us. It is in prayer, in living contact with God in living faith, that faith—the power to trust God, and in that trust, to accept everything He says, to accept every possibility He has offered to our faith—will become strong in us. Many Christians cannot understand what is meant by the much prayer they sometimes heard spoken of. They can form no conception of, nor do they feel the need of, spending hours with God. But what the Master says, the experience of His people has confirmed: Men of strong faith are men of much prayer.

> *It is in prayer, in the exercise of the faith I have in fellowship with the living God, that faith can increase. Faith can only live by feeding on what is divine—on God Himself.*

This just brings us back again to the lesson we learned when Jesus, before telling us to believe that we receive what we ask for, first said, "Have faith in God." It is God, the living God, into whom our faith must sink its roots deeply and broadly. Then it will be strong enough to move mountains and cast out demons. "If you have faith. . .nothing will be impossible for you." If we could only give ourselves up to the work God has for us in the world, coming into contact with the mountains and the demons there are to be cast away and cast out, we would soon comprehend the need there is for much faith and for much prayer, which are the only soil in which faith can be cultivated. Christ Jesus is our life, the life of our faith, too. It is His life in us that makes us strong and makes us ready to believe. It is in the dying to self, which much prayer implies, in closer union to Jesus, that the spirit of faith will come in power. *Faith needs prayer* for its full growth.

And *prayer needs fasting* for its full growth: This is the second lesson. Prayer is the one hand with which we grasp the invisible. Fasting is the other hand, with which we let loose and cast away the visible. In nothing is man more closely connected with the world of sense than in his need for and enjoyment of food. It was the fruit, good for food, with which man was tempted and fell in Paradise. It was with bread to be made of stones that Jesus, when He hungered, was tempted in the wilderness, and in fasting that He triumphed. The body has been redeemed to be a temple of the Holy Spirit. It is in body as well as spirit, it is very specially, scripture says, in eating and drinking, that we are to glorify God. It is to be feared that there are many Christians to whom this eating to the glory of God has not yet become a spiritual reality. And the first thought suggested by Jesus' words in regard to fasting and prayer is that it is only in a life of moderation and self-control and self-denial that there will there be sufficient heart and strength to pray much.

But then there is also its more literal meaning. Sorrow and anxiety cannot eat, but joy celebrates its feasts with eating and drinking. There may come times of intense desire, when it is strongly felt how the body, with its appetites, still hinder the spirit in its battle with the powers of darkness, and the need is felt of keeping it subdued. We are creatures of the senses. Our mind is helped by what comes to us in concrete form. Fasting helps to express, to deepen, and to confirm the resolution that we are ready to sacrifice anything, to sacrifice ourselves, to attain what we seek for the kingdom of God. And He who accepted the fasting and sacrifice of the Son knows to value and accept and reward with spiritual power the soul that is therefore ready to give up everything for Christ and His kingdom.

And then follows a still a wider application. Prayer is reaching out for God and the unseen, and fasting is the letting go of everything that is of the seen and temporal. While ordinary Christians imagine that everything that is not positively forbidden and sinful is permissible to them, and seek to retain as much as possible of this world—with its prosperity, its literature, its enjoyments—the truly consecrated soul is like a soldier who carries only what he needs for battle. Laying aside every weight, as well as the easily entangling sin, afraid of entangling himself with the affairs of this life, he seeks to lead a Nazarite life, as one specially set apart for the Lord and His service. Without such voluntary separation, even from what is lawful, no one will attain power in prayer. This kind does not go out except by prayer and fasting.

Disciples of Jesus! You who have asked the Master to teach you to pray, come now and accept His lessons. He tells you that prayer is the path to faith, strong faith that can cast out demons. He tells you: "If you have faith, nothing shall be impossible to you." Let this glorious promise encourage you to pray much. Isn't the prize worth the price? Shall we not give up all to follow Jesus in the path He opens to us here? Shall we not, if need be, fast? Shall we not do anything so that neither the body nor the world can hinder us in our great life work—communicating with our God in prayer so that we may become men of faith He can use in His work of saving the world?

"LORD, TEACH US TO PRAY."

O Lord Jesus! How continually You must reprimand us for our unbelief. How strange it must appear to You, this terrible inability of trusting our Father and His promises. Lord, Let Your reprimand, with its searching, "Because of your unbelief," sink into the very depths of our hearts and reveal to us how much of the sin and suffering around us is our fault. Then teach us, blessed Lord, that there is a place where faith can be learned and gained—even in the prayer and fasting that brings us into living fellowship with Yourself and the Father.

O Savior! You are the Author and the Perfecter of our faith. Teach us what it means to let You live in us by Your Holy Spirit. Lord! Our efforts and prayers for grace to believe have been so ineffective. We know why it was: We sought for strength in ourselves to be given from You. Holy Jesus! Teach us at length the mystery of Your life in us and how You, by Your Spirit, work to live in us the life of faith, to see to it that our faith shall not fail. Let us see that our faith will just be a part of that wonderful prayer life You give in those who expect their training for the ministry of intercession, not in word and thought only, but in the holy anointing You give, the inflowing of the Spirit of Your own life. And teach us how, in fasting and prayer, we can mature in the faith for which nothing shall be impossible. Amen.

For Further Thought

1. *Why could the disciples not cast out the demon, even though they spoke against it in Jesus' name? Can you see that same source of failure in your own prayer life?*
2. *What kind of relationship with God do you need to cultivate in order to have the kind of faith that can move mountains?*
3. *What does fasting in conjunction with prayer express to God? What kind of power does fasting give to your own prayer life?*

NOTE

AT the time when Blumhardt was passing through his terrible conflict with the evil spirits in those who were possessed, and seeking to cast them out by prayer, he often wondered what it was that hindered the answer. One day a friend to whom he had spoken of his trouble directed his attention to our Lord's words about fasting. Blumhardt resolved to give himself to fasting, sometimes for more than thirty hours. From reflection and experience, he gained the conviction that it is of more importance than is generally thought. He says, "Inasmuch as the fasting is before God a practical proof that the thing we ask is to us a matter of true and pressing interest, and inasmuch as in a high degree it strengthens the intensity and power of the prayer and becomes the unceasing practical expression of a prayer without words, I could believe that it would not be without effectiveness, especially as the Master's words had reference to a case like the present. I tried it without telling anyone, and in truth the later conflict was extraordinarily lightened by it. I could speak with much greater restfulness and decision. I did not need to be so long present with the sick one, and I felt that I could influence without being present."

LESSON 14

"WHEN YOU STAND PRAYING, FORGIVE," OR, PRAYER AND LOVE

*"And whenever you stand praying, if you have anything
against anyone, forgive him, that your Father in
heaven may also forgive you your trespasses"*
MARK 11:25

THESE words follow immediately on the great prayer promise, "Whatever things you ask when you pray, believe that you receive them, and you will have them" (Mark 11:24). We have already seen how the words that preceded that promise, "Have faith in God," taught us that in prayer everything depends on our relationship with God being clear. These words that follow it remind us that our relationships with our fellowmen must be clear, too. Love of God and love of our neighbor are inseparable. The prayer from a heart that is either not right with God on one side, or with men on the other, cannot succeed. Faith and love are essential to each other.

We find that this is a thought to which our Lord frequently gave expression. In the Sermon on the Mount, when speaking of the sixth commandment, He taught His disciples how impossible acceptable worship of the Father was if everything was not right with the brother: "Therefore if you bring your gift to the altar, and there remember that your brother has something against you, leave your gift there before the altar, and go your way. First be reconciled to your brother, and then come and offer your gift" (Matt. 5:23–24). And so later, when speaking of prayer to God, after having taught us to pray, "Forgive us our debts, as we forgive our debtors" (Matt. 6:12), He added at the close of the prayer: "If you do not forgive men their trespasses, neither will your Father forgive your trespasses" (6:15). At the close of the parable of the unmerciful servant, He applies His teaching in the words, "So My heavenly Father also will do to you if each of you, from his heart, does not forgive his brother his trespasses" (Matt. 18:35).

And so here, beside the dried-up fig tree, where Jesus speaks of the wonderful power of faith and the prayer of faith, He all at once, apparently without connection, introduces the thought, "And whenever you stand praying, if you have anything against anyone, forgive him, that your Father in heaven may also forgive you your trespasses" (Mark 11:25). It is as if the Lord had learned during His life at Nazareth and afterwards that disobedience to the law of brotherly love to men was the great sin even of praying people—and the great cause of the weakness of their prayer. And it is as if He wanted to lead us into His own blessed experience that nothing gives such liberty of access and such power in believing as the consciousness that we have given ourselves in love and compassion for those whom God loves.

> *L*ove of God and love of our neighbor are inseparable. The prayer from a heart that is either not right with God on one side, or with men on the other, cannot succeed. Faith and love are essential to each other.

The first lesson we are taught here is that of a forgiving disposition. We pray, "Forgive us *just as* we have forgiven others." Scripture says to forgive one another, "even as God in Christ forgave you" (Eph. 4:32). God's full and free forgiveness is to be the rule of ours with men. Otherwise, our reluctant, halfhearted forgiveness, which is not forgiveness at all, will be God's rule with us. Every prayer depends on our faith in God's pardoning grace. If God dealt with us as our sins deserved, not one prayer could be heard. Pardon opens the door to all God's love and blessing. Because God has pardoned all our sins, our prayer can prevail to receive all we need.

The deep, sure ground of answer to prayer is God's forgiving love. When it has taken possession of the heart, we pray in faith. But also, when it has taken possession of our hearts, we live in love. God's forgiving nature, revealed to us in His love, becomes our nature. As the power of His forgiving love shed abroad dwells in us, we forgive just as He forgives. If there is a great and grievous injury or injustice done to us, we seek first of all to possess a Godlike disposition—to be kept from a sense of wounded honor, from a desire to maintain or rights, or from rewarding the offender as he has deserved. In the little annoyances of daily life, we are careful not to excuse the hasty temper, the sharp word, or the quick judgment with the thought that we mean no harm, that we do not keep the anger long, or that it would be too much to expect feeble human nature to really forgive the way God and Christ do. Take the command literally: "*Forgive, even as* God in Christ forgave you." The blood that cleanses the conscience from dead works cleanses from selfishness, too. The love it reveals is pardoning love that takes possession of us and flows through us to others. Our forgiving love toward men is the evidence of God's forgiving love in us and, therefore, the condition of the prayer of faith.

There is a second, more general lesson: Our daily life in the world is the test of our communication with God in prayer. How often the Christian, when he comes to pray, does his utmost to cultivate certain frames of mind that he thinks will be pleasing. He doesn't understand, or he forgets, that life does not consist of many loose pieces, of which now the one then the other can be taken up. Life is a whole, and the spiritual frame of the hour of prayer is judged by God from the ordinary frame of the daily life, of which the hour of prayer is but a small part. Not the feeling I call up, but the tone of my life during the day is God's criterion of what I really am and desire.

My drawing near to God is of one piece with my relationships with men. Failure in one will cause failure in the other. That's not only when there is the distinct consciousness of something wrong between my neighbor and myself, but in the ordinary current of my thinking and judging. The unloving thoughts and words I allow to pass unnoticed can hinder my prayer. The effective prayer of faith comes from a life given up to the will and the love of God. Not according to what I try to be when praying, but what I am when I'm not praying is my prayer dealt with by God.

> *Our forgiving love toward men is the evidence of God's forgiving love in us and, therefore, the condition of the prayer of faith.*

We may gather all these thoughts into a third lesson: In our life with men, the one thing on which everything depends is love. The spirit of forgiveness is the spirit of love. Because God is love, He forgives. It is only when we are dwelling in love that we can forgive as God forgives. In love to the brethren we have the evidence of love to the Father, the basis for confidence before God, and the assurance that our prayer will be heard. "Let us. . .love. . .in deed and in truth. And *by this*. . .we assure our hearts before Him. . . . if our heart does not condemn us, we have confidence toward God. And whatever we ask we receive from Him (1 John 3:18–22). Neither faith nor work will profit us if we don't have love. It is love that unites with God and proves the reality of faith. As essential as in the word that precedes the great prayer-promise of Mark 11:24, "Have faith in God," is the one that follows it, "Have love for men." The right relationships with the living God above me and the living men around me are the conditions for effective prayer.

This love is of special consequence when we labor for such men and pray for them. We sometimes commit ourselves to work for Christ out of zeal for His cause, as we call it, or for our own spiritual health, without giving ourselves in personal self-sacrificing love for those whose souls we seek. No wonder that our faith is weak and does not conquer. To look at each wretched one, however unlovable he is, in the light of the tender love of Jesus the Shepherd searching for the lost, to see Jesus Christ in him, and to take him up, for Jesus' sake, in a heart that really loves—this, this is the secret of believing prayer and successful effort. Jesus, in speaking of forgiveness, speaks of love as its root. Just as in the Sermon on the Mount He connected His teaching and promises about prayer with the call to be merciful, as the Father in heaven is merciful (Matt. 5:7, 9, 22, 38–48), so we see it here: A loving life is the condition of believing prayer.

It has been said that there is nothing as heart-searching as believing prayer, or even the honest effort to pray in faith. O let us not turn the edge of that self-examination by the thought that God does not hear our prayers for reasons known to Himself alone. By no means! "You ask and do not receive, because you ask amiss" (James 4:3). Let that Word of God search us. Let us ask whether our prayer is indeed the expression of a life wholly given over to the will of God and the love of man.

> *As love throws its arms up and opens its heart heavenward, the Father always looks to see if it has them opened toward the evil and the unworthy, too.*

Love is the only soil in which faith can take root and thrive. As love throws its arms up and opens its heart heavenward, the Father always looks to see if it has them opened toward the evil and the unworthy, too. In that love, not indeed the love of perfect attainment but the love of fixed purpose and sincere obedience, faith can alone obtain the blessing. It is he who gives himself to let the love of God dwell in him, and in the practice of daily life to love as God loves, who will have the power to believe in the love that hears his every prayer. It is *the Lamb*, who is in the midst of the throne: It is suffering and patient love that prevails with God in prayer. The merciful shall obtain mercy; the meek shall inherit the earth.

"LORD, TEACH US TO PRAY."

Blessed Father! You are love, and only he who abides in love abides in You and in fellowship with You. The blessed Son has this day again taught me how deeply true this is of my fellowship with You in prayer. O my God! Let Your love, shed abroad in my heart by the Holy Spirit, be in me a fountain of love to all around me, so that out of a life in love may spring the power of believing prayer. O my Father! Grant by the Holy Spirit that this may be my experience, that a life in love to all around me is the gate to a life in the love of my God. And give me especially to find in the joy with which I forgive day by day whoever might offend me the proof that Your forgiveness is to me a power and a life.

Lord Jesus! My blessed Teacher! Teach me how to forgive and to love. Let the power of Your blood make the pardon of my sins such a reality that forgiveness, as shown by You to me, and by me to others, may be the very joy of heaven. Show me anything in my relationships with my fellowmen that might hinder my fellowship with God, so that my daily life in my own home and in society may be the school in which strength and confidence are gathered for the prayer of faith. Amen.

FOR FURTHER THOUGHT

1. Who is the model or example of the kind of forgiveness you must extend those who have offended or hurt you in order for your prayers to be heard and answered? In what ways has this person forgiven others?
2. What are the evidences of God's forgiving love within you? How can you make those evidences a more prominent part of your life of faith and, therefore, pray more effectively?
3. Whom should you forgive in order that God may forgive you and hear your prayers? From whom should you withhold God's forgiveness?

LESSON 15

"IF TWO OF YOU AGREE," OR,

THE POWER OF UNITED PRAYER

"Again I say to you that if two of you agree on earth concerning
anything that they ask, it will be done for them by My Father in
heaven. For where two or three are gathered together
in My name, I am there in the midst of them."
MATTHEW 18:19–20

ONE of the first lessons of our Lord in His school of prayer was: not to be seen by men. Go into your closet and be alone with the Father. When He has through this taught us that the meaning of prayer is personal, individual contact with God, He comes with a second lesson: You don't need just secret, solitary prayer, but also public, united prayer. And He gives us a very special promise for the united prayer of two or three who agree in what they ask. Just as a tree has its root hidden in the ground and its stem growing up into the sunlight, likewise prayer needs equally for its full development the hidden secrecy in which the soul meets God alone, as well as the public fellowship with those who find in the name of Jesus their common meeting place.

The reason why this must be so is plain. The bond that unites a man with his fellowmen is no less real and close than that which unites him to God: He is one with them. Grace renews not only our relationship with God but to man, too. We not only learn to say "My Father" but also "Our Father." Nothing would be more unnatural than for the children of a family to always meet with their father separately, but never in the united expression of their desires or their love. Believers are not only members of one family, but even of one body. Just as each member of the body depends on the other, and the full action of the spirit dwelling in the body depends on the union and cooperation of all, so Christians cannot reach the full blessing God is ready to bestow through His Spirit until they seek and receive it in fellowship with each other. It is in the union and fellowship of believes that the Spirit can manifest His full power. It was to the 120 staying in one place together and praying in one accord that the Spirit came from the throne of the glorified Lord (see Acts 1:15, 2:1–4).

The marks of true, united prayer are given to us in these words of our Lord. The first is *agreement* as to the thing asked. There must not only be generally the consent to agreement with anything another may ask, there must also be some special thing—a matter of distinct, united desire. And the agreement must be, as in all prayer, in spirit and in truth. In such agreement it will become very clear to us what exactly we are asking for, whether we may confidently ask for it according to God's will, and whether we are ready to believe that we have received what we ask.

> *G*race renews not only our relationship with God but to man, too. We not only learn to say "My Father" but also "Our Father."

The second mark is the gathering in, or into, the name of Jesus. We shall later have much more to learn about the need and the power of the name of Jesus in prayer, but here our Lord teaches us that His name must be the center of union to which believers gather, the bond of union that makes them one, just as a home contains and unites all who are in it. "The name of the LORD is a strong tower; the righteous run to it and are safe" (Prov. 18:10). That name is such a reality to those who understand and believe in it that to meet within it is to have Himself present. The love and unity of His disciples have infinite attraction to Jesus: "For where two or three are gathered together in My name, *I am there in the midst of them*" (Matt. 18:20). It is the living presence of Jesus, in the fellowship of His loving, praying disciples that gives united prayer its power.

The third mark is the sure answer: "It will be done for them by My Father in heaven." A prayer meeting for maintaining religious fellowship, or for our own edification, may have its use, but this was not the Savior's reason for its appointment. He meant it as a means of securing *special answer to prayer.* A prayer meeting without recognized answer to prayer ought to be an anomaly. When any of us have distinct desires in regard to which we feel too weak to exercise the needed faith, we ought to seek strength in the help of others. In the unity of faith, of love, and of the Spirit, the power of the name and the presence of Jesus acts more freely, and the answer comes more surely. The evidence that there has been true united prayer is the fruit, the answer, the receiving of the thing we have asked for: "I say to you. . .*it will be done* for them by My Father in heaven."

What an extraordinary privilege united prayer is, and what a power it might be! If the believing husband and wife knew they were joined together in the name of Jesus to experience His presence and power in united prayer (1 Peter); if friends believed what mighty help two or three praying in concert could give each other; if in every prayer meeting the coming together in the name, the faith in the presence, and the expectation of the answer stood in the foreground; if in every Church united effective prayer were regarded as one of the chief purposes for which they are banded together, the highest exercise of their power as a Church; if in the Church universal the coming of the kingdom, the coming of the King Himself, first in the mighty outpouring of His Holy Spirit, then in His own glorious person, were really a matter of unceasing united crying to God—O who can say what blessing might come to, and through, those who agreed to prove God this way in the fulfillment of His promise.

In the apostle Paul we see very distinctly what a reality his faith in the power of united prayer was. To the Romans he writes, "Now I beg you, brethren, through. . .the love of the Spirit, that *you strive together with me* in prayers to God for me" (15:30). He expects in answer to those prayers to be delivered from his enemies, and to prosper in his work. To the Corinthians, "He will still deliver us, you also helping together in prayer for us" (2 Cor. 1:10–11). He expects their prayer to have a real share in his deliverance. To the Ephesians he writes, "Praying always with all prayer and supplication in the Spirit. . .perseverance and supplication for all the saints—and for me, that utterance may be given to me" (6:18–19). His power and success in his ministry he makes dependent on their prayers. With the Philippians he expects that his trials will turn to his salvation and increase the progress of the gospel, "*through your prayer and* the supply of the Spirit of Jesus Christ" (1:19). To the Colossians he adds to the injunction to continue steadfast in prayer, "Meanwhile praying also for us, that God would open to us a door for the word" (4:3). And to the Thessalonians he writes, "Finally, brethren, pray for us, that the word of the Lord may run swiftly and be glorified. . .and that we may be delivered from unreasonable and wicked men" (2 Thess. 3:1–2).

> *In the unity of faith, of love, and of the Spirit, the power of the name and the presence of Jesus acts more freely, and the answer comes more surely.*

It is everywhere evident that Paul saw himself as the member of a body, on whose sympathy and cooperation he depended, and that he counted on the prayers of these churches to gain for him what otherwise might not be given. The prayers of the Church were to him as real a factor in the work of the kingdom as the power of God.

Who can say what power a Church could develop and exercise if it gave itself to the work of praying day and night for the coming of the kingdom, for God's power on His servants and His Word, and for the glorifying of God through the salvation of souls? Most churches think their members are gathered into one simply to take care of and build up each other. They don't know that God rules the world by the prayers of His saints, that prayer is the power by which Satan is conquered, and that through prayer the Church on earth has access to the powers of the heavenly world. They do not remember that Jesus has, by His promise, consecrated every assembly in His name to be a gate to heaven, where His presence is to be felt and His power experience by the Father fulfilling their desires.

We cannot sufficiently thank God for the blessed week of united prayer, with which Christianity, in our days, opens every year. As proof of our unity and our faith in the power of united prayer, as a training school for the enlargement of our hearts to take in all the needs of the Church universal, and as a help to united persevering prayer, it is of unspeakable value. But very specially as a stimulus to continued union in prayer in the smaller circles, its blessing has been great. And it will become even greater, as God's people realize what it means to meet as one in the name of Jesus, to have His presence in the midst of a body all united in the Holy Spirit, and to boldly to claim the promise that it shall be done of the Father what they agree to ask.

"LORD, TEACH US TO PRAY."

Blessed Lord, who in Your high-priestly prayer asked so earnestly for the unity of Your people, teach us how You invite and urge us to this unity by Your precious promise given to united prayer. It is when we are one in love and desire that our faith has Your presence and the Father's answer.

> Who can say what power a church could develop and exercise if it gave itself to the work of praying day and night for the coming of the kingdom, and for the glorifying of God through the salvation of souls?

O Father! We pray for Your people, and for every smaller circle of those who meet together, that they may be one. Remove, we pray, all selfishness and self-interest, all narrowness of heart and estrangement by which unity is hindered. Cast out the spirit of the world and the flesh, through which Your promise loses all its power. Let the thought of Your presence and the Father's favor draw us all nearer to each other.

Grant especially, blessed Lord, that Your Church may believe that it is by the power of united prayer that she can bind and loose in heaven, that Satan can be cast out, that souls can be saved, that mountains can be moved, that the kingdom can be hastened. And grant, good Lord, that in the circle in which I pray, the prayer of the Church may indeed be the power through which Your name and Word are glorified. Amen.

For Further Thought

1. *What did Jesus teach about personal, individual prayer, and what did He teach about united prayer? Is one more important or effective than the other?*
2. *What did the apostle Paul teach about united prayer, and how can you apply what he taught to your prayer life?*
3. *What are the benefits of the Church of united, believing, agreeing prayer? Which of those benefits do you recognize as needed today?*

Lesson 16

"Speedily, Though Bearing Long," or, The Power of Persevering Prayer

Then He spoke a parable to them, that men always
ought to pray and not lose heart. . . . Then the Lord said, "Hear
what the unjust judge said. And shall God not avenge His own
elect who cry out day and night to Him, though He bears long
with them? I tell you that He will avenge them speedily."
LUKE 18:1, 6–8

OF all the mysteries of the prayer world, the need for persevering prayer is one of the greatest. That the Lord, who is so loving and longing to bless, should have to be petitioned time after time, sometimes year after year, before the answer comes, we cannot easily understand. It is also one of the greatest practical difficulties in the exercise of believing prayer. When, after persevering prayer, our repeated prayer remains unanswered, it is easy for our complacent flesh—and it has all the appearance of devout submission—to think that we must stop praying because God may have a secret reason for withholding His answer to our request.

It is by faith alone that the difficulty is overcome. Once faith has taken its stand on God's Word and on the name of Jesus, and has yielded itself to the leading of the Spirit to seek God's will and honor alone in its prayer, it need not be discouraged by delay. It knows from scripture that the power of believing prayer is irresistible, that real faith can never be disappointed. It knows how, just as water, to exercise the irresistible power it can have. Water must be gathered up and accumulated until the stream can come down in full force. Likewise, there must often be a heaping up of prayer, until God sees that the measure is full, and then the answer comes. It knows how, just as the farmer has to take his ten thousand steps and sow his ten thousand seeds, each one a part of the preparation for the final harvest, there is a need for often-repeated persevering prayer, all working out some desired blessing. It knows for certain that not a single believing prayer can fail to affect heaven, but has its influence and is treasured up to work out an answer in due time to he who perseveres to the end. It knows that it has nothing to do with human thoughts and possibilities, but with the word of the living God.

And so, even as Abraham through so many years "contrary to hope, in hope believed" (Rom. 4:18) and then "through faith *and patience* inherit the promise" (Heb. 6:12), it accounts that the bearing long of the Lord is salvation, *waiting* and *hastening* for the coming of its Lord to fulfill His promise.

To enable us, when the answer to our prayer does not come right away, we should combine quiet patience and joyful confidence in our persevering prayer. We must especially try to understand that two words with which our Lord sets forth the character and conduct, not of the unjust judge but of our God and Father toward those He allows to cry day and night to Him: "He *bears long* with them. . .He will avenge them *speedily*."

He will avenge them *speedily*, the Master says. The blessing is all prepared. He is not only willing but eager to give them what they ask. Everlasting love burns with the longing desire to reveal itself fully to its beloved and to satisfy their needs. God will not delay one moment longer than is absolutely necessary. He will do everything in His power to hasten and speed the answer.

But why, if this is true and His power is infinite, does it often take so long to get an answer to prayer? And why must God's own elect so often, in the midst of suffering and conflict, cry day and night? "He bears long with them." "See how the farmer waits for the precious fruit of the earth, waiting patiently for it until it receives the early and latter rain" (James 5:7). The farmer indeed longs for his harvest, but he knows it must have its full time of sunshine and rain, so he has plenty of patience. A child so often wants to pick the half-ripe fruit, but the farmer knows to wait until the proper time. Man, in his spiritual nature, too, is under the law of gradual growth that reigns in all created life. It is only in the path of development that can he reach his divine destiny. And it is the Father, in whose hands are the times and seasons, who alone knows the moment when the soul or the Church is ripened to that fullness of faith in which it can really take and keep the blessing. As a father who longs to have his only child home from school, and yet waits patiently until the time of training is completed, so it is with God and His children: He is the longsuffering One and answers speedily.

The insight into this truth leads the believer to cultivate the corresponding dispositions: *Patience* and *faith*, *waiting* and *praise* are the secret of his perseverance. By faith in the promise of God, we know that we *have* the petitions we have asked of Him. Faith takes and holds the answer in the promise as an unseen spiritual possession, rejoices in it and praises for it. But there is a difference between the faith that holds the word and knows it has the answer, and the clearer, fuller, riper faith that obtains the promise as a present experience. It is in persevering, not unbelieving, but confident and praising prayer that the soul grows up into full union with its Lord in which it can enter into the possession of the blessing in Him.

There may be in these around us, there may be in that great system of being of which we are part, there may be in God's government, things that have to be put right through our prayer before the answer can fully come. The faith that has, according to the command, believed that it has received, can allow God to take His time, for it knows it has succeeded and must succeed. In quiet, persistent, and determined perseverance it continues in prayer and thanksgiving until the blessing comes. And so we see a combination of what at first sight appears to be so contradictory: the faith that rejoices in God's answer as a present possession, with the patience that cries day and night until it is revealed. The *speedily* of God's *bearing long* is met by the triumphant but patient faith of His waiting child.

> *O*nce faith has taken its stand on God's Word and on the name of Jesus, and has yielded itself to the leading of the Spirit to seek God's will and honor alone in its prayer, it need not be discouraged by delay.

Our great danger in this school of the answer delayed is the temptation to think that, after all, it may not be God's will to give us what we ask. If our prayer is according to God's Word, and under the leading of the Spirit, let us not give way to these fears. Let us learn to give God time. God needs time with us. If we only give Him time—that is, time in the daily fellowship with Himself, for Him to exercise the full influence of His presence on us, and time, day by day, in the course of our being kept waiting for faith to prove its reality and to fill our whole being, He Himself will lead us from faith to vision. Then we shall see the glory of God. Let no delay shake our faith. Of faith it holds true: first the blade, then the ear, then the full corn in the ear. Each believing prayer is a step nearer to the final victory. Each believing prayer helps to ripen the fruit and bring us nearer to it. It fills up the measure of prayer and faith known to God alone. It conquers the unseen world and hastens the end.

Child of God! Give the Father time. He bears long over you. He wants the blessing to be rich, full, and sure. Give Him time while you cry day and night. Only remember the word, "I say to you. . .He will avenge them speedily."

The blessing of such persevering prayer is unspeakable. There is nothing so heart-searching as the prayer of faith. It teaches you to discover and confess and then to give up everything that hinders the coming of the blessing, everything not in accordance with the Father's will. It leads to closer fellowship with Him who alone can teach you to pray, to a more entire surrender to draw near under no covering but that of the blood and the Spirit. It calls to a closer and simpler abiding in Christ alone. Christian! Give God time! He will perfect whatever concerns you! "Bearing long—speedily": This is God's watchword as you enter the gates of prayer. Let it be yours, too.

Let it be this way, whether you pray for yourself, or for others. All labor, bodily or mental, needs time and effort. We must give *ourselves* up to it. Nature reveals her secrets and yields her treasures only to diligent and thoughtful labor. However little we can understand it, in the spiritual farming is the same: The seed we sow in the soil of heaven, the efforts we put forth, and the influence we seek to exert in the world above, all need our whole being. We must *give ourselves* to prayer. But let us maintain the great confidence that when the time is right, we will reap abundantly if we do not lose heart.

And let us specially learn the lesson as we pray for the Church of Christ. She is indeed like a poor widow in the absence of her Lord, apparently at the mercy of her adversary and helpless to correct the situation. Let us, when we pray for His Church or any portion of it that is under the power of the world, ask Him to visit her with mighty workings of His Spirit to prepare her for His coming. Let us pray in the assured faith that prayer does help. Praying always and not losing heart will bring the answer. Just give God time. And then keep crying day and night. "Hear what the unjust judge said. And shall God not avenge His own elect who cry out day and night to Him, though *He bears long* with them? I tell you that *He will avenge them speedily.*"

"LORD, TEACH US TO PRAY."

O Lord my God! Teach me how to know Your way, and in faith to learn what Your beloved Son has taught: "He will avenge them speedily." Let Your tender love, and the delight You have in hearing and blessing Your children, lead me implicitly to accept Your promise that we may receive what we believe, that we have the petitions we ask, that the answer will in due time be seen. Lord! We understand the seasons in nature, and we know to wait with patience for the fruit we long for. O fill us with the assurance that You won't delay one moment longer than is necessary, and that faith will hasten the answer.

> *T*he faith that has, *according to the command,* believed that it has received, can allow God to take His time, for it knows it has succeeded and must succeed.

Blessed Master! You have said that it is a sign of God's elect that they cry day and night. Please teach us to understand this. You know how quickly we lose heart and grow weary. It is as if the divine Majesty is so beyond the need or the reach of our continued prayer that it isn't fitting for us to be too persistent. O Lord! Teach me how real the labor of prayer is! I know how here on earth, when I have failed in an undertaking, I can often succeed by renewed and more continuous effort, by taking more time and thought. Show me how, by giving myself more entirely to prayer and to live in prayer, I shall obtain what I ask.

And above all, O blessed Teacher, Author, and Perfecter of my faith, by Your grace let my whole life be one of faith in the Son of God, who loved me and gave Himself for me—in whom my prayer gains acceptance, in whom I have assurance of the answer, in whom the answer will be mine. Lord Jesus! In this faith I will pray always and not lose heart. Amen.

For Further Thought

1. *How can you maintain your faith and faithfulness in prayer when God seems to delay in answering? Should you cease praying for something you believe is His will when that delay happens, or should you persevere?*

2. *What four dispositions or attitudes in prayer are essential to persevering in prayer when God seems to be delaying in answering?*

3. *What sorts of blessings do you believe if you give Him time and don't grow weary of praying for what you know is His will?*

THE need of persevering prayer appears to some to be at odds with the faith that knows that it has received what it asks (Mark 11:24). One of the mysteries of the divine life is the harmony between the gradual and the sudden, immediate full possession and slow, imperfect appropriation. And so here, persevering prayer appears to be the school in which the soul is strengthened for the boldness of faith. And with the diversity of operations of the Spirit, there may be some in whom faith takes the form of persistent waiting, while to others triumphant thanksgiving appears the only proper expression of the assurance of having been heard.

In a very remarkable way, the need for persevering prayer, and the gradual rising into greater ease in obtaining the answer, is illustrated in the life of Blumhardt. Complaints had been lodged against him of neglecting his work as a minister of the gospel and of devoting himself to the healing of the sick—especially his unauthorized healing of the sick belonging to other congregations. In his defense, he writes:

"I simply ventured to do what is fitting for one who has the charge of souls, and to pray according to the command of the Lord in James 1:6–7. In no way did I trust to my own power or imagine that I had any gift that others did not have. But this is true: I set myself to the work as a minister of the gospel who has a right to pray. But I speedily discovered that the gates of heaven were not fully open to me. Often I was inclined to retire in despair. But the sight of the sick ones, who could find help nowhere, gave me no rest. I thought of the word of the Lord: 'Ask, and it will be given to you' (Luke 11:9). And further, I thought that if the Church and her ministers had, through unbelief, complacency, and disobedience, lost what was needed for the overcoming of the power of Satan, it was just for such times of leanness and famine that the Lord had spoken the parable of the friend at midnight and his three loaves. I felt that I was not worthy thus at midnight, in a time of great darkness, to appear before God as His friend and ask for a member of my congregation what he needed. And yet, to leave him uncared for I could not do either. And so I kept knocking, as the parable directs, or, as some have said, with great presumption and tempting of God. Be this as it may, I could not leave my guest unprovided for. At this time, the parable of the widow became very precious to me. I saw that the Church was the widow, and I was the minister of the church. I had the right to be her mouthpiece against the adversary. But for a long time the Lord would not. I asked nothing more than the three loaves—what I needed for my guest. At last the Lord listened to the persistent beggar and helped me. Was it wrong of me to pray this way? The two parables must surely be applicable somewhere, and where was greater need to be conceived?

And what was the fruit of my prayer? The friend who was at first unwilling did not say, 'Go now; I will myself give to your friend what he needs; I do not require you but to give it to me as His friend, to give to my guest.' And so I used the three loaves and had some to spare. But the supply was small, and new guests came, because they saw I had a heart to help them and that I would take the trouble even at midnight to go to my friend. When I asked for them, too, I got what I needed again, and there was again some to spare. How could I help that the needy continually came to my house? Was I to harden myself and say, 'Why do you come to me? There are larger and better homes in the city. Go there.' Their answer was, 'Dear sir, we cannot go there. We have been there, and they were very sorry to send us away so hungry, but they could not undertake to go and ask a friend for what we wanted. Do go and get us bread, for we suffer great pain.' What would I do? They spoke the truth, and their suffering touched my heart. However much labor it cost me, I went each time again, and got the three loaves. Often I got what I asked much quicker than at first, and also much more abundantly. But all did not care for this bread, and so some left my home hungry."[30]

In his first struggles with the evil spirits, it took him more than eighteen months of much prayer and labor before the final victory was gained. Afterwards, he had such ease of access to the throne, and stood in such close communication with the unseen world, that often, when letters came asking prayer for sick people, he could, after just looking upward of for a single moment, obtain the answer as to whether they would be healed.

[30] From *Johann Christophe Blumhardt, Ein Lebensbild von F. Zündel.*

LESSON 17

"I KNOW THAT YOU ALWAYS HEAR ME," OR, PRAYER IN HARMONY WITH THE BEING OF GOD

"Father, I thank You that You have heard Me.
And I know that You always hear Me."
JOHN 11:41–42

"You are My Son, today I have begotten
You. Ask of Me, and I will give You."
PSALM 2:7–8

IN the New Testament we find a distinction made between faith and knowledge. "For to one is given the word of *wisdom* through the Spirit, to another the word of *knowledge* through the same Spirit, to another *faith* by the same Spirit" (1 Cor.12:8–9). In a child or a simple-minded Christian there may be much faith with little knowledge. Childlike simplicity accepts the truth without difficulty, and often cares little to give any reason for its faith but this: God said it. But it is the will of God that we should love and serve Him, not only with all the heart but also with all the mind, that we should grow up into an insight into the divine wisdom and beauty of all His ways and words and works.

It is only this way that the believer will be able to fully approach and rightly adore the glory of God's grace, only this way that our hearts can intelligently understand the treasures of wisdom and knowledge there are in redemption and be prepared to join in the highest note of the song that rises before the throne: "Oh, the depth of the riches both of the wisdom and knowledge of God!" (Rom. 11:33).

In our prayer life this truth has its full application. While prayer and faith are so simple that the newborn convert can pray with power, true Christian science finds in the doctrine of prayer some of its deepest problems. In how far is the power of prayer a reality? If so, how can God grant to prayer such mighty power? How can the action of prayer be harmonized with the will and the decrees of God? How can God's sovereignty and our will, God's liberty and ours be reconciled? These and similar questions are appropriate subjects for Christian meditation and inquiry. The more earnestly and reverently we approach such mysteries, the more shall we in adoring wonder fall down to praise Him who has in prayer given such power to man.

One of the secret difficulties with regard to prayer—one that, though not expressed, does often really hinder prayer—is derived from the perfection of God, in His absolute independence of all that is outside Himself. Is He not an infinite Being who owes what He is to Himself alone, who determines Himself, and whose wise and holy will has determined all that is to be? How can prayer influence Him, or He be moved by prayer, to do what otherwise would not be done? Is not the promise of an answer to prayer simply a condescension to our weakness? Is what is said of the power—the much-availing power—of prayer anything more than an accommodation to our mode of thought, because the Deity never can be dependent of any outside action for its doings? And isn't the real blessing of prayer simply the influence it exerts on ourselves?

> *It is the will of God that we should love and serve Him, not only with all the heart but also with all the mind, that we should grow up into an insight into the divine wisdom and beauty of all His ways and words and works.*

In seeking answers to such questions, we find the key in the very being of God, in the mystery of the holy Trinity. If God were only one Person, shut up within Himself, there could be no thought of nearness to Him or influence on Him. But in God there are three Persons. In God we have Father and Son, who have in the Holy Spirit their living bond of unity and fellowship. When eternal love fathered the Son, and the Father gave the Son as the Second Person a place next to Himself as His equal and His counselor, there was a way opened for prayer and its influence into the very innermost life of Deity itself.

Just as on earth, so in heaven the whole relationship between Father and Son is that of giving and taking. And if that taking is to be as voluntary and self-determined as the giving, there must be on the part of the Son an asking and receiving. In the holy fellowship of the divine Persons, this asking of the Son was one of the great operations of the thrice-blessed life of God. That's why it says in Psalm 2, "You are My Son, today I have begotten You. Ask of Me, and I will give You" (7–8). The Father gave the Son the place and the power to act upon Him. The Son's asking was no mere show or shadow, but one of those life movements in which the love of the Father and the Son met and completed each other. The Father had determined that He would not be alone in His plans. There was a Son on whose asking and accepting their fulfillment should depend. And so there was in the very Being and life of God an asking of which prayer on earth was to be the reflection and the outflow.

It was not without including this that Jesus said, "I know that You always hear Me" (John 11:42). Just as the sonship of Jesus on earth cannot be separated from His sonship in heaven, even so with His prayer on earth, it is the continuation and the counterpart of His asking in heaven. The prayer of the man Christ Jesus is the link between the eternal asking of the only-begotten Son in the bosom of the Father and the prayer of men on earth. Prayer has its rise and its deepest source in the very being of God. In the bosom of Deity nothing is ever done without prayer—the asking of the Son and the giving of the Father.[31]

> *Prayer has its rise and its deepest source in the very being of God. In the bosom of Deity nothing is ever done without prayer—the asking of the Son and the giving of the Father.*

This may help us somewhat to understand how the prayer of man, coming through the Son, can have an effect on God. The decrees of God are not made without reference to the Son, His petition, or the petition sent up through Him. By no means. The Lord Jesus is the first-begotten, the Head and Heir of all things. All things were created *through Him* and *for Him*, and all things consist *in Him*. In the plans of the Father, the Son, as the Representative of all creation, always had a voice. In the decrees of eternal purpose, there was always room left for the liberty of the Son as Mediator and Intercessor, and so for the petitions of all who draw near to the Father through the Son.

And if the thought come that this liberty and power to influence the Father seems to be at odds with the unchangeableness of the divine decrees, let us remember that there is not with God, as with man, a past by which He is irrevocably bound. God does not live in time with its past and future; the distinctions of time have no meaning to Him who inhabits eternity. And eternity is an ever-present now, in which the past is never past and the future is always present. To meet our human weakness, scripture must speak of past decrees and a coming future.

In reality, the unchanging nature of God's plan is still in perfect harmony with His liberty to do whatever He will. Not so were the prayers of the Son and His people taken up into the eternal decrees simply so that their effect should only be an apparent one; but so that the Father-heart holds itself open and free to listen to every prayer that rises through the Son, and that God does indeed allow Himself to be moved by prayer to do what He otherwise would not have done.

This perfect harmony and union of divine sovereignty and human liberty is an unfathomable mystery, because God as the *Eternal One* transcends all our thoughts. But let it be our comfort and strength to be assured that in the eternal fellowship of the Father and the Son, the power of prayer has its origin and

---

[31] See this thought developed in R. Löber, *Die Lehre vom Gebet.*

certainty, and that through our union with the Son, our prayer is taken up and can have its influence in the inner life of the blessed Trinity. God's decrees are no iron framework against which man's liberty would vainly seek to struggle. No! God Himself is the living Love, who in His Son as man has entered into the most tender relationship with all that is human, who through the Holy Spirit takes up all that is human into the divine life of love and keeps Himself free to give every human prayer its place in His government of the world.

> *This perfect harmony and union of divine sovereignty and human liberty is an unfathomable mystery, because God as the eternal One transcends all our thoughts.*

It is in the daybreak light of such thoughts that the doctrine of the blessed Trinity is no longer an abstract speculation, but the living manifestation of the way in which it is possible for man to be taken up into the fellowship of God, and his prayers becoming a real factor in God's rule of this earth. We can, at a distance, catch a glimpse of the light shining out from the eternal world in words such as these: "*Through Him* we both have access *by one Spirit to the Father*" (Eph. 2:18).

"LORD, TEACH US TO PRAY."

Everlasting God! The Three-One and thrice Holy! In deep reverence and with veiled face I worship before the holy mystery of Your divine Being. And if it pleases You, most glorious God, to reveal some of that mystery, I would bow with fear and trembling rather than sin against You, as I meditated on Your glory.

Father! I thank You that You bear this name not only as the Father of Your children here on earth, but as having from eternity existed as the Father with Your only-begotten Son. I thank You that as Father You can hear our prayer, because You have from eternity given a place in Your plans for the asking of Your Son. I thank You that we have seen in Him on earth what the blessed communication was He had with You in heaven, and how from eternity in all Your plans and decrees there had been room left for His prayers and their answers. And I thank You above all that through His true human nature on Your throne above, and through Your Holy Spirit in our human nature here below, a way has been opened by which every human cry of need can be received into and touch the life and love of God, and receive in answer whatever it shall ask.

Blessed Jesus, in whom as the Son the path of prayer has been opened, and who gives us assurance of the answer, we ask you to teach Your children how to pray. Let every day be the sign of our sonship so that we, like You, may know that the Father always hears us. Amen.

FOR FURTHER THOUGHT

1. *How firmly are you convinced that prayer indeed can change the course of human events—including the salvation of sinners? Who does that conviction affect your life of prayer?*
2. *Why do you think God, who exists in and of Himself, allows prayer to influence Him or move Him to do what otherwise would not be done?*
3. *How and why does God leave Himself free to give human prayers a place in His rule of the world? How does knowing the "how" and "why" motivate you to persevere in prayer?*

G OD *hears prayer.'* This simplest view of prayer is taken throughout scripture. It does not dwell on the reflex influence of prayer on our heart and life, although it abundantly shows the connection between prayer as an act and prayer as a state. It rather fixes with great definiteness the objective or real purposes of prayer, to obtain blessing, gifts, and deliverances from God. 'Ask, and it will be given,' Jesus says.

"However true and valuable the reflection may be, that God, foreseeing and foreordaining all things, has also foreseen and foreordained our prayers as links in the chain of events, of cause and effect, as a real power, yet we feel convinced that this is not the light in which the mind can find peace in this great subject, nor do we think that there is the attractive power to draw us in prayer. We feel rather that such a reflection *diverts* the attention from the Object from whom comes the impulse, life, and strength of prayer. The living God, *contemporary and not merely eternal,*[32] the living, merciful, holy One, God manifesting Himself to the soul, God saying, 'Seek My face'—this is the magnet that draws us, this alone can open heart and lips. . . .

"In Jesus Christ the Son of God we have the full solution for the difficulty. He prayed on earth, and that not merely as a man, but as the Son of God incarnate. His prayer on earth is only the manifestation of His prayer from all eternity, when in the divine plan He was set up as the Christ. . . . The Son was appointed to be heir of all things. From all eternity the Son of God was the Way, the Mediator. He was, to use our imperfect language, from eternity speaking to the Father on behalf of the world."

—SAPHIR, *The Hidden Life*, Chap. 6.

[32] Should it not be *contemporary, because eternal,* in the proper meaning of this latter word?

LESSON 18

"WHOSE IMAGE IS THIS?"

OR, PRAYER IN HARMONY

WITH THE DESTINY OF MAN

And He said to them,
"Whose image and inscription is this?"
MATTHEW 22:20

Then God said, "Let Us make man in
Our image, according to Our likeness"
GENESIS 1:26

WHOSE image and inscription is this?" It was with this question that Jesus foiled His enemies when they tried to take Him, and also settled the matter of duty in regard to the tax. The question and the principle it involves are of universal application. Nowhere more truly than in man himself. The image he bears decides his destiny. Bearing God's image, he belongs to God, and prayer to God is what he was created for. Prayer is part of the wondrous likeness he bears to His divine original. Of the deep mystery of the fellowship of love in which the Three-One has its blessedness, prayer is the earthly image and likeness.

The more we meditate on what prayer is, and on the wonderful power it has with God, the more we feel it necessary to ask who and what man is that such a place in God's plans has been allotted to him. Sin has so degraded him, that from what he is now we can form no conception of what he was meant to be. We must turn back to God's own record of man's creation to discover there what God's purpose was, and what the capacities with which man was endowed for the fulfillment of that purpose.

Man's destiny appears clearly in God's language at creation. It was to *fill*, to *subdue*, and to *have dominion* over the earth and everything in it. These three expressions show us that man was intended, as God's representative, to hold rule here on earth. As God's appointed ruler, he was to fill God's place: Himself subject to God, man was to keep all else in subjection to Him. It was the will of God that all that was to be done on earth should be done through him. The history of the earth was to be entirely in his hands.

In accordance with such a destiny was the position he was to occupy and the power at his disposal. When an earthly ruler sends a representative to a distant land, it is understood that he advises the ruler as to the policy to be adopted, and that the advice is acted on, and that the representative is at liberty to apply for troops and other means needed for carrying out the policy or maintaining the dignity of the empire. If his policy is not approved of, he is recalled to make way for someone who better understands his ruler's desires. But as long as the representative is trusted, his advice is carried out.

As God's representative, man was to have ruled. Everything was to have been done under his will and rule. On his advice and at his request, heaven was to have bestowed its blessing on earth. His prayer was to have been the wonderful, though simple and most natural, channel in which the communication between the King in heaven and His faithful servant, man, as lord of this world, was to have been maintained. The destinies of the world were given into the power of the wishes, the will, and the prayers of man.

> *Man's destiny appears clearly in God's language at creation. It was to fill, to subdue, and to have dominion over the earth and everything in it.*

With sin, all this underwent a terrible change. Man's fall brought all creation under the curse. With redemption, the beginning was seen of a glorious restoration. No sooner had God begun in Abraham to make for Himself a people from whom kings—especially the great King—would emerge than we see what power the prayer of God's faithful servant has to decide the destinies of those who came into contact with him. In Abraham we see how prayer is not only, or even chiefly, the means of obtaining blessing for ourselves but is the exercise of his royal prerogative to influence the destinies of men and the will of God that rules them. We do not once find Abraham praying for himself. His prayers for Sodom and Lot, for Abimelech, and for Ishmael prove what power a man who is God's friend has to make the history of those around him.

This had been man's destiny from the beginning. Scripture not only tells us this, but also teaches us how it was that God could entrust man with such a high calling. It was because He had created him *in His own image and likeness*. The external rule was not committed to him without the inner fitness. The bearing of God's image in having dominion, in being lord of all, had its root in the inner likeness, in his nature. There was an inner agreement and harmony between God and man, an incipient Godlikeness, which gave man a real fitness for being the mediator between God and His world, for he was to be prophet, priest, and king, and to interpret God's will, to represent nature's needs, to receive and dispense God's bounty. It was in bearing God's image that he could bear God's rule. He was indeed so much like God, so capable of entering into God's purposes and carrying out His plans that God could trust him with the wonderful privilege of asking for and obtaining what the world might need.

Although sin has for a time frustrated God's plans, prayer still remains what it would have been if man had never fallen: the proof of man's Godlikeness, the vehicle of his communication with the infinite, unseen One, and the power that is allowed to hold the hand that holds the destinies of the universe. Prayer is not merely the cry of the supplicant for mercy, but also the highest forth-putting of his will by man, who knows himself to be of divine origin, created for and capable of being, in kinglike liberty, the executor of the plans of the Eternal.

> *The destinies of the world were given into the power of the wishes, the will, and the prayers of man.*

What sin destroyed, grace has restored. What the first Adam lost, the second has won back. In Christ, man regains his original position, and the Church, abiding in Christ, inherits the promise: "Ask what you desire, and it shall be done for you" (John 15:7). Such a promise by no means, in the first place, refers to the grace or blessing we need for ourselves. It has reference to our position as the fruit-bearing branches of the heavenly Vine, who, like Him, only lives for the work and glory of the Father. It is for those who abide in Him, who have forsaken self to make their home in Him with His life of obedience and self-sacrifice, who have lost their life and found it in Him, who are now entirely given up to the interests of the Father and His kingdom. These are they who understand how their new creation has brought them back to their original destiny, has restored God's image and likeness, and with it the power to have dominion. Such indeed have the power, each in his own circle, to obtain and dispense the powers of heaven here on earth. With holy boldness they may make known what they desire. They live as priests in God's presence. As kings, the powers of the world to come begin to be at their disposal.[33] They enter into the fulfillment of the promise: "Ask what you desire, and it shall be done for you"

Church of the living God! Your calling is higher and holier than you know.

---

[33] "God is seeking priests among the sons of men. A human priesthood is one of the essential parts of His eternal plan. To *rule* creation by man is His design; to carry on the worship of creation by man is no less part of His design.

"Priesthood is the appointed link between heaven and earth, the channel of communication between the sinner and God. Such a priesthood, insofar as expiation is concerned, is in the hands of the Son of God alone; insofar as it is to be the medium of communication between Creator and creature, is also in the hands of redeemed men—of the Church of God.

"God is seeking kings. Not out of the ranks of angels. Fallen man must furnish Him with the rulers of His universe. Human hands must wield the scepter, human heads must wear the crown."
—*The Rent Veil*, by Dr. H. Bonar.

Through your members, as kings and priests to God, God wants to rule the world; your prayers bestow and withhold the blessings of heaven. Through His elect who are not content just to be saved themselves but who yield themselves wholly, that through them, even as through the Son, the Father may fulfill all His glorious plans, in these His elect, who cry day and night to Him, God wants to prove how wonderful man's original destiny was. As the image-bearer of God on earth, the earth was indeed given into his hand. When he fell, all fell with him, and now the whole creation groans and labors in pain together.

> *A*s image-bearer and representative of God on earth, redeemed man will by his prayers determine the history of this earth.

But now man is redeemed, and the restoration of the original dignity has begun. It is in very deed God's purpose that the fulfillment of His eternal purpose, and the coming of His kingdom, should depend on His people, who, abiding Christ, are ready to accept Him as their Head, the great Priest-King, and in their prayers are bold enough to say what they want their God to do. As image-bearer and representative of God on earth, redeemed man will by his prayers determine the history of this earth. Man was created and has now again been redeemed to pray, and by his prayer to have dominion.

"LORD, TEACH US TO PRAY."

Lord! "What is man that You are mindful of him, and the son of man that You visit him? For You have made him a little lower than the angels, and You have crowned him with glory and honor. You have made him to have dominion over the works of Your hands; You have put all *things* under his feet.... O LORD, our Lord, how excellent *is* Your name in all the earth!" (Psalm 8:4–6, 9).

Lord God! How low sin has made man to sink. And how terribly it has darkened his mind, so that he doesn't even know his divine destiny: to be Your servant and representative. How sad it is that even Your people, when their eyes are opened, are so unready to accept their calling and seek to have power with God so that they may have power with men too to bless them.

Lord Jesus! It is in You the Father has again crowned man with glory and honor, and opened the way for us to be what He wants us to be. O Lord! Have mercy on Your people and visit Your heritage! Work mightily in Your Church, and teach Your believing disciples to accept and to go out in their royal priesthood, and, in the power of prayer, about which You have given such wonderful promises, to serve Your Kingdom, to have rule over the nations, and to make the name of God glorious on the earth. Amen.

FOR FURTHER THOUGHT

1. *What was God's purpose in creating man and placing him in the world? How does that relate to prayer today?*
2. *What makes you fit to be a mediator between God and His world? In what does that role consist for you?*
3. *What must you do to be a part of God's purpose of fulfilling His eternal purpose and the coming of His kingdom?*

LESSON 19

"I GO TO MY FATHER," OR, POWER
FOR PRAYING AND WORKING

*"Most assuredly, I say to you, he who believes in Me, the
works that I do he will do also; and greater works than these he
will do, because I go to My Father. And whatever you ask in
My name, that I will do, that the Father may be glorified in
the Son. If you ask anything in My name, I will do it."*
JOHN 14:12–14

AS the Savior opened His public ministry with His disciples by the Sermon
on the Mount, so He closes it by the parting address from the Gospel of John. In
both He speaks more than once of prayer. But there is a difference. The Sermon
on the Mount is directed at disciples who have only just entered His school, who
hardly know that God is their Father, and whose prayer chiefly has reference to
their personal needs. In His closing address, He speaks to disciples whose training time has now coming to an end, and who are ready as His messengers to take
His place and His work.

In the former, the chief lesson is: Be childlike, pray believingly, and trust the
Father to give you all good gifts. Here He points to something higher. The disciples are now His friends to whom He has made known all He has heard from
the Father, and His messengers, who have entered into His plans and into whose
hand the care of His work and kingdom on earth is to be entrusted. They are now
to go out and do His works, and, in the power of His approaching exaltation,
even greater works. Prayer is now to be the channel through which that power is
received for their work. With Christ's ascension to the Father, a new epoch begins
for both their working and their praying.

See how clearly this connection comes out in our text. As His Body here on
earth, as those who are one with Him in heaven, the disciples are now to do greater works than He had done. Their successes and their victories are to be greater
than His. He mentions two reasons for this. The one was because He was to go to
the Father to receive all power, the other that they could now ask for and expect
all in His Name. "Because I go to My Father. And"—notice this *and*—"whatever

you ask in My name, that I will do." His going to the Father would therefore bring a double blessing: They would ask and receive everything in His Name, and, consequently, they would do the greater works. This first mention of prayer in our Savior's parting words teaches us two most important lessons. He who desires to do the works of Jesus *must pray* in His Name. He who desires to pray in His Name *must work* in His Name.

> *A*s His Body here on earth, as those who are one with Him in heaven, the disciples are now to do greater works than He had done.

He who desires to work *must pray*. It is in prayer that the power for work is obtained. He who in faith wants to do the works that Jesus did must pray in His name. As long as Jesus was here on earth, He did the greatest works Himself: Demons the disciples could not cast out fled at His word. When He went to the Father, He was no longer here in body to work directly. The disciples were now His body, and all His work from the throne in heaven must and could be done here on earth through them. One might have thought that now that He was leaving the scene Himself, and could only work through commissioners, the works might be fewer and weaker. But He assures us that just the opposite would be true: "*Most assuredly*, I say to you, he who believes in Me, the works that I do he will do also; and greater works than these he will do" (John 14:12). His approaching death was to be a real breaking down and end of the power of sin. With the resurrection, the powers of the eternal life were truly to take possession of the human body and to obtain supremacy over human life. With His ascension, He was to receive the power to communicate the Holy Spirit so fully to own. The union—the oneness between Himself on the throne and those on earth—was to be so intensely and divinely perfect that He meant it as the literal truth: "Greater works than these he will do, because I go to My Father."

And the results proved how true it was. While Jesus, during three years of personal labor on earth, gathered few more than five hundred disciples, most of whom were so powerless that they were of little use to His cause, it was given to men like Peter and Paul manifestly to do greater things than He had done. From the throne He could do through them what He Himself in His humiliation could not yet do.

But there was one condition: "He who believes in Me, the works that I do he will do also; and greater works than these he will do, because I go to My Father. *And whatever you ask in My name, that I will do.*" His going to the Father would give Him new power to hear prayer. For the doing of these greater works, two things were needed: His going to the Father to receive all power from Him again, and our prayer in His name to receive all power from Him again. As He asks the Father, He receives and bestows on us the power of the new dispensation for greater works. As we believe and ask in His name, the power comes and takes possession of us to do the greater works.

Sadly, there is much work of God attempted in which there is little or nothing to be seen of the power to do anything like Christ's works, not to mention greater works. There can only be one reason: The believing in Him and the believing prayer in His Name are so much lacking. O that every laborer and leader in church, in school, in the work of home philanthropy or foreign missions might learn that lesson: Prayer in the name of Jesus is the only way to share in the mighty power that Jesus has received from the Father for His people. It is in this power alone that he who believes can do greater works.

> *As He asks the Father, He receives and bestows on us the power of the new dispensation for greater works. As we believe and ask in His name, the power comes and takes possession of us to do the greater works.*

To every complaint about weaknesses or unfitness, or about difficulties or lack of success, Jesus gives this one answer: "*He who believes* in Me. . .greater works than these he will do, because I go to My Father. And *whatever you ask* in My name, *that I will do.*" We must understand that the first and chief thing for everyone who desires to do the work of Jesus is to believe and so to get linked to Him, the almighty One, and then to pray the prayer of faith in His name. Without this, our work is just human and carnal. It may have some use in restraining sin or in preparing the way for a blessing, but the real power is missing. Effective working needs first effective prayer.

And now the second lesson: He who desires to pray *must work.* It is for power to work that prayer has such great promises. It is in working that the power for the effective prayer of faith will be gained. In these parting words of our blessed Lord, we find that no fewer than six times (John 14:13–14; 15:7, 16; 16:23–24) He repeats those unlimited prayer promises that have so often awakened our anxious questions as to their real meaning: "*whatever*," "*anything*," "*what you desire*," "*ask, and you will receive.*" Many a believer has read these with joy and hope, and in deep earnestness of soul has tried to plead them for his own need. And he has come out disappointed. The simple reason was this: He had separated the promise from its surrounding context.

The Lord gave the wonderful promise of the free use of His name with the Father in connection with the *doing of His works.* It is the disciple who gives himself wholly to live for Jesus' work and kingdom, for His will and honor, to whom the power will come to appropriate the promise. He who would simply grasp the promise when he wants something very special for himself will be disappointed, because he is making Jesus the servant of his own comfort. But to him who seeks to pray the effective prayer of faith because he needs it for the work of the Master will learn it, because he has made himself the servant of his Lord's interests. Prayer not only teaches and strengthens for work, but work teaches and strengthens to pray.

This is in perfect harmony with what holds true both in the natural and in the spiritual worlds. "To everyone who has (more) will be given" (Luke 19:26); or, "He who is faithful in what is least is faithful also in much" (Luke 16:10). Let us with the small amount of grace already received give ourselves to the Master for His work. This work will be to us a real school of prayer. It was when Moses had to take full charge of a rebellious people that he felt the need, but also the courage, to speak boldly to God and to ask great things from Him (Exod. 33:12, 15, 18). As you give yourself entirely to God for His work, you will feel that nothing less than these great promises are what you need, that nothing less is what you may most confidently expect.

Believer in Jesus! You are called, you are appointed to do the works of Jesus, and even greater works, because He has gone to the Father to receive the power to do them in and through you.

"*Whatever* you ask in My name, that *I will do*." Give yourself, and live, to do the works of Christ, and then you will learn to pray in such a way that you obtain wonderful answers to prayer. Give yourself, and live, to pray, and then you will learn to do the works He did, and greater works. With disciples full of faith in Himself and bold in prayer to ask great things, Christ can conquer the world.

"Lord, teach us to pray."

O my Lord! I have this day again heard words from You that are beyond my comprehension. And yet I can do nothing but in simple childlike faith accept them as Your gift to me, too. You have said that because You go to Your Father, he who believes in You will do the works You have done, and greater works. Lord! I worship You as the glorified One, and I look forward to the fulfillment of Your promise. May my whole life be one of continued believing in You. So purify and sanctify my heart, make it so tenderly susceptible to Yourself and Your love, that believing in You will become the very life it breathes.

You have said that because You went to the Father, You will do whatever we ask You to do. From Your throne of power, You desire to make Your people share the power given You, and work through them as the members of Your Body, in response to their believing prayer in Your name. Power in prayer with You, and power in work with men, You have promised Your people and me, too.

Blessed Lord! Forgive us all that we have so little believed You and Your promise, and so little proved Your faithfulness in fulfilling it. Please forgive us that we have so little honored Your all-prevailing name in heaven or on earth.

Lord! Teach me to pray so that I can prove that Your name is indeed all-powerful with God, with men, and with demons. Yes, teach me to work and to pray in such a way that You, the omnipotent One, can glorify Yourself in me, and do Your great works through me too. Amen.

For Further Thought

1. *How and why would the disciples be able to do greater works than Jesus Himself had done during His earthly ministry?*
2. *What is the channel through which the disciples—the original twelve and you today—are to receive power for the work Jesus called them to do?*
3. *What are the conditions for your learning to pray in such a way that you obtain answers to prayer?*

LESSON 20

"THAT THE FATHER MAY BE GLORIFIED,"OR, THE CHIEF PURPOSE OF PRAYER

I go to My Father. And whatever you ask in My name,
that I will do, that the Father may be glorified in the Son.
If you ask anything in My name, I will do it."
JOHN 14:12–14

THAT *the Father may be glorified in the Son*: It is for this purpose that Jesus on His throne in glory will do everything we ask in His Name. Every answer to prayer He gives will have this as its object: When there is no prospect of this object being obtained, He will not answer. It follows as a matter of course that with us, as with Jesus, the essential element in our petitions: The glory of the Father must be the aim and purpose, the very soul and life of our prayer.

It was so with Jesus when He was on earth: "I don't seek my own honor; I seek the honor of Him who sent me." In such words we have the keynote of His life. In the first words of the high-priestly prayer, He gives voice to it: "Father...glorify Your Son, *that Your Son also may glorify You.... I have glorified You on the earth....* Glorify Me together with Yourself" (John 17:1, 4, 5). The ground on which He asks to be taken up into the glory He had with the Father is a twofold one: He has glorified Him on earth, and He will still glorify Him in heaven. What He asks is only to enable Him to glorify the Father more.

It is as we enter into agreement with Jesus on this point, and please Him by making the Father's glory our chief object in prayer, too, that our prayer cannot fail to get an answer. There is nothing of which the beloved Son has said will glorify the Father more than this: His doing what we ask. He will not, therefore, miss any opportunity to secure this object. Let us make His aim ours! Let the glory of the Father be the link between our asking and His doing! Such prayer must prevail.[34]

This word of Jesus comes indeed as a sharp two-edged sword, piercing even to the dividing of soul and spirit, and quick to discern the thoughts and intents

---

[34] See in the note on George Müller, at the close of this volume, how he was led to make God's glory his first objective.

of the heart (see Heb. 4:12). Jesus, in His prayers on earth, in His intercession in heaven, and in His promise of an answer to our prayers from there, makes His first object—the glory of the Father. Is it so with us, too? Or are not, in large measure, self-interest and self-will the strongest motives urging us to pray? Or, if we cannot see that this is the case, have we not acknowledged that the distinct, conscious longing for the glory of the Father is not what animates our prayers? And yet it must be so.

It is not as if the believer does not at times desire it. But he has to mourn that he has so little attained it. And he knows the reason for his failure, too. It was because the separation between the spirit of daily life and the spirit of the hour of prayer was too wide. We begin to see that the desire for the glory of the Father is not something we can arouse and present to our Lord when we prepare ourselves to pray. No! It is only when the whole life in all its parts is given up to God's glory that we can really pray to His glory, too. "*Do all* to the glory of God" (1 Cor. 10:31), and "*Ask all* to the glory of God." These twin commands are inseparable. Obedience to the former is the secret of grace for the latter. A life to the glory of God is the condition of the prayers that Jesus can answer, "that the Father may be glorified."

> There is nothing of which the beloved Son has said will glorify the Father more than this: His doing what we ask. He will not, therefore, miss any opportunity to secure this object.

This demand in connection with prevailing prayer—that it should be to the glory of God—is no more than right and natural. There is no one glorious but the Lord; there is no glory but His and what He allots to His creatures. Creation exists to show forth His glory. All that is not for His glory is sin and darkness and death. It is only in the glorifying of God that the creatures can find glory. What the Son of Man did—giving Himself wholly, His whole life, to glorify the Father—is nothing but the simple duty of every redeemed one. And Christ's reward will be his, too. Because He gave Himself so entirely to the glorifying of the Father, the Father crowned Him with glory and honor and gave the kingdom into His hands, with the power to ask what He desired and, as Intercessor, to answer our prayers. And just as we become one with Christ in this, and as our prayer is part of a life completely surrendered to God's glory, will the Savior be able to glorify the Father in us by the fulfillment of the promise: "Whatever you ask in My name, that I will do."

To such a life, one with God's glory our only aim, we cannot attain by any effort of our own. It is only in the man Christ Jesus that such a life is to be seen. In Him it is to be found for us. Yes, blessed be God! His life is our life. He gave

Himself for us, and He Himself is now our life. The discovery, the confession, and the denial of self, as taking the place of God, and of self-seeking and self-trusting is essential, and yet is what we cannot accomplish in our own strength. It is the incoming and indwelling, the presence and the rule in the heart, of our Lord Jesus, who glorified the Father on earth and is now glorified with Him, so that He might glorify Him in us—it is Jesus Himself coming in, who can cast out all self-glorification and give us instead His own God-glorifying life and Spirit. It is Jesus, who longs to glorify the Father in hearing our prayers, who will teach us to live and to pray to the glory of God.

And what motive and what power is there that can urge our complacent hearts to yield themselves to our Lord to work this in us? Surely nothing more is needed than a glimpse of how glorious, how alone worthy of glory the Father is. Let our faith learn to bow in adoring worship before Him and ascribe to Him alone the kingdom, the power, and the glory, and to yield ourselves to live in the light of the always-blessed, always-loving One. Surely we shall be stirred to say, "To Him alone be glory." And we shall look to our Lord Jesus with new intensity of desire for a life that refuses to see or seek out anything but the glory of God. When there is only little prayer that can be answered, the Father is not glorified. It is our duty, for the glory of God, to live and pray so that our prayer can be answered. For the sake of God's glory, let us learn to pray well.

What a humbling thought it is that so often there is earnest prayer for a child or a friend, or for a work or a circle, in which the desire for our own joy or pleasure was far stronger than any yearnings for God's glory. No wonder there are so many unanswered prayers: Here we have the secret. God would not be glorified when that glory was not our objective. He who desires to pray the prayer of faith must give himself to live literally so that the Father in all things may be glorified in him. This must be his aim, for without it there cannot be a prayer of faith.

> *I*t is our duty, for the glory of God, to live and pray so that our prayer can be answered. For the sake of God's glory, let us learn to pray well.

"How can you believe," asked Jesus, "who receive honor from one another, and do not seek the honor that comes from the only God?" (John 5:44). All seeking of our own glory with men makes faith impossible. It is the deep, intense self-sacrifice that gives up its own glory, and seeks the glory of God alone, that awakens in the soul that spiritual susceptibility of the divine, which is faith. The surrender to God and the expectation that He will show His glory in hearing us are inseparable. Only he who seeks God's glory will see it in the answer to his prayer.

And how, we ask again, shall we accomplish it? Let us begin with confession.

How little has the glory of God been an all-absorbing passion; how little our lives and our prayers have been full of it. How little have we lived in the likeness of the Son and in agreement with Him—for God and His glory alone. Let us take time, until the Holy Spirit shows us, and we will see how lacking we have been in this. True knowledge and confession of sin is the sure path to deliverance.

And then let us look to Jesus. In Him we can see by what death we can glorify God. In death He glorified Him, and through death He was glorified with Him. It is by dying, being dead to self and living to God, that we can glorify Him. And this—this death to self, this life to the glory of God—is what Jesus gives and lives in each one who can trust Him for it. Let nothing less than these—the desire and the decision to live only for the glory of the Father, just as Christ did; the acceptance of Him with His life and strength working in us; and the joyful assurance that we can live to the glory of God, because Christ lives in us—let these be the spirit of our daily life.

Jesus stands as the surety for our living this way. The Holy Spirit is given, and is waiting to make it our experience, if we will only trust and let Him. Let us not hold back through unbelief but confidently take as our watchword—All to the glory of God! The Father accepts the will, the sacrifice is well-pleasing. The Holy Spirit will seal us within with the consciousness that we are living for God and His glory.

And then what quiet peace and power there will be in our prayers as we know ourselves, through His grace, in perfect harmony with Him who says to us when He promises to do what we ask: "That the Father may be glorified in the Son." With our whole being consciously yielded to the inspiration of the Word and Spirit, our desires will no longer be ours but His, and their chief purpose will be the glory of God.

With increasing liberty we shall be able in prayer to say: "Father! You know we ask it only for Your glory." And the condition of prayer answers, instead of being like a mountain we cannot climb, will give us greater confidence that we are heard, because we have seen that prayer has no higher beauty or blessedness than this, that it glorifies the Father. And the precious privilege of prayer will become doubly precious because it brings us into perfect unity with the beloved Son in the wonderful partnership He proposes: "*You ask*, and *I do*, that the Father may be glorified in the Son."

"LORD, TEACH US TO PRAY."

Blessed Lord Jesus! I come again to You. Every lesson you give me convinces me all the more deeply how little I know how to pray properly. But every lesson also inspires me with hope that You are going to teach me, that You are teaching me not only to know what prayer should be, but actually to pray as I should. O my Lord! I look with courage to You, the great Intercessor who prayed and hears prayer only that the Father may be glorified, to teach me, too, to live and pray to the glory of God.

Savior! For this purpose I yield myself to You again. I want to be nothing. I have given self, as already crucified with You, to death. Through the Spirit, its works are mortified and made dead. Your life and Your love of the Father are taking possession of me. A new longing begins to fill my soul so that every day, every hour, and in every prayer the glory of the Father may be everything to me. O my Lord! I am in Your school to learn. Please teach me this!

God of glory, Father of glory, my God and my Father, accept the desire of Your child who has seen that Your glory is indeed alone worth living for. O Lord! Show me Your glory. Let it fill the temple of my heart. Let me live in it as revealed in Christ. And do Yourself fulfill in me Your own good pleasure so that Your child should find his glory in seeking the glory of his Father. Amen.

FOR FURTHER THOUGHT

1. *What is the one thing Jesus taught that you can do to glorify the Father?*
2. *What is the only way a life for the glory of God can be found?*
3. *What will happen when you yield your whole being to the inspiration of the Word and Spirit? What will then be your purpose and desire in life?*

LESSON 21

"IF YOU ABIDE IN ME," OR,
THE ALL-INCLUSIVE CONDITION

*"If you abide in Me, and My words abide in you, you
will ask what you desire, and it shall be done for you."*
JOHN 15:7

IN all God's communication with us, the promise and its conditions are inseparable. If we fulfill the conditions, He fulfills the promise. What He is to be to us depends on what we are willing to be to Him. "Draw near to God and He will draw near to you" (James 4:8). And so in prayer, the unlimited promise, *Ask what you desire*, has one simple and natural condition: *If you abide in Me*. It is Christ whom the Father always hears. God is *in Christ*, and can only be reached by being in Him. To be *in Him* is the way to have our prayer heard. Fully and wholly *abiding in Him*, we have the right to ask whatever we desire and the promise that we will get an answer.

When we compare this promise with the experience of most believers, we are startled by a terrible discrepancy. Who can number the countless prayers that rise up but bring no answer? The cause must be either that we do not fulfill the condition, or that God does not fulfill the promise. Believers are not willing to admit either, and have therefore devised a way of escape from the dilemma. They put into the promise the qualifying clause our Savior did not put there—"If it is God's will"—and so maintain both God's integrity and their own. If they would only accept it and hold it firmly as it stands, trusting trust Christ to vindicate His truth, God's Spirit would lead them to see the divine appropriateness of such a promise to those who really abide in Christ in the sense in which He means it, and also to confess that the failure to fulfill the condition is the one sufficient explanation of unanswered prayer. And how the Holy Spirit would then make our weakness in prayer one of the mightiest motivations to urge us on to discover the secret and obtain the blessing of fully abiding in Christ.

"If you abide in Me." As a Christian grows in grace and knowledge of the Lord Jesus, he is often surprised to find how the words of God grow, too—in the new and deeper meaning with which they come to him. He can look back

to the day when some word of God was opened up to him, and he rejoiced in the blessing he had found in it. After a time, some deeper experience gave the word a new meaning, and it was as if he never had seen what it contained. And yet once again, as he advanced in the Christian life, the same word stood before him again as a great mystery, until one more the Holy Spirit led him still deeper into its divine fullness.

One of these ever-growing, never-exhausted words, opening up to us step by step the fullness of the divine life, is the Master's precious "Abide in Me." As the union of the branch with the vine is one of growth, never-ceasing growth and increase, so our abiding in Christ is a life process in which the divine life takes fuller and fuller and more complete possession of us. The young and weak believer may really be abiding in Christ up to the measure of his light, but it is he who reaches onward to the full abiding, in the sense in which the Master meant the words, who inherits all the promises connected with it.

> *A*s a Christian grows in grace and knowledge of the Lord Jesus, he is often surprised to find how the words of God grow, too—in the new and deeper meaning with which they come to him.

In the growing life of abiding in Christ, the first stage is that of faith. As the believer sees that, with all his weakness, the command is really meant for him, his great aim is simply to believe that, as he knows he is in Christ, so now—notwithstanding unfaithfulness and failure—abiding in Christ is his immediate duty, and a blessing is within his reach. He is specially occupied with the love, power, and faithfulness of the Savior. He feels his one need is to believe.

It is not long before he sees something more is needed. Obedience and faith must go together. Not that he needed to add obedience to faith, but that faith must be demonstrated or revealed in obedience. Faith is obedience at home and looking to the Master, and obedience is faith going out to do His will. He sees how he has been more occupied with the privilege and the blessings of this abiding than with its duties and its fruit. There has been much self and self-will that has been unnoticed or tolerated. The peace that as a young and weak disciple he could enjoy in believing goes from him. It is in practical obedience that the abiding must be maintained: "If you keep My commandments, you will abide in My love" (John 15:10). As before, his great aim was through the *mind*, and the truth it took hold of, to let the heart rest on Christ and His promises, so now, in this stage, his chief effort is to get his *will* united with the will of his Lord, with his heart and life brought entirely under His rule.

And yet it is as if there is something lacking. The will and the heart are on Christ's side, and he obeys and loves his Lord. But still, why is it that the fleshly nature still has so much power, that the spontaneous motions and emotions of the innermost begin are not what they should be? The will does not approve or allow, but here is a region beyond control of the will. And why also, even when there is not much of positive commission of sin to condemn, is there so much of omission, the deficiency of that beauty of holiness, that zeal of love, that conformity to Jesus and to His death, in which the life of self is lost, and which is certainly implied in the abiding, as the Master meant it? There must certainly be something in our abiding in Christ, and Christ abiding in us, that he has not yet experienced.

It is so. Faith and obedience is just the pathway to blessing. Before giving us the parable of the vine and the branches, Jesus had very distinctly told what that full blessing is to which faith and obedience are to lead. Three times over He had said, "If you love Me, keep My commandments," and spoken of the threefold blessing with which He would crown such obedient love: The Holy Spirit would come from the Father, the Son would manifest Himself, and the Father and the Son would come and make their home. It is as our faith grows into obedience, and in obedience and love our whole being goes out and clings itself to Christ, that our inner life opens up, and the capacity is formed within us of receiving the life, the Spirit, of the glorified Jesus, as a distinct and conscious union with Christ and with the Father. The word is fulfilled in us: "At that day you will know that I am in My Father, and you in Me, and I in you" (John 14:20). We understand how, just as Christ is in God and God in Christ—one together not only in will and in love, but in identity of nature and life, because they exist in each other—so we are in Christ and Christ is in us, in union not only of will and love, but of life and nature, too.

> t is in practical obedience that the abiding must be maintained: "If you keep My commandments, you will abide in My love"

It was after Jesus had spoken of us thus through the Holy Spirit knowing that He is in the Father, and likewise we are in Him and He in us, that He said, "Abide in me, and I in you. Accept, consent to receive that divine life of union with Myself, in virtue of which, as you abide in Me, I also abide in you, just as I abide in the Father. So that your life is Mine and Mine is yours." This is true abiding, the occupying of the position into which Christ can come and abide. It is so abiding in Him that the soul has come away from self to find that He has taken its place and become our life. It is the becoming like little children who have no care, and who find their happiness in trusting and obeying the love that has done all for them.

To those who abide this way comes as their rightful heritage: "Ask what you desire." It cannot be otherwise. Christ has taken full possession of them. Christ dwells in their love, their will, and their life. Not only has their will been given up, but Christ has entered it and dwells and breathes in it by His Spirit. He whom the Father always hears prays in them, and they pray in Him, so what they ask will be done for them.

Beloved fellow believer! Let us confess that it is because we do not abide in Christ as He would like us to that the Church lacks power in the presence of infidelity, worldliness, and heathendom, in the midst of which the Lord is able to make her more than a conqueror. Let us believe that He means what He promises, and accept the condemnation the confession implies.

But let us not be discouraged. The abiding of the branch in the Vine is a life of never-ceasing growth. The abiding, as the Master meant it, is within our reach, for He lives to give it to us. Let us just be ready to count all things as loss and to say, "Not that I have already attained. . .but I press on, that I may lay hold of that for which Christ Jesus has also laid hold of me" (Phil. 3:12). Let us not be so much occupied with the abiding as with *Him* to whom the abiding links us, and His fullness. Let it be *Him*, the whole Christ—in His obedience and humiliation, in His exaltation and power—in whom our soul moves and acts. Then He Himself will fulfill His promise in us.

> *A*s we abide, and grow into fuller and fuller abiding, let us exercise our right, the will to enter into God's will. Obeying what that will commands, let us claim what it promises.

And then as we abide, and grow into fuller and fuller abiding, let us exercise our right, the will to enter into God's will. Obeying what that will commands, let us claim what it promises. Let us yield to the teaching of the Holy Spirit, who will show each of us, according to his own growth and strength, what the will of God is that we may claim in power. And let us rest content with nothing less than the personal experience of what Jesus gave when He said, "If you abide in Me. . .ask what you desire, and it shall be done for you."

"LORD, TEACH US TO PRAY."

Beloved Lord! Teach me to take this promise anew in all its simplicity, and to be sure that the only measure of Your holy giving is our holy willing. Lord! Let each word of Your promise be, in a new way, made living and powerful in my soul.

You say, *Abide in me!* O my Master, my Life my All, I do abide in You. Allow me to grow up into all your fullness. It is not the effort of faith, trying to cling to You, nor even the rest of faith, trusting You to protect me; it is not the obedience of the will, nor the keeping of the commandments. It is Yourself living in me as in the Father that alone can satisfy me. It is You, my Lord, no longer before me and above me, but one with me and abiding in me. It is this I need and this I seek. It is this I trust You for.

You say, *Ask whatever you desire*! Lord! I know that a life of full, deep abiding will so renew and sanctify and strengthen the will that I shall have the light and the liberty to ask great things. Lord! Let my will—dead in Your death, living in Your life—be bold and large in its requests.

You say, *It shall be done*! O Jesus! You who are the Amen, the faithful and true Witness: Give me in Yourself the joyous confidence that You will make this word still more wonderfully true to me than ever, because it has not entered into the heart of man to conceive what God has prepared for those who love Him. Amen.

For Further Thought

1. *Under what condition do you have the God-given right to ask whatever you desire with the promise that You will get an answer?*
2. *What did Jesus say three times, and what three promises did He make in connection with His thrice-repeated statement?*
3. *Why, according to this lesson, does the Church lack power in the presence of infidelity and worldliness? What must you do to receive that power?*

ON a thoughtful comparison between what we mostly find in books or sermons on prayer, and the teaching of the Master, we shall find one great difference: The importance assigned to the answer to prayer is by no means the same. In the former, we find a great deal on the blessing of prayer as a spiritual exercise, even when there is no answer, and on the reasons why we should be content without it. God's fellowship ought to be more important to us than the gift we ask for. God's wisdom only knows what is best. God may give something better than what He withholds.

Though this teaching looks very high and spiritual, it is remarkable that we find nothing of it from our Lord. The more carefully we gather together all He spoke on prayer, the clearer it becomes that He wished us to think of prayer simply as the means to an end, and that prayer was to be the proof that we and our prayer are acceptable to the Father in heaven. It is not that Christ wants us to consider the gifts of higher value than the fellowship and favor of the Father. By no means! But the Father intends the answer to be evidence of His favor and of the reality of our fellowship with Him. "Today your servant knows that I have found favor in your sight, my lord, O king, in that the king has fulfilled the request of his servant" (2 Sam. 14:22).

A life marked by daily answer to prayer is the proof of our spiritual maturity. It shows that we have indeed attained the true abiding in Christ, that our will is truly at one with God's will, that our faith has grown strong enough to see and take what God has prepared for us, that the name of Christ and His nature have taken full possession of us, that we have been found fit to take a place among those whom God admits to His counsels, and according to whose prayer He rules the world. These are they in whom something of man's original dignity has been restored, in whom, as they abide in Christ, His power as the all-prevailing Intercessor can manifest itself, in whom the glory of His Name is shown forth. Prayer is very blessed, but *the answer is more blessed still*, as the response from the Father that our prayer, our faith, and our will are indeed as He would wish them to be.

I make these remarks with the one desire of leading my readers to put together for themselves everything Christ has said about prayer and to yield themselves to the full impression of the truth that when prayer is what it should be, or rather when we are what we should be—abiding in Christ—the answer must be expected. It will bring us out from those refuges where we have comforted ourselves with unanswered prayer. It will reveal to us the place of power to which Christ has appointed His Church, but which it occupies so little. It will reveal the terrible weakness of our spiritual life as the cause of our not knowing to pray boldly in Christ's name. It will urge us mightily to rise to a life in full union with Christ, and in the fullness of the Spirit, as the secret of effective prayer. And it will so lead us to realize our destiny: "*At that day*. . .most assuredly, I say to you, whatever you ask the Father in My name He will give you. . . . Ask, and you will receive, that your joy may be full" (John 14:20; 16:23–24). Prayer that is really, spiritually, *in union with Jesus* is always answered.

LESSON 22

"MY WORDS IN YOU," OR,
THE WORD AND PRAYER

"If you abide in Me, and My words abide in you, you
will ask what you desire, and it shall be done for you."
JOHN 15:7

THE vital connection between the word and prayer is one of the simplest and earliest lessons of the Christian life. As that newly converted heathen put it: "I pray—I speak to my Father; I read—my Father speaks to me." Before prayer, it is God's Word that prepares me for it by revealing what the Father wants me to ask. In prayer, it is God's Word that strengthens me by giving my faith its warrant and its plea. And after prayer, it is God's Word that brings me the answer when I have prayed, for in it the Spirit allows me to hear the Father's voice.

Prayer is not monologue but dialogue. God's voice in response to mine is its most essential part. Listening to God's voice is the secret of the assurance that He will listen to mine. "Incline your ear and hear," "Give ear to Me," and "Hear My voice" are words that God speaks to man as well as man to God. His hearing will depend on ours. The entrance His words find with me will be the measure of the power of my words with Him. What God's words are to me is the test of what He Himself is to me, and therefore of the uprightness of my desire for Him in prayer.

It is this connection between His Word and our prayer that Jesus points to when He says, "If you abide in Me, *and My words abide in you,* you will ask what you desire, and it shall be done for you." The deep importance of this truth becomes clear if we notice the other expression this one has replaced. More than once Jesus had said, "Abide in Me, and *I in you.*" His abiding in us was the complement and the crown of our abiding in Him. But here, instead of "You in Me, *and I in you,*" He says, "You in Me, *and My words in you.*" His words abiding are the equivalent of Himself abiding.

What a view is here opened up to us of the place the words of God in Christ are to have in our spiritual life, especially in our prayer. In a man's words, *he reveals himself.* In his promises, *he gives himself away* and binds himself to the one who receives his promises. In his commands, he proclaims his will and seeks to *make himself master* of him whose obedience he claims, to guide and use him as if he were part of himself. It is through our words that spirit holds fellowship with spirit, so that the spirit of one man passes over and transfers itself to another. It is though the words of man, heard and accepted and held firmly and obeyed, that he can impart himself to another. But all this in a very relative and limited sense.

But when God, the infinite Being in whom everything is life, power, spirit, and truth, in the very deepest meaning of the words—when God speaks forth Himself in His words, He does indeed give *Himself*, His love and His life, His will and His power, to those who receive these words in a reality passing comprehension. In every promise, He puts *Himself* in our power to lay hold of and posses. In every command, He puts *Himself* in our power for us to share with Him His will, His holiness, and His perfection. In God's Word, God gives us *Himself*. His word is nothing less than the eternal Son, Christ Jesus. And so, all Christ's words are God's words, full of a divine quickening life and power. "The words that I speak to you are spirit, and they are life" (John 6:63).

Those who have made the deaf and mute their study tell us how much the power of speaking depends on that of hearing, and how the loss of hearing in children is followed by that of speaking, too. This is also true in a wider sense: As we hear, so we speak. This is true in the highest sense of our communication with God. To offer a prayer—to give utterance to certain wishes and to appeal to certain promises—is an easy thing and can be learned by man through human wisdom. But to pray in the Spirit, to speak words that reach and touch God and affect and influence the powers of the unseen world—such praying, such speaking depends entirely on our hearing God's voice. Just as much as we listen to the voice and language that God speaks, and in the words of God receive His thoughts, His mind, and His life into our heart, we shall learn to speak in the voice and the language God hears. It is the ear of the learner, awakened morning by morning, that prepares the tongue of the learned to speak to God as well as men, as should be (see Isa. 1:4).

This hearing the voice of God is something more than the thoughtful study of the Word. There may be a study and knowledge of the Word in which there is little real fellowship with the living God. But there is also a reading of the Word, in the very presence of the Father and under the leading of the Spirit, in which the Word comes to us in living power from God Himself. This is to us the very voice of the Father, a real, personal fellowship with Himself. It is the living voice of God that enters the heart, that brings blessing and strength, and that awakens the response of a living faith that reaches the heart of God again.

It is on this hearing the voice that the power both to obey and believe depends. The chief thing is not to know *what* God has said we must do, but that *God Himself* says it to us. It is not the law, and not the book, not the knowledge of what is right that works obedience, but the personal influence of God and His living fellowship. Likewise, it is not the knowledge of *what* God has promised, but the presence of God Himself as the Promiser that awakens faith and trust in prayer. It is only in the full presence of God that disobedience and unbelief become impossible.

"If you abide in Me, *and My words abide in you*, you will ask what you desire, and it shall be done for you." We see what this means. In the words, the Savior gives Himself. We must have the words *in us*, taken up into our wills and lives and reproduced in our inner natures and conduct. We must have them *abiding* in us—our whole life one continuous display of the words that are within and filling us; the words revealing Christ within us, and our life revealing Him without. It is as the words of Christ enter our very heart and become our life and influence it that our words will enter His heart and influence Him. My prayer will depend on my life: What God's words are to me and in me, my words will be to God and in God. If I do what God says, God will do what I say.

How well the Old Testament saints understood this connection between God's words and ours, and how really prayer with them was the loving response to what they had heard God speak! If the word was a promise, they counted *on God to do as He had spoken*. "Do as You have said," "For You, Lord, have spoken it," "According to Your promise," "According to Your word": In such expressions they showed that what God spoke in promise was the root and the life of what they spoke in prayer. If the word was a command, they simply *did* as the Lord had spoken: "So Abram departed as the LORD had spoken" (Gen. 12:4). Their life was fellowship with God, the interchange of word and thought. What God spoke they heard and did; what they spoke God heard and did. In each word He speaks to us, the whole Christ gives Himself to fulfill it for us. For each word He asks no less than that we give the whole man to keep that word and to receive its fulfillment.

> *To* pray in the Spirit, to speak words that reach and touch God and affect and influence the powers of the unseen world—such praying, such speaking depends entirely on our hearing God's voice.

"If My words abide in you": The condition is simple and clear. In His words His will is revealed. As the words abide in me, His will rules me. My will becomes the empty vessel that His will fills, the willing instrument that His will rules. He fills my inner being. In the exercise of obedience and faith, my will becomes stronger and stronger and is brought into deeper inner harmony with Him. He can fully trust it to will nothing but what He wills, so He is not afraid to give the promise, "If My words abide in you, you will ask what you desire, and it shall be done for you." To all who believe it and act on it, He will make it literally true.

Disciples of Christ! Is it not becoming clearer and clearer to us that while we have been excusing our unanswered prayers and our powerlessness in prayer with a fancied submission to God's wisdom and will, the real reason has been that our own weak life has been the cause of our weak prayers? Nothing can make men strong but the word coming from God's mouth. By that we must live. It is the word of Christ loved, lived in, abiding in us, becoming through obedience and action part of our being, that makes us one with Christ and prepares us spiritually for touching and taking hold of God. All that is of the world will pass away, but he who does the will of God abides forever.

Let us yield heart and life to the words of Christ, the words in which He gives *Himself*, the personal living Savior. Then His promise will be our rich experience: "If you abide in Me, and My words abide in you, you will ask what you desire, and it shall be done for you."

"Lord, teach us to pray."

Blessed Lord! Your lesson today has again revealed my foolishness. I see how it is that my prayer has not been more believing and prevailing. I was more occupied with my speaking to You than with Your speaking to me. I did not understand that the secret of faith is this: There can be only as much faith as there is of the living Word dwelling in the soul.

Your Word has taught me so clearly: "Let every man be swift to hear, slow to speak" (James 1:19), and "let not your heart utter anything hastily before God" (Eccl. 5:2). Lord, teach me that it is only with Your Word taken into my life that my words can be taken into Your heart, that Your Word, if it is a living power within me, will be a living power with You, and that what Your mouth has spoken Your hand will perform.

Lord! Deliver me from the uncircumcised ear. Give me the opened ear of the learner who is awakened morning by morning to hear the Father's voice. Just as You spoke only what You heard, may my speaking be the echo of Your speaking to me. "When Moses went into the tabernacle of meeting to speak with Him, he heard the voice of One speaking to him from above the mercy seat" (Num. 7:89). Lord, may it be so with me, too. Let a life and character bearing the one mark, that Your words abide and are seen in me, be the preparation for the complete blessing: "You will ask what you desire, and it shall be done for you." Amen.

For Further Thought

1. *Of what must you have knowledge in order to awaken faith and trust in prayer?*
2. *What kind of prayer depends entirely on hearing God's voice? How can you pray that way in your own life of prayer?*
3. *What effect will it have when you allow Christ's words to abide in you?*

Lesson 23

"Bear Fruit, That the Father Will Give You What You Ask," or, Obedience: The Path to Power in Prayer

"You did not choose Me, but I chose you and appointed you that you should go and bear fruit, and that your fruit should remain, that whatever you ask the Father in My name He may give you."
John 15:16

The effective, fervent prayer of a righteous man avails much.
James 5:16

THE promise of the Father's giving whatever we ask is here once again repeated, in such a connection as to show us to whom such wonderful influence in the council chamber of the Most High is to be granted. "I chose you," the Master says, "and appointed you that you should go and bear fruit, and that your fruit should remain." He then adds, *at the end* "that whatever you," the fruit-bearing ones, "ask the Father in My name He may give you."

This is nothing but the fuller expression of what He had spoken in the words, "If you abide in Me." He had spoken of the object of this abiding as the bearing of "fruit," "more fruit," and "much fruit." In this God was to be glorified, and the mark of discipleship would be seen. No wonder that He now adds that where the reality of the abiding is seen in fruit abounding and abiding, this would be the qualification for praying so as to obtain what we ask. Entire dedication to the fulfillment of our calling is the condition to effective prayer and the unlimited blessings of Christ's wonderful prayer promises.

There are Christians who fear that such a statement is add odds with the doctrine of free grace. But surely it doesn't disagree with free grace rightly understood or with so many express statements of God's blessed Word. Take the words of St.

John, "Let us. . .love. . .in deed and in truth. And *by this* we know that we are of the truth, and shall assure our hearts before Him. . . . And whatever we ask we receive from Him, *because* we keep His commandments and do those things that are pleasing in His sight" (1 John 3:18–19, 22). Or take the often-quoted words of James: "The effective, fervent prayer of a *righteous* man avails much" (5:16); that is the man of whom, according to the definition of the Holy Spirit, it can be said, "He who practices righteousness is righteous, just as He is righteous" (1 John 3:7).

Mark the spirit of so many of the psalms with their confident appeal to the integrity and righteousness of the one praying. In Psalm 18 David says: "The LORD rewarded me according to my righteousness; according to the cleanness of my hands He has recompensed me. . . . I was also blameless before Him, and I kept myself from my iniquity. Therefore the LORD has recompensed me according to my righteousness" (18:20, 23–24; also see Pss. 7:3–5; 15:1–2; 17:3, 6; 26:16; 119:121, 153).

If we carefully consider such words in the light of the New Testament, we find them in perfect harmony with the explicit teaching of the Savior's parting words: "*If you keep* my commandments, you will abide in My love" (John 15:10) and "You are My friends *if you do* whatever I command you" (15:14). The words are indeed meant literally: "I chose you and appointed you that you should go and bear fruit. . .*that*," then, "whatever you ask the Father in My name He may give you."

Let us seek to enter into the spirit of what the Savior teaches us here. There is a danger in our evangelical religion of looking too much at what it offers from one side, as a certain experience obtained in prayer and faith. There is another side that God's Word puts very strongly, that of obedience as the only path to blessing. What we need to realize is that in our relationship to the infinite Being we call God, who has created and redeemed us, the first sentiment that should motivate us is that of subjection, the surrender to His supremacy, His glory, His will, and His pleasure. This ought to be the first and uppermost thought of our life.

The question is not, however, how we are to obtain and enjoy His favor, for in this the main thing may still be self. What this Being in the very nature of things rightfully claims, and is infinitely and unspeakably worthy of, is that His glory and pleasure should be my only objective. Surrender to His perfect and blessed will—a life of service and obedience—is the beauty and the charm of heaven. Service and obedience were the thoughts that were uppermost in the mind of the Son when He was on earth. Service and obedience must become the chief objects of our desire and aim, even more so than rest, light, joy, or strength. In them we will find the path to all the higher blessedness that awaits us.

Just note what a prominent place the Master gives it, not only in this fifteenth chapter, in connection with the abiding, but in the fourteenth, where He speaks of the indwelling of the three-one God. John 14:15 says: "*If you* love Me, *keep My commandments*," and the Spirit will be given to you by the Father. Then verse 21:

"He who has *My commandments and keeps them*, it is he who loves Me," and he will have the special love of My Father and the special manifestation of Myself. Verse 23 is one of the highest of all the great and precious promises: "If anyone loves Me, *he will keep My word*; and My Father will love him, and We will come to him and make Our home with him." Could words put it more clearly that obedience is the way to the indwelling of the Spirit, to His revealing the Son within us, and to His preparing us to be the home of the Father? The indwelling of the three-one God is the heritage of those who obey.

Obedience and faith are just two parts of one act—surrender to God and His will. As faith strengthens for obedience, it is in turn strengthened by it. Faith is made perfect by works. It is to be feared that often our efforts to believe are unsuccessful because we have not taken up the only position in which a large faith is legitimate or possible—that of entire surrender to the honor and the will of God. It is the man who is entirely consecrated to God and His will who will find the power to claim everything that his God has promised to be for him.

The application of this in the school of prayer is very simple but very solemn. "I chose you," the Master says, "and appointed you that you should go and bear fruit," "much fruit" (John 15:8,16), "and that your fruit should remain," that your life might be one of abiding fruit and abiding fruitfulness, "that" as fruitful branches abiding in Me, "Whatever you ask the Father in my name, He may give you."

> *E*ntire dedication to the fulfillment of our calling is the condition to effective prayer and the unlimited blessings of Christ's wonderful prayer promises.

How often we've sought to be able to pray the effective prayer for much grace to bear fruit, and then wondered why the answer didn't come. It was because we were reversing the Master's order. We wanted to have the comfort, the joy, and the strength first, so we could do the work easily and without any feeling of difficulty or self-sacrifice. But He wanted us in faith, without asking whether we felt weak or strong, or whether the work was hard or easy, in the obedience of faith to do what He said. The path of fruit-bearing would have led us to the place and the power of successful prayer.

Obedience is the only path that leads to the glory of God. Not obedience instead of faith, nor obedience to overcome the shortcomings of faith, but faith's obedience gives access to all the blessings our God has for us. The baptism of the Spirit (John 14:16), the manifestation of the Son (14:21), the indwelling of the Father (14:23), the abiding in Christ's love (15:10), the privilege of His holy friendship (15:14), and the power of effective prayer (15:16)—all wait for the obedient.

Let us take home the lessons. Now we know the great reason why we have not had power in faith to pray successfully. Our life wasn't as it should have been. Simple, absolute obedience and abiding fruitfulness were not its chief objectives. And with our whole heart we approve of the divine appointment: men to whom God is to give such influence in the rule of the world, as at their request to do otherwise would not have taken place, men whose will is to guide the path in which God's will is to work, must be men who have themselves learned obedience, whose loyalty and submission to authority must be above all suspicion. Our whole soul approves the law: Obedience and fruit-bearing are the path to prevailing prayer. And with shame we acknowledge how little our lives have borne this stamp.

Let us yield ourselves to take up the appointment the Savior gives us. Let us study His relationship to us as Master. Let us seek no more with each new day to think first of comfort, joy, or blessing. Our first thought should be: I belong to the Master. In my every moment and every movement, I must act as His property, as a part of Himself, as one who only seeks to know and do His will. A servant, a slave of Jesus Christ—let this be the spirit that animates me. If He says, "No longer do I call you servants. . .but I have called you friends" (John 15:15), let us accept the place of friends, because, "Your are My friends if you do whatever I command you."

The one thing He commands us as His branches is to bear fruit. Live to bless others, to testify of the life and the love there is in Jesus. Let us in faith and obedience give our whole life to that which Jesus chose us for and appointed us to— fruit-bearing. As we think of His electing us to this and take up our appointment as coming from Him who always gives all He demands of us, we will grow strong in the confidence that a life of fruit-bearing, abounding, and abiding is within our reach. And we will understand why this fruit-bearing alone can be the path to the place of all-prevailing prayer. It is the man who, in obedience to the Christ of God, proves that he is doing what his Lord wills, for whom the Father will do whatever he desires: "And whatever we ask we receive from Him, because we keep His commandments and do those things that are pleasing in His sight" (1 John 3:22).

"LORD, TEACH US TO PRAY."

Blessed Master! Teach me to understand fully what I only partly realize, that it is only through the will of God, accepted and acted out in obedience to His commands, that we obtain the power to grasp His will in His promises and fully to appropriate them in our prayers. And teach me that it is in the path of fruit-bearing that the deeper growth of the branch into the Vine can be perfected. We desire and seek that perfect oneness with You in which we ask whatever we desire.

O Lord! Reveal to us, we ask You, how with all the hosts of heaven, and with Yourself the Son on earth, and with all the men of faith who have glorified You on earth, *obedience to God is our highest privilege, because it gives access to oneness with Himself in that which is His highest glory—His all-perfect will.* And we ask You to show us how, in keeping Your commandments and bearing fruit according to Your will, our spiritual nature will grow to the full stature of a perfect man who has power to ask and receive anything he desires.

O Lord Jesus! Reveal Yourself to us, and reveal the reality of Your purpose and power to make these wonderful promises the daily experience of everyone who completely yields himself to You and Your words. Amen.

FOR FURTHER THOUGHT

1. *Read 1 John 3:18–19, 22. What is the condition for receiving what you ask for in prayer?*
2. *Why is that the believer's prayers for grace to bear fruit fail to receive an answer? How can you make sure that your prayers for God's grace are answered?*
3. *What is the one thing that Jesus the Vine commands us as His branches to do? How do you begin do what He has commanded?*

LESSON 24

"IN MY NAME," OR,
THE ALL-POWERFUL PLEA

"And whatever you ask in My name, that I will do. . . .
If you ask anything in My name, I will do it. . .that whatever you
ask the Father in My name He may give you. . . . Most assuredly,
I say to you, whatever you ask the Father in My name
He will give you. Until now you have asked
nothing in My name. Ask, and you will receive. . . .
In that day you will ask in My name."
JOHN 14:13–14; 15:16; 16:23–24, 26

UNTIL now the disciples had not asked in the name of Christ, nor had He Himself ever used the expression. The nearest approach is, "met together in My Name" (see Matt. 18:20). Here in His parting words, He repeats the word repeatedly in connection with those promises of unlimited meaning: "*Whatever*," "*Anything*," "*What you desire*," to teach them and us that His name is our only, but also our completely sufficient, plea. The power of prayer and its answer depend on the right use of the name.

What is a person's name? That word or expression the person is called or represented to us. When I mention or hear a name, it brings to mind the whole man, what I know of him, and also the impression he has made on me. The name of a king includes his honor, his power, and his kingdom. His name is the symbol of his power. And so each name of God embodies and represents some part of the glory of the unseen One. And the name of Christ is the expression of all He has done and all He is and lives to do as our Mediator.

And what does it mean to do a thing in the name of another? It is to come with his power and authority of that other as his representative and substitute. We know how such use of another's name always presupposes a common interest. No one would give another the free use of his name without first being assured that his honor and interests were as safe with that other person as with himself.

And what does it mean when Jesus gives us power over His name, the free use of it, with the assurance that whatever we ask in it will be given to us? The ordinary comparison of one person giving another, on some special occasion, the liberty to ask something in his name, comes altogether short here—Jesus solemnly gives to *all* His disciples a general and unlimited power to freely use His name at *all* times for *all* they desire. He could not do this if He did not know that He could trust us with His interests and that His honor would be safe in our hands. The free use of the name of another is always evidence of great confidence and close union. He who gives his name to another stands aside to let that person act for him. He who takes the name of another gives up his own as of no value. When I go in the name of another, I deny myself. I take not only his name, but himself and what he is, instead of myself and what I am.

Such use of the name of a person may be the result of a *legal union*. A merchant leaving his home and business gives his chief clerk a general power by which he can withdraw thousands of dollars in the merchant's name. The clerk does this, not for himself but only in the interests of the business. It is because the merchant knows and trusts him as wholly devoted to his interests and business that he dares put his name and property at his command.

> *Each name of God embodies and represents some part of the glory of the unseen One. And the name of Christ is the expression of all He has done and all He is and lives to do as our Mediator.*

When the Lord Jesus went to heaven, He left His work—the management of His kingdom on earth—in the hands of His servants. He could not do otherwise than also to give them His name to draw all the supplies they needed for the due conduct of His business. And they have the spiritual power to use the name of Jesus just to the extent to which they yield themselves to live only for the interests and the work of the Master. The use of the name always supposes the surrender of our interests to Him whom we represent.

Or such a use of the name may be in virtue of a *life union*. In the case of the merchant and his clerk, the union is temporary. But we know how oneness of life on earth gives oneness of name. A child has the father's name because he has his life. Often the child of a good father is honored or helped by others for the sake of the name he bears. But this would not last long if it were found that it was only a name, and that the father's character was lacking. The name and the character or spirit must be in harmony. When such is the case, the child will have a double claim on the father's friends. The character secures and increases the love and esteem extended first for the name's sake. So it is with Jesus and the believer. We are one and have one life and one Spirit with Him. For this reason we may come in His name. Our power in using that name, whether with God, or men, or devils, *depends on the measure of our spiritual life-union*. The use of the name rests on the unity of life. The name and the Spirit of Jesus are one.[35]

Or the union that gives power to the use of the name may be *the union of love*. When a bride whose life has been one of poverty becomes united to the bridegroom, she gives up her own name to be called by his, and now has the full right to use it. She purchases in his name, and that name is not refused. This is done because the bridegroom has chosen her for himself, counting on her to care for his interests. They are now one. And so the heavenly Bridegroom could do nothing less. Having loved us and made us one with Himself, what can He do but give those who bear His name the right to present it before the Father, or to come with it to Himself for all they need? And there is no one who really gives himself up to live in the name of Jesus who does not receive in ever-increasing measure the spiritual capacity to ask and receive in that name whatever he desires. The bearing of the name of another shows my having given up my own, and with it my own independent life. But it also shows, just as surely, my possession of all there is in the name I have taken instead of my own.

Such illustrations show us how defective the common view is of a messenger sent to ask in the name of another, or of a guilty one appealing to the name of a guardian. No, Jesus Himself is with the Father. He is not an absent one in whose name we come. Even when we pray to Jesus Himself, it must be in His name. The name represents the person, and to ask in the name is to ask in full union of interest, life, and love with Himself, as one who lives in and for Him. Let the name of Jesus only have undivided supremacy in my heart and life! My faith will grow to the assurance that what I ask for in that name cannot be refused. The name and the power of asking go together. When the name of Jesus has become the power that rules my life, its power in prayer with God will be seen, too.

We see, therefore, that everything depends on our own relationship to the name. The power it has on my life is the power it will have in my prayers. There is more than one expression in scripture that can make this clear to us. When it says, "*Do all* in the name of the Lord Jesus" (Col. 3:17), we see how this is the counterpart of the other: "*Ask all.*" To do all and ask all in His name go together. When we read, "We will walk in the name of the LORD our God" (Micah 4:5), we see how the power of the name must rule in the whole life. Only then will it have power in prayer. It is not the lips but to the life that God looks to see what the name is to us. When scripture speaks of men who have given their lives for the name of the Lord Jesus, or of one ready to die for the name of the Lord Jesus, we see what our relationship to the name must be. When it is everything to me, it will obtain everything for me. If I let it have all I have, it will let me have all it has.

"*Whatever* you ask in My name, that I will do" (John 14:13). Jesus means that promise literally. Christians have sought to limit it because it looked too free. It

[35] "Whatever you ask in My name," that is, in My nature; for things with God are called according to their nature. We ask in Christ's name, not when at the end of some request we say, "This I ask in the name of Jesus Christ," but when we pray *according to His nature*, which is love, which seeks not its own desires, but only the will of God and the good of all creatures. Such asking is the cry of His own Spirit in our hearts.—Jukes, *The New Man*.

was hardly safe to trust man so unconditionally. We did not understand that the phrase "in My name" is its own safeguard. It is a spiritual power that no one can use further than he obtains the capacity for, by his living and acting in that name. As we bear the name before men, we have the power to use it before God. Let us plead for God's Holy Spirit to show us what the name means, and what the right use of it is. It is through the Spirit that the name, which is above every name in heaven, will take the place of supremacy in our hearts and lives, too.

> *Let each disciple of Jesus seek to avail himself of the rights of his royal priesthood, and use the power placed at his disposal for his work.*

Disciples of Jesus! Let the lessons of this day enter deeply into your hearts. The Master says, "Only pray in my name; whatever you ask will be given. Heaven is opened to you! The treasures and power of the spiritual world are placed at your disposal to help those around you." Let us learn to pray in the name of Jesus. He says to us as He said to the disciples, "Until now you have asked nothing in My name. Ask, and you will receive" (John 16:24). Let each disciple of Jesus seek to avail himself of the rights of his royal priesthood, and use the power placed at his disposal for his work. Let Christians awake and hear this message: your prayer can obtain what would otherwise be withheld and can accomplish what would otherwise remain undone. O awake, and use the name of Jesus to open the treasures of heaven for this perishing world. Learn as the servants of the King to use His Name: "*Whatever* you ask in My name, *that I will do.*"

"Lord, teach us to pray."

Blessed Lord! It is as if each lesson You give me has such fullness and depth of meaning that if I can only learn that one, I shall know how to pray properly. Today I feel again as if I needed but one prayer every day. Lord, teach me what it is to pray in Your name. Teach me so to live and act, to walk and speak, and to do all in the name of Jesus, so that my prayer cannot be anything else but in that blessed name, too.

Lord! Teach me to hold firmly the precious promise that *Whatever* we ask in Your name, that you will do and the Father will give. Though I do not yet fully understand, and still less have fully attained, the wondrous union You mean when You say, "*In My Name,*" I would yet hold firmly the promise until it fills my heart with the undoubting assurance that I can ask for anything in the name of Jesus.

O my Lord! Let the Holy Spirit teach me this! You did say of Him, "the Helper, whom the Father will send *in My name*" (John 14:26). He knows what it is to be sent from heaven in Your name, to reveal and to honor the power of that name in Your servants, and to use that name alone to glorify You. Lord Jesus! Let Your Spirit dwell in me and fill me. I want to, I do yield my whole being to His rule and leading. Your name and Your Spirit are one. Through Him, Your name will be the strength of my life and my prayer. Then I will be able for Your name's sake to forsake everything, in Your name to speak to men and to God, and to prove that Yours is indeed the name above every name.

Lord Jesus! Please teach me by Your Holy Spirit to pray in Your name. Amen.

FOR FURTHER THOUGHT

1. *On what does the power of prayer and the answer to prayer depend? How can you learn to do that one thing?*
2. *Read John 14:13. What does it mean to you that Jesus said, "Whatever you ask in My name, that I will do"? What, in your own life, is included in the "whatever"?*
3. *What are the results of praying in the name of Jesus Christ? What do you attain when you pray in His name?*

NOTE

WHAT is meant by praying in Christ's name? It cannot mean simply appearing before God with faith in the mediation of the Savior. When the disciples asked Jesus to teach them to pray, He supplied them with petitions. And afterwards Jesus said to them, 'Until now you have asked nothing in My Name.' Until the Spirit came, the seven petitions of the Lord's Prayer lay as it were dormant within them. When by the Holy Spirit Christ descended into their hearts, they desired the very blessings that Christ as our High Priest obtains for us by His prayer from the Father. And such petitions are always answered. The Father is always willing to give what Christ asks. The Spirit of Christ always teaches and influences us to offer the petitions that Christ ratifies and presents to the Father. To pray in Christ's name is therefore to be identified with Christ as to our righteousness, and *to be identified with Christ in our desires by the indwelling of the Holy Spirit*. To pray *in the Spirit*, to pray *according to the will of the Father*, to pray *in Christ's name, are identical expressions*. The Father Himself loves us, and is willing to hear us: two intercessors, Christ the Advocate above, and the Holy Ghost, the Advocate within, are the gifts of His love.

"This view may appear at first less comforting than a more prevalent one, which refers prayer in Christ's name chiefly to our trust in Christ's merit. The defect of this opinion is that it does not combine the intercession of the Savior with the will of the Father, and the indwelling Spirit's aid in prayer. Nor does it fully realize the mediation of Christ, for the mediation consists not merely in that for Christ's sake the Holy Father is able to regard me and my prayer, but also in that Christ Himself presents my petitions as His petitions, desired by Him for me, just as all blessings are purchased for me by His precious blood.

In all prayer, the one essential condition is that we are able to offer it in the name of Jesus, as according to His desire for us, according to the Father's will, according to the Spirit's teaching. And praying like this in Christ's name is impossible without self-examination, without reflection, without self-denial; in short, without the aid of the Spirit."—*Saphir, The Lord's Prayer*.

Lesson 25

"In That Day," or,

The Holy Spirit and Prayer

"And in that day you will ask Me nothing. Most assuredly,
I say to you, whatever you ask the Father in My name He will give
you. Until now you have asked nothing in My name. Ask, and you
will receive, that your joy may be full. . . . In that day you will ask
in My name, and I do not say to you that I shall pray the
Father for you; for the Father Himself loves you."
JOHN 16:23–24, 26–27

Praying in the Holy Spirit,
keep yourselves in the love of God.
JUDE 20–21

THE words of John (1 John 2:12–14) to little children, to young men, and to fathers suggest the thought that there often are in the Christian life three great stages of experience. The first, that of the newborn child, with the assurance and the joy of forgiveness. The second, the transitional stage of struggle and growth in knowledge and strength: young men growing strong and God's Word doing its work in them and giving them victory over the Evil One. And then the final stage of maturity and ripeness: the fathers, who have entered deeply into the knowledge and fellowship of the eternal One.

In Christ's teaching on prayer, there appear to be three stages in the prayer-life, all somewhat similar. In the Sermon on the Mount we have the initial stage. His teaching is all comprised in one word: Father. Pray to your Father, for your Father sees, hears, knows, and will reward—*how much more* than any earthly father! Only be childlike and trustful. Then comes later on something like the transition stage of conflict and conquest, in words like these: "This kind can come out by nothing but prayer and fasting" (Mark 9:29), and "Shall God not avenge His own elect who cry out day and night to Him?" (Luke 18:7). And then we have in the parting words a higher stage. The children have become men: They are now the Master's friends, from whom He has no secrets, to whom He says, "All things that I heard from

My Father I have made known to you" (John 15:15), and to whom, in the often-repeated "Whatever you desire," He hands over the keys of the kingdom. Now the time has come for the power of prayer in His name to be proved.

The contrast between this final stage and the previous preparatory ones our Savior marks most distinctly in the words we are to meditate on: "*Until now* you have asked nothing in my name," and "*In that day*, you will ask in My name." We know what *in that day* means. It is the day of the outpouring of the Holy Spirit. The great work Christ was to do on the cross, the mighty power and the complete victory to be manifested in His resurrection and ascension were both to allow, in the coming down from heaven, as never before, of the glory of God to dwell in men. The Spirit of the glorified Jesus was to come and be the life of His disciples. And one of the marks of that wonderful spirit-dispensation was to be a power in prayer until then unknown—prayer in the name of Jesus, asking and obtaining whatever they desired, is to be the manifestation of the reality of the Spirit's indwelling.

> *T*o understand how the coming of the Holy Spirit was indeed to commence a new epoch in the prayer world, we must remember who He is, what His work is, and what the significance is of His not being given until Jesus was glorified.

To understand how the coming of the Holy Spirit was indeed to commence a new epoch in the prayer world, we must remember who He is, what His work is, and what the significance is of His not being given until Jesus was glorified. It is in the Spirit that God exists, for He is Spirit. It is in the Spirit that the Son was begotten of the Father, and it is in the fellowship of the Spirit that the Father and the Son are one. The eternal never-ceasing giving to the Son, which is the Father's prerogative, and the eternal asking and receiving, which is the Son's right and blessedness—it is through the Spirit that this communion of life and love is maintained. It has been so from all eternity. It is so especially now, when the Son as Mediator always lives to pray.

The great work Jesus began on earth of reconciling in His own body God and man, He carries on in heaven. To accomplish this He took up into His own person the conflict between God's righteousness and our sin. On the cross He once and for all ended the struggle in His own body. And then He ascended to heaven, so that from there He might, in each member of His body, carry out the deliverance and manifest the victory He had obtained. It is to do this that He always lives to pray. In His unceasing intercession, He places Himself in living fellowship with the unceasing prayer of His redeemed ones. In other words, it is His unceasing intercession that shows itself in their prayers and gives them a power they never had before.

And He does this through the Holy Spirit. The Holy Spirit, the Spirit of the glorified Jesus, was not (John 7:39) and could not be until He had been glorified. This gift of the Father was something distinctively new and entirely different from what Old Testament saints had known. The work that the blood effected in heaven when Christ entered within the veil was something so true and new, the redemption of our human nature into fellowship with His resurrection-power and His exaltation-glory was so intensely real, and the taking up of our humanity in Christ into the life of the three-one God was an event of such inconceivable significance, that the Holy Spirit, who had to come from Christ's exalted humanity to testify in our hearts of what Christ had accomplished, was indeed no longer only what He had been in the Old Testament.

> The Spirit prays for us without words. In the depths of a heart, where even thoughts are at times without form, the Spirit takes us up into the wonderful flow of the life of the three-one God.

It was literally true that "the Holy Spirit was not yet given, because Jesus was not yet glorified" (John 7:39). He came now first as the Spirit of the glorified Jesus. Even as the Son, who was from eternity God, had entered into a new existence as man and returned to heaven with what He did not have before, so the blessed Spirit, whom the Son, on His ascension, received from the Father (see Acts 2:33) into His glorified humanity, came to us with a new life, which He had not previously communicated. Under the Old Testament, He was invoked as the Spirit of God, but at Pentecost He descended as the Spirit of the glorified Jesus, bringing down and communicating to us the full fruit and power of the accomplished redemption.

It is in the intercession of Christ that the continued effectiveness and application of His redemption is maintained. And it is through the Holy Spirit descending from Christ to us that we are drawn up into the great stream of His always-ascending prayers. The Spirit prays for us without words. In the depths of a heart, where even thoughts are at times without form, the Spirit takes us up into the wonderful flow of the life of the three-one God. Through the Spirit, Christ's prayers become ours, and ours are made His. We ask what we desire, and it is given to us. We then understand from experience, "Until now you have asked nothing in My name. . . . *In that* day you will ask in My name."

Brother! What we need to pray in the name of Christ, to ask to receive so that our joy may be full, is the baptism of this Holy Spirit. This is more than the Spirit of God under the Old Testament. This is more than the Spirit of conversion and regeneration the disciples had before Pentecost. This is more than the Spirit with a measure of His influence and working. This is the Holy Spirit, the Spirit of the glorified Jesus in His exaltation-power, coming on us as the Spirit of the indwelling

Jesus, revealing the Son and the Father within us (see John 14:16–23).

It is when this Spirit is the Spirit not of our hours of prayer, but of our whole life and walk, when this Spirit glorifies Jesus in us by revealing the completeness of His work and making us completely one with Him and like Him, that we can pray in His name, because we are in very deed one with Him. It is then that we have that immediateness of access to the Father of which Jesus says, "I do not say to you that I shall pray the Father for you" (John 16:26). O how we need to understand and believe that to be filled with this, the Spirit of the glorified One, is the one need of God's believing people! Then we will realize what it is, "praying always with all prayer and supplication in the Spirit" (Eph. 6:18), and what it is to be, "Praying in the Holy Spirit, keep (ourselves) in the love of God" (Jude 20–21). "*In that day* you will ask in My name."

> *W*hat our prayer benefits depends on what we are and what our life is. It is living in the name of Christ that is the secret of praying in the name of Christ and living in the Spirit that makes us fit for praying in the Spirit.

So once again the lesson comes: What our prayer benefits depends on what we are and what our life is. It is living in the name of Christ that is the secret of praying in the name of Christ and living in the Spirit that makes us fit for praying in the Spirit. It is abiding in Christ that gives us the right and power to ask what we desire. The extent of the abiding is the exact amount of the power in prayer. It is the Spirit dwelling within us who prays, not in words and thoughts always, but in a breathing and being deeper than words. Only as much as there is of Christ's Spirit in us is there real prayer. Our lives, our lives—O let our lives be full of Christ and full of His Spirit, and then the wonderfully unlimited promises to our prayer will no longer appear strange. "Until now you have asked nothing in My name. Ask, and you will receive, that your joy may be full. . . . In that day you will ask in My Name. . . . Most assuredly, I say to you, whatever you ask the Father in My name He will give you."

"LORD, TEACH US TO PRAY."

O my God! In holy awe I bow before You, the Three in One. Again I have seen how the mystery of prayer is the mystery of the holy Trinity. I adore the Father who ever hears, and the Son who ever lives to pray, and the Holy Spirit who proceeds from the Father and the Son to lift us up into the fellowship of that ever-blessed, never-ceasing asking and receiving. I bow, my God, in adoring worship, before the infinite reaching down that in this way, through the Holy Spirit, takes us and our prayers into the divine life and its fellowship of love.

O my Blessed Lord Jesus! Teach me to understand Your lesson, that it is the indwelling Spirit who streams from You, is united to You, and who is the Spirit of prayer. Teach me what it is as an empty, completely dedicated vessel and to yield myself to His being my life. Teach me to honor and trust Him, as a living Person, to lead my life and my prayer. Teach me specifically in prayer to wait in holy silence and give Him place to breathe within me His unspeakable intercession. And teach me that through Him it is possible to pray without ceasing and without failing, because He makes me a partaker of the never-ceasing and never-failing intercession in which You, the Son, appears before the Father. Yes, Lord, fulfill in me Your promise: "In that day you will ask in My Name. Most assuredly, I say to you, whatever you ask the Father in My name He will give you." Amen.

FOR FURTHER THOUGHT

1. *What are the three great stages of the Christian experience, and what marks each one of them? What does the final stage—maturity—look like in the believer?*
2. *What are the three stages of prayer that Christ teaches, and what are the marks of each of them? What is the most important part of the third stage?*
3. *On what do the benefits you receive from prayer depend? What steps must you take to receive those benefits?*

PRAYER has often been compared to breathing: We need only carry out the comparison fully to see how wonderful the place is that the Holy Spirit occupies. With every breath we expel the impure air that would soon cause our death, and then inhale again the fresh air to which we owe our life. Likewise, we give out from us, in confession the sins, in prayer the needs and the desires of our heart. And in drawing in our breath again, we inhale the fresh air of the promises and the love and the life of God in Christ. We do this through the Holy Spirit, who is the breath of our life.

And this is because He is the breath of God. The Father breathes Him into us to unite Himself with our life. And then, just as on every exhale there follows again the inhaling or drawing in of the breath, so God draws in again His breath, and the Spirit returns to Him carrying the desires and needs of our hearts. And this is the way in which the Holy Spirit is the breath of the life of God—and the breath of the new life in us. As God breathes Him out, we receive Him in answer to prayer. As we breathe Him back again, He rises to God carrying our requests.

As the Spirit of God, in whom the Father and the Son are one, and in whom the intercession of the Son reaches the Father, He is to us the Spirit of prayer. True prayer is the living experience of the truth of the holy Trinity. The Spirit's breathing, the Son's intercession, and the Father's will—these three become one in us.

LESSON 26

"I HAVE PRAYED FOR YOU,"
OR, CHRIST THE INTERCESSOR

"But I have prayed for you,
that your faith should not fail."
LUKE 22:32

"I do not say to you that I shall pray the Father for you."
JOHN 16:26

He always lives to make intercession for them.
HEBREWS 7:25

ALL growth in the spiritual life is connected with the clearer insight into what Jesus is to us. The more I realize that Christ must be all to me and in me, that all in Christ is indeed for me, the more I learn to live the real life of faith, which, dying to self, lives wholly in Christ. The Christian life is no longer the futile struggle to live right, but the resting in Christ and finding strength in Him as our life to fight the fight and gain the victory of faith.

This is especially true of the life of prayer. As it, too, comes under the law of faith alone, and is seen in the light of the fullness and completeness there is in Jesus, the believer understands that it no longer needs to be a matter of strain or anxious care, but an experience of what Christ will do for him and in him—a participation in that life of Christ that, as on earth and so in heaven, always ascends to the Father as prayer. And he begins to pray, not only trusting in the merits of Jesus or in the intercession by which our unworthy prayers are made acceptable, but in that near and close union in virtue of which He prays in us and we in Him.[36] The whole of salvation is Christ Himself: He has given *Himself* to us; He Himself lives in us. Because He prays, we pray too. As the disciples, when they saw Jesus pray, asked Him to make them partakers of what He knew of prayer, so we now see Him as intercessor on the throne and know

---

[36] See on the difference between having Christ as an Advocate or Intercessor who stands outside of us, and the having Him within us, we abiding in Him and He in us through the Holy Spirit perfecting our union with Him, so that we ourselves can come directly to the Father in His Name—the note from Beck of Tubingen.

that He makes us participate with Himself in the life of prayer.

How clearly this comes out in the last night of His life. In His high-priestly prayer (John 17), He shows us how and what He has to pray to the Father—and will pray once He ascended to heaven. And yet He had in His parting address so repeatedly also connected His going to the Father with *their* new life of prayer. The two would be ultimately connected: His entrance into the work of His eternal intercession *would be the beginning and the power of their new prayer-life in His Name*. It is the sight of Jesus in His intercession that gives us power to pray in His Name; all right and power of prayer is Christ's, and He makes us share in His intercession.

To understand this, think first of *His intercession:* He always lives to make intercession. The work of Christ on earth as Priest was just a beginning. It was as Aaron He shed His blood, and it is as Melchizedek that He now lives within the veil to continue His work, after the power of the eternal life. As Melchizedek is more glorious than Aaron, so it is in the work of intercession that the atonement has its true power and glory. "It is Christ who died. . .*and furthermore*. . .who is even at the right hand of God, who also makes intercession for us" (Rom. 8:34). That intercession is an intense reality, a work that is absolutely necessary, and without which the continued application of redemption cannot take place. In the incarnation and resurrection of Jesus, the wondrous reconciliation took place, by which man became a partaker of the divine life and blessedness. But the real personal appropriation of this reconciliation in each of His members here on earth cannot take place without the unceasing exercise of His divine power by the head in heaven. In all conversion and sanctification, in every victory over sin and the world, there is a real demonstration of the power of Him who is mighty to save.

And this exercise of His power only takes place through His prayer. He asks of the Father, and receives from the Father. "*He is also able* to save to the uttermost. . .*since* He always lives to make intercession" (Heb. 7:25). There is not a need of His people in which He doesn't receive in intercession what the Godhead has to give: His mediation on the throne is as real and indispensable as on the cross. Nothing takes place without His intercession, which engages all His time and powers and is His unceasing occupation at the right hand of the Father.

And we participate not only in the benefits of this His work, but in the work itself. This because we are His body. Body and members are one: "The head (cannot say) to the feet, 'I have no need of you'" (1 Cor. 12:21). We share with Jesus in all He is and has: "And the glory which You gave Me I have given them" (John 17:22). We are partakers of His life, His righteousness, and His work. We share with Him in His intercession, too; it is not a work He does without us.

We do this because we are partakers of His life: "Christ is our life" (Col. 3:4), "It is no longer I who live, but Christ lives in me" (Gal. 2:20). The life in Him and in us is identical, one and the same. His life in heaven is an *always-praying* life. When it descends and takes possession of us, it does not lose its character. In us, too, it is the *always-praying* life—a life that without ceasing asks and receives from God. And this not as if there were two separate currents of prayer rising upwards—one from Him, and one from His people. No, but the substantial life-union is also prayer-union; what He prays passes through, and what we pray passes through Him. He is the angel with the golden censer: "*He* was given much incense," the secret of acceptable prayer, "that he should offer it with the prayers of all the saints upon the golden altar" (Rev. 8:3). We live and abide in Him, the interceding One.

The Only-Begotten is the only one who has the right to pray. To Him alone it was said, "Ask, and it shall be given You" (Matt. 7:7). As in all other things the fullness dwells in Him, so the true prayerfulness, too. He alone has the power of prayer. And just as the growth of the spiritual life consists in the clearer insight that all the treasures are *in Him*, and that we too are *in Him* to receive each moment what we possess in Him, grace for grace, so it is with the prayer-life, too. Our faith in the intercession of Jesus must not only be that He prays in our place—when we do not or cannot pray—but that, as the Author of our life and our faith, He draws us on to pray in unison with Himself. Our prayer must be a work of faith in this sense too—that as we know that Jesus communicates His whole life in us, He also out of that prayerfulness, which is His alone, breathes into us our praying.

> *We* are partakers of His life, His righteousness, and His work. We share with Him in His intercession, too; it is not a work He does without us.

To many a believer it was a new chapter in his spiritual life when it was revealed to him how truly and entirely Christ was his life, standing good as a promise for his remaining faithful and obedient. It was then that he first really began to life a *faith-life*. No less blessed will be the discovery that Christ is surety for our prayer-life, too—the center and embodiment of all prayer, which is to be communicated by Him through the Holy Spirit to His people. He always lives to make intercession as the Head of the body, as the Leader in that new and living way that He has opened up, and as the "Author and the Finisher of our faith" (Heb. 12:2). He provides everything for the life of His redeemed ones by giving His own life in them. He cares for their life of prayer by taking them up into His heavenly prayer-life, by giving and maintaining His prayer-life within them. "I have prayed for you," not to render your faith needless, "but that *your faith* should not fail" (see Luke 22:32). Our faith and prayer of faith is rooted in His. It is, "If you abide in Me," the ever-living Intercessor, and pray with Me and in Me, "ask what you desire, and it shall be done for you" (see John 15:7).

The thought of our fellowship in the intercession of Jesus reminds us of what He has taught us more than once before: how all these wonderful prayer promises have as their aim and their justification the glory of God in the manifestation of His kingdom and the salvation of sinners. As long as we only or chiefly pray for ourselves, the promises of the last night must remain a sealed book to us.

It is to the fruit-bearing branches of the Vine—to disciples sent into the world as the Father sent Him to live for perishing men, to His faithful servants and intimate friends who take up the work He leaves behind and who have like their Lord become as the seed corn, losing its life to multiply it manifold—that the promises are given. Let us each find out what the work is and who the souls are entrusted to our special prayers. Let us make our intercession for them our life of fellowship with God, and we shall not only find the promises of power in prayer made true to us, but we shall then first begin to realize how our abiding in Christ and His abiding in us makes us share in His own joy of blessing and saving men.

> How wonderful is the intercession of our blessed Lord Jesus, to which we not only owe everything, but in which we are taken up as active partners and fellow workers!

How wonderful is the intercession of our blessed Lord Jesus, to which we not only owe everything, but in which we are taken up as active partners and fellow workers! Now we understand what it is to pray in the name of Jesus, and why it has such power. In His name, in His Spirit, in Himself, in perfect union with Him. O wondrous, ever-active, and most effectual intercession of the man Christ Jesus! When shall we be completely taken up into it and always pray in it?

"LORD, TEACH US TO PRAY."

Blessed Lord! In humble adoration I again bow before You. Your whole redemption work has now passed into prayer. All that now occupies You in maintaining and dispensing what You purchased with Your blood is only prayer. You always live to pray. And because we are and abide in You, the direct access to the Father is always open, and our life can be one of unceasing prayer and the sure answer to our prayer.

Blessed Lord! You have invited Your people to be Your fellow workers in a life of prayer. You have united Yourself with Your people and make them as Your body share with You in that ministry of intercession, through which alone the world can be filled with the fruit of Your redemption and the glory of the Father. With more liberty than ever, I come to You, my Lord, and beg You: Teach me to pray. Your life is prayer, Your life is mine. Lord! Teach me to pray, in You and like You.

And, O my Lord! Teach me especially to know, as You promised Your disciples, that You are in the Father, that I am in You and You in me. Let the uniting power of the Holy Spirit make my whole life an abiding in You and Your intercession, so that my prayer may be its echo, and that the Father hears me in You and You in me. Lord Jesus! Let Your mind in everything be in me, and my life in everything be in You. So shall I be prepared to be the channel through which Your intercession pours its blessing on the world. Amen.

FOR FURTHER THOUGHT

1. *You are to trust in the merits of Jesus Christ and in His intercession, which makes our unworthy prayers acceptable to God. What else must you trust in?*
2. *What is the aim of the prayer promises Jesus spoke to His disciples when He was on earth and which He speaks to you now?*
3. *What specifically are you, as an intercessor for Jesus Christ, responsible to do for those souls who are entrusted to your special prayers?*

THE new epoch of prayer in the name of Jesus is pointed out by Christ as the time of the outpouring of the Spirit, in which the disciples enter into a more enlightened understanding of the plan of redemption and become as clearly conscious of their oneness with Jesus as of His oneness with the Father. Their prayer in the name of Jesus is now directly to the Father Himself. 'I do not say to you that I shall pray the Father for you; for the Father Himself loves you' (John 16:26–27), Jesus says, though He had previously spoken of the time before the Spirit's coming: 'I will pray the Father, and He will give you another Helper' (John 14:16). This prayer therefore has as its central thought the insight into our being united to God in Christ as on both sides the living bond of union between God and us (John 17:23: 'I in them, and You in Me.'), so that in Jesus we see the Father as united to us and ourselves as united to the Father. Jesus Christ must have been revealed to us, not only through the truth in the mind but in our innermost personal consciousness as the living personal reconciliation, as He in whom God's fatherhood and Father-love have been perfectly united with human nature and it with God. Not that with the immediate prayer to the Father, the mediatorship of Christ is set aside. But it is no longer looked at as something external, existing outside of us, but as a real living spiritual existence within us, so that the Christ *for us*, the Mediator, has really become Christ *in us*.

"When the consciousness of this oneness between God in Christ and us in Christ is still lacking, or has been darkened by the sense of guilt, then the prayer of faith looks to our Lord as the Advocate who pays the Father *for us*. (Compare John 16:26 with John 14:16, 17; 9:20; Luke 22:32, 1 John 2:1) To take Christ this way in prayer as Advocate is, according to John 16:26, not perfectly the same as the prayer in His Name. Christ's advocacy is meant to lead us on to that inner self-standing life-union with Him, and with the Father in Him, in virtue of which Christ is He in whom God enters into immediate relationship and unites Himself with us, and in whom we in all circumstances enter into immediate relationship with God.

"Even so, the prayer in the name of Jesus does not consist in our prayer at His command. The disciples had prayed that way ever since the Lord had given them His 'Our Father,' and yet He says, 'Until now you have not prayed in my name.' Only when the mediation of Christ has become, through the indwelling of the Holy Spirit, life and power within us—and so *His mind, as it found expression in His word and work, has taken possession of and filled our personal consciousness and will*, so that in faith and love we have Jesus in us as the Reconciler who has actually made us one with God—only then His Name, which included His nature and His work, will become truth and power in us (not only for us), and we have in the Name of Jesus the free, direct access to the Father, who is sure of being heard.

"Prayer in the name of Jesus is the liberty of a son with the Father, just as Jesus had this as the First-Begotten. We pray in the place of Jesus, not as if we could put ourselves in His place, but in as far as we are in Him and He in us. We go directly to the Father, but only as the Father is in Christ, not as if He were separate from Christ. Wherever, therefore, the inner man does not live in Christ and does not have Him present as the Living One, where His word is not ruling in the heart in its Spirit-power, where His truth and life have not become the life of our soul, it is wrong to think that a formula like 'for the sake of Your dear Son' will succeed."
—*Christliche Ethik, von Dr. I. T. Beck, Tubingen.*

LESSON 27

"FATHER, I DESIRE," OR,

CHRIST THE HIGH PRIEST

"Father, I desire that they also whom
You gave Me may be with Me where I am."
JOHN 17:24

IN His parting address, Jesus gives His disciples the full revelation of what the new life was to be, once the kingdom of God had come in power. In the indwelling of the Holy Spirit, in union with Him the heavenly Vine, and in their going out to witness and to suffer for Him, they were to find their calling and their blessedness. In between His setting forth of their future new life, the Lord had repeatedly given the most unlimited promises as to the power their prayers might have. And now in closing, He Himself proceeds to pray. To let His disciples have the joy of knowing what His intercession for them in heaven as their High Priest will be, He gives this precious legacy of His prayer to the Father. He does this at the same time because they as priests are to share in His work of intercession so that they and we might know how to perform this holy work.

In the teaching of our Lord on this last night, we have learned to understand that these astonishing prayer promises have not been given on our own behalf, but in the interest of the Lord and His kingdom. It is from the Lord Himself alone that we can learn what the prayer in His name is to be and to obtain. We have understood that to pray in His name is to pray in perfect unity with Himself, that the high-priestly prayer recorded in John 17 will teach all that the prayer in the name of Jesus may ask and expect.

This prayer is ordinarily divided into three parts. Our Lord first prays for Himself (17:1–5), then for His disciples (17:6–19), and last for all the believing people through all ages (17:20–26). The follower of Jesus, who gives himself to the work of intercession, and who would desire to see how much blessing he can pray down on his circle in the name of Jesus, will in all humility let himself be led by the Spirit to study this wonderful prayer as one of the most important lessons of the school of prayer.

First of all, Jesus prays for Himself, for His being glorified, that so He may glorify the Father. "Father...glorify Your Son.... And now, O Father, glorify Me" (17:1, 5). And He brings forward the grounds on which He prays this way. A holy covenant had been concluded between the Father and the Son in heaven. The Father had promised Him power over all flesh as the reward of His work. He had done the work. He had glorified the Father, and His one purpose is now to glorify Him still further. With the utmost boldness He asks that the Father may glorify Him, so that He may now be and do for His people all He has undertaken.

> *It is from the Lord Himself alone that we can learn what the prayer in His Name is to be and to obtain.*

Disciple of Jesus! Here you have the first lesson in your work of priestly intercession, which is to be learned from the example of your great High Priest. To pray in the name of Jesus is to pray in unity, in agreement with Him. As the Son began His prayer by making clear His relationship to the Father, pleading His work and obedience and His desire to see the Father glorified, do so, too. Draw near and appear before the Father in Christ. Plead His finished work. Say that you are one with it, that you trust in it and live in it. Say that you, too, have given yourself to finish the work the Father has given you to do and to live alone for His glory. And then confidently ask that the Son may be glorified in you. This is praying in the name, in the very words, in the Spirit of Jesus, in union with Jesus Himself. Such prayer has power. If with Jesus you glorify the Father, the Father will glorify Jesus by doing what you ask in His Name. It is only when your own personal relation on this point, like Christ's, is clear with God, when you are glorifying Him and seeking all for His glory, that, like Christ, you will have power to intercede for those around you.

Our Lord next prays for the circle of His disciples. He speaks of them as those the Father has given Him. Their chief mark is that they have received Christ's word. He says of them that He now sends them into the world in His place, just as the Father had sent Him. And He asks two things for them: that the Father keep them from the evil one, and that He sanctify them through His Word, because He sanctifies Himself for them (17:15–19).

Just like the Lord, each believing intercessor has his own immediate circle for whom he first prays. Parents have their children, teachers their pupils, pastors their flocks, all workers their special charge, all believers those whose care lies upon their hearts. It is of great importance that intercession should be personal, pointed, and definite. And then our first prayer must always be that they may receive the Word. But this prayer will not succeed unless with our Lord we say, "I have given them Your word" (17:14). It is this that gives us liberty and power in intercession for souls. Not only pray for them, but speak to them. And when they have received the Word, let us pray much for their being kept from the evil one and for their being sanctified through that word. Instead of being hopeless or judging or giving up those who fall, let us pray for our circle, "Father, keep them in Your name; sanctify them by Your truth." Prayer in the name of Jesus prevails much. What you desire will be done for you.

And then follows our Lord's prayer for a still wider circle. "I do not pray for these alone, but also for those who will believe" (17:20). His priestly heart enlarges itself to embrace all places and all time, and He prays that all who belong to Him may everywhere be one, as God's proof to the world of the divinity of His mission, and then that they may ever be with Him in His glory. Until then, "that the love with which You loved Me may be in them, and I in them" (17:26).

The disciple of Jesus who has first in his own circle proved the power of prayer cannot confine himself within its limits, but prays for the Church universal and its different branches. He prays specifically for the unity of the Spirit and of love. He prays for its being one in Christ as a witness to the world that Christ, who has accomplished such a wonder as making love triumph over selfishness and separation, is indeed the Son of God sent from heaven. Every believer should pray greatly that the unity of the Church, not in external organizations, but in spirit and in truth, may be made a reality.

Draw near and appear before the Father in Christ. Plead His finished work. Say that you are one with it, that you trust in it and live in it. Say that you, too, have given yourself to finish the work the Father has given you to do and to live alone for His glory.

So much for the subject of the prayer. Now for its method. Jesus says, *Father, I desire*" (17:24). On the ground of His right as Son, and the Father's promise to Him, and His finished work, He can do this. The Father had said to Him, "Ask of Me, and I will give You" (Ps. 2:8). He simply claimed for Himself the Father's promise. Jesus has given us an identical promise: "*Whatever you desire* shall be done for you." He asks me in His name to say what I desire. Abiding in Him, in a living union with Him in which man is nothing and Christ all, the believer has the liberty to take up that word of His High Priest and, in answer to the question "What do you desire?" to say, "*Father, I desire* all You have promised." This is nothing but true faith; this is honoring to God: To be assured that such confidence in saying what I desire is indeed acceptable to Him. At first sight, our heart shrinks from that expression because we feel neither the liberty nor the power to speak this way. It is a word for which alone in the most entire renunciation of our will grace will be given, but for which grace will most assuredly be given to each one who loses his will in his Lord's. He who loses his will shall find it, and he who gives up his will entirely shall find it again renewed and strengthened with a divine strength.

Father, I desire: this is the keynote of the everlasting, ever-active, all-prevailing intercession of our Lord in heaven. It is only in union with Him that our prayer succeeds. In union with Him it accomplishes much. If we simply abide in Him—living and walking and doing all things in His name—if we simply come and bring each separate request, tested and touched by His Word and Spirit and cast it into the mighty stream of intercession that goes up from Him to be borne upward and presented before the Father, then we shall have the full confidence that we receive the petitions we ask. The "Father, I *desire*" will be breathed into us by the Spirit Himself. We shall lose ourselves in Him and become nothing, to find that, despite our own helplessness, we have power and victory.

The disciple of Jesus who has first in his own circle proved the power of prayer cannot confine himself within its limits, but prays for the Church universal and its different branches.

Disciples of Jesus, called to be like your Lord in His priestly intercession: when, O when shall we awaken to the glory, passing all human understanding, of our destiny to plead and prevail with God for perishing men? O when shall we shake off the idleness that clothes itself with the pretence of humility, and yield ourselves wholly to God's Spirit, so that He may fill our wills with light and with power to know and to take and to possess all that our God is waiting to give to a will that lays hold on Him?

"LORD, TEACH US TO PRAY."

O my blessed High Priest! Who am I that You should invite me to share with You in Your power of prevailing intercession? And why, O my Lord, am I so slow of heart to understand and believe and exercise this wonderful privilege for which You have redeemed Your people? O Lord, give Your grace so that this may increasingly be my unceasing life work: praying without ceasing to draw down the blessing of heaven on all my surroundings on earth.

Blessed Lord! I come now to accept this my calling. For this I would give up all and follow You. Into Your hands I would believingly yield my whole being. Form, train, and inspire me to be one of Your prayer legion, wrestlers who watch and strive in prayer, Israel's, God's princes who have power and who prevail. Take possession of my heart and fill it with the one desire for the glory of God in the ingathering, sanctification, and union of those the Father has given You. Take my mind and let this be my study and my wisdom to know when prayer can bring a blessing. Take

889

me completely and fit me as a priest to stand constantly before God and to bless in His name.

Blessed Lord! Let it be here, as through all the spiritual life: You everything, I nothing. And let it be here my experience, too, that he who has and seeks nothing for himself receives all, especially the wonderful grace of sharing with You in Your everlasting ministry of intercession. Amen.

For Further Thought

1. *What had the Father promised Jesus in return for His obediently completing the work He had been sent to do?*
2. *God places people in every believer's life with the responsibility of praying, of interceding on their behalf by name. What is the first thing you should pray for those God has placed in your circle of influence?*
3. *What two words are the keynote for everlasting, effective intercession of Jesus Christ in heaven? How does that relate to the success of our own intercession for others?*

LESSON 28

"FATHER. . .NOT WHAT I WILL,"

OR, CHRIST THE SACRIFICE

He said, "Abba, Father, all things are possible for You.
Take this cup away from Me; nevertheless,
not what I will, but what You will."
MARK 14:36

WHAT a contrast within the space of a few hours! What a transition from the quiet elevation of that, "Jesus. . .lifted up His eyes to heaven, and said. . .*Father, I desire*" (John 17:1, 24), to that falling on the ground and crying in agony, "My Father! Not what I will." In the one we see the High Priest within the veil in His all-prevailing intercession; in the other, the sacrifice on the altar opening the way through the torn veil. The high-priestly "Father! I desire," in order of time precedes the sacrificial "Father! Not what I will." But this was only by anticipation, to show what the intercession would be when once the sacrifice was brought.

In reality it was that prayer at the altar, "Father! Not what I will," in which the prayer before the throne, "Father! I desire," had its origin and its power. It is from the entire surrender of His will in Gethsemane that the High Priest on the throne has the power to ask what He desires and the right to make His people share in that power, too, and ask what they desire.

For all who want to learn to pray in the school of Jesus, this Gethsemane lesson is one of the most sacred and precious. To a superficial student, it may appear to take away the courage to pray in faith. If even the earnest prayer of the Son was not heard, if even the Beloved had to say, *Not what I will!* how much more do we need to speak this way. And therefore it appears impossible that the promises the Lord had given only a few hours previously, "*Whatever you ask*," AND "*what you desire*," could have been meant literally.

A deeper insight into the meaning of Gethsemane would teach us that we have just here the sure ground and the open way to the assurance of an answer to our prayer. Let us draw near in reverent and adoring wonder and look intently on this great sight—God's Son offering up prayer and supplications with strong crying and tears, but not obtaining what He asks. He Himself is our

Teacher, and He will open up to us the mystery of His holy sacrifice as revealed in this wondrous prayer.

To understand the prayer, let us note the infinite difference between what our Lord prayed a short time ago as a royal High Priest, and what He here requests in His weakness. *There* it was for the glorifying of the Father He prayed, as well as for the glorifying of Himself and His people as the fulfillment of distinct promises that had been given Him. He asked what He knew to be according to the word and the will of the Father. He might boldly say, "*Father, I desire.*" *Here* He prays for something in regard to which the Father's will is not yet clear to Him. As far as He knows, it is the Father's will that He should drink the cup. He had told His disciples of the cup He must drink, and a little later He would again say, "Shall I not drink the cup which My Father has given Me?" (John 18:11). It was for this He had come to this earth. But when, in the unspeakable agony of soul that burst upon Him as the power of darkness came upon Him, as He began to taste the first drops of death as the wrath of God against sin, His human nature, as it shuddered in the presence of the awful reality of being made a curse, gave utterance in this cry of anguish, to its desire that, if God's purpose could be accomplished without it, He might be spared the awful cup: "Take this cup away from Me."

*L*et us draw near in reverent and adoring wonder and look intently on this great sight—God's Son offering up prayer and supplications with strong crying and tears, but not obtaining what He asks.

That desire was the evidence of the intense reality of His humanity. The "Not as I will" kept that desire from being sinful. As He pleadingly cries, "All things are possible for You," and returns again to still more earnest prayer that the cup may be removed, it is His thrice-repeated "*Not what I will*" that constitutes the very essence and worth of His sacrifice. He had asked for something of which He could not say: "I know it is Your will." He had pleaded God's power and love, and had then withdrawn it in His final, "*Your will be done.*" The prayer that the cup should be taken away could not be answered, and the prayer of submission that God's will be done was heard and gloriously answered in His victory first over the fear, and then over the power of death.

It is in this denial of His will, this complete surrender of His desires to the will of the Father, that Christ's obedience reached its highest perfection. It is from the sacrifice of the will in Gethsemane that the sacrifice of the life on Calvary derives its value. It is here, as scripture says, that He learned obedience and became the author of everlasting salvation to all who obey Him (Heb. 5:8–9). It was because He there, in that prayer, became obedient to the point of death, even death on the cross, that God has highly exalted Him and gave Him the power to ask what He desired (Phil. 2:8–9). It was in that "Father, not what I will," that He obtained the power for that other "*Father*, I will." It was by Christ's submission at Gethsemane to have not His will done that He secured for His people the right to say to them, "Ask whatever you desire."

Let me look again at the deep mysteries Gethsemane offers to my view. There is the first: The Father offers His Well-Beloved the cup, the cup of wrath. The second: The Son, always so obedient, shrinks back and begs that He may not have to drink it. The third: The Father does not grant the Son His request, but still gives the cup. And then the last: The Son yields His will, is content that His will not be done, and goes to Calvary to drink the cup. O Gethsemane! In you I see how my Lord could give me such unlimited assurance of an answer to my prayers. As my assurance He won it for me, and by His consent to have His petition unanswered.

This is in harmony with the whole plan of redemption. Our Lord always wins for us the opposite of what He suffered. He was bound so that we might go free. He was made sin so that we might become the righteousness of God. He died so that we might live. He bore God's curse so that God s blessing might be ours. He endured no answer to His prayer so that our prayers might find an answer. Yes, He said, "*Not as I will*" so that He might say to us, "If you abide in Me…you will *ask what you desire*, and it shall be done for you" (John 15:7).

Yes, "If You abide in Me"—here in Gethsemane the word acquires new force and depth. Christ is our Head, who as surety stands in our place and bears what we must forever have borne. We had deserved that God should turn a deaf ear to us and never listen to our cry. Christ comes and suffers this, too, for us. He suffers what we had deserved. For our sins He suffers beneath the burden of that unanswered prayer. But now His suffering this benefits me: What He has borne is taken away for me, and His obedience has won for me the answer to every prayer—if I abide in Him.

Yes, in Him, as He bows there in Gethsemane, I must abide. As my Head, He not only once suffered for me, but always lives in me, breathing and working His own nature in me, too. The eternal Spirit, through which He offered Himself to God, is the Spirit that dwells in me, too, and makes me a partaker of the very same obedience, as well as the sacrifice of my will to God. That Spirit teaches me to yield my will entirely to the will of the Father, to give it up even to the point of death, and in Christ to be dead to it.

Whatever is my own mind and thought and will, even though it may not be directly sinful, He teaches me to fear and flee. He opens my ear to wait in great gentleness and teachability of soul for what the Father has day by day to speak and to teach. He shows me how union with God's will in the love of it is union with God Himself, how entire surrender to God's will is the Father's claim, the Son's example, and the true blessedness of the soul. He leads my will into the fellowship of Christ's death and resurrection, my will dies in Him and in Him, in Him to be made alive again. He breathes into it, as a renewed and quickened will, a holy insight into God's perfect will, a holy joy in yielding itself to be an instrument of that will, a holy liberty and power to lay hold of God's will to answer prayer.

With my whole being I will learn to live for the interests of God and His kingdom, to exercise the power of that will—crucified but risen again—in nature and in prayer, on earth and in heaven, with men and with God. The more deeply I enter into the "*Father, not what I will*" of Gethsemane and into Him who prayed it, and to abide in Him, the fuller is my spiritual access into the power of His "*Father, I will*." And the soul experiences that it is the will, which has become nothing so that God's will may be everything, which now becomes inspired with a divine strength to truly will what God wills, and to claim what has been promised it in the name of Christ.

> *We had deserved that God should turn a deaf ear to us and never listen to our cry. Christ comes and suffers this, too, for us. He suffers what we had deserved.*

O let us listen to Christ in Gethsemane, as He calls, "If you abide in Me... ask what you desire, and it shall be done for you." Being of one mind and spirit with Him in His giving up everything to God's will, living like Him in obedience and surrender to the Father—this is abiding in Him as well as the secret of power in prayer.

"LORD, TEACH US TO PRAY."

Blessed Lord Jesus! Gethsemane was Your school where You learned to pray and to obey. It is still Your school, where You lead all Your disciples who desire to learn to obey and to pray as You did. Lord! Teach me there to pray, in the faith that You have atoned for and conquered our self-will and can indeed give us grace to pray like You.

O Lamb of God! I desire to follow You to Gethsemane, to become one with You there, and to abide in You as You to the very point of death yield Your will to the Father. With You, through You, and in You, I yield my will in absolute and entire surrender to the will of the Father. Conscious of my own weakness and of the secret power with which self-will can assert itself and again take its place on the throne, I claim in faith the power of Your victory. You triumphed over it and delivered me from it. In Your death I desire to daily live; in Your life I desire to daily die. Abiding in You, let my will, through the power of Your eternal Spirit, be the tuned instrument that yields to every touch of the will of my God. With my whole soul I say with You and in You, "Father! Not what I will, but what You will."

And then, blessed Lord! Open my heart and the hearts of all Your people to take in fully the glory of the truth that a will given up to God is a will accepted by God to be used in His service to desire, purpose, determine, and will what is according to God's will. A will that, in the power of the Holy Spirit the indwelling God, is to exercise its royal prerogative in prayer, to loose and to bind in heaven and on earth, to ask whatever it desires, and to say it shall be done.

O Lord Jesus! Teach me to pray. Amen.

FOR FURTHER THOUGHT

1. *In what ways were Christ's high-priestly prayer and His prayer at Gethsemane different? What is the significance of those differences for you today?*
2. *What four points of Jesus' suffering at Gethsemane is most important for believers, for you, to understand, and why are they important to you today?*
3. *What did Christ suffer in His prayer at Gethsemane that you deserve now? What did His obedience in the face of the Father's silence accomplish for you?*

LESSON 29

"IF WE ASK ACCORDING TO HIS WILL," or, Our Boldness in Prayer

Now this is the confidence that we have in Him, that if we ask
anything according to His will, He hears us. And if we know
that He hears us, whatever we ask, we know that we
have the petitions that we have asked of Him.
1 JOHN 5:14–15

ONE of the greatest hindrances to believing prayer for many is undoubtedly this: They don't know if what they ask is according to the will of God. As long as they are in doubt on this point, they cannot have the boldness to ask in the assurance that they certainly will receive. And they soon begin to think that if once they have made their requests known and receive no answer, it is best to leave it to God to do according to His good pleasure. The words of John, "If we ask anything *according to His will*, He hears us," as they understand them, make certainty as to answer to prayer impossible, because they cannot be sure of what really may be the will of God. They think of God's will as His hidden plan—how should man be able to fathom what really may be the purpose of the all-wise God.

This is the very opposite of what John aimed at when he wrote this. He wished to move us toward boldness, toward confidence, and toward full assurance of faith in prayer. He says, "*This is the confidence that we have in Him,*" that we can say, "Father, You know and I know that I ask according to Your will. I know You hear me."

"Now this is the confidence that we have in Him, that if we ask anything according to His will, He hears us." To this point He adds at once: "And if we know that He hears us, whatever we ask, we *know*," through this faith, "that we have," that we know while we pray receive, "the petitions," the special things, "that we have asked of Him" (1 John 5:15). John starts with the premise that when we pray, we first find out if our prayers are according to the will of God. They may be according to God's will, and yet not come at once, or without the persevering prayer of faith. It is to give us courage to persevere this way and to be strong in faith that He tells us: "This gives us boldness or confidence in prayer, if we ask anything according to His will, He hears us." It is evident that if there is a matter of uncertainty to us whether our petitions are according to His will, we cannot have the comfort of what he says, "We know that we have the petitions that we have asked of Him."

But just this is the difficulty. More than one believer says: "I do not know if what I desire is according to the will of God. God's will is the purpose of His infinite wisdom, so it is impossible for me to know whether He may not consider something else better for me than what I desire, or may not have some reasons for withholding what I ask." Everyone feels how with such thoughts, the prayer of faith, of which Jesus said, "Whoever. . .believes that *those things he says* will be done, he will have *whatever* he says" (Mark 11:23), becomes an impossibility. There may be the prayer of submission and of trust in God's wisdom, but there cannot be the prayer of faith. The great mistake here is that God's children do not really believe that it is possible to know God's will. Or if they believe this, they do not take the time and trouble to find it out. What we need is to see clearly in what way the Father leads His waiting, teachable child to know that his petition is according to His will.[37] It is through God's holy Word, taken up and kept in the heart, the life, the will, and through God's Holy Spirit, accepted in His indwelling and leading, that we shall learn to know that our petitions are according to His will.

> *It is through God's holy Word, taken up and kept in the heart, the life, the will, and through God's Holy Spirit, accepted in His indwelling and leading, that we shall learn to know that our petitions are according to His will.*

Through the Word. There is a secret will of God with which we often fear that our prayers may be at odds. It is not with this will of God, but His will as revealed in His Word, that we have to do in prayer. Our notions of what the secret will may have decreed, and of how it might make the answers to our prayers impossible, are mostly very erroneous. Childlike faith as to what He is willing to do for His children simply holds to the Father's assurance that it is His will to hear prayer and to do what faith in His Word desires and accepts. In the Word the Father has revealed in general promises the great principles of His will with His people. The child has to take the promises and apply them to the special circumstances in His life to which they are related. Whatever he asks within the limits of that revealed will, he can know to be according to the will of God, and he may confidently expect an answer.

In His Word, God has given us the revelation of His will and plans with us, with His people, and with the world with the most precious promises of the grace

---

[37] See this illustrated in the extracts from George Müller at the end of this volume.

and power with which, through His people, He will carry out His plans and do His work. As faith becomes strong and bold enough to claim the fulfillment of the general promise in the special case, we may have the assurance that our prayers are heard, because they are according to God's will. Take the words of John in the verse following our text as an illustration: "If anyone sees his brother sinning a sin which does not lead to death, he will ask, and *He will give him life*" (1 John 5:16). Such is the general promise; and the believer who pleads on the ground of this promise, prays according to the will of God, and John wants to give him boldness to know that he has the petition he asks.

> *In the heart the Word and the Spirit must meet. It is only by their indwelling that we can experience their teaching.*

But this understanding of God's will is something spiritual and must be spiritually discerned. It is not as a matter of logic that we can argue it out: God has said it; I must have it. Nor has every Christian the same gift or calling. While the general will revealed in the promise is the same for all, there is for each one a special different will according to God's purpose. And in this is the wisdom of the saints—to know this special will of God for each of us, according to the measure of grace given us, and to ask in prayer just what God has prepared and made possible for each. It is to communicate this wisdom *that the Holy Spirit dwells in us*. The personal application of the general promises of the Word to our special personal needs—*it is for this that the leading of the Holy Spirit is given to us.*

It is this union of the teaching of the Word and Spirit that many do not understand, and so there is a twofold difficulty in knowing what God's will may be. Some seek the will of God in an inner feeling or conviction, and want to have the Spirit lead them without the Word. Others seek it in the Word, but without the living leading of the Holy Spirit. The two must be united. Only in the Word, only in the Spirit, but in these most surely, can we know the will of God and learn to pray according to it. In the heart the Word and the Spirit must meet. It is only by their indwelling that we can experience their teaching. The Word must dwell and must abide in us. Heart and life must daily be under its influence. Not from without, but from within comes the quickening of the Word by the Spirit. It is only he who yields himself entirely in his whole life to the supremacy of the Word and the will of God who can expect in special cases to discern what that Word and will permit him to boldly to ask for.

And even as with the Word, it is just so with the Spirit: if I want to have the leading of the Spirit in prayer to assure me what God's will is, my whole life must be yielded to that leading. That's the only way mind and heart can become spiritual and capable of knowing God's holy will. It is he who, through Word and Spirit, *lives in the will* of God by doing it who will know to pray according to that will in the confidence that He hears us.

Christians need to see what incalculable harm they do themselves by thinking that because possibly their prayer is not according to God's will, they must be content without an answer. God's Word tells us that the great reason of unanswered prayer is that we do not pray correctly: "You ask and do not receive, because you ask amiss" (James 4:3). In not granting an answer, the Father tells us that there is something wrong in our praying. He wants to teach us to find it out and confess it, and so to educate us to true believing and prevailing prayer. He can only attain His objective when He brings us to see that we are to blame for the withholding of the answer, because our aim, our faith, or our life is not what it should be. But this purpose of God is frustrated as long as we are content to say: "It is perhaps because my prayer is not according to His will that He does not hear me."

O let us no longer throw the blame of our unanswered prayers on the secret will of God, but on our praying amiss. Let that word, "You ask and do not receive, because you ask amiss," be like the lantern of the Lord, searching heart and life to prove that we are indeed among those to whom Christ gave His promises of certain answers. Let us believe that we *can know* if our prayer is according to God's will. Let us yield our heart to have the Word of the Father dwell richly there, to have Christ's Word abiding in us. Let us live day by day with the anointing that teaches us all things. Let us yield ourselves unreservedly to the Holy Spirit as He teaches us to abide in Christ and to dwell in the Father's presence. When we do that, we shall soon understand how the Father's love longs for His child to know His will, and how he should, in the confidence that that will includes all that His power and love have promised to do, know, too, that He hears the petitions that we ask of Him. "*This is* the confidence that we have in Him, that if we ask anything according to His will, He hears us."

"LORD, TEACH US TO PRAY."

Blessed Master! With my whole heart I thank You for this blessed lesson that the path to a life full of answers to prayer is through the will of God. Lord! Teach me to know this blessed will by living it, loving it, and always doing it. So shall I learn to offer prayers according to that will, and to find in their harmony with God's blessed will my boldness in prayer and my confidence in accepting the answer.

Father! *It is Your will* that Your child should enjoy Your presence and blessing. *It is Your will* that everything in the life of Your child should be in accordance with Your will, and that the Holy Spirit should work this in Him. *It is Your will* that Your child should live in the daily experience of specific answers to prayer, and therefore enjoy living and direct fellowship with Yourself. *It is Your will* that Your Name should be glorified in and through Your children, and that it will be in those who trust You. O my Father! Let Your will be my confidence in all I ask.

Blessed Savior! Teach me to believe in the glory of this will. That will is the eternal love, which with Divine power works out its purpose in each human will that yields itself to it. Lord! Teach me this. You can make me see how every promise and every command of the Word is indeed the will of God, and that its fulfillment is secured to me by God Himself. Let, therefore, the will of God become to me the sure rock on which my prayer and my assurance of an answer always rest. Amen.

FOR FURTHER THOUGHT

1. *Read 1 John 5:14–15. What blessing do you receive when you ask anything of God that you know is according to His will?*
2. *How can you have a perfect understanding of God's will? What part do the mind and logic play in knowing His will? What part does spiritual discernment play?*
3. *The apostle James wrote, "You ask and do not receive, because you ask amiss" (4:3). In what ways do believers "ask amiss," and how can you know you are asking God for the right things and in the right way?*

THERE is often great confusion as to the will of God. People think that what God wills must inevitably take place. This is by no means the case. God wills a great deal of blessing to His people that never comes to them. He wills it most earnestly, but they do not will it, so it cannot come to them. It is the great mystery of man's creation with a free will—and also of the renewal of his will in redemption—that God has made the execution of His will, in many things, dependent on the will of man. Of God's will revealed in His promises, so much will be fulfilled only as our faith accepts it. Prayer is the power by which comes to pass that which otherwise would not take place. And faith is the power by which it is decided how much of God's will be done in us. When once God reveals to a soul what He is willing to do for it, the responsibility for the execution of that will rests with us.

Some are afraid that this is putting too much power into the hands of man. But all power is put into the hands of man in Christ Jesus. The key of all prayer and all power is His, and when we learn to understand that He is just as much with us as with the Father, that we are also just as much one with Him as He with the Father, we shall see how natural and right and safe it is that God gives to those who abide in Him, as He in the Father, such power. It is Christ the Son who has the right to ask what He will, and it is through abiding in Him and His abiding in us (in a divine reality of which we have too little understanding) that His Spirit breathes in us what He wants to ask and obtain through us. We pray in His Name, and the prayers are really ours and as really His.

Others again fear that to believe that prayer has such power is limiting the liberty and the love of God. O if we only knew how we are limiting His liberty and His love by not allowing Him to act in the only way in which He chooses to act, now that He has taken us up into fellowship with Himself—through our prayers and our faith. As we were speaking on the subject, a brother in the ministry once asked whether there was not a danger of our thinking that our love for souls and our willingness to see them blessed were to move God's love and God's willingness to bless them. We were just passing some large water pipes, by which water was being carried over hill and dale from a large mountain stream to a town some distance away. "Just look at these pipes," was the answer. They did not make the water willing to flow downward from the hills, nor did they give it its power of blessing and refreshment. That is water's very nature. All that they could do is to determine its direction, and by that direction the inhabitants of the town said they want the blessing there. And just so, it is the very nature of God to love and to bless. Downward and ever downward His love longs to come with its life-giving and refreshing streams. But He has left it to prayer to say where the blessing is to come. He has committed it to His believing people to bring the living water to the desert places. The will of God to bless is dependent on the will of man to say where the blessing must descend. "This honor have all His saints" (Ps. 149:9). "Now this is *the confidence* that we have in Him, that if we ask anything according to His will, He hears us. And if *we know* that He hears us, whatever we ask, *we know that we have* the petitions that we have asked of Him."

LESSON 30

"A HOLY PRIESTHOOD," OR,

THE MINISTRY OF INTERCESSION

A holy priesthood, to offer up spiritual sacrifices
acceptable to God through Jesus Christ.
1 PETER 2:5

"But you shall be named the priests of the LORD."
ISAIAH 61:6

"THE Spirit of the Lord GOD is upon Me, because the LORD has anointed Me" (Isa. 61:1). These are the words of Jesus in Isaiah. As the fruit of His work, all redeemed ones are priests and fellow partakers with Him of His anointing with the Spirit as High Priest. "It is like the precious oil upon. . .the beard of Aaron, running down on the edge of his garments" (Ps. 133:2). As with every son of Aaron, so every member of Jesus' body has a right to the priesthood. But not every one exercises it. Many are still entirely ignorant of it. And yet it is the highest privilege of a child of God, the mark of greatest nearness and likeness to Him who always lives to pray. Do you doubt if this is really true? Think of what constitutes priesthood.

There is, first, the *work of the priesthood.* This has two sides: one Godward, the other manward. "Every priest. . .is *appointed for men* in things *pertaining to God*" (Heb. 5:1); or, as it is said by Moses: "The LORD separated the tribe of Levi. . .to *stand before the LORD* to minister to Him and *to bless in His name*" (Deut. 10:8; also see 21:5, 33:10; Mal. 2:6). On the one hand, the priest had the power to draw near to God, to dwell with Him in His house, and to present before Him the blood of the sacrifice or the burning incense. This work he did not do, however, on his own behalf, but for the sake of the people he represented. This is the other side of his work. He received from the people their sacrifices, presented them before God, and then came out to bless in His name, to give the assurance of His favor and to teach them His law.

A priest is therefore a man who does not live at all for himself. *He lives with God and for God.* As God's servant, his work is to care for His house, His honor, and His worship, to make known to men His love and His will. *He lives with men and for men* (see Heb. 5:2). His work is to find out their sin and need and to bring it before God, to offer sacrifice and incense in their name in order to obtain forgiveness and blessing for them, and then to come out and bless them in His name. This is the high calling of every believer: "This honor have all His saints" (Ps. 149:9). They have been redeemed with the one purpose to be in the midst of the perishing millions around them God's priests who, in conformity to Jesus the Great High Priest, are to be the ministers and stewards of the grace of God to all around them.

And then there is *the walk of the priesthood*, in harmony with its work. Just as God is holy, so the priest was to be especially holy. This means not only separated from everything unclean, but *holy to their God* (Lev. 21:6), being set apart and given up to God for His use. The separation from the world and setting apart to God was indicated in many ways.

It was seen in the clothing: The holy garments, made after God's own order, marked them as His (see Exod. 28). It was seen in the command regarding their special purity and freedom from all contact from death and defilement (see Lev. 11:22). Much that was allowed to an ordinary Israelite was forbidden to them. It was seen in the command that the priest must have no bodily defect or blemish, because bodily perfection was to be the type of wholeness and holiness in God's service. And it was seen in the arrangement by which the priestly tribes were to have no inheritance with the other tribes, because God alone was to be their inheritance. Their life was to be one of faith—set apart to God, they were to live on Him as well as for Him.

All this is the emblem of what the character of the New Testament priest is to be. Our priestly power with God depends on our personal life and walk. We must be of them of whose walk on earth Jesus says, they "have not defiled their garments" (Rev. 3:4).

In the surrender of what may appear lawful to others in our separation from the world, we must prove that our dedication to be holy to the Lord is whole-hearted and entire. The bodily perfection of the priest must have its counterpart in our, too, being "without spot or blemish;" "the man of God may be complete, thoroughly equipped for every good work," "perfect and complete, lacking nothing" (Lev. 21:17–21, Eph. 5:27, 2 Tim. 3:17, James 1:4). And above all, we agree to give up all inheritance on earth and to forsake all, and like Christ to have only God as our portion—to possess as not possessing, and hold all for God alone. It is this that marks the true priest, the man who only lives for God and his fellowmen.

And now *the way to the priesthood*. In Aaron God had chosen all his sons to be priests; each of them was a priest by birth. And yet he could not enter into his work without a special act of ordinance—his consecration. Every child of God is priest in right of his birth and his blood relationship to the Great High Priest.

But this is not enough. He will exercise his power only as he accepts and realizes his consecration.

With Aaron and his sons, it took place like this (see Exod. 29): After being washed and clothed, they were anointed with the holy oil. Sacrifices were then offered, and the right ear, the right hand, and the right foot were touched with blood. And then they and their garments were once again sprinkled with the blood and the oil together. And so it is as the child of God enters more fully into what *the Blood and the Spirit*, of which he already is a partaker, are to him that the power of the holy priesthood will work in him. The blood will take away all sense of unworthiness, the Spirit all sense of unfitness.

> *A*s with every son of Aaron, so every member of Jesus' body has a right to the priesthood. But not every one exercises it.

Let us notice what there was new in the application of the blood to the priest. If ever he had as a penitent brought a sacrifice for his sin, seeking forgiveness, the blood was sprinkled on the altar, but not on his person. But now, for priestly consecration, there was to be closer contact with the blood. Ear and hand and foot were by a special act brought under its power, and the whole being taken possession of and sanctified for God. Likewise, when the believer, who had been content to think chiefly of the blood sprinkled on the mercy seat as what he needs for pardon, is led to seek full priestly access to God, he feels the need of a fuller and more abiding experience of the power of the blood, as really sprinkling and cleansing the heart from an evil conscience so that he has "no more conscience of sins" (Heb. 10:2), as cleansing from all sin. And it is as he gets to enjoy this that the consciousness is awakened of his wonderful right of most intimate access to God, and of the full assurance that his intercessions are acceptable.

And as the blood gives the right, the Spirit gives the power, and fits for believing intercession. He breathes into us the priestly spirit—burning love for God's honor and the saving of souls. He makes us so one with Jesus that prayer in His name is a reality. He strengthens us for believing, persistent prayer. The more the Christian is truly filled with the Spirit of Christ, the more spontaneous will be his giving himself up to the life of priestly intercession.

Beloved fellow Christians! God needs—greatly needs—priests who can draw near to Him, who live in His presence, and who, by their intercession, draw down the blessings of His grace on others. And the world needs—greatly needs—priests who will bear the burden of the perishing ones and intercede on their behalf.

Are you willing to offer yourself for this holy work? You know the surrender it demands: nothing less than the Christlike giving up of all, so that the saving purposes of God's love may be accomplished among men. Oh, be no longer one of those who are content to have salvation and just do work enough to keep themselves warm and lively. Let nothing keep you back from giving yourselves to be wholly and only priests—nothing else, nothing less than the priests of the Most High God. The thought of unworthiness, of unfitness, need not keep you back. In *the Blood*, the objective power of the perfect redemption works in you. In *the Spirit* its full subjective personal experience as a divine life is secured. *The Blood* provides an infinite worthiness to make your prayers most acceptable. *The Spirit* provides a divine fitness, teaching you to pray just according to the will of God. *Every priest knew that when he presented a sacrifice according to the law of the sanctuary, it was accepted.* Under the covering of the Blood and Spirit, you have the assurance that all the wonderful promises of prayer in the name of Jesus will be fulfilled in you.

> *he more the Christian is truly filled with the Spirit of Christ, the more spontaneous will be his giving himself up to the life of priestly intercession.*

Abiding in union with the Great High Priest, "You shall ask what you desire, and it shall be done for you." You will have power to pray the effectual prayer "of the righteous man that accomplishes much" (see James 5:16). You will not only join in the general prayer of the Church for the world, but you will be able in your own sphere to take up your special work in prayer as priests—to transact it with God, to receive and know the answer, and so to bless in His name. Come, brother, come and be a priest—*only* priest, *all* priest. Seek now to walk before the Lord in the full consciousness that you have been set apart for the holy ministry of intercession. This is the true blessedness of conformity to the image of God's Son.

"Lord, teach us to pray."

O my blessed High Priest, accept the consecration in which my soul now would respond to Your message.

I believe in the *Holy Priesthood of Your Saints*, and that I, too, am a priest, with power to appear before the Father, and in the prayer that accomplishes much bring down blessing on the perishing around me.

I believe in the *Power of Your Precious Blood* to cleanse from all sin, to give me perfect confidence toward God, and to bring me near in the full assurance of faith that my intercession will be heard.

I believe in the *Anointing of the Spirit*, coming down daily from You, my Great High Priest, to sanctify me, to fill me with the consciousness of my priestly calling, and, with love to souls, to teach me what is according to God's will and how to pray the prayer of faith.

I believe that, as You my Lord Jesus are Yourself in all things my life, so You, too, are *The surety for My Prayer Life*, and will Yourself draw me up into the fellowship of Your wondrous work of intercession.

In this faith I yield myself today to my God, as one of His anointed priests, to stand before His face to intercede in behalf of sinners, and to come out and bless in His name.

Holy Lord Jesus! Accept and seal my consecration. Yes, Lord, do lay Your hands on me and Yourself consecrate me to Your holy work. And let me walk among men with the consciousness and the character of a priest of the Most High God.

To Him who loved us and washed us from our sins *In His Own Blood And Has Made Us* kings and priests to God and His Father, TO *Him* be glory and authority forever and ever. Amen.

FOR FURTHER THOUGHT

1. Read 1 Peter 2:5. As a member of Jesus' body on earth, what right do you have in relation to intercession for others?

2. As a child of God, what must you do in order for the power of the holy priesthood to work in you and through you?

3. What privilege and power do you have when you abide in union with Jesus Christ, your Great High Priest?

Lesson 31

"Pray without Ceasing,"
or, A Life of Prayer

Rejoice always, pray without ceasing, in everything give thanks.
1 Thessalonians 5:16–18

O UR Lord spoke the parable of the widow and the unjust judge (Luke 18:1–8) to teach us that men ought to pray always and not grow tired and give up. Because the widow persevered in seeking one definite thing, the parable appears to have reference to persevering prayer for one particular blessing, even when God delays or appears to refuse.

The words in the Epistles—which speak of continuing spontaneously in prayer, continuing and watching in prayer, of praying always in the Spirit—appear to refer more to the whole life being one of prayer. As the soul is filling with the longing for the manifestation of God's glory to us and in us, through us and around us, and with the confidence that He hears the prayers of His children—the inmost life of the soul is continually rising upward in dependence and faith, and in longing desire and trustful expectation.

At the close of our meditations, it will not be difficult to say what is needed to live such a life of prayer. The first thing is undoubtedly the entire sacrifice of the life to God's kingdom and glory. He who seeks to pray without ceasing because he wants to be very devout and good will never accomplish it. It is the forgetting of self and yielding ourselves to live for God and His honor that enlarges the heart, that teaches us to regard everything in the light of God and His will, and that instinctively recognizes in everything around us the need of God's help and blessing and an opportunity for His being glorified.

Because everything is weighed and tested by the one thing that fills the heart— the glory of God—and because the soul has learned that only what is of God can really be to Him and His glory, the whole life becomes a looking up, a crying from the innermost heart for God to prove His power and love and so show forth His glory. The believer awakes to the consciousness that he is one of the watchmen on Zion's walls, one of the Lord's "remembrancers," whose call really touches and moves the King in heaven to do what would otherwise not be done. He understands how real was Paul's exhortation, "praying always with all prayer and supplication in the Spirit. . .for all the saints—and for me. . . . Continue earnestly in prayer. . . meanwhile praying also for us" (Eph. 6:18, 19; Col. 4:2, 3). To forget oneself, to live for God and His kingdom among men, is the way to learn to pray without ceasing.

This life devoted to God must be accompanied by the deep confidence that our prayer is effective. We have seen how our blessed Lord insisted on nothing so much in His prayer lessons as faith in the Father as a God who most certainly does what we ask. "Ask, and you will receive" and counting confidently on an answer is with Him the beginning and the end of His teaching (compare Matt. 7:8 and John 16:24). In the proportion that this assurance masters us, and it becomes a settled thing that our prayers do tell and that God does what we ask, we do not dare neglect the use of this wonderful power. Then the soul turns wholly to God, and our life becomes prayer.

We see that the Lord needs and takes time, because we and all around us are the creatures of time, under the law of growth. But knowing that not one single prayer of faith can possibly be lost, that there is sometimes a need for the storing up and accumulating of prayer, that persevering prayer is irresistible, prayer becomes the quiet, persistent living of our life of desire and faith in the presence of our God.

O let us not any longer by our human reasoning limit and weaken such free and sure promises of the living God, thus robbing them of their power and ourselves of the wonderful confidence they are meant to inspire. Not in God, not in His secret will, and not in the limitations of His promises, but in us, in ourselves is the hindrance. We are not what we should be to obtain the promise. Let us open our whole heart to God's words of promise in all their simplicity and truth, for they will search us and humble us and will lift us up and make us glad and strong. And to the faith that knows it gets what it asks, prayer is not a work or a burden, but a joy and a triumph—it becomes a necessity and a second nature.

This union of strong desire and firm confidence again is nothing but the life of the Holy Spirit within us. The Holy Spirit dwells in us, hides Himself in the depths of our being, and stirs the desire after the unseen and the divine—after God Himself. Now in "groanings which cannot be uttered" (Rom. 8:26), then in clear and conscious assurance; now in special distinct petitions for the deeper revelation of Christ to ourselves, then in pleadings for a soul, for a work, for the Church or the world, it is always and alone the Holy Spirit who draws out the heart to thirst for God and to long for His being made known and glorified.

Where the child of God really lives and walks in the Spirit, where he is not content to remain carnal but seeks to be spiritual—in everything a fit organ for the divine Spirit to reveal the life of Christ and Christ Himself, there the never-ceasing intercession life of the blessed Son cannot but reveal and repeat itself in our experience. Because it is the Spirit of Christ who prays in us, our prayer must be heard. Because it is we who pray in the Spirit, there is need for time and patience and continual renewing of the prayer until every obstacle is conquered and the harmony between God's Spirit and ours is perfect.

But the chief thing we need for such a life of unceasing prayer is this: to know that Jesus teaches us to pray. We have begun to understand a little what *His* teaching is. Not the communication of new thoughts or views, not the discovery of failure or error, not the stirring up of desire and faith, however important all this be, but the taking us up into the fellowship of His own prayer-life before the Father—this it is by which Jesus really teaches.

It was the sight of the praying Jesus that made the disciples long and ask to be taught to pray. It is the faith of the ever-praying Jesus, whose power alone it is to pray, that teaches us truly to pray. We know why: He who prays is our Head and our life. All He has is ours and is given to us when we give ourselves all to Him. By His blood, He leads us into the immediate presence of God. The inner sanctuary is our home, and we dwell there. And He who lives so near God, and knows that He has been brought near to bless those who are far, can't help but pray.

Christ makes us partakers with Himself of His prayer-power and prayer-life. We understand, then, that our true aim must not be to work much and have prayer enough to keep the work going, but to pray much and then to work enough for the power and blessing obtained in prayer to find its way through us to men. It is Christ who always lives to pray and who saves and reigns. He communicates His prayer-life to us. He demonstrates it in us if we trust Him. He is assurance for our praying without ceasing. Yes, Christ teaches us to pray by showing how He does it, by doing it in us, by leading us to do it in Him and like Him. Christ is all, the life and the strength too for a never-ceasing prayer-life.

> To forget oneself, to live for God and His kingdom among men, is the way to learn to pray without ceasing.

It is the sight of the ever-praying Christ as our life that enables us to pray without ceasing. Because His priesthood is the power of an endless life, that resurrection life never fades and never fails, and because His life is our life, praying without ceasing can become to us nothing less than the life joy of heaven. So the apostle says: "Rejoice *always*, pray *without ceasing, in everything* give thanks" (1 Thess. 5:16–18). Borne up between the never-ceasing joy and the never-ceasing praise, never-ceasing prayer is the manifestation of the power of the eternal life, and it's where Jesus always prays.

The union between the Vine and the branch is indeed very much a prayer-union. The highest conformity to Christ, the most blessed participation in the glory of His heavenly life, is that we take part in His work of intercession: He and we live always to pray. In the experience of our union with Him, praying without ceasing becomes a possibility, a reality, and the holiest and most blessed part of our holy and blessed fellowship with God.

We have our home within the veil, in the presence of the Father. What the Father says, we do, and what the Son says, the Father does. Praying without ceasing is the earthly manifestation of heaven come down to us, the foretaste of the life where they don't rest day or night in the song of worship and adoration.

"LORD, TEACH US TO PRAY."

O my Father, with my whole heart I praise You for this wondrous life of never-ceasing prayer, never-ceasing fellowship, never-ceasing answers, and never-ceasing experience of my oneness with Him who always lives to pray. O my God! Keep me always dwelling and walking in the presence of Your glory, so that prayer may be the spontaneous expression of my life with You.

> The chief thing we need for such a life of unceasing prayer is this: to know that Jesus teaches us to pray.

Blessed Savior! With my whole heart I praise You that You came from heaven to share with me in my needs and cries, so that I might share with You in Your all-prevailing intercession. And I thank You that You have taken me into the school of prayer to teach the blessedness and the power of a life that is all prayer. And most of all, that You have taken me up into the fellowship of Your life of intercession, so that through me, too, Your blessings may be dispensed to those around me.

Holy Spirit! With deep reverence I thank You for Your work in me. It is through You that I am lifted up into a share in the fellowship between the Son and the Father, and therefore enter into the fellowship of the life and love of the Holy Trinity. Spirit of God! Perfect Your work in me and bring me into perfect union with Christ my Intercessor. Let Your unceasing indwelling make my life one of unceasing intercession. And let likewise my life become one that is unceasingly to the glory of the Father and to the blessing of those around me. Amen.

FOR FURTHER THOUGHT

1. *What must you do to learn to "pray without ceasing"? What is the right motivation for learning to pray that way, and what is the wrong motivation?*
2. *How, specifically, does Jesus teach you to pray? What must your attitude and disposition toward Him be as you allow Him to teach you?*
3. *In relation to prayer, what is the union between yourself and Christ, your heavenly Vine? When you intercede, what are you taking part in here on earth?*

GEORGE MÜLLER, AND THE

SECRET OF HIS POWER IN PRAYER

WHEN God wishes to freshly teach His Church a truth that is not currently understood or practiced, He does so mostly by raising a man to be, in word and deed, a living witness to its blessedness. And so God has raised up in this nineteenth century, among others, George Müller to be His witness that He is indeed the Hearer of prayer. I know of no way in which the principal truths of God's Word in regard to prayer can be more effectually illustrated and established than a short review of his life and of what he tells of his prayer experiences.

He was born in Prussia on September 25, 1805, and is now eighty years of age. His early life, even after having entered the University of Halle as a theological student, was wicked in the extreme. Led by a friend one evening, when just twenty years of age, to a prayer meeting, he was deeply impressed, and was soon after brought to know the Savior. Not long after, he began reading missionary papers, and after a time he offered himself to the London Society for promoting Christianity to the Jews. He was accepted as a student, but soon found that he could not in all things submit to the rules of the Society, which left too little liberty for the leading of the Holy Spirit. The connection was dissolved in 1830 by mutual consent, and he became the pastor of a small congregation at Teignmouth. In 1832, he was led to Bristol, and it was as pastor of Bethesda Chapel that he was led to the Orphan Home and other work, in connection with which God has so remarkably led him to trust His Word and to experience how God fulfills that Word.

A few extracts in regard to his spiritual life will prepare the way for what we specially wish to quote of his experiences in reference to prayer:

"In connection with this, I would mention that the Lord very graciously gave me, from the very commencement of my divine life, a measure of simplicity and of childlike disposition in spiritual things, so that while I was exceedingly ignorant of the scriptures and was still from time to time overcome even by outward sins, I was still enabled to carry most minute matters to the *Lord in prayer*. And I have found 'godliness is profitable for all things, having promise of the life that now is and of that which is to come' (1 Tim. 4:8). Though very weak and ignorant, yet I had now, by the grace of God, some desire to benefit others, and he who so faithfully had once served Satan, sought now to win souls for Christ."

It was at Teignmouth that he was led to know how to use God's Word and to trust the Holy Spirit as the Teacher given by God to make that word clear. He writes:

"God then began to show me that the Word of God alone is our standard of judgment in spiritual things; that it can be explained only by the Holy Spirit; and that in our day, as well as in former times. He is the Teacher of His people. The office of the Holy Spirit I had not experientially understood before that time.

"It was my beginning to understand this latter point in particular, which had a great effect on me, for the Lord enabled me to put it to the test of experience by laying aside commentaries and almost every other book and simply reading the Word of God and studying it.

"The result of this was, that the first evening that I shut myself into my room, to give myself to prayer and meditation over the scriptures, I learned more in a few hours than I had done during a period of several months previously.

"*But the particular difference was that I received real strength for my soul in so doing.* I now began to try by the test of the scriptures the things that I had learned and seen, and found that only those principles that stood the test were of real value."

Of obedience to the Word of God, in connection with his being baptized, he writes as follows:

"It had pleased God, in His abundant mercy, to bring my mind into such a state, that I was willing to carry out into my life whatever I should find in the scriptures. I could say, 'I will do His will,' and it was on that account, I believe, that I saw which '*doctrine is of God.*'—And I would observe here, by the way, that the passage to which I have just alluded (John 7:17) has been a most remarkable comment to me on many doctrines and precepts of our most holy faith. For instance: 'But I tell you not to resist an evil person. But whoever slaps you on your right cheek, turn the other to him also. If anyone wants to sue you and take away your tunic, let him have your cloak also. And whoever compels you to go one mile, go with him two. Give to him who asks you, and from him who wants to borrow from you do not turn away. You have heard that it was said, "You shall love your neighbor and hate your enemy." But I say to you, love your enemies, bless those who curse you, do good to those who hate you, and pray for those who spitefully use you and persecute you' (Matt. 5:39–44). 'Sell what you have and give alms' (Luke 12:33). 'Owe no one anything except to love one another' (Rom. 13:8).

"It may be said, 'Certainly these passages cannot be taken literally, for how would the people of God be able to pass through the world?' The state of mind commanded in John 7:17 will cause such objections to vanish: *Whoever is willing to act out* these commandments of the Lord *literally*, will, I believe, be led with me to see that to take them *literally* is the will of God. Those who do take them *that way* will no doubt often be brought into difficulties, which are hard for the flesh to bear. But these will have a tendency to make them constantly feel that they are strangers and pilgrims here, that this world is not their home, and thus to throw them more on God, who will assuredly help us through any difficulty into which we may be brought by seeking to act in obedience to His Word."

This implicit surrender to God's Word led him to certain views and conduct in regard to money, which mightily influenced his future life. They had their root in the conviction that money was a divine stewardship, and that all money had therefore to be received and dispensed in direct fellowship with God Himself. This led him to the adoption of the following four great rules:

1. *Not to receive any fixed salary*, both because in the collecting of it there was often much that was at odds with the freewill offering with which God's service is to be maintained, and in the receiving of it a danger of placing more dependence on human sources of income than in the living God Himself.

2. *Never to ask any human being for help*, however great the need might be, but to make his wants known to the God who has promised to care for His servants and to hear their prayer.

3. To take this command literally, "*Sell what you have and give alms*," and never to save money but to spend all God entrusted to him on God's poor and on the work of His kingdom.

4. Also to take "*Owe no one anything*" (Rom. 13:8) literally, and never to buy on credit or be in debt for anything, but to trust God to provide.

This mode of living was not easy at first. But Müller testifies it was most blessed in bringing the soul to rest in God and drawing it into closer union with Himself when tempted to backslide. "*For it will not do, it is not possible, to live in sin, and at the same time, by communion with God, to draw down from heaven everything one needs for the life that now is.*"

Not long after his settlement at Bristol, THE SCRIPTURAL KNOWLEDGE INSTITUTION FOR HOME AND ABROAD was established for aiding in Day, Sunday School, Mission, and Bible work. Of this Institution, the Orphan Home work, by which Mr. Müller is best known, became a branch. It was in 1834 that his heart was touched by the case of an orphan brought to Christ in one of the schools, but who had to go to a poorhouse where its spiritual needs would not be cared for. Meeting shortly after with a life of Franke, he writes (Nov, 20, 1835): "Today I have had it very much laid on my heart no longer merely to *think* about the establishment of an Orphan Home, but actually to set about it, and I have been very much in prayer respecting it, in order to ascertain the Lord's mind. May God make it plain." And again, Nov. 25: "I have been again much in prayer yesterday and today about the Orphan Home, and am more and more convinced that it is of God. May He in mercy guide me. The three chief reasons are: 1. That God may be glorified, should He be pleased to furnish me with the means, in its being seen that it is not a futile thing to trust Him; and that thus the faith of His children may be strengthened. 2. The spiritual welfare of fatherless and motherless children. 3. Their temporal welfare."

After some months of prayer and waiting on God, a house was rented, with room for thirty children, and in course of time three more, containing in all 120 children. The work was carried on in this way for ten years, the supplies for the needs of the orphans being asked and received from God alone. It was often a time of sore need and much prayer, but a trial of faith more precious than of gold was found to praise and honor and glory of God. The Lord was preparing His servant for greater things. By His providence and His Holy Spirit, Mr. Müller was led to desire, and to wait on God until he received from Him, the sure promise of 15,000 pounds for a home to contain 300 children. This first home was opened in 1849. In 1858, a second and third home, for 950 more orphans, was opened, costing 35,000 pounds. And in 1869 and 1870, a fourth and a fifth home, for 850 more, at an expense of 50,000 pounds, making the total number of the orphans 2,100.

In addition to this work, God has given him almost as much as for the building of the Orphan Homes, and the maintenance of the orphans, for other work, the support of schools and missions, Bible and tract circulation. In all he has received from God, to be spent in His work, during these fifty years, more than one million pounds sterling. How little he knew, let us carefully notice, that when he gave up his little salary of 35 pounds a year in obedience to the leading of God's word and the Holy Spirit, what God was preparing to give him as the reward of obedience and faith; and how wonderfully the word was to be fulfilled to him: "You have been faithful over a few things, I will make you ruler over many things" (Matt. 25:23).

And these things have happened for an example to us. God calls us to be followers of George Müller, even as he is of Christ. His God is our God, and the same promises are for us. The same service of love and faith in which he labored is calling for us on every side. Let us in connection with our lessons in the school of prayer study the way in which God gave George Müller such power as a man of prayer. We shall find in it the most remarkable illustration of some of the lessons which we have been studying with the blessed Master in the Word. We shall especially have impressed upon us His first great lesson, that if we will come to Him in the way He has pointed out, with definite requests—made known to us by the Spirit through the word as being according to the will of God—we may most confidently believe that whatever we ask will be done.

PRAYER AND THE WORD OF GOD

We have more than once seen that God's listening to our voice depends on our listening to His voice (See Lessons 22 and 23). We must not only have a special promise to plead when we make a special request, but our whole life must be under the supremacy of the word; the word must be dwelling in us. The testimony of George Müller on this point is most instructive. He tells us how the discovery of the true place of the Word of God, and the teaching of the Spirit with it, was the commencement of a new era in his spiritual life. Of it he writes:

"Now the scriptural way of reasoning would have been: God Himself has reached down to become an author, and I am ignorant about that precious book that His Holy Spirit has caused to be written through the instrumentality of His servants, and it contains that which I ought to know, and the knowledge of which will lead me to true happiness. Therefore, I ought to read again and again this most precious book, this Book of books, most earnestly and most prayerfully and with much meditation. And in this practice, I should continue all the days of my life. For I was aware, though I read it but little, that I knew scarcely anything of it. But instead of acting this way and being led by my ignorance of the Word of God to study it more, my difficulty in understanding it and the little enjoyment I had in it made me careless in reading it (for much prayerful reading of the Word gives not merely more knowledge, but increases the delight we have in reading it). Therefore, like many believers, I practically preferred, for the first four years of my divine life, the works of uninspired men to the oracles of the living God. The victory was that I remained a baby, both in knowledge and grace. In knowledge, I say, for all *true* knowledge must be derived, by the Spirit, from the Word. And as I neglected the Word, I was for nearly four years so ignorant that I did not *clearly* know even the *fundamental* points of our holy faith. And, most sadly, this lack of knowledge kept me back from walking steadily in the ways of God. For when it pleased the Lord in August 1829 to bring me really to the scriptures, my life and walk became very different. And though ever since that I have very much fallen short of what I might and ought to be, yet by the grace of God I have been enabled to live much nearer to Him than before.

"If any believers read this who practically prefer other books to the holy scriptures—and who enjoy the writings of men much more than the Word of God—may they be warned by my loss. I shall consider this book to have been the means of doing much good, should it please the Lord, through its usefulness, to lead some of His people to no longer to neglect the holy scriptures, but to give them that preference that they have before now bestowed on the writings of men.

"Before I leave this subject, I would only add: If the reader understands very little of the Word of God, he ought to read it very much, for the Spirit explains the Word by the Word. And if he enjoys the reading of the word little, that is just the reason why he should read it much, for the frequent reading of the scriptures creates a delight in them, so that the more we read them, the more we desire to do so.

"Above all, he should seek to have it settled in his own mind that God alone by His Spirit can teach him, and that therefore, as God will be inquired of for blessings, it becomes him to seek God's blessing previous to reading, and also while he reads it.

"He should have it, furthermore, settled in his mind that although the Holy Spirit is the *best* and *sufficient* Teacher, yet that this Teacher does not always teach immediately *when* we desire it, and that therefore we may have to ask Him again and again for the explanation of certain passages, but that He will surely teach us at last, if indeed we are seeking for light prayerfully, patiently, and with a view to the glory of God."[38]

We find in his journal frequent mention made of his spending two and three hours in prayer over the Word for the feeding of his spiritual life. As the fruit of this, when he had need of strength and encouragement in prayer, the individual promises were not to him so many arguments from a book to be used with God, but living words that he had heard the Father's living voice speak to him, and that he could now bring to the Father in living faith.

PRAYER AND THE WILL OF GOD

One of the greatest difficulties with young believers is to know how they can find out whether what they desire is according to God's will. I count it one of the most precious lessons God wants to teach through the experience of George Müller, that He is willing to make known, of things of which His word says nothing directly, that they are His will for us, and that we may ask them. The teaching of the Spirit—not without or against the word, but as something above and beyond it and in addition to it, without which we cannot see God's will—is the heritage of every believer. It is through the *Word and the Word alone* that the Spirit teaches, applying the general principles or promises to our special need. And it is *The Spirit and the Spirit alone* who can really make the word a light on our path, whether the path of duty in our daily walk, or the path of faith in our approach to God. Let us try to notice in what childlike simplicity and teachableness that it was that the discovery of God's will that was so surely and so clearly made known to His servant.

With regard to the building of the first home and the assurance he had of its being God's will, he writes in May 1850, just after it had been opened, speaking of the great difficulties there were, and how little likely it appeared to nature that they would be removed: "But while the prospect before me would have been overwhelming had I looked at it naturally, I was never even for once permitted to question how it would end. For as from the beginning I was sure *it was the will of God* that I should go to the work of building for Him this large orphan home, so also from the beginning I was as certain that the whole would be finished as if the home had been already filled."

The way in which he found out what was God's will comes out with special clearness in his account of the building of the second home. I ask the reader to study with care the lesson the narrative conveys:

"*Dec.* 5, 1850—Under these circumstances I can only pray that the Lord in His tender mercy would not allow Satan to gain an advantage over me. By the grace of God my heart says: Lord, if I could be sure that it is Your will that I should go forward in this matter, I would do so cheerfully. And, on the other hand, if I could be sure that these are vain, foolish, proud thoughts, that they are not

[38] The extracts are from a work in four volumes, *The Lord's Dealings with George Müller*. J. Nisbet & Co., London.

from You, I would, by Your grace, hate them and entirely put them aside.

"My hope is in God. He will help and teach me. Judging, however, from His former dealings with me, it would not be a strange thing to me, nor surprising, if He called me to labor yet still more largely in this way.

"The thoughts about enlarging the orphan work have not yet arisen on account of an abundance of money having come in lately, for I have had of late to wait for about seven weeks on God, while little—very little comparatively—came in, *i.e.* about four times as much was going out as came in; and, had not the Lord previously sent me large sums, we should have been distressed indeed.

"Lord! How can Your servant know Your will in this matter? Will You be pleased to teach him!

"*December* 11—During the last six days, since writing the above, I have been, day after day, waiting on God concerning this matter. It has generally been more or less all the day on my heart. When I have been awake at night, it has not been far from my thoughts. Yet all this without the least excitement. I am perfectly calm and quiet about it. My soul would rejoice to go forward in this service, could I be sure that the Lord would have me to do so. For then, notwithstanding the numberless difficulties, all would be well, and His name would be magnified.

"On the other hand, were I assured that the Lord would have me to be satisfied with my present sphere of service, and that I should not pray about enlarging the work, by His grace I could, *without an effort*, cheerfully yield to it. For He has brought me into such a state of heart that I only desire to please Him in this matter. Moreover, before now I have not spoken about this thing even to my beloved wife, the sharer of my joys, sorrows, and labors for more than twenty years, nor is it likely that I shall do so for some time to come—for I prefer quietly to wait on the Lord without conversing on this subject, in order that in this way I may be kept more easily, by His blessing, from being influenced by things from outside. The burden of my prayer concerning this matter is that the Lord would not allow me to make a mistake, and that He would teach me to do His will.

"*December* 26. Fifteen days have elapsed since I wrote the preceding paragraph. Every day since then I have continued to pray about this matter, and that with a good measure of earnestness, by the help of God. There has passed hardly an hour during these days in which, while awake, this matter has not been more or less before me. But all without even a shadow of excitement. I converse with no one about it. Until now, I have not even done so with my dear wife. For this I refrain still, and deal with God alone about the matter, in order that no outward influence and no outward excitement may keep me from attaining to *a clear discovery of His will. I have the fullest and most peaceful assurance that He will clearly show me His will.*

"This evening I have had again an especially solemn season for prayer to seek to know the will of God. But while I continue to plead with and ask the Lord that He would not allow me to be deluded in this business, I may say I have scarcely any doubt remaining on my mind as to what will be the issue, even that I should go forward in this matter. As this, however, is one of the most momentous steps that I have ever taken, I believe I cannot go about this matter with too much caution, prayerfulness, and deliberation. I am in no hurry about it. I could wait for years, by God's grace, were this His will, before even taking one single step toward this thing or even speaking to anyone about it. On the other hand, I would get to work tomorrow, were the Lord to command me do so.

"This calmness of mind, this having no will of my own in the matter, this only wishing to please my heavenly Father in it, this only seeking His and not my honor in it, this state of heart, I say, is the fullest assurance to me that my heart is not under a fleshly excitement, and that, if I am helped to go on this way, *I shall know the will of God to the full*. But, while I write this, I can't help but add at the same time that I crave the honor and the glorious privilege to be more and more used by the Lord.

"I desire to be allowed to provide scriptural instruction for a thousand orphans, instead of doing so for 300. I desire to teach the holy scriptures regularly to a thousand orphans, instead of doing so to 300. I desire that it may be yet more abundantly demonstrated that God is still the Hearer and Answerer of prayer, and that He is the living God now as He ever was and ever will be, when He shall simply, in answer to prayer, have reached down and provided me with a house for 700 orphans and with means to support them. This last consideration is the most important point in my mind. The Lord's honor is the principal point with me in this whole matter. And just because this is the case, if He would be more glorified by not going forward in this business, I should by His grace be perfectly content to give up all thoughts about another Orphan House. Surely in such a state of mind, obtained by the Holy Spirit, You, my heavenly Father, *will not allow Your child to be mistaken, much less deluded.* By the help of God, I shall continue further day by day to wait on Him in prayer concerning this thing—until He shall move me to act.

"*Jan. 2, 1851*—A week ago I wrote the preceding paragraph. During this week I have still been helped day by day, and more than once every day, to seek the guidance of the Lord about another Orphan House. The burden of my prayer has still been that He in His great mercy would keep me from making a mistake. During the last week the Book of Proverbs has come in the course of my scripture reading, and my heart has been refreshed in reference to this subject by the following passages: "Trust in the Lord with all your heart, and lean not on your own understanding; in all your ways acknowledge Him, and He shall direct your paths" (Prov. 3:5–6). By the grace of God I do acknowledge the Lord in all my ways, and in this thing in particular. I have, therefore, the comfortable assurance that He will direct my paths concerning this part of my service, as to whether I shall be occupied in it or not. Further: "The integrity of the upright will guide them" (Prov. 11:3). By the grace of God I am upright in this business. My honest purpose is to get glory to God. Therefore I expect to be guided in the right direction. Further: "Commit your works to the Lord, and your thoughts will be established" (Prov. 16:3). I do commit my works to the Lord, and therefore expect that my thoughts will be established. My heart is more and more coming to a calm, quiet, and set-tled assurance that the Lord will reach down to use me still further in the orphan work. Here, Lord, is Your servant."

When later he decided to build two additional houses, Nos. 4 and 5, he writes again:

"Twelve days have passed away since I wrote the last paragraph. I have still day by day been enabled to wait on the Lord with reference to enlarging the or-phan work and have been during the whole of this period also in perfect peace, which is the result of seeking in this thing only the Lord's honor and the temporal and spiritual benefit of my fellowmen. Without an effort I could by His grace put aside all thoughts about this whole affair, if only assured that it is the will of God that I should do so. But, on the other hand, I immediately could go forward, if He desired to have it be so.

"I have still kept this matter entirely to myself. Though it is now about seven weeks since, day by day, more or less, my mind has been pondering it, and since I have been daily praying about it, not one human being knows of it. As yet I have not even mentioned it to my dear wife, in order that, by quietly waiting on God, I might not be influenced by what might be said to me on the subject.

"This evening has been particularly set apart for prayer, asking the Lord once more not to allow me to be mistaken in this thing, and much less to be deluded by the devil. I have also sought to let all the reasons *against* building another Orphan House, and all the reasons *for* doing so pass before my mind. And now for the clearness and definiteness, I write them down. . . .

"As much, however, as the nine previous reasons weigh with me, yet they would not influence me were there not one more. It is this. After having for months pondered the matter, and having looked at it in all its bearings and with all its difficulties, and then having been finally led, after much prayer, to decide on this enlargement, my mind is at peace. The child who has again and again asked His heavenly Father not to allow him to be deluded, nor even to make a mistake, is at peace, perfectly at peace concerning this decision, and has the assurance that the decision come to, after much prayer during weeks and months, is the leading of the Holy Spirit. And it therefore purposes to go forward, assuredly believing that he will not be frustrated, for he trusts in God. Many and great may be his dif-ficulties, and thousands and ten thousands of prayers may have ascended to God before the full answer may be obtained. Much exercise of faith and patience may be required, but in the end it will again be seen, so that His servant, who trusts in Him, has not been frustrated."

Prayer and the Glory of God

We have sought more than once to enforce the truth that while we ordinarily seek the reasons for our prayers not being heard in the thing we ask not being according to the will of God, scripture warns us to find the cause in ourselves: in our not being in the right state or not asking in the right spirit. The thing may be in full accordance with His will, but the asking, the spirit of the supplicant, isn't. Then we are not heard. As the great root of all sin is self and self-seeking, so there is nothing that even in our more spiritual desires so effectively hinders God in answering as this: We pray for our own pleasure or glory. Prayer to have power and prevail must ask for the glory of God, and he can only do this as he is living for God's glory.

In George Müller we have one of the most remarkable instances on record of God's Holy Spirit leading a man deliberately and systematically, at the outset of a course of prayer, to make the glorifying of God his first and only objective. Let us ponder well what he says, and learn the lesson God wants to teach us through him:

"I had cases constantly brought before me that proved that one of the things that the children of God especially needed in our day was *to have their faith strengthened*.

"I longed, therefore, to have something to point my brethren to as a visible proof that our God and Father is the same faithful God as ever He was, the one who is as willing as ever to *Prove* Himself to be the *Living God* in our day, as before, *to all who put their trust in Him*.

"My spirit longed to be instrumental in strengthening their faith, by giving them not only instances from the Word of God of His willingness and ability to help all who rely upon Him, but to *show* them *by proofs* that He is the same in our day. I knew that the Word of God ought to be enough, and it was by grace enough for me. But still I believed I ought to lend a helping hand to my brethren.

"I therefore judged myself bound to be the servant of the Church of Christ, in the particular point in which I had obtained mercy—namely, in being able to take God at His word and rely on it. The first object of the work was, and is still: *that God might be magnified* by the fact that the orphans under my care are provided with all they need, *only by prayer and faith*, without anyone being asked. In this, it may be seen that God is *faithful still, and hears prayer still*.

"I have again these last several days prayed much about the Orphan House, and have frequently examined my heart—that if it were at all my desire to establish it for the sake of gratifying myself I might find it out. For as I desire only the Lord's glory, and I shall be glad to be instructed through the use of my brother if the matter is not of Him.

"When I began the orphan work in 1835, my chief objective was the glory of God, by giving a practical demonstration as to what could be accomplished simply through the instrumentality of prayer and faith, in order to benefit the Church at large and to lead a careless world to see the reality of the things of God by showing them in this work that the living God is still, as 4,000 years ago, the living God. My aim has been abundantly honored. Multitudes of sinners have been converted, and multitudes of the children of God in all parts of the world have been benefited by this work, just as I had anticipated. But the larger the work has grown, the greater has been the blessing—and bestowed in the very way in which I looked for blessing—for the attention of hundreds of thousands has been drawn to the work, and many tens of thousands have come to see it.

"All this leads me to desire further and further to labor on in this way, in order to bring yet greater glory to the name of the Lord. *That He may be looked at, magnified, admired, trusted in,* relied on at all times, is my aim in this service; and so particularly in this intended enlargement. That it may be seen how one very poor man, simply by trusting in God, can bring about by prayer, and that through this other children of God may be led to carry on the work of God in dependence upon Him, and that children of God may be led increasingly to trust in Him in their individual positions and circumstances—therefore I am led to this further enlargement."

Prayer and Trust in God

There are other points on which I would be glad to point out what is to be found in Mr. Müller's narrative, but one more must suffice. It is the lesson of firm and un-wavering trust in God's promise as the secret of persevering prayer. If once we have, in submission to the teaching of the Spirit in the word, taken hold of God's promise and believed that the Father has heard us, we must not allow ourselves by any delay or unfavorable appearances to be shaken in our faith:

"The full answer to my daily prayers was far from being realized, yet there was abundant encouragement granted by the Lord to continue in prayer. But suppose that far less had come in than was received, still after having come to the conclusion, on scriptural grounds and after much prayer and self-examination, I ought to have gone on without wavering in the exercise of faith and patience concerning this object. And therefore all the children of God, who were once satisfied that anything that they bring before God in prayer, is according to His will, ought to continue in believing and expecting and persevering prayer until the blessing is granted.

"Therefore I am myself now waiting on God for certain blessings for which I have daily sought Him for ten years and six months without one day's rest. Still the full answer is not yet given concerning the conversion of certain individuals, though in the meantime I have received many thousands of answers to prayer. I have also prayed daily without rest for the conversion of other individuals about ten years—for others six or seven years, for others from three or two years—and still the answer is not yet granted concerning those persons, while in the mean-time many thousands of my prayers have been answered, and also souls converted for whom I had been praying.

"I lay particular stress on this for the benefit of those who may suppose that I need only to ask of God and receive immediately, or that I might pray concerning anything, and the answer would surely come. One can only expect to obtain answers to prayers that are according to the mind of God. Even then, patience and faith may be exercised for many years, even as mine are exercised, in the matter to which I have referred. And yet I am daily continuing in prayer and expecting the answer—so surely expecting the answer—that I have often thanked God that He will surely give it, though now for nineteen years, faith and patience have been exercised this way. Be encouraged, dear Christians, with fresh earnestness to give yourselves to prayer, if you can only be sure that you ask things which are for the glory of God.

"But the most remarkable point is this, that £6, 6s. 6d. from Scotland supplied me, as far as can be known now, with all the means necessary for fitting up and promoting the new Orphan Houses. Six years and eight months I have been daily, usually several times daily, asking the Lord to give me the needed means for this enlargement of the orphan work, which, according to calculations made in the spring of 1861, appeared to be about fifty thousand pounds—the total of this amount I had now received. I praise and glorify the Lord for putting this enlargement of the work into my heart and for giving me courage and faith for it—and above all, for sustaining my faith daily without wavering.

"When the last portion of the money was received, I was no more assured concerning the whole than I was at the time I had not received one single donation towards this large sum. I was at the beginning, after at one time having learned His mind—through most patient and heart-searching waiting upon God—was fully assured that He would bring it about, as if the two houses, with their hundreds of orphans occupying them, had been already before me.

"I make a few remarks here for the sake of young believers in connection with this subject: 1. Be slow to take new steps in the Lord's service, or in your business, or in your families: weigh everything well; weigh all in the light of the holy scriptures and in the fear of God. 2. Seek to have no will of your own, in order to ascertain the mind of God, regarding any steps you propose taking, so that you can honestly say you are willing to do the will of God, if He will only please to instruct you. 3. But when you have found out what the will of God is, seek for His help, and seek it earnestly, perseveringly, patiently, believingly, and expectantly, and you will surely in His own time and way obtain it.

"To suppose that we have difficulty with money only would be a mistake. There occur hundreds of other wants and of other difficulties. It is a rare thing that a day passes without some difficulty or some need, but often there are many difficulties and many needs to be met and overcome the same day. All these are met by prayer and faith, our universal remedy. And we have never been confounded. Patient, persevering, believing prayer, offered up to God, in the Name of the Lord Jesus, has always, sooner or later, brought the blessing. I do not doubt, by God's grace, that I will obtain any blessing, provided I can be sure it would be for any real good, and for the glory of God."

THE MINISTRY OF INTERCESSION

Contents

INTRODUCTION

I have been asked by a friend who heard of this book being published what the difference would be between it and the previous one on the same subject, *With Christ in the School of Prayer*. An answer to that question may be the best introduction I can give to the present volume.

Any acceptance the former work has had must be attributed, as far as the contents go, to the prominence given to two great truths. The one was the certainty that prayer will be answered. There is with some an idea that to ask and expect an answer is not the highest form of prayer. Fellowship with God, apart from any request, is more than supplication. About the petition, there is something of selfishness and bargaining—to worship is more than to beg. With others, the thought that prayer is so often unanswered is so prominent that they think more of the spiritual benefit derived from the exercise of prayer than the actual gifts to be obtained by it.

While admitting the measure of truth in these views, when kept in their true place, *The School of Prayer* points out how our Lord continually spoke of prayer as a means of obtaining what we desire, and how He seeks in every possible way to waken in us the confident expectation of an answer. I was led to show how prayer, in which a man could enter into the mind of God, could assert the royal power of a renewed will and bring down to earth what without prayer would not have been given, in the highest proof of his having been made in the likeness of God's Son. He is found worthy of entering into fellowship with Him, not only in adoration and worship, but in having his will actually taken up into the rule of the world and becoming the intelligent channel through which God can fulfill His eternal purpose. The book sought to reiterate and enforce the precious truths Christ preaches so continually: The blessing of prayer is that you can ask and receive what you desire, and the highest exercise and the glory of prayer is that persevering importunity can prevail and obtain what God at first could not and would not give.

With this truth, there was a second one that came out very strongly as we studied the Master's words. In answer to the question, *But why, if the answer to prayer is so positively promised, why are there such numberless unanswered prayers?* We found that Christ taught us that the answer depended on certain conditions. He spoke of faith, of perseverance, of praying in His Name, of praying in the will of God. But all these conditions were summed up in the one central one: "*If you abide in Me. . .you will ask what you desire, and it shall be done for you*" (John 15:7). It became clear that the power to pray the effectual prayer of faith depended *on the life*. It is only to a man given up to live as entirely in Christ and for Christ as the branch in the vine and for the vine that these promises can come true. "*In that day*," Christ said, the day of Pentecost, "you will ask in My name" (John 16:26). It is only in a life full of the Holy Spirit that the true power to ask in Christ's name can be known.

This led to the emphasizing of the truth that the ordinary Christian life cannot appropriate these promises. It needs a spiritual life, altogether sound and vigorous, to pray in power. The teaching naturally led to press the need of a life of entire consecration. More than one has told me how it was in the reading of the book that he first saw what the better life was that could be lived, and must be lived, if Christ's wonderful promises are to come true to us.

In regard to these two truths, there is no change in the present volume. One only wishes that one could put them with such clearness and force as to help every beloved fellow Christian to some right impression of the reality and the glory of our privilege as God's children: "Ask what you desire, and it shall be done for you." The present volume owes its existence to the desire to enforce two truths, of which formerly I had no such impression as now.

The one is—that Christ actually meant prayer to be the great power by which His Church should do its work, and that the neglect of prayer is the great reason the Church does not have greater power over the masses in Christian and in heathen countries. In the first chapter, I have stated how my convictions in regard to this have been strengthened, and what gave occasion to the writing of the book. It is meant to be, on behalf of myself and my brethren in the ministry and all God's people, a confession of shortcoming and of sin, and, at the same time, a call to believe that things can be different, and that Christ waits to fit us by His Spirit to pray as He would have us.

This call, of course, brings me back to what I spoke of in connection with the former volume: that there is a life in the Spirit, a life of abiding in Christ, within our reach, in which the power of prayer—both the power to pray and the power to obtain the answer—can be realized in a measure that we could not have thought possible before. Any failure in the prayer-life, any desire or hope really to take the place Christ has prepared for us, brings us to the very root of the doctrine of grace as manifested in the Christian life.

It is only by a full surrender to the life of abiding, by the yielding to the fullness of the Spirit's leading and quickening, that the prayer-life can be restored to a truly healthy state. I feel deeply how little I have been able to put this in the volume as I could wish. I have prayed and am trusting that God, who chooses the weak things, will use it for His own glory.

The second truth that I have sought to enforce is that we have far too little concept of the place that intercession, as distinguished from prayer for ourselves, ought to have in the Church and the Christian life. In intercession, our King upon the throne finds His highest glory, and in it we shall find our highest glory, too. Through it, He continues His saving work, and can do nothing without it. Through it alone, we can do our work, and nothing benefits without it. In it, He always receives from the Father the Holy Spirit and all spiritual blessings to impart, and in it, we too are called to receive in ourselves the fullness of God's Spirit, with the power to impart spiritual blessing to others.

The power of the Church truly to bless rests on intercession—asking and receiving heavenly gifts to carry to men. Because this is so, it is no wonder that where, due to lack of teaching or spiritual insight, we put trust in our own diligence and effort, to the influence of the world and the flesh, and work more than we pray, the presence and power of God are not seen in our work as we would wish.

Such thoughts have led me to wonder what could be done to rouse believers to a sense of their high calling in this and to help and train them to take part in it. And so this book differs from the former one in the attempt to open a practicing school, and to invite all who have never taken systematic part in the great work of intercession to begin and give themselves to it. There are tens of thousands of workers who have known and are proving wonderfully what prayer can do. But there are tens of thousands who work with but little prayer, and as many more who do not work because they do not know how or where, who might all be won to swell the host of intercessors who are to bring down the blessings of heaven to earth. For their sakes, and the sake of all who feel the need of help, I have prepared helps and hints for a school of intercession for a month (see the Appendix). I have asked those who would join to begin by giving at least ten minutes a day definitely to this work. It is in doing that we learn to do. It is as we take hold and begin that the help of God's Spirit will come. It is as we daily hear God's call, and at once put it into practice, that the consciousness will begin to live in us—*I, too, am an intercessor*—and that we shall feel the need of living in Christ and being full of the Spirit if we are to do this work correctly.

Nothing will so test and stimulate the Christian life as the honest attempt to be an intercessor. It is difficult to conceive how much we ourselves and the Church will be the gainers if with our whole heart we accept the post of honor God is offering us. With regard to the school of intercession, I am confident that the result of the first month's course will be to wake the feeling of how little we know how to intercede. And a second and a third month may only deepen the sense of ignorance and unfitness. This will be an unspeakable blessing. The confession, "We do not know how to pray as we ought," is the introduction to the experience, "The Spirit Himself makes intercession for us" (Rom. 8:26)—our sense of ignorance will lead us to depend on the Spirit praying in us, to feel the need of living in the Spirit.

We have heard a great deal of systematic Bible study, and we praise God for thousands upon thousands of Bible classes and Bible readings. Let all the leaders of such classes see whether they could not open prayer classes—helping their students to pray in secret, and training them to be, above everything, men of prayer. Let ministers ask what they can do in this. The faith in God's word can nowhere be so exercised and perfected as in the intercession that asks and expects and looks out for the answer. Throughout scripture, in the life of every saint, of God's own Son, throughout the history of God's Church, God is, first of all, a prayer-hearing God. Let us try to help God's children to know their God and encourage all God's servants to labor with the assurance: the chief and most blessed part of my work is to ask and receive from my Father what I can bring to others.

It will now easily be understood how what this book contains will be nothing but the confirmation and the call to put into practice the two great lessons of the former one.

"Ask what you desire, and it shall be done for you"; "Whatever things you ask. . .believe that you receive" (Mark 11:24): These great prayer promises, as part of the Church's provision of power for her work, are to be taken as literally and actually true. "If you abide in Me, and My words abide in you"; "In that day you will ask in My Name": These great prayer conditions are universal and unchangeable. A life abiding in Christ and filled with the Spirit, a life entirely given up as a branch for the work of the vine, has the power to claim these promises and to pray the effectual prayer that accomplishes much. Lord, teach us to pray.

ANDREW MURRAY
Wellington, September 1, 1897

THE LACK OF PRAYER

You do not have because you do not ask.
JAMES 4:2

He saw that there was no man,
and wondered that there was no intercessor.
ISAIAH 59:16

There is no one who calls on Your name,
who stirs himself up to take hold of You.
ISAIAH 64:7

AT our last Wellington Convention for the Deepening of the Spiritual Life, in April, the morning meetings were devoted to prayer and intercession. Great blessing was found, both in listening to what the Word teaches of their need and power, and in joining in continued united supplication. Many felt that we know too little of persevering importunate prayer, and that it is indeed one of the greatest needs of the Church.

During the past two months, I have been attending a number of conventions. At the first, a Dutch Missionary Conference at Langlaagte, prayer had been chosen as the subject of the addresses. At the next, at Johannesburg, a brother in business gave expression to his deep conviction that the great lack of the Church of our day was more of the spirit and practice of intercession. A week later, we had a Dutch Ministerial Conference in the Free State, where three days were spent—after two days' services in the congregation on the work of the Holy Spirit—in considering the relation of the Spirit to prayer. At the ministerial meetings held at most of the succeeding conventions, we were led to take up the subject, and everywhere there was the confession: We pray too little! And with this there appeared to be a fear that, with the pressure of duty and the force of habit, it was almost impossible to hope for any great change.

I cannot say what a deep impression was made on me by these conversations. Most of all, by the thought that there should be anything like hopelessness on the part of God's servants as to the prospect of an entire change being effected, and real deliverance found from a failure that cannot but hinder our own joy in God and our power in His service. And I prayed to God to give me words that might not only help to direct attention to the evil, but, specially, that might stir up faith and waken the assurance that God by His Spirit will enable us to pray as we should.

Let me begin, for the sake of those who have never had their attention directed to the matter, by stating some of the facts that prove how universal is the sense of shortcoming in this respect.

Last year there appeared a report of an address to ministers by Dr. Whyte, of Free St. George's Edinburgh. In that, he said that as a young minister, he had thought that, of the time he had over from pastoral visitation, he ought to spend as much as possible with his books in his study. He wanted to feed his people with the very best he could prepare for them. But he had now learned that prayer was of more importance than study. He reminded his brethren of the election of deacons to take charge of the collections, that the twelve might give themselves "to prayer and the ministry of the word" (Acts 6:4), and said that at times, when the deacons brought him his salary, he had to ask himself whether he had been as faithful in his engagement as the deacons had been to theirs. He felt as if it were almost too late to regain what he had lost, and he urged his brethren to pray more. What a solemn confession and warning from one of the high places: We pray too little!

During the Regent Square Convention two years ago, the subject came up in conversation with a well-known London minister. He urged that if so much time must be given to prayer, it would involve the neglect of the imperative calls of duty. "There is the morning post, before breakfast, with ten or twelve letters that *must* be answered. Then there are committee meetings waiting, with numberless other engagements, more than enough to fill up the day. It is difficult to see how it can be done."

My answer was, in substance, that it was simply a question of whether the call of God for our time and attention was of more importance than that of man. If God was waiting to meet us and to give us blessing and power from heaven for His work, it was a shortsighted policy to put other work in the place that God and waiting on Him should have.

At one of our ministerial meetings, the superintendent of a large district put the case this way: "I rise in the morning and have half an hour with God, in the Word and prayer, in my room before breakfast. I go out, and am occupied all day with a multiplicity of engagements. I do not think many minutes elapse without my breathing a prayer for guidance or help. After my day's work, I return in my evening devotions and speak to God of the day's work. But of the intense, definite, persistent prayer of which scripture speaks one knows little." What, he asked, must I think of such a life?

We all know the difference between a man whose profits are just enough to maintain his family and keep up his business, and another whose income enables him to extend the business and to help others. There may be an earnest Christian life in which there is prayer enough to keep us from going back and just maintain the position we have attained to, without much of growth in spirituality or Christlikeness. The attitude is more defensive, seeking to ward off temptation, than aggressive, reaching out after higher attainment.

If there is indeed to be a going from strength to strength, with some large experience of God's power to sanctify ourselves and to bring down real blessing on others, there must be more definite and persevering prayer. The Scripture teaching about crying day and night, continuing steadfastly in prayer, watching unto prayer, being heard for his importunity, must in some degree become our experience if we are really to be intercessors.

At the very next convention the same question was put in somewhat different form. "I am at the head of a station, with a large outlying district to care for. I see the importance of much prayer, and yet my life hardly leaves room for it. Are we to submit? Or tell us how we can attain to what we desire?" I admitted that the difficulty was universal. I recalled the words of one of our most honored South African missionaries, now gone to his rest. He had the same complaint: "In the morning at five the sick people are at the door waiting for medicine. At six the printers come, and I have to set them to work and teach them. At nine the school calls me, and until late at night I am kept busy with a large correspondence." In my answer, I quoted a Dutch proverb: "What is heaviest must weigh heaviest," or must have the first place.

> *If there is indeed to be a going from strength to strength, with some large experience of God's power to sanctify ourselves and to bring down real blessing on others, there must be more definite and persevering prayer.*

The law of God is unchangeable: As on earth, so in our traffic with heaven, we only get as we give. Unless we are willing to pay the price and sacrifice time and attention and what appear legitimate or necessary duties, for the sake of the heavenly gifts, we need not look for a large experience of the power of the heavenly world in our work. The whole company present joined in the sad confession. It had been thought over, and mourned over, times without number, and yet, somehow, there they were, all these pressing claims, and all the ineffectual resolves to pray more, barring the way. I need not now say to what further thoughts our conversation led. The substance of them will be found in some of the later chapters in this volume.

Let me call just one more witness. In the course of my journey, I met with one of the Cowley Fathers, who had just been holding retreats for clergy of the English church. I was interested to hear from him the line of teaching he follows.

In the course of conversation he used the expression "the distraction of business," and it came out that he found it one of the great difficulties he had to deal with in himself and others. Of himself, he said that by the vows of his Order he was bound to give himself specially to prayer. But he found it exceedingly difficult. Every day he had to be at four different points of the town he lived in. His predecessor had left him the charge of a number of committees where he was expected to do all the work. It was as if everything conspired to keep him from prayer.

All this testimony surely suffices to make clear that prayer has not the place it ought to have in our ministerial and Christian life, that the shortcoming is one of which all are willing to make confession, and that the difficulties in the way of deliverance are such as to make a return to a time and full prayer-life almost impossible. Blessed be God—"The things which are impossible with men are possible with God!" (Luke 18:27). "God is able to make all grace abound toward you, that you, always having all sufficiency in all things, may have an abundance for every good work" (2 Cor. 9:8).

> *Christ lives in us in such reality that His life of prayer on earth, and of intercession in heaven, is breathed into us in just such measure as our surrender and our faith allow and accept it.*

Do let us believe that God's call to much prayer need not be a burden and cause of continual self-condemnation. He means it to be a joy. He can make it an inspiration, giving us strength for all our work and bringing down His power to work through us in our fellowmen. Let us not fear to admit to the full the sin that shames us, and then to face it in the name of our Mighty Redeemer. *The light that shows us our sin and condemns us for it will show us the way out of it, into the life of liberty that is well-pleasing to God.* If we allow this one matter, unfaithfulness in prayer, to convict us of the lack in our Christian life that lies at the root of it, God will use the discovery to bring us not only the power to pray that we long for, but the joy of a new and healthy life, of which prayer is the spontaneous expression.

And what is now the way by which our sense of the lack of prayer can be made the means of blessing, the entrance on a path in which the evil may be conquered? How can our communication with the Father in continual prayer and intercession become what it ought to be, if we and the world around us are to be blessed? As it appears to me, we must begin by going back to God's Word to study what the place is God means prayer to have in the life of His child and His Church. A fresh sight of what prayer is according to the will of God, of what our prayers can be, through the grace of God, will free us from those feeble defective views, in regard to the absolute necessity of continual prayer, which lie at the root of our failure.

As we get an insight into the reasonableness and rightness of this divine appointment and come under the full conviction of how wonderfully it fits in with God's love and our own happiness, we shall be freed from the false impression of its being an arbitrary demand. We shall with our whole heart and soul consent to it and rejoice in it as the one only possible way for the blessing of heaven to come to earth. All thought of task and burden, of self-effort and strain, will pass away in the blessed faith that as simple as breathing is in the healthy natural life, will praying be in the Christian life that is led and filled by the Spirit of God.

As we occupy ourselves with and accept this teaching of God's Word on prayer, we shall be led to see how our failure in the prayer-life was due to failure in the Spirit-life. Prayer is one of the most heavenly and spiritual of the functions of the Spirit-life. How could we try or expect to fulfill it so as to please God, except as our soul is in perfect health and our life truly possessed and moved by God's Spirit? The insight into the place God means prayer to take, and which it only can take, in a full Christian life will show us that we have not been living the true, the abundant life, and that any thought of praying more and effectually will be vain, except when we are brought into a closer relationship to our blessed Lord Jesus.

Christ is our life. Christ lives in us in such reality that His life of prayer on earth, and of intercession in heaven, is breathed into us in just such measure as our surrender and our faith allow and accept it. Jesus Christ is the Healer of all diseases, the Conqueror of all enemies, the Deliverer from all sin, and if our failure teaches us to turn afresh to Him, and find in Him the grace He gives to pray as we ought, this humiliation may become our greatest blessing.

Let us all unite in praying God that He would visit our souls and fit us for that work of intercession, which is at this moment the greatest need of the Church and the world. It is only by intercession that power can be brought down from heaven that will enable the Church to conquer the world. Let us stir up the slumbering gift that is lying unused, and seek to gather and train and band together as many as we can, to be God's remembrancers, and to give Him no rest until He makes His Church a joy in the earth. Nothing but intense believing prayer can meet the intense spirit of worldliness, of which complaint is everywhere made.

FOR FURTHER THOUGHT

1. *In your own Christian life, what do you think is the cause for a lack of prayer? How can you overcome those things that keep you from praying consistently and persistently?*
2. *What is the condition for receiving a large inflowing of power from heaven in your work here on earth?*
3. *When it comes to intercession, what is the benefit of having Christ living within you—truly living within you?*

2

THE MINISTRATION OF
THE SPIRIT AND PRAYER

"If you then, being evil, know how to give good gifts to
your children, how much more will your heavenly Father
give the Holy Spirit to those who ask Him!"
LUKE 11:13

CHRIST had just said (11:9), "Ask, and it will be given": God's giving is inseparably connected with our asking. He applies this especially to the Holy Spirit. As surely as a father on earth gives bread to his child, so God gives the Holy Spirit to those who ask Him. The whole ministration of the Spirit is ruled by the one great law: God must give, we must ask. When the Holy Spirit was poured out at Pentecost with a flow that never ceases, it was in answer to prayer. The inflow into the believer's heart, and His outflow in the rivers of living water, always still depend upon the law: "Ask, and it will be given."

In connection with our confession of the lack of prayer, we have said that what we need is some due apprehension of the place it occupies in God's plan of redemption. We shall perhaps nowhere see this more clearly than in the first half of the Acts of the Apostles. The story of the birth of the Church in the outpouring of the Holy Spirit, and of the first freshness of its heavenly life in the power of that Spirit, will teach us how prayer on earth, whether as cause or effect, *is the true measure of the presence of the Spirit of heaven.*

We begin with the well-known words (1:14), "These all continued with one accord in prayer and supplication." And then there follows: "When the Day of Pentecost had fully come, they were all with one accord in one place.... And they were all filled with the Holy Spirit...and that day about three thousand souls were added to them" (2:1, 4, 41). The great work of redemption had been accomplished. The Holy Spirit had been promised by Christ "not many days from now" (1:5). He had sat down on His throne and received the Spirit from the Father. But all this was not enough. One thing more was needed: the ten days' united continued supplication of the disciples. It was intense, continued prayer that prepared the disciples' hearts, that opened the windows of heaven, that brought down the promised gift. As little as the power of the Spirit could be given without Christ sitting on the throne, *could it descend without the disciples on the footstool of the throne.* For all the ages the law is laid down here, at the birth of the Church, that whatever else may be found on earth, the power of the Spirit must be prayed down from heaven. The measure of believing, continued prayer will be the measure of the Spirit's working in the Church. Direct, definite, determined prayer is what we need.

See how this is confirmed in Acts 4. Peter and John had been brought before the Council and threatened with punishment. When they returned to their brethren, and reported what had been said to them, "they raised their voice to God with one accord" (4:24) and prayed for boldness to speak the word. "And when they had prayed, the place where they were assembled together was shaken; and they were all filled with the Holy Spirit, and they spoke the word of God with boldness. Now the multitude of those who believed were of one heart and one soul. . . . And with great power the apostles gave witness to the resurrection of the Lord Jesus. And great grace was upon them all" (4:31–33). It is as if the story of Pentecost is repeated a second time over, with the prayer, the shaking of the house, the filling with the Spirit, the speaking God's Word with boldness and power, the great grace upon all, the manifestation of unity and love—to imprint it ineffaceably on the heart of the Church: It is prayer that lies at the root of the spiritual life and power of the Church. The measure of God's giving the Spirit is our asking. He gives as a father to him who asks as a child.

Go on to the sixth chapter. There we find that, when murmurings arose as to the neglect of the Grecian Jews in the distribution of alms, the apostles proposed the appointment of deacons to serve the tables. "We," they said, "will give ourselves continually to prayer and to the ministry of the word" (6:2). It is often said, and rightly said, that there is nothing in honest business, when it is kept in its place as entirely subordinate to the kingdom, that must ever be first, that need prevent fellowship with God. Least of all ought a work like ministering to the poor hinder the spiritual life. And yet the apostles felt it would hinder them in their giving themselves to the ministry of prayer and the Word.

What does this teach? That the maintenance of the spirit of prayer, such as is consistent with the claims of much work, is not enough for those who are the leaders of the Church. To keep up the communication with the King on the throne and the heavenly world clear and fresh; to draw down the power and blessing of that world, not only for the maintenance of our own spiritual life, but for those around us; continually to receive instruction and empowerment for the great work to be done—the apostles, as the ministers of the Word, felt the need of being free from other duties, that they might give themselves to much prayer.

James writes: "Pure and undefiled religion before God and the Father is this: to visit orphans and widows in their trouble" (1:27). If ever any work were a sacred one, it was that of caring for these Grecian widows. And yet, even such duties might interfere with the special calling to give themselves to prayer and the ministry of the Word. As on earth, so in the kingdom of heaven, there is power in the division of labor. And while some, like the deacons, had specially to care for serving the tables and ministering the alms of the Church here on earth, others had to be set free for that steadfast continuance in prayer that would uninterruptedly secure the downflow of the powers of the heavenly world. The minister of Christ is set apart to give himself as much to prayer as to the ministry of the word. In faithful obedience to this law is the secret of the Church's power and success. As before, so after Pentecost, the apostles were men given up to prayer.

In chapter 8 we have the intimate connection between the Pentecostal gift and prayer, from another point of view. At Samaria, Philip had preached with great blessing, and many had believed. But the Holy Spirit was, as yet, fallen on none of them. The apostles sent down Peter and John to pray for them so that they might receive the Holy Spirit. The power for such prayer was a higher gift than preaching—the work of the men who had been in closest contact with the Lord in glory, the work that was essential to the perfection of the life that preaching and baptism, faith and conversion had only begun. Surely of all the gifts of the early Church for which we should long, there is none more needed than the gift of prayer—prayer that brings down the Holy Spirit on believers. This power is given to the men who say: "We will give ourselves to prayer."

> *he measure of believing, continued prayer will be the measure of the Spirit's working in the Church. Direct, definite, determined prayer is what we need.*

In the outpouring of the Holy Spirit in the house of Cornelius at Caesarea (Acts 10), we have another testimony to the wondrous interdependence of the action of prayer and the Spirit, and another proof of what will come to a man who has given himself to prayer. Peter went up at midday to pray on the housetop. And what happened? He saw heaven opened, and there came the vision that revealed to him the cleansing of the Gentiles. With that came the message of the three men from Cornelius, a man who "prayed to God always" (Acts 10:2) and had heard from an angel, "Your prayers and alms have come up before God" (10:4). Then the voice of the Spirit was heard saying, "Go with them" (10:20). It is Peter praying, to whom the will of God is revealed, to whom guidance is given as to going to Caesarea, and who is brought into contact with a praying and prepared company of hearers. No wonder that in answer to all this prayer a blessing comes beyond all expectation, and the Holy Ghost is poured out upon the Gentiles (10:44–46).

A much-praying minister will receive an entrance into God's will he would otherwise know nothing of. He will be brought to praying people where he does not expect them and will receive blessing above all he asks or thinks. The teaching and the power of the Holy Spirit are alike unalterably linked to prayer.

Our next reference will show us faith in the power that the Church's prayer has with its glorified King, as it is found, not only in the apostles, but in the Christian community. In chapter 12, we have the story of Peter in prison on the eve of execution. The death of James had aroused the Church to a sense of real danger, and the thought of losing Peter, too, wakened up all its energies. It roused itself to prayer: "Constant prayer was offered to God for him by the church" (12:5). That prayer accomplished much, and Peter was delivered. When he came to the house of Mary, he found "many. . .gathered together praying" (12:12).

> *T*he minister of Christ is set apart to give himself as much to prayer as to the ministry of the Word. In faithful obedience to this law is the secret of the Church's power and success.

Stone walls and double chains, soldiers and keepers, and the iron gate, all gave way before the power from heaven that prayer brought down to Peter's rescue. The whole power of the Roman Empire, as represented by Herod, was powerless in the presence of the power the Church of the Holy Spirit wielded in prayer. They stood in such close and living communication with their Lord in heaven. They knew so well that the words, "all authority has been given to Me" and "Lo, I am with you always" (Matt. 28:18, 20) were absolutely true. They had such faith in His promise to hear them whatever they asked that they prayed in the assurance that the powers of heaven could work on earth and would work at their request and on their behalf. The Pentecostal church believed in prayer and practiced it.

Just one more illustration of the place and the blessing of prayer among men filled with the Holy Spirit. In chapter 13 we have the names of five men at Antioch who had given themselves specially to ministering to the Lord with prayer and fasting (13:1). Their giving themselves to prayer was not in vain. As they ministered to the Lord, the Holy Spirit met them and gave them new insight into God's plans. He called them to be fellow workers with Himself. There was a work to which He had called Barnabas and Saul. Their part and privilege would be to separate these men with renewed fasting and prayer, and to let them go, "sent out by the Holy Spirit" (13:4).

God in heaven would not send forth His chosen servants without the cooperation of His Church. Men on earth were to have a real partnership in the work of God. It was prayer that made them fit and prepared them for this, and it was to praying men the Holy Spirit gave authority to do His work and use His name. It was to prayer the Holy Spirit was given.

It is still prayer that is the only secret of true Church extension, that is guided from heaven to find and send forth God-called and God-empowered men. To prayer the Holy Spirit will show the men He has selected, to prayer that sets them apart under His guidance He will give the honor of knowing that they are men, "sent out by the Holy Spirit." It is prayer that is the link between the King on the throne and the Church at His footstool—the human link that has its divine strength in the power of the Holy Spirit, who comes in answer to it.

As one looks back upon these chapters in the history of the Pentecostal church, how clear the two great truths stand out: Where there is much prayer there will be much of the Spirit, and where there is much of the Spirit there will be ever-increasing prayer. So clear is the living connection between the two that when the Spirit is given in answer to prayer, it always wakens more prayer to prepare for the fuller revelation and communication of His Divine power and grace.

> *Heaven is still as full of stores of spiritual blessing as it was then. God still delights to give the Holy Spirit to them that ask Him.*

If prayer was in this way the power by which the primitive Church flourished and triumphed, is it not the one need of the Church of our days? Let us learn what ought to be counted axioms in our Church work:

Heaven is still as full of stores of spiritual blessing as it was then. God still delights to give the Holy Spirit to them that ask Him.

Our life and work are still as dependent on the direct impartation of divine power as they were in Pentecostal times. Prayer is still the appointed means for drawing down these heavenly blessings in power on ourselves and those around us. God still seeks for men and women who will, with all their other work of ministering, specially give themselves to persevering prayer.

And we—you, my reader, and I—may have the privilege of offering ourselves to God to labor in prayer, and bring down these blessings to this earth. Shall we not ask God to make all this truth so living in us that we may not rest until it has mastered us, and our whole heart is so filled with it that the practice of intercession shall be counted by us our highest privilege, and we find in it the sure and only measure for blessing on ourselves, on the Church, and on the world?

FOR FURTHER THOUGHT

1. *With what has God connected the Holy Spirit's working in the Church? What should you do to play a part in that working?*
2. *As recorded in Acts 13, what was the result of the five men of Antioch who gave themselves to ministering to the Lord in prayer and fasting? What do you think can happen in your life and in the lives of those around you if you give yourself to the same thing?*
3. *What is God's appointed means for bringing down heavenly blessings on yourself and on those around you?*

3

A MODEL OF INTERCESSION

And He said to them, "Which of you shall have a friend,
and go to him at midnight and say to him, 'Friend, lend me three
loaves; for a friend of mine has come to me on his journey, and I have
nothing to set before him'; and he will answer from within and say,
'Do not trouble me; the door is now shut, and my children are with
me in bed; I cannot rise and give to you'? I say to you, though he will
not rise and give to him because he is his friend, yet because of his
persistence he will rise and give him as many as he needs."
LUKE 11:5–8

"I have set watchmen on your walls, O Jerusalem; they shall
never hold their peace day or night. You who make mention
of the LORD, do not keep silent, and give Him no rest."
ISAIAH 62:6–7

WE have seen in our previous chapter what power prayer has. It is the one power on earth that commands the power of heaven. The story of the early days of the Church is God's great object lesson to teach His Church what prayer can do, how it alone, but it most surely, can draw down the treasures and powers of heaven into the life of earth.

Just remember the lessons we learned of how prayer is both indispensable and irresistible. Did we not see how unknown and untold power and blessing is stored up for us in heaven? How that power will make us a blessing to men, and make us fit to do any work or face any danger? How it is to be sought in prayer continually and persistently? How they who have the heavenly power can pray it down upon others? How in all the interaction of ministers and people, in all the ministrations of Christ's Church, it is the one secret of success? How it can defy all the power of the world, and fit men to conquer that world for Christ? It is the power of the heavenly life, the power of God's own Spirit, the power of Omnipotence, that waits for prayer to bring it down.

In all this prayer there was little thought of personal need or happiness. It was the desire to witness for Christ and bring Him and His salvation to others, it was the thought of God's kingdom and glory, that possessed these disciples. If we would be delivered from the sin of restraining prayer, we must enlarge our hearts for the work of intercession. The attempt to pray constantly for ourselves must be a failure, but it is in intercession for others that our faith and love and perseverance will be aroused, and that power of the Spirit be found that can make us fit for saving men. We are asking how we may become more faithful and successful in prayer. Let us see how the Master teaches us, in the parable of the Friend at Midnight, that intercession for the needy calls forth the highest exercise of our power of believing and prevailing prayer. Intercession is the most perfect form of prayer: It is the prayer Christ always lives to pray on His throne. Let us learn what the elements of true intercession are.

> *It is the power of the heavenly life, the power of God's own Spirit, the power of omnipotence, that waits for prayer to bring it down.*

1. Notice the *urgent need*: Here intercession has its origin. The friend came at midnight—an untimely hour. He was hungry but could not buy bread. If we are to learn to pray rightly, we must open eye and heart to the need around us. We hear continually of the thousand millions of heathens and Mohammedans living in midnight darkness, perishing for lack of the bread of life. We hear of hundreds of millions of nominal Christians, the great majority of them almost ignorant and indifferent as the heathen. We see millions in the Christian Church, not ignorant or indifferent, and yet knowing little of a walk in the light of God or in the power of a life fed by bread from heaven. We have each of us our own circles—congregations, schools, friends, missions—in which the great complaint is that the light and life of God are too little known. Surely, if we believe what we profess, that God alone is able to help, that God certainly will help in answer to prayer—all this need ought to make intercessors of us, people who give their lives to prayer for those around them.

Let us take time to consider and realize the need. Each Christless soul going down into outer darkness, perishing of hunger, with bread enough and to spare! Thirty millions a year dying without the knowledge of Christ! Our own neighbors and friends, souls entrusted to us, dying without hope! Christians around us living a sickly, weak, fruitless life! Surely there is need for prayer. Nothing, nothing but prayer to God for help, will avail.

2. Note the *willing love*—the friend took his weary, hungry friend into his house, and into his heart too. He did not excuse himself by saying he had no bread. He gave himself at midnight to seek it for him. He sacrificed his night's rest, his comfort, to find the needed bread. "Love does not seek its own" (1 Cor. 13:5). It is the very nature of love to give up and forget itself for the sake of others. It takes their needs and makes them its own. It finds its real joy in living

and dying for others as Christ did.

It is the love of a mother to her prodigal son that makes her pray for him. True love to souls will become in us the spirit of intercession. It is possible to do a great deal of faithful, earnest work for our fellowmen without true love to them. Just as a lawyer or a physician, from a love of his profession and a high sense of faithfulness to duty, may interest himself most thoroughly in clients or patients without any special love to each, so servants of Christ may give themselves to their work with devotion and even self-sacrificing enthusiasm without the Christlike love to souls being strong. It is this lack of love that causes so much shortcoming in prayer. It is as love of our profession and work, delight in thoroughness and diligence, sink away in the tender compassion of Christ that love will compel us to prayer, because we cannot rest in our work if souls are not saved. True love must pray.

3. Note the *sense of powerlessness*—We often speak of the power of love. In one sense this is true, and yet the truth has its limitations that must not be forgotten. The strongest love may be utterly powerless. A mother might be willing to give her life for her dying child and yet not be able to save it. The friend at midnight was most willing to give his friend bread, but he had none. It was this sense of powerlessness, of his inability to help, that sent him begging: "A friend of mine has come to me on his journey, and *I have nothing* to set before him." It is this sense of powerlessness with God's servants that is the very strength of the life of intercession.

> *I*t is the very nature of love to give up and forget itself for the sake of others. It takes their needs and makes them its own. It finds its real joy in living and dying for others as Christ did.

"I have nothing to set before them": As this consciousness takes possession of the minister or missionary, the teacher or worker, intercession will become their only hope and refuge. I may have knowledge and truth, a loving heart, and the readiness to give myself for those under my charge. But the bread of heaven I cannot give them. With all my love and zeal, "I have nothing to set before them." Blessed is the man who has made that "I have nothing" the motto of his ministry. As he thinks of the judgment day and the danger of souls, as he sees what a supernatural power and life is needed to save men from sin, as he feels how utterly insufficient all he can ever do is to give them life, that *"I have nothing"* urges him to pray. Intercession appears to him, as he thinks of the midnight darkness and the hungry souls, as his only hope, the one thing in which his love can take refuge.

Let us take the lesson to heart, for a warning to all who are strong and wise to work, for the encouragement of all who are feeble. The sense of our powerlessness is the soul of intercession. The simplest, weakest Christian can pray down blessing from an Almighty God.

4. Note *the faith in prayer*—What he has not himself, another can supply. He

has a rich friend near who will be both able and willing to give the bread. He is sure that if he only asks, he will receive. This faith makes him leave his home at midnight. If he does not have the bread himself to give, he can ask another.

It is this simple, confident faith that God will give that we need. Where it really exists, there will surely be no mistake about our not praying. And in God's word we have everything that can stir and strengthen such faith in us. Just as the heaven our natural eye can see is one great ocean of sunshine, with its light and heat, giving beauty and fruitfulness to earth. Scripture shows us God's true heaven, filled with all spiritual blessings—divine light and love and life, heavenly joy and peace and power, all shining down upon us. It reveals to us God waiting, delighting to bestow these blessings in answer to prayer. By a thousand promises and testimonies, it calls and urges us to believe that prayer will be heard, that what we cannot possibly do ourselves for those whom we want to help, *can be got by prayer*. Surely there can be no question as to our believing that prayer will be heard, that through prayer the poorest and weakest can dispense blessings to the needy, and each of us, though poor, may yet be making many rich.

5. Note the *persistence that prevails*—The faith of the friend met a sudden and unexpected check: the rich friend refuses to hear—"I cannot rise to give to you." How little the loving heart had counted on this disappointment; it cannot consent to accept it. The supplicant presses his threefold plea: here is my needy friend, you have abundance, I am your friend; and refuses to accept a denial. The love that opened his house at midnight, and then left it to seek help, must win.

This is the central lesson of the parable. In our intercession, we may find that there is difficulty and delay with the answer. It may be as if God says, "I cannot give to you." It is not easy, against all appearances, to hold firmly our confidence that He will hear and to persevere in full assurance that we will have what we ask. And yet this is what God looks for from us. He so highly prizes our confidence in Him, it is so essentially the highest honor the creature can render the Creator, that He will do anything to train us in the exercise of this trust in Him. Blessed is the man who is not staggered by God's delay, or silence, or apparent refusal, but is strong in faith, giving glory to God. Such faith perseveres, persistently, if need be, and cannot fail to inherit the blessing.

6. Note, last, *the certainty of a rich reward*—"I say to you, because of his persistence, he will give him as many as he needs." Oh that we might learn to believe in the certainty of an abundant answer. A prophet said of old: "Do not let your hands be weak, for *your work shall be rewarded*!" (2 Chron. 15:7). If only all who feel it difficult to pray much would fix their eye on the payment of the reward, and in faith learn to count upon the Divine assurance that their prayer cannot be vain. If we will just believe in God and His faithfulness, intercession will become to us the very first thing we take refuge in when we seek blessing for others, and the very last thing for which we cannot find time. And it will become a thing of joy and hope, because, all the time we pray, we know that we are sowing seed that will bring forth fruit a

hundredfold. Disappointment is impossible: "I say to you, he will rise and give him as many as he needs."

Let all lovers of souls, and all workers in the service of the gospel, take courage. Time spent in prayer will yield more than that given to work. Prayer alone gives work its worth and its success. Prayer opens the way for God Himself to do His work in us and through us. Let our chief work, as God's messengers, be intercession, for in it we secure the presence and power of God to go with us.

"Which of you shall have a friend at midnight and say to him, 'Friend, lend me three loaves?'" This friend is none other but our God. Let us learn that in the darkness of midnight, at the most unlikely time, and in the greatest need, when we have to say of those we love and care for, "I have nothing to set before them," we have a rich Friend in heaven, the Everlasting God and Father, who only waits to be asked rightly. Let us confess before Him our lack of prayer. Let us admit that the lack of faith, of which it is the proof, is the symptom of a life that is not spiritual, that is yet all too much under the power of self and the flesh and the world. Let us in the faith of the Lord Jesus, who spoke this parable, and Himself waits to make every trait of it true in us, give ourselves to be intercessors. Let every sight of souls needing help, let every stirring of the spirit of compassion, let every sense of our own inability to bless, let every difficulty in the way of our getting an answer, just combine to urge us to do this one thing: with persistence to cry to the God who alone can help, who, in answer to our prayer, will help. And let us, if we indeed feel that we have failed, do our utmost to train a young generation of Christians who profit by our mistake and avoid it.

Moses could not enter the land of Canaan, but there was one thing he could do: He could at God's bidding "command Joshua, and encourage him and strengthen him" (Deut. 3:28). If it is too late for us to make good our failure, let us at least encourage those who come after us to enter into the good land, the blessed life of unceasing prayer.

The model intercessor is the model Christian worker. First to get from God, and then to give to men what we ourselves secure from day to day, is the secret of successful work. Between our powerlessness and God's omnipotence, intercession is the blessed link.

FOR FURTHER THOUGHT

1. *What powers will intercessory prayer bring down on you as an individual believer and on the church as a whole?*

2. *What is the importance of love—love for God and for humankind—in a life of intercessory prayer? How can love motivate you to pray this way?*

3. *How should you respond in your life of intercessory prayer when there is difficulty or delay in an answer, when it seems as if God is saying, "I cannot give to you"?*

4

BECAUSE OF HIS PERSISTENCE

*"I say to you, though he will not rise and give to him
because he is his friend, yet because of his persistence he
will rise and give him as many as he needs."*
LUKE 11:8

*Then He spoke a parable to them, that men always ought to pray
and not lose heart.... "Hear what the unjust judge said. And shall
God not avenge His own elect who cry out day and night
to Him, though He bears long with them? I tell you
that He will avenge them speedily."*
LUKE 18:1–8

OUR Lord Jesus thought it of such importance that we should know the
need of perseverance and persistence in prayer, that He spoke two parables to
teach us this. This is proof sufficient that in this aspect of prayer we have both its
greatest difficulty and its highest power. He would have us know that in prayer all
will not be easy and smooth, that we must expect difficulties, which can only be
conquered by persistent, determined perseverance.

In the parables, our Lord represents the difficulty as existing on the side of
the persons to whom the petition was addressed, and the persistence as needed to
overcome their reluctance to hear. In our communication with God, the difficulty
is not on His side but on ours. In connection with the first parable He tells us
that our Father is more willing to give good things to those who ask Him than
any earthly father is to give his child bread. In the second, He assures us that God
longs to avenge His elect speedily. The need of urgent prayer cannot be because
God must be made willing or disposed to bless: The need lies altogether in ourselves. But because it was not possible to find any earthly illustration of a loving
father or a willing friend from whom the needed lesson of importunity could be
taught, He takes the unwilling friend and the unjust judge to encourage in us the
faith that perseverance can overcome every obstacle.

The difficulty is not in God's love or power, but in ourselves and our own
incapacity to receive the blessing. And yet, because there is this difficulty with us,

this lack of spiritual preparedness, there is a difficulty with God, too. His wisdom, His righteousness, yes, His love, dare not give us what would do us harm, if we received it too soon or too easily. The sin, or the consequence of sin, that makes it impossible for God to give at once is a barrier on God's side as well as ours, and to break through this power of sin in ourselves, or those for whom we pray, is what makes the striving and the conflict of prayer such a reality.

And so in all ages men have prayed, and that rightly, too, under a sense that there were difficulties in the heavenly world to overcome. As they pleaded with God for the removal of the unknown obstacles, and in that persevering supplication were brought into a state of utter brokenness and helplessness, of entire resignation to Him, of union with His will, and of faith that could take hold of Him, the hindrances in themselves and in heaven were together overcome. As God conquered them, they conquered God. As God prevails over us, we prevail with God.

God has so constituted us that the clearer our insight is into the reasonableness of a demand, the more hearty will be our surrender to it. One great cause of our negligence in prayer is that there appears to be something arbitrary, or at least something incomprehensible, in the call to such continued prayer. If we could be brought to see that this apparent difficulty is a divine necessity, and in the very nature of things the source of unspeakable blessing, we should be more ready with gladness of heart to give ourselves to continue in prayer. Let us see if we cannot understand how the difficulty that the call to persistence throws in our way is one of our greatest privileges.

I do not know whether you have ever noticed what a part difficulties play in our natural life. They call out man's powers as nothing else can. They strengthen and ennoble character. We are told that one reason of the superiority of the northern nations, like Holland and Scotland, in strength of will and purpose, over those of the sunny south, as Italy and Spain, is that the climate of the latter has been too beautiful, and the life it encourages too easy and relaxing—the difficulties the former had to contend with have been their greatest benefit. How all nature has been so arranged by God that in sowing and reaping, in seeking coal or gold, nothing is found without labor and effort.

What is education but a daily developing and disciplining of the mind by new difficulties presented to the pupil to overcome? The moment a lesson has become easy, the pupil is moved on to one that is higher and more difficult. With the race and the individual, it is in the meeting and the mastering of difficulties that our highest attainments are found.

It is even so in our communication with God. Just imagine what the result would be if the child of God had only to kneel down and ask, and get, and go away. What unspeakable loss to the spiritual life would ensue! It is in the difficulty and delay that calls for persevering prayer that the true blessing and blessedness of the heavenly life will be found. We there learn how little we delight in fellowship with God, how little we have of living faith in Him. We discover how earthly and unspiritual our heart still is, how little we have of God's Holy Spirit. We there are brought to know our own weakness and unworthiness, and to yield to God's Spirit to pray in us, to take our place in Christ Jesus and abide in Him as our only plea with the Father. There our own will and strength and goodness are crucified. There we rise in Christ to newness of life, with our whole will dependent on God and set upon His glory. Do let us begin to praise God for the need and the difficulty of persistent prayer as one of His choicest means of grace.

> *The sin, or the consequence of sin, that makes it impossible for God to give at once is a barrier on God's side as well as ours, is what makes the striving and the conflict of prayer such a reality.*

Just think what our Lord Jesus owed to the difficulties in His path. In Gethsemane it was as if the Father would not hear: He prayed yet more earnestly, until He "was heard" (Heb. 5:7). In the way He opened up for us, He learned obedience by the things He suffered, and so was made perfect (see Heb. 5:8–9). His will was given up to God, and His faith in God was proved and strengthened. The prince of this world, with all his temptation, was overcome. This is the new and living way He consecrated for us. It is in persevering prayer we walk with and are made partakers of His very Spirit.

Prayer is one form of crucifixion, of our fellowship with Christ's Cross of our giving up our flesh to the death. O Christians! Shall we not be ashamed of our reluctance to sacrifice the flesh and our own will and the world, as it is seen in our reluctance to pray much? Shall we not learn the lesson that nature and Christ alike teach? The difficulty of persistent prayer is our highest privilege, and the difficulties to be overcome in it bring us our richest blessings.

In persistence there are various elements. Of these the chief are perseverance, determination, intensity. It begins with the refusal to immediately accept a denial. It grows to the determination to persevere, to spare no time or trouble, until an answer comes. It rises to the intensity in which the whole being is given to God in supplication, and the boldness comes to lay hold of God's strength. At one time it is quiet and restful, at another passionate and bold. Now it takes time and is patient, then again it claims right now what it desires. In whatever different shape, it always means and knows—God hears prayer: I must be heard.

Remember the wonderful instances we have of it in the Old Testament saints. Think of Abraham, as he pleads for Sodom. Time after time he renews his prayer until the sixth time he has to say, "Let not the Lord be angry" (Gen. 18:32). He does not cease until he has learned to know God's condescension in each time consenting to his petition, until he has learned how far he can go, has entered into God's mind, and now rests in God's will. And for his sake Lot was saved. "God remembered Abraham, and sent Lot out of the midst of the overthrow" (Gen.

19:29). And shall not we, who have a redemption and promises for the nonbelievers that Abraham never knew, begin to plead more with God on their behalf.

Think of Jacob, when he feared to meet Esau. The angel of the Lord met him in the dark and wrestled with him. And when the angel saw that he had not prevailed, he said, "Let Me go." And Jacob said, "I will not let You go" (Gen. 32:26). And he blessed him there. And that boldness that said, "I will not," and forced from the reluctant angel the blessing, was so pleasing in God's sight that a new name was there given to him: "Israel; for you have struggled with God and with men, and have prevailed" (32:28).

And through all the ages God's children have understood what Christ's two parables teach, that God holds Himself back and seeks to get away from us until what is of flesh and self and laziness in us is overcome and we so prevail with Him that He can and must bless us. Oh, why is it that so many of God's children have no desire for this honor—being princes of God, strivers with God, and prevailing? What our Lord taught us, "Whatever things you ask. . .*believe that you receive them*" (Mark 11:24), is nothing but His putting of Jacob's words, "I will not let You go unless You bless me." This is the persistence He teaches and we must learn: to claim and take the blessing.

Think of Moses when Israel had made the golden calf. "Moses returned to the LORD and said, 'Oh, these people have committed a great sin! . . . Yet now, if You will forgive their sin—but if not, I pray, blot me out of Your book which You have written'" (Exod. 32:31–32). That was persistence that would rather die than not have his people given to him. Then, when God had heard him and said He would send His angel with the people, Moses came again, and would not be content until, in answer to his prayer that God Himself should go with them (Exod. 33:12–13, 15–16), He had said, "I will also do this thing that you have spoken" (33:17). After that, when in answer to his prayer, "Show me Your glory" (33:18), God made His goodness pass before him, he immediately again began pleading, "Let my Lord, I pray, go among us" (34:9). And he was there with the Lord forty days and forty nights (34:28). Of these days he says, "And I fell down before the LORD, as at the first, forty days and forty nights; I neither ate bread nor drank water, because of all your sin which you committed" (Deut. 9:18). As an intercessor, Moses used persistence with God, and prevailed. He proves that the man who truly lives near to God, and with whom God speaks face-to-face, becomes partaker of that same power of intercession that there is in Him who is at God's right hand and always lives to pray.

Think of Elijah in his prayer, first for fire, and then for rain. In the former you have the persistence that claims and receives an immediate answer. In the latter, bowing himself down to the earth, his face between his knees, his answer to the servant who had gone to look toward the sea, and come with the message, "There is nothing," was "Go again" seven times (1 Kings 18:43). Here was the persistence of perseverance. He had told Ahab there would be rain. He knew it was coming; and yet he prayed until the seven times were fulfilled. And it is of this Elijah and this prayer we are taught, "Pray for one another. . . . Elijah was a man with a nature like ours. . . . The effective, fervent prayer of a righteous man avails much" (James 5:16–17). Will there not be some who feel constrained to cry out, "Where is the LORD God of Elijah?" (2 Kings 2:14)—this God who draws forth such effectual prayer, and hears it so wonderfully. His name be praised: He is still the same. Let His people just believe that He still waits to be inquired of! Faith in a prayer-hearing God will make a prayer-loving Christian.

We remember the marks of the true intercessor as the parable taught us them. A sense of the need of souls, a Christlike love in the heart, a consciousness of personal powerlessness, faith in the power of prayer, courage to persevere in spite of refusal, and the assurance of an abundant reward—these are the dispositions that constitute a Christian as intercessor and call forth the power of prevailing prayer. These are the dispositions that constitute the beauty and the health of the Christian life, that fit a man for being a blessing in the world, that make him a true Christian worker who does indeed get from God the bread of heaven to dispense to the hungry. These are the dispositions that call forth the highest, the heroic virtues of the life of faith.

There is nothing to which the nobility of natural character owes so much as the spirit of enterprise and daring that in travel or war, in politics or science, battles with difficulties and conquers. No labor or expense is grudged for the sake of victory. And shall we who are Christians not be able to face the difficulties that we meet in prayer? It is as we "labor" and "strive" in prayer that the renewed will asserts its royal right to claim in the name of Christ what it will and wields its God-given power to influence the destinies of men.

Shall men of the world sacrifice ease and pleasure in their pursuits, and shall we be such cowards and sluggards as not to fight our way through to the place where we can find liberty for the captive and salvation for the perishing? Let each servant of Christ learn to know his calling. His King always lives to pray. The Spirit of the King always lives in us to pray. It is from heaven the blessings, which the world needs, must be called down in persevering, persistent, believing prayer. It is from heaven, in answer to prayer, the Holy Spirit will take complete possession of us to do His work through us. Let us acknowledge how vain our much work has been due to our little prayer. Let us change our method, and let from now on more prayer, much prayer, unceasing prayer, be the proof that we look for all to God, and that we believe that He hears us.

FOR FURTHER THOUGHT

1. *What are some of the reasons God delays in giving you what you ask for, even when you know that it is His will to give it to you?*
2. *What must you rid yourself of in order for God to give Himself to answering your prayers and giving you what you ask for?*
3. *What heart attitude is necessary for you to be a prayer-loving Christian?*

5

THE LIFE THAT CAN PRAY

*"If you abide in Me, and My words abide in you, you
will ask what you desire, and it shall be done for you."*
JOHN 15:7

The effective, fervent prayer of a righteous man avails much.
JAMES 5:16

*Beloved, if our heart does not condemn us, we have confidence
toward God. And whatever we ask we receive from Him,
because we keep His commandments and do those
things that are pleasing in His sight.*
1 JOHN 3:21–22

HERE on earth the influence of one who asks a favor for others depends entirely on his character and on the relationship he bears to him with whom he is interceding. It is what he is that gives weight to what he asks. It is not otherwise with God. Our power in prayer depends upon our life. Where our life is right we shall know how to pray so as to please God, and prayer will secure the answer.

The texts quoted above all point in this direction. *"If you abide in Me,"* our Lord says, you shall ask, and it shall be done for you. It is the prayer of a *righteous man*, according to James, that avails much. We receive whatever we ask, John says, because we obey and please God. All lack of power to pray rightly and perseveringly, all lack of power in prayer with God, points to some lack in the Christian life. It is as we learn to live the life that pleases God that God will give what we ask.

Let us learn from our Lord Jesus, in the parable of the vine, what the healthy, vigorous life is that may ask and receive what it will. Hear His voice, "If you abide in Me, and My words abide in you, you will ask what you desire, and it shall be done for you." And again at the close of the parable: "You did not choose Me, but I chose you and appointed you that you should go and bear fruit, and that your fruit should remain, that *whatever you ask* the Father in My name *He may give you*" (John 15:16).

And what is now, according to the parable, the life that one must lead to bear fruit, and then ask and receive what we desire? What is it we are to be or do that will enable us to pray as we should and to receive what we ask? The answer is in one word: It is the branch life that gives power for prayer. We are branches of Christ, the Living Vine. We must simply live like branches and abide in Christ, and then we will ask what we desire, and it shall be done for us.

We all know what a branch is, and what its essential characteristic. It is simply a growth of the vine, produced by it and appointed to bear fruit. It has only one reason for existence. It is there at the bidding of the vine, that through it the vine may bear and ripen its precious fruit. Just as the vine only and solely and wholly lives to produce the sap that makes the grape, so the branch has no other aim and object but this alone: to receive that sap and bear the grape. Its only work is to serve the vine, that through it the vine may do its work.

And the believer, the branch of Christ the heavenly Vine, is it to be understood that he is as literally, as exclusively, to live only that Christ may bear fruit through him? Is it meant that a true Christian as a branch is to be just as absorbed in and devoted to the work of bearing fruit to the glory of God as Christ the Vine was on earth, and is now in heaven? This, and nothing less, is indeed what is meant. It is to such that the unlimited prayer promises of the parable are given. It is the branch-life, existing solely for the Vine, that will have the power to pray rightly. With our life abiding in Him, and His words abiding, kept and obeyed, in our heart and life, transmuted into our very being, there will be the grace to pray rightly and the faith to receive whatever we desire.

Let us connect the two things and take them both in their simple, literal truth, and their infinite, divine grandeur. The promises of our Lord's farewell discourse, with their wonderful sixfold repetition of the unlimited, *anything*, *whatever* (John 14:13–14; 15:7, 16; 16:23–24), appear to us altogether too large to be taken literally, and they are qualified down to meet our human ideas of what appears fitting. It is because we separate them from that life of absolute and unlimited devotion to Christ's service to which they were given. God's covenant is always: Give all and take all. He who is willing to be fully branch and nothing but branch, who is ready to place himself absolutely at the disposal of Jesus the Vine of God to bear His fruit through him and to live every moment only for Him, will receive a divine liberty to claim Christ's *whatever* in all its fullness, and a divine wisdom and humility to use it correctly. He will live and pray and claim the Father's promises, even as Christ did, only for God's glory in the salvation of men. He will use his boldness in prayer only with a view to power in intercession and getting men blessed. The unlimited devotion of the branch life to fruit-bearing and the unlimited access to the treasures of the Vine life are inseparable. It is the life abiding wholly in Christ that can pray the effectual prayer in the name of Christ.

Just think for a moment of the men of prayer in scripture, and see in them what the life was that could pray in such power. We spoke of Abraham as intercessor. What gave Him such boldness? He knew that God had chosen and called him away from his home and people to walk before Him so that all nations might be blessed in him. He knew that he had obeyed and forsaken all for God. Implicit obedience, to the very sacrifice of his son, was the law of his life. He did what God asked: He dared to trust God to do what he asked. We spoke of Moses as intercessor. He, too, had forsaken all for God, "esteeming the reproach of Christ greater riches than the treasures in Egypt" (Heb. 11:26). He lived at God's disposal: "faithful in all His house as a servant" (Heb. 3:5). How often it is written of him, "According to all that the LORD commanded Moses, so he did." No wonder that he was very bold: His heart was right with God, so he knew God would hear him. No less true is this of Elijah, the man who stood up to plead for the Lord God of Israel. The man who is ready to risk all for God can count on God to do all for him.

It is as men live that they pray. It is the life that prays. It is the life that, with wholehearted devotion, gives up all for God and to God that can claim all from God. Our God longs exceedingly to prove Himself the faithful God and mighty Helper of His people. He only waits for hearts wholly turned from the world to Himself and open to receive His gifts. The man who loses all will find all, and he dares ask and take it. The branch that only and truly lives abiding in Christ, the heavenly Vine, entirely given up, like Christ, to bear fruit in the salvation of men, and has His words taken up into and abiding in its life, may dare ask what it will—it shall be done.

> We are branches of Christ, the living Vine. We must simply live like branches and abide in Christ, and then we will ask what we desire, and it shall be done for us.

And where we have not yet attained to that full devotion to which our Lord had trained His disciples, and cannot equal them in their power of prayer, we may, nevertheless, take courage in remembering that, even in the lower stages of the Christian life, every new onward step in the striving after the perfect branch life, and every surrender to live for others in intercession, will be met from above by a corresponding liberty to draw near with greater boldness and expect larger answers. The more we pray, and the more conscious we become of our unfitness to pray in power, the more we shall be urged and helped to press on toward the secret of power in prayer—a life abiding in Christ entirely at His disposal.

And if any are asking, with somewhat of a hopelessness of attainment, what the reason may be for the failure in this blessed branch life, so simple and yet so mighty, and how they can come to it, let me point them to one of the most precious lessons of the parable of the Vine. It is one that is all too little noticed. Jesus spoke, "I am the true vine, *and My Father is the vinedresser*" (John 15:1). We have not only Himself, the glorified Son of God, in His divine fullness, out of whose fullness of life and grace we can draw—this is very wonderful—but there is something more blessed still. We have the Father, as the Vinedresser, watching over our abiding in the Vine, over our growth and fruit-bearing.

It is not left to our faith or our faithfulness to maintain our union with Christ. The God, who is the Father of Christ, who united us with Him—God Himself will see to it that the branch is what it should be. He will enable us to bring forth just the fruit we were appointed to bear. Hear what Christ said of this, "Every branch that bears fruit He prunes, that it may bear more fruit" (John 15:2). More fruit is what the Father seeks; more fruit is what the Father will Himself provide. It is for this that He, as the Vinedresser, cleanses the branches.

> *he branch that only and truly lives abiding in Christ, the heavenly Vine, entirely given up, like Christ, to bear fruit in the salvation of men*

Just think a moment what this means. It is said that of all fruit-bearing plants on earth, there is none that produces fruit so full of spirit, from which spirit can be so abundantly distilled, as the vine. And of all fruit-bearing plants, there is none that is so ready to run into wild wood, and for which pruning and cleansing are so indispensable. The one great work that a vinedresser has to do for the branch every year is to prune it. Other plants can for a time dispense with it and yet bear fruit, but the vine must have it.

And likewise, the one thing the branch that desires to abide in Christ and bring forth much fruit, and to be able to ask whatever it desires, must do, is to trust in and yield itself to this Divine cleansing. What is it that the Vinedresser cuts away with his pruning knife? Nothing but the wood that the branch has produced—true, honest wood, with the true vine nature in it. This must be cut away. And why? Because it draws away the strength and life of the vine and hinders the flow of the juice to the grape. The more it is cut down, the less wood there is in the branch, the more all the sap can go to the grape. The wood of the branch must decrease so that the fruit for the vine may increase. In obedience to the law of all nature, that death is the way to life, that gain comes through sacrifice, the rich and luxuriant growth of wood must be cut off and cast away so that the life more abundant may be seen in the cluster.

Even so, child of God, branch of the heavenly Vine, there is in you that which appears perfectly innocent and legitimate, and which yet so draws out your interest and your strength, that it must be pruned and cleansed away.

We saw what power in prayer men like Abraham and Moses and Elijah had, and we know what fruit they bore. But we also know what it cost them, how

God had to separate them from their surroundings and ever again to draw them from any trust in themselves, to seek their life in Him alone. It is only as our own will and strength and effort and pleasure, even where these appear perfectly natural and sinless, are cut down, so that the whole energies of our being are free and open to receive the sap of the heavenly Vine, the Holy Spirit, that we shall bear much fruit. It is in the surrender of what nature holds firmly, it is in the full and willing submission to God's holy pruning knife, that we shall come to what Christ chose and appointed us for—to bear fruit, that whatever we ask the Father in Christ's name, He may give to us.

What the pruning-knife is, Christ tells us in the next verse. "You are *already clean because of the word* which I have spoken to you" (John 15:3). As He says later, "Sanctify them by Your truth. Your word is truth" (John 17:17). "The word of God *is* living and powerful, and sharper than any two-edged sword, piercing even to the division of soul and spirit" (Heb. 4:12). What heart-searching words Christ had spoken to His disciples on love and humility, on being the least and, like Himself, the servant of all, on denying self, and taking the cross, and losing the life. Through His Word, the Father had cleansed them, cut away all confidence in themselves or the world, and prepared them for the inflowing and filling of the Spirit of the heavenly Vine. It is not we who can cleanse ourselves but God is the Vinedresser. We may confidently entrust ourselves to His care.

> The one great work that a vinedresser has to do for the branch every year is to prune it. Other plants can for a time dispense with it and yet bear fruit, but the vine must have it.

Beloved brethren—ministers, missionaries, teachers, workers, believers old and young—are you mourning your lack of prayer, and, as a consequence, your lack of power in prayer? Oh, come and listen to your beloved Lord as He tells you, "only be a branch, united to, identified with, the heavenly Vine, and your prayers will be effectual and much availing." Are you mourning that just this is your trouble—you do not, cannot, live this branch-life, abiding in Him? Oh! Come and listen again. "More fruit" is not only your desire, but the Father's, too. He is the Vinedresser who cleanses the fruitful branch so that it may bear more fruit. Cast yourself on God, to do in you what is impossible to man. Count upon a Divine pruning to cut down and take away all that self-confidence and self-effort, which has been the cause of your failure. The God who gave you His beloved Son to be your Vine, who made you His branch, will He not do His work of cleansing to make you fruitful in every good work—in the work of prayer and intercession, too?

Here is the life that can pray. A branch entirely given up to the Vine and its aims, with all responsibility for its cleansing cast on the Vinedresser. A branch abiding in Christ, trusting and yielding to God for His cleansing, can bear much fruit. In the power of such a life we shall love prayer, we shall know how to pray, we shall pray, and receive whatever we ask.

For Further Thought

1. *What, according to the parable of the Vine, the life you must lead to bear fruit and to receive from God what you desire? What is it you are to be or do that will enable you to pray as you should and to receive what you ask?*

2. *What is required of you in your relationship to Jesus Christ in order for you to receive from Him the power to pray rightly? What must you do to make your relationship with Him one of asking and receiving what you desire?*

3. *What should you do when you recognize in your own life a lack of power in prayer? How can you access the power that has until now been missing?*

6

RESTRAINING PRAYER: IS IT SIN?

"You. . .restrain prayer before God."
JOB 15:4

"And what profit do we have if we pray to Him?"
JOB 21:15

*"Far be it from me that I should sin against
the LORD in ceasing to pray for you."*
1 SAMUEL 12:23

*"Neither will I be with you anymore,
unless you destroy the accursed from among you."*
JOSHUA 7:12

ANY deep quickening of the spiritual life of the Church will always be accompanied by a deeper sense of sin. This will not begin with theology; that can only give expression to what God works in the life of His people. Nor does it mean that that deeper sense of sin will only be seen in stronger expressions of self-reproach or penitence: That is sometimes found to consist with a harboring of sin and unbelief as to deliverance. But the sense of the hatefulness of sin, the hatred of it, will be proved by the intensity of desire for deliverance and the struggle to know to the very utmost what God can do in saving from it—a holy jealousy, in nothing to sin against God.

If we are to deal effectually with the lack of prayer, we must look at it from this point of view and ask, Restraining prayer, is it sin? And if it is, how is it to be dealt with, to be discovered, confessed, cast out by man, and cleansed away by God? Jesus is a Savior from sin. It is only as we know sin truly that we can truly know the power that saves from sin. The life that can pray effectually is the life of the cleansed branch—the life that knows deliverance from the power of self. To see that our prayer sins are indeed sins, is the first step to a true and divine deliverance from them.

In the story of Achan (Josh. 7) we have one of the strongest proofs in scripture that it is sin that robs God's people of His blessing, and that God will not tolerate it. At the same time we have the dearest indication of the principles under which God deals with it and removes it. Let us see in the light of the story if we can learn how to look at the sin of prayerlessness and at the sinfulness that lies at the root of it. The words I have quoted above, "Neither will I be with you anymore, unless you destroy the accursed from among you," take us into the very heart of the story and suggest a series of the most precious lessons around the truth they express: that the presence of sin makes the presence of God impossible.

1. *The presence of God is the great privilege of God's people and their only power against the enemy*—God had promised to Moses, *I will bring you in*, into the land. Moses proved that he understood this when God, after the sin of the golden calf, spoke of withdrawing His presence and sending an angel. He refused to accept anything less than God's presence. "For how then will it be known that Your people and I have found grace in Your sight, except *You go with us*?" (Exod. 33:16). It was this that gave Caleb and Joshua their confidence: The Lord is with us. It was this that gave Israel their victory over Jericho: the presence of God. This is throughout scripture the great central promise: I am with you. This marks off the wholehearted believer from the worldling and worldly Christians around him: He lives consciously hidden in the secret of God's presence.

> *This marks off the wholehearted believer from the worldling and worldly Christians around him: He lives consciously hidden in the secret of God's presence.*

2. *Defeat and failure are always due to the loss of God's presence*—It was like that at Ai. God had brought His people into Canaan with the promise to give them the land. When the defeat at Ai took place, Joshua felt immediately that the cause must be in the withdrawal of God's power. He had not fought for them. His presence had been withheld.

In the Christian life and the work of the Church, defeat is always a sign of the loss of God's presence. As we apply this to our failure in the prayer-life, and as a result of that to our failure in work for God, we are led to see that all is simply due to our not standing in clear and full fellowship with God. His nearness, His immediate presence, has not been the chief thing sought after and trusted in. He could not work in us as He desires. Loss of blessing and power is always caused by the loss of God's presence.

3. *The loss of God's presence is always due to some hidden sin*—Just as pain is ordered in nature to warn of some hidden evil in the system, defeat is God's voice telling us there is something wrong. He has given Himself so wholly to His people. He delights so in being with them, and would so desire to reveal in them His love and power that He never withdraws Himself unless they compel Him by sin.

Throughout the Church there is a complaint of defeat. The Church has so little power over the masses or the educated classes. Powerful conversions are comparatively rare. The fewness of holy, consecrated, spiritual Christians, devoted to the service of God and their fellowmen, is felt everywhere. The power of the Church for the preaching of the gospel to the unreached is paralyzed by the scarcity of money and men—and all due to the lack of the effectual prayer that brings the Holy Spirit in power, first on ministers and believers, then on missionaries and the unreached. Can we deny it that the lack of prayer is the sin on account of which God's presence and power are not more noticeably seen among us?

4. *God Himself will discover the hidden sin*—We may think we know what the sin is, but it is only God who can discover its real deep meaning. When He spoke to Joshua, before naming the sin of Achan, God first said, "They have. . .transgressed My covenant which I commanded them" (Josh. 7:11). God had commanded that all the booty of Jericho, gold and silver and all that was in it, was to be a devoted thing, consecrated unto the Lord, and to come into His treasury (6:19). And Israel had broken this consecration vow: It had not given God His due. It had robbed God.

It is this we need: God must reveal to us how the lack of prayer is the indication of unfaithfulness to our consecration vow, that God should have all our heart and life. We must see that this restraining prayer, with the excuses we make for it, is greater sin than we have thought. For what does it mean? That we have little taste or relish for fellowship with God, that our faith rests more on our own work and efforts than on the power of God, that we have little sense of the heavenly blessing God waits to shower down, that we are not ready to sacrifice the ease and confidence of the flesh for persevering waiting on God, that the spirituality of our life, and our abiding in Christ, is altogether too feeble to make us prevail in prayer.

When the pressure of work for Christ is allowed to be the excuse for our not finding time to seek and secure His own presence and power in it as our chief need, it surely proves that there is no right sense of our absolute dependence upon God—no deep apprehension of the divine and supernatural work of God in which we are only His instruments, no true entrance into the heavenly, altogether otherworldly, character of our mission and aims, no full surrender to and delight in Christ Jesus Himself.

If we were to yield to God's Spirit to show us that all this is in very deed the meaning of remissness in prayer, and of our allowing other things to crowd it out, all our excuses would fall away, and we should fall down and cry, "We have sinned! We have sinned!" Samuel once said, "As for me, far be it from me that I should sin against the Lord in ceasing to pray for you" (1 Sam. 12:23). Ceasing from prayer is sin against God. May God reveal this to us. (Appendix 1.)

5. *When God reveals sin, it must be confessed and cast out*—When the defeat at Ai came, Joshua and Israel were ignorant of the cause. God dealt with Israel as a nation, as one body, and the sin of one member was visited on all. Israel as a whole was ignorant of the sin, and yet suffered for it.

The Church may be ignorant of the greatness of this sin of restraining prayer, and individual ministers or believers may never have looked at it as actual transgression, but nonetheless does it bring its punishment. But when the sin is no more hidden, when the Holy Spirit begins to convince of it, then comes the time of heart-searching. In our story, the combination of individual and united responsibility is very solemn. The individual: as we find it in the expression, "man by man" (Josh. 7:17). Each man felt himself under the eye of God, to be dealt with. And when Achan had been taken, he had to make confession. The united: as we see it in all Israel first suffering and dealt with by God, then taking Achan, his family, and the accursed thing and destroying them out of their midst.

> *If we were to yield to God's Spirit to show us that all this is in very deed the meaning of remissness in prayer, and of our allowing other things to crowd it out, all our excuses would fall away*

If we have reason to think this is the sin that is in the camp, let us begin with personal and united confession. And then let us come before God to put away and destroy the sin. Here stands at the very threshold of Israel's history in Canaan the heap of stones in the valley of Achor, to tell us that God cannot bear sin, that God will not dwell with sin, and that if we really want God's presence in power, sin must be put away (see Josh. 7:26).

Let us look the solemn fact in the face. There may be other sins, but here is certainly one that causes the loss of God's presence—we do not pray as Christ and scripture teaches us. Let us bring it out before God and give up this sin to the death. Let us yield ourselves to God to obey His voice. Let no fear of past failure, let no threatening array of temptations, duties, or excuses keep us back. It is a simple question of obedience. Are we going to give up ourselves to God and His Spirit to live a life in prayer, well-pleasing to Him?

Surely, if it is God who has been withholding His presence, who has been revealing the sin, who is calling for its destruction and a return to obedience, surely we can count on His grace to accept and strengthen for the life He asks of us. It is not a question of what you can do, but the question of whether you now, with your whole heart, turn to give God His due and give yourself to let His will and grace have their way with you.

6. *With sin cast out, God's presence is restored*—From this day onwards there is not a word in Joshua of defeat in battle. The story shows them going on from victory to victory. God's presence secured gives power to overcome every enemy.

This truth is so simple that the very ease with which we acquiesce in it robs it of its power. Let us pause and think what it implies. God's presence restored means victory secured. Then, we are responsible for defeat. Then, there must be sin somewhere causing it. Then, we ought at once to find out and put away the sin. We may confidently expect God's presence the moment the sin is put away. Surely each one is under the solemn obligation to search his life and see what part he may have in this evil.

God never speaks to His people of sin except with a view to saving them from it. *The same light that shows the sin will show the way out of it.* The same power that breaks down and condemns will, if humbly yielded to and waited on in confession and faith, give the power to rise up and conquer. It is God who is speaking to His Church and to us about this sin: "*He. . .wondered* that there was no intercessor" (Isa. 59:16). "I *wondered* that there was no one to uphold" (Isa. 63:5). "I *sought* for a man among them who would. . .stand in the gap before Me. . .but I found no one" (Ezek. 22:30). The God who speaks these things is He who will work the change for His children who seek His face. He will make the valley of Achor, of trouble and shame, of sin confessed and cast out, a door of hope.

Let us not fear, let us not cling to the excuses and explanations that circumstances suggest, but simply confess, "We have sinned; we are sinning; we dare not sin longer." In this matter of prayer we are sure God does not demand of us impossibilities. He does not weary us with an impracticable ideal. He asks us to pray no more than He gives grace to enable us to. He will give the grace to do what He asks, and so to pray that our intercessions shall, day by day, be a pleasure to Him and to us, a source of strength to our conscience and our work and a channel of blessing to those for whom we labor.

God dealt personally with Joshua, with Israel, with Achan. Let each of us allow Him to deal personally with us concerning this sin of restraining prayer and its consequences in our life and work, concerning the deliverance from sin, its certainty and blessedness. Just bow in stillness and wait before God until, as God, He overshadows you with His presence, leads you out of that region of argument as to human possibilities, where conviction of sin can never be deep and full deliverance can never come. Take quiet time and be still before God so that He may take this matter in hand. "Sit still, for He will not be in rest until He has concluded the matter this day" (see Ruth 3:18). Leave yourself in God's hands.

FOR FURTHER THOUGHT

1. *What is meant by "restraining prayer?" Have you recognized this in your own Christian life and prayer life?*

2. *The Bible teaches that the loss of God's presence is due to sin. How can you have that sin revealed? When it is revealed, what must you do with it in order to have God's presence restored to you?*

3. *What will happen in your Christian life once sin is discovered and dealt with? What kind of changes can you expect?*

7

WHO SHALL DELIVER?

"Is there no balm in Gilead, is there no physician there?
Why then is there no recovery for the health
of the daughter of my people?"
JEREMIAH 8:22

"Return, you backsliding children, and I will heal
your backslidings." "Indeed we do come to You,
for You are the LORD our God."
JEREMIAH 3:22

Heal me, O LORD, and I shall be healed.
JEREMIAH 17:14

O wretched man that I am! Who will deliver me from this body
of death? I thank God—through Jesus Christ our Lord! . . .
For the law of the Spirit of life in Christ Jesus has made
me free from the law of sin and death.
ROMANS 7:24–25, 8:2

DURING one of our conventions a gentleman called upon me to ask advice and help. He was evidently an earnest and well-instructed Christian man. He had for some years been in most difficult surroundings, trying to witness for Christ. The result was a sense of failure and unhappiness. His complaint was that he had no enjoyment for the Word, and that though he prayed, it was as if his heart was not in it. If he spoke to others or gave a tract, it was under a sense of duty: The love and the joy were not present. He longed to be filled with God's Spirit, but the more he sought it, the farther off it appeared to be. What was he to think of his state, and was there any way out of it?

My answer was that the whole matter appeared to me very simple: He was living under the law and not under grace. As long as he did so, there could be no change. He listened attentively, but could not exactly see what I meant.

I reminded him of the difference, the utter contrariety between law and grace.

Law demands, but grace bestows. Law commands, but gives no strength to obey, but grace promises and performs, does all we need to do. Law burdens and casts down and condemns, but grace comforts and makes strong and glad. Law appeals to self to do its utmost, but grace points to Christ to do all. Law calls to effort and strain and urges us towards a goal we never can reach, but grace works in us all God's blessed will. I pointed out to him how his first step should be, instead of striving against all this failure, fully to accept it and the lesson of his own power-lessness, as God had been seeking to teach it to him, and, with this confession, to sink down before God in utter helplessness. There would be the place where he would learn that unless grace gave him deliverance and strength, he never could do better than he had done, and that grace would indeed work all for him. He must come out from under law and self and effort, and take his place under grace, allowing God to do all.

In later conversations, he told me the diagnosis of the disease had been correct. He admitted grace must do all. And yet, so deep was the thought that we must do something, that we must at least bring our faithfulness to secure the work of grace, he feared that his life would not be very different; he would not be equal to the strain of new difficulties into which he was now going. There was, amid all the intense ear-nestness, an undertone of despair. He could not live as he knew he ought to.

I have already said, in the opening chapter, that in some of our meetings I had noticed this tone of hopelessness. And no minister who has come into close con-tact with souls seeking to live wholly for God, to "walk worthy of the Lord, fully pleasing Him" (Col. 1:10), but knows that this renders the progress impossible. To speak specially of the lack of prayer and the desire of living a fuller prayer life, how many are the difficulties to be met! We have so often resolved to pray more and better, and have failed. We do not have the strength of will some have, with one resolve to turn around and change our habits. The press of duty is as great as ever it was, and it is so difficult to find time for more prayer. Real enjoyment in prayer, which would enable us to persevere, is what we do not feel. We do not possess the power to supplicate and to plead as we should. Our prayers, instead of being a joy and a strength, are a source of continual self-condemnation and doubt. We have at times mourned and confessed and resolved, but, to tell the honest truth, we do not expect, for we do not see the way to any great change.

It is evident that as long as this spirit prevails, there can be very little prospect of improvement. Discouragement must bring defeat. One of the first objects of a physician is always to awaken hope, for without this he knows his medicine will often profit little. No teaching from God's Word as to the duty, the urgent need, the blessed privilege of more prayer, of effectual prayer, will avail while the secret whisper is heard: *There is no hope*.

Our first care must be to find out the hidden cause of the failure and despair, and then to show how divinely sure deliverance is. We must, unless we are to rest content with our state, listen to and join in the question, "Is there no balm in

Gilead, is there no physician there? Why then is there no recovery for the health of the daughter of my people?" We must listen and receive into our heart the divine promise with the response it met with: "Return, you backsliding children, and I will heal your backslidings. . . . Indeed we do come to You, for You are the Lord our God." We must come with the personal prayer and with the faith that there will be a personal answer. Shall we not even now begin to claim it in regard to the lack of prayer and believe that God will help us: "Heal me, O Lord, and I shall be healed."

It is always of consequence to distinguish between the symptoms of a disease and the disease itself. Weakness and failure in prayer is a sign of weakness in the spiritual life. If a patient were to ask a physician to give him something to stimulate his weak pulse, he would be told that this would do him little good. The pulse is the index of the state of the heart and the whole system, but the physician strives to have health restored. What everyone who would desire to pray more faithfully and effectually must learn is this: that his whole spiritual life is in a sickly state and needs restoration. It is as he comes to look not only at his shortcomings in prayer, but at the lack in the life of faith, of which this is the symptom, that he will become fully alive to the serious nature of the disease. He will then see the need of a radical change in his whole life and walk, if his prayer life, which is simply the pulse of the spiritual system, is to indicate health and vigor. God has so created us that the exercise of every healthy function causes joy. Prayer is meant to be as simple and natural as breathing or working to a healthy man. The reluctance we feel and the failure we confess are God's own voice calling us to acknowledge our disease and to come to Him for the healing He has promised.

> *It is always of consequence to distinguish between the symptoms of a disease and the disease itself. Weakness and failure in prayer is a sign of weakness in the spiritual life.*

And what is now the disease of which the lack of prayer is the symptom? We cannot find a better answer than is pointed out in the words, "You are not under the law but under grace" (Rom. 6:14).

Here we have suggested the possibility of two types of Christian life. There may be a life partly under the law and partly under grace—or a life entirely under grace in the full liberty from self-effort, and the full experience of the divine strength that it can give. A true believer may still be living partly under the law, in the power of self-effort, striving to do what he cannot accomplish. The continued failure in his Christian life to which he confesses is due to this one thing: He trusts in himself and tries to do his best. He does, indeed, pray and look to God for help, but still it is he in his strength, helped by God, who is to do the work.

In the Epistles to the Romans, the Corinthians, and the Galatians, we know how Paul tells them that they have not received the spirit of bondage again, that they are free from the law, that they are no more servants but sons, that they must beware of nothing so much as to be entangled again with the yoke of bondage. Everywhere it is the contrast between the law and grace, between the flesh, which is under the law, and the Spirit, who is the gift of grace, and through whom grace does all its work. In our days, just as in those first ages, the great danger is living under the law and serving God in the strength of the flesh. With the great majority of Christians, it appears to be the state in which they remain all their lives. Therefore the lack to such a large extent of true holy living and power in prayer. They do not know that all failure can have but one cause: Men seek to do themselves what grace alone can do in them, what grace most certainly will do.

> *aul writes: "Much more those who receive abundance of grace and of the gift of righteousness will reign in life through the One, Jesus Christ." That reigning in life, as conqueror over sin, is even here on earth.*

Many will not be prepared to admit that this is their disease, that they are not living "under grace." Impossible, they say. "From the depth of my heart," a Christian cries, "I believe and know that there is no good in me, and that I owe everything to grace alone." "I have spent my life," a minister says, "and found my glory in preaching and exalting the doctrines of free grace." "And I," a missionary answers, "how could I ever have thought of seeing the heathen saved, if my only confidence had not been in the message I brought, and the power I trusted, of God's abounding grace." Surely you cannot say that our failures in prayer, and we sadly confess to them, are due to our not living "under grace"? This cannot be our disease.

We know how often a man may be suffering from a disease without knowing it. What he counts a slight ailment turns out to be a dangerous complaint. Do not let us be too sure that we are not, to a large extent, still living "under the law," while considering ourselves to be living fully "under grace." Very frequently the reason for this mistake is the limited meaning attached to the word *grace*. Just as we limit God Himself by our little or unbelieving thoughts of Him, so we limit His grace at the very moment that we are delighting in terms like the "riches of grace," "grace exceedingly abundant." Has not the very term, "grace abounding," from Bunyan's book downward, been confined to the one great blessed truth of free justification with ever-renewed pardon and eternal glory for the vilest of sinners, while the other equally blessed truth of "grace abounding" in sanctification is not fully known.

Paul writes: "Much more those who receive abundance of grace and of the gift of righteousness will reign in life through the One, Jesus Christ" (Rom. 5:17). That reigning in life, as conqueror over sin, is even here on earth. "Where sin abounded" in the heart and life, "grace abounded much more, so that. . .grace might reign through righteousness" (Rom. 5:20–21) in the whole life and being of the believer. It is of this reign of grace in the soul that Paul asks, "Shall we sin because we are. . .under grace?" and answers, "God forbid" (Rom. 6:15). Grace is not only pardon of, but power over sin. Grace takes the place sin had in the life, and undertakes, as sin had reigned within in the power of death, to reign in the power of Christ's life. It is of this grace that Christ spoke, "My grace is sufficient for you," and Paul answered, "I will rather boast in my infirmities. . .For when I am weak, then I am strong" (2 Cor. 12:9–10). It is of this grace, which, when we are willing to confess ourselves utterly powerless and helpless, comes in to work all in us, that Paul elsewhere teaches, "God is able to make *all grace* abound toward you, that you, *always* having *all sufficiency* in all things, may have an abundance for *every good work*" (2 Cor. 9:8).

> The law of God could only deliver us into the power of the law of sin and death. The grace of God can bring us into, and keep us in, the liberty of the Spirit.

It has often happened that a seeker after God and salvation has read his Bible long, and yet never seen the truth of a free and full and immediate justification by faith. When once his eyes were opened and he accepted it, he was amazed to find it everywhere. Even so, many believers who hold the doctrines of free grace as applied to pardon have never seen its wondrous meaning as it undertakes to work our whole life in us and *actually give us strength every moment* for whatever the Father would have us be and do. When God's light shines into our heart with this blessed truth, we know what Paul means by, "Not I, but the grace of God" (1 Cor. 15:10). There again you have the twofold Christian life. The one, in whom that "Not I"—I am nothing, I can do nothing—has not yet become a reality. The other, when the wondrous exchange has been made and grace has taken the place of our effort, and we say and know, "It is no longer I who live, but Christ lives in me" (Gal. 2:20). It may then become a lifelong experience: "The grace of our Lord was exceedingly abundant, with faith and love which are in Christ Jesus" (1 Tim. 1:14).

Beloved child of God! Do you think it is possible that this has been the lack in your life, the cause of your failure in prayer? You did not know how grace would enable you to pray, if once the whole life were under its power. You sought by earnest effort to conquer your reluctance or deadness in prayer, but you failed. You strove by every motive of shame or love you could think of to stir yourself to it, but it would not help. Is it not worthwhile asking the Lord whether the message I bring you as His servant may not be more true for you than you think? Your lack of prayer is due to a diseased state of life, and the disease is nothing but this—you have not accepted, for daily life and every duty, the full salvation that word brings: "You are not under the law but under grace." As universal and deep-reaching as the demand of the law and the reign of sin, yes, more exceedingly abundant is the provision of grace and the power by which it makes us reign in life. (Appendix 2)

In the chapter that follows that in which Paul wrote, "You are not under the law but under grace," he gives us a picture of a believer's life under law, with the bitter experience in which it ends: "O wretched man that I am! Who will deliver me from this body of death?" His answer to the question, "I thank God—through Jesus Christ our Lord!" shows that there is deliverance from a life held captive under evil habits that have been struggled against in vain. That deliverance is by the Holy Spirit giving the full experience of what the life of Christ can work in us: "The law of the Spirit of life in Christ Jesus has made me free from the law of sin and death" (Rom. 8:2). The law of God could only deliver us into the power of the law of sin and death. The grace of God can bring us into, and keep us in, the liberty of the Spirit. We can be made free from the sad life under the power that led us captive, so that we did not do what we desired. The Spirit of life in Christ can free us from our continual failure in prayer and enable us in this, too, to walk worthy of the Lord to all well-pleasing.

Oh! Do not be hopeless, do not be despondent, for there is a balm in Gilead. There is a Physician there, and there is healing for our sickness. What is impossible with man is possible with God. What you see no possibility of doing grace will do. Confess the disease, trust the Physician, claim the healing, and pray the prayer of faith, "Heal me, and I shall be healed." You, too, can become a man of prayer and pray the effectual prayer that avails much.[39]

FOR FURTHER THOUGHT

1. *How can you know that God has called you personally and individually to a life of intercessory prayer?*
2. *What is the connection between "living under the law," "living under grace," and a life of effective, powerful intercessory prayer?*
3. *The apostle Paul wrote to the Romans, "O wretched man that I am! Who will deliver me from this body of death?" What was his answer, and how does it apply to you today?*

---

[39] I ought to say for the encouragement of all that the gentleman of whom I spoke, at a convention two weeks later, saw and claimed the rest of faith in trusting God for all, and a letter from England tells that he has found that His grace is sufficient.

8

Do You Want to
Be Made Whole?

He said to him, "Do you want to be made well?"
The sick man answered Him, "Sir, I have no man to put me
into the pool. . . . Jesus said to him, "Rise, take up your
bed and walk." And immediately the man was
made well, took up his bed, and walked.
JOHN 5:6–9

Peter said, "In the name of Jesus Christ of Nazareth,
rise up and walk.". . . "The faith which comes through Him
has given him this perfect soundness in the presence of you all."
ACTS 3:6, 16

And Peter said to him, "Aeneas, Jesus the Christ heals you.
Arise and make your bed." Then he arose immediately.
ACTS 9:34

WEAKNESS in prayer is the mark of disease. Powerlessness to walk is, in the Christian as in the natural life, a terrible proof of some evil in the system that needs a physician. The lack of power to walk joyfully in the new and living way that leads to the Father and the throne of grace is especially grievous.

Christ is the Great Physician who comes to every Bethesda where sickly people are gathered and speaks out His loving, searching question: Do you want to be made well? For all who are still clinging to their hope in the pool or are looking for some man to put them in, who are hoping, in course of time somehow to be helped by just continuing in the use of the ordinary means of grace, His question points to a better way. He offers them healing in a way of power they have never understood.

And to all who are willing to confess, not only their own powerlessness but their failure to find any man to help them, His question brings the sure and certain hope of a near deliverance. We have seen that our weakness in prayer is part of a life smitten with spiritual sickness. Let us listen to our Lord as He offers to restore our spiritual strength so we can walk like healthy, strong men in all the ways of the Lord and so be made fit to fill our place in the great work of intercession. As we see what the wholeness is He offers, how He gives it, and what He asks of us, we shall be prepared for giving a willing answer to His question.

What Is the Health That Jesus Offers?

I might mention many proofs of spiritual health. Our text leads us to take one—walking. Jesus said to the sick man, Rise and walk, and with that restored him to his place among men in full health and vigor, able to take his part in all the work of life. It is a wonderfully suggestive picture of the restoration of spiritual health. To the healthy, walking is a pleasure, but to the sick a burden, if not an impossibility. How many Christians there are to whom, like the maimed and the hobbled and the lame and the sickly, movement and progress in God's way is indeed an effort and a weariness. Christ comes to say, and with the word He gives the power, Rise and walk.

Just think of this walk to which He restores and empowers us. It is a life like that of Enoch and Noah, who "walked with God" (Gen. 5:22, 6:9). A life like that of Abraham, to whom God said, "Walk before Me" (Gen. 17:1), and who himself said, "The Lord, before whom I walk" (Gen. 24:40). A life of which David sings, "They walk in the light of Your countenance" (Ps. 89:15), and Isaiah prophesies, "Those who wait on the LORD shall renew their strength...they shall run and not be weary, they shall walk and not faint" (Isa. 40:31). Even as God the Creator does not faint nor become weary, shall they who walk with Him, waiting on Him, never be exhausted or weak. It is a life concerning which it could be said of the last of the Old Testament saints, Zacharias and Elizabeth, "They were both righteous before God, walking in all the commandments and ordinances of the Lord blameless" (Luke 1:6). This is the walk Jesus came to make possible and true to His people in greater power than ever before.

Hear what the New Testament speaks of it: "That just as Christ was raised from the dead by the glory of the Father, even so we also should walk in newness of life" (Rom. 6:4). It is the Risen One who says to us, Rise and walk, for He gives the power of the resurrection life. It is a walk in Christ "As you therefore have received Christ Jesus the Lord, so walk in Him" (Col. 2:6). It is a walk like Christ. "He who says he abides in Him ought himself also to walk just as He walked" (1 John 2:6) It is a walk by the Spirit and after the Spirit. "Walk in the Spirit, and you shall not fulfill the lust of the flesh" (Gal. 5:16). "Who do not walk according to the flesh, but according to the Spirit" (Rom. 8:1). It is a walk worthy of God and well-pleasing to Him. "That you may walk worthy of the Lord, fully pleasing Him, being fruitful in every good work" (Col. 1:10). "We urge and exhort in the Lord Jesus that you should abound more and more, just as you received from us how you ought to walk and to please God" (1 Thess. 4:1). It is a walk in heavenly love. "Walk in love, as Christ also has loved us" (Eph. 5:2). It is a "walk in the light as He is in the light" (1 John 1:7). It is a walk of faith, all its power coming simply from God and Christ and the Holy Spirit, to the soul turned away from the world. "We walk by faith, and not by sight" (2 Cor. 5:7).

How many believers there are who regard such a walk as an impossible thing—so impossible that they do not feel it a sin that they "walk otherwise," and so they do not long for this walk in newness of life. They have become so accustomed to the life of powerlessness that the life and walk in God's strength has little attraction. But some there are with whom it is not this way. They do wonder if these words really mean what they say, if the wonderful life each one of them speaks of is simply an unattainable ideal, or meant to be realized in flesh and blood. The more they study them, the more they feel that they are spoken as for daily life. And yet they appear too high. Oh that they would believe that God sent His Mighty Son and His Holy Spirit indeed to bring us and make us fit for a life and walk from heaven beyond all that man could dare to think or hope for.

How Jesus Makes Us Whole

When a physician heals a patient he acts on him from the outside and does something that is, if possible, after that to render him independent of his aid. He restores him to perfect health and leaves him. With the work of our Lord Jesus, it is in both respects the very opposite. Jesus works not from the outside but from within by entering Himself in the power of His Spirit into our very life. And instead of, as in the bodily healing, being rendered, if possible, independent of a physician for the future, Christ's one purpose in healing is, as we said, the exact opposite. His one condition of success is to bring us into *such dependence upon Himself that we will not be able one single moment to do without Him.*

> *Let us listen to our Lord as He offers to restore our spiritual strength so we can walk like healthy, strong men in all the ways of the Lord and so be made fit to fill our place in the great work of intercession.*

Christ Jesus Himself is our life, in a sense that many Christians have no conception of. The prevailing weak and sickly life is entirely due to the lack of the apprehension of the divine truth that as long as we expect Christ continually to do something for us from heaven, in single acts of grace from time to time, and each time trust Him to give us what will last a little while, we cannot be restored to perfect health. But when once we see how there is to be nothing of our own for a single moment and it is to be all Christ moment by moment, and learn to accept it from Him and trust Him for it, the life of Christ becomes the health of our soul. Health is nothing but life in its normal, undisturbed action. Christ gives us health by giving us Himself as our life. That is how He becomes our strength for our walk. Isaiah's words find their New Testament fulfillment: Those who wait on the Lord shall walk and not faint because Christ is now the strength of their life.

> *It is a walk of faith, all its power coming simply from God and Christ and the Holy Spirit, to the soul turned away from the world.*

It is strange how believers sometimes think this life of dependence is too great a strain and a loss of our personal liberty. They admit a need of dependence, of much dependence, but with room left for their own will and energy. They do not see that even a partial dependence makes us debtors and leaves us nothing to boast of. They forget that our relationship to God and cooperation with Him are not that He does the larger part and we the lesser, but that God does all and we do all—God all in us, we all through God. This dependence upon God secures our true independence. When our will seeks nothing but the divine will, we reach a divine nobility, the true independence of all that is created. He who has not seen this must remain a sickly Christian, letting self do part and Christ part. He who accepts the life of unceasing dependence on Christ, as life and health and strength, is made whole. As God, Christ can enter and become the life of His creature. As the glorified One who received the Holy Spirit from the Father to bestow, He can renew the heart of the sinful creature and make it His home and by His presence maintain it in find health and strength.

You who would desire to walk and please God and in your prayer life not have your heart condemn you, listen to Christ's words: "Do you want to be made well?" He can give soul-health. He can give a life that can pray and know that it is well-pleasing to the Father. If you desire to have this, come and hear how you can receive it.

What Christ Asks of Us

The story invites us to notice three things very specially. Christ's question first appeals to the will and asks for the repression of its consent. He then listens to man's confession of his utter helplessness. Then comes the ready obedience to Christ's command that rises up and walks.

1. Do you want to be made well? About the answer of the sickly man there could be no doubt. Who would not be willing to have his sickness removed? But, sadly, in the spiritual life what need there is to press the question. Some will not admit that they are so sick. And some will not believe that Christ can make a man well. And some will believe it for others, but they are sure it is not for them. At the root of all lies the fear of the self-denial and the sacrifice that will be needed. They are not willing to forsake entirely the walk after the course of this world, to

give up all self-will, self-confidence, and self-pleasing. The walk in Christ and like Christ is too straight and hard, and they do not desire it, they do not desire to be made whole. My brother, if you are willing, speak it out: "Lord! At any price, I will!" From Christ's side, the act is one of the will: "I will! Be clean." From your side equally: "Be it done to you as you desire." If you would be delivered from your sickness—oh, do not be afraid to say, "I will, I will!"

Then comes the second step. Christ wants us to look up to him as our only Helper. "I have no man to put me in," must be our cry. Here on earth there is no help for me. Weakness may grow into strength in the ordinary use of means if all the organs and functions are in a sound state. Sickness needs special measures. Your soul is sick. Your inability to walk joyfully the Christian walk in God's way is a sign of disease. Do not be afraid to confess it and to admit that there is no hope for restoration except by an act of Christ's mercy healing you. Give up the idea of growing out of your sickliness into a healthy state, of growing out from under the law into a life under grace.

A few days ago I heard a student plead the cause of the Volunteer Pledge. "The pledge calls you," he said, "to a decision. Do not think of growing into a missionary. Unless God forbids you, take the step, and the decision will bring joy and strength, will set you free to grow up in all needed for a missionary, and will be a help to others." It is like that in the Christian life. Delay and struggle will equally hinder you. Do confess that you cannot bring yourself to pray as you desire because you cannot give yourself the healthy, heavenly life that loves to pray and that knows to count upon God's Spirit to pray in us. Come to Christ to heal you. He can in one moment make you whole. Not in the sense of working a sudden change in your feelings or in what you are in yourself, but in the heavenly reality of coming in response to your surrender and faith, taking charge of your inner life, and filling it with Himself and Spirit.

As the glorified One who received the Holy Spirit from the Father to bestow, He can renew the heart of the sinful creature and make it His home and by His presence maintain it in find health and strength.

The third thing Christ asks is this: the surrender of faith. When He spoke to the helpless man, His word of command had to be obeyed. The man believed that there was truth and power in Christ's word, and in that faith he rose and walked. By faith he obeyed. And what Christ said to others was for him, too—"Go your way. Your faith has made you well" (Luke 17:19). Of us, too, Christ asks this faith that His word changes our weakness into strength and makes us fit for that walk in newness of life for which we have been awakened in Him. If we do not believe this, if we will not take courage and say, with Paul, "I can do all things through

Christ who strengthens me" (Phil. 4:13), then we cannot obey. But if we will listen to the word that tells us of the walk that is not only possible, but has been proved and seen in God's saints from of old, if we will fix our eye on the mighty, living, loving Christ who speaks in power, "Rise and walk," we shall take courage and obey. We shall rise and begin to walk in Him and His strength. In faith, apart from and above all feeling; we shall accept and trust an unseen Christ as our strength, and go on in the strength of the Lord God. We shall know Christ as the strength of our life. We shall know, and tell, and prove that Jesus Christ has made us whole.

> *D*o confess that you cannot bring yourself to pray as you desire because you cannot give yourself the healthy, heavenly life that loves to pray and that knows to count upon God's Spirit to pray in us.

Can it indeed be? Yes, it can. He has done it for many, and He will do it for you. Beware of forming wrong conceptions of what must take place. When the sickly man was made whole, he had still all to learn as to the use of his new-found strength. If he wanted to dig or build or learn a trade, he had to begin at the beginning. Do not expect at once to be proficient in prayer or any part of the Christian life. No, but expect and be confident of this one thing: that as you have trusted yourself to Christ to be your health and strength, He will lead and teach you. Begin to pray in a quiet sense of your ignorance and weakness, but in a joyful assurance that He will work in you what you need. Rise and walk each day in a holy confidence that He is with you and in you. Just accept Jesus Christ the Living One and trust Him to do His work.

Will you do it? Have you done it? Even now Jesus speaks, "Rise and walk." "Amen, Lord! At Your word I come. I rise to walk with You, and in You, and like You."

For Further Thought

1. *What is Jesus' one condition for making you whole? What must you do to meet that condition?*
2. *What three things does Christ ask of you so that you can be made "well," and made able and ready to live and pray with the overcoming power He has promised those who abide in Him?*
3. *What will you need to do in order to learn to walk and live in power once Christ has made you well? What attitude will this require?*

9

The Secret of Effectual Prayer

"What things soever ye desire, when ye pray,
believe that ye receive them, and ye shall have them."
Mark 11:24 kjv

Here we have a summary of the teaching of our Lord Jesus on prayer. Nothing will so much help to convince us of the sin of our remissness in prayer, to discover its causes, and to give us courage to expect entire deliverance as the careful study and then the believing acceptance of that teaching.

The more heartily we enter into the mind of our blessed Lord and set ourselves simply just to think about prayer as He thought, the more surely will His words be as living seeds. They will grow and produce in us their fruit—a life and practice exactly corresponding to the divine truth they contain. Do let us believe this: Christ, the living Word of God, gives in His words a divine quickening power that brings what they say, that works in us what He asks, that actually makes us fit and enables for all He demands. Learn to look upon His teaching on prayer as a definite promise of what He, by His Holy Spirit dwelling in you, is going to work into your very being and character.

Our Lord gives us the five marks, or essential elements, of true prayer. There must be, first, the heart's *desire*; then the expression of that desire is *prayer*; with that, the *faith* that carries the prayer to God; in that faith, *the acceptance of God's answer*; then comes the *experience* of the desired blessing. It may help to give definiteness to our thought if we each take a definite request in regard to which we would desire to learn to pray believingly. Or, perhaps better still, we might all unite and take the one thing that has been occupying our attention. We have been speaking of failure in prayer, so why should we not take as the object of desire and supplication the "grace of supplication" (Zech. 12:10 kjv) and say, "I want to ask and receive in faith the power to pray just as, and as much as, my God expects of me?" Let us meditate on our Lord's words, in the confidence that He will teach us how to pray for this blessing.

1. "What things soever *ye desire*"—Desire is the secret power that moves the whole world of living men and directs the course of each. And so desire is the soul of prayer, and the cause of insufficient or unsuccessful prayer is very much to be

found in the lack or weakness of desire. Some may doubt this. They are sure that they have very earnestly desired what they ask. But if they consider whether their desire has indeed been as wholehearted as God would have it, as the heavenly worth of these blessings demands, they may come to see that it was indeed the lack of desire that was the cause of failure.

What is true of God is true of each of His blessings, and is the more true the more spiritual the blessing: "And you will seek Me and find Me, when you search for Me with all your heart" (Jer. 29:13). Of Judah in the days of Asa it is written, "They sought Him with their whole desire" (2 Chron. 15:15 KJV). A Christian may often have very earnest desires for spiritual blessings. But alongside of these there are other desires in his daily life occupying a large place in his interests and affections. The spiritual desires are not all-absorbing. He wonders that his prayer is not heard. It is simply that God wants the whole heart. "The LORD our God, the LORD is one! You shall love the LORD your God with all your heart" (Deut. 6:4–5). The law is unchangeable: God offers Himself, gives Himself away, to the whole-hearted who give themselves wholly away to Him. He always gives us according to our heart's desire. But not as we think it, but as He sees it. If there are other desires that are more at home with us, that have our heart more than Himself and His presence, He allows these to be fulfilled, and the desires that engage us at the hour of prayer cannot be granted.

> The more heartily we enter into the mind of our blessed Lord and set ourselves simply just to think about prayer as He thought, the more surely will His words be as living seeds.

We desire the gift of intercession, the grace and power to pray rightly. Our hearts must be drawn away from other desires. We must give ourselves wholly to this one. We must be willing to live wholly in intercession for the kingdom. By fixing our eye on the blessedness and the need of this grace, by thinking of the certainty that God will give it to us, by giving ourselves up to it for the sake of the perishing world, desire may be strengthened and the first step taken toward the possession of the coveted blessing. Let us seek the grace of prayer as we seek the God with whom it will link us, "with our whole desire." Then we may depend upon the promise, "He will fulfill the desire of those who fear Him" (Ps. 145:19). Let us not fear to say to Him, "I desire it with my whole heart."

2. What things soever ye desire when *ye pray*—The desire of the heart must become the expression of the lips. Our Lord Jesus more than once asked those who cried to Him for mercy, "What do you want?" He wanted them to say what they wanted. To speak it out roused their whole being into action, brought them into contact with Him, and wakened their expectation. To pray is to enter into God's

presence, to claim and secure His attention, to have distinct dealing with Him in regard to some request, to commit our need to His faithfulness, and to leave it there. It is in so doing that we become fully conscious of what we are seeking.

There are some who often carry strong desires in their heart without bringing them to God in the clear expression of definite and repeated prayer. There are others who go to the Word and its promises to strengthen their faith, but do not give sufficient place to that pointed asking of God that helps the soul to the assurance that the matter has been put into God's hands. Still others come in prayer with so many requests and desires that it is difficult for them to say what they really expect God to do. If you would obtain from God this great gift of faithfulness in prayer and power to pray rightly, begin by exercising yourself in prayer in regard to it. Say of it to yourself and to God: "Here is something I have asked, and am continuing to ask until I receive. As plain and pointed as words can make it, I am saying, 'My Father! I do desire, I do ask of You and expect of You the grace of prayer and intercession.'"

> To pray is to enter into God's presence, to claim and secure His attention, to have distinct dealing with Him in regard to some request, to commit our need to His faithfulness, and to leave it there.

3. "What things soever ye desire, when ye pray, *believe*"—As it is only by faith that we can know God, receive Jesus Christ, or live the Christian life, so faith is the life and power of prayer. If we are to enter upon a life of intercession, in which there is to be joy and power and blessing, if we are to have our prayer for the grace of prayer answered, we must learn anew what faith is and begin to live and pray in faith as never before.

Faith is the opposite of sight, and the two are contrary to one another. "We walk by faith, not by sight" (2 Cor. 5:7). If the unseen is to get full possession of us, and if heart and life and prayer are to be full of faith, there must be a withdrawal from, a denial of, the visible. The spirit that seeks to enjoy as much as possible of what is innocent or legitimate, that gives the first place to the calls and duties of daily life, is inconsistent with a strong faith and close interaction with the spiritual world. "We do not look at the things which are seen"—The negative side needs to be emphasized if the positive—"but at the things which are not seen" (2 Cor. 4:18)—is to become natural to us. In praying, faith depends upon our living in the invisible world.

This faith has especially to do with God. The great reason for our lack of faith is our lack of knowledge of God and communication with Him. "Have faith in God," Jesus said when He spoke of removing mountains (Mark 11:22–24). It is as a soul knows God and is occupied with His power, love, and faithfulness, and comes away out of self and the world and allows the light of God to shine on it that unbelief will become impossible. All the mysteries and difficulties connected with answers to prayer will, however little we may be able to solve them intellectually, be swallowed up in the adoring assurance: "This God is our God. He will bless us. He does indeed answer prayer. And the grace to pray I am asking for He will delight to give." (Appendix 3)

4. "What things soever ye desire, when ye pray, believe that ye *have received*," now as you pray—*Faith has to accept the answer, as given by God in heaven, before it is found or felt upon earth.* This point causes difficulty, and yet it is of the very essence of believing prayer, its real secret. Try and take it in. Spiritual things can only be spiritually apprehended or appropriated. The spiritual heavenly blessing of God's answer to your prayer must be spiritually recognized and accepted before you feel anything of it. It is faith that does this. A soul that not only seeks an answer but seeks first the God who gives the answer receives the power to know that it has what it has asked of Him. If it knows that it has asked according to His will and promises, and that it has come to and found Himself to give it, it does believe that it has received. "We know that He hears us" (1 John 5:15).

There is nothing so heart-searching as this faith, "*Believe that you have received.*" As we strive to believe and find we cannot, it leads us to discover what there is that hinders. Blessed is the man who holds nothing back and lets nothing hold him back, but, with his eye and heart on God alone, refuses to rest until he has believed what our Lord promises him, "that he has received." Here is the place where Jacob becomes Israel, where the power of prevailing prayer is born out of human weakness and despair. Here comes in the real need for persevering and ever-persistent prayer that will not rest, go away, or give up until it knows it is heard and believes that it has received.

You pray for "the Spirit of grace and supplication" (Zech. 12:10)? As you ask for it in strong desire and believe in God who hears prayer, do not be afraid to press on and believe that your life can indeed be changed, that the world with its press of duties, whether religious or not, hindering prayer can be overcome and that God gives you your heart's desire: grace to pray both in measure and in spirit, just as the Father would have His child do. "Believe that you have received."

5. "What things soever ye desire, when ye pray, believe that ye have received, and *ye shall have them*"—The receiving from God in faith, the believing acceptance of the answer with the perfect, praising assurance that it has been given, is not necessarily the experience or subjective possession of the gift we have asked for. At times there may be a considerable or even a long interval. In other cases the believing supplicant may at once enter on the actual enjoyment of what he has received. It is especially in the former case that we have need of faith and patience—faith to rejoice in the assurance of the answer bestowed and received and to begin and act upon that answer though nothing is felt, and patience to wait if there be for the present no sensible proof of its presence. We can count

on it: *You shall have*, in actual enjoyment.

If we apply this to the prayer for the power of faithful intercession, the grace to pray earnestly and perseveringly for souls around us, let us learn to hold firmly the divine assurance that as surely as we believe we receive and that faith, therefore, apart from all failing, may rejoice in the certainty of an answered prayer. The more we praise God for it, the sooner will the experience come. We may begin immediately to pray for others in the confidence that grace will be given us to pray more perseveringly and more believingly than we have done before.

If we do not find any special enlargement or power in prayer, this must not hinder or discourage us. We have accepted, apart from feeling, a spiritual divine gift by faith, and in that faith we are to pray, nothing doubting. The Holy Spirit may for a little time be hiding Himself within us, but we may count on Him, even though it is with groanings that cannot find expression, to pray in us. In due time, we shall become conscious of His presence and power. As sure as there is desire and prayer and faith, and faith's acceptance of the gift, there will be, too, the manifestation and experience of the blessing we sought.

Beloved brother! Do you truly desire that God should enable you so to pray that your life may be free from continual self-condemnation and that the power of His Spirit may come down in answer to your petition? Come and *ask God for it*. Kneel down and pray for it in a single definite sentence. When you have done so, kneel still in faith, believing in God who answers. Believe that you do now receive what you have prayed: believe that you have received. If you find it difficult to do this, kneel still, and say that you do it on the strength of His own word. If it cost time, struggle, and doubt—do not be afraid, for at His feet, looking up into His face, faith will come. "Believe that you have received": at His bidding you dare claim the answer. Begin in that faith, even though it is weak, a new prayer-life with this one thought as its strength: "You have asked and received grace in Christ to prepare you, step by step, to be faithful in prayer and intercession. The more simply you hold to this, and expect the Holy Spirit to work it in you, the more surely and fully will the word be made true to you: You shall have it. God Himself who gave the answer will work it in you."

For Further Thought

1. What five essential elements of true prayer did Jesus give His disciples—the original disciples and disciples today, including you?

2. What must happen within you before you can receive, find, or feel God's answer to your prayers here on earth?

3. You know that you are to believe that will receive that for which you have prayed. What should you do when you find it difficult to believe, when you feel that your faith is too weak to receive from God the things you request?

10

THE SPIRIT OF SUPPLICATION

"I will pour on the house of David. . .
the Spirit of grace and supplication."
ZECHARIAH 12:10

Likewise the Spirit also helps in our weaknesses.
For we do not know what we should pray for as we ought,
but the Spirit Himself makes intercession for us with groanings
which cannot be uttered. Now He who searches the hearts
knows what the mind of the Spirit is, because He makes
intercession for the saints according to the will of God.
ROMANS 8:26–27

With all prayer and supplication in the Spirit,
being watchful to this end with all perseverance
and supplication for all the saints.
EPHESIANS 6:18

Praying in the Holy Spirit.
JUDE 20

THE Holy Spirit has been given to every child of God to be his life. He dwells in him, not as a separate Being in one part of his nature, but as his very life. He is the divine power or energy by which his life is maintained and strengthened. All that a believer is called to be or to do, the Holy Spirit can and will work in him. If he does not know or yield to the Holy Guest, the blessed Spirit cannot work, and his life is a sickly one, full of failure and of sin. As he yields and waits, and obeys the leading of the Spirit, God works in him all that is pleasing in His sight.

This Holy Spirit is, in the first place, a Spirit of prayer. He was promised as a "Spirit of grace and supplication," the grace for supplication. He was sent forth into our hearts as "the Spirit of adoption by whom we cry out, 'Abba, Father'" (Rom. 8:15). He enables us to say, in the faith and growing apprehension of its meaning, Our Father in heaven. "He makes intercession for the saints according

THE MINISTRY OF INTERCESSION

to...God" (Rom. 8:27). And as we pray in the Spirit, our worship is as God seeks it to be: "in spirit and in truth" (John 4:23). Prayer is just the breathing of the Spirit in us. Power in prayer comes from the power of the Spirit in us, waited on and trusted in. Failure in prayer comes from weakness of the Spirit's work in us. Our prayer is the index of the measure of the Spirit's work in us. To pray rightly, the life of the Spirit must be right in us. For praying the effectual, much-availing prayer of the righteous man everything depends on being full of the Spirit.

> *To pray rightly, the life of the Spirit must be right in us. For praying the effectual, much-availing prayer of the righteous man everything depends on being full of the Spirit.*

There are three very simple lessons that the believer who wants to enjoy the blessing of being taught to pray by the Spirit of prayer must know. The first is: *Believe that the Spirit dwells in you* (Eph. 1:13). Deep in the innermost recesses of his being, hidden and unfelt, every child of God has the holy, mighty Spirit of God dwelling in him. He knows it by faith, the faith that, accepting God's Word, realizes that of which he sees as yet no sign. "We receive the promise of the Spirit through faith" (Gal. 3:14). As long as we measure our power for praying rightly and perseveringly by what we feel or think we can accomplish, we shall be discouraged when we hear of how much we ought to pray. But when we quietly believe that, in the midst of all our conscious weakness, the Holy Spirit as a Spirit of supplication is dwelling within us *for the very purpose of enabling us to pray in such manner and measure as God would have us,* our hearts will be filled with hope. We shall be strengthened in the assurance that lies at the very root of a happy and fruitful Christian life, and that God *has made an abundant provision for our being what He wants us to be.* We shall begin to lose our sense of burden and fear and discouragement about our ever praying sufficiently because we see that the Holy Spirit Himself will pray, is praying, in us.

The second lesson is: *Beware above everything of grieving the Holy Spirit* (Eph. 4:30). If you do, how can He work in you the quiet, trustful, and blessed sense of that union with Christ that makes your prayers well pleasing to the Father? Beware of grieving Him by sin, by unbelief, by selfishness, by unfaithfulness to His voice in conscience. Do not think grieving Him is a necessity, for that cuts away the very sinews of your strength. Do not consider it impossible to obey the command, "Do not grieve the Holy Spirit." He Himself is the very power of God to make you obedient.

The sin that comes up in you against your will—the tendency to laziness, pride, self-will, or passion that rises in the flesh—your will can, in the power of the Spirit, immediately reject and cast upon Christ and His blood, and your communion with God is immediately restored. Accept each day the Holy Spirit as your leader and life and strength. Then you can count on Him to do in your heart all that ought to be done there. He, the unseen and unfelt One—but known by faith—gives there, unseen and unfelt, the love and the faith and the power of obedience you need because He reveals Christ unseen within you as actually your life and strength. Do not grieve the Holy Spirit by distrusting Him because you do not feel His presence in you.

Especially in the matter of prayer do not grieve Him. Do not expect, when you trust Christ to bring you into a new, healthy prayer life, that you will be able all at once to pray as easily and powerfully and joyfully as you would desire to do. No, it may not come instantly. But just bow quietly before God in your ignorance and weakness. That is the best and truest prayer: to put yourself before God just as you are and to count on the hidden Spirit praying in you. "We do not know what we should pray for as we ought," for ignorance, difficulty, and struggle marks our prayer all along. But, "the Spirit also helps in our weaknesses." How? "The Spirit Himself," deeper down than our thoughts or feelings, "makes intercession for us with groanings which cannot be uttered." When you cannot find words, when your words appear cold and weak, just believe: *The Holy Spirit is praying in me.* Be quiet before God and give Him time and opportunity, and in due season you will learn to pray. Beware of grieving the Spirit of prayer by not honoring Him in patient, trustful surrender to His intercession in you.

> *B*e quiet before God and give Him time and opportunity, and in due season you will learn to pray. Beware of grieving the Spirit of prayer by not honoring Him in patient, trustful surrender to His intercession in you.

The third lesson: *"Be filled with the Spirit"* (Eph. 5:18). I think that we have seen the meaning of the great truth: It is only the healthy spiritual life that can pray rightly. The command comes to each of us: "Be filled with the Spirit." That implies that while some rest content with the beginning, with a small measure of the Spirit's working, it is God's will that we should be filled with the Spirit. That means, from our side, that our whole being ought to be entirely yielded up to the Holy Spirit, to be possessed and controlled by Him alone. And from God's side, that we may count on and expect the Holy Spirit to take possession and fill us.

Has not our failure in prayer evidently been due to our not having accepted the Spirit of prayer to be our life, to our not having yielded fully to Him, whom the Father gave as the Spirit of His Son to work the life of the Son in us? Let us, to say the very least, be willing to receive Him, to yield ourselves to God and trust Him for it. Let us not again willfully grieve the Holy Spirit by declining, by neglecting, by hesitating to seek to have Him as fully as He is willing to give Himself to us. If we have at all seen that prayer is the great need of our work and of the Church, if we have at all desired or resolved to pray more, let us turn to the very source of all power and blessing—let us believe that the Spirit of prayer, even in His fullness, is for us.

We all admit the place the Father and the Son have in our prayer. It is to the Father we pray, and from whom we expect the answer. It is in the merit, name, and life of the Son, abiding in Him and He in us, that we trust to be heard. But have we understood that in the holy Trinity, all the three Persons have an equal place in prayer, and that the faith in the Holy Spirit of intercession as praying in us is as indispensable as the faith in the Father and the Son? How clearly we have this in the words, "Through (Christ) we both have access by one Spirit to the Father" (Eph. 2:18).

As much as prayer must be *to* the Father and *through* the Son, it must be *by* the Spirit. And the Spirit can pray in no other way in us than as He lives in us. It is only as we give ourselves to the Spirit living and praying in us that the glory of the prayer-hearing God and the ever-blessed and most effectual mediation of the Son can be known by us in their power. (Appendix 4)

> *W*hen the Spirit of intercession takes full possession of us, all selfishness, as if we wanted Him separate from His intercession for others and have Him for ourselves alone, is banished, and we begin to take advantage of our wonderful privilege to plead for men.

Our last lesson: *Pray in the Spirit for all saints* (Eph. 6:18). The Spirit, who is called "the Spirit of supplication," is also and very specially the Spirit of intercession. It is said of Him, "the Spirit Himself makes intercession for us with groanings that cannot be uttered." "He makes intercession for the saints." It is the same word as is used of Christ, "who also makes intercession for us" (Rom. 8:34). The thought is essentially that of mediation—one pleading for another. When the Spirit of intercession takes full possession of us, all selfishness, as if we wanted Him separate from His intercession for others and have Him for ourselves alone, is banished, and we begin to take advantage of our wonderful privilege to plead for men. We long to live the Christ-life of self-consuming sacrifice for others, as our heart unceasingly yields itself to God to obtain His blessing for those around us. Intercession then becomes not an incident or an occasional part of our prayers, but our one great object. Prayer for ourselves then takes its true place, simply as a means for fitting us better for exercising our ministry of intercession more effectually.

May I be allowed to speak a very personal word to each of my readers? I have humbly sought God to give me what I may give them—divine light and help them to forsake the life of failure in prayer and to enter, even now and at once, into the life of intercession that the Holy Spirit can enable them to lead. It can be done by a simple act of faith: claiming the fullness of the Spirit—that is, the full measure of the Spirit that you are capable in God's sight of receiving and that He is therefore willing to bestow. Will you not even now accept of this by faith?

Let me remind you of what takes place at conversion. Most of us—you probably, too—for a time sought peace in efforts and struggles to give up sin and please God. But you did not find it this way. The peace of God's pardon came by faith, by trusting God's word concerning Christ and His salvation. You had heard of Christ as the gift of His love, and you knew that He was for you, too. You had felt the movings and drawings of His grace. But never until, in faith in God's Word, you accepted Him as God's gift to you did you know the peace and joy that He can give. Believing in Him and His saving love made all the difference. It changed your relationship from one who had always grieved Him to one who loved and served Him. And yet, after a time, you have a thousand times wondered why you love and serve Him so ill.

> *W*ithout the Holy Spirit, no man can call Jesus Lord, or cry, "Abba, Father," or worship in spirit and truth, or pray without ceasing.

At the time of your conversion, you knew little about the Holy Spirit. Later on you heard of His dwelling in you and of His being the power of God in you for all the Father intends you to be. And yet His indwelling and in working have been something vague and indefinite, hardly a source of joy or strength. At conversion, you did not yet know your need for Him, and still less what you might expect of Him. But your failures have taught it to you. And now you begin to see how you have been grieving Him by not trusting and not following Him, by not allowing Him to work in you all God's pleasure.

All this can be changed. Just as you, after seeking Christ, praying to Him, and trying without success to serve Him, found rest in accepting Him by faith, just so you may even now yield yourself to the full guidance of the Holy Spirit and claim and accept Him to work in you what God would have. Will you not do it? Just accept Him in faith as Christ's gift to be the Spirit of your whole life, of your prayer-life, too, and you can count on Him to take charge. You can then begin, however weak you feel and unable to pray rightly, to bow before God in silence with the assurance that He will teach you to pray.

My dear brother, as you consciously by faith accepted Christ to pardon, you can consciously now in the same kind of faith accept of Christ who gives the Holy Spirit to do His work in you. "Christ has redeemed us. . .that we might receive the promise of the Spirit through faith" (Gal. 3:13–14). Kneel down, and simply believe that the Lord Christ, who baptizes with the Holy Spirit, does now, in response to your faith, begin in you the blessed life of a full experience of the power of the indwelling Spirit. Depend most confidently on Him, apart from all feeling or experience, as the Spirit of supplication and intercession to do His work. Renew that act of faith each morning, each time you pray. Trust Him, against all appearances, to work in you—be sure He is working—and He will teach you to know what the joy of the Holy Spirit is as the power of your life.

"I will pour out the Spirit of supplication." Do you not begin to see that the mystery of prayer is the mystery of the divine indwelling? God in heaven gives His Spirit in our hearts to be there the divine power praying in us and drawing us upward to our God. God is a Spirit, and nothing but a like life and Spirit within us can hold communion with Him. It was for this that man was created, that God might dwell and work in Him and be the life of his life. It was this divine indwelling that sin lost. It was this that Christ came to exhibit in His life to win back for us in His death and then to impart to us by coming again from heaven in the Spirit to live in His disciples. It is this, the indwelling of God through the Spirit, that alone can explain and enable us to appropriate the wonderful promises given to prayer. God gives the Spirit as a Spirit of supplication, too, to maintain His divine life within us as a life out of which prayer ever rises upward.

Without the Holy Spirit, no man can call Jesus Lord, or cry, "Abba, Father," or worship in spirit and truth, or pray without ceasing. The Holy Spirit is given the believer to be and do in him all that God wants him to be or do. He is given him especially as the Spirit of prayer and supplication. Is it not clear that everything in prayer depends on our trusting the Holy Spirit to do His work in us, yielding ourselves to His leading, and depending only and wholly on Him?

We read, "Stephen was a man full of faith and the Holy Spirit" (Acts 6:5). The two always go together, in exact proportion to each other. As our faith sees and trusts the Spirit in us to pray and waits on Him, He will do His work. It is the longing desire, the earnest supplication, and the definite faith the Father seeks. Let us know Him, and in the faith of Christ who unceasingly gives Him, cultivate the assured confidence that we can learn to pray as the Father would have us.

FOR FURTHER THOUGHT

1. *What are the three simple lessons you must learn if you desire to enjoy the blessing of being taught to pray by the Spirit of prayer?*
2. *What happens when the Spirit of intercession takes full possession of you? What visible changes will result?*
3. *What is the role of the Holy Spirit in, among other spiritual blessings, learning to pray without ceasing?*

11

IN THE NAME OF CHRIST

*"Whatever you ask in My name, that I will do. . . . If you ask
anything in My name, I will do it. . . . I chose you and appointed
you. . .that whatever you ask the Father in My name He may give
you. . . . Most assuredly, I say to you, whatever you ask the Father
in My name He will give you. Until now you have asked
nothing in My name. Ask, and you will receive, that your joy
may be full. . . . In that day you will ask in My name."*
JOHN 14:13–14, 15:16, 16:23–24, 26

I N *My Name*—repeated six times over. Our Lord knew how slow our hearts
would be to take it in, and He so longed that we should really believe that His
name is the power in which every knee should bow, and in which every prayer
should be heard, that He did not weary of saying it over and over: *In My name!*
Between the wonderful *whatever you ask*, and the nivine *I will do it, the Father will
give it*, this one word is the simple link: *In My name.* Our asking and the Father's
giving are to be equally in the name of Christ. Everything in prayer depends upon
our grasping this—*In My name.*

We know what a name is: a word by which we call up to our mind the whole
being and nature of an object. When I speak of a lamb or a lion, the name at once
suggests the different nature peculiar to each. The name of God is meant to express
His whole divine nature and glory. And so the name of Christ means His whole nature. His person and work. His disposition and Spirit. To ask in the name of Christ
is to pray in union with Him.

When first a sinner believes in Christ, he only knows and thinks of His merit
and intercession. And to the very end that is the one foundation of our confidence. And yet, as the believer grows in grace and enters more deeply and truly
into union with Christ—that is, as he abides in Him—he learns that to pray in
the name of Christ also means in His Spirit and in the possession of His nature
as the Holy Spirit imparts it to us. As we grasp the meaning of the words, *"In that
day you will ask in My name"*—the day when in the Holy Spirit, Christ came
to live in His disciples—we shall no longer be staggered at the greatness of the
promise: *"Whatever you shall ask in My name, I will do it."*

We shall get some insight into the unchangeable necessity and certainty of the law: What is asked in the name of Christ, in union with Him, out of His nature and Spirit, must be given. As Christ's prayer-nature lives in us, His prayer power becomes ours, too. Not that the measure of our attainment or experience is the ground of our confidence, but the honesty and wholeheartedness of our surrender to all that we see that Christ seeks to be in us will be the measure of our spiritual fitness and power to pray in His name. "If you abide in Me," He says, "you will ask what you desire" (John 15:7). As we live in Him, we get the spiritual power to avail ourselves of His name. As the branch fully given up to the life and service of the Vine can count on all its sap and strength for its fruit, so the believer who in faith has accepted the fullness of the Spirit to possess his whole life can indeed avail himself of all the power of Christ's name.

Here on earth, Christ as man came to reveal what prayer is. To pray in the Name of Christ, we must pray as He prayed on earth, as He taught us to pray, and in union with Him, just as He now prays in heaven. We must in love study and in faith accept Him as our Example, our Teacher, our Intercessor.

CHRIST OUR EXAMPLE

Prayer in Christ on earth and in us cannot be two different things. Just as there is but one God, who is a Spirit, who hears prayer, there is but one spirit of acceptable prayer. When we realize what time Christ spent in prayer and how the great events of His life were all connected with special prayer, we learn the necessity of absolute dependence on and unceasing direct communication with the heavenly world—if we are to live a heavenly life or to exercise heavenly power around us. We see how foolish and fruitless the attempt must be to do work for God and heaven without in the first place in prayer getting the life and the power of heaven to possess us. Unless this truth lives in us, we cannot avail ourselves rightly of the mighty power of the name of Christ. His example must teach us the meaning of His name.

> *The name of Christ means His whole nature. His person and work. His disposition and Spirit. To ask in the name of Christ is to pray in union with Him.*

Of His baptism we read, "Jesus also was baptized; *and while He prayed*, the heaven was opened" (Luke 3:21). It was in prayer that heaven was opened to Him, that heaven came down to Him with the Spirit and the voice of the Father. In the power of these He was led into the wilderness, in fasting and prayer to have them tested and fully appropriated. Early in Jesus' ministry, Mark records (1:35), "Now in the morning, having risen a long while before daylight, He went out and departed to a solitary place; *and there He prayed*." And somewhat later, Luke tells (5:15–16), "Multitudes came together to hear, and to be healed.... *So*

He Himself often withdrew into the wilderness and prayed." He knew how the holiest service, preaching, and healing, can exhaust the spirit, how too much interaction with men could cloud the fellowship with God, how time, time, full time, is needed if the spirit is to rest and root in Him, how no pressure of duty among men can free from the absolute need of much prayer. If anyone could have been satisfied with always living and working in the spirit of prayer, it would have been our Master. But He could not. He needed to have His supplies replenished by continual and long-continued seasons of prayer. To use Christ's name in prayer surely includes this: to follow His example and to pray as He did.

Of the night before choosing His apostles we read (Luke 6:12), "He went out to the mountain *to pray, and continued all night in prayer to God."* The first step toward the constitution of the Church and the separation of men to be His witnesses and successors called Him to special long continued prayer. All had to be done according to the pattern on the mount. "The Son can do nothing of Himself. . . the Father. . .shows Him all things that He Himself does" (John 5:19–20). It was in the night of prayer it was shown Him.

> o use Christ's name in prayer surely includes this: to follow His example and to pray as He did.

In the night between the feeding of the five thousand—when Jesus knew that they wanted to take Him by force and make Him King—and the walking on the sea, "He went up on the mountain by Himself *to pray*" (Matt. 14:23, Mark 6:46, John 6:15). It was God's will He was come to do and God's power He was to show forth. He had it not as a possession of His own; it had to be prayed for and received from above. The first announcement of His approaching death, after He had elicited from Peter the confession that He was the Christ, is introduced by the words (Luke 9:18), "And it happened, as *He was alone praying."* The introduction to the story of the Transfiguration is (Luke 9:28), "He. . .went up on the mountain to pray." The request of the disciples, "Lord, teach us to pray' (Luke 11:1), follows on, "it came to pass, *as He was praying in a certain place."* In His own personal life, in His communication with the Father, in all He is and does for men, the Christ whose name we are to use is a Man of prayer. It is prayer that gives Him His power of blessing and transfigures His very body with the glory of heaven. It is His own prayer life that makes Him the teacher of others how to pray. How much more must it be prayer, prayer alone, much prayer, that can make us fit to share His glory of a transfigured life or make us the channel of heavenly blessing and teaching to others. To pray in the name of Christ is to pray as He prays.

As the end approaches, it is still more prayer. When the Greeks asked to see Him, and He spoke of His approaching death, He prayed. At Lazarus' grave He prayed. In the last night He prayed His prayer as our High Priest, that we might know what His sacrifice would win and what His everlasting intercession on the throne would be. In Gethsemane He prayed His prayer as victim, the Lamb giving itself to the slaughter. On the cross it is still all prayer—the prayer of compassion for His murderers, the prayer of atoning suffering in the thick darkness, the prayer in death of confiding resignation of His spirit to the Father. (Appendix 5)

Christ's life and work, His suffering and death—it was all prayer, all dependence on God, trust in God, receiving from God, surrender to God. Your redemption, O believer, is a redemption accomplished by prayer and intercession. Your Christ is a praying Christ. The life He lived for you, the life He lives in you, is a praying life that delights to wait on God and receive all from Him. To pray in His name is to pray as He prayed. Christ is only our example because He is our Head, our Savior, and our life. In virtue of His Deity and of His Spirit, He can live in us. We can pray in His name, because we abide in Him and He in us.

CHRIST OUR TEACHER

Christ was what He taught. All His teaching was just the revelation of how He lived, and—praise God—of the life He was to live in us. His teaching of the disciples was first to awaken desire and so prepare them for what He would by the Holy Spirit be and work in them. Let us believe very confidently: All He was in prayer and all He taught, He Himself will give. He came to fulfill the law, and much more will He fulfill the gospel in all He taught us as to what to pray and how.

What to pray—It has sometimes been said that direct petitions, as compared with the exercise of fellowship with God, are but a subordinate part of prayer, and that "in the prayer of those who pray best and most, they occupy but an inconsiderable place." If we carefully study all that our Lord spoke of prayer, we shall see that this is not His teaching. In the Lord's Prayer, in the parables on prayer, in the illustration of a child asking for bread, of our seeking and knocking, in the central thought of the prayer of faith, "Whatever you pray, believe that you have received," in the oft-repeated "whatsoever" of the last evening—everywhere our Lord urges and encourages us to offer definite petitions and to expect definite answers.

It is only because we have too much confined prayer to our own needs that it has been thought needed to free it from the appearance of selfishness by giving the petitions a subordinate place. If once believers were to awake to the glory of the work of intercession, and to see that in it and the definite pleading for definite gifts on definite spheres and persons lie our highest fellowship with our glorified Lord—and our only real power to bless men—it would be seen that there can be no truer fellowship with God than these definite petitions and their answers, by which we become the channel of His grace and life to men. Then our fellowship with the Father is even such as the Son has in His intercession.

How to pray—Our Lord taught us to pray in secret, in simplicity, with the eye on God alone, in humility, in the spirit of forgiving love. But the chief truth He reiterated was always this: to pray in faith. And He defined that faith not only as a trust in God's goodness or power, but as the definite assurance that we have received the very thing we ask. And then, in view of the delay in the answer, He insisted on perseverance and urgency. We must be followers of those "who through faith and patience inherit the promises" (Heb. 6:12)—the faith that accepts the promise and knows it has what it has asked—the patience that obtains the promise and inherits the blessing. We shall then learn to understand why God, who promises to avenge His elect speedily, bears with them in apparent delay. It is that their faith may be purified from all that is of the flesh and tested and strengthened to become that spiritual power that can do all things—can even cast mountains into the heart of the sea.

CHRIST AS OUR INTERCESSOR

We have gazed on Christ in His prayers. We have listened to His teaching as to how we must pray. To know fully what it is to pray in His Name, we must know Him, too, in His heavenly intercession.

Just think what it means: that all His saving work accomplished from heaven is still carried on, just as on earth, in unceasing communication with and direct intercession to the Father, who works all in all, who is All in All. Every act of grace in Christ has been preceded by, and owes its power to, intercession. God has been honored and acknowledged as its Author. On the throne of God, Christ's highest fellowship with the Father, and His partnership in His rule of the world, is in intercession. Every blessing that comes down to us from above bears upon it the stamp from God: through Christ's intercession. His intercession is nothing but the fruit and the glory of His atonement. When He gave Himself a sacrifice to God for men, He proved that His whole heart had the one object: the glory of God in the salvation of men. In His intercession this great purpose is realized: He glorifies the Father by asking and receiving all of Him. He saves men by bestowing what He has obtained from the Father. Christ's intercession is the Father's glory, His own glory, our glory.

And now, this Christ, the Intercessor, is our life—He is our Head and we are His body. His Spirit and life breathe in us. As in heaven so on earth, intercession is God's chosen, God's only channel of blessing. Let us learn from Christ what glory there is in it, what the way to exercise this wondrous power, and what the part it is to take in work for God.

The glory of it—By it, beyond anything, we glorify God. By it we glorify Christ. By it we bring blessing to the Church and the world. By it we obtain our highest nobility—the Godlike power of saving men.

The way to it—Paul writes, "Walk in love, as Christ also has loved us and given Himself for us, an offering and a sacrifice to God" (Eph. 5:2). If we live as Christ lived, we will, as He did, give ourselves, for our whole life, to God to be used by Him for men. When once we have done this, given ourselves, no more to seek anything for ourselves but for men, and that to God for Him to use us and to impart to us what we can bestow on others, intercession will become to us, as it is in Christ in heaven, the great work of our life. And if ever the thought comes that the call is too high or the work too great, the faith in Christ, the Interceding Christ who lives in us, will give us the victory. We will listen to Him who said, "The works that I do he will do also; and greater works than these he will do" (John 14:12). We shall remember that we are not under the law, with its powerlessness, but under grace with its omnipotence, working all in us. We shall believe again in Him who said to us, Rise and walk, and gave us—and we received it—His life as our strength. We shall claim afresh the fullness of God's Spirit as His sufficient provision for our need and count Him to be in us the Spirit of intercession, who makes us one with Christ in His. Oh! Let us only keep our place—giving up ourselves, like Him, in Him, to God for men.

> When He gave Himself a sacrifice to God for men, He proved that His whole heart had the one object: the glory of God in the salvation of men.

Then we shall understand the part intercession is to take in God's work through us. We shall no longer try to work for God and ask Him to follow it with His blessing. We shall do what the friend at midnight did, what Christ did on earth and always does in heaven—we shall first get from God, and then turn to men to give what He gave us. As with Christ, we shall make our chief work—we shall count no time or trouble too great—to receive from the Father. Then, giving to men will then be in power.

Servants of Christ! Children of God! Be of good courage. Let no fear of weakness or poverty make you afraid—ask in the name of Christ. His name is Himself, in all His perfection and power. He is the living Christ and will Himself make His name a power in you. Do not be afraid to plead the name. His promise is a threefold cord that cannot be broken: Whatever you ask—in My Name—*it shall be done for you.*

FOR FURTHER THOUGHT

1. *What does the name of Christ truly mean? What does it mean to pray in His name? What are the results of praying in His name?*
2. *Jesus taught His followers, including you, to pray in secret, in simplicity, in humility, and in forgiving love. But what is the foundation of all prayer, and how is it defined?*
3. *Read Ephesians 5:2. What will be the marks of your life when you commit yourself to walking as Jesus walked, when you allow Him through His Holy Spirit to take control of you?*

12

MY GOD WILL HEAR ME

Therefore the LORD will wait, that He may be
gracious to you.... Blessed are all those who wait for Him....
He will be very gracious to you at the sound of your cry;
when He hears it, He will answer you.
ISAIAH 30:18–19

The LORD will hear when I call to Him.
PSALM 4:3

I have called upon You, for You will hear me, O God.
PSALM 17:6

Therefore I will look to the LORD;
I will wait for the God of my salvation; my God will hear me.
MICAH 7:7

THE power of prayer rests in the faith that God hears it. In more than one sense this is true. It is this faith that gives a man courage to pray. It is this faith that gives him power to prevail with God. The moment I am assured that God hears me, too, I feel drawn to pray and to persevere in prayer. I feel strong to claim and to take in faith the answer God gives.

One great reason of lack of prayer is the lack of the living, joyous assurance: "My God will hear me." If once God's servants got a vision of the living God waiting to grant their request and to bestow all the heavenly gifts of the Spirit they are in need of, for themselves or those they are serving, how everything would be set aside to make time and room for this one and only power that can ensure heavenly blessing—the prayer of faith!

When a man can and does say in living faith, "My God will hear me!" surely nothing can keep him from prayer. He knows that what he cannot do or get done on earth, can and will be done for him from heaven. Let each one of us bow in stillness before God and wait on Him to reveal Himself as the prayer-hearing God. In His presence the wondrous thoughts gathering round the central truth will unfold themselves to us.

1. *"My God will hear me."—What a blessed certainty!*—We have God's word for it in numberless promises. We have thousands of witnesses to the fact that they have found it true. We have had experience of it in our lives. We have had the Son of God come from heaven with the message that if we ask, the Father will give. We have had Himself praying on earth and being heard. And we have Him in heaven now, sitting at the right hand of God and making intercession for us. God hears prayer—God delights to hear prayer. He has allowed His people a thousand times over to be tried so that they might be compelled to cry to Him and learn to know Him as the Hearer of Prayer.

Let us confess with shame how little we have believed this wondrous truth, in the sense of receiving it into our heart and allowing it to possess and control our whole being. That we accept a truth is not enough. The living God of whom the truth speaks must in its light so be revealed that our whole life is spent in His presence, with the consciousness as clear as in a little child toward its earthly parent—I know for certain my father hears me.

Beloved child of God! You know by experience how little an intellectual apprehension of truth has profited you. Ask God to reveal Himself to you. If you want to live a different prayer-life, bow each time before you pray in silence to worship this God—to wait until there rests on you some right sense of His nearness and readiness to answer. So will you begin to pray with the words, "My God will hear me!"

2. *"My God will hear me." What a wondrous grace!*—Think of God in His infinite majesty, His altogether incomprehensible glory, His unapproachable holiness, sitting on a throne of grace, waiting to be gracious, inviting, encouraging you to pray with His promise: "Call to Me, and I will answer you" (Jer. 33:3). Think of yourself in your nothingness and helplessness as a creature—in your wretchedness and transgressions as a sinner, in your feebleness and unworthiness as a saint—and praise the glory of that grace that allows you to say boldly of your prayer for yourself and others, "My God will hear me." Think of how you are not left to yourself, of what you can accomplish in this wonderful communication with God.

God has united you with Christ. In Him and His name you have your confidence. On the throne He prays with you and for you, and on the footstool of the throne you pray with Him and in Him. His worth and the Father's delight in hearing Him are the measure of your confidence, your assurance of being heard. There is more. Think of the Holy Spirit, the Spirit of God's own Son, sent into your heart to cry, "Abba, Father," and to be in you a Spirit of supplication when you know not what to pray as you should. Think, in all your insignificance and unworthiness, of your being as acceptable as Christ Himself. Think in all your ignorance and weakness, of the Spirit making intercession according to God within you, and cry out, "What wondrous grace! Through Christ I have access to the Father, by the Spirit. I can, I do believe it: My God will hear me."

3. *"My God will hear me."*—*What a deep mystery!*—There are difficulties that cannot but at times arise and perplex even the honest heart. There is the question as to God's sovereign, all-wise, all-disposing will. How can our wishes, often so foolish, and our will, often so selfish, overrule or change that perfect will? Were it not better to leave all to His disposal, who knows what is best and loves to give us the very best? Or how can our prayer change what He has ordained before?

Then there is the question as to the need of persevering prayer and long waiting for the answer. If God is Infinite Love and delighting more to give than we to receive, where is the need for the pleading and wrestling, the urgency, and the long delay of which scripture and experience speak? Arising out of this there is still another question—that of the multitude of apparently vain and unanswered prayers. How many have pleaded for loved ones who die unsaved. How many cry for years for spiritual blessing, and no answer comes. To think of all this tries our faith, and makes us hesitate as we say, "My God will hear me."

Beloved! Prayer, in its power with God and His faithfulness to His promise to hear it is a deep spiritual mystery. To the questions put above, answers can be given that remove some of the difficulty. But, after all, the first and the last that must be said is this: As little as we can comprehend God can we comprehend this, one of the most blessed of His attributes, that He hears prayer. It is a spiritual mystery—nothing less than the mystery of the Holy Trinity. God hears because we pray in His Son, because the Holy Spirit prays in us.

If we have believed and claimed the life of Christ as our health and the fullness of the Spirit as our strength, let us not hesitate to believe in the power of our prayer too. The Holy Spirit can enable us to believe and rejoice in it, even where every question is not yet answered. He will do this as we lay our questionings in God's bosom, trust His faithfulness, and give ourselves humbly to obey His command to pray without ceasing.

Every art unfolds its secrets and its beauty only to the man who practices it. To the humble soul who prays in the obedience of faith, who practices prayer and intercession diligently, because God asks it, the secret of the Lord will be revealed, and the thought of the deep mystery of prayer, instead of being a weary problem, will be a source of rejoicing, adoration, and faith, in which the unceasing refrain is ever heard: "My God will hear me!"

4. *"My God will hear me." What a solemn responsibility!*—How often we complain of darkness, of weakness, of failure as if there was no help for it. And God has promised in answer to our prayer to supply our every need and give us His light and strength and peace. We need to realize the responsibility of having such a God and such promises, with the sin and shame of not availing ourselves of them to the utmost. How confident we should feel that the grace, which we have accepted and trusted to enable us to pray as we should, will be given.

There is more. This access to a prayer-hearing God is specially meant to make us intercessors for our fellowmen. Even as Christ obtained His right of prevailing intercession by His giving Himself a sacrifice to God for men—and through it receives the blessings He dispenses—so if we have truly with Christ given ourselves to God for men, we share His right of intercession, and are able to obtain the powers of the heavenly world for them, too. The power of life and death is in our hands (1 John 5:16). In answer to prayer, the Spirit can be poured out, souls can be converted, believers can be established. In prayer, the kingdom of darkness can be conquered, souls brought out of prison into the liberty of Christ, and the glory of God be revealed. Through prayer, the sword of the Spirit, which is the Word of God, can be wielded in power, and, in public preaching as in private speaking, the most rebellious made to bow at Jesus' feet.

What a responsibility on the Church to give herself to the work of intercession! What a responsibility on every minister, missionary, worker, set apart for the saving of souls, to yield himself wholly to act out and prove his faith: "My God will hear me!" And what a call on every believer, instead of burying and losing this talent, to seek to the very utmost to use it in prayer and supplication for all saints and for all men. My God will hear me: The deeper our entrance into the truth of this wondrous power God has given to men, the more wholehearted will be our surrender to the work of intercession.

5. *"My God will hear me." What a blessed prospect!*—I see it—all the failures of my past life have been due to the lack of this faith. My failure, especially in the work of intercession, has had its deepest root in this—I did not live in the full faith of the blessed assurance, *"My God will hear me!"* Praise God! I begin to see it—I believe it. All can be different. Or, rather, I see Him, I believe Him. *"My God will hear me!"* Yes, me, even me! Commonplace and insignificant though I be, filling but a very little place so that I will hardly be missed when I go—even I have access to this Infinite God, with the confidence that He hears me. One with Christ, led by the Holy Spirit, I dare to say: "I will pray for others, for I am sure my God will listen to me: *'My God will hear me.'*" What a blessed prospect before me—every earthly and spiritual anxiety exchanged for the peace of God, who cares for all and hears prayer. What a blessed prospect in my work—to know that even when the answer is long delayed and there is a call for much patient, persevering prayer, the truth remains infallibly sure—*"My God will hear me!"*

And what a blessed prospect for Christ's Church if we could only all give prayer its place, give faith in God its place, or, rather, *give the prayer-hearing God His place!* Is not this the one great thing those who in some little measure begin to see the urgent need of prayer ought in the first place to pray for? When God at the first, time after time, poured forth the Spirit on His praying people, He laid down the law for all time: as much of prayer, so much of the Spirit. Let each one who can say, "*My God will hear me,*" join in the fervent supplication so that throughout the Church that truth may be restored to its true place and the blessed prospect will be realized: a praying Church endued with the power of the Holy Spirit.

6. *"My God will hear Me." What a need of Divine teaching!*—We need this, both

to enable us to hold this word in living faith and to make full use of it in intercession. It has been said, and it cannot be said too often or too earnestly, that the one thing needed for the Church of our day is the power of the Holy Spirit. It is just because this is so, from the divine side, that we may also say as truly that, from the human side, the one thing needed is more prayer, more believing, persevering prayer. In speaking of lack of the Spirit's power and the condition for receiving it, someone used the expression—the block is not on the perpendicular, but on the horizontal line. It is to be feared that it is on both. There is much to be confessed and taken away in us if the Spirit is to work freely. But it is especially on the perpendicular line that the block is—the upward look, the deep dependence, the strong crying to God, and the effectual prayer of faith that avails—all this is sadly lacking. And just this is the one thing needed.

Shall we not all set ourselves to learn the lesson that will make prevailing prayer possible—the lesson of a faith that always sings, "*My God will hear me*"? Simple and elementary as it is, it needs practice and patience. It needs time and heavenly teaching to learn it correctly. Under the impression of a bright thought or a blessed experience, it may look as if we knew the lesson perfectly. But ever again the need will recur of making this our first prayer—that God who hears prayer would teach us to believe it, and so to pray rightly. If we desire it, we can count on Him He who delights in hearing prayer and answering it. He who gave His Son so that He might always pray for us and with us, and His Holy Spirit to pray in us—we can be sure there is not a prayer that He will hear more certainly than this: that He so reveal Himself as the prayer-hearing God that our whole being may respond, "*My God will hear me*."

FOR FURTHER THOUGHT

1. *How do you know for certain that God hears you when you pray and bring your requests before Him?*
2. *How does knowing that God hears you when you pray strengthen you and motivate you to pray?*
3. *What is our access to a prayer-hearing heavenly Father meant to enable and motivate us to do? In what ways was Christ an example of this?*

13

PAUL: A PATTERN OF PRAYER

"Go. . .and inquire. . .for one called Saul of Tarsus,
for behold, he is praying."
ACTS 9:11

For this reason I obtained mercy, that in me first Jesus Christ might
show all longsuffering, as a pattern to those who
are going to believe on Him for everlasting life.
1 TIMOTHY 1:16

GOD took His own Son and made Him our Example and our Pattern. It sometimes is as if the power of Christ's example is lost in the thought that He in whom there is no sin is not man as we are. Our Lord took Paul, a man of like passions with ourselves, and made him a pattern of what he could do for one who was the chief of sinners (see 1 Tim. 1:15). And Paul, the man who more than any other has set his mark on the Church, has ever been appealed to as a pattern man. In his mastery of divine truth and his teaching of it, in his devotion to his Lord and his self-consuming zeal in His service, in his deep experience of the power of the indwelling Christ and the fellowship of His cross, in the sincerity of his humility and the simplicity and boldness of his faith, in his missionary enthusiasm and endurance—in all this and so much more, "the grace of our Lord Jesus was exceeding abundant" in him (1 Tim. 1:14). Christ gave him, and the Church has accepted him, as a pattern of what Christ would have, of what Christ would work. Seven times Paul speaks of believers following him: "Therefore I urge you, imitate me" (1 Cor. 4:16), "Imitate me, just as I also imitate Christ" (1 Cor. 11:1)—also see Philippians 3:17, 4:9; 1 Thessalonians 1:6; 2 Thessalonians 3:7–9.

If Paul as a pattern of prayer is not as much studied or appealed to as he is in other respects, it is not because he is not in this, too, as remarkable a proof of what grace can do, or because we do not in this respect as much stand in need of the help of his example. A study of Paul as a pattern of prayer will bring a rich reward of instruction and encouragement. The words our Lord used of him at his conversion, "Behold, he is praying" (Acts 9:11), may be taken as the keynote of his life. The heavenly vision that brought him to his knees ever after ruled his life. Christ at the right hand of God, in whom we are blessed with all spiritual blessings, was everything to him. To pray and expect the heavenly power in his work and on his work, from heaven direct by prayer, was the simple outcome of his faith in the glorified One. In this, too, Christ meant him to be a pattern, that we might learn that just in the measure in which the heavenliness of Christ and His gifts—the unworldliness of the powers that work for salvation—are known and believed will prayer become the spontaneous rising of the heart to the only source of its life.

Let us see what we know of Paul.

PAUL'S HABITS OF PRAYER

These are revealed almost unconsciously. He writes, (Rom. 1:9, 11): "God is my witness, whom I serve with my spirit in the gospel of His Son, that without ceasing I make mention of you always in my prayers. . . . For I long to see you, that I may impart to you some spiritual gift, so that you may be established." "*My heart's desire and prayer to God* for Israel is that they may be saved. ... I have great sorrow and *continual grief in my heart.* For I could wish that I myself were accursed from Christ for my brethren" (Rom. 10:1, 9:2–3). "I thank my God *always* concerning you for the grace of God which was given to you by Christ Jesus" (1 Cor. 1:4). "We commend ourselves as ministers of God. . .*in sleeplessness, in fastings*" (2 Cor. 6:4–5). "My little children, for whom I *labor in birth again* until Christ is formed in you" (Gal. 4:19). "I *do not cease* to give thanks for you, making mention of you *in my prayers*" (Eph. 1:16). "I *bow my knees* to the Father. . .that He would grant you. . .to be strengthened with might through His Spirit in the inner man" (Eph. 3:14, 16). "I thank my God *upon every remembrance of you*, always in every prayer of mine making request for you all with joy. . . . For God is my witness, how greatly I long for you all with the affection of Jesus Christ. And this I pray" (Phil. 1:3–4, 8–9). "We give thanks to the God and Father of our Lord Jesus Christ, *praying always for you.* . . . For this reason we also, since the day we heard it, do not cease to pray for you, and to ask. . ." (Col. 1:3, 9). "I want you to know what a *great conflict* I have for you and those in Laodicea, and for as many as have not seen my face in the flesh" (Col. 2:1). "We give thanks to God always for you all, making mention of you *in our prayers*" (1 Thess. 1:2). "We rejoice for your sake before our God, *night and day praying exceedingly* that we may see your face and perfect what is lacking in your faith" (1 Thess. 3:9–10). "We are bound to thank God *always* for you. . . . Therefore *we also pray always* for you" (2 Thess. 1:3, 11). "I thank God. . . as *without ceasing* I remember you in my prayers night and day" (2 Tim. 1:3). "I thank my God, making mention of you *always in my prayers*" (Philem. 4).

These passages taken together give us the picture of a man whose words, "Pray without ceasing" (1 Thess. 5:17), were simply the expression of his daily life. He had such a sense of the insufficiency of simple conversion, of the need of the grace and the power of heaven being brought down for the young converts in prayer, of the need of much and unceasing prayer day and night to bring it down, and of the certainty that prayer would bring it down—that his life was continual and most definite prayer. He had such a sense that everything must come from above and such a faith that it would come in answer to prayer that prayer was neither a duty nor a burden, but the natural turning of the heart to the only place from where it could possibly obtain what it sought for others.

THE CONTENTS OF PAUL'S PRAYERS

It is of as much importance to know *what* Paul prayed as how frequently and earnestly he did so. Intercession is a spiritual work. Our confidence in it will depend much on our knowing that we ask according to the will of God. The more distinctly we ask heavenly things, which we feel at once God alone can bestow and which we are sure He will bestow, the more direct and urgent will our appeal be to God alone. The more impossible the things are that we seek, the more we will turn from all human work to prayer and to God alone.

In the Epistles, in addition to expressions in which he speaks of his praying, we have a number of distinct prayers in which Paul gives utterance to his heart's desire for those to whom he writes. In these, we see that his first desire was always that they might be "established" in the Christian life. Much as he praised God when he heard of conversion, he knew how weak the young converts were and how for their establishing nothing would be accomplished without the grace of the Spirit prayed down. If we notice some of the principals of these prayers we shall see what he asked and obtained.

Take the two prayers in Ephesians—the one for light, the other for strength. In the former (1:15), he prays for the Spirit of wisdom to enlighten them to know what their calling was, what their inheritance, what the mighty power of God working in them. Spiritual enlightenment and knowledge was their great need, to be obtained for them by prayer. In the latter (3:15) he asks that the power they had been led to see in Christ might work in them and that they be strengthened with divine might so as to have the indwelling Christ, the love that passes knowledge, and the fullness of God actually come on them. These were things that could only come directly from heaven, and these were things he asked and expected. If we want to learn Paul's art of intercession, we must ask nothing less for believers in our days.

Look at the prayer in Philippians (1:9–11). There, too, it is first for spiritual knowledge. Then comes a blameless life, and then a fruitful life to the glory of God. So also in the beautiful prayer in Colossians (1:9–11). First, spiritual knowledge and understanding of God's will, then the strengthening with all might to all patience and joy.

Or take the two prayers in 1 Thessalonians (3:12–13 and 5:23). The one: "May the Lord make you increase and abound in love to one another...that He may establish your *hearts blameless in holiness*." The other: "God...sanctify *you completely*; and may your whole spirit, soul, and body be preserved blameless." The very words are so high that we hardly understand—still less believe, still less experience—what they mean. Paul so lived in the heavenly world, he was so at home in the holiness and omnipotence of God and His love, that such prayers were the natural expression of what he knew God could and would do.

> *T*hese were things that could only come directly from heaven, and these were things he asked and expected. If we want to learn Paul's art of intercession, we must ask nothing less for believers in our days.

"The Lord establish your hearts blameless in holiness," "God sanctify you completely"—the man who believes in these things and desires them will pray for them for others. The prayers are all a proof that he seeks for them the very life of heaven on earth. No wonder that he is not tempted to trust in any human means but looks for it from heaven alone. Again, I say, the more we take Paul's prayers as our pattern and make his desires our own for believers for whom we pray, the more will prayer to the God of heaven become as our daily breath.

PAUL'S REQUESTS FOR PRAYER

These are no less instructive than his own prayers for the saints. They prove that he does not count prayer any special prerogative of an apostle. Rather, he calls the humblest and simplest believer to claim his right. They prove that he does not think that only the new converts or feeble Christians need prayer. He himself is, as a member of the body, dependent upon his brethren and their prayers. After he had preached the gospel for twenty years, he still asks for prayer so that he may speak as he ought to speak. Not once for all, not for a time, but day by day, and that without ceasing, must grace be sought and brought down from heaven for his work. United, continued waiting on God is to Paul the only hope of the Church. With the Holy Spirit a heavenly life, the life of the Lord in heaven, entered the world, and nothing but unbroken communication with heaven can keep it up.

Listen how he asks for prayer and with what earnestness—Romans 15:30–32: "I beg you, brethren, through the Lord Jesus Christ, and through the love of the Spirit, that you strive together with me in prayers to God for me, that I may be delivered from those in Judea who do not believe ... that I may come to you with joy by the will of God." How remarkably both prayers were answered: Romans 15:5–6, 13. The remarkable fact that the Roman world power, which in Pilate with Christ, in Herod with Peter, and at Philippi had proved its antagonism to God's kingdom, all at once becomes Paul's protector and secures him a safe convoy to Rome, can only be accounted for by these prayers.

"In whom we trust that He will still deliver us, *you also helping together in prayer for us*" (2 Cor. 1:10–11). "Praying always with all prayer and supplication in the Spirit...for all the saints—*and for me*...that I may open my mouth boldly. . .that in it I may speak boldly, as I ought to speak" (Eph. 6:18–20). "I know that this (trouble) will turn out for my deliverance *through your prayer* and the supply of the Spirit of Jesus Christ" (Phil. 1:19). "Continue earnestly in prayer. . .meanwhile *praying also for us,* that God would open to us a door for the word, to speak the mystery of Christ. . .that I may make it manifest, as I ought to speak" (Col. 4:2–4). "Brethren, pray for us" (1 Thess. 5:25). "I trust that through your prayers I shall be granted to you" (Philem. 22).

We saw how Christ prayed and taught His disciples to pray. We see how Paul prayed and taught the churches to pray. As the Master, so the servant calls us to believe and to prove that prayer is the power alike of the ministry and the Church. Of his faith we have a summary in these remarkable words concerning something that caused him grief: "This will turn out for my deliverance through your prayer and the supply of the Spirit of Jesus Christ." As much as he looked to his Lord in heaven did he look to his brethren on earth to secure the supply of that Spirit for him. The Spirit from heaven and prayer on earth were to him, as to the twelve after Pentecost, inseparably linked. We speak often of apostolic zeal and devotion and power—may God give us a revival of apostolic prayer.

Let me once again ask the question: Does the work of intercession take the place in the Church it ought to have? Is it a thing commonly understood in the Lord's work, that everything depends upon getting from God that "supply of the Spirit of Christ" for and in ourselves that can give our work its real power to bless? This is Christ's divine order for all work. His own and that of His servants. This is the order Paul followed: First come every day, as having nothing, and receive from God "the supply of the Spirit" in intercession—then go and impart what has come to you from heaven.

> *he Spirit from heaven and prayer on earth were to him, inseparably linked. We speak often of apostolic zeal and devotion and power—may God give us a revival of apostolic prayer.*

In all His instructions, our Lord Jesus spoke much more often to His disciples about their praying than their preaching. In the farewell discourse, He said little about preaching, but much about the Holy Spirit and their asking whatever they would in His Name. If we are to return to this life of the first apostles and of Paul and really accept the truth every day—my first work, my only strength is intercession, to secure the power of God on the souls entrusted to me—we must have the courage to confess past sin, and to believe that there is deliverance. To break through old habits, to resist the clamor of pressing duties that have always had their way, to make every other call subordinate to this one, whether others approve or not, will not be easy at first. But the men or women who are faithful will not only have a reward themselves, but become benefactors to their brethren. "You shall be called the Repairer of the Breach, the Restorer of Streets to Dwell in" (Isa. 58:12).

But is it really possible? Can it indeed be that those who have never been able to face, much less to overcome the difficulty can yet become mighty in prayer? Tell me, was it really possible for Jacob to become Israel—a prince who prevailed with God? It was. The things that are impossible with men are possible with God. Have you not in very deed received from the Father, as the great fruit of Christ's redemption, the Spirit of supplication, the Spirit of intercession? Just pause and think what that means. And will you still doubt whether God is able to make you "strivers with God," princes who prevail with Him? Oh, let us banish all fear and in faith claim the grace for which we have the Holy Spirit dwelling in us, the grace of supplication, the grace of intercession. Let us quietly, perseveringly believe that He lives in us and will enable us to do our work. Let us in faith not fear to accept and yield to the great truth that intercession, as it is the great work of the King on the throne, *is the great work of His servants on earth.* We have the Holy Spirit who brings the Christ-life into our hearts, to make us fit for this work. Let us immediately begin and stir up the gift within us. As we set aside each day our time for intercession and count upon the Spirit's enabling power, the confidence will grow that we can, in our measure, follow Paul even as he followed Christ.

FOR FURTHER THOUGHT

1. *What was the outcome of Paul's faith in the glorified Jesus Christ? How did faith affect His prayer life?*
2. *Read Paul's prayers in Philippians 1:9–11 and Colossians 1:9–11. What was the content of those prayers, and how important is it for you today to pray for the same things?*
3. *How should you personally pray so that the ministry of intercession has its rightful place in the Church and in your own prayer life? How did Paul pray so that this would happen in the Church of his day?*

14

God Seeks Intercessors

I have set watchmen on your walls, O Jerusalem;
they shall never hold their peace day or night. You who make
mention of the Lord, do not keep silent, and give Him
no rest till He establishes and till He makes
Jerusalem a praise in the earth.
Isaiah 62:6–7

He saw that there was no man,
and wondered that there was no intercessor.
Isaiah 59:16

"I looked, but there was no one to help,
and I wondered that there was no one to uphold."
Isaiah 63:5

There is no one who calls on Your name,
who stirs himself up to take hold of You.
Isaiah 64:7

"So I sought for a man among them who would make a wall,
and stand in the gap before Me on behalf of the land,
that I should not destroy it; but I found no one."
Ezekiel 22:30

"I chose you and appointed you that you should go
and bear fruit. . .that whatever you ask the
Father in My name He may give you."
John 15:16

In the study of the starry heavens, how much depends upon a due apprehension of magnitudes. Without some sense of the size of the heavenly bodies that appear so small to the eye and yet are so great, and of the almost illimitable extent of the regions in which they move, though they appear so near and so familiar, there can be no true knowledge of the heavenly world or its relation to this earth. It is even so with the spiritual heavens and the heavenly life in which we are called to live. It is especially so in the life of intercession, that most wondrous communication between heaven and earth. Everything depends upon the due apprehension of magnitudes.

Just think of the three that come first: There is a world, with its needs entirely dependent on and waiting to be helped by intercession. There is a God in heaven, with His all-sufficient supply for all those needs, waiting to be asked. And there is a Church, with its wondrous calling and its sure promises, waiting to be roused to a sense of its wondrous responsibility and power.

God seeks intercessors—There is a world with its perishing millions, with intercession as its only hope. How much of love and work is comparatively vain because there is so little intercession. A thousand millions living as if there never had been a Son of God to die for them. Thirty millions every year passing into the outer darkness without hope. Fifty millions bearing the Christian name, and the great majority living in utter ignorance or indifference. Millions of weak, sickly Christians and thousands of wearied workers, who could be blessed by intercession, could help themselves to become mighty in intercession. Churches and missions sacrificing life and labor often with little result, for lack of intercession. Souls, each one worth more than worlds, worth nothing less than the price paid for them in Christ's blood, and within reach of the power that can be won by intercession. We surely have no conception of the magnitude of the work to be done by God's intercessors, or we should cry to God above everything to give from heaven the spirit of intercession.

God seeks intercessors—There is a God of glory able to meet all these needs. We are told that He delights in mercy, that He waits to be gracious, that He longs to pour out His blessing, that the love that gave the Son to death is the measure of the love that each moment hovers over every human being. And yet He does not help. And there they perish, a million a month in China alone, and it is as if God does not move. If He does so love and long to bless, there must be some inscrutable reason for His holding back. What can it be? Scripture says, because of your unbelief. It is the faithlessness and consequent unfaithfulness of God's people. He has taken them up into partnership with Himself. He has honored them and bound Himself by making their prayers one of the standard measures of the working of His power. Lack of intercession is one of the chief causes of lack of blessing. Oh, that we would turn eye and heart from everything else and fix them on this God who hears prayer, until the magnificence of His promises, His power, and His purpose of love overwhelmed us! How our whole life and heart would become intercession.

God seeks intercessors—There is a third magnitude to which our eyes must be opened: the wondrous privilege and power of the intercessors. There is a false humility that makes a great virtue of self-depreciation, because it has never seen its utter nothingness. If it knew that, it would never apologize for its feebleness but glory in its utter weakness as the one condition of Christ's power resting on it. It would judge of itself, its power and influence before God in prayer, as little by what it sees or feels, as we judge of the size of the sun or stars by what the eye can see.

Faith sees man created in God's image and likeness to be God's representative in this world and have dominion over it. Faith sees man redeemed and lifted into union with Christ, abiding in Him, identified with Him, and clothed with His power in intercession. Faith sees the Holy Spirit dwelling and praying in the heart, making, in our sighings, intercession according to God. Faith sees the intercession of the saints to be part of the life of the holy Trinity—the believer as God's child asking of the Father, in the Son, through the Spirit. Faith sees something of the divine fitness and beauty of this scheme of salvation through intercession, wakens the soul to a consciousness of its wondrous destiny, and girds it with strength for the blessed self-sacrifice it calls to.

> *God* seeks intercessors—He longs to dispense larger blessings. He longs to reveal His power and glory as God, His saving love, more abundantly. He seeks intercessors in larger number, in greater power, to prepare the way of the Lord.

God seeks intercessors—When He called His people out of Egypt, He separated the priestly tribe to draw near to Him, stand before Him, and bless the people in His name. From time to time He sought and found and honored intercessors, for whose sake He spared or blessed His people. When our Lord left the earth, He said to the inner circle He had gathered around Him—an inner circle of special devotion to His service, to which access is still free to every disciple: "I chose you and appointed you that. . .that whatever you ask the Father in My name He may give you" (John 15:16).

We have already noticed the six times repeated three wonderful words— *Whatever—In My name—It shall be done.* In them Christ placed the powers of the heavenly world at their disposal—not for their own selfish use, but in the interests of His kingdom. How wondrously they used it we know. And since that time, down through the ages, these men have had their successors, men who have proved how surely God works in answer to prayer. And we may praise God that, in our days, too, there is an ever-increasing number who begin to see and prove that in church and mission, in large societies and little circles and individual effort, intercession is the chief thing, the power that moves God and opens heaven. They are learning, and long to learn better, and that all may learn, that in all work for souls intercession must take the first place, and that those who in it have received from heaven, in the power of the Holy Spirit, what they are to communicate to others, will be best able to do the Lord's work.

God seeks intercessors—Though God had His appointed servants in Israel, watchmen set by Himself to cry to Him day and night and give Him no rest. He often had to wonder and complain that there was no intercessor, none to stir himself up to take hold of His strength. And He still waits and wonders in our day that there are not more intercessors, that all His children do not give themselves to this highest and holiest work, that many of them who do so do not engage in it more intensely and perseveringly. He wonders to find ministers of His gospel complaining that their duties do not allow them to find time for this, which He counts their first, their highest, their most delightful, their alone effective work. He wonders to find His sons and daughters who have forsaken home and friends for His sake and the gospel's, come so short in what He meant to be their abiding strength—receiving day by day all they needed to impart to the dark heathen. He wonders to find multitudes of His children who have hardly any idea of what intercession is. He wonders to find multitudes more who have learned that it is their duty and seek to obey it, but confess that they know but little of taking hold on God or prevailing with Him.

> *The* effort to bring this message of God may cause much heart-searching and humiliation. All the better. The best practice in doing a thing is helping others to do it.

God seeks intercessors—He longs to dispense larger blessings. He longs to reveal His power and glory as God, His saving love, more abundantly. He seeks intercessors in larger number, in greater power, to prepare the way of the Lord. He seeks them. Where could He seek them but in His Church? And how does He expect to find them? He entrusted to His church the task of telling of their Lord's need, the task of encouraging and training and preparing them for His holy service. And He constantly comes again, seeking fruit, seeking intercessors. In His Word, He has spoken of "she who is really a widow...trusts in God and continues in supplications and prayers night and day" (1 Tim. 5:5). He looks if the Church is training the great army of aged men and women whose time of outward work is past but who can strengthen the army of the "elect who cry out day and night to Him" (Luke 18:7). He looks to the great host of the Christian Endeavor, the three or four million of young lives that have given themselves away in the solemn pledge, "I promise the Lord Jesus Christ that I will strive to do whatever He would like to have me do," and wonders how many are being trained to pass from the brightness of the weekly prayer meeting and its confession of loyalty to swell the secret intercession that is to save souls. He looks to the thousands of young men and young women in training for the work of ministry and mission, and gazes longingly to see if the Church is teaching them that intercession, power with God, must be their first care, and in seeking to train and help them to it. He looks to see whether ministers and missionaries are understanding their opportunity, and laboring to train the believers of their congregation into those who can "help together" by their prayer, and can "strive with them in their prayers" (see Rom. 15:30). As Christ seeks the lost sheep until He finds it, Gods seeks intercessors. (Appendix 6)

God seeks intercessors—He will not, He cannot, take the work out of the hands of His Church. And so He comes, calling and pleading in many ways. Now by a man whom He raises up to live a life of faith in His service and to prove how actually and abundantly He answers prayer. Then by the story of a church that makes prayer for souls its starting point and bears testimony to God's faithfulness. Sometimes in a mission that proves how special prayer can meet special need and bring down the power of the Spirit. And sometimes again by a season of revival coming in answer to united urgent supplication. In these and many other ways, God is showing us what intercession can do and asking us to waken up and train His great host to be, every one, a people of intercessors.

God seeks intercessors—He sends His servants out to call them. Let ministers make this a part of their duty. Let them make their church a training school of intercession. Give the people definite objects for prayer. Encourage them to take a definite time to it, even if it were only ten minutes every day. Help them to understand the boldness they may use with God. Teach them to expect and look out for answers. Show them what it is first to pray and get an answer in secret, and then carry the answer and impart the blessing. Tell everyone who is master of his own time that he is as the angels—free to tarry before the throne and then go out and minister to the heirs of salvation. Sound out the blessed tidings that this honor is for all God's people. There is no difference. That servant girl, this day laborer, that bedridden invalid, this daughter in her mother's home, these men and young men in business—all are called, all, all are needed. God seeks intercessors.

God seeks intercessors—As ministers take up the work of finding and training them, it will urge themselves to pray more. Christ gave Paul to be a pattern of His grace before He made him a preacher of it. It has been well said, "The first duty of a clergyman is humbly to beg of God that all he would have done in his people may be first truly and fully done in himself." The effort to bring this message of God may cause much heart-searching and humiliation. All the better. The best practice in doing a thing is helping others to do it.

O ye servants of Christ set as watchmen to cry to God day and night, let us awake to our holy calling. Let us believe in the power of intercession. Let us practice it. Let us seek on behalf of our people to get from God Himself the Spirit and the life we preach. With our spirit and life given up to God in intercession, the Spirit and life that God gives them through us cannot fail to be the life of intercession, too.

FOR FURTHER THOUGHT

1. *For what specific purposes does God seek intercessors, people who will pour out their hearts and offer their requests on behalf of others, in the church today?*
2. *For what specific needs is God calling you to be an intercessor today? How can you know that He has called you to pray for those needs?*
3. *Why can't and won't God take the work of intercession out of the hands of His people today?*

15

The Coming Revival

Will You not revive us again,
that Your people may rejoice in You?
PSALM 85:6

O LORD, revive Your work in the midst of the years!
HABAKKUK 3:2

Though I walk in the midst of trouble, You will
revive me. . .and Your right hand will save me.
PSALM 138:7

"I dwell. . .with him who has a contrite and humble spirit. . .
to revive the heart of the contrite ones."
ISAIAH 57:15

Come, and let us return to the LORD; for He has torn,
but He will heal us. . .He will revive us.
HOSEA 6:1–2

THE coming revival—one frequently hears the word. There are more than a few teachers who see the signs of its approach and confidently herald its speedy appearance. In the increase of mission interest, in the tidings of revivals in places where all were dead or cold, in the hosts of our young gathered into Students' and other Associations or Christian Endeavor Societies, in doors everywhere opened in the Christian and the heathen world, in victories already secured in the fields white to the harvest, wherever believing, hopeful workers enter, they find the assurance of a time of power and blessing such as we have not known. The Church is about to enter on a new era of increasing spirituality and larger extension.

There are others who, while admitting the truth of some of these facts, yet fear that the conclusions drawn from them are one-sided and premature. They see the interest in missions increased, but point out to how small a circle it is confined and how utterly out of proportion it is to what it ought to be. To the great majority of

Church members, to the greater part of the Church, it is as yet anything but a life question. They remind us of the power of worldliness and formality, of the increase of the money-making and pleasure-loving spirit among professing Christians, to the lack of spirituality in so many of our churches, and the continuing and apparently increasing estrangement of multitudes from God's Day and Word as proof that the great revival has certainly not begun, and is hardly thought of by the most. They say that they do not see the deep humiliation, the intense desire, the fervent prayer that appear as the forerunners of every true revival.

There are right-hand and left-hand errors that are equally dangerous. We must seek as much to be kept from the superficial optimism, which never is able to gauge the extent of the evil, as from the hopeless pessimism, which can neither praise God for what He has done nor trust Him for what He is ready to do. The former will lose itself in a happy self-congratulation as it rejoices in its zeal and diligence and apparent success, and never see the need of confession and great striving in prayer before we are prepared to meet and conquer the hosts of darkness. The latter virtually gives over the world to Satan and almost prays and rejoices to see things get worse, to hasten the coming of Him who is to put all right. May God keep us from either error, and fulfill the promise, "Your ears shall hear a word behind you, saying, 'This is the way, walk in it,' whenever you turn to the right hand or whenever you turn to the left" (Isa. 30:21). Let us listen to the lessons suggested by the passages we have quoted. They may help us to pray the prayer rightly: "Revive Your work, O Lord!"

1. *"Revive Thy work, O Lord!"*—Read again the passages of scripture and see how they all contain the one thought: Revival is God's work, He alone can give it, and it must come from above. We are frequently in danger of looking to what God has done and is doing and to count on that as the pledge that He will at once do more. And all the time it may be true that He is blessing us up to the measure of our faith or self-sacrifice and cannot give larger measure until there has been a new discovery and confession of what is hindering Him. Or we may be looking to all the signs of life and good around us and congratulating ourselves on all the organizations and agencies that are being created, while the need of God's mighty and direct interposition is not rightly felt, and the entire dependence upon Him not cultivated.

Regeneration, the giving of divine life, we all acknowledge to be God's act, a miracle of His power. The restoring or reviving of the divine life, in a soul or a Church, is as much a supernatural work. To have the spiritual discernment that can understand the signs of the heavens and prognosticate the coming revival, we need to enter deeply into God's mind and will as to its conditions, and the preparedness of those who pray for it or are to be used to bring it about. "Surely the Lord GOD does nothing, unless He reveals His secret to His servants the prophets" (Amos 3:7). It is God who is to give the revival. It is God who reveals His secret, and it is the spirit of absolute dependence upon God, giving Him the honor and the glory, that will prepare for it.

2. *"Revive Your work, O Lord!"*—A second lesson suggested is that the revival God is to give will be given in answer to prayer. It must be asked and received directly from God Himself. Those who know anything about the history of revivals will remember how often this has been proved—both larger and more local revivals have been distinctly traced to special prayer. In our own day, there are numbers of congregations and missions where special or permanent revivals are—all glory be to God—connected with systematic, believing prayer. The coming revival will be no exception. An extraordinary spirit of prayer, urging believers to much secret and united prayer, pressing them to "labor fervently" in their supplications, will be one of the surest signs of approaching showers and floods of blessing.

Let all who are burdened with the lack of spirituality, with the low state of the life of God in believers, listen to the call that comes to all. If there is to be revival—a mighty, divine revival—it will need, on our part, corresponding whole-heartedness in prayer and faith. Let not one believer think of himself as too weak to help, or imagine that he will not be missed. If he first begin, the gift that is in him may be so stirred that, for his circle or neighborhood, he shall be God's chosen intercessor. Let us think of the need of souls, of all the sins and failings among God's people, of the little power there is in so much of the preaching, and begin to cry every day, "Will You not revive us again, that Your people may rejoice in You?" And let us have the truth graven deep in our hearts: every revival comes, as Pentecost came, as the fruit of united, continued prayer. The coming revival must begin with a great prayer revival. It is in the closet, with the door shut, that the sound of abundance of rain will be first heard. An increase of secret prayer with ministers and members will be the sure harbinger of blessing.

3. *"Revive Your work, O Lord!"*—A third lesson our texts teach is that it is to the humble and contrite that the revival is promised. We want the revival to come upon the proud and the self-satisfied, to break them down and save them. God will give this, but only on the condition that those who see and feel the sin of others take their burden of confession and bear it, and that all who pray for and claim in faith God's reviving power for His Church shall humble themselves with the confession of its sins. The need of revival always points to previous decline, and decline was always caused by sin. Humiliation and contrition have always been the conditions of revival. In all intercession, confession of man's sin and God's righteous judgment is always an essential element.

Throughout the history of Israel we continually see this. It comes out in the reformations under the pious Kings of Judah. We hear it in the prayer of men like Ezra and Nehemiah and Daniel. In Isaiah and Jeremiah and Ezekiel, as well as in the minor prophets, it is the keynote of all the warning as of all the promise. If there is no humiliation and forsaking of sin, there can be no revival or deliverance: "These men have set up their idols in their hearts.... Should I let Myself be inquired of at all by them?" (Ezek. 14:3). "On this one will I look: On him who is poor and of a contrite spirit, and who trembles at My word" (Isa. 66:2). Amid the most gracious promises of divine visitation there is ever this note: "Be ashamed and confounded for your own ways, O house of Israel!" (Ezek. 36:32).

We find the same in the New Testament. The Sermon on the Mount promises the kingdom to the poor and those who mourn. In the Epistles to the Corinthians and Galatians, the religion of man, of worldly wisdom and confidence in the flesh, is exposed and denounced. Without its being confessed and forsaken, all the promises of grace and the Spirit will be vain. In the Epistles to the seven churches, we find five of which He, out of whose mouth goes the sharp, two-edged sword, says, that He has something against them. In each of these the keyword of His message is—not to the unconverted, but to the Church—Repent! All the glorious promises that each of these Epistles contain, down to the last one, with its "Open the door and I will come in" (see Rev. 3:20) and "He who overcomes shall sit with Me on My throne" (see Rev. 3:21) are dependent on that one word—Repent!

> Read again the passages of scripture and see how they all contain the one thought: Revival is God's work, He alone can give it, and it must come from above.

And if there is to be a revival, not among the unsaved but in our churches, to give a holy, spiritual membership, will not that trumpet sound need to be heard—Repent? Was it only in Israel, in the ministry of kings and prophets, that there was so much evil in God's people to be cleansed away? Was it only in the church of the first century that Paul and James and our Lord Himself had to speak such sharp words? Or is there not in the Church of our days an idolatry of money and talent and culture, a worldly spirit, making it unfaithful to its one only Husband and Lord, a confidence in the flesh which grieves and resists God's Holy Spirit? Is there not almost everywhere a confession of the lack of spirituality and spiritual power?

Let all who long for the coming revival and seek to hasten it by their prayers, pray above everything that the Lord may prepare His prophets to go before Him at His bidding: "Cry aloud, spare not; lift up your voice like a trumpet; tell My people their transgression" (Isa. 58:1). Every deep revival among God's people must have its roots in a deep sense and confession of sin. Until those who want to lead the Church in the path of revival bear faithful testimony against the sins of the Church, it is feared that it will find people unprepared. Men would desire to have a revival as the outgrowth of their agencies and progress. God's way is the opposite: It is out of death, acknowledged as the desert of sin, confessed as utter helplessness, that He revives. He revives the heart of the contrite one.

4. *"Revive Your work, O Lord!"*— There is a last thought, suggested by the text from Hosea. It is as we return to the Lord that revival will come, for if we had not wandered from Him, His life would be among us in power. "Come, and let us return to the LORD; for He has torn, but He will heal us; He has stricken, but He will bind us up. . . . *He will revive us. . .*that we may live in His sight" (6:1–2). As we have said, there can be no return to the Lord, where there is no sense or confession of wandering.

Let us return to the Lord must be the keynote of the revival. Let us return, acknowledging and forsaking whatever there has been in the Church that is not entirely according to His mind and spirit. Let us return, yielding up and casting out whatever there has been in our religion or along with it of the power of God's two great enemies—confidence in the flesh or the spirit of the world. Let us return in the acknowledgment of how undividedly God must have us, to fill us with His Spirit and use us for the kingdom of His Son. Oh, let us return, in the surrender of a dependence and a devotion that has no measure but the absolute claim of Him who is the Lord! Let us return to the Lord with our whole heart so that He may make and keep us wholly His. He will revive us, and we shall live in His sight. Let us turn to the God of Pentecost, as Christ led His disciples to turn to Him, and the God of Pentecost will turn to us.

It is for this returning to the Lord that the great work of intercession is needed. It is here the coming revival must find its strength. Let us begin as individuals in secret to plead with God, confessing whatever we see of sin or hindrance in ourselves or others. If there were not one other sin, surely in the lack of prayer there is matter enough for repentance and confession and returning to the Lord. Let us seek to foster the spirit of confession and supplication and intercession in those around us. Let us help to encourage and to train those who think themselves too weak. Let us lift up our voice to proclaim the great truths. The revival must come from above. The revival must be received in faith from above and brought down by prayer. The revival comes to the humble and contrite, for them to carry to others if we return to the Lord with our whole heart. He will revive us. On those who see these truths rests the solemn responsibility of giving themselves up to witness for them and to act them out.

And as each of us pleads for the revival throughout the Church, let us especially, at the same time, cry to God for our own neighborhood or sphere of work. Let, with every minister and worker, there be "great searchings of heart" (see Ps. 139:23) as to whether they are ready to give such proportion of time and strength to prayer as God would have. Let them, even as in public they are leaders of their larger or smaller circles, give themselves in secret to take their places in the front rank of the great intercession host that must prevail with God before the great revival, the floods of blessing, can come. Of all who speak or think of, or long for, revival, let not one hold back in this great work of honest, earnest, definite pleading: Revive Your work, O Lord! Will You not revive us again?

Come and let us return to the Lord: He will revive us! And let us know, let us follow on to know the Lord. "*His going forth* is established as the morning; *He will come to us* like the rain, like the latter and former rain to the earth" (Hos. 6:3). Amen. So be it.

FOR FURTHER THOUGHT

1. *What part should prayer play in bringing in spiritual revival among the people of God? What part do you think He wants you to play?*
2. *What heart attitude must we as a church and as individuals approach God if we are to see spiritual revival today?*
3. *God promises His people revival if they will meet certain conditions. What are those conditions, and what can you personally do to meet them?*

APPENDICES

Just this day I have been meeting a very earnest lady missionary from India. She confesses and mourns the lack of prayer. But—in India at least—it can hardly be otherwise. You have only the morning hours, from six to eleven, for your work. Some have attempted to rise at four and get the time they think they need, and have suffered and had to give it up. Some have tried to take time after lunch and been found asleep on their knees. You are not your own master, and must act with others. No one who has not been in India can understand the difficulty. Sufficient time for much intercession cannot be secured.

Were it only in the heat of India the difficulty existed, one might be silent. But, sadly, in the coldest winter in London, and in the moderate climate of South Africa, there is the same trouble everywhere. If once we really felt—*intercession is the most important part of our work*, the securing of God's presence and power in full measure is the essential thing, this is one first duty—our hours of work would all be made subordinate to this one thing.

May God show us all whether there indeed is an insurmountable difficulty for which we are not responsible, whether it is only a mistake we are making, or a sin by which we are grieving Him and hindering His Spirit!

If we ask the question George Müller once asked of a Christian who complained that he could not find time sufficient for the study of the Word and prayer, whether an hour less work, say four hours, with the soul dwelling in the full light of God, would not be more prosperous and effective than five hours with the depressing consciousness of unfaithfulness, and the loss of the power that could be obtained in prayer, the answer will not be difficult. The more we think of it, the more we feel that when earnest, godly workers allow, against their better will, the spiritual to be crowded out by incessant occupation and the fatigue it brings, it must be because the spiritual life is not sufficiently strong in them to command the lever stand aside until the presence of God in Christ and the power of the Spirit have been fully secured.

Let us listen to Christ saying, "Render to Caesar the things that are Caesar's"—let duty and work have their place—"and to God the things that are God's" (Mark 12:17). Let the worship in the Spirit, the entire dependence and continued waiting upon God for the full experience of His presence and power every day, and the strength of Christ working in us, always have the first place. The whole question is simply this. Is God to have the place, the love, the trust, the time for personal fellowship He claims, so that all our working shall be God working in us?

Let me tell here a story that occurs in one of Dr. Boardman's works. He had been invited by a lady of good position, well known as a successful worker among her husband's dependents, to come and address them. "And then," she added, "I want to speak to you about a bit of bondage of my own." When he had addressed her meeting and found many brought to Christ through her, he wondered what her trouble might be. She soon told him. God had blessed her work, but, sadly, the enjoyment she once had had in God's Word and secret prayer had been lost. And she had tried her utmost to get it back, and had failed. "Ah! that is just your mistake," he said. "How is that? Ought I not to do my best to have the coldness removed?" "Tell me," he said, "were you saved by doing your best?" "Oh, no! I tried long to do that, but only found rest when I ceased trying and trusted Christ." "And that is what you need to do now. Enter your closet at the appointed time, however dull you feel, and place yourself before your Lord. Do not try to rouse an earnestness you do not feel, but quietly say to Him that He sees how all is wrong, how helpless you are, and trust Him to bless you. He will do it as you trust quietly. His Spirit will work."

The simple story may teach many a Christian a most blessed lesson in the life of prayer. You have accepted of Christ Jesus to make you whole and give you strength to walk in newness of life. You have claimed the Holy Spirit to be in you the Spirit of supplication and intercession. But do not wonder if your feelings are not all at once changed, or if your power of prayer does not come in the way you would like. It is a life of faith. By faith we receive the Holy Spirit and all His workings. Faith regards neither sight nor feeling, but rests, even when there appears to be no power to pray, in the assurance that the Spirit is praying in us as we bow quietly before God. He who waits this way in faith and honors the Holy Spirit and yields himself to Him will soon find that prayer will begin to come. And he who perseveres in the faith that through Christ and by the Spirit each prayer, however weak, is acceptable to God, will learn the lesson that it is possible to be taught by the Spirit and led to walk worthy of the Lord to all well pleasing.

APPENDIX 3 (CHAPTER 9)

Just yesterday again—three days after the conversation mentioned in the Appendix to chapter 7—I met a devoted young missionary lady from the interior. As a conversation on prayer was proceeding, she interposed unasked with the remark, "But it is really impossible to find the time to pray as we wish to." I could only answer, "Time is a quantity that accommodates itself to our will. What our hearts really consider of first importance in the day we will soon succeed in finding time for."

It must surely be that the ministry of intercession has never been put before our students in Theological Halls and Missionary Training Homes as the most important part of their life-work. We have thought of our work in preaching or visiting as our real duty, and of prayer as a subordinate means to do this work successfully. Would not the whole position be changed if we regarded the ministry of intercession as the chief thing—*getting the blessing and power of God* for the souls entrusted to us? Then our work would take its right place and become the subordinate one of really dispensing blessings which we had received from God.

It was when the friend at midnight, in answer to his prayer, had received from Another as much as he needed that he could supply his hungry friend. It was the intercession, going out and persisting, that was the difficult work. Returning home with his rich supply to impart was easy, joyful work. This is Christ's divine order for all your work, my brother: First come in utter poverty, every day, and get from God the blessing in intercession, then go rejoicingly to impart it.

APPENDIX 4 (CHAPTER 10)

Let me once again refer my readers to William Law and repeat what I have said before, that no book has so helped me to an insight into the place and work of the Holy Spirit in the economy of redemption as his *Address to the Clergy*.[40]

The way in which he opens up how God's one object was to dwell in man, making him partaker of His goodness and glory, other way than by Himself living and working in him, gives one the key to what Pentecost and the sending forth of the Spirit of God's Son into our hearts really means. It is Christ in God's name really regaining and retaking possession of the home He had created for Himself. It is God entering into the secret depths of one nature there to "work to will and to do" (Phil. 2:13) and to "work in you what is well pleasing in His sight though Christ Jesus" (Heb. 13:21). It is as this truth enters into us and we see that there is and can be no good in us but what God works, that we shall see light on the divine mystery of prayer and believe in the Holy Spirit as breathing within us desires that God will fulfill when we yield to them and believingly present them in the name of Christ. We shall then see that just as wonderful and prevailing as the intercession and prayer passing from the Incarnate Son to the Father in heaven is one communication with God—the Spirit, who is God, breathing and praying in us amid all our weakness His heaven-born divine petitions. What a heavenly thing prayer becomes.

The latter part of the above-mentioned book consists of extracts from Law's letters. These have been published separately as a little shilling volume.[41] No one who will take the time quietly to read and master the so simple but deep teaching they contain, without being wonderfully strengthened in the confidence that is needed if we are to pray much and boldly. As we learn that the Holy Spirit is within us to reveal Christ there, to make us in living reality partakers of His death, His life, His merit, and His disposition so that He is formed within us, we will begin to see how divinely right and sure it is that our intercessions in His name must be heard. His own Spirit maintains the living union with Himself, in whom we are brought near to God and gives us boldness of access. What I have so weakly

---

[40] *The Power of the Spirit: An Address to the Clergy*. By William Law. With additional Extracts and an Introduction by Rev. A.M. James Nisbet & Co.

[41] *The Divine Indwelling. Selections from the Letters of William Law*. With introduction by A.M. James Nisbet & Co.

said in the chapter on the Spirit of supplication will get new meaning, and, what is more, the exercise of prayer a new attractiveness—its solemn divine mystery will humble us, its unspeakable privilege lift us up in faith and adoration.

APPENDIX 5 (CHAPTER 11)

There is a question, the deepest of all, on which I have not entered in this book. I have spoken of the lack of prayer in the individual Christian as a symptom of a disease. But what shall we say of it that there is such a widespread prevalence of this failure to give a due proportion of time and strength to prayer? Do we not need to inquire how comes it that the Church of Christ, provided with the Holy Ghost, cannot train its ministers and workers and members to place first what is first? How comes it that the confession of too little prayer and the call for more prayer is so frequently heard, and yet the evil continues?

The Spirit of God, the Spirit of supplication and intercession, is in the Church and in every believer. There must surely be some other spirit of great power resisting and hindering this Spirit of God. It is indeed so. The spirit of the world, which under all its beautiful and even religious activities is the spirit of the god of this world, is the great hindrance. Everything that is done on earth, whether within or without the Church, is done by either of these two spirits. What is in the individual, the flesh, is in mankind as a whole the spirit of the world, and all the power the flesh has in the individual is due to the place given to the spirit of this world in the Church and in Christian life. It is the spirit of the world that is the great hindrance to the spirit of prayer. All our most earnest calls to men to pray more will be vain unless this evil is acknowledged and combated and overcome. The believer and the Church must be entirely freed from the spirit of the world.

And how is this to be done? There is but one way—the Cross of Christ, "by whom," as Paul says, "the world is crucified to me, and I to the world" (Gal. 6:14). It is only through death to the world that we can be freed from its spirit. The separation must be vital and entire. It is only through the acceptance of our crucifixion with Christ that we can live out this confession and, as crucified to the world, maintain the position of irreconcilable hostility to whatever is of its spirit and not of the Spirit of God. And it is only God Himself who, by His divine power, can lean us into and keep us daily dead to sin and alive unto God in Christ Jesus. The cross, with its shame and its separation from the world and its death to all that is of flesh and of self, is the only power that can conquer the spirit of the world.

I have felt so strongly that the truth needs to be newly asserted that I hope, if it please God, to publish a volume, *The Cross of Christ*, with the inquiry into what God's Word teaches as to our actual participation with Christ in His crucifixion. Christ prayed on the way to the cross. He prayed Himself to the cross. He prayed on the cross. He prays always as the fruit of the cross. As the Church lives on the cross and the cross lives in the Church, the spirit of prayer will be given. In Christ it was the crucifixion spirit and death that was the source of the intercession spirit and power. With us it cannot be otherwise.

APPENDIX 6 (CHAPTER 14)

I have more than once spoken of the need for training Christians in the work of intercession. In a previous note, I have asked the question whether, in the teaching of our Theological Halls and Mission Training Houses, sufficient attention is given to prayer as the most important, and in some senses the most difficult, part of the work for which the students are being prepared. I have wondered whether it might not be possible to offer those who are willing, during their student life, to put themselves under a course of training, some help in the way of hints and suggestions as to what is needed to give prayer the place and the power in our ministry it ought to have.

As a rule, it is in the student life that the character must be formed for future years, and it is in the present student world that the Church of the future must be influenced. If God allows me to carry out a plan that is hardly quite mature yet, I would wish to publish a volume, *The Student's Prayer Manual*, combining the teaching of scripture as to what is most needed to make men of prayer of us, with such practical directions as may help a young Christian preparing to devote his life to God's service successfully, to cultivate such a spirit and habit of prayer as shall abide with him through all his coming life and labors.

PRAY WITHOUT CEASING

PREFACE

PRAY WITHOUT CEASING. Who can do this? How can one do it who is surrounded by the cares of daily life? How can a mother love her child without ceasing? How can the eyelid without ceasing hold itself ready to protect the eye? How can I breathe and feel and hear without ceasing? Because all these are the functions of a healthy, natural life. And likewise, if the spiritual life is healthy, under the full power of the Holy Spirit, praying without ceasing will be natural.

PRAY WITHOUT CEASING. Does it refer to continual acts of prayer, in which we are to persevere until we obtain, or to the spirit of prayerfulness that should animate us all the day? It includes both. The example of our Lord Jesus shows us this. We have to enter our closet for special seasons of prayer, and we are at times to persevere there in persistent prayer. We are also all the day to walk in God's presence, with the whole heart set upon heavenly things. Without set times of prayer, the spirit of prayer will be dull and weak. Without the continual prayerfulness, the set times will not benefit us.

PRAY WITHOUT CEASING. Does that refer to prayer for ourselves or others? To both. It is because many confine it to themselves that they fail so in practicing it. It is only when the branch gives itself to bear fruit—more fruit, much fruit— that it can live a healthy life and expect a rich inflow of sap. The death of Christ brought Him to the place of everlasting intercession. Your death with Him to sin and self sets you free from the care of self and elevates you to the dignity of intercessor—one who can get life and blessing from God for others. Know your calling; begin this your work. Give yourself completely to it, and before you know it, you will be finding something of this *"Praying always"* within you.

PRAY WITHOUT CEASING. How can I learn it? The best way of learning to do a thing—in fact the only way—is *to do it*. Begin by setting apart some time every day, say ten or fifteen minutes, in which you say to God, and to yourself, that you come to Him now as an intercessor for others. Let it be after your morning or evening prayer, or any other time. If you cannot secure the same time every day, do not be troubled. Only see that you do your work. Christ chose you and appointed you to pray for others. If at first you do not feel any special urgency or faith or power in your prayers, do not let that hinder you. Quietly tell your Lord Jesus of your weakness. Believe that the Holy Spirit is in you to teach you to pray, and be assured that if you begin, God will help you. God cannot help you unless you begin and keep on.

PRAY WITHOUT CEASING. How do I know what to pray for? If once you begin, and think of all the needs around you, you will soon find enough. But to help you, this little book is filled with subjects and hints for prayer for a month. It is meant that we should use it month by month, until we know more fully how to follow the Spirit's leading, and have learned, if need be, to make our own list of subjects, and then can dispense with it. In regard to the use of these helps, a few words may be needed.

1. How to Pray. You notice for every day two headings—the one *What to Pray*, the other, *How to Pray*. If the subjects only were given, one might fall into the routine of mentioning names and things before God, and the work would become a burden. The hints under the heading *How to Pray*, are meant to remind you of the spiritual nature of the work, of the need for divine help, and to encourage faith in the certainty that God, through the Spirit, will give us grace to pray rightly and will also hear our prayer. One does not at once learn to take his place boldly and to dare to believe that he will be heard. Therefore, take a few moments each day to listen to God's voice reminding you of how certainly even you will be heard and calling on you to pray in that faith in your Father, to claim and take the blessing you plead for. And let these words about *How to Pray* enter your hearts and occupy your thoughts at other times, too. The work of intercession is Christ's great work on earth, entrusted to Him because He gave Himself as a sacrifice to God for men. The work of intercession is the greatest work a Christian can do. Give yourself as a sacrifice to God for men, and the work will become your glory and your joy, too.

2. What to Pray. Scripture calls us to pray for many things: for all saints, for all men, for kings and all rulers, for all who are in adversity, for the sending forth of laborers, for those who labor in the gospel, for all converts, for believers who have fallen into sin, for one another in our own immediate circles. The Church is now so much larger than when the New Testament was written, the number of forms of work and workers so much greater, and the needs of the Church and the world so much better known that we need to take time and thought to see where prayer is needed, and to what our hearts are most drawn out. The scripture calls to prayer demand a large heart, taking in all saints and all men and all needs. An attempt has been made in these helps to indicate what the chief subjects are that need prayer and that ought to interest every Christian.

It will be felt difficult by many to pray for such large spheres as are sometimes mentioned. Let it be understood that in each case we may make special intercession for our own circle of interest coming under that heading. And it is hardly necessary to say, further, that where one subject appears of more special interest or urgency than another, we are free for a time, day after day, to take up that subject. If only time be really given to intercession, and the spirit of believing intercession be cultivated, the object is attained. While, on the one hand, the heart must be enlarged at times to take in all, the more pointed and definite our prayer can be, the better. With this view, paper is left blank on which we can write down special petitions we desire to urge before God.

3. ANSWERS TO PRAYER. More than one little book has been published in which Christians may keep a register of their petitions and note when they are answered. Room has been left on every page for this so that more definite petitions with regard to individual souls or special spheres of work may be recorded, and the answer expected. When we pray for all saints, or for missions in general, it is difficult to know when or how our prayer is answered, or whether our prayer has had any part in bringing the answer. It is of extreme importance that we should prove that God hears us, and to this end take note of what answers to look for and when they come. On the day of praying for all saints, take the saints of your congregation or in your prayer meeting, and ask for a revival among them. Take, in connection with missions, some special station or missionary you are interested in, or more than one, and plead for blessing. And expect and look for its coming, that you may praise God.

4. PRAYER CIRCLES. There is no desire in publishing this invitation to intercession to add another to the many existing prayer unions or praying bands. The first object is to stir the many Christians who practically, through ignorance of their calling or unbelief as to their prayer accomplishing much, take but very little part in the work of intercession, and then to help those who do pray to some fuller apprehension of the greatness of the work and the need of giving their whole strength to it. There is a circle of prayer that asks for prayer on the first day of every month for the fuller manifestation of the power of the Holy Spirit throughout the Church. I have given the words of that invitation as subject for the first day, and taken the same thought as keynote throughout. The more one thinks of the need and the promise—and the greatness of the obstacles to be overcome in prayer—the more one feels it must become our life work day by day, that to which every other interest is subordinated.

But while not forming a large prayer union, it is suggested that it may be found helpful to have small prayer circles to unite in prayer, either for one month, with some special object introduced daily along with the others, or through a year or longer, with the view of strengthening each other in the grace of intercession. If a minister were to invite some of his neighboring brethren to join for some special requests along with the printed subjects for supplication, or a number of the more earnest members of his congregation to unite in prayer for revival, some might be trained to take their place in the great work of intercession who now stand idle because no man has hired them.

5. WHO IS SUFFICIENT FOR THESE THINGS? The more we study and try to practice this grace of intercession, the more we become overwhelmed by its greatness and our feebleness. Let every such impression lead us to listen: "My grace is sufficient for you" (2 Cor. 12:9), and to answer truthfully: Our sufficiency is from God. Take courage, for it is in the intercession of Christ you are called to take part. The burden and the agony, the triumph and the victory are all His. Learn from Him, yield to His Spirit in you, to know how to pray. He gave Himself a sacrifice to God for men so that He

might have the right and power of intercession. "He bore the sin of many, and made intercession for the transgressors" (Isa. 53:12). Let faith rest boldly on His finished work. Let your heart wholly identify itself with Him in His death and His life. *Like Him,* give yourself to God a sacrifice for men; it is your highest nobility; it is your true and full union with Him; it will be to you, as to Him, your power of intercession. Beloved Christian! Come and give your whole heart and life to intercession, and you will know its blessedness and its power. God asks nothing less; the world needs nothing less; Christ asks nothing less; let us offer to God nothing less.

DAY 1

What to Pray—For the Power of the Holy Spirit

I bow my knees to the Father. . .that He would grant you,
according to the riches of His glory, to be strengthened
with might through His Spirit. —EPHESIANS 3:14, 16
Wait for the Promise of the Father. —ACTS 1:4

"The fuller manifestation of the grace and energy of the blessed Spirit of God, in the removal of all that is contrary to God's revealed will, so that we do not grieve the Holy Spirit, but that He may work in mightier power in the Church, for the exaltation of Christ and the blessing of souls."

God has one promise to and through His exalted Son; our Lord has one gift to His Church; the Church has one need; all prayer unites in the one petition— the power of the Holy Spirit. Make it your one prayer.

How to Pray—As a Child Asks a Father

"If a son asks for bread from any father among you, will he give him
a stone?. . .How much more will your heavenly Father give the
Holy Spirit to those who ask Him!" —LUKE 11:11, 13

Ask as simply and trustfully as a child asks for bread. You can do this because "God has sent forth the Spirit of His Son into your hearts, crying out, 'Abba, Father!'" (Gal. 4:6). This Spirit is in you to give you childlike confidence. In the faith of His praying in you, ask for the power of that Holy Spirit everywhere. Mention places or circles where you specially ask it to be seen.

Day 2

What to Pray—For the Spirit of Supplication

The Spirit Himself makes
intercession for us. —Romans 8:26

"I will pour on. . .the Spirit of. . .
supplication." —Zechariah 12:10

"The evangelization of the world depends first of all upon a revival of prayer. Deeper than the need of men—yes, deep down at the bottom of our spiritless life—is the need for the forgotten secret of prevailing, world wide prayer."

Every child of God has the Holy Spirit in him to pray. God waits to give the Spirit in full measure. Ask for yourself, and all who join, the outpouring of the Spirit of Supplication. Ask it for your own prayer circle.

How to Pray—In the Spirit

Praying always with all prayer and
supplication in the Spirit. —Ephesians 6:18

Praying in the Holy Spirit. —Jude 20

Our Lord gave His disciples on His resurrection day the Holy Spirit to enable them to wait for the full outpouring on the day of Pentecost. It is only in the power of the Spirit already in us, acknowledged and yielded to, that we can pray for His fuller manifestation. Say to the Father, it is the Spirit of His Son in you urging you to plead His promise.

DAY 3

WHAT TO PRAY—FOR ALL SAINTS

> *Praying always with all prayer and supplication in the Spirit,*
> *being watchful to this end with all perseverance and*
> *supplication for all the saints.* —EPHESIANS 6:18

Every member of a body is interested in the welfare of the whole, and exists to help and complete the others. Believers are one body, and ought to pray, not so much for the welfare of their own church or society, but, first of all, for all saints. This large, unselfish love is the proof that Christ's Spirit and love are teaching them to pray. Pray first for all and then for the believers around you.

HOW TO PRAY—IN THE LOVE OF THE SPIRIT

> *"By this all will know that you are My disciples,*
> *if you have love for one another."* —JOHN 13:35
> *"That they all may be one. . .that the world may*
> *believe that You sent Me."* —JOHN 17:21
> *Now I beg you, brethren, through the Lord Jesus Christ,*
> *and through the love of the Spirit, that you strive together*
> *with me in prayers to God for me.* —ROMANS 15:30
> *Above all things have fervent love*
> *for one another.* —1 PETER 4:8

If we are to pray, we must love. Let us say to God we do love all His saints; let us say we love especially every child of His we know. Let us pray with fervent love, in the love of the Spirit.

DAY 4

WHAT TO PRAY—FOR THE SPIRIT OF HOLINESS

God is the Holy One. His people are a holy people. He speaks: I am holy: I am the Lord who makes you holy. Christ prayed: Sanctify them. Make them holy through Your Truth. Paul prayed: "He may establish your hearts blameless in holiness before our God" (1 Thess. 3:13). God sanctify you wholly!

Pray for all saints—God's holy ones—throughout the Church, that the Spirit of holiness may rule them. Specially for new converts. For the saints in your own neighborhood or congregation. For any you are specially interested in. Think of their special need, weakness, or sin, and pray that God may make them holy.

HOW TO PRAY—TRUSTING IN GOD'S OMNIPOTENCE

The things that are impossible with men are possible with God. When we think of the great things we ask for, of how little likelihood there is of their coming, of our own insignificance, prayer is not only wishing or asking, but believing and accepting. Be still before God and ask Him to let you know Him as the Almighty One, and leave your petitions with Him who does wonders.

Day 5

What to Pray—That God's People May Be Kept from the World

> *"Father, keep through Your name those whom You have given Me. . . . I do not pray that You should take them out of the world, but that You should keep them from the evil one. They are not of the world, just as I am not of the world."*
> —John 17:11, 15–16

In the last night, Christ asked three things of His disciples: that they might be kept as those who are not of the world, that they might be sanctified, and that they might be one in love. You cannot do better than pray as Jesus prayed. Ask for God's people that they may be kept separate from the world and its spirit so that they, by the Spirit, may live as those who are not of the world.

How to Pray—Having Confidence before God

> *Beloved, if our heart does not condemn us, we have confidence toward God. And whatever we ask we receive from Him, because we keep His commandments and do those things that are pleasing in His sight.*
> —1 John 3:21–22

Learn these words by heart. Get them into your heart. Join the ranks of those who, with John, draw near to God with an assured heart, that does not condemn them, having confidence toward God. In this spirit pray for your brother who sins (1 John 5:16). In the quiet confidence of an obedient child, plead for those of your brethren who may be giving way to sin. Pray for all to be kept from the evil. And say often, "What we ask, we receive, because we keep and do."

Day 6

WHAT TO PRAY—FOR THE SPIRIT OF LOVE IN THE CHURCH

> *"That they may be one just as We are one: I in them,*
> *and You in Me. . .that the world may know that You have*
> *sent Me, and have loved them as You have loved Me. . .*
> *that the love with which You loved Me may be in them,*
> *and I in them."* —JOHN 17:22–23, 26
>
> *The fruit of the Spirit is love.* —GALATIANS 5:22

Believers are one in Christ, as He is one with the Father. The love of God rests on them and can dwell in them. Pray that the power of the Holy Spirit may so work this love in believers, that the world may see and know God's love in them. Pray much for this.

HOW TO PRAY—AS ONE OF GOD'S REMEMBRANCERS

> *I have set watchmen upon thy walls, O Jerusalem;*
> *they shall never hold their peace day nor night:*
> *ye that are the LORD's remembrancers,*
> *take ye no rest.* —ISAIAH 62:6 ERV

Study these words until your whole soul be filled with the consciousness, I am appointed intercessor. Enter God's presence in that faith. Study the world's need with that thought—it is my work to intercede; the Holy Spirit will teach me for what and how. Let it be an abiding consciousness: My great lifework, like Christ's, is intercession—to pray for believers and those who do not yet know God.

DAY 7

WHAT TO PRAY—FOR THE POWER OF THE HOLY SPIRIT ON MINISTERS

Now I beg you, brethren. . .that you strive together
with me in prayers to God for me. —ROMANS 15:30

He will still deliver us, you also helping together
in prayer for us. —2 CORINTHIANS 1:10–11

What a great host of ministers there is in Christ's Church. What need they have of prayer. What a power they might be, if they were all clothed with the power of the Holy Sprit. Pray definitely for this; long for it. Think of your minister, and ask it very specially for him. Connect every thought of the ministry, in your town or neighborhood or the world, with the prayer that all may be filled with the Spirit. Plead for them the promise, "Tarry. . .until you are endued with power from on high" (Luke 24:49). "You shall receive power when the Holy Spirit has come upon you" (Acts 1:8).

HOW TO PRAY—IN SECRET

"But you, when you pray, go into your room,
and when you have shut your door, pray to your
Father who is in the secret place." —MATTHEW 6:6

He went up on the mountain by Himself to pray.
—MATTHEW 14:23, JOHN 6:15

Take time to realize, when you are alone with God: Here am I now, face-to-face with God, to intercede for His servants. Do not think you have no influence, or that your prayer will not be missed. Your prayer and faith will make a difference. Cry in secret to God for His ministers.

Day 8

WHAT TO PRAY—FOR THE SPIRIT ON ALL CHRISTIAN WORKERS

> *You also helping together in prayer for us, that thanks may be*
> *given by many persons on our behalf for the gift granted*
> *to us through many.* —2 CORINTHIANS 1:11

What multitudes of workers in connection with our churches and missions, our railways and postmen, our soldiers and sailors, our young men and young women, our fallen men and women, our poor and sick! God be praised for this! What could they not accomplish if each were living in the fullness of the Holy Spirit? Pray for them; it makes you a partner in their work, and you will praise God each time you hear of blessing anywhere.

HOW TO PRAY—WITH DEFINITE PETITIONS

> *"What do you want Me to do for you?"* —LUKE 18:41

The Lord knew what the man wanted, and yet He asked him. The utterance of our wish gives point to the transaction in which we are engaged with God, and so awakens faith and expectation. Be very definite in your petitions, so as to know what answer you may look for. Just think of the great host of workers, and ask and expect God definitely to bless them in answer to the prayer of His people. Then ask still more definitely for workers around you. Intercession is not the breathing out of pious wishes; its aim is—in believing, persevering prayer—to receive and bring down blessing.

DAY 9

WHAT TO PRAY—FOR GOD'S SPIRIT ON OUR MISSION WORK

"The evangelization of the world depends first of all upon a revival of prayer. Deeper than the need for men—yes, deep down at the bottom of our spiritless life is the need for the forgotten secret of prevailing, worldwide prayer."

> *As they ministered to the Lord and fasted, the Holy Spirit said, "Now separate to Me Barnabas and Saul for the work to which I have called them." Then, having fasted and prayed, and laid hands on them, they sent them away. So, being sent out by the Holy Spirit, they went down to Seleucia.* —ACTS 13:2-4

Pray that our mission work may all be done in this spirit—waiting on God, hearing the voice of the Spirit, sending forth men with fasting and prayer. Pray that in our churches our mission interest and mission work may be in the power of the Holy Spirit and of prayer. It is a Spirit-filled, praying Church that will send out Spirit-filled missionaries, mightily in prayer.

HOW TO PRAY—TAKE TIME

> *I give myself to prayer.* —PSALM 109:4
> "*We will give ourselves continually to prayer.*" —ACTS 6:4
> "*Do not be rash with your mouth, and let not your heart utter anything hastily before God.*" —ECCLESIASTES 5:2
> *And (He) continued all night in prayer to God.* —LUKE 6:12

Time is one of the chief standards of value. The time we give is a proof of the interest we feel.

We need time with God—to realize His presence, to wait for Him to make Himself known, to consider and feel the needs we plead for, to take our place in Christ, to pray until we can believe that we have received. Take time in prayer, and pray down blessing on the mission work of the Church.

Day 10

What to Pray—For God's Spirit on Our Missionaries

"What the world needs today is not only more missionaries, but the outpouring of God's Spirit on everyone whom He has sent out to work for Him in the foreign field."

> *"But you shall receive power when the Holy Spirit has*
> *come upon you; and you shall be witnesses to Me...*
> *to the end of the earth." —*Acts 1:8

God always gives His servants power equal to the work He asks of them. Think of the greatness and difficulty of this work—casting Satan out of his strongholds—and pray that everyone who takes part in it may receive and do all his work in the power of the Holy Spirit. Think of the difficulties of your missionaries, and pray for them.

How to Pray—Trusting God's Faithfulness

> *He who promised is faithful.... She judged Him faithful*
> *who had promised. —*Hebrews 10:23, 11:11

Just think of God's promises to His Son concerning His kingdom, to the Church concerning the heathen, to His servants concerning their work, to yourself concerning your prayer, and pray in the assurance that He is faithful and only waits for prayer and faith to fulfill them. "He who calls you is faithful" (to pray), "who also will do it" (what He has promised). Take up individual missionaries, make yourself one with them, and pray until you know that you are heard. Oh, begin to live for Christ's kingdom as the one thing worth living for!

DAY 11

WHAT TO PRAY—FOR MORE LABORERS

*"Therefore pray the Lord of the harvest to send out
laborers into His harvest."* —MATTHEW 9:38

What a remarkable call of the Lord Jesus for help from His disciples in getting the need supplied. What an honor put upon prayer. What a proof that God wants prayer and will hear it.

Pray for laborers, for all students in theological seminaries, training homes, Bible institutes, that they may not go unless He fits them and sends them forth. Pray that our churches may train their students to seek for the sending forth of the Holy Spirit and that all believers may hold themselves ready to be sent forth, or to pray for those who can go.

HOW TO PRAY—IN FAITH, NOTHING DOUBTING

*So Jesus answered and said to them, "Have faith in God. . . .
Whoever says to this mountain, 'Be removed and be cast
into the sea,' and does not doubt in his heart, but believes
that those things he says will be done, he will have
whatever he says."* —MARK 11:22–23

Have faith in God! Ask Him to make Himself known to you as the faithful mighty God, who works all in all, and you will be encouraged to believe that He can give suitable and sufficient laborers, however impossible this appears. But, remember, in answer to prayer and faith.

Apply this to every opening where a good worker is needed. The work is God's. He can give the right workman. But He must be asked and waited on.

Day 12

WHAT TO PRAY—FOR THE SPIRIT TO CONVINCE THE WORLD OF SIN

"I will send (a Helper) to you. And when He has come,
He will convict the world of sin." —JOHN 16:7–8

God's one desire, the one object of Christ's being manifested, is to take away sin. The first work of the Spirit on the world is conviction of sin. Without that, no deep or abiding revival, no powerful conversion. Pray for it, that the gospel may be preached in such power of the Spirit that men may see that they have rejected and crucified Christ, and cry out, What shall we do?

Pray most earnestly for a mighty power of conviction of sin wherever the gospel is preached.

HOW TO PRAY—STIR UP YOURSELF TO TAKE HOLD OF GOD'S STRENGTH

"Let him take hold of My strength, that he
may make peace with Me." —ISAIAH 27:5
And there is no one who calls on Your name,
who stirs himself up to take hold of You. —ISAIAH 64:7
Stir up the gift of God which is in you. —2 TIMOTHY 1:6

First, take hold of God's strength. God is a Spirit. I cannot take hold of Him and hold Him firmly except by the Spirit. Take hold of God's strength, and hold on until it has done for you what He has promised. Pray for the power of the Spirit to convict of sin.

Second, stir up yourself, the power that is in you by the Holy Spirit, to take hold. Give your whole heart and will to it and say, "I will not let You go unless You bless me" (Gen. 32:26).

DAY 13

WHAT TO PRAY—FOR THE SPIRIT OF BURNING

And it shall come to pass that he who is left in Zion. . .will
be called holy. . . . When the Lord has washed away the filth
of the daughters of Zion. . .by the spirit of judgment
and by the spirit of burning. —ISAIAH 4:3–4

A washing by fire! A cleansing by judgment! He who has passed through this shall be called holy. The power of blessing for the world, the power of work and intercession that will avail, depends on the spiritual state of the Church, and that can only rise higher as sin is discovered and put away. Judgment must begin at the house of God. There must be conviction of sin for sanctification. Ask God to give His Spirit as a spirit of judgment and a spirit of burning—to discover and burn out sin in His people.

HOW TO PRAY—IN THE NAME OF CHRIST

"Whatever you ask in My name, that I will do. . . .
If you ask anything in My name, I will do it.
—JOHN 14:13–14

Ask in the name of your Redeemer God who sits upon the throne. Ask what He has promised, what He gave His blood for so that sin may be put away from among His people. Ask—the prayer is after His own heart—for the spirit of deep conviction of sin to come among His people. Ask for the spirit of burning. Ask in the faith of His name—the faith of what He wills, of what He can do—and look for the answer. Pray that the Church may be blessed, to be made a blessing in the world.

Day 14

WHAT TO PRAY—FOR THE CHURCH OF THE FUTURE

And may not be like their fathers. . .a generation
that did not set its heart aright, and whose spirit
was not faithful to God. —PSALM 78:8

"I will pour My Spirit on your descendants,
and My blessing on your offspring." —ISAIAH 44:3

Pray for the rising generation who are to come after us. Think of the young men and women and children of this age, and pray for all the agencies at work among them; that in associations and societies and unions, in homes and schools, Christ may be honored, and the Holy Spirit get possession of them. Pray for the young of your own neighborhood.

HOW TO PRAY—WITH THE WHOLE HEART

May He grant you according to
your heart's desire. —PSALM 20:4

You have given him his heart's desire. —PSALM 21:2

I cry out with my whole heart;
hear me, O LORD! —PSALM 119:145

God lives and listens to every petition with His whole heart. Each time we pray, the whole infinite God is there to hear. He asks that in each prayer the whole man shall be there, too, that we shall cry with our whole heart. Christ gave Himself to God for men, and so He takes up every need into His intercession. If once we seek God with our whole heart, the whole heart will be in every prayer with which we come to this God. Pray with your whole heart for the young.

DAY 15

WHAT TO PRAY—FOR SCHOOLS AND COLLEGES

> *"As for Me," says the LORD, "this is My covenant with them:*
> *My Spirit who is upon you, and My words which I have*
> *put in your mouth, shall not depart from your mouth,*
> *nor from the mouth of your descendants, nor from the*
> *mouth of your descendants' descendants," says the LORD,*
> *"from this time and forevermore."* —ISAIAH 59:21

The future of the Church and the world depends, to an extent we little conceive, on the education of the day. The Church may be seeking to evangelize the heathen, and be giving up her own children to secular and materialistic influences. Pray for schools and colleges, and that the Church may realize and fulfill its momentous duty of caring for its children. Pray for godly teachers.

HOW TO PRAY—NOT LIMITING GOD

> *They. . .limited the Holy One of Israel.* —PSALM 78:41
> *He did not do many mighty works there because*
> *of their unbelief.* —MATTHEW 13:58
> *"Is anything too hard for the LORD?"* —GENESIS 18:14
> *"Ah, Lord GOD! Behold, You have made the heavens and the earth by*
> *Your great power and outstretched arm. There is nothing too hard for*
> *You. . . . Behold, I am the LORD, the God of all flesh.*
> *Is there anything too hard for Me?"* —JEREMIAH 32:17, 27

Beware, in your prayer, above everything, of limiting God, not only by unbelief, but by fancying that you know what He can do. Expect unexpected things, above all that we ask or think. Each time you intercede, be quiet first and worship God in His glory. Think of what He can do, of how He delights to hear Christ, of your place in Christ, and expect great things.

DAY 16

WHAT TO PRAY—FOR THE POWER OF THE HOLY SPIRIT IN OUR
SUNDAY SCHOOLS

*But thus says the LORD: "Even the captives of the mighty shall
be taken away, and the prey of the terrible be delivered;
for I will contend with him who contends with you,
and I will save your children." —*ISAIAH 49:25

Every part of the work of God's Church is His work. He must do it. Prayer is the
confession that He will—the surrender of ourselves into His hands to let Him—
work in us and through us. Pray for the hundreds of thousands of Sunday School
teachers, that those who know God may be filled with His Spirit. Pray for your
own Sunday School. Pray for the salvation of the children.

HOW TO PRAY—BOLDLY

*We have a great High Priest. . .Jesus the Son of God. . . .
Let us therefore come boldly to the throne
of grace. —*HEBREWS 4:14, 16

These hints to help us in our work of intercession—what are they doing for us?
Making us conscious of our feebleness in prayer? Thank God for this. It is the very
first lesson we need on the way to pray the effectual prayer that avails much. Let
us persevere, taking each subject boldly to the throne of grace. As we pray, we shall
learn to pray and to believe and to expect with increasing boldness. Hold firmly your
assurance: It is at God's command you come as an intercessor. Christ will give you
grace to pray rightly.

DAY 17

WHAT TO PRAY—FOR KINGS AND RULERS

> *Therefore I exhort first of all that supplications, prayers,*
> *intercessions, and giving of thanks be made for all men,*
> *for kings and all who are in authority, that we may*
> *lead a quiet and peaceable life in all godliness*
> *and reverence.* —1 TIMOTHY 2:1–2

What a faith in the power of prayer! A few weak and despised Christians are to influence the mighty Roman emperors and help in securing peace and quietness. Let us believe that prayer is a power that is taken up by God in His rule of the world. Let us pray for our country and its rulers, for all the rulers of the world, for rulers in cities or districts in which we are interested. When God's people unite in this, they may count upon their prayers effecting in the unseen world more than they know. Let faith hold this fast.

HOW TO PRAY—THE PRAYER BEFORE GOD AS INCENSE

> *Then another angel, having a golden censer, came and stood*
> *at the altar. He was given much incense, that he should offer it with*
> *the prayers of all the saints upon the golden altar which was before*
> *the throne. And the smoke of the incense, with the prayers of the*
> *saints, ascended before God from the angel's hand. Then the angel*
> *took the censer, filled it with fire from the altar, and threw it to*
> *the earth. And there were noises, thunderings, lightnings,*
> *and an earthquake.* —REVELATION 8:3–5

The same censer brings the prayer of the saints before God and casts fire upon the earth. The prayers that go up to heaven have their share in the history of this earth. Be sure that your prayers enter God's presence.

DAY 18

Therefore I exhort first of all that supplications, prayers, intercessions, and giving of thanks be made for all men, for kings and all who are in authority, that we may lead a quiet and peaceable life in all godliness and reverence. For this is good and acceptable in the sight of God our Savior. —1 TIMOTHY 2:1–3

He makes wars cease to the end of the earth. —PSALM 46:9

What a terrible sight!—the military armaments in which the nations find their pride. What a terrible thought!—the evil passions that may at any moment bring on war. And what a prospect for suffering and desolation that must come. God can, in answer to the prayer of His people, give peace. Let us pray for it, and for the rule of righteousness on which alone it can be established.

HOW TO PRAY—WITH THE UNDERSTANDING

What is the conclusion then? I will pray with the spirit, and I will also pray with the understanding.
—1 CORINTHIANS 14:15

We need to pray with the spirit, as the vehicle of the intercession of God's Spirit, if we are to take hold of God in faith and power. We need to pray with the understanding, if we are really to enter deeply into the needs we bring before Him. Take time to grasp intelligently, in each subject, the nature, the extent, the urgency of the request, the ground and way and certainty of God's promise as revealed in His Word. Let the mind affect the heart. Pray with the understanding and with the spirit.

DAY 19

WHAT TO PRAY—FOR THE HOLY SPIRIT ON CHRISTENDOM

Having a form of godliness but denying its power.
—2 TIMOTHY 3:5

"You have a name that you are alive, but you are dead."
—REVELATION 3:1

There are hundreds of millions of nominal Christians. The state of the majority is unspeakably awful. Formality, worldliness, ungodliness, rejection of Christ's service, ignorance, and indifference—to what an extent does all this prevail. We pray for the unreached—oh! do let us pray for those bearing Christ's name—many in worse than heathen darkness.

Does not one feel as if one ought to begin to give up his life, and to cry day and night to God for souls? In answer to prayer, God gives the power of the Holy Spirit.

HOW TO PRAY—IN DEEP STILLNESS OF SOUL

Truly my soul silently waits for God;
from Him comes my salvation. —PSALM 62:1

Prayer has its power in God alone. The nearer a man comes to God Himself, the deeper he enters into God's will. The more he takes hold of God, the more power in prayer.

God must reveal Himself. If it pleases Him to make Himself known, He can make the heart conscious of His presence. Our posture must be that of holy reverence, of quiet waiting and adoration.

As your month of intercession passes on, and you feel the greatness of your work, be still before God. That is how you will get power to pray.

DAY 20

WHAT TO PRAY—FOR GOD'S SPIRIT ON THE UNREACHED

> *"Surely these shall come from afar...*
> *and these from the land of Sinim." —*ISAIAH 49:12
> *Envoys will come out of Egypt; Ethiopia will*
> *quickly stretch out her hands to God. —*PSALM 68:31
> *"I, the LORD, will hasten it in its time." —*ISAIAH 60:22

Pray for the unreached who are yet without the Word. Think of China, with her three hundred millions—a million a month dying without Christ. Think of Dark Africa, with its two hundred millions. Think of thirty millions a year going down into the thick darkness. If Christ gave His life for them, will you not do so? You can give yourself up to intercede for them. Just begin, if you have never yet begun, with this simple monthly school of intercession. The ten minutes you give will make you feel this is not enough. God's Spirit will draw you on. Persevere, however weak you are. Ask God to give you some country or tribe to pray for. Can anything be nobler than to do as Christ did? Give your life for the unreached.

HOW TO PRAY—WITH CONFIDENT EXPECTATION OF AN ANSWER

> *"Call to Me, and I will answer you, and show you great and mighty*
> *things, which you do not know." —*JEREMIAH 33:3
> *"Thus says the Lord GOD: 'I will also let the house of Israel inquire of*
> *Me to do this for them.'" —*EZEKIEL 36:37

Both texts refer to promises definitely made, but their fulfillment would depend upon prayer: God would be inquired of to do it.

Pray for God's fulfillment of His promises to His Son and His Church, and expect the answer. Plead for the unreached: Plead God's promises.

Day 21

WHAT TO PRAY—FOR GOD'S SPIRIT ON THE JEWS

> *"And I will pour on the house of David and on the inhabitants of*
> *Jerusalem the Spirit of grace and supplication; then they will look on*
> *Me whom they pierced."* —ZECHARIAH 12:10
> *Brethren, my heart's desire and prayer to God for Israel*
> *is that they may be saved.* —ROMANS 10:1

Pray for the Jews. Their return to the God of their fathers stands connected, in a way we cannot tell, with wonderful blessing to the Church, and with the coming of our Lord Jesus. Let us not think that God has foreordained all this, and that we cannot hasten it. In a divine and mysterious way God has connected His fulfillment of His promise with our prayer. His Spirit's intercession in us is God's forerunner of blessing. Pray for Israel and the work done among them. And pray, too: Amen. Even so, come Lord Jesus!

HOW TO PRAY—WITH THE INTERCESSION OF THE HOLY SPIRIT

> *For we do not know what we should pray for as we ought,*
> *but the Spirit Himself makes intercession for us with groanings*
> *which cannot be uttered.* —ROMANS 8:26

In your ignorance and feebleness, believe in the secret indwelling and intercession of the Holy Spirit within you. Yield yourself to His life and leading habitually. He will help your infirmities in prayer. Plead the promises of God even where you do not see how they are to be fulfilled. God knows the mind of the Spirit, because He makes intercession for the saints according to the will of God. Pray with the simplicity of a little child. Pray with the holy awe and reverence of one in whom God's Spirit dwells and prays.

Day 22

Remember the prisoners as if chained with them—
those who are mistreated—since you yourselves
are in the body also. —HEBREWS 13:3

What a world of suffering we live in! How Jesus sacrificed all and identified Himself with it! Let us in our measure do so, too. The persecuted, the Jews, the famine-stricken millions of India, the hidden slavery of Africa, the poverty and wretchedness of our great cities—and so much more: what suffering among those who know God and who don't know Him. And then in smaller circles, in ten thousand homes and hearts, what sorrow. In our own neighborhood, how many needing help or comfort. Let us have a heart for, let us think of the suffering. It will stir us to pray, to work, to hope, to love more. And in a way and time we don't know God will hear our prayer.

HOW TO PRAY—PRAYING ALWAYS AND NOT FAINTING

Then He spoke a parable to them, that men always
ought to pray and not lose heart. —LUKE 18:1

Do you not begin to feel prayer is really the help for this sinful world? What a need there is of unceasing prayer! The very greatness of the task makes us despair! What can our ten minutes' intercession accomplish? It is right we feel this, for this is the way in which God is calling and preparing us to give our life to prayer. Give yourself completely to God for men, and amid all your work, your heart will be drawn out to men in love and drawn up to God in dependence and expectation. To a heart led this way by the Holy Spirit, it is possible to pray always and not to faint.

DAY 23

WHAT TO PRAY—FOR THE HOLY SPIRIT IN YOUR OWN WORK

I also labor, striving according to His working
which works in me mightily. —COLOSSIANS 1:29

You have your own special work; make it a work of intercession. Paul labored, striving according to the working of God in him. Remember, God is not only the Creator, but the great Workman who works all in all. You can only do your work in His strength, by His working in you through the Spirit. Intercede much for those among whom you work until God gives you life for them. Let us all intercede too for each other, for every worker throughout God's Church, however solitary or unknown.

HOW TO PRAY—IN GOD'S VERY PRESENCE

Draw near to God and He will draw near to you.
—JAMES 4:8

The nearness of God gives rest and power in prayer. The nearness of God is given to him who makes it his first object. "Draw near to God." Seek the nearness to Him, and He will give it: "He will draw near to you." Then it becomes easy to pray in faith. Remember that when first God takes you into the school of intercession it is almost more for your own sake than that of others. You have to be trained to love and wait and pray and believe. Only persevere. Learn to set yourself in His presence, to wait quietly for the assurance that He draws near. Enter His holy presence, wait there, and spread your work before Him. Intercede for the souls you are working among. Get a blessing from God, His Spirit into your own heart, for them.

DAY 24

WHAT TO PRAY—FOR THE SPIRIT ON YOUR OWN CONGREGATION

Beginning at Jerusalem.
—LUKE 24:47

Each one of us is connected with some congregation or circle of believers who are to us the part of Christ's body with which we come into most direct contact. They have a special claim on our intercession. Let it be a settled matter between God and you that you are to labor in prayer on its behalf. Pray for the minister and all leaders or workers in it. Pray for the believers according to their needs. Pray for conversions. Pray for the power of the Spirit to manifest itself. Band yourself with others to join in secret in definite petitions. Let intercession be a definite work, carried on as systematically as preaching or Sunday school. And pray, expecting an answer.

HOW TO PRAY—CONTINUALLY

"Watchmen. . .they shall never hold
their peace day or night." —ISAIAH 62:6
His own elect who cry out day and night to Him.
—LUKE 18:7
Night and day praying exceedingly that we may
see your face and perfect what is lacking in
your faith. —1 THESSALONIANS 3:10
Now she who is really a widow, and left alone,
trusts in God and continues in supplications and
prayers night and day. —1 TIMOTHY 5:5

When the glory of God and the love of Christ and the need of souls are revealed to us, the fire of this unceasing intercession will begin to burn in us for those who are near and those who are far off.

DAY 25

WHAT TO PRAY—FOR MORE CONVERSIONS

He is also able to save to the uttermost. . .
*since He always lives to make intercession. —*HEBREWS 7:25
"We will give ourselves continually to prayer and to the ministry of
the word.". . . Then the word of God spread, and the number of the
*disciples multiplied greatly. —*ACTS 6:4, 7

Christ's power to save, and save completely, depends on His unceasing intercession. The apostles' withdrawing themselves from other work to give themselves
continually to prayer was followed by the number of the disciples multiplying exceedingly. As we, in our day, give ourselves to intercession, we shall have more and
mightier conversions. Let us plead for this. Christ is exalted to give repentance.
The Church exists with the divine purpose and promise of having conversions.
Let us not be ashamed to confess our sins and weakness, and cry to God for more
conversions in Christian and heathen lands, of those, too, whom you know and
love. Plead for the salvation of sinners.

HOW TO PRAY—IN DEEP HUMILITY

"Yes, Lord, yet even the little dogs eat the crumbs. . ."
"O woman, great is your faith! Let it be to you as you desire."
—MATTHEW 15:27–28

You feel unworthy and unable to pray rightly. To accept this heartily, and to be
content still to come and be blessed in your unworthiness, is true humility. It
proves its integrity by not seeking for anything, but simply trusting His grace.
And so it is the very strength of a great faith and gets a full answer. "Yet even the
dogs"—let that be your plea as you persevere for someone possibly possessed by
the devil. Do not let your littleness hinder you for a moment.

Day 26

What to Pray—For the Holy Spirit on Young Converts

*(Peter and John) prayed for them that they might receive
the Holy Spirit. For as yet He had fallen upon none of them.
They had only been baptized in the name of the Lord Jesus.*
—Acts 8:15–16

*Now He who establishes us with you in Christ and has
anointed us is God, who also has sealed us and given
us the Spirit in our hearts as a guarantee.*
—2 Corinthians 1:21–22

How many new converts who remain weak, how many who fall into sin, how many who backslide entirely! If we pray for the Church, its growth in holiness and devotion to God's service, pray especially for the young converts. How many stand alone, surrounded by temptation. How many have no teaching on the Spirit in them and the power of God to establish them. How many in heathen lands, surrounded by Satan's power. If you pray for the power of the Spirit in the Church, pray especially that every young convert may know that he may claim and receive the fullness of the Spirit.

How to Pray—Without Ceasing

*"As for me, far be it from me that I should sin against the
Lord in ceasing to pray for you."* —1 Samuel 12:23

It is sin against the Lord to cease praying for others. When once we begin to see how absolutely indispensable intercession is, just as much a duty as loving God or believing in Christ, and how we are called and bound to it as believers, we shall feel that to cease intercession is grievous sin. Let us ask for grace to take up our place as priests with joy and give our lives to bring down the blessing of heaven.

DAY 27

WHAT TO PRAY—THAT GOD'S PEOPLE MAY REALIZE THEIR CALLING

"I will bless you. . .and you shall be a blessing. . . . And in you all the
families of the earth shall be blessed." —GENESIS 12:2–3
God be merciful to us and bless us, and cause His face to
shine upon us, that Your way may be known on earth,
Your salvation among all nations. —PSALM 67:1–2

Abraham was only blessed so that he might be a blessing to all the earth. Israel prays for blessing so that God may be known among all nations. Every believer, just as much as Abraham, is only blessed so that he may carry God's blessing to the world.

Cry to God that His people may know this so that every believer is only to live for the interests of God and His kingdom. If this truth were preached and believed and practiced, what a revolution it would bring in our mission work! What a host of willing intercessors we should have! Plead with God to work it by the Holy Spirit.

HOW TO PRAY—AS ONE WHO HAS ACCEPTED FOR HIMSELF WHAT HE
ASKS FOR OTHERS

Peter said. . ."What I do have I give you?". . .
The Holy Spirit fell upon them, as upon us at the beginning. . . .
God gave them the same gift as He gave us." —ACTS 3:6; 11:15, 17

As you pray for this great blessing on God's people—the Holy Spirit taking entire possession of them for God's service—yield yourself to God and claim the gift anew in faith. Let each thought of weakness or shortcoming only make you the more urgent in prayer for others. Then, as the blessing comes to them, you, too, will be helped. With every prayer for conversions or mission work, pray that God's people may know how completely they belong to Him.

Day 28

What to Pray—That All God's People May Know the Holy Spirit

"The Spirit of truth, whom the world cannot receive. . .
but you know Him, for He dwells with you
and will be in you." —John 14:17

Do you not know that your body is the temple
of the Holy Spirit? —1 Corinthians 6: 19

The Holy Spirit is the power of God for the salvation of men. He only works as He dwells in the Church. He is given to enable believers to live wholly as God would have them live, in the full experience and witness of Him who saves completely. Pray and ask God that every one of His people may know the Holy Spirit! That He, in all His fullness, is given to them! That they cannot expect to live as their Father would have without having Him in His fullness, without being filled with Him! Pray that all God's people, even away in churches gathered out of heathendom, may learn to say: "I believe in the Holy Spirit."

How to Pray—Laboring Fervently in Prayer

Epaphras, who is one of you, a bondservant of Christ,
greets you, always laboring fervently for you in prayers,
that you may stand perfect and complete in all the will of God.
—Colossians 4:12

To a healthy man labor is a delight, and in what interests him he labors fervently. The believer who is in full health, whose heart is filled with God's Spirit, labors fervently in prayer. For what? That his brethren may stand perfect and complete in all the will of God, that they may know what God wills for them and how He calls them to live, and to be led and walk by the Holy Spirit. Labor fervently in prayer that all God's children may know this as possible, as divinely sure.

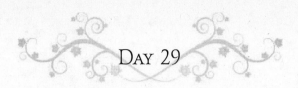

DAY 29

> *"I chose you and appointed you that you should go and*
> *bear fruit. . .that whatever you ask the Father in*
> *My name He may give you."* —JOHN 15:16
> *"Until now you have asked nothing in My name. . . .*
> *In that day you will ask in My name."*
> —JOHN 16:24, 26

Has not our school of intercession taught us how little we have prayed in the name of Jesus? He promised His disciples: "In that day, when the Holy Spirit comes upon you, you shall ask in My name." Are there not tens of thousands with us mourning the lack of the power of intercession? Let our intercession today be for them and all God's children, that Christ may teach us that the Holy Spirit is in us, what it is to live in His fullness, and to yield ourselves to His intercessional work within us. The Church and the world need nothing so much as a mighty Spirit of Intercession to bring down the power of God on earth. Pray for the descent from heaven of the Spirit of Intercession for a great prayer revival.

HOW TO PRAY—ABIDING IN CHRIST

> *"If you abide in Me, and My words abide in you,*
> *you will ask what you desire, and it shall be done for you."*
> —JOHN 15:7

Our acceptance with God, our access to Him, is all in Christ. As we consciously abide in Him, we have the liberty, not a liberty to our old nature or self-will but the Divine liberty from all self-will, to ask what we desire, in the power of the new nature, and it shall be done. Let us keep this place and believe even now that our intercession is heard and that the Spirit of supplication will be given all around us.

DAY 30

WHAT TO PRAY—FOR THE HOLY SPIRIT WITH THE WORD OF GOD

Our gospel did not come to you in word only, but also in power,
and in the Holy Spirit and in much assurance.
—1 THESSALONIANS 1:5

Those who have preached the gospel to you by the
Holy Spirit sent from heaven. —1 PETER 1:12

What numbers of Bibles are being circulated. What numbers of sermons on the Bible are being preached. What numbers of Bibles are being read in home and school. How little blessing when it comes "in word" only, and what divine blessing and power when it comes "in the Holy Spirit," when it is preached "with the Holy Spirit sent from heaven." Pray for Bible circulation, and preaching and teaching and reading, that it may all be in the Holy Spirit, with much prayer. Pray for the power of the Spirit with the word, in your own neighborhood, wherever it is being read or heard. Let every mention of "The Word of God" awaken intercession.

HOW TO PRAY—WATCHING AND PRAYING

Continue earnestly in prayer, being vigilant in it with thanksgiving;
meanwhile praying also for us, that God would open
to us a door for the word. —COLOSSIANS 4:2–3

Do you not see how all depends upon God and prayer? As long as He lives and loves and hears and works, as long as there are souls with hearts closed to the word, as long as there is work to be done in carrying the Word—Pray without ceasing. Continue steadfastly in prayer, watching your prayers with thanksgiving. These words are for every Christian.

Day 31

WHAT TO PRAY—FOR THE SPIRIT OF CHRIST IN HIS PEOPLE

"I am the vine, you are the branches."
—JOHN 15:5
"That you should do as I have done to you."
—JOHN 13:15

As branches, we are to be so like the Vine, so entirely identified with it, that all may see that we have the same nature and life and Spirit. When we pray for the Spirit, let us not only think of a Spirit of power, but the very disposition and temper of Christ Jesus. Ask and expect nothing less—for yourself, and all God's children, cry for it.

HOW TO PRAY—STRIVING IN PRAYER

Strive together with me in prayers
to God for me. —ROMANS 15:30
I want you to know what a great conflict
I have for you. —COLOSSIANS 2:1

All the powers of evil seek to hinder us in prayer. Prayer is a conflict with opposing forces. It needs the whole heart and all our strength. May God give us grace to strive in prayer until we prevail.

ABSOLUTE SURRENDER

CONTENTS

"I and all that I have are yours."
1 KINGS 20:4

1

ABSOLUTE SURRENDER

*Now Ben-Hadad the king of Syria gathered all his forces together;
thirty-two kings were with him, with horses and chariots. And he
went up and besieged Samaria, and made war against it. Then he
sent messengers into the city to Ahab king of Israel, and said to him,
"Thus says Ben-Hadad: 'Your silver and your gold are mine; your
loveliest wives and children are mine.'" And the king of Israel
answered and said, "My lord, O king, just as you say,
I and all that I have are yours."*
1 KINGS 20:1–4

WHAT Ben-Hadad asked was *absolute surrender*, and what Ahab gave was what was asked of him—*absolute surrender*. I want to use these words: "My lord, O king, just as you say, I and all that I have are yours," as the words of absolute surrender with which every child of God ought to yield himself to his Father. We have heard it before, but we need to hear it very definitely—the condition of God's blessing is absolute surrender of all into His hands. Praise God! If our hearts are willing for that, there is no end to what God will do for us, and to the blessing God will bestow.

Absolute surrender—let me tell you where I got those words. I used them myself often, and you have heard them numberless times. But in Scotland once I was in a company where we were talking about the condition of Christ's Church and what the great need of the Church and of believers is. There was in our company a godly worker who has much to do in training workers, and I asked him what he would say was the great need of the Church and the message that ought to be preached. He answered very quietly and simply and determinedly: *"Absolute surrender to God is the one thing."*

The words struck me as never before. And that man began to tell how, in the workers with whom he had to deal, he finds that if they are sound on that point, even though they are backward, they are willing to be taught and helped, and they always improve; whereas others who are not sound there very often go back and leave the work. The condition for obtaining God's full blessing is *absolute surrender* to Him.

And now, I desire by God's grace to give to you this message—that your God in heaven answers the prayers that you have offered for blessing on yourselves and for blessing on those around you by this one demand: *Are you willing to surrender yourselves absolutely into His hands?* What is our answer to be? God knows there are hundreds of hearts who have said it, and there are hundreds more who long to say it but hardly dare to do so. And there are hearts who have said it, but who have yet miserably failed, and who feel themselves condemned because they did not find the secret of the power to live that life. May God have a word for all!

Let me say, first of all, God claims it from us.

Yes, it has its foundation in the very nature of God. God cannot do otherwise. Who is God? He is the fountain of life, the only source of existence and power and goodness, and throughout the universe there is nothing good but what God works. God has created the sun, the moon, the stars, the flowers, the trees, and the grass. Are they not all absolutely surrendered to God? Do they not allow God to work in them just what He pleases? When God clothes the lily with its beauty, is it not yielded up, surrendered, given over to God as He works in it its beauty?

And God's redeemed children, oh, can you think that God can work His work if there is only half or a part of them surrendered? God cannot do it. God is life, love, blessing, power, and infinite beauty, and God delights to communicate Himself to every child who is prepared to receive Him. But this one lack of absolute surrender is just the thing that hinders God. And now He comes, and as God He claims it.

You know in daily life what absolute surrender is. You know that everything has to be given up to its special, definite object and service. I have a pen in my pocket, and that pen is absolutely surrendered to the one work of writing, and that pen must be absolutely surrendered to my hand if I am to write properly with it. If another holds it partly, I cannot write properly. This coat is absolutely given up to me to cover my body. This building is entirely given up to religious services. And now, do you expect that in your immortal being, in the divine nature that you have received by regeneration, God can work His work, every day and every hour, unless you are entirely given up to Him? God cannot. The temple of Solomon was absolutely surrendered to God when it was dedicated to Him. And every one of us is a temple of God, in which God will dwell and work mightily on one condition—absolute surrender to Him. God claims it, God is worthy of it, and without it God cannot work His blessed work in us.

But secondly, God not only claims it, but God will accomplish it Himself.

I am sure there is many a heart that says: "Ah, but that absolute surrender implies so much!" Someone says: "Oh, I have passed through so much trial and suffering, and there is so much of the self-life still remaining, and I do not dare face the entire giving of it up, because I know it will cause so much trouble and agony."

How sad it is that God's children have such thoughts of Him, such cruel thoughts. Oh, I come to you with a message, a fearful and anxious one. God does not ask you to give the perfect surrender in your strength, or by the power of your will. Rather, God is willing to work it in you. Do we not read: "It is God who works in you both to will and to do for His good pleasure" (Phil. 2:13)? And that is what we should seek for—to get on our faces before God until our hearts learn to believe that the everlasting God Himself will come to get rid of what is wrong, to conquer what is evil, and to work what is well-pleasing in His blessed sight. God Himself will work it in you.

Look at the men in the Old Testament, like Abraham. Do you think it was by accident that God found that man—the father of the faithful and the friend of God—and that it was Abraham himself, apart from God, who had such faith and such obedience and such devotion? You know it is not so. God raised him up and prepared him as an instrument for His glory.

Did not God say to Pharaoh: "For this purpose I have raised you up, that I may show My power" (Exod. 9:16)?

And if God said that of him, will not God say it far more of every child of His?

Oh, I want to encourage you, and I want you to cast away every fear. Come with that weak desire, and if there is the fear that says, "Oh, my desire is not strong enough. I am not willing for everything that may come. I do not feel bold enough to say I can conquer everything"—I encourage you, learn to know and trust your God now. Say: "My God, I am willing that You would make me willing." If there is anything holding you back or any sacrifice you are afraid of making, come to God now and prove how gracious your God is. And do not be afraid that He will command from you what He will not bestow.

God comes and offers to work this absolute surrender in you. All these searchings and hungerings and longings that are in your heart—I tell you, they are the drawings of the divine magnet, Christ Jesus. He lived a life of absolute surrender, He has possession of you, and He is living in your heart by His Holy Spirit. You have hindered and hindered Him terribly, but He desires to help you to get hold of Him entirely. And He comes and draws you now by His message and words. Will you not come and trust God to work in you that absolute surrender to Himself? Yes, bless God, He can do it, and He will do it.

The third thought: God not only claims it and works it, but God accepts it when we bring it to Him.

God works it in the secret of our heart. God urges us by the hidden power of His Holy Spirit to come and speak it out, and we have to bring and to yield to Him that absolute surrender. But remember, when you come and bring God that absolute surrender, it may, as far as your feelings or your consciousness go, be a thing of great imperfection, and you may doubt and hesitate and say: "Is it absolute?"

But remember, there was once a man to whom Christ had said: "If you can believe, all things *are* possible to him who believes" (Mark 9:23).

And his heart was afraid, and he cried out: "Lord, I believe; help my unbelief!" (Mark 9:24).

That was a faith that triumphed over the devil, and the evil spirit was cast out. And if you come and say: "Lord, I yield myself in absolute surrender to my God," even though it is with a trembling heart and with the consciousness, "I do not feel the power, I do not feel the determination, I do not feel the assurance," it will succeed. Do not be afraid, but come just as you are, and even in the midst of your trembling, the power of the Holy Spirit will work.

Have you never yet learned the lesson that the Holy Spirit works with mighty power, while on the human side everything appears weak? Look at the Lord Jesus Christ in Gethsemane. We read that He, "through the eternal Spirit" (Heb. 9:14), offered Himself a sacrifice to God. The Almighty Spirit of God was enabling Him to do it. And yet what agony and fear and exceeding sorrow came over Him! And how He prayed! Externally, you can see no sign of the mighty power of the Spirit, but the Spirit of God was there. And likewise, while you are weak and fighting and trembling, in faith in the hidden work of God's Spirit do not fear but yield yourself.

> *And God's redeemed children, oh, can you think that God can work His work if there is only half or a part of them surrendered? God cannot do it.*

And when you yield yourself in absolute surrender, let it be in the faith that God does now accept of it. That is the great point, and that is what we so often miss—that believers should be occupied this way with God in this matter of surrender. I encourage you, be occupied with God. We want to get help, every one of us, so that in our daily life God shall be clearer to us, so that God shall have the right place and be "all in all" (1 Cor. 15:28). And if we are to have that throughout life, let us begin now and look away from ourselves and look up to God. Let each believe—*While I, a poor worm on earth and a trembling child of God, full of failure and sin and fear, bow here, and no one knows what passes through my heart, and while I in simplicity say, "O God, I accept Your terms. I have pleaded for blessing on myself and others, and I have accepted Your terms of absolute surrender."* While your heart says that in deep silence, remember there is a God present who takes note of it and writes it down in His book, and there is a God present who at that very moment takes possession of you. You may not feel it, and you may not realize it, but God takes possession if you will trust Him.

A fourth thought: God not only claims it, works it, and accepts it when I bring it, but God maintains it.

That is the great difficulty with many. People say: "I have often been stirred at a meeting or a convention, and I have consecrated myself to God, but it has passed away. I know it may last for a week or for a month, but away it fades, and after a time it is all gone."

But listen! It is because you do not believe what I am now going to tell you and remind you of. When God has begun the work of absolute surrender in you, and when God has accepted your surrender, then God holds Himself bound to care for it and to keep it. Will you believe that?

> *When God has begun the work of absolute surrender in you, and when God has accepted your surrender, then God holds Himself bound to care for it and to keep it.*

In this matter of surrender, there are two: God and I—I a worm, God the everlasting and omnipotent Jehovah. Worm, will you be afraid to trust yourself to this mighty God now? God is willing. Do you not believe that He can keep you continually, day by day, and moment by moment?

Moment by moment I'm *kept* in His love; moment by moment I've life from above.

If God allows the sun to shine on you moment by moment, without intermission, will not God let His life shine on you every moment? And why have you not experienced it? Because you have not trusted God for it, and because you do not surrender yourself absolutely to God in that trust.

A life of absolute surrender has its difficulties. I do not deny that. Yes, it has something far more than difficulties. It is a life that with men is absolutely impossible. But by the grace of God, by the power of God, and by the power of the Holy Spirit dwelling in us, it is a life to which we are destined, a life that is possible for us, praise God! Let us believe that God will maintain it.

Some of you have read the words of that aged saint who, on his ninetieth birthday, told of all God's goodness to him—I mean George Müller. What did he say he believed to be the secret of his happiness and of all the blessing that God had given him? He said he believed there were two reasons. The one was that he had been enabled by grace to maintain a good conscience before God day by day, and the other was that he was a lover of God's Word. Ah, yes, a good conscience is complete obedience to God day by day, and fellowship with God every day in His Word and prayer—that is a life of absolute surrender.

Such a life has two sides—on the one side, *absolute surrender to work what God wants you to do*; on the other side, *to let God work what He wants to do*.

First, *to do what God wants* you *to do*.

Give up yourselves absolutely to the will of God. You know something of that will, but not enough—far from all. But say absolutely to the Lord God: "By Your grace I desire to do Your will in everything, every moment of every day." Say:

"Lord God, not a word on my tongue but for Your glory, not a movement of my temper but for Your glory, not an affection of love or hate in my heart but for Your glory, and according to Your blessed will."

Someone says: "Do you think that possible?"

I ask, what has God promised you, and what can God do to fill a vessel absolutely surrendered to Him? Oh, God wants to bless you in a way beyond what you expect. From the beginning, ear has not heard, neither has the eye seen, what God has prepared for those who wait for Him (see 1 Cor. 2:9). God has prepared unheard-of things, blessings much more wonderful than you can imagine, more mighty than you can conceive. They are divine blessings. Oh, say now: "I give myself absolutely to God, to His will, to do only what God wants."

It is God who will enable you to carry out the surrender.

And, on the other side, come and say: "I give myself absolutely to God, *to let Him work in me to will and to do of His good pleasure,* as He has promised to do."

Yes, the living God wants to work in His children in a way that we cannot understand, but that God's Word has revealed, and He wants to work in us every moment of the day. God is willing to maintain our life. Only let our absolute surrender be one of simple, childlike, and unbounded trust.

> We are members of that sickly body, and the sickliness of the body will hinder us and break us down, unless we come to God, and in confession separate ourselves from partnership with worldliness.

The last thought: This absolute surrender to God will wonderfully bless us. What Ahab said to his enemy, King Ben-hadad—"O king, just as you say, I and all that I have are yours"—shall we not say to our God and loving Father? If we do say it, God's blessing will come upon us. God wants us to be separate from the world. We are called to come out from the world that hates God. Come out for God and say: "Lord, anything for You." If you say that with prayer and speak that into God's ear, He will accept it and He will teach you what it means.

I say again, God will bless you. You have been praying for blessing. But do remember, there must be absolute surrender. At every tea table you see it. Why is tea poured into that cup? Because it is empty and given up for the tea. But put ink, vinegar, or wine into it, and will they pour the tea into the vessel? And can God fill you, can God bless you if you are not absolutely surrendered to Him? He cannot. Let us believe God has wonderful blessings for us—if we will but stand up for God and say, be it with a trembling will, yet with a believing heart: "O God, I accept Your demands. I and all I have are Yours. Absolute surrender is what my soul yields to You by divine grace."

You may not have such strong and clear feelings of deliverances as you would desire to have, but humble yourselves in His sight, and acknowledge that you have grieved the Holy Spirit by your self-will, self-confidence, and self-effort. Bow humbly before Him in the confession of that, and ask Him to break the heart and to bring you into the dust before Him. Then, as you bow before Him, just accept God's teaching that in your flesh "nothing good dwells" (Rom. 7:18), and that nothing will help you except another life that must come in. You must deny self once for all. Denying self must every moment be the power of your life, and then Christ will come in and take possession of you.

When was Peter delivered? When was the change accomplished? The change began with Peter weeping, and then the Holy Spirit came down and filled his heart.

God the Father loves to give us the power of the Spirit. We have the Spirit of God dwelling within us. We come to God confessing that and praising God for it, and yet confessing how we have grieved the Spirit. And then we bow our knees to the Father to ask that He would strengthen us with all might by the Spirit in the inner man, and that He would fill us with His mighty power. And as the Spirit reveals Christ to us, Christ comes to live in our hearts forever, and the self-life is cast out.

Let us bow before God in humility, and in that humility confess before Him the state of the whole Church. No words can tell the sad state of the Church of Christ on earth. I wish I had words to speak what I sometimes feel about it. Just think of the Christians around you. I do not speak of nominal Christians, or of professing Christians, but I speak of hundreds and thousands of honest, earnest Christians who are not living a life in the power of God or to His glory. So little power, so little devotion or consecration to God, so little perception of the truth that a Christian is a man utterly surrendered to God's will! Oh, we want to confess the sins of God's people around us, and to humble ourselves. We are members of that sickly body, and the sickliness of the body will hinder us and break us down, unless we come to God and in confession separate ourselves from partnership with worldliness, with coldness toward each other, unless we give up ourselves to be entirely and wholly for God.

How much Christian work is being done in the spirit of the flesh and in the power of self! How much work, day by day, in which human energy—our will and our thoughts about the work—is continually demonstrated, and in which there is but little of waiting on God and on the power of the Holy Spirit! Let us confess. But as we confess the state of the Church and the weakness and sinfulness of work for God among us, let us come back to ourselves. Who is there who truly longs to be delivered from the power of the self-life, who truly acknowledges that it is the power of self and the flesh, and who is willing to cast all at the feet of Christ? There is deliverance.

I heard of one who had been an earnest Christian who spoke about the "cruel" thought of separation and death. But you do not think that, do you? What are we to think of separation and death? This: Death was the path to glory for Christ (Phil. 2:5–11). For the joy set before Him He endured the cross (Heb. 12:2). The cross was the birthplace of His everlasting glory. Do you love Christ? Do you long to be *in* Christ, and not just *like* Him? Let death be to you the most desirable thing on earth—death to self, and fellowship with Christ. Separation—do you think of it as a hard thing to be called to be entirely free from the world, and by that separation to be united to God and His love, by separation to become prepared for living and walking with God every day? Surely one ought to say: "Anything to bring me to separation—to death—for a life of full fellowship with God and Christ."

Come and cast this self-life and flesh-life at the feet of Jesus. Then trust Him. Do not worry yourselves with trying to understand all about it, but come in the living faith that Christ will come into you with the power of His death and the power of His life. Then the Holy Spirit will bring the whole Christ—Christ crucified and risen and living in glory—into your heart.

For Further Thought

1. *What is the one thing that can keep God from doing His work? What can you do in your own life of faith to make sure God can do that work?*
2. *What things within you will Christ use to draw you closer to Himself?*
3. *As an individual member of Christ's body—the Church—what must you do as an individual in order to heal the sicknesses within the Church today?*

2

"THE FRUIT OF
THE SPIRIT IS LOVE"

I want to look at the fact of a life filled with the Holy Spirit more from the practical side, and to show how this life will show itself in our daily walk and conduct.

You know that under the Old Testament the Holy Spirit often came upon men as a divine Spirit of revelation to reveal the mysteries of God, or for power to do the work of God. But He did not then dwell in them. Now, many just want the Old Testament gift of power for work but know very little of the New Testament gift of the indwelling Spirit, animating and renewing the whole life. When God gives the Holy Spirit, His great object is the formation of a holy character. It is a gift of a holy mind and spiritual disposition, and what we need above everything else is to say: "I must have the Holy Spirit sanctifying my whole inner life if I am really to live for God's glory."

You might say that when Christ promised the Spirit to the disciples, He did so that they might have power to be witnesses. True, but then they received the Holy Spirit in such heavenly power and reality that He took possession of their whole being at once and so prepared them as holy men for doing the work with power as they had to do it. Christ spoke of power to the disciples, but it was the Spirit filling their whole being that worked the power.

I wish now to focus on the passage found in Galatians 5:22: "The fruit of the Spirit is love."

We read that "Love is the fulfillment of the law" (Rom. 13:10), and my desire is to speak on love as a fruit of the Spirit with a twofold object. One is that this word may be a searchlight in our hearts and give us a test by which to try all our thoughts about the Holy Spirit and all our experience of the holy life. Let us try ourselves by this word. Has it been our daily habit to seek being filled with the Holy Spirit as the Spirit of love? "The fruit of the Spirit is love." Has it been our experience that the more we have of the Holy Spirit, the more loving we become? In claiming the Holy Spirit, we should make this the first object of our expectation. The Holy Spirit comes as a Spirit of love.

Oh, if this were just true in the Church of Christ, how different her state would be! May God help us to get hold of this simple, heavenly truth—that the fruit of the Spirit is a love that appears in the life, that just as the Holy Spirit gets real possession of the life, the heart will be filled with real, divine, universal love.

One of the great causes why God cannot bless His Church is *the lack of love*. When the body is divided, there cannot be strength. In the time of their great religious wars, when Holland stood out so nobly against Spain, one of their mottoes was: "Unity gives strength." It is only when God's people stand as one body—one before God in the fellowship of love, one toward another in deep affection, one before the world in a love that the world can see—it is only then that they will have power to secure the blessing that they ask of God.

Remember that if a vessel that ought to be one whole is cracked into many pieces, it cannot be filled. You can take a potsherd, one part of a vessel, and dip out a little water into that, but if you want the vessel full, the vessel must be whole. That is literally true of Christ's Church, and if there is one thing we must pray still, it is this: "Lord, melt us together into one by the power of the Holy Spirit. Let the Holy Spirit, who at Pentecost made them all of one heart and one soul, do His blessed work among us." Praise God, we can love each other in a divine love, for "the fruit of the Spirit is love." Give yourselves up to love, and the Holy Spirit will come. Receive the Spirit, and He will teach you to love more.

1. Now, why is it that the fruit of the Spirit is love? *Because God is love* (1 John 4:8).

And what does that mean?

> *H*as it been our experience that the more we have of the Holy Spirit, the more loving we become? In claiming the Holy Spirit, we should make this the first object of our expectation.

It is the very nature and being of God to delight in communicating Himself. God has no selfishness, and God keeps nothing to Himself. God's nature is to be always giving. In the sun and the moon and the stars, in every flower you see it, in every bird in the air, in every fish in the sea. God communicates life to His creatures. And the angels around His throne, the seraphim and cherubim who are flames of fire—why do they have their glory? It is because God is love, and He imparts to them of His brightness and His blessedness. And we, His redeemed children—God delights to pour His love into us. And why? Because, as I said, God keeps nothing for Himself. From eternity, God had His only begotten Son, and the Father gave Him all things, and nothing that God had was kept back. "God is love."

One of the old Church fathers said that we cannot better understand the trinity than as a revelation of divine love—the Father, the loving One, the fountain of love; the Son, the beloved one, the reservoir of love, in whom the love was poured out; and the Spirit, the living love who united both and then overflowed into this world. The Spirit of Pentecost, the Spirit of the Father, and the Spirit of the Son is love. And when the Holy Spirit comes to us and to other men, will He be less a Spirit of love than He is in God? It cannot be, because He cannot change His nature. The Spirit of God is love, and "the fruit of the Spirit is love."

2. Why is that so? That was the one great need of mankind, the thing that Christ's redemption came to accomplish: *to restore love to this world.*

When man sinned, why was it that he sinned? Selfishness triumphed—he sought self instead of God. And just look! Adam immediately begins to accuse the woman of having led him astray. Love to God had gone, love to man was lost. Look again: of the first two children of Adam the one becomes a murderer of his brother.

Does that not teach us that sin had robbed the world of love? Yes, what a proof the history of the world has been of love having been lost! There may have been beautiful examples of love even among the heathen, but only as a little remnant of what was lost. One of the worst things sin did for man was to make him selfish, for selfishness cannot love.

The Lord Jesus Christ came down from heaven as the Son of God's love. "God so loved the world that He gave His only begotten Son" (John 3:16). God's Son came to show what love is, and He lived a life of love here on earth in fellowship with His disciples, in compassion over the poor and miserable, in love even to His enemies, and He died the death of love. And when He went to heaven, whom did He send down? The Spirit of love, to come and banish selfishness and envy and pride, and to bring the love of God into the hearts of men. "The fruit of the Spirit is love."

And what was the preparation for the promise of the Holy Spirit? You know that promise as found in the fourteenth chapter of John's Gospel. But remember what precedes it in the thirteenth chapter. Before Christ promised the Holy Spirit, He gave a new commandment, and about that new commandment He said wonderful things. One thing was: "As I have loved you. . .you also love one another" (13:34). To them, His dying love was to be the only law of their conduct and interaction with each other. What a message to those fishermen, to those men full of pride and selfishness! "Learn to love each other," said Christ, "as I have loved you." And by the grace of God they did it. When Pentecost came, they were of one heart and one soul. Christ did it for them.

And now He calls us to dwell and to walk in love. He demands that though a man hate you, still you love him. True love cannot be conquered by anything in heaven or on the earth. The more hatred there is, the more love triumphs through it all and shows its true nature. This is the love that Christ commanded His disciples to exercise.

What more did He say? "By this all will know that you are My disciples, if you have love for one another" (John 13:35).

You all know what it is to wear a badge. And Christ said to His disciples in effect: "I give you a badge, and that badge is love. That is to be your mark. It is the only thing in heaven or on earth by which men can know Me."

Do we not begin to fear that love has fled from the earth? That if we were to ask the world: "Have you seen us wear the badge of love?" the world would say: "No! What we have heard of the Church of Christ is that there is not a place where there is no quarreling and separation." Let us ask God with one heart that we may wear the badge of Jesus' love. God is able to give it.

3. "The fruit of the Spirit is love." Why? Because *nothing but love can expel and conquer our selfishness.*

Self is the great curse, whether in its relation to God, to our fellowmen in general, or to fellow Christians—thinking of ourselves and seeking our own. Self is our greatest curse. But, praise God, Christ came to redeem us from self. We sometimes talk about deliverance from the self-life—and thank God for every word that can be said about it to help us—but I am afraid some people think deliverance from the self-life means that now they are no longer going to have any trouble in serving God. Then they forget that deliverance from self-life means to be a vessel overflowing with love to everybody all the day.

> *There may have been beautiful examples of love even among the heathen, but only as a little remnant of what was lost.*

And there you have the reason why many people pray for the power of the Holy Spirit and get something, but oh, so little! It's because they prayed for power for work and power for blessing, but they have not prayed for power for full deliverance from self. That means not only the righteous self in their relationship with God, but the unloving self in relationships with men. And there *is* deliverance. "The fruit of the Spirit is love." I bring you the glorious promise of Christ that He is able to fill our hearts with love.

A great many of us try hard at times to love. We try to force ourselves to love, and I do not say that is wrong. It is better than nothing! But the end of it is always very sad. "I fail continually," such a one must confess. And what is the reason? The reason is simply this: Because they have never learned to believe and accept the truth that the Holy Spirit can pour God's love into their heart. How often that blessed text has been limited!—"The love of God is shed abroad in our hearts" (Rom. 5:5 KJV). It has often been understood in this sense: It means the love of God *to me.* Oh, what a limitation! That is only the beginning. The love of God is always the love of God in its entirety, in its fullness as an indwelling power, a love of God to me that leaps back to Him in love and overflows to my fellowmen in love—God's love to me, my love to God, and my love to my fellowmen. The three are one. You cannot separate them.

Do believe that the love of God can be shed abroad in your heart and mine so that we can love all the day.

"Ah!" you say, "how little I have understood that!"

Why is a lamb always gentle? Because that is its nature. Does it cost the lamb any trouble to be gentle? No. Why not? It is so beautiful and gentle. Does a lamb need to study to be gentle? No. Why does that come so easy? It is its nature. And a wolf—why does it cost a wolf no trouble to be cruel, to put its fangs into the poor lamb or sheep? Because that is its nature. It doesn't need to summon up its courage, for the wolf-nature is there.

And how can I learn to love? Never until the Spirit of God fills my heart with God's love, and I begin to long for God's love in a very different sense from which I have sought it so selfishly, as a comfort and a joy and a happiness and a pleasure to myself. Never until I begin to learn that "God is love," and to claim it and receive it as an indwelling power for self-sacrifice. Never until I begin to see that my glory, my blessedness, is to be like God and like Christ in giving up everything in myself for my fellowmen. May God teach us that! Oh, the divine blessedness of the love with which the Holy Spirit can fill our hearts! "The fruit of the Spirit is love."

4. Once again I ask, Why must this be so? And my answer is: *Without this we cannot live the daily life of love.*

> *T*he love of God is always the love of God in its entirety, in its fullness as an indwelling power, a love of God to me that leaps back to Him in love and overflows to my fellowmen in love.

How often when we speak about the consecrated life that we have to speak about *temper*, and some people have sometimes said: "You make too much of temper."

I do not think we can make too much of it. Think for a moment of a clock and of what its hands mean. The hands tell me what is within the clock. If I see that the hands stand still or that they point wrong or that the clock is slow or fast, I say that something inside the clock is not working properly. And temper is just like the revelation that the clock gives of what is within. Temper is a proof whether or not the love of Christ is filling the heart.

How many there are who find it easier in church, in prayer meeting, or in work for the Lord—diligent, earnest work—to be holy and happy than in the daily life with wife and children, easier to be holy and happy outside the home than in it! Where is the love of God? In Christ. God has prepared for us a wonderful redemption in Christ, and He longs to make something supernatural of us. Have we learned to long for it, to ask for it, and to expect it in its fullness?

Then there is the *tongue!* We sometimes speak of the tongue when we talk of the better life and the restful life, but just think what liberty many Christians give to their tongues. They say: "I have a right to think what I like."

When they speak about each other, when they speak about their neighbors, when they speak about other Christians, how often there are sharp remarks! God keep me from saying anything that would be unloving. God shut my mouth if I am not to speak in tender love. But what I am saying is a fact. How often there are found among Christians who are banded together in work sharp criticism, sharp judgment, hasty opinion, unloving words, secret contempt of each other, secret condemnation of each other!

Oh, just as a mother's love covers her children and delights in them and has the most tender compassion with their foibles or failures, so there ought to be in the heart of every believer a motherly love toward every brother and sister in Christ. Have you aimed at that? Have you sought it? Have you ever pleaded for it? Jesus Christ said: "As I have loved you. . .love one another" (John 13:34). And He did not put that among the other commandments, but He said in effect: "That is a *new* commandment, the one commandment: Love one another as I have loved you."

It is in our daily life and conduct that the fruit of the Spirit is love. From that there come all the graces and virtues in which love is manifested: joy, peace, long-suffering, gentleness, and goodness, and no sharpness or hardness in your tone, no unkindness or selfishness, but meekness before God and man. You see that all these are the gentler virtues.

I have often thought as I read those words in Colossians, "Therefore, as the elect of God, holy and beloved, put on tender mercies, kindness, humility, meekness, longsuffering" (Col. 3:12), that if we had written this, we would have put in the foreground the manly virtues, such as zeal, courage, and diligence. But we need to see how the gentler, the most womanly virtues are especially connected with dependence on the Holy Spirit. These are indeed heavenly graces. They never were found in the heathen world. Christ was needed to come from heaven to teach us. Your blessedness is longsuffering, meekness, and kindness, and your glory is humility before God. The fruit of the Spirit that He brought from heaven out of the heart of the crucified Christ, and that He gives in our heart, is first and foremost—love.

> God keep me from saying anything that would be unloving. God shut my mouth if I am not to speak in tender love.

You know what John says: "No one has seen God at any time. If we love one another, God abides in us" (1 John 4:12). That is, I cannot see God, but as a compensation, I can see my brother, and if I love him, God dwells in me. Is that really true? That I cannot see God, but I must love my brother, and then God will dwell in me? Loving my brother is the way to real fellowship with God. You know what

John further says in that most solemn test: "If someone says, 'I love God,' and hates his brother, he is a liar; for he who does not love his brother whom he has seen, how can he love God whom he has not seen?" (1 John 4:20). There is a brother, a most unlovable man. He worries you every time you meet him. He is of the very opposite disposition to yours. You are a careful businessman, and you have to do with him in your business. He is most untidy, unbusinesslike. You say: "I cannot love him."

Oh, friend, you have not learned the lesson that Christ wanted to teach above everything. Let a man be what he will, but you are to love him. Love is to be the fruit of the Spirit all the day and every day. Yes, listen! If a man doesn't love his brother whom he has seen—if you don't love that unlovable man whom you have seen, how can you love God whom you have not seen? You can deceive yourself with beautiful thoughts about loving God. You must prove your love to God by your love to your brother. That is the one standard by which God will judge your love for Him. If the love of God is in your heart, you will love your brother. The fruit of the Spirit is love.

> *The children of God, wherever they come together, to whatever church or mission or society they belong, must love each other intensely, or the Spirit of God cannot do His work.*

And what is the reason that God's Holy Spirit cannot come in power? Is it not possible?

You remember the comparison I used in speaking of the vessel. I can dip a little water into a potsherd—a bit of a vessel. But if a vessel is to be full, it must be unbroken. And the children of God, wherever they come together, to whatever church or mission or society they belong, must love each other intensely, or the Spirit of God cannot do His work. We talk about grieving the Spirit of God by worldliness and ritualism and formality and error and indifference, but, I tell you, the one thing above everything that grieves God's Spirit is this lack of love. Let every heart search itself and ask that God may search it.

5. Why are we taught that "the fruit of the Spirit is love"? *Because the Spirit of God has come to make our daily life an exhibition of divine power and a revelation of what God can do for His children.*

In the second and the fourth chapters of Acts, we read that the disciples were of one heart and of one soul. During the three years they had walked with Christ they never had been in that spirit. All Christ's teaching could not make them of one heart and one soul. But the Holy Spirit came from heaven and shed the love of God in their hearts, and they were of one heart and one soul. The same Holy Spirit who brought the love of heaven into their hearts must fill us, too. Nothing less will do. Even as Christ did, one might preach love for three years with the tongue of an angel, but that would not teach any man to love unless the power of the Holy Spirit comes upon him to bring the love of heaven into his heart.

Think of the church at large. What divisions! Think of the different bodies. Take the questions of holiness, of the cleansing blood, of the baptism of the Spirit—what differences are caused among dear believers by such questions! That there are differences of opinion does not trouble me. We do not have the same constitution and temperament and mind. But how often hate, bitterness, contempt, separation, unlovingness are caused by the holiest truths of God's Word! Our doctrines and creeds have been more important than love. We often think we are valiant for the truth, but we forget God's command to speak the truth *in love* (Eph. 4:15). And it was so in the time of the Reformation between the Lutheran and Calvinistic churches. What bitterness there was then in regard to the holy supper, which was meant to be the bond of union among all believers! And so, down the ages, the very dearest truths of God have become mountains that have separated us.

If we want to pray in power, and if we want to expect the Holy Spirit to come down in power, and if we want indeed that God shall pour out His Spirit, we must enter into a covenant with God that we love one another with a heavenly love.

> *I*f my vow—absolute surrender to God—was true, then it must mean absolute surrender to the divine love to fill me so that I can be a servant of love to love every child of God around me.

Are you ready for that? Only that is true love that is large enough to take in all God's children, the most unloving and unlovable, and unworthy, and unbearable, and trying. If my vow—absolute surrender to God—was true, then it must mean absolute surrender to the divine love to fill me so that I can be a servant of love to love every child of God around me. "The fruit of the Spirit is love."

Oh, God did something wonderful when He gave Christ, at His right hand, the Holy Spirit to come down out of the heart of the Father and His everlasting love. And how we have degraded the Holy Spirit into a mere power by which we have to do our work! God forgive us! Oh, that the Holy Spirit might be held in honor as a power to fill us with the very life and nature of God and of Christ!

6. "The fruit of the Spirit is love." I ask once again, Why is it so? And the answer comes: *That is the only power in which Christians really can do their work.*

Yes, it is that we need. We lack not only love that is to bind us to each other, but we lack a divine love in our work for the lost around us. Oh, do we not often undertake a great deal of work, just as men undertake work of philanthropy, from a natural spirit of compassion for our fellowmen? Do we not often undertake Christian work because our minister or friend calls us to it? And do we not often perform Christian work with a certain zeal but without having had a baptism of love?

People often ask: "What is the baptism of fire?"

I have answered more than once: I know no fire like the fire of God, the fire of everlasting love that consumed the sacrifice on Calvary. The baptism of love is what the Church needs. To get that we must begin immediately to get down on our faces before God in confession and plead: "Lord, let love from heaven flow down into my heart. I am giving up my life to pray and live as one who has given himself up for the everlasting love to dwell in and fill him."

Ah, yes, if the love of God were in our hearts, what a difference it would make! There are hundreds of believers who say: "I work for Christ, and I feel I could work much harder, but I don't have the gift. I do not know how or where to begin. I do not know what I can do."

Brother, sister: Ask God to baptize you with the Spirit of love, and then love will find its way. Love is a fire that will burn through every difficulty. You may be a shy, hesitating man who cannot speak well, but love can burn through everything. God fill us with love! We need it for our work.

You have read many a touching story of love expressed, and you have said, "How beautiful!" I heard one not long ago. A lady had been asked to speak at a Rescue Home where there were a number of poor women. As she arrived there and got to the window with the matron, she saw outside a wretched object sitting, and asked: "Who is that?"

The matron answered: "She has been into the house thirty or forty times, and she has always gone away again. Nothing can be done with her, she is so low and hard."

But the lady said: "She must come in."

The matron then said: "We have been waiting for you, and the company is assembled, and you have only an hour for the address."

The lady replied: "No, this is of more importance," and then she went outside where the woman was sitting and said: "My sister, what is the matter?"

"I am not your sister," was the reply.

Then the lady laid her hand on her and said: "Yes, I am your sister, and I love you." She spoke this way until the heart of the poor woman was touched.

The conversation lasted some time, and the company was waiting patiently. Ultimately the lady brought the woman into the room. There was the poor wretched, degraded creature, full of shame. She would not sit on a chair but sat down on a stool beside the speaker's seat, and she let her lean against her, with her arms around the poor woman's neck, while she spoke to the assembled people. And that love touched the woman's heart, and she had found one who really loved her, and that love gave access to the love of Jesus.

Praise God! There is love on earth in the hearts of God's children. But oh, that there were more!

O God, baptize our ministers with a tender love, and our missionaries, and our Bible readers, and our workers, and our young men's and young women's associations. Oh, that God would begin with us now and baptize us with heavenly love!

7. Once again: *It is only love that can make us fit for the work of intercession.*

I have said that love must make us fit for our work. Do you know what the hardest and the most important work is that has to be done for this sinful world? It is the work of intercession, the work of going to God and taking time to lay hold on Him.

A man may be an earnest Christian, an earnest minister, and a man may do good. But, sadly, how often he has to confess that he knows very little of what it is to wait with God. May God give us the great gift of an intercessory spirit, a spirit of prayer and supplication! Let me ask you in the name of Jesus not to let a day pass without praying for all saints, and for all God's people.

> *raise God! There is love on earth in the hearts of God's children. But oh, that there were more!*

I find there are Christians who think little of that. I find there are prayer unions where they pray for the members, and not for all believers. I encourage you, take time to pray for the Church of Christ. It is right to pray for the heathen, as I have already said. God help us to pray more for them. It is right to pray for missionaries, for evangelistic work, and for the unconverted. But Paul did not tell people to pray for the heathen or the unconverted. Paul told them to pray for believers. Do make this your first prayer every day: "Lord, bless Your saints everywhere."

The state of Christ's Church is indescribably low. Plead for God's people that He would visit them. Plead for each other. Plead for all believers who are trying to work for God. Let love fill your heart. Ask Christ to pour it out freshly into you every day. Try to get it into you by the Holy Spirit of God: I am separated to the Holy Spirit, and the fruit of the Spirit is love. God help us to understand it.

May God grant that we learn day by day to wait more quietly on Him. Do not wait on God only for ourselves, or the power to do so will soon be lost. Instead, give ourselves up to the ministry and the love of intercession, and pray more for God's people, for God's people around about us, for the Spirit of love in ourselves and in them, and for the work of God we are connected with. Then the answer will surely come, and our waiting on God will be a source of untold blessing and power. "The fruit of the Spirit is love."

Have you a lack of love to confess before God? Then make confession and say before Him, "O Lord, my lack of heart, my lack of love—I confess it." And then, as you cast that lack at His feet, believe that the blood cleanses you, that Jesus comes in His mighty, cleansing, saving power to deliver you, and that He will give His Holy Spirit.

"THE FRUIT OF THE SPIRIT IS LOVE."

For Further Thought

1. What does the biblical truth that "God is love" mean to you personally? How does God identifying Himself as love move you toward absolute surrender to Him?
2. Why is it so hard at times to love? Why do your efforts at loving others fail? What is the remedy for that failure?
3. Why does the Bible teach that the fruit of the Spirit is love? What kind of difference is that to make in your daily walk of faith in and love for God? What kind of difference is that to make in your relationships with other people?

3

SEPARATED TO
THE HOLY SPIRIT

Now in the church that was at Antioch there were certain
prophets and teachers: Barnabas, Simeon who was called Niger,
Lucius of Cyrene, Manaen. . .and Saul. As they ministered to
the Lord and fasted, the Holy Spirit said, "Now separate to Me
Barnabas and Saul for the work to which I have called them."
Then, having fasted and prayed, and laid hands on them, they
sent them away. So, being sent out by the Holy Spirit,
they went down to Seleucia.
ACTS 13:1–4

IN the story of our text we shall find some precious thoughts to guide us as to what God desires to have of us, and what God desires to do for us. The great lesson of the verses quoted is this: *The Holy Spirit is the director of the work of God on the earth.* And what we should do if we are to work rightly for God, and if God is to bless our work, is to see that we stand in a right relationship to the Holy Spirit, that we give Him every day the place of honor that belongs to Him, and that in all our work and (what is more) in all our private inner life, the Holy Spirit shall always have the first place. Let me point out to you some of the precious thoughts our passage suggests.

First of all, we see that *God has His own plans with regard to His kingdom.*

His church at Antioch had been established. God had certain plans and intentions with regard to Asia and with regard to Europe. He had conceived them. They were His, and He made them known to His servants.

Our great commander organizes every campaign, and His generals and officers do not always know the great plans. They often receive sealed orders, and they have to wait on Him for what He gives them as orders. God in heaven has wishes and a will in regard to any work that ought to be done, and to the way in which it has to be done. Blessed is the man who gets into God's secrets and works under God.

Some years ago, at Wellington, South Africa, where I live, we opened a

Mission Institute—what is counted there a fine large building. At our opening services the principal said something that I have never forgotten. He remarked:

"Last year we gathered here to lay the foundation stone, and what was there then to be seen? Nothing but rubbish and stones and bricks and ruins of an old building that had been pulled down. There we laid the foundation stone, and very few knew what the building was that was to rise. No one knew it perfectly in every detail except one man, the architect. In his mind it was all clear, and as the contractor and the mason and the carpenter came to their work, they took their orders from him, and the humblest laborer had to be obedient to orders, and the structure rose, and this beautiful building has been completed. And just so," he added, "this building that we open today is but laying the foundation of a work of which only God knows what is to become."

But God has His workers and His plans clearly mapped out, and our position is to wait, so that God would communicate to us as much of His will as each time needs.

We need simply to be faithful in obedience, in carrying out His orders. God has a plan for His Church on earth. But, sadly, we too often make our plan, and we think that we know what ought to be done. We ask God first to bless our weak efforts, instead of absolutely refusing to go unless God goes before us. God has planned for the work and the extension of His kingdom. The Holy Spirit has had that work given in charge to Him. "The work to which I have called them." May God, therefore, help us all to be afraid of touching "the ark of God" except as we are led by the Holy Spirit.

Then the *second* thought—*God is willing and able to reveal to His servants what His will is.*

Yes, blessed be God, communications still come down from heaven! As we read here what the Holy Spirit said, so the Holy Spirit will still speak to His Church and His people. In these later days He has often done it. He has come to individual men, and by His divine teaching He has led them out into fields of labor that others could not at first understand or approve, and into ways and methods that did not seem right to the majority. But the Holy Spirit does still in our time teach His people. Thank God, in our foreign missionary societies, in our home missions, and in a thousand forms of work, the guiding of the Holy Spirit is known, but (we are all ready, I think, to confess) *too little* known. We have not learned enough to wait on Him, and so we should make a solemn declaration before God: "O God, we want to wait more for You to show us Your will."

Do not ask God only for power. Many a Christian has his own plan of working, but God must send the power. The man works in his own will, and God must give the grace—that is the one reason why God often gives so little grace and so little success. But let us all take our place before God and say: "What is done in the will of God, the strength of God will not be withheld from it. What is done in the will of God must have the mighty blessing of God."

And so let our first desire be to have the will of God revealed.

If you ask me, "Is it an easy thing to get these communications from heaven, and to understand them?" I can give you the answer. It is easy to those who are in right fellowship with heaven, and who understand the art of waiting on God.

How often we ask: "How can a person know the will of God?" And people want, when they are confused, to pray very earnestly that God would answer them immediately. But God can only reveal His will to a heart that is humble and tender and empty. God can only reveal His will in perplexities and special difficulties to a heart that has learned to obey and honor Him loyally in little things and in daily life.

That brings me to the *third* thought—*Note the disposition to which the Spirit reveals God's will.*

What do we read here? There were a number of men ministering to the Lord and fasting, and the Holy Spirit came and spoke to them. Some people understand this passage very much as they would in reference to a missionary committee of our day. We see there is an open field. We have had our missions in other fields, and we are going to get on to that field. We have virtually settled that, and we pray about it. But the position was a very different one in those former days. I doubt whether any of them thought of Europe, for later on even Paul himself tried to go back into Asia, until the night vision called him by the will of God. Look at those men. God had done wonders. He had extended the Church to Antioch, and He had given rich and large blessing. Now, here were these men ministering to the Lord, serving Him with prayer and fasting. What a deep conviction they have: "It must all come directly from heaven. We are in fellowship with the risen Lord. We must have a close union with Him, and somehow He will let us know what He wants." And there they were—empty, ignorant, helpless, glad and joyful, but deeply humbled.

> *W*e need simply to be faithful in obedience, in carrying out His orders. God has a plan for His Church on earth.

"O Lord," they seem to say, "we are Your servants, and in fasting and prayer we wait on You. What is Your will for us?"

Was it not the same with Peter? He was on the housetop, fasting and praying, and little did he think of the vision and the command to go to Caesarea. He was ignorant of what his work might be (see Acts 10:9–23).

It is in hearts entirely surrendered to the Lord Jesus, in hearts separating themselves from the world, and even from ordinary religious exercises, and giving themselves up in intense prayer to look to their Lord—it is in such hearts that the heavenly will of God will be made known.

You know that word *fasting* occurs a second time (in the third verse): "They fasted and prayed." When you pray, you love to go into your closet, according to the command of Jesus, and shut the door. You shut out business and company and pleasure and anything that can distract, and you want to be alone with God. But in one way, even the material world follows you there. You must eat. These men wanted to shut themselves out from the influences of the material and the visible, and so they fasted. What they ate was simply enough to supply the wants of nature, and in the intensity of their souls they thought to give expression to their letting go of everything on earth in their fasting before God.

> *It is in hearts entirely surrendered to the Lord Jesus, in hearts separating themselves from the world—it is in such hearts that the heavenly will of God will be made known.*

Oh, may God give us that intensity of desire, that separation from everything, because we want to wait on God so that the Holy Spirit may reveal to us God's blessed will.

The *fourth* thought—*What is now the will of God as the Holy Spirit reveals it?* It is contained in one phrase: *Separation to the Holy Spirit.* That is the keynote of the message from heaven.

"Separate to Me Barnabas and Saul for the work to which I have called them. The work is mine, and I care for it, and I have chosen these men and called them, and I want you who represent the Church of Christ on earth to set them apart to Me."

Look at this heavenly message in its twofold aspect. The men were to be *set apart* to the Holy Spirit, and *the Church was to do this separating work.* The Holy Spirit could trust these men to do it in a right spirit. There they were abiding in fellowship with the heavenly, and the Holy Spirit could say to them, "Do the work of separating these men." And these were the men the Holy Spirit had prepared, and He could say of them, "Let them be separated to Me."

Here we come to the very root, to the very life of the need of Christian workers. The question is: What is needed so that the power of God should rest on us more mightily, that the blessing of God should be poured out more abundantly among those poor, wretched people and perishing sinners among whom we labor? And the answer from heaven is: "I want men separated to the Holy Spirit."

What does that imply? You know that there are two spirits on earth. Christ said, when He spoke about the Holy Spirit: "The world cannot receive [Him]" (John 14:17). Paul said: "Now we have received, not the spirit of the world, but the Spirit who is from God" (1 Cor. 2:12). That is the great need in every worker—the spirit of the world going out, and the Spirit of God coming in to take possession of the inner life and of the whole being.

I am sure there are workers who often cry to God for the Holy Spirit to come on them as a Spirit of power for their work, and when they feel that measure of power and get blessing, they thank God for it. But God wants something more and something higher. God wants us to seek for the Holy Spirit as a Spirit of power in our own heart and life, to conquer self and cast out sin, and to work the blessed and beautiful image of Jesus into us.

There is a difference between the power of the Spirit as a gift, and the power of the Spirit for the grace of a holy life. A man may often have a measure of the power of the Spirit, but if there is not a large measure of the Spirit as the Spirit of grace and holiness, the defect will be seen in his work. He may be made the means of conversion, but he never will help people on to a higher standard of spiritual life, and when he passes away, a great deal of his work may pass away, too. But a man who is separated to the Holy Spirit is a man who is given up to say: "Father, let the Holy Spirit have full dominion over me—in my home, in my temper, in every word of my tongue, in every thought of my heart, in every feeling toward my fellowmen. Let the Holy Spirit have entire possession."

Is that what has been the longing and the covenant of your heart with your God—to be a man or a woman separated and given up to the Holy Spirit? I pray you listen to the voice of heaven. "Separate to Me," said the Holy Spirit. Yes, *separated* to the Holy Spirit. May God grant that the Word may enter into the very depths of our being to search us, and if we discover that we have not come out from the world entirely, if God reveals to us that the self-life, self-will, self-exaltation are there, let us humble ourselves before Him.

Man, woman, brother, sister: You are a worker separated to the Holy Spirit. Is that true? Has that been your longing desire? Has that been your surrender? Has that been what you have expected through faith in the power of our risen and almighty Lord Jesus? If not, here is the call of faith, and here is the key of blessing—*separated to the Holy Spirit*. God write the word in our hearts!

I said the Holy Spirit spoke to that church as a church capable of doing that work. The Holy Spirit trusted them. God grant that our churches, our missionary societies, and our workers' unions, that all our directors and councils and committees may be men and women who are *fit for the work of separating workers to the Holy Spirit*. We can ask God for that, too.

Then comes my *fifth* thought, and it is this: *This holy partnership with the Holy Spirit in this work becomes a matter of consciousness and of action.*

These men, what did they do? They set apart Paul and Barnabas, and then it is written of the two that they, being sent out by the Holy Spirit, went down to Seleucia. Oh, what fellowship! The Holy Spirit in heaven doing part of the work, men on earth doing the other part. After the ordination of the men on earth, it is written in God's inspired Word that they were sent out by the Holy Spirit.

And see how this partnership calls to new prayer and fasting. They had for a certain time been ministering to the Lord and fasting—perhaps for days. And the Holy Spirit speaks, and they have to do the work and to enter into partnership, and immediately they come together for more prayer and fasting. That is the spirit in which they obey the command of their Lord. And that teaches us that it is not only in the beginning of our Christian work, but all along that we need to have our strength in prayer.

If there is one thought with regard to the Church of Christ, which at times comes to me with overwhelming sorrow; if there is one thought in regard to my own life of which I am ashamed; if there is one thought of which I feel that the Church of Christ has not accepted it and not grasped it; if there is one thought that makes me pray to God: "Oh, teach us by Your grace new things"—it is the wonderful power that prayer is meant to have in the kingdom. We have so little availed ourselves of it.

We have all read the expression of Christian in Bunyan's great work, when he found he had the key in his breast that would unlock the dungeon. We have the key that can unlock the dungeon of atheism and of heathendom. But we are far more occupied with our work than we are with prayer. We believe more in speaking to men than we believe in speaking to God. Learn from these men that the work that the Holy Spirit commands must call us to new fasting and prayer, to new separation from the spirit and the pleasures of the world, to new consecration to God and to His fellowship.

Those men gave themselves up to fasting and prayer, and if in all our ordinary Christian work there were more prayer, there would be more blessing in our own inner life. If we felt and proved and testified to the world that our only strength lay in keeping every minute in contact with Christ, every minute allowing God to work in us—if that were our spirit, would not, by the grace of God, our lives be holier? Would not they be more abundantly fruitful?

I hardly know a more solemn warning in God's Word than that which we find in the third chapter of Galatians, where Paul asked: "Having begun in the Spirit, are you now being made perfect by the flesh?" (3:3).

Do you understand what that means? A terrible danger in Christian work, just as in a Christian life that is begun with much prayer, begun in the Holy Spirit, is that it may be gradually moved off on to the lines of the flesh. And the word comes: "Having begun in the Spirit, are you now being made perfect by the flesh?" In the time of our first perplexity and helplessness we prayed much to God, and God answered and God blessed, and our organization became perfected, and our band of workers became large. But gradually the organization and the work and the rush have so taken possession of us that the power of the Spirit, in which we began when we were a small company, has almost been lost. Oh, I encourage you, note it well! It was with new prayer and fasting, with more prayer and fasting, that this company of disciples carried out the command of the Holy Spirit. "My soul, wait silently for God alone" (Ps. 62:5). That is our highest and most important work. The Holy Spirit comes in answer to believing prayer.

You know when the exalted Jesus had ascended to the throne, for ten days the footstool of the throne was the place where His waiting disciples cried to Him.

And that is the law of the kingdom—the King on the throne, the servants on the footstool. May God find us there unceasingly!

Then comes the *last* thought—*What a wonderful blessing comes when the Holy Spirit is allowed to lead and to direct the work, and when it is carried on in obedience to Him!*

You know the story of the mission on which Barnabas and Saul were sent out. You know what power there was with them. The Holy Spirit sent them, and they went on from place to place with large blessing. The Holy Spirit was their leader further on. You recollect how it was by the Spirit that Paul was hindered from going again into Asia and was led away over to Europe. Oh, the blessing that rested on that little company of men and on their ministry to the Lord!

> *I*s that what has been the longing and the covenant of your heart with your God—to be a man or a woman separated and given up to the Holy Spirit? I pray you listen to the voice of heaven. "Separate to Me," said the Holy Spirit.

I encourage you, let us learn to believe that God has a blessing for us. The Holy Spirit, into whose hands God has put the work, has been called "the executive of the Holy Trinity." The Holy Spirit has not only power, but He has the Spirit of love. He is brooding over this dark world and every sphere of work in it, and He is willing to bless. And why is there not more blessing? There can be but one answer. We have not honored the Holy Spirit as we should have done. Is there one who can say that that is not true? Is not every thoughtful heart ready to cry: "God forgive me that I have not honored the Holy Spirit as I should have done, that I have grieved Him, that I have allowed self and the flesh and my own will to work where the Holy Spirit should have been honored! May God forgive me that I have allowed self and the flesh and the will actually to have the place that God wanted the Holy Spirit to have."

Oh, the sin is greater than we know! No wonder that there is so much weakness and failure in the Church of Christ!

FOR FURTHER THOUGHT

1. *God is willing and able to reveal to His servants—including you—what His will is. How does He reveal that will?*
2. *What must be your heart attitude to receive the revelation of His will? What must be your relationship with God before you can know what His will is?*
3. *The Holy Spirit has been called "the executive of the Holy Trinity." What does that mean, and how does it affect your approach to His work in your life?*

4

PETER'S REPENTANCE

And the Lord turned and looked at Peter. Then Peter
remembered the word of the Lord, how He had said to him,
"Before the rooster crows, you will deny Me three times."
So Peter went out and wept bitterly.
LUKE 22:61–62

THAT was the turning point in the history of Peter. Christ had said to him: "You cannot follow Me now" (John 13:36). Peter was not in a fit state to follow Christ, because he had not been brought to an end of himself. He did not know himself, and he therefore could not follow Christ. But when he went out and wept bitterly, then came the great change. Christ previously said to him: "When you have returned to Me, strengthen your brethren" (Luke 22:32). Here is the point where Peter was converted from self to Christ.

I thank God for the story of Peter. I do not know a man in the Bible who gives us greater comfort. When we look at his character, so full of failures, and at what Christ made him by the power of the Holy Spirit, there is hope for every one of us. But remember, before Christ could fill Peter with the Holy Spirit and make a new man of him, he had to go out and weep bitterly—he had to be humbled. If we want to understand this, I think there are four points that we must look at. First, let us look at *Peter the devoted disciple of Jesus*; next, at *Peter as he lived the life of self*; then at *Peter in his repentance*; and last, at *what Christ made of Peter by the Holy Spirit*.

1. First, then, look at Peter the devoted disciple of Christ. Christ called Peter to forsake his nets and follow Him. Peter did it at once, and he afterward could say rightly to the Lord: "We have left all and followed You" (Matt. 19:27).

Peter was a man of *absolute surrender*, because he gave up all to follow Jesus. Peter was also a man of *ready obedience*. You remember Christ said to him, "Launch out into the deep and let down your nets for a catch." Peter the fisherman knew there were no fish there, for they had been toiling all night and had caught nothing; but he said: "At Your word I will let down the net" (Luke 5:4–5). He submitted to the word of Jesus. Further, he was a man *of great faith*. When he saw Christ walking on the sea, he said: "Lord, if it is You, command me to come to You" (Matt. 14:28), and at the voice of Christ he stepped out of the boat and walked on the water.

And Peter was a man of *spiritual insight*. When Christ asked the disciples: "Who do you say I am?" Peter was able to answer: "You are the Christ, the Son of the living God." And Christ said: "Blessed are you, Simon Bar-Jonah, for flesh and blood has not revealed this to you, but My Father who is in heaven" (Matt. 16:15–17). And Christ spoke of him as the *rock* man and of his having the keys of the kingdom. Peter was a splendid man, a devoted disciple of Jesus, and if he were living nowadays, everyone would say that he was an advanced Christian. And yet how much there was lacking in Peter!

2. Look next at Peter living the life of self, pleasing self, and trusting self, and seeking the honor of self.

You recollect that just after Christ had said to him: "Flesh and blood has not revealed this to you, but My Father who is in heaven," Christ began to speak about His sufferings, and Peter dared to say: "Far be it from You, Lord; this shall not happen to You!" Then Christ had to say: "Get behind Me, Satan! ...for you are not mindful of the things of God, but the things of men" (Matt. 16:22–23).

There was Peter in his self-will, trusting his own wisdom, and actually forbidding Christ to go and die. From where did that come? Peter trusted in himself and his own thoughts about divine things. We see later on, more than once, that among the disciples there was a questioning who would be the greatest, and Peter was one of them, and he thought he had a right to the very first place. He sought his own honor even above the others. It was the life of self strong in Peter. He had left his boats and his nets, but not his old self.

When Christ had spoken to him about His sufferings and said: "Get behind me, Satan," He followed it up by saying: "If anyone desires to come after Me, let him deny himself, and take up his cross, and follow Me" (Matt. 16:24). No man can follow Him unless he does that. Self must be utterly denied. What does that mean? When Peter denied Christ, we read that he said three times: "I do not know the man"—in other words, "I have nothing to do with Him. He and I are not friends. I deny having any connection with Him." Christ told Peter that he must deny self. Self must be ignored, and its every claim rejected. That is the root of true discipleship, but Peter did not understand it and could not obey it. And what happened? When the last night came, Christ said to him: "Before the rooster crows twice, you will deny Me three times" (Mark 14:30).

But with what self-confidence Peter said: "Though all should forsake You, I will not. Lord, I am ready to go with You, both to prison and to death" (Luke 22:33).

Peter meant it honestly, and Peter really intended to do it, but Peter did not know himself. He did not believe he was as bad as Jesus said he was.

We perhaps think of individual sins that come between us and God, but what are we to do with that self-life, which is all unclean, with our very nature? What are we to do with that flesh, which is entirely under the power of sin? Deliverance from that is what we need. Peter didn't know that, and therefore it was that in his self-confidence he went forth and denied his Lord.

> *eter was a splendid man, a devoted disciple of Jesus, and if he were living nowadays, everyone would say that he was an advanced Christian. And yet how much there was lacking in Peter!*

Notice how Christ uses that word *deny* twice. He said to Peter the first time, "*Deny self,*" and He said to Peter the second time, "*You will deny me.*" It is either of the two. There is no choice for us. We must either deny self or deny Christ. There are two great powers fighting each other—the self-nature in the power of sin, and Christ in the power of God. Either of these must rule within us.

It was self that made the devil. He was an angel of God, but he wanted to exalt self. He became a devil in hell. Self was the cause of the fall of man. Eve wanted something for herself, and so our first parents fell into all the wretchedness of sin. We their children have inherited an awful nature of sin.

3. Look now at Peter's repentance. Peter denied his Lord three times, and then the Lord looked at him. That look of Jesus broke the heart of Peter, and all at once there opened up before him the terrible sin that he had committed, the terrible failure that had come, and the depth into which he had fallen, and "Peter went out and wept bitterly."

Oh! who can tell what that repentance must have been? During the following hours of that night and the next day, when he saw Christ crucified and buried, and the next day, the Sabbath—oh, in what hopeless despair and shame he must have spent that day!

"My Lord is gone, and my hope is gone, and I denied my Lord. After that life of love, after that blessed fellowship of three years, I denied my Lord. God have mercy on me!"

I do not think we can realize into what a depth of humiliation Peter sank then. But that was the turning point and the change, and on the first day of the week Peter saw Christ, and in the evening He met him with the others. Later on at the Lake of Galilee, He asked him: "Do you love Me?" until Peter was made sad by the thought that the Lord reminded him of having denied Him three times, and said in sorrow, but in uprightness: "Lord, You know all things; You know that I love You" (John 21:17).

4. And then Peter was prepared for the deliverance from self, and that is my last thought. You know Christ took him with others to the footstool of the throne and told them to wait there, and then on the day of Pentecost the Holy Spirit came, and Peter was a changed man. I do not want you to think only of

the change in Peter—in that boldness, and that power, and that insight into the scriptures, and that blessing with which he preached that day. Thank God for that. But there was something for Peter deeper and better. Peter's whole nature was changed. The work that Christ began in Peter when He looked at him was perfected when he was filled with the Holy Spirit.

If you want to see that, read the First Epistle of Peter. You know where Peter's failings lay. When he said to Christ, in effect: "You never can suffer; it cannot be"—it showed he had no conception of what it was to pass through death into life. Christ said: *"Deny yourself,"* and in spite of that he denied his Lord. When Christ warned him: "You will deny Me," and he insisted that he never would, Peter showed how little he understood what there was in himself. But when I read his epistle and hear him say: "If you are reproached for the name of Christ, blessed are you, for the Spirit of glory and of God rests upon you" (1 Pet. 4:14), then I say that it is not the old Peter, but that is the very Spirit of Christ breathing and speaking within him.

> *I* do not think we can realize into what a depth of humiliation Peter sank then. But that was the turning point and the change, and on the first day of the week Peter saw Christ, and in the evening He met him with the others.

I read again how he says: "For to this you were called, because Christ also suffered" (1 Pet. 2:21). I understand what a change had come over Peter. Instead of denying Christ, he found joy and pleasure in having self denied and crucified and given up to the death. And therefore it is in the Acts we read that, when he was called before the Council, he could boldly say: "We must obey God rather than men" (Acts 5:29), and that he could return with the other disciples and rejoice that they were counted worthy to suffer for Christ's name.

You remember his self-exaltation, but now he has found out that "the incorruptible beauty of a gentle and quiet spirit, which is very precious in the sight of God" (1 Pet. 3:4). Again he tells us to be "submissive to one another, and be clothed with humility" (1 Pet. 5:5).

Dear friend, I ask you to look at Peter utterly changed—the self-pleasing, the self-trusting, the self-seeking Peter, full of sin, continually getting into trouble, foolish and impetuous, but now filled with the Spirit and the life of Jesus. Christ had done it for him by the Holy Spirit.

And now, what is my object in having thus very briefly pointed to the story of Peter? That story must be the history of every believer who is really to be made a blessing by God. That story is a prophecy of what everyone can receive from God in heaven.

Now let us just glance hurriedly at what these lessons teach us.

The *first lesson* is this: You may be a very earnest, godly, devoted believer, in whom the power of the flesh is yet very strong.

That is a very solemn truth. Peter, before he denied Christ, had cast out demons and had healed the sick, and yet the flesh had power, and the flesh had room in him. Oh, beloved, we have to realize that it is just because there is so much of that self-life in us that the power of God cannot work in us as mightily as God is willing that it should work.

Do you realize that the great God is longing to double His blessing, to give tenfold blessing through us? But there is something hindering Him, and that something is a proof of nothing but the self-life. We talk about the pride of Peter, and the impetuosity of Peter, and the self-confidence of Peter. It all rooted in that one word: *self*. Christ had said, "Deny self," and Peter had never understood and never obeyed, and his every failing came out of that.

What a solemn thought, and what an urgent plea for us to cry: "O God, reveal this to us, so that none of us may be living the self-life!" It has happened to many an individual who had been a Christian for years, who had perhaps occupied a prominent position, that God found him out and taught him to find himself out, and he became utterly ashamed, falling down broken before God. Oh, the bitter shame and sorrow and pain and agony that came to him, until at last he found that there was deliverance! Peter went out and wept bitterly, and there may be many a godly one in whom the power of the flesh still rules.

> *O*h, beloved, we have to realize that it is just because there is so much of that self-life in us that the power of God cannot work in us as mightily as God is willing that it should work.

And then my *second lesson* is: It is the work of our blessed Lord Jesus to reveal the power of self.

How was it that Peter—the carnal Peter, self-willed Peter, Peter with the strong self-love—ever became a man of Pentecost and the writer of his epistles? It was because Christ had him in charge, and Christ watched over him, and Christ taught and blessed him. The warnings that Christ had given him were part of the training. And last of all there came that look of love. In His suffering, Christ did not forget him but turned around and looked at him, and "Peter went out and wept bitterly." And the Christ who led Peter to Pentecost is waiting today to take charge of every heart that is willing to surrender itself to Him.

Are there not some saying: "Yes, that is the problem with me. It is always the self-life, and self-comfort, and self-consciousness, and self-pleasing, and self-will. How do I get rid of it?"

My answer is: It is Christ Jesus who can rid you of it. No one else but Christ Jesus can give deliverance from the power of self. And what does He ask you to do? He asks that you would humble yourself before Him.

FOR FURTHER THOUGHT

1. *How was Peter's absolute surrender to Jesus Christ demonstrated prior to his fall? What about Peter can you take as an example to follow?*

2. *How did Peter's denial of Jesus Christ affect him immediately? What was the long-term benefit he received from the humiliation of falling where he told Jesus he would never fall? What did his failure prepare him for?*

3. *In what ways was Peter an example to you of being rid of self-life, self-comfort, self-consciousness, and self-will? How can you follow that example?*

5

IMPOSSIBLE WITH MAN, POSSIBLE WITH GOD

But He said, "The things which are
impossible with men are possible with God."
LUKE 18:27

CHRIST had said to the rich young ruler, "Sell all that you have. . .and come, follow Me" (Luke 18:22). The young man went away sorrowful. Christ then turned to the disciples and said: "How hard it is for those who have riches to enter the kingdom of God!" (18:24). The disciples, we read, were greatly astonished and answered: "If it is so difficult to enter the kingdom, who, then, can be saved?" And Christ gave this blessed answer: "The things which are impossible with men are possible with God."

The text contains two thoughts—that *in religion, in the question of salvation and of following Christ by a holy life, it is impossible for man to do it.* And then alongside that is the thought—*What is impossible with man is possible with God.*

The two thoughts mark the two great lessons that man has to learn in the religious life. It often takes a long time to learn the first lesson, that in religion man can do nothing, that salvation is impossible to man. And often a man learns that, and yet he does not learn the second lesson—what has been impossible to him is possible with God. Blessed is the man who learns both lessons! The learning of them marks stages in the Christian's life.

1. The one stage is when a man is trying to do his utmost and fails, when a man tries to do better and fails again, when a man tries much more and always fails. And yet very often he does not even then learn the lesson: *With man it is impossible to serve God and Christ.* Peter spent three years in Christ's school, and he never learned that word, *It is impossible,* until he had denied his Lord and went out and wept bitterly. Then he learned it.

Just look for a moment at a man who is learning this lesson. At first he fights against it, and then he submits to it, but reluctantly and in despair. At last he accepts it willingly and rejoices in it. At the beginning of the Christian life, the young convert has no conception of this truth. He has been converted, he has the joy of the

Lord in his heart, and he begins to run the race and fight the battle. He is sure he can conquer, for he is earnest and honest, and God will help him. Yet, somehow, very soon he fails where he did not expect it, and sin gets the better of him. He is disappointed, but he thinks, *I was not watchful enough, and I did not make my resolutions strong enough*. And again he vows, and again he prays, and yet he fails. He thought: *Am I not a regenerate man? Have I not the life of God within me?* And he thinks again: *Yes, and I have Christ to help me, so I can live the holy life.*

At a later period he comes to another state of mind. He begins to see such a life is impossible, but he does not accept it. There are multitudes of Christians who come to this point: "I cannot," and then think God never expected them to do what they cannot do. If you tell them that God does expect it, it appears to them a mystery. A good many Christians are living a low life—a life of failure and of sin, instead of rest and victory—because they began to see: "I cannot; it is impossible." And yet they do not understand it fully, and so, under the impression, *I cannot*, they give way to despair. They will do their best, but they never expect to get on very far.

But God leads His children on to a third stage, when a man comes to take that, *It is impossible*, in its full truth, and yet at the same time says: "I must do it, and I will do it—it is impossible for man, and yet I must do it." And when the renewed will begins to exercise its whole power, and in intense longing and prayer begins to cry to God: "Lord, what is the meaning of this?—how am I to be freed from the power of sin?"

It is the state of the regenerate man in Romans 7. There you will find the Christian man trying his very utmost to live a holy life. God's law has been revealed to him as reaching down into the very depth of the desires of the heart, and the man can dare to say: "I delight in the law of God according to the inward man. To will what is good is present with me. My heart loves the law of God, and my will has chosen that law."

Can a man like that fail, with his heart full of delight in God's law and with his will determined to do what is right? Yes. That is what Romans 7 teaches us. There is something more needed. Not only must I delight in the law of God after the inward man, and will what God wills, but I need a divine omnipotence to work it in me. And that is what the apostle Paul teaches in Philippians 2:13: "It is God who works in you both to will and to do."

Note the contrast. In Romans 7 the regenerate man says: "To will is present with me, but *how* to perform what is good I do not find" (7:18). But in Philippians 2 you have a man who has been led on further, a man who understands that when God has worked the renewed will, God will give the power to accomplish what that will desires. Let us receive this as the first great lesson in the spiritual life: "It is impossible for me, my God. Let there be an end of the flesh and all its powers, an end of self, and let it be my glory to be helpless."

Praise God for the divine teaching that makes us helpless!

When you thought of absolute surrender to God, were you not brought to an end of yourself and made to feel that you could see how you actually could live as a man absolutely surrendered to God every moment of the day—at your table, in your house, in your business, in the midst of trials and temptations? I pray you learn the lesson now. If you felt you could not do it, you are on the right road—if you let yourselves be led. Accept that position, and maintain it before God: "My heart's desire and delight, O God, is absolute surrender, but I cannot perform it. It is impossible for me to live that life. It is beyond me." Fall down and learn that when you are utterly helpless, God will come to work in you not only to will, but also to do.

2. Now comes the second lesson. "The things which *are impossible with men are possible with God.*"

I said a little while ago that there is many a man who has learned the lesson, *It is impossible with men*, and then he gives up in helpless despair and lives a wretched Christian life, one without joy, strength, or victory. And why? Because he does not humble himself to learn that other lesson: *With God all things are possible.*

> *God leads His children on to a third stage, when a man comes to take that, It is impossible, in its full truth, and yet at the same time says: "I must do it, and I will do it—it is impossible for man, and yet I must do it."*

Your religious life is every day to be a proof that God works impossibilities. Your religious life is to be a series of impossibilities made possible and actual by God's almighty power. That is what the Christian needs. He has an almighty God whom he worships, and he must learn to understand that he does not need a little of God's power, but he needs—with reverence be it said—the whole of God's omnipotence to keep him right, and to live like a Christian.

The whole of Christianity is a work of God's omnipotence. Look at the birth of Christ Jesus. That was a miracle of divine power, and it was said to Mary: "With God nothing will be impossible" (Luke 1:37). It was the omnipotence of God. Look at Christ's resurrection. We are taught that it was according to the "exceeding greatness of His mighty power" that God raised Christ from the dead (see Eph. 1:19–20).

Every tree must grow on the root from which it springs. An oak tree three hundred years old grows all the time on the one root from which it had its beginning. Christianity had its beginning in the omnipotence of God, and in every soul it must have its continuance in that omnipotence. All the possibilities of the higher Christian life have their origin in a new understanding of Christ's power to work all God's will in us.

I want to call on you now to come and worship an almighty God. Have you learned to do it? Have you learned to deal so closely with an almighty God that you know omnipotence is working in you? In outward appearance there is often so little sign of it. The apostle Paul said: "I was with you in weakness, in fear, and in much trembling. And. . .my preaching [was]. . .in demonstration of the Spirit and of power" (1 Cor. 2:3–4). From the human side there was weakness, from the divine side there was divine omnipotence. And that is true of every godly life, and if we would only learn that lesson better and give a wholehearted, undivided surrender to it, we would learn what blessedness there is in dwelling every hour and every moment with an almighty God.

Have you ever studied in the Bible the attribute of God's omnipotence? You know that it was God's omnipotence that created the world, created light out of darkness, and created man. But have you studied God's omnipotence in the works of redemption?

Look at Abraham. When God called him to be the father of that people out of which Christ was to be born, God said to him: "I am Almighty God; walk before Me and be blameless" (Gen. 17:1). And God trained Abraham to trust Him as the omnipotent One, and whether it was his going out to a land that he didn't know, or his faith as a pilgrim amidst the thousands of Canaanites—his faith that said, "This is my land"—or whether it was his faith in waiting twenty-five years for a son in his old age, against all hope, or whether it was the raising up of Isaac from the dead on Mount Moriah when he was going to sacrifice him, Abraham believed God. He was strong in faith, giving glory to God, because he accounted Him who had promised able to perform. The cause of the weakness of your Christian life is that you want to work it out partly, and to let God help you. And that cannot be. You must come to be utterly helpless, to let God work, and God will work gloriously.

It is this that we need if we are indeed to be workers for God. I could go through scripture and prove to you how Moses, when he led Israel out of Egypt; how Joshua, when he brought them into the land of Canaan; how all God's servants in the Old Testament counted on the omnipotence of God doing impossibilities. And this God lives today, and this God is the God of every child of His. And yet there are some of us wanting God to give us a little help while we do our best, instead of coming to understand what God wants and to say: "I can do nothing. God must and will do all."

Have you said: "In worship, in work, in sanctification, in obedience to God, I can do nothing of myself, and so my place is to worship the omnipotent God and to believe that He will work in me every moment"? Oh, may God teach us this! Oh, that God would by His grace show you what a God you have and to what a God you have entrusted yourself—an omnipotent God, willing with His whole omnipotence to place Himself at the disposal of every child of His! Shall we not take the lesson of the Lord Jesus and say: "Amen! The things which are impossible with men are possible with God"?

Remember what we have said about Peter—about his self-confidence, self-power, self-will, and how he came to deny his Lord. You feel: "Ah, there is the self-life, there is the flesh-life that rules in me!" And now, have you believed that there is deliverance from that? Have you believed that Almighty God is able so to reveal Christ in your heart, so to let the Holy Spirit rule in you, that the self-life shall not have power or dominion over you? Have you coupled the two together, and with tears of penitence and with deep humiliation and weakness cried out: "O God, it is impossible to me! Man cannot do it, but, glory to Your name, it is possible with God"? Have you claimed deliverance? Do it now. Put yourself afresh in absolute surrender into the hands of a God of infinite love. And as infinite as His love is His power to do it.

But again, we came to the question of absolute surrender and felt that that is what the Church of Christ lacks, and that is why the Holy Spirit cannot fill us, and why we cannot live as people entirely separated to the Holy Spirit. That is why the flesh and the self-life cannot be conquered. We have never understood what it is to be absolutely surrendered to God as Jesus was. I know that many a one earnestly and honestly says, "Amen! I accept the message of absolute surrender to God" and yet thinks, "Will that ever be mine? Can I count on God to make me one of whom it shall be said in heaven and on earth and in hell, he lives in absolute surrender to God?"

> *C*hristianity had its beginning in the omnipotence of God, and in every soul it must have its continuance in that omnipotence.

Brother, sister: "The things which are impossible with men are possible with God." Do believe that when He takes charge of you in Christ, it is possible for God to make you a man of absolute surrender. And God is able to maintain that. He is able to let you rise from bed every morning of the week with that blessed thought directly or indirectly: "I am in God's charge. My God is working out my life for me."

Some are weary of thinking about sanctification. You prayed, you longed and cried for it, and yet it appeared so far off! The holiness and humility of Jesus—you are so conscious of how distant it is. Beloved friends, the one doctrine of sanctification that is scriptural and real and effectual is: "The things which are impossible with men are possible with God." God can sanctify men, and by His almighty and sanctifying power every moment, God can keep them. Oh, that we might get a step nearer to our God now! Oh, that the light of God might shine, and that we might know our God better!

I could go on to speak about the life of Christ in us—living like Christ, taking Christ as our Savior from sin and as our life and strength. It is God in heaven who can reveal that in you. What does that prayer of the apostle Paul say: "That he would grant you, according to riches of his glory"—it is sure to be something very wonderful if it is according to the riches of His glory—"to be strengthened with might by his Spirit in the inner man" (Eph. 3:16)? Do you not see that it is an omnipotent God working by His omnipotence in the heart of His believing children, so that Christ can become an indwelling Savior? You have tried to grasp it and to seize it, and you have tried to believe it, and it would not come. It was because you had not been brought to believe that "the things which are impossible with men are possible with God."

And so, I trust that the word spoken about love may have brought many to see that we must have an inflowing of love in quite a new way, that our heart must be filled with life from above, from the fountain of everlasting love, if it is going to overflow all the day. Then it will be just as natural for us to love our fellowmen as it is natural for the lamb to be gentle and the wolf to be cruel. Until I am brought to such a state that the more a man hates and speaks evil of me, the more unlikable and unlovable a man is, I shall love him all the more; until I am brought to such a state that the more the obstacles and hatred and ingratitude, the more can the power of love triumph in me—until I am brought to see that, I am not saying: "It is impossible with men." But if you have been led to say: "This message has spoken to me about a love utterly beyond my power; it is absolutely impossible"—then we can come to God and say: "It is possible with You."

Some are crying to God for a great revival. I can say that that is the unceasing prayer of my heart. Oh, if God would only revive His believing people! I cannot think in the first place of the unconverted formalists of the Church, or of the infidels and skeptics, or of all the wretched and perishing around me, my heart prays in the first place: "My God, revive Your Church and people." It is not for nothing that there are in thousands of hearts yearnings after holiness and consecration, for it is a forerunner of God's power. God works *to will* and then He works *to do* (see Phil. 2:13). These yearnings are a witness and a proof that God has worked *to will*. Oh, let us in faith believe that the omnipotent God will work *to do* among His people more than we can ask. "Now to Him," Paul said, "who is able to do exceedingly abundantly above all that we ask or think. . .to him be glory" (Eph. 3:20–21). Let our hearts say that. Glory to God, the omnipotent One, who can do above what we dare to ask or think!

"The things which are impossible with men are possible with God." All around you there is a world of sin and sorrow, and the devil is there. But remember, Christ is on the throne. Christ is stronger, Christ has conquered, and Christ will conquer. But wait on God. My text casts us down: "The things which are *impossible with men*," but it ultimately lifts us up high—"are *possible with God*." Get linked to God. Adore and trust Him as the omnipotent One, not only for your own life, but for all the souls that are entrusted to you. Never pray without adoring His omnipotence, saying: *"Mighty God, I claim Your almightiness."* And the answer to the prayer will come, and, like Abraham, you will become strong in faith, giving glory to God, because you account Him who has promised able to perform.

FOR FURTHER THOUGHT

1. *Read Luke 18:27. What is the first great lesson in the spiritual life that Jesus' words teach? How can you apply them to your own life of faith?*
2. *What should be your position with God in Christ in order to make and keep you a believer of absolute surrender?*
3. *What is the primary cause of weakness in your Christian life and in the lives of other believers? How can that cause be overcome?*

6

"O Wretched Man That I Am!"

*O wretched man that I am! Who will deliver me from this body
of death? I thank God—through Jesus Christ our Lord!*
Romans 7:24–25

YOU know the wonderful place that this text has in the wonderful epistle to the Romans. It stands here at the end of the seventh chapter as the gateway into the eighth. In the first sixteen verses of the eighth chapter, the name of the Holy Spirit is found sixteen times. You have there the description and promise of the life that a child of God can live in the power of the Holy Spirit. This begins in the second verse: "For the law of the Spirit of life in Christ Jesus has made me free from the law of sin and death" (8:2). From that Paul goes on to speak of the great privileges of the child of God, who is to be led by the Spirit of God.

The gateway into all this is in the twenty-fourth verse of the seventh chapter: "O wretched man that I am!"

There you have the words of a man who has come to the end of himself. He has in the previous verses described how he had struggled and wrestled in his own power to obey the holy law of God, and had failed. But in answer to his own question he now finds the true answer and cries out: "I thank God—through Jesus Christ our Lord." From there he goes on to speak of what that deliverance is that he has found.

I want from these words to describe the path by which a man can be led out of the spirit of bondage into the spirit of liberty. You know how distinctly it is said: "You did not receive the spirit of bondage again to fear" (Rom. 8:15). We are continually warned that this is the great danger of the Christian life, to go again into bondage. And I want to describe the path by which a man can get out of bondage into the glorious liberty of the children of God. Rather, I want to describe the man himself.

First, these words are the language of a *regenerate* man; *second,* of a powerless man; *third,* of a *wretched* man; and *fourth,* of a man *on the borders of complete liberty.*

In the first place, then, we have here the words of a regenerate man.

You know how much evidence there is of that from the fourteenth verse of the chapter on to the twenty-third. "It is no longer I who do it, but sin that dwells in me"

(7:20). That is the language of a regenerate man, a man who knows that his heart and nature have been renewed and that sin is now a power in him that is not himself. "I delight in the law of God according to the inward man" (7:22): That again is the language of a regenerate man. He dares to say when he does evil: "It is no longer I who do it, but sin that dwells in me." It is of great importance to understand this.

In the first two great sections of the epistle, Paul deals with justification and sanctification. In dealing with justification, he lays the foundation of the doctrine in the teaching about sin, not in the singular sin, but in the plural, "sins"—the actual transgressions. In the second part of the fifth chapter he begins to deal with sin, not as actual transgression, but as a power. Just imagine what a loss it would have been to us if we did not have this second half of the seventh chapter of the Epistle to the Romans, if Paul had omitted in his teaching this vital question of the sinfulness of the believer. We would have missed the question we all want answered as to sin in the believer. What is the answer? The regenerate man is one in whom the will has been renewed, and who can say: "I delight in the law of God according to the inward man."

But secondly: *The regenerate man is also* a powerless man.

> *T*he regenerate man is one in whom the will has been renewed, and who can say: "I delight in the law of God according to the inward man."

Here is the great mistake made by many Christian people. They think that when there is a renewed will, it is enough. But that is not the case. This regenerate man tells us: "For *to will* is present with me, but *how to perform* what is good I do not find" (Rom. 7:18). How often people tell us that if you set yourself determinedly, you can perform what you desire! But this man was as determined as any man can be, and yet he made the confession: "For to will is present with me, but how to perform what is good I do not find."

But, you ask, how is it that God makes a regenerate man utter such a confession, with a right will, with a heart that longs to do good, and longs to do its very utmost to love God?

Let us look at this question. What has God given us our will for? Had the angels who fell, in their own will, the strength to stand? Truly, no. The will of the creature is nothing but an empty vessel in which the power of God is to be made manifest. The creature must seek in God all that it is to be. You have it in the second chapter of the epistle to the Philippians, and you have it here also, that God's work is to work in us both *to will* and *to do* of His good pleasure. Here is a man who appears to say: "God has not worked to do in me." But we are taught that God works both to will and to do. How is the apparent contradiction to be reconciled?

You will find that in this passage (Rom. 7:6–25) the name of the Holy Spirit does not appear once, nor does the name of Christ appear. The man is wrestling and struggling to fulfill God's law. Instead of the Holy Spirit and of Christ, the law is mentioned nearly twenty times. In this chapter, it shows a believer doing his very best to obey the law of God with his regenerate will. Not only this, but you will find the little words, *I, me, my,* appear more than forty times. It is the regenerate *I* in its powerlessness seeking to obey the law without being filled with the Spirit. This is the experience of almost every saint. After conversion, a man begins to do his best, and he fails. But if we are brought into the full light, we need fail no longer. Nor need we fail at all if we have received the Spirit in His fullness at conversion.

God allows that failure so that the regenerate man can be taught his own utter powerlessness. It is in the course of this struggle that there comes to us this sense of our utter sinfulness. It is God's way of dealing with us. He allows that man to strive to fulfill the law so that as he strives and wrestles, he may be brought to this: "I am a regenerate child of God, but I am utterly helpless to obey His law." See what strong words are used all through the chapter to describe this condition: "I am carnal, sold under sin" (7:14), "I see another law in my members. . .bringing me into captivity" (7:23), and last of all, "O wretched man that I am! Who will deliver me from this body of death?" (7:24). This believer who bows here in deep contrition is utterly unable to obey the law of God.

> *I*f we are brought into the full light, we need fail no longer. Nor need we fail at all if we have received the Spirit in His fullness at conversion.

But thirdly, *Not only is the man who makes this confession a regenerate and a powerless man, but he is also* a wretched man.

He is utterly unhappy and miserable. And what is it that makes him so utterly miserable? It is because God has given him a nature that loves Himself. He is deeply wretched because he feels he is not obeying his God. He says, with brokenness of heart: "It is not I who do it, but I am under the awful power of sin, which is holding me down. It is I, and yet not I: sadly, it is myself, for so closely am I bound up with it, and so closely is it intertwined with my very nature." Blessed be God when a man learns to say: "O wretched man that I am!" from the depth of his heart. He is on the way to the eighth chapter of Romans.

There are many who make this confession a pillow for sin. They say that since Paul had to confess his weakness and helplessness in this way, what are they that they should try to do better? So the call to holiness is quietly set aside. God desires that every one of us had learned to say these words in the very spirit in which they are written here! When we hear sin spoken of as the abominable thing that God hates, do not many of us wince before the word? If only all Christians who go on sinning and sinning would take this verse to heart! If ever you utter a sharp word, say: "O wretched man that I am!" And every time you lose your temper, kneel down and understand that it never was meant by God that this was to be the state in which His child would remain. God desires that we would take this word into our daily life and say it every time we are touched about our own honor, and every time we say sharp things, and every time we sin against the Lord God and against the Lord Jesus Christ in His humility, in His obedience, and in His self-sacrifice! God desires that you could forget everything else, and cry out to Him: "O wretched man that I am! Who will deliver me from the body of this death?"

Why should you say this whenever you commit sin? Because it is when a man is brought to this confession that deliverance is at hand.

> *G*od works to will, and He is ready to work to do, but, sadly, many Christians misunderstand this. They think because they have the will, it is enough, and that now they are able to do.

And remember it was not only the sense of being powerless and taken captive that made him wretched, but it was above all the sense of sinning against his God. The law was doing its work, making sin *exceeding sinful* in his sight. The thought of continually grieving God became utterly unbearable—it was this brought forth the piercing cry: "O wretched man!" As long as we talk and reason about our powerlessness and our failure, and only try to find out what Romans 7 means, it will profit us but little. But when once *every sin* gives new intensity to the sense of wretchedness, and we feel our whole state as one of not only helplessness, but actual exceeding sinfulness, we shall be pressed not only to ask: "Who shall deliver us?" but to cry out: "I thank God through Jesus Christ my Lord."

Fourthly: *When a man comes here he is* on the very brink of deliverance.

The man has tried to obey the beautiful law of God. He has loved it, he has wept over his sin, he has tried to conquer, and he has tried to overcome fault after fault—but every time he has ended in failure.

What did he mean by "the body of this death"? Did he mean, my body when I die? Truly, no. In the eighth chapter you have the answer to this question in the words: "If by the Spirit you put to death the deeds of the body, you will live" (Rom. 8:13). That is the body of death from which he is seeking deliverance.

And now he is on the brink of deliverance! In the twenty-third verse of the seventh chapter we have the words: "I see another law in my members, warring against the law of my mind, and bringing me into *captivity* to the law of sin which is in my members." It is a *captive* that cries: "O wretched man that I am! Who will deliver me from the body of this death?" He is a man who feels himself bound. But look to the contrast in the second verse of the eighth chapter: "The law of the Spirit of life in Christ Jesus *has made me free* from the law of sin and death." That is the deliverance through Jesus Christ our Lord—the *liberty* to the captive that the Spirit brings. Can you keep captive any longer a man made free by the "law of the Spirit of life in Christ Jesus"?

But, you say, didn't the regenerate man have the Spirit of Jesus when he spoke in the sixth chapter? Yes, *but he did not know what the Holy Spirit could do for him.*

God does not work by His Spirit as He works by a blind force in nature. He leads His people on as reasonable, intelligent beings. Therefore when He wants to give us that Holy Spirit whom He has promised, He brings us first to the end of self, to the conviction that though we have been striving to obey the law, we have failed. When we have come to the end of that, then He shows us that in the Holy Spirit we have the power of obedience, the power of victory, and the power of real holiness.

God works *to will*, and He is ready to work *to do*, but, sadly, many Christians misunderstand this. They think because they have the will, it is enough, and that now they are able to do. This is not so. The new will is a permanent gift, an attribute of the new nature. The power to do is not a permanent gift, but must be each moment received from the Holy Spirit. It is the man who is conscious *of his own powerlessness as a believer* who will learn that by the Holy Spirit *he can live a holy life.* This man is on the brink of that great deliverance, because the way has been prepared for the glorious eighth chapter. I now ask this solemn question: Where are you living? Is it with you, "O wretched man that I am! Who will deliver me?" with now and then a little experience of the power of the Holy Spirit? Or is it, "I thank God through Jesus Christ! The law of the Spirit has made me free from the law of sin and death"?

What the Holy Spirit does is to give the victory. "If by the Spirit you put to death the deeds of the body, you will live." It is the Holy Spirit who does this— the third Person of the Godhead. He it is who, when the heart is opened wide to receive Him, comes in and reigns there and puts to death the deeds of the body, day by day, hour by hour, and moment by moment.

I want to bring this to a point. Remember, dear friend, what we need is to come to decision and action. There are in scripture two very different sorts of Christians. The Bible speaks in *Romans, Corinthians,* and *Galatians* about yielding to the flesh, and that is the life of tens of thousands of believers. All their lack of joy in the Holy Spirit, and their lack of the liberty He gives, is just because of the flesh. The Spirit is within them, but the flesh rules the life. To be led by the Spirit of God is what they need.

God desires that I could make every child of His realize what it means that the everlasting God has given His dear Son, Christ Jesus, to watch over you every day, and that what you have to do is to trust, and that the work of the Holy Spirit is to enable you every moment to remember Jesus and to trust Him! The Spirit has come to keep the link with Him unbroken every moment. Praise God for the Holy Spirit! We are so accustomed to think of the Holy Spirit as a luxury, for special times, or for special ministers and men. But the Holy Spirit is necessary for every believer, every moment of the day. Praise God you have Him, and that He gives you the full experience of the deliverance in Christ as He makes you free from the power of sin.

Who longs to have the power and the liberty of the Holy Spirit? Oh, brother, bow before God in one final cry of despair: "O God, must I go on sinning this way forever? Who will deliver me, O wretched man that I am, from the body of this death?"

Are you ready to sink before God in that cry and seek the power of Jesus to dwell and work in you? Are you ready to say: "I thank God through Jesus Christ"?

> *There is deliverance and the liberty of the Holy Spirit. The kingdom of God is "joy in the Holy Spirit."*

What good does it do that we go to church or attend conventions, that we study our Bibles and pray, unless our lives are filled with the Holy Spirit? That is what God wants. Nothing else will enable us to live a life of power and peace. You know that when a minister or parent is using the catechism, when a question is asked an answer is expected. How sad it is that so many Christians are content with the question put here: "O wretched man that I am! Who will deliver me from the body of this death?" but never give the answer. Instead of answering, they are silent. Instead of saying: "I thank God through Jesus Christ our Lord," they are forever repeating the question without the answer.

If you want the path to the full deliverance of Christ and the liberty of the Spirit, the glorious liberty of the children of God, take it through the seventh chapter of Romans, and then say: "I thank God through Jesus Christ our Lord." Don't be content to remain always groaning, but say: "I, a wretched man, thank God, through Jesus Christ. Even though I do not see it all, I am going to praise God."

There is deliverance and the liberty of the Holy Spirit. The kingdom of God is "joy in the Holy Spirit" (Rom. 14:17).

FOR FURTHER THOUGHT

1. *When the apostle Paul wrote, "O wretched man that I am!" what kind of "man" is he referring to himself as being? What has he failed to do that has brought him to the end of himself? How does he answer his own question, "Who will deliver me from this body of death?"*
2. *The Bible speaks in Romans, Corinthians, and Galatians about yielding to the flesh. Those who do that lack the joy of the Holy Spirit and the liberty He gives. What must they do and what (whom) must they receive and be led by in order to have that joy and liberty?*
3. *What kind of relationship must you walk in with the Holy Spirit in order to have His power, His joy, and His liberty?*

7

"HAVING BEGUN IN THE SPIRIT"

THE words from which I wish to address you, you will find in the epistle to the Galatians, the third chapter, the third verse; let us read the second verse also: "This only I want to learn from you: Did you receive the Spirit by the works of the law, or by the hearing of faith? Are you so foolish?" And then comes my text— "Having begun in the Spirit, are you now being made perfect by the flesh?"

When we speak of the quickening or the deepening or the strengthening of the spiritual life, we are thinking of something that is weak and wrong and sinful, and it is a great thing to take our place before God with the confession: "O God, our spiritual life is not what it should be!"

May God work that in your heart, reader.

As we look around at the church, we see so many indications of weakness and of failure, and of sin, and of shortcoming, that we are compelled to ask: Why is it? Is there any necessity for the church of Christ to be living in such a low state? Or is it actually possible that God's people should be living always in the joy and strength of their God?

Every believing heart must answer: It is possible.

Then comes the great question: Why is it, how is it to be accounted for, that God's church as a whole is so weak, and that the great majority of Christians are not living up to their privileges? There must be a reason for it. Has God not given Christ His almighty Son to be the keeper of every believer, to make Christ an ever-present reality, and to impart and communicate to us all that we have in Christ? God has given His Son, and God has given His Spirit. How is it that believers do not live up to their privileges?

We find in more than one of the epistles a very solemn answer to that question. There are epistles, such as the first to the Thessalonians, where Paul writes to the Christians, in effect: "I want you to grow, to abound, to increase more and more." They were young, and there were things lacking in their faith, but their state was so far satisfactory and gave him great joy, and he writes time after time: "I ask God that you may abound more and more; I write to you to increase more and more" (see 1 Thess. 4:10–11).

But there are other epistles where he takes a very different tone, especially the epistles to the Corinthians and to the Galatians, where he tells them in many different ways what the one reason was why they were not living as Christians ought to live, why many were under the power of the flesh. My text is one example. He reminds them that by the preaching of faith they had received the Holy Spirit. He had preached Christ to them, and they had accepted that Christ and had received the Holy Spirit in power. But what happened? Having begun in the Spirit, they tried to perfect the work that the Spirit had begun in the flesh by their own effort. We find the same teaching in the epistle to the Corinthians.

> *H*as God not given Christ His almighty Son to be the keeper of every believer, to make Christ an ever-present reality, and to impart and communicate to us all that we have in Christ?

Now, we have here a solemn discovery of what the great lack is in the Church of Christ. God has called the Church of Christ to live in the power of the Holy Spirit, and the church is living for the most part in the power of human flesh, and of will and energy and effort apart from the Spirit of God. I do not doubt that that is the case with many individual believers. And if God will use me to give you a message from Him, my one message will be this: "If the Church will return to acknowledge that the Holy Spirit is her strength and her help, and if the Church will return to give up everything, and wait on God to be filled with the Spirit, her days of beauty and gladness will return, and we shall see the glory of God revealed among us." This is my message to every individual believer: "Nothing will help you unless you come to understand that you must live every day under the power of the Holy Spirit."

God wants you to be a living vessel in whom the power of the Spirit is to be manifested every hour and every moment of your life, and God will enable you to be that.

Now let us try to learn that this word to the Galatians teaches us some very simple thoughts. It shows us how (1) *the beginning of the Christian life is receiving the Holy Spirit.* It shows us (2) what *great danger there is of forgetting that we are to live by the Spirit* and not live after the flesh. It shows us (3) *what are the fruits and the proofs of our seeking perfection in the flesh.* And then it suggests to us (4) *the way of deliverance from this state.*

1. First of all, Paul says: *"Having begun in the Spirit."* Remember, the apostle not only preached justification by faith, but he preached something more. He preached this—the epistle is full of it—that justified men can only live by the Holy Spirit, and that therefore God gives to every justified man the Holy Spirit to seal him. The apostle says to them in effect more than once: "How did you receive the Holy Spirit? Was it by the preaching of the law, or by the preaching of faith?"

He could point back to that time when there had been a mighty revival under his teaching. The power of God had been manifested, and the Galatians were compelled to confess: "Yes, we have received the Holy Spirit. Accepting Christ by faith, by faith we received the Holy Spirit."

Now, it is to be feared that there are many Christians who hardly know that when they believed, they received the Holy Spirit. A great many Christians can say: "I received pardon and I received peace." But if you were to ask them: "Have you received the Holy Spirit?" they would hesitate, and many, if they were to say "Yes," would say it with hesitation, and they would tell you that they hardly knew what it was, since that time, to walk in the power of the Holy Spirit. Let us try to take hold of this great truth: The beginning of the true Christian life is to receive the Holy Spirit. And the work of every Christian minister is that which was the work of Paul—to remind his people that they received the Holy Spirit and must live according to His guidance and in His power.

If those Galatians who received the Holy Spirit in power were tempted to go astray by that terrible danger of perfecting in the flesh what had been begun in the Spirit, how much more danger do those Christians run who hardly ever know that they have received the Holy Spirit, or who, if they know it as a matter of belief, hardly ever think of it and hardly ever praise God for it!

2. But now look, in the second place, at *the great danger*.

You all know what shunting is on a railway. A locomotive with its train may be run in a certain direction, and the points at some place may not be properly opened or closed, and unobservingly it is shunted off to the right or to the left. And if that takes place, for instance, on a dark night, the train goes in the wrong direction, and the people might never know it until they have gone some distance.

And just so God gives Christians the Holy Spirit with this intention that every day all their life would be lived in the power of the Spirit. A man cannot live one hour a godly life unless it is by the power of the Holy Spirit. He may live a proper, consistent life, as people call it, an irreproachable life, a life of virtue and diligent service. But to live a life acceptable to God, in the enjoyment of God's salvation and God's love, to live and walk in the power of the new life—he cannot do it unless he is guided by the Holy Spirit every day and every hour.

But now listen to the danger. The Galatians received the Holy Spirit, but what was begun by the Spirit they tried to perfect in the flesh. How? They fell back again under Judaizing teachers who told them they must be circumcised. They began to seek their religion in external observances. And so Paul uses that expression about those teachers who had them circumcised, that "they sought to boast in their flesh" (see Gal. 6:13).

You sometimes hear the expression used, *religious flesh*. What is meant by that? It is simply an expression made to give utterance to this thought: My human nature and my human will and my human effort can be very active in religion, and after being converted, and after receiving the Holy Spirit, I may begin in my own strength to try to serve God.

I may be very diligent and doing a great deal, and yet all the time it is more the work of human flesh than of God's Spirit. What a solemn thought that man can, without noticing it, be shunted off from the line of the Holy Spirit on to the line of the flesh, that he can be most diligent and make great sacrifices, and yet it is all in the power of the human will! Ah, the great question for us to ask of God in self-examination is that we may be shown whether our religious life is lived more in the power of the flesh than in the power of the Holy Spirit. A man may be a preacher who works most diligently in his ministry, another man may be a Christian worker others say makes great sacrifices—and yet you can feel there is a lacking about it. You feel that he is not a spiritual man, that there is no spirituality about his life. How many Christians there are about whom no one would ever think of saying: "What a spiritual man he is!" Ah! there is the weakness of the Church of Christ. It is all in that one word: flesh.

Now, the flesh may manifest itself in many ways. It may be manifested in fleshly wisdom. My mind may be most active about religion. I may preach or write or think or meditate, and I may delight in being occupied with things in God's book and in God's kingdom, and yet the power of the Holy Spirit may be markedly absent.

I fear that if you take the preaching throughout the Church of Christ and ask why there is, sadly, so little converting power in the preaching of the Word, why there is so much work and often so little result for eternity, why the Word has so little power to build up believers in holiness and in consecration—the answer will come: It is the absence of the power of the Holy Spirit. And why is this? There can be no other reason but that the flesh and human energy have taken the place that the Holy Spirit ought to have. That was true of the Galatians, and it was true of the Corinthians. You know Paul said to them: "I cannot speak to you as to spiritual men; you ought to be spiritual men, but you are carnal" (see 1 Cor. 3:1–3). And you know how often in the course of his epistles he had to scold and condemn them for strife and for divisions.

3. A third thought: *What are the proofs or indications that a church like the Galatians, or a Christian, is serving God in the power of the flesh—is perfecting in the flesh what was begun in the Spirit?*

The answer is very easy. Religious self-effort always ends in sinful flesh. What was the state of those Galatians? Striving to be justified by the works of the law. And yet they were quarreling and in danger of devouring one another. Count up the expressions that the apostle uses to indicate their lack of love, and you will find more than twelve—envy, jealousy, bitterness, strife, and all sorts of expressions. Read in the fourth and fifth chapters what he says about that. You see how they tried to serve God in their own strength, and how they failed utterly. All this religious effort resulted in failure. The power of sin and the sinful flesh got the better of them, and their whole condition was one of the saddest that could be thought of.

This comes to us with unspeakable solemnity. There is a complaint everywhere in the Christian church of the lack of a high standard of integrity and godliness, even among the professing members of Christian churches. I remember a sermon I heard preached by Dr. Dykes on commercial morality. He spoke of what was to be found in London. And oh, if we speak not only of the commercial morality or immorality, but if we go into the homes of Christians, and if we think of the life to which God has called His children and which He enables them to live by the Holy Spirit, and if we think of how much, nevertheless, there is of unlovingness and temper and sharpness and bitterness, and if we think how much there is very often of strife among the members of churches, and how much there is of envy and jealousy and sensitiveness and pride, then we are compelled to say: "Where are marks of the presence of the Spirit of the Lamb of God?" Lacking, sadly lacking!

> *U*ntil we learn to make confession, and until we begin to see that we must somehow or other get God's Spirit in power back to His Church, we must fail.

Many people speak of these things as though they were the natural result of our weakness and cannot well be helped. Many people speak of these things as sins, yet have given up the hope of conquering them. Many people speak of these things in the church around them, and do not see the least prospect of ever having the things changed. There is no prospect until there comes a radical change, until the Church of God begins to see that every sin in the believer comes from the flesh, from a fleshly life amid our religious activities, from a striving in self-effort to serve God. Until we learn to make confession, and until we begin to see that we must somehow or other get God's Spirit in power back to His church, we must fail. Where did the Church begin in Pentecost? There they began in the Spirit. But, sadly, how the Church of the next century went off into the flesh! They attempted to perfect the Church in the flesh.

Do not let us think that because the blessed Reformation restored the great doctrine of justification by faith that the power of the Holy Spirit was then fully restored. If it is our faith that God is going to have mercy on His Church in these last ages, it will be because the doctrine and the truth about the Holy Spirit will not only be studied, but sought after with a whole heart—and not only because that truth will be sought after, but because ministers and congregations will be found bowing before God in deep abasement with one cry: "We have grieved God's Spirit. We have tried to be Christian churches with as little as possible of God's Spirit. We have not sought to be churches filled with the Holy Spirit."

All the weakness in the Church is due to the refusal of the Church to obey its God.

And why is that so? I know your answer. You say: "We are too weak and too helpless. We try to obey, and we vow to obey, but somehow we fail."

Ah, yes; *you fail because you do not accept the strength of God.* God alone can work out His will in you. You cannot work out God's will, but His Holy Spirit can. And until the Church and believers grasp this and cease trying by human effort to do God's will, and wait on the Holy Spirit to come with all His omnipotent and enabling power, the Church will never be what God wants her to be and what God is willing to make of her.

4. I come now to my last thought, the question: *What is the way to restoration?*

Beloved friend, the answer is simple and easy. If that train has been shunted off, there is nothing for it but to come back to the point at which it was led away. The Galatians had no other way in returning but to come back to where they had gone wrong, to come back from all religious effort in their own strength, and from seeking anything by their own work, and to yield themselves humbly to the Holy Spirit. There is no other way for us as individuals.

> The Father in heaven loves to fill His children with His Holy Spirit. God longs to give each one individually and separately the power of the Holy Spirit for daily life.

Is there any brother or sister whose heart is conscious: "Sadly, my life knows but little of the power of the Holy Spirit"? I come to you with God's message that you can have no conception of what your life would be in the power of the Holy Spirit. It is too high and too blessed and too wonderful, but I bring you the message that just as truly as the everlasting Son of God came to this world and accomplished His wonderful works, that just as truly as on Calvary He died and worked out your redemption by His precious blood, so, just as truly can the Holy Spirit come into your heart so that with His divine power He may sanctify you and enable you to do God's blessed will and fill your heart with joy and with strength.

But, sadly, we have forgotten, we have grieved, we have dishonored the Holy Spirit, and He has not been able to do His work. But I bring you the message: The Father in heaven loves to fill His children with His Holy Spirit. God longs to give each one individually and separately the power of the Holy Spirit for daily life. The command comes to us individually, unitedly. God wants us as His children to arise and place our sins before Him and to call on Him for mercy. Oh, are you so foolish? Having begun in the Spirit, are you now perfecting in the flesh that which was begun in the spirit? Let us bow in shame and confess before God how our fleshly religion, our self-effort, and our self-confidence have been the cause of every failure.

I have often been asked by young Christians: "Why is it that I fail so? I so solemnly vowed with my whole heart, and desired to serve God. Why have I failed?"

To such I always give the one answer: "My dear friend, you are trying to do in your own strength what Christ alone can do in you."

And when they tell me: "I am sure I knew Christ alone could do it, and I was not trusting in myself," my answer always is: "You were trusting in yourself or you could not have failed. If you had trusted Christ, He could not fail."

Oh, this perfecting in the flesh what was begun in the Spirit runs far deeper through us than we know. Let us ask God to reveal to us that it is only when we are brought to utter shame and emptiness that we shall be prepared to receive the blessing that comes from on high.

And so I come with these two questions. Are you living, beloved brother-minister—I ask it of every minister of the Gospel—are you living under the power of the Holy Spirit? Are you living as an anointed, Spirit-filled man in your ministry and in your life before God? O brethren, our place is an awful one. We have to show people what God will do for us, not in our words and teaching, but in our life. God help us to do it!

> God alone can effect the change. God alone, who gave us the Holy Spirit, can restore the Holy Spirit in power into our life.

I ask it of every member of Christ's Church and of every believer: Are you living a life under the power of the Holy Spirit day by day, or are you attempting to live without that? Remember you cannot. Are you consecrated, given up to the Spirit to work in you and to live in you? Oh, come and confess every failure of temper, every failure of tongue however small, every failure due to the absence of the Holy Spirit and the presence of the power of self. Are you consecrated, are you given up to the Holy Spirit?

If your answer is *No*, then I come with a second question—Are you *willing* to be consecrated? Are you willing to give up yourself to the power of the Holy Spirit?

You well know, I trust, that the human side of consecration will not help you. I may consecrate myself a hundred times with all the intensity of my being, and that will not help me. What will help me is this: that God from heaven accepts and seals the consecration.

And now are you willing to give yourselves up to the Holy Spirit? You can do it now. A great deal may still be dark and dim and beyond what we understand, and you may feel nothing. But come. God alone can effect the change. God alone, who gave us the Holy Spirit, can restore the Holy Spirit in power into our life. God alone can strengthen us "with might by his Spirit in the inner man" (Eph. 3:16). And to every waiting heart that will make the sacrifice, that will give up everything and give time to cry and pray to God, the answer will come. The blessing is not far off. Our God delights to help us. He will enable us to perfect, not in the flesh, but in the Spirit, what was begun in the Spirit.

For Further Thought

1. *God has given Christ His almighty Son to be the keeper of every believer. Why, then, is God's church as a whole so weak? Why are individual believers not living up to their privileges as children of God through Christ?*
2. *What are the evidences that a church or an individual believer is attempting to serve God through the power of the flesh?*
3. *What must happen after you consecrate yourself to God in order for you to be able to walk in God's power and to have victory in all things?*

8

KEPT BY THE
POWER OF GOD

THE words from which I speak you will find in 1 Peter 1:5. The third, fourth, and fifth verses are: "Blessed be the God and Father of our Lord Jesus Christ, who. . .has begotten us again to a living hope through the resurrection of Jesus Christ from the dead, to an inheritance incorruptible. . .reserved in heaven for you, who are kept by the power of God through faith for salvation." The words of my text are: "Kept by the power of God through faith."

There we have two wonderful, blessed truths about the keeping by which a believer is kept for salvation. One truth is, *Kept by the power of God*, and the other truth is, *Kept through faith*. We should look at the two sides—at God's side and His almighty power offered to us to be our keeper every moment of the day, and at the human side, we having nothing to do but in faith to let God do His keeping work. We are begotten again to an inheritance kept in heaven for us, and we are kept here on earth by the power of God. We see there is a double keeping—*the inheritance kept for me* in heaven, and *I on earth kept for the inheritance there.*

Now, as to the first part of this keeping, there is no doubt and no question. God keeps the inheritance in heaven very wonderfully and perfectly, and it is waiting there safely. And the same God keeps me for the inheritance. That is what I want to understand.

You know it is very foolish of a father to take great trouble to have an inheritance for his children, and to keep it for them, if he does not keep them for it. What would you think of a man spending his whole time and making every sacrifice to amass money, and as he gets his tens of thousands, you ask him why it is that he sacrifices himself so, and his answer is: "I want to leave my children a large inheritance, and I am keeping it for them"—if you were then to hear that that man takes no trouble to educate his children, that he allows them to run on the street wild, and to go on in paths of sin and ignorance and folly? Would not you say: "Poor man! He is keeping an inheritance for his children, but he is not keeping or preparing his children for the inheritance!" And there are so many Christians who think, "My God is keeping the inheritance for me," but they cannot believe, "My God is keeping me for that inheritance." The same power, the same love, the same God doing the double work.

Now, I want to speak about a work God does on us—keeping us for the inheritance. I have already said that we have two very simple truths: the one the divine side—*we are kept by the power of God;* the other, the human side—*we are kept through faith.*

1. First, look at the divine side—kept by the power of God. Think, first of all, that *this keeping is all-inclusive.*

What is kept? You are kept. How much of you? The whole being. Does God keep one part of you and not another? No. Some people have the idea that this is a sort of vague, general keeping, and that God will keep them in such a way that when they die they will get to heaven. But they do not apply that word *kept* to everything in their being and nature. And yet that is what God wants.

Here I have a watch. Suppose that this watch had been borrowed from a friend, and he said to me: "When you go to Europe, I will let you take it with you, but mind you, keep it safely and bring it back."

And suppose I damaged the watch and had the hands broken, the face defaced, and some of the wheels and springs spoiled, and then took it back in that condition and handed it to my friend. He would say: "Ah, but I gave you that watch on condition that you would keep it."

"Have I not kept it? There is the watch."

"But I did not want you to keep it in that general way, so that you should bring me back only the shell of the watch or the remains. I expected you to keep every part of it."

And likewise God does not want to keep us in this general way, so that at the last, somehow or other, we shall be saved as by fire and just get into heaven. But the keeping power and the love of God applies to every particular of our being.

There are some people who think God will keep them in spiritual things, but not in temporal things. This latter, they say, lies outside of His line. Now, God sends you to work in the world, but He did not say: "I must now leave you to go and earn your own money and to get your livelihood for yourself." He knows you are not able to keep yourself. But God says: "My child, there is no work you are to do, and no business in which you are engaged, and not a cent which you are to spend, but that I, your Father, will take that up into My keeping." God not only cares for the spiritual, but for the temporal also. The greater part of the life of many people must be spent, sometimes eight or nine or ten hours a day, amid the temptations and distractions of business. But God will care for you there. The keeping of God includes all.

There are other people who think: "Ah! In time of trial God keeps me, but in times of prosperity I do not need His keeping. Then I forget Him and let Him go." Others, again, think the very opposite. They think: "In time of prosperity, when things are smooth and quiet, I am able to cling to God, but when heavy trials come, somehow or other my will rebels, and God does not keep me then."

Now, I bring you the message that in prosperity as in adversity, in the sunshine as in the dark, your God is ready to keep you all the time.

Then again, there are others who think of this keeping this way: "God will keep me from doing very great wickedness, but there are small sins I cannot expect God to keep me from. There is the sin of temper. I cannot expect God to conquer that."

When you hear of some man who has been tempted and gone astray or fallen into drunkenness or murder, you thank God for His keeping power. "I might have done the same as that man," you say, "if God had not kept me." And you believe He kept you from drunkenness and murder.

And why do you not need believe that God can keep you from outbreaks of temper? You thought that this was of less importance. You did not remember that the great commandment of the New Testament is, "Love one another as I have loved you." And when your temper and hasty judgment and sharp words came out, you sinned against the highest law—the law of God's love. And yet you say: "God will not, God cannot"—no, you will not say, "God cannot," but you say, "God does not keep me from that." You perhaps say: "He can, but there is something in me that cannot attain to it, and which God does not take away."

> *G*od keeps the inheritance in heaven very wonderfully and perfectly, and it is waiting there safely. And the same God keeps me for the inheritance.

I want to ask you, can believers live a holier life than is generally lived? Can believers experience the keeping power of God all the day to keep them from sin? Can believers be kept in fellowship with God? And I bring you a message from the Word of God, in these words: *Kept by the power of God.* There is no qualifying clause to them. The meaning is that if you will entrust yourself entirely and absolutely to the omnipotence of God, He will delight to keep you.

Some people think that they never can get so far as that every word of their mouth would be to the glory of God. But it is what God wants of them, what God expects of them. God is willing to set a watch at the door of their mouth, and if God will do that, cannot He keep their tongue and their lips? He can, and that is what God is going to do for those who trust Him. God's keeping is all-inclusive, so let everyone who longs to live a holy life think out all their needs, all their weaknesses, all their shortcomings, and all their sins, and then say deliberately: "Is there any sin that my God cannot keep me from?" And the heart will have to answer: "No! God can keep me from every sin."

Secondly, if you want to understand this keeping, remember that it is not only an all-inclusive keeping, but it is an almighty keeping.

I want to get that truth burned into my soul. I want to worship God until my whole heart is filled with the thought of His omnipotence. God is almighty, and the almighty God offers Himself to work in my heart, to do the work of keeping me. And I want to get linked with omnipotence, or rather, linked to the omnipotent One, to the living God, and to have my place in the hollow of His hand.

You read the Psalms, and you think of the wonderful thoughts in many of the expressions that David uses—as, for instance, when he speaks about God being *our God, our fortress, our refuge, our strong tower, our strength,* and *our salvation.* David had very wonderful views of how the everlasting God is Himself the hiding place of the believing soul, and of how He takes the believer and keeps him in the very hollow of His hand, in the secret of His tent, under the shadow of His wings, under His very feathers. And there David lived. And oh, we who are the children of Pentecost, we who have known Christ and His blood and the Holy Spirit sent down from heaven, why is it we know so little of what it is to walk tremblingly step by step with the almighty God as our keeper?

> *The greater part of the life of many people must be spent, sometimes eight or nine or ten hours a day, amid the temptations and distractions of business. But God will care for you there.*

Have you ever thought that in every action of grace in your heart you have the whole omnipotence of God engaged to bless you? When I come to a man and he gives me a gift of money, I get it and go away with it. He has given me something of his, and the rest he keeps for himself. But that is not the way with the power of God. God can part with nothing of His own power, and therefore I can experience the power and goodness of God only so far as I am in contact and fellowship with Himself. And when I come into contact and fellowship with Him, I come into contact and fellowship with the whole omnipotence of God and have the omnipotence of God to help me every day.

A son has, perhaps, a very rich father, and as the former is about to commence business, the father says: "You can have as much money as you want for your undertaking." All the father has is at the disposal of the son. And that is the way with God, your almighty God. You can hardly take it in. You feel yourself such a little worm. His omnipotence needed to keep a little worm! Yes, His omnipotence is needed to keep every little worm that lives in the dust, and also to keep the universe, and therefore His omnipotence is much more needed in keeping your soul and mine from the power of sin.

Oh, if you want to grow in grace, do learn to begin here. In all your judgings and meditations and thoughts and deeds and questionings and studies and prayers, learn to be kept by your almighty God. What is almighty God not going to do for the child who trusts Him? The Bible says: "Above all that we can ask

ABSOLUTE SURRENDER

or think" (Eph. 3:20). It is omnipotence you must learn to know and trust, and then you will live as a Christian ought to live. How little we have learned to study God, and to understand that a godly life is a life full of God, a life that loves God and waits on Him, and trusts Him, and allows Him to bless it! We cannot do the will of God except by the power of God. God gives us the first experience of His power to prepare us to long for more, and to come and claim all that He can do. God help us to trust Him every day.

Another thought. This keeping is not only all-inclusive and omnipotent, but also continuous and unbroken.

People sometimes say: "For a week or a month God has kept me very wonderfully. I have lived in the light of His countenance, and I cannot say what joy I have not had in fellowship with Him. He has blessed me in my work for others. He has given me souls, and at times I felt as if I were carried heavenward on eagle wings. But it did not continue. It was too good. It could not last." And some say: "It was necessary that I should fall to keep me humble." And others say: "I know it was my own fault, but somehow you cannot always live up in the heights."

> *I* want to get that truth burned into my soul. I want to worship God until my whole heart is filled with the thought of His omnipotence.

Oh, beloved, why is it? Can there be any reason why the keeping of God should not be continuous and unbroken? Just think. All life is in unbroken continuity. If my life were stopped for half an hour, I would be dead and my life gone. Life is a continuous thing, and the life of God is the life of His Church, and the life of God is His almighty power working in us. And God comes to us as the almighty One, and without any condition He offers to be my keeper, and His keeping means that day by day, moment by moment, God is going to keep us.

If I were to ask you the question, "Do you think God is able to keep you one day from actual transgression?" you would answer, "I not only know He is able to do it, but I think He has done it. There have been days in which He has kept my heart in His holy presence, when, though I have always had a sinful nature within me, He has kept me from conscious, actual transgression."

Now, if He can do that for an hour or a day, why not for two days? Let us make God's omnipotence as revealed in His Word the measure of our expectations! Has God not said in His Word, "I, the LORD, keep it, I water it every moment" (Isa. 27:3)? What can that mean? Does "every moment" mean every moment? Did God promise of that vineyard or red wine that every moment He would water it so that the heat of the sun and the scorching wind might never dry it up? Yes. In South Africa they sometimes make a graft, and above it they tie a bottle of water, so that now and then there shall be a drop to saturate what they have put about

1120

it. And so the moisture is kept there unceasingly until the graft has had time to strike and resist the heat of the sun.

Will our God, in His tenderhearted love toward us, not keep us every moment when He has promised to do so? Oh! if we once got hold of the thought: Our whole religious life is to be God's doing—"It is God who works in you both to will and to do for His good pleasure" (Phil. 2:13)—and when once we get faith to expect that from God, God will do all for us.

The keeping is to be continuous. Every morning God will meet you as you wake. It is not a question of, "If I forgot to wake in the morning with the thought of Him, what will come of it?" If you trust your waking to God, God will meet you in the morning as you wake with His divine sunshine and love, and He will give you the consciousness that through the day you have God to take charge of you continuously with His almighty power. And God will meet you the next day and every day. And never mind if in the practice of fellowship there comes failure sometimes. If you maintain your position and say: "Lord, I am going to expect You to do Your utmost, and I am going to trust You day by day to keep me absolutely," your faith will grow stronger and stronger, and you will know the keeping power of God in unbrokenness.

2. And now the other side—*Believing.* "Kept by the power of God *through faith.*" How must we look at this faith?

Let me say, first of all, that this faith means utter powerlessness and helplessness before God.

> *God comes to us as the almighty One, and without any condition He offers to be my keeper, and His keeping means that day by day, moment by moment, God is going to keep us.*

At the bottom of all faith there is a feeling of helplessness. If I have a bit of business to transact, perhaps to buy a house, the conveyancer must do the work of getting the transfer of the property in my name and making all the arrangements. I cannot do that work, and in trusting that agent I confess I cannot do it. And so faith always means helplessness. In many cases, it means I can do it with a great deal of trouble, but another can do it better. But in most cases, it is utter helplessness—another must do it for me. And that is the secret of the spiritual life. A man must learn to say: "I give up everything. I have tried and longed, and thought and prayed, but failure has come. God has blessed me and helped me, but still, in the long run, there has been so much of sin and sadness." What a change comes when a man is broken down this way into utter helplessness and self-despair, and says: "I can do nothing!"

Remember Paul. He was living a blessed life, and he had been taken up into the third heaven, and then the thorn in the flesh came, "a messenger of Satan to buffet me" (2 Cor. 12:7). And what happened? Paul could not understand it, and he begged the Lord three times to take it away (12:8), but the Lord said, in effect: "No, it is possible that you might exalt yourself, and therefore I have sent you this trial to keep you weak and humble."

And Paul then learned a lesson that he never forgot, and that was to rejoice in his infirmities. He said that the weaker he was the better it was for him, for when he was weak, he was strong in his Lord Christ (12:10).

Do you want to enter what people call "the higher life?" Then go a step lower down. I remember Dr. Boardman telling how that once he was invited by a gentleman to go to see some works where they made fine shot, and I believe the workmen did so by pouring down molten lead from a great height. This gentleman wanted to take Dr. Boardman up to the top of the tower to see how the work was done. The doctor came to the tower, he entered by the door and began going upstairs, but when he had gone a few steps the gentleman called out: "That is the wrong way. You must come down this way. That stair is locked up."

The gentleman took him downstairs a good many steps, and there an elevator was ready to take him to the top, and he said: "I have learned a lesson that going down is often the best way to get up."

Ah, yes, God will have to bring us very low down. There will have to come on us a sense of emptiness and despair and nothingness. It is when we sink down in utter helplessness that the everlasting God will reveal Himself in His power, and then that our hearts will learn to trust God alone.

What is it that keeps us from trusting Him perfectly?

Many say, "I believe what you say, but there is one difficulty. If my trust were perfect and always abiding, all would come right, for I know God will honor trust. But how am I to get that trust?"

My answer is: "By the death of self. The great hindrance to trust is self-effort. So long as you have your own wisdom and thoughts and strength, you cannot fully trust God. But when God breaks you down, when everything begins to grow dim before your eyes, and you see that you understand nothing, then God is coming near, and if you will bow down in nothingness and wait on God, He will become all."

As long as we are something, God cannot be all, and His omnipotence cannot do its full work. That is the beginning of faith—utter despair of self, a ceasing from man and everything on earth, and finding our hope in God alone.

And then, next, we must understand that faith is rest.

In the beginning of the faith-life, faith is struggling. But as long as faith is struggling, faith has not attained its strength. But when faith in its struggling gets to the end of itself and just throws itself on God and rests on Him, then comes joy and victory.

Perhaps I can make it plainer if I tell the story of how the Keswick Convention began. Canon Battersby was an evangelical clergyman of the Church of

England for more than twenty years. He was a man of deep and tender godliness, but he didn't have the consciousness of rest and victory over sin, and often was deeply sad at the thought of stumbling and failure and sin. When he heard about the possibility of victory, he felt it was desirable, but it was as if he could not attain it. On one occasion, he heard an address on "Rest and Faith" from the story of the nobleman who came from Capernaum to Cana to ask Christ to heal his child (John 4:46–54). In the address, it was shown that the nobleman believed that Christ could help him in a general way, but he came to Jesus a good deal by way of an experiment. He hoped Christ would help him, but he had not any assurance of that help. But what happened? When Christ said to him: "Go your way; your son lives" (John 4:50), that man believed the word that Jesus spoke, and he rested in that word. He had no proof that his child was well again, and he had to walk back seven hours' journey to Capernaum. He walked back, and on the way met his servant and received the first news that the child was well, that at one o'clock on the afternoon of the previous day—at the very time that Jesus spoke to him—the fever left the child. That father rested on the word of Jesus and His work, and he went down to Capernaum and found his child well. And he praised God, and became with his whole house a believer and disciple of Jesus.

Oh, friends, that is faith! When God comes to me with the promise of His keeping, and I have nothing on earth to trust in, I say to God: "Your word is enough; kept by the power of God." That is faith. That is rest.

When Canon Battersby heard that address, he went home that night, and in the darkness of the night found rest. He rested on the word of Jesus. And the next morning, in the streets of Oxford, he said to a friend: "I have found it!" Then he went and told others, and asked that the Keswick Convention might be begun, and those at the convention with himself would testify simply what God had done.

It is a great thing when a man comes to rest on God's almighty power for every moment of his life, in the prospect of temptations to temper and haste and anger and unlovingness and pride and sin. It is a great thing in prospect of these to enter into a covenant with the omnipotent Jehovah, not on account of anything that any man says, or of anything that my heart feels, but on the strength of the Word of God: "Kept by the power of God through faith."

Oh, let us say to God that we are going to prove Him to the very uttermost. Let us say: "We ask You for nothing more than You can give, but we want nothing less." Let us say: "My God, let my life be a proof of what the omnipotent God can do." Let these be the two dispositions of our souls every day—deep helplessness, and simple, childlike rest.

That brings me to just one more thought in regard to faith—faith implies fellowship with God.

Many people want to take the Word and believe that, and they find they cannot believe it. Ah, no! You cannot separate God from His Word. No goodness or power can be received separate from God, and if you want to get into this life of godliness, you must take time for fellowship with God.

People sometimes tell me: "My life is one of such hurry and bustle that I have no time for fellowship with God." A dear missionary said to me: "People do not know how we missionaries are tempted. I get up at five o'clock in the morning, and there are the natives waiting for their orders for work. Then I have to go to the school and spend hours there. And then there is other work, and sixteen hours rush along, and I hardly get time to be alone with God."

Ah, there is the need! I encourage you, remember two things. I have not told you to trust the omnipotence of God as a thing, and I have not told you to trust the Word of God as a written book, but I have told you to go to the God of omnipotence and the God of the Word. Deal with God as that nobleman dealt with the living Christ. Why was he able to believe the word that Christ spoke to him? Because in the very eyes and tones and voice of Jesus, the Son of God, he saw and heard something that made him feel that he could trust Him. And that is what Christ can do for you and me.

Do not try to stir and arouse faith from within. How often I have tried to do that, and made a fool of myself! You cannot stir up faith from the depths of your heart. Leave your heart and look into the face of Christ, and listen to what He tells you about how He will keep you. Look up into the face of your loving Father, and take time every day with Him. Begin a new life with the deep emptiness and poverty of a man who has nothing, and who wants to get everything from Him—with the deep restfulness of a man who rests on the living God, the omnipotent Jehovah. And try God, and ask Him if He will not open the windows of heaven and pour out such a blessing that there shall not be room to receive it.

> *As long as we are something, God cannot be all, and His omnipotence cannot do its full work.*

I close by asking if you are willing to experience to the very full the heavenly keeping for the heavenly inheritance? Robert Murray M'Cheyne says, somewhere: "Oh, God, make me as holy as a pardoned sinner can be made." And if that prayer is in your heart, come now, and let us enter into a covenant with the everlasting and omnipotent Jehovah afresh, and in great helplessness, but in great restfulness, place ourselves in His hands. And then as we enter into our covenant, let us have the one prayer—that we may believe fully that the everlasting God is going to be our companion, holding our hand every moment of the day; our keeper, watching over us without a moment's interval; our Father, delighting to reveal Himself in our souls always. He has the power to let the sunshine of His love be with us all the day. Do not be afraid that because you have your business that you cannot have God with you always. Learn the lesson that the natural sun shines on you all the day, and you enjoy its light, and wherever you are you have got the sun. God takes care that it shines on you. And God will take care that His own divine light shines on you, and that you shall abide in that light, if you will only trust Him for it. Let us trust God to do that with a great and entire trust.

Here is the omnipotence of God, and here is faith reaching out to the measure of that omnipotence. Shall we not say: "All that that omnipotence can do, I am going to trust my God for"? Are not the two sides of this heavenly life wonderful? God's omnipotence covers me, and my will in its littleness rests in that omnipotence and rejoices in it!

> Moment by moment, I'm kept in His love;
> Moment by moment, I've life from above;
> Looking to Jesus, the glory doth shine;
> Moment by moment, Oh, Lord, I am Thine!

FOR FURTHER THOUGHT

1. *What are the two sides of the work God does on and in you in keeping you for the inheritance?*
2. *How can you be sure that God will keep you continuously without interruption? What should you do to ensure that this happens?*
3. *How are you to gain the trust it takes in order for God to keep you perfectly? What part do you play, and what part does God play in giving you this trust?*

9

"YOU ARE THE BRANCHES": AN ADDRESS TO CHRISTIAN WORKERS

EVERYTHING depends on our being right ourselves in Christ. If I want good apples, I must have a good apple tree. And if I care for the health of the apple tree, the apple tree will give me good apples. And it is just so with our Christian life and work. *If our life with Christ is right,* all will come right. There may be the need of instruction and suggestion and help and training in the different departments of the work, and all that has value. But in the long run, the greatest essential is to have the full life in Christ—in other words, to have Christ in us, working through us. I know how much there often is to disturb us or to cause anxious questionings, but the Master has such a blessing for every one of us, and such perfect peace and rest, and such joy and strength, if we can only come into, and be kept in, the right attitude toward Him.

I will take my text from the parable of the vine and the branches, in John 15:5: "I am the vine, you are the branches." Especially these words: "You are the branches."

What a simple thing it is to be a branch—the branch of a tree, or the branch of a vine! The branch grows out of the vine or out of the tree, and there it lives and grows and, in due time, bears fruit. It has no responsibility except just to receive from the root and stem sap and nourishment. And if we only by the Holy Spirit knew our relationship to Jesus Christ, our work would be changed into the brightest and most heavenly thing on earth. Instead of there ever being soul-weariness or exhaustion, our work would be like a new experience, linking us to Jesus as nothing else can.

Sadly, is it not often true that our work comes between us and Jesus? What folly! The very work that He has to do in me, and I for Him, I take up in such a way that it separates me from Christ. Many a laborer in the vineyard has complained that he has too much work and not time for close communion with Jesus, and that his usual work weakens his inclination for prayer, and that his too much interaction with men darkens the spiritual life. Sad thought, that the bearing of fruit would separate the branch from the vine! That must be because we have looked at our work as something other than the branch bearing fruit. May God deliver us from every false thought about the Christian life.

Now, just a few thoughts about this blessed branch-life. In the first place, it is a life of absolute dependence. The branch has nothing; it just depends on the vine for everything. That phrase *absolute dependence* is one of the most solemn and large and precious of thoughts. A great German theologian wrote two large volumes some years ago to show that the whole of Calvin's theology is summed up in that one principle of *absolute dependence* on God—and he was right. Another great writer has said that *absolute, unalterable dependence on God* alone is the essence of the religion of angels, and should be that of men also. God is everything to the angels, and He is willing to be everything to the Christian. If I can learn every moment of the day to depend on God, everything will come right. You will get the higher life if you depend absolutely on God.

Now, here we find it with the vine and the branches. Every vine you ever see, or every bunch of grapes that comes upon your table, let it remind you that the branch is absolutely dependent on the vine. The vine has to do the work, and the branch enjoys the fruit of it.

What has the vine to do? It has to do a great work. It has to send its roots out into the soil and hunt under the ground—the roots often extend a long way out—for nourishment and to drink in the moisture. Put certain elements of fertilizer in certain directions, and the vine sends its roots there, and then in its roots or stems it turns the moisture and fertilizer into that special sap that is to make the fruit that is borne. The vine does the work, and the branch has just to receive from the vine the sap, which is changed into grapes.

I have been told that at Hampton Court, London, there is a vine that sometimes bore a couple of thousand bunches of grapes, and people were astonished at its large growth and rich fruitage. Afterward it was discovered what was the cause of it. Not so very far away runs the River Thames, and the vine had stretched its roots away hundreds of yards under the ground, until it had come to the riverside. There in all the rich slime of the riverbed, it had found rich nourishment and obtained moisture, and the roots had drawn the sap all that distance up and up into the vine, and as a result there was the abundant, rich harvest. The vine had the work to do, and the branches had just to depend on the vine and receive what it gave.

Is that literally true of my Lord Jesus? Must I understand that when I have to work, when I have to preach a sermon, or address a Bible class, or to go out and visit the poor, neglected ones, that all the responsibility of the work is on Christ?

That is exactly what Christ wants you to understand. Christ wants that in all your work, the very foundation should be the simple, blessed consciousness: Christ must care for all.

And how does He fulfill the trust of that dependence? He does it by sending down the Holy Spirit—not now and then only as a special gift, for remember the relationship between the vine and the branches is such that hourly, daily, unceasingly there is the living connection maintained. The sap does not flow for a time, then stop, and then flow again, but from moment to moment the sap flows from the vine to the branches. And just so, my Lord Jesus wants me to take that blessed position as a worker, and morning by morning and day by day and hour by hour and step by step, in every work I have to go out to, just to abide before Him in the simple utter helplessness of one who knows nothing, and is nothing, and can do nothing. Oh, beloved workers, study that word *nothing*. You sometimes sing: "Oh, to be nothing, nothing," but have you really studied that word and prayed every day and worshiped God in the light of it? Do you know the blessedness of that word *nothing*?

If I am something, then God is not everything. But when I become *nothing*, God can become all, and the everlasting God in Christ can reveal Himself fully. That is the higher life. We need to become nothing. Someone has well said that the seraphim and cherubim are flames of fire because they know they are nothing, and they allow God to put His fullness and His glory and His brightness into them. Oh, become nothing in deep reality, and, as a worker, study only one thing—to become poorer and lower and more helpless, so that Christ may work all in you.

If we only by the Holy Spirit knew our relationship to Jesus Christ, our work would be changed into the brightest and most heavenly thing on earth.

Workers, here is your first lesson: Learn to be nothing, learn to be helpless. The man who has got something is not absolutely dependent, but the man who has got nothing is absolutely dependent. Absolute dependence on God is the secret of all power in work. The branch has nothing but what it gets from the vine, and you and I can have nothing but what we get from Jesus.

But secondly, the life of the branch is not only a life of entire dependence, but of deep restfulness.

That little branch, if it could think, and if it could feel, and if it could speak—that branch away in Hampton Court vine, or on some of the million vines that we have in South Africa, in our sunny land—if we could have a little branch here today to talk to us, and if we could say: "Come, branch of the vine, I want to learn from you how I can be a true branch of the living Vine," what would it answer? The little branch would whisper:

"Man, I hear that you are wise, and I know that you can do a great many wonderful things. I know you have much strength and wisdom given to you, but I have one lesson for you. With all your hurry and effort in Christ's work, you never prosper. The first thing you need is to come and rest in your Lord Jesus. That is what I do. Since I grew out of that vine I have spent years and years, and all I have done is just to rest in the vine. When the time of spring came, I had no anxious thought or care. The vine began to pour its sap into me, and to give the bud and leaf. And when the time of summer came, I had no care, and in the great heat I trusted the vine to bring moisture to keep me fresh. And in the time of harvest, when the owner came to pluck the grapes, I had no care. If there was anything in the grapes not good, the owner never blamed the branch, for the blame was always on the vine. And if you desire to be a true branch of Christ, the living Vine, just rest on Him. Let Christ bear the responsibility."

You say, "Won't that make me lazy?"

> *Christ wants that in all your work, the very foundation should be the simple, blessed consciousness: Christ must care for all.*

I tell you it will not. No one who learns to rest on the living Christ can become lazy, for the closer your contact with Christ, the more of the Spirit of His zeal and love will be borne in upon you. But begin to work in the midst of your entire dependence by adding to that *deep restfulness*. A man sometimes tries and tries to be dependent on Christ, but he worries himself about this absolute dependence. He tries and he cannot get it. But let him sink down into entire restfulness every day.

In Thy strong hand I lay me down. So shall the work be done; for who can work so wondrously as the almighty One?

Worker, take your place every day at the feet of Jesus, in the blessed peace and rest that come from the knowledge—I have no care, my cares are His! I have no fear, He cares for all my fears.

Come, children of God, and understand that it is the Lord Jesus who wants to work through you. You complain of the lack of fervent love. It will come from Jesus. He will give the divine love in your heart with which you can love people. That is the meaning of the assurance: "The love of God has been poured out in our hearts by the Holy Spirit" (Rom. 5:5), and of that other word: "The love of Christ compels us" (2 Cor. 5:14). Christ can give you a fountain of love, so that you cannot help loving the most wretched and the most ungrateful, or those who have wearied you before.

Rest in Christ, who can give wisdom and strength, and you do not know how that restfulness will often prove to be the very best part of your message. You plead with people and you argue, and they get the idea: "There is a man arguing and striving with me." They only feel, "Here are two men dealing with each other." But if you will let the deep rest of God come over you, the rest in Christ Jesus, the peace and rest and holiness of heaven, that restfulness will bring a blessing to the heart, even more than the words you speak.

But a third thought: the branch teaches a lesson of much fruitfulness.

The Lord Jesus Christ repeated that word *fruit* often in that parable. He spoke, first, of *fruit,* and then of *more fruit,* and then of *much fruit.* Yes, you are ordained not only to bear fruit, but to bear much fruit. "By this My Father is glorified, that you bear much fruit" (John 15:8). In the first place, Christ said: "I am the true vine, and My Father is the vinedresser" (15:1)—"My Father is the vinedresser who has charge of me and you." He who will watch over the connection between Christ and the branches is God, and it is in the power of God through Christ we are to bear fruit.

Oh Christians, you know this world is perishing for the lack of workers. And it wants not only more workers. The workers are saying, some more earnestly than others, "We need not only more workers, but we need our workers to have a new power, a different life, so that we workers would be able to bring more blessing." Children of God, I appeal to you. You know what trouble you take, say, in a case of sickness. You have a beloved friend apparently in danger of death, and nothing can refresh that friend so much as a few grapes, and they are out of season. But what trouble you will take to get the grapes that are to be the nourishment of this dying friend! And, there are around you people who never go to church, and so many who go to church but do not know Christ. And yet the heavenly grapes, the grapes of Eshcol, the grapes of the heavenly Vine are not to be had at any price, except as the child of God bears them out of his inner life in fellowship with Christ.

> *I*f I am something, then God is not everything. But when I become nothing, God can become all, and the everlasting God in Christ can reveal Himself fully.

Unless the children of God are filled with the sap of the heavenly Vine, unless they are filled with the Holy Spirit and the love of Jesus, they cannot bear much of the real heavenly grape. We all confess there is a great deal of work, a great deal of preaching and teaching and visiting, a great deal of machinery, a great deal of earnest effort of every kind. But there is not much manifestation of the power of God in it.

What is lacking? There is lacking the close connection between the worker and the heavenly Vine. Christ, the heavenly Vine, has blessings that He could pour on tens of thousands who are perishing. Christ, the heavenly Vine, has power to provide the heavenly grapes. But "You are the branches," and you cannot bear heavenly fruit unless you are in close connection with Jesus Christ.

Do not confuse *work* and *fruit.* There may be a good deal of work for Christ that is not the fruit of the heavenly Vine. Do not seek for work only. Yes, study this question of fruit-bearing. It means the very life and the very power and the very spirit and the very love within the heart of the Son of God—it means the heavenly Vine Himself coming into your heart and mine.

You know there are different sorts of grapes, each with a different name, and every vine provides exactly that peculiar aroma and juice that gives the grape its particular flavor and taste. Just so, there is in the heart of Christ Jesus a life, and a love, and a Spirit, and a blessing, and a power for men that are entirely heavenly and divine, and that will come down into our hearts. Stand in close connection with the heavenly Vine and say: "Lord Jesus, nothing less than the sap that flows through You, nothing less than the Spirit of Your divine life is what we ask. Lord Jesus, I ask You to let Your Spirit flow through me in all my work for You."

> *Rest in Christ, who can give wisdom and strength, and you do not know how that restfulness will often prove to be the very best part of your message.*

I tell you again that the sap of the heavenly Vine is nothing but the Holy Spirit. The Holy Spirit is the life of the heavenly Vine, and what you must get from Christ is nothing less than a strong inflow of the Holy Spirit. You need it exceedingly, and you lack nothing more than that. Remember that. Do not expect Christ to give a bit of strength here, and a bit of blessing there, and a bit of help over there. As the vine does its work in giving its own peculiar sap to the branch, so expect Christ to give His own Holy Spirit into your heart, and then you will bear much fruit. And if you have only begun to bear fruit, and are listening to the word of Christ in the parable—"more fruit," "much fruit"—remember that in order for you to bear more fruit, you just require more of Jesus in your life and heart.

We ministers of the gospel, how we are in danger of getting into a condition of *work, work, work*! And we pray over it, but the freshness and buoyancy and joy of the heavenly life are not always present. Let us seek to understand that the life of the branch is a life of much fruit, because it is a life rooted in Christ, the living, heavenly Vine.

A fourth thought: The life of the branch is a life of close communion.

Let us again ask: What has the branch to do? You know that precious, inexhaustible word that Christ used: *Abide*. Your life is to be an abiding life. And how is the abiding to be? It is to be just like the branch in the vine, abiding every minute of the day. There are the branches in close communion, in unbroken communion, with the vine, from January to December. And cannot I live every day—it is to me an almost terrible thing that we should ask the question—cannot I live in abiding communion with the heavenly Vine?

You say: "But I am so much occupied with other things."

You may have ten hours' hard work daily, during which your brain has to be occupied with temporal things. God orders it so. But the abiding work is the work of the *heart*, not of the brain—the work of the heart clinging to and resting in Jesus, a work in which the Holy Spirit links us to Christ Jesus. Oh, do believe that deeper down than the brain, deep down in the inner life, you can abide in Christ, so that every moment you are free, the consciousness will come: "Blessed Jesus, I am still in You."

If you will learn for a time to put aside other work and to get into this abiding contact with the heavenly Vine, you will find that fruit will come.

What is the application to our life of this abiding communion? What does it mean?

It means *close fellowship with Christ in secret prayer.* I am sure there are Christians who do long for the higher life, and who sometimes have received a great blessing and have at times found a great inflow of heavenly joy and a great outflow of heavenly gladness. And yet, after a time, it has passed away. They have not understood that close personal actual communion with Christ is an absolute necessity for daily life. Take time to be alone with Christ. Nothing in heaven or earth can free you from the necessity for that, if you are to be happy and holy Christians.

Oh, how many Christians look at it as a burden and a tax, and a duty, and a difficulty to be often alone with God! That is the great hindrance to our Christian life everywhere. We need more quiet fellowship with God, and I tell you in the name of the heavenly Vine that you cannot be healthy branches—branches into which the heavenly sap can flow—unless you take plenty of time for communion with God. If you are not willing to sacrifice time to get alone with Him, to give Him time every day to work in you, and to keep up the link of connection between you and Himself, He cannot give you that blessing of His unbroken fellowship. Jesus Christ asks you to live in close communion with Him. Let every heart say: "O Christ, it is this I long for. It is this I choose." And He will gladly give it to you.

And then my last thought: the life of the branch is a life of absolute surrender. This word, absolute surrender, is a great and solemn word, and I believe we do not understand its meaning. But yet the little branch preaches it.

"Have you anything to do, little branch, besides bearing grapes?"

"No, *nothing.*"

"Are you fit for nothing?"

Fit for nothing! The Bible says that a bit of vine cannot even be used as a pen, that it is fit for nothing but to be burned (John 15:6).

"And now, what do you understand, little branch, about your relationship to the vine?"

"My relationship is just this: I am utterly given up to the vine, and the vine can give me as much or as little sap as it chooses. Here I am at its disposal, and the vine can do with me what it likes."

Oh, friends, we need this absolute surrender to the Lord Jesus Christ. The more I speak, the more I feel that this is one of the most difficult points to make clear, and one of the most important and needed points to explain—what this absolute surrender is. It is often an easy thing for a man or a number of men to come out and offer themselves up to God for entire consecration, and to say: "Lord, it is my desire to give up myself entirely to You." That is of great value, and it often brings very rich blessing. But the one question I ought to study quietly is: what is meant by absolute surrender?

It means that just as literally as Christ was given up entirely to God, I am given up entirely to Christ. Is that too strong? Some think so. Some think that never can be—that just as entirely and absolutely as Christ gave up His life to do nothing but seek the Father's pleasure and depend on the Father absolutely and entirely, I am to do nothing but to seek the pleasure of Christ. But that is actually true. Christ Jesus came to breathe His own Spirit into us, to make us find our very highest happiness in living entirely for God, just as He did.

Oh, beloved brethren, if that is the case, then I ought to say: "Yes, as true as it is of that little branch of the vine, so true, by God's grace, I want to have it to be of me. I want to live day by day that Christ may be able to do with me what He will."

But here comes the terrible mistake that lies at the bottom of so much of our own religion. A man thinks: "I have my business and family duties and my relationships as a citizen, and all this I cannot change. And now alongside all this I am to take in religion and the service of God as something that will keep me from sin. God help me to perform my duties properly!"

This is not right. When Christ came, He came and bought the sinner with His blood. If there were a slave market here and I were to buy a slave, I would take that slave away to my own house from his old surroundings, and he would live at my house as my personal property, and I could order him about all the day. And if he were a faithful slave, he would live as having no will and no interests of his own, his one care being to promote the well-being and honor of his master. And in like manner I, who have been bought with the blood of Christ, have been bought to live every day with the one thought—How can I please my Master?

Oh, we find the Christian life so difficult because we seek for God's blessing while we live in our own will. We would be glad to live the Christian life according to our own liking. We make our own plans and choose our own work, and then we ask the Lord Jesus to come in and take care that sin shall not conquer us too much, and that we shall not go too far wrong. We ask Him to come in and give us so much of His blessing. But our relationship to Jesus ought to be such that we are entirely at His disposal, and every day we ought to come to Him humbly and straightforwardly and say: "Lord, is there anything in me that is not according to Your will, that has not been ordered by You, or that is not entirely given up to You?"

Oh, if we would wait and wait patiently, I tell you what the result would be.

There would spring up a relationship between us and Christ so close and so tender that we would afterward be amazed at how we formerly could have lived with the idea: "I am surrendered to Christ." We would feel how far distant our relationship with Him had previously been, and that He can, and does indeed, come and take actual possession of us, and gives unbroken fellowship all the day. The branch calls us to absolute surrender.

I do not speak now so much about the giving up of sins. There are people who need that, people who have violent tempers, bad habits, and actual sins that they from time to time commit, and that they have never given up into the very bosom of the Lamb of God. I encourage you, if you are branches of the living Vine, do not keep one sin back. I know there are a great many difficulties about this question of holiness. I know that all do not think exactly the same with regard to it. That would be to me a matter of comparative indifference if I could see that all are honestly longing to be free from every sin. But I am afraid that unconsciously there are in hearts often compromises with the idea that we cannot be without sin, that we must sin a little every day because we cannot help it. Oh, that people would actually cry to God: "Lord, keep me from sin!" Give yourself utterly to Jesus and ask Him to do His very utmost for you in keeping you from sin.

If you will learn for a time to put aside other work and to get into this abiding contact with the heavenly Vine, you will find that fruit will come.

There is a great deal in our work, in our church, and in our surroundings that we found in the world when we were born into it, and it has grown all around us, and we think that it is all right, that it cannot be changed. We do not come to the Lord Jesus and ask Him about it. Oh! I advise you, Christians, *bring everything into relationship with Jesus* and say: "Lord, everything in my life has to be in most complete harmony with my position as a branch of You, the blessed Vine."

Let your surrender to Christ be absolute. I do not understand that word *surrender* fully. It gets new meanings every now and then. It enlarges immensely from time to time. But I advise you to speak it out: "Absolute surrender to You, O Christ, is what I have chosen." And Christ will show you what is not according to His mind and lead you on to deeper and higher blessedness.

In conclusion, let me gather up all in one sentence. Christ Jesus said: "I am the Vine, you are the branches." In other words: "I, the living One who has so completely given Myself to you, am the Vine. You cannot trust Me too much. I am the almighty Worker, full of a divine life and power." You are the branches of the Lord Jesus Christ. If there is in your heart the consciousness that you are not a strong, healthy, fruit-bearing branch, not closely linked with Jesus, not living in Him as you should be—then listen to Him say: "I am the Vine, I will receive you,

I will draw you to Myself, I will bless you, I will strengthen you, I will fill you with My Spirit. I, the Vine, have taken you to be My branches, I have given Myself utterly to you. Children, give yourselves utterly to Me. I have surrendered Myself as God absolutely to you. I became man and died for you that I might be entirely yours. Come and surrender yourselves entirely to be Mine."

What shall our answer be? Oh, let it be a prayer from the depths of our heart that the living Christ may take each one of us and link us close to Himself. Let our prayer be that He, the living Vine, shall so link each of us to Himself that we shall go away with our hearts singing: "He is my Vine, and I am His branches—I want nothing more—now I have the everlasting Vine." Then, when you get alone with Him, worship and adore Him, praise and trust Him, love Him and wait for His love. "You are my Vine, and I am Your branch. It is enough—my soul is satisfied."

Glory to His blessed name!

For Further Thought

1. *What is most essential in order for your work to bear much real and lasting fruit for the kingdom of God?*
2. *What exactly is wrong with looking at your already busy life and asking God to help you begin and to continue your duties of service properly? Where does asking for His "help" fall short?*
3. *What does it mean to you when you read Jesus' words, "I am the the Vine, you are the branches"? How does knowing you are one of Christ's branches change your outlook on service to Him and to your fellowman?*

WAITING ON GOD

CONTENTS

"Wait Thou Only Upon God"

My soul, wait silently
for God alone.
PSALM 62:5

A God. . .who acts for the one
who waits for Him.
ISAIAH 64:4

"Wait only upon God"; my soul, be still,
And let thy God unfold His perfect will.
Thou fain would'st follow Him throughout this year,
Thou fain with listening heart His voice would'st hear,
Thou fain would'st be a passive instrument
Possessed by God, and ever Spirit-sent
Upon His service sweet—then be thou still,
For only thus can He in thee fulfill
His heart's desire. Oh, hinder not His hand
From fashioning the vessel He hath planned.
"Be silent unto God," and thou shalt know
The quiet, holy calm He doth bestow
On those who wait on Him; so shalt thou bear
His presence, and His life and light e'en where
The night is darkest, and thine earthly days
Shall show His love, and sound His glorious praise.
And He will work with hand unfettered, free
His high and holy purposes through thee.
First on thee must that hand of power be turned,
Till in His love's strong fire thy dross is burned,
And thou come forth a vessel for thy Lord,
So frail and empty, yet, since He hath poured
Into thine emptiness His life, His love,

Henceforth through thee the power of God shall move
And He will work for thee. Stand still and see
The victories thy God will gain for thee;
So silent, yet so irresistible,
Thy God shall do the thing impossible.
Oh, question not henceforth what thou canst do;
Thou canst do nought. But He will carry through
The work where human energy had failed,
Where all thy best endeavors had availed
Thee nothing. Then, my soul, wait and be still;
Thy God shall work for thee His perfect will.
If thou wilt take no less, His best shall be
Thy portion now and through eternity.

FREDA HANBURY

Extract from Address in Exeter Hall

May 31, 1895

I have been surprised at nothing more than at the letters that have come to me from missionaries and others from all parts of the world—devoted men and women, testifying to the need they feel in their work of being helped to a deeper and a clearer insight into all that Christ could be to them. Let us look to God to reveal Himself among His people in a measure very few have realized. Let us expect great things of our God. At all our conventions and assemblies too little time is given to waiting on God. Is He not willing to put things right in His own divine way? Has the life of God's people reached the utmost limit of what God is willing to do for them? Surely not. We want to wait on Him, to put away our experiences, however blessed they have been, our conceptions of truth, however sound and scriptural we think they seem, our plans, however needed and suitable they appear, and give God time and place to show us what He could do, what He will do. God has new developments and new resources. He can do new things, unheard-of things, hidden things. Let us enlarge our hearts and not limit Him. "When You did awesome things for which we did not look, You came down, the mountains shook at Your presence" (Isa. 64:3).

A. M.

PREFACE

PREVIOUS to my leaving home for England last year, I had been much impressed by the thought of how, in all our religion, personal and public, we need more of God. I had felt that we needed to train our people in their worship more to wait on God and to make the cultivation of a deeper sense of His presence, of more direct contact with Him, of entire dependence on Him, a definite aim of our ministry. At a "welcome" breakfast in Exeter Hall, I gave very simple expression to this thought in connection with all our religious work. I have already said elsewhere that I was surprised at the response the sentiment met with. I saw that God's Spirit had been working the same desire in many hearts.

The experiences of the past year, both personal and public, have greatly deepened the conviction. It is as if I myself am only beginning to see the deepest truth concerning God, and our relation to Him, center in this waiting on God, and how very little, in our life and work, we have been surrounded by its spirit. The following pages are the outcome of my conviction, and of the desire to direct the attention of all God's people to the one great remedy for all our needs. More than half the pieces were written onboard ship, so I fear they bear the marks of being somewhat crude and hasty. I have felt, in looking them over, as if I could wish to write them over again. But this I cannot now do. And so I send them out with the prayer that He who loves to use the feeble may give His blessing with them.

I do not know if it will be possible for me to put into a few words what are the chief things we need to learn. But what I want to say here is this: The great lack of our religion is that *we do not know God*. The answer to every complaint of weakness and failure, the message to every congregation or convention seeking instruction on holiness, ought to be simply, What is the matter: *Have you not God?* If you really believe in God, He will put all right. God is willing and able by His Holy Spirit. Cease from expecting the least good from yourself or the least help from anything there is in man, and just yield yourself unreservedly to God to work in you: He will do all for you.

How simple this looks! And yet this is the gospel we so little know. I feel ashamed as I send forth these very defective meditations. I can only cast them on the love of my brethren and of our God. May He use them to draw us all to Himself, to learn in practice and experience the blessed art of WAITING ONLY ON GOD. God desires that we might get some right conception of what the influence would be on a life spent not in thought or imagination or effort, but in the power of the Holy Spirit, fully waiting on God.

With my greeting in Christ to all God's saints it has been my privilege to meet, and no less to those I have not met, I subscribe myself, your brother and servant,

ANDREW MURRAY

Day 1

The God of

Our Salvation

My soul silently waits for God;
from Him comes my salvation.
PSALM 62:1

IF salvation indeed comes from God and is entirely His work, just as Creation was, it follows, as a matter of course, that our first and highest duty is to wait on Him to do the work that pleases Him. Waiting becomes then the only way to the experience of a full salvation, the only way, truly, to know God as the God of our salvation.

All the difficulties that are brought forward as keeping us back from full salvation have their cause in this one thing: the defective knowledge and practice of waiting on God. All that the Church and its members need for the manifestation of the mighty power of God in the world is the return to our true place, the place that belongs to us, both in creation and redemption, the place of absolute and unceasing dependence on God. Let us strive to see what the elements are that make up this most blessed and needed waiting on God. It may help us to discover the reasons why this grace is so little cultivated and to feel how infinitely desirable it is that the Church, that we ourselves, should at any price learn its blessed secret.

The deep need for this waiting on God lies equally in the nature of man and the nature of God. God, as Creator, formed man to be a vessel in which He could show forth His power and goodness. Man was not to have in himself a fountain of life, or strength, or happiness: The ever-living and only living One was each moment to be the communicator to him of all that he needed. Man's glory and blessedness was not to be independent or dependent on himself, but dependent on a God of such infinite riches and love. Man was to have the joy of receiving every moment out of the fullness of God. This was his blessedness as an unfallen creature.

When he fell from God, he was even more absolutely dependent on Him. There was not the slightest hope of his recovery out of his state of death but in God, in

His power and mercy. It is God alone who began the work of redemption, and it is God alone who continues and carries it on each moment in each individual believer. Even in the regenerate man, there is no power of goodness in himself. He has and can have nothing that he does not each moment receive. Waiting on God is just as indispensable and must be just as continuous and unbroken as the breathing that maintains his natural life.

It is, then, because Christians do not know their relation to God of absolute poverty and helplessness that they have no sense of the need of absolute and unceasing dependence or the unspeakable blessedness of continual waiting on God. But when once a believer begins to see it and consent to it that he by the Holy Spirit must each moment receive what God each moment works, waiting on God becomes his brightest hope and joy. As he apprehends how God, as God, as infinite love, delights to impart His own nature to His child as fully as He can, how God is not weary of each moment keeping charge of his life and strength, he wonders that he ever thought otherwise of God than as a God to be waited on all the day. God unceasingly giving and working and His child unceasingly waiting and receiving: this is the blessed life.

> *Man's glory and blessedness was not to be independent or dependent on himself, but dependent on a God of such infinite riches and love.*

"Truly my soul silently waits for God; from Him comes my salvation." First we wait on God for salvation. Then we learn that salvation is only to bring us to God and teach us to wait on Him. Then we find what is better still, that waiting on God is itself the highest salvation. It is the ascribing to Him the glory of being All. It is the experiencing that He is All to us. May God teach us the blessedness of waiting on Him.

"MY SOUL, WAIT SILENTLY FOR GOD ALONE!"

FOR FURTHER THOUGHT

1. *What is your highest duty in your relationship with God through Jesus Christ? Why is it your highest duty?*
2. *On what is your glory and blessedness to depend upon? How does knowing that affect your relationship with God?*
3. *What are the three things you learn when it comes to waiting on God? What does waiting on God demonstrate in your relationship to Him?*

DAY 2

THE KEYNOTE OF LIFE

"I have waited for Your salvation, O LORD!"
GENESIS 49:18

IT is not easy to say exactly in what sense Jacob used these words in the midst of his prophecies in regard to the future of his sons. But they do certainly dictate that both for himself and for them, his expectation was from God alone. It was God's salvation he waited for, a salvation that God had promised and that God Himself alone could work out. He knew himself and his sons to be under God's charge. Jehovah the everlasting God would show in them what His saving power is and does. The words point forward to that wonderful history of redemption that is not yet finished and to the glorious future in eternity where it is leading. They suggest to us how there is no salvation but God's salvation, and how waiting on God for that, whether for our personal experience or in wider circles, is our first duty, our true blessedness.

Let us think of ourselves and the inconceivably glorious salvation God has accomplished for us in Christ and is now purposing to work out and to perfect in us by His Spirit. Let us meditate until we somewhat realize that every participation of this great salvation, from moment to moment, must be the work of God Himself. God cannot part with His grace, goodness, or strength as an external thing that He gives us, as He gives the raindrops from heaven. No, He can only give it, and we can only enjoy it, as He works it Himself directly and unceasingly. And the only reason that He does not work it more effectually and continuously is that we do not let Him. We hinder Him either by our indifference or by our self-effort, so that He cannot do what He would.

What He asks of us, in the way of surrender, obedience, desire, and trust is all comprised in this one word: waiting on Him, waiting for His salvation. It combines the deep sense of our entire helplessness of ourselves to work what is divinely good, and our perfect confidence that our God will work it all in His divine power.

Again I say, let us meditate on the divine glory of the salvation God purposes working out in us until we know the truths it implies. Our heart is the scene of a divine operation more wonderful than Creation. We can do as little toward the work as toward creating the world, except as God works in us to will and to do.

God only asks of us to yield, to consent, to wait on Him, and then He will do it all. Let us meditate and be still until we see how fitting and right and blessed it is that God alone do all, and our soul will by itself sink down in deep humility to say: "I have waited for Your salvation, O Lord." And the deep blessed background of all our praying and working will be: "Truly my soul waits for God."

The application of the truth to wider circles, to those we labor among or intercede for, to the Church of Christ around us, or throughout the world is not difficult. There can be no good except what God works. To wait on God and have the heart filled with faith in His working, and in that faith to pray for His mighty power to come down is our only wisdom. Oh, for the eyes of our heart to be opened to see God working in ourselves and in others, and to see how blessed it is to worship and just to wait for His salvation!

> *What He asks of us, in the way of surrender, obedience, desire, and trust is all comprised in this one word: waiting on Him, waiting for His salvation.*

Our private and public prayer is our chief expression of our relation to God. It is in them chiefly that our waiting on God must be exercised. If our waiting begins by quieting the activities of nature and being still before God, if it bows and seeks to see God in His universal and almighty operation, alone able and always ready to work all good, if it yields itself to Him in the assurance that He is working and will work in us, if it maintains the place of humility and stillness and surrenders until God's Spirit has quickened the faith that He will perfect His work: it will indeed become the strength and the joy of the soul. Life will become one deep blessed cry: "I have waited for Your salvation, O Lord."

"MY SOUL, WAIT SILENTLY FOR GOD ALONE!"

FOR FURTHER THOUGHT

1. To what specifically do Jacob's words recorded in Genesis 49:18 point? How can you apply his words to your own life of faith?
2. How would you define waiting on God, waiting for His salvation? What does waiting on God include?
3. How should your prayers—both in private and in public—express a heart attitude of waiting on God?

DAY 3

THE TRUE PLACE

OF THE CREATURE

These all wait for You, that You may give them their food
in due season. What You give them they gather in;
you open Your hand, they are filled with good.
PSALM 104:27–28

THIS Psalm, in praise of the Creator, has been speaking of the birds and the beasts of the forest, of the young lions and man going forth to his work, of the great sea where there are things creeping innumerable, both small and great beasts. And it sums up the whole relation of all creation to its Creator, and its continuous and universal dependence on Him in the one word: "*These all wait for You.*" Just as it was God's work to create, it is His work to maintain. As little as the creature could create itself, it is left to provide for itself. The whole creation is ruled by the one unalterable law of—*waiting on God!*

The word is the simple expression of that for the sake of which alone the creature was brought into existence, the very groundwork of its constitution. The one object for which God gave life to creatures was that in them He might prove and show forth His wisdom, power, and goodness in His being each moment their life and happiness, and pouring forth to them, according to their capacity, the riches of His goodness and power. And just as this is the very place and nature of God, to be unceasingly the supplier of every need in the creature, so the very place and nature of the creature is nothing but this—to wait on God and receive from Him what He alone can give, what He delights to give.

If we are in this little book at all to apprehend what *waiting on God* is to be to the believer, to practice it and to experience its blessedness, it is of consequence that we begin at the very beginning and see the deep reasonableness of the call that comes to us. We shall understand how the duty is no arbitrary command. We shall see how it is not only rendered necessary by our sin and helplessness. It is simply and truly our restoration to our original destiny and our highest nobility, to our true place and glory as creatures blessedly dependent on the All-Glorious God.

If once our eyes are opened to this precious truth, all nature will become a preacher, reminding us of the relationship that, founded in Creation, is now taken in grace. As we read this Psalm and learn to look on all life in nature as continually maintained by God Himself, waiting on God will be seen to be the very necessity of our being. As we think of the young lions and the ravens crying to Him, of the birds and the fishes and every insect waiting on Him until He gives them their food in due season, we shall see that it is the very nature and glory of God that He is a God who is to be waited on. Every thought of what nature is, and what God is, will give new force to the call: "Wait only on God." "These all wait for You, that You may *give*." It is God who gives all. Let this faith enter deeply into our hearts. Before yet we fully understand all that is implied in our waiting on God, before we have even been able to cultivate the habit, let the truth enter our souls: waiting on God, unceasing and entire dependence on Him, is, in heaven and earth, the one only true religion, the one unalterable and all-comprehensive expression for the true relationship to the ever-blessed One in whom we live.

> Every thought of what nature is, and what God is, will give new force to the call: "Wait only on God."

Let us resolve now that it shall be the one characteristic of our life and worship—a continual, humble, truthful waiting on God. We may rest assured that He who made us for Himself so that He might give Himself to us and in us, that *He* will never disappoint us. In waiting on Him we shall find rest and joy and strength and the supply of every need.

"My soul, wait silently for God alone!"

For Further Thought

1. *Why is it important in your personal Christian life to make waiting on God the foundation of everything you do, say, and pray?*
2. *How does looking at and contemplating the God-created nature so strongly emphasize the importance of the command, the call to "wait only on God?"*
3. *Why do you think God made you in the first place? What kind of assurance does knowing why He made you give you? What blessings will God give you if you only wait on Him?*

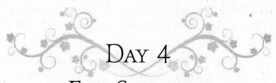

Day 4

For Supplies

The LORD upholds all who fall, and raises up all who are bowed down. The eyes of all look expectantly to You, and You give them their food in due season.
PSALM 145:14–15

PSALM 104 is a psalm of Creation, and the words "*These all wait for You*" were used with reference to the animal creation. Here we have a Psalm of the kingdom, and "*The eyes of all look expectantly to You*" appears specifically to point to the needs of God's saints, of all who fall and those who be bowed down. What the universe and the animal creation do unconsciously, God's people are to do intelligently and voluntarily. Man is to be the interpreter of nature. He is to prove that there is nothing nobler or more blessed in the exercise of our free will than to use it in waiting on God.

If an army has been sent out to march into an enemy's country, and news is received that it is not advancing, the question is immediately asked, What may be the cause of delay? The answer will very often be: "Waiting for supplies." All the stores of provisions or clothing or ammunition have not arrived, and without these it dare not proceed. It is no different in the Christian life: day by day, at every step, we need our supplies from above. And there is nothing so needed as to cultivate that spirit of dependence on God and of confidence in Him, which refuses to go on without the needed supply of grace and strength.

If the question be asked, whether this be anything different from what we do when we pray, the answer is that there may be much praying with but very little waiting on God. In praying we are often occupied with ourselves, with our own needs and our own efforts in the presentation of them. In waiting on God, the first thought is of *the God on whom we wait*. We enter His presence and feel we need just to be quiet, so that He, as God, can overshadow us with Himself. God longs to reveal Himself, to fill us with Himself. Waiting on God gives Him time in His own way and divine power to come to us.

It is especially at the time of prayer that we ought to set ourselves to cultivate this spirit.

Before you pray, bow quietly before God, just to remember and realize who He is, how near He is, how certainly He can and will help. Just be still before

1153

Him and allow His Holy Spirit to waken and stir up in your soul the childlike disposition of absolute dependence and confident expectation. Wait on God as a living Being, as the living God who notices you and is just longing to fill you with His salvation. Wait on God until you know you have met Him. Prayer will then become so different.

> *God longs to reveal Himself, to fill us with Himself. Waiting on God gives Him time in His own way and divine power to come to us.*

And when you are praying, let there be intervals of silence, reverent stillness of soul, in which you yield yourself to God, in case He may have something He wishes to teach you or to work in you. Waiting on Him will become the most blessed part of prayer, and the blessing obtained this way will be doubly precious as the fruit or such fellowship with the Holy One. God has so ordained it, in harmony with His holy nature and with ours, that waiting on Him should be the honor we give Him. Let us bring Him the service gladly and truthfully. He will reward it abundantly.

"The eyes of all look expectantly to You, and You give them their food in due season." Dear soul, God provides in nature for the creatures He has made. How much more will He provide in grace for those He has redeemed. Learn to say of every need, every failure, and every lack of needed grace: "I have waited too little on God, or He would have given me in due season all I needed." And say then too—

"MY SOUL, WAIT SILENTLY FOR GOD ALONE!"

FOR FURTHER THOUGHT

1. *How should your life of prayer and your life of waiting on God be related? What does waiting on God accomplish in your prayer life?*
2. *What should you do before you pray so you can be assured how near He is to you and how certainly He can and will give you what you need?*
3. *What should you do while you pray in order that He can teach you or accomplish something within you?*

DAY 5

FOR INSTRUCTION

*Show me Your ways, O Lord; teach me Your paths. Lead
me in Your truth and teach me, for You are the God
of my salvation; on You I wait all the day.*
PSALM 25:4–5

I spoke of an army on the point of entering an enemy's territories. Answering the question as to the cause of delay: *"Waiting for supplies."* The answer might also have been: *"Waiting for instructions,"* or *"Waiting for orders."* If the last dispatch had not been received, with the final orders of the commander-in-chief, the army dared not move. It is like that in the Christian life. As deep as the need is of *waiting for supplies* is that of *waiting for instructions.*

See how beautiful this comes out in Psalm 25. The writer knew and loved God's law exceedingly and meditated in that law day and night. But he knew that this was not enough. He knew that for the right spiritual apprehension of the truth, and for the right personal application of it to his own peculiar circumstances, he needed a direct divine teaching.

The psalm has at all times been a very peculiar one because of its repeated expression of the felt need of the divine teaching and of the childlike confidence that that teaching would be given. Study the psalm until your heart is filled with the two thoughts—the absolute need and the absolute certainty of divine guidance. And with these how entirely it is in this connection that he speaks, *"On You I wait all the day."* Waiting for guidance, waiting for instruction all the day is a very blessed part of waiting on God.

The Father in heaven is so interested in His child and so longs to have his life at every step in His will and His love that He is willing to keep his guidance entirely in His own hand. He knows so well that we are unable to do what is really holy and heavenly, unless He works it in us, that He means His very demands to become promises of what He will do in watching over and leading us all the day. Not only in special difficulties and times of perplexity, but in the common course of everyday life, we may count on Him to teach us *His* way and show us *His* path.

And what is needed in us to receive this guidance? One thing: waiting for instructions, waiting on God. "On You I wait all the day." We want in our times of

1155

prayer to give clear expression to our sense of need and to our faith in His help. We want definitely to become conscious of our ignorance as to what God's way may be, and the need of the divine light shining within us if our way is to be as of the sun, shining more and more to the perfect day. And we want to wait quietly before God in prayer until the deep, restful assurance fills us: It will be given—"the humble He teaches His way" (Ps. 25:9).

> The Father in heaven is so interested in His child and so longs to have his life at every step in His will and His love that He is willing to keep his guidance entirely in His own hand.

"On You I wait all the day." The special surrender to the divine guidance in our seasons of prayer must cultivate, and be followed up by, the habitual looking upwards "all the day." As simple as it is to one who has eyes to walk all the day in the light of the sun, just as simple and delightful can it become to a soul practiced in waiting on God to walk all the day in the enjoyment of God's light and leading. What is needed to help us to such a life is just one thing: the real knowledge and faith of God as the one and only source of wisdom and goodness, as ever ready and longing much to be to us all that we can possibly require—yes! this is the one thing we need. If we only saw our God in His love, if we just believed that He waits to be gracious, that He waits to be our life and to work all in us—how this waiting on God would become our highest joy, the natural and spontaneous response of our hearts to His great love and glory!

"MY SOUL, WAIT SILENTLY FOR GOD ALONE!"

FOR FURTHER THOUGHT

1. *Read Psalm 25:4–5 again. What was the psalmist praying for? Why should you pray for the very same thing?*
2. *Why does your Father in heaven keep your guidance entirely in His own hand? What does He know about you that moves and motivates Him to do so?*
3. *What must you do to receive your heavenly Father's guidance? How can you apply that need to your daily prayer?*

DAY 6

FOR ALL SAINTS

Let no one who waits on You be ashamed.
PSALM 25:3

LET us now, in our meditation of today, each one forget himself, to think of the great company of God, saints throughout the world, who are all with us waiting on Him. And let us all join in the fervent prayer for each other, "Let no one who waits on You be ashamed."

Just think for a moment of the multitude of waiting ones who need that prayer—how many there are sick and weary and solitary, to whom it is as if their prayers are not answered, and who sometimes begin to fear that their hope will be put to shame. And then, how many servants of God—ministers or missionaries, teachers or workers, of various name—whose hopes in their work have been disappointed and whose longing for power and blessing remains unsatisfied. And then, too, how many, who have heard of a life of rest and perfect peace, of abiding light and fellowship, of strength and victory, and who cannot find the path. With all these, it is nothing but that they have not yet learned the secret of full waiting on God. They just need what we all need: the living assurance that waiting on God can never be in vain. Let us remember all who are in danger of fainting or being weary, and all unite in the cry, "Let no one who waits on You be ashamed!"

If this intercession for all who wait on God becomes part of our waiting on Him for ourselves, we shall help to bear each other's burdens, and so fulfill the law of Christ.

There will be introduced into our waiting on God that element of unselfishness and love, which is the path to the highest blessing and the fullest communion with God. Love to the brethren and love to God are inseparably linked. In God, the love for His Son *and for us* are one: "That the love with which You loved Me may be in them, and I in them" (John 17:26). In Christ, the love of the Father for Him and *His love for us* are one: "As the Father loved Me, I also have loved you" (John 15:9). In us, He asks that His love for us shall be *ours* for the brethren: "As I have loved you, that you also love one another" (John 13:34). All the love of God and of Christ are inseparably linked with love to the brethren. And how can we, day by day, prove and cultivate this love otherwise than by daily praying for each other? Christ did not seek to enjoy the Father's love for Himself; He passed it all on to us. All true seeking of God and His love for ourselves will be inseparably linked with the thought and the love of our brethren in prayer for them.

"Let no one who waits on You be ashamed." Twice in the psalm, David speaks of his waiting on God for himself, but here he thinks of *all* who wait on Him. Let this page take the message to all God's tried and weary ones that there are more praying for them than they know. Let it stir them and us in our waiting to make a point of at times forgetting ourselves and to enlarge our hearts and say to the Father, "These all wait on You, and You give them their food in due season." Let it inspire us all with new courage—for who is there who is not at times ready to faint and be weary? "Let no one who waits on You be ashamed" is a promise in a prayer, "Those who wait on You will not be ashamed"!

> *All true seeking of God and His love for ourselves will be inseparably linked with the thought and the love of our brethren in prayer for them.*

From many and many a witness, the cry comes to every one who needs the help—brother, sister, tried one: "Wait on the LORD; be of good courage, and He shall strengthen your heart; wait, I say, on the LORD! Be of good courage, and He shall strengthen your heart, all you who hope in the LORD" (Ps. 27:14, 31:24).

Blessed Father! We humbly ask You, let no one who waits on You be ashamed; no, not one. Some are weary, and the time of waiting appears long. And some are weak and scarcely know how to wait. And some are so entangled in the effort of their prayers and their work that they think that they can find no time to wait continually. Father, teach us all how to wait. Teach us to think of each other and pray for each other. Teach us to think of You, the God of all waiting ones. Father! Let no one who waits on You be ashamed. For Jesus' sake. Amen.

"My soul, wait silently for God alone!"

For Further Thought

1. *Read Jesus' words in John 17:26 and 15:9. What is the connection between God's love for His Son, Jesus, and God's love for you?*
2. *Read Psalm 25. What guarantees does God give in that psalm to those who wait on Him? How can those guarantees motivate you to committing yourself to waiting on God?*
3. *Read Psalm 27:14. What additional promise does God give those who wait on Him? How does that apply to your personal spiritual life?*

DAY 7

A PLEA IN PRAYER

Let integrity and uprightness preserve me,
for I wait for You.
PSALM 25:21

FOR the third time in this psalm, we have the word *wait*. As before in verse 5, "On You I wait all the day," so here, too, the believing supplicant appeals to God to remember that he is waiting on Him, looking for an answer. It is a great thing for a soul not only to wait on God, but to be filled with such a consciousness that its whole spirit and position is that of a waiting one that it can, in childlike confidence, say, "Lord! You know I wait on You." It will prove a mighty plea in prayer, giving ever-increasing boldness of expectation to claim the promise, "Those who wait on Me shall not be ashamed!"

The prayer in connection with which the plea is put forth here is one of great importance in the spiritual life. If we draw near to God, it must be with a true heart. There must be perfect integrity, wholeheartedness, in our dealing with God. As we read in the next psalm (26:1, 11), "Vindicate me, O LORD, for I have walked in my integrity," "As for me, I walk in my integrity," there must be perfect uprightness or singleheartedness before God, as it is written, "His righteousness is for the upright in heart" (see Ps. 36:10). The soul must know that it allows nothing sinful, nothing doubtful. If it is indeed to meet the Holy One and receive His full blessing, it must be with a heart fully and singly given up to His will. The whole spirit that animates us in the waiting must be, "Let integrity and uprightness"—You see that I desire to come so to You, You know I am looking to You to work them perfectly in me—let them "preserve me, for I wait for You" (Ps. 25:21).

And if at our first attempt truly to live the life of fully and always waiting on God, we begin to discover how much that perfect integrity is lacking, this will just be one of the blessings that the waiting was meant to work. *A soul cannot seek close fellowship with God or attain the abiding consciousness of waiting on Him all the day without a very honest and entire surrender to all His will.*

"For I wait for You": It is not only in connection with the prayer of our text but with every prayer that this plea may be used. To use it often will be a great blessing to ourselves. Let us therefore study the words well until we know all their

1159

bearings. It must be clear to us *what we are waiting for.* There may be very different things. It may be waiting for God in our times of prayer to take His place as God and to work in us the sense of His holy presence and nearness. It may be a special petition to which we are expecting an answer. It may be our whole inner life, in which we are on the lookout for God's putting forth of His power. It may be the whole state of His Church and saints, or some part of His work, for which our eyes are constantly toward Him. It is good that we sometimes count up to ourselves exactly what the things are we are waiting for, and as we say definitely of each of them, "On You I wait," we shall be emboldened to claim the answer, "*For on You I wait.*"

> *It* must be clear to us what we are waiting for. It may be waiting for God in our times of prayer to take His place as God and to work in us the sense of His holy presence and nearness.

It must also be clear to us on whom we are waiting. Not an idol, a god of whom we have made an image by our conceptions of what He is. No, but the living God, such as He really is in His great glory, His infinite holiness, His power, wisdom, and goodness, in His love and nearness. It is the presence of a beloved or a dreaded master that wakens up the whole attention of the servant who waits on him. It is the *presence of God, as He can in Christ by His Holy Spirit make Himself known* and keep the soul under its covering and shadow, that will waken and strengthen the true waiting spirit. Let us be still and wait and worship until we know how near He is, and then say, "On You I wait."

And then, let it be very clear, too, that *we are waiting.* Let that become so much our consciousness that the utterance comes spontaneously, "On You I wait all the day; I wait for You." This will indeed imply sacrifice and separation, a soul entirely given up to God as its all, its only joy. This waiting on God has hardly yet been acknowledged as the only true Christianity. And yet, if it is true that God alone is goodness and joy and love, if it is true that our highest blessedness is in having as much of God as we can, if it is true that Christ has redeemed us wholly for God and made a life of continual abiding in His presence possible, then nothing less ought to satisfy than to be ever breathing this blessed atmosphere, "I wait for You."

"MY SOUL, WAIT SILENTLY FOR GOD ALONE!"

For Further Thought

1. *What does the psalmist's prayer in Psalm 25:21 tell you about your spiritual life in general and your relationship with God Himself in particular?*
2. *What is God's condition for seeking and having close fellowship with God or attaining the abiding consciousness of waiting on Him?*
3. *How exactly does God waken and strengthen your spirit as you wait on Him?*

Day 8

Strong and of Good Courage

Wait on the Lord; be of good courage,
and He shall strengthen your heart;
wait, I say, on the Lord!
PSALM 27:14

THE psalmist had just said, "I would have lost heart, unless I had believed that I would see the goodness of the Lord in the land of the living" (Ps. 27:13). If it had not been for his faith in God, he would have lost heart. But in the confident assurance in God that faith gives, he urges himself and us to remember one thing above all—to wait on God. "Wait on the Lord; be of good courage, and He shall strengthen your heart; wait, I say, on the Lord." One of the chief needs in our waiting on God, one of the deepest secrets of its blessedness and blessing, is a quiet, confident persuasion that it is not in vain—courage to believe that God will hear and help and that we are waiting on a God who never could disappoint His people.

"Be strong and of good courage." These words are frequently found in connection with some great and difficult enterprise, in prospect of the combat with the power of strong enemies, and the utter insufficiency of all human strength. Is waiting on God a work so difficult that for that, too, such words are needed, "Be strong and let your heart take courage"? Yes, indeed. The deliverance for which we often have to wait is from enemies, in the presence of whom we are powerless. The blessings for which we plead are spiritual and all unseen—things impossible with men, heavenly, supernatural, divine realities. Our heart may well faint and fail.

Our souls are so little accustomed to hold fellowship with God; the God on whom we wait so often *appears* to hide Himself. We who have to wait are often tempted to fear that we do not wait right, that our faith is too weak, that our desire is not as upright or as earnest as it should be, that our surrender is not complete. Amid all these causes of fear or doubt, how blessed to hear the voice of God, "Wait on the Lord! Be of good courage, and He shall strengthen your heart! WAIT, I SAY, on the Lord!" Let nothing in heaven or earth or hell—let nothing keep you from waiting on your God in the full assurance that it cannot be in vain.

The one lesson our text teaches us is this: that when we set ourselves to wait on God we ought beforehand to resolve that it shall be with the most confident expectation of God's meeting and blessing us. We ought to make up our minds that nothing was ever so sure as that waiting on God will bring us untold and unexpected blessing. We are so accustomed to judge of God and His work in us by *what we feel* that the great probability is that when we begin more to cultivate the waiting on Him, we shall be discouraged because we do not find any special blessing from it. The message comes to us, "Above everything, when you wait on God, do so in the spirit of abounding hopefulness. It is God in His glory, in His power, in His love longing to bless you whom you are waiting on."

> *We* ought to make up our minds that nothing was ever so sure as that waiting on God will bring us untold and unexpected blessing.

If you say that you are afraid of deceiving yourself with vain hope because you do not see or feel any warrant in your present state for such special expectations, my answer is, it is God who is the guarantee for your expecting great things. Oh, do learn the lesson. You are not going to wait on yourself to see what you feel and what changes come to you. You are going to WAIT ON GOD, to know *first what* HE IS, and then, after that, what He will do. The whole duty and blessedness of waiting on God has its root in this: that He is such a blessed Being, full to overflowing of goodness and power and life and joy that we, however wretched, cannot for any time come into contact with Him without that life and power secretly, silently beginning to enter into him and blessing him. God is love! That is the one only and all-sufficient warrant of your expectation. Love seeks out its own: God's love is just *His delight to impart Himself and His blessedness* to His children.

Come, and however weak you feel, just wait in His presence. As a weak, sickly invalid is brought out into the sunshine to let its warmth go through him, come with all that is dark and cold in you *into the sunshine of God's holy, omnipotent love*, and sit and wait there with the one thought: Here I am, in the sunshine of His love. Just as the sun does its work in the weak one who seeks its rays, *God will do His work in you*. Oh, do trust Him fully. "Wait on the Lord! Be of good courage, and He shall strengthen your heart; wait, I say, on the Lord!"

"MY SOUL, WAIT SILENTLY FOR GOD ALONE!"

For Further Thought

1. *Read Psalm 27:14. What kept the psalmist from losing heart in the face of his difficulties? How can you continue to keep heart, even when you are faced with severe trials and tribulations in this life?*
2. *What should you confidently expect and wait for as you set yourself to wait on God during difficult times?*
3. *How does today's lesson define God's love? What confidence can that definition give you personally?*

DAY 9

WITH THE HEART

Be of good courage,
and He shall strengthen your heart,
all you who hope in the LORD.
PSALM 31:24

THE words are nearly the same as in our last meditation. But I gladly make use of them again to press home a much-needed lesson for all who desire to learn truly and fully what waiting on God is. The lesson is this: It is with the heart we must wait on God. "He shall strengthen *your heart*."

All our waiting depends on the state of the heart. As a man's heart is, so is he before God. We can advance no further or deeper into the holy place of God's presence to wait on Him there, than our heart is prepared for it by the Holy Spirit. The message is, "He shall strengthen your heart, all you who hope in the LORD."

The truth appears so simple that some may ask, Do not all admit this? Where is the need of insisting on it so specially? Because very many Christians have no sense of the great difference between the religion of the mind and the religion of the heart, and the former is far more diligently cultivated than the latter. They do not know how infinitely greater the heart is than the mind. It is in this that one of the chief causes must be sought of the weakness of our Christian life, and it is only as this is understood that waiting on God will bring its full blessing.

A text in Proverbs (3:5) may help to make my meaning plain. Speaking of a life in the fear and favor of God, it says, "Trust in the LORD with all your heart, and lean not on your own understanding." In all religion, we have to use these two powers. The mind as to gather knowledge from God's Word and prepare the food by which the heart with the inner life is to be nourished. But here comes in a terrible danger, that of our leaning to our own understanding and trusting in our apprehension of divine things.

People imagine that if they are occupied with the truth, the spiritual life will as a matter of course be strengthened. And this is by no means the case. The understanding deals with conceptions and images of divine things, but it cannot reach the real life of the soul. That is the reason for the command, "Trust in the LORD with all your heart, and lean not on your own understanding." It is with the heart man believes and comes into touch with God. It is in the heart God has given His Spirit to be there to us the presence and the power of God working in us. In all our religion, it is the heart that must trust and love and worship and obey. My mind is utterly helpless in creating or maintaining the spiritual life within me: the heart must wait on God for Him to work it in me.

It is in this even as in the physical life. My reason may tell me what to eat and drink and how the food nourishes me. But in the eating and feeding my reason, I can do nothing. The body has its organs for that special purpose. Just so, reason may tell me what God's Word says, but it can do nothing to the feeding of the soul on the bread of life—this the heart alone can do by its faith and trust in God. A man may be studying the nature and effects of food or sleep. When he wants to eat or sleep, he sets aside his thoughts and study and uses the power of eating or sleeping. And so the Christian needs always, when he has studied or heard God's word, to cease from his thoughts, to put no trust in them, and to waken up his heart to open itself before God and seek the living fellowship with Him.

> *My mind is utterly helpless in creating or maintaining the spiritual life within me: the heart must wait on God for Him to work it in me.*

This is now the blessedness of waiting on God, that I confess the helplessness of all my thoughts and efforts and set myself still to bow my heart before Him in holy silence and to trust Him to renew and strengthen His own work in me. And this is just the lesson of our text, "Be of good courage, and He shall *strengthen your heart*, all you who hope in the LORD." Remember the difference between knowing with the mind and believing with the heart. Beware of the temptation of leaning on your understanding, with its clear, strong thoughts. They only help you to know what the heart must get from God. In themselves they are only images and shadows.

"Be of good courage, and He shall *strengthen your heart*, all you who hope in the LORD." Present it before Him as that wonderful part of your spiritual nature in which God reveals Himself, and by which you can know Him. Cultivate the greatest confidence that though you cannot see into your heart, God is working there by His Holy Spirit. Let the heart wait at times in perfect silence and quiet, and in its hidden depths God will work. Be sure of this, and just wait on Him. Give your whole heart, with its secret workings, into God's hands continually. He wants the heart, and takes it, and as God dwells in it. "Be of good courage, and He shall strengthen your heart, all you who hope in the LORD."

"MY SOUL, WAIT SILENTLY FOR GOD ALONE!"

FOR FURTHER THOUGHT

1. *How specifically can you prepare your heart to wait on God?*
2. *What should you do in order for the truth of what God's Word says to penetrate your heart, your whole being, and give you the blessings associated with waiting on God?*
3. *What is the promised blessing for you when you are of good courage and keep your hope in the Lord?*

Day 10

In Humble Fear and Hope

Behold, the eye of the Lord is on those who fear Him,
on those who hope in His mercy, to deliver their soul from death,
and to keep them alive in famine. Our soul waits for the Lord;
He is our help and our shield. For our heart shall rejoice in Him,
because we have trusted in His holy name. Let Your mercy,
O Lord, be upon us, just as we hope in You.
PSALM 33:18–22

GOD'S eye is upon His people; their eye is upon Him. In waiting on God, our eye, looking up to Him, meets His looking down upon us. This is the blessedness of waiting on God: that it takes our eyes and thoughts away from ourselves, even our needs and desires, and occupies us with our God. We worship Him in His glory and love, with His all-seeing eye watching over us so that He may supply our every need. Let us consider this wonderful meeting between God and His people, and mark well what we are taught here of those on whom God's eye rests, and of Him on whom our eye rests.

"The eye of the Lord is on those who fear Him, on those who hope in His mercy." Fear and hope are generally thought to be in conflict with each other, but in the presence and worship of God they are found side by side in perfect and beautiful harmony. And this because in God Himself all apparent contradictions are reconciled. Righteousness and peace, judgment and mercy, holiness and love, infinite power and infinite gentleness, a majesty that is exalted above all heaven, and a condescension that bows very low, meet and kiss each other.

There is indeed a fear that torments that is cast out entirely by perfect love. But there is a fear that is found in the very heavens. In the song of Moses and the Lamb they sing, "Who shall not fear You, O Lord, and glorify Your name?" (Rev. 15:4). And out of the very throne the voice came, "Praise our God, all you His servants and those who fear Him!" (Rev. 19:5). Let us in our waiting ever seek to "fear this glorious and awesome name, THE LORD YOUR GOD" (Deut. 28:58). The deeper we bow before His holiness in holy fear and adoring awe, in deep reverence and humble self-abasement, even as the angels veil their faces before the throne, the more will His holiness rest on us, and the soul be filled to have God reveal Himself. The deeper we enter into the truth "that no flesh should glory in His

1168

presence" (1 Cor. 1:29), the more will it be given us to see His glory. "The eye of the Lord is on those who fear Him."

"On those who hope in His mercy." So far will the true fear of God be from keeping us back from hope, it will stimulate and strengthen it. The lower we bow, the deeper we feel we have nothing to hope in but His mercy. The lower we bow, the nearer God will come and make our hearts bold to trust Him. Let every exercise of waiting, let our whole habit of waiting on God be pervaded by abounding hope—a hope as bright and boundless as God's mercy. The fatherly kindness of God is such that in whatever state we come to Him, we may confidently hope in His mercy.

> *That eye sees the danger, sees in tender love His trembling, waiting child, sees the moment when the heart is ripe for the blessing, and sees the way in which it is to come.*

Such are God's waiting ones. And now, think of the God on whom we wait. "The eye of the LORD is on those who fear Him, on those who hope in His mercy, to deliver their soul from death, and to keep them alive in famine." Not to prevent the danger of death and famine—this is often needed to stir the waiting on Him—but to deliver and to keep alive. For the dangers are often very real and dark. The situation, whether in the temporal or spiritual life, may appear to be utterly hopeless. There is always one hope: *God's eye is on them.*

That eye sees the danger, sees in tender love His trembling, waiting child, sees the moment when the heart is ripe for the blessing, and sees the way in which it is to come. This living, mighty God—oh, let us fear Him and hope in His mercy. And let us humbly but boldly say, "Our soul waits for the LORD; He is our help and our shield. Let Your mercy, O LORD, be upon us, just as we [wait for] You" (Ps. 33:20, 22).

Oh, the blessedness of waiting on such a God! A very present help in every time of trouble; a shield and defense against every danger. Children of God! Will you not learn to sink down in entire helplessness and powerlessness and in stillness to wait and see the salvation of God?

In the utmost spiritual famine, and when death appears to prevail, oh, wait on God. He does deliver, He does keep alive. Say it not only in solitude, but say it to each other—the psalm speaks not of one but of God's people—"*Our* soul waits for the LORD; He is *our* help and *our* shield." Strengthen and encourage each other in the holy exercise of waiting so that each may not only say of it himself, but of his brethren, "*We* have waited for Him. . .*we* will be glad and rejoice in His salvation" (Isa. 25:9).

"MY SOUL, WAIT SILENTLY FOR GOD ALONE!"

FOR FURTHER THOUGHT

1. *What does today's lesson tell you is the true blessedness of waiting on God?*
2. *"The eye of the LORD is on those who fear Him, on those who hope in His mercy, to deliver their soul from death, and to keep them alive in famine." From what specifically does God promise to deliver you?*
3. *What approach and attitude should you take to God in order to see His salvation?*

DAY 11

PATIENTLY

Rest in the LORD, and wait patiently for Him;
those who wait on the LORD, they shall inherit the earth.
PSALM 37:7, 9

"BY your patience possess your souls" (Luke 21:19). "[You] have need of patience" (Heb. 10:36 KJV). "Let patience have its perfect work, that you may be perfect and complete" (James 1:4). Such words of the Holy Spirit show us what an important element in the Christian life and character patience is. And nowhere is there a better place for cultivating or displaying it than in waiting on God. There we discover how impatient we are and what our impatience means.

We confess at times that we are impatient with men and circumstances that hinder us, or with ourselves and our slow progress in the Christian life. If we truly set ourselves to wait on God, we shall find that it is with Him we are impatient, because He does not immediately, or as soon as we would wish, do our bidding. It is in waiting on God that our eyes are opened to believe in His wise and sovereign will, and to see that the sooner and the more completely we yield absolutely to it, the more surely His blessing can come to us.

"So then it is not of him who wills, nor of him who runs, but of God who shows mercy" (Rom. 9:16). We have as little power to increase or strengthen our spiritual life as we had to originate it. We "were born, not of blood, nor of the will of the flesh, nor of the will of man, but of God" (John 1:13). Even so, our willing and running, our desire and effort, accomplish nothing, for all is "of God who shows mercy."

All the exercises of the spiritual life—our reading and praying, our willing and doing—have their very great value. But they can go no further than this: that they point the way and prepare us in humility to look to and to depend alone on God Himself, and in patience to wait His good time and mercy. The waiting is to teach us our absolute dependence on God's mighty working and to make us in perfect patience place ourselves at His disposal. Those who wait on the Lord, they shall inherit the earth; the promised land and its blessing. The heirs must wait; they can afford to wait.

"Rest in the LORD, and wait patiently for Him." The margin gives for "Rest in the Lord," "Be silent to the Lord," or in the Revised Version, "Be still before the Lord." It is resting in the Lord—in His will, His promise, His faithfulness, and His love—that makes patience easy. And the resting in Him is nothing but being silent to Him, still before Him. Having our thoughts and wishes, our fears and hopes, hushed into calm and quiet in that great peace of God that passes all understanding. That peace guards the heart and mind when we are anxious for anything, because we have made our request known to Him. The rest, the silence, the stillness, and the patient waiting—all find their strength and joy in God Himself.

> *The waiting is to teach us our absolute dependence on God's mighty working and to make us in perfect patience place ourselves at His disposal.*

The needs for patience, and the reasonableness and the blessedness of patience will be opened up to the waiting soul. Our patience will be seen to be the counterpart of God's patience. He longs far more to bless us fully than we can desire it. But, as the vinedresser has long patience until the fruit is ripe, so God bows Himself to our slowness and bears long with us. Let us remember this and wait patiently: of each promise and every answer to prayer the word is true: "I, the LORD, will hasten it in its time" (Isa. 60:22).

"Rest in the LORD, and wait patiently for Him." Yes, *for Him*. Do not seek only the help, the gift; you need seek *Himself*. Wait for *Him*. Give God His glory by resting in Him, by trusting Him fully, by waiting patiently for Him. This patience honors Him greatly. It leaves Him, as God on the throne, to do His work. It yields self fully into His hands. It lets God *be God*. If your desire is for some special request, wait patiently. If your waiting is more the exercise of the spiritual life seeking to know and have more of God, wait patiently. Whether it is in the shorter specific periods of waiting, or as the continuous habit of the soul, rest in the Lord, be still before the Lord, and wait patiently. "Those who wait on the LORD, they shall inherit the earth."

"MY SOUL, WAIT SILENTLY FOR GOD ALONE!"

FOR FURTHER THOUGHT

1. *Why is patience such an important element in the Christian life? How is your own impatience revealed when you wait on God?*
2. *What spiritual benefit do you receive when you wait patiently on God? What does this waiting teach you about how He answers pray and how He blesses those who are patient?*
3. *For what should you seek as you patiently wait on God and God alone?*

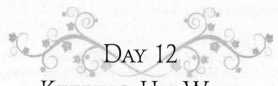

Day 12
Keeping His Ways

Wait on the LORD, and keep His way,
and He shall exalt you to inherit the land.
Psalm 37:34

IF we desire to find a man whom we long to meet, we inquire where the places and the ways are where he is to be found. When waiting on God, we need to be very careful that we keep His ways, for outside of these we never can expect to find Him. "You meet him who rejoices and does righteousness, who remembers You *in Your ways*" (Isa. 64:5). We may be sure that God is never and nowhere to be found but in His ways. And that there by the soul who seeks and patiently waits He is always most surely to be found. "Wait on the LORD, and keep His ways, and He shall exalt you."

How close the connection between the two parts of the injunction, "Wait on the LORD"—that has to do with worship and disposition; "and keep His ways"—that deals with walk and work. The outer life must be in harmony with the inner, and the inner must be the inspiration and the strength for the outer. It is our God who has made known His ways in His Word for our conduct, and who invites our confidence for His grace and help in our heart. If we do not keep His ways, our waiting on Him can bring no blessing. The surrender to full obedience to all His will is the secret of full access to all the blessings of His fellowship.

Notice how strongly this comes out in the psalm. It speaks of the evildoer who prospers in his way, and calls on the believer not to worry himself. When we see men around us prosperous and happy while they forsake God's ways, and ourselves left in difficulty or suffering, we are in danger of first worrying at what appears so strange, and then gradually yielding to seek our prosperity in their path. The psalm says, "Do not fret. . . Trust in the LORD, and do good. . . . Rest in the LORD, and wait patiently for Him. . .Cease from anger, and forsake wrath. . . . Depart from evil, and do good. . . . For the LORD does not forsake His saints. . . . The righteous shall inherit the land. . . . The law of his God *is* in his heart; none of his steps shall slide." And then follows—the word occurs for the third time in the psalm—"*Wait* on the LORD, *and keep His way*" (Ps. 37:34). Do what God asks you to do, and God will do more than you can ask Him to do.

And let no one give way to the fear: I cannot keep His way. It is this that robs one of every confidence. It is true you do not have the strength yet to keep all His ways. But keep carefully those for which you have received strength already. Surrender yourself willingly and trustingly to keep all God's ways, in the strength that will come in waiting on Him. Give up your whole being to God without reserve and without doubt. Then He will prove Himself God to you and work in you that which is pleasing in His sight through Jesus Christ. Keep His ways, as you know them in the Word. Keep His ways, as nature teaches them, in always doing what appears right. Keep His ways, as Providence points them out. Keep His ways, as the Holy Spirit suggests. Do not think of waiting on God while you say you are not willing to work in His path. However weak you feel, only be willing, and He who has worked to will, will work to *do* by His power.

> *It is true you do not have the strength yet to keep all His ways. But keep carefully those for which you have received strength already.*

"Wait on the LORD, and keep His way." It may be that the consciousness of shortcoming and sin makes our text look more like a hindrance than a help in waiting on God. Let it not be so. Have we not said more than once that the very starting point and groundwork of this waiting is utter and absolute powerlessness? Why then not come with everything evil you feel in yourself, every memory of unwillingness, unwatchfulness, unfaithfulness, and all that causes such unceasing self-condemnation? Put your power in God's omnipotence and find in waiting on God your deliverance.

Your failure has been due to only one thing: you sought to conquer and obey in your own strength. Come and bow before God until you learn that He is the God who alone is good, and alone can work any good thing. Believe that in you, and all that nature can do, there is no true power. Be content to receive from God each moment the inworking of His mighty grace and life, and then waiting on God will become the renewal of your strength to run in His ways and not be weary, to walk in His paths and never faint. "Wait on the LORD, and keep His way" will be command and promise in one.

"MY SOUL, WAIT SILENTLY FOR GOD ALONE!"

FOR FURTHER THOUGHT

1. *According to Isaiah 64:5, what does God do for you when you rejoice and do righteousness and remember God and His ways?*
2. *The Bible teaches that no one has the strength in his or her own power to keep all God's ways. What should you do in order to receive that strength from God?*
3. *What should you do with the evil within yourself, every memory of unwillingness, unwatchfulness, unfaithfulness, and all that causes you to condemn yourself?*

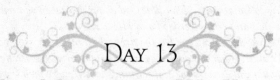

DAY 13

FOR MORE THAN WE KNOW

"And now, Lord, what do I wait for?
My hope is in You. Deliver me from all my transgressions."
PSALM 39:7–8

THERE may be times when we feel as if we didn't know what we are waiting for. There may be other times we think we know, and when it would just be so
good for us to realize that we do not know what to ask as we should. God is able
to do for us exceeding abundantly above what we ask or think, and we are in danger of limiting Him when we confine our desires and prayers to our own thoughts
of them. It is a great thing at times to say, as our psalm says: "And now, Lord, what
do I wait for?" I scarcely know or can tell. All I can is—"My hope is in You."

How we see this limiting of God in the case of Israel! When Moses promised
them food in the wilderness, they doubted, saying, "Can God prepare a table in
the wilderness? Behold, He struck the rock, so that the waters gushed out, and the
streams overflowed. Can He give bread also? Can He provide meat for His people?" (Ps. 78:19–20). If they had been asked whether God could provide streams
in the desert, they would have answered, Yes. God had done it, and He could do
it again. But when the thought came of God doing something new, they limited
Him. Their expectation could not rise beyond their past experience, or their own
thoughts of what was possible.

Even so we may be limiting God by our conceptions of what He has promised
or is able to do. Do let us beware of limiting the Holy One of Israel in our very
prayer. Let us believe that the very promises of God we plead have a divine meaning infinitely beyond our thoughts of them. Let us believe that His fulfillment of
them can be, in a power and an abundance of grace, beyond our largest grasp of
thought. And let us therefore cultivate the habit of waiting on God, not only for
what we think we need, but for all His grace and power are ready to do for us.

In every true prayer there are two hearts in exercise. The one is your heart,
with its little, dark, human thoughts of what you need and God can do. The
other is God's great heart, with its infinite, its divine purposes of blessing. What
think you? To which of these two ought the larger place to be given in your approach to Him? Undoubtedly, to the heart of God, for everything depends on
knowing and being occupied with that. But how little this is done. This is what

waiting on God is meant to teach you. Just think of God's wonderful love and redemption in the meaning these words must have to Him. Confess how little you understand what God is willing to do for you, and say each time as you pray: "And now, what do I wait for?" My heart cannot say, God's heart knows and waits to give. "My hope is in You." Wait on God to do for you more than you can ask or think.

*D*o let us beware of limiting the Holy One of Israel in our very prayer. Let us believe that the very promises of God we plead have a divine meaning infinitely beyond our thoughts of them.

Apply this to the prayer that follows: "Deliver me from all my transgressions." You have prayed to be delivered from temper, pride, or self-will. It is as if it is in vain. May it not be that you have had your own thoughts about the way or the extent of God's doing it, and have never waited on the God of glory, according to the riches of His glory, to do for you what has not entered the heart of man to conceive? Learn to worship God as the God who does wonders, who wishes to prove in you that He can do something supernatural and divine. Bow before Him and wait on Him until your soul realizes that you are in the hands of a divine and almighty worker. Consent just to know what and how He will work. Expect it to be something altogether godlike, something to be waited for in deep humility and received only by His divine power. Let the "And now, LORD, what do I wait for? My hope is in You" become the spirit of every longing and every prayer. He will in His time do His work.

Dear soul, in waiting on God you may often be ready to be weary because you hardly know what you have to expect. I encourage you, be of good courage—this ignorance is often one of the best signs. He is teaching you to leave all in His hands and to wait on Him alone. "Wait on the LORD! Be of good courage, and He shall strengthen your heart; wait, I say, on the LORD."

"MY SOUL, WAIT SILENTLY FOR GOD ALONE!"

FOR FURTHER THOUGHT

1. *What do believers do that puts them in danger of keeping God from doing for them exceeding abundantly above what they ask or think? How can you avoid limiting God that way?*

2. *In prayer, there are two hearts in action. What are they, and to which of them should you give a larger place in your approach to Him?*

3. *What must you do in order to learn to trust God to do for you what has not entered your heart to conceive or understand?*

Day 14

The Way to the New Song

I waited patiently for the LORD;
and He inclined to me, and heard my cry. . . .
He has put a new song in my mouth—praise to our God.
PSALM 40:1, 3

COME and listen to the testimony of one who can speak from experience of the sure and blessed outcome of patient waiting on God. True patience is so foreign to our self-confident nature. But it is so indispensable in our waiting on God, it is such an essential element of true faith that we may well once again meditate on what the word has to teach us.

The word *patience* is derived from the Latin word for suffering. It suggests the thought of being under the constraint of some power from which we would desire to be free. At first we submit against our will, but experience teaches us that when it is vain to resist, patient endurance is our wisest course. In waiting on God, it is of infinite consequence that we not only submit because we are compelled to, but because we lovingly and joyfully consent to be in the hands of our blessed Father. Patience then becomes our highest blessedness and our highest grace. It honors God and gives Him time to have His way with us. It is the highest expression of our faith in His goodness and faithfulness. It brings the soul perfect rest in the assurance that God is carrying on His work. It is the evidence of our full consent that God should deal with us in such a way and time as He thinks best. True patience is the losing of our self-will in His perfect will.

Such patience is needed for the true and full waiting on God. Such patience is the growth and fruit of our first lessons in the school of waiting. To many individuals it will appear strange how difficult it is truly to wait on God. The great stillness of soul before God that sinks into its own helplessness and waits for Him to reveal Himself, the deep humility that is afraid to let own will or own strength work anything except as God works to will and to do, the meekness that is content to be and to know nothing except as God gives His light, the entire resignation of the will that only wants to be a vessel in which His holy will can move and mold: all these elements of perfect patience are not found immediately. But they will come in measure as the soul maintains its position and always again says: "Truly my soul silently waits for God; from HIM comes my salvation. He only is my rock and my salvation" (Ps. 62:1–2).

Have you ever noticed what proof we have that patience is a grace for which very special grace is given, in these words of Paul: "Strengthened with all might, according to His glorious power, for all"—what? "patience and longsuffering with joy" (Col. 1:11). Yes, we need to be strengthened with all God's might, and that according to the measure of His glorious power, if we are to wait on God in all patience. It is God revealing Himself in us as our life and strength that will enable us with perfect patience to leave all in His hands. If any are inclined to become disheartened because they do not have such patience, let them be of good courage, for it is in the course of our weak and very imperfect waiting that God Himself by His hidden power strengthens us and works out in us the patience of the saints, the patience of Christ Himself.

> *Yes, we need to be strengthened with all God's might, and that according to the measure of His glorious power, if we are to wait on God in all patience.*

Listen to the voice of one who was deeply tried: "I waited patiently for the LORD; and He inclined to me, and heard my cry." Hear what he passed through: "He also brought me up out of a horrible pit, out of the miry clay, and set my feet upon a rock, *and* established my steps. He has put a new song in my mouth—praise to our God" (Ps. 40:2–3). Patient waiting on God brings a rich reward: the deliverance is sure, and God Himself will put a new song into your mouth. O soul! Do not be impatient, whether it is in the exercise of prayer and worship that you find it difficult to wait, or in the delay in respect of definite requests, or in the fulfilling of your heart's desire for the revelation of God Himself in a deeper spiritual life—do not fear, but rest in the Lord and wait patiently for Him.

And if you sometimes feel as if patience is not your gift, then remember it is God's gift, and take that prayer (2 Thess. 3:5): "The Lord direct your hearts...into the patience of Christ." Into the patience with which you are to wait on God, He Himself will guide you.

"My soul, wait silently for God alone!"

For Further Thought

1. *What, according to today's lesson, does the word patience literally mean? How does that relate to your waiting patiently on God?*
2. *Read Colossians 1:11. What is the proof that patience is a grace for which God gives very special grace?*
3. *What should you do when you feel that patience is not your strength or one of your special gifts? How can you acquire that patience?*

DAY 15

FOR HIS COUNSEL

They soon forgot His works;
they did not wait for His counsel.
PSALM 106:13

THIS is said of the sin of God's people in the wilderness. He had wonderfully redeemed them and was prepared as wonderfully to supply their every need. But when the time of need came, "they did not wait for His counsel." They did not think that the almighty God was their leader and provider, so they did not ask what His plans might be. They simply thought the thoughts of their own heart and tempted and provoked God by their unbelief. "They did not wait for His counsel."

How this has been the sin of God's people in all ages! In the land of Canaan, in the days of Joshua, the only three failures of which we read were due to this one sin. In going up against Ai, in making a covenant with the Gibeonites, in settling down without going up to possess the whole land, they did not wait for His counsel. And likewise, even the advanced believer is in danger from this most subtle of temptations—taking God's Word and thinking his own thoughts of them and not waiting for His counsel. Let us take the warning and see what Israel teaches us. And let us very specially regard it not only as a danger to which the individual is exposed, but as one against which God's people, in their collective capacity, need to be on their guard.

Our whole relationship to God is ruled in this: that His will is to be done in us and by us as it is in heaven. He has promised to make known His will to us by His Spirit, the guide into all truth. And our position is to be that of waiting for His counsel as the only guide of our thoughts and actions. In our church worship, in our prayer meetings, in our conventions, in all our gatherings as managers, directors, committees, or helpers in any part of the work for God, our first object ought always to be to ascertain the mind of God. God always works according to the counsel of His will, and the more that counsel of His will is sought and found and honored, the more surely and mightily will God do His work for us and through us.

The great danger in all such assemblies is that in our consciousness of having our Bible, and our past experience of God's leading, and our sound creed, and our

1180

honest wish to do God's will, we trust in these and do not realize that with every step we need and may have a heavenly guidance. There may be elements of God's will, applications of God's Word, experiences of the close presence and leading of God, manifestations of the power of His Spirit, of which we know nothing as yet. God may be willing, no, God *is* willing to open up these to the souls who are intently set on allowing Him to have His way entirely, and who are willing in patience to wait for His making it known.

> *Our whole relationship to God is ruled in this: that His will is to be done in us and by us as it is in heaven.*

When we come together praising God for all He has done and taught and given, we may at the same time be limiting Him by not expecting greater things. It was when God had given the water out of the rock that they did not trust Him for bread. It was when God had given Jericho into his hands that Joshua thought the victory over Ai was sure, and did not wait for counsel from God. And so, while we think that we know and trust the power of God for what we may expect, we may be hindering Him by not giving time, and not definitely cultivating the habit of waiting for His counsel.

A minister has no more solemn duty than teaching people to wait on God. Why was it that in the house of Cornelius, when "Peter was still speaking these words, the Holy Spirit fell upon all those who heard the word" (Acts 10:44)? They had said, "We are all present *before God*, to hear all the things commanded you *by God*" (10:33). We may come together to give and to listen to the most earnest exposition of God's truth with little spiritual profit if there is not the waiting for God's counsel.

And so in all our gatherings we need to believe in the Holy Spirit as the guide and teacher of God's saints when they wait to be led by Him into the things which God has prepared, and which the heart cannot conceive.

More stillness of soul to realize God's presence, more consciousness of ignorance of what God's great plans may be, more faith in the certainty that God has greater things to show us so that He Himself will be revealed in new glory: these must be the marks of the assemblies of God's saints if they want to avoid the reproach, "They did not wait for His counsel."

"MY SOUL, WAIT SILENTLY FOR GOD ALONE!"

For Further Thought

1. *What was the sin of God's people, the Israelites, in the wilderness—even though He had miraculously delivered them and met their every need? Have you found that you are guilty of that same sin in your own Christian life?*
2. *How can you best keep from forgetting the wonderful works God has done in you? How will remembering those things affect your own spiritual life?*
3. *What should be the characteristics and attitudes of individual believers and of congregations who are waiting on God and listening to Him?*

DAY 16

AND HIS LIGHT

IN THE HEART

I wait for the LORD, my soul waits,
and in His word I do hope. My soul waits for the Lord
more than those who watch for the morning—yes,
more than those who watch for the morning.
PSALM 130:5–6

WITH what intense longing the morning light is often waited for. By the mariners in a shipwrecked vessel, by a traveler overtaken by darkness in a dangerous country, by an army that finds itself surrounded by an enemy. The morning light will show what hope of escape there may be. The morning may bring life and liberty. And likewise the saints of God in darkness have longed for the light of His countenance, more than watchmen for the morning. They have said, "My soul waits for the Lord more than those who watch for the morning." Can we say that, too? Our waiting on God can have no higher object than simply having His light shine on us, in us, and through us all the day.

God is light. God is a sun. Paul says: "[God] has shone in our hearts to give the light." What light? "The light of. . .the glory of God in the face of Jesus Christ" (2 Cor. 4:6). Just as the sun shines its beautiful, life-giving light on and into our earth, so God shines into our hearts the light of His glory, of His love in Christ His Son. Our heart is meant to have that light filling and gladdening it all the day. It can have it because God is our sun, and it is written, "Your sun shall no longer go down" (Isa. 60:20). God's love shines on us without ceasing.

But can we indeed enjoy it all the day? We can. And how can we? Let nature give us the answer. Those beautiful trees and flowers with all this green grass—what do they do to keep the sun shining on them? They do nothing. They simply bask in the sunshine when it comes. The sun is millions of miles away, but over all that distance it comes, its own light and joy, and the tiniest flower that lifts its little head upwards is met by the same exuberance of light and blessing as flood the widest landscape. We need not care for the light we need for our day's work, because the sun cares and provides and shines the light around us all the day. We simply count on it, receive it, and enjoy it.

The only difference between nature and grace is this: that what the trees and the flowers do unconsciously as they drink in the blessing of the light is to be with us a voluntary and a loving acceptance. Faith, simple faith in God's Word and love, is to be the opening of the eyes, the opening of the heart to receive and enjoy the unspeakable glory of His grace. And just as the trees, day by day and month by month, stand and grow into beauty and fruitfulness, just welcoming whatever sunshine the sun may give, so it is the very highest exercise of our Christian life just to abide in the light of God and let it, and let Him, fill us with the life and the brightness it brings.

And if you ask, "But can it really be that just as naturally and heartily as I recognize and rejoice in the beauty of a bright sunny morning, I can rejoice in God's light all the day?" It can, indeed. From my breakfast table I look out on a beautiful valley, with trees and vineyards and mountains. In our spring and autumn months the light in the morning is exquisite, and almost involuntarily we say, "How beautiful!" And the question comes, "Is it only the light of the sun that is to bring such continual beauty and joy? And is there no provision for the light of God being just as much an unceasing source of joy and gladness?" There is, indeed, if the soul will just be still and wait on Him, ONLY LET GOD SHINE.

> *Faith, simple faith in God's word and love, is to be the opening of the eyes, the opening of the heart to receive and enjoy the unspeakable glory of His grace.*

Dear soul! Learn to wait on the Lord more than watchers for the morning. All within you may be very dark, but is that not the very best reason for waiting for the light of God? The first beginnings of light may be just enough to reveal the darkness and painfully to humble you on account of sin. Can you not trust the light to expel the darkness? Do believe it will. Just bow, even now, in stillness before God, and wait on Him to shine into you. Say, in humble faith, God is light, infinitely brighter and more beautiful than that of the sun. God is light: the Father. The eternal, inaccessible, and incomprehensible light: the Son. The light concentrated, embodied, and manifested: the Spirit, the light entering and dwelling and shining in our hearts. God is light and is here shining on my heart. I have been so occupied with the candles of my thoughts and efforts that I have never opened the shutters to let His light in. Unbelief has kept it out.

I bow in faith; God, light, is shining into my heart. The God of whom Paul wrote, "God has shone into our hearts," is my God. What would I think of a sun that could not shine? What shall I think of a God that does not shine? No, God shines! God is light! I will take time and just be still and rest in the light of God.

My eyes are weak, and the windows are not clean, but I will wait on the Lord. The light does shine, and the light will shine in me and make me full of light. And I shall learn to walk all the day in the light and joy of God. My soul waits for the Lord more than those who watch for the morning.

"MY SOUL, WAIT SILENTLY FOR GOD ALONE!"

FOR FURTHER THOUGHT

1. *What is the light, according to 2 Corinthians 4:6, that God shines into your heart?*
2. *What is the benefit of the light God shines on and into you, and how can you know He is shining into your heart?*
3. *How can you know you can trust the light of God to expel the darkness that was within you? What must you do for that to happen?*

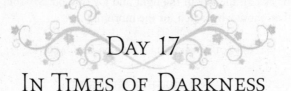

Day 17

In Times of Darkness

And I will wait on the LORD,
who hides His face from the house of Jacob;
and I will hope in Him.
ISAIAH 8:17

HERE we have a servant of God waiting on Him, not on behalf of himself, but of his people, from whom God was hiding His face. It suggests to us how our waiting on God, though it commences with our personal needs, with the desire for the revelation of Himself or for the answer to personal petitions, need not, may not stop there. We may be walking in the full light of God's countenance, and God yet be hiding His face from His people around us. Far from being content to think that this is nothing but the just punishment of their sin or the consequence of their indifference, we are called with tender hearts to think of their sad state and to wait on God on their behalf.

The privilege of waiting on God is one that brings great responsibility. Even as Christ, when He entered God's presence, at once used His place of privilege and honor as intercessor, so we, no less, if we know what it is really to enter in and wait on God, must use our access for our less-favored brethren. "I will wait on the LORD, who hides His face from the house of Jacob."

You worship with a certain congregation. Possibly there is not the spiritual life or joy either in the preaching or in the fellowship that you could desire. You belong to a church, with its many congregations. There is so much of error or worldliness, of seeking after human wisdom and culture or trust in ordinances and observances that you do not wonder that God hides His face, in many cases, and that there is but little power for conversion or true edification.

Then there are branches of Christian work with which you are connected—a Sunday school, a gospel hall, a young men's association, a mission work abroad—in which the weakness of the Spirit's working appears to indicate that God is hiding His face. You think, too, you know the reason, There is too much trust in men and money, too much formality and self-indulgence, too little faith and prayer, too little love and humility, and too little of the spirit of the crucified Jesus. At times you feel as if things were hopeless, that nothing will help.

Do believe that God can help and will help. Let the spirit of the prophet come into you, as you value his words and set yourself to wait on God on behalf of His erring children. Instead of the tone of judgment or condemnation, of despondency or despair, realize your calling to wait on God. If others fail in doing it, give yourself doubly to it. The deeper the darkness, the greater the need of appealing to the one and only deliverer. The greater the self-confidence around you that knows not that it is poor and wretched and blind, the more urgent the call on you, who professes to see the evil and to have access to Him who alone can help, to be at your post waiting on God. Say on each new occasion when you are tempted to speak or to sigh: "I will wait on the LORD, who hides His face from the house of Jacob."

There is a still larger circle—the Christian church throughout the world. Think of Greek, Roman Catholic, and Protestant churches, and the state of the millions that belong to them. Or think only of the Protestant churches with their open Bible and orthodox creeds. How much nominal profession and formality, how much of the rule of the flesh and of man in the very temple of God! And what abundant proof that God does hide His face!

> *Let the spirit of the prophet come into you, as you value his words and set yourself to wait on God on behalf of His erring children.*

What are those who see and mourn this to do? The first thing to be done is this: "I will wait on the LORD, who hides His face from the house of Jacob." Let us wait on God in the humble confession of the sins of His people. Let us take time and wait on Him in this exercise. Let us wait on God in tender, loving intercession for all saints, our beloved brethren, however wrong their lives or their teaching may appear. Let us wait on God in faith and expectation until He shows us that He will hear. Let us wait on God with the simple offering of ourselves to Himself, and the earnest prayer that He would send us to our brethren. Let us wait on God and give Him no rest until He makes Zion a joy in the earth.

Yes, let us rest in the Lord and wait patiently for Him who now hides His face from so many of His children. And let us say of the lifting up of the light of His countenance we long for all His people, "I wait for the LORD, my soul waits, and in His word I do hope. My soul waits for the Lord more than those who watch for the morning—yes, more than those who watch for the morning" (Ps. 130:5–6).

"MY SOUL, WAIT SILENTLY FOR GOD ALONE!"

For Further Thought

1.   How should you use the privilege of waiting on God? What does Jesus do now that sets an example of what you should do as you wait on Him?
2.   Why do you think God hides His face from His own children? What is He trying to teach or to correct when He hides His face?
3.   What should you do as you recognize and grieve over the nominal practice of the faith and the formality that is such a part of the Christian church as a whole today? What specific steps should you take as you see these things?

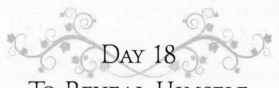

DAY 18
TO REVEAL HIMSELF

And it will be said in that day:
"Behold, this is our God; we have waited for Him,
and He will save us. This is the LORD; we have waited for Him;
we will be glad and rejoice in His salvation."
ISAIAH 25:9

IN this passage, we have two precious thoughts. The one, that it is the language of God's people who have been in unison waiting on Him. The other, that the fruit of their waiting has been that God has so revealed Himself that they could joyfully say, BEHOLD, THIS IS OUR GOD...THIS IS THE LORD. The power and the blessing of united waiting is what we need to learn.

Note that this phrase is repeated twice, "We have waited for him." In some time of trouble, the hearts of the people had been drawn together and they had, ceasing from all human hope or help, with one heart set themselves to wait for their God. Is this not just what we need in our churches and conventions and prayer meetings? Is not the need of the church and the world great enough to demand it? Are there not in the church of Christ evils to which no human wisdom is equal? Have we not ritualism and rationalism, formalism and worldliness, robbing the church of its power? Have we not culture and money and pleasure threatening its spiritual life? Are not the powers of the church utterly inadequate to cope with the powers of infidelity and iniquity and wretchedness in Christian countries and in heathendom? And is there not, in the promise of God and in the power of the Holy Spirit, a provision made that can meet the need and give the church the restful assurance that she is doing all her God expects of her? And would not united waiting on God for the supply of His Spirit most certainly seem the needed blessing? We cannot doubt it.

The object of a more definite waiting on God in our gatherings would be very much the same as in personal worship. It would mean a deeper conviction that God must and will do all. It would require a more humble and abiding entrance into our deep helplessness and the need of entire and unceasing dependence on Him. We need a more living consciousness that the essential thing is to give God His place of honor and of power. We must have a confident expectation that to those who wait on Him, God will, by His Spirit, give the secret of His acceptance and presence, and then, in due time, the revelation of His saving power. The great aim would be to bring everyone in a praying and worshiping company under a deep sense of God's presence, so that when they part there will be the consciousness of having met God Himself, of having left every request with Him, and of now waiting in stillness while He works out His salvation.

It is this experience that is indicated in our text. The fulfillment of the words may, at times, be in such striking interpositions of God's power that all can join in the cry, "BEHOLD, THIS IS OUR GOD. . .THIS IS THE LORD." They may equally become true in spiritual experience when God's people, in their waiting times, become so conscious of His presence that, in holy awe, souls feel, "BEHOLD, THIS IS OUR GOD. . .THIS IS THE LORD."

> *We must have a confident expectation that to those who wait on Him, God will, by His Spirit, give the secret of His acceptance and presence, and then, in due time, the revelation of His saving power.*

It is this, sadly, that is too much missed in our meetings for worship. The godly minister has no more difficult, no more solemn, no more blessed task than to lead his people out to meet God. And, before he preaches, he must bring each one into contact with Him. "We are all present before God"—these words of Cornelius show the way in which Peter's audience was prepared for the coming of the Holy Spirit (see Acts 10:33). Waiting *before* God, waiting *for* God, and waiting *on* God are the conditions of God showing His presence.

A company of believers gathered with the one purpose, helping each other by little intervals of silence, to wait on God alone, opening the heart for whatever God may have of new discoveries of evil, of His will, and of new openings in work or methods of work would soon have reason to say, "BEHOLD, THIS IS OUR GOD; we have waited for Him, and He will save us. THIS IS THE LORD; we have waited for Him; we will be glad and rejoice in His salvation."

"MY SOUL, WAIT SILENTLY FOR GOD ALONE!"

For Further Thought

1. What, according to Isaiah 25:9, will God do for His people when they simply wait on Him? What will be our response when God reveals Himself?
2. What can you confidently expect God to do for you when you set yourself to waiting on Him?
3. What is any minister's most important and solemn—yet most difficult—task? How can you, even if you are not a fulltime minister, accomplish this in the lives of those God has placed in your circle of influence?

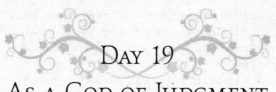

Day 19

As a God of Judgment

Yes, in the way of Your judgments, O LORD, we have waited
for You. . . . For when Your judgments are in the earth,
the inhabitants of the world will learn righteousness.
ISAIAH 26:8–9

For the LORD is a God of justice;
blessed are all those who wait for Him.
ISAIAH 30:18

GOD is a God of mercy and a God of judgment. Mercy and judgment are forever together in His dealings. In the flood, in the deliverance of Israel out of Egypt, in the overthrow of the Canaanites, we constantly see mercy in the midst of judgment. In these, the inner circle of His own people, we see it, too. The judgment punishes the sin, while mercy saves the sinner. Or, rather, mercy saves the sinner, not in spite of, but by means of, the very judgment that came upon his sin. In waiting on God, we must be careful not to forget—as we wait, we must expect Him as a God of judgment.

"In the way of Your judgments, O LORD, we have waited for You." That will prove true in our inner experience. If we are honest in our longing for holiness—in our prayers to be completely the Lord's—His holy presence will stir up and reveal hidden sin, and bring us very low in the bitter conviction of the evil of our nature, its opposition to God's law, and its inability to fulfill that law. The words will come true: "Who can endure the day of His coming? . . . For He is like a refiner's fire" (Mal. 3:2). "Oh, that You would. . .come down! . . . As fire burns" (Isa. 64:1–2). In great mercy, God executes within the soul His judgments on sin as He makes it feel its wickedness and guilt. Many try to flee from these judgments. The soul that longs for God and for deliverance from sin bows under them in humility and in hope. In silence of soul, it says, "Rise up, O LORD! Let Your enemies be scattered" (Num. 10:35). "In the way of Your judgments, we have waited for You" (Isa. 26:8).

Let no one who seeks to learn the blessed art of waiting on God wonder if at first the attempt to wait on Him only reveals more of sin and darkness. Let no one despair because unconquered sins, evil thoughts, or great darkness appear to hide God's face. Was not, in His own beloved Son, the gift and bearer of His mercy on Calvary, the mercy as hidden and lost in the judgment? Oh, submit and sink down deep under the judgment of your every sin. Judgment prepares the way and breaks out in wonderful mercy. It is written, "Zion shall be redeemed with judgment" (Isa. 1:27 KJV). Wait on God in the faith that His tender mercy is working out His redemption in the midst of judgment. Wait for Him; He will be gracious to you.

> *L*et no one who seeks to learn the blessed art of waiting on God wonder if at first the attempt to wait on Him only reveals more of sin and darkness.

There is another application still, one of unspeakable solemnity. We are expecting God, in the way of His judgments, to visit His earth, and we are waiting for Him. What a thought! We know of these coming judgments. We know that there are tens of thousands of professing Christians who live on in carelessness and who, if no change comes, must perish under God's hand. Oh, will we not do our utmost to warn them, to plead with and for them, if God may have mercy on them! If we feel our lack of boldness, zeal, and power, will we not begin to wait on God more definitely and persistently as a God of judgment? Will we not ask Him to so reveal Himself in the judgments that are coming on our very friends, that we may be inspired with a new fear of Him and them, and constrained to speak and pray as never yet before? Verily, waiting on God is not meant to be a spiritual self-indulgence. Its object is to let God and His holiness, Christ and the love that died on Calvary, the Spirit and fire that burns in heaven and came to earth, get possession of us to warn and arouse men with the message that we are waiting for God in the way of His judgments. Oh, Christian! Prove that you really believe in the God of judgment!

"My soul, wait silently for God alone!"

For Further Thought

1. *What is the connection of God's mercy and God's judgment in the life of the individual believer? How does He demonstrate those parts of His character?*

2. *The Bible teaches that God, in His great mercy, executes judgment on the sin of His people. Knowing that, how should you respond to God's promise to execute those judgments?*

3. *Do you recognize in your own Christian life a lack of boldness, zeal, and power? What should you do if you desire to have those things?*

DAY 20

WHO WAITS ON US

Therefore the LORD will wait, that He may be gracious to you;
and therefore He will be exalted, that He may have
mercy on you. For the LORD is a God of justice;
blessed are all those who wait for Him.
ISAIAH 30:18

WE must not only think of our waiting on God, but also of what is more wonderful still: of God's waiting on us. The vision of Him waiting on us will give new impulse and inspiration to our waiting on Him. It will give us an unspeakable confidence that our waiting cannot be in vain. If He waits for us, then we may be sure that we are more than welcome—that He rejoices to find those He has been seeking for. Let us seek even now at this moment, in the spirit of lowly waiting on God, to find out something of what it means. "Therefore the LORD will wait, that he may be gracious to you." We will accept and echo back the message, "Blessed *are all those* who wait for him."

Look up and see the great God on His throne. He is love—an unceasing and inexpressible desire to communicate His own goodness and blessedness to all His creatures. He longs and delights to bless. He has inconceivably glorious purposes concerning every one of His children, by the power of His Holy Spirit, to reveal in them His love and power. He waits with all the longings of a father's heart. He waits that He may be gracious to you. And each time you come to wait on Him or seek to maintain in daily life the holy habit of waiting, you may look up and see Him ready to meet you. He will be waiting so that He may be gracious unto you. Yes, connect every exercise, every breath of the life of waiting, with faith's vision of your God waiting for you.

And if you ask, "How is it, if He waits to be gracious, that even after I come and wait on Him, He does not give the help I seek but waits on longer and longer?" There is a double answer. The one is this. God is a wise vinedresser who "waits for the precious fruit of the earth, waiting patiently for it" (James 5:7). He cannot gather the fruit until it is ripe. He knows when we are spiritually ready to receive the blessing to our profit and His glory. Waiting in the sunshine of His love is what will ripen the soul for His blessing. Waiting under the cloud of trial, which breaks in showers of blessing, is as needed. Be assured that if God waits longer than you could wish, it is only to make the blessing doubly precious. God waited four thousand years, until the fullness of time, before He sent His Son. Our times are in His hands. He will avenge His elect speedily. He will make haste for our help and not delay one hour too long.

The other answer points to what has been said before. The giver is more than the gift—God is more than the blessing. And our being kept waiting on Him is the only way for our learning to find our life and joy in *Himself*. Oh, if God's children only knew what a glorious God they have, and what a privilege it is to be linked in fellowship with Him, then they would rejoice in Him! Even when He keeps them waiting, they will learn to understand better than ever. "Therefore the LORD will wait, that He may be gracious to you." His waiting will be the highest proof of His graciousness.

> *Look up and see the great God on His throne. He is love—an unceasing and inexpressible desire to communicate His own goodness and blessedness to all His creatures.*

"Blessed are all those who wait for Him." A queen has her ladies-in-waiting. The position is one of subordination and service, and yet it is considered one of the highest dignity and privilege because a wise and gracious sovereign makes them companions and friends. What a dignity and blessedness to be attendants-in-waiting on the everlasting God, always on the watch for every indication of His will or favor, always conscious of His nearness, His goodness, and His grace! "The LORD is good to those who wait for Him" (Lam. 3:25). "Blessed are all those who wait for Him." Yes, it is blessed when a waiting soul and a waiting God meet each other. God cannot do His work without His and our waiting His time. Let waiting be our work, as it is His. And if His waiting is nothing but goodness and graciousness, let ours be nothing but a rejoicing in that goodness and a confident expectancy of that grace. And let every thought of waiting become to us the simple expression of unmingled and unutterable blessedness, because it brings us to a God who waits so that He may make Himself known to us perfectly as the gracious One.

"MY SOUL, WAIT SILENTLY FOR GOD ALONE!"

For Further Thought

1. *For what purpose does God wait on those who are His own? What does knowing how and why He waits on you inspire and encourage you to wait on Him?*
2. *God waits and desires to be gracious to His people. Why, then, does He not always immediately give you the help you need, but instead waits longer and longer?*
3. *What is the nature of God's waiting on you? What should be yours in waiting on Him?*

Day 21

The Almighty One

*But those who wait on the Lord shall renew their strength;
they shall mount up with wings like eagles, they shall
run and not be weary, they shall walk and not faint.*
Isaiah 40:31

WAITING always partakes of the character of our thoughts of the one on whom we wait. Our waiting on God will depend greatly on our faith of what He is. In our text, we have the close of a passage in which God reveals Himself as the everlasting and almighty One. It is as that revelation enters into our soul that the waiting will become the spontaneous expression of what we know Him to be—a God altogether most worthy to be waited on.

Listen to the words "Why do you say, O Jacob. . .'My way is hidden from the Lord'?" (Isa. 40:27). Why do you speak as if God does not hear or help?

"Have you not known? Have you not heard? The everlasting God, the Lord, the Creator of the ends of the earth, *neither faints nor is weary*?" (40:28). So far from it, "He gives power to the weak, and to those who have no might He increases strength. Even the youths" (40:29–30)—"The glory of young men is their strength" (Prov. 20:29)—"even the youths shall faint and be weary, and the young men shall utterly fall": all that is considered strong with man shall come to nothing. "*But* those who wait on the Lord," on the everlasting One who does not faint nor is weary, they "shall renew their strength; they shall mount up with wings like eagles, they shall run and"—listen now, they will be strong with the strength of God and, even as He, "*shall not be weary*; and they shall walk, and," even as he, "shall not be weary; they shall walk and," even as He, "*not faint*."

Yes, "they shall mount up with wings like eagles." You know what eagles' wings mean. The eagle is the king of birds. It soars the highest into the heavens. Believers are to live a heavenly life in the very presence and love and joy of God. They are to live where God lives. They need God's strength to rise there. To those who wait on Him it shall be given.

You know how the eagles' wings are obtained. Only in one way—by the eagle birth. You are born of God. You *have* the eagles' wings. You may not have known it, and you may not have used them. But God can and will teach you how to use them.

You know how the eagles are taught the use of their wings. See yonder cliff rising a thousand feet out of the sea. See high up a ledge on the rock, where there is an eagle's nest with its treasure of two young eaglets. See the mother bird come and stir up her nest and with her beak push the timid birds over the precipice. See how they flutter and fall and sink toward the depth. See now how it "hovers over its young, spreading out its wings, taking them up, carrying them on its wings" (Deut. 32:11), and so, as they ride upon her wings, brings them to a place of safety. And so, she does this once and again, each time casting them out over the precipice, and then again taking and carrying them. "So the LORD alone led him" (32:12). Yes, the instinct of that eagle mother was God's gift, a single ray of that love in which the Almighty trains His people to mount as on eagles' wings.

> *Believers are to live a heavenly life in the very presence and love and joy of God. They are to live where God lives.*

He stirs up your nest. He disappoints your hopes. He brings down your confidence. He makes you fear and tremble, as all your strength fails and you feel utterly weary and helpless. And all the while He is spreading His strong wings for you to rest your weakness on, and offering His everlasting Creator strength to work in you. And all He asks is that you sink down in your weariness and *wait on Him*. Allow Him in His Jehovah strength to carry you as you ride upon the wings of His omnipotence.

Dear child of God, I encourage you, lift up your eyes, and behold your God! Listen to Him who says that He "neither faints, nor is weary," who promises that you, too, will neither faint nor be weary, who asks nothing but this one thing: that you should wait on Him. And let your answer be, With such a God, so mighty, so faithful, so tender,

"MY SOUL, WAIT SILENTLY FOR GOD ALONE!"

FOR FURTHER THOUGHT

1. *How is your waiting on God related to taking on His character and thoughts? How is waiting related to your faith in who and what God is?*
2. *How are the instinctual actions of an eagle mother very much like those of God toward you, His child?*
3. *Why would a God who loves you disappoint your hopes, bring down your confidence, and make you fear and tremble? What is He trying to accomplish in doing those things?*

DAY 22

ITS CERTAINTY OF BLESSING

"Then you will know that I am the LORD,
for they shall not be ashamed who wait for Me."
ISAIAH 49:23

Blessed are all those who wait for Him.
ISAIAH 30:18

WHAT promises! How God seeks to draw us to waiting on Him by the most positive assurance that it never can be in vain; "they shall not be ashamed who wait for Me." How strange that, though we should so often have experienced it, we are yet so slow to learn that this blessed waiting must and can be the very breath of our life, a continuous resting in God's presence and His love, an unceasing yielding of ourselves for Him to perfect His work in us. Let us once again listen and meditate until our heart says with new conviction, "*Blessed are all those who wait for Him.*"

In our sixth day's lesson, we found in the prayer of Psalm 25: "Let no one who waits on You be ashamed" (25:3). The very prayer shows how we fear that it might be true. Let us listen to God's answer until every fear is banished, and we send back to heaven the words God speaks, Yes, Lord, we believe what You say: "All those who wait for Me will not be ashamed." "Blessed are all those who wait for Him."

The context of each of these two passages points us to times when God's church was in great straits and to the human eye there were no possibilities of deliverance. But God interposes with His word of promise and pledges His almighty power for the deliverance of His people. And it is as the God who has Himself undertaken the work of their redemption that He invites them to wait on Him and assures them that disappointment is impossible.

We, too, are living in days when there is much in the state of the church, with its profession and its formalism, that is indescribably sad. Amid all we praise God for, there is, sadly, much to mourn over! Were it not for God's promises, we might well despair. But in His promises, the living God has given and bound Himself to us. He calls us to wait on Him. He assures us we will not be put to shame.

Oh, that our hearts might learn to wait before Him until He Himself reveals to us what His promises mean, and in the promises reveals Himself in His hidden glory! We will be irresistibly drawn to wait on Him alone. May God increase the company of those who say: "Our soul waits for the LORD; He *is* our help and our shield" (Ps. 33:20).

This waiting on God on behalf of His church and people will depend greatly on the place that waiting on Him has taken in our personal life. The mind may often have beautiful visions of what God has promised to do, and the lips may speak of them in stirring words, but these are not really the measure of our faith or power. No, it is what we really know of God in our personal experience, conquering the enemies within, reigning and ruling, revealing Himself in His holiness and power in our innermost being—it is this that will be the real measure of the spiritual blessing we expect from Him, and which we bring to our fellowmen.

> The living God has given and bound Himself to us. He calls us to wait on Him. He assures us we will not be put to shame.

It is as we know how blessed the waiting on God has become to our own souls that we will confidently hope in the blessing to come on the Church around us, and the keyword of all our expectations will be, He has said: "All those who wait on Me will not be ashamed." From what He has done in us, we will trust Him to do mighty things around us. "Blessed are all those who wait for Him." Yes, blessed even now in the waiting. The promised blessings for ourselves or for others may wait. The unutterable blessedness of knowing and having Him who has promised—the divine blesser, the living fountain of the coming blessings—is even now ours. Let this truth acquire full possession of your souls: that waiting on God is itself the highest privilege of man, the highest blessedness of His redeemed child.

Even as the sunshine enters with its light and warmth, with its beauty and blessing, into every little blade of grass that rises upward out of the cold earth, so the everlasting God meets, in the greatness and the tenderness of His love, each waiting child to shine in his heart "the light of the knowledge of the glory of God in the face of Jesus Christ" (2 Cor. 4:6). Read these words again until your heart learns to know what God waits to do to you. Who can measure the difference between the great sun and that little blade of grass? And yet the grass has all of the sun it can need or hold.

Believe that in waiting on God, His greatness and your littleness suit and meet each other most wonderfully. Just bow in emptiness and poverty and utter helplessness, in humility and meekness, and surrender to His will before His great glory, and be still. As you wait on Him, God draws near. He will reveal

Himself as the God who will mightily fulfill His every promise. And, let your heart continually take up the song: "Blessed are all those who wait for Him."

"MY SOUL, WAIT SILENTLY FOR GOD ALONE!"

FOR FURTHER THOUGHT

1. *Read Isaiah 49:23. What positive assurance does God give you as He commands you, and encourages you, to wait on Him?*
2. *Why would a believer fear to wait on God? What promises does He give to assure you that you need never fear to wait on Him?*
3. *Why is waiting on God your highest privilege and your highest blessedness, as His redeemed child?*

DAY 23

FOR UNLOOKED-FOR THINGS

*For since the beginning of the world men have not heard nor
perceived by the ear, nor has the eye seen any God besides You,
who acts for the one who waits for Him.*

ISAIAH 64:4

THE Revised Version has: "*Neither hath the eye seen a God besides Thee, which
worketh for him that waiteth for Him.*" In the Authorized Version, the thought is
that no eye has seen *the thing* that God has prepared. In the Revised Version, no
eye has seen a God, besides our God, who works for him who waits for Him. To
both, the two thoughts are common: that our place is to wait on God, and that
what the human heart cannot conceive—the difference is: in the Revised Version, it is *the God* who works, but in the Authorized Version, *the thing* He is to
work. In 1 Corinthians 2:9, the citation is in regard to the things that the Holy
Spirit is to reveal, as in the Authorized Version, and in this meditation we will
keep to that.

The previous verses in Isaiah, especially Isaiah 63:15, refer to the low state of
God's people. The prayer has been poured out, "Look down from heaven" (63:15).
"Why have you. . .hardened our heart from Your fear? Return for Your servants'
sake" (63:17). And 64:1–2, still more urgent, "Oh, that You would rend the heavens! That You would come down! . . .As fire burns. . .to make Your name known
to Your adversaries." Then follows the plea from the past, "When You did awesome things for which we did not look, You came down, the mountains shook
at Your presence" (64:3). "For"—this is now the faith that has been awakened by
the thought of things for which we did not look. He is still the same God—"nor
has the eye seen any God besides You, who acts for the one who waits for Him."
God alone knows what He can do for His waiting people. As Paul expounds and
applies it: "No one knows the things of God except the Spirit of God" (1 Cor.
2:11). "But God has revealed them unto us through His Spirit" (2:10).

The need of God's people, and the call for God's intervention, is as urgent in
our days as it was in the time of Isaiah. There is now, as there was then, as there
has been at all times, a few who seek after God with their whole hearts. But, if
we look at Christianity as a whole, at the state of the Church of Christ, there is
infinite cause for begging God to open the heavens and come down. Nothing but

a special interposition of almighty power will avail. I fear we do not have a proper conception of what the so-called Christian world is in the sight of God. Unless God comes down "as when the melting fire burns, to make known His name to His adversaries" (see Isa. 64:2 KJV), our labors are comparatively fruitless.

> *I* f we look at Christianity as a whole, at the state of the Church of Christ, there is infinite cause for begging God to open the heavens and come down

Look at the ministry—how much it is in the wisdom of man and of literary culture—how little in demonstration of the Spirit and of power. Think of the unity of the body—how little there is of the manifestation of the power of a heavenly love binding God's children into one. Think of holiness—the holiness of Christlike humility and crucifixion to the world—how little the world sees that they have men among them who live in Christ in heaven, in whom Christ and heaven live.

What is to be done? There is only one thing. We must wait on God. And what for? We must cry, with a cry that never rests, "Oh, that You would rend the heavens! That You would come down! That the mountains might shake at Your presence" (see Isa. 64:1). We must desire and believe, we must ask and expect, that God will do unlooked-for things. We must set our faith on a God of whom men do not know what He has prepared for them who wait for Him. The wonder-doing God, who can surpass all our expectations, must be the God of our confidence.

Yes, let God's people enlarge their hearts to wait on a God able to do exceeding abundantly above what we can ask or think (see Eph. 3:20). Let us band ourselves together as His elect who cry day and night to Him for things men have not seen. He is able to arise and to make His people a name and a praise in the earth. "The LORD will wait, that He may be gracious to you...blessed are all those who wait for Him" (Isa. 30:18).

"MY SOUL, WAIT SILENTLY FOR GOD ALONE!"

FOR FURTHER THOUGHT

1. *How can looking at the state of your own spiritual life, and the spiritual life of the Church as a whole, motivate you to wait on God? What specifically are you waiting on God to do in you and through you?*
2. *For what must you wait for God to do in order for His Spirit to work for you in mighty ways, ways you can't even fully understand or expect right now?*
3. *What are you waiting and asking for God to do in your personal spiritual life right now?*

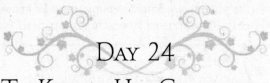

DAY 24

TO KNOW HIS GOODNESS

The LORD is good to those who wait for Him.
LAMENTATIONS 3:25

NO one is good but. . .God" (Matt. 19:17). His goodness is in the heavens. "Oh, how great is Your goodness, which You have laid up for those who fear You" (Ps. 31:19). "Oh, taste and see that the LORD is good" (Ps. 34:8). And here is now the true way of entering into and rejoicing in this goodness of God—waiting on Him. The Lord is good—even His children often do not know it, for they do not wait in quietness for Him to reveal it. But, to those who persevere in waiting, whose souls do wait, it will come true. One might think that it is just those who have to wait who might doubt it. But this is only when they do not wait but grow impatient. The truly waiting ones will all say, "The LORD is good to those who wait for Him." If you want to fully know the goodness of God, give yourself more than ever to a life of waiting on Him.

At our first entrance into the school of waiting on God, the heart is chiefly set on the blessings that we wait for. God graciously uses our needs and desires for help to educate us for something higher than we were thinking of. We were seeking gifts. He, the Giver, longs to give Himself and to satisfy the soul with His goodness. It is just for this reason that He often withholds the gifts and that the time of waiting is made so long. He is constantly seeking to win the heart of His child for Himself. He wishes that we would not only say, when He bestows the gift, "How good is God!" but that long before it comes, and even if it never comes, we should all the time be experiencing: *It is good* that a man should quietly wait— "The LORD is *good* to those who wait for Him."

What a blessed life the life of waiting then becomes—the continual worship of faith, adoring, and trusting His goodness. As the soul learns its secret, every act or exercise of waiting becomes just a quiet entering into the goodness of God to let it do its blessed work and satisfy our every need. And every experience of God's goodness gives the work of waiting new attractiveness, and instead of only taking refuge in time of need, there comes a great longing to wait continually and all the day. And however duties and engagements occupy the time and the mind, the soul gets more familiar with the secret art of always waiting. Waiting becomes the habit and disposition, the very second nature and breath of the soul.

Dear Christian! Do you not begin to see that waiting is not one among a number of Christian virtues, to be thought of from time to time, but that it expresses that disposition that lies at the very root of the Christian life. It gives a higher value and a new power to our prayers and worship, to our faith and surrender, because it links us, in unalterable dependence, to God Himself. And, it gives us the unbroken enjoyment of the goodness of God: "The LORD is good to those who wait for Him."

> *A*s the soul learns its secret, every act or exercise of waiting becomes just a quiet entering into the goodness of God to let it do its blessed work and satisfy our every need.

Let me press upon you once again to take time and trouble to cultivate this so-much-needed element of the Christian life. We get too much of religion at second hand from the teaching of men. That teaching has great value if, even as the preaching of John the Baptist sent his disciples away from himself to the living Christ, if it leads us to God Himself. What our faith needs is—*more of God.*

Many of us are too occupied with our work. As with Martha, the very service we want to render the Master separates us from Him. It is neither pleasing to Him nor profitable to ourselves. The more work, the more need of waiting on God. The doing of God's will would then be, instead of exhausting, our food and drink, our nourishment and refreshment and strength. "The LORD is good to those who wait for Him." How good none can tell but those who prove it by waiting on Him. How good none can fully tell but those who have proved Him to the utmost.

"MY SOUL, WAIT SILENTLY FOR GOD ALONE!"

FOR FURTHER THOUGHT

1. *What does the "goodness" of God mean to you? How does He demonstrate that goodness to you? What should you do in order to more fully know God's goodness?*
2. *How does God graciously use your needs and desires to give you something higher than the gifts you asked for and to educate you to something higher than you had asked Him to reveal?*
3. *What should you do in order to allow God to demonstrate His goodness in your own life and in the lives of those you pray for, care for, and love?*

Day 25

Quietly

It is good that one should hope and wait
quietly for the salvation of the LORD.
LAMENTATIONS 3:26

TAKE heed, and be quiet; do not fear or be fainthearted" (Isa. 7:4). "In quietness and confidence shall be your strength" (Isa. 30:15). Such words reveal to us the close connection between quietness and faith. They show us what a deep need there is of quietness as an element of true waiting on God. If we are to have our whole heart turned toward God, we must have it turned away from creature, from all that occupies and interests, whether of joy or sorrow.

God is a being of such infinite greatness and glory, and our nature has become so estranged from Him, that it requires our whole heart and desires set on Him, even in some little measure, to know and receive Him. Everything that is not God, that excites our fears or stirs our efforts or awakens our hopes or makes us glad hinders us in our perfect waiting on Him. The message is one of deep meaning: "Take heed, and be quiet"; "In quietness. . .shall be your strength"; "It is good that a man should. . .wait quietly."

How the very thought of God in His majesty and holiness should silence us, scripture abundantly testifies.

"The LORD is in His holy temple. Let all the earth keep silence before Him" (Hab. 2:20).

"Be silent in the presence of the Lord GOD" (Zeph. 1:7).

"Be silent, all flesh, before the LORD, for He is aroused from His holy habitation!" (Zech. 2:13).

As long as the waiting on God is chiefly regarded as an end toward more effectual prayer, and the obtaining of our petitions, this spirit of perfect quietness will not be obtained. But, when it is seen that waiting on God is itself an unspeakable blessedness—one of the highest forms of fellowship with the Holy One—the adoration of Him in His glory will of necessity humble the soul into a holy stillness, making way for God to speak and reveal Himself. Then it comes to the fulfillment of the precious promise, that all of self and self-effort will be humbled: "The haughtiness of men shall be bowed down, and the LORD alone shall be exalted in that day" (Isa. 2:11).

Let everyone who wants to learn the art of waiting on God remember the lesson, "Take heed, and be quiet." "It is good that one. . .wait quietly." Take time to be separate from all friends and all duties, all cares and all joys—time to be still and quiet before God. Take time not only to secure stillness from man and the world, but from self and its energy. Let the Word and prayer be very precious, but remember, even these may hinder the quiet waiting. The activity of the mind in studying the Word or giving expression to its thoughts in prayer, the activities of the heart, with its desires and hopes and fears, may so engage us that we do not come to the still waiting on the all-glorious One with our whole being prostrate in silence before Him. Though at first it may appear difficult to know how quietly to wait this way, with the activities of mind and heart for a time subdued, every effort after it will be rewarded. We will find that it grows on us, and the little season of silent worship will bring a peace and a rest that give a blessing not only in prayer, but all the day.

> *L*et everyone who wants to learn the art of waiting on God remember the lesson, "Take heed, and be quiet." "It is good that one. . .wait quietly."

"*It is good* that one should. . .quietly for the salvation of the LORD." Yes, it is good. The quietness is the confession of our helplessness. That with all our willing and running, with all our thinking and praying, it will not be done. We must receive it from God. It is the confession of our trust that our God will in His time come to our help—the quiet resting in Him alone. It is the confession of our desire to sink into our nothingness and to let Him work and reveal Himself. Let us wait quietly. In daily life, let there be, in the soul that is waiting for the great God to do His wondrous work, a quiet reverence, an abiding watching against too deep engrossment with the world. Then, the whole character will come to bear the beautiful stamp: quietly waiting for the salvation of God.

"MY SOUL, WAIT SILENTLY FOR GOD ALONE!"

FOR FURTHER THOUGHT

1. *What, according to today's lesson, is the connection between quietness before God and faith in God?*
2. *What hinders your having this spirit of quietness before God? What must you do in order to learn to be quiet before Him?*
3. *What does your quietness before God confess to Him? What can He do in and for you once you make that confession?*

Day 26

In Holy Expectancy

Therefore I will look to the LORD;
I will wait for the God of my salvation;
my God will hear me.
MICAH 7:7

HAVE you ever heard of a little book, *Expectation Corners*? If not, get it, for you will find in it one of the best sermons on our text. It tells of a king who prepared a city for some of his poor subjects. Not far from them were large store-houses, where everything they could need was supplied if they sent in their requests. But on one condition—that they should be on the lookout for the answer, so that when the king's messengers came with the answer to their petitions, they should always be found waiting and ready to receive them. The sad story is told of one desponding person who never expected to get what he asked for because he was too unworthy. One day he was taken to the king's storehouses, and there, to his amazement, he saw, with his address on them, all the packages that had been made up for him and sent. There was the garment of praise, the oil of joy, the eye salve, and so much more. They had been to his door but found it closed; he was not on the lookout. From that time on, he learned the lesson Micah would teach us today. "I will look to the LORD; I will wait for the God of my salvation; my God will hear me."

We have said more than once: Waiting for the answer to prayer is not the whole of waiting, but only a part. Today we want to take in the blessed truth that it is a part, and a very important one. When we have special petitions, in connection with which we are waiting on God, our waiting must be very definitely in the confident assurance, "My God will hear me."

A holy, joyful expectancy is of the very essence of true waiting. And this is not only true in reference to the many varied requests every believer has to make, but most especially to the one great petition that ought to be the chief thing every heart seeks for itself—that the LIFE OF GOD in the soul may have full sway, that Christ may be fully formed within, and that we may be filled to all the fullness of God. This is what God has promised. This is what God's people too little seek, very often because they do not believe it is possible. This is what we ought to seek and dare to expect, because God is able and waiting to work it in us.

But GOD HIMSELF must work it. And for this end our working must cease. We must see how entirely it is to be the faith of the operation of God, who raised Jesus from the dead—just as much as the resurrection, the perfecting of God's life in our souls is to be directly His work. And waiting has to become, more than ever, a tarrying before God in stillness of soul, counting on Him who raises the dead and calls the things that are not as though they were (see Rom. 4:17).

> *Everything that is salvation, everything that is good and holy, must be the direct, mighty work of God Himself within us.*

Just notice how the threefold use of the name of God in our text points us to Himself as the one from whom alone is our expectation. "I will look to THE LORD; I will wait for THE GOD OF MY SALVATION; MY GOD will hear me." Everything that is salvation, everything that is good and holy, must be the direct, mighty work of God Himself within us. In every moment of a life in the will of God, there must be the immediate operation of God. And, the one thing I have to do is this: to look to the Lord, to wait for the God of my salvation, to hold fast the confident assurance that "my God will hear me."

God says, "Be still, and know that I am God" (Ps. 46:10).

There is no stillness like that of the grave. In the grave of Jesus, in the fellowship of His death, in death to self with its own will and wisdom, its own strength and energy, there is rest. As we cease from self and our soul becomes still to God, God will arise and show Himself. "Be still, and know," then you will know "that I am God." There is no stillness like the stillness Jesus gives when He speaks, "Peace, be still!" (Mark 4:39). In Christ, in His death, and in *His life*, in His perfected redemption, the soul may be still, and God will come in, take possession, and do His perfect work.

"MY SOUL, WAIT SILENTLY FOR GOD ALONE!"

FOR FURTHER THOUGHT

1. *What about the character of God assures you that He will hear you when you pray, that He will grant your petitions when you pray in faith? How does—or should—that assurance affect your prayer life?*
2. *What does today's lesson tell you is the very essence of true waiting on God? What are the benefits of waiting on God this way?*
3. *Where should you go and what should you do in order to find rest in the Lord? What will happen to you and in you when you rest in that place?*

DAY 27

FOR REDEMPTION

Simeon. . .was just and devout, waiting for the Consolation
of Israel, and the Holy Spirit was upon him. . . .
Anna, a prophetess. . .spoke of Him to all those
who looked for redemption in Jerusalem.
LUKE 2:25, 36, 38

HERE we have the mark of a waiting believer. *Just*, righteous in all his conduct; *devout*, devoted to God, always walking as in His presence; *waiting for the Consolation of Israel*, looking for the fulfillment of God's promises: *and the Holy Spirit was upon him*. In the devout waiting, he had been prepared for the blessing. And Simeon was not the only one. Anna spoke to all who looked for redemption in Jerusalem. This was the one mark, amid surrounding formalism and worldliness, of a godly band of men and women in Jerusalem. They were waiting on God, looking for His promised redemption.

And now that the consolation of Israel has come and the redemption has been accomplished, do we still need to wait? We do indeed. But will not our waiting—we who now look back to it as come—differ greatly from those who looked forward to it as coming? It will, especially in two aspects. We now wait on God in the full power of the redemption, and we wait for its full revelation.

Our waiting is now in the full power of the redemption. Christ said, "At that day you will know that. . .you are *in Me*. Abide in Me" (John 14:20, 15:4). The epistles teach us to present ourselves to God as "dead indeed to sin, but alive to God in *Christ Jesus*" (Rom. 6:11), "blessed. . .with every spiritual blessing in heavenly places in *Christ*" (Eph. 1:3). Our waiting on God may now be in the wonderful consciousness begun and maintained by the Holy Spirit within us that we are accepted in the Beloved, that the love that rests on Him rests on us, that we are living in that love in the very nearness and presence and sight of God.

The old saints took their stand on the Word of God, and waiting, hoping on that Word, we rest on the Word, too—but, oh, under what exceedingly greater privileges, as one with Christ Jesus! In our waiting on God, let this be our confidence: in Christ we have access to the Father. How sure, therefore, we may be that our waiting cannot be in vain.

Our waiting differs, too, in this: while they waited for a redemption to come, we see it accomplished and now wait for its revelation in *us*. Christ not only said, "Abide in Me," but also "*I in you*" (John 15:4). The Epistles not only speak of us in Christ, but of Christ in us as the highest mystery of redeeming love. As we maintain our place in Christ day by day, God waits to reveal Christ in us in such a way that He is formed in us, that His mind and disposition and likeness acquire form and substance in us, so that by each it can in truth be said, "Christ lives in me" (Gal. 2:20).

> *In our waiting on God, let this be our confidence: in Christ we have access to the Father.*

My life in Christ up there in heaven and Christ's life in me down here on earth—these two are the complement of each other. And the more my waiting on God is marked by the living faith *I in Christ*, the more the heart thirsts for and claims the Christ in me. The waiting on God, which began with special needs and prayer, will increasingly be concentrated, as far as our personal life is concerned, on this one thing: Lord, reveal Your redemption fully in me; let Christ live in me.

Our waiting differs from that of the old saints in the place we take and the expectations we entertain. But at root it is the same: waiting on God, from whom alone is our expectation.

Learn one lesson from Simeon and Anna. How utterly impossible it was for them to do anything toward the great redemption—toward the birth of Christ or His death. *It was God's work. They could do nothing but wait.* Are we as absolutely helpless in regard to the revelation of Christ in us? We are indeed. God did not work out the great redemption in Christ as a whole and leave its application in detail to us.

The secret thought that it is so is the root of all our feebleness. The revelation of Christ in every individual believer, and in each one the daily revelation, step by step and moment by moment, is as much the work of God's omnipotence as the birth or resurrection of Christ. Until this truth enters and fills us, and we feel that we are just as dependent on God for each moment of our life in the enjoyment of redemption as they were in their waiting for it, our waiting on God will not bring its full blessing. The sense of utter and absolute helplessness and the confidence that God can and will do all are the marks of our waiting as it was of theirs. As gloriously as God proved Himself to them as the faithful and wonder-working God, He will to us too.

"MY SOUL, WAIT SILENTLY FOR GOD ALONE!"

FOR FURTHER THOUGHT

1. *In what two ways does your waiting for your redemption differ from how the saints before Christ waited for theirs?*
2. *How has God reveal to you that you are in Christ, that the love of the Son rests on you, that you are living in the very nearness and presence and sight of God? How does that revelation relate to waiting on God?*
3. *What truth must enter and fill you before your waiting on God can bring its full blessing? How is that truth revealed within you?*

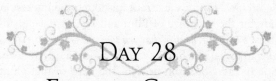

DAY 28

FOR THE COMING

OF HIS SON

"You yourselves be like men who
wait for their master."
LUKE 12:36

Until our Lord Jesus Christ's appearing, which He will manifest
in His own time, He who is the blessed and only Potentate,
the King of kings and Lord of lords.
1 TIMOTHY 6:14–15

Turned to God from idols to serve the living and true God,
and to wait for His Son from heaven.
1 THESSALONIANS 1:9–10

WAITING on God in heaven and waiting for His Son from heaven—these two God has joined together and no man may separate. The waiting on God for His presence and power in daily life will be the only true preparation for waiting for Christ in humility and true holiness. The waiting for Christ coming from heaven to take us to heaven will give the waiting on God its true tone of hopefulness and joy. The Father, who in His own time will reveal His Son from heaven, is the God who, as we wait on Him, prepares us for the revelation of His Son. The present life and the coming glory are inseparably connected in God and in us.

There is sometimes a danger of separating them. It is always easier to be engaged with the Christianity of the past or the future than to be faithful in the Christianity of today. As we look to what God has done in the past, or will do in time to come, the personal claim of present duty and present submission to His working may be escaped. Waiting on God must always lead to waiting for Christ as the glorious consummation of His work. And waiting for Christ must always remind us of the duty of waiting on God as our only proof that the waiting for Christ is in spirit and in truth.

There is such a danger of our being more occupied with the things that are coming than *with Him* who is to come. There is such scope in the study of coming events for imagination and reason and human ingenuity that nothing but deeply humble waiting on God can save us from mistaking the interest and pleasure of intellectual study for the true love of Him and His appearing. All you who say you wait for Christ's coming, *be sure that you wait on God now.* All you who seek to wait on God now to reveal His Son in you, see to it that you do so as men waiting for the revelation of His Son from heaven. The hope of that glorious appearing will strengthen you in waiting on God for what He is to do in you now. The same omnipotent love that is to reveal that glory is working in you even now to prepare you for it.

"The blessed hope and glorious appearing of our great God and Savior Jesus Christ" (Titus 2:13) is one of the great bonds of union given to God's church throughout the ages. "When He comes, in that Day, to be glorified in His saints and to be admired among all those who believe" (2 Thess. 1:10). Then we will all meet, and the unity of the body of Christ will be seen in its divine glory. It will be the meeting place and the triumph of divine love. Jesus receiving His own and presenting them to the Father. His own meeting Him and worshiping, in speechless love, that blessed face. His own meeting each other in the ecstasy of God's own love. Let us wait for, long for, and love the appearing of our Lord and heavenly Bridegroom. Tender love for Him and tender love for each other is the true and only bridal spirit.

> *All you who seek to wait on God now to reveal His Son in you, see to it that you do so as men waiting for the revelation of His Son from heaven.*

I fear greatly that this is sometimes forgotten. A beloved brother in Holland was speaking about the expectancy of faith being the true sign of the bride. I ventured to express a doubt. An unworthy bride about to be married to a prince might only be thinking of the position and the riches that she was to receive. The expectancy of faith might be strong while true love utterly lacking. It is not when we are most occupied with prophetic subjects, but when in humility and love we are clinging close to our Lord and His followers that we are in the bride's place. Jesus refuses to accept our love except as it is love to His disciples. Waiting for His coming means waiting for the glorious coming manifestation of the unity of the body, while we seek here to maintain that unity in humility and love. Those who love most are the most ready for His coming. Love for each other is the life and beauty of His bride, the Church.

And how is this to be brought about? Beloved child of God! If you want to learn how to properly wait for His Son from heaven, live even now waiting on God in heaven. Remember how Jesus lived always waiting on God. He could do nothing by Himself. It was God who perfected His Son through suffering and then exalted Him. It is God alone who can give you the deep spiritual life of one who is really waiting for His Son. Wait on God for it. Waiting for Christ Himself is so different from waiting for things that may come to pass! The latter any Christian can do, but the former God must work in you every day by His Holy Spirit. Therefore, all you who wait on God, look to Him for grace to wait for His Son from heaven in the Spirit that is from heaven. And you who want to wait for His Son, wait on God continually to reveal Christ in you.

The revelation of Christ in us as it is given to those who wait on God is the true preparation for the full revelation of Christ in glory.

"MY SOUL, WAIT SILENTLY FOR GOD ALONE!"

FOR FURTHER THOUGHT

1. *How are waiting on God in heaven and waiting for His Son from heaven inseparably joined together? Why is the connection between the two important in your spiritual life?*
2. *What must you do now as you wait for Christ's coming? What must you do as you seek to wait on God to reveal His Son in you now?*
3. *What is the connection between loving your fellow believers, and others, and waiting for Christ's coming?*

DAY 29

FOR THE PROMISE

OF THE FATHER

He commanded them not to depart from Jerusalem,
but to wait for the Promise of the Father.
ACTS 1:4

IN speaking of the saints in Jerusalem at Christ's birth, with Simeon and Anna, we saw how, though the redemption they had waited for has arrived, the call to waiting is no less urgent now than it was then. We wait for the full revelation in us of what came to them but what they could scarcely comprehend. It is the same way with waiting for the promise of the Father. In one sense, the fulfillment can never come again as it came at Pentecost. In another sense, and that in as deep a reality as with the first disciples, we need to wait daily for the Father to fulfill His promise in us.

The Holy Spirit is not a person distinct from the Father in the way two persons on earth are distinct. The Father and the Spirit are never without or separate from each other. The Father is always in the Spirit, and the Spirit works nothing but as the Father works in Him. Each moment, the same Spirit who is in us is in God, too, and he who is most full of the Spirit will be the first to wait on God most earnestly to further fulfill His promise and still strengthen him mightily by His Spirit in the inner man. The Spirit in us is not a power at our disposal. Nor is the Spirit an independent power, acting apart from the Father and the Son. The Spirit is *the real, living presence and the power of the Father* working in us. Therefore, it is just he who knows that the Spirit is in him who waits on the Father for the full revelation and experience of what the Spirit's indwelling is: for His increase and abounding more and more.

See this in the apostles. They were filled with the Spirit at Pentecost. When they, not long after, on returning from the council where they had been forbidden to preach, prayed afresh for boldness to speak in His name, a fresh coming down of the Holy Spirit was the Father's fresh fulfillment of His promise.

At Samaria, by the word and the Spirit, many had been converted, and the whole city was filled with joy. At the apostles' prayer, the Father once again fulfilled the promise (see Acts 8:14–17). Even so to the waiting company—"We are all present before God" (see Acts 10:33)—in Cornelius's house. And so, too, in Acts 13. It was when men, filled with the Spirit, prayed and fasted that the promise of the Father was newly fulfilled, and the leading of the Spirit was given from heaven: "Separate to Me Barnabas and Saul" (Acts 13:2).

So also we find Paul, in Ephesians, praying for those who have been sealed with the Spirit that God would grant them the spirit of illumination. And later on, that He would grant them, according to the riches of His glory, to be strengthened with might by the Spirit in the inner man.

> When He gives grace or strength or life, He gives it by giving Himself to work it—it is all inseparable from Himself. Much more so is the Holy Spirit.

The Spirit given at Pentecost was not something that God failed with in heaven, and then sent out of heaven to earth. God does not, cannot, give away anything in that manner. When He gives grace or strength or life, He gives it by giving Himself to work it—it is all inseparable from Himself.[42] Much more so is the Holy Spirit. He is God, present and working in us. The true position in which we can count on that working with an unceasing power is as we, praising for what we have, still unceasingly wait for the Father's promise to be still more mightily fulfilled.

What new meaning and promise does this give to our lives of waiting! It teaches us to continually keep the place where the disciples waited at the footstool of the throne. It reminds us that as helpless as they were to meet their enemies or to preach to Christ's enemies until they were endued with power, we, too, can only be strong in the life of faith, or the work of love, as we are in direct communication with God and Christ. They must maintain the life of the Spirit in us. This assures us that the omnipotent God will, through the glorified Christ, work in us a power that can bring unexpected things to pass, impossible things. Oh, what the Church will be able to do when her individual members learn to live their lives waiting on God, when together, with all of self and the world sacrificed in the fire of love, they unite in waiting with one accord for the promise of the Father, once so gloriously fulfilled but still unexhausted!

Come and let each of us be still in the presence of the inconceivable grandeur of this prospect: the Father waiting to fill the Church with the Holy Spirit. "And willing to fill me," let each one say.

With this faith, let a hush and a holy fear come over the soul as it waits in stillness to take it all in. And let life increasingly become a deep joy in the hope of the ever fuller fulfillment of the Father's promise.

"MY SOUL, WAIT SILENTLY FOR GOD ALONE!"

For Further Thought

1. What is the true relationship of the Holy Spirit to the Father and to the Son? What specific roles does the Holy Spirit play in your life as a believer?
2. How does God give away any of His gifts—including His gift of the Holy Spirit—to those who are His own people? What does that tell you about seeking and accepting the gifts of God?
3. What heart attitude is necessary if you are to count on God's working, and continuing to work, with unceasing power within you and through you?

Day 30

Continually

So you, by the help of your God, return; observe mercy
and justice, and wait on your God continually.
Hosea 12:6

CONTINUITY is one of the essential elements of life. Interrupt it for a single hour in a man, and it is lost and he is dead. Continuity, unbroken and ceaseless, is essential to a healthy Christian life. God wants me to be, and God waits to make me—I want to be and I wait on Him to make me every moment—what He expects of me and what is well pleasing in His sight. If waiting on God is the essence of true religion, the maintenance of the spirit of entire dependence must be continuous. The call of God, "wait on your God continually," must be accepted and obeyed. Although there may be times of special waiting, the disposition and habit of soul must be there unchangeably and uninterrupted.

This waiting continually is indeed a necessity. To those who are content with a powerless Christian life, it appears to be a luxury beyond what is essential to be a good Christian. But, all who are praying the prayer, "Lord, make me as holy as a pardoned sinner can be made! Keep me as near to You as it is possible for me to be! Fill me as full of Your love as You are willing to do!" feel at once that it is something that must be had. They feel that there can be no unbroken fellowship with God, no full abiding in Christ, no maintaining of victory over sin and readiness for service, without waiting continually on the Lord.

The continual waiting is a possibility. Many think that with the duties of life it is out of the question. They cannot always be thinking of it. Even when they wish to, they forget.

They do not understand that it is a matter of the heart and that what the heart is full of occupies it, even when the thoughts are otherwise engaged. A father's heart may be continuously filled with intense love and longing for a sick wife or child at a distance, even though pressing business requires all his thoughts. When *the heart* has learned how entirely powerless it is for one moment to keep itself or bring forth any good, when it has learned how surely and truly God will keep it when it has, in despair of itself, accepted God's promise to do for it the impossible, it learns to rest in God. In the midst of occupations and temptations, it can wait continually.

This waiting is a promise. God's precepts are enablings. Gospel precepts are all promises, revelations of what our God will do for us. When you first begin waiting on God, it is with frequent intermission and failure. But do believe God is watching over you in love and secretly strengthening you in it. There are times when waiting appears like just losing time, but it is not so. Waiting, even in darkness, is unconscious advance because it is God you have to do with, and He is working in you. God, who calls you to wait on Him, sees your weak efforts and works it in you. Your spiritual life is in no respect your own work; as little as you begin it can you continue it. It is God's Spirit who has begun the work in you of waiting on God. He will enable you to wait continually.

> *When you first begin waiting on God, it is with frequent intermission and failure. But do believe God is watching over you in love and secretly strengthening you in it.*

Waiting continually will be met and rewarded by God Himself working continually. We are coming to the end of our lessons. I hope that you and I might learn one thing: God must, God will work continually. He always works continually, but the experience of it is hindered by unbelief. But He who by His Spirit teaches you to wait continually will bring you also to experience how, as the Everlasting One, His work is never-ceasing. In the love and the life and the work of God, there can be no break, no interruption.

Do not limit God in this by your thoughts of what may be expected. Do fix your eyes upon this one truth: in His very nature, God, as the only giver of life, *cannot do anything other than work in His child every moment.* Do not look only at the one side: "If I wait continually, God will work continually." No, look at the other side. Place God first and say, "*God works continually, so every moment I can wait on Him continually.*" Take time until the vision of your God working continually, without one moment's intermission, fills your being. Your waiting continually will then come of itself. Full of trust and joy, the holy habit of the soul will be: "On You I wait *all the day*" (Ps. 25:5). The Holy Spirit will keep you always waiting.

"MY SOUL, WAIT SILENTLY FOR GOD ALONE!"

o naa,.

FOR FURTHER THOUGHT

1. *Why is it important that you not only wait on God, but you wait on Him continually—without break or interruption?*
2. *How does God enable you as a believer to wait on Him in this manner? What does He do within you to make possible what otherwise is impossible: waiting on Him continually?*
3. *What are the rewards of waiting on God continually? In what ways does God work on and in you continually?*

MOMENT BY MOMENT

"I, the LORD, keep it,
I water it every moment."
ISAIAH 27:3

Dying with Jesus, by death reckoning mine;
Living with Jesus, a new life divine;
Looking to Jesus till glory doth shine,
Moment by moment, O Lord, I am Thine.

Chorus— Moment by moment I'm kept in His love;
Moment by moment I've life from above;
Looking to Jesus till glory doth shine;
Moment by moment, O Lord, I am Thine.

Never a battle with wrong for the right,
Never a contest that He doth not fight;
Lifting above us His banner so white,
Moment by moment, I'm kept in His sight.

Never a trial that He is not there,
Never a burden that He doth not bear,
Never a sorrow that He doth not share,
Moment by moment, I'm under His care.

Never a heartache, and never a groan,
Never a teardrop, and never a moan;
Never a danger but there on the throne,
Moment by moment, He thinks of His own.

Never a weakness that He doth not feel,
Never a sickness that He cannot heal;
Moment by moment, in woe or in weal,
Jesus, my Savior, abides with me still.

(Music in *Sankey's Sacred Songs and Solos*)

Day 31

Only

My soul, wait silently for God alone,
for my expectation is from Him.
He only is my rock and my salvation.
PSALM 62:5–6

IT is possible to be waiting continually on God, but not only on Him. There may be other secret confidences intervening and preventing the blessing that was expected. And so the word *only* must come to throw its light on the path to the fullness and certainty of blessing. "My soul, wait silently for God *alone*. . .HE *only* is my rock."

Yes, "My soul, wait silently for God alone." There is only one God, only one source of life and happiness for the heart. He *only* is my rock; my soul, wait silently for God *alone*. You desire to be good. "No one is good but. . .God" (Matt. 19:17), and there is no possible goodness except what is received directly from Him. You have sought to be holy. "No one is holy like the LORD" (1 Sam. 2:2), and there is no holiness except what He by His Spirit of holiness every moment breathes in you. You desire to live and work for God and His kingdom, for men and their salvation. Hear how He says: "The everlasting God, the LORD, the Creator of the ends of the earth, (He only) neither faints nor is weary. . . . He gives power to the weak, and to those who have no might He increases strength. . . . But those who wait on the LORD shall renew their strength" (see Isaiah 40:28–31). He only is God, He only is your Rock. "My soul, wait silently for God alone."

"My soul, wait silently for God alone." You will not find many who can help you in this. There will be enough of your brothers to draw you to put trust in churches and doctrines, in schemes and plans and human appliances, in means of grace and divine appointments. But, "My soul, wait silently for God Himself." His most sacred appointments become a snare when trusted in. The brazen serpent becomes Nehushtan (see 2 Kings 18:4); the ark and the temple a vain confidence. Let the living God alone, none and nothing but He, be your hope.

"*My soul*, wait silently for God alone." Eyes and hands and feet, mind and thought, may have to be intently engaged in the duties of this life. "*My soul*, wait silently for God alone." You are an immortal spirit, created not for this world but for eternity and for God. Oh, my soul, realize your destiny! Know your privilege, and "wait for *God alone*." Do not let the interest of spiritual thoughts and exercises deceive you, for they very often take the place of waiting on God. My soul, wait, your very self, your innermost being, with all its power, "wait for God alone." God is for you, and you are for God. Wait only on Him.

Yes, "my soul, wait silently for God alone." Beware of two great enemies: the world and self. Beware of allowing any earthly satisfaction or enjoyment, however innocent it appears, to keep you back from saying, "I will go...to God my exceeding joy" (Ps. 43:4). Remember and study what Jesus said about denying self: "Let a man deny himself" (see Matt. 16:24). Tersteegen says: "The saints deny themselves in everything." Pleasing self in little things may be strengthening it to assert itself in greater things. "My soul, wait silently for God *alone*." Let Him be all your salvation and all your desire. Say continually and with an undivided heart, "From Him comes my [expectation]. He only is my rock...I shall not be greatly moved" (Ps. 62:1–2). Whatever your spiritual or temporal needs are, whatever the desire or prayer of your heart, whatever your interest in connection with God's work in the Church or the world—in solitude or in the rush of the world, in public worship or other gatherings of the saints, "my soul, wait silently for God *alone*." Let your expectations be from Him alone. He only is your rock.

> *You* are an immortal spirit, created not for this world but for eternity and for God. Oh, my soul, realize your destiny! Know your privilege, and "wait for God alone."

"My soul, wait silently for God alone." Never forget the two foundational truths on which this blessed waiting rests. If you are ever inclined to think this "waiting for God only" is too hard or too high, they will bring you back at once. They are your absolute helplessness and the absolute sufficiency of your God. Oh, enter deeply into the entire sinfulness of all that is of self, and do not think of letting self have anything to say one single moment. Enter deeply into your utter and unceasing inability to ever change what is evil in you or to bring forth anything that is spiritually good. Enter deeply into your relationship of dependence on God to receive from Him every moment what He gives. Enter deeper still into His covenant of redemption, with His promise to restore more gloriously than ever what you have lost. Then, by His Son and Spirit, He will unceasingly give you His actual divine presence and power. And thus, wait on your God continually and only.

"My soul, wait silently for God alone." No words can tell, no heart can conceive, the riches of the glory of this mystery of the Father and of Christ. Our God, in the infinite tenderness and omnipotence of His love, waits to be our life and joy. Oh, my soul, let it no longer be necessary that I repeat the words, "Wait on God."

But let all that is in me rise and sing, "Truly my soul silently waits for God. On You I wait all the day."

"MY SOUL, WAIT SILENTLY FOR GOD ALONE!"

FOR FURTHER THOUGHT

1. *Why do you think God commands you to wait on Him only? What blessings does He desire to impart to you when you obey?*
2. *God commands you to wait on Him alone. On what two other things can you be tempted to wait on when you should be waiting only on God? Why are they a danger to waiting on God alone?*
3. *What are the two foundational truths on which this blessed waiting on God rests? How will these truths bless you during those times when you think that waiting for God alone is too difficult for you to accomplish?*

LIKE CHRIST

CONTENTS

Preface

IN sending forth this little book on the image of our blessed Lord, and the likeness to Him to which we are called, I have only two remarks by way of preface.

The one is that no one can be more conscious than myself of the difficulty of the task I have undertaken, and of its very defective execution. There were two things I had to do. The one was to draw such a portrait of the Son of God, as "in all things He had to be made like His brethren" (Heb. 2:17), as to show how, in the reality of His human life, we have indeed an exact pattern of what the Father wants us to be. What was wanted was such a portrait as should make likeness to Him infinitely and mightily attractive, should rouse desire, awaken love, inspire hope, and strengthen faith in all who are seeking to imitate Jesus Christ. And then I had to sketch another portrait—that of the believer as he really, with some degree of spiritual exactness, reflects this image, and amid the trials and duties of daily life proves that likeness to Christ is no mere ideal, but through the power of the Holy Spirit a most blessed reality.

How often and how deeply I have felt, after having sought to delineate some one trait of the blessed life, how utterly insufficient human thoughts are to grasp, or human words to express that spiritual beauty of which one at best has seen only faint glimpses! And how often our very thoughts deceive us, as they give us some human conception in the mind of what the Word reveals, while we lack that true vision of the spiritual glory of Him who is the brightness of the Father's glory!

The second remark I wish to make is a suggestion as to what I think is needed really to behold the glory of the blessed image into which we are to be changed. I was very much struck some time ago, in an infant school examination, with the practice a little class in object lessons was put through. A picture was shown them, which they were told to look at carefully. They then had to shut their eyes and take time to think and remember everything they had seen. The picture was now removed, and the little ones had to tell all they could. Again the picture was shown, and they had to try to notice what they had not observed before; again to shut their eyes and think, and again to tell what more they had noticed. And so once more, until every line of the picture had been taken in. As I looked at the keen interest with which the little eyes now gazed on the picture, and then were pressed so tightly shut as they tried to realize, and take in, and keep what they had been looking at, I felt that if our Bible reading were more of such an object lesson, the unseen spiritual realities pictured to us in the Word would take much deeper hold of our inner life. We are too easily content with the thoughts suggested by the words of the Bible, though these are but forms of truth, without giving time for the substantial spiritual reality, which the Word as the truth of God contains, to get lodged and rooted in the heart. Let us, in meditating on the image of God in Christ, to which we are to be conformed, remember this. When some special trait has occupied our thoughts, let us shut our eyes and open our hearts. Let us think, and pray, and believe in the working of the Holy Spirit, until we really see the blessed Master in that special light in which the Word has been setting Him before us, until we can carry away for that day the deep and abiding impression of that heavenly beauty in Him which we know is to be reproduced in us. Let us gaze, and gaze again, let us worship and adore, for the more we see Him as He is, the more like Him we must become. To study the image of God in the man Christ Jesus, to yield and set open our inmost being for that image to take possession and live in us, and then to go forth and let the heavenly likeness reflect itself and shine out in our life among our fellowmen—this is what we have been redeemed for, let this be what we live for.

And now I entrust the little book to the gracious care of the blessed Lord of whose glory it seeks to tell. May He allow us to see that there is no beauty or blessedness like that of a Christlike life. May He teach us to believe that in union with Him the Christlike life is indeed for us. And as each day we listen to what His Word tells us of His image, may each one of us have grace to say, "O my Father! Just as Your beloved Son lived in You, with You, for You on earth, even so I desire to also live."

ANDREW MURRAY
Wellington, Cape of Good Hope

P.S.—As the tone of the meditations is mostly personal, I have, at the close of the volume, added some more general thoughts: "On Preaching Christ Our Example."

"Do just as I have done."
JOHN 13:15 ESV

DAY 1
BECAUSE WE ABIDE IN HIM

He who says he abides in Him ought
himself also to walk just as He walked.
1 JOHN 2:6

ABIDING *in Christ* and *walking like Christ:* these are the two blessings of the new life that are here set before us in their essential unity. The fruit of a life *in Christ* is a life *like Christ*.

To the first of these expressions, *abiding in Christ*, we are no strangers. The wondrous parable of the vine and the branches, with the accompanying command, "Abide in Me, and I in you" (John 15:4), has often been to us a source of rich instruction and comfort. And though we feel as if we had but very imperfectly learned the lesson of abiding in Him, yet we have tasted something of the joy that comes when the soul can say: "Lord, You know all things, and You know that I do abide in You." And He knows, too, how often the fervent prayer still arises: "Blessed Lord, do grant me the complete unbroken abiding."

The second expression, *walking like Christ*, is not less significant than the first. It is the promise of the wonderful power that the abiding in Him will exert. As the fruit of our surrender to live wholly in Him, His life works so mightily in us that our walk, the outward expression of the inner life, becomes like His. The two are inseparably connected. The abiding in always precedes the walking like Him. And yet the aim to walk like Him must equally precede any large measure of abiding. Only then is the need for a close union fully realized, or is the heavenly Giver free to bestow the fullness of His grace, because He sees that the soul is prepared to use it according to His design. Many a one will discover that just here is the secret of his failure in abiding in Christ: he did not seek it with the view of walking like Christ. The words of St. John invite us to look at the two truths in their vital connection and dependence on each other.

The first lesson they teach is: He who seeks to abide in Christ must *walk just as He walked*. We all know that it is a matter of course that a branch bears fruit of the same sort as the vine to which it belongs. The life of the vine and the branch is so completely identical that the manifestation of that life must be identical, too. When the Lord Jesus redeemed us with His blood and presented us to the Father in His righteousness, He did not leave us in our old nature to serve God as best we could.

1233

No! In Him dwelled the eternal life, the holy divine life of heaven, and everyone who is in Him receives from Him that same eternal life in its holy heavenly power. That's why nothing can be more natural than the claim that he who abides in Him, continually receiving life from Him, must *also so* walk *even as He* walked.

This mighty life of God in the soul does not, however, work as a blind force, compelling us ignorantly or involuntarily to act like Christ. On the contrary, the walking like Him must come as the result of a deliberate choice, sought in strong desire, accepted by a living will. With this view, the Father in heaven showed us in Jesus' earthly life what the life of heaven would be when it came down into the conditions and circumstances of our human life. And with the same object the Lord Jesus, when we receive the new life from Him, when He calls us to abide in Him so that we may receive that life more abundantly, always points us to His own life on earth and tells us that it is to walk just as He walked that the new life has been bestowed. "Do just as I have done to you" (John 13:15 ESV): that word of the Master takes His whole earthly life and very simply makes it the rule and guide of all our conduct. If we abide in Jesus, we may not act otherwise than He did. "Like Christ" gives in one short, all-inclusive word the blessed law of the Christian life. He is to think, to speak, to act as Jesus did; as Jesus was, *just so* is he to be.

> he abiding in always precedes the walking like Him. And yet the aim to walk like Him must equally precede any large measure of abiding.

The second lesson is the complement of the first: He who seeks to walk like Christ must *abide in Him.*

There is a twofold need for this lesson. With some there is the earnest desire and effort to follow Christ's example, without any sense of the impossibility of doing so, except by deep, real abiding in Him. They fail because they seek to obey the high command to live like Christ, but without the only power that can do so—the living in Christ. With others there is the opposite error. They know their own weakness and believe walking like Christ is an impossibility. Those who seek to do it and fail need the lesson we are enforcing just as much as those who do not seek because they expect to fail. To walk like Christ one must abide in Him, for he who abides in Him has the power to walk like Him, and that not indeed in himself or his own efforts, but in Jesus, who perfects His strength in our weakness. It is just when I feel my utter powerlessness most deeply, and fully accept Jesus in His wondrous union to myself as my life, that His power works in me. Then I am able to lead a life completely beyond what my power could obtain. I begin to see that abiding in Him is not a matter of moments or special seasons, but the deep life process in which, by His keeping grace, I continue without a moment's intermission, and from which I act out all my Christian life. And I feel emboldened really to take Him in everything as my example, because I am sure that the hidden inner union and likeness must work itself out into a visible likeness in walk and conduct.

> o walk like Christ one must abide in Him, for he who abides in Him has the power to walk like Him, and that not indeed in himself or his own efforts, but in Jesus, who perfects His strength in our weakness.

Dear reader! If God gives us grace, in the course of our meditations, to truly enter into the meaning of these His words and what they teach of a life in very deed like Christ's, we shall more than once come into the presence of heights and depths that will make us cry out, "How can these things be?" If the Holy Spirit reveals to us the heavenly perfection of the humanity of our Lord as the image of the unseen God, and speaks to us, "ought himself also to walk just as He walked," the first effect will be that we shall begin to feel at what a distance we are from Him. We shall be ready to give up hope, and to say with so many, "It does not benefit to attempt it. I never can walk like Jesus." At such moments we shall find our strength in the message, *He who abides in Him, he* must, *he* can also walk just as He walked. The word of the Master will come with new meaning as the assurance of sufficient strength: "He who abides in Me. . .bears much fruit" (John 15:5).

Therefore, brother, abide in Him! Every believer is in Christ, but not every one abides in Him, in the consciously joyful and trustful surrender of the whole being to His influence. You know what abiding in Him is. It is to consent with our whole soul to His being our life, to rely on Him to inspire us in all that goes to make up life, and then to give up everything most absolutely for Him to rule and work in us. It is the rest of the full assurance that He does, each moment, work in us what we are to be, and so Himself enables us to maintain that perfect surrender in which He is free to do all His will. Let all who indeed long to walk like Christ take courage at the thought of what He is and will prove Himself to be if they trust Him. He is the *true Vine*, and no vine ever did so fully for its branches what He will do for us. We need only consent to be branches. Honor Him by a joyful trust that He is, beyond all conception, the *true Vine*, holding you by His almighty strength, supplying you from His infinite fullness. And as your faith looks this way to Him, instead of sighing and failure, the voice of praise will be heard repeating the language of faith: Thanks be to God! He who abides in Him does walk just as He walked. Thanks be to God! I abide in Him, and I walk as He walked. Yes, thanks be to God! In the blessed life of God's redeemed these two are inseparably one: abiding in Christ and walking like Christ.

Blessed Savior! You know how often I have said to You, Lord, I do abide in You! And yet I sometimes feel that the full joy and power of life in You is lacking. Your Word this day has reminded me of what may be the reason of failure. I sought to abide in You more for my own comfort and growth than for Your glory. I did not understand fully how the hidden union with You had for its object perfect conformity to You, and how only he who wholly yields himself to serve and obey the Father as completely as You did can fully receive all that the heavenly love can do for him. I now see something of it: the entire surrender to live and work like You must precede the full experience of the wondrous power of Your life.

> *hanks be to God! He who abides in Him does walk just as He walked. Thanks be to God! I abide in Him, and I walk as He walked.*

Lord, I thank You for the discovery. With my whole heart I would accept Your calling and yield myself in everything to walk just as You walked. To be Your faithful follower in all You were and did on earth is the one desire of my heart.

Blessed Lord! He who truly yields himself to walk as You did will receive grace to wholly abide in You. O my Lord! Here I am. *To walk like Christ!* For this I do indeed consecrate myself to You. *To abide in Christ!* For this I trust in You with full assurance of faith. Perfect in me Your own work.

And let Your Holy Spirit help me, O my Lord, each time I meditate on what it is to walk like You, to hold fast the blessed truth: as one who abides in *Christ*, I have the strength to walk like *Christ*. Amen.

For Further Thought

1. *What does it literally mean to "walk just as He walked"? In what ways did Jesus "walk" when He was on earth?*

2. *How are abiding in Christ and walking like Christ related? What is the mutual importance of doing one if you want to do the other?*

3. *What is the definition in today's lesson of abiding in Christ? What does abiding in Christ give you the power to do consistently?*

DAY 2

HE HIMSELF CALLS US TO IT

"I have given you an example,
that you also should do just as I have done to you."
JOHN 13:15 ESV

IT is Jesus Christ, the beloved redeemer of our souls, who speaks this. He had just—humbling Himself to do the work of the slave—washed His disciples' feet. In doing so, His love had rendered to the body the service of which it stood in need at the supper table. At the same time He had shown, in a striking symbol, what He had done for their souls in cleansing them from sin. In this twofold work of love, He had thus set before them, just before parting, in one significant act, the whole work of His life as a ministry of blessing to body and to soul. And as He sits down, He says: "*I have given you an example,* THAT YOU *also should do* JUST AS I *have done to you.*" All that they had seen in Him, and experienced from Him, is thus made the rule of their life: "YOU SHOULD DO JUST AS I have done."

The word of the blessed Savior is for us, too. To each one who knows that the Lord has washed away his sin, the command comes with all the touching force of one of the last words of Him who is going out to die for us: "YOU SHOULD DO JUST AS I have done to you." Jesus Christ does indeed ask every one of us in everything to act just as we have seen Him do. What He has done to ourselves, and still does each day, we are to do over again to others. In His condescending, pardoning, saving love, He is our example, and each of us is to be the copy and image of the Master.

The thought comes at once: Sadly, how little have I lived this way; how little have I even known that I was expected to live this way! And yet, He is my lord. He loves me, and I love Him, so I dare not entertain the thought of living otherwise than He would have me. What can I do but open my heart to His Word and fix my gaze on His example, until it exercises its divine power on me and draws me with irresistible force to cry: "Lord, just as You have done, I will do also."

The power of an example depends chiefly on two things. The one is the attractiveness of what it gives us to see, the other the personal relationship and influence of him in whom it is seen. In both aspects, what power there is in our Lord's example!

Or, is there really anything very attractive in our Lord's example? I ask it in all earnest, because, in order to judge by the conduct of many of His disciples, it would really seem as if it were not so. Oh, that the Spirit of God would open our eyes to see the heavenly beauty of the likeness of the only begotten Son!

We know who the Lord Jesus is. He is the Son of the all-glorious God, one with the Father in nature and glory and perfection. When He was on earth it could be said about Him, "We show you that eternal life which was with the Father and was manifested to us" (see 1 John 1:2). In Him we see God. In Him we see how God would act were He here in our place on earth. In Him all that is beautiful and lovely and perfect in the heavenly world is revealed to us in the form of an earthly life. If we want to see what is really counted noble and glorious in the heavenly world, if we want to see what is really divine, we have only to look at Jesus, for in all He does the glory of God is shown forth.

But oh, the blindness of God's children: this heavenly beauty has to many of them no attraction. There is no form or comeliness that they should desire it.

> *Jesus Christ does indeed ask every one of us in everything to act just as we have seen Him do. What He has done to ourselves, and still does each day, we are to do over again to others.*

The manners and the way of living in the court of an earthly king exercise influence throughout the empire. The example it gives is imitated by all who belong to the nobility or the higher classes. But the example of the King of heaven, who came and dwelled in the flesh, so that we might see how we might here on earth live a God-like life—sadly, with how few of His followers does it really find imitation. When we look at Jesus, at His obedience to the will of the Father, at His humiliation to be a servant of the most unworthy, and at His love as manifested in the entire giving up and sacrifice of Himself, we see the most wondrous and glorious thing heaven has to show. In heaven itself we shall see nothing greater or brighter. Surely such an example, given by God on very purpose to make the imitation attractive and possible, ought to win us. Is it not enough to stir all that is within us with a holy jealousy and with joy unutterable as we hear the message, "I have given you an example, that you also should do just as I have done to you"?

This is not all. The power of an example consists not only in its own intrinsic excellence, but also in the personal relationship to him who gives it. Jesus had not washed the feet of others in the presence of His disciples. It was when He had washed *their feet* that He said: "You also should do just as I have done to *you*." It is the consciousness of a personal relationship to Christ that enforces the command: Do as I have done. It is the experience of what Jesus has done to me that is the strength in which I can go and do the same to others. He does not ask that I shall do more than has been done to me. But not less either: JUST AS I have done to you. He does not ask that I shall humble myself as a servant deeper than He has done. It would not have been strange if He had asked this of such a worm. But this is not His wish. He only demands that I shall just do and be what He, the King, has done and been. He humbled Himself as low as humiliation could go to love and to bless me. He counted this *His highest honor and blessedness*. And now He invites me to partake of the same honor and blessedness, in loving and serving as He did. Truly, if I indeed know the love that rests on me, and the humiliation through which alone that love could reach me, and the power of the cleansing that has washed me, nothing can keep me back from saying: "Yes, blessed Lord, just as You have done to me, I will also do." The heavenly loveliness of the great Example, and the divine lovingness of the great Exemplar, combine to make the example above everything attractive.

> *It is the consciousness of a personal relationship to Christ that enforces the command: Do as I have done.*

Only there is one thing I must not forget. It is not the remembrance of what Jesus has once done to me, but the living experience of what He is now to me that will give me the power to act like Him. His love must be a present reality, the inflowing of a life and a power in which I can love like Him. It is only as by the Holy Spirit I realize WHAT Jesus is doing for me, and HOW He does it, and that it is HE who does it, that it is possible for me to do to others what He is doing to me.

"YOU ALSO SHOULD DO JUST AS *I* have done to you!" What a precious word! What a glorious prospect! Jesus is going to show forth in me the divine power of His love so that I may show it forth to others. He blesses me so that I may bless others. He loves me so that I may love others. He becomes servant to me so that I may become a servant to others. He saves and cleanses me so that I may save and cleanse others. He gives Himself wholly for and to me so that I may wholly give myself for and to others. I have only to be doing over to others what He is doing to me—nothing more. I can do it, just because He is doing it to me. What I do is nothing but the repeating, the showing forth of what I am receiving from Him.[42]

Wondrous grace that calls us to be like our Lord in that which constitutes His highest glory! Wondrous grace that prepares us for this calling by Himself first being to us and in us what we are to be to others! Shall not our whole heart joyously respond to His command? Yes, blessed Lord, just as You do to me I will also do to others.

Gracious Lord! What can I now do but praise and pray? My heart feels overwhelmed with this wondrous offer, that You will reveal all Your love and power in me if I will yield myself to let it flow through me to others. Though with fear and

---

[42] How beautifully the principle is expressed in the words of Moses to Hobab (Num. 10:32), "And it shall be, if you go with us—indeed it shall be—that *whatever good the Lord will do to us, the same we will* do to you."

trembling, yet in deep and grateful adoration, with joy and confidence, I want to accept the offer and say: Here I am! Show me how much You love me, and I will show it to others by loving them just so.

And that I may be able to do this, blessed Lord, grant me these two things. Grant me, by Your Holy Spirit, a clear insight into Your love to me, that I may know how You love me, how Your love to me is Your delight and blessedness, how in that love You give Yourself so completely to me, that You are indeed mine to do for me all I need. Grant this, Lord, and I shall know how to love and how to live for others, just as You love and live for me.

> *hall not our whole heart joyously respond to His command? Yes, blessed Lord, just as You do to me I will also do to others.*

And then grant me to see, as often as I feel how little love I have, that it is not with the love of my little heart, but with Your love shed abroad in me, that I have to fulfill the command of loving like You. Am I not Your branch, O my heavenly Vine? It is the fullness of Your life and love that flows through me in love and blessing to those around. It is Your Spirit that, at the same moment, reveals what You are to me, and strengthens me for what I am to be to others in Your name. In this faith I dare to say, Amen, Lord, just as You do to me, I also do. Yes, amen.

FOR FURTHER THOUGHT

1. *What does Jesus ask you to do in response to all the wonderful things He has done for you? How can you accomplish this in a practical, meaningful way?*
2. *How can your consciousness of a personal relationship with the Lord Jesus Christ motivate and empower you to do the things He did when He was on earth?*
3. *What does Jesus give you and do in you so that you can walk as He walked and serve others as He so selflessly served others?*

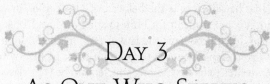

Day 3

As One Who Serves

*"If I then, your Lord and Teacher, have washed your feet,
you also ought to wash one another's feet."*
John 13:14

"I am among you as the One who serves."
Luke 22:27

YESTERDAY we thought of the right that the Lord has to demand and expect that His redeemed ones should follow His example. Today we will more specially consider in what it is we have to follow Him.

"You also ought to wash one another's feet" is the word of which we want to understand the full meaning. The form of a servant in which we see Him, the cleansing that was the object of that service, the love that was its motive power—these are the three chief thoughts.

First, the form of a servant. All was ready for the last supper, to the very water to wash the feet of the guests, according to custom. But there was no slave to do the work. Each one waits for the other, for none of the twelve thinks of humbling himself to do the work. Even at the table they were full of the thought, who should be greatest in the kingdom they were expecting (see Luke 22:26–27). All at once Jesus rises (they were already reclining at the table), lays aside His garments, girds Himself with a towel, and begins to wash their feet.

What a wondrous spectacle, on which angels gazed with adoring wonder! Christ, the Creator and King of the universe, at whose order legions of angels are ready to serve Him, who might with one word of love have said which one of the twelve must do the work—Christ chooses the slave's place for His own, takes the soiled feet in His own holy hands, and washes them. He does it in full consciousness of His divine glory, for John says, "Jesus, knowing that the Father had given all things into His hands, and that He had come from God and was going to God, rose" (John 13:3–4). For the hands into which God had given all things, nothing is common or unclean.

The lowliness of a work never lowers the person; rather the person honors and elevates the work and imparts his own worth even to the lowliest service. In such deep humiliation, as we men call it, our Lord finds divine glory, and is in this the Leader of His Church in the path of true blessedness. It is as the Son that He is the servant. Just because He is the beloved of His Father, in whose hands all things are given, it is not difficult for Him to stoop so low. In taking the form of a servant this way, Jesus proclaims the law of rank in the Church of Christ. The higher one wishes to stand in grace, the more it must be his joy to be servant of all. "Whosoever desires to be first among you, let him be your slave" (Matt. 20:27); "He who is greatest among you shall be your servant" (Matt. 23:11).

> or love, nothing is too hard. Love never speaks of sacrifice. To bless the loved one, however unworthy, it willingly gives up all.

A servant is one who is always caring for the work and interest of his master, is always ready to let his master see that he only seeks to do what will please or profit him. This is how Jesus lived: "For even the Son of Man did not come to be served, but to serve, and to give His life a ransom for many" (Mark 10:45): "I am among you as the One who serves" (Luke 22:27). This is how I must live, moving about among God's children as the servant of all. If I seek to bless others, it must be in the humble, loving readiness with which I serve them, not caring for my own honor or interest, if I can but be a blessing to them. I must follow Christ's example in washing the disciples' feet. A servant counts it no humiliation and is not ashamed of being counted an inferior. It is his place and work to serve others. The reason why we so often do not bless others is that we wish to address them as their superiors in grace or gifts, or at least their equals. If we first learned from our Lord to associate with others in the blessed spirit of a servant, what a blessing we would become to the world! When once this example is admitted to the place it ought to have in the Church of Christ, the power of His presence would soon make itself felt.

And what is now the work the disciple has to perform in this spirit of lowly service? The foot washing speaks of a double work—the one for the cleansing and refreshing of the body, the other for the cleansing and saving of the soul. During the whole of our Lord's life on earth these two things were always united: "The sick were healed, to the poor the gospel was preached" (see Luke 7:22). As with the paralytic, so with many others, blessing to the body was the type and promise of life to the spirit.

The follower of Jesus may not lose sight of this when he receives the command, "You also ought to wash one another's feet." Remembering that the external and bodily is the gate to the inner and spiritual life, he makes the salvation of the soul the first object in his holy ministry of love, at the same time, however, seeking the way to the hearts by the ready service of love in the little and common things of daily life. It is not by reproof and censure that he shows that he is a servant, but by the friendliness and kindliness with which he proves in his daily interactions that he always thinks how he can help or serve, that he becomes the living witness of what it is to be a follower of Jesus. From such a one the word when spoken comes with power and finds easy entrance. And then, when he comes into contact with the sin and perverseness and contradiction of men, instead of being discouraged, he perseveres as he thinks with how much patience Jesus has borne with him, and still daily cleanses him. He realizes himself to be one of God's appointed servants, one called to stoop to the lowest depth to serve and save men, even to bow at the feet of others if this is needed.

> *To love and serve like Jesus is the highest blessedness and joy, as well as the way, like Jesus, to be a blessing and a joy to others.*

The spirit that will enable one to live such a life of loving service can be learned from Jesus alone. John writes, "Having loved His own who were in the world, He loved them to the end" (John 13:1). For love, nothing is too hard. Love never speaks of sacrifice. To bless the loved one, however unworthy, it willingly gives up all. It was love that made Jesus a servant. It is love alone that will make the servant's place and work such blessedness to us, that we shall persevere in it at all costs. We may perhaps, like Jesus, have to wash the feet of some Judas who rewards us with ingratitude and betrayal. We shall probably meet many a Peter, who first, with his "Never my feet," refuses, and then is dissatisfied when we do not comply with his impatient "Not my feet only, but also *my* hands and *my* head!" (John 13:9). Only love, a heavenly unquenchable love, gives the patience, the courage, and the wisdom for this great work the Lord has set before us in His holy example: "Wash one another's feet."

O my soul, your love cannot attain to this. Therefore listen to Him who says, "Abide in *My love*" (John 15:10). Our one desire must be that He may show us how He loves us, and that He Himself may keep us abiding in *"His love."* Live every day, as the beloved of the Lord, in the experience that His love washes and cleanses, bears and blesses you all the day long. This love of His flowing into you will flow out again from you and make it your greatest joy to follow His example in washing the feet of others. Do not complain much of the lack of love and humility in others, but pray much that the Lord would awaken His people to their calling, truly so to follow in His footsteps that the world may see that they have taken Him for their example. And if you do not see it as soon as you wish in those around you, let it only urge you to more earnest prayer, that in you at least the Lord may have one who understands and proves that to love and serve like Jesus is the highest blessedness and joy, as well as the way, like Jesus, to be a blessing and a joy to others.

My Lord, I give myself to You, to live this blessed life of service. In You I have seen it, the spirit of a servant is a kingly spirit, come from heaven and lifting up to heaven, yes, the Spirit of God's own Son. Jesus, everlasting Love, dwell in me, and my life shall be like Yours, and the language of my life to others as Yours, "I am among you as the One who serves."

O glorified Son of God, You know how little of Your Spirit dwells in us, how this life of a servant is opposed to all that the world sees as honorable or proper. But You have come to teach us new lessons of what is right, to show us what is thought in heaven of the glory of being the least, of the blessedness of serving. My Lord, who not only gives new thoughts but implant new feelings, give me a heart like Yours, a heart full of the Holy Spirit, a heart that can love as You do. O Lord, Your Holy Spirit dwells within me, and Your fullness is my inheritance. In the joy of the Holy Spirit I can be as You are. I do yield myself to a life of service like Yours. Let the same mind be in me that was also in You, when You made Yourself of no reputation and took upon You the form of a servant, and being found in fashion as a man, humbled Yourself (see Phil. 2:5–8). Yes, Lord, that very same mind is in me, too, by Your grace. As a son of God, let me be the servant of men. Amen.

FOR FURTHER THOUGHT

1. *Jesus humbly served His disciples by washing their feet. In what specific ways can you selflessly and humbly serve others just as He served others?*
2. *What does it take for you to be a blessing to others, just as Jesus was a blessing to others?*
3. *How can you best bless and serve a loved one who is "unworthy"—just as Jesus loved and served Judas, the man He knew would betray Him? How can you bless and serve those who are ungrateful or who intentionally mistreat you?*

DAY 4

OUR HEAD

For to this you were called, because Christ also suffered for us,
leaving us an example, that you should follow His steps. . .
who Himself bore our sins in His own body on the tree,
that we, having died to sins, might live for righteousness.
1 PETER 2:21, 24

THE call to follow Christ's example, and to walk in His footsteps, is so high that there is every reason to ask with wonder, "How can it be expected of sinful men that they should walk like the Son of God?" The answer that most people give is, practically, that it cannot really be expected, for the command sets before us an ideal, beautiful but unattainable.[43]

The answer scripture gives is different. It points us to the wonderful relationship in which we stand to Christ. Because our union to Him sets in operation within us a heavenly life with all its powers, therefore the claim may be made in downright earnest that we should live as Christ did. The realization of this relationship between Christ and His people is necessary for everyone who is in earnest in following Christ's example.

And what is now this relationship? It is threefold. Peter speaks in this passage of Christ as our *surety*, our *example*, and our *head*.

Christ is our *surety*. "Christ also suffered for us"— "who Himself bore our sins in His own body on the tree." As surety, Christ suffered and died in our *stead*. He bore our sin and broke at once its curse and power. As surety, He did what we could not do, what we now need not do.

Christ is also our *example*. In one sense His work is unique, but in another we have to follow Him in it: we must do as He did, live and suffer like Him. "Christ also suffered for us, leaving us an example that we should follow in His steps." His suffering as my surety calls me to a suffering like His as my example. But is this reasonable? In His suffering, as surety He had the power of the divine nature, and how can I be expected in the weakness of the flesh to suffer as He did? Is there not an impassable gulf between these two things that Peter unites so closely, the suffering as surety and the suffering as example? No, there is a blessed third aspect of Christ's work, which bridges that gulf, which is the connecting link between Christ as surety

[43] See note.

and Christ as example, which makes it possible for us in very deed to take the surety as example, and live and suffer and die like Him.

Christ is also our *head*. In this His suretyship and His example have their root and unity. Christ is the second Adam (see 1 Cor. 15:45). As a believer, I am spiritually one with Him. In this union He lives in me and imparts to me the power of His finished work, the power of His sufferings and death and resurrection. It is on this ground we are taught in Romans 6 and elsewhere that the Christian is indeed dead to sin and alive to God. The very life that Christ lives, the life that passed through death and the power of that death, work in the believer so that he is dead and has risen again with Christ. It is this thought Peter gives utterance to when he says: "Who Himself bore our sins. . .on the tree," not alone that we through His death might receive forgiveness, but "that we, having *died to sins, might live* for righteousness." As we have part in the spiritual death of the first Adam, having really died to God in him, so we have part in the second Adam, having really died to sin in Him, and in Him being made alive again to God. Christ is not only our surety who lived and died for us, our example who showed us how to live and die, but also our head, with whom we are one, in whose death we have died, with whose life we now live. This gives us the power to follow our surety as our example: Christ being our head is the bond that makes the believing on the surety and the following of the example inseparably one.

These three are one. The three truths may not be separated from each other. And yet this happens but too often. There are some who wish to follow Christ's example without faith in His atonement. They seek within themselves the power to live like Him, but their efforts must be vain. There are others who hold firmly to the suretyship but neglect the example. They believe in redemption through the blood of the cross, but neglect the footsteps of Him who bore it. Faith in the atonement is indeed the foundation of the building, but it is not all. Theirs, too, is a deficient Christianity, with no true view of sanctification, because they do not see how, along with faith in Christ's atonement, following His example is indispensably necessary.

There are still others who have received these two truths—Christ as surety and Christ as example—and yet lack something. They feel constrained to follow Christ as example in what He did as surety, but lack the power. They do not rightly understand how this following His example can really be attained. What they need is the clear insight as to what scripture teaches of Christ as head. Because the surety is not someone outside of me, but One in whom I am, and who is in me, therefore it is that I can become like Him. His very life lives in me. He lives Himself in me, whom He bought with His blood. To follow His footsteps is a duty, because it is a possibility, the natural result of the wonderful union between head and members. It is only when this is rightly understood that the blessed truth of Christ's example will take its rightful place. If Jesus Himself through His life union will work in me the life likeness, then my duty becomes plain, but glorious. I have, on the one side, to gaze on His example so as to know and follow it. On the other side, to abide in Him and open my heart to the blessed workings of His life in me. As surely as He conquered sin and its curse for me will He conquer it in its power in me. What He began by His death for me, He will perfect by His life in me. Because my surety is also my head, His example must and will be the rule of my life.

> If Jesus Himself through His life union will work in me the life likeness, then my duty becomes plain, but glorious.

There is a saying of Augustine that is often quoted: "Lord, give what You command, and command what You will." This holds true here. If the Lord, who lives in me, *gives* what He requires of me, then no requirement can be too high. Then I have the courage to gaze on His holy example in all its height and breadth, and to accept of it as the law of my conduct. It is no longer merely a command telling what I must be, but a promise of what I shall be.

There is nothing that weakens the power of Christ's example so much as the thought that we cannot really walk like Him. Do not listen to such thoughts. The perfect likeness in heaven is begun on earth, and it can grow with each day and become more visible as life goes on. As certain and mighty as the work of surety that Christ, your head, completed once for all, is the renewal after His own image, which He is still working out. Let this double blessing make the cross doubly precious: Our head suffered as a surety so that in union with us He might bear sin for us. Our head offered as an example so that He might show us what the path is in which, in union with Himself, He would lead us to victory and to glory. The suffering Christ is our head, our surety, and our example.

And so the great lesson I have to learn is the wonderful truth that it is just in that mysterious path of suffering, in which He accomplished our atonement and redemption, that we are to follow His footsteps, and that the full experience of that redemption depends on the personal fellowship in that suffering. "Christ suffered for us, leaving us an example." May the Holy Spirit reveal to me what this means.

Precious Savior! How shall I thank You for the work that You have done as surety? Standing in the place of me, a guilty sinner, You have borne my sins in Your body on the cross. That cross was my due. You took it and were made like me, that the cross might be changed this way into a place of blessing and life.

And now You call me to the place of crucifixion as the place of blessing and life, where I may be made like You and may find in You power to suffer and to cease from sin. As my head, You were my surety to suffer and die with me. As my head, You are my example that I might suffer and die with You.

Precious Savior! I confess that I have too little understood this. Your surety-ship was more to me than Your example. I rejoiced much that You have borne the cross for me, but too little that I, like You and with You, might also bear the cross. The atonement of the cross was more precious to me than the fellowship of the cross, the hope in Your redemption more precious than the personal fellowship with Yourself.

> *C*hrist suffered for us, leaving us an example."
> May the Holy Spirit reveal to me what this means.

Forgive me for this, dear Lord, and teach me to find my happiness in union with You, my head, not more in Your suretyship than in Your example. And grant that, in my meditations as to how I am to follow You, my faith may become stronger and brighter. Jesus is my example because He is my life. I must and can be like Him, because I am one with Him. Grant this, my blessed Lord, for Your love's sake. Amen.

FOR FURTHER THOUGHT

1. *How do most believers respond to the call and command to walk as Jesus walked, to live the way He lived? How is that response different from what you read in the Bible about walking as He walked?*
2. *In suffering for you, Jesus Christ set for you a perfect example of obedience, service, and love. How can you learn to follow that example?*
3. *What is your duty in response to Jesus working in you His likeness? How can you best carry out that duty?*

THOMAS à Kempis has said, 'All men wish to be with Christ, and to belong to His people, but few are really willing to follow the life of Christ.' There are many who imagine that to imitate Jesus Christ is an especially advanced state in the Christian life, to which only a few elect can attain. They think that one can be a real Christian if he only confesses his weakness and sin, and holds firmly to the Word and sacrament, *without attaining any real confirm to the life of Christ*. They even count it pride and fanaticism if one venture to say that *conformity to the likeness of Jesus Christ is an indispensable sign of the true Christian*. And yet our Lord says to all without exception: 'He who does not take his cross and follow after Me is not worthy of Me' (Matt. 10:38). He mentions expressly the most difficult thing in His life—the cross, that which includes all else. And Peter writes not to some but to the whole Church: Christ also suffered for us, leaving us an example, that you should follow His steps.

"It is a sad sign that these unmistakable commands have been so darkened in our modern Christianity that our leading ministers and church members have quietly, as by common consent, agreed to rob these words of their sting. A false dogmatic must bear no small share of the blame. To defend the divinity of our Savior against unbelief, men have presented and defended His divine nature with such exclusiveness that it became impossible to form any real living conception of His humanity. It is not enough that we admit that Christ was a true man. No one can form any true idea of this humanity who is ever afraid to lose the true Christ, if he does not every moment ascribe to Him divine power and omniscience. For, of a truth, if Christ's suffering and cross are only and altogether something supernatural, we must cease to speak of the imitation of Christ in any true or real sense of the word.

"Oh, the gulf of separation which comes between the life of Christ and the life of Christians when the relationship between them is only an external one! And how slow and complacent the Church of our day is to apply the great and distinct rule so clearly laid down in the life of Christ to the filling of these gulfs and the correcting of the disorders of our modern life. The church of Christ will not be brought again out of her confusions until *the faithful actual imitation of her Lord and Head again become the banner round which she rallies His disciples*." [44]

---

[44] From M. Diemer, *Een nieuw boek over de navolging van Jesus Christus* (A New Book on the Imitation of Jesus Christ).

DAY 5

IN SUFFERING WRONG

For this is commendable, if because of conscience toward God one
endures grief, suffering wrongfully. For what credit is it if,
when you are beaten for your faults, you take it patiently?
But when you do good and suffer, if you take
it patiently, this is commendable before God.
1 PETER 2:19–20

IT is in connection with a very everyday matter that Peter gave utterance to those weighty words concerning Christ as our surety and example. He is writing to servants, who, at that time were mostly slaves. He teaches them "to be submissive to your masters with all fear" (1 Pet. 2:18), not only to the good and gentle, but also to the harsh. For, so he writes, if any one does wrong and is punished for it, to bear it patiently is no special grace. No, but if one does well and suffers for it and takes it patiently, this is acceptable with God, for such bearing of wrong is Christlike. In bearing our sins as surety, Christ suffered wrong from man, and after His example we must be ready to suffer wrongfully, too.

There is almost nothing harder to bear than injustice from our fellow men. It is not only the loss of pain, but there is the feeling of humiliation and injustice, and the consciousness of our rights asserts itself. In what our fellow creatures do to us, it is not easy at once to recognize the will of God, who allows us to be tried this way to see if we have truly taken Christ as our example. Let us study that example. From Him we may learn what it was that gave Him the power to bear injuries patiently.

Christ believed in suffering as the will of God. He had found it in scripture that the servant of God should suffer. He had made Himself familiar with the thought, so that when suffering came, it did not take Him by surprise. He expected it. He knew that through it He must be perfected, and so His first thought was not how to be delivered from it, but how to glorify God in it. This enabled Him to bear the greatest injustice quietly. He saw God's hand in it.

Christian! Do you desire to have strength to suffer wrong in the spirit in which Christ did? Accustom yourself in everything that happens to recognize the hand and will of God. This lesson is of more consequence than you think. Whether it is some great wrong that is done you, or some little offense that you meet in daily life, before you fix your thoughts on the person who did it, first be still, and remember, *God allows me to come into this trouble to see if I shall glorify Him in it.* Then in the rest of soul which this gives, I shall receive wisdom to know how to behave in it. With my eye turned from man to God, suffering wrong is not so hard as it seems.

> *C*hrist believed in suffering as the will of God. He had found it in scripture that the servant of God should suffer. He had made Himself familiar with the thought, so that when suffering came, it did not take Him by surprise.

Christ also believed that God would care for His rights and honor. There is an innate sense of right within us that comes from God. But he who lives in the visible wants his honor to be vindicated at once here below. He who lives in the eternal, and as seeing the invisible, is satisfied to leave the vindication of his rights and honor in God's hands, for he knows that they are safe with Him. It was that way with the Lord Jesus. Peter writes, "He committed Himself to Him who judges righteously" (1 Pet. 2:23). It was a settled thing between the Father and the Son that the Son was not to care for His own honor, but only for the Father's. The Father would care for the Son's honor. Let the Christian just follow Christ's example in this, and it will give him such rest and peace. Give your right and your honor into God's keeping. Meet every offense that man commits against you with the firm trust that God will watch over and care for you. Commit it to Him who judges righteously.

Further, *Christ believed in the power of suffering love.* We all admit that there is no power like that of love. Through it Christ overcomes the enmity of the world. Every other victory gives only a forced submission, but love alone gives the true victory over an enemy, by converting him into a friend. We all acknowledge the truth of this as a principle, but we shrink from the application. Christ believed it, and acted accordingly. He said, too, "I shall have my revenge," but His revenge was that of love, bringing enemies as friends to His feet. He believed that by silence and submission, and suffering and bearing wrong, He would win the cause, because through these things love would have its triumph.

And this is what He desires of us, too. In our sinful nature there is more faith in might and right than in the heavenly power of love. But he who would be like Christ must follow Him in this also, that He seeks to conquer evil with good. *The more another does him wrong, the more he feels called to love him.* Even if it be needed for the public welfare that justice should punish the offender, he takes care that there be in it nothing of personal feeling. As far as he is concerned, he forgives and loves.

Ah, what a difference it would make in Christianity and in our churches if

Christ's example were followed! If each one who was reviled "did not revile in return," if each one who suffered "did not threaten, but committed himself to Him who judges righteously." Fellow Christians, this is literally what the Father would have us do. Let us read and read again the words of Peter, until our soul is filled with the thought, "But when you do good and suffer, if you take it patiently, *this is commendable before God*."[45]

In ordinary Christian life, where we mostly seek to fulfill our calling as redeemed ones in our own strength, such a conformity to the Lord's image is an impossibility. But in a life of full surrender, where we have given all into His hands, in the faith that He will work all in us, there the glorious expectation is awakened, that the imitation of Christ in this is indeed within our reach. For the command to suffer like Christ has come in connection with the teaching, "Christ also suffered for us...that we, having died to sins, might live for righteousness" (1 Pet. 2:21, 24).

> *L*et us read and read again the words of Peter, until our soul is filled with the thought, "But when you do good and suffer, if you take it patiently, this is commendable before God."

Beloved fellow Christian! Would you not love to be like Jesus, and in bearing injuries act as He Himself would have acted in your place? Is it not a glorious prospect in everything, even in this, too, to be conformed to Him? For our strength it is too high, but in His strength it is possible. Only surrender yourself day by day to Him to be in all things just what He wants to have you to be. Believe that He lives in heaven to be the life and the strength of each one who seeks to walk in His footsteps. Yield yourself to be one with the suffering, crucified Christ so that you may understand what it is to be dead to sins and to live to righteousness. And it will be your joyful experience what wonderful power there is in Jesus' death, not only to atone for sin, but to break its power; and in His resurrection, to make you live to righteousness. You shall find it *equally blessed to follow fully the footsteps of the suffering Savior* as it has been to trust fully and only in that suffering for atonement and redemption. Christ will be as precious as your example as He has ever been as your surety. Because He took your sufferings upon Himself, you will lovingly take His sufferings on yourself. And bearing wrong will become a glorious part of the fellowship with His holy sufferings, a glorious mark of being conformed to His most holy likeness, a most blessed fruit of the true life of faith.

O Lord my God, I have heard Your precious word: If one endures grief, suffering wrongfully, and takes it patiently, this is commendable before God. This is indeed a sacrifice that is well-pleasing to You, a work that Your own grace alone

---

[45] See note.

has accomplished, a fruit of the suffering of Your beloved Son, of the example He left, and the power He gives in virtue of His having destroyed the power of sin.

O my Father, teach me and all Your children to aim at nothing less than complete conformity to Your dear Son in this trait of His blessed image. Lord my God, I want to now, once for all, give up the keeping of my honor and my rights into Your hands, never more again myself to take responsibility for them. You will care for them most perfectly. May my only care be the honor and the rights of my Lord!

I specially ask You to fill me with faith in the conquering power of suffering love. Allow me to understand fully how the suffering Lamb of God teaches us that patience and silence and suffering accomplish more with God, and therefore with man, too, than might or right. O my Father, I must, I want to walk in the footsteps of my Lord Jesus. Let Your Holy Spirit, and the light of Your love and presence, be my guide and strength. Amen.

FOR FURTHER THOUGHT

1. *What was Jesus' approach to enduring His own suffering? From where did He get that approach? What does His approach teach you about enduring your own suffering?*
2. *How can you acquire the strength to suffer the wrong done to you in just the same way as Jesus suffered the wrongs done to Him?*
3. *What is the wrong way to be conformed to the image of Jesus Christ? What is the right way?*

WHAT is it you say, My son? Cease from complaining, when you consider My passion and the sufferings of My other saints. Do not say, 'To suffer this from such a one, it is more than I can or may do. He has done me great wrong, and accused me of things I never thought of. Of another I might bear it, if I thought I deserved it, but not from him!' Such thoughts are very foolish. Instead of thinking of patience in suffering, or of Him by whom it will be crowned, we only are occupied with the injury done to us and the person who has done it. No, he does not deserve the name of patient *who is only willing to suffer as much as he thinks proper, and from whom he pleases*. The truly patient man does not ask from whom he suffers—his superior, his equal, or his inferior—or whether from a good and holy man, or one who is perverse and unworthy. But from whomever, how much, or how often wrong is done to him, he accepts it all as from the hand of God and counts it gain. For with God it is impossible that anything suffered for His sake should pass without its reward.

"O Lord, let that become possible to me by Your grace which by nature seems impossible. Grant that the suffering wrong may by Your love be made pleasant to me. To suffer for Your sake is most healthful to my soul."[46]

[46] From Thomas à Kempis, *Of the Imitation of Christ*. That the suffering of wrong is the proof of true patience.

DAY 6
CRUCIFIED WITH HIM

I have been crucified with Christ; it is no longer I who live,
but Christ lives in me. . . . But God forbid that I should boast
except in the cross of our Lord Jesus Christ, by whom the
world has been crucified to me, and I to the world.
GALATIANS 2:20, 6:14

TAKING up the cross was always spoken of by Christ as the test of discipleship. On three different occasions (Matt. 10:38, 16:24; Luke 14:27) we find the words repeated, "If anyone desires to come after Me, let him. . .take up his cross, and follow Me." While the Lord was still on His way to the cross, this expression—taking up the cross—was the most appropriate to indicate that conformity to Him to which the disciple is called.[47] But now that He has been crucified, the Holy Spirit gives another expression, in which our entire conformity to Christ is still more powerfully set forth—the believing disciple is himself crucified with Christ. The cross is the chief mark of the Christian as of Christ: the crucified Christ and the crucified Christian belong to each other. The chief element of likeness to Christ consists in being crucified with Him. Whoever wishes to be like Him must seek to understand the secret of fellowship with His cross.

At first sight the Christian who seeks conformity to Jesus is afraid of this truth. He shrinks from the painful suffering and death with which the thought of the cross is connected. As His spiritual discernment becomes clearer, however, this word becomes all his hope and joy, and he glories in the cross, because it makes him a partner in a death and victory that has already been accomplished, and in which the deliverance from the powers of the flesh and of the world has been secured to him. To understand this we must notice carefully the language of scripture.

"I have been crucified with Christ," Paul says; "it is no longer I who live, but Christ lives in me." Through faith in Christ we become partakers of Christ's life.

---

[47] See note. Christians entirely miss the point of the Lord's command when they refer the taking up of the cross only to the crosses or trials of life. It means much more. The cross means death. Taking up the cross means going out to die. It is just in the time of prosperity that we most need to bear the cross. Taking up the cross and following Him is nothing less than living every day with our own life and will given up to death.

That life is a life that has passed through the death of the cross, and in *which the power of that death is always working*. When I receive that life, I receive at the same time the full power of the death on the cross working in me in its never-ceasing energy. "I have been crucified with Christ; yet I live; and yet no longer I, but Christ liveth in me" (RV); the life I now live is not my own life, but the life of the Crucified One, is the life of the cross." The being crucified is a thing past and done: "Knowing this, that our old man *was* crucified with Him" (Rom. 6:6); "Those who are Christ's *have* crucified the flesh" (Gal. 5:24); "God forbid that I should boast except in the cross of our Lord Jesus Christ, by whom the world *has been* crucified to me, and I to the world" (Gal. 6:14). These texts all speak of something that has been done in Christ, and into which I am admitted by faith.

> *T*hrough faith in Christ we become partakers of Christ's life. That life is a life that has passed through the death of the cross, and in which the power of that death is always working.

It is of great consequence to understand this and to give bold utterance to the truth that I have been crucified with Christ, that I have crucified the flesh. I learn through this how perfectly I share in the finished work of Christ. If I am crucified and dead with Him, then I am a partner in His life and victory. I learn to understand the position I must take to allow the power of that cross and that death to manifest itself in mortifying or making dead the old man and the flesh in destroying the body of sin (see Rom. 6:6).

For there is still a great work for me to do. But that work is not to crucify myself, for I have been crucified; the old man was crucified, so the scripture speaks. But what I have to do is always to regard and treat it as crucified, and not to allow it to come down from the cross. I must maintain my crucifixion position. I must keep the flesh in the place of crucifixion. To realize the force of this I must notice an important distinction. I have been crucified and am dead. The old Adam was crucified but is not yet dead. When I gave myself to my crucified Savior, sin and flesh and all, He took me wholly, and I with my evil nature was taken up with Him in His crucifixion. But here a separation took place. In fellowship with Him, I was freed from the life of the flesh, and I myself died with Him. In the innermost center of my being, I received new life, and Christ lives in me.

But the flesh, in which I yet am, the old man that was crucified with Him remained condemned to an accursed death but is not yet dead. And now it is my calling, in fellowship with and in the strength of my Lord, to see that the old nature be kept nailed to the cross until the time comes that it is entirely destroyed. All its desires and affections cry out, "Come down from the cross. Save yourself and us." It is my duty to glory in the cross, and with my whole heart to maintain the dominion of the cross, and to set my seal to the sentence that has been pronounced, to make dead every uprising of sin, as already crucified, and so not to suffer it to have dominion. This is what scripture means when it says, "If by the Spirit you put to death the deeds of the body, you will live" (Rom. 8:13). "Make dead therefore your members which are upon the earth." Doing this, I continually and voluntarily acknowledge that in my flesh dwells no good thing, that my Lord is Christ the crucified One, that I have been crucified and am dead in Him, and that the flesh has been crucified and, though not yet dead, has been forever given over to the death of the cross. And so I live like Christ, in very deed crucified with Him.

In order to enter fully into the meaning and the power of this fellowship of the crucifixion of our Lord, two things are especially necessary to those who are Christ's followers. The first is the clear consciousness of their fellowship with the crucified One through faith. At conversion they became partakers of it without fully understanding it. Many remain in ignorance all their life long through a lack of spiritual knowledge.

> In fellowship with Him, I was freed from the life of the flesh, and I myself died with Him. In the innermost center of my being, I received new life, and Christ lives in me.

Brother, pray that the Holy Spirit may reveal to you your union to the crucified One. "I have been crucified with Christ," "I boast in the cross of Christ, through which I have been crucified to the world." Take such words of holy scripture, and by prayer and meditation make them your own, with a heart that expects and asks the Holy Spirit to make them living and effectual within you. Look at yourself in the light of God as what you really are, "crucified with Christ."

Then you will find the grace for the second thing you need to enable you to live as a crucified one, in whom Christ lives. You will be able always to look upon and to treat the flesh and the world as nailed to the cross. The old nature seeks continually to assert itself, to make you feel as if it is expecting too much that you should always live this crucifixion life. Your only safety is in fellowship with Christ.

"Through Him and His cross," says Paul, "I have been crucified to the world." In Him the crucifixion is an accomplished reality; in Him you have died, but also have been made alive. Christ lives in you. With this fellowship of His cross let it be with you the deeper the better, for it brings you into deeper communion with His life and His love. To be crucified with Christ means being freed from the power of sin, being a redeemed one, a conqueror. Remember that the Holy Spirit has been specially provided to glorify Christ in you, to reveal within you and make your very own all that is in Christ for you.

Do not be satisfied, as with so many others, only to know the cross in its power to atone, for the glory of the cross is that it was not only to Jesus the path to life, but that each moment it can become to us the power that destroys sin and death and keeps us in the power of the eternal life. Learn from your Savior the holy art of using it for this. Faith in the power of the cross and its victory will day by day make dead the deeds of the body, the lusts of the flesh. This faith will teach you to count the cross, with its continual death to self, all your glory. Because you regard the cross, not as one who is still on the way to crucifixion, with the prospect of a painful death, but as one to whom the crucifixion is past, who already lives in Christ and now only bears the cross as the blessed instrument through which the body of sin is done away (see Rom. 6:6). The banner under which complete victory over sin and the world is to be won is the cross.

Above all, remember what still remains the chief thing. It is Jesus, the living, loving Savior, who Himself enables you to be like Him in all things. His sweet fellowship, His tender love, His heavenly power—make it a blessedness and joy to be like Him, the crucified One, make the crucifixion life a life of resurrection joy and power. In Him the two are inseparably connected. In Him you have the strength to be always singing the triumphant song: God forbid that I should boast except in the cross of our Lord Jesus Christ, by whom the world has been crucified to me, and I to the world.

> *Faith in the power of the cross and its victory will day by day make dead the deeds of the body, the lusts of the flesh.*

Precious Savior, I humbly ask You to show me the hidden glory of the fellowship of Your cross. The cross was my place, the place of death and curse. You became like us and have been crucified with us. And now the cross is Your place, the place of blessing and life. And You call me to become like You, and as one who is crucified with You, to experience how entirely the cross has made me free from sin.

Lord, teach me to know its full power. It is long since I knew the power of the cross to redeem from the curse. But how long I strove in vain as a redeemed one to overcome the power of sin and to obey the Father as You have done! I could not break the power of sin. But now I see that this comes only when Your disciple yields himself entirely to be led by Your Holy Spirit into the fellowship of Your cross. There You allow him to see how the cross *has broken forever* the power of sin and has made him free. There You, the crucified One, live in him and impart to him Your own Spirit of wholehearted self-sacrifice in casting out and conquering sin. Oh, my Lord, teach me to understand this better. In this faith I say, "I have been crucified with Christ." Oh, You who loved me to the death, not Your cross, but Yourself the crucified One, You are He whom I seek, and in whom I hope. Take me, crucified One, and hold me firmly, and teach me from moment to moment to look upon all that is of self as condemned and only worthy to be crucified. Take me, hold me, and teach me, from moment to moment, that in You I have all I need for a life of holiness and blessing. Amen.

FOR FURTHER THOUGHT

1. *Read Matthew 10:38, 16:24, and Luke 14:27. What is your test of true discipleship?*
2. *What do you lose in fellowship with Christ and His suffering? What amazing blessing do you gain in that fellowship?*
3. *The Bible teaches that in the cross is the power to atone for your sins. For what else does the cross have power for you?*

JESUS has now many lovers of His heavenly kingdom, but few bearers of His cross. He has many who desire His comfort, but few His tribulation; many who are willing to share His table, few His fasting. All are willing to rejoice with Him, few will endure anything for Him. Many follow Jesus into the breaking of bread, but few to drink of the cup from which He drank. Many glory in His miracles, few in the shame of His cross."[48]

"To many it seems a hard speech, 'Deny yourself, take up your cross, and follow Jesus.' But it will be much harder to bear that other word, 'Depart from me, you cursed' (Matt. 25:41), for only they who now hear and follow the word of the cross shall then have no fear of the word of condemnation. For the sign of the cross will be seen in the heaven when the Lord comes to judgment, and all the servants of the cross, who in their lifetime have been conformed to Christ crucified, will then draw near to Christ their judge with great confidence. Why, then, do you fear to take up the cross that makes you fit for the kingdom? In the cross is life, in the cross is salvation. The cross defends against all enemies. In the cross there is the infusion of all heavenly sweetness. In the cross is strength of mind, joy of spirit. The cross is the height of virtue and the perfection of sanctity. There is no happiness for the soul but in the cross. Take up, therefore, your cross and follow Jesus, and you shall live forever.

"If you bear the cross cheerfully, it will bear you. If you bear it unwillingly, you make for yourself a burden that you still have to bear. What saint was there ever who did not bear the cross? Even Christ must suffer. How then do you seek any other way than this, which is the royal way, the way of the sacred cross?

"He who willingly submits to the cross, to him its whole burden is changed into a sweet assurance of divine comfort. And the more the flesh is broken down by the cross, the more the spirit is strengthened by inward grace. It is not in man by nature to bear the cross, to love the cross, to deny self, to bring the body into subjection, and willingly to endure suffering. If you look to yourself, you can accomplish none of this. But if you trust in the Lord, strength shall be given you from heaven, and the world and the flesh shall be made subject to your rule. Set yourself, therefore, to bear manfully the cross of your Lord, who out of love was crucified for you.

"Know for certain that you should lead a dying life, for the more any man dies to himself, the more he lives to God. Surely, if there had been any better thing, and more profitable to man's salvation, than bearing the cross, Christ would have showed it us by word and example. But now He calls all who would follow Him plainly to do this one thing, daily to bear the cross."[49]

---

[48] From Thomas à Kempis, *Of the Imitation of Christ.* That the lovers of the cross of Jesus are few.
[49] From Thomas à Kempis, *Of the Imitation of Christ.* Of the royal way of the sacred cross.

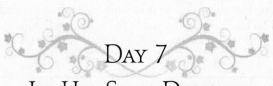

Day 7
In His Self-Denial

We then who are strong ought to bear with the scruples
of the weak, and not to please ourselves. Let each of us please his
neighbor for his good, leading to edification. For even Christ did
not please Himself; but as it is written, "The reproaches of those who
reproached You fell on Me."...Therefore receive one another,
just as Christ also received us, to the glory of God.
Romans 15:1-3, 7

"If anyone desires to come after Me,
let him deny himself, and take up his cross, and follow Me."
Matthew 16:24

EVEN *Christ did not please Himself:* He bore the reproaches, with which men reproached and dishonored God, so patiently so that He might glorify God and save man. Christ pleased not Himself: with reference both to God and man, this word is the key of His life. In this, too, His life is our rule and example; we who are strong ought not to please ourselves.

To deny self—this is the opposite of pleasing self. When Peter denied Christ, he said: "I do not know the man. I have nothing to do with Him and His interests. I do not wish to be counted His friend." In the same way the true Christian denies himself, the old man: "I do not know this old man. I will have nothing to do with him and his interests." And when shame and dishonor come upon him, or anything be demanded that is not pleasant to the old nature, he simply says: "Do as you like with the old ties of the Adam, for I will take no notice of it. Through the cross of Christ I am crucified to the world, and the flesh, and self. To the friendship and interest of this old man I am a stranger. I deny him to be my friend, and I deny his every claim and wish. I do not know him."

The Christian who only thinks of his salvation from curse and condemnation cannot understand this, so he finds it impossible to deny self. Although he may sometimes try to do so, his life mainly consists in pleasing himself. The Christian who has taken Christ as his pattern cannot be content with this. He has surrendered himself to seek the most complete fellowship with the cross of Christ.

The Holy Spirit has taught him to say, "I have been crucified with Christ, and so am dead to sin and self." In fellowship with Christ he sees the old man crucified, a condemned troublemaker he is ashamed to have as a friend. It is his fixed purpose—and he has received the power for it, too—no longer to please his old nature, but to deny it. *Because the crucified Christ is his life, self-denial is the law of his life.*

> *Through the cross of Christ I am crucified to the world, and the flesh, and self. To the friendship and interest of this old man I am a stranger.*

This self-denial extends itself over the whole domain of life. It was so with the Lord Jesus and is so with everyone who longs to follow Him perfectly. This self-denial has not so much to do with what is sinful, and unlawful, and contrary to the laws of God, as with what is lawful, or apparently indifferent. To the self-denying spirit the will and glory of God and the salvation of man are always more than our own interests or pleasure.

Before we can know how to please our neighbor, self-denial must first exercise itself in our own personal life. It must rule the body. The holy fasting of Him who said, "Man shall not live by bread alone, but by every word that proceeds from the mouth of God" (Matt. 4:4), and who would not eat until His Father gave Him food, and until His Father's work was done, teaches the believer a holy self-control in eating and drinking. The holy poverty of Him who had no place to lay His head teaches him so to regulate the possession, and use, and enjoyment of earthly things that he may always possess as not possessing. After the example of the holy suffering of Him who bore all our sins in His own body on the tree, he learns to bear all suffering patiently. Even in the body as the temple of the Holy Spirit, he desires to bear about the dying of the Lord Jesus. With Paul he keeps under the body and brings it into subjection—all its desires and appetites he would have ruled by the self-denial of Jesus. He does not please himself.

This self-denial keeps watch over the spirit, too. His own wisdom and judgment the believer brings into subjection to God's Word; he gives up his own thoughts to the teaching of the Word and the Spirit. Toward man he manifests the same self-denial of his own wisdom in a readiness to hear and learn, in the meekness and humility with which, even when he knows he is in the right, he gives his opinion in the desire always to find and to acknowledge what is good in others.

And then self-denial has special reference to the heart. All the affections and desires are placed under it. The will, the kingly power of the soul, is especially under its control. As little as self-pleasing could be a part of Christ's life, may

Christ's follower allow it always to influence his conduct. "We ought not to please ourselves. For even Christ did not please Himself" (see Rom. 15:1, 3). Self-denial is the law of his life.

Nor does he find it hard when once he has truly surrendered himself to it. To one who, with a divided heart, seeks to force himself to a life of self-denial, it is hard indeed, but to one who has yielded himself to it unreservedly, because he has with his whole heart accepted the cross to destroy the power of sin and self, the blessing it brings more than compensates for apparent sacrifice or loss. He hardly dares any longer speak of self-denial, for there is such blessedness in becoming conformed to the image of Jesus.

Self-denial does not have its value with God, as some think, from the measure of pain it causes. No, for this pain is very much caused by the remaining reluctance to practice it. But it has its highest worth in that meek or even joyful acquiescence which counts nothing a sacrifice for Jesus' sake, and feels surprised when others speak of self-denial.

> *B*efore we can know how to please our neighbor, self-denial must first exercise itself in our own personal life. It must rule the body.

There have been ages when men thought they must fly to the wilderness or monastery to deny themselves. The Lord Jesus has shown us that the best place to practice self-denial is in our ordinary interaction with men. So Paul also says here, "We *ought not to please ourselves. Let each of us please his neighbor for his good, leading to edification. For even Christ did not please Himself.* . . . Therefore receive one another, *just as Christ* also received us" (Rom. 15:1–3, 7). Nothing less than the self-denial of our Lord, who did not please Himself, is our law. What He was we must be. What He did we must do.

What a glorious life it will be in the Church of Christ when this law prevails! Each one considers it the object of existence to make others happy. Each one denies himself, seeks not his own, esteems others better than himself. All thought of taking offense, of wounded pride, of being slighted or passed by, would pass away. As a follower of Christ, each would seek to bear the weak and to please his neighbor. The true self-denial would be seen in this, that no one would think of himself but would live in and for others.

"If anyone desires to *come after Me,* let him deny himself, and take up his cross, and *follow Me.*" This word not only gives us the will but also the power for self-denial. He who does not simply wish to reach heaven through Christ, but comes after Him for His own sake, will *follow* Him. And in his heart Jesus speedily takes the place that self had. *Jesus only* becomes the center and object of such a life. The undivided surrender to follow Him is crowned with this wonderful blessing, that

Christ by His Spirit Himself becomes his life. Christ's spirit of self-denying love is poured out on him, and to deny self is the greatest joy of his heart, and the means of the deepest communion with God. Self-denial is no longer a work he simply does as a means of attaining perfection for himself. Nor is it merely a negative victory, of which the main feature is the keeping self in check. Christ has taken the place of self, and His love and gentleness and kindness flow out to others, now that self is parted with. No command becomes more blessed or more natural than this: "*We ought not to please ourselves, for even Christ did not please Himself.*" "If any man desires to come after Me, let him deny himself, and FOLLOW ME."

> *I*f anyone desires to come after Me, let him deny himself, and take up his cross, and follow Me." This word not only gives us the will but also the power for self-denial.

Beloved Lord, I thank You for this new call to follow You and not to please myself, just as You did not please Yourself. I thank You that I have now no longer, as once, to hear it with fear. Your commandments are no longer grievous to me, for Your yoke is easy and Your burden light (see Matt. 11:30). What I see in Your life on earth as my example is the certain pledge of what I receive from Your life in heaven. I did not always so understand it. Long after I had known You, I dared not think of self-denial. But for him who has learned what it is to take up the cross, to be crucified with You, and to see the old man nailed to the cross, it is no longer terrible to deny it. Oh, my Lord! Who would not be ashamed to be the friend of a crucified and accursed criminal? Since I have learned that You are my life, and that You wholly take charge of the life that is wholly entrusted to You, to work both to will and to do, I do not fear, for You will give me the love and wisdom in the path of self-denial joyfully to follow Your footsteps. Blessed Lord, Your disciples are not worthy of this grace. But since You have chosen us to it, we will gladly seek not to please ourselves, but everyone his neighbor, as You have taught us. And may Your Holy Spirit work it in us mightily. Amen.

FOR FURTHER THOUGHT

1. *Read Romans 15:1–3, 7. What are we who are strong in the faith to do for those who are weak? How did Christ set an example of this?*
2. *God's Word commands us to please our neighbor and not ourselves. What are the evidences that you are living to please and to bless others and not just yourself?*
3. *What exactly did Jesus mean when He said, "If anyone desires to come after Me, let him deny himself, and take up his cross, and follow Me"? What does understanding His meaning give you?*

Day 8

In His Self-Sacrifice

*And walk in love, as Christ also has loved us and
given Himself for us, an offering and a sacrifice
to God for a sweet-smelling aroma.*
EPHESIANS 5:2

*By this we know love, because He laid down His life for us.
And we also ought to lay down our lives for the brethren.*
1 JOHN 3:16

WHAT is the connection between self-sacrifice and self-denial? The former is the root from which the latter springs. In self-denial, self-sacrifice is tested, and thus strengthened and prepared each time again to renew its entire surrender. That is how it was with the Lord Jesus. His incarnation was a self-sacrifice, and His life of self-denial was the proof of it. Through this, again, He was prepared for the great act of self-sacrifice in His death on the cross. This is how it is with the Christian. His conversion is to a certain extent the sacrifice of self, though but a very partial one, due to ignorance and weakness. From that first act of self-surrender arises the obligation to the exercise of daily self-denial. The Christian's efforts to do so show him his weakness and prepare him for that new and more entire self-sacrifice, in which he first finds strength for more continuous self-denial.

Self-sacrifice is of the very essence of true love. The very nature and blessedness of love consist in forgetting self and seeking its happiness in the loved one. Where in the beloved there is a desire or need, love is impelled by its very nature to offer up its own happiness for that of the other, to unite itself to the beloved one, and at any sacrifice to make him the sharer of its own blessedness.

Who can say whether this is not one of the secrets that eternity will reveal, that sin was permitted because otherwise God's love could never so fully have been revealed? The highest glory of God's love was manifested in the self-sacrifice of Christ. It is the highest glory of the Christian to be like his Lord in this. Without entire self-sacrifice the new command, the command of love, cannot be fulfilled. Without entire self-sacrifice we cannot love as Jesus loved. "Be imitators of God," says the apostle, "and walk in love, as Christ also has loved us and given Himself for us, an offering and a sacrifice" (Eph. 5:1–2). Let all your walk and conversation be, according to Christ's example, in love. It was this love that made His sacrifice acceptable in God's sight, a sweet-smelling aroma. As His love exhibited itself in self-sacrifice, let your love prove itself to be conformable to His in the daily self-sacrifice for the welfare of others, and so will it also be acceptable in the sight of God. "We also ought to lay down our lives for the brethren."

Self-sacrifice is of the very essence of true love. The very nature and blessedness of love consist in forgetting self and seeking its happiness in the loved one.

Down even into the daily affairs of home life, in the relationship between husband and wife, in the relationship of master and servant, Christ's self-sacrifice must be the rule of our walk. "Husbands, love your wives, just as Christ also loved the church and *gave Himself for her*" (Eph. 5:25).

And mark specially the words, "Has given Himself *for us*, an offering *to God*." We see that self-sacrifice has here two sides. Christ's self-sacrifice had a Godward as well as a manward aspect. It was *for us*, but it was *to God* that He offered Himself as a sacrifice. In all our self-sacrifice there must be these two sides in union, though now the one and then again the other may be more prominent.[50]

It is only when we sacrifice ourselves *to God* that there will be the power for an entire self-sacrifice. The Holy Spirit reveals to the believer the right of God's claim on us, how we are not our own, but His. The realization of how absolutely we are God's property, bought and paid for with blood, of how we are loved with such a wonderful love, and of what blessedness there is in the full surrender to Him, leads the believer to yield himself a whole burnt offering. He lays himself on the altar of consecration, and he finds it his highest joy to be a sweet-smelling aroma *to his God*, God-devoted and God-accepted. And then it becomes his first and most earnest desire to know how God would have him show this entire self-sacrifice in life and walk.

God points him to Christ's example. He was a sweet-smelling aroma to God when He gave Himself a sacrifice *for us*. For every Christian who gives himself entirely to His service, God has the same honor as He had for His Son. He uses him as an instrument of blessing to others. Therefore John says, "He who does not love his brother whom he has seen, how can he love God whom he has not seen?" (1 John 4:20). The self-sacrifice in which you have devoted yourself to God's service binds you also to serve your fellowmen, for the same act that makes you entirely God's makes you entirely theirs.

It is just this surrender to God that gives the power for self-sacrifice toward others, and even makes it a joy. When faith has first appropriated the promise,

[50] See note.

"inasmuch as you did it to one of the least of these My brethren, you did it to Me" (Matt. 25:20), I understand the glorious harmony between sacrifice *to God* and sacrifice *for men*. My interaction with my fellowmen, instead of being, as many complain, a hindrance to unbroken communion with God, becomes an opportunity of offering myself unceasingly to Him.

Blessed calling! To walk in love JUST AS Christ loved us and gave Himself for us a sacrifice and sweet-smelling aroma to God. Only this way can the church fulfill her destiny and prove to the world that she is set apart to continue Christ's work of self-sacrificing love, and fill up that which remains behind of the afflictions of Christ.

But does God really expect us to deny ourselves so entirely for others? Is it not asking too much? Can anyone really sacrifice himself so entirely? Christian! God does expect it. Nothing less than this is the conformity to the image of His Son, to which He predestinated you from eternity. This is the path by which Jesus entered into His glory and blessedness, and by no other way can the disciple enter into the joy of His Lord. *It is in very deed our calling to become exactly like Jesus in His love and self-sacrifice.* "Walk in love, AS Christ loved" (see Eph. 5:2).

> *It is only when we sacrifice ourselves to God that there will be the power for an entire self-sacrifice.*

It is a great thing when a believer sees and acknowledges this. That God's people and even God's servants understand it so little is one great cause of the powerlessness of the Church. In this matter the Church indeed needs a second reformation. In the great Reformation centuries ago, the power of Christ's atoning death and righteousness were brought to light, to the great comfort and joy of anxious souls. But we need a second reformation to lift on high the banner of Christ's example as our law, to restore the truth of the power of Christ's resurrection as it makes us partakers of the life and the likeness of our Lord. Christians must not only believe in the full union with their surety for their reconciliation, but with their head as their example and their life. They must really represent Christ on earth and let men *see in the members* how the Head lived when He was in the flesh. Let us earnestly pray that God's children everywhere may be taught to see their holy calling.

And all you who already long after it, oh, do not be afraid to yield yourselves to God in the great act of a Christlike self-sacrifice! In conversion you gave yourself to God. In many acts of self-surrender since then, you have again given yourselves to Him. But experience has taught you how much is still lacking. Perhaps you never knew how entire the self-sacrifice must be and could be. Come now and see in Christ your example, and in His sacrifice of Himself on the cross, *what your Father expects of you.* Come now and see in Christ—for He is your head and life—*what He will enable you to be and do.* Believe in Him, so that what

He accomplished on earth in His life and death as your example, He will now accomplish in you from heaven. Offer yourself to the Father in Christ, with the desire to be, as entirely and completely as He, an offering and a sacrifice to God. Expect Christ to work this in you and to maintain it. Let your relationship to God be clear and distinct; you, like Christ, wholly given up to Him. Then it will no longer be impossible to walk in love as Christ loved us. Then all your fellowship with the brethren and with the world will be the most glorious opportunity of proving before God how completely you have given yourself to Him, an offering and a sacrifice for a sweet-smelling aroma.

> *Come now and see in Christ your example, and in His sacrifice of Himself on the cross, what your Father expects of you.*

O my God, who am I that You should have chosen me to be conformed to the image of Your Son in His self-sacrificing love? In this is His divine perfection and glory, that He did not love His own life, but freely offered it for us to You in death. And in this I may be like Him. In a walk in love I may prove that I, too, have offered myself wholly to God.

O my Father, Your purpose is mine. At this solemn moment I affirm anew my consecration to You. Not in my own strength, but in the strength of Him who gave Himself for me. Because Christ, my example, is also my life, I venture to say it: Father, in Christ, like Christ, I yield myself a sacrifice to You for men.

Father, teach me how You want to use me to manifest Your love to the world. You will do it by filling me full of Your love. Father, do it so that I may walk in love, *just as* Christ loved us. May I live every day as one who has the power of Your Holy Spirit to enable me to love everyone with whom I come into contact, under every possible circumstance, to love with a love that is not of me but of Yourself. Amen.

FOR FURTHER THOUGHT

1. What are the distinctions between self-sacrifice and self-denial? How are the two inseparably linked and related?
2. Of what is self-sacrifice the very essence? For whom does God call you to live in that kind of self-sacrifice?
3. What must you do before you can live a life of practical and effective self-sacrifice for others—the kind of self-sacrifice God calls you to walk in daily?

ONE of the most earnest and successful laborers in the work of saving the lost writes as follows: "If I had not been led to a clearer and fuller experience of what salvation is, I never could have gone through the work of the last few years. But, at the same time, one thing has continually been becoming clearer: that we cannot speak of unbroken *fellowship* with our Lord unless we give up ourselves, and that *without ceasing*, to a world lying in the wicked one, to save in the strength of our Lord what He gives us to save. A consecration to the Lord without a *consecration to our neighbor* becomes an illusion or leads to fanaticism. It is this giving up of ourselves to the world to be its light and salt, to love it, even when it hates us, that constitutes for all really consecrated souls the true battle of life. To find in labor our rest, and in fighting the sin around us in the power of Jesus our highest joy, to rejoice more in the happiness of others than our own, and so not to seek anything for ourselves, but everything for others, this, this is our holy calling."

May God help us not only to admire such thoughts, but immediately to join the little bands among His children who are really giving up everything and making their life's work the winning of souls for Jesus.

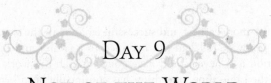

DAY 9

NOT OF THE WORLD

*"These are in the world. . . . The world has hated them
because they are not of the world, just as I am not of the world. . . .
They are not of the world, just as I am not of the world."*
JOHN 17:11, 14, 16

Because as He is, so are we in this world.
1 JOHN 4:17

IF Jesus was not of the world, why was He in the world? If there was no sympathy between Him and the world, why was it that He lived in it and did not remain in that high and holy and blessed world to which He belonged? The answer is, The Father had sent Him into the world. In these two expressions, "In the world" and "Not of the world," we find the whole secret of His work as Savior, of His glory as the God-man.

"In the world"—in human nature, because God wants to show that this nature belonged to Him, and not to the god of this world, so that it was most fit to receive the divine life, and in this divine life to reach its highest glory.

"In the world"—in fellowship with men, to enter into loving relationship with them, to be seen and known by them, and thus to win them back to the Father.

"In the world"—in the struggle with the powers that rule the world, to learn obedience, and so to perfect and sanctify human nature.

"Not of the world"—but of heaven, to manifest and bring near the life that is in God, and which man had lost, so that men might see and long for it.

"Not of the world"—witnessing against its sin and departure from God, its powerlessness to know and please God.

"Not of the world"—founding a kingdom entirely heavenly in origin and nature, entirely independent of all that the world holds desirable or necessary, with principles and laws the very opposite of those that rule in the world.

"Not of the world"—in order to redeem all who belong to Him and bring them into that new and heavenly kingdom that He had revealed.

"In the world," "not of the world." In these two expressions we have revealed to us the great mystery of the person and work of the Savior. "Not *of* the world," in the

power of His divine holiness judging and overcoming it, but still *in* the world, and through His humanity and love seeking and saving all that can be saved. The most entire separation from the world, with the closest fellowship with those in the world: these two extremes meet in Jesus, in His own person He has reconciled them. And it is the calling of the Christian in his life to prove that these two dispositions, however much they may seem at odds, can in our life, too, be united in perfect harmony. In each believer there must be seen a heavenly life shining out through earthly forms.

To take one of these two truths and exclusively cultivate it is not so difficult. So you have those who have taken "Not of the world" as their motto. From the earliest ages, when people thought they must fly to monasteries and deserts to serve God, to our own days, when some seek to show the earnestness of their spirituality by severely judging all that is in the world, there have been those who counted this the only true religion. There was separation from sin, but then there was also no fellowship with sinners. The sinner could not feel that he was surrounded with the atmosphere of a tender heavenly love. It was a one-sided and therefore a defective religion.

> "In the world," "not of the world." In these two expressions we have revealed to us the great mystery of the person and work of the Savior.

Then there are those who, on the other side, lay stress on "In the world," and very specially appeal to the words of the apostle, "Since then you would need to go out of the world" (1 Cor. 5:10). They think that by showing that religion does not make us unfriendly or unfit to enjoy all that there is to enjoy, they will induce the world to serve God. It has often happened that they have indeed succeeded in making the world very religious, but at too high a price—religion became very worldly.

The true follower of Jesus must combine both. If he does not clearly show that he is not of the world, and prove the greater blessedness of a heavenly life, how will he convince the world of sin, or prove to her that there is a higher life, or teach her to desire what she does not yet possess? Earnestness, holiness, and separation from the spirit of the world must characterize him. His heavenly spirit must demonstrate that he belongs to a kingdom not of this world. An unworldly, an otherworldly, a heavenly spirit must breathe in him.

And still he must live as one who is "in the world." Expressly placed here by God, among those who are of the world, to win their hearts, to acquire influence over them, and to communicate to them of the Spirit who is in him, it must be the great study of his life how he can fulfill this his mission. Not, as the wisdom of the world would teach, by yielding, complying, and softening down the solemn realities of religion will he succeed. No, but only by walking in the footsteps of Him who alone can teach how to be in the world and yet not of it. Only by a life of serving and suffering love, in which the Christian distinctly confesses that the glory of God is the aim of his existence, and in which, full of the Holy Spirit, he brings men into direct contact with the warmth and love of the heavenly life, can he be a blessing to the world.

Oh, who will teach us the heavenly secret of uniting every day in our lives what is so difficult to unite—to be in the world, and not of the world? He can do it who has said: "They are not of the world, JUST AS I am not of the world." That "JUST AS" has a deeper meaning and power than we know. If we allow the Holy Spirit to unfold that word to us, we shall understand what it is to be in the world as He was in the world. That "JUST AS" has its root and strength in a life union. In it we shall discover the divine secret, that the *more entirely one is not of the world, the more fit he is to be in the world.* The freer the Church is of the spirit and principles of the world, the more influence she will exert in it.

> *hat "just as" has its root and strength in a life union. In it we shall discover the divine secret, that the more entirely one is not of the world, the more fit he is to be in the world.*

The life of the world is self-pleasing and self-exaltation. The life of heaven is holy, self-denying love. The weakness of the life of many Christians who seek to separate themselves from the world is that they have too much of the spirit of the world. They seek their own happiness and perfection more than anything else. Jesus Christ was not of the world and had nothing of its spirit. This is why He could love sinners, could win them and save them. The believer is as little of the world as Christ. The Lord says: "Not of the world, JUST AS I am not of the world." In his new nature he is born from heaven, has the life and love of heaven in him, and his supernatural heavenly life gives him power to be in the world without being of it. The disciple who believes fully in the Christlikeness of his inner life will experience the truth of it. He cultivates and gives utterance to the assurance: "JUST AS Christ, so am I not of the world, because I am in Christ." He understands that alone in close union with Christ can his separation from the world be maintained. Just as much as Christ lives in him can he lead a heavenly life. He sees that the only way to answer to his calling is, on the one side, as crucified to the world to withdraw himself from its power; and, on the other, as living in Christ to go into it and bless it. He lives in heaven and walks on earth.

Christians! See here the true imitation of Jesus Christ. "Therefore 'come out from among them and be separate, says the Lord'" (2 Cor. 6:17). Then the promise is fulfilled, "I will dwell in them and walk among them" (2 Cor. 6:16). Then Christ sends you, as the Father sent Him, to be in the world as the place ordained by your Father to glorify Him and to make known His love.

"Not of the world" is not only separation from and testimony against the world, but is the living manifestation of the spirit, and the love, and the power of the other world, of the heaven to which we belong, in its divine work of making this world partaker of its blessedness.

O great High Priest, who in Your high priestly power prayed for us to the Father, as those who, no more than Yourself, belong to the world, and still must remain in it, let Your all-prevailing intercession now be effectual in our behalf.

> *Not of the world" is not only separation from and testimony against the world, but is the living manifestation of the spirit, and the love, and the power of the other world, of the heaven to which we belong*

The world still has entrance to our hearts, and its selfish spirit is still too much within us. Through unbelief the new nature does not always have full power. Lord, we ask of You, as fruit of Your all-powerful intercession, let that word be fully realized in us: "Not of the world, JUST AS I am not of the world." In our likeness to You is our only power against the world.

Lord, we can only be like You when we are one with You. We can only walk like You when we abide in You. Blessed Lord, we surrender ourselves to abide in You alone. You take entire possession of a life entirely given to You. Let Your Holy Spirit, who dwells in us, unite us so closely with Yourself that we may always live as not of the world. And let Your Spirit so make known to us Your work in the world that it may be our joy in deep humility and fervent love to exhibit to all what a blessed life there is in the world for those who are not of the world. May the proof that we are not of the world be the tenderness and fervency with which, like You, we sacrifice ourselves for those who are in the world. Amen.

FOR FURTHER THOUGHT

1. *Jesus said that you, like the original disciples, are in this world but not of it. What does that mean, and for what purpose does God leave you in the world?*

2. *What are some of the ways men have misapplied the words "not of the world"? What did their approach fail in doing in and for the world?*

3. *How can you learn the heavenly secret of being in the world but not of it as well as the true purpose for God commanding you to be in the world but not of it?*

DAY 10

IN HIS HEAVENLY MISSION

"As You sent Me into the world,
I also have sent them into the world."
JOHN 17:18

"As the Father has sent Me, I also send you."
JOHN 20:21

THE Lord Jesus lived here on earth under a deep consciousness of having a mission from His Father to fulfill. He continually used the expression, "The Father has sent Me."[51] He knew what this mission was. He knew the Father had chosen Him and sent Him into the world with the one purpose of fulfilling that mission, and He knew the Father would give Him all that He needed for it. Faith in the Father having sent Him was the motive and power for all that He did.

In earthly things, it is a great help if an ambassador knows clearly what his mission is, that he has nothing to do but to care for its accomplishment, and that he has given himself undividedly to do this one thing. For the Christian it is of no less consequence that he should know that he has a mission, what its nature is, and how he is to accomplish it.

Our heavenly mission is one of the most glorious parts of our conformity to our Lord. He says it plainly in the most solemn moments of His life, "that JUST AS the Father sent Him," so He sends His disciples. He says it to the Father in His high priestly prayer, as the ground upon which He asks for their keeping and sanctification. He says it to the disciples after His resurrection, as the ground on which they are to receive the Holy Spirit. Nothing will help us more to know and fulfill our mission than to realize how perfectly it corresponds to the mission of Christ, how they are, in fact, identical.

Our mission is like His *in its object*. Why did the Father send His Son? To make known His love and His will in the salvation of sinners. He was to do this, not alone by word and instruction, but in His own person, disposition, and conduct to exhibit the Father's holy love. He was so to represent the unseen Father in

---

[51] It will repay the trouble to compare carefully the following passages: John 5:24, 30, 37–38; 6:38, 40 , 44; 7:16, 28–29, 33; 8:16, 18, 26, 29, 42; 9:4; 11:42; 12:44–45, 49; 13:20; 14:24; 15:21; 16:25; 17:8, 18, 21, 23, 25; 20:21. Christ wanted men to know that He did not act independently, but on behalf of another who had sent Him. The consciousness of a mission never left Him for a moment.

heaven, so that men on earth might know what "like the Father" was.

After the Lord had fulfilled His mission, He ascended into heaven and became to the world like the Father, the Unseen One. And now He has given over His mission to His disciples, after having shown them how to fulfill it. They must so represent Him, the Invisible One, that from seeing them men can judge what He is. Every Christian must so be the image of Jesus—must so exhibit in his person and conduct the same love to sinners, and desire for their salvation, as animated Christ, that from them the world may know what "like Christ" is. Oh, my soul! Take time to realize these heavenly thoughts: Our mission is like Christ's in its object, the showing forth of the holy love of heaven in earthly form.

> *O*ur heavenly mission is one of the most glorious parts of our conformity to our Lord. He says it plainly in the most solemn moments of His life, "that just as the Father sent Him," so He sends His disciples.

Like Christ's *in its origin, too*. It was the Father's love that chose Christ for this work and counted Him worthy of such honor and trust. We also are chosen by Christ for this work. Every redeemed one knows that it was not he who sought the Lord, but the Lord who sought and chose him. In that seeking and drawing, the Lord had expressly this heavenly mission in view. "You did not choose Me, but I chose you and appointed you that you should go and bear fruit" (John 15:16).

Believer! Whoever you are, and wherever you live, the Lord, who knows You and Your surroundings, has need of You and has chosen You to be His representative in the circle in which you move. Fix your heart on this. He has fixed His heart on you and saved you, in order that you should bear and exhibit to those who surround you the very image of His unseen glory. Oh, think of this origin of your heavenly mission in His everlasting love, as His had its origin in the love of the Father. Your mission is in very truth just like His.

Like it, too, *in the preparing for it*. Every ambassador expects to be supplied with all that he needs for his embassy. "He who sent Me is with Me. The Father has not left Me alone" (John 8:29). That word tells us how, when the Father sent the Son, He was always with Him, His strength and comfort. Likewise, the Church of Christ in her mission: "Go therefore and make disciples of all the nations" (Matt. 28:19), has the promise: "Lo, I am with you always" (Matt. 28:20). The Christian need never hold back because of unfitness. The Lord does not demand anything that He does not give the power to perform. Every believer may depend on it, that as the Father gave His Holy Spirit to the Son to prepare Him for His work, so the Lord Jesus will give His people, too, all the preparation they need. The grace to show forth Christ evermore, to exhibit the lovely light of His example and likeness, and like Christ Himself to be a fountain of love and life and blessing to all around, is given to everyone who only heartily and believingly takes up his heavenly calling. In this, too, that the sender cares for all that is needed for the sent ones, is our mission like His.

And like also *in the consecration that it demands*. The Lord Jesus gave Himself entirely and undividedly over to accomplish His work and lived for it alone. "I must work the works of Him who sent Me while it is day; the night is coming when no one can work" (John 9:4). The Father's mission was the only reason for His being on earth. For that alone He would live: to reveal to mankind what a glorious blessed God the Father in heaven was.

As with Jesus, so with us. Christ's mission is *the only reason for our being on earth*. Were it not for that, He would take us away. Most believers do not believe this. To fulfill Christ's mission is with them at best something to be done along with other things, for which it is difficult to find time and strength. And yet it is so certainly true: to accomplish Christ's mission is the only reason for my being on earth. Then first when I believe this, and like my Lord in His mission consecrate myself undividedly to it, shall I indeed live well-pleasing to Him. This heavenly mission is so great and glorious that without an entire consecration to it we cannot accomplish it. Without this, the powers that prepare us for it cannot take possession of us. Without this, we have no liberty to expect the Lord's wonderful help and the fulfillment of all His blessed promises. Just as with Jesus, our heavenly mission demands nothing less than entire consecration. Am I prepared for this? Then I have indeed the key through which the holy hidden glories of this word of Jesus will be revealed to my experience: "As the Father has sent Me, I also send you."

> he Christian need never hold back because of unfitness. The Lord does not demand anything that He does not give the power to perform.

O brothers! This heavenly mission is indeed worthy that we devote ourselves entirely to it as the only thing we live for.

O Lord Jesus! You descended from heaven to earth to show us what the life of heaven is. You could do this because You were of heaven. You brought with You the image and Spirit of the heavenly life to earth. Therefore You so gloriously exhibited what constitutes the very glory of heaven: the will and love of the unseen Father.

Lord! You are now the Invisible One in heaven, and You send us to represent You in Your heavenly glory as Savior. You ask that we should so love men that from us they may form some idea of how You love them in heaven.

Blessed Lord! Our heart cries out: How can You send us with such a calling? How can You expect it of us who have so little love? How can we, who are of the earth earthly, show what the life of heaven is?

Precious Savior! Our souls bless You that we know that You do not demand more than You give. You who are Yourself the life of heaven, You live Yourself in Your disciples. Blessed be Your holy name, they have from You Your Holy Spirit from heaven as their life-breath. He is the heavenly life of the soul, and whoever surrenders himself to the leading of the Spirit can fulfill his mission. In the joy and power of the Holy Spirit we can be Your image-bearers, can show to men in some measure what Your likeness is. Lord, teach me and all Your people to understand that we are not of the world, as You were not of the world, and therefore we are sent by You, even as You were sent by the Father, to prove in our life that we are of that world, full of love, and purity, and blessing, of which You were. Amen.

For Further Thought

1. *For what specific purpose has God sent you as a disciple of Jesus Christ into the world? How can you obediently and effectively fulfill that assignment in your part of the world today?*

2. *What is the connection between God's choosing you for salvation and His choosing you for the purpose and mission for which He leaves you in the world?*

3. *What must you do before you can successfully accomplish the purpose, the mission for which God has sent you into the world around you?*

DAY 11

AS THE ELECT OF GOD

Predestined to be conformed to the image of His Son,
that He might be the firstborn among many brethren.
ROMANS 8:29

SCRIPTURE teaches us a personal election. It does this not only in single passages, but its whole history of the working out here in time of the plans of eternity proves it. We see continually how the whole future of God's kingdom depends on the faithful filling of His place by some single person, how the only security for the carrying out of God's purpose is His foreordaining of the individual. In predestination alone the history of the world and of God's kingdom, as of the individual believer, has its sure foundation.

There are Christians who cannot see this. They are so afraid of interfering with human responsibility that they reject the doctrine of divine predestination, because it appears to rob man of his liberty of will and action. Scripture does not share this fear. It speaks in one place of man's free will as though there were no election, in another of election as though there were no free will. Thus it teaches us that we must hold firmly both these truths alongside each other, even when we cannot understand them or make them perfectly to harmonize. In the light of eternity, the solution of the mystery will be given. He who grasps both in faith will speedily experience how little they are in conflict. He will see that the stronger his faith is in God's everlasting purpose, the more his courage for work will be strengthened, while, on the other side, the more he works and is blessed, the clearer it will become that all is of God.

For this reason it is of so much consequence for a believer to make his election sure. The scriptures give the assurance that if we do this, "we shall never stumble" (see 2 Pet. 1:10). The more I believe not only in general that I am elected by God, but see how this election has reference to every part of my calling, the more shall I be strengthened in the conviction that God Himself will perfect His work in me, and that therefore it is possible for me to be all that God really expects. With every duty scripture lays upon me, with every promise for whose fulfillment I long, I will go to find in God's purposes the firm footing on which my expectations may rest, and the true measure by which they are to be guided. I shall understand that my life on earth is to be a copy of the heavenly life-plan, which the Father has drawn out, of what I am to be on earth. Christian! Make your calling and election sure. Let it become clear to you that you are elected, and to what: "If you do these things, you will never stumble." Quiet communion with God on the ground of His unchangeable purpose imparts to the soul an immoveable firmness that keeps from stumbling.

One of the most blessed expressions in regard to God's purpose concerning us in Christ is this word: "Predestinated to be conformed to the image of His Son." The man Christ Jesus is the elect of God. In Him election has its beginning and ending. "In Him we are chosen." For the sake of our union with Him and to His glory our election took place. The believer who seeks in election merely the certainty of his own salvation, or relief from fear and doubt, knows very little of its real glory. The purposes of election embrace all the riches that are prepared for us in Christ, and reach to every moment and every need of our lives. "He chose us in Him before the foundation of the world, that we should be holy and without blame before Him in love" (Eph. 1:4). It is only when the connection between election and sanctification is rightly understood in the Church that the doctrine of election will bring its full blessing (see 2 Thess. 2:13; 1 Pet. 1:2). It teaches the believer how it is God who must work all in him, who will work all in him, and how he may rely even in the smallest matters upon the unchangeable purpose of God to work out itself in the accomplishment of everything that He expects of His people. In this light, the word "Predestinated to be conformed to the image of His Son" gives new strength to everyone who has begun to take *what Christ is* as the rule of *what he himself is to be.*

> The more I believe not only in general that I am elected by God, but see how this election has reference to every part of my calling, the more shall I be strengthened in the conviction that God Himself will perfect His work in me,

Christian! If you desire in very deed to be *like Christ,* fix your mind on the thought of how certainly this is God's will concerning you, how the whole of redemption has been planned with the view of your becoming so, and how God's purpose is the guarantee that your desires must be fulfilled. There, where your name is written in the book of life, there stands also, "Predestinated to be conformed to the image of His Son." All the powers of the deity that have already accomplished together in the accomplishment of the first part of the eternal purpose, the revealing of the Father's perfect likeness in the man Christ Jesus, are equally engaged to accomplish the second part, and work that likeness in each of God's children. In the work of Christ there is the most perfect provision possible for the carrying out of God's purposes in this. Our union to Christ, held firmly in a living faith, will be an all-prevailing power. We can depend on it as something ordained with a divine certainty, and that must come if we yield ourselves to it. Has not God elected us to be conformed to the image of His Son?

It can easily be understood what a powerful influence the living consciousness of this truth will have. It teaches us to give up ourselves to the eternal will so that it may, with divine power, effect its purpose in us. It shows us how useless and powerless our own efforts are to accomplish this work, for all that is *of* God must also be *through* Him. He who is the beginning must be the middle and the end. In a very wonderful manner it strengthens our faith with a holy boldness to glory in God alone, and to expect from God Himself the fulfillment of every promise and every command, of every part of the purpose of His blessed will.

Believer! Take time and prayer to take in this truth, and let it exercise its full power in your soul. Let the Holy Spirit write it into your innermost being that you are predestined to be conformed to the image of His Son. The Father's object was the honor of His Son, "that He might be the firstborn among many brethren" (Rom. 8:29). Let this be your object, too, in all your life, so to show forth the image of your Elder Brother that other Christians may be pointed to Him alone, may praise Him alone, and seek to follow Him more closely, too.

> *T*here, where your name is written in the book of life, there stands also, "Predestinated to be conformed to the image of His Son."

Let it be the fixed and only purpose of your life, the great object of your believing prayer, that "Christ will be magnified in my body" (Phil. 1:20). This will give you new confidence to ask and expect all that is necessary to live like Christ. Your conformity to Christ will be one of the links connecting the eternal purpose of the Father with the eternal fulfillment of it in the glorifying of the Son. Your conformity to Christ becomes then such a holy, heavenly, divine work that you realize that it can come only from the Father, but that from Him you can and shall most certainly receive it. What God's purpose has decreed, God's power will perform. What God's love has ordained and commanded, God's love will most certainly accomplish. A living faith in His eternal purpose will become one of the mightiest powers in urging and helping us to live LIKE CHRIST.

O incomprehensible Being, I bow before You in deepest humility. It has been such a strength to know that Your Son has chosen me, in order to send me into the world as You had sent Him. But here You have led me still higher and shown that this mission to be as He was in the world was from eternity decreed by Yourself. O my God, my soul bows prostrate in the dust before You.

Lord God, now that Your child comes to You for the fulfillment of Your own purpose, he dares confidently look for an answer. Your will is stronger than every hindrance. The faith that trusts You will not be put to shame. Lord, in holy reverence and worship, but with childlike confidence and hope, I utter this prayer: "Father, give me the desire of my soul, conformity to the image of Your Son. Father, likeness to Jesus, this is what my soul desires of You. Let me, like Him, be Your holy child."

O my Father, write it in Your book of remembrance, and write it in my remembrance, too, that I have asked it from You as what I desire above all things, conformity to the image of Your Son.

Father, to this You have chosen me, and You will give it me, for Your own and His glory. Amen.

For Further Thought

1. *How and why can you be sure that God will perfect the work He began in you?*
2. *"Elected us to be conformed to the image of His Son." What does this verse tell you about God's intentions concerning what He will do for you in the future—what He is indeed doing right now?*
3. *Read Philippians 1:20. How does the promise of this passage give you confidence to boldly ask and confidently expect God to give you everything you need to live like Christ?*

DAY 12

IN DOING GOD'S WILL

"For I have come down from heaven, not to do
My own will, but the will of Him who sent Me."
JOHN 6:38

IN the will of God we have the highest expression of His divine perfection, and at the same time the highest energy of His divine power. Creation owes its being and its beauty to it, for it is the manifestation of God's will. In all nature the will of God is done. In heaven the angels find their highest blessedness in doing God's will. For this man was created with a free will, in order that he might have the power to choose, and of his own accord do God's will. And, deceived by the devil, man committed the great sin of rather doing his own than God's will. *Yes, rather his own than God's will!* In this is the root and the wretchedness of sin.

Jesus Christ became man to bring us back to the blessedness of *doing God's will.* The great object of redemption was to make us and our will free from the power of sin, and to lead us again to live and do the will of God. In His life on earth He showed us what it is to live only for the will of God, and in His death and resurrection He won for us the power to live and do the will of God as He had done.

"Behold, I have come. . .to do Your will, O God" (Heb. 10:7). These words, uttered through the Holy Spirit by the mouth of one of His prophets long ages before Christ's birth, are the key to His life on earth. At Nazareth in the carpenter's shop, at the Jordan with John the Baptist, in the wilderness with Satan, in public with the multitude, in living and dying, it was this that inspired and guided and gladdened Him—the glorious will of the Father was to be accomplished in Him and by Him.

Let us not think that this cost Him nothing. He says repeatedly, *"Not My will,* but the will of the Father," to let us understand that there was in very deed a denial of His own will. In Gethsemane the sacrifice of His own will reached its height, but what took place there was only the perfect expression of what had rendered His whole life acceptable to the Father. The sin is not that man has a creature-will different from the Creator's, but in this, that he clings to his own will when it is seen to be contrary to the will of the Creator. As man, Jesus had a human will, the natural, though not sinful desires that belong to human nature. As man, His did not always know beforehand what the will of God was. He had to wait, and be taught by God, and learn from time to time what that will was. But when the will of His Father was once known to Him, then He was always ready to give up His own human will and do the will of the Father. It was this that constituted the perfection and the value of His self-sacrifice. He had once for all surrendered Himself as a man, to live only in and for the will of God, and was always ready, even to the sacrifice of Gethsemane and Calvary, to do that will alone.

It is *this life of obedience*, demonstrated by the Lord Jesus in the flesh, that is not only imputed to us, but *imparted through the Holy Spirit*. Through His death our Lord Jesus has atoned for our self-will and disobedience. It was by conquering it in His own perfect obedience that He atoned for it. He has in this respect not only blotted out the guilt of our self-will before God, but broken its power in us. In His resurrection He brought from the dead a life that had conquered and destroyed all self-will. And the believer who knows the power of Jesus' death and resurrection has the power to consecrate himself entirely to God's will. He knows that the call to follow Christ means nothing less than to take and speak the words of the Master as his own solemn vow, "I do not seek my own will but the will of the Father" (John 5:30).

> *The* great object of redemption was to make us and our will free from the power of sin, and to lead us again to live and do the will of God.

To attain this we must begin by taking the same stand that our Lord did. Take God's will as one great whole, as the only thing for which you live on earth. Look at the sun and moon, the grass and flowers, what glory each of them has, only because they are just doing God's will. But they do it without knowing it. You can do it still more gloriously, because you know and will to do it. Let your heart be filled with the thought of the glory of God's will concerning His children, and concerning you, and say that it is your one purpose that that will should be done in you. Yield yourself to the Father frequently and distinctly, with the declaration that with you, as with Jesus, it is a settled thing that His beautiful and blessed will must and shall be done. Say it frequently in your quiet meditations, with a joyful and trusting heart: *Praise God! I may live only to do the will of God.*

Let no fear keep us back from this. Do not think that this will is too hard for us to do, for God's will only seems hard as long as we look at it from a distance and are unwilling to submit to it. Just look again how beautiful the will of God makes everything in nature. Ask yourself, now that He loves and blesses you as a child, if it is right to distrust Him. The will of God is the will of His love, so how can you fear to surrender yourself to it?

Nor let the fear that you will not be able to obey that will keep you back. The

Son of God came to earth to show what the life of man must and may become. His resurrection life gives us power to live as He lived. Jesus Christ enables us, through His Spirit, to walk not after the flesh but according to the will of God (see Rom. 8:4).

"I have come to do Your will, O God": Before the Lord Jesus ever came down to earth, a believer in the Old Testament was able, through the Spirit, to speak that word of himself as well as for Christ (see Ps. 40:6–8). Christ took it up and filled it with new life-power. And now He expects of His redeemed ones that since He has been on earth, they will even more heartily and entirely make it their choice. Let us do so. We must not first try and see whether, in single instances, we succeed in doing God's will, in the hope of afterwards attaining to the entire consecration that can say: "I have come to do Your will." No, this is not the right way. Let us first recognize God's will as a whole, and the claims it has upon us, as well as its blessedness and glory. Let us surrender ourselves to it as to God Himself, and consider it as one of the first articles of our creed: I am in the world, like Christ, only to do the Father's will.

This surrender will teach us with joy to accept every command and every providence as part of the will we have already yielded ourselves to. This surrender will give us courage to wait for God's sure guidance and strength, because the man who lives only for God's will may depend on it that God takes him for his reckoning. This surrender will lead us deeper into the consciousness of our utter powerlessness, but also deeper into the fellowship and the likeness of the beloved Son, and make us partakers of all the blessedness and love that the Son has prepared for us. There is nothing that will bring us closer to God in union to Christ than loving and keeping and doing the will of God.

Child of God! One of the first marks of conformity to Christ is obedience, simple and implicit obedience to all the will of God. Let it be the most marked thing in your life. Begin by a willing and wholehearted keeping of every one of the commands of God's holy Word. Go on to a very tender yielding to everything that conscience tells you to be right, even when the Word does not directly command it. Then you will rise higher, for a hearty obedience to the commandments, as far as you know them, and a ready obedience to conscience wherever it speaks, are the preparation for that divine teaching of the Spirit.

This will lead you deeper into the meaning and application of the Word, and into a more direct and spiritual insight into God's will with regard to yourself personally. It is to those *who obey* Him God gives the Holy Spirit, through whom the blessed will of God becomes the light that shines always more brightly on our path. "If any man wills to *do His* will, he shall know" (John 7:17). Blessed will of God! Blessed obedience to God's will! Oh, that we knew to count and keep these as our most precious treasures!

O my God, I thank You for this wondrous gift: Your Son become man, to teach us how man may do the will of his God. I thank You for the glorious calling to be like Him in this, too, with Him to taste the blessedness of a life in perfect harmony with Your glorious and perfect will. I thank You for the power given in Christ to do and to bear all that will. I thank You that in this, too, I may be like the first-begotten Son.

I come now, O my Father, afresh to take up this my calling in childlike, joyous trust and love. Lord, I want to live wholly and only to do Your will. I want to abide in the Word and wait on the Spirit. I want to, like Your Son, live in fellowship with You in prayer, in the firm confidence that You will day by day make me to know Your will more clearly. O my Father, let this my desire be acceptable in Your sight. Keep it in the thoughts of my heart forever. Give me grace with true joy continually to say: "Not my will, but the will of my Father must be done. I am here on the earth only to do the will of my God." Amen.

For Further Thought

1. *Why was it necessary for Jesus to come to earth as a man of flesh and blood? What did He demonstrate as He lived a life committed to doing the will of God?*
2. *Why can doing the will of God seem too difficult or beyond your reach? How can you overcome that error in thinking, thus making obedience easier?*
3. *What blessing does God give you when you obey Him? How does this blessing teach you the blessings of further obedience?*

DAY 13

IN HIS COMPASSION

Now Jesus called His disciples to Himself and said,
"I have compassion on the multitude."
MATTHEW 15:32

"Should you not also have had compassion on your
fellow servant, just as I had pity on you?"
MATTHEW 18:33

ON three different occasions Matthew tells us that our Lord was moved with compassion on the multitude. His whole life was a manifestation of the compassion with which He had looked at the sinner from everlasting, and of the tenderness with which He was moved at the sight of misery and sorrow. He was in this the true reflection of our compassionate God, of the father who, moved with compassion toward his prodigal son, fell on his neck and kissed him.

In this compassion of the Lord Jesus we can see how He did not look at the will of God He came to do as a duty or an obligation, but had that divine will dwelling within Him as His own, inspiring and ruling all His sentiments and motives. After He had said, "I have come down from heaven, *not to do My own will*, but the will of Him who sent Me" (John 6:38), He immediately added, "*This is the will* of the Father who sent Me, that of all He has given Me I should lose nothing, but should raise it up at the last day" (6:39). "And *this is the will* of Him who sent Me, that everyone who sees the Son and believes in Him may have everlasting life" (6:40).

For the Lord Jesus, the will of God consisted not in certain things that were forbidden or commanded. No, He had entered into that which truly forms the very heart of God's will, and that is that to lost sinners He should give eternal life. Because God Himself is love, His will is that love should have full scope in the salvation of sinners. The Lord Jesus came down to earth in order to manifest and accomplish this will of God. He did not do this as a servant obeying the will of a stranger. In His personal life and all His dispositions He proved that the loving will of His Father to save sinners was His own. Not only His death on Golgotha, but just as much the compassion in which He took and bore the need of all the wretched, and the tenderness of His interaction with them, was the proof that the Father's will had truly become His own. In every way He showed that life was of no value to Him except as the opportunity of doing the will of His Father.

Beloved followers of Christ, who have offered yourselves to imitate Him, let the will of the Father be to you what it was to your Lord. The will of the Father in the mission of His Son was the manifestation and the triumph of divine compassion in the salvation of lost sinners. Jesus could not possibly accomplish this will in any other way than by having and showing this compassion. *God's will is for us what it was for Jesus: the salvation of the perishing.* It is impossible for us to fulfill that will other than by having, carrying with us, and showing in our lives the compassion of our God. The seeking of God's will must not be only denying ourselves certain things that God forbids, and doing certain works that God commands, but must consist especially in this: that we surrender ourselves to have the same mind and disposition toward sinners as God has, and that we find our pleasure and joy alone in living for this. By the most personal devotion to each poor perishing sinner around us, and by our helping them in compassionate love, we can show that the will of God has become our will. With the compassionate God as our Father, with Christ who was so often moved with compassion as our life, nothing can be more just than the command that the life of every Christian should be one of compassionate love.

> Because God Himself is love, His will is that love should have full scope in the salvation of sinners.

Compassion is the spirit of love that is awakened by the sight of need or wretchedness. What abundant occasion is there every day for the practice of this heavenly virtue, and what a need of it in a world so full of misery and sin! Every Christian ought therefore by prayer and practice to cultivate a compassionate heart as one of the most precious marks of likeness to the blessed Master. Everlasting love longs to give itself to a perishing world and to find its satisfaction in saving the lost. *It seeks for vessels that it may fill with the love of God and send out among the dying so that they may drink and live forever.* It asks hearts to fill with its own tender compassion at the sight of all the need in which sinners live, hearts that will consider it their highest blessedness, as the dispensers of God's compassion, to live entirely to bless and save sinners. O my brother, the everlasting compassion that has had mercy on you calls you, as one who has obtained mercy, to come and let it fill you. It will fit you, in your compassion on all around, to be a witness to God's compassionate love.

The opportunity for showing compassion we have all around us. How much there is of need in the world! There are the poor and the sick, widows and orphans, distressed and despondent souls who need nothing so much as the refreshment a compassionate heart can bring. They live in the midst of Christians, and sometimes complain that it is as if there are children of the world who have more sympathy than those who are only concerned about their own salvation. O brothers, pray earnestly for a compassionate heart, always on the lookout for an opportunity for doing some work of love, always ready to be an instrument of the divine compassion. It was the compassionate sympathy of Jesus that attracted so many to Him upon earth. That same compassionate tenderness will still, more than anything, draw souls to you and to your Lord.[52]

> The opportunity for showing compassion we have all around us. How much there is of need in the world!

And how much of spiritual misery surrounds us on all sides! Here is a poor rich man. There is a foolish, thoughtless youth. There is again a poor drunkard, or a hopeless unfortunate. Or perhaps none of these, but simply people entirely wrapped up in the follies of the world that surround them. How often are words of unloving indifference, or harsh judgment, or apathetic hopelessness heard concerning all these! The compassionate heart is lacking. Compassion looks at the deepest misery as the place prepared for her by God, and is attracted by it. Compassion never wearies, never gives up hope. Compassion will not allow itself to be rejected, for it is the self-denying love of Christ that inspires it.

The Christian does not confine his compassion to his own circle, for he has a large heart. His Lord has shown him the whole heathen world as his field of labor. He seeks to be acquainted with the circumstances of the heathen, and he carries their burden on his heart. He is really moved with compassion, and means to help them. Whether the heathenism is near or far off, whether he witnesses it in all its filth and degradation, or only hears of it, compassionate love lives only to accomplish God's will in saving the perishing.

LIKE CHRIST *in His compassion:* let this now be our motto. After uttering the parable of the compassionate Samaritan, who, "moved with compassion," helped the wounded stranger, the Lord said, "Go and do likewise" (Luke 10:37). He is Himself the compassionate Samaritan, who speaks to every one of us whom He has saved, "Go and do likewise." JUST AS I have done to you, you do likewise. We, who owe everything to His compassion, who profess ourselves His followers, who walk in His footsteps and bear His image, oh, let us exhibit His compassion to the world. We can do it. He lives in us. His Spirit works in us. Let us with much prayer and firm faith look to *His example* as the sure promise of what we can be. It will be to Him an unspeakable joy if He finds us prepared for it, not only to show His compassion to us, but through us to the world. And ours will be the unutterable joy of having a

[52] See note.

Christlike heart, full of compassion and of great mercy.

O my Lord! My calling is becoming almost too high. In Your compassionate love, too, I must follow and imitate and reproduce Your life. In the compassion with which I see and help every bodily and spiritual misery, in the gentle, tender love with which every sinner feels that I long to bless men, must the world form some idea of Your compassion. Most merciful One! Forgive me that the world has seen so little of it in me. Most mighty Redeemer! Let Your compassion not only save me, but so take hold of me and dwell in me that compassion may be the very breath and joy of my life. May Your compassion toward me be within me a living fountain of compassion toward others.

Lord Jesus, I know You can only give this on one condition: that I let go of my own life and my efforts to keep and sanctify that life, and allow You to live in me and to be my life. Most merciful One, I yield myself to You! You have a right to me, You alone. There is nothing more precious to me than Your compassionate countenance. What can be more blessed than to be like You!

> *We, who owe everything to His compassion, who profess ourselves His followers, who walk in His footsteps and bear His image, oh, let us exhibit His compassion to the world.*

Lord, here I am. I have faith in You, that You Yourself will teach and fit me to obey Your word: "You should have had compassion, just as I had compassion on You." In that faith I go out this very day to find in my interactions with others the opportunity of showing how You have loved me. In that faith it will become the great object of my life to win men to You. Amen.

FOR FURTHER THOUGHT

1. *The Lord Jesus lived a life of compassion toward those God had sent Him to reach. What does the compassion of Jesus teach you about His commitment to doing the will of God? What does it teach you about your doing His will?*

2. *What was God's will for Jesus in sending Him into the world? What is His will for you? (Hint: They are the same thing.)*

3. *What can you do to effectively demonstrate the compassion of Jesus Christ—the kind He demonstrated to you—to the world around you?*

NOTE

EVIL can only be overcome by the contact of a most personal self-devotion, never by a love that stands at a distance. 'You are the salt of the earth,' Jesus said (Matt. 5:13). *You yourselves* just as you are, in the midst of society, in every place and every moment a sanctifying power must flow out from you and your presence. Christ *Himself* is the life and the light. In all that He does, says, or suffers, it is always *Himself*, so whoever separates anything from Himself no longer preserves it, and it vanishes in his hands. And just this is the radical error of our modern Christianity. Men separate the words and works of Christ from Himself, and so it comes that many, with all they do as Christians, have never found Christ Himself. So there are many who trust in His suffering and merit, but who cannot show that they have any real fellowship with Him or truly follow Him. Christ had His home not only in Cana of Galilee, but also in Gethsemane and on Calvary. Sadly, are there not many who make their boast of the cross, and yet are more afraid of the real cross than they are of the devil? They have so wisely arranged their profession of Christ's cross that no loss to their honor, their goods, or their liberty can ever come from it. Christ's true and actual imitation must once again, as in the olden times, become the standard of Christianity. Only and alone in this way will faith again conquer unbelief and superstition. Many are laboring hard at present to prove to a doubting world the inspiration of holy scripture, the truth of the words and the life of the Lord Jesus. It is labor in vain, to try and prove by words and argument that which can alone *be made known by its own self-evidencing power and its actual presence!* Let the proof be given in your deeds that the spirit of the miracles dwells in you. *Prove above all in your life that Jesus Christ is continuing in you His heavenly eternal life*, and then your words will bring many to believe. But if you are lacking in this demonstration of the Spirit and of power, do not be surprised if the world gives little attention to your eloquent arguments. The hour has come that all Christianity must rise up as one man, and in *the power of Christ repeat over again what Christ Himself did to a perishing world*. This is the need there is for the imitation of Jesus Christ; this is the only valid proof for the truth of Christianity."[53]

[53] From M. Diemer, *Een nieuw boek van de navolging van Jesus Christus.*

DAY 14

IN HIS ONENESS

WITH THE FATHER

"Holy Father, keep through Your name those whom You have
given Me, that they may be one as We are. . . . That they all may
be one, as You, Father, are in Me, and I in You; that they also may
be one in Us, that the world may believe that You sent Me.
And the glory which You gave Me I have given them,
that they may be one just as We are one: I in them, and You in Me;
that they may be made perfect in one, and that the
world may know that You have sent Me, and have
loved them as You have loved Me."
JOHN 17:11, 21–23

WHAT an unspeakable treasure we have in this high-priestly prayer! There the heart of Jesus is laid open to our view, and we see what His love desires for us. There the heavens are opened to us, and we learn what He as our intercessor is continually asking and obtaining for us from the Father.

In that prayer the mutual union of believers has a larger place than anything else. In His prayer for all who in future shall believe, this is the chief petition, John 16:20–26. Three times He repeats this prayer for their unity.

The Lord tells us plainly why He desires it so strongly. *This unity is the only convincing proof to the world that the Father had sent Him.* With all its blindness, the world knows that selfishness is the curse of sin. It helps but little that God's children tell that they are born again, and that they are happy, that they can do wonders in Jesus' name, or prove that what the scriptures teach is the truth. When the world sees a church from which selfishness is banished, then it will acknowledge the divine mission of Christ, because He has accomplished such a wonder: a community of men who truly and heartily love one another.

The Lord speaks of this unity three times as the reflection of His own oneness with the Father. He knew that this was the perfection of the Godhead: the Father and Son, as persons separate and yet perfectly one in the living fellowship of the Holy Spirit. And He cannot imagine anything higher than this: that His believing people should with Him and in Him be one with each other, JUST AS He and the Father are one.

The intercession of the Lord Jesus accomplishes much; it is all-prevailing. What He asks He receives of His Father. But understand that the blessing that descends finds no entrance in hearts where there is no open door, no place prepared to receive it. How many believers there are who do not even desire to be one even as the Father and the Son are one! They are so accustomed to a life of selfishness and imperfect love that they do not even long for such perfect love. Instead they put off that union until they meet in heaven. And yet the Lord thought of a life on earth when He twice said, "That the world may know."

That "they may be one, JUST AS We are one." The Church must be awakened to understand and to value this prayer rightly. This union is one of life and love at once. Some explain it as having reference to the hidden life-union that binds all believers even under external divisions. But this is not what the Lord means. He speaks of something that the world can see, something that resembles the union between God the Father and God the Son. The hidden unity of life must be manifest in the visible unity and fellowship of love. Only when it becomes impossible for believers, in the different smaller circles in which they are associated, not to live in the full oneness of love with the children of God around them; only when they learn that a life in love to each other, such as Christ's to us, and the Father's to Him, is simple duty, and begin to cry to God for His Holy Spirit to work it in them, then only will there be a hope of change in this respect. The fire will spread from circle to circle and from church to church, until all who truly do the will of God will consecrate themselves to abide in love, even as God is love.

> When the world sees a church from which selfishness is banished, then it will acknowledge the divine mission of Christ

And what are we to do now, while we wait for and wish to hasten that day? Let everyone who takes up earnestly the word of the Master, "JUST AS I, you also do," let him begin with his own circle. And in that circle with himself first. However weak or sickly, however perverse or trying the members of Christ's body may be with whom he is surrounded, let him live with them in close fellowship and love. Whether they are willing for it or not, whether they accept or reject, let him love them with a Christlike love. Yes, to love them as Christ does must be the purpose of his life. This love will find an echo in some hearts at least, and awaken in them the desire, too, to seek after the life of love and perfect oneness.

But what discoveries such effort will bring of the powerlessness of the believer, who has been before now satisfied with the ordinary Christian life, at all to reach this standard! He will soon find that nothing will succeed but a personal, undivided consecration. To have a love like Christ's, I must truly have a life like Christ's: *I must live with His life.* The lesson must be learned anew that Christ in the fullest sense of the word will be the life of those who dare to trust Him for it. Those who cannot trust with a full trust cannot love with a full love.

Believer, listen once more to the simple way to such a life. First of all, acknowledge your calling to live and love just like Christ. Confess your inability to fulfill this calling, even in the very least. Listen to the word that Christ is waiting to prepare you to fulfill this calling if you will give yourself unreservedly to Him. Make the surrender in this, that, conscious of being utterly unable to do anything in your own strength, you offer yourself to your Lord to work in you both to will and to do. And count then most confidently on Him, who in the power of His unceasing intercession can save completely, to do in you what He has asked of His Father for you. Yes, count on Him who has said to the Father, "You in Me and I in them, that they may be one, JUST AS We are one," that He will manifest His life in you with heavenly power. As you live with His life, you will love with His love.

> *Make the surrender in this, that, conscious of being utterly unable to do anything in your own strength, you offer yourself to your Lord to work in you both to will and to do.*

Beloved fellow Christians, the oneness of Christ with the Father is our model; just as they, so must we be one. Let us love one another, serve one another, bear with one another, help one another, live for one another. For this our love is too small, but we will earnestly pray that Christ gives us His love with which to love. With God's love shed abroad in our hearts through the Holy Spirit, we shall be so one that the world will know that it is indeed the truth that the Father sent Christ into the world and that Christ has given in us the very life and love of heaven.

Holy Father, we know now with what petitions He, who always lives to make intercession, continually approaches You. It is for the perfect unity of His disciples. Father, we, too, would cry to You for this blessing. Sadly, how divided is Your Church! It is not the division of language or country that we deplore, not even the difference of doctrine that so much grieves us. But, Lord, the lack of that unity of spirit and love whereby Your Church should convince the world that she is from heaven.

O Lord! We desire to confess before You with deep shame the coldness, selfishness, distrust, and bitterness that is still at times to be seen among Your children. We confess before You our own lack of that fervent and perfect love to which You have called us. Oh, forgive, and have mercy upon us.

Lord God! Visit Your people. It is through the one Spirit that we can know and show our unity in the one Lord. Let Your Holy Spirit work powerfully in Your believing people to make them one. Let it be felt in every circle where God's children meet each other how indispensable a close union in the love of Jesus is. And let my heart, too, be delivered from self, to realize, in the fellowship with Your children, how we are one, JUST AS You, Father, and Your Son are one. Amen.

FOR FURTHER THOUGHT

1. *Jesus prayed to the Father that believers "may be one just as We are one." What was the nature of Christ's "oneness" with the Father, and how can that oneness be demonstrated in the Church today?*

2. *Of what benefit is it for the world to see the unity and the lack of selfishness in the Church of Christ? How will seeing this in the Church affect the world's view of the work of Jesus Christ?*

3. *What heart attitude must you have to love like Jesus loved—to give yourself fully to your fellow believers in selfless love and compassion?*

Day 15

In His Dependence

on the Father

Then Jesus answered and said to them,
"Most assuredly, I say to you, the Son can do nothing of Himself,
but what He sees the Father do; for whatever He does, the Son also
does in like manner. For the Father loves the Son, and shows Him
all things that He Himself does; and He will show Him
greater works than these, that you may marvel."
John 5:19–20

"I know my own and my own know me,
just as the Father knows me and I know the Father."
John 10:14–15 esv

OUR relationship to Jesus is the exact counterpart of His to the Father. And so the words in which He sets forth His fellowship with the Father have their truth in us, too. And as the words of Jesus in John 5 describe the natural relationship between every father and son, whether on earth or in heaven, they are applicable not only to the Only Begotten, but to every one who in and like Jesus is called a son of God.

We cannot better catch the simple truth and force of the illustration than by thinking of Jesus with His earthly father in the carpenter's shop learning his trade. The first thing you notice is the entire *dependence*: "The Son can do nothing of Himself, but what He sees the Father do." Then you are struck by the implicit *obedience* that just seeks to imitate the father: "for whatever He does, the Son also does in like manner." You then notice the loving *intimacy* to which the father admits him, keeping back none of his secrets: "For the Father loves the Son, and shows Him all things that He Himself does." And in this dependent obedience on his son's part, and the loving teaching on the father's part, you have the pledge of an ever-growing advance to greater works. Step by step, the son will be led up to all that the father himself can do: "He will show Him greater works than these, that you may marvel."

In this picture we have the reflection of the relationship between God the Father and the Son in His blessed humanity. If His human nature is to be something real and true, and if we are to understand how Christ is in very deed to be our example, we must believe fully in what our blessed Lord here reveals to us of the secrets of His inner life. The words He speaks are literal truth. His dependence on the Father for each moment of His life was absolutely and intensely real: "The Son can do nothing of Himself, but what He sees the Father do." He counted it no humiliation to wait on Him for His commands; He rather considered it His highest blessedness to let Himself be led and guided by the Father as a child. And accordingly, He held Himself bound in strictest obedience to say and do only what the Father showed Him: "Whatever (the Father) does, the Son also does in like manner."

> *he words He speaks are literal truth. His dependence on the Father for each moment of His life was absolutely and intensely real: "The Son can do nothing of Himself, but what He sees the Father do."*

The proof of this is the exceeding carefulness with which in everything He seeks to keep to holy scripture. In His sufferings, He will endure all in order that the scriptures may be fulfilled. For this He remained the whole night in prayer. In such continued prayer He presents His thoughts to the Father, and waits for the answer, so that He may know the Father's will. No child in his ignorance, no slave in his bondage was ever so anxious to keep to what the father or master had said as the Lord Jesus was to follow the teaching and guidance of His heavenly Father. On this account the Father kept nothing hidden from Him. The entire dependence and willingness always to learn were rewarded with the most perfect communication of all the Father's secrets. "For the Father loves the Son, and shows Him all things that He Himself does; and He will show Him greater works than these, that you may marvel." The Father had formed a glorious life plan for the Son, so that in Him the divine life might be shown forth in the conditions of human existence. This plan was shown to the Son piece by piece until at last all was gloriously accomplished.

Child of God, it is not only for the only-begotten Son that a life plan has been arranged, but for each one of His children. Just in proportion as we live in more or less entire dependence on the Father will this life plan be more or less perfectly worked out in our lives. The nearer the believer comes to this entire dependence of the Son, "doing nothing but what He sees the Father do," and then to His implicit obedience, "whatever He does, doing these in like manner," so much more will the promise be fulfilled to us: "The Father shows Him all things that He Himself does; and He will show Him greater works than these." LIKE CHRIST! That word calls us to a life of conformity to the Son in His blessed dependence on the Father.

Each one of us is invited to live this way.

To such a life in dependence on the Father, the first thing that is necessary is a firm faith that He will make known His will to us. I think this is something that keeps many back, for they cannot believe that the Lord cares for them so much that He will indeed give Himself the trouble every day to teach them and to make known to them His will, just as He did to Jesus. Christian, you are of more value to the Father than you know. You are as much worth as the price He paid for you—that is, the blood of His Son, and He therefore attaches the highest value to the least thing that concerns you, and will guide you even in what is most insignificant. He longs more for close and constant fellowship with you than you can conceive. He can use you for His glory and make something of you higher than you can understand. The Father loves His child and shows him what He does. That He proved in Jesus, and He will prove it in us, too. There must only be the surrender to expect His teaching. Through His Holy Spirit He gives this most tenderly. Without removing us from our circle, the Father can so conform us to Christ's image that we can be a blessing and joy to all. Do not let unbelief of God's compassionate love prevent us from expecting the Father's guidance in all things.

Like Christ! That word calls us to a life of conformity to the Son in His blessed dependence on the Father. Each one of us is invited to live this way.

Let the unwillingness to submit yourself as little keep you back. This is the second great hindrance. The desire for independence was the temptation in paradise, is the temptation in each human heart. It seems hard to be nothing, to know nothing, to will nothing. And yet it is so blessed. This dependence brings us into most blessed communion with God. Of us it becomes true as of Jesus, "The Father loves the Son, and shows Him all things that He Himself does." This dependence takes from us all care and responsibility, for we have only to obey orders. It gives real power and strength of will, because we know that He works in us to will and to do. It gives us the blessed assurance that our work will succeed, because we have allowed God alone to take charge of it.

My brother, if you have before now known only little of this life of conscious dependence and simple obedience, begin today. Let your Savior be your example in this. It is His blessed will to live in you, and in you to be again what He was here on earth. He only longs for your submission, which He will work in you. Offer yourself to the Father this day, after the example of the First-begotten, to do nothing of yourself but only what the Father shows you. Fix your gaze on Jesus as also in this the example and promise of what you shall be. Adore Him who, for your sake, humbled Himself and showed how blessed the dependent life can be.

Blessed dependence! It is indeed the disposition that becomes us toward such a God. It gives Him the glory that belongs to Him as God. It keeps the soul in peace and rest, for it allows God to care for all. It keeps the mind quiet and prepared to receive and use the Father's teaching. And it is so gloriously rewarded in the deeper experience of holy fellowship, and the continued ever-advancing discoveries of His will and work with which the Father crowns it. Blessed dependence, in which the Son lived on earth, you are the desire of my soul.

> *lessed dependence! It is indeed the disposition that becomes us toward such a God. It gives Him the glory that belongs to Him as God. It keeps the soul in peace and rest, for it allows God to care for all.*

O my Father, the longer I fix my gaze on the image of the Son, the more I discover the fearful ruin of my nature, and how far sin has estranged me from You. To be dependent on You: there can be no higher blessedness than this—to trust in all things in a God such as You are, so wise and good, so rich and powerful. And it has become the most difficult thing there can be. We would rather be dependent on our own folly than the God of all glory. Even Your own children, O most blessed Father, often think it so hard to give up their own thoughts and will, to believe that absolute dependence on God, to the very least things, is alone true blessedness.

Lord! I come to You with the humble prayer: teach me this. He who purchased with His own blood for me the everlasting, blessedness, has shown me in His own life where that blessedness consists. And I know He will now lead and keep me in it. O my Father! In Your Son I yield myself to You, to be made like Him, like Him to do nothing of myself but what I see the Father doing. Father! You will take even me, too, like the Firstborn, and for His sake, into Your training, and show me what You do. Amen.

For Further Thought

1. *What did Jesus' words, "The Son can do nothing of Himself, but what He sees the Father do," demonstrate about His relationship with the Father?*
2. *To what kind of relationship with the Father does Jesus invite you to live today and every day? What must you do in order to live in that kind of relationship?*
3. *What are the benefits and blessings you will most certainly receive when your relationship with Jesus and with the Father is like that of Jesus' relationship with His Father?*

Day 16

In His Love

*"A new commandment I give to you, that you love one another:
just as I have loved you, you also are to love one another."*
John 13:34 ESV

*"This is My commandment, that you
love one another as I have loved you."*
John 15:12

JUST AS: We begin to understand somewhat of the blessedness of that little phrase. It is not the command of a law that only convinces of sin and powerlessness, but a new command under a new covenant that is established on better promises. It is the command of Him who asks nothing that He has not provided, and now offers to bestow. It is the assurance that He expects nothing from us, that He does not work in us: JUST AS I have loved you, and every moment am pouring out that love upon you through the Holy Spirit, IN THE SAME WAY do you love one another. The measure, the strength, and the work of your love you will find in My love to you.

JUST AS I have loved you: that phrase gives us the *measure* of the love with which we must love each other. True love knows no measure; it gives itself entirely. It may take into consideration the time and measure of showing it, but love itself is always whole and undivided. This is the greatest glory of divine love that we have, in the Father and Son, two persons, who in love remain one Being, each losing Himself in the other. This is the glory of the love of Jesus, who is the image of God, that He loves us just as the Father loves Him. And this is the glory of brotherly love, that it will know of no other law than to love just as God and Christ.

He who desires to be like Christ must unhesitatingly accept this as his rule of life. He knows how difficult, how impossible it often is to in this way love brethren, in whom there is so much that is offensive or unamiable. Before going out to meet them in circumstances where his love may be tested, he goes in secret to the Lord, and with his eye fixed on his own sin and unworthiness asks: "How much do you owe your Lord?" He goes to the cross and seeks there to fathom the love with which the Lord has loved him. He lets the light of the immeasurable love of Him who is in heaven, his Head and his Brother, shine in upon his soul, until he learns to feel divine love has but one law: Love does not seeks its own, love gives itself wholly. And he lays himself on the altar before his Lord: "Just as You have loved me, so will I love the brethren. In virtue of my union with Jesus, and in Jesus with them, there can be no question of anything less: I love them as Christ did." Oh, that Christians would close their ears to all the reasonings of their own hearts and fix their eyes only on the law that He who loves them has promulgated in His own example. Then they would realize that there is nothing for them to do but this—to accept His commands and to obey them.

Our love may recognize no other measure than His, because His love is *the strength* of ours. The love of Christ is no mere idea or sentiment; it is a real divine life power. As long as the Christian does not understand this, it cannot exert its full power in him. But when his faith rises to realize that Christ's love is nothing less than the imparting of Himself and His love to the beloved, and he becomes rooted in this love as the source from where his life derives its sustenance, then he sees that his Lord simply asks that he should allow His love to flow through him. He must live in a Christ-given strength, for the love of Christ constrains him and enables him to love as He did.

> *J*ust as I have loved you: that word gives us the measure of the love with which we must love each other.

From this love of Christ the Christian also learns what *the work* of his love to the brethren must be. We have already had occasion to speak of many manifestations of love: its loving service, its self-denial, its meekness. Love is the root of all these. It teaches the disciple to look at himself as really called on to be, in his little circle, just like Jesus, the one who lives solely to love and help others. Paul prays for the Philippians: "That your love may abound still more and more in knowledge and all discernment" (Phil. 1:9). Love does not comprehend immediately what the work is that it can do. The believer who prays that his love may abound in knowledge and really takes Christ's example as his rule of life will be taught what a great and glorious work there is for him to do. The Church of God, and every child of God, as well as the world, has an unspeakable need of love, of the manifestation of Christ's love. The Christian who really takes the Lord's word, "Love one another, *just as* I have loved you," as a command that must be obeyed, carries about a power for blessing and life for all with whom he comes in contact. Love is the explanation of the whole wonderful life of Christ, and of the wonder of His death. Divine love in God's children will still work its mighty wonders.

"Behold what manner of love!" (1 John 3:1). "See how He loved!" (John 11:36). These words are the superscription over the love of the Father and of the Son. They must yet become the keywords to the life of every Christian. They will be so where in living faith and true consecration the command of Christ to love, just as He loved, is accepted as the law of life. As early as the call of Abraham, this principle was deposited as a living seed in God's kingdom, that what God is for us we must be for others. "I will bless you...and you shall be a blessing" (Gen. 12:2). If "I have loved you" is the highest manifestation of what God is for us, then "Just as I, you" must be the first and highest expression of what the child of God must be. In preaching, as in the life, of the church, it must be understood: *The love that loves like Christ is the sign of true discipleship.*

Beloved Christians! Christ Jesus longs for you in order to make you, amid those who surround you, a very fountain of love. The love of heaven desires to take possession of you in order that, in and through you, it may work its blessed work on earth. Yield to its rule. Offer yourself unreservedly to its indwelling. Honor it by the confident assurance that it can teach you to love as Jesus loved. As conformity to the Lord Jesus must be the chief mark of your Christian walk, so love must be the chief mark of that conformity. Do not be disheartened if you do not attain it immediately. Only keep firm hold of the command, "Love, just as I have loved you." It takes time to grow into it. Take time in secret to gaze on that image of love. Take time in prayer and meditation to fan the desire for it into a burning flame. Take time to survey all around you, whoever they are and whatever may happen, with this one thought, "I must love them." Take time to become conscious of your union with your Lord so that every fear as to the possibility of this kind of loving may be met with the word: "Have not I commanded you: Love as I have loved"? Christian, take time in loving communion with Jesus your loving example, and then you will joyfully fulfill this command, too, to love just as He did.

> *The Church of God, and every child of God, as well as the world, has an unspeakable need of love, of the manifestation of Christ's love.*

Lord Jesus, who has loved me so wonderfully and now commands me to love just as You, look at me at Your feet. Joyfully would I accept Your commands, and now go out in Your strength to demonstrate Your love to all.

In Your strength, O my Lord, be therefore pleased to reveal Your love to me. Shed abroad Your love in my heart through Your Holy Spirit. Let me live each moment in the experience that I am the beloved of God.

Lord, let me understand that I can love, not with my own but with Your love. You live in me, and Your Spirit dwells and works in me. From You there streams into me the love with which I can love others. You only ask of me that I understand and accept my calling, and that I surrender myself to live as You did. You desire that I look at my old nature with its selfishness and unlovingness as crucified, and in faith prepare to do as You command.

Lord, I do it. In the strength of my Lord, I desire to live *to love just as You have loved me.* Amen.

FOR FURTHER THOUGHT

1. *What is the nature of the love God calls you to live in toward your Christian brethren and toward people who are still in and of the world?*
2. *What can you do in order to more observably and effectively love your Christian brothers, even those who are difficult to love?*
3. *In what ways did Jesus model for you the kind of love He commanded you to demonstrate toward others while you live among them on this earth?*

Day 17

In His Prayer

Now in the morning, having risen a long while
before daylight, He went out and departed to
a solitary place; and there He prayed.
MARK 1:35

And He said to them, "Come aside by
yourselves to a deserted place and rest a while."
MARK 6:31

IN His life of secret prayer, too, my Savior is my example. He could not maintain the heavenly life in His soul without continually separating Himself from man and communing with His Father. With the heavenly life in me it is no different, for it has the same need of entire separation from man, the need not only of single moments, but of time enough for fellowship with the fountain of life, the Father in heaven.

It was at the commencement of His public ministry that the event happened that so attracted the attention of His disciples that they wrote it down. After a day full of wonders and of work at Capernaum (Mark 1:21–32), the press in the evening became still greater. The whole town is before the door. Sick are healed and devils are cast out. It is late before they get to sleep, and in the throng there is little time for quiet or for secret prayer. And indeed, as they rise early in the morning, they find Him gone. In the silence of the night, He has gone out to seek a place of solitude in the wilderness. When they find Him there, He is still praying.

And why did my Savior need these hours of prayer? Did He not know the blessedness of silently lifting up His soul to God in the midst of the most pressing business? Did not the Father dwell in Him? And did He not in the depth of His heart enjoy unbroken communion with Him? Yes, that hidden life was indeed His portion. But that life, as subject to the law of humanity, had need of continual refreshing and renewing from the fountain. It was a life of dependence, and just because it was strong and true, it could not bear the loss of direct and constant fellowships with the Father, with whom and in whom it had its being and its blessedness.

What a lesson for every Christian! Much fellowship with man is dissipating and dangerous to our spiritual life, for it brings us under the influence of the visible and temporal. Nothing can make up for the loss of secret and direct fellowship with God. Even work in the service of God and of love is exhausting. We cannot bless others without power going out from us, so this must be renewed from above. The law of the manna, that what is heavenly cannot remain good long upon earth but must day by day be renewed afresh from heaven, still holds true. Jesus Christ teaches it to us: I need every day time to have communion with my Father in secret. My life is like His, a life hidden in heaven, in God, and it needs time day by day to be fed from heaven. It is *from heaven* alone that the power to lead a *heavenly life* on earth can come.

And what may have been the prayers that occupied our Lord there so long? If I could hear Him pray, how I might learn how I, too, must pray! Praise God, of His prayers we have more than one recorded, so that in them, too, we might learn to follow His holy example. In the high-priestly prayer (see John 17) we hear Him speak, as in the deep calm of heaven, to His Father. In His Gethsemane prayer, a few hours later, we see Him call out of the depths of trouble and darkness to God. In these two prayers we have all: the highest and the deepest that there is to be found in the communion of prayer between Father and Son.

> *Even work in the service of God and of love is exhausting. We cannot bless others without power going out from us, so this must be renewed from above.*

In both these prayers we see how He addresses God. Each time it is *Father! O my Father!* In that word lies the secret of all prayer. The Lord knew that He was a Son, and that the Father loved Him. With that word He placed Himself in the full light of the Father's countenance. This was to Him the greatest need and greatest blessing of prayer, to enter into the full enjoyment of the Father's love. Let it be this way with me, too. Let the principal part of my prayer be the holy silence and adoration of faith, in which I wait on God until He reveals Himself to me and gives me, through His Spirit, the loving assurance that He looks down on me as a Father, that I am well-pleasing to Him.

He who in prayer does not have time in quietness of soul, and in full consciousness of its meaning, to say "Abba Father," has missed the best part of prayer. It is in prayer that the witness of the Spirit that we are children of God and that the Father draws near and delights in us must be exercised and strengthened. "If our heart does not condemn us, we have confidence toward God. And whatever we ask we receive from Him, because we keep His commandments and do those things that are pleasing in His sight" (1 John 3:21–22).

In both these prayers I also see what He desired: *that the Father may be glorified*. He speaks: "I have glorified You; glorify Your Son, that Your Son *also may glorify You*" (John 17:1, 4). That will assuredly have been the spirit of every prayer: the entire surrender of Himself only to live for the Father's will and glory. All that He asked had but one object, "That God might be glorified." In this, too, He is my example. I must seek to have the spirit of each prayer I offer: "Father! Bless Your child, and glorify Your grace in me, only that Your child may glorify You." Everything in the universe must show forth God's glory. The Christian who is inspired with this thought, and makes use of prayer to express it, until he is thoroughly filled with it, will have power in prayer. Even of His work in heaven our Lord says: "Whatever you ask in My name, that I will do, *that the Father may be glorified in the Son*" (John 14:13). O my soul, learn from Your Savior, before you ever pour out Your desires in prayer, first to yield Yourself as a whole burnt offering, with the one object that God may be glorified in You.

> *I*t is in prayer that the witness of the Spirit that we are children of God and that the Father draws near and delights in us must be exercised and strengthened.

Then you have sure ground on which to pray. You will feel the strong desire, as well as the full liberty, to ask the Father that in each part of Christ's example, in each feature of Christ's image, you may be made like Him, that so God may be glorified. You will understand how, only in continually renewed prayer, the soul can surrender itself to wait so that God may from heaven do in it what will be to His glory. Because Jesus surrendered Himself so entirely to the glory of His Father, He was worthy to be our mediator and could in His high-priestly prayer ask such great blessings for His people. Learn like Jesus only to seek God's glory in prayer, and you will become a true intercessor, one who can not only approach the throne of grace with his own needs, but can also pray for others the effective, fervent prayer of a righteous man that avails much (see James 5:16). The words that the Savior put into our mouth in the Lord's Prayer: "Your will be done," because He was made like His brethren in all things, He took from our lips again and made His own in Gethsemane, so that from Him we might receive them back again, in the power of His atonement and intercession, and so be able to pray them just as He had done. You, too, shall become Christlike in that priestly intercession, on which the unity and prosperity of the Church and the salvation of sinners so much depend.

And he who in every prayer makes God's glory the chief object will also, if God calls him to it, have strength for the prayer of Gethsemane. Every prayer of Christ was intercession, because He had given Himself for us. All He asked and received was in our interest, and every prayer He prayed was in the spirit of self-sacrifice. Give yourself, too, wholly to God for man, and as with Jesus so with us, the entire sacrifice of ourselves to God in every prayer of daily life is the only preparation for those single hours of soul-struggle in which we may be called to some special act of the surrender of the will that costs us tears and anguish. But he who has learned the former will surely receive strength for the latter.

O my brother! If you and I want to be like Jesus, we must especially contemplate Jesus praying alone in the wilderness. *There is the secret of His wonderful life.* What He did and spoke to man *was first spoken and lived through with the Father.* In communion with Him the anointing with the Holy Spirit was each day renewed. He who wants to be like Him in his walk and conversation must simply begin here, that he follows Jesus into solitude. Even though it cost the sacrifice of night's rest, of business, of fellowship with friends, *the time must be found to be alone with the Father.* Besides the ordinary hour of prayer, he will feel at times irresistibly drawn to enter into the holy place, and not to come there until it has newly been revealed to him that God is his portion. In his secret chamber, with closed door, or in the solitude of the wilderness, God must be found every day, and our fellowship with Him renewed. If Christ needed it, how much more we! What it was to Him it will be for us.

What it was to Him is apparent from what is written of His baptism: "It came to pass that Jesus also was baptized; and while He prayed, the heaven was opened. And the Holy Spirit descended in bodily form like a dove upon Him, and a voice came from heaven which said, 'You are My beloved Son; in You I am well pleased'" (Luke 3:21–22). Yes, this will be to us the blessing of prayer: the opened heaven, the baptism of the Spirit, the Father's voice, the blessed assurance of His love and good pleasure. *As with Jesus, so with us: from above, from above must it all come in answer to prayer.*

Christlike praying in secret will be the secret of Christlike living in public. O let us rise and avail ourselves of our wonderful privilege—the Christlike boldness of access into the Father's presence, the Christlike liberty with God in prayer.

O my blessed Lord, You have called me, and I have followed You, that I may bear Your image in all things. Daily I desire to seek Your footsteps, so that I may be led by You wherever You go. This day I have found them, wet with the dew of night, leading to the wilderness. There I have seen You kneeling for hours before the Father. There I have heard You, too, in prayer. You give up all to the Father's glory, and from the Father You ask, expect, and receive all. Impress, I ask You, this wonderful vision deep into my soul: my Savior rising up a great while before day to seek communion with His Father, and to ask and obtain in prayer all that He needed for His life and work.

O my Lord! Who am I that I may listen to You this way? Yes, who am I that You call me to pray, even as You have done? Precious Savior, from the depths of my heart I ask You to awaken in me the same strong need of secret prayer. Convince me more deeply that, as with You so with me, the divine life cannot attain its full growth without much secret communion with my heavenly Father, so that my soul may indeed dwell in the light of His countenance. Let this conviction awaken in me such burning desire that I may not rest until each day afresh my soul has been baptized in the streams of heavenly love. You, who are my example and intercessor, teach me to pray like You. Amen.

FOR FURTHER THOUGHT

1. *Why do you think that Jesus, the only begotten Son of God in whom the Father dwelled, needed time alone with His Father to pray? What does His need for personal prayer tell you about your need for the same thing?*

2. *Read 1 John 3:21–22. What does this passage teach you about the importance of personal prayer, of spending time alone with God?*

3. *If you want to be like Jesus in all ways, what must you do when it comes to your prayer life? What kind of changes would that mean in how you have approached prayer in the past?*

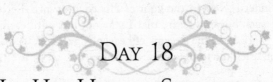

DAY 18

IN HIS USE OF SCRIPTURE

*"That all things must be fulfilled which were written
in the Law of Moses and the Prophets
and the Psalms concerning Me."*

LUKE 24:44

WHAT the Lord Jesus accomplished here on earth as man He owed greatly to His use of the scriptures. He found in them the way marked in which He had to walk, the food and the strength on which He could work, the weapon by which He could overcome every enemy. The scriptures were indeed indispensable to Him through all His life and passion. From beginning to end, His life was the fulfillment of what had been written of Him in the volume of the Book.

It is scarcely necessary to cite proofs of this. In the temptation in the wilderness (Matt. 4:1–11), it was by His *"It is written"* that He conquered Satan. In His conflicts with the Pharisees, He continually appealed to the Word: *"What does the scripture say?" "Have you not read?" "Is it not written?"* In His interactions with His disciples, it was always from the scriptures that He proved the certainty and necessity of His sufferings and resurrection: *"How otherwise can the scriptures be fulfilled?"* And in His communication with His Father in His last sufferings, it is in the words of scripture that He pours out the complaint of being forsaken, and then again entrusts His spirit into the Father's hands. All this has a very deep meaning. He was Himself the living Word. He had the Spirit without measure. If anyone could have done without the written Word, it was Him. And yet we see that it is everything to Him. More than anyone else, He shows us through this that *the life of God in human flesh and the word of God in human speech* are inseparably connected. Jesus would not have been what He was, could not have done what He did, had He not yielded Himself step by step to be led and sustained by the Word of God.

Let us try to understand what this teaches us. The Word of God is more than once called Seed; it is the seed of the divine life. We know what seed is. It is that wonderful organism in which the life, the invisible essence of a plant or tree, is so concentrated and embodied that it can be taken away and made available to impart the life of the tree elsewhere. This use may be twofold. As fruit we eat it.

For instance, in the corn that gives us bread, the life of the plant becomes our nourishment and our life. Or we plant it, and the life of the plant reproduces and multiplies itself. In both aspects, the Word of God is seed.

True life is found only in God. But that life cannot be imparted to us unless it is set before us in some shape in which we know and apprehend it. It is in the Word of God that the invisible divine life takes shape, brings itself within our reach, and becomes communicable. The life, the thoughts, the sentiments, the power of God—all are embodied in His words. And it is only through His Word that the life of God can really enter into us. His Word is the seed of the heavenly life.

As the bread of life we eat it, we feed upon it. In eating our daily bread, the body takes in the nourishment that visible nature, the sun and the earth, prepared for us in the seed-corn. We assimilate it, and it becomes our very own, part of ourselves, our life. In feeding on the Word of God, the powers of the heavenly life enter into us and become our very own. We assimilate them, and they become a part of ourselves, the life of our life.

Or we use the seed to plant. The words of God are sown in our heart. They have a divine power of reproduction and multiplication. The very life that is in them, the divine thought, disposition, or powers that each of them contains, takes root in the believing heart and grows up. Then the very thing of which the word was the expression is produced within us. The words of God are the seeds of the fullness of the divine life.

> Jesus would not have been what He was, could not have done what He did, had He not yielded Himself step by step to be led and sustained by the Word of God.

When the Lord Jesus was made man, He became entirely dependent on the Word of God, and He submitted Himself wholly to it. His mother taught it to Him. The teachers of Nazareth instructed Him in it. In meditation and prayer, in the exercise of obedience and faith, He was led, during His silent years of preparation, to understand and appropriate it. The Word of the Father was to the Son the life of His soul. What He said in the wilderness was spoken from His inmost personal experience: "Man shall not live by bread alone, but by every word of God" (see Luke 4:4). He felt He could not live unless the Word brought Him the life of the Father. His whole life was a life of faith, a depending on the Word of the Father. The Word was to Him not instead of the Father, but the vehicle for the living fellowship with the living God. And He had His whole mind and heart so filled with it that the Holy Spirit could at each moment find within Him, all ready for use, the right word to suggest just as He needed it.

Child of God! If you desire to become a man of God, strong in faith, full of blessing, rich in fruit to the glory of God, be full of the Word of God. Like Christ, make the Word your bread. Let it dwell richly in you. Have your heart full of it. Feed on it. Believe it. Obey it: It is only by believing and obeying that the Word can enter into our inward parts, into our very being. Take it day by day as the Word that proceeds, not has proceeded, but proceeds and is proceeding out of the mouth of God, as the Word of the living God, who in it holds living fellowship with His children and speaks to them in living power. Take your thoughts of God's will, and God's work, and God's purpose with you and the world, not from the Church and not from Christians around you, but from the Word taught you by the Father, and then, like Christ, you will be able to fulfill all that is written in the scripture concerning you.

> *Child of God! If you desire to become a man of God, strong in faith, full of blessing, rich in fruit to the glory of God, be full of the Word of God.*

In Christ's use of scripture, the most remarkable thing is this: *He found Himself there, and He saw there His own image and likeness.* And He gave Himself to the fulfillment of what He found written there. It was this that encouraged Him under the bitterest sufferings and strengthened Him for the most difficult work. Everywhere He saw traced by God's own hand the divine plan and direction: *through suffering to glory.* He had but one thought: to be what the Father had said He should be, to have His life correspond exactly to the image of what He should be as He found it in the Word of God.

Disciple of Jesus, in the scriptures *your likeness, too, is to be found,* a picture of what the Father means you to be. Seek to have a deep and clear impression of what the Father says in His word that you should be. If this is once fully understood, it is inconceivable what courage it will give to conquer every difficulty. To know that it is ordained of God, that I have seen what has been written concerning me in God's Book, and that I have seen the image of what I am called in God's plans to be: this thought inspires the soul with a faith that conquers the world.

The Lord Jesus found His own image not only in the institutions, but especially in the believers of the Old Testament. Moses and Aaron, Joshua, David, and the Prophets, were types. And so He is Himself again the image of believers in the New Testament. It is especially in *Him and His example* that we must find our own image in the scriptures. "Being transformed into the same image from glory to glory, just as by the Spirit of the Lord" (2 Cor. 3:18), we must in the scripture-glass gaze on that image as our own. In order to accomplish His work in us, the Spirit teaches us to take Christ as in very deed our example, and to gaze on every feature as the promise of what we can be.

Blessed is the Christian who has truly done this, who has not only found Jesus in the scriptures, but also in His image the promise and example of what he is to become. Blessed is the Christian who yields himself to be taught by the Holy Spirit not to indulge in human thoughts as to scripture and what it says of believers, but in simplicity to accept what it reveals of God's thoughts about His children.

Child of God! It was "according to the scriptures" that Jesus Christ lived and died. It was "according to the scriptures" that He was raised again. All that the scriptures said He must do or suffer He was able to accomplish, because He knew and obeyed them. All that the scriptures had promised that the Father should do for Him, the Father did. Oh, give yourself up with an undivided heart to learn in the scriptures what God says and seeks of you. Let the scriptures in which Jesus found every day the food of His life be your daily food and meditation. Go to God's Word each day with the joyful and confident expectation that through the blessed Spirit who dwells in us the Word will indeed accomplish its divine purpose in you. Every word of God is full of a divine life and power. Be assured that when you seek to use the scriptures as Christ used them, they will do for you what they did for Him. God has marked out the plan of your life in His Word, and each day you will find some portion of it there. Nothing makes a man more strong and courageous than the assurance that he is just living out the will of God. God Himself, who had your image portrayed in the scriptures, will see to it that the scriptures are fulfilled in you, if like His Son you will just surrender yourself to this as the highest object of your life.

> *Every word of God is full of a divine life and power. Be assured that when you seek to use the scriptures as Christ used them, they will do for you what they did for Him.*

O Lord, my God! I thank You for Your precious Word, the divine glass of all unseen and eternal realities. I thank You that I have in it the image of Your Son, who is Your image, and also—O wonderful grace!—my image. I thank You that as I gaze on Him I may also see what I can be.

O my Father! Teach me rightly to understand what a blessing Your Word can bring me. To Your Son, when here on earth, it was the manifestation of Your will, the communication of Your life and strength, the fellowship with Yourself. In the acceptance and the surrender to Your Word, He was able to fulfill all Your plans. May Your Word be all this to me, too. Make it to me, each day freshly through the anointing of the Holy Spirit, the Word proceeding from the mouth of God, the voice of Your living presence speaking to me. May I feel with each word of Yours that it is God coming to impart to me somewhat of His own life. Teach me to keep it hidden in my heart as a divine seed, which in its own time will spring up and reproduce in me in divine reality the very life that was hidden in it, the very thing which I at first saw in it only as a thought. Teach me above all, O my God, to find in it Him who is its center and substance, Himself the Eternal Word. Finding Him, and myself in Him, as my head and example, I shall learn like Him to consider Your Word my food and my life.

I ask this, O my God, in the name of our blessed Christ Jesus. Amen.

For Further Thought

1. *In what specific ways and for what specific purposes did Jesus use scripture? What benefits did He receive from doing so, and what benefits would you receive by following His example?*
2. *What were the results of Christ's using scripture in His dealings with His disciples, with His earthly enemies, and with the devil?*
3. *Read 2 Corinthians 3:18. What must you do in order to make that verse's promise a reality in your Christian life?*

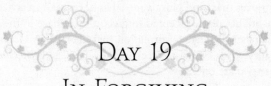

Day 19

In Forgiving

Bearing with one another, and forgiving one another,
if anyone has a complaint against another;
even as Christ forgave you, so you also must do.
COLOSSIANS 3:13

IN the life of grace, forgiveness is one of the first blessings we receive from God. It is also one of the most glorious. It is the transition from the old to the new life, the sign and pledge of God's love, for with it we receive the right to all the spiritual gifts that are prepared for us in Christ. The redeemed saint can never forget, either here or in eternity, that he is a forgiven sinner. Nothing works more mightily to inflame his love, to awaken his joy, or to strengthen his courage than the experience, continually renewed by the Holy Spirit as a living reality, of God's forgiving love. Every day, yes, every thought of God reminds him: I owe everything to pardoning grace.

This forgiving love is one of the greatest marvels in the manifestation of the divine nature. In it God finds His glory and blessedness. And it is in this glory and blessedness God wants His redeemed people to share, when He calls on them, as soon and as much as they have received forgiveness, also to bestow it upon others.

Have you ever noticed how often and how expressly the Lord Jesus spoke of it? If we read thoughtfully our Lord's words (Matt. 6:12, 15; 18:2–25; Mark 11:25), we shall understand how inseparably the two are united: God's forgiveness of us and our forgiveness of others. After the Lord was ascended to grant repentance and forgiveness of sins, the scriptures say of Him just what He had said of the Father, so we must forgive like Him. As our text expresses it, *even as Christ* forgave you, *so you also must do.* We must be like God, like Christ, in forgiving.

It is not difficult to find the reason for this. When forgiving love comes to us, it is not only to deliver us from punishment. No, much more: it seeks to win us for its own, to take possession of us and to dwell in us. And when it has come down to dwell in us like this, it does not lose its own heavenly character and beauty. It still is forgiving love seeking to do its work not alone toward us, but in us and through, leading and enabling us to forgive those who sin against us. So much so is this the case that we are told that not to forgive is a sure sign that one has himself not been forgiven. He who only seeks forgiveness from selfishness and as freedom from punishment, but has not truly accepted forgiving love to rule his heart and life, proves that God's forgiveness has never really reached him. He who, on the other hand, has really accepted forgiveness will have in the joy with which he forgives others a continual confirmation that his faith in God's forgiveness of himself is a reality. *From* Christ to receive forgiveness, and *like Christ* to bestow it on others: these two are one.

> *This forgiving love is one of the greatest marvels in the manifestation of the divine nature. In it God finds His glory and blessedness.*

This is what the scriptures and the Church teach. But what do the lives and experience of Christians say? It is sad how many there are who hardly know that it is written this way, or who, if they know it, think it is more than can be expected from a sinful being, or who, if they agree in general to what has been said, always find a reason in their own particular case why it should not be so. Others might be strengthened in evil, assuming that the offender would never forgive had the injury been done to him, or that there are very many eminent Christians who do not act so. Such excuses are never lacking. And yet the command is so very simple, and its sanction so very solemn: "Even as Christ forgave you, so you also must do." "If you do not forgive, neither will your Father in heaven forgive you" (Mark 11:26). With such human reasonings the Word of God is made ineffective. As though it were not just through forgiving love that God seeks to conquer evil, and therefore forgives even up to seventy times seven (see Matt. 18:21–22). As though it were not plain that it is not what the offender would do to me, *but what Christ has done* that must be the rule of my conduct. As though conformity to the example not of Christ Himself but of pious Christians were the sign that I have truly received the forgiveness of sins.

Sadly, what Church or Christian circle is there in which the law of forgiving love is not grievously transgressed? How often in our church assemblies, in philanthropic undertakings as well as in ordinary social interactions, and even in domestic life, proof is given that to many Christians the call to forgive, just as Christ did, has never yet become a ruling principle of their conduct. On account of a difference of opinion or of opposition to a course of action that appeared to us right, on the ground of a real or an imagined slight or the report of some unkind or thoughtless word, feelings of resentment, contempt, or estrangement have been harbored, instead of loving, forgiving, and forgetting like Christ. In such, the thought has never yet taken possession of mind and heart that the law of compassion and love and forgiveness, in which the relationship of the head to the members is rooted, must rule the whole relation of the members to each other.

Beloved followers of Jesus, who are called to manifest His likeness to the world, learn that as forgiveness of your sins was one of the first things Jesus did for you, forgiveness of others is one of the first that you can do for Him. And remember that to the new heart there is a joy even sweeter than that of being forgiven, and that is the joy of forgiving others. The joy of being forgiven is only that of a sinner and of earth, but the joy of forgiving is Christ's own joy, the joy of heaven. Oh, come and see that it is nothing less than the work that Christ Himself does, and the joy with which He Himself is satisfied that you are called to participate in.

It is this way that you can bless the world. It is as the forgiving One that Jesus conquers His enemies and binds His friends to Himself. It is as the forgiving One that Jesus has set up His kingdom and continually extends it. It is through the same forgiving love, not only preached but *shown in the life of His disciples*, that the Church will convince the world of God's love. If the world sees men and women loving and forgiving as Jesus did, it will be compelled to confess that God is with them of a truth.

> Beloved followers of Jesus, learn that as forgiveness of your sins was one of the first things Jesus did for you, forgiveness of others is one of the first that you can do for Him.

And if it still appears too hard and too high, remember that this will only be as long as we consult the natural heart. A sinful nature has no taste for this joy, and it never can attain it. But in union with Christ we can do it. He who abides in Him walks just as He walked. If you have surrendered yourself to follow Christ in everything, then He will by His Holy Spirit enable you to do this, too. Before you come into temptation, accustom yourself to fixing your gaze on Jesus, in the heavenly beauty of His forgiving love as your example: "Beholding. . .the glory of the Lord, [we] are being transformed into the same image from glory to glory" (2 Cor. 3:18). Every time you pray or thank God for forgiveness, make the vow that to the glory of His name you will manifest the same forgiving love to all around you. Before ever there is a question of forgiveness of others, let your heart be filled with love to Christ, love to the brethren, and love to enemies, for a heart full of love finds it blessed to forgive. Let, in each little circumstance of daily life when the temptation not to forgive might arise, the opportunity be joyfully welcomed to show how truly you live in God's forgiving love, how glad you are to let its beautiful light shine through you on others, and how blessed a privilege you feel it to be thus, too, to bear the image of your beloved Lord.

To forgive like You, blessed Son of God! I take this as the law of my life. You who have given the command give also the power. You who had love enough to forgive me will also fill me with love and will teach me to forgive others. You who gave me the first blessing, in the joy of having my sins forgiven, will surely give me the second blessing: the deeper joy of forgiving others as You have forgiven me. Oh, fill me for this purpose with faith in the power of Your love in me, to make me like Yourself, to enable me to forgive the seventy times seven, and so to love and bless all around me.

O my Jesus! Your example is my law: I must be like You. And Your example is my gospel, too: I can be as You are. You are at once my law and my life. What You demand of me by Your example, You work in me by Your life. I shall forgive like You.

Lord, only lead me deeper into my dependence on You, into the all-sufficiency of Your grace and the blessed keeping, which comes from Your indwelling. Then shall I believe and prove the all-prevailing power of love. I shall forgive just as Christ has forgiven me. Amen.

FOR FURTHER THOUGHT

1. *"Even as Christ forgave you, so you also must do." Why is it so important to God that we forgive one another in the very same way Christ has forgiven us? What blessings does God promise to those who walk with an attitude of forgiveness?*

2. *What is Christ's response to you when you consistently forgive those who offend you—even intentionally?*

3. *What must your relationship with Christ look like in order for you to receive the power and the proper motivation to obey God's command to forgive those who sin against you?*

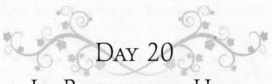

Day 20

In Beholding Him

*But we all, with unveiled face, beholding as in a mirror the glory of
the Lord, are being transformed into the same image from glory to
glory, just as by the Spirit of the Lord.*
2 Corinthians 3:18

MOSES had been forty days on the mount in communion with God. When
he came down, his face shone with divine glory. He did not know it himself, but
Aaron and the people saw it (Exod. 34:30). It was so evidently God's glory that
Aaron and the people feared to approach him.

In this we have an image of what takes place in the New Testament. The
privilege Moses there alone enjoyed is now the portion of every believer. When
we behold the glory of God in Christ, in the glass of the holy scriptures, His glory
shines on us and into us and fills us until it shines out from us again. By gazing on
His glory, the believer is changed through the Spirit into the same image. *Beholding Jesus makes us like Him.*

It is a law of nature that the eye exercises a mighty influence on mind and
character. The education of a child is carried on greatly through the eye, for he
is molded very much by the manners and habits of those he sees continually. To
form and mold our character, the heavenly Father shows us His divine glory in
the face of Jesus. He does it in the expectation that it will give us great joy to gaze
on it, and because He knows that when we gaze on it, we shall be conformed to
the same image. Let every one who desires to be like Jesus note how he can attain
to it.

Look continually to the divine glory as seen in Christ. What is the special
characteristic of that glory? *It is the manifestation of divine perfection in human
form.* The chief marks of the image of the divine glory in Christ are these two: His
humiliation and His love.

There is the glory of His humiliation. When you see how the eternal Son
emptied Himself and became man, and how as man He humbled Himself as a
servant and was obedient even the point of the death of the cross, you have seen
the highest glory of God. The glory of God's omnipotence as Creator, and the
glory of God's holiness as King, is not so wonderful as this: the glory of grace
that humbled itself as a servant to serve God and man. We must learn to look

at this humiliation as really glory. *To be humbled like Christ must be to us the only thing worthy of the name of glory on earth.* It must become in our eyes the most beautiful, the most wonderful, the most desirable thing that can be imagined—a very joy to look upon or to think of. The effect of gazing on it and admiring it will be that you will not be able to conceive of any glory greater than to be and act like Jesus, and then you will long to humble yourself just as He did. Gazing on Jesus, admiring, and adoring Him will work in us the same mind that there was in Him, and so we shall be changed into His image.

Inseparable from this is the glory of His love. The humiliation leads you back to the love as its origin and power. It is from love that the humiliation has its beauty. Love is the highest glory of God. But this love was a hidden mystery, until it was manifest in Christ Jesus. It is only in His humanity, in His gentle, compassionate, and loving fellowship with men—with foolish, sinful, hostile men—that the glory of divine love was first really seen. The soul that gets a glimpse of this glory, that understands that *to love like Christ is alone worthy of the name of glory,* will long to become like Christ in this. Beholding this glory of the love of God in Christ, he is changed to the same image.

> *By* gazing on His glory, the believer is changed through the Spirit into the same image. Beholding Jesus makes us like Him.

Do you desire to be like Christ? Here is the path: Gaze on the glory of God in Him. In Him, that is to say: do not look only to the words and the thoughts and the graces in which His glory is seen, but look to Himself, the living, loving Christ. Behold Him, look into His very eye, look into His face, as a loving friend, as the living God.

Look to Him in adoration. Bow before Him as God. His glory has an almighty living power to impart itself to us, to pass over into us and to fill us.

Look to Him in faith. Exercise the blessed trust that He is yours, that He has given Himself to you, and that you have a claim to all that is in Him. It is His purpose to work out His image in you. Behold Him with the joyful and certain expectation: the glory that I behold in Him is destined for me. He will give it to me, and as I gaze and wonder and trust, I become like Christ.

Look to Him with strong desire. Do not yield to the slothfulness of the flesh that is satisfied without the full blessing of conformity to the Lord. Pray and ask God to free you from all carnal resting content with present attainments, and to fill you with the deep unquenchable longing for His glory. Pray most fervently the prayer of Moses, "show me Your glory" (Exod. 33:18). Let nothing discourage you, not even the apparently slow progress you make, but press onwards with ever growing desire after the blessed prospect that God's Word holds out to you: "We are transformed into the same image from glory to glory."

And as you behold Him, above all, let the look of love not be lacking. Tell Him continually how He has won your heart, how you do love Him, how entirely you belong to Him. Tell Him that to please Him, the beloved One, is your highest, your only joy. Let the bond of love between you and Him be drawn continually closer. Love unites and makes like.

Like Christ! We can be it, we shall be it, each in our measure. The Holy Spirit is the pledge that it shall be. God's holy Word has said, "We are transformed into the same image from glory to glory, just as *by the Spirit of the Lord.*" This is the Spirit who was in Jesus, and through whom the divine glory lived and shone on Him. This Spirit is called "the Spirit of Glory." This Spirit is in us as in the Lord Jesus, and it is His work, in our silent, adoring contemplation, to bring over into us and work within us what we see in our Lord Jesus. Through this Spirit we have already Christ's life in us, with all the gifts of His grace. But that life must be stirred up and developed. It must grow up, pass into our whole being, take possession of our entire nature, and penetrate and pervade it all. We can count on the Spirit to work this in us, if we but yield ourselves to Him and obey Him.

> *Look to Him in adoration. Bow before Him as God. His glory has an almighty living power to impart itself to us, to pass over into us and to fill us.*

As we gaze on Jesus in the Word, He opens our eyes to see the glory of all that Jesus does and is. He makes us willing to be like Him. He strengthens our faith, so that what we behold in Jesus can be in us, because Jesus Himself is ours. He works in us unceasingly the life of abiding in Christ, a wholehearted union and communion with Him. He does according to the promise: "[The Spirit] will glorify Me, for He will take of what is Mine and declare it to you" (John 16:14). We are changed into the image on which we gaze, from glory to glory, *as by the Spirit of the Lord.* Let us only understand that the fullness of the Spirit is given to us, and that he who believingly surrenders himself to be filled with Him will experience how gloriously He accomplishes His work of stamping on our souls and lives the image and likeness of Christ.

Brother! Beholding Jesus and His glory, you can confidently expect to become like Him. Only trust yourself in quietness and restfulness of soul to the leading of the Spirit. "*The Spirit of glory. . .rests upon you*" (1 Pet. 4:14). Gaze on and adore the glory of God in Christ, and then you will be changed with divine power from glory to glory. In the power of the Holy Spirit, the mighty transformation will be accomplished by which your desires will be fulfilled, and *like Christ* will be the blessed God-given experience of your life.

O my Lord! I do thank You for the glorious assurance that while I am engaged with You in my work of beholding Your glory, the Holy Spirit is engaged with me in His work of changing me into that image, of the laying of Your glory on me.

> eholding Jesus and His glory, you can confidently expect to become like Him. Only trust yourself in quietness and restfulness of soul to the leading of the Spirit.

Lord! Grant me to behold Your glory rightly. Moses had been forty days with You when Your glory shone on Him. I acknowledge that my communion with You has been too short and passing, that I have taken too little time to come under the full impression of what Your image is. Lord, teach me this. Draw me in these my meditations, too, to surrender myself to contemplate and adore, until my soul at every line of that image may exclaim: This is glorious! This is the glory of God! O my God, show me Your glory.

And strengthen my faith, blessed Lord, so that, even when I am not conscious of any special experience, the Holy Spirit will do His work. Moses did not know that his face shone. Lord, keep me from looking at self. May I be so taken up only with You that I forget and lose myself in You. Lord! It is he who is dead to self who lives in You.

O my Lord, as often as I gaze upon Your image and Your example, I want to do it in the faith that Your Holy Spirit will fill me, will take entire possession of me, and so work Your likeness in me that the world may see in me somewhat of Your glory. In this faith I will venture to take Your precious word, "FROM GLORY TO GLORY," as my watchword, to be to me the promise of a grace that grows richer every day, of a blessing that is always ready to surpass itself and to make what has been given only the pledge of the better that is to come. Precious Savior! Gazing on You it shall indeed be so, "From glory to glory." Amen.

FOR FURTHER THOUGHT

1. *What are the results of your gazing on God's glory? What kind of changes will gazing on Him that way make in your spiritual life?*
2. *What attitudes or dispositions should you look on Christ with if you are to receive all the benefits and blessings of gazing on Him?*
3. *What does Jesus do in you and for you when you take the time to gaze on Him in the written Word? What does doing that accomplish in your life of faith?*

NOTE

I have left the preceding piece as it was originally published in Dutch. The English Revised Version translates: "But we all, with unveiled face reflecting as in a mirror the glory of the Lord, are transformed into the same image, from glory to glory, even as from the Lord the Spirit," and gives in the margin "beholding as in a mirror." It is difficult to settle which is the better translation, as the original can bear both meanings. I confess that beholding appears to me better to suit the passage: the reflecting the image can only come after we have been, or at least as we are being, "transformed into the same image." It is only as we are transformed into it that we can reflect it, so the means of the transformation appear to be almost better expressed by *beholding* than *reflecting*. However this may be, even if we prefer to translate reflecting, what has been said on beholding does not lose its force. It is the intent, longing, loving, adoring gaze on the glory of God in the face of the beloved Son that transforms.

What rich instruction in regard to the divine photography of which the text speaks there is in what we see in the human art! In the practice of the photographer, we see two things: faith in the power and effects of light, and the wise adjustment of everything in obedience to its laws. With what care the tenderly sensitive plate is prepared to receive the impression! With what precision its relative position to the object to be portrayed is adjusted! How still and undisturbed it is then held face to face with that object! Having done this, the photographer leaves the light to do its wonderful work: his work is indeed a work of faith.

May we learn the precious lessons. Let us believe in the light, in the power of the light of God, to transcribe Christ's image on our heart. "We are *changed* into the same image as by the Spirit of the Lord." Let us not seek to do the work the Spirit must do, rather let us simply trust Him to do it. Our duty is to seek the prepared heart—waiting, longing, praying for the likeness; to take our place face to face with Jesus, studying, gazing, loving, worshipping, and believing that the wonderful vision of that Crucified One is the sure promise of what we can be; and then, putting aside all that can distract, in stillness of soul, silent to God, just to allow the blessed Spirit as the Light of God to do the work. Not less surely or wonderfully than in the light-printing that is done here on earth will our souls receive and show the impress of that wonderful likeness.

I feel tempted to add one thought: what a solemn calling that of ministers as the servants of this heavenly photography, "ministers of the Spirit" in His work (see 2 Cor. 4:6): to lead believers on and point them to Jesus and every trait in that blessed face and life as what they are to be changed to; to help them to that wistful longing, that deep thirsting for conformity to Jesus, which is the true preparation of soul; to teach them how, both in public worship and private prayer, they have just to place themselves face to face with their Lord, and give Him time, as they unbare and expose their whole inner being to the beams of His love and His glory, to come in and take possession, by His Spirit to transform them into His own likeness.

"Who is sufficient for these things? . . . Our sufficiency is from God, who also made us sufficient as ministers of the. . .the Spirit" (2 Cor. 2:16; 3:5–6).

DAY 21

IN HIS HUMILITY

With humility of mind regard one another as more important than
yourselves. . . . Have this attitude in yourselves which was also in
Christ Jesus, who, although He existed in the form of God. . .
emptied Himself, taking the form of a bond-servant, and being
made in the likeness of men. Being found in appearance as
a man, He humbled Himself by becoming obedient
to the point of death, even death on a cross.
PHILIPPIANS 2:3–8 NASB

IN this wonderful passage we have a summary of all the most precious truths that cluster around the person of the blessed Son of God. There is, first, His adorable divinity: *"in the form of God," "equal with God."* Then comes the mystery of His incarnation, in that word of deep and inexhaustible meaning: *"He emptied Himself."* The atonement follows, with the humiliation, and obedience, and suffering, and death, whence it derives its worth: *"He humbled Himself by becoming obedient to the point of death, even death on a cross."* And all is crowned by His glorious exaltation: *"God has highly exalted Him"* (see Phil 2:9). Christ as God, Christ becoming man, Christ as man in humiliation working out our redemption, and Christ in glory as Lord of all: such are the treasures of wisdom this passage contains.

Volumes have been written on the discussion of some of the words the passage contains. And yet sufficient attention has not always been given to the connection in which the Holy Spirit gives this wondrous teaching. It is not in the first place as a statement of truth for the refutation of error, or the strengthening of faith. The object is a very different one. Among the Philippians there was still pride and lack of love. It is with the distinct view of setting Christ's example before them, and teaching them to humble themselves as He did, that this portion of inspiration was given: "With humility of mind regard one another as more important than yourselves. Have this attitude in yourselves which was also in Christ Jesus." He who does not study this portion of God's Word with the wish to become lowly as Christ was has never used it for the one great purpose for which God gave it. Christ descending from the throne of God, and seeking His way back there as man through the humiliation of the cross, reveals the only way by which we ever can reach that throne. The faith that, with His atonement, accepts His example, too, is alone true faith. Each soul that desires to truly belong to Him must in union with Him have His Spirit, His disposition, and His image.

"Have this attitude in yourselves which was also in Christ Jesus, who, although He existed in the form of God. . .emptied Himself. Being found in appearance as a man, He humbled Himself." We must be like Christ in His self-emptying and self-humiliation. The first great act of self-denial in which as God He emptied Himself of His divine glory and power and laid it aside was followed up by the no less wondrous humbling of Himself as man, to the death of the cross. And in this amazing twofold humiliation, the astonishment of the universe and the delight of the Father, holy scripture with the utmost simplicity tells us we must, as a matter of course, be like Christ.

> *E*ach soul that desires to truly belong to Him must in union with Him have His Spirit, His disposition, and His image.

And does Paul, and do the scriptures, and does God really expect this of us? Why not? Or rather, how can they expect anything else? They know indeed the fearful power of pride and the old Adam in our nature. But they know also that Christ has redeemed us not only from the curse but from the power of sin, and that He gives us His resurrection life and power to enable us to live as He did on earth. They say that He is not only our surety, but our example also, so that we not only live through Him, but like Him. And further, not only our example but also our Head, who lives in us and continues in us the life He once led on earth. With such a Christ and such a plan of redemption, can it be otherwise? The follower of Christ must have the same mind as was in Christ; he must especially be like Him in His humility.

Christ's example teaches us that it is not sin that must humble us. This is what many Christians think. They consider daily falls necessary to keep us humble. This is not so. There is indeed a humility that is very lovely, and so of great worth, as the beginning of something more, consisting in the acknowledgment of transgression and shortcomings. But there is a humility that is more heavenly still, even like Christ, which consists, even when grace keeps us from sinning, in the self-abasement that can only wonder that God should bless us, and also that delights to be as nothing before Him to whom we owe all. It is grace we need, and not sin, to make and keep us humble. The heaviest-laden branches always bow the lowest. The greatest flow of water makes the deepest riverbed. The nearer the soul comes to God, the more His majestic presence makes it feel its littleness. It is this alone that makes it possible for each to count others better than himself. Jesus Christ, the Holy One of God, is our example of humility: it was while knowing that the Father had given all things into His hands, and that He was come from God and went to God, that He washed the disciples' feet. It is the divine presence, the consciousness of the divine life and the divine love in us, that will make us humble.

It appears to many Christians an impossibility to say: "I will not think of self, I will esteem others better than myself." They ask grace to overcome the worst outpourings of pride and vainglory, but an entire self-renunciation, such as Christ's, is too difficult and too high for them. If they only understood the deep truth and blessedness of the word, "He who humbles himself shall be exalted" (Luke 14:11), "Whoever loses his life...will find it" (Matt. 16:25), they would not be satisfied with anything less than entire conformity to their Lord in this. And they would find that there is a way to overcome self and self-exaltation: to see it nailed to Christ's cross, and there keep it crucified continually through the Spirit (see Gal. 5:24, Rom. 8:13). He only can grow to such humility who heartily yields himself to live in the fellowship of Christ's death.

> *It is the divine presence, the consciousness of the divine life and the divine love in us, that will make us humble.*

To attain this, two things are necessary. The first is a fixed purpose and surrender from now on to be nothing and seek nothing for oneself, but to live only for God and our neighbor. The other is the faith that appropriates the power of Christ's death in this also, as our death to sin and our deliverance from its power. This fellowship of Christ's death brings an end to the life where sin *is too strong for us;* it is the commencement of a life in us where *Christ is too strong for sin.*

It is only under the teaching and powerful working of the Holy Spirit that one can realize, accept, and keep hold of this truth. But, thank God, we have the Holy Spirit. Oh, that we may trust ourselves fully to His guidance. He *will* guide us, for it is His work, and He will glorify Christ in us. He will teach us to understand that we are dead to sin and the old self, that Christ's life and humility are ours.

This is how Christ's humility is appropriated in faith. This may take place instantly. But the appropriation in experience is gradual. Our thoughts and feelings, our very manners and conversation, have been so long under the dominion of the old self that it takes time to instill and permeate and transfigure them with the heavenly light of Christ's humility. At first the conscience is not perfectly enlightened, for the spiritual taste and the power of discernment have not yet been exercised. But with each believing renewal of the consecration in the depth of the soul: "I have surrendered myself to be humble like Jesus," power will go out from Him to fill the whole being, until in face, and voice, and action, the sanctification of the Spirit will be observable, and the Christian will truly be clothed with humility.

The blessedness of a Christlike humility is unspeakable. It is of great worth in the sight of God: "He gives grace to the humble" (Prov. 3:34, James 4:6). In the spiritual life it is the source of rest and joy. To the humble all God does is right and good. Humility is always ready to praise God for the least of His mercies. Humility does not find it difficult to trust. It submits unconditionally to all that God says. The two whom Jesus praises for their great faith are just those who thought least of themselves. The centurion had said, "I am not worthy that You should come under my roof" (Matt. 8:8), and the Syrophenician woman was content to be numbered with the dogs (Matt. 15:26–28). In relationships with men it is the secret of blessing and love. The humble man does not take offense, and he is very careful not to give it. He is always ready to serve his neighbor, because he has learned from Jesus the divine beauty of being a servant. He finds favor with God and man.

Oh, what a glorious calling for the followers of Christ! To be sent into the world by God to prove that there is nothing more divine than self-humiliation. The humble glorifies God, he leads others to glorify Him, and he will at last be glorified with Him. Who doesn't desire to be humble like Jesus?

> *The humble man does not take offense, and he is very careful not to give it. He is always ready to serve his neighbor, because he has learned from Jesus the divine beauty of being a servant.*

O Lord, who descended from heaven and humbled Yourself to the death of the cross: You call me to take Your humility as the law of my life.

Lord, teach me to understand the absolute need of this. A proud follower of the humble Jesus—this I cannot, I may not be. In the secrecy of my heart, of my closet, in my house, in presence of friends or enemies, in prosperity or adversity, I want to be filled with Your humility.

O my beloved Lord! I feel the need of a new and deeper insight into Your crucifixion and my part in it. Reveal to me how my old proud self is crucified with You. Show me in the light of Your Spirit how I, God's regenerate child, am dead to sin and its power, and how when I am in communion with You, sin has no power over me. Lord Jesus, who has conquered sin, strengthen in me the faith that You are my life, and that You will fill me with Your humility if I will submit to be filled with Yourself and Your Holy Spirit.

Lord, my hope is in You. In faith in You I go into the world to show how the same attitude that was in You is also in Your children, that it teaches us in lowliness of mind each to regard others better than himself. May God help us. Amen.

For Further Thought

1. Read Philippians 2:3–8. What was the purpose of the apostle Paul's writing this passage to the Philippian church? What does it teach you about your relationship with God and with others?
2. What exactly has God given you in order to keep you humble?
3. What are the evidences of your humility as you deal with others—with those who offend you, whose actions or attitudes might give you cause to take offense or "stand up for yourself?"

DAY 22

IN THE LIKENESS OF HIS DEATH

For if we have been united together in the likeness of His death,
certainly we also shall be in the likeness of His resurrection. . . .
For the death that He died, He died to sin once. . .
Likewise you also, reckon yourselves to be dead indeed to sin,
but alive to God in Christ Jesus our Lord.
ROMANS 6:5, 10–11

IT is to the death of Christ we owe our salvation. The better we understand the meaning of that death, the richer will be our experience of its power. In these words we are taught what it is to be one with Christ in the likeness of His death. Let everyone who truly longs to be like Christ in his life seek to understand aright what the likeness of His death means.

Christ had a double work to accomplish in His death. The one was to work out righteousness for us, the other to obtain life for us. When scripture speaks of the first part of this work, it uses the expression *Christ died for our sin* (1 Cor. 15:3), meaning He took sin on Himself, bore its punishment, and, in doing so, He made atonement and brought in a righteousness in which we could stand before God. When scripture speaks of the second part of this work, it uses the expression *He died to sin* (Rom. 6:10). Dying *for sin* has reference to the judicial relationship between Him and sin: God laid our sin upon Him, and through His death atonement is made for sin before God. *Dying to sin* has reference to a personal relationship: through His death, the connection in which He stood to sin was entirely dissolved. During His life, sin had great power to cause Him conflict and suffering. But His death made an end of this. Sin had now no more power to tempt or to hurt Him. He was beyond its reach. Death had completely separated between Him and sin. Christ died to sin.

Like Christ, the believer, too, has died to sin; he is one with Him in the likeness of His death. And as the knowledge that Christ died for sin as our atonement is indispensable to our justification, so the knowledge that Christ and we with Him, in the likeness of His death, are dead to sin is indispensable to our sanctification. Let us endeavor to understand this.

It was as the second Adam that Christ died. With the first Adam we had been united together in the likeness of *his* death. He died, and we with him, and the power of his death works in us. We have in very deed died in him, as truly as he himself died. We understand this. Just so we are one with Christ in the likeness of His death. He died to sin, and we in Him, and now the power of His death works in us. We are indeed dead to sin, as truly so as He Himself is.

Through our first birth we were made partakers in Adam's death, but through our second birth we become partakers in the death of the second Adam. Every believer who accepts of Christ is partaker of the power of His death and is dead to sin. But a believer may have much of which he is ignorant. Most believers are in their conversion so occupied with Christ's death *for sin* as their justification that they do not seek to know what it means that in Him they are dead *to sin*. When they first learn to feel their need of Him as their sanctification, then the desire is awakened to understand this likeness of His death. They find the secret of holiness in it: that like Christ, they also have died to sin.

The Christian who does not understand this always imagines that sin is too strong for him, that sin still has power over him, and that he must sometimes obey it. But he thinks this because he does not know that he, like Christ, is dead to sin. If he only believed and understood what this means, his language would be, "Christ has died to sin. Sin has nothing more to say to Him. In His life and death, sin had power over Him, for it was sin that caused Him the sufferings of the cross and the humiliation of the grave. But He is dead to sin, so it has lost all claim over Him. He is entirely and forever freed from its power. Even so, I as a believer. The new life that is in me is the life of Christ from the dead, a life that has been begotten through death, a *life that is entirely dead to sin*." The believer as a new creature in Christ Jesus can glory and say: "Like Christ I am dead to sin. Sin has no right or power over me whatsoever. I am freed from it, and therefore I do not need to sin."

> *C*hrist had a double work to accomplish in His death. The one was to work out righteousness for us, the other to obtain life for us.

And if the believer still sins, it is because he does not use his privilege to live as one who is dead to sin. Through ignorance or unwatchfulness or unbelief, he forgets the meaning and the power of this likeness of Christ's death, and so he sins. But if he holds firmly what his participation with Christ's death signifies, he has the power to overcome sin. He marks well that it is not said, "Sin is dead." No, sin is not dead. Sin lives and works still in the flesh. But he himself is dead to sin and alive to God, and so sin cannot for a single moment, without his consent, have dominion over him. If he sins, it is because he allows it to reign and submits himself to obey it.

Beloved Christian, who seeks to be like Christ, take the likeness of His death as one of the most glorious parts of the life you covet. Appropriate it first of all in faith. Reckon that you are indeed dead to sin. Let it be a settled thing; God says it to every one of His children, even the weakest—say it before Him, too: "Like Christ, I am dead to sin." Do not be afraid to say it, for it is the truth. Ask the Holy Spirit earnestly to enlighten you with regard to this part of your union with Christ, so that it may not only be a doctrine, but power and truth.

Endeavor to understand more deeply what it says to live as dead to sin as one who, in dying, has been freed from its dominion, and who can now reign in life through Jesus Christ over it. Then there will follow on the likeness of His death, accepted in faith, the conformity to His death (see Philem. 3:10)[54], something that is gradually and increasingly appropriated, as Christ's death manifests its full power in all the faculties and powers of your life.

And in order to have the full benefit of this likeness of Christ's death, notice particularly two things. The one is the obligation under which it brings you, "How shall we who died to sin live any longer in it?" (Rom. 6:2). Endeavor to enter more deeply into the meaning of this death of Christ into which you have been baptized. His death meant: Rather die than sin; willing to die in order to overcome sin; dead, and therefore released from the power of sin. Let this also be your position: "Do you not know that as many of us as were baptized into Christ Jesus were baptized into His death?" (Rom. 6:3). Let the Holy Spirit baptize you continually deeper into His death, until the power of God's Word, dead to sin, until the conformity to Christ's death, is discernible in all your walk and conversation.

> *The believer as a new creature in Christ Jesus can glory and say: "Like Christ I am dead to sin. Sin has no right or power over me whatsoever."*

The other lesson is this: The likeness of Christ's death is not only an obligation but a power. O Christian longing to be Christlike, if there be one thing you need more than and above all else, it is this: to know the exceeding greatness of God's power that works in you. It was in the power of eternity that Christ in His death wrestled with and conquered the powers of hell. You have part with Christ in His death, so you have part in all the powers by which He conquered. Yield yourself joyfully and believingly to be led more deeply into the conformity to Christ's death. Then you cannot but become like Him.

O my Lord! How little I have understood Your grace. I have often read the

---

[54] *The likeness of Christ's death* in Roman 6 precedes the likeness of His resurrection; no one can be made alive in Him who has not given himself up to die with Him. *The conformity to Christ's death* in Philemon 3 is spoken of as coming after the knowing Him in the power of His resurrection: the growth of the resurrection life within us leads to a deeper experience of the death. The two continually act and react.

words "united into the likeness of His death," and seen that as You died to sin, so it is said to Your believing people, "Likewise you also." But I have not understood its power. And so it came that, not knowing the likeness of Your death, I did not know that I was free from the power of sin, and as a conqueror could have dominion over it. Lord, You have indeed opened to me a glorious prospect. The man who believingly accepts the likeness of Your death, and according to Your Word reckons himself dead to sin—sin shall not have dominion over him, and he has power to live for God.

Lord, let Your Holy Spirit reveal this to me more perfectly. I wish to take Your Word in simple faith, to take the position You assign me as one who in You is dead to sin. Lord, *in You* I am dead to sin. Teach me to hold it firmly, or rather to hold You firmly in faith, until my whole life is a proof of it. O Lord, take me up and keep me in communion with Yourself, that, abiding in You, I may find *in You* the death to sin and the life to God. Amen.

FOR FURTHER THOUGHT

1. *What are the two parts of the work Christ accomplished for you in His death? What does scripture say about each (see 1 Cor. 15:3, Rom. 6:10)?*
2. *What has the death of Christ accomplished for you in regards to the power of sin in your life?*
3. *What does it mean to you as a believer to have been baptized into the death of Christ?*

NOTE

AT a meeting of ministers, where these words in Romans 6:11 were being discussed, the question was asked by the reader, which of the five different thoughts of the verse was the most important. He pointed out what these thoughts were. The first, *likewise you also*, suggesting the complete likeness to Him of whom it had just been said, "For the death that He died, He died to sin once for all; but the life that He lives, He lives to God" (6:10). The second, *reckon yourselves*, the command in which the duty of a large but simple faith is laid on us. Then, *dead indeed to sin*, the truth in which the teaching of the previous verses is summed up. Next, *alive to God*, the never-failing accompaniment and the blessing of the death to sin. And then, *in Christ Jesus our Lord*, in Him who is always root and center of all scripture teaching. Which of these clauses must be considered as that, the right understanding of which is most essential to the full experience of the whole?

The first answer was immediately given, *"dead to sin."* It is certainly this expression, the leader remarked, that above all has created such deep interest in this verse and stirred so much earnest striving to realize what it implies. And yet it does not appear to me the most important.

"Alive to God" was the answer of a second. For it is the life of Jesus given to us in regeneration that makes its partakers of His death and its power over sin. "Dead to sin" is only the negative aspect of what we have as a positive reality in being alive to God. If we looked more at the "alive to God," the "dead to sin" would be better understood.

"Reckon yourselves" was suggested by a third. Is not this command to act faith in what has been prepared us of God the chief thought of the verse, and that, therefore, to which our chief attention must be given?

Another brother now said, *"Through Christ Jesus our Lord."* Our leader said: "I think I have lately been taught that this is indeed that on the right apprehension of which the power of the whole verse depends."

How many have been looking most earnestly for the full insight into the blessedness of being dead to sin and alive to God, and yet have failed! How often we have heard them pray, "Lord, we are not yet utterly dead, but we long to be so!" How many others, who have better understood the text and have seen that everything depends on the "Reckon yourselves to be dead," upon the faith that accepts God's statement of what is already true and sure, yet confess that their faith is not followed by the power and the blessing they hoped for!

The mistake has been this: they have been more occupied with the blessings to be had in Jesus, "dead to sin," "alive to God," and the question as to their experience of them, or even with the effort to exercise a strong abiding faith in these blessings as theirs, than with Jesus Himself, in whom both the blessings, and the faith that sees them are ours. The death to sin, the life to God, are *His* (see 6:10), are IN HIM, accomplished, living, actual, mighty realities. It is as *we are* IN HIM, and know ourselves to be in Him, and so come away out of ourselves to be and abide in Him only and always, that the blessings that there are in Him will, in the most simple and natural way possible, spontaneously become ours in experience, and that we shall be strengthened in faith to claim and enjoy them. It must be Christ Jesus first and Christ Jesus last. He must be all.

See how clearly this comes out in the third verse of the chapter: "Do you not know that as many of us as were baptized into Christ Jesus were baptized into His death?" The baptism into Jesus Christ was the first thing—*that* they had understood and accepted; the baptism into His death followed from it—*this* they were now yet to learn the meaning of. The Lord Jesus had been baptized with water and with the Holy Spirit, and yet He spoke of a baptism yet to come. The full outcome of His first baptism was to be the death of the cross. Even so it is with us. When baptized unto Christ we "put on Christ" (Gal. 3:27), we are made partakers of Him and all He is and was, of His death, too. But it is only in course of time that we got to understand this, and really to claim the power of *His* death to sin and His living to God. But we can do this successfully only as we hold fast the initial all-comprehensive blessing, baptized INTO CHRIST. It is the faith that goes away out to take its home consciously and permanently *in Jesus* that will have the power to say, "IN CHRIST JESUS" we are dead to sin, and alive to God; "I in Christ Jesus," we do boldly reckon ourselves dead to sin and alive to God.

"Baptized into His death." What a word! The death of our Lord Jesus was the chief thing about Him, for it gives Him His beauty, His glory, His victory, His power. In the complete conformity to this, the highest privilege of the Christian consists. To be immersed, plunged into, steeped in the death of Christ—the whole being penetrated with the spirit of that death, its obedience, its self-sacrifice, its utter giving up of everything that is of nature, that has been in contact with sin, to pass through the death into the new life that God gives—this must be the highest longing of the Christian.

He has been baptized into the death, and he yields himself to the Holy Spirit to have all that it contains unfolded and applied. And he does this in simple faith, for he knows that in *Christ Jesus* he is dead to sin and alive to God. Just as the life to God is a complete and perfect thing, and yet subject to the law of growth and increase, so that he goes on to life more abundant, so with the death to sin. In Christ he *is dead* to sin, completely and entirely, and yet the full enjoyment of what that death means and works in all its extent is a matter of growing intelligence and experience.

But let us beware of wearying ourselves—how often we have done so!—with trying more to comprehend exactly, and to realize feelingly, what this death to sin is, and what the conscious reckoning ourselves dead is, than to remember that all this comes only as we are and abide IN CHRIST JESUS, IN WHOM alone these blessings are ours. I may be so occupied with the blessings and their pursuit that I lose sight and hold of Him in whom I must be abiding most entirely if I am to enjoy them. Let my first aim be in wholehearted faith and obedience to dwell in *Jesus*, in whom are the death to sin and the life to God: the whole state of being which is implied in these words is His—*He lives it, it is His alone*—as I lose myself *in Him*, I may rest assured that the blessing I long for will come, or rather, I shall know that *in Him* I have the thing itself, that divine life out of death working in me, even when I do not know exactly to describe it in words. And I shall see how the whole power and blessedness of the command gathers itself into the closing clause, "Likewise you also, reckon yourselves to be dead indeed to sin, but alive to God IN CHRIST JESUS." IN CHRIST is the root of LIKE CHRIST.[55]

---

[55] At the close of the volume see extract from Marshall, *On Sanctification.*

Day 23

In the Likeness of
His Resurrection

For if we have been united together in the likeness of His death,
certainly we also shall be in the likeness of His resurrection . . .
that just as Christ was raised from the dead by the glory of the
Father, even so we also should walk in newness of life.
ROMANS 6:4-5

ON the likeness of His death there follows necessarily the likeness of His resurrection. To speak alone of the likeness of His death, of bearing the cross, and of self-denial gives a one-sided view of following Christ. It is only the power of His resurrection that gives us strength to go on from that likeness of His death as what we receive immediately by faith, to that conformity to His death that comes as the growth of the inner life. Being dead with Christ refers more to the death of the old life to sin and the world which we abandon; risen with Christ refers to the new life through which the Holy Spirit expels the old. To the Christian who earnestly desires to walk as Christ did, the knowledge of this likeness of His resurrection is indispensable. Let us see if we do not here get the answer to the question as to where we shall find strength to live in the world as Christ did.

We have already seen how our Lord's life before His death was a life of weakness. As our surety, sin had great power over Him. It had also power over His disciples, so that He could not give them the Holy Spirit or do for them what He wished. But with the resurrection all was changed. Raised by the almighty power of God, His resurrection life was full of the power of eternity. He had not only conquered death and sin for Himself but for His disciples, so that He could from the first day make them partakers of His Spirit, of His joy, and of His heavenly power.

When the Lord Jesus now makes us partakers of His life, then it is not the life that He had before His death, but the resurrection life that He won through death. A life in which sin is already made an end of and put away, a life that has already conquered hell and the devil, the world and the flesh, a life of divine power in human nature, this is the life that likeness to His resurrection gives us: "The life that He lives, He lives to God. *Likewise you also*, reckon yourselves to be...alive to God in Christ Jesus our Lord" (Rom. 6:10–11). Oh, that through the Holy Spirit God might reveal to us the glory of the life in the likeness of Christ's resurrection! In it we find the secret of power for a life of conformity to Him.

> *B*eing dead with Christ refers more to the death of the old life to sin and the world which we abandon; risen with Christ refers to the new life through which the Holy Spirit expels the old.

To most Christians this is a mystery, and therefore their life is full of sin and weakness and defeat. They believe in Christ's resurrection as the sufficient proof of their justification. They think that He had to rise again to continue His work in heaven as mediator. But that He rose again, in order that His glorious resurrection life might now be *the very power of their daily life*—of this they have no idea. Hence their hopelessness when they hear of following Jesus fully, and being perfectly conformed to His image. They cannot imagine how it can be required of a sinner that he should in all things act as Christ would have done. They do not know Christ in the power of His resurrection, or the mighty power with which His life now works in those who are willing to count all things but loss for His sake (Phil. 3:8, Eph. 1:19–20).

Come, all you who are weary of a life unlike Jesus, and who long to walk always in His footsteps, who begin to see that there is in the scriptures a better life for you than you have until now known—come and let me try to show you the unspeakable treasure that is yours in your likeness to Christ in His resurrection. Let me ask three questions.

The first is: Are you ready to surrender your life to the rule of Jesus and His resurrection life? I do not doubt that the contemplation of Christ's example has convinced you of sin in more than one point. In seeking your own will and glory instead of God's, in ambition and pride and selfishness and lack of love toward man, you have seen how far you are from the obedience and humility and love of Jesus. And now it is the question, whether in view of all these things, in which you have acknowledged sin, you are willing to say: "If Jesus will take possession of my life, then I resign all right or wish ever in the least to have or to do my own will. I give my life with all I have and am entirely to Him, always to do what He through His Word and Spirit commands me. If He will live and rule in me, I promise unbounded and hearty obedience."

For such a surrender faith is needed. Therefore the second question is: Are you prepared to believe that Jesus will take possession of the life entrusted to Him, and that He will rule and keep it? When the believer entrusts his entire spiritual and temporal life completely to Christ, then he learns to rightly understand Paul's words: "I am dead; it is no longer I who live, but Christ lives in me" (see Gal. 2:20). Dead with Christ and risen again, the living Christ in His resurrection life takes possession of and rules my new life. The resurrection life is not a thing that I may have if I can undertake to keep it. No, just this is what I cannot do. But blessed be God! JESUS CHRIST HIMSELF *is the resurrection and the life,* is the resurrection life. *He Himself will from day to day and hour to hour see to it and ensure that I live as one who is risen with Him.* He does it through that Holy Spirit who is the Spirit of His risen life. The Holy Spirit is in us, and He will, if we trust Jesus for it, maintain within us every moment the presence and power of the risen Lord. We need not fear that we never can succeed in leading such a holy life as becomes those who are temples of the living God. *We are indeed not able.* But it is not required of us. The living Jesus, who is the resurrection, has shown His power over all our enemies. He Himself, who so loves us, He will work it in us. He gives us the Holy Spirit as our power, and He will perform His work in us with divine faithfulness, if we will only trust Him; *Christ Himself is our life.*

*A*re you prepared to believe that Jesus will take possession of the life entrusted to Him, and that He will rule and keep it?

And now comes the third question: Are you ready to use this resurrection life for the purpose for which God gave it to Him, and gives it to you, as a power of blessing to the lost? All desires after the resurrection life will fail if we are only seeking our own perfection and happiness. God raised up and exalted Jesus to give repentance and remission of sins. He always lives to pray for sinners. Yield yourself to receive His resurrection life with the same aim. Give yourself wholly to working and praying for the perishing; then you will become a fit vessel and instrument in which the resurrection life can dwell and work out its glorious purposes.

Brother! Your calling is to live like Christ. For this purpose *you have already been made one with Him* in the likeness of His resurrection. The only question is now whether you desire the full experience of His resurrection life, whether you are willing to surrender your whole life that He Himself may manifest resurrection power in every part of it. I encourage you, do not draw back. Offer yourself unreservedly to Him, with all your weakness and unfaithfulness. Believe that as His resurrection was a wonder above all thought and expectation, so He as the Risen One will still work in you exceeding abundantly above all you could think or desire.

What a difference there was in the life of the disciples before Jesus' death and after His resurrection! Then all was weakness and fear, self and sin, but with the resurrection all was power and joy, life and love, and glory. Just as great will the change be when a believer, who has known Jesus' resurrection only as the ground of his justification but has not known of the *likeness* of His resurrection, discovers how the Risen One will Himself be his life, and in very deed take on Himself the responsibility for the whole of that life. Oh, brother, you who have not yet experienced this, who has been troubled and weary because you are called to walk like Christ but cannot do it, come and taste the blessedness of giving your whole life to the risen Savior in the assurance that He will live it for you.

I encourage you, do not draw back. Offer yourself unreservedly to Him, with all your weakness and unfaithfulness.

O Lord! My soul adores You as the Prince of life! On the cross You conquered each one of my enemies—the devil, the flesh, the world, and sin. As Conquerer You rose to manifest and maintain the power of Your risen life in Your people. You have made them one with Yourself in the likeness of Your resurrection, and now You will live in them and show forth in their earthly life the power of Your heavenly life.

Praise Your name for this wonderful grace. Blessed Lord, I come at Your invitation to offer and surrender to You my life, with all it implies. Too long have I striven in my own strength to live like You, and not succeeded. The more I sought to walk like You, the deeper was my disappointment. I have heard of Your disciples who tell how blessed it is to cast all care and responsibility for their life on You. Lord, I am risen with You, one with You in the likeness of Your resurrection. Come and take me entirely for Your own, and be Yourself my life.

Above all, I ask You, O my risen Lord, reveal Yourself to me, as You did to Your first disciples, in the power of Your resurrection. It was not enough that after Your resurrection You appeared to Your disciples; they did not know You until You made Yourself known. Lord Jesus! I do believe in You; *be pleased, O be pleased to make Yourself known to me as my Life.* It is Your work, and You alone can do it. I trust You for it. And so shall my resurrection life be, like Your own, a continual source of light and blessing to all who are needing You. Amen.

FOR FURTHER THOUGHT

1. *What does it mean to you to be dead with Christ? To what does that refer? What does risen with Christ mean to you?*
2. *What does it mean to surrender your life to the rule of Jesus and His resurrection life? For what purpose did God give Jesus Christ, and you, the resurrection life?*
3. *What were the differences in the lives of the disciples before Jesus' death and after His resurrection? What does that tell you about the power and effect of His resurrection?*

DAY 24

BEING MADE CONFORMABLE
TO HIS DEATH

*That I may know Him and the power
of His resurrection, and the fellowship of His sufferings,
being conformed to His death.*
PHILIPPIANS 3:10

WE know that the death of Christ was the death of the cross. We know that that death of the cross is His chief glory. Without that death He would not be the Christ. The distinguishing characteristic, the one mark by which He is separated here in earth and in heaven, from all other persons, both in the divine Being and in God's universe, is this one: He is the crucified Son of God. Of all the articles of conformity, this must necessarily be the chief and most glorious one—conformity to His death.

This is what made it so attractive to Paul. What were Christ's glory and blessedness must be his glory, too, for he knows that the most intimate likeness to Christ is conformity to His death. What that death had been to Christ it would be to him as he grew conformed to it.

Christ's death on the cross had been the end of sin. During His life it could tempt Him, but when He died on the cross, He died to sin, and it could no more reach Him. Conformity to Christ's death is the power to keep us from the power of sin. As I by the grace of the Holy Spirit am kept in my position as crucified with Christ, and live out my crucifixion life as the Crucified One lives it in me, I am kept from sinning.

Christ's death on the cross was to the Father a sweet-smelling sacrifice, infinitely pleasing. Oh, if I want to dwell in the favor and love of the Father, and be His delight, I am sure there is nothing that gives such deep and perfect access to it as being conformable to Christ's death. There is nothing in the universe to the Father so beautiful, so holy, so heavenly, and so wonderful as this sight, the crucified Jesus. And the closer I can get to Him, and the more like and the more conformed to His death I can become, the more surely shall I enter into the very bosom of His love.

Christ's death on the cross was the entrance to the power of the resurrection life, the unchanging life of eternity. In our spiritual life we often have to mourn the breaks, and failures, and intervals that prove to us that there is still something lacking that prevents the resurrection life from asserting its full power. The secret is here: there is still some subtle self-life that has not yet been brought into the perfect conformity of Christ's death. We can be sure of it, nothing is needed but a fuller entrance into the fellowship of the cross to make us the full partakers of the resurrection joy.

Above all, it was Christ's death on the cross that made Him the life of the world, gave Him the power to bless and to save (John 12:24–25). In the conformity to Christ's death there is an end of self. We give up ourselves to live and die for others, and we are full of the faith that our surrender of ourselves to bear the sin of others is accepted of the Father. Out of this death we rise, with the power to love and to bless.

And now, what is this conformity to the death of the cross that brings such blessings, and in what does it consist? We see it in Jesus. The cross means entire self-denial. The cross means the death of self—the utter surrender of our own will and our life to be lost in the will of God, to let God's will do with us what it pleases. This was what the cross meant to Jesus. It cost Him a terrible struggle before He could give Himself up to it. When He was greatly amazed and very heavy, and His soul exceedingly sorrowful to the point of death, it was because His whole being shrank back from that cross and its curse. Three times He had to pray before He could fully say, "Yet not My will, but Yours be done." But He did say it. And His giving Himself up to the cross is to say: Let Me do anything rather than that God's will would not be done. I give up everything—only God's will must be done.

> *O*f all the articles of conformity, this must necessarily be the chief and most glorious one—conformity to His death.

And this is being made conformable to Christ's death, that we so give away ourselves and our whole life, with its power of willing and acting, to God, that we learn to be and work, and do nothing but what God reveals to us as His will. And such a life is called conformity to the death of Christ, not only because it is somewhat similar to His, but because it is Himself by His Holy Spirit just repeating and acting over again in us the life that animated Him in His crucifixion. Were it not for this, the very thought of such conformity would be akin to blasphemy.

But now it is not so. In the power of the Holy Spirit, as the Spirit of the crucified Jesus, the believer knows that the blessed resurrection life has its power and its glory from its being a crucifixion life, begotten from the cross. He yields himself to it, believing that it has possession of him. Realizing that he himself does not have the power to think or do anything that is good or holy—no, that the power of the flesh asserts itself and defiles everything that is in him—he yields and holds every power of his being, as far as his disposal of them goes, in the place of crucifixion and condemnation. And so he yields and holds every power of his being, every faculty of body, soul, and spirit, at the disposal of Jesus. The distrust and denial of self in everything, and the trust of Jesus in everything mark his life. The very spirit of the cross breathes through his whole being.

> *Christ's death on the cross was the entrance to the power of the resurrection life, the unchanging life of eternity.*

And so far is it from being, as might appear, a matter of painful strain and weary effort to maintain the crucifixion position this way—to one who knows Christ in the power of His resurrection, for Paul puts this first, and so is made conformed to His death, it is rest and strength and victory. Because it is not the dead cross, not self's self-denial, not a work in his own strength, that he has to do with, but the living Jesus, in whom the crucifixion is an accomplished thing, already passed into the life of resurrection. "I have been crucified with Christ: Christ lives in me" (Gal. 2:20): this it is that gives the courage and the desire for an ever-growing, ever-deeper entrance into most perfect conformity with His death.

And how is this blessed conformity to be attained? Paul will give us the answer. "*What things were gain to me*, these I have counted loss for Christ. Yet indeed I also count all *things* loss for the excellence of the knowledge of Christ Jesus my Lord. . .that I may know Him. . .being conformed to His death" (Phil. 3:7–8, 10). The pearl is of great price; but oh, it is worth the purchase. Let us give up all, yes, all, to be admitted by Jesus to a place with Him on the cross.

And if it appears hard to give up all, and then as our reward only have a whole lifetime on the cross, oh, let us listen again to Paul as he tells us what made him so willingly give up all, and so intently choose the cross. It was Jesus—Christ Jesus, my Lord. The cross was the place where he could get into fullest union with his Lord. To know *Him*, to win *Him*, to be found in *Him*, to be made *like to Him*—this was the burning passion that made it easy to cast away all, that gave the cross such mighty attractive power. Anything to come nearer to Jesus. All for Jesus, was his motto. It contains the twofold answer to the question, How to attain this conformity to Christ's death? The one is, Cast out all. The other, And let Jesus come in. ALL for JESUS.

Yes, it is only knowing Jesus that can make the conformity to His death at all possible. But let the soul win HIM, and be found in HIM, and know HIM in the power of the resurrection, and it becomes more than possible, but a blessed reality.

Therefore, beloved follower of Jesus, look to Him, look to Him, the crucified One. Gaze on Him until your soul has learned to say: "O my Lord, I must be like You." Gaze until you have seen how He Himself, the Crucified One, in His ever-present omnipotence, draws near to live in you and breathe through your being His crucifixion life.

It was through the eternal Spirit that He offered Himself to God. That Spirit brings and imparts all that that death on the cross is, means, and effected to you as your life. By that Holy Spirit, Jesus Himself maintains in each soul, who can trust Him for it, the power of the cross as an abiding death to sin and self, and a never-ceasing source of resurrection life and power. Therefore, once again, look to Him, the living, crucified Jesus.

But remember, above all, that while you have to seek the best and the highest with all your might, the full blessing does not come as the fruit of your efforts, but unsought, a free gift to whom it is given from above. It is as it pleases the Lord Jesus to reveal Himself that we are made conformable to His death. Therefore, seek and get it FROM HIMSELF.

> *I have been crucified with Christ: Christ lives in me": this it is that gives the courage and the desire for an ever-growing, ever-deeper entrance into most perfect conformity with His death.*

O Lord, such knowledge is too wonderful for me. It is so high, I cannot attain to it. To know You in the power of Your resurrection, and to be made conformable to Your death: these are of the things which are hidden from the wise and prudent, and are revealed to babes, to those elect souls alone to whom it is given to know the mysteries of the kingdom.

O my Lord! I see more than ever what utter folly it is to think of likeness to You as an attainment through my effort. I cast myself on Your mercy. Look at me according to the greatness of Your lovingkindness, and of Your free favor reveal Yourself to me. If You will be pleased to come forth from Your heavenly dwelling place, and to draw near to me, and to prepare me, and take me up into the full fellowship of Your life and death, O my Lord, then will I live and die for You, and for the souls You have died to save.

Blessed Savior! I know You are willing. Your love to each of Your redeemed ones is infinite. Oh, teach me, draw me to give up all for You, and take eternal possession of me for Yourself. And let some measure of conformity to Your death, in its self-sacrifice for the perishing, be the mark of my life. Amen.

For Further Thought

1. Read Philippians 3:10. What, according to the apostle Paul, is the most intimate likeness to Christ?
2. What are the two things you must do to attain conformity to Christ's death?
3. What two things must you remember above all as you seek conformity to Christ's death, as you seek God's highest and best for you?

Day 25

Giving His Life
for Men

"Whoever desires to become great among you, let him be your servant.
And whoever desires to be first among you, let him be your
slave—just as the Son of Man did not come to be served,
but to serve, and to give His life a ransom for many."
MATTHEW 20:26–28

By this we know love, because He laid down His life for us.
And we also ought to lay down our lives for the brethren.
1 JOHN 3:16

IN speaking of the likeness of Christ's death, and of being made conformable to it, of bearing the cross and being crucified with Him, there is one danger to which even the earnest believer is exposed, and that is of seeking after these blessings for his own sake or, as he thinks, for the glory of God in His own personal perfection. The error would be a fatal one, for he would never attain the close conformity to Jesus' death he hoped for, for he would be leaving out just that which is the essential element in the death of Jesus, and in the self-sacrifice it inculcates. That characteristic is its absolute unselfishness, its reference to others.

To be made conformable to Christ's death implies a dying to self, a losing sight of self altogether in giving up and laying down our lives for others. To the question, how far we are to go in living for, in loving, in serving, in saving men, the scriptures do not hesitate to give the unequivocal answer: We are to go as far as Jesus, even to the laying down of our life. We are to consider this so entirely as the object for which we are redeemed, and are left in the world, the one object for which we live, that the laying down of the life in death follows as a matter of course. Like Christ, the only thing that keeps us in this world is to be the glory of God in the salvation of sinners. Scripture does not hesitate to say that it is in His path of suffering, as He goes to work out atonement and redemption, that we are to follow Him.[56]

[56] Compare Matt. 20:28 with Eph. 5:2, 25–26; Phil. 2:5–8; 1 Pet. 2:21–23, and note how distinctly it is in connection with His redemptive work that Christ is set before us as our example: the giving His life away for others is its special significance.

How clearly this comes out in the words of the Master Himself: "Whoever desires to be first among you, let him be your slave—JUST AS the Son of Man did not come to be served, but to serve, and to give His life a ransom for many." The highest in glory will be he who was lowest in service, and most like the Master in His giving His life as a ransom. And so again, a few days later, after having spoken of His own death in the words: "The hour has come that the Son of Man should be glorified. Most assuredly, I say to you, unless a grain of wheat falls into the ground and dies, it remains alone; but if it dies, it produces much grain" (John 12:23–24), He at once applied to His disciples what He had said by repeating what they had already heard spoken to themselves, "He who loves his life will lose it, and he who hates his life in this world will keep it for eternal life" (12:25).

The grain of wheat dying to rise again, losing its life to regain it multiplied manifold, is clearly set forth as the emblem not only of the Master but of each one of His followers. Loving life, refusing to die, means remaining alone in selfishness, but losing life to bring forth much fruit in others is the only way to keep it for ourselves. There is no way to find our life but as Jesus did, in giving it up for the salvation of others. In this is the Father, in this shall we be glorified. The deepest underlying thought of conformity to Christ's death is giving our life to God for saving others. Without this, the longing for conformity to that death is in danger of being a refined selfishness.

> To be made conformable to Christ's death implies a dying to self, a losing sight of self altogether in giving up and laying down our life for others.

How remarkable the exhibition we have in the apostle Paul of this spirit, and how instructive the words in which the Holy Spirit in him expressed to us its meaning! To the Corinthians he says: "Always carrying about in the body the dying of the Lord Jesus, that the life of Jesus also may be manifested in our body. For we who live are always delivered to death for Jesus' sake, that the life of Jesus also may be manifested in our mortal flesh. So then *death is working in us, but life in you*" (2 Cor. 4:10–12). "Though *He was crucified in weakness*, YET HE LIVES BY THE POWER OF GOD. For *we also are weak in Him*, but we shall LIVE WITH HIM BY THE POWER OF GOD TOWARD YOU" (2 Cor. 13:4). "I now rejoice in *my sufferings for you*, and fill up in my flesh what is lacking in the afflictions of Christ, for the sake of His body, which is the Church" (Col. 1:24).

These passages teach us how the vicarious element of the suffering that Christ bore in His body on the tree to a certain extent still characterizes the sufferings of His body the Church. Believers who give themselves up to bear the burden of the sins of men before the Lord, who suffer reproach and shame, weariness and pain, in the effort to win souls, are filling up that which is lacking of the afflictions of Christ in their flesh. The power and the fellowship of His suffering and death work in them, the power of Christ's life through them in those for whom they labor in love. There is no doubt that in the fellowship of His sufferings, and the conformity to His death in Philemon 3, Paul had in view not only the inner spiritual, but also the external bodily participations in the suffering of Christ.

And so it must be with each of us in some measure. Self-sacrifice not merely for the sake of our own sanctification, but for the salvation of our fellowmen is what brings us into true fellowship with the Christ who gave Himself for us.

> *Believers who give themselves up to bear the burden of the sins of men before the Lord, who suffer reproach and shame, weariness and pain, in the effort to win souls, are filling up that which is lacking of the afflictions of Christ in their flesh.*

The practical application of these thoughts is very simple. Let us first of all try to see the truth the Holy Spirit seeks to teach us. As the most essential thing in likeness to Christ is likeness to His death, so the most essential thing in likeness to His death is the giving up our life to win others to God. It is a death in which all thought of saving self is lost in that of saving others. Let us pray for the light of the Holy Spirit to show us this, until we learn to feel that we are in the world just as Christ was, to give up self, to love and serve, to live and die, "JUST AS the Son of Man did not come to be served, but to serve, and to give His life a ransom for many." Oh, that God would teach His people to know their calling: that they do not belong to themselves but to God and *to their fellowmen*, that, just as Christ, they are only to live to be a blessing to the world.

Then let us *believe* in the grace that is waiting to make our experience of this truth a reality. Let us believe that God accepts of our giving up of our whole life for His glory in the saving of others. Let us believe that conformity to the death of Jesus in this, its very life-principle, is what the Holy Spirit will work out in us. Let us above all believe in Jesus, for it is He Himself who will take up every soul that in full surrender yields itself to Him, into the full fellowship of His death, of His dying, in love to bring forth much fruit. Yes, let us believe, and believing seek from above, as the work end the gift of Jesus, likeness to Jesus in this, too.

And let us at once begin and *act* this faith. Let us put it into practice. Looking on ourselves now as wholly given up, just like Christ, to live and die for God in our fellowmen, let us with new zeal exercise the ministry of love in winning souls. As we wait for Christ to work out His likeness, as we trust the Holy Spirit to give His mind in us more perfectly, let us in faith begin immediately to act as followers of Him who only lived and died to be a blessing to others. Let our love open the way to the work it has to do by the kindness, and gentleness, and helpfulness with which it shines out on all whom we meet in daily life. Let it give itself to the work of intercession, and look up to God to use us as one of His instruments in the answering of those prayers. Let us speak and work for Jesus as those who have a mission and a power from on high which make us sure of a blessing. Let us make soul-winning our object. Let us band ourselves with the great army of reapers the Lord is sending out into His harvest. And before we thought of it, we shall find that giving our life to win others for God is the most blessed way of dying to self, of being even as the Son of man was, a servant and a Savior of the lost.

O most wonderful and inconceivably blessed likeness to Christ! He gave Himself to men but could not really reach them until, giving Himself *a sacrifice to God* for them, the seed-corn died, the life was poured out. Then the blessing flowed forth in mighty power. I may seek to love and serve men, but I can only really influence and bless them as I yield myself *to God* and give up my life into His hands for them. As I lose myself as an offering on the altar, I become in His spirit and power in very deed a blessing. My spirit given into His hands, He can use and bless me.

O most blessed God! Do You in very deed ask me to come and give myself, my very life, wholly, even to the death, to You for my fellowmen? If I have heard the words of the Master correctly, You indeed seek nothing less.

> *He gave Himself to men but could not really reach them until, giving Himself a sacrifice to God for them, the seed-corn died, the life was poured out.*

O God! Will You indeed have me? Will You in very deed in Christ permit me, like Him, as a member of His body, to live and die for those around me? To lay myself, I say it in deep reverence, beside Him on the altar of death, crucified with Him, and be a living sacrifice to You for men? Lord! I do praise You for this most wonderful grace. And now I come, Lord God, and give myself. Oh, for the grace of Your Holy Spirit to make the transaction definite and real! Lord! Here I am, given up to You, to live only for those whom You are seeking to save.

Blessed Jesus! Come Yourself, and breathe Your own mind and love within me. Take possession of me—my thoughts to think, my heart to feel, my powers to work, my life to live—as given away to God for men. Write it in my heart: It is done, I am given away to God, and He has taken me. Keep me each day as in His hands, expecting and assured that He will use me. On Your giving up Yourself followed the life in power, the outbreaking of the blessing in fullness and power. It will be so in Your people, too. Glory to Your name. Amen.

FOR FURTHER THOUGHT

1. What is the connection between being made conformable to Christ's death and losing sight of yourself, giving yourself up for others?
2. Read 2 Corinthians 4:10–12, 13:4; and Colossians 1:24. What do these passages teach you about Christ giving Himself up to death on a cross and the power He imparts to you for service to others?
3. What must you do in order that God may really use you to influence and bless others? What must be your position in God in order for Him to use and bless you this way?

DAY 26

IN HIS MEEKNESS

"Behold, thy King cometh unto thee, meek."
MATTHEW 21:5 KJV

"Learn of me; for I am meek and lowly in heart:
and ye shall find rest unto your souls."
MATTHEW 11:29 KJV

IT is on His way to the cross that we find the first of these two words written of our Lord Jesus. It is in His sufferings that the meekness of Jesus is specially manifested. Follower of Jesus, one who is so ready to take your place under the shadow of His cross, there to behold the Lamb slain for your sins: is it not a precious thought, that there is one part of His work, as the suffering Lamb of God, in which You may bear His image and be like Him every day? You can be meek and gentle, just as He was.

Meekness is the opposite of all that is hard or bitter or sharp. It has reference to the disposition that animates us toward our inferiors. "With meekness" ministers must instruct those who oppose themselves, teach and bring back the erring (Gal. 6:1, 2 Tim. 2:25). It expresses our disposition toward superiors: we must "receive the word with meekness" (see James 1:21). If the wife is to be in subjection to her husband, it must be in a meek and quiet spirit, which is in the sight of God of great price (1 Pet. 3). As one of the fruits of the Spirit, meekness ought to characterize all our daily interactions with fellow-Christians, and extend to all with whom we have to do (Eph. 4:2, Gal. 5:22, Col. 3:12, Titus 3:2). It is mentioned in scripture along with humility, because that is the inward disposition concerning oneself out of which meekness toward others springs.

There is perhaps none of the lovely virtues that adorn the image of God's Son that is more seldom seen in those who ought to be examples. There are many servants of Jesus, in whom much love to souls, much service for the salvation of others, and much zeal for God's will are visible, and yet who continually come short in this. How often, when offense comes unexpectedly, whether at home or abroad, they are carried away by temper and anger, and have to confess that they have lost the perfect rest of soul in God! There is no virtue, perhaps, for which some have prayed more earnestly. They feel they would give anything if in their interactions with partner, or children, or servants, in company or in business, they could always keep their temper perfectly and exhibit the meekness and gentleness of Christ. Unspeakable is the grief and disappointment experienced by those who have learned to long for it, and yet have not discovered where the secret of meekness lies.

The self-command needed for this seems to some so impossible that they seek comfort in the belief that this blessing belongs to a certain natural temperament, and is too contrary to their character for them ever to expect it. To satisfy themselves, they find all sorts of excuses. They do not mean it so ill. Though the tongue or the temper is sharp, there is still love in their hearts. It would not be good to be too gentle, for evil would be strengthened by it. And through these things the call to entire conformity to the holy gentleness of the Lamb of God is robbed of all its power. And the world is strengthened in its belief that Christians are after all not very much different from other people, because, though they do indeed say, they do not show that Christ changes the heart and life after His own image. And the soul suffers itself and causes unspeakable harm in Christ's Church, through its unfaithfulness in appropriating this blessing of salvation: the bearing the image and likeness of God.

> Is it not a precious thought, that there is one part of His work, as the suffering Lamb of God, in which You may bear His image and be like Him every day? You can be meek and gentle, just as He was.

This grace is of great price in the sight of God. In the Old Testament there are many glorious promises for the meek, which were by Jesus gathered up into this one, "Blessed are the meek, for they shall inherit the earth" (Matt. 5:5; also see Pss. 25:9, 76:9; Prov. 3:34; Jer. 2:3). In the New Testament, its praise consists in this, that it is His meekness that gives its supernatural incomparable beauty to the image of our Lord. A meek spirit is of great value in God's sight; it is the choicest ornament of the beloved Son. The Father could surely offer no higher inducement to His children to seek it above all things.

For everyone who longs to possess this spirit, Christ's word is full of comfort and encouragement: "Learn of Me; for I am meek." And what will it profit us to learn that *He is meek*? Will not just the experience of His meekness make the discovery of our want of it all the more painful? What we ask, Lord, is that You shouldest teach us how we may be meek. The answer is again: "Learn of *Me*; for I AM MEEK."

We are in danger of seeking meekness and the other graces of our Lord Jesus as gifts of which we must be conscious before we practice them. This is not the path of faith. "Moses did not know that the skin of his face shone" (Exod. 34:29), for he had only seen the glory of God. The soul that seeks to be meek must learn that Jesus is meek. We must take time to gaze on His meekness, until the heart has received the full impression: He only is meek, and with Him alone can meekness be found. When we begin to realize this, we next fix our hearts on the truth: This meek One is *Jesus the Savior*. All He is, all He has, is for His redeemed ones, and His meekness is to be communicated to us. But He does not impart it by giving, as it were from Himself, something of it away to us. No! We must learn that He alone is meek, and that only when He enters and takes possession of heart and life, He brings His meekness with Him. It is with the meekness of Jesus that we can be meek.

We know how little He succeeded in making His disciples meek and lowly while on earth. It was because He had not yet obtained the new life, and could not yet bestow, through His resurrection, the Holy Spirit. But now He can do it. He has been exalted to the power of God from which to reign in our hearts, to conquer every enemy, and continue in us His own holy life. Jesus was our visible example on earth that we might see in Him what the hidden life is like that He would give us from heaven, that He Himself would be within us.

"Learn of Me, for I am meek and lowly of heart." Without ceasing, the word sounds in our ears as our Lord's answer to all the sad complaints of His redeemed ones, as to the difficulty of restraining temper. O my brother! Why is Jesus, your Jesus, your life, and your strength, why is He the meek and lowly One, if it is not to impart to you, to whom He so wholly belongs, His own meekness?

Therefore, only believe! Believe that Jesus is able to fill your heart with His own spirit of meekness. Believe that Jesus Himself will, through His own Spirit, accomplish in you the work that you have in vain endeavored to do. "BEHOLD! YOUR KING COMES TO YOU, MEEK." Welcome Him to dwell in your heart. Expect Him to *reveal Himself to* you. Everything depends on this. Learn from Him that He is meek and lowly of heart, and you shall find rest to your soul.

> We must take time to gaze on His meekness, until the heart has received the full impression: He only is meek, and with Him alone can meekness be found.

Precious Savior, grant me now, under the overshadowing of Your Holy Spirit, to draw near to You and to appropriate Your heavenly meekness as my life. Lord, You have not shown me Your meekness as a Moses who demands but does not give. You are Jesus who saves from all sin, giving in its place Your heavenly holiness. Lord, I claim Your meekness as a part of the salvation that You have given me. I cannot do without it. How can I glorify You if I do not possess it? Lord, I will learn from You that You are meek. Blessed Lord, teach me. And teach me that You are always with me, always in me as my life. Abiding in You, with You abiding in me, I have You the meek One to help me and make me like Yourself. O holy meekness! You have not come down to earth only for a short visit, then to disappear again in the heavens. You have come to seek a home. I offer You my heart; come and dwell in it.

Blessed Lamb of God, my Savior and Helper, I count on You. You will make Your meekness to dwell in me. Through Your indwelling You conform me to Your image. Oh, come, and as an act of Your rich free grace even now, as I wait on You, reveal Yourself as my King, meek, and coming in to take possession of me for Yourself.

> "Precious, gentle, holy Jesus,
> Blessed bridegroom of my heart,
> In Your secret inner chamber,
> You wilt show me what You art. Amen."

FOR FURTHER THOUGHT

1. *In what way can you best—and most easily and effectively—bear Jesus' image and be like Him every day?*
2. *In what ways did Jesus demonstrate His meekness and gentleness, thus setting for you the perfect example to follow?*
3. *What must you do in order for Christ's meekness and gentleness to be imparted in you and be seen in you by God Himself and by others?*

DAY 27

ABIDING IN THE
LOVE OF GOD

"As the Father loved Me, I also have loved you; abide in My love.
If you keep My commandments, you will abide in My love, just as I
have kept My Father's commandments and abide in His love."
JOHN 15:9–10

O UR blessed Lord not only said, "Abide in Me," but also, "Abide in My love." Of the abiding in Him, the principal part is the entering into and dwelling and being rooted in that wonderful love with which He loves us and gives Himself to us. "Love does not seek its own" (1 Cor. 13:5); it always goes out of itself to live and be at one with the beloved; it always opens itself and stretches its arms wide to receive and hold firmly the object of its desire. Christ's love longs to possess us. The abiding in Christ is an intensely personal relationship, the losing ourselves in the fellowship of an infinite love, finding our life in the experience of being loved by Him, being nowhere at home but in His love.

To reveal this life in His love to us in all its divine beauty and blessedness, Jesus tells us that this love of His to us in which we are to abide is just the same as the Father's love to Him in which He abides. Surely, if anything were needed to make the abiding in His love more wonderful and attractive, this ought to do so. "As the Father loved me, so also have I loved you; abide in My love." Our life may be Christlike, unspeakably blessed in the consciousness of an infinite love embracing and delighting in us.

We know how this was the secret of Christ's wonderful life, and His strength in prospect of death. At His baptism the voice was heard, the divine message that the Spirit brought and unceasingly maintained in living power, "This is My BELOVED Son, in whom I am well pleased" (Matt. 3:17). More than once we read: "The Father loves the Son" (John 3:35, 5:20). Christ speaks of it as His highest blessedness: "That the world may know that You. . .have loved them as *You have loved Me. . . . You loved Me* before the foundation of the world" (John 17:23–24); "That *the love with which You loved Me* may be in them" (17:26). Just as we day by day walk and live in the light of the sun shining around us, so Jesus just lived in the light of the glory of the Father's love shining on Him all the day. It was as THE BELOVED OF GOD that He was able to do God's will and finish His work. He dwelled in the love of the Father.

And just so we are THE BELOVED OF JESUS. As the Father loved Him, He loves us. And what we need is just to take time, and, shutting our eyes to all around us, to worship and to wait until we see the infinite love of God in all its power and glory streaming forth on us through the heart of Jesus, seeking to make itself known, and to get complete possession of us, offering itself to us as our home and resting place. Oh, if the Christian would just take time to let the wondrous thought fill him, "I AM THE BELOVED OF THE LORD, Jesus loves me every moment, just as the Father loved Him," how the faith would grow, that one who is loved as Christ was must walk as He walked!

> *Our life may be Christlike, unspeakably blessed in the consciousness of an infinite love embracing and delighting in us.*

But there is a second point in the comparison. Not only is the love we are to abide in like that in which He abode, but the way to our abiding is the same as His. As Son, Christ was in the Father's love when He came into the world. But it was only through obedience He could secure its continued enjoyment, could abide in it. Nor was this an obedience that cost Him nothing. No, it was in giving up His own will and learning obedience by what He suffered, in becoming obedient to the death, even the death of the cross, that He kept the Father's commandments and *abode in His love.* "Therefore My Father loves Me, *because* I lay down My life. . . . This command I have received from My Father" (John 10:17–18). "The Father has not left Me alone, *for I always do* those things that please Him" (John 8:29). And having this way given us His example, and proved how surely the path of obedience takes us up into the presence and love and glory of God, He invites us to follow Him. "If you keep My commandments, you will abide in My love, JUST AS I have kept My Father's commandments and abide in His love."

Christlike obedience is the way to a Christlike enjoyment of love divine. How it secures our boldness of access into God's presence! "Let us love in *deed* and in *truth. By this* we. . .assure our hearts before Him" (see 1 John 3:18–19). "Beloved, if our heart does not condemn us, we have confidence toward God. And whatever we ask we receive from Him, because we keep His commandments and do those things that are pleasing in His sight" (3:21–22). How it gives us boldness before men and lifts us above their approval or contempt, because we move at God's bidding and feel that we have just to obey orders! And what boldness, too, in the face of difficulty or danger we are doing God's will and dare leave to Him all responsibility as to failure or success. The heart filled with the thought of direct and entire obedience to God alone rises above the world into the will of God, into the place where God's love rests on him. Like Christ, he has his abode in the love of God.

Let us seek to learn from Christ what it means to have this spirit of obedience ruling our life. It implies the spirit of dependence, the confession that we have neither the right nor the desire in anything to do our own will. It involves teachableness of spirit. Conscious of the blinding influence of tradition, and prejudice, and habit, it takes its law not from men but from God Himself. Conscious of how little the most careful study of the Word can reveal God's will in its spiritual power, it seeks to be led, and for this purpose to be entirely under the rule of the Holy Spirit. It knows that its views of truth and duty are very partial and deficient, and it counts on being led by God Himself to deeper insight and higher attainment.

> The heart filled with the thought of direct and entire obedience to God alone rises above the world into the will of God, into the place where God's love rests on him.

It has marked God's word, "If you diligently *heed the voice* of the LORD your God and do what is right in His sight" (Exod. 15:26), and understood that it is only when the commands do not come from conscience, or memory, or the book, but from the *living voice* of the Lord heard speaking through the Spirit, that the obedience will be possible and acceptable. It sees that it is only as a following out of the Father's personal directions, and as a service rendered to Himself, that obedience has its full value and brings its full blessing. Its great care is to live on the altar, given up to God, to keep eye and ear open to God for every indication of His blessed will. It is not content with doing right for its own sake. Rather it brings everything in personal relation to God Himself, doing it as for the Lord. It wants every hour and every step in life to be a fellowship with God. It longs in little things and daily life to be consciously obeying the Father, because this is the only way to be prepared for higher work. Its one desire is the glory of God in the triumph of His will; its one means for obtaining that desire, with all its heart and strength to be working out that will each moment of the day. And its one but sufficient reward is this, it knows that through the will of God lies the road, opened up by Christ Himself, deeper into the love of God: "If you keep My commandments, you will abide in My love."

Oh, this blessed Christlike obedience, leading to a Christlike abiding in the divine love! To attain it we must just study Christ more. He emptied Himself, and humbled Himself, and *became obedient*. May He empty us and humble us, too! He *learned obedience* in the school of God, and being made perfect, became the author of eternal salvation to all *who obey Him*. We must yield ourselves to be taught obedience by Him! We just need to listen to what He has told us how He did nothing of Himself, but only what He saw and heard from the Father; how entire dependence and continual waiting on the Father was the root of implicit obedience, and this again the secret of ever-growing knowledge of the Father's deeper secrets (John 5:19–20; see Day 15). God's love and man's obedience there are as the lock and key fitting into each other. It is God's grace that has fitted the key to the lock, and it is man who uses the key to unlock the treasures of love.

In the light of Christ's example and words, what new meaning comes to God's words spoken to His people from of old! "Blessing I will bless you, and multiplying I will multiply your descendants. . .*because you have obeyed My voice*" (Gen. 22:17–18). "If you will indeed *obey My voice* and keep My covenant, then you shall be a special treasure to Me" (Exod. 19:5). "The LORD will greatly bless you. . .*only if you carefully obey* the voice of the LORD your God, to observe with care all these commandments" (Deut. 15:4–5). Love and obedience indeed become the two great factors in the wonderful relationship between God and man. The love of God, giving Himself and all He has to man; the obedience of the believer in that love, giving himself and all he has to God.

We have heard a good deal in these later years of full surrender and entire consecration, and thousands praise God for all the blessing He has given them through these words. Only let us beware that we be not led too much, in connection with them, to seek for a blessed experience to be enjoyed, or a state to be maintained, while the simple downright doing of God's will to which they point is overlooked. Let us take hold and use this word that God loves to use: obedience. "To obey is better than sacrifice" (1 Sam. 15:22): self-sacrifice is nothing without, is nothing but, obedience. It was the meek and lowly obedience of Christ, as of a servant and a son, that made His sacrifice such a sweet-smelling aroma, and it is humble, childlike obedience, first listening gently to the *Father's voice*, and then doing that which is right *in His sight*, that will bring us the witness that we please Him.

Dear reader! Shall not this be our life? So simple and sublime: obeying Jesus and abiding in His Love.

> *I*f you will indeed obey My voice and keep My covenant, then you shall be a special treasure to Me." "The Lord will greatly bless you. . .only if you carefully obey the voice of the Lord your God, to observe with care all these commandments"

O my God! What shall I say to the wonderful interchange between the life of heaven and the life of earth You have set before me? Your Son, our blessed Lord, has shown and proved to us how it is possible on this earth of ours, and how unspeakably blessed, for a man to live with the love of God always surrounding him, by just yielding himself to obey Your voice and will. And because He is ours, our head and our life, we know that we can indeed in our measure live and walk as we see Him do; our souls every moment abiding and rejoicing in Your divine love, because You accept our feeble keeping of Your commandments for His sake. O my God, it is indeed too wonderful that we are called to this Christlike dwelling in love through the Christlike obedience Your Spirit works!

Blessed Jesus! How can I praise You for coming and bringing such a life on earth and making me a sharer in it? O my Lord, I can only yield myself afresh to You to keep Your commandments, as You kept the Father's. Lord! Only impart to me the secret of Your own blessed obedience: the open ear, the watchful eye, the meek and lowly heart, the childlike giving up of all as the beloved Son to the beloved Father. Savior! Fill my heart with Your love. In the faith and experience of that love I will do it, too. Yes, Lord, this only is my life: keeping Your commandments and abiding in Your love. Amen.

For Further Thought

1. *Read Jesus' own words in John 15:9–10. What must you do in order to consistently and uninterruptedly abide in the love of Christ and, therefore, of the Father?*

2. *The Bible teaches that though Jesus was the Son of God, He learned obedience through the things He suffered (see Heb. 5:8). What must you do in order for Him to teach you the kind of obedience He walked in every day of His life on earth?*

3. *What are the two great factors in the relationship between you and God? How does God demonstrate His side in the equation, and how should you demonstrate yours?*

Day 28

Led by the Spirit

Then Jesus, being filled with the Holy Spirit,
returned from the Jordan and was
led by the Spirit into the wilderness.
Luke 4:1

Be filled with the Spirit.
Ephesians 5:18

For as many as are led by the Spirit of God,
these are sons of God.
Romans 8:14

FROM His very birth, the Lord Jesus had the Spirit dwelling in Him. But there were times when He needed special communications of the Spirit from the Father. Thus it was with His baptism. The descent of the Holy Spirit on Him, the baptism of the Spirit, given in the baptism with water, was a real transaction. He was filled with the Spirit, and He returned from the Jordan full of the Holy Spirit, and experienced more manifestly than ever the leading of the Spirit. In the wilderness He wrestled and conquered, not in His own divine power, but as a man who was strengthened and led by the Holy Spirit. In this also "He had to be made *like* His brethren" (Heb. 2:17).

The other side of the truth also holds true: the brethren are in all things made like Him. They are called to live like Him. This is not demanded from them without their having the same power. This power is the Holy Spirit dwelling in us, whom we have of God. Just as Jesus was filled with the Spirit and then led by the Spirit, so must we be also filled with the Spirit and be led by the Spirit.

More than once, in our meditations on the different traits of Christ's character, it has seemed to us almost impossible to be like Him. We have lived so little for it, and we feel so little able to live this way. Let us take courage in the thought: Jesus Himself could only live that way through the Spirit. It was after He was filled with the Spirit that He was led out by that Spirit to the place of conflict and of victory. And this blessing is ours as surely as it was His. We may be filled with the Spirit, and we may be led by the Spirit. Jesus, who was Himself baptized with the Spirit, to set us an example how to live, has ascended into heaven to baptize us into the likeness with Himself. He who desires to live like Jesus must begin here: he must be baptized with the Spirit. What God demands from His children He first gives. He demands entire likeness to Christ because He will give us, as He did Jesus, the fullness of the Spirit. We must be filled with the Spirit.

> *Just as Jesus was filled with the Spirit and then led by the Spirit, so must we be also filled with the Spirit and be led by the Spirit.*

We have here the reason why the teaching of the imitation and likeness to Christ has so little prominence in the Church of Christ. Men sought it in their own strength, with the help of some workings of the Holy Spirit. They did not understand that nothing less was needed than being filled with the Spirit. No wonder that they thought that real conformity to Christ could not be expected of us, because they had mistaken thoughts about being *filled with the Spirit*. It was thought to be the privilege of a few, and not the calling and duty *of every child of God*. It was not sufficiently realized that "Be filled with the Spirit" (Eph. 5:18) is a command to every Christian.

Only when the Church first gives the baptism of the Spirit, and Jesus, as the Savior *who baptizes with the Spirit* each one who believes in Him, their right place, only then will likeness to Christ be sought after and attained. People will then understand and acknowledge: to be like Christ, we must be led by the same Spirit, and to be led by the Spirit as He was, we must be filled with the Spirit. Nothing less than the fullness of the Spirit is absolutely necessary to live a truly Christian, Christlike life.

The way to arrive at it is simple. It is Jesus who baptizes with the Spirit, and whoever comes to Him desiring it will get it. All that He requires of us is the surrender of faith to receive what He gives.

The surrender of faith. What He asks is whether we are indeed in earnest to follow in His footsteps, and for this to be baptized of the Spirit. Do not let there be any hesitation as to our answer. First, look back on all the glorious promises of His love and of His Spirit, in which the blessed privilege is set forth: JUST AS I, YOU ALSO. Remember that it was of this likeness to Himself in everything He said to the Father: "The glory which You gave Me I have given them" (John 17:22). Think how the love of Christ and the true desire to please Him, how the glory of God and the needs of the world, plead with us not through our apathy to despise this heavenly birthright of being Christlike. Acknowledge the sacred right of ownership Christ has in you, His blood-bought ones, and let nothing prevent your answering: "Yes, dear Lord, as far as is allowed to a child of dust, I will be like

You. I am entirely Yours. I must, I will, in all things bear Your image. It is for this I ask to be filled with the Spirit."

The surrender of faith: only this, but nothing less than this He demands. Let us give what He asks. If we yield ourselves to be like Him, in all things, let it be in the quiet trust that He accepts, and immediately begins in secret to make the Spirit work more mightily in us. Let us believe it although we do not immediately experience it. To be filled with the Holy Spirit, we must wait on our Lord in faith. We can depend on it that His love desires to give us more than we know. Let our surrender be made in this assurance.

> *he surrender of faith. What He asks is whether we are indeed in earnest to follow in His footsteps, and for this to be baptized of the Spirit. Do not let there be any hesitation as to our answer.*

And let this surrender of faith be entire. The fundamental law of following Christ is this: "He who loses his life shall find it" (see Matt. 10:39). The Holy Spirit comes to take away the old life and to give in its place the life of Christ in you. Renounce the old life of self-working and self-watching, and believe that, as the air you breathe renews your life every moment, so naturally and continually the Holy Spirit will renew your life. In the work of the Holy Spirit in you there are no breaks or interruptions. You are in the Spirit as your vital air; the Spirit is in you as your life-breath. Through the Spirit, God works in you both to will and to do according to His good pleasure.

Oh, Christian, have a deep reverence for the work of the Spirit who dwells within you. Believe in God's power, which works in you through the Spirit, to conform you to Christ's life and image moment by moment. Be occupied with Jesus and His life, that life that is at the same time your example and your strength, in the full assurance that the Holy Spirit knows in deep quiet to fulfill His office of communicating Jesus to you. Remember that the fullness of the Spirit is yours in Jesus, a real gift that you accept and hold in faith, even when there is not such feeling as you could wish, and on which you count to work in you all you need. The feeling may be weakness and fear and much trembling, and yet the speaking, and working, and living in demonstration of the Spirit and of power. Live in the faith that the fullness of the Spirit is yours, and that you will not be disappointed if, looking unto Jesus, you rejoice every day in the blessed trust that the care of your spiritual life is in the hands of the Holy Spirit the Comforter. Thus, with the loving presence of Jesus in you, the living likeness to Jesus will be seen on you. The Spirit of life in Christ Jesus dwelling within, the likeness of the life of Christ Jesus will shine around.

And if it does not appear that in believing and obeying this way your desires are fulfilled, remember that it is in the fellowship with the members of Christ's body, and in the full surrender to Christ's service in the world, that the full power of the Spirit is made manifest. It was when Jesus gave Himself to enter into full fellowship with men around Him, and like them to be baptized with water, that He was baptized with the Holy Spirit. And it was when He had given Himself in His second baptism of suffering, a sacrifice for us, that He received the Holy Spirit to give to us. Seek fellowship with God's children, who will with you plead and believe for the baptism of the Spirit. The disciples received the Spirit not singly, but when they were with one accord in one place. Band yourself with God's children around you to work for souls. The Spirit is the power from on high to prepare for that work, and the promise will be fulfilled to the believing servants who want Him not for their enjoyment, but for that work. Christ was filled with the Spirit so that He might be prepared to work and live and die for us. Give yourself to such a Christlike living and dying for men, and you may depend upon it that a Christlike baptism of the Spirit, a Christlike fullness of the Spirit, will be your portion.

Blessed Lord! How wondrously You have provided for our growing likeness to Yourself, in giving us Your own Holy Spirit. You have told us that it is His work to reveal You, to give us Your real presence within us. It is by Him that all You have won for us, all the life and holiness and strength we see in You, is brought over and imparted and made our very own. He takes of Yours, and shows it to us, and makes it ours. Blessed Jesus! We thank You for the gift of the Holy Spirit.

> Be occupied with Jesus and His life, that life that is at the same time your example and your strength, in the full assurance that the Holy Spirit knows in deep quiet to fulfill His office of communicating Jesus to you.

And now, we ask You, fill us, oh, fill us full, with Your Holy Spirit! Lord! Nothing less is sufficient. We cannot be led like You, we cannot fight and conquer like You, we cannot love and serve like You, we cannot live and die like You, unless like You we are full of the Holy Spirit. Blessed, blessed be Your name! You have commanded, You have promised it. It may, it can, it shall be.

Holy Savior! Draw Your disciples together to wait and plead for this. Let their eyes be opened to see the wondrous unfulfilled promises of floods of the Holy Spirit. Let their hearts be drawn to give themselves, like You, to live and die for men. And we know it will be Your delight to fulfill Your office, as He who baptizes with the Holy Spirit and with fire. Glory to Your name. Amen.

FOR FURTHER THOUGHT

1. *What was the nature of Jesus' relationship to the Holy Spirit, and how important to you is it that you walk in that very same relationship? How can you make sure that happens in your Christian life?*
2. *What, according to today's lesson, is the fundamental law of following Christ? What steps are involved in following that fundamental law?*
3. *How exactly does God's power work in you day by day, moment by moment? What is your part in seeing to it that this happens?*

Day 29

In His Life

through the Father

*"I live because of the Father, so he who
feeds on Me will live because of Me."*
John 6:57

EVERY contemplation of a walk in the footsteps of Christ, and in His likeness, reveals anew the need of fixing the eye on the deep living union between the Forerunner and His followers. *Like Christ:* the longer we meditate on the word, the more we realize how impossible it is without that other: *In Christ.* The outward likeness can only be the manifestation of a living inward union. To do the same works as Christ, I must have the same life. The more earnestly I take Him for my example, the more I am driven to Him as my head. Only an inner life essentially like His can lead us to a visible walk like His.

What a blessed word we have here, to assure us that His life on earth and ours are really like each other: "I live *because* of the Father, *so* he who feeds on Me will live because of Me." If you desire to understand your life in Christ, what He will be for you and how He will work in you, you have only to contemplate what the Father was for Him, and how He worked in Him. Christ's life in and through the Father is the image and the measure of what your life in and through the Son may be. Let us meditate on this.

As Christ's life was a life *hidden in God in heaven,* so must ours be. When He emptied Himself of His divine glory, He laid aside the free use of His divine attributes. He needed thus as a man to live by faith; He needed to wait on the Father for such communications of wisdom and power, as it pleased the Father to impart to Him. He was entirely dependent on the Father, and His life was hidden in God. Not in virtue of His own independent Godhead, but through the operations of the Holy Spirit He spoke and acted as the Father from time to time taught Him.

Exactly so, believer, must your life be hidden with Christ in God. Let this encourage you. Christ calls you to a life of faith and dependence, because it is the life He Himself led. He has tried it and proved its blessedness. He is willing now to live over again His life in you, to teach you also to live in no other way. He knew that the Father was His life, and that He lived through the Father, and that the Father supplied His need moment by moment. And now He assures you that as He lived through the Father, even so you shall live through Him. Take this assurance in faith. Let your heart be filled with the thought of the blessedness of this fullness of life, which is prepared for you in Christ, and will be abundantly supplied as you need it. Do not think any more of your spiritual life as something that you must watch over and nourish with care and anxiety. Rejoice every day that you need not live in your own strength, but in your Lord Jesus, just as He lived through His Father.

Just as Christ's life was a *life of divine power*, although a life of dependence, so ours will *also be*. He never regretted having laid aside His glory to live before God as a man on earth. The Father never disappointed His confidence, but gave Him all He needed to accomplish His work. Christ experienced that as blessed as it was to be like God in heaven, and to dwell in the enjoyment of divine perfection, it was no less blessed to live in the relationship of entire dependence on earth, and to receive everything day by day from His hands.

Christ calls you to a life of faith and dependence, because it is the life He Himself led. He has tried it and proved its blessedness. He is willing now to live over again His life in you, to teach you also to live in no other way.

Believer, if you will have it so, your life can be the same. The divine power of the Lord Jesus will work in and through us. Do not think that your earthly circumstances make a holy life to God's glory impossible. It was just to manifest, in the midst of earthly surroundings that were even more difficult, the divine life that Christ came and lived on earth. As He lived so blessed an earthly life through the Father, so may you also live your earthly life through Him. Only cultivate large expectations of what the Lord will do for you. Let it be your sole desire to attain to an entire union with Him. *It is impossible to say what the Lord Jesus would do for a soul who is truly willing to live as entirely through Him as He through the Father.* Because just as He lived through the Father, and the Father made that life with all its work so glorious, so will you experience in all your work how entirely He has undertaken to work all in you.

As the life of Christ was the *manifestation of His real union with the Father, so ours also*. Christ says, "As the Father has sent Me, and I live by the Father" (see John 6:57). When the Father desired to manifest Himself on earth in His love, He could entrust that work to no one less than His beloved Son, who was one with Him. It was because He was *Son* that the Father sent Him. It was because the Father had sent Him that it could not be otherwise, but He must care for His life. In the union on which the mission rested, rested the blessed certainty that Jesus would live on earth through the Father.

"Even so," Christ said, "He who feeds on Me will live because of Me" (John 6:57). He had said before, "He who eats My flesh and drinks My blood abides in Me, and I in him" (John 6:56). In death He had given His flesh and blood for the life of the world. Through faith the soul partakes of the power of His death and resurrection, and receives its right to His life, as He had a right to His Father's life. In the words, "Whosoever feeds on Me," is expressed the intimate union and unbroken communion with the Lord Jesus, which is the power of a life in Him. The one great work for the soul who truly longs to live entirely and only by Christ is to eat Him, daily to feed on Him, to make Him his own.[57]

> *Just as He lived through the Father, and the Father made that life with all its work so glorious, so will you experience in all your work how entirely He has undertaken to work all in you.*

To attain this, seek continually to have your heart filled with a believing and lively assurance that all Christ's fullness of life is truly yours. Rejoice in the contemplation of His humanity in heaven, and in the wonderful provision God has made through the Holy Spirit for the communication of this life of your Head in heaven to flow unbroken and unhindered down upon you. Thank God unceasingly for the redemption in which He opened the way to the life of God, and for the wonderful life now provided for you in the Son. Offer yourself unreservedly to Him with an open heart and consecrated life that seeks His service alone. In such trust and consecration of faith, in the outpouring of love and cultivation of communion, with His words abiding in you, let Jesus be your daily food. He who feeds on Me shall live by Me: even as the Father has sent Me, and I live by the Father.

Beloved Christian! What think you? Does not the imitation of Christ begin to seem possible in the light of this promise? He who lives through Christ can also live like Him. Therefore let this wonderful life of Christ on earth through the Father be the object of our adoring contemplation, until our whole heart understands and accepts the word, "So he who feeds on Me will live because of Me." Then we shall dismiss all care and anxiety, because the same Christ who set us the example works in us from heaven that life that can live out the example. And our life will become a continual song: To Him who lives in us, in order that we may live like Him, is the love and praise of our hearts. Amen.

O my God! How shall I thank You for this wonderful grace! Your Son became man to teach us the blessedness of a life of human dependence on the Father. He lived through the Father. It has been given us to see in Him how the divine life can live and work and conquer on earth. And now He is ascended into heaven, and has

[57] For the application of our text to the Lord's Supper, see Note.

all power to let that life work in us. We are called to live just as He did on earth, and we live through Him. O God, praise Your name for this unspeakable grace.

Lord, my God, hear the prayer that I now offer to You. If it may be, show me more, much more of Christ's life through the Father. I need to know it, O my God, if I am to live as He did! Oh, give me the spirit of wisdom in the knowledge of Him. Then shall I know what I may expect from Him, what I can do through Him. It will then no longer be a struggle and an effort to live according to Your will and His example. Because I shall then know that this blessed life on earth is now mine, according to the word, "Just as I through the Father, so you through Me." Then shall I daily feed on Christ in the joyful experience: I live through Him. O my Father! Grant this in full measure for His name's sake. Amen.

FOR FURTHER THOUGHT

1.   *What is the connection between becoming like Christ and living in Christ? What does it mean to be "in Christ," and how can you live and walk consistently in Him?*

2.   *Jesus said, "He who eats My flesh and drinks My blood abides in Me, and I in him." What is the literal meaning and practical application of eating Christ's flesh and drinking His blood?*

3.   *What steps should you take to "eat Christ's flesh and drink His blood"? What attitudes and actions toward Christ are essential to attaining this?*

NOTE

THOUGH the words of our Lord Jesus in the sixth of John were not spoken directly of the Lord's Supper, they are yet applicable to it, because they set forth that spiritual blessing of which the Holy Supper is the communication in a visible form. In eating the bread and drinking the wine, our spiritual life is not only strengthened because in these the pardon of our sins is signified and sealed to us, but because the Holy Spirit does indeed make us partakers of the very body and blood of our Lord Jesus as a spiritual reality. So one of our Reformed Church Catechisms, the Heidelberg (Qu. 78), puts it, "What is it then to eat the broken body and drink the shed blood of Christ?" "It is *not only* to embrace with a believing heart the sufferings and death of Christ, and so to obtain the pardon of sin and life eternal; but *moreover also* that we are united *to His sacred body* by the Holy Spirit, who dwells both in Christ and in us, *so that we*, though Christ be in heaven and we on earth, are nevertheless *flesh of His flesh and bones of His bones.*"

It is known that there are in our Protestant churches three views of the Lord's Supper. On the one hand, the Lutheran with its consubstantiation, teaching that the body of our Lord is so present *in the bread*, that even an unbeliever eats no longer only bread, but the body of the Lord. On the other the Zwinglian view, according to which the effect of the sacrament is a very impressive exhibition of the truth that the death of Christ is to us what wine and bread are to the body, and a very expressive confession of our faith in this truth, and so of our interest in the blessings of that death. As the Holy Spirit in the Word speaks to us through the ear, so in the sacrament through the eye. Midway between these views is that of Calvin, who strongly urges that there is in it a mysterious blessing, not well to be expressed in words; that it is not enough to speak of the life that the Spirit gives to our spirit through faith, but that there is a real communication by the Holy Spirit of the very flesh and blood of Jesus in heaven to our very body, so that in virtue of this we are called members of His body, and have His body in us as the seed of the spiritual body of the resurrection. While avoiding, on the one hand, the sacramentarian view of a change in the bread, it seeks to hold firmly, on the other, the reality of a spiritual substantial participation of the very body and blood of our Lord Jesus.

This is not the place to enter on this more fully. But I am persuaded that, when a more scriptural view prevails as to the relation between *body* and *spirit*, it will not be thought strange to believe that without anything like a real presence in the bread itself, we are indeed fed with the very body and blood of our Lord Jesus. The *body* of our Lord is now a spiritual body, transfigured and glorified into the spirit-life of the heavenly world, the spirit and the body in perfect unity and harmony, so that now the Holy Spirit can freely dispense and communicate that body as He will. Our *body* is the temple of the Holy Spirit who dwells in us; our *bodies* are members of Christ; our *mortal bodies* are even now being quickened and prepared by the indwelling Spirit for the resurrection (Rom. 8:11). Why, then, should it be thought strange that by the Holy Spirit the communion of the body of Christ, so distinctly promised, should be, not an Old Testament symbol or shadow, but a blessed heavenly reality?

Calvin's words are as follows: "I am not satisfied with the view of those who, while acknowledging that we have some kind of communion with Christ, only make us partakers of the Spirit, omitting all mention of flesh and blood." "In His humanity also the fullness of life resides, so that everyone who communicates in His flesh and blood, at the same time enjoys the participation of life. *The flesh* of Christ is like a perennial fountain that transfuses into us the life flowing forth from the Godhead into itself. The communion of the flesh and blood of Christ is necessary to all who aspire to the Christian life. Hence these expressions: 'The Church is "the body of Christ."' "Our bodies are 'the members of Christ.'" "We are members of His body, of His flesh and His bones." What our mind does not comprehend, let faith receive, that the Spirit unites things separated by space. That sacred communion of flesh and blood by which Christ transfuses His life into us, just as if it penetrated our bones and marrow, He testifies and seals in the Supper, not by representing a vain or empty sign, but by these exerting an efficacy of the Spirit by which He fulfills what He promises." "I willingly admit anything that helps to express the true and substantial communication of the body and blood of the Lord, as exhibited to believers under the sacred symbols of the Supper, understanding that they are not received by the imagination or the intellect merely, but are enjoyed in reality as the food of eternal life." "We say that Christ descends to us, as well by the external symbol as by His Spirit, that He may truly quicken our souls by the substance of His flesh and blood." "Such is the corporeal presence that the sacrament requires, and which we say is here displayed in such power and efficacy that it not only gives our minds undoubted assurance of heavenly life, but also secures the immortality of our flesh."[58]

To the soul who seeks fully to live by Christ as He did by the Father, the sacrament is a real spiritual blessing, something more than what faith in the Word gives. Let all the praying and believing and living in which we seek to realize the wonderful blessing of living just as Christ did by the Father ever culminate in our communion of the body and blood at the Lord's table. And let us go forth from each such celebration with new confidence that what has been given and confirmed on the great day of the feast will by Jesus Himself be maintained in power in the daily life through the more ordinary channels of His grace—the blessed fellowship with Himself in the word and prayer.

[58] Calvin's *Institutes* 4:17, § 7, 9, 10, 19, 24.

DAY 30

IN GLORIFYING THE FATHER

"Father, the hour has come. Glorify Your Son,
that Your Son also may glorify You. . . .
I have glorified You on the earth."
JOHN 17:1, 4

"By this My Father is glorified, that you
bear much fruit; so you will be My disciples."
JOHN 15:8

THE glory of an object is, that in its sort its intrinsic worth and excellence answers perfectly to all that is expected of it. That excellence or perfection may be so hidden or unknown that the object has no glory to those who behold it. To *glorify* is to remove every hindrance, and so to reveal the full worth and perfection of the object, that its glory is seen and acknowledged by all.

The highest perfection of God, and the deepest mystery of Godhead, is His holiness. In it righteousness and love are united. As the Holy One He hates and condemns sin. As the Holy One He also frees the inner from its power, and raises him to communion with Himself. His name is, "The Holy One of Israel, your Redeemer" (see Isa. 48:17). The song of redemption is: "Great is the Holy One of Israel in your midst!" (Isa. 12:6). To the blessed Spirit, whose special work it is to maintain the fellowship of God with man, the title of Holy in the New Testament belongs more than to the Father or the Son. It is this holiness, judging sin and saving sinners, that is the glory of God. For this reason the two words are often found together. So in the song of Moses: "Who is like You. . .*glorious* in *holiness*?" (Exod. 15:11). So in the song of the Seraphim: "*Holy, Holy, Holy* is the LORD God of hosts; the whole earth is full of His *glory*" (Isa. 6:3). And so in the song of the Lamb: "Who shall not. . .*glorify* Your name? For You alone are *holy*" (Rev. 15:4). As has been well said: "God's glory is His manifested holiness; God's holiness is His hidden glory."

When Jesus came to earth, it was that He might glorify the Father, that He might again show forth in its true light and beauty that glory that sin had so entirely hidden from man. Man himself had been created in the image of God, that God might lay of His glory on him, to be shown forth in him—that God might be glorified in him. The Holy Spirit says, "Man is the image and glory of God." Jesus came to restore man to his high destiny. He laid aside the glory that He had with the Father and came in our weakness and humiliation, so that He might teach us how to glorify the Father on earth. God's glory is perfect and infinite. Man cannot contribute any new glory to God above what He has. He can only serve as a glass in which the glory of God is reflected. God's holiness is His glory. As the holiness of God is seen in him, God is glorified; His glory as God is shown forth.

> The highest perfection of God, and the deepest mystery of Godhead, is His holiness. In it righteousness and love are united.

Jesus glorified God *by obeying Him*. In giving His commandments to Israel, God continually said, "Be holy, for I am holy." In keeping the commandments they would be transformed into a life of harmony with Him, they would enter into fellowship with Him as the Holy One. In His conflict with sin and Satan, in His sacrifice of His own will, in His waiting for the Father's teaching, in His unquestioning obedience to the Word, Christ showed that He counted nothing worth living for, but that men might understand what a blessed thing it is to let this holy God really BE GOD, His will alone acknowledged and obeyed. Because He alone is holy, His will alone should be done, and so His glory is shown in us.

Jesus glorified God *by confessing Him*. He not only in His teaching made known the message God had given Him and showed us who the Father is. There is something far more striking. He continually spoke of His own personal relationship to the Father. He did not trust to the silent influence of His holy life; He wanted men distinctly to understand what the root and aim of that life was. Time after time He told them that He came as a servant sent from the Father, that He depended on Him and owed everything to Him, that He only sought the Father's honor, and that all His happiness was to please the Father and to secure His love and favor.

Jesus glorified God *by giving Himself for the work of His redeeming love*. God's glory is His holiness, and God's holiness is His redeeming love—love that triumphs over sin by conquering the sin and rescuing the sinner. Jesus not only told of the Father being the righteous One whose condemnation must rest on sin, and the loving One who saves everyone who turns from his sin, but He gave Himself to be a sacrifice to that righteousness, a servant to that love, even to the death. It was not only in acts of obedience or words of confession that He glorified God, but in giving Himself to magnify the holiness of God, to vindicate at once His law and His love by His atonement. He gave Himself, His whole life and being,

HIMSELF wholly, to show how the Father loved and longed to bless, how the Father must condemn the sin and yet would save the sinner. He counted nothing too great a sacrifice. He lived and died only for this, that the glory of the Father, the glory of His holiness, of His redeeming love, might break through the dark veil of sin and flesh, and shine into the hearts of the children of men. As He Himself expressed it in the last week of His life, when the approaching anguish began to press in on Him: "Now My soul is troubled, and what shall I say? 'Father, save Me from this hour'? But for this purpose I came to this hour. FATHER, GLORIFY YOUR NAME." And the assurance came that the sacrifice was well-pleasing and accepted, in the answer: "I have both glorified it and will glorify it again" (John 12:28).

It was in this that Jesus as man was prepared to have part in the glory of God: He sought it in the humiliation on earth, and He found it on the throne of heaven. And so He has become our forerunner, leading many children to glory. He shows us that the sure way to the glory of God in heaven is to live only for the glory of God on earth. Yes, this is the glory of a life on earth: glorifying God here, we are prepared to be glorified with Him forever.

> God's glory is His holiness, and God's holiness is His redeeming love—love that triumphs over sin by conquering the sin and rescuing the sinner.

Beloved Christian! Is it not a wonderful calling, blessed beyond all conception, like Christ to live only to glorify God, to let God's glory shine out in every part of our life? Let us take time to take in the wondrous thought: our daily life, down to its most ordinary acts, may be transparent with the glory of God. Oh, let us study this trait as one that makes the wondrous image of our Jesus especially attractive to us: He glorified the Father. Let us listen to Him as He points us to the high aim, *that your Father in heaven may be glorified,* and as He shows us the way, *By this is my Father glorified.* Let us remember how He told us that, when in heaven He answers our prayer, this would still be His object, and in every breathing of prayer and faith let it be our object, too: *"That the Father may be glorified in the Son."* Let our whole life, like Christ's, be animated by this as its ruling principle, growing stronger until in a holy enthusiasm our watchword has become: *All, all to the glory of God.* And let our faith hold firmly the confidence that in the fullness of the Spirit there is the sure provision for our desire being fulfilled: "Do you not know that your body is the temple of the Holy Spirit who is in you...*therefore* glorify God in your body and in your spirit" (1 Cor. 6:19–20).

If we want to know the way, let us again study Jesus. He obeyed the Father. Let simple downright obedience mark our whole life. Let a humble, childlike waiting for direction, a soldier-like looking for orders, a Christlike dependence on the Father's showing us His way, be our daily attitude. Let everything be done to the Lord, according to His will, for His glory, in direct relationship to Himself. Let God's glory shine out in the holiness of our life.

He confessed the Father. He did not hesitate to speak often of His personal relationship and fellowship, just as a little child would do of an earthly parent. It is not enough that we live right before men. How can they understand, if there is no interpreter? They need, not as a matter of preaching but as a personal testimony, to hear that what we are and do is *because we love the Father and are living for Him.* The witness of the life and the words must go together.[59]

And He gave Himself to the Father's work. So He glorified Him. He showed sinners that God has a right to have us wholly and only for Himself, that God's glory alone is worth living and dying for, and that as we give ourselves to this, God will most wonderfully use and bless us in leading others to see and confess His glory, too. It was that men might glorify the Father in heaven, might find their blessedness also in knowing and serving this glorious God, that Jesus lived, and that we must live, too. Oh, let us give ourselves to God for men. Let us plead, and work, and live, and die, so that men, our fellowmen, may see that God is glorious in holiness, that the whole earth may be filled with His glory.

Believer! "The Spirit of God and of glory, the spirit of holiness, rests upon you" (see 1 Pet. 4:14). Jesus delights to do in you His beloved work of glorifying the Father. Fear not to say: "O my Father, in Your Son, *like Your Son*, I will only live to glorify You."

> *J*esus delights to do in you His beloved work of glorifying the Father. Fear not to say: "O my Father, in Your Son, like Your Son, I will only live to glorify You."

O my God! I do pray, show me Your glory! I feel deeply how utterly impossible it is, by any resolution or effort of mine, to lift myself up or bind myself to live for Your glory alone. But if You will reveal to me Your glory, if You will make all Your goodness pass before me, and show me how glorious You are, how there is no glory but Yours; if, O my Father, You will let Your glory shine into my heart and take possession of my innermost being, I never will be able to do anything but glorify You, but live to make known what a glorious, holy God You are.

Lord Jesus, who came to earth to glorify the Father in our sight, and ascend to heaven leaving us to do it now in Your name and stead, give us by Your Holy Spirit a sight of how You did it. Teach us the meaning of Your obedience to the Father, Your acknowledgment that, at any cost, His will must be done. Teach us to mark Your confession of the Father, and how You in personal testimony told men of what He was to You, and what You felt for Him, and let our lips, too, tell out what we taste of the love of the Father, that men may glorify Him. And above

[59] See note.

all, teach us that it is in saving sinners that redeeming love has its triumph and its joy, that it is in holiness casting out sin that God has His highest glory. And do so take possession of our whole hearts that we may love and labor, live and die, for this one thing, "That every tongue should confess that Jesus Christ is Lord, TO THE GLORY OF GOD THE FATHER" (Phil. 2:11).

O my Father, let the whole earth, let my heart, be filled with Your glory. Amen.

FOR FURTHER THOUGHT

1. *"To glorify is to remove every hindrance, and so to reveal the full worth and perfection of the object, that its glory is seen and acknowledged by all."* In light of that, what does it mean to glorify the Father, just as Christ did in His every word, thought, and action?

2. What is the nature of God's holiness? How does His holiness reveal and demonstrate itself? In His holiness, what does He do to sin and for those who are His, including you?

3. In what specific ways did Christ glorify the Father? How does He enable you, though you are weak and powerless, to glorify the Father in exactly the same way?

Note

LET us begin by considering what was the groundwork of the whole beauty and harmony of our blessed Savior's character. Love to the Father was the ruling motive of His life. It so pervaded His nature as to find expression, directly or indirectly, in every word as well as every action. It will be well if we try to realize something of the perfect simplicity with which that love was so continually shown forth in daily life.

"We especially need to remind ourselves of how entirely this was the case, because, in these days of artificial manners, and of false shame, we are so frequently tempted to conceal our true motives and to think it a disgrace if we are led into any sign of betraying our deepest religious feelings. We conceal them from those who would not understand them, unless by chance they should scorn our judgment and wound our self-respect; and we too frequently even hide them from those who are of like mind with ourselves, lest they, too, might think us lacking in good taste. Self fears the slightest rebuke, the merest breath of disapproval. So long as our love to God is weak enough to allow of its being hidden, self will carefully hide it, rather than run the least risk of being considered deficient in discretion.

"Of true discretion, which is quite a different thing, we shall find abundant examples in our Master's life. But that false discretion, which strives to divert notice, not from ourselves, but from the deepest principles of our conduct, and in order to save our own selfish feelings from being wounded, finds no counterpart whatever in the life of our Lord. In His earthly nature, as man, Christ loved the Lord His God with all His heart and with all His strength. And this all-pervading love could not but assert itself continually. Our Lord simply and unhesitatingly referred to it as a simple fact, whenever the slightest occasion for doing so arose. It was His avowed object *that the world should know that He loved the Father*. He frequently and emphatically alluded to *His personal connection with the Father* as the means by which He lived. It was His consciousness of that union that gave Him unfailing support.

"Jesus Christ made known the Father's love. He was sent that He might reveal *the deep blessedness of belonging wholly to God*. Even so are we sent, each one of us into the world, in order that we may make the Savior known to those around us. Through our own intimate and personal connection with Himself, we are each one of us to reveal the Son, just as He revealed the Father. And this we can only do by acting as He did, by continually *proving how all-sufficient is the sense of union with Himself*."[60]

---

[60] From a chapter on the example left us by Christ, in a little book containing many precious thoughts, *Steps on the Upward Path; or, Holiness unto the Lord*. By A. M. James. Religious Tract Society.

Day 31
In His Glory

We know that when He is revealed,
we shall be like Him, for we shall see Him as He is.
And everyone who has this hope in Him
purifies himself, just as He is pure.
1 John 3:2–3

"And I bestow upon you a kingdom,
just as My Father bestowed one upon Me."
Luke 22:29

GOD'S glory is His holiness. To glorify God is to yield ourselves so that God in us may show forth His glory. It is only by yielding ourselves to be holy, to let His holiness fill our life, that His glory can shine forth from us. The one work of Christ was to glorify the Father, to reveal what a glorious, holy God He is. Our one work is, like Christ's, so by our obedience, and testimony, and life, to make known our God as "glorious in holiness," that He may be glorified in heaven and earth.

When the Lord Jesus had glorified the Father on earth, the Father glorified Him with Himself in heaven. This was not only His just reward; it was a necessity in the very nature of things. There is no other place for a life given up to the glory of God, as Christ's was, than in that glory. The law holds true for us, too: a heart that yearns and thirsts for the glory of God, that is ready to live and die for it, becomes prepared and fitted to live in it. *Living to God's glory* on earth is the gate to *living in God's glory* in heaven. If with Christ we glorify the Father, the Father will with Christ glorify us, too. Yes, we shall be like Him in His glory.

We shall be like Him in *His spiritual glory*, the glory of His holiness. In the union of the two words in the name of the Holy Spirit, we see that what is HOLY and what is *spiritual* stand in the closest connection with each other. When Jesus as man had glorified God by revealing, and honoring, and giving Himself up to His holiness, He was as man taken up into and made partaker of the divine glory.

And so it will be with us. If here on earth we have given ourselves to have

God's glory take possession of us, and God's holiness, God's Holy Spirit, dwell and shine in us, then our human nature with all our faculties, created in the likeness of God, shall have poured into and transfused through it, in a way that passes all conception, the purity and the holiness and the life, the very brightness of the glory of God.

We shall be like Him in *His glorified body*. It has been well said: "Embodiment is the end of the ways of God." The creation of man was to be God's masterpiece. There had previously been spirits without bodies and animated bodies without spirits, but in man there was to be a spirit in a body lifting up and spiritualizing the body into its own heavenly purity and perfection. Man as a whole is God's image, his body as much as his spirit. In Jesus a human body—O mystery of mysteries!—is set on the throne of God, is found a worthy partner and container of the divine glory.

> *If with Christ we glorify the Father, the Father will with Christ glorify us, too. Yes, we shall be like Him in His glory.*

Our bodies are going to be the objects of the most astonishing miracle of divine transforming power: "(He) will transform our lowly body that it may be conformed to His glorious body, according to the working by which He is able even to subdue all things to Himself" (Phil. 3:21). The glory of God as seen in our bodies, made like Christ's glorious body, will be something almost more wonderful than in our spirits. We are "waiting for the adoption, to wit, the redemption of our body."

We shall be like Him in *His place of honor*. Every object must have a fit place for its glory to be seen. Christ's place is the central one in the universe: the throne of God. He spoke to His disciples, "Where I am, there My servant will be also. If anyone serves Me, *him My Father will honor*" (John 12:26). "I bestow upon you a kingdom, JUST AS My Father bestowed one upon Me, that you may eat and drink at My table in My kingdom, and sit on thrones judging the twelve tribes of Israel" (Luke 22:29–30). To the church at Thyatira He says: "He who overcomes, and keeps My works until the end, to him I will give power over the nations—*as I also* have received from My Father" (Rev. 2:26–27). And to the church at Laodicea: "To him who overcomes I will grant to sit with Me on My throne, AS I ALSO overcame and sat down with My Father on His throne" (Rev. 3:21). Higher and closer it cannot be: "AND AS WE have borne the image of the man of dust, we shall also bear the image of the heavenly Man" (1 Cor. 15:49). The likeness will be complete and perfect.

Such divine God-given glimpses into the future reveal to us, more than all our thinking, what intense truth, what divine meaning there is in God's creative word:

"Let us make man in Our image, according to Our likeness" (Gen. 1:26). To show forth the likeness of the invisible, to be partaker of the divine nature, to share with God His rule of the universe, is man's destiny. His place is indeed one of unspeakable glory. Standing between two eternities, the eternal purpose in which we were predestinated to be conformed to the image of the firstborn Son, and the eternal realization of that purpose when we shall be like Him in His glory, we hear the voice from every side: You image-bearers of God! On the way to share the glory of God and of Christ, live a Godlike, live a Christlike life!

"I shall be satisfied when I awake in YOUR LIKENESS," so the psalmist sang of old (17:15). Nothing can satisfy the soul but God's image, because for that it was created. And this not as something external to it, only seen but not possessed; it is as partaker of that likeness that we shall be satisfied. Blessed are they who here long for it with insatiable hunger, for they shall be filled. This, the very likeness of God, this will be the glory, streaming down on them from God Himself, streaming through their whole being, streaming out from them through the universe. "When Christ who is our life appears, then you also will appear with Him in glory" (Col. 3:4).

Beloved fellow Christians! Nothing can be revealed in that day that has not a real existence here in this life. If the glory of God is not our life here, it cannot be hereafter. It is impossible. Him alone who glorifies God here can God glorify hereafter. "Man is the image and glory of God" (see 1 Cor. 11:7). It is as you bear the image of God here, as you live in the likeness of Jesus, who is the brightness of His glory, and the express image of His person, that you will be fitted for the glory to come. If we are to be as the image of the heavenly, the Christ in glory, we must first bear the image of the earthly, the Christ in humiliation.

> *L*ike Christ, let us pray for each other, and for all God's children, that in ever-growing measure this may be the one aim of our faith, the one desire of our heart, the one joy of our life.

Child of God! Christ is the uncreated image of God. Man is His created image. On the throne in the glory the two will be eternally one. You know what Christ did, how He drew near, how He sacrificed all, to restore us to the possession of that image. Oh, shall we not at length yield ourselves to this wonderful love, to this glory inconceivable, and give our life wholly to manifest the likeness and the glory of Christ. Shall we not, like Him, make the Father's glory our aim and hope, living to His glory here, as the way to live in His glory there.

Beloved brethren! You who have accompanied me this far in these meditations on the image of our Lord and the Christlike life in which it is to be reflected: the time is now come for us to part. Let us do so with the word, "We shall be LIKE Him, for we shall see Him as He is. And everyone who has this hope in Him purifies himself, JUST AS He is pure" (1 John 3:2–3). LIKE CHRIST, let us pray for each other, and for all God's children, that in ever-growing measure this may be the one aim of our faith, the one desire of our heart, the one joy of our life. Oh, what will it be when we meet in the glory, when we see Him as He is, and see each other all like Him!

Ever blessed and most glorious God! What thanks shall we render You for the glorious gospel of Christ, who is the image of God, and for the light of Your glory that shines on us in Him! And what thanks shall we render You, that in Jesus we have seen the image not only of Him, but of our glory, the pledge of what we are to be with You through eternity!

O God! Forgive us, forgive us for Jesus' blood's sake, that we have so little believed this, that we have so little lived this. And we ask You that You would reveal to all who have had fellowship with each other in these meditations, what THE GLORY is in which they are to live eternally, in which they can be living, even now, as they glorify You. O Father! Awaken us and all Your children to see and feel what Your purpose with us is. We are indeed to spend eternity in Your glory. Your glory is to be around us, and on us, and in us, and we are to be like Your Son in His glory. Father! We ask You, oh, visit Your Church! Let Your Holy Spirit, the Spirit of glory, work mightily in her, and let this be her one desire, the one mark by which she is known: the glory of God resting on her.

Our Father! Grant it for Jesus' sake. Amen.

FOR FURTHER THOUGHT

1. *What was the one work for which Christ came to earth? What is your one work as a disciple of Christ living here on earth?*
2. *Read 1 John 3:2–3. In what specific ways will we be like Christ when we are glorified in heaven?*
3. *As a created image-bearer of God, what does God call and command you to do on the way to sharing in the glory of Christ? How does He empower you to obey that command, and how will He reward your obedience?*

ON PREACHING CHRIST
OUR EXAMPLE

Let us make man IN OUR IMAGE, ACCORDING TO OUR LIKENESS" (Gen. 1:26). In these words of the council of Creation, with which the Bible history of man opens, we have the revelation of the eternal purpose to which man owes his existence, of the glorious eternal future to which he is destined. God proposes to make a GODLIKE CREATURE, a being who shall be His very image and likeness, the visible manifestation of the glory of the invisible One.

To have a being, at the same time created and yet Godlike, was indeed a task worthy of infinite wisdom. It is the nature and glory of God that He is absolutely independent of all else, having life in Himself, owing His existence to none but Himself alone. If man is to be Godlike, he must bear His image and likeness in this, too, that he must become what he is to be, of his own free choice; he must make himself. It is the nature and glory of the creature to be dependent, to owe everything to the blessed Creator. How can the contradiction be reconciled?—a being at the same time dependent and yet self-determined, created and yet God-like. In man the mystery is solved. As a creature God gives him life, but endows him with the wonderful power of a free will. It is only in the process of a personal and voluntary appropriation that anything so high and holy as likeness to God can really become his very own.

When sin entered and man fell from his high destiny, God did not give up His purpose. Of His revelation in Israel the central thought was: "Be holy, as I am holy." Likeness to God in that which constitutes His highest perfection is to be Israel's hope. Redemption had no higher ideal than Creation had revealed; it could only take up and work out the eternal purpose.

It was with this in view that the Father sent to the earth the Son who was the express image of His person. In Him, the Godlikeness to which we had been created, and which we had personally to appropriate and make our own, was revealed in human form. He came to show to us at once the image of God and our own image. In looking at Him, the desire after our long-lost likeness to God was to be awakened, and that hope and faith birthed that gave us courage to yield ourselves to be renewed after that image.

To accomplish this, there was a twofold work He had to do. The one was *to reveal in His life the likeness of God,* so that we might know what a life in that likeness was, and understand what it was we had to expect and accept from Him as our redeemer. When He had done this, and shown us the *likeness of the life of God* in human form, He died so that He might win for us, and impart to us, His own life as *the life of the likeness of God*, that in its power we might live in the likeness of what we had seen in Him. And when He ascended to heaven, it was to give us in the Holy Spirit the power of that life He had first set before us and then won to impart to us.

It is easy to see how close the connection is between these two parts of the work of our Lord, and how the one depends on the other. For what as our example He had in His life revealed, He as our redeemer by His death purchased the power. His earthly life showed the path, and His heavenly life gives the power in which we are to walk. What God has joined together no man may separate. Whoever does not stand in the full faith of the redemption does not have the strength to follow the example. And whoever does not seek conformity to the image as the great object of the redemption cannot fully enter into its power. Christ lived on earth so that He might show forth *the image of God in His life*; He lives in heaven so that we may show forth *the image of God in our lives*.

The Church of Christ has not always maintained the due relationship of these two truths. In the Catholic church the former of the two was placed in the foreground, and the following of Christ's example pressed with great earnestness. As the fruit of this, she can point to no small number of saints who, notwithstanding many errors, with admirable devotion sought literally and entirely to bear the Master's image. But to the great loss of earnest souls, the other half of the truth was neglected, that only they who in the power of Christ's death receive His life within them are able to imitate His life as set before them.

The Protestant churches owe their origin to the revival of the second truth. The truth of God's pardoning and quickening grace took its true place to the great comfort and joy of thousands of anxious souls. And yet here the danger of one-sidedness was not entirely avoided. The doctrine that Christ lived on earth, not only to die for our redemption but to show us how we were to live, did not receive sufficient prominence. While no orthodox church will deny that Christ is our example, *the absolute necessity* of following the example of His life is not preached with the same distinctness as that of trusting the atonement of His death. Great pains are taken, and that most justly, to lead men to accept the merits of His death. As great pains are not taken, and this is what is not right to lead men to accept the imitation of His life as the one mark and test of true discipleship.

It is hardly necessary to point out what influence the mode of presenting this truth will exercise in the life of the Church. If atonement and pardon are everything, and the life in His likeness something secondary, that is to follow as a matter of course, the chief attention will be directed to the former. Pardon and peace will be the great objects of desire, and with these attained, there will be a tendency to rest content. If, on the other hand, conformity to the image of God's Son is the chief object, and the atonement the means to secure this end, as the fulfillment of God's purpose in creation, then in all the preaching of repentance and pardon, the true aim will always be kept in the foreground. Faith in Jesus and conformity to character will be regarded as inseparable. Such a Church will produce real followers of the Lord.

In this respect the Protestant churches need still to go on to perfection. Then only will the Church put on her beautiful garments and truly shine in the light of God's glory, when these two truths are held in that wondrous unity in which they appear in the life of Christ Himself. *In all He suffered for us, He left us an example* that we should follow in His footsteps. As the banner of the cross is lifted high, *the atonement of the cross* and *the fellowship of the cross* must equally be preached as the condition of true discipleship.

It is remarkable how distinctly this comes out in the teaching of the blessed Master Himself. In fact, in speaking of the cross, He gives its fellowship more prominence than its atonement. How often He told the disciples that they must bear it with Him and like Him, that this was the only way they could be disciples and share in the blessings His cross-bearing was to win. When Peter rebuked Him as He spoke of His being crucified, He did not argue as to the need of the cross in the salvation of men, but simply insisted on its being borne, because to Him as to us the death of self is the only path to the life of God. The disciple must be as the Master. He spoke of it as the instrument of self-sacrifice, the mark and the means of giving up our own life to the death, the only path for the entrance into the new divine life He came to bring. It is not only I who must die, He said, but you, too. The cross, the spirit of daily self-sacrifice, is to be the badge of your allegiance to Me.

How well Peter learned the lesson we see in his epistle. Both the remarkable passages in which he speaks of the Savior suffering for us—("Christ also suffered for us; who bore our sins upon the tree" (1 Pet. 2:21, 24); "He suffered. . .the *just for the unjust*" (1 Pet. 3:18)—are brought in almost incidentally in connection with our suffering like Him. He tells us that as we gaze at the crucified One, we are not only to think of the cross as the path in which Christ found His way to glory, but as that in which each of us is to follow Him.

The same thought comes out with great prominence in the writing of the apostle Paul. To take one epistle, that to the Galatians, we find four passages in which the power of the cross is set forth. In one we have one of the most striking expressions of the blessed truth of substitution and atonement: "Having become *a curse for us* (for it is written, 'Cursed is everyone who hangs on a tree')" (Gal. 3:13). This is indeed one of the foundation stones on which the faith of the Church and the Christian rests. But a house needs more than foundation stones.

And so we find that no less than three times in the epistle the fellowship of the cross, as a personal experience, is spoken of as the secret of the Christian life.

"I have been crucified with Christ" (2:20). "Those who are Christ's have crucified the flesh with its passions and desires" (5:24). "But God forbid that I should boast except in the cross of our Lord Jesus Christ, by whom the world has been crucified to me, and I to the world" (6:14). That Christ bore the cross for us is not all; it is but the beginning of His work. It just opens the way to the full exhibition of what the cross can do as we are taken up into a lifelong fellowship with Him the crucified One, and in our daily life we experience and prove what it is to be crucified to the world. And yet how many earnest and eloquent sermons have been preached on glorying in the cross of Christ, in which Christ's dying on the cross for us has been expounded, but our dying with Him, in which Paul so gloried, has been forgotten!

The Church does indeed need to have this second truth sounded out as clearly as the first. Christians need to understand that bearing the cross does not in the first place refer to the trials which we call crosses, but to that daily giving up of life, of dying to self, which must mark us as much as it did Jesus, which we need in times of prosperity almost more than in adversity, and without which the fullness of the blessing of the cross cannot be disclosed to us. It is the cross, not only as exhibited on Calvary, but as gloried in on account of its crucifying us, its spirit breathing through all our life and actions, that will be to the Christian and the Church, as it was to Christ, the path to victory and to glory, the power of God for the salvation of men.

The redemption of the cross consists of two parts—Christ bearing the cross, Christ's crucifixion for us, as our atonement, the opening up of the way of life; and our crucifixion, our bearing the cross with Christ, as our sanctification, our walking in the path of conformity to His blessed likeness. Christ the Surety and Christ the example must equally be preached.

But it will not be sufficient that these two truths be set forth as separate doctrines. They can exercise their full power only as their inner unity is found in the deeper truth of Christ our head. As we see how union with the Lord Jesus is the root in which the power of both the surety and the example has its life, and how the one Savior makes us partakers both of the atonement and the fellowship of His cross, we shall understand how wonderful their harmony is, and how indispensable both are to the welfare of the Church. We shall see that as it is Jesus who opened up the way to heaven *as much by the footsteps He left us to tread in as by the atonement He gave us to trust in*, so it is the same Jesus who gives us pardon through His blood and conformity to Himself through His Spirit. And we shall understand how for both, faith is the only possible path. The life-power of this atonement comes through faith alone; the life-power of the example no less so. Our evangelical Protestantism cannot fulfill its mission until the grand central truth of *salvation by faith alone* has been fully applied, not only to justification, but to sanctification, too—that is, to the conformity to the likeness of Jesus.

The preacher who desires in this matter to lead his people in the path of entire conformity to the Savior's likeness will find a very wide field indeed opened up to him. The Christlike life is like a tree, in which we distinguish the *fruit*, the *root*, and the *stem* that connects the two. As in individual effort, so in the public ministry, THE FRUIT will probably first attract attention. The words of Christ, "Do just as I have done," and the frequent exhortations in the epistles to love, and forgive, and forbear, even as Christ did, lead first to a comparison of the actual life of Christians with His, and to the unfolding and setting up of that only rule and standard of conduct which the Savior's example is meant to supply. The need will be awakened of taking time and looking distinctly at each of the traits of that wonderful portrait, so that some clear and exact impressions are obtained from it of what God actually desires to have us be.

Believers must be brought to feel that the life of Christ is in very deed the law of their life, and that complete conformity to His example is what God expects of them. There may be a difference in measure between the sun shining in the heavens and a lamp lighting our home here on earth. But still the light is the same in its nature, and in its little sphere the lamp may be doing its work as beautifully as "the sun itself." The conscience of the Church must be educated to understand that the humility and self-denial of Jesus, His entire devotion to His Father's work and will, His ready obedience, His self-sacrificing love and kindly beneficence, are nothing more than what each believer is to consider it his simple duty as well as his privilege to exhibit, too. There is not, as so many think, one standard for Christ and another for His people. No! As branches of the vine, as members of the body, as partakers of the same spirit, we may and therefore must bear the image of the Elder Brother.

The great reason why this conformity to Jesus is so little seen, and in fact so little sought after among a large majority of Christians, is undoubtedly to be found in erroneous views as to our powerlessness and what we may expect divine grace to work in us. Men have such strong faith in the power of sin, and so little faith in the power of grace, that they at once dismiss the thought of our being expected to be just as loving, and just as forgiving, and just as devoted to the Father's glory as Jesus was, as an ideal far beyond our reach—beautiful indeed, but never to be realized. God cannot expect us to be or do what is so entirely beyond our power. They confidently point to their own failure in earnest attempts to curb temper and to live wholly for God as the proof that the thing cannot be.

It is only by the persistent preaching of Christ our example, in all the fullness and glory of this blessed truth, that such unbelief can be overcome. Believers must be taught that God does not reap where He has not sown, that the fruit and THE ROOT are in perfect harmony. God expects us to strive to speak and think and act exactly like Christ, because *the life that is in us is exactly the same as that which was in Him*. We have a life like His, within us, so what more natural than that the outward life should be like His, too? Christ living in us is the root and strength of Christ's acting and speaking through us, shining out from us so as to be seen by the world.

It is specially the preaching of Christ our example, *to be received by faith alone*, that will be needed to lead God's people on to what their Lord desires to have them be. The prevailing idea is that we have to believe in Jesus as our atonement and our Savior, and then, under the influence of the strong motives of gratitude and consistency, to strive to imitate His example. But motives cannot supply the strength, and the sense of powerlessness remains. We are brought again under the law: we ought to, but cannot. These souls must be taught what it means *to believe in Christ their example.* That is, to claim by faith His example, His holy life, as part of the salvation He has prepared for them. They must be taught to believe that this Example is not a something, not even a someone outside of them, but the living Lord Himself, their very life, who will work in them what He first gave them to see in His earthly life. They must learn to believe that if they will submit themselves to Him, He will manifest Himself in them and their life-walk in a way passing all their thoughts—to believe that *the example of Jesus and the conformity to Him* is a part of that eternal life that came down from heaven, and *is freely given to everyone who believes.* It is because we are one with Christ and abide in Him, because we have in us the same divine life He had, that we are expected to walk like Him.

The full insight into this truth, and the final acceptance of it, is no easy matter. Christians have become so accustomed to a life of continual stumbling and unfaithfulness that the very thought of their being able with at least such a measure of resemblance as the world must recognize to show forth the likeness of Christ has become strange to them. The preaching that will conquer their unbelief, and lead God's people to victory, must be animated by a joyous and triumphant faith. For it is only to faith, a faith larger and deeper than Christians ordinarily think needed for salvation, that the power of Christ's example taking possession of the whole life will be given. But when Christ in His fullness, Christ as the law and the life of the believer, is preached, this deeper faith, penetrating to the very root of our oneness of life with Him, will come, and with it the power to manifest that life.

The growth of this faith may in different cases vary much. To some it may come in the course of quiet, persevering waiting on God. To others it may come as a sudden revelation, after seasons of effort, of struggling and failure; just one full sight of what Jesus as the example really is, *Himself being and giving* all He claims. To some it may come in solitude—where there is none to help but the living God Himself alone. To others it will be given, as it has been so often, in the communion of the saints, where amid the enthusiasm and love that the fellowship of the Spirit creates, hearts are melted, decision is strengthened, and faith is stirred to grasp what Jesus offers when He reveals and gives Himself to make us like Himself. But, in whatever way it come, it will come when Christ in the power of the Holy Spirit is preached as God's revelation of what His children are to be. And believers will be led, in the deep consciousness of utter sinfulness and powerlessness, to yield themselves and their life as never before into the hands of an almighty Savior, and to realize in their experience the beautiful harmony between the apparently contradictory words: "In me (that is, in my flesh) nothing good dwells" (Rom. 7:18), and, "I can do all things through Christ who strengthens me" (Phil. 4:13).

But root and fruit are ever connected by a STEM, with its branches and leaves. In the life of Christ this was so, too. The connection between His hidden life rooted in God, and that life manifesting itself in the fruit of holy words and works, was maintained by His life of conscious and continual personal fellowship with the Father. In His waiting on the Father to see and hear what He had to make known, in His yielding Himself to the leadings of the Spirit, in His submission to the teachings of the Word that He came to fulfill, in His watching to prayer, and in His whole life of dependence and faith, Christ became our example. He had so truly been made like us in all things, become one with us in the weakness of the flesh, that it was only through these things that the life of the Father could be kept flowing freely into Him and manifesting itself in the works He did.

And just so it will be with us. Our union to Jesus, and His life in us, will most certainly secure a life like His. This not, however, in the way of an absolute necessity, as a blind force in nature works out its end, but in the way of an intelligent, willing, loving cooperation—a continual coming and receiving from Him in the surrender of faith and prayer, a continual appropriating and exercising of what we receive in watchful obedience and earnest effort, a continual working because we know He works in us. The faith in the vitality and the energy of the life in which we are eternally rooted will not lead to complacency or carelessness, but, as with Christ, rouse our energies to their highest power. It is the faith in the glorious possibilities that open up to us in Christ our life, that will lead to the cultivation of all that constitutes true personal fellowship and waiting on God.

It is in these three points of similarity that the Christlike life must be known: our life like Christ's hidden *in God*, maintained like His in fellowship *with God*, will in its external manifestation be like His, too, a life *for God*. As believers rise to apprehend the truth that we are indeed like Christ in the life we have in God through Him, that we can be like Christ in the keeping up and strengthening of that life in fellowship with God, and that we shall be like Christ in the fruits which such a life must bear, the name of followers of Christ, the imitation of Christ, will not be a profession but a reality, and the world will know that the Father has indeed loved us as He loved the Son.

I venture to suggest to all ministers and Christians who may read this, the inquiry whether, in the teaching and the thought of the Church, we have sufficiently lifted up Christ as the divine model and pattern, in likeness to whom alone we can be restored to the Image of God in which we were created. The more clearly the teachers of the church realize the eternal ground on which a truth rests, its essential importance to other truths for securing their complete healing and development, and the share it has in leading into the full enjoyment of that wonderful salvation God has prepared for us, the better will they be able to guide God's people into the blessed possession of that glorious life of high privilege and holy practice that will prepare them for becoming such a blessing to the world as God meant them to be. It is the one thing that the world needs in these latter days—men and women of Christlike lives, who prove that they are in the world as He was in the world, that the one object of their existence is nothing other than what was Christ's object—the glorifying of the Father and the saving of men.

One word more. Let us above all beware lest in the preaching and seeking of Christlikeness that secret but deadly selfishness creeps in which leads men to seek it for the sake of getting for themselves as much as is to be had, and because they desire to be as eminent in grace and as high in the favor of God as may be. God is love: the image of God is Godlike love. When Jesus said to His disciples: "You shall be perfect, just as your Father in heaven is perfect" (Matt. 5:48), He told them that perfection was loving and blessing the unworthy. His very names tell us that all the other traits of Christlikeness must be subordinate to this one: seeking the will and glory of God in loving and saving men. He is Christ the anointed. The Lord has anointed Him—for whom? For the brokenhearted and the captive, for those who are bound and those who mourn. He is Jesus—living and dying to save the lost.

There may be a great deal of Christian work with little of true holiness or of the spirit of Christ. But there can be no large measure of real Christlike holiness without a distinct giving up oneself to make the salvation of sinners for the glory of God the object of our life. He gave HIMSELF FOR US so that He might claim US FOR HIMSELF, a peculiar people, zealous of good works. HIMSELF FOR US, and US FOR HIMSELF: an entire exchange, a perfect union, a complete identity in interest and purpose. HIMSELF FOR US as Savior, US FOR HIMSELF still as Savior; like Him and for Him to continue on earth the work He began. Whether we preach the Christlike life in its deep inner springs, where it has its origin in our oneness with Him in God, or in its growth and maintenance by a life of faith and prayer, of dependence and fellowship with the Father, or in its fruits of humility and holiness and love, let us always keep this in the foreground. The one chief mark and glory of the Christ is that He lived and died and lives again for this one thing alone: THE WILL AND THE GLORY OF THE GOD OF LOVE IN THE SALVATION OF SINNERS. And to be Christlike means simply this: To seek the life and favor and Spirit of God only, that we may be entirely given up to the same object: THE WILL AND THE GLORY OF THE GOD OF LOVE IN THE SALVATION OF SINNERS.

I add here an extract from Marshall's *On Sanctification*, in which the reality of our being partakers with Jesus of the very nature in which He lived and died and rose again is very clearly put.

I have often regretted that the somewhat antiquated style of this writer, and the introduction of questions not of immediate interest to the soul seeking the path of holiness, prevents his book from being as well known as it deserves to be. It is on all hands acknowledged to be the one standard work on the subject. It has been given him by God's Spirit with wonderful simplicity to set forth the great truth that holiness is a new life, a new nature, prepared for us in Christ Jesus, and that therefore every step in the pathway of holiness, whether in the use of the means of grace or in obeying God's commands, must be one of faith. I have thought that an abridgment of the work, in which all that is essential is provided in the author's own words, would supply a real need and might be a blessing to many. I have prepared such an abridgment, which has been issued by the publishers of the present work, under the title of *The Highway of Holiness*.

The end of Christ's incarnation, death, and resurrection was *to prepare and form a holy nature and frame for us in Himself, to be communicated to us by union* and fellowship with Him; and not to enable us to produce in ourselves the first original of such a holy nature by our own endeavors.

1. By His *incarnation* there was a man created in a new holy frame, after the holiness of the first Adam's frame had been marred and abolished by the first transgression. And this *new frame* was far more excellent than ever the first Adam's was, because man was really joined to God by a close, inseparable union of the divine and human nature in one person—Christ—so that these natures had communion each with the other in their actings, and Christ was able to act in His human nature by power proper to the divine nature, in which He was one God with the Father.

Why was it that Christ set up the fallen *nature of man in such a wonderful frame of holiness, in bringing it to live and act by communion with God living and acting in it?* One great purpose was, *that He might communicate this excellent frame to His seed* that should by His Spirit be born of Him and be in Him as the last Adam, as the quickening Spirit; that, as we have borne the image the earthly man, so we might also bear the image of the heavenly (1 Cor. 15:45, 49), in holiness here and in glory hereafter. For this reason, He was born Emmanuel, God with us; because *the fullness of the Godhead with all holiness did first dwell* in Him bodily, even in *His* human nature, that we might be filled with that fullness in Him (Matt. 1:23, Col. 2:9–10). For this reason, He came down from heaven as living bread, that, as He lives by the Father, so those who eat Him may live by Him (John 6:51, 57); by the *same life of God* in them that was first in Him.

2. By His *death* He freed Himself from the guilt of our sins imputed to Him, and from all that innocent weakness of human nature which He had borne for a time for our sakes. And, by freeing Himself, *He prepared a freedom for us from our whole natural condition*, which is both weak as His was, and also polluted with our guilt and sinful corruption. In this way the corrupt natural state that is called in scripture the "old man" was crucified together with Christ, so that the body of sin might be destroyed. And it is destroyed in us, not by any wounds that we ourselves can give it, but by our partaking of that freedom from it, and death to it, that *is already accomplished for us* by the death of Christ, as is signified by our baptism, in which we are buried with Christ by the application of His death to us (Rom. 6:2–4, 10–11).

God "sending His own Son in the likeness of sinful flesh, on account of sin [or "by a sacrifice for sin," as in the margin]. . .condemned sin in the flesh, that the righteous requirement of the law might be fulfilled in us who do not walk according to the flesh but according to the Spirit" (Rom. 8:3–4). Observe here that though Christ died that we might be justified by the righteousness of God and of faith, not by our own righteousness, which is of the law (Rom. 10:4–6; Phil. 3:9), yet *He died also*, that the righteousness of the law might be fulfilled in us, and that by walking after His Spirit, as those who are in Christ (Rom. 8:4). He is resembled in His death to a corn of wheat dying in the earth so that it may propagate its own nature by bringing forth much fruit (John 12:24); to the Passover that was slain so that a feast might be kept on it, and to be broken that it may be nourishment to those who eat it (1 Cor. 5:7–8, 11:24); to the rock struck so that water might gush out of it for us to drink (1 Cor. 10:4).

He died that He might make of Jew and Gentile one new man in Himself (Eph. 2:15); and that He might see His seed, i.e., such as derive their holy nature from Him (Isa. 53:10). Let these scriptures be well observed, and they will sufficiently demonstrate that Christ died, not that we might be able to form a holy nature in ourselves, but that we might *receive one ready prepared and formed in Christ for* us, by union and fellowship with Him.

3. By His resurrection He took possession of spiritual life for us, as now fully procured for us, and made to be our right and property by the merit of His death, and therefore we are said to be raised to life together with Christ. His resurrection was our resurrection to the life of holiness, as Adam's fall was our fall into spiritual death. And we are not ourselves the first makers and formers of our new holy nature, any more than of our original corruption, but both are formed ready for

us to partake of them. And, by union with Christ, we partake of that spiritual life that He took possession of for us at His resurrection, and thereby we are enabled to bring forth the fruit of it; as the scripture shows by the similitude of a marriage union: "You may be married to another—to Him who was raised from the dead, that we should bear fruit to God" (Romans 7:4).

THE END

Scripture Index

24:12—16
26:40-41—152
26:42—19

Numbers
3:12—390
3:13—389, 390
5:7—151
6:5—414
6:8—414, 416
7:89—861
8:16—390
8:17—389, 390
10:32—1239
10:35—1192
12:11—151
13:30—344, 596
14:8—596
14:17-18—131
14:20—131
15:40—400
19:12—156
21:7—151
23:19—132, 232
25:10-13—81
31:23-24—156

Deuteronomy
1:30—459
3:22—173
3:28—947
4:1—26
4:13—25
4:29—111
5:29—41
6:2—226
6:4—111, 977
6:5—92, 111, 273,
  736, 977
7:6—228
7:9—17, 41, 172
7:12—25
8:2—519
8:17-18—149
9:18—951
10:8—903
10:12—111
10:17—227

10:20-21—227
11:10—129
11:13—111
11:18—128
11:26-28—683
13:3—111
15:4-5—250, 1357
20:3—202
20:4—173
20:8—202
21:5—903
24:8—266
26:16—111
26:17-18—141
26:27-28—231
27:26—148
28:1—129, 251
28:2—129
28:9—591
28:47—214
28:58—1168
30:2—111
30:6—41, 70, 91,
  111, 695, 730
30:8—41, 70, 695,
  730
30:9-10—111
30:14—128
32:10—172
32:11-12—1198
32:46-47—135
33:8-11—80
33:10—81, 903

Joshua
1:7—135
1:9—135, 173, 207
3:4—123
4:24—227
5:14—201
6:19—961
6:20—202
7—959
7:11—961
7:12—219, 959
7:13—214
7:17—962
7:26—962

21:45—132
22:5—111
23:14—129, 132
24:15—229
24:19—418

Judges
5:31—126
7:3—202
10:10—151
10:15-16—151
17:3—263

Ruth
1:16—229
3:18—963

1 Samuel
2:2—368, 395, 422,
  1224
3:9-10—273
8:18—219
10:8—683
12:20—112
12:23—959, 961,
  1052
12:24—112, 227
13:8-14—684
14:37-38—219
15:3—684
15:11—684
15:13—684
15:20—684
15:22—251, 684,
  1357
15:23—684
18:14—260
27:1—276
28:6—219
28:15—219

2 Samuel
3:17-18—604
5:3—604
6:7—260
7:25—132
7:29—132
12:13—151, 152

14:22—857
15:21—228
22:21—156
22:25—156
23:4—214
24:10—151

1 Kings
2:4—112
8:48-49—112
14:8—112
18:24—223
18:34—951
18:37—223
20:1-4—1063
20:4—145, 1061

2 Kings
2:14—952
6:17—73
10:30-31—112
23:3—91, 112
23:25—112

1 Chronicles
8:15—132
8:24—132
18:4—1224
19:12—185
20:20—131
28:20—227
29:6—265
29:9—265
29:14—264
29:18—591

2 Chronicles
5:3—206
5:10—156
6:4—798, 802
7:2—178
9:8—591
15:7—207, 946
15:12—91
15:14—91
15:15—91, 977
16:9—175
17:14—151

59:16—176
59:17—176
61:8—602
62:1—616, 619, 1045, 1147, 1225
62:2—185, 201, 241, 1225
62:3—201
62:5—617, 1087, 1141, 1224
62:6—185, 201, 241, 1224
64:1-2—1178
64:11—162
65:3—219
66:16—206
66:19—219, 769
67:1-2—1053
68:4—162, 214
68:19—602
68:31—1046
68:34-35—176
69:6—171
71:8—206
71:15—206
71:16—176
71:24—206
73:1—156
73:25—137
76:9—1351
78:8—1040
78:19-20—1176
78:41—42, 1041
84:7—481
84:8—126
85:6—1010
89:5—232
89:15—213, 971
89:16—213
89:17—213
89:18—176, 523
89:20—523
89:29—276
89:33—172
89:34—172, 277
89:35-36—276
92:10—527
92:13—126, 162

92:14—126, 270
94:12—216
95:8—359
96:9—388
97:11—162
97:12—162, 395
99—396, 422
99:3—388
103:2-3—153, 154
103:12—153
104—1153
104:27-28—1151
106:12—460
106:13—1180
106:16—436
106:32-33—260
109:4—1035
111:1—112
112:1—225
112:5—203
112:7-8—225
112:9—203
115:13—225, 227
116:1—769
118:14—176
119—112, 274
119:1—274
119:2—274
119:5—274
119:6—274
119:8—274
119:10—272, 274
119:11—128, 129, 214, 272, 274
119:12—274
119:14—126, 129, 274
119:15—128, 273
119:16—128
119:17—274
119:18—126
119:24—274
119:26—274
119:22—274
119:32—274
119:33—274
119:34—128, 274
119:36—128, 274

119:40—273
119:41—274
119:42—274
119:44—274
119:45—129, 274
119:47—126, 274
119:48—126, 273
119:49—132, 217, 274
119:50—217
119:54—274
119:58—274
119:67—216
119:69—129, 273
119:71—216
119:72—274
119:76—274
119:77—274
119:92—217
119:93—274
119:97—99, 126, 129, 272, 274
119:98—129
119:100—126
119:102—274
119:105—274
119:106—274, 642
119:107—274
119:110—274
119:111—126
119:112—274
119:116—274
119:117—274
119:121—274, 863
119:127—126
119:128—274, 642
119:129—274
119:130—274
119:133—274
119:135—274
119:143—217
119:144—274
119:145—1040
119:146—274
119:153—863
119:159—274
119:165—129, 172
119:166—162

119:168—162, 274
119:170—274
119:176—274
121:5—172, 332
121:7—172, 596
126:6-7—207
127:11—227
130:5-6—1183, 1187
131:2—185
132:14—242
133:1—222
133:2—527, 614, 903
133:3—222
135:20—226
138:1—112
138:7—1010
138:8—276, 277, 590
139:6—558
139:7—181
139:23—150, 182, 1014
139:24—150
141:3—261
141:8—172
142:6—137
143:2—161
143:8—123
144:2—201
144:8—162
145:9—220
145:14-15—1153
145:19—227, 977
147:11—225
149:9—902, 904

Proverbs
1:1—227
1:7—225
1:8—227
1:13-14—227
1:27—227
2:2—261
2:4—274
2:5—226, 274
2:10—260

58:5-6—148
58:7-8—210
58:10—214
58:12—1003
59:1-2—148, 214
59:9—214
59:12-13—151
59:16—933, 963, 1004
59:21—1041
60:1—210, 214
60:2—210
60:3—211, 211
60:11—211
60:16—211
60:19—215
60:20—214, 215, 1183
60:22—348, 1046, 1172
61:1—217, 699, 903
61:2—217
61:3—476
61:6—903
62:2—211
62:6—943, 1004, 1032, 1050
62:7—943, 1004
63:5—251, 963, 1004
63:15—1202
63:17—1202
64:1—1192, 1203
64:2—1192, 1203
64:3—1202
64:4—123, 1141, 1202
64:5—1143, 1173, 1175
64:7—933, 1004, 1037
65:5—167
66:2—1013

Jeremiah
1:2—273
1:6-7—207
1:9—172
2:3—1351
3:12-14—711
3:21—151
3:22—712, 715, 964
3:25—151
4:1—712
4:13—270

5:22—227
7:4—167
7:22—684
7:23—26, 39, 684, 698
8:13—21
8:22—964
10:6-7—227
11:4—26, 39
11:27—26
12:12—176
15:16—273
17:14—964
23:6—574
24:7—30, 91, 113
26:3-4—172
27:8—148
29:13—91, 113, 977
31—642
31:3—566, 633
31:18-19—152
31:31–32—21, 25
31:32—22, 70
31:33—29, 67, 172, 261, 714
31:34—29
31:34—85, 153
32:17—173, 1041
32:27—173, 1041
32:38—39
32:39—113, 222
32:40—39, 91, 113, 225, 667, 714
32:41—91, 113
33:3—220, 994, 1046
33:25-26—277
44:4—148

Lamentations
3:25—1195, 1204
3:26—1206

Ezekiel
1:8—719
3:10—128
3:18—162
3:20—162
14:3—1013
18:21—162
18:23—162

20:12—240
20:20—240
22:13—963
22:30—1004
24:14—89, 110
30:25—157
33:6—151
33:12—162
34:25—41
36:23—763
36:25—55, 348, 349
36:26—39, 718
36:27—37, 39, 41, 70, 348, 349, 667, 695, 718
36:32—1013
36:37—1046
37:9—307, 344
37:23—55
37:26—39, 41, 55
37:27-28—241

Daniel
4:35—253, 501
9:4-5—151
9:20—151

Hosea
6:1-2—1010, 1014
6:3—1015
7:14-15—216
11:9—158, 423
12:6—1219
14:4—153
14:5—153
14:6-7—184
14:8—624
14:16—270

Joel
2:12—113
2:16-17—222
2:28—780

Amos
3:7—1011

Micah
3:4—220

5:4—1089
5:5—178, 251, 1089
5:8—168
5:15—988
5:16—988
6:12—989, 1035
6:31—188
6:32—165
6:35—165
6:40—234
7:22—1242
7:36-39—617
7:38—148
7:40—206
7:47—154
7:50—141
8:1—824
8:6-8—824
8:48—141
8:50—341
9:1—808
9:18—222, 989
9:23—256
9:24—257
9:28—222, 989
9:48—168
10:18—197
10:22—766
10:30-37—497
10:37—617, 1288
10:39—617
11:1—747, 989
11:5—783, 943
11:6—783, 943
11:7—783, 943
11:8—783, 789, 943, 948
11:9—829, 938
11:10—829
11:11—1027
11:13—341, 778, 938, 1027
11:28—273
12:4—225
12:7—225
12:29-30—1377
12:31—264
12:33—913

12:35—170
12:36—1213
13:16—197
13:24—200
13:26—151
14:11—168, 433, 1325
14:26—229, 712
14:27—229, 256, 1255, 1259
14:33—228, 229, 299, 312
15:22—153
15:31—348
16:8—260
16:10—845
16:21—264
17:5-6—134
17:19—141, 974
18:1-8—908, 948
18:1—286, 1048
18:2—226
18:4—226
18:7—873, 1007, 1050
18:8—219
18:14—168
18:20—711
18:22—145, 229, 1095
18:24—1095
18:27—173, 235, 936, 1095, 1101
18:29—229
18:41—793, 1034
18:42—141
19:2—264
19:7-8—148
19:10—148
19:26—845
21:19—1171
21:24—209
21:34—261
21:36—260
22:3—197
22:19—248
22:20—21
22:24—293

22:26—165, 1241
22:27—165, 168, 1241, 1242
22:29—1376
22:31—197
22:32—197, 879, 881, 884, 1089
22:33—1090
22:53—197
22:61-62—1089
23:41—151
24:16—73, 234
24:19—699
24:44—1308
24:47—209, 1050
24:49—203, 346, 658, 1033

John
1:4—614
1:12—122, 137, 138, 142
1:13—122
1:14—75, 137, 159, 449, 754
1:16—75, 137, 142, 159
1:17—75, 449, 754
1:33—754
1:42—206
1:43—539
1:46—206
3:1-8, 144
3:3—206, 244
3:5—122, 244
3:7—122
3:14, 144
3:15—122, 144
3:16—122, 132, 137, 144, 716, 1073
3:17—132, 144
3:18—144
3:20-21—145
3:33—132, 231
3:35—633, 1354
3:36—122, 132, 178
4:7—206
4:13—232

4:14—442
4:21—753
4:22—752
4:23—752, 982
4:24—752
4:28—206
4:34—254, 403, 693
4:39—206
4:46-54—1123
4:50—132, 1123
5:4-5—171
5:6-9—970
5:10—122
5:19—109, 175, 637, 989, 1295, 1357
5:20—637, 989, 1295, 1354, 1357
5:23—108
5:24—122
5:26—108
5:28—122
5:30—108, 254, 339, 685, 694, 697, 1283
5:38—128
5:39—272
5:44—237, 257, 630, 849
6:12—724
6:15—989, 1033
6:25—122
6:26—122, 148
6:29—141
6:35—141, 328
6:37—277
6:38—254, 339, 693, 1282, 1286
6:39—505, 1286
6:40—122, 253, 505, 1286
6:45—31, 525
6:51—122, 247, 1389
6:53—55
6:54-55—247
6:56—55, 247, 248, 1366
6:57—234, 247, 540,

987, 1055, 1290
16:27—884
16:33—149, 238
17—130, 629, 646,
  880, 886, 1304
17:1—847, 887, 891,
  1305, 1370
17:4—847, 1305,
  1370
17:5—670, 847, 887
17:6—129
17:8—129, 447
17:11—450, 1031,
  1270
17:13—646
17:14—237, 887,
  1270
17:15—263, 1031
17:16—88, 237, 263,
  306, 1031, 1270
17:17—129, 447,
  448, 450, 888, 957
17:18—209, 732,
  1274
17:19—88, 235, 450,
  451, 507, 578
17:20—450
17:21—648, 1029
17:22—556, 636,
  880, 1032, 1360
17:23—137, 141,
  636, 648, 884,
  1032, 1354
17:24—886, 888,
  891, 1354
17:25—137
17:26—141, 766,
  888, 1032, 1157,
  1158, 1354
18:11—892
19:30—241, 454
19:37—274
20:1—241
20:19—240, 241
20:21—211, 324,
  732, 1274
20:22—211, 352
20:23—324
20:26—241

20:28—137
20:29—132, 178
21:17—145, 229,
  1091
21:19—539

Acts
1:2—734
1:4—181, 185, 778,
  1027, 1216
1:5—938
1:8—185, 206, 209,
  241, 308, 346, 658,
  732, 1033, 1036
1:14—222, 302, 938
1:15—296, 819
1:18-19—151
2:1—819, 938
2:2—819
2:3—819
2:4—292, 819, 938
2:15—265
2:33—181, 754, 875
2:38—289
2:41—938
2:43—658
3:6—970, 1053
3:14-15—456
3:16—289, 970
3:17—289
4:13—207, 658
4:24—222, 939
4:31-33—939
4:34—265
5:13—658
5:29—294, 686,
  1092
5:32—185, 251, 324,
  686
5:39—200
6:2—939
6:4—934, 1035,
  1051
6:5—986
6:7—251, 1051
7:51—187
8—940
8:2—209
8:4—209

8:14—1217
8:15—1052, 1217
8:16—1052, 1217
8:17—1217
8:30—128
8:37—128
9:11—998
9:17—288, 290
9:31—225
9:34—970
10—940
10:2—940
10:4—940
10:9-23—1084
10:20—940
10:33—1181, 1190,
  1217
10:35—227
10:38—197, 523
10:44-46—940
10:44—940, 1181
10:45-46—940
11:12—209
11:15—1053
11:17—1053
11:19—206
11:23-24—209
12—941
12:5—222, 223, 941
12:12—941
13—941, 942
13:1—941, 1082
13:2—286, 1035,
  1082, 1217
13:3—286, 1035,
  1082
13:4—941, 1035,
  1082
13:5—1082
13:52—473
14:27—209
15:4-5—209
15:9—491
16:31—246
17:11—274
17:21—261
17:28—108
19:1—287
19:2—185, 287

19:6—287
19:36—260
20:7—241
20:35—264
22:19-20—151
22:21—209
26:18—153, 199,
  457
27:25—131, 132,
  231

Romans
1:3—136, 462
1:4—88, 159, 182,
  462, 780
1:5—251, 686
1:7—88, 367
1:9—999
1:11—999
1:17—132, 161, 194,
  559, 574
1:18—148
1:21—167
1:23—167
2:29—192
3:10—161
3:15—141
3:19—26
3:20—26, 161
3:21—689
3:22—161
3:24—161
3:28—178
3:31—162
4:4—175
4:5—132, 175, 178,
  192
4:14—191
4:15—26, 191, 267,
  473
4:16—78, 141, 178
4:17—194, 384, 424,
  609, 1209
4:18—825
4:19—178
4:20—131, 141, 179,
  231, 718
4:21—131, 141, 173,
  179, 231, 718

15:30—821, 1008, 1029, 1033, 1057
16:2—530
16:6—136
16:20—197
16:25—591
16:26—251, 686
16:27—592

1 Corinthians
1:2—88, 159, 367, 372, 508
1:4—999
1:8—173
1:9—173, 590
1:10-11—187
1:12—272
1:17—256
1:18-19—123
1:21—593
1:22—593
1:23—570
1:24—175, 482, 570
1:27—175, 256, 272
1:28—175
1:30—87, 138, 158, 159, 161, 442, 458, 479, 565, 569, 573, 574, 577
1:31—479
2—68, 86
2:3—84, 1098
2:4—85, 304, 1098
2:5—304
2:6—237, 256, 272
2:7—123
2:8—181, 237
2:9—159, 248, 1068, 1202
2:10—123, 159, 181, 184, 1203
2:11—1203
2:12—123, 181, 234, 237, 248, 272, 206, 480, 1085
2:13—234
2:14—184
2:15—191

3:1—125, 190, 191, 193, 234, 442, 1111
3:2—234, 442, 1111
3:3—187, 190, 442, 1111
3:6—67
3:13—125
3:14—442
3:16—125, 159, 181, 185, 228, 464, 484
3:17—159, 182, 228, 406
4:16—998
5:5—198
5:7-8—1389
5:10—1271
6:9-10—491
6:13—247, 484, 491
6:15—247, 248, 491
6:17—248
6:19—141, 159, 182, 184, 188, 247, 289, 406, 442, 484, 486, 1054, 1372
6:20—141, 154, 184, 188, 247, 484, 486, 1372
7:1—388, 490
7:5—198
7:19—165
7:22—469
7:23—268
7:31—263
7:34—484, 487
8:8—268
8:9—262
8:13—229
9:4-5—268
9:9-10—93
9:12—93
9:19—472
9:21—268
9:25—229, 256
9:27—229, 256, 488
10:4—1389
10:16—247
10:17—248

10:22—200
10:23—229, 257
10:24—257
10:31—167, 848
10:32—262
11:1—235, 998
11:7—168, 1378
11:8—248
11:14—416
11:24—1389
11:25—53, 248
11:32—217
12:3—181
12:8-9—831
12:11—126
12:13—248
12:20—229
12:21—209, 229, 880
12:26—296
13:1—187
13:3—187
13:4—168
13:5—203, 337, 499, 500, 944, 1354
13:8—442, 500
13:13—165, 326, 500
13:14-15—165
14:4—442
14:15—1044
14:24-25—181
15:3—1328, 1331
15:9—168
15:10—77, 149, 168, 175, 195, 230, 661, 968
15:17—466
15:28—354, 1066
15:45—1246, 1388
15:49—1377, 1388
15:56—76, 267, 468
15:58—203
16:2—241

2 Corinthians
1:3-4—217
1:9—170, 175, 195

1:10—821, 1001, 1033
1:11—223, 821, 1001, 1033, 1034
1:20—332, 667, 722
1:21—590, 1052
1:22—182, 1052
1:24—171
2:10—198
2:14—201, 268, 475, 645
2:16—1322
3—68, 86
3:2-6—83
3:3—44
3:5—207, 257, 465
3:6-10—44
3:7—26, 48
3:10-12—27, 142
3:13—137, 142
3:16—142
3:17—182, 267, 469
3:18—235, 1310, 312, 1315, 1317
4:4—197
4:6—1183, 1185, 1200, 1321
4:7—659
4:10—455, 484, 13461349
4:11—484, 1346, 1349
4:12—1346, 1349
4:13—779
4:18—237, 534, 978
5:5—185
5:7—178, 237, 972, 978
5:8—137
5:14—1129
5:15—138, 145, 237
5:17—292
5:21—161, 574
6:2—200, 603
6:4-5—999
6:9—433, 475
6:10—142, 213, 433, 475, 645

10:23—346, 1036
10:24—207
10:29—53, 187, 779
10:35—132, 170, 277
10:36—254, 1171
10:38—123, 194
11:1—132, 458
11:6—196, 759
11:7—682
11:8—72, 123, 250, 251, 717
11:11—132, 1036
11:12—278
11:13—785
11:18—132, 173
11:23—202
11:26—955
11:33—131
11:35—131
11:38—194
11:39—785
12:1—270
12:2—881
12:10—216, 462, 517, 621
12:11—217
12:14—517, 529
12:15—158
12:24—57
13:3—1048
13:5-6—217, 277
13:12-13—414
13:15—206
13:16—227
13:20—48, 50, 53, 170, 277, 493
13:21—48, 50, 170, 254, 277, 493, 721, 1018

James
1:2—216
1:3—216
1:4—170, 218, 493, 903, 1171
1:6—220
1:15—268
1:19—861

1:20-24—686
1:21—134, 136, 168, 272, 1350
1:25—273
1:27—939
2:12—268
2:20—459
2:21—459
2:22—232, 459, 640, 785, 787
2:23—785, 787
3:2—170
3:9-10—188
3:14—187
3:16—179
4:2—933
4:3—148, 220, 631, 767, 817, 899, 900
4:4—238
4:5—168
4:6—1325
4:8—157, 223, 852, 1049
5:7—270, 825, 953, 1194
5:16—152, 220, 223, 863, 906, 952
5:17—223, 952

1 Peter
1:2—88, 148, 159, 182, 250, 367, 441, 501, 686, 1279
1:3—462
1:4—132
1:5—132, 179
1:7—179
1:8—132, 179, 213, 215
1:10—1278
1:12—84, 700, 1056
1:13—170
1:14—125, 143, 250, 686
1:15—148, 158, 241, 367, 368, 388, 458, 686
1:16—148, 158, 241, 367, 577

1:17—143, 154, 171, 388
1:18—54, 154, 171
1:19—54, 125, 496
1:22—100, 156, 165, 229, 250, 687
1:23—125, 135, 273
2:2—125
2:5—145, 506, 903, 907
2:6—329
2:9—79, 506, 707
2:10—125, 141
2:14—148
2:16—268
2:18-20—1250
2:21—1092, 1245, 1252, 1345, 1382
2:22—1345
2:23—1251, 1345
2:24—148, 1252, 1382
2:25—125
3—1350
3:3—488
3:4—488, 1092
3:5—226, 488
3:14—225
3:18—513, 1382
4:1—513
4:2—190
4:7—260
4:8—1029
4:13—522
4:14—522, 780, 1092, 1319, 1373
5:5—168, 1092
5:7—277
5:8—170, 476
5:9—170
5:10—170, 277, 592, 593

2 Peter
1:4—170
1:7—165
1:8—170
1:10—170
2:7—162

2:19—267
3:11—529
3:14—496, 531, 534
3:18—126

1 John
1:2—122, 1238
1:3—122
1:5—214, 423
1:7—156, 182, 492, 972
1:8—652
1:9—151, 156, 157, 171, 350, 491
1:10—652
1:13—1171
2:1—171, 884
2:2—653
2:4—162, 687
2:6—234, 971, 1233
2:10—214
2:11—162
2:12—152, 873
2:13—173, 873
2:14—129, 176, 873
2:16—237, 485
2:17—254
2:20—523
2:24—129, 173, 562
2:27—446, 523, 612, 614
2:29—161, 162
3:1—122, 143, 165, 1301
3:2—125, 1377, 1378
3:3—157, 1377, 1378
3:4—201
3:5—148, 201, 652, 655
3:6—148, 149, 652, 655
3:7—575, 863
3:8—148, 197
3:9—161
3:10—143, 161, 162, 166, 198, 440
3:14—122, 125, 232